BRITISH WRITERS

BRITISH WRITERS

GEORGE STADE

General Editor

CAROL HOWARD

Associate Editor

SUPPLEMENT III

JAMES M. BARRIE

TO

MARY WOLLSTONECRAFT

CHARLES SCRIBNER'S SONS
MACMILLAN LIBRARY REFERENCE USA
SIMON & SCHUSTER MACMILLAN
NEW YORK

SIMON & SCHUSTER AND PRENTICE HALL INTERNATIONAL
LONDON   MEXICO CITY   NEW DELHI   SINGAPORE   SYDNEY   TORONTO

Charles Scribner's Sons
An Imprint of Simon & Schuster Macmillan
866 Third Avenue
New York, NY 10022

Library of Congress Cataloging-in-Publication Data

British writers. Supplement III, James M. Barrie to Mary
    Wollstonecraft / George Stade, general editor : Carol Howard,
    associate editor.
        p.   cm.
    Includes bibliographical references and cumulative index.
    ISBN 0-684-19593-3 (alk. paper : full set). — ISBN 0684-19714-6
(alk. paper)
    1. English literature—History and criticism.   2. English
literature—Bio-bibliography.   3. Authors, English—Biography.
I. Stade, George.   II. Howard, Carol, 1963-
PR85.B688   Suppl. 3
820.9—dc20
[B]   95-38155
                                                                                   CIP

1 3 5 7 9 11 13 15 17 19 V/C 20 18 16 14 12 10 8 4 2

Printed in the United States of America

The paper used in this publication meets the minimum requirements of the American National Standard for Information Sciences—Permanence of Paper for Printed Library Materials, ANSI Z39.48–1984.

Acknowledgments

Acknowledgment is gratefully made to those publishers and individuals who permitted the use of the following materials in copyright.

APHRA BEHN Excerpts from *"To the fair* Clarinda, *who made Love to me, imagin'd more than Woman,"* "Song," "Those Arbitrary Rulers over men," and "A Pindaric Poem to the Reverend Doctor Burnet" from *The Works of Aphra Behn*, edited by Janet Todd. Copyright © 1992 by Pickering & Chatto, Ltd. Reprinted by permission.

FRANCES BURNEY Excerpts from *Camilla; or, A Picture of Youth*, ed. by E. A. Bloom and L. D. Bloom. Copyright © 1972 by Oxford University Press. Reprinted by permission of Oxford University Press. Excerpts from *Cecelia; or, Memoirs of an Heiress*, ed. by P. Sabor and M. Doody. Copyright © 1988 by Oxford University Press. Reprinted by permission of Oxford University Press. Excerpts from *The Early Journal and Letters of Fanny Burney*, ed. by Lars Troide et al. Copyright © 1988 by Oxford University Press. Reprinted by permission of Oxford University Press.

ANGELA CARTER From *Love* by Angela Carter. Copyright © 1972, 1987 by Angela Carter. Used by permission of Penguin, a division of Penguin Books USA, Inc. Excerpts from *Heroes and Villains, Nothing Sacred, The Pasion of New Eve, The Sadeian Woman, Several Perceptions*, and *Shadow Dance* by Angela Carter. Copyright © 1969, 1982, 1977, 1979, 1968, and 1966 by Angel Carter. Reprinted by permission of the estate in care of Rogers, Coleridge & White, Ltd.

CYRIL CONNOLLY Excerpt from review by Donald Stauffer, *New York Times*, 28 July 1946. Copyright © 1946 by The New York Times Company. Reprinted by permission. Excerpts from *Enemies of Promise* by Cyril Connolly. Copyright © 1948 by Routledge. Reprinted by permission.

CECIL DAY LEWIS Excerpt from *The Buried Day* by C. Day Lewis. Copyright © 1960 by C. Day Lewis. Reprinted by permission of the Peters Fraser & Dunlop Group, Ltd., on behalf of the estate. Excerpts from *The Complete Poems of C. Day Lewis*. Copyright © 1992 by Reed Books. Reprinted by permission of Sinclair-Stevenson.

C. S. LEWIS Excerpts from *The Abolition of Man* by C. S. Lewis. Copright © 1943. Reprinted by permission of HarperCollins Publishers, Ltd. Excerpts from *The Allegory of Love* by C. S. Lewis. Copyright © 1936. Reprinted by permission of Oxford University Press. Selected quotations from *A Grief Observed* by C. S. Lewis. Copyright © 1961 by N. W. Clerk. Reprinted by per-

mission of HarperCollins Publishers, Inc., and of Faber and Faber, Ltd. Excerpts from *Out of the Silent Planet* by C. S. Lewis. Copyright © 1938. Reprinted by permission of the estate of C. S. Lewis and The Bodley Head, a division of Random House U.K., Ltd. Excerpts from *Perelandra* by C. S. Lewis. Copyright © 1943. Reprinted by permission of the estate of C. S. Lewis and The Bodley Head, a division of Random House U.K., Ltd. Excerpts from *The Screwtape Letters* by C. S. Lewis. Copyright © 1942. Reprinted by permission of HarperCollins Publishers, Ltd. Excerpts from *The Silver Chair* by C. S. Lewis. Copyright © 1953. Reprinted by permission of HarperCollins Publishers, Ltd. Excerpts from *Till We Have Faces: A Myth Retold*, copyright © 1957, 1956 by C. S. Lewis and renewed 1985, 1984 by Arthur Owen Barfield, reprinted by permission of Harcourt Brace & Company and of HarperCollins Publishers, Ltd.

MALCOLM LOWRY Excerpts from *The Collected Poetry of Malcolm Lowry*, ed. by Kathleen Dorothy Scherf. Copyright © 1992 by University of British Columbia Press. Reprinted with permission of the publisher. All rights reserved by the publisher.

BEATRIX POTTER Excerpts from *The Journal of Beatrix Potter, 1881-1897*, transcribed by Leslie Linder. Copyright © Frederick Warne & Co., 1966. Reproduced by permission of Frederick Warne & Co. Excerpts from *Beatrix Potter's Letters*, selected by Judy Taylor. Copyright © Frederick Warne & Co., 1989. Reproduced by permission of Frederick Warne & Co.

MARY SHELLEY Excerpts from *The Journal of Mary Shelley* by Paula R. Feldman and D. Scott-Kelvert. Copyright © 1987. Reprinted by permission of Oxford University Press.

BRAM STOKER Excerpts from *The Man Who Wrote Dracula* by Daniel Farson. Copyright © 1976 by Daniel Farson. Reprinted by permission of A. M. Heath on behalf of the author. Excerpts from *Hollywood Gothic* by David J. Skal. Copyright © 1990, 1995. Reprinted by permission of W. W. Norton & Company and of Malaga Baldi Literary Agency by arrangement of the author.

EDWARD THOMAS Excerpts from *Letters from Edward Thomas to Gordon Bottomley*, ed. by R. George Thomas. Copyright © 1968. Reprinted by permission of Oxford University Press. Excerpts from *The Collected Poems of Edward Thomas*. Copyright © 1978. Reprinted by permission of Oxford University Press.

v

ACKNOWLEDGMENTS

JAMES THOMSON   Approximately ten sentences have been adapted from Frans De Bruyn, "Hooking the Leviathan: The Eclipse of the Heroic and the Emergence of the Sublime in Eighteenth-Century British Literature," in *The Eighteenth Century* 28, no. 3.

REBECCA WEST   From *Black Lamb and Grey Falcon* by Rebecca West. Copyright © 1941 by Rebecca West. Used by permission of Viking Penguin, a division of Penguin Books USA, Inc. From *The Fountain Overflows* by Rebecca West. Copyright © 1956 by Rebecca West; Renewed Copyright © 1985 by the Executors of the Estate of Rebecca West. Used by permission of Viking Penguin, a division of Penguin Books USA, Inc. Ex-cerpt from *H. G. Wells and Rebecca West* by Gordon N. Ray. Copyright © 1974 by Yale University Press. Reprinted by permission of Yale University Press. Excerpts from *A Train of Powder* by Rebecca West. Copyright © 1955. Reprinted by permission of the Peters Fraser & Dunlop Group, Ltd. Excerpts from *Saint Augustine,* in *Rebecca West: A Celebration.* Copyright © 1977. Reprinted by permission of the Peters Fraser & Dunlop Group, Ltd.

MARY WOLLSTONECRAFT   Excerpts from *The Proper Lady and the Woman Writer* by Mary Poovey. Copyright © 1984 by The University of Chicago. Reprinted by permission of The University of Chicago Press. All rights reserved.

Editorial Staff

Contents

Introduction

The twenty-five articles in *British Writers* Supplement III are on writers who for one reason or another were not represented in the initial seven-volume *British Writers* (1979–1984) or in Supplements I (1987) or II (1992). From its inception, *British Writers* was designed as a companion to the ongoing *American Writers* set (1974–   ). These two sets were followed by *Ancient Writers: Greece and Rome* (2 vols., 1982), by *European Writers* (13 vols., 1983–1991), and by *Latin American Writers* (3 vols., 1989). These reference works constitute, so far, the Scribner World Literature Series. And related to this series are works such as *Science Fiction Writers* (1982), *Supernatural Fiction Writers,* (2 vols., 1985), *William Shakespeare: His World, His Work, His Influence* (3 vols., 1985), *Writers for Children* (1988), *The Books of the Bible* (1989), *Modern American Women Writers* (1991), and *African American Writers* (1991).

Each article in Supplement III is devoted to a single writer and is between 12,000 and 15,000 words long. Each article offers an account of the writer's works, his or her life, literary relations, and operative ideas. But from article to article the emphasis varies, just as from writer to writer the relative importance of his or her life or reading or situation varies. Whatever the relative emphasis, the works come first; other matters are taken up to the extent that they form or inform the works.

In style and scope, the articles are expressly written for that mythical but inspiring figure, the general reader, rather than for the specialist. They are written, that is, for high school, undergraduate, and graduate students, as well as for their teachers; for librarians and editors; for reviewers, scholars, critics; for literary browsers; for anyone who wants to repair an erosion or gap in his or her reservoir of knowledge; for anyone who wants to know more about a writer whose name is in the air. The article that can at once inform the beginner and interest the specialist has achieved its goal.

Above all, the editors asked themselves whether a writer under consideration for inclusion was someone whom English-speaking readers were likely to look up, both at the time of publication and twenty years thereafter. The editors took into account a shift in reader interest and critical activity and classroom attention that has not yet worked itself out. That shift, which is often thought of as a process of decanonization, includes an erosion of the distinction between popular literature and the other kind, whatever we call it, as well as a recovery of women writers who had fallen into neglect between their own times and the recent past. Thus there are articles on "popular" writers such as Bram Stoker, H. Rider Haggard, James M. Barrie, Beatrix Potter, P. G. Wodehouse, Dorothy L. Sayers, and Daphne du Maurier; and there are articles on rediscovered women writers such as Aphra Behn, Frances Burney, Mary Wollstonecraft, Maria Edgeworth, Mary Shelley, and Rebecca West. (Some of these writers, of course, have a place in both categories.) And as in earlier volumes, the editors have included articles on writers who were not in the narrow sense literary, but who were powerful prose stylists and powerfully influential on writers of poems, plays, and novels, as well as writers who were by themselves whole climates of opinion, such as David Hume and James George Frazer.

In accordance with a practice that evolved early in the series, not all the writers represented in Supplement III are "British" in one or another restricted sense of the term. Bram Stoker, for example, was Irish-born; Malcolm Lowry, though born in England, wrote most of his works while living in Canada. But their relation to British literary culture was continuous and formative; their work shows up most vividly for what it is against a background of that English literary tradition of which it has become a part. In any case, the editors felt that readers would want to look Stoker and Lowry up, but could not do so elsewhere in articles like the ones included in this volume. That last justification, however, could apply to all the articles in this volume: they are all about writers who are well worth looking up.

GEORGE STADE

Complete British Writers Chronology

CHRONOLOGY

CHRONOLOGY

1565	Mary Queen of Scots marries Lord Darnley
1566	William Painter's *Palace of Pleasure*, a miscellany of prose stories, the source of many dramatists' plots
1567	Darnley murdered at Kirk o'Field
	Mary Queen of Scots marries the earl of Bothwell
1569	Rebellion of the English northern earls suppressed
1570	Roger Ascham's *The Schoolmaster*
1571	Defeat of the Turkish fleet at Lepanto
ca. 1572	Ben Jonson born
1572	St. Bartholomew's Day massacre
	John Donne born
1574	The earl of Leicester's theater company formed
1576	The Theatre, the first permanent theater building in London, opened
	The first Blackfriars Theatre opened with performances by the Children of St. Paul's
1576–1578	Martin Frobisher's voyages to Labrador and the northwest
1577–1580	Sir Francis Drake sails around the world
1577	Holinshed's *Chronicles of England, Scotlande, and Irelande*
1579	John Lyly's *Euphues: The Anatomy of Wit*
	Thomas North's translation of *Plutarch's Lives*
1581	The Levant Company founded
	Seneca's *Ten Tragedies* translated
1582	Richard Hakluyt's *Divers Voyages Touching the Discoverie of America*
1584–1585	Sir John Davis' first voyage to Greenland
1585	First English settlement in America, the "Lost Colony" comprising 108 men under Ralph Lane, founded at Roanoke Island, off the coast of North Carolina
1586	Kyd's *Spanish Tragedy*
	Marlowe's *Tamburlaine*
	William Camden's *Britannia*
	The Babington conspiracy against Queen Elizabeth
	Death of Sir Philip Sidney

1587	Mary Queen of Scots executed
	Birth of Virginia Dare, first English child born in America, at Roanoke Island
1588	Defeat of the Spanish Armada
	Marlowe's *Dr. Faustus*
1590	Spenser's *The Faerie Queen*, Cantos 1–3
1592	Outbreak of plague in London: the theaters closed
1593	Death of Christopher Marlowe
1594	The Lord Chamberlain's Men, the company to which Shakespeare belonged, founded
	The Swan Theatre opened
	Death of Thomas Kyd
1595	Ralegh's expedition to Guiana
	Sidney's *Apology for Poetry*
1596	The earl of Essex's expedition captures Cadiz
	The second Blackfriars Theatre opened
ca. 1597	Death of George Peele
1597	Bacon's first collection of *Essays*
1598	Jonson's *Every Man in His Humor*
1598–1600	Richard Hakluyt's *Principal Navigations, Voyages, Traffics, and Discoveries of the English Nation*
1599	The Globe Theatre opened
	Death of Edmund Spenser
1600	Death of Richard Hooker
1601	Rebellion and execution of the earl of Essex
1602	The East India Company founded
	The Bodleian Library reopened at Oxford
1603–1625	**Reign of James I**
1603	John Florio's translation of Montaigne's *Essays*
1605	Bacon's *Advancement of Learning*
	Cervantes' *Don Quixote* (Part 1)
	The Gunpowder Plot
	Thomas Browne born
1606	Shakespeare's *Macbeth*
	Jonson's *Volpone*
	Death of John Lyly
	Edmund Waller born
1607	The first permanent English colony established at Jamestown, Virginia
1608	John Milton born
1609	Kepler's *Astronomia nova*
	John Suckling born

CHRONOLOGY

CHRONOLOGY

1640 The Long Parliament assembled
The king's advisers, Archbishop Laud and the earl of Strafford, impeached
Aphra Behn born

1641 Strafford executed
Acts passed abolishing extraparliamentary taxation, the king's extraordinary courts, and his power to order a dissolution without parliamentary consent
The Grand Remonstrance censuring royal policy passed by eleven votes
William Wycherley born

1642 Parliament submits the nineteen Propositions, which King Charles rejects as annihilating the royal power
The Civil War begins
The theaters close
Royalists victory at Edgehill; King Charles established at Oxford
Death of Sir John Suckling

1643 Parliament concludes the Solemn League and Covenant with the Scots
Louis XIV becomes king of France
Charles Sackville, earl of Dorset, born

1644 Parliamentary victory at Marston Moor
The New Model army raised
Milton's *Areopagitica*

1645 Parliamentary victory under Fairfax and Cromwell at Naseby
Fairfax captures Bristol
Archbishop Laud executed

1646 Fairfax besieges King Charles at Oxford
King Charles takes refuge in Scotland; end of the First Civil War
King Charles attempts negotiations with the Scots
Parliament's proposals sent to the king and rejected

1647 Conflict between Parliament and the army
A general council of the army established that discusses representational government within the army

The Agreement of the People drawn up by the Levelers; its proposals include manhood suffrage
King Charles concludes an agreement with the Scots
George Fox begins to preach
John Wilmot, earl of Rochester, born

1648 Cromwell dismisses the general council of the army
The Second Civil War begins
Fairfax defeats the Kentish royalists at Maidstone
Cromwell defeats the Scots at Preston
The Thirty Years' War ended by the treaty of Westphalia
Parliament purged by the army

1649–1660 **Commonwealth**

1649 King Charles I tried and executed
The monarchy and the House of Lords abolished
The Commonwealth proclaimed
Cromwell invades Ireland and defeats the royalist Catholic forces
Death of Richard Crashaw

1650 Cromwell defeats the Scots at Dunbar

1651 Charles II crowned king of the Scots, at Scone
Charles II invades England, is defeated at Worcester, escapes to France
Thomas Hobbes's *Leviathan*

1652 War with Holland

1653 The Rump Parliament dissolved by the army
A new Parliament and council of state nominated; Cromwell becomes Lord Protector
Walton's *The Compleat Angler*

1654 Peace concluded with Holland
War against Spain

1655 Parliament attempts to reduce the army and is dissolved
Rule of the major-generals

1656 Sir William Davenant produces *The Siege of Rhodes,* one of the first English operas

1657 Second Parliament of the Protectorate
Cromwell is offered and declines the throne
Death of Richard Lovelace

CHRONOLOGY

1658   Death of Oliver Cromwell
Richard Cromwell succeeds as Protector

1659   Conflict between Parliament and the army

1660   General Monck negotiates with Charles II
Charles II offers the conciliatory Declaration of Breda and accepts Parliament's invitation to return
Will's Coffee House established
Sir William Davenant and Thomas Killigrew licensed to set up two companies of players, the Duke of York's and the King's Servants, including actors and actresses
Pepys's *Diary* begun

1660–1685   **Reign of Charles II**

1661   Parliament passes the Act of Uniformity, enjoining the use of the Book of Common Prayer; many Puritan and dissenting clergy leave their livings

1662   Peace Treaty with Spain
King Charles II marries Catherine of Braganza
The Royal Society incorporated (founded in 1660)

1664   War against Holland
New Amsterdam captured and becomes New York
John Vanbrugh born

1665   The Great Plague
Newton discovers the binomial theorem and invents the integral and differential calculus, at Cambridge

1666   The Great Fire of London
Bunyan's *Grace Abounding*
London Gazette founded

1667   The Dutch fleet sails up the Medway and burns English ships
The war with Holland ended by the Treaty of Breda
Milton's *Paradise Lost*
Thomas Sprat's *History of the Royal Society*
Death of Abraham Cowley

1668   Sir Christopher Wren begins to rebuild St. Paul's Cathedral
Triple Alliance formed with Holland and Sweden against France
Dryden's *Essay of Dramatick Poesy*

1670   Alliance formed with France through the secret Treaty of Dover
Pascal's *Pensées*
The Hudson's Bay Company founded
William Congreve born

1671   Milton's *Samson Agonistes* and *Paradise Regained*

1672   War against Holland
Wycherley's *The Country Wife*
King Charles issues the Declaration of Indulgence, suspending penal laws against Nonconformists and Catholics

1673   Parliament passes the Test Act, making acceptance of the doctrines of the Church of England a condition for holding public office

1674   War with Holland ended by the Treaty of Westminster
Deaths of John Milton, Robert Herrick, and Thomas Traherne

1676   Etherege's *The Man of Mode*

1677   Baruch Spinoza's *Ethics*
Jean Racine's *Phèdre*
King Charles's niece, Mary, marries her cousin William of Orange

1678   Fabrication of the so-called popish plot by Titus Oates
Bunyan's *Pilgrim's Progress*
Dryden's *All for Love*
Death of Andrew Marvell
George Farquhar born

1679   Parliament passes the Habeas Corpus Act
Rochester's *A Satire Against Mankind*

1680   Death of John Wilmot, earl of Rochester

1681   Dryden's *Absalom and Achitophel* (Part 1)

1682   Dryden's *Absalom and Achitophel* (Part 2)
Thomas Otway's *Venice Preserv'd*
Philadelphia founded
Death of Sir Thomas Browne

1683   The Ashmolean Museum, the world's first public museum, opens at Oxford
Death of Izaak Walton

CHRONOLOGY

CHRONOLOGY

1713	War with France ended by the Treaty of Utrecht
	The *Guardian* founded
	Swift becomes dean of St. Patrick's, Dublin
	Addison's *Cato*
	Laurence Sterne born
1714–1727	**Reign of George I**
1714	Pope's expanded version of *The Rape of the Lock* (Cantos 1–5)
1715	The Jacobite rebellion in Scotland
	Pope's translation of Homer's *Iliad* (1715–1720)
	Death of Louis XIV
1716	Death of William Wycherley
	Thomas Gray born
1717	Pope's *Eloisa to Abelard*
	David Garrick born
	Horace Walpole born
1718	Quadruple Alliance (Britain, France, the Netherlands, the German Empire) in war against Spain
1719	Defoe's *Robinson Crusoe*
	Death of Joseph Addison
1720	Inoculation against smallpox introduced in Boston
	War against Spain
	The South Sea Bubble
	Defoe's *Captain Singleton* and *Memoirs of a Cavalier*
1721	Tobias Smollett born
	William Collins born
1722	Defoe's *Moll Flanders*, *Journal of the Plague Year*, and *Colonel Jack*
1724	Defoe's *Roxana*
	Swift's *The Drapier's Letters*
1725	Pope's translation of Homer's *Odyssey* (1725–1726)
1726	Swift's *Gulliver's Travels*
	Voltaire in England (1726–1729)
	Death of Sir John Vanbrugh
1727–1760	**Reign of George II**
1728	Gay's *The Beggar's Opera*
	Pope's *The Dunciad* (Books 1–2)
	Oliver Goldsmith born
1729	Swift's *A Modest Proposal*
	Edmund Burke born
	Deaths of William Congreve and Sir Richard Steele
1731	Navigation improved by introduction of the quadrant
	Pope's *Moral Essays* (1731–1735)

	Death of Daniel Defoe
	William Cowper born
1732	Death of John Gay
1733	Pope's *Essay on Man* (1733–1734)
	Lewis Theobald's edition of Shakespeare
1734	Voltaire's *Lettres philosophiques*
1737	Edward Gibbon born
1738	Johnson's *London*
1740	War of the Austrian Succession, 1740–1748 (King George's War in America, 1744–1748)
	George Anson begins his circumnavigation of the world (1740–1744)
	Frederick the Great becomes king of Prussia (1740–1786)
	Richardson's *Pamela* (1740–1741)
	James Boswell born
1742	Fielding's *Joseph Andrews*
	Edward Young's *Night Thoughts* (1742–1745)
	Pope's *The New Dunciad* (Book 4)
1744	Johnson's *Life of Mr. Richard Savage*
	Death of Alexander Pope
1745	Second Jacobite rebellion, led by Charles Edward, the Young Pretender
	Death of Jonathan Swift
1746	The Young Pretender defeated at Culloden
	Collins' *Odes on Several Descriptive and Allegorical Subjects*
1747	Richardson's *Clarissa Harlowe* (1747–1748)
	Franklin's experiments with electricity announced
	Voltaire's *Essai sur les moeurs*
1748	War of the Austrian Succession ended by the Peace of Aix-la-Chapelle
	Smollett's *Adventures of Roderick Random*
	David Hume's *Enquiry Concerning Human Understanding*
	Montesquieu's *L'Esprit des lois*
1749	Fielding's *Tom Jones*
	Johnson's *The Vanity of Human Wishes*
	Bolingbroke's *Idea of a Patriot King*
1750	The *Rambler* founded (1750–1752)

CHRONOLOGY

1751 Gray's *Elegy Written in a Country Churchyard*
Fielding's *Amelia*
Smollett's *Adventures of Peregrine Pickle*
Denis Diderot and Jean le Rond d'Alembert begin to publish the *Encyclopédie* (1751–1765)
Richard Brinsley Sheridan born

1752 Frances Burney and Thomas Chatterton born

1753 Richardson's *History of Sir Charles Grandison* (1753–1754)
Smollett's *The Adventures of Ferdinand Count Fathom*

1754 Hume's *History of England* (1754–1762)
Death of Henry Fielding
George Crabbe born

1755 Lisbon destroyed by earthquake
Fielding's *Journal of a Voyage to Lisbon* published posthumously
Johnson's *Dictionary of the English Language*

1756 The Seven Years' War against France, 1756–1763 (the French and Indian War in America, 1755–1760)
William Pitt the Elder becomes prime minister
Johnson's proposal for an edition of Shakespeare

1757 Robert Clive wins the battle of Plassey, in India
Gray's "The Progress of Poesy" and "The Bard"
Burke's *Philosophical Enquiry into the Origin of Our Ideas of the Sublime and Beautiful*
Hume's *Natural History of Religion*
William Blake born

1758 The *Idler* founded (1758–1760)

1759 Capture of Quebec by General James Wolfe
Johnson's *History of Rasselas, Prince of Abyssinia*
Voltaire's *Candide*
The British Museum opens
Sterne's *The Life and Opinions of Tristram Shandy* (1759–1767)
Death of William Collins
Mary Wollenstonecraft born
Robert Burns born

1760–1820 **Reign of George III**

1760 James Macpherson's *Fragments of Ancient Poetry Collected in the Highlands of Scotland*
William Beckford born

1761 Jean Jacques Rousseau's *Julie, ou la nouvelle Héloïse*
Death of Samuel Richardson

1762 Rousseau's *Du Contrat social* and *Émile*
Catherine the Great becomes czarina of Russia (1762–1796)

1763 The Seven Years' War ended by the Peace of Paris
Smart's *A Song to David*

1764 James Hargreaves invents the spinning jenny

1765 Parliament passes the Stamp Act to tax the American colonies
Johnson's edition of Shakespeare
Walpole's *The Castle of Otranto*
Thomas Percy's *Reliques of Ancient English Poetry*
Blackstone's *Commentaries on the Laws of England* (1765–1769)

1766 The Stamp Act repealed
Swift's *Journal to Stella* first published in a collection of his letters
Goldsmith's *The Vicar of Wakefield*
Smollett's *Travels Through France and Italy*
Lessing's *Laokoon*
Rousseau in England (1766–1767)

1768 Sterne's *A Sentimental Journey Through France and Italy*
The Royal Academy founded by George III
First edition of the *Encyclopaedia Britannica*
Maria Edgeworth born
Death of Laurence Sterne

1769 David Garrick organizes the Shakespeare Jubilee at Stratford-upon-Avon
Sir Joshua Reynolds' *Discourses* (1769–1790)
Richard Arkwright invents the spinning water frame

1770 Boston Massacre
Burke's *Thoughts on the Cause of the Present Discontents*

CHRONOLOGY

Oliver Goldsmith's *The Deserted Village*

Death of Thomas Chatterton

William Wordsworth born

1771 Arkwright's first spinning mill founded

Deaths of Thomas Gray and Tobias Smollett

Walter Scott born

1772 Samuel Taylor Coleridge born

1773 Boston Tea Party

Goldsmith's *She Stoops to Conquer*

Johann Wolfgang von Goethe's *Götz von Berlichingen*

1774 The first Continental Congress meets in Philadelphia

Goethe's *Sorrows of Young Werther*

Death of Oliver Goldsmith

Robert Southey born

1775 Burke's speech on American taxation

American War of Independence begins with the battles of Lexington and Concord

Samuel Johnson's *Journey to the Western Islands of Scotland*

Richard Brinsley Sheridan's *The Rivals* and *The Duenna*

Beaumarchais's *Le Barbier de Séville*

James Watt and Matthew Boulton begin building steam engines in England

Births of Jane Austen, Charles Lamb, Walter Savage Landor, and Matthew Lewis

1776 American Declaration of Independence

Edward Gibbon's *Decline and Fall of the Roman Empire* (1776–1788)

Adam Smith's *Inquiry into the Nature & Causes of the Wealth of Nations*

Thomas Paine's *Common Sense*

Death of David Hume

1777 Maurice Morgann's *Essay on the Dramatic Character of Sir John Falstaff*

Sheridan's *The School for Scandal* first performed (published 1780)

General Burgoyne surrenders at Saratoga

1778 The American colonies allied with France

Britain and France at war

Captain James Cook discovers Hawaii

Death of William Pitt, first earl of Chatham

Deaths of Jean Jacques Rousseau and Voltaire

William Hazlitt born

1779 Johnson's *Prefaces to the Works of the English Poets* (1779–1781); reissued in 1781 as *The Lives of the Most Eminent English Poets*

Sheridan's *The Critic*

Samuel Crompton invents the spinning mule

Death of David Garrick

1780 The Gordon Riots in London

1781 Charles Cornwallis surrenders at Yorktown

Burney's *Cecilia*

Immanuel Kant's *Critique of Pure Reason*

Friedrich von Schiller's *Die Räuber*

1782 William Cowper's "The Journey of John Gilpin" published in the *Public Advertiser*

Pierre de Laclos's *Les Liaisons dangereuses*

Rousseau's *Confessions* published posthumously

1783 American War of Independence ended by the Definitive Treaty of Peace, signed at Paris

William Blake's *Poetical Sketches*

George Crabbe's *The Village*

William Pitt the Younger becomes prime minister

Henri Beyle (Stendhal) born

1784 Beaumarchais's *Le Mariage de Figaro* first performed (published 1785)

Death of Samuel Johnson

1785 Warren Hastings returns to England from India

James Boswell's *The Journey of a Tour of the Hebrides, with Samuel Johnson, LL.D.*

Cowper's *The Task*

Edmund Cartwright invents the power loom

Thomas De Quincey born

Thomas Love Peacock born

CHRONOLOGY

1786 William Beckford's *Vathek* published in English (originally written in French in 1782)

Robert Burns's *Poems Chiefly in the Scottish Dialect*

Wolfgang Amadeus Mozart's *The Marriage of Figaro*

Death of Frederick the Great

1787 The Committee for the Abolition of the Slave Trade founded in England

The Constitutional Convention meets at Philadelphia; the Constitution is signed

1788 The trial of Hastings begins on charges of corruption of the government in India

The Estates-General of France summoned

U.S. Constitution is ratified

George Washington elected president of the United States

Giovanni Casanova's *Histoire de ma fuite* (first manuscript of his memoirs)

The *Daily Universal Register* becomes the *Times* (London)

George Gordon, Lord Byron born

1789 The Estates-General meets at Versailles

The National Assembly (Assemblée Nationale) convened

The fall of the Bastille marks the beginning of the French Revolution

The National Assembly draws up the Declaration of Rights of Man and of the Citizen

First U.S. Congress meets in New York

Blake's *Songs of Innocence*

Jeremy Bentham's *Introduction to the Principles of Morals and Legislation* introduces the theory of utilitarianism

Gilbert White's *Natural History of Selborne*

1790 Congress sets permanent capital city site on the Potomac River

First U.S. Census

Burke's *Reflections on the Revolution in France*

Blake's *The Marriage of Heaven and Hell*

Edmund Malone's edition of Shakespeare

Wollstonecraft's *A Vindication of the Rights of Men*

Death of Benjamin Franklin

1791 French royal family's flight from Paris and capture at Varennes; imprisonment in the Tuileries

Bill of Rights is ratified

Paine's *The Rights of Man* (1791–1792)

Boswell's *The Life of Johnson*

Burns's *Tam o'Shanter*

The *Observer* founded

1792 The Prussians invade France and are repulsed at Valmy

September massacres

The National Convention declares royalty abolished in France

Washington reelected

New York Stock Exchange opens

Mary Wollstonecraft's *Vindication of the Rights of Woman*

William Bligh's voyage to the South Sea in HMS *Bounty*

Percy Bysshe Shelley born

1793 Trial and execution of Louis XVI and Marie Antoinette

France declares war against England

The Committee of Public Safety (Comité de Salut Public) established

Eli Whitney devises the cotton gin

William Godwin's *An Enquiry Concerning Political Justice*

Blake's *Visions of the Daughters of Albion and America*

Wordsworth's *An Evening Walk* and *Descriptive Sketches*

1794 Execution of Georges Danton and Maximilien de Robespierre

Paine's *The Age of Reason* (1794–1796)

Blake's *Songs of Experience*

Ann Radcliffe's *The Mysteries of Udolpho*

Death of Edward Gibbon

1795 The government of the Directory established (1795–1799)

Hastings acquitted

CHRONOLOGY

Landor's *Poems*
Death of James Boswell
John Keats born
Thomas Carlyle born

1796 Napoleon Bonaparte takes command in Italy
Matthew Lewis' *The Monk*
John Adams elected president
Death of Robert Burns

1797 The peace of Campo Formio: extinction of the Venetian Republic
XYZ Affair
Mutinies in the Royal Navy at Spithead and the Nore
Blake's *Vala, Or the Four Zoas* (first version)
Mary Shelley born
Deaths of Edmund Burke, Mary Wollstonecraft, and Horace Walpole

1798 Napoleon invades Egypt
Horatio Nelson wins the battle of the Nile
Wordsworth's and Coleridge's *Lyrical Ballads*
Landor's *Gebir*
Thomas Malthus' *Essay on the Principle of Population*

1799 Napoleon becomes first consul
Pitt introduces first income tax in Great Britain
Sheridan's *Pizarro*
Honoré de Balzac born
Thomas Hood born
Alexander Pushkin born

1800 Thomas Jefferson elected president
Alessandro Volta produces electricity from a cell
Library of Congress established
Death of William Cowper
Thomas Babington Macaulay born

1801 First census taken in England

1802 The Treaty of Amiens marks the end of the French Revolutionary War
The *Edinburgh Review* founded

1803 England's war with France renewed
The Louisiana Purchase
Robert Fulton propels a boat by steam power on the Seine

1804 Napoleon crowned emperor of the French
Jefferson reelected
Blake's *Milton* (1804–1808) and *Jerusalem*
The Code Napoleon promulgated in France
Beethoven's *Eroica* Symphony
Schiller's *Wilhelm Tell*
Benjamin Disraeli born

1805 Napoleon plans the invasion of England
Battle of Trafalgar
Battle of Austerlitz
Beethoven's *Fidelio* first produced
Scott's *Lay of the Last Minstrel*

1806 Scott's *Marmion*
Death of William Pitt
Death of Charles James Fox
Elizabeth Barrett born

1807 France invades Portugal
Aaron Burr tried for treason and acquitted
Byron's *Hours of Idleness*
Charles and Mary Lamb's *Tales from Shakespeare*
Thomas Moore's *Irish Melodies*
Wordsworth's *Ode on the Intimations of Immortality*

1808 National uprising in Spain against the French invasion
The Peninsular War begins
James Madison elected president
Covent Garden theater burned down
Goethe's *Faust* (Part 1)
Beethoven's Fifth Symphony completed
Lamb's *Specimens of English Dramatic Poets*

1809 Drury Lane theater burned down and rebuilt
The *Quarterly Review* founded
Byron's *English Bards and Scotch Reviewers*
Byron sails for the Mediterranean
Goya's *Los Desastres de la guerra* (1809–1814)
Alfred Tennyson born
Edward Fitzgerald born

1810 Crabbe's *The Borough*
Scott's *The Lady of the Lake*
Elizabeth Gaskell born

xxiv

CHRONOLOGY

1811–1820 **Regency of George IV**
1811 Luddite Riots begin
Coleridge's *Lectures on Shakespeare* (1811–1814)
Jane Austen's *Sense and Sensibility*
Shelley's *The Necessity of Atheism*
John Constable's *Dedham Vale*
William Makepeace Thackeray born
1812 Napoleon invades Russia; captures and retreats from Moscow
United States declares war against England
Henry Bell's steamship *Comet* is launched on the Clyde river
Madison reelected
Byron's *Childe Harold* (Cantos 1–2)
The Brothers Grimm's *Fairy Tales* (1812–1815)
Hegel's *Science of Logic*
Robert Browning born
Charles Dickens born
1813 Wellington wins the battle of Vitoria and enters France
Jane Austen's *Pride and Prejudice*
Byron's *The Giaour* and *The Bride of Abydos*
Shelley's *Queen Mab*
Southey's *Life of Nelson*
1814 Napoleon abdicates and is exiled to Elba; Bourbon restoration with Louis XVIII
Treaty of Ghent ends the war between Britain and the United States
Jane Austen's *Mansfield Park*
Byron's *The Corsair* and *Lara*
Scott's *Waverley*
Wordsworth's *The Excursion*
1815 Napoleon returns to France (the Hundred Days); is defeated at Waterloo and exiled to St. Helena
USS *Fulton*, the first steam warship, built
Scott's *Guy Mannering*
Schlegel's *Lectures on Dramatic Art and Literature* translated
Wordsworth's *The White Doe of Rylstone*
Anthony Trollope born
1816 Byron leaves England permanently
The Elgin Marbles exhibited in the British Museum

James Monroe elected president
Jane Austen's *Emma*
Byron's *Childe Harold* (Canto 3)
Coleridge's *Christabel. Kubla Khan: A Vision. The Pains of Sleep*
Benjamin Constant's *Adolphe*
Goethe's *Intalienische Reise*
Peacock's *Headlong Hall*
Scott's *The Antiquary*
Shelley's *Alastor*
Rossini's *Il Barbiere di Siviglia*
Death of Richard Brinsley Sheridan
Charlotte Brontë born
1817 *Blackwood's Edinburgh* magazine founded
Jane Austen's *Northanger Abbey* and *Persuasion*
Byron's *Manfred*
Coleridge's *Biographia Literaria*
Hazlitt's *The Characters of Shakespeare's Plays* and *The Round Table*
Keats's *Poems*
Peacock's *Melincourt*
David Ricardo's *Principles of Political Economy and Taxation*
Death of Jane Austen
Death of Mme de Staël
Branwell Brontë born
Henry David Thoreau born
1818 Byron's *Childe Harold* (Canto 4) and *Beppo*
Hazlitt's *Lectures on the English Poets*
Keat's *Endymion*
Peacock's *Nightmare Abbey*
Scott's *Rob Roy* and *The Heart of Mid-Lothian*
Mary Shelley's *Frankenstein*
Percy Shelley's *The Revolt of Islam*
Emily Brontë born
Karl Marx born
Ivan Sergeyevich Turgenev born
1819 The *Savannah* becomes the first steamship to cross the Atlantic (in 26 days)
Peterloo massacre in Manchester
Byron's *Don Juan* (1819–1824) and *Mazeppa*
Crabbe's *Tales of the Hall*
Géricault's *Raft of the Medusa*
Hazlitt's *Lectures on the English Comic Writers*

CHRONOLOGY

Arthur Schopenhauer's *Die Welt als Wille und Vorstellung* (*The World as Will and Idea*)

Scott's *The Bridge of Lammermoor* and *A Legend of Montrose*

Shelley's *The Cenci,* "The Masque of Anarchy," and "Ode to the West Wind"

Wordsworth's *Peter Bell*

Queen Victoria born

George Eliot born

1820–1830   **Reign of George IV**

1820   Trial of Queen Caroline

Cato Street Conspiracy suppressed; Arthur Thistlewood hanged

Monroe reelected

Missouri Compromise

The *London* magazine founded

Keats's *Lamia, Isabella, The Eve of St. Agnes, and Other Poems*

Hazlitt's *Lectures Chiefly on the Dramatic Literature of the Age of Elizabeth*

Charles Maturin's *Melmoth the Wanderer*

Scott's *Ivanhoe* and *The Monastery*

Shelley's *Prometheus Unbound*

Anne Brontë born

1821   Greek War of Independence begins

Liberia founded as a colony for freed slaves

Byron's *Cain, Marino Faliero, The Two Foscari,* and *Sardanapalus*

Hazlitt's *Table Talk* (1821–1822)

Scott's *Kenilworth*

Shelley's *Adonais* and *Epipsychidion*

Death of John Keats

Death of Napoleon

Charles Baudelaire born

Feodor Dostoyevsky born

Gustave Flaubert born

1822   The Massacres of Chios (Greeks rebel against Turkish rule)

Byron's *The Vision of Judgment*

De Quincey's *Confessions of an English Opium-Eater*

Peacock's *Maid Marian*

Scott's *Peveril of the Peak*

Shelley's *Hellas*

Death of Percy Bysshe Shelley

Matthew Arnold born

1823   Monroe Doctrine proclaimed

Byron's *The Age of Bronze* and *The Island*

Lamb's *Essays of Elia*

Scott's *Quentin Durward*

1824   The National Gallery opened in London

John Quincy Adams elected president

The *Westminster Review* founded

Beethoven's Ninth Symphony first performed

James Hogg's *The Private Memoirs and Confessions of a Justified Sinner*

Landor's *Imaginary Conversations* (1824–1829)

Scott's *Redgauntlet*

Death of George Gordon, Lord Byron

1825   Inauguration of steam-powered passenger and freight service on the Stockton and Darlington railway

Bolivia and Brazil become independent

Alessandro Manzoni's *I Promessi Sposi* (1825–1826)

1826   André-Marie Ampère's *Mémoire sur la théorie mathématique des phénomènes électrodynamiques*

James Fenimore Cooper's *The Last of the Mohicans*

Disraeli's *Vivian Grey* (1826–1827)

Scott's *Woodstock*

1827   The battle of Navarino ensures the independence of Greece

Josef Ressel obtains patent for the screw propeller for steamships

Heinrich Heine's *Buch der Lieder*

Death of William Blake

1828   Andrew Jackson elected president

Henrik Ibsen born

George Meredith born

Dante Gabriel Rossetti born

Leo Tolstoy born

1829   The Catholic Emancipation Act

Robert Peel establishes the metropolitan police force

Greek independence recognized by Turkey

Balzac begins *La Comédie humaine* (1829–1848)

CHRONOLOGY

Peacock's *The Misfortunes of Elphin*
J. M. W. Turner's *Ulysses Deriding Polyphemus*

1830–1837 Reign of William IV

1830 Charles X of France abdicates and is succeeded by Louis-Philippe
The Liverpool-Manchester railway opened
Tennyson's *Poems, Chiefly Lyrical*
Death of William Hazlitt
Christina Rossetti born

1831 Michael Faraday discovers electromagnetic induction
Charles Darwin's voyage on HMS *Beagle* begins (1831–1836)
The Barbizon school of artists' first exhibition
Nat Turner slave revolt crushed in Virginia
Peacock's *Crotchet Castle*
Stendhal's *Le Rouge et le noir*
Edward Trelawny's *The Adventures of a Younger Son*

1832 The first Reform Bill
Samuel Morse invents the telegraph
Jackson reelected
Disraeli's *Contarini Fleming*
Goethe's *Faust* (Part 2)
Tennyson's *Poems, Chiefly Lyrical*, including "The Lotus-Eaters" and "The Lady of Shalott"
Death of Johann Wolfgang von Goethe
Death of Sir Walter Scott
Lewis Carroll born

1833 Robert Browning's *Pauline*
John Kemble launches the Oxford Movement
The Factory Act
American Anti-Slavery Society founded
Lamb's *Last Essays of Elia*
Carlyle's *Sartor Resartus* (1833–1834)
Pushkin's *Eugene Onegin*
Mendelssohn's *Italian Symphony* first performed

1834 Abolition of slavery in the British Empire
Louis Braille's alphabet for the blind
The Factory Act

Balzac's *Le Père Goriot*
Nikolai Gogol's *Dead Souls* (Part 1, 1834–1842)
Death of Samuel Taylor Coleridge
Death of Charles Lamb
William Morris born

1835 Hans Christian Andersen's *Fairy Tales* (1st ser.)
Robert Browning's *Paracelsus*
Samuel Butler born
Alexis de Tocqueville's *De la Democratie en Amerique* (1835–1840)

1836 Martin Van Buren elected president
Dickens' *Sketches by Boz* (1836–1837)
Landor's *Pericles and Aspasia*

1837–1901 Reign of Queen Victoria

1837 Carlyle's *The French Revolution*
Dickens' *Oliver Twist* (1837–1838) and *Pickwick Papers*
Disraeli's *Venetia* and *Henrietta Temple*

1838 Chartist movement in England
National Gallery in London opened
Elizabeth Barrett Browning's *The Seraphim and Other Poems*
Dickens' *Nicholas Nickleby* (1838–1839)

1839 Louis Daguerre perfects process for producing an image on a silver-coated copper plate
Faraday's *Experimental Researches in Electricity* (1839–1855)
First Chartist riots
Opium War between Great Britain and China

1840 Canadian Act of Union
Queen Victoria marries Prince Albert
Charles Barry begins construction of the Houses of Parliament (1840–1852)
William Henry Harrison elected president
Robert Browning's *Sordello*

1841 New Zealand proclaimed a British colony
James Clark Ross discovers the Antarctic continent
Punch founded
John Tyler succeeds to the presidency after the death of Harrison
Carlyle's *Heroes and Hero-Worship*
Dickens' *The Old Curiosity Shop*

CHRONOLOGY

CHRONOLOGY

1852 The Second Empire proclaimed with Napoleon III as emperor
David Livingstone begins to explore the Zambezi (1852–1856)
Franklin Pierce elected president
Arnold's *Empedocles on Etna*
Thackeray's *The History of Henry Esmond, Esq.*

1853 Crimean War (1853–1856)
Arnold's *Poems,* including "The Scholar Gypsy" and "Sohrab and Rustum"
Charlotte Brontë's *Villette*
Elizabeth Gaskell's *Ruth*

1854 Frederick D. Maurice's Working Men's College founded in London with more than 130 pupils
Battle of Balaklava
Dickens' *Hard Times*
James George Frazer born
Theodor Mommsen's *History of Rome* (1854–1856)
Tennyson's "The Charge of the Light Brigade"
Florence Nightingale in the Crimea (1854–1856)

1855 David Livingstone discovers the Victoria Falls
Robert Browning's *Men and Women*
Elizabeth Gaskell's *North and South*
Olive Schreiner born
Tennyson's *Maud*
Thackeray's *The Newcomes*
Trollope's *The Warden*

1856 The Treaty of Paris ends the Crimean War
Henry Bessemer's steel process invented
James Buchanan elected president
H. Rider Haggard born

1857 The Indian Mutiny begins; crushed in 1858
The Matrimonial Causes Act
Charlotte Brontë's *The Professor*
Elizabeth Barrett Browning's *Aurora Leigh*
Dickens' *Little Dorritt*
Elizabeth Gaskell's *The Life of Charlotte Brontë*
Thomas Hughes's *Tom Brown's School Days*
Trollope's *Barchester Towers*

1858 Carlyle's *History of Frederick the Great* (1858–1865)
George Eliot's *Scenes of Clerical Life*
Morris' *The Defense of Guinevere*
Trollope's *Dr. Thorne*

1859 Charles Darwin's *The Origin of Species*
Dickens' *A Tale of Two Cities*
Arthur Conan Doyle born
George Eliot's *Adam Bede*
Fitzgerald's *The Rubáiyát of Omar Khayyám*
Meredith's *The Ordeal of Richard Feverel*
Mill's *On Liberty*
Samuel Smiles's *Self-Help*
Tennyson's *Idylls of the King*

1860 Abraham Lincoln elected president
The *Cornhill* magazine founded with Thackeray as editor
James M. Barrie born
William Wilkie Collins' *The Woman in White*
George Eliot's *The Mill on the Floss*

1861 American Civil War begins
Louis Pasteur presents the germ theory of disease
Arnold's *Lectures on Translating Homer*
Dickens' *Great Expectations*
George Eliot's *Silas Marner*
Meredith's *Evan Harrington*
Francis Turner Palgrave's *The Golden Treasury*
Trollope's *Framley Parsonage*
Peacock's *Gryll Grange*
Death of Prince Albert

1862 George Eliot's *Romola*
Meredith's *Modern Love*
Christina Rossetti's *Goblin Market*
Ruskin's *Unto This Last*
Trollope's *Orley Farm*

1863 Thomas Huxley's *Man's Place in Nature*

1864 The Geneva Red Cross Convention signed by twelve nations
Lincoln reelected
Robert Browning's *Dramatis Personae*
John Henry Newman's *Apologia pro vita sua*
Tennyson's *Enoch Arden*
Trollope's *The Small House at Allington*

CHRONOLOGY

CHRONOLOGY

CHRONOLOGY

Stoker's *Dracula*
Wells's *The Invisible Man*

1898 Kitchener defeats the Mahdist forces at Omdurman: the Sudan reoccupied
Hardy's *Wessex Poems*
Henry James's *The Turn of the Screw*
C. S. Lewis born
Shaw's *Caesar and Cleopatra*
Wells's *The War of the Worlds*
Wilde's *The Ballad of Reading Gaol*

1899 The Boer War begins
Elizabeth Bowen born
Noël Coward born
Elgar's *Enigma Variations*
Kipling's *Stalky and Co.*

1900 McKinley reelected
British Labour party founded
Boxer Rebellion in China
Reginald A. Fessenden transmits speech by wireless
First Zeppelin trial flight
Max Planck presents his first paper on the quantum theory
Conrad's *Lord Jim*
Elgar's *The Dream of Gerontius*
Sigmund Freud's *The Interpretation of Dreams*
V. S. Pritchett born
William Butler Yeats's *The Shadowy Waters*

1901–1910 Reign of King Edward VII

1901 William McKinley assassinated; Theodore Roosevelt succeeds to the presidency
First transatlantic wireless telegraph signal transmitted
Chekhov's *Three Sisters*
Freud's *Psychopathology of Everyday Life*
Rudyard Kipling's *Kim*
Thomas Mann's *Buddenbrooks*
Potter's *The Tale of Peter Rabbit*
Shaw's *Captain Brassbound's Conversion*
August Strindberg's *The Dance of Death*

1902 Barrie's *The Admirable Crichton*
Arnold Bennett's *Anna of the Five Towns*
Cézanne's *Le Lac D'Annecy*
Conrad's *Heart of Darkness*

Henry James's *The Wings of the Dove*
William James's *The Varieties of Religious Experience*
Kipling's *Just So Stories*
Maugham's *Mrs. Cradock*
Stevie Smith born
Times Literary Supplement begins publishing

1903 At its London congress the Russian Social Democratic Party divides into Mensheviks, led by Plekhanov, and Bolsheviks, led by Lenin
The treaty of Panama places the Canal Zone in U.S. hands for a nominal rent
Motor cars regulated in Britain to a 20-mile-per-hour limit
The Wright brothers make a successful flight in the United States
Burlington magazine founded
Samuel Butler's *The Way of All Flesh* published posthumously
Cyril Connolly born
George Gissing's *The Private Papers of Henry Ryecroft*
Thomas Hardy's *The Dynasts*
Henry James's *The Ambassadors*
Alan Paton born
Shaw's *Man and Superman*
Synge's *Riders to the Sea* produced in Dublin
Yeat's *In the Seven Woods* and *On Baile's Strand*

1904 Roosevelt elected president
Russo-Japanese war (1904–1905)
Construction of the Panama Canal begins
The ultraviolet lamp invented
The engineering firm of Rolls Royce founded
Barrie's *Peter Pan* first performed
Cecil Day Lewis born
Chekhov's *The Cherry Orchard*
Conrad's *Nostromo*
Henry James's *The Golden Bowl*
Kipling's *Traffics and Discoveries*
Georges Rouault's *Head of a Tragic Clown*
G. M. Trevelyan's *England Under the Stuarts*

Puccini's *Madame Butterfly*
First Shaw-Granville Barker season
at the Royal Court Theatre
The Abbey Theatre founded in
Dublin

1905 Russian sailors on the battleship
Potemkin mutiny
After riots and a general strike the
czar concedes demands by the
Duma for legislative powers, a
wider franchise, and civil liber-
ties
Albert Einstein publishes his first
theory of relativity
The Austin Motor Company
founded
Bennett's *Tales of the Five Towns*
Claude Debussy's *La Mer*
E. M. Forster's *Where Angels Fear to
Tread*
Henry Green born
Richard Strauss's *Salome*
H. G. Wells's *Kipps*
Oscar Wilde's *De Profundis*

1906 Liberals win a landslide victory in
the British general election
The Trades Disputes Act legitimizes
peaceful picketing in Britain
Captain Dreyfus rehabilitated in
France
J. J. Thomson begins research on
gamma rays
The U.S. Pure Food and Drug Act
passed
Churchill's *Lord Randolph Churchill*
William Empson born
Galsworthy's *The Man of Property*
Kipling's *Puck of Pook's Hill*
Shaw's *The Doctor's Dilemma*
Yeats's *Poems 1899–1905*

1907 Exhibition of cubist paintings in
Paris
Henry Adams' *The Education of
Henry Adams*
Henri Bergson's *Creative Evolution*
Conrad's *The Secret Agent*
Daphne du Maurier born
Forster's *The Longest Journey*
Christopher Fry born
André Gide's *La Porte étroite*
Shaw's *John Bull's Other Island* and
Major Barbara

Synge's *The Playboy of the Western
World*
Trevelyan's *Garibaldi's Defence of the
Roman Republic*

1908 Herbert Asquith becomes prime
minister
David Lloyd George becomes
chancellor of the exchequer
William Howard Taft elected presi-
dent
The Young Turks seize power in Is-
tanbul
Henry Ford's Model T car pro-
duced
Bennett's *The Old Wives' Tale*
Pierre Bonnard's *Nude Against the
Light*
Georges Braque's *House at L'Es-
taque*
Chesterton's *The Man Who Was
Thursday*
Jacob Epstein's *Figures* erected in
London
Forster's *A Room with a View*
Anatole France's *L'Ile des Pingouins*
Henri Matisse's *Bonheur de Vivre*
Elgar's First Symphony
Ford Madox Ford founds the *En-
glish Review*

1909 The Young Turks depose Sultan
Abdul Hamid
The Anglo-Persian Oil Company
formed
Louis Bleriot crosses the English
Channel from France by mono-
plane
Admiral Robert Peary reaches the
North Pole
Freud lectures at Clark University
(Worcester, Mass.) on psycho-
analysis
Serge Diaghilev's Ballets Russes
opens in Paris
Galsworthy's *Strife*
Hardy's *Time's Laughingstocks*
Malcolm Lowry born
Claude Monet's *Water Lilies*
Stephen Spender born
Trevelyan's *Garibaldi and the Thou-
sand*
Well's *Tono-Bungay* first published
(in book form, 1909)

CHRONOLOGY

1910–1936 **Reign of King George V**
1910 The Liberals win the British general election
Marie Curie's *Treatise on Radiography*
Arthur Evans excavates Knossos
Edouard Manet and the first post-impressionist exhibition in London
Filippo Marinetti publishes "Manifesto of the Futurist Painters"
Norman Angell's *The Great Illusion*
Bennett's *Clayhanger*
Forster's *Howards End*
Galsworthy's *Justice* and *The Silver Box*
Kipling's *Rewards and Fairies*
Rimsky-Korsakov's *Le Coq d'or*
Stravinsky's *The Firebird*
Vaughan Williams' *A Sea Symphony*
Wells's *The History of Mr. Polly*
Wells's *The New Machiavelli* first published (in book form, 1911)
1911 Lloyd George introduces National Health Insurance Bill
Suffragette riots in Whitehall
Roald Amundsen reaches the South Pole
Bennett's *The Card*
Chagall's *Self Portrait with Seven Fingers*
Conrad's *Under Western Eyes*
D. H. Lawrence's *The White Peacock*
Katherine Mansfield's *In a German Pension*
Edward Marsh edits *Georgian Poetry*
Moore's *Hail and Farewell* (1911–1914)
Flann O'Brien born
Strauss's *Der Rosenkavalier*
Stravinsky's *Petrouchka*
Trevelyan's *Garibaldi and the Making of Italy*
Wells's *The New Machiavelli*
Mahler's *Das Lied von der Erde*
1912 Woodrow Wilson elected president
SS *Titanic* sinks on its maiden voyage
Five million Americans go to the movies daily; London has four hundred movie theaters
Second post-impressionist exhibition in London
Bennett's and Edward Knoblock's *Milestones*
Constantin Brancusi's *Maiastra*
Wassily Kandinsky's *Black Lines*
D. H. Lawrence's *The Trespasser*
1913 Second Balkan War begins
Henry Ford pioneers factory assembly technique through conveyor belts
Epstein's *Tomb of Oscar Wilde*
New York Armory Show introduces modern art to the world
Alain-Fournier's *Le Grand Meaulnes*
Freud's *Totem and Tabu*
D. H. Lawrence's *Sons and Lovers*
Mann's *Death in Venice*
Proust's *Du Côte de Chez Swann* (first volume of *À la recherche du temps perdu*, 1913–1922)
Barbara Pym born
Ravel's *Daphnis and Chloé*
1914 The Panama Canal opens (formal dedication on 12 July 1920)
Irish Home Rule Bill passed in the House of Commons
Archduke Franz Ferdinand assassinated at Sarajevo
World War I begins
Battles of the Marne, Masurian Lakes, and Falkland Islands
Joyce's *Dubliners*
Shaw's *Pygmalion* and *Androcles and the Lion*
Yeats's *Responsibilities*
Wyndham Lewis publishes *Blast* magazine and *The Vorticist Manifesto*
1915 The Dardanelles campaign begins
Britain and Germany begin naval and submarine blockades
The *Lusitania* is sunk
Hugo Junkers manufactures the first fighter aircraft
Poison gas used for the first time
First Zeppelin raid in London
Brooke's *1914: Five Sonnets*
Norman Douglas' *Old Calabria*
D. W. Griffith's *The Birth of a Nation*
Gustav Holst's *The Planets*
D. H. Lawrence's *The Rainbow*

CHRONOLOGY

Wyndham Lewis's *The Crowd*
Maugham's *Of Human Bondage*
Pablo Picasso's *Harlequin*
Sibelius' Fifth Symphony

1916 Evacuation of Gallipoli and the Dardanelles
Battles of the Somme, Jutland, and Verdun
Britain introduces conscription
The Easter Rebellion in Dublin
Asquith resigns and David Lloyd George becomes prime minister
The Sykes-Picot agreement on the partition of Turkey
First military tanks used
Wilson reelected
Henri Barbusse's *Le Feu*
Griffith's *Intolerance*
Joyce's *Portrait of the Artist as a Young Man*
Jung's *Psychology of the Unconscious*
Moore's *The Brook Kerith*
Edith Sitwell edits *Wheels* (1916–1921)
Wells's *Mr. Britling Sees It Through*

1917 United States enters World War I
Czar Nicholas II abdicates
The Balfour Declaration on a Jewish national home in Palestine
The Bolshevik Revolution
Georges Clemenceau elected prime minister of France
Lenin appointed chief commissar; Trotsky appointed minister of foreign affairs
Conrad's *The Shadow-Line*
Douglas' *South Wind*
Eliot's *Prufrock and Other Observations*
Modigliani's *Nude with Necklace*
Sassoon's *The Old Huntsman*
Prokofiev's *Classical Symphony*
Yeats's *The Wild Swans at Coole*

1918 Wilson puts forward Fourteen Points for World Peace
Central Powers and Russia sign the Treaty of Brest-Litovsk
Execution of Czar Nicholas II and his family
Kaiser Wilhelm II abdicates
The Armistice signed

Women granted the vote at age thirty in Britain
Brooke's *Collected Poems*
Gerard Manley Hopkins' *Poems*
Joyce's *Exiles*
Lewis's *Tarr*
Sassoon's *Counter-Attack*
Oswald Spengler's *The Decline of the West*
Strachey's *Eminent Victorians*
Béla Bartók's *Bluebeard's Castle*
Charlie Chaplin's *Shoulder Arms*

1919 The Versailles Peace Treaty signed
J. W. Alcock and A. W. Brown make first transatlantic flight
Ross Smith flies from London to Australia
National Socialist party founded in Germany
Benito Mussolini founds the Fascist party in Italy
Sinn Fein Congress adopts declaration of independence in Dublin
Eamon De Valera elected president of Sinn Fein party
Communist Third International founded
Lady Astor elected first woman Member of Parliament
Prohibition in the United States
John Maynard Keynes's *The Economic Consequences of the Peace*
Eliot's *Poems*
Maugham's *The Moon and Sixpence*
Shaw's *Heartbreak House*
The Bauhaus school of design, building, and crafts founded by Walter Gropius
Amedeo Modigliani's *Self-Portrait*

1920 The League of Nations established
Warren G. Harding elected president
Senate votes against joining the League and rejects the Treaty of Versailles
The Nineteenth Amendment gives women the right to vote
White Russian forces of Denikin and Kolchak defeated by the Bolsheviks
Karel Čapek's *R.U.R.*
Galsworthy's *In Chancery* and *The Skin Game*

Sinclair Lewis' *Main Street*
Katherine Mansfield's *Bliss*
Matisse's *Odalisques* (1920–1925)
Ezra Pound's *Hugh Selwyn Mauberly*
Paul Valéry's *Le Cimetière Marin*
Yeats's *Michael Robartes and the Dancer*

1921　Britain signs peace with Ireland
First medium-wave radio broadcast in the United States
The British Broadcasting Corporation founded
Braque's *Still Life with Guitar*
Chaplin's *The Kid*
Aldous Huxley's *Crome Yellow*
Paul Klee's *The Fish*
D. H. Lawrence's *Women in Love*
John McTaggart's *The Nature of Existence* (vol. 1)
Moore's *Héloïse and Abélard*
Eugene O'Neill's *The Emperor Jones*
Luigi Pirandello's *Six Characters in Search of an Author*
Shaw's *Back to Methuselah*
Strachey's *Queen Victoria*

1922　Lloyd George's Coalition government succeeded by Bonar Law's Conservative government
Benito Mussolini marches on Rome and forms a government
William Cosgrave elected president of the Irish Free State
The BBC begins broadcasting in London
Lord Carnarvon and Howard Carter discover Tutankhamen's tomb
The PEN club founded in London
The *Criterion* founded with T. S. Eliot as editor
Kingsley Amis born
Eliot's *The Waste Land*
A. E. Housman's *Last Poems*
Joyce's *Ulysses*
D. H. Lawrence's *Aaron's Rod* and *England, My England*
Sinclair Lewis' *Babbitt*
O'Neill's *Anna Christie*
Pirandello's *Henry IV*
Edith Sitwell's *Façade*
Virginia Woolf's *Jacob's Room*
Yeats's *The Trembling of the Veil*

1923　The Union of Soviet Socialist Republics established
French and Belgian troops occupy the Ruhr in consequence of Germany's failure to pay reparations
Mustafa Kemal (Ataturk) proclaims Turkey a republic and is elected president
Warren G. Harding dies; Calvin Coolidge becomes president
Stanley Baldwin succeeds Bonar Law as prime minister
Adolf Hitler's attempted coup in Munich fails
Time magazine begins publishing
E. N. da C. Andrade's *The Structure of the Atom*
Brendan Behan born
Bennett's *Riceyman Steps*
Churchill's *The World Crisis* (1923–1927)
J. E. Flecker's *Hassan* produced
Nadine Gordimer born
Paul Klee's *Magic Theatre*
Lawrence's *Kangaroo*
Rainer Maria Rilke's *Duino Elegies* and *Sonnets to Orpheus*
Sibelius' Sixth Symphony
Picasso's *Seated Woman*
William Walton's *Façade*

1924　Ramsay MacDonald forms first Labour government, loses general election, and is succeeded by Stanley Baldwin
Calvin Coolidge elected president
Noël Coward's *The Vortex*
Forster's *A Passage to India*
Mann's *The Magic Mountain*
Shaw's *St. Joan*

1925　Reza Khan becomes shah of Iran
First surrealist exhibition held in Paris
Alban Berg's *Wozzeck*
Chaplin's *The Gold Rush*
John Dos Passos' *Manhattan Transfer*
Theodore Dreiser's *An American Tragedy*
Sergei Eisenstein's *Battleship Potemkin*
F. Scott Fitzgerald's *The Great Gatsby*
André Gide's *Les Faux Monnayeurs*
Hardy's *Human Shows and Far Phantasies*

Huxley's *Those Barren Leaves*
Kafka's *The Trial*
O'Casey's *Juno and the Paycock*
Virginia Woolf's *Mrs. Dalloway* and *The Common Reader*
Brancusi's *Bird in Space*
Shostakovich's First Symphony
Sibelius' *Tapiola*

1926 Ford's *A Man Could Stand Up*
Gide's *Si le grain ne meurt*
Hemingway's *The Sun Also Rises*
Kafka's *The Castle*
D. H. Lawrence's *The Plumed Serpent*
T. E. Lawrence's *Seven Pillars of Wisdom* privately circulated
Maugham's *The Casuarina Tree*
O'Casey's *The Plough and the Stars*
Puccini's *Turandot*

1927 General Chiang Kai-shek becomes prime minister in China
Trotsky expelled by the Communist party as a deviationist; Stalin becomes leader of the party and dictator of the Soviet Union
Charles Lindbergh flies from New York to Paris
J. W. Dunne's *An Experiment with Time*
Freud's *Autobiography* translated into English
Albert Giacometti's *Observing Head*
Ernest Hemingway's *Men Without Women*
Fritz Lang's *Metropolis*
Wyndham Lewis' *Time and Western Man*
F. W. Murnau's *Sunrise*
Proust's *Le Temps retrouvé* posthumously published
Stravinsky's *Oedipus Rex*
Virginia Woolf's *To the Lighthouse*

1928 The Kellogg-Briand Pact, outlawing war and providing for peaceful settlement of disputes, signed in Paris by sixty-two nations, including the Soviet Union
Herbert Hoover elected president
Women's suffrage granted at age twenty-one in Britain
Alexander Fleming discovers penicillin

Bertolt Brecht and Kurt Weill's *The Three-Penny Opera*
Eisenstein's *October*
Huxley's *Point Counter Point*
Christopher Isherwood's *All the Conspirators*
D. H. Lawrence's *Lady Chatterley's Lover*
Wyndham Lewis' *The Childermass*
Matisse's *Seated Odalisque*
Munch's *Girl on a Sofa*
Shaw's *Intelligent Woman's Guide to Socialism*
Virginia Woolf's *Orlando*
Yeats's *The Tower*

1929 The Labour party wins British general election
Trotsky expelled from the Soviet Union
Museum of Modern Art opens in New York
Collapse of U.S. stock exchange begins world economic crisis
Robert Bridges's *The Testament of Beauty*
William Faulkner's *The Sound and the Fury*
Robert Graves's *Goodbye to All That*
Hemingway's *A Farewell to Arms*
Ernst Junger's *The Storm of Steel*
Hugo von Hoffmansthal's *Poems*
Henry Moore's *Reclining Figure*
J. B. Priestley's *The Good Companions*
Erich Maria Remarque's *All Quiet on the Western Front*
Shaw's *The Applecart*
R. C. Sheriff's *Journey's End*
Edith Sitwell's *Gold Coast Customs*
Thomas Wolfe's *Look Homeward, Angel*
Virginia Woolf's *A Room of One's Own*
Yeats's *The Winding Stair*
Second surrealist manifesto; Salvador Dali joins the surrealists
Epstein's *Night and Day*
Mondrian's *Composition with Yellow Blue*

1930 Allied occupation of the Rhineland ends
Mohandas Gandhi opens civil disobedience campaign in India

The Daily Worker, journal of the British Communist party, begins publishing

J. W. Reppe makes artificial fabrics from an acetylene base

John Arden born

Auden's *Poems*

Coward's *Private Lives*

Eliot's *Ash Wednesday*

Wyndham Lewis' *The Apes of God*

Maugham's *Cakes and Ale*

Ezra Pound's *XXX Cantos*

Evelyn Waugh's *Vile Bodies*

1931 The failure of the Credit Anstalt in Austria starts a financial collapse in Central Europe

Britain abandons the gold standard; the pound falls by twenty-five percent

Mutiny in the Royal Navy at Invergordon over pay cuts

Ramsay MacDonald resigns, splits the Cabinet, and is expelled by the Labour party; in the general election the National Government wins by a majority of five hundred seats

The Statute of Westminster defines dominion status

Ninette de Valois founds the Vic-Wells Ballet (eventually the Royal Ballet)

Coward's *Cavalcade*

Dali's *The Persistence of Memory*

John le Carré born

O'Neill's *Mourning Becomes Electra*

Anthony Powell's *Afternoon Men*

Antoine de Saint-Exupéry's *Vol de nuit*

Walton's *Belshazzar's Feast*

Virginia Woolf's *The Waves*

1932 Franklin D. Roosevelt elected president

Paul von Hindenburg elected president of Germany; Franz von Papen elected chancellor

Sir Oswald Mosley founds British Union of Fascists

The BBC takes over development of television from J. L. Baird's company

Basic English of 850 words designed as a prospective international language

The Folger Library opens in Washington, D.C.

The Shakespeare Memorial Theatre opens in Stratford-upon-Avon

Faulkner's *Light in August*

Huxley's *Brave New World*

F. R. Leavis' *New Bearings in English Poetry*

Boris Pasternak's *Second Birth*

Ravel's *Concerto for Left Hand*

Rouault's *Christ Mocked by Soldiers*

Waugh's *Black Mischief*

Yeats's *Words for Music Perhaps*

1933 Roosevelt inaugurates the New Deal

Hitler becomes chancellor of Germany

The Reichstag set on fire

Hitler suspends civil liberties and freedom of the press; German trade unions suppressed

George Balanchine and Lincoln Kirstein found the School of American Ballet

Lowry's *Ultramarine*

André Malraux's *La Condition humaine*

Orwell's *Down and Out in Paris and London*

Gertrude Stein's *The Autobiography of Alice B. Toklas*

1934 The League Disarmament Conference ends in failure

The Soviet Union admitted to the League

Hitler becomes Führer

Civil war in Austria; Engelbert Dollfuss assassinated in attempted Nazi coup

Frédéric Joliot and Irene Joliot-Curie discover artificial (induced) radioactivity

Einstein's *My Philosophy*

Fitzgerald's *Tender Is the Night*

Graves's *I, Claudius* and *Claudius the God*

Toynbee's *A Study of History* begins publication (1934–1954)

Waugh's *A Handful of Dust*

CHRONOLOGY

1935 Grigori Zinoviev and other Soviet leaders convicted of treason
Stanley Baldwin becomes prime minister in National Government; National Government wins general election in Britain
Italy invades Abyssinia
Germany repudiates disarmament clauses of Treaty of Versailles
Germany reintroduces compulsory military service and outlaws the Jews
Robert Watson-Watt builds first practical radar equipment
Karl Jaspers' *Suffering and Existence*
Ivy Compton-Burnett's *A House and Its Head*
Eliot's *Murder in the Cathedral*
Barbara Hepworth's *Three Forms*
George Gershwin's *Porgy and Bess*
Greene's *England Made Me*
Isherwood's *Mr. Norris Changes Trains*
Malraux's *Le Temps du mépris*
Yeats's *Dramatis Personae*
Klee's *Child Consecrated to Suffering*
Benedict Nicholson's *White Relief*

1936 Edward VII accedes to the throne in January; abdicates in December

1936–1952   Reign of George VI

1936 German troops occupy the Rhineland
Ninety-nine percent of German electorate vote for Nazi candidates
The Popular Front wins general election in France; Léon Blum becomes prime minister
Roosevelt reelected
The Poplar Front wins general election in Spain
Spanish Civil War begins
Italian troops occupy Addis Ababa; Abyssinia annexed by Italy
BBC begins television service from Alexandra Palace
Auden's *Look, Stranger!*
Auden and Isherwood's *The Ascent of F-6*
A. J. Ayer's *Language, Truth and Logic*
Chaplin's *Modern Times*

Greene's *A Gun for Sale*
Huxley's *Eyeless in Gaza*
Keynes's *General Theory of Employment*
F. R. Leavis' *Revaluation*
Mondrian's *Composition in Red and Blue*
Dylan Thomas' *Twenty-five Poems*
Wells's *The Shape of Things to Come* filmed

1937 Trial of Karl Radek and other Soviet leaders
Neville Chamberlain succeeds Stanley Baldwin as prime minister
China and Japan at war
Frank Whittle designs jet engine
Picasso's *Guernica*
Shostakovich's Fifth Symphony
Magritte's *La Reproduction interdite*
Hemingway's *To Have and Have Not*
Malraux's *L'Espoir*
Orwell's *The Road to Wigan Pier*
Priestley's *Time and the Conways*
Virginia Woolf's *The Years*

1938 Trial of Nikolai Bukharin and other Soviet political leaders
Austria occupied by German troops and declared part of the Reich
Hitler states his determination to annex Sudetenland from Czechoslovakia
Britain, France, Germany, and Italy sign the Munich agreement
German troops occupy Sudetenland
Edward Hulton founds *Picture Post*
Cyril Connolly's *Enemies of Promise*
du Maurier's *Rebecca*
Faulkner's *The Unvanquished*
Graham Greene's *Brighton Rock*
Hindemith's *Mathis der Maler*
Jean Renoir's *La Grande Illusion*
Jean-Paul Sartre's *La Nausée*
Yeats's *New Poems*
Anthony Asquith's *Pygmalion* and Walt Disney's *Snow White*

1939 German troops occupy Bohemia and Moravia; Czechoslovakia incorporated into Third Reich
Madrid surrenders to General Franco; the Spanish Civil War ends

CHRONOLOGY

Italy invades Albania

Spain joins Germany, Italy, and Japan in anti-Comintern Pact

Britain and France pledge support to Poland, Romania, and Greece

The Soviet Union proposes defensive alliance with Britain; British military mission visits Moscow

The Soviet Union and Germany sign nonaggression treaty, secretly providing for partition of Poland between them

Germany invades Poland; Britain, France, and Germany at war

The Soviet Union invades Finland

New York World's Fair opens

Eliot's *The Family Reunion*

Seamus Heaney born

Isherwood's *Good-bye to Berlin*

Joyce's *Finnegans Wake* (1922–1939)

MacNeice's *Autumn Journal*

Powell's *What's Become of Waring?*

1940   Churchill becomes prime minister

Italy declares war on France, Britain, and Greece

General de Gaulle founds Free French Movement

The Battle of Britain and the bombing of London

Roosevelt reelected for third term

Betjeman's *Old Lights for New Chancels*

Angela Carter born

Chaplin's *The Great Dictator*

Disney's *Fantasia*

Greene's *The Power and the Glory*

Hemingway's *For Whom the Bell Tolls*

C. P. Snow's *Strangers and Brothers* (retitled *George Passant* in 1970, when entire sequence of ten novels, published 1940–1970, was entitled *Strangers and Brothers*)

1941   German forces occupy Yugoslavia, Greece, and Crete and invade the Soviet Union

Lend-Lease agreement between the United States and Britain

President Roosevelt and Winston Churchill sign the Atlantic Charter

Japanese forces attack Pearl Harbor; United States declares war on Japan, Germany, Italy; Britain on Japan

Auden's *New Year Letter*

James Burnham's *The Managerial Revolution*

F. Scott Fitzgerald's *The Last Tycoon*

Huxley's *Grey Eminence*

Shostakovich's Seventh Symphony

Tippett's *A Child of Our Time*

Orson Welles's *Citizen Kane*

Virginia Woolf's *Between the Acts*

1942   Japanese forces capture Singapore, Hong Kong, Bataan, Manila

German forces capture Tobruk

U.S. fleet defeats the Japanese in the Coral Sea, captures Guadalcanal

Battle of El Alamein

Allied forces land in French North Africa

Atom first split at University of Chicago

William Beveridge's *Social Insurance and Allied Services*

Albert Camus's *L'Étranger*

Joyce Cary's *To Be a Pilgrim*

Edith Sitwell's *Street Songs*

Waugh's *Put Out More Flags*

1943   German forces surrender at Stalingrad

German and Italian forces surrender in North Africa

Italy surrenders to Allies and declares war on Germany

Cairo conference between Roosevelt, Churchill, Chiang Kai-shek

Teheran conference between Roosevelt, Churchill, Stalin

Eliot's *Four Quartets*

Henry Moore's *Madonna and Child*

Sartre's *Les Mouches*

Vaughan-Williams' Fifth Symphony

1944   Allied forces land in Normandy and southern France

Allied forces enter Rome

Attempted assassination of Hitler fails

Liberation of Paris

U.S. forces land in Philippines

xl

German offensive in the Ardennes
halted
Roosevelt reelected for fourth term
Education Act passed in Britain
Pay-as-You-Earn income tax introduced
Beveridge's *Full Employment in a
Free Society*
Cary's *The Horse's Mouth*
Huxley's *Time Must Have a Stop*
Maugham's *The Razor's Edge*
Sartre's *Huis Clos*
Edith Sitwell's *Green Song and
Other Poems*
Graham Sutherland's *Christ on the
Cross*
Trevelyan's *English Social History*

1945 British and Indian forces open offensive in Burma
Yalta conference between Roosevelt, Churchill, Stalin
Mussolini executed by Italian partisans
Roosevelt dies; Harry S. Truman
becomes president
Hitler commits suicide; German
forces surrender
The Potsdam Peace Conference
The United Nations Charter ratified in San Francisco
The Labour Party wins British General Election
Atomic bombs dropped on Hiroshima and Nagasaki
Surrender of Japanese forces ends
World War II
Trial of Nazi war criminals opens
at Nuremberg
All-India Congress demands British
withdrawal from India
de Gaulle elected president of
French Provisional Government;
resigns the next year
Betjeman's *New Bats in Old Belfries*
Britten's *Peter Grimes*
Orwell's *Animal Farm*
Russell's *History of Western Philosophy*
Sartre's *The Age of Reason*
Edith Sitwell's *The Song of the
Cold*
Waugh's *Brideshead Revisited*

1946 Bills to nationalize railways, coal
mines, and the Bank of England
passed in Britain
Nuremberg Trials concluded
United Nations General Assembly
meets in New York as its permanent headquarters
The Arab Council inaugurated in
Britain
Frederick Ashton's *Symphonic Variations*
Britten's *The Rape of Lucretia*
David Lean's *Great Expectations*
O'Neill's *The Iceman Cometh*
Roberto Rosselini's *Paisà*
Dylan Thomas' *Deaths and Entrances*

1947 President Truman announces program of aid to Greece and Turkey
and outlines the "Truman Doctrine"
Independence of India proclaimed;
partition between India and Pakistan and communal strife between Hindus and Moslems
follow
General Marshall calls for a European recovery program
First supersonic air flight
Britain's first atomic pile at Harwell comes into operation
Edinburgh festival established
Discovery of the Dead Sea Scrolls
in Palestine
Princess Elizabeth marries Philip
Mountbatten, duke of Edinburgh
Auden's *Age of Anxiety*
Camus's *La Peste*
Chaplin's *Monsieur Verdoux*
Lowry's *Under the Volcano*
Priestley's *An Inspector Calls*
Edith Sitwell's *The Shadow of Cain*
Waugh's *Scott-King's Modern Europe*

1948 Gandhi assassinated
Czech Communist Party seizes
power
Pan-European movement (1948–
1958) begins with the formation
of the permanent Organization
for European Economic Cooperation (OEEC)
Berlin airlift begins as the Soviet
Union halts road and rail traffic
to the city

British mandate in Palestine ends; Israeli provisional government formed

Yugoslavia expelled from Soviet bloc

Columbia Records introduces the long-playing record

Truman elected for second term

Greene's *The Heart of the Matter*

Huxley's *Ape and Essence*

Leavis' *The Great Tradition*

Pound's *Cantos*

Priestley's *The Linden Tree*

Waugh's *The Loved One*

1949 North Atlantic Treaty Organization established with headquarters in Brussels

Berlin blockade lifted

German Federal Republic recognized; capital established at Bonn

Konrad Adenauer becomes German chancellor

Mao Tse-tung becomes chairman of the People's Republic of China following Communist victory over the Nationalists

Simone de Beauvoir's *The Second Sex*

Cary's *A Fearful Joy*

Arthur Miller's *Death of a Salesman*

Orwell's *Nineteen Eighty-four*

1950 Korean War breaks out

Nobel Prize for literature awarded to Bertrand Russell

R. H. S. Crossman's *The God That Failed*

T. S. Eliot's *The Cocktail Party*

Fry's *Venus Observed*

Doris Lessing's *The Grass Is Singing*

C. S. Lewis' *The Chronicles of Narnia* (1950–1956)

Wyndham Lewis' *Rude Assignment*

George Orwell's *Shooting an Elephant*

Carol Reed's *The Third Man*

Dylan Thomas' *Twenty-six Poems*

1951 Guy Burgess and Donald Maclean defect from Britain to the Soviet Union

The Conservative party under Winston Churchill wins British general election

The Festival of Britain celebrates both the centenary of the Crystal Palace Exhibition and British postwar recovery

Electric power is produced by atomic energy at Arcon, Idaho

W. H. Auden's *Nones*

Samuel Beckett's *Molloy* and *Malone Dies*

Greene's *The End of the Affair*

Akira Kurosawa's *Rashomon*

Lewis' *Rotting Hill*

Anthony Powell's *A Question of Upbringing* (first volume of *A Dance to the Music of Time*, 1951–1975)

J. D. Salinger's *The Catcher in the Rye*

C. P. Snow's *The Masters*

Igor Stravinsky's *The Rake's Progress*

1952– **Reign of Elizabeth II**

At Eniwetok Atoll the United States detonates the first hydrogen bomb

The European Coal and Steel Community comes into being

Radiocarbon dating introduced to archaeology

Michael Ventris deciphers Linear B script

Dwight D. Eisenhower elected president

Beckett's *Waiting for Gadot*

Charles Chaplin's *Limelight*

Ernest Hemingway's *The Old Man and the Sea*

Arthur Koestler's *Arrow in the Blue*

F. R. Leavis' *The Common Pursuit*

Lessing's *Martha Quest* (first volume of *The Children of Violence*, 1952–1965)

C. S. Lewis' *Mere Christianity*

Thomas' *Collected Poems*

Evelyn Waugh's *Men at Arms* (first volume of *Sword of Honour*, 1952–1961)

Angus Wilson's *Hemlock and After*

1953 Constitution for a European political community drafted

Julius and Ethel Rosenberg executed for passing U.S. secrets to the Soviet Union

CHRONOLOGY

Cease-fire declared in Korea

Edmund Hillary and his Sherpa guide, Tenzing Norkay, scale Mt. Everest

Nobel Prize for literature awarded to Winston Churchill

General Mohammed Naguib proclaims Egypt a republic

Beckett's *Watt*

Joyce Cary's *Except the Lord*

Robert Graves's *Poems 1953*

1954   First atomic submarine, *Nautilus*, is launched by the United States

Dien Bien Phu captured by the Vietminh

Geneva Conference ends French dominion over Indochina

U.S. Supreme Court declares racial segregation in schools unconstitutional

Nasser becomes president of Egypt

Nobel Prize for literature awarded to Ernest Hemingway

Kingsley Amis' *Lucky Jim*

John Betjeman's *A Few Late Chrysanthemums*

William Golding's *Lord of the Flies*

Christopher Isherwood's *The World in the Evening*

Koestler's *The Invisible Writing*

Iris Murdoch's *Under the Net*

C. P. Snow's *The New Men*

Thomas' *Under Milk Wood* published posthumously

1955   Warsaw Pact signed

West Germany enters NATO as Allied occupation ends

The Conservative party under Anthony Eden wins British general election

Cary's *Not Honour More*

Greene's *The Quiet American*

Philip Larkin's *The Less Deceived*

F. R. Leavis' *D. H. Lawrence, Novelist*

Vladimir Nabokov's *Lolita*

Patrick White's *The Tree of Man*

1956   Nasser's nationalization of the Suez Canal leads to Israeli, British, and French armed intervention

Uprising in Hungary suppressed by Soviet troops

Khrushchev denounces Stalin at Twentieth Communist Congress

Eisenhower reelected

Anthony Burgess' *Time for a Tiger*

Golding's *Pincher Martin*

Murdoch's *Flight from the Enchanter*

John Osborne's *Look Back in Anger*

Snow's *Homecomings*

Edmund Wilson's *Anglo-Saxon Attitudes*

1957   The Soviet Union launches the first artificial earth satellite, *Sputnik I*

Eden succeeded by Harold Macmillan

Suez Canal reopened

Eisenhower Doctrine formulated

Parliament receives the Wolfenden Report on Homosexuality and Prostitution

Nobel Prize for literature awarded to Albert Camus

Beckett's *Endgame* and *All That Fall*

Lawrence Durrell's *Justine* (first volume of *The Alexandria Quartet,* 1957–1960)

Ted Hughes's *The Hawk in the Rain*

Murdoch's *The Sandcastle*

V. S. Naipaul's *The Mystic Masseur*

Eugene O'Neill's *Long Day's Journey into Night*

Osborne's *The Entertainer*

Muriel Spark's *The Comforters*

White's *Voss*

1958   European Economic Community established

Khrushchev succeeds Bulganin as Soviet premier

Charles de Gaulle becomes head of France's newly constituted Fifth Republic

The United Arab Republic formed by Egypt and Syria

The United States sends troops into Lebanon

First U.S. satellite, *Explorer 1,* launched

Nobel Prize for literature awarded to Boris Pasternak

Beckett's *Krapp's Last Tape*

John Kenneth Galbraith's *The Affluent Society*

Greene's *Our Man in Havana*

xliii

Murdoch's *The Bell*
Pasternak's *Dr. Zhivago*
Snow's *The Conscience of the Rich*

1959   Fidel Castro assumes power in Cuba
St. Lawrence Seaway opens
The European Free Trade Association founded
Alaska and Hawaii become the forty-ninth and fiftieth states
The Conservative party under Harold Macmillan wins British general election
Brendan Behan's *The Hostage*
Golding's *Free Fall*
Graves's *Collected Poems*
Koestler's *The Sleepwalkers*
Harold Pinter's *The Birthday Party*
Snow's *The Two Cultures and the Scientific Revolution*
Spark's *Memento Mori*

1960   South Africa bans the African National Congress and Pan-African Congress
The Congo achieves independence
John F. Kennedy elected president
The U.S. bathyscaphe *Trieste* descends to 35,800 feet
Publication of the unexpurgated *Lady Chatterley's Lover* permitted by court
Auden's *Hommage to Clio*
Betjeman's *Summoned by Bells*
Pinter's *The Caretaker*
Snow's *The Affair*
David Storey's *This Sporting Life*

1961   South Africa leaves the British Commonwealth
Sierra Leone and Tanganyika achieve independence
The Berlin Wall erected
The New English Bible published
Beckett's *How It Is*
Greene's *A Burnt-Out Case*
Koestler's *The Lotus and the Robot*
Murdoch's *A Severed Head*
Naipaul's *A House for Mr Biswas*
Osborne's *Luther*
Spark's *The Prime of Miss Jean Brodie*
White's *Riders in the Chariot*

1962   John Glenn becomes first U.S. astronaut to orbit earth

The United States launches the spacecraft *Mariner* to explore Venus
Algeria achieves independence
Cuban missile crisis ends in withdrawal of Soviet missiles from Cuba
Adolf Eichmann executed in Israel for Nazi war crimes
Second Vatican Council convened by Pope John XXIII
Nobel Prize for literature awarded to John Steinbeck
Edward Albee's *Who's Afraid of Virginia Woolf?*
Beckett's *Happy Days*
Anthony Burgess' *A Clockwork Orange* and *The Wanting Seed*
Aldous Huxley's *Island*
Isherwood's *Down There on a Visit*
Lessing's *The Golden Notebook*
Nabokov's *Pale Fire*
Aleksandr Solzhenitsyn's *One Day in the Life of Ivan Denisovich*

1963   Britain, the United States, and the Soviet Union sign a test-ban treaty
Britain refused entry to the European Economic Community
The Soviet Union puts into orbit the first woman astronaut, Valentina Tereshkova
Paul VI becomes pope
President Kennedy assassinated; Lyndon B. Johnson assumes office
Nobel Prize for literature awarded to George Seferis
Britten's *War Requiem*
John Fowles's *The Collector*
Murdoch's *The Unicorn*
Spark's *The Girls of Slender Means*
Storey's *Radcliffe*
John Updike's *The Centaur*

1964   Tonkin Gulf incident leads to retaliatory strikes by U.S. aircraft against North Vietnam
Greece and Turkey contend for control of Cyprus
Britain grants licenses to drill for oil in the North Sea
The Shakespeare Quatercentenary celebrated

CHRONOLOGY

Lyndon Johnson elected president

The Labour party under Harold Wilson wins British general election

Nobel Prize for literature awarded to Jean-Paul Sartre

Saul Bellow's *Herzog*

Burgess' *Nothing Like the Sun*

Golding's *The Spire*

Isherwood's *A Single Man*

Stanley Kubrick's *Dr. Strangelove*

Larkin's *The Whitsun Weddings*

Naipaul's *An Area of Darkness*

Peter Shaffer's *The Royal Hunt of the Sun*

Snow's *Corridors of Power*

1965   The first U.S. combat forces land in Vietnam

The U.S. spacecraft *Mariner* transmits photographs of Mars

British Petroleum Company finds oil in the North Sea

War breaks out between India and Pakistan

Rhodesia declares its independence

Ontario power failure blacks out the Canadian and U.S. east coasts

Nobel Prize for literature awarded to Mikhail Sholokhov

Robert Lowell's *For the Union Dead*

Norman Mailer's *An American Dream*

Osborne's *Inadmissible Evidence*

Pinter's *The Homecoming*

Spark's *The Mandelbaum Gate*

1966   The Labour party under Harold Wilson wins British general election

The Archbishop of Canterbury visits Pope Paul VI

Florence, Italy, severely damaged by floods

Paris exhibition celebrates Picasso's eighty-fifth birthday

Fowles's *The Magus*

Greene's *The Comedians*

Osborne's *A Patriot for Me*

Paul Scott's *The Jewel in the Crown* (first volume of *The Raj Quartet*, 1966–1975)

White's *The Solid Mandala*

1967   Thurgood Marshall becomes first black U.S. Supreme Court justice

Six-Day War pits Israel against Egypt and Syria

Biafra's secession from Nigeria leads to civil war

Francis Chichester completes solo circumnavigation of the globe

Dr. Christiaan Barnard performs first heart transplant operation, in South Africa

China explodes its first hydrogen bomb

Golding's *The Pyramid*

Hughes's *Wodwo*

Isherwood's *A Meeting by the River*

Naipaul's *The Mimic Men*

Tom Stoppard's *Rosencrantz and Guildenstern Are Dead*

Orson Welles's *Chimes at Midnight*

Angus Wilson's *No Laughing Matter*

1968   Violent student protests erupt in France and West Germany

Warsaw Pact troops occupy Czechoslovakia

Violence in Northern Ireland causes Britain to send in troops

Tet offensive by Communist forces launched against South Vietnam's cities

Theater censorship ended in Britain

Robert Kennedy and Martin Luther King, Jr., assassinated

Richard M. Nixon elected president

Booker Prize for fiction established

Durrell's *Tunc*

Graves's *Poems 1965–1968*

Osborne's *The Hotel in Amsterdam*

Snow's *The Sleep of Reason*

Solzhenitsyn's *The First Circle* and *Cancer Ward*

Spark's *The Public Image*

1969   Humans set foot on the moon for the first time when astronauts descend to its surface in a landing vehicle from the U.S. spacecraft *Apollo 11*

The Soviet unmanned spacecraft *Venus V* lands on Venus

Capital punishment abolished in Britain

Colonel Muammar Qaddafi seizes power in Libya

Solzhenitsyn expelled from the Soviet Union

Nobel Prize for literature awarded to Samuel Beckett

Carter's *The Magic Toyshop*

Fowles's *The French Lieutenant's Woman*

Storey's *The Contractor*

1970 Civil war in Nigeria ends with Biafra's surrender

U.S. planes bomb Cambodia

The Conservative party under Edward Heath wins British general election

Nobel Prize for literature awarded to Aleksandr Solzhenitsyn

Durrell's *Nunquam*

Hughes's *Crow*

F. R. Leavis and Q. D. Leavis' *Dickens the Novelist*

Snow's *Last Things*

Spark's *The Driver's Seat*

1971 Communist China given Nationalist China's UN seat

Decimal currency introduced to Britain

Indira Gandhi becomes India's prime minister

Nobel Prize for literature awarded to Heinrich Böll

Bond's *The Pope's Wedding*

Naipaul's *In a Free State*

Pinter's *Old Times*

Spark's *Not to Disturb*

1972 The civil strife of "Bloody Sunday" causes Northern Ireland to come under the direct rule of Westminster

Nixon becomes the first U.S. president to visit Moscow and Beijing

The Watergate break-in precipitates presidential scandal in the United States

Eleven Israeli athletes killed by terrorists at Munich Olympics

Nixon reelected

Bond's *Lear*

Snow's *The Malcontents*

Stoppard's *Jumpers*

1973 Britain, Ireland, and Denmark enter European Economic Community

Egypt and Syria attack Israel in the Yom Kippur War

Energy crisis in Britain reduces production to a three-day week

Nobel Prize for literature awarded to Patrick White

Bond's *The Sea*

Greene's *The Honorary Consul*

Lessing's *The Summer Before the Dark*

Murdoch's *The Black Prince*

Shaffer's *Equus*

White's *The Eye of the Storm*

1974 Miners strike in Britain

Greece's military junta overthrown

Emperor Haile Selassie of Ethiopia deposed

President Makarios of Cyprus replaced by military coup

Nixon resigns as U.S. president and is succeeded by Gerald R. Ford

Betjeman's *A Nip in the Air*

Bond's *Bingo*

Durrell's *Monsieur* (first volume of *The Avignon Quintet*, 1974–1985)

Larkin's *The High Windows*

Solzhenitsyn's *The Gulag Archipelago*

Spark's *The Abbess of Crewe*

1975 The U.S. *Apollo* and Soviet *Soyuz* spacecrafts rendezvous in space

The Helsinki Accords on human rights signed

U.S. forces leave Vietnam

King Juan Carlos succeeds Franco as Spain's head of state

Nobel Prize for literature awarded to Eugenio Montale

1976 New U.S. copyright law goes into effect

Israeli commandos free hostages from hijacked plane at Entebbe, Uganda

British and French SST Concordes make first regularly scheduled commercial flights

The United States celebrates its bicentennial

Jimmy Carter elected president

Byron and Shelley manuscripts discovered in Barclay's Bank, Pall Mall

CHRONOLOGY

Hughes's *Seasons' Songs*
Koestler's *The Thirteenth Tribe*
Scott's *Staying On*
Spark's *The Take-over*
White's *A Fringe of Leaves*

1977   Silver jubilee of Queen Elizabeth II celebrated

Egyptian president Anwar el-Sadat visits Israel

"Gang of Four" expelled from Chinese Communist party

First woman ordained in the U.S. Episcopal church

After twenty-nine years in power, Israel's Labour party is defeated by the Likud party

Fowles's *Daniel Martin*
Hughes's *Gaudete*

1978   Treaty between Israel and Egypt negotiated at Camp David

Pope John Paul I dies a month after his coronation and is succeeded by Karol Cardinal Wojtyla, who takes the name John Paul II

Former Italian premier Aldo Moro murdered by left-wing terrorists

Nobel Prize for literature awarded to Isaac Bashevis Singer

Greene's *The Human Factor*
Hughes's *Cave Birds*
Murdoch's *The Sea, The Sea*

1979   The United States and China establish diplomatic relations

Ayatollah Khomeini takes power in Iran and his supporters hold U.S. embassy staff hostage in Teheran

Rhodesia becomes Zimbabwe

Earl Mountbatten assassinated

The Soviet Union invades Afghanistan

The Conservative party under Margaret Thatcher wins British general election

Nobel Prize for literature awarded to Odysseus Elytis

Golding's *Darkness Visible*
Hughes's *Moortown*
Lessing's *Shikasta* (first volume of *Canopus in Argos, Archives*)
Naipaul's *A Bend in the River*
Spark's *Territorial Rights*
White's *The Twyborn Affair*

1980   Iran-Iraq war begins

Strikes in Gdansk give rise to the Solidarity movement

Mt. St. Helen's erupts in Washington State

British steelworkers strike for the first time since 1926

More than fifty nations boycott Moscow Olympics

Ronald Reagan elected president

Burgess's *Earthly Powers*
Golding's *Rites of Passage*
Shaffer's *Amadeus*
Storey's *A Prodigal Child*
Angus Wilson's *Setting the World on Fire*

1981   Greece admitted to the European Economic Community

Iran hostage crisis ends with release of U.S. embassy staff

Twelve Labour MPs and nine peers found British Social Democratic party

Socialist party under François Mitterand wins French general election

Rupert Murdoch buys *The Times* of London

Turkish gunman wounds Pope John Paul II in assassination attempt

U.S. gunman wounds President Reagan in assassination attempt

President Sadat of Egypt assassinated

Nobel Prize for literature awarded to Elias Canetti

Spark's *Loitering with Intent*

1982   Britain drives Argentina's invasion force out of the Falkland Islands

U.S. space shuttle makes first successful trip

Yuri Andropov becomes general secretary of the Central Committee of the Soviet Communist party

Israel invades Lebanon

First artificial heart implanted at Salt Lake City hospital

Bellow's *The Dean's December*
Greene's *Monsignor Quixote*

xlvii

1983   South Korean airliner with 269 aboard shot down after straying into Soviet airspace

U.S. forces invade Grenada following left-wing coup

Widespread protests erupt over placement of nuclear missiles in Europe

The £1 coin comes into circulation in Britain

Australia wins the America's Cup

Nobel Prize for literature awarded to William Golding

Hughes's *River*

Murdoch's *The Philosopher's Pupil*

1984   Konstantin Chernenko becomes general secretary of the Central Committee of the Soviet Communist party

Prime Minister Indira Gandhi of India assassinated by Sikh bodyguards

Reagan reelected

Toxic gas leak at Bhopal, India, plant kills 2,000

British miners go on strike

Irish Republican Army attempts to kill Prime Minister Thatcher with bomb detonated at a Brighton hotel

World Court holds against U.S. mining of Nicaraguan harbors

Golding's *The Paper Men*

Lessing's *The Diary of Jane Somers*

Spark's *The Only Problem*

1985   United States deploys cruise missiles in Europe

Mikhail Gorbachev becomes general secretary of the Soviet Communist party following death of Konstantin Chernenko

Riots break out in Handsworth district (Birmingham) and Brixton

Republic of Ireland gains consultative role in Northern Ireland

State of emergency is declared in South Africa

Nobel Prize for literature awarded to Claude Simon

A. N. Wilson's *Gentlemen in England*

Lessing's *The Good Terrorist*

Murdoch's *The Good Apprentice*

Fowles's *A Maggot*

1986   U.S. space shuttle *Challenger* explodes soon after takeoff

United States attacks Libya

Atomic power plant at Chernobyl destroyed in accident

Corazon Aquino becomes president of the Philippines

Giotto spacecraft encounters Comet Halley

Nobel Prize for literature awarded to Wole Soyinka

Final volume of *Oxford English Dictionary* supplement published

Amis' *The Old Devils*

Ishiguro's *An Artist of the Floating World*

A. N. Wilson's *Love Unknown*

Powell's *The Fisher King*

1987   Gorbachev begins reform of Communist party of the Soviet Union

Stock market collapses

Iran-contra affair reveals that Reagan administration used money from arms sales to Iran to fund Nicaraguan rebels

Palestinian uprising begins in Israeli-occupied territories

Nobel Prize for literature awarded to Joseph Brodsky

Golding's *Close Quarters*

Burgess' *Little Wilson and Big God*

Drabble's *The Radiant Way*

1988   Soviet Union begins withdrawing troops from Afghanistan

Iranian airliner shot down by U.S. Navy over Persian Gulf

War between Iran and Iraq ends

George Bush elected president

Pan American flight 103 destroyed over Lockerbie, Scotland

Nobel Prize for literature awarded to Naguib Mafouz

Greene's *The Captain and the Enemy*

Amis' *Difficulties with Girls*

Rushdie's *Satanic Verses*

1989   Ayatollah Khomeini pronounces death sentence on Salman Rushdie; Great Britain and Iran sever diplomatic relations

F. W. de Klerk becomes president of South Africa

Chinese government crushes student demonstration in Tiananmen Square

Communist regimes are weakened or abolished in Poland, Czechoslovakia, Hungary, East Germany, and Romania

Lithuania nullifies its inclusion in Soviet Union

Nobel Prize for literature awarded to José Cela

Second edition of *Oxford English Dictionary* published

Drabble's *A Natural Curiosity*

Murdoch's *The Message to the Planet*

Amis' *London Fields*

Ishiguro's *The Remains of the Day*

1990   Communist monopoly ends in Bulgaria

Riots break out against community charge in England

First women ordained priests in Church of England

de Klerk announces end of South African emergency measures and freeing of political prisoners, including Nelson Mandela

East and West Germany united

Iraq invades Kuwait

Margaret Thatcher resigns as prime minister and is succeeded by John Major

Nobel Peace Prize awarded to Mikhail Gorbachev

Nobel Prize for literature awarded to Octavio Paz

Amis' *The Folks that Live on the Hill*

Byatt's *Possession*

Pritchett's *Complete Short Stories*

1991   American-led coalition forces Iraqi withdrawal from Kuwait in Persian Gulf War

Rajiv Gandhi assassinated

Civil war breaks out in Yugoslavia; Croatia and Slovenia declare independence.

Bush and Gorbachev sign START agreement to reduce nuclear-weapons arsenals

President Jean-Baptiste Aristide overthrown by military in Haiti

Boris Yeltsin elected president of Russia

Dissolution of the Soviet Union

Nobel Prize for literature awarded to Nadine Gordimer

1992   U.N. Conference on Environment and Development (the "Earth Summit") meets in Rio de Janeiro

Prince Charles and Princess Diana separate

War in Bosnia-Herzegovina intensifies

Bill Clinton elected president in three-way race with Bush and independent candidate H. Ross Perot

Nobel Prize for literature awarded to Derek Walcott

1993   Czechosolvakia divides into the Czech Republic and Slovakia; playwright Vaclav Havel elected president of the Czech Republic.

Britain ratifies Treaty of European Union (the "Maastricht Treaty")

U.S. troops provide humanitarian aid amid famine in Somalia

United States, Canada, and Mexico sign North American Free Trade Agreement

Nobel Prize for literature awarded to Toni Morrison

1994   Nelson Mandela elected president in South Africa's first post-apartheid election

Jean-Baptiste Aristide restored to presidency of Haiti

Clinton health care reforms rejected by Congress

Civil war in Rwanda

Republicans win control of both houses of Congress for first time in forty years

Prime Minister Albert Reynolds of Ireland meets with Gerry Adams, president of Sinn Fein

Nobel Prize for literature awarded to Kenzaburō Ōe

Amis' *You Can't Do Both*

Naipaul's *A Way in the World*

CHRONOLOGY

1995   Britian and Irish Republican Army engage in diplomatic talks
Barings Bank forced into bankruptcy as a result of a maverick bond trader's losses

United States restores full diplomatic relations with Vietnam
NATO initiates air strikes in Bosnia
Death of Stephen Spender
Nobel Prize for literature awarded to Seamus Heaney

List of Contributors

BROOKE ALLEN. Writer and critic. Author of articles on Henry Green, George Bernard Shaw, Wilkie Collins, Evelyn Waugh, David Livingstone, and other nineteenth- and twentieth-century writers. Has contributed reviews and essays to numerous publications, including the *Wall Street Journal, New York Times Book Review, New Criterion, Nineteenth-Century Prose, Common Knowledge, Twentieth-Century Literature,* and *The Encyclopaedia of British Humorists.* She has also been an editor and written for television and the theater. **Rupert Brooke**

NINA AUERBACH. John Welsh Centennial Professor of History and Literature, University of Pennsylvania. Visiting Professor, University of Washington and University of California, Los Angeles. Coeditor of *Forbidden Journeys: Fairy Tales and Fantasies by Victorian Woman Writers.* Books include *Communities of Women; Woman and the Demon; Romantic Imprisonment; Ellen Terry, Player in Her Time; Private Theatricals;* and *Our Vampires, Ourselves.* **Daphne du Maurier**

RICHARD BRAVERMAN. Professor of English and Comparative Literature, Columbia University. Author of *Plots and Counterplots: Sexual Politics and the Body Politic in English Literature, 1660–1730* and of numerous articles on Restoration and eighteenth-century literature in *English Literary History, Clio, Studies in English Literature, British Journal for Eighteenth-Century Studies, Philological Quarterly,* and elsewhere. **Maria Edgeworth**

MASON COOLEY. Professor of English, College of Staten Island (CUNY). Senior Fellow, Columbia University. Author of *The Comic Art of Barbara Pym,* articles in the Scribner Writers Series on Roland Barthes, Barbara Pym, and Hippolyte Taine, and numerous reviews. **Cyril Connolly**

DAVID DAMROSCH. Professor of English and Comparative Literature, Columbia University. Author of articles on ancient, medieval, and modern literature and literary theory and of two books, *The Narrative Covenant* and *We Scholars: Changing the Culture of the University.* General editor of the forthcoming *HarperCollins Anthology of British Literature.* **P. G. Wodehouse**

FRANS DE BRUYN. Associate Professor of English, University of Ottawa. Author of essays on Burke, the eighteenth-century novel, and georgic poetry and agricultural writing. Writer of a forthcoming book on Edmund Burke. **James Thomson**

JOSEPH DONAHUE. Assistant Professor of English, Stevens Institute of Technology. Writer of three books of poetry: *Before Creation, Monitions of the Approach,* and *World Well Broken.* Coeditor of *Primary Trouble: An Anthology of Contemporary American Poetry.* **James George Frazer**

MARGARET ANNE DOODY. Andrew W. Mellon Professor of Humanities and Professor of English, Vanderbilt University. Director of Program in Comparative Literature, Vanderbilt University. Author of *A Natural Passion: A Study of the Novels of Samuel Richardson; Aristotle Detective; The Daring Muse: Augustan Poetry Reconsidered; Frances Burney: The Life in the Works;* and *The True Story of the Novel* (forthcoming). **Frances Burney**

DAVID GALEF. Associate Professor of English, University of Mississippi. Author of *The Supporting Cast: A Study of Flat and Minor Characters* and *Flesh,* a novel. Specialist in British Modernism; also essayist and reviewer for *The Columbia History of the British Novel, Twentieth-Century Literature, Journal of Modern Literature, New York Times, Verbatim,* and many other publications. **Malcolm Lowry**

DAVID GLOVER. Research Fellow in History, Rutgers University. Has published widely on mass communication and popular culture. Author of essays on Wilkie Collins, Bram Stoker, Charles Bukowski, and William S. Burroughs. Coauthor of *The Sociology of Knowledge.* Author of *The Sociology of the Mass Media* and the forthcoming *Vampires, Mummies, and Liberals: Bram Stoker and the Politics of Popular Fiction.* **Dorothy L. Sayers**

CAROL HOWARD. Preceptor in English and Writing, Columbia University; Adjunct Lecturer in Literature and Women's Studies, Purchase College. Has contributed reviews to the *Romanic Review* and the *Women's Review of Books*. Author of a forthcoming study on liberty, authority, and the harem in British women's writing, 1688–1818. Associate Editor of this volume. **Aphra Behn**

CORA KAPLAN. Professor of English, Rutgers University. Author of *Sea Changes: Essays on Culture and Feminism*. Has published widely on feminist theory, women's writing in the nineteenth and twentieth centuries, and popular culture. **Dorothy L. Sayers**

GLENN LONEY. Professor of Theatre, City University of New York, Graduate Center, and Brooklyn College. Editor, the *Modernist*, the quarterly publication of the Art Deco Society of New York. Publications include *Twentieth Century Theatre, American Musical Theatre,* and *The House of Mirth: The Play of the Novel.* **Christopher Fry**

LISA HERMINE MAKMAN. Doctoral candidate, Department of English and Comparative Literature, Columbia University. Preceptor in Literature and the Humanities, Columbia University. **Beatrix Potter**

GITA MAY. Professor of French, Columbia University. Has published extensively on French Enlightenment, post-revolutionary era, eighteenth-century aesthetics, and women in literature, history, and art. Author of *Diderot et Baudelaire, critiques d'art; Stendhal and the Age of Napoleon;* and *Madame Roland and the Age of Revolution.* Publications also include articles on Rousseau, Germaine de Staël, George Sand, and Simone de Beauvoir. **Rebecca West**

ANNE K. MELLOR. Professor of English and Women's Studies, University of California, Los Angeles. Author of *Blake's Human Form Divine; English Romantic Irony; Mary Shelley: Her Life, Her Fiction, Her Monsters;* and *Romanticism and Gender.* **Mary Shelley**

TYRUS H. MILLER. Assistant Professor of Comparative Literature and English, Yale University. Author of essays on Walter Benjamin, John Cage, Ezra Pound, William Empson, Samuel Beckett, Andrea Zanzotto, Michel Leiris, and Georges Bataille. **Cecil Day Lewis**

MARY POOVEY. Professor of English, Johns Hopkins University. Author of *The Proper Lady and the Woman Writer: Ideology as Style in the Works of Mary Wollstonecraft, Mary Shelley, and Jane Austen; Uneven Developments: The Ideological Work of Gender in Mid-Victorian England;* and *Making a Social Body: British Cultural Formation, 1830–1864.* Has also written extensively on late-twentieth-century feminist issues. **Mary Wollstonecraft**

JOHN RICHETTI. Leonard Sugarman Professor of English, University of Pennsylvania. Coeditor of Cambridge University Press Studies in Eighteenth-Century Literature and Thought and editor of *The Columbia History of the British Novel.* Author of books and essays on the early English novel and philosophical prose in the eighteenth century. Books include *Popular Fiction Before Richardson: Narrative Patterns, 1700–1739; Defoe's Narratives: Situations and Structures;* and *Philosophical Writing: Locke, Berkeley, Hume.* **David Hume**

SANFORD SCHWARTZ. Associate Professor of English, Pennsylvania State University, University Park. Author of *The Matrix of Modernism: Pound, Eliot, and Early-Twentieth-Century Thought* and of various essays on modern literary, cultural, and intellectual history. **C. S. Lewis**

ROBERT SQUILLACE. Visiting Assistant Professor, Wittenberg University. Author of "Bennett, Wells, and the Persistence of Realism," in *The Columbia History of the British Novel* and of the forthcoming *Modernity, Modernism, and Arnold Bennett.* Coeditor (with Edward Mendelson) of *Riceyman Steps* by Arnold Bennett. Has also published on Thomas Hardy. **V. S. Pritchett**

HOWARD STEIN. Professor Emeritus, Columbia University. Formerly chairman, Oscar Hammerstein II Center for Theatre Studies. Author of *A Time to Speak* and coeditor of *The Best American Short Plays* series. **James M. Barrie**

JOHN L. TUCKER. Professor of English, Nassau Community College (SUNY). Adjunct Assistant Professor, Department of English and Comparative Literature, Columbia University. **H. Rider Haggard**

ANTHONY WHITING. Independent scholar. Author of a forthcoming study of Wallace Stevens, *The*

Never-Resting Mind: Wallace Stevens' Romantic Theory. **Edward Thomas**

LEONARD WOLF. Emeritus Professor of English Literature and Creative Writing, San Francisco State University. Publications on terror literature and film include *A Dream of Dracula; The Annotated Dracula* (reissued as *The Essential Dracula*); *The Annotated Frankenstein* (reissued as *The Essential Frankenstein*); *Wolf's Complete Book of Terror; Horror: A Connoisseur's Guide to Literature and Film; The Essential Jekyll and Hyde;* and *Doubles, Dummies, and Dolls: A Horror Anthology.* **Bram Stoker**

MICHAEL WOOD. Professor of English, Princeton University. Author of *Stendhal; America in the Movies; García Márquez: One Hundred Years of Solitude;* and *The Magician's Doubts.* **Angela Carter**

BRITISH WRITERS

JAMES M. BARRIE

(1860–1937)

Howard Stein

DURING A LITERARY career that spanned fifty years (1887–1937), Sir James M. Barrie was frequently characterized as a genius. Sir John Hammerton described Barrie's life as "the story of a genius," the subtitle of his 1929 work on the writer; Patrick Braybrooke, commenting in 1924 on *The Little Minister* (1891), noted, "its writer happened to be a genius"; Sir Walter Raleigh, Regius Professor of English Literature at Oxford, when asked to work with Barrie, said, "Of course. Why ever not? After all, Jimmie is a genius, and it isn't every day you're invited to help a genius" (quoted in Asquith, p. 5); and William Lyon Phelps, Lampson Professor of English Literature at Yale University, wrote in 1922, "In the plays of J. M. Barrie, we see the perfect combination—the combination of original genius with mastery of dramatic devices." But it was Robert Louis Stevenson, Barrie's fellow Scotsman, who most appropriately applied the term "genius" to Barrie: in a letter to Henry James, Stevenson said of Barrie, "[there is] stuff in that young man, but he must see and not be too funny. Genius [is] in him, but there's a journalist at his elbow" (quoted in Roy, pp. 60–61). Stevenson was accurate (Barrie had, after all, started out writing for a newspaper), and although Sir Ian Hamilton could say that Barrie wrote like an angel, and the famed actress Mrs. Patrick Campbell could say that Jimmie was a magician, the fact is that no one commenting on his work or talent ever said he was a poet.

The enthusiasm for the label "genius" was inspired by Barrie's wit, his fantasy and inventiveness, his literacy. His journalism was on a very high level; but one seldom associates journalism with genius. Phelps is quite right in assessing Barrie's dramatic technique as extraordinarily well developed, and the fertility with which Barrie invented situations, allowed dramatic discoveries and reversals, and created a population worth re-

membering is indeed impressive. In the mid-1990s, however, just as one would not associate the word "genius" with the work of Alan Ayckbourn or A. R. Gurney, Jr., so today's critical club would not be apt to assign that label to Barrie. Nevertheless, it was Barrie who stood out at Thomas Hardy's funeral where Rudyard Kipling, John Galsworthy, A. E. Housman, Stanley Baldwin, and Ramsay MacDonald were the pallbearers. George Bernard Shaw described the scene: "I looked very well myself, but Barrie, blast him: looked far the most effective. He made himself look 'specially small'" (quoted in Asquith, p. 2).

LIFE

ALTHOUGH Barrie's literary life was almost exclusively that of a writer of comedy, his personal life was plagued with considerable tragedy. When James was six years old, his brother David died as a result of a fall on the ice. Barrie's mother, Margaret Ogilvy, never recovered from that loss, and her son James fanatically began to concentrate on taking David's place in his mother's heart. That relationship, commentators later surmised, was the critical experience in determining the writer. On his thirty-second birthday, James Barrie suffered a second major death in his life, that of his sister's fiancé, James Winter, who died after falling from a horse that Barrie had given him as a wedding present. Barrie then spent the next years constantly blaming himself for having provided Mr. Winter with the cause of his death and deliberately promised to take care of his sister for the rest of her life, a promise he kept until his sister married James Winter's brother. In 1909, after five years of a childless marriage to Mary Ansell, Barrie was informed by his gardener that Mrs. Barrie was carrying on with a constant houseguest, Gilbert Cannan. When Barrie confronted his wife with the charge, she acknowledged its validity, and he demanded a divorce. She later confessed that the marriage had never been consummated and that Barrie had suffered from impotence, for which she encouraged him to seek medical advice. He refused to discuss the matter. After their divorce later that year, Mary married Cannan; Barrie never remarried.

In 1921 yet another tragedy overtook Barrie with the accidental drowning of his adopted son, Michael Davies, one of the children who had inspired the fantasy *Peter Pan*. Barrie had functioned as substitute father for the Davies children after the death of their parents. Cynthia Asquith reports, "Ever since Michael was a little boy Barrie had especially loved him. For many years now he had made him the chief object of his care, his hopes—his dreams. What his death dealt Barrie in shock and in horror cannot—should not—be told" (p. 135). This series of deaths, impotence in his marriage, and betrayal by his wife contributed to the personality of a man frequently given to chronic migraine, increasing short temper, and dramatic swing of moods.

Barrie's losses in life were, however, perhaps softened by the successes he enjoyed. He was born on 9 May 1860 in Kirriemuir, Scotland, into a working-class family that believed in education. Despite the Barries' limited living conditions, James had the good fortune of being educated at Dumfries Academy and Edinburgh University. After receiving a master of arts degree at Edinburgh in 1882, he took up a happy and productive residence as leader writer and subeditor of the *Nottingham Journal* in England. After two years there he was prepared for the great leap to London, where his literary ambitions were soon established.

By the end of his career, Barrie was knighted and made chancellor of Edinburgh University, a strange turn for a literary man. It was not that he had written himself out, nor did he need a regular source of income or university benefits. Before he ascended to the office of chancellor, he had been made a baronet by George V, approved to the order of merit in 1922, and he had received a plethora of honors: LL.D. degrees from Edinburgh and St. Andrews universities, Litt.D. from Oxford and Cambridge. He was recognized as a major literary figure on both sides of the Atlantic and had

amassed a fortune from his theater successes. He had written plays for Charles Frohman, the American impresario, until Frohman's death on the *Lusitania* put an end to his theatrical enterprise. Barrie was known worldwide for *Peter Pan* (1906; first performance 1904) and for his fantasies as well as for his comedies of manners. He took the position of chancellor, then, to give something back. Barrie was a genuine democrat, but unlike Shaw he never engaged in political organizations or battles, never participated in social movements, and never wrote plays or fiction that argued for justice, equality, or conscience, as one would imagine a journalist might. Instead he wrote as an observer, but he took that job as an advocate. He intended to contribute to the democratic nature of Edinburgh's heritage.

EARLY WRITING: PROSE AND FICTION

ALTHOUGH Barrie is best remembered for his dramatic works, he was recognized first as a writer of prose and of fiction, both of which came from his journalistic impulse and experience. *Better Dead* (1888), which was a reworking of a tale by Robert Louis Stevenson, owes as much to Barrie's journalistic background as it does to his familiarity with Stevenson. (When asked in 1930 about seeing the book still in print, Barrie replied, "Better dead.") *Auld Licht Idylls* (1888), on the other hand, was indebted to his mother's tales and anecdotes about the Scottish church into which both mother and son were born:

The reason my books deal with the past instead of with the life I myself have known is simply this, that I soon grow tired of writing tales unless I can see a little girl, of whom my mother has told me, wandering confidently through the pages.

(*Margaret Ogilvy*, p. 25)

The people I see passing up and down these wynds, sitting night-capped on their barrow shafts, hobbling in their blacks to church on Sunday, are less those I saw in my childhood than their fathers and mothers who did these things in the same way when my mother was young.

(quoted in Roy, p. 60)

The influence of his mother's tales on the young James can be found in his book about his mother,

Margaret Ogilvy, published in 1896. Harry Geduld analyzes the psychological influences of Barrie's mother on his writing in *Sir James Barrie* (1971). One commentator, George Blake, said that their mother-son relationship was not only oedipal, but positively fetal. Regardless of the psychological tension that resulted from their relationship, the fact is that the early books, *Auld Licht Idylls, When a Man's Single* (1888), *A Window in Thrums* (1889), *Sentimental Tommy* (1896), and *Margaret Ogilvy,* all owe a considerable debt to the stories and anecdotes passed on to Barrie by his mother. The son with a journalist's gift turned the stories and anecdotes into vignettes packed with wit and charm and color, with the result that he announced himself to the literary scene much like the American writer Sherwood Anderson did with his *Winesburg, Ohio* (1919). With *The Little Minister,* a novel made possible by his mother's stories, convictions, and memories, Barrie not only aroused excitement in the literary community but began to assemble his fortune. With his adaptation of that novel to the stage in 1897 he also established himself internationally as a playwright of consequence.

It was Stevenson once again who saw the limits in the novelist as well as in the person:

The Little Minister ought to have ended badly; we all know it did; and we are infinitely grateful to you for the grace and good feeling with which you lied about it. . . . If you are going to make a book end badly, it must end badly from the beginning. Now your book began to end well. You let yourself fall in love with, and fondle, and smile at your puppets. Once you had done that your honour was committed—at the cost of truth to life you were bound to save them.

(quoted in Roy, pp. 120–121)

Barrie's predilection for happy endings, for providing agreeable experiences for his audience, who came to expect joyous occasions in the theater and in the easy chair, catapulted him to fame and fortune. *The Little Minister* was a success. The novel is composed of three generations and two plots, the whole narrated by the dominie of Glen Quharity, Gavin Ogilvy, to his six-year-old granddaughter. The first plot centers on a love triangle involving Gavin Ogilvy, Margaret Ogilvy, and Adam Dishart. Despite her love for Gavin, an unassertive bookish man, Margaret marries the braggart, masterful Adam. Subsequently Adam disappears, assumed to have drowned at sea but in actuality free to live a life of pleasure. Margaret

marries Gavin and they have a son named Gavin, who makes up the center of the second plot.

The story of Gavin—the little minister—and Babbie, his audacious gypsy, is engaging in the way that an excellent soap opera is engaging; events pile up on top of events, incident after incident, and the suspense is without cease. The novel is filled with mystery, danger, secrets, trickery, and surprise, culminating in a plot twist that provides the desired happy ending. Stevenson correctly cites Rob Dow's martyrdom, which saves Gavin's life at the end of the story, as an artistic lion, what the ancients would have termed a "deus ex machina."

The novel was first published in the monthly magazine *Good Words,* and then collected and received by an eagerly enthusiastic readership. The kind of reception is clear in J. A. Hammerton's review in the *National Observer*:

Here is another book of genius. 'Tis a big word, and one not often used in this place. But we use it now with a full sense of the weight of it, and a clear perception of our own responsibility. Mr. Barrie has played many parts in his time—brief as that time has been— and has played them all well. But he has not given his true measure heretofore. That he had with gaiety, charm, and admirable gift of observation, humor the quaintest and oddest, a singular command of certain sorts of characters—all this we knew. But it is a great and delightful surprise to find him writing what cannot fail to prove the novel of the year: a year, be it remarked, that has witnessed the production of work by such men as George Meredith, Thomas Hardy, and Rudyard Kipling.

(Hammerton, p. 232)

The positive reception encouraged Barrie to adapt the novel to the stage, where he was assured an audience concerned not so much with something well made as with something that might be entertaining. His decision proved to be an inspired choice, for the play, a major commercial success, catapulted Barrie to preeminence in the London theater and made him famous and rich. The dramatic version of *The Little Minister* inspired three movie versions, including the last with Katharine Hepburn as Babbie, the gypsy Lady Rintoul. After the success of the stage version of *The Little Minister,* Barrie devoted himself mainly to the theater, although not exclusively, and the theater took him to its heart; audiences emptied their purses and sang his praises.

EMERGING PLAYWRIGHT

ALTHOUGH *The Little Minister* was not Barrie's first venture into the theater, it was his seminal venture. Earlier plays, such as *Walker, London* (1907; first performed 1892) and *A Professor's Love Story* (first performed 1894), had been commercially acceptable, but they did not capture Barrie for the theater. His experience in America with the producer Charles Frohman, however, was crucial in revealing Barrie's impulses, ambivalence, and ambitions; the experience also dictated his future as a dramatist. When *The Little Minister* was brought to Frohman as a project, his first reaction was to reject it because it was a male actor's play. Frohman wanted a play for rising stage star Maude Adams. Elisabeth Marbury, Barrie's American agent, told the producer that she would get the author to rewrite the play and change the main character from the minister to his wife, the gypsy.

Barrie at first refused outright; but even after he consented to making the necessary changes, the problem of dramatizing *The Little Minister* was by no means solved. Barrie was convinced that no actress in the world could perform his Babbie. Frohman was stymied. He needed to persuade Barrie that not only could an actress master the role but that a specific actress under contract to him, Maude Adams, could do it. He outwitted the innocent, naive, inexperienced Barrie by maneuvering him into a rehearsal space where Barrie would "just happen" to catch sight of Adams performing. Barrie was smitten, thrilled by what he saw, and came rushing back to Frohman with the news that he had found the perfect actress to play Babbie.

The James M. Barrie whose theatrical career was launched under the influence of producer-impresario Charles Frohman was not the James M. Barrie who first entered the London stage. That first entrance was short-lived, but it provides an insight into an aspect of Barrie that was seldom heard from again. The event was a burlesque on Henrik Ibsen, then the rage in the London theater of 1891. Ibsen's plays had been produced in London before, but the harsh and negative reaction to the plays reached the level of scandal in 1891. In January, *A Doll's House* was produced, followed in rapid succession by *Rosmersholm* and *Ghosts*. The accumulation of disgust and outrage was evident in the critical responses to *Ghosts*, which included such phrases as "revoltingly suggestive and blasphemous," "as foul and filthy a concoction as has ever been allowed to disgrace the boards," "a loathsome sore unbandaged, a dirty act done publicly." While the theater was exercising its vituperation, the literary world was being amused by a translator's war between William Archer and Edmond Gosse, two literary figures vying for the championship in a fight for the master's voice. On the heels of all this Sturm und Drang entered the meek and mild James Barrie with his burlesque of Ibsen, which he shyly offered to the great comic actor and producer J. L. Toole.

Ibsen's Ghost; or, Toole Up to Date (published in 1975 as *Ibsen's Ghost: A Play in One Act*) was slipped in after a short farce at Toole's Theatre, on 30 May 1891. It played to packed houses until July of that year and then was not seen again on the stage until November 1960, when it played for a single performance at the Turn of the Centuries Celebration in Liverpool. The play is an outrageous parody. Unaware of the poet in Ibsen, unflustered by the fashionable appeal of plays about women's rights, Barrie ridicules the Ibsen canon mercilessly by offering a play in which Tesman is married to Thea some six years after the death of Hedda Gabler. Barrie also introduces the characters of Thea's grandparents, whose literary ancestry is grounded in Ibsen's *The Wild Duck* and *A Doll's House* and maybe a bit of *Ghosts*. In *Ibsen's Ghost*, Barrie is a satirist of fertile anger, a luxury he seldom allowed himself once his success in the theater was established:

PETER   [Thea's grandfather]: Have we not been happy, Delia?

DELIA   [Peter's Doll]: Because we knew no better. Go on Peter Terence, cast my innocence in my teeth—I know what you will say, that you have been faithful to me. Yes, you have been faithful, and yet you call yourself a man—

PETER: A virtuous woman—

DELIA: Virtuous! Have I ever had a chance of being anything else? I am your wife. We were to be complement and supplement—it was on that understanding you got me, and how have you kept your trust? Peter Terence answer me this. Did you ever take me into low society? Dare you answer yes? You dare not. Of the women who have come to our house during these forty years of ridiculous happiness, was there one who was not a lady? Peter Terence, there was not. You know the world, you see it in all its colours, and yet did you ever bring home a disreputable man to dinner? Not one—Peter Terence. Did you ever make a remark in my presence that was not fit for a lady's ear? Never—When I should have been living my own life, I bore you six children, and did you propose that they should be sent out to nurse because a true woman cannot be bothered with children? I had to bring them all up myself, they called me mother, you stood by and let them call me mother.

PETER: Brandy—
THEA: No!
PETER: But my Duck—
DELIA: No!
PETER: I mean my Wild Duck—

(pp. 41–43)

In a much later play, *Dear Brutus* (1923; first performance 1917), we get something of this almost-savage spirit in a dialogue between a husband, mistress, and wife:

JOANNA [mistress]: That man—he suspects! . . .
PURDIE [husband]: No one minds Lob. My dear, oh my dear!
JOANNA (*faltering*): Yes, but he saw you kiss my hand. Jack, if Mabel were to suspect!
PURDIE (*happily*): There is nothing for her to suspect.
JOANNA (*eagerly*): No, there isn't, is there? . . . Jack, I am not doing anything wrong, am I?
PURDIE: You! (*With an adorable gesture she gives him one of her hands, and manlike he takes the other also.*)
JOANNA: Mabel is your wife, Jack. I should so hate myself if I did anything that was disloyal to her.
. . .
JOANNA: Was that any one in the garden?
PURDIE (*returning from a quest*): There is no one there now.
JOANNA: I am sure I heard some one. If it was Mabel!
. . .
[Mabel enters]
MABEL (*apologetically*): I am so so sorry to interrupt you, Jack; but please wait a moment before you kiss her again.
. . .
JOANNA (*guardedly*): I insist on an explanation. . . . What were you doing in the garden, Mabel?
MABEL (*who has not been so quiet all day*): I was looking for something I had lost.
PURDIE (*hope springing eternal*): Anything important?

MABEL: I used to fancy it, Jack. It is my husband's love. You don't happen to have picked it up, Joanna? If so and you don't set a great store by it I should like it back—the pieces, I mean.

(act 1)

Meanwhile, however, this brand of biting satire appeared in only one other Barrie play, *The Adored One* (first performance 1913; revised as *Seven Women*, first performance 1917), a complete commercial flop.

In *The Adored One*, a lady of magnetic charm, whom everyone calls Leonora, travels in a train with a young daughter who suffers from a cold. A gentleman sitting opposite her refuses to let the window be closed. The mother insists, but the man remains obdurate. At last she opens the door, pushes him out to his death, closes the door, draws up the window, and calmly continues on her journey.

At the inquest she glories in her deed; and in the dock of the Old Bailey, charged with murder, she sits smiling across her bouquet at her friends, quoting Horace to the judge, and obstinately answering the prosecuting counsel's charge with the cry, "But my little girl had a cold!" In the end she is triumphantly acquitted.

This court scene, which occupies the second and third acts, is Gilbertian burlesque. When the accused takes her place in the dock, the whole assembly reverently rises; the counsel for the defense offers the woman his hand in marriage as she stands in the witness box; the judge flirts with her, eyeing her amorously; and the jury begs for her to be allowed to sit with them while they consider the verdict. Could all this be considered amusing as the sequel to an act of murder?

The audience thought not. In his 1941 biography of Barrie, Denis Mackail reports the opening-night response to *The Adored One*. After the first interval a happy audience returned to its seats prepared to enjoy the last two acts of a murder story, but over the course of the evening the climate in the theater cooled considerably:

In the second interval, short as it is, there is a hushed and horrible silence. And as the curtain falls on the last act, something [occurs] that has never happened to the author before. . . . The pink placard of *The Globe* . . . will put the catastrophe into two words: "Baronet Booed."

Such was the verdict on *The Adored One*.

(p. 459)

In rewriting *The Adored One*, Barrie tried desperately to salvage both this script and the evening and to repay the play's producer, Charles Frohman, for the failure by imposing on the last two acts a dream sequence. The audience did not buy the trip to fantasyland, and the play closed as an anomaly in the Barrie canon and in his commercial ventures.

Although Barrie remained, perhaps, a satirist at heart, and although Asquith describes him as carrying an anger that bordered on rage, after the failure of *The Adored One*, Barrie's fury had no outlet in his writing. Avoiding the acerbic expression of Jonathan Swift or Alexander Pope, and without the instincts toward social philosophy of his contemporary George Bernard Shaw, Barrie settled for something more acceptable and charming.

Barrie's significance resides in his plays—*What Every Woman Knows* (1918; first performance 1908) *The Admirable Crichton* (1914; first performance 1902), *Quality Street* (1901; first performance 1902), *Dear Brutus*, *The Twelve-Pound Look* (1914; first performance 1910), *The Old Lady Shows Her Medals* (first performance 1917), and *Shall We Join The Ladies?* (1927; first performance 1921). His immortality, however, resides as the creator of *Peter Pan; or, The Boy Who Would Not Grow Up* (1928; first performance 1904). That play contains the essence of Barrie as a dramatist and as a literary smithy.

PETER PAN

FLIGHT is the operative word in *Peter Pan*, and it is a word that plays a major role throughout Barrie's oeuvre. Instead of confronting reality and sustaining the repercussions, Barrie provides his audience with leaps of fancy that take them to a blessed or haunted island, a mythical kingdom lorded over by either Peter Pan or Captain Hook, a fanciful garden in the domain of a Puck-like character who has nothing to gain nor anything to lose. Barrie's impulse, contrary to Shaw's, is to escape, and his greatest escape of all is *Peter Pan*.

Although written especially for young audiences (the dedication is "To the Five," a reference to the five sons of Arthur and Sylvia Llewelyn Davies on whom he lavished affection), and played throughout the years as a children's play for Christmas, the play has always had a great appeal to adult audiences. In fact, Shaw took seriously the challenge created by Max Beerbohm's critique of the play (the only negative critique from either side of the Atlantic). Shaw told his biographer, Hesketh Pearson:

When *Peter Pan* was in its first great vogue, Max Beerbohm caricatured Barrie reading it to a circle of elderly people and children. The elderlies were beaming with enjoyment: the children were all asleep. I agreed, and wrote *Androcles* to show what a play for children should be like. It should never be childish; nothing offends children more than to play down to them.

(quoted in Geduld, p. 65)

Despite Shaw's gasconade, *Peter Pan* continues to draw audiences all over the world—by 1950, before the musical version with Mary Martin, the play had drawn worldwide audiences of fifteen million people—while *Androcles* has only a limited audience, if an audience at all. *Peter Pan* offers one of those rare aesthetic experiences in which audiences respond in proportion to the development of their own aesthetic and human development. Children experience the play's adventure and its danger while adults smile and sweat at a tale in which the hero is a boy who refuses to become an adult. Peter's desire for eternal youth touches all those who know that great loss occurs in giving up the freedom of a child's world to become an adult. Melville's Bartleby knew that; Goncharov's Oblomov knew that; all those who refuse to accept the responsibility to get a job, get married, and raise a family know that. In Arnold Grisman's story "Rockabye Baby," Willy responds to all the relatives who tell him to "get a job, get married, and raise a family" by asking "Why?" Their response is silence, and Willy says, "They all looked as if I had spit at them."

Beyond the issues of family responsibility and raising children, *Peter Pan* plays with the darker side of human experience, the side that deals with danger, adventure, risk, and excitement. What could be more thrilling to the human spirit than to traffic with pirates and fairies, battle and warfare, unlimited freedom and brutal revenge—and all with the promised return to safety. While playing with fire, Barrie simultaneously plays with water; his device of "believing" in Tinker Bell cuts across both audiences. The children find believing participatory and romantic; the adults discover the power of belief in their own lives, a quality that contemporary audiences find somewhat weak. In the second half of the twentieth century, Barrie's work touches on humanity's loss of the power to believe in anything.

Few if any other theater pieces so engage an audience of both children and adults and provide both with such pleasure. For nearly a hundred years, Peter, Tinker Bell, Captain Hook, Wendy, and all the other characters in *Peter Pan* have brought joy to audiences. They encourage and inspire us to fly away from reality and into another world—to change our lives—and to confront danger and encourage adventure as a means of thrilling our spirits with the possibility of victory and excitement.

The Darlings cannot afford a nurse for their three children and instead have as their guardian angel a Newfoundland dog named Nana. (In his description of the nursery, Barrie says that the Darlings could not, in fact, afford children.) Nana rises at six o'clock and does everything that a good nurse would do. She "turns down" the beds, carries the various articles on the fireguard to the children, escorts the two older children to school with an umbrella in her mouth, and carries the youngest of the children on her back.

Nana reflects the limits in Barrie's metaphor. A metaphor compares the unfamiliar with the familiar in order to illuminate the familiar. Barrie provides us with no illumination by this dog-as-nurse comparison, but he does provide us with a reflection of the Darling household and the family scenes of the day. Nana's first act is to bathe Michael, who in the opening act screams as all children do at bedtime: "I won't go to bed, I won't, I won't. Nana, it isn't six o'clock yet. Two minutes more, please, one minute more? Nana, I won't be bathed, I tell you I will not be bathed." Barrie introduces the family to the audience in a familiar situation and with the most familiar language imaginable. Every parent and every child knows the scene and the words. Nothing is left to the imagination except for the oddity of a dog that functions as a parent (or nurse) and hears English as if it is dog language.

Familiarity is followed by suspense because as Mrs. Darling enters the nursery, she is "startled to see a strange little face outside the window and a hand groping as if it wanted to come in." "Who are you?" she asks, as the unknown disappears. With the entrance of the children, we are in the company of "imaginary" offspring pretending to be parents having a new child. All the audience smiles with recognition. That recognition is rein-

forced by the entrance of Mr. Darling, the father, who cannot tie his tie, who needs the skillful hand of his wife, the master fixer in the household. Mrs. Darling is the one who keeps the family functioning. This turn-of-the-century drama announces that marriage is a woman's job and that the family is her career. But with the tie incident, Mrs. Darling is put to a test, because tying the tie properly around Mr. Darling's neck will free him to go out to dinner, which in turn will free him to go to the office tomorrow, which in turn will free him to keep providing for his children and wife, which will ultimately keep the Darling family from being thrown out into the street, impoverished and homeless. So the drama starts out in a rapid succession of familiarity, suspense, and then a test.

Peter Pan himself represents the human desire both to change one's life and to keep the life of a child. After all, what alternatives do we have? We are programmed by society to grow into responsibility, subordinating our own lives to those of our newly made families, accepting the accountability for our children and living a life of tension and anxiety, because poverty waits in the wings and misfortune just around the corner. Wendy and her brothers see their father's anxiety, and their mother's, and intelligently enough suggest that the play's audience have no part in such a life, by staying young and thereby avoiding it. Peter Pan's fantasy is one part of every human being's fantasy, the other part perhaps being in battle with Captain Hook. The play touches us in many ways, on a practical level: What should we do with our lives? What should we do with our well-nurtured self-interest; can we possibly indulge our every whim and fancy and still remain connected to some community, namely, the family? The classic conflict is dramatized: self-interest in battle with the interests of others. The play continues with many aspects of human desire: love, freedom, danger, adventure, dreams, imagination, and choice. This play requires audiences to announce their belief or lack of belief and to see the results of their vote. What could satisfy an audience more?

Barrie's fertile imagination in the context of the familiar knows no bounds. He takes the stereotypical pirate captain, adds his own hook, and provides Captain Hook with an array of cohorts who are like ordinary people. He invents the crocodile with a ticking clock, an adversary of Hook, who, with the assistance of Peter Pan's superreal talents, manages to capture the pirate chief. He creates from the clichéd Indian stories an Indian princess, Tiger Lily, who is captured and ready to be hoisted onto the rock and left to drown. Barrie describes a stereotypical picture of Indians: "To one of her race this is an end darker than death by fire or torture, for it is written in the laws of the Pickaninnies that there is no path through water to the happy hunting ground. Yet her face is impassive; she is the daughter of a chief and must die as a chief's daughter; it is enough" (act 3).

Barrie's use of the terms "redskins" and "pickaninnies," whatever their source, fall on unsympathetic ears today: boycotts and canceled performances have for the first time entered the life of *Peter Pan*. Whether this reaction will continue to occupy the future of the play remains to be seen.

The rescue of Tiger Lily is accomplished through the trickery and cleverness of Peter Pan, who even adds to her escape the war cry she had forgotten to utter. Barrie uses everything, exploiting the familiar by his addition of imaginative details. The only moment in the play where his dramaturgy falters is in Peter's last and crucial decision, the decision to give up Mother Wendy and let her remain with her own Mrs. Darling. Peter is so moved by the sight of Mrs. Darling's tears that despite his cry— "You will never see Wendy again, lady, for the window is barred!"—within seconds he has changed his mind. He says to Tinker Bell, "Come on, Tink; we don't want any silly mothers." This decision is the major discovery and reversal in the play. Barrie permits the director and the performer to convince us of his choice to leave Wendy behind. The drama only persuades us.

Peter Pan has been created in the first four acts as a character from another reality, fairyland, angel land. When he discovers the joy of having Wendy in his world as mother, he has no reason to let her leave and return to her regular life, leaving him abandoned.

As Barrie was guilty of ending *The Little Minister* with an artistic lie, so he is once again guilty in *Peter Pan. Peter Pan* ends with Peter, a supernatural creation not subject to human nature, succumbing to a human feature, human compassion, in bowing to the tear in Mrs. Darling's eye. He has not been endowed with such human feeling by his creator until that very moment. The moment then becomes artistically suspect. The audience will and does love Barrie's choice; the director and the actor can make that choice into a moving stage moment

for both the children and adults. But in reality, Peter should be no more subject to the tears of Mrs. Darling than Iago would be subject to tears of Desdemona. Those fictional creations have an aesthetic reality that must be honored, and Barrie fails to honor it in this case. The aesthetic truth of the story all hangs together with Hook and Smee and Tiger Lily and the crocodile and Peter and Wendy and the house and all the magical inventiveness. But this final moment escapes that aesthetic reality and strikes a false note: pity.

The author's virtuosity and imagination are constantly on display. The yarn spins relentlessly, one invention topping another. The author even provides us with a third-act curtain line that approaches the best of that tradition: "To die will be an awfully big adventure." With all the goodies, the fact remains that an illumination of the human condition, rather than just a reflection of it, is nowhere to be found.

The idea of flight, with its many variant meanings, so important in *Peter Pan*, is prevalent in Barrie's comedies of manners. The parents in *Alice Sit-by-the-Fire* (1938; first performance 1905) return from their flight to India where they have lived for some time without the burden of raising their own children. The second act of *Dear Brutus* is a flight of fancy, a midsummer night's dream in which everyone in the garden is provided a "second chance" in their lives, presumably to make up for the mistake of the first chance. *Mary Rose* (1938; first performance 1920) is a fantasy in which the major character has a flight so severe and total that it passes with the speed of a moment despite the fact that in our reality it has taken decades. In *The Twelve-Pound Look*, Kate has flown the family coop, leaving Harry Sims behind while she makes her own way with her typing skills. At the end of that play we are left with the second Lady Sims quite seduced by the possibility of her own flight in exactly the same way. There is a dream sequence based on the Cinderella legend in the second act of *A Kiss for Cinderella* (1938; first performance 1916), a wartime story with a reality of war, poverty, disease, abandonment, devastation, even hopelessness. Barrie thus uses flight as a character choice, as a writer's device, and as a theatrical technique.

At the same time, he also gives us plays that speak to endurance, to sustaining. In *Quality Street*, Phoebe and her sister maintain their dignity, courage, and integrity as they endure hardship and betrayal. Led into poverty by a well-meaning but incompetent investment adviser named Valentine, they are suddenly bereft of any assistance in their lives. They exercise ingenuity and imagination in keeping their lives secret, their pain to themselves, and their survival on Quality Street a reality. Rather than fly, they endure. Few characters in dramatic literature reflect more of the sense of endurance than does Crichton in *The Admirable Crichton.* Having displayed his talents as a servant to his masters, he then turns the tables and exercises his talents as the leader of his former masters. He displays his superior character by his ability to survive on an abandoned island and to be solely responsible for the survival of his entire entourage. When he and his original masters finally are saved and returned to their former life, Crichton picks up where he left off as servant to his masters. He returns with grace, dignity, integrity, and conviction. Likewise, at the end of *Alice Sit-by-the-Fire*, Alice faces her own reality and accepts her role as mother, wife, and an aging member of the human race. The characters in *Dear Brutus*, following their adventure in the garden during the second act, return to their lives with resignation and awareness that their characters have determined their experience, and that second chances are like turning over a new leaf when, lo and behold, what you find is the old one flourishing beneath.

CHARACTER AS THEME

CHARACTER as defined by Aristotle in his discussion of the six parts of a tragedy is the "ethical habit of action." Such a definition carries with it a suggestion of integrity, honesty, and courage as well as a moral imperative. This description helps separate character from personality, for personality expresses not ethical behavior but color, charm, wit, and the prevailing mood and temperament of a particular person in either fiction or real life. Barrie has many colorful personalities in his canon, from Babbie, Nana, Lob, Captain Hook, Colonel Grey, and Lady Sybil to all of the fifteen people who inhabit *Shall We Join the Ladies?* But character is equally, if not more, significant to Barrie, as demonstrated by his creation of John Shand, Maggie, Crichton, Kate, Phoebe, and Susan Throssel and the cast of *Dear Brutus*. On a superficial reading of Barrie, one might get the

impression because of his drawing-room comedies that he concentrates on a stereotypical level of characterization by his frequent depiction of stuffy, upper-class, haughty, boring, and even dumb personalities such as Ernest Wooley, Sir Harry Sims, Lord Loam, and the ladies Catherine and Agatha. The list is indeed extensive. But a more careful reading of the plays will give the reader the chance to take pleasure in Barrie's sympathetic nature and compassion for the people he chose to write about.

In *What Every Woman Knows*, Maggie certainly performs with an honorable, virtuous habit of action. This is equally true for Crichton in *The Admirable Crichton*. In *The Twelve-Pound Look*, Kate is a model for virtuous habit, as is Mrs. Dowey in *The Old Lady Shows Her Medals*. In *A Kiss for Cinderella*, Cinderella is an extraordinarily good human being who takes risks caring for four small children, one of whom is German, in her London home when Britain is at war with Germany. Although some have interpreted such creations as expressions of Barrie's sentimentality, one can also recognize Barrie's approval of people who act with an admirable habit of action. Despite John Shand's use in *What Every Woman Knows* of an unethical method—illegal trespassing—to gain his objective of reading books, a luxury his poverty does not allow, he is nevertheless shown to be an honorable Scotsman willing to face his discovery and willing to accept the consequences. He is not unlike Cameron in *Mary Rose* and the venerable Scotsman in Barrie's early journalism, and not unlike Barrie himself who, in his "Address Delivered on Installation as Chancellor of Edinburgh University," said, "I wish I was a little less unworthy of this gown. I will do my best."

Such a population provided for Barrie the means by which to dramatize his plays about the manners, values, behavior, and morals of the upper-crust society he adopted in Great Britain. Barrie's targets are general: hypocrisy, snobbism, indifference, narrow-mindedness. He never establishes specific targets such as the system, war, social class, religion, capitalism, middle-class morality. He is gentle with his attack, if an attack it is, for nothing vicious or harsh informs the lack of character of the upper classes in *Dear Brutus*, *Shall We Join the Ladies?*, *Mary Rose*, or *Alice Sit-by-the-Fire*. Barrie's satire never again reaches the proportions of *Ibsen's Ghost* or *The Adored One*. Members of his audience might have recognized themselves and their failings, but they were not threatened by the display. They were not chastised as they would be in the hands of Shaw.

WHAT EVERY WOMAN KNOWS

BY his own admission Barrie was no preacher. But he had strong ideas about education and society if not about politics and society:

But our universities must remain what our forebears conceived with such great travail, men of the smiddies and the plough, the loom and the bothies, as well as scholars, they must remain, first and foremost something to supply the needs of the genius of the Scottish people. Those needs are that every child born in this country shall as far as possible have an equal chance.
(*The Entrancing Life*, pp. 12–13)

For Barrie, "genius" was defined by Thomas Carlyle, a fellow Scotsman, who described it as "an infinite capacity for taking pains." Barrie's devotion to his heritage as well as to education is expressed in his own words:

Their [various nations] student from his earliest age is being brought up to absorb the ideas of his political rulers. This is all of his education, not merely in his academic studies but in all his social life, all his mind, all his relaxation; they are in control from his birth, and he is to emerge into citizenship with rigid convictions which it is trusted will last his lifetime. The systems vary in different lands, but that seems to be their trend, and I tell you that they are being carried out with thoroughness. Nothing can depart more from the Scottish idea, which I take to be to educate our men and women primarily not for their country's good but for their own, not so much to teach them what to think as how to think, not preparing them to give as little trouble as possible in the future but sending them into it in the hope that they will give trouble.
(*The Entrancing Life*, pp. 13–14)

One of Barrie's most accomplished and famous plays, *What Every Woman Knows*, was inspired by just such convictions, and John Shand is just such a Scotsman, an ambitious young man with an appetite for learning. Barrie sympathetically describes his quality of character when David Wylie responds to Maggie's question, "Is that the student Shand?" "It's true he is a student at Glasgow University in the winter months, but in the summer he's just the railway porter here; and I think it's very presumptuous of a young lad like that to make a speech when he hasn't a penny to bless himself with" (act 1). The conflict between Shand and the Wylies is established immediately. Shand has been sneaking into the Wylie house to read the books the Wylies have stacked in their library: "I'm desperate for want of books. You have all I want here; no use to you but for display; well, I came here to study. I come twice weekly . . . by the window" (act 1). The Wylies are obliged to deal with a situation that they could turn over to the police or turn to their own advantage. Among the three siblings is a marriageable daughter who claims to have no charm, no qualities that would appeal to a marriageable man. The two sons want their sister to marry. They come upon a happy idea: John Shand can use the library, read the books to his heart's content, if he will accept their proposition. David says, "We're willing, the three of us, to lay out 300 pounds on your education if . . . five years from now, Maggie Wylie, if still unmarried, can claim to marry you, should such be her wish; the thing to be perfectly open on her side, but you to be strictly tied down" (act 1).

From that offer springs the drama. John completes his studies, enters politics, extends the agreement for one full year pending the outcome of his campaign for a Parliament seat, wins the election, and despite some political complications, agrees to fulfill his end of the bargain by marrying Maggie. After some few years their marriage is threatened by Lady Sybil, a woman popular with the other politicos and a woman known to have charm; but the marriage survives the intrusion because of Maggie's cleverness, wit, talent, insight, and courage. Although the play is about what every woman knows, it is also about love, marriage, women, and the reckless upper classes.

Barrie invents considerable impediments to the wedding: postponement until Shand succeeds in his ambitions, political colleagues who try to determine Shand's future, Maggie's willingness to give up John by tearing up the contract, John's infatuation with the agreeable Lady Sybil. But in the end, Shand will allow none of the obstacles to deter him from fulfilling his obligations. He marries Maggie and the two remain married. Although Maggie's married life is threatened considerably, in the play's third act, when Maggie is hoisted on the shoulders of her brother, she shouts to all the assembled, including the audience in the theater, "my constituency." And indeed it is her constituency.

John Shand's rise to political office is a direct result of Maggie's having provided humor, levity, and wit to his speeches, although he thinks his strength has been his outspokenness, which is dangerously close to demagoguery. John does not know how to laugh, knows neither humor nor wit, is earnest and good but lacks lightheartedness. Left to his own devices, he would never extract the votes from the public. But Maggie's spirit, infused in his rhetoric, is irresistible, and John is the richer for that.

What every woman knows, then, is that behind every successful man is a determined, brighter, and patient woman. Maggie is the model of such a character. When Lady Sybil and John Shand, who have had an affair, are caught in an embrace, their adventure becomes public knowledge. John wishes to give up his career in order to remain with Lady Sybil. The Wylies are outraged at the possible abandonment of Maggie. Maggie withdraws knowing full well that John will go under if Lady Sybil is the new caretaker of John's sturdy but dull prose. She knows she is necessary for his success and that he will soon see Lady Sybil's limitations. The events turn out just as she anticipates, and John again prospers from Maggie's wit and charm while Lady Sybil tires of John and his earnestness. John discovers the truth about his wife's role in crafting his speeches, and by the end she has helped him find the power to laugh.

What Every Woman Knows is exactly what it says it is: no metaphysics, no lectures on social conscience, no admonitions, no scorn or irreverence. The tale is the tender story of an unattractive twenty-seven-year-old woman with no apparent charm, seemingly doomed to spinsterhood. The Maggie Shand whom we leave at the end of the play is the same Maggie Wylie whom we met at the beginning of the play, but she has found her niche, has dug out of her spirit the very charm that she had been unable to expose in her daily traffic with her community. She has, with courage, exercised her strengths, has found a way to be of use and of value, and has mustered the ability to fight for her own rights and desires. She does not confront battles so much as she employs strategies in order to gain her objectives, strategies that are informed by her own intelligence and insight. No one in the play really gets hurt: Lady Sybil recovers her life after John, the Wylie family survives

the threat to their plans, and the Scottish political scene is not damaged by the turmoil created by John Shand. All of the characters work out a complicated plot sequence that titillates the audience and provides it with just a little bit to think about. Who, indeed, should have the books available? Is marriage a woman's job and the family her career? Audiences might see the questions, but they are unlikely to leave the theater disturbed, uncomfortable, or indifferent. They will leave entertained rather than inspired; charmed rather than aroused.

DEAR BRUTUS

Dear Brutus is a more ambitious play than *What Every Woman Knows*. Although Barrie's style becomes journalistic, intent upon a message, at a critical moment in the play, the play aspires to truth rather than lingering with mere fact. He presents facts in act 3 with the following dialogue that justifies the title of the play:

PURDIE: . . . I haven't the stuff in me to take warning. My whole being is corroded. Shakespeare knew what he was talking about—"The fault, dear Brutus, is not in our stars, but in ourselves, that we are underlings."

JOANNA: For "dear Brutus" we are to read "dear audience," I suppose?

PURDIE: You have it.

JOANNA: Meaning that we have the power to shape ourselves?

PURDIE: We have the power right enough.

JOANNA: But isn't that rather splendid?

PURDIE: For those that have the grit in them, yes.

In *Dear Brutus*, no one has the grit, but the audience has its message.

Rather than put the audience through an experience that would leave them inspired, mystified, anxious, and aroused, Barrie leaves them startled by an imaginary trip through a mysterious wood, amused but baffled with the different realities he has placed before the audience, and thoughtful about their own second chances. The audience may feel as if they have been put through a personal examination of their own self-delusion, but they have not been witness to a struggle with the dark forces of destiny or individual evil. Still, in the Barrie canon, this play comes closest to a willingness to examine the nature of the human spirit, "character" rather than personality, human drives rather than human behavior.

Although the play calls forth parallels with *The Ghost Sonata* of August Strindberg, *The Iceman Cometh* of Eugene O'Neill, and *The Wild Duck* of Ibsen, it does not probe on the same level as those dramas. Rather than unmask its characters, it simply schematizes them. Their second-chance behavior reveals only what they have already demonstrated—their habit of behavior rather than their ethical habit of action. They have experienced discomfort and embarrassment during their adventure in the dream-garden-wood, but they have not been wrung and tattered and torn as have the people in Strindberg, O'Neill, or Ibsen. In fact, a secret resides in a line spoken by Joanna: "You know, we are not people worth being sorrowful about—so let us laugh."

In Strindberg's *Dream Play*, Indra's daughter says over and over again, "Human beings are to be pitied." Strindberg knew that human beings, all human beings doomed and destined to live a lifetime, were to be pitied. He did not distinguish them by social status, intelligence, or profession. Down deep where all human activity resides, the locale for the human condition, human beings were to be pitied for their endurance of an endless series of days and nights. Barrie, like Joanna, presumably did not share the human compassion demonstrated by Strindberg.

Although Barrie remains on the surface, he does not fall into the trap of pretending to be profound. Barrie described himself to a gathering of London critics: "None of your adjectives get to the mark as much as the one I have found for myself—'Inoffensive Barrie.' A bitter pill; but it looks as if on one subject I were the best critic in the room" (in *M'Connachie and J. M. B.*, p. 54). This "inoffensive Barrie" is the author of *Dear Brutus*.

He offers us in this play the familiar once again, but with a twist: What would we change if we were given the opportunity to rectify our mistakes through a second chance? The question is interesting enough, and though it is certainly asked by most human beings during the course of their lives, it makes the audience think that they are thinking on an unfamiliar level. Barrie's scheme seems to smack of a profound experience. In reality, however, the playwright has simply worked out a design, of which he warns us in the very first lines of his stage directions at the beginning

of the play: "Our object is to catch our two chief characters unawares; they are Darkness and Light." The people who struggle with darkness and light seem to be subordinate. Joanna, in fact, at the end of the event, gives us the playwright's, the craftsman's, message: "A strange experiment, Matey; does it ever have a permanent effect?" Matey's answer: "So far as I know, not often, Miss; but I believe once in a while." The audience takes away its own answer; people will indeed take the question out of the theater into their homes. The play may not be as profound as those of other playwrights with a similar subject, but it is a provocative piece.

For a playwright beholden to Aristotle, to examine the "character" of a character in a play, he must invent an unfamiliar situation by which to test a given ethical habit. Claudius, for example, in *Hamlet*, prior to the opening of the play, has solved his ethical choices or made his ethical decisions by sneaky, indirect, secretive, and deceptive methods: pouring poison in the king's ear, usurping the throne, marrying Gertrude. His habit in solving crisis situations is a sneaky, nonconfrontational, unethical habit. In acts 3 and 4, after sending his words to the Lord, after lamenting his own corruption and unethical behavior, after rising from his knees, he is told about Hamlet's having slain Polonius. Claudius' immediate impulse is to solve the problem in a sneaky fashion: send Hamlet off to England on a pretext and then have him slain by pirates. When tested, Claudius reverts to his former convenient habit, just as he does in the last act by poisoning Laertes' foil and by poisoning the glass from which Hamlet is expected to drink.

But Barrie provides a different opportunity for his population. He lets them live out their fantasies, their thoughts of self-deception, and watches them repeat their errors with neither consequences nor revelations. He brings together his cast at a country home in which resides Lob, a Puck-like character—mysterious, bizarre, and as much of a mystery as Robin Goodfellow himself. This group of people, ignorant of the reason for their convening, soon discover that they all have something in common and that they are threatened to have a mysterious experience if they wander out into the garden, which might become a woodland. The members of the group, including Lob's butler, do wander out and experience the mystery of the dream-garden-wood, which in fact is the opportunity for a second chance in life to rectify one's mistakes. With their second chance in act 2, however, each person ends up actually repeating the types of choices they had made in their "first" life, leaving them at the end of the play in much the same condition as when we first met them.

Although the play provides precious little, if any, illumination, and although it offers no real testing of the characters, the play is nevertheless intriguing in the working out of the scheme. Barrie does approach a major question when it comes to examining the human condition. For in "character" resides destiny. However, he provides no one in the play a chance to alter decisions or habits. He is a total fatalist, although he denies his people in the play the experience of danger. He protects them for the sake of his plan. The people in the play do not suffer threat. Their future is not at stake. They are safe from harm, especially since they are not the main concern of the story. They are the instruments on which Barrie plays his tune of the game between darkness and light. Although he may possess something of the tragic vision of Strindberg and O'Neill and Ibsen, his play does not dramatize the tragic vision. It remains on a level of comedy. The answer in Barrie's play may prove to be discouraging, just as in those of the other playwrights, but the journey in Barrie is quite different from that taken in the others.

Lady Caroline, for example, in the first act, the act in which we see all the gathering as they live their real lives, is snobbish, pretentious, haughty, and disdainful in a manner stereotypical of her upper-class station. Matey, Lob's butler, in contrast, behaves in the obsequious manner appropriate to his station. In the dream-garden-wood, Matey becomes Lady Caroline's mate, her choice a direct result of Matey's booming career as a business tycoon. When Matey is discovered to be a jewel thief in act 1, he maintains that he steals only because he was born and raised as a poor child and as a man he has had to resort to burglary in order to support himself. But Matey discovers in the new life of the dream-garden-wood that he steals once again, only now he steals the way a big businessman steals. The fault is not in his stars but in his "character." Lady Caroline's snobbishness turns to servility, for she will do anything to keep a rich husband. The three married couples—the Coades, the Dearths, and the Purdies—are exposed to similar adventures. The Coades (the oldest of the group) learn to live with their unfulfilled lives. Mr. Coade has blamed his second marriage and the loss he feels from the death of his first wife for his procrastination in completing his magnum opus. In the dream-garden-wood, he procrastinates despite no outside stimuli or reasons, just his own desire to procrastinate by dancing and prancing about. Purdie replaces his real-life wife, Mabel, with real-life mistress Joanna; the choice Purdie would have made had he ever been given the opportunity (as he now has) reveals that Purdie is the same philanderer with Joanna as he was with Mabel.

The Dearths undergo a similar dramatic experience, perhaps the most interesting of the couples (and triangles). Mr. Dearth is an unsuccessful artist, one who blames his lack of success on the fact that he and his wife have failed to have a child. Mrs. Dearth is sarcastic, nasty, unrelenting, bitter, and wracked with pain. She blames herself for not having married Freddy Fallow-Finch, with whom she is sure she would have had a much more satisfying life. In the dream-garden-wood she does indeed have as her mate Fred Fallow-Finch, but the marriage ends up as wretched as the marriage with Dearth. In the dream-garden-wood she is an old hag begging for morsels from any who will give them to her. Fred has left her with nothing. During this adventure, she comes upon Dearth and his dream-garden-wood daughter, Margaret, the child he yearned for and never had in his real life, from whom she manipulates some money. She pretends humility, but in actuality is unyielding in her resentment and constant irritation. The sarcastic, embittered Alice Dearth of true life is again possessed of those qualities in her wood life, but the circumstances are very different. She is reduced to poverty and begging in her wood life, and she leaves her generous supporters, Dearth and Margaret, with a kind of curse:

ALICE   (*speaking to Dearth at his easel*): What is her name, Mister?
DEARTH: Margaret.
ALICE: Margaret. You drew something good out of the lucky bag when you got her, Mister.
DEARTH: Yes.
ALICE: Take care of her; they are easily lost.

(act 2)

And Dearth does lose Margaret, first in his realization that the child will become a woman and leave him for her own life and family, and second as the light in Lob's house tempts him into a separation from Margaret. Margaret, on the other hand, is frightened of being alone without her father and without any identity yet and calls out: "Daddy, come back; I don't want to be a might-have-been." Dearth himself has emerged as a might-have-been, an unsuccessful artist. The encounter with Margaret, Dearth's most successful episode in the play, is an anomaly in his life and an engaging episode in the drama. There he does have for a brief time a very happy encounter with his wishes, hopes, and dreams. In act 3 Alice discovers that it is better for her to be with Dearth than with Fallow-Finch, while Dearth discovers that his wife may be a major reason for his having been a waster and an unfulfilled human being. Dearth thanks Lob for the hour he has had with his imaginary daughter. Maybe it offered a little change in his life, maybe even in his wife's life, but of very little consequence. Still the interlude was rich and different. For Barrie the master craftsman, this interlude is not at all well made, but instead a flight of dramaturgy that comes from a warm and compassionate impulse to grant Dearth some satisfaction in his life, even if it throws the drama into a little chaos.

Barrie's *Dear Brutus* shares similarities with Shakespeare's *A Midsummer Night's Dream*—most obvious the day and time that the plays takes place and the presence of the drama maker, Lob—but the most accurate connection between the two may be found in Shakespeare's line, "Lord, what fools these mortals be!"

THE ADMIRABLE CRICHTON

The Admirable Crichton also is a play about "character," but in this case, Barrie does have the play's population undergo a serious test of character. Crichton's integrity, competence, amorous feelings, compassion, and responsibility are tested. He meets the challenge, saving an entire household shipwrecked on an uninhabited island. He maintains their civilized life by building a domicile, cooking the food, organizing the living duties, and finding the means of survival. The butler has become the master, but not only the master in action, the master in love. His servile position at the beginning of the play is handled with distinction, but he is nevertheless a servant in a master's home. On the island he works and performs as the master of the castaways' fate, and everyone else is obliged to accept the position of serving Crichton humbly in order to accomplish the practical tasks of surviving hunger, finding shelter, and creating community. In the third act, the islanders are saved after two years, and as the schematic tendency of Barrie would have it, everything reverts back to its original form: the master is again master, the servant (butler) is again butler, and the love of Crichton's life is again destined for someone from her own class. When Crichton is left with the decision at the end of the play to leap from his social position into a higher realm, he refuses, and demands to remain once again in his "natural" position of serving the upper classes.

Crichton is not just stubborn or stereotypical (the butler who is smarter and more capable than the master is as old as Greek and Roman drama); he is a man with integrity, spirit, wit, and insight. His function in the play is to dramatize Barrie's conviction that civilized society must have classes, one to command, the other to obey.

Although Barrie's target is the indulgent, incompetent, and hypocritical upper-class British society, his message is Darwinian in spirit—it is a representation of the survival of the fittest and of Barrie's conviction that nature has established that the human race will be divided between servants and masters, hammers and nails, haves and have-nots. Just as character to Barrie seems to be an intrinsic quality, a biological determinism, leadership is not determined by master or manservant. It is determined by nature. Cream will rise to the top; those who can drive the carts will appropriate them; the capable will survive, and the infirm will fall or falter.

Lord Loam, Crichton's master, is a man who fancies liberal attitudes. In the 1960s he would have been called an example of radical chic; at the very end of the twentieth century he would have been called politically correct. Believing in the fundamental equality of all human beings, he puts aside his upper-class station once a month to invite his manservant, Crichton, and the "between maid" Tweeny to behave as and to be treated as equals with their master. Crichton detests Lord Loam's habit and dreads the once-a-month occasion. The play opens on such a day, and an upper-class guest named Ernest joins the Loams, Crichton, Tweeny, and the Reverend Treherne on a sea voyage. The voyage ends in a shipwreck, and the fate of the aristocratic household falls into the hands of the one competent member of the group with an ability to survive. The next two acts work out the life on the island, and the fourth act returns to the original house and to the original order of social class. During the middle two acts Lady Mary and Crichton fall in love, but in the fourth act, when Mary encourages Crichton to continue his masterful ways and his secret love for her, Crichton reverts to his true self. In the play's opening act, Crichton is described in such a way as to distinguish him from his master:

To be an indoor servant at all is to Crichton a badge of honour; to be a butler at thirty is the realisation of his proudest ambitions. He is devotedly attached to his master, who, in his opinion, has but one fault, he is not sufficiently contemptuous of his inferiors. We are immediately to be introduced to this solitary failing of a great English peer.

Ladies Catherine and Agatha are the two daughters of the house. Catherine is twenty, and Agatha two years younger. They are very fashionable young women, who might wake up for a dance, but they are otherwise very lazy.

Earl of Loam is a widower, a philanthropist, and a peer of advanced ideas:

He takes in all the weightiest monthly reviews, and prefers those that are uncut, because he perhaps never looks better than when he is cutting them; but he does not read them, and save for the cutting it would suit him as well merely to take in the covers. He writes letters to the papers, which are printed in a type to scale with himself, and he is very jealous of those other correspondents who get his type. Let laws and learning, art and commerce die, but leave the big type to an intellectual aristocracy. He is really the reformed House of Lords which will come some day.

(act 1)

Barrie is quite contemptuous of the values in this house and of the people who parade those values. But getting them shipwrecked on a deserted island does not unmask them; Barrie has unmasked them from the outset. All the island adventure does is provide the audience with more of what they already know about the Loam house.

The Admirable Crichton is arguably the most accomplished of Barrie's plays. A comedy of manners in the classical British sense, its source the Restoration drama, the story of a butler and his master with a cast of fumbling, bumbling people including maids and ladies, provides a satire on the upper-class society of Britain, their fashion, habits, and hypocrisy. Barrie says of Ernest (aptly derived from Oscar Wilde) that he is impervious to satire. Indeed, Barrie demonstrates that all the household of the Earl of Loam is impervious to satire. And in this case Barrie is unrelenting. His target is the fake quality of the British peerage, the radical chic, the haughtiness, indolence, and slothfulness. Ernest is a liar and a fraud: he publishes a book on their island adventures that is totally fabricated; it depicts the upper class as heroes, and the butler and maid as insignificant to their survival. This class demonstrates no humility, no gratitude, no generosity of spirit, no awareness, no humanity, no honor; only unadulterated selfishness, self-interest, vanity, self-preoccupation. Their entire world is their own little island, an island of self. Even more so than in *Dear Brutus*, Barrie reveals this class of British aristocracy as being a sham, without virtue or dignity, but only fashionable and corrupt. The target in this play is clearer and more unrelentingly pursued than in any of the other satire pieces except *Ibsen's Ghost* and *The Adored One*:

LADY MARY: You are the best man among us.
CRICHTON: On an island, my lady, perhaps; but not in England, no.
                        . . .
CRICHTON: My lady, not even from you can I listen to a word against England.

(act 5)

But Lady Mary concludes: "Then there's something wrong with England."

SHORT PLAYS

THREE of Barrie's short plays have substantial value and can justifiably be considered among his best work. *The Twelve-Pound Look*, his own *A Doll's House*, has been hailed by generations of playwriting teachers as a model of the perfect short play. The play is not a well-made play in the tradition of nineteenth-century French farce and melodrama, but a play that is made well in the tradition of *Oedipus* and *Tartuffe*. Kate, yearning for an independent life as a modern English woman, rejecting her role as the Lady Sims, rebels against her chauvinistic mate, Harry. After saving twelve pounds, with which she buys a typewriter, she flies the coop. She later returns to her former home as a typist who has been called to do work for none other than Lord Harry Sims. There she meets the new Lady Sims, who, by the end of the play, expresses wonder about the amount of money one needs to purchase a typewriter. She now has that same twelve-pound look that catapulted Kate out onto the street.

Barrie's craft is in top form. Kate is a woman of courage, ability, independence, and spirit. Sir Harry is the stereotypical upper-class snob. The new Lady Sims is the typical downtrodden lady of the house. Although today not as immediately relevant to the countries of the Western world as at the time of its original presentation, *The Twelve-Pound Look* still stands as the expression of the New Woman's rebellion of the late nineteenth century. The play recognizes early the role that economic freedom would play in the future of women's freedom. It has a position in the British drama comparable to that of Clifford Odets' *Waiting for Lefty* in the American drama. Both plays are "message plays" offering a solution to a social problem, offering good guys and bad guys, with the good guys being victorious. But *The Twelve-Pound Look* gives more energy and attention to the character of Kate than *Waiting for Lefty* gives to either Joe or Edna. Barrie is more generous to his characters, and his sympathy for Kate and the new Lady Sims is obvious. An essay in dramatic form, the play survives and flourishes.

The Old Lady Shows Her Medals is a comedy of manners about the lower economic class of Londontown. But unlike the comedies that satirized the upper classes and their fashionable behavior, this play treats sympathetically the virtuous charwomen and their progeny in their struggle for survival and dignity. Mrs. Dowey and her charmates, her adopted son, Kenneth, and her messenger of good fortune, Mr. Willings, are people of courage, warmth, generosity, color, and resilience.

Mrs. Dowey has no family and no way to contribute to the war effort in World War I. She invents a son, a pen pal, a young soldier about whom she talks to her fellow chars. Soon a Mr. Willings comes to tell Mrs. Dowey and her lady friends that Mrs. Dowey's son is returning home on a five-day leave. The play is about the soldier's visit, his willingness to accept this stranger as his surrogate mother, and their adventures on the furlough that provide her with a reason to live. At the end of the play she is left with the knowledge that he has been killed in the war. In a moving scene, she touches and caresses all the medals (the mementos) from the five-day leave, all the memories of that young man's visit and his attachment to her. The play is an outstanding vehicle for an actress and has endeared itself to a theatergoing community.

The third short piece that deserves attention is *Shall We Join the Ladies?*, the first act of what Barrie intended as a longer play. Barrie never finished the drama, despite the grand reception of its initial presentation, in celebration of the opening of the Royal Academy of Dramatic Art on 27 May 1921, and its subsequent 407 performances at St. Martin's Theatre in 1923. The play, which is a detective mystery story, is itself a mystery. Patrick Braybrooke prefaced his 1924 volume on Barrie, subtitled *A Study in Fairies and Mortals,* with an author's note suggesting that Barrie might finish *Shall We Join the Ladies?*, an appeal that voiced the hopes of many others. But Barrie never budged, and the play remains an unfinished drama in one act.

The story is similar in form to *Dear Brutus:* a collection of people who do not know why they have been invited by a Pickwickian figure to congregate for a week at a country home soon discover the explanation. They have something in common: they all had been in Monte Carlo when the host's brother died. The host, Sam Smith, believes that his brother had been murdered and has assembled all of the prime suspects. The ladies go off to their room while the men remain in theirs. At the end of the act, the men are asked to join the ladies. At that very moment, we hear a "dreadful scream" from the ladies' room. The butler, Dolphin, reappears in the doorway unable to speak, but livid with "mingled horror and appeal" as he looks at his master, Sam Smith, who sits with a glass of brandy, "his rigid little back merciless." As he rises to follow the others, the curtain falls, ending act 1 and the play itself. That someone is going to die that night is in the air, but the air remains forever engulfed in a dense fog.

The play is impeccably constructed with clues and innuendo so abundant that no one is above suspicion. By the end of the act, in fact, everyone among the thirteen guests is a suspect, each having revealed some self-incriminating clue. Barrie's power as a theatrical wizard is at its peak. It is especially important to note that this play is a precursor of J. B. Priestley's *An Inspector Calls* (1947) and the mystery writing of Agatha Christie. The real debt that both Barrie and Priestley owe is to Nikolay Gogol, whose *Government Inspector* (1836) is an unmasking of the political community of nineteenth-century Russia. Gogol's play is based on the same premise as that expressed by Sam Smith in the early scene of Barrie's play. Smith asks Sir Joseph, "Do you really know me? Does any person ever know another absolutely?" *Shall We Join the Ladies?* gives a clue to James M. Barrie's preoccupation with the mask that hides the face.

CONCLUSION

JAMES M. Barrie holds a minor place in nineteenth-century English literature, but he holds a major place in the theatrical world of Western dramatic writing. He has provided us with masterpieces of value and even brilliance. His comedies of manners rank among the very best examples of that genre, which had its beginnings in the second half of the seventeenth century. His limits are real, but his strengths outshine those limits. Would that "inoffensive Barrie" been willing to be more offensive! Had that been the case, we may indeed be celebrating here a genius of the order of W. S. Gilbert. As reality would have it, however, we instead celebrate a talent of considerable, even significant, gift who leaves a major legacy on which the theater of the English-speaking world can build.

SELECTED BIBLIOGRAPHY

I. BIBLIOGRAPHY. Herbert Garland, *A Bibliography of the Writings of Sir James Matthew Barrie* (London, 1928); Carl Markgraf, *J. M. Barrie: An Annotated Secondary Bibliography* (Greensboro, N.C., 1989).

II. COLLECTED WORKS. *The Kirriemuir Edition of the Works of J. M. Barrie*, 10 vols. (London, 1913); *The Plays of J. M. Barrie* (London, 1918–1938), the Uniform edition; *The Works of J. M. Barrie*, 10 vols. (New York, 1918); *The Works of J. M. Barrie*, 14 vols. (New York, 1929), known as the Peter Pan edition; *The Plays of J. M. Barrie: In One Volume* (New York, 1933); A. E. Wilson, ed., *The Plays of J. M. Barrie* (London, 1947).

III. SEPARATE WORKS. *Auld Licht Idylls* (London, 1888); *Better Dead* (London, 1888); *When a Man's Single: A Tale of Literary Life* (London, 1888; New York, 1889); *An Edinburgh Eleven* (London, 1889); *A Window in Thrums* (London, 1889); *My Lady Nicotine* (London, 1890); *The Little Minister* (London, 1891), a novel, later adapted as a play; *Margaret Ogilvy* (London and New York, 1896); *Sentimental Tommy* (London, 1896); *Tommy and Grizel* (London, 1900); *The Little White Bird* (London and New York, 1902); *Peter Pan in Kensington Gardens* (London and New York, 1906; repr. New York, 1975), illustrated by Arthur Rackham; *Peter and Wendy* (London and New York, 1911), illustrated by F. D. Bedford; *Peter Pan; or, The Boy Who Would Not Grow Up* (London and New York, 1928), the original play version; *The Entrancing Life* (London and New York, 1930), a speech; *Farewell, Miss Julie Logan: A Wintry Tale* (London, 1932), first published in a Christmas supplement to *The* (London) *Times*, 24 December 1931; *The Greenwood Hat: Being a Memoir of James Anon, 1885–1887* (London, 1938); *M'Connachie and J. M. B.: Speeches by J. M. Barrie* (London, 1938; New York, 1939), with a preface by Hugh Walpole.

IV. LETTERS. Viola Meynell, ed., *Letters* (New York, 1947).

IV. PLAYS. *Richard Savage* (London, 1891); *The Little Minister* (London, 1897), published originally as a novel in 1891; *The Wedding Guest: A Comedy in Four Acts* (London and New York, 1900); *Quality Street: A Comedy in Four Acts* (London, 1901); *Walker, London: A Farcical Comedy in Three Acts* (London, 1907); *The Admirable Crichton* (London, 1914); *Der Tag; or, The Tragic Man* (New York, 1914); *Half Hours* (London and New York, 1914), includes *Pantaloon, The Twelve-Pound Look, Rosalind*, and *The Will* in the New York edition; *Echoes of the War* (London and New York, 1918), includes *The Old Lady Shows Her Medals, The New Word, Barbara's Wedding*, and *A Well-Remembered Voice; Representative Plays by J. M. Barrie* (New York, 1922), with an intro. by William Lyon Phelps, contains *Quality Street, The Admirable Crichton, What Every Woman Knows, Dear Brutus, The Twelve-Pound Look*, and *The Old Lady Shows Her Medals*; Penelope Griffin, ed., *Ibsen's Ghost: A Play in One Act* (London, 1975), with an intro. by J. M. Barrie.

V. BIOGRAPHICAL AND CRITICAL STUDIES. H. M. Walbrook, *J. M. Barrie and the Theatre* (London, 1922); Patrick Braybrooke, *J. M. Barrie: A Study in Fairies and Mortals* (London, 1924); Sir John A. Hammerton, *Barrie: The Story of a Genius* (London and New York, 1929); James A. Roy, *James Matthew Barrie: An Appreciation* (London, 1937; New York, 1938); Denis G. Mackail, *The Story of J. M. B.: A Biography* (London and New York, 1941); George Blake, *Barrie and the Kailyard School* (London, 1951); Lady Cynthia Asquith, *Portrait of Barrie* (London, 1954); Janet Dunbar, *J. M. Barrie: The Man Behind the Image* (Boston, 1970); Harry M. Geduld, *Sir James Barrie* (New York, 1971).

APHRA BEHN

(1640–1689)

Carol Howard

IN 1928, NEARLY two and a half centuries after the death of Aphra Behn, Virginia Woolf wrote in *A Room of One's Own*: "All women together ought to let flowers fall upon the tomb of Aphra Behn which is, most scandalously but rather appropriately, in Westminster Abbey, for it was she who earned them the right to speak their minds" (New York, 1989, p. 66). Woolf's inclusion of an almost gossipy parenthetical tidbit, the site of Behn's burial, amid a hyperbolic pronouncement on Behn's role in women's history is no mere instance of Woolf's curious mock-heroic style, of her unflagging habit of yoking together the trivial and the grand. Behn's burial in Westminster Abbey—or, to be more particular than Woolf, not inside that ancient and venerable institution, and tellingly not in Poets' Corner among the company of the great English bards, but outside the Abbey proper, on the edge of a courtyard at the entrance to the cloisters—is a perfect tribute to the life Behn led and a perfect emblem of the position she has come to occupy in British literary history. It is also perfectly scandalous.

Aphra Behn was the first professional woman writer in England. That is to say, she was the first Englishwoman to make a fairly steady, if sometimes meager, living from writing, at a time when writing was just becoming a profession or trade. During her lifetime, she achieved wide recognition and high acclaim as a playwright, poet, translator, and fiction writer. She was also vilified for these very achievements. Using her customary poetic pseudonym, verse panegyrics hailed Behn as "the Incomparable Astrea" or "the Lovely Witty Astrea," while verse satires dwelled upon the "ruin of her face" and her "lewdness." A woman who wrote publicly, for money, and without apology flew in the face of seventeenth-century convention. That Behn, like so many of her male colleagues, wrote a bawdy play or poem now and again made it all the worse. Drawing upon a familiar cliché most often used to describe actresses of the period, satirists and moralists regularly compared her to a prostitute. She was a public scandal to some, a scandalous genius to others. But in Restoration England (Charles II was "restored" to the throne in 1660, following the Puritan rule of Oliver Cromwell, and little more than a decade after the beheading of Charles I), when indolence and questionable morals reigned at court, scandals garnered little more than a wink and a nod.

It was not so much her contemporaries, then, but the more judgmental voices of subsequent generations that banished Behn to obscurity. The censure remained fairly constant for more than two hundred years. In the moment of high Victorianism, when inquisitive scholars, not satisfied to leave well enough alone, shamelessly began dusting off Behn's bindings, an onslaught of reprimands ensued: "If Mrs. Behn is read at all, it can only be from a love of impurity for its own sake, for rank indecency of the dullest, stupidest, grossest kind, unrelieved by the faintest gleam of wit and sensibility. . . . it is a pity her books did not rot with her bones" ("Literary Garbage," *Saturday Review*, 27 January 1872, pp. 109–110). Only in recent years has she begun to assume her rightful place in literary history, in the company of John Dryden and other male writers who were her friends and associates, men who have long received the attention that might likewise have been accorded to Behn. If it is a scandal that she crossed the bounds of womanly modesty by writing for publication and writing racy material to boot, and yet was buried on the hallowed grounds of Westminster Abbey, then we may say, in retrospect, it is a worse scandal that a writer as talented and prolific as almost any of her generation went virtually unread and entirely unappreciated for the two centuries following her death. It is a scandal that no stone in Poets' Corner bears her name. Still, as a symbol of the historical position she has come thus far to hold, her resting place at the doorway of the cloisters is appropriate. It reminds us of her actual liminal status in life and in death, poised as she is on the threshold of established greatness, waiting, perhaps, for the tide of opinion to turn further to her favor.

LIFE AND TIMES

APHRA Behn's life spanned what is arguably the most tumultuous era of English history. She was born shortly before the beginning of the English Civil War in 1642, died on 16 April 1689, just after the Glorious Revolution, and witnessed in between the dissolution and subsequent restoration of the monarchy, three wars with the Netherlands, nation-shaking political plots and intrigues, a devastating outbreak of bubonic plague, the Great Fire of London, and the first actresses upon the London stage. We have almost no sure knowledge of Behn's first twenty-three years, the years that coincided with the period of civil war and its immediate aftermath. We do know from her later literary work, which on occasion takes the form of outright royalist propaganda, that at some point she became a staunch supporter of Charles II, although she sometimes offered oblique criticism of his actions or judgment. It is hard to say, however, whether the monarchical fervor that characterized her later years represented a longstanding personal conviction or an immediate and shrewd professional opportunism. If her political sympathies were consistent and firmly entrenched throughout her life, then she and her family may well have had difficulties in the Cromwell years. Yet during this period she does seem to have had close ties not only to distinguished royalists but to the family of Thomas Scot, a member of Parliament intimately involved in the overthrow of Charles I. At the Restoration, Scot was executed as a regicide; his son William, who had earlier fled into exile, would later become Behn's lover.

If letters and other documents left to posterity offer proof of Behn's aristocratic connections on both sides of the political divide, there is little evidence apart from untrustworthy fictional accounts concerning the identity of her own family. It is generally agreed that her birth name was Johnson (Behn is the name of the unknown man she is presumed to have married) and that she was born somewhere in the county of Kent, possibly in Canterbury. She was long thought to have been a barber's daughter, but the evidence supporting this claim has been refuted. Another account declares her the daughter of a wet nurse employed by the prominent Culpepper family, but it seems unlikely that a member of Behn's supposed birth class would be adopted and educated along with the aristocratic family's natural children, as the account suggests. The testimony for this claim comes primarily from a memoir in which one of the Culpepper children, later the avid royalist Colonel Thomas Culpepper, calls Behn his "foster sister." What is already a murky story becomes murkier still when we consider that the deaths in 1643 of Sir Thomas Culpepper and his wife, Dame Barbara, left the young Culpepper children, as well as the three-year-old Aphra and any siblings she may have had, to be reared by friends or relations whose identity remains uncertain. In any case, a more credible version of Behn's birth and early life, which makes her seem something of a female counterpart to Henry Fielding's eighteenth-century fictional hero Tom Jones, is that she was the illegitimate child of a genteel parent who knew the Culpeppers, and that, in an effort to avoid exposure, she was represented to be the child of a wet nurse or of a dead relative. This story would explain the persistent mystery surrounding her birth, her distinguished connections, and her fine education.

It is worth pausing for a moment on this last attribute: Behn's education. Throughout the seventeenth century, girls and women had fairly limited educational opportunities. Since the law and social custom judged a woman to be the appendage, if not exactly the property, of her husband or father, to many men it seemed unnecessary, potentially dangerous even, to train women to think independently. And yet some degree of education could prove useful: an elementary ability to read, write, or keep accounts would be invaluable in maintaining a household. Some men thought an ability to read the Bible would promote piety in their wives or daughters; others deemed a woman's firsthand knowledge of Scripture to be inappropriate. Wealthy families who did wish to educate girls had several options: they could tutor them at home, dispatch them as boarders to another private home, or send them to boarding school. In addition to reading and writing, girls from affluent families learned French, music, dancing, and needlework. Girls from poorer families could attend charity schools, the numbers of which increased as the eighteenth century approached. These girls might learn reading, writing, and other skills considered useful for household employment. But girls of whatever background who did manage to obtain a formal or informal education were almost never taken as seriously as their male counterparts. A girl's course of study was never as long as that of her brother and was always of less consequence. Where boys learned Greek and Latin, the languages of knowledge and state, girls learned to first catch and then please a husband. To admit women to the universities was, at least to the minds of most men, simply unthinkable.

Behn's talent as a writer makes it quite clear that she was afforded at least a rudimentary education and quite possibly a tolerably good one. And while she of course did not attend university, in her later years she surrounded herself with men who had been at Oxford and Cambridge, men whose conversation and collegiality helped this enterprising and independent woman develop her knowledge and talents as much as any formal education could—or almost as much. Even as her drama parodied the fustian prose of classically trained university men, Behn resented her inability to read classical languages, and she was forced to become especially resourceful when "translating" classical texts (she worked from literal renderings in English and possibly from French translations).

Nor was she the only woman of her generation angered by the constraints of a female education. Several women (as well as some men) wrote treatises in favor of improving women's education in matters academic and practical. Concerning herself primarily with educating daughters of the aristocracy in religion, philosophy, and ancient and modern languages, Bathsua Makin, governess to the children of Charles I and, later, head of a school for young gentlewomen, published *An Essay to Revive the Antient Education of Gentlewomen* in 1673, three years after Behn had produced her first play. During the same period, a more catholic-minded governess, Hannah Woolley, offered practical advice for household maintenance to rich and poor women alike; the most famous of her several works is *The Gentlewoman's Companion*.

A number of women formed intellectual friendship circles, precursors to the eighteenth-century "bluestocking" circles. The most celebrated group surrounded Mary Astell, who, in the years immediately following Behn's death, advanced the first comprehensive system of feminist thought in English. Despite her own explicit complaints against gender inequities, Behn does not seem to have become affiliated with any group of intellectual women, although she certainly developed associations with a number of talented individuals. The London theater scene, as well as her own predilections, undoubtedly led her to focus her social and intellectual energies elsewhere.

Whatever activities Behn's formal and informal education may have included, one significant component of the latter consisted of travels abroad. It is now generally agreed that Behn arrived with her family or guardians in the English, later Dutch, South American colony of Surinam in the autumn of 1663 and remained there until the spring of 1664. In the early decades of the twentieth century, however, scholars spiritedly debated whether Behn went to Surinam at all, since a good deal of the evidence concerning her presence there derives from her most famous work of fiction, *Oroonoko; or, The Royal Slave* (1688), the second half of which is set in Surinam. On the one hand, some readers have taken Behn's fictional female narrator, who claims "eye-witness" authority for the events of the novella, to represent Behn herself and have accepted as historical fact much of the narrative detail. The problem is that since we unluckily have scant knowledge external to the novella of Behn's activities in Surinam, the fictional account all too readily serves as the mine supplying an impoverished biography with unsubstantiated nuggets of fact. On the other hand, skeptical literary historians have rightly mistrusted Behn's romantic story of an African prince's enslavement, rebellion, and eventual death on a South American colonial plantation to be a chronicle of actual historical events recorded by Behn herself. The problem here is that rather than sift the historical elements from the fictional account, skeptics have sometimes dismissed the entire Surinam episode, kit and caboodle, as—to preserve one detractor's terse vitriol—a lie. Truth be told, external evidence in the form of letters from the deputy governor of Surinam, William Byam (a scurrilous figure in Behn's novella), and Sir Robert Harley, who owned property in Surinam, as well as correspondence between Harley and his Surinam agents, corroborate Behn's presence there, although they do not document the specific events Behn's narrative persona claims to have witnessed. Yet slave resistance, which is central to the plot of *Oroonoko,* was common enough on colonial plantations, and while in Surinam Behn could easily have witnessed or discussed or read of a situation comparable to the one she recounts.

Little as is known of Behn's Surinam sojourn, there is reason to believe she read fiction (perhaps the French authors of historical romance—Madeleine de Scudéry, Honoré d'Urfé, and La Calprenède—whose influence is conspicuous in her own work), wrote early drafts of poetry and prose to be developed later on, and sustained a romantic liaison with the regicide Thomas Scot's son William, who was by then in his mid-thirties (there is no hint of the affair in *Oroonoko*). Shortly before the Restoration, Scot ran into trouble with the Parliamentarian regime of which his father was a key figure and, despite the family connection, was unable to extricate himself from what became a considerable political and financial plight. Scot fled to his brother Richard's plantation in Surinam, where he seems to have encountered Behn. We know almost nothing of the substance of this relationship, only that it existed, since references to it appear now and again in documentary evidence. When Scot's difficulties pursued him to South America, he eventually escaped to the European continent, but not before Behn herself had returned to England. Behn would again meet up with Scot two years later in Antwerp.

Sometime shortly after she left Surinam, perhaps during the return voyage, Aphra most likely met and married the mysterious Mr. Behn. Most likely, but not certainly, because one fairly untenable conjecture has been advanced that Aphra, with native expediency, invented Mr. Behn and then—as though he were a functional cipher dotting the page of a seventeenth-century French romance—unceremoniously killed him off: a widow of Behn's class would be accorded a measure of social mobility and esteem a never-married woman never would. But this is pure speculation, strongly disputed by Behn's most recent biographer, Angeline Goreau (1980). The marriage, assuming that it took place, does not appear to have lasted long, and the match, like most during this period, did not issue from mutual love or affection but was arranged for economic convenience.

Sources claim Mr. Behn to have been a London merchant of Dutch ancestry and—by way of accounting for the brevity of the marriage—possibly a victim of the Great Plague of 1665–1666, the catastrophic scourge described in Daniel Defoe's realist fiction *A Journal of the Plague Year* (1722). The marriage was surely a low point in Aphra Behn's life: in the plays written during the 1670s, she lampooned foppish Dutchmen and avaricious merchants alike and built comic plots upon young lovers' aversion to arranged marriages (her first play is frankly entitled *The Forc'd Marriage; or, The Jealous Bridegroom,* 1671).

Aphra Behn bore no children, never remarried, and was therefore a free agent when summoned as a secret agent to the service of king and country in July 1666. At the time, England was embroiled in the second of three wars waged against the Netherlands. England precipitated all three conflicts (1652–1654, 1665–1667, 1673–1674) by enacting a series of Navigation Acts establishing trade monopoly with British overseas colonies. As the Duke of Albemarle (to whose son, the second duke, Behn would one day address a Pindaric ode) put it, slicing deftly through parliamentary ideology to the realpolitik core: "What matters is not this or that reason. . . . What we want is more of the trade the Dutch now have" (quoted in Christopher Hill, *The Century of Revolution, 1603–1714,* New York, 1966, pp. 210–211). In the case of the second war, England added injury to the insult of hostile trade legislation by wresting from Dutch control West African coastal slave trading posts, as well as the American territory of New Amsterdam, afterward dubbed New York. Behn's own nagging antipathy toward all things Dutch (husbands, merchants, and, eventually, parvenu royalty in the person of William III included) would saturate a career's worth of drama, fiction, and poetry; yet these particular maneuvers, these key territorial jugglings of the 1660s, would form an especially vivid backdrop to *Oroonoko*: Behn considered the English capitulation of Surinam to the Dutch during this period terribly injudicious. She responded publicly by translating her general fascination with and pointed criticism of England's political, military, and economic policy toward the Netherlands into the conventions and embellishments of romantic intrigue. The narrator of Behn's tale at one point ventures so far as to attribute the hero Oroonoko's deplorable obscurity (assuming, as she does, his actual historical existence) to the Dutch acquisition of Surinam; this untoward episode in Anglo-Dutch relations, she tells us, produced a dearth of worthy historians: "it [Oroonoko's fame] had lived from others Endeavours, if the *Dutch,* who immediately after his [Oroonoko's] time took that Country, had not killed, banished and dispersed all those that were capable of giving the World this great Man's Life, much better than I have done" (vol. 5, p. 40).[1]

The ministers of Charles II dispatched Behn to Antwerp to reestablish connections with her erstwhile lover, William Scot. Scot—along with assorted renegade Englishmen and sometime republicans—was now in Holland feeding the enemy information concerning English military and trade maneuvers (what ships were sailing where and when, which turncoats were reliable, and so forth). Behn fairly succeeded at her task of convincing Scot to shift allegiance to Charles II, for which he was to be paid with ample money and full amnesty. Given that Behn was a tyro in the intelligence work she also conducted, her indiscretion and impetuousness were only partly attributable to the poverty that dogged her. Nevertheless, she did collect and ferry home significant tidings, including the unheeded early rumor of Dutch plans to bombard English ships docked in the Thames. The actual debacle of June 1667—the Dutch sailed unimpeded up the Medway to demolish a bemused English fleet—was as cruel a blow to England's morale as it was to its navy.

When the English government repeatedly ignored Behn's plea for pecuniary support, she borrowed a badly needed sum of money, discharged her debts, and sailed home in and across dire straits (it seems the Channel waters, like Behn's finances, were remarkably turbulent that season). Safely back in England, yet still unremunerated for her Antwerp service and therefore unable to satisfy her sizable debt, Behn was consigned to debtor's prison, where she served a brief term beginning sometime around the end of 1668. The government may have responded to her importunate letters by actually paying the debt incurred in its service and obtaining her reasonably quick release, or her wealthy connections may have intervened. Whatever the circumstances, Behn was soon thereafter rooming in London and trying her hand at a new profession: writing.

DRAMA

WHEN Charles II returned to the throne of England in 1660, he brought the theater with him. The oppositional Parliament had darkened the London stage in 1642 at the outset of the Civil War, thereby marking the culmination of a formidable late-Renaissance tradition of Puritan antitheatrical literature and thought, typified by William Prynne's *Histriomastix* (1633), which attributed to the corrupting influence of the stage any number of existing or potential moral and political "abuses." The restored theater incorporated a number of technical and other innovations, the most significant of which, for our purposes, was London's first public performance by an actress (putatively, she who played Desdemona in a production of *Othello* on 8 December 1660): the public production of plays written by women would be the next step. Prior to the Civil War, the commercial theater, as opposed to the court theater, exclusively employed boys to play women characters—a circumstance of which we to this day are reminded when, in the epilogue of *As You Like It,* Shakespeare's heroine Rosalind enticingly declares to the men in the audience: "If I were a woman, I would kiss as many of you as had beards that pleased me." By contrast, at the court theater of Charles I, women were better tolerated as players: in the late 1620s and early 1630s, Queen Henrietta Maria herself was known to have appeared on the stage, as had James's Queen Anne before her. That women were prohibited from the London stage ostensibly follows the belief that public performance or exhibition is indecent or even whorish, yet this very opinion issues from a redoubtable web of religious, economic, and political pressures that conspire to restrict women's activities. The ascent of actresses and female playwrights during the Restoration has partly to do with a general restructuring of this web, but specifically with the unprecedented tie between the court and the public theater. Since Stuart monarchs had traditionally supported women players (as had the European continent where Charles II was long exiled), the interest and patronage the restored king brought to the public

[1]References to Behn's prose and drama are from the Montague Summers edition except for *Love-Letters Between a Nobleman and His Sister,* which are from the Virago Press edition. All italics within quotations are Behn's own.

stage naturally brought women artists to the theater as well.

While logic does not necessarily dictate that female actresses lead to female playwrights, the presence of women on the stage seems to have facilitated the possibility of women writing for the stage. One decade after the first actress performed publicly, Aphra Behn became the first female playwright fully to embrace public exposure and acclaim, and to succeed extraordinarily well in her chosen career. To be sure, other women of the period—Katherine Philips, Elizabeth Polwhele, Frances Boothby—were writing or translating plays, but either the novelty of women's drama hampered their acceptance by the theater world or modesty bade them shirk publicity. Nor was any other woman of the century (and no man of the Restoration, excepting Dryden) nearly so prolific as Behn, to whom twenty plays have been attributed. However, for the record, a handful of women dramatists, famous in their day, who directly succeeded Behn—Mary Pix, Catharine Trotter, Delarivier Manley, Susannah Centlivre—did yield a respectable output; their failure to rival Behn in productivity may be attributed to the relative decline of the theater after 1682.

The recipe for success as an artist is one tablespoon talent, another of persistence, and a heaping portion of being in the right place at the right time. Behn clearly had the ingredients, but how she ended up where she did is anybody's guess. At the Restoration, Charles II licensed two theaters. Although Behn had connections to Charles's close friend Thomas Killigrew, patent holder for the King's Company (whose premier house playwright was Dryden), she somehow became exclusively affiliated with the Duke's Company at Dorset Garden, which flourished under the guidance of the brilliant Restoration actor and comanager Thomas Betterton (this theater, located at Lincoln's Inn before Behn's time, had first been licensed to the renowned royalist playwright William Davenant, who died in 1668).

Behn's first play, *The Forc'd Marriage; or, The Jealous Bridegroom*, ran a respectable six nights in September 1670, respectable because even the most wildly successful plays, given the limited audience pool, did not last beyond two weeks (that a play ran three nights was of utmost importance to the author, whose fee—aside from any special deals he or she may have negotiated—usually consisted of third-night receipts). Al-

though it was a commercial success, critics have generally considered *The Forc'd Marriage* to be among Behn's worst dramatic efforts: the form and content largely want originality; the language (a hodgepodge of prose, blank verse, and rhymed couplets) is sometimes stilted; the wit, dull and obvious; the characters, shallow; the plot and subplots, loosely woven. Yet despite its several flaws, the play is undeniably engaging: literature that least fulfills our standards for artistic greatness can sometimes be the most visually and emotionally satisfying (as a bonus, this play features a baroque masque in act 5 to feast audience eyes). Moreover, the recent interest feminist critics have shown in Behn's work may oblige us to reassess the merits of this early attempt—the play's prologue, an astute and witty commentary on sex, power, and the theater, has already begun to attract a good deal of critical attention.

The Forc'd Marriage belongs to the genre of romantic tragicomedy popular during the Jacobean period and revived with the Restoration. Like most romantic comedies, the plot concerns the efforts of the young and the restless to marry, preferably the right person, and ideally with parental approval. In this instance, the noblewoman Erminia and the prince Philander love each other; Philander's sister, the princess Galatea, loves the brave warrior Alcippus, but Alcippus desires Erminia. The failure of the individuals to divvy themselves neatly into pairs makes for comic tension: we expect the couples to sort themselves out eventually, but how? The tension is heightened from the outset, since Alcippus, having just returned triumphant from a military campaign, requests and secures as his prize Erminia's hand in marriage. The script leaves some room for doubt as to whether Alcippus is fully ignorant of his comrade-in-arms the prince's love for Erminia, and were the plot richer and characters deeper, the antagonism foaming beneath the men's congenial hail-fellow-well-met exteriors might have yielded exciting drama.

It will come as no surprise that fathers with occluded judgment have sanctioned the ill-wrought match: such is the standard fare of comedy. In this case, as with many plays of the tragicomic variety, parental and monarchical authority overlap, the king being father to a potential bride and bridegroom. Where a pure comedy might nudge royalty to the background, concentrating instead on the actions of lesser mortals, the foregrounded royalty here adds the requisite lofty and, therefore, potentially tragic element to the hybrid genre. However, the presence of royalty in Behn's plays never exists solely for artistic or generic effect; in her later drama, the veil covering political allusion would be diaphanous at best. One of her last plays, *The Roundheads; or, The Good Old Cause* (1682), provides the most pointed example. While ostensibly a farcical historical treatment of republican Parliamentarians on the eve of the Restoration, the show was produced in the aftermath of the Exclusion Crisis (1679–1681), during which Parliament sought to ratify a bill excluding Charles's younger brother James from the throne. Contemporary audiences would certainly have read the play as an attack on this most recent Parliamentary presumption.

While the political content of *The Forc'd Marriage* is considerably more diffuse than that of *The Roundheads*, we may at least glean from it the crude grain of Behn's future preoccupation. The arranged match is bad business. Erminia is daughter to the aging General Orgulius, long banished for an attempted military coup, but lately returned, thanks to the king's liberal mercy and Erminia's propitiating beauty. One would think the king had inexplicably jeopardized his own sovereignty by consenting to a blood alliance between a former traitor, Orgulius, and a potential one, Alcippus—two ambitious men who between them command the allegiance of an entire army. Political wisdom dictates the king should consolidate his rule by wedding his daughter to Alcippus, his son to Erminia. But these considerations, once and future treason, are so far removed from the action and energy of the play as to seem negligible. Orgulius and Alcippus appear steadfastly loyal; no inkling gives evidence to the contrary. That we learn of Orgulius' former treachery only in the middle of act 3 might seem to prove Behn's inexperience as a storyteller, since this background information appears indispensable to our understanding of both character and plot. Until this point, when an embittered princess Galatea angrily reminds Erminia of her father's embroiled past, we might just as well assume—given the cordial dialogue of act 1—that some regrettable spat between the king and his general, some pardonable act of insubordination, had escalated into Orgulius' exile. Yet burying this essential political history amid what seems the wholly unrelated action of romantic intrigue may represent Behn's de-liberate choice to weight family romance above national politics and to make the former determine the course of the latter. Then again, it is worth considering that the name Orgulius—a variation of Orgoglio, the haughty giant of Spenser's *The Faerie Queene*—means "pride" and could well remind Restoration audience members of Cromwell's officer, Colonel Thomas Pride, who removed dissident members from the House of Commons in December 1648, thereby facilitating the parliamentary mandate to execute Charles I a month later. The event is remembered as "Pride's purge."

The actual wedding between Erminia and Alcippus piques our curiosity. How to amend the lovers' predicament once the holy ritual has transpired? Here begins the inevitable contest between love and honor, the sundry aspects of which form the theme of the play. Erminia's determination to remain faithful to her beloved Philander by refusing to consummate her marriage wounds the honor of her lawful husband, Alcippus. In a fit of jealousy, Alcippus strangles Erminia yet—unbeknownst to everyone except Erminia's maid—fails to kill her. In addition to providing the brush with death required of tragicomedy, this incident confers the necessary change of fortune by giving the upper hand to the heretofore thwarted lovers. The benighted fathers begin to see the light. Alcippus regrets his nearly fatal error, relinquishes Erminia to Philander, and effects a happy ending for all by conveniently falling in love with Galatea. The comic figures of the underdeveloped and poorly integrated subplots follow suit; the social fabric is everywhere mended; the balance of power restored.

The question remains: What of this play, if anything, is innovative? Most plays of the Restoration, including those by Behn, freely borrow plots, characters, and themes from Elizabethan, Jacobean, French, or Spanish drama; or they adapt material from nondramatic forms. There was far less regard then than now for originality in the modern sense of the word. In fact, the very concept of the "original" was still in transition: the word could mean, as it currently does, "unprecedented"; but it could also mean, paradoxically, "derivative," that is, traceable to a model. Behn was to become an expert at adaptation, although she once suffered a public accusation of plagiarism—no mean feat in an age whose notions of intellectual property were not nearly so rigorous as they are today. Significantly enough, her defense was not to deny she had plundered the source, but to insist she had vastly improved it.

Although *The Forc'd Marriage* imitates its Jacobean models to little advantage, Behn's minor alterations nevertheless reveal her own burgeoning commitment to investigating gender roles. The heroine Erminia can hardly be said to emulate Behn's later feminist models—the saucy, clever, enterprising women who would cut bold and witty figures in some of Behn's best plays, including *The Rover; or, The Banish'd Cavaliers* (1677) and *The Lucky Chance; or, An Alderman's Bargain* (1687). The difficulty has much to do with the Restoration's customary preference for fast action and faster talk: powerless and perplexed heroines are never as engaging as pert, plotting ones. And yet Erminia's moral dilemma, her apparently unreconcilable conflict not just between love and honor, but between competing claims of honor, discloses the kernel that would yield the great and the complex, the virtuous and the duty-bound heroines of the eighteenth-century novel, heroines epitomized by Samuel Richardson's Clarissa.

The seventeenth-century definition of honor varies according to gender. For women, honor means sexual chastity and duty to father or husband. For men, honor signifies position and rank, as well as a broad spectrum of obligations and responsibilities between the individual and society and between the individual and the sovereign state. Moreover, where men contract honorable relationships of their own volition, women's honor is contracted for them by the fathers and husbands who negotiate marriage arrangements, which, in Behn's plays, often mean political as well as social and economic alliances. (It is no accident that mothers are very nearly invisible throughout Behn's oeuvre, the mother's parental authority being decidedly vitiated by her gender.) Erminia's difficulty is that her love for the prince Philander is not entirely a secret and exalted passion, born of unauthorized trysts, meaningful glances, longing sighs. If it were, the play would replicate the classic dramatic theme of youth's sublime love at odds with the mundane and frustrating reality of social and familial obligation. Instead, when Orgulius compels Erminia to marry Alcippus, Erminia and Philander reveal a genuine sense of indignation—although one the conventional seventeenth-century dialogue cannot fully articulate—that a private contract, publicly binding, has been violated. The implication is that

while Erminia bears a relationship of love to Philander, she bears one of honor to him as well, although the code of woman's honor, the duty she owes her husband and father, would seem to render this independently contracted honor logically untenable. And yet Erminia is obdurate: her obligation to Philander comes into conflict with the one she concedes to owe Alcippus. That the conflict is evinced through Erminia's irresolute resolution to forsake Alcippus' bed while honoring him in every other respect suggests the play's inability to sustain a woman's presumption to dispose of her own person as she sees fit. The problem is a generic one: while high-Restoration comedy and nascent feminist prose polemics can accommodate—although not necessarily vindicate—the language of women's freedom, the tragicomic hybrid cannot. Apart from the playful subplots, within whose borders fops and brazen women are strictly confined, the tenor of dialogue here is too serious, too traditional to indulge liberal speech. Behn's sustained arguments for women's rights and equality—invariably hazarded in a playful, teasing, or satiric form—would come later. Here, she registers dissent negatively and violently through the play's title, *The Forc'd Marriage,* and through Erminia's failed strangulation, both of which instances smack more of vulgar barbarism than hint at elevated tragedy.

Behn's second play, *The Amorous Prince; or, The Curious Husband* (1671), and her third, *The Dutch Lover* (1673), comprise her next and last efforts to remain solidly within the vein of romantic tragicomedy. With both, however, she leans closer to the comic element that would ultimately become her forte. The plot of *The Amorous Prince* is more sophisticated than that of *The Forc'd Marriage,* although the vexed-love themes of both are equally hackneyed. By contrast, *The Dutch Lover,* while lacking the brilliance of Behn's high comedy, is more polished than its two predecessors in every respect, especially in its brisk pace and complex network of plot lines. And although the play was commercially unsuccessful (which Behn mainly attributes to undisciplined actors), the ridicule aimed at the bumbling fop of a title character, the Dutch lover, Haunce van Ezel, would have satisfied the contemporary English audience whose beleaguered country was again at war with the Netherlands.

Of more interest to modern scholars than *The Dutch Lover* itself is the arresting epistle to the reader—Behn's best of several ironic meditations on life and literature—prefacing the published version of the play. Adopting a persona whose piquant, beguiling attitude she would later bestow upon her comic heroines, Behn hails her audience as "Good, Sweet, Honey, Sugar-candied READER," a greeting that serves simultaneously as ironic shield and mischievous invitation. The epistle opens as a general exercise in anti-intellectualism and as a particular attack on Puritan antitheatricalism:

> I have heard the most of that which bears the name of Learning, and which has abused such quantities of Ink and Paper, and continually employs so many ignorant, unhappy souls for ten, twelve, twenty years in the University (who yet poor wretches think they are doing something all the while) as Logick etc. and several other things (that shall be nameless lest I misspell them) are much more absolutely nothing than the errantest Play that e'er was writ.
>
> (vol. 1, p. 221)

For fear the reader might suppose Behn means to defend drama as the preferred refuge of truth and morality, or playwrights as the sage wardens of human nature, she hastily launches an indictment of dramatic theory, thereby gently and covertly taunting her colleague Dryden, whose outstanding feat of the genre, *An Essay of Dramatick Poesy* (1668), takes drama too seriously for Behn's tastes. Where Dryden thoughtfully weighs ancients and moderns, French and English, or the three unities, Behn dispenses the lot and proclaims instead an undiscriminating pleasure principle: "I think a Play the best divertisement that wise men have: but I do also think them nothing so who do discourse as formallie about the rules of it, as if 'twere the grand affair of humane life" (p. 223).

To what end, this sentiment? Behn seldom offers gratuitous thoughts on anything, but parcels out personal opinion and common wisdom always to immediate, practical effect. Her interest, in this case, is to defend her own dramatic practice against those who would and do reproach her for taking up the pen. Indeed, she shows no mercy in unleashing a fierce torrent of invective at the particular audience member ("a long, lither, phlegmatick, white, ill-favour'd, wretched Fop") bold enough to criticize her publicly. She regains her composure, however, by shifting from the personal to the universal. A backhanded feminism bolsters the self-serving purpose: "For waving the

examination why women having equal education with men, were not as capable of knowledge, of whatsoever sort as well as they: I'll only say as I have touch'd before, that Plays have no great room for that which is men's great advantage over women, that is Learning" (p. 224).

Behn's quirky enthymeme is staggeringly pragmatic: the drama is unsuitable for erudition, and men are better educated than women. The implied conclusion is that women are equally (or perhaps better) suited to the vocation of playwright. Whether women's minds are innately inferior to men's is neither here nor there for Behn's immediate aim, and she therefore declines to engage an argument to which early feminist polemicists devote so much critical attention.

Behn's next play, *Abdelazer; or, The Moor's Revenge* (1677), which was not produced until 1676, initiated Behn's most productive period as a playwright. Between 1676 and 1682 she would write more than a dozen plays. *Abdelazer* is Behn's only adventure with romantic tragedy, a form quite popular during the period and better explored by Dryden. A study of lust, revenge, and empire, the play echoes *Othello* and vaguely anticipates Behn's great achievement in prose fiction, *Oroonoko*. Although during this period Behn also authored what might be described as history plays, such as the farcical *The Roundheads,* she excelled at the comedy of intrigue and manners, a mode to which she added a pinch of history, a dash of politics. Behn's most famous play, one of her comic masterpieces, is *The Rover; or, The Banish'd Cavaliers,* which received tremendous critical and popular acclaim and was succeeded in 1681 by a less stellar sequel, *The Second Part of the Rover* (the two parts derive from Thomas Killigrew's *Thomaso*). Here Behn displays a number of well-polished comic devices: elaborate disguises and fight scenes augment rapid dialogue, action, and scene changes; and with consummate skill Behn links the main plot to the several secondary plots. The latter, unlike the subplots in *The Forc'd Marriage,* are indispensable to the main story line and serve as felicitous complements to the former.

The Rover describes the exploits of a company of English cavaliers who, having been exiled with Charles II during the Cromwell years and finding themselves in Naples during carnival time, set about looking for women. Willmore, the hero and rover, so called because he roves from place to place and woman to woman, bears resemblance both to Charles II and to the randy pornographer-poet and theater-devotee Earl of Rochester. He encounters the virginal heroine Hellena (played in the original production by Rochester's mistress, the illustrious actress Elizabeth Barry), who is destined for a convent but who, desiring sexual experience, dons masquerade gear and ventures to the carnival celebration, accompanied by her kinswomen. The principal plot, inseparable from the scarcely less central story of frustrated courtship between the virtuous Florinda and faithful Belvile, concerns the flirtatious banter, witty negotiations, and artful intrigue of Hellena and Willmore: she wants (or, rather, her reputation requires) marriage first and sex thereafter; he, sex first and marriage never. Willmore's coincident seduction of the famous courtesan Angelica Bianca—who, having fallen in love with him, grants sexual favors gratis—makes for a raucous triangle of desire, jealousy, and plotting.

A habit of comedy, masterfully engineered in *The Rover* and central to its plot, is to debase the exalted love ethos that motivates romantic tragedy and romantic prose fiction by exposing the economic underpinnings of marriage and the crass profit motive that governs courtship. An effective way for the more daring variety of comedy to achieve this effect is to confuse marriage with prostitution and, thereby, to imply all women are commodities for sale. Snippets of this confusion are manifest in *The Rover* when male characters mistake virgins for whores: the ingenuous Florinda's difficulty in adroitly managing intrigue (secret trysts, disguises) leads her into compromising situations in which predatory men, not recognizing her quality, assume her to be sexually available. In one instance, Frederick, a cavalier who, along with his cohort Ned Blunt, temporarily has Florinda in his power and begins to suspect she is not the loose woman he assumed her to be, carries the coarse logic of the play to its nadir: "'twou'd anger us vilely to be truss'd up for a Rape upon a Maid of Quality, when we only believe we ruffle a Harlot" (vol. 1, p. 85). That is, it would be a shame to pay the price (in this case, to be hanged or, at least, arrested) for what is both a brand-new model and another man's property (thus far, her father's), when he thinks he merely enjoys used and public goods. That Frederick cannot discern the difference between a "maid of quality" and a "harlot," or rather, that he expects appearances to make the difference

clear, confirms the play's tantalizing proposition that appearances are everything, and that—contrary to the ideals if not the conventions of both romance and propriety—advertising, packaging, and distribution make the quality of the woman.

Several feminist literary critics have argued that Behn most intriguingly complicates the issue of appearances during an early scene in which an impoverished Willmore, unable to pay the thousand crowns asked for Angelica Bianca's favors, is satisfied to steal a small painting of her. By coveting and possessing the representation, Willmore inadvertently manages to gain what he calls the "original," as if the woman herself were a painting to be copied. The theft of the painting at last leads Angelica Bianca, the woman who theretofore trafficked exclusively in appearances, or in surfaces, to expose her depths, her hidden self, to the one man who surely will forsake her. Given that the prostitute's initials correspond to those of the playwright, and given Behn's habitual manipulation of the playwright-as-prostitute trope, Angelica Bianca's sober game of hide-and-seek becomes self-consciously mapped onto the macrocosm of the theater, the world that puts a premium on appearances and the playwright's ability to sustain them or purposefully to betray them.

The confusion of marriage and prostitution also drives the main plot: the virgin-whore-rake triangle ingeniously complicates the relationships between sex, love, and money. At the same time, Behn is particularly astute in comically inverting the direction of desire, so that women become the buyers and men the goods, and in exploding the myth that good girls have no sexual desires, while bad girls have nothing else. Whereas the convent-bound virgin Hellena vows to find "some mad companion or other that will spoil my [religious] devotion" and ultimately achieves this goal with Willmore, the prostitute Angelica Bianca fears her own love for Willmore will spoil "my virgin heart." This inversion may represent the woman playwright's effort to explore women's desire, even as it exploits, and perhaps confirms, a common strain of misogynistic Restoration opinion that regards all women, even good girls, as fundamentally—and redoubtably—insatiable and scheming creatures warranting restraint. Whether the play finally celebrates or censures women's desire is debatable, especially since Restoration culture, which defines desire as a chiefly masculine prerogative, has no positive means of accommodating women's desire and no language to express it. Angelica Bianca gets a broken and bitter heart for her efforts, while the witty Hellena appears to win her heart's, as well as her body's, desire. Then again, Hellena's victory seems compromised. Within the economy of marriage, Hellena must be constant, but Willmore, or rather "will more," the man whose very name suggests insatiable desire, will continue to rove. And yet Willmore's roving nature is his appeal: his inconstancy has whetted Hellena's desire from the outset. In the end, the audience must decide whether feminine desire fueled by the prospect of masculine infidelity is cheapened desire or whether it is enhanced desire—desire heightened by the thrill of the chase.

In 1682 waning patronage and assorted circumstantial disasters forced the King's Company to unite with the Duke's: the heyday of Restoration drama had reached its gloaming. Thereafter, Behn's dramatic output declined precipitously, although *The Lucky Chance; or, The Alderman's Bargain,* one of her finest comedies, was quite successful in its original production. However, Behn's new reticence in the theater was not entirely the result of the reconfigured London theater scene nor of broader changes in the cultural climate. In August 1682, having criticized Charles II's rebellious illegitimate son, the Duke of Monmouth, in the epilogue to the anonymous play, *Romulus and Hersilia; or, The Sabine War,* Behn was arrested (along with the actress, Lady Slingsby, who recited the offending lines) and may have been incarcerated for a short spell. Behn's fervent preference for the future James II backfired: even as Charles fought Parliament to defend James's right to accession, he retained a soft spot for, and brooked little criticism of, the insurgent Monmouth (Dryden's 1681 epic satire on these events, *Absalom and Achitophel,* was rather more circumspect than Behn's reproof). With the theater in decline and her political commentary temporarily squelched, Behn turned to new literary pursuits. Other genres would provide marketable alternatives and newer venues to unleash her political views.

FICTION

IT is difficult comfortably to assign Behn's prose, or, for that matter, any late-seventeenth-century prose, to modern categories of genre. The basic

characteristics of form and content we recognize today, as well as the generic distinctions we make between fact and fiction and among history, romance, novel, and tale, were in Behn's period in the process of becoming stabilized. Today we regard Behn's more than a dozen prose works, which range in length from a few pages to a few hundred pages, as novels, novellas, romances, or tales. However, Behn called her works "history" (a word whose definition was in flux and that could refer to what we consider fact, fiction, or both) and often insisted that she offered "eyewitness" accounts of the events she described. On the occasions when she identified her work as "story," she made sure to preface the classification with claims to veracity: "true story." In the dedicatory epistle prefacing *The Fair Jilt; or, The Amours of Prince Tarquin and Miranda* (1688), a fifty-page work she distinguishes as "history," but one that we would probably ascribe to the category of romance or novella, she protests, "For however it may be imagin'd that Poetry (my talent) has so greatly the Ascendant over me, that all I write must pass for Fiction, I now desire to have it understood that this is Reality, and Matter of Fact, and acted in this our latter Age" (vol. 5, p. 70). Since, as she maintains, she has a reputation as someone whose literary inventions are the products of her own imagination (a poet, or, for that matter, a dramatist), she wants to assure her reader that her prose works constitute faithful and scrupulously reported accounts of actual events.

While Behn's insistent journalistic posturing reflects her generation's increasing preoccupation with printed accounts of current events or "news" (although printed "news," which often included romance or tales, was not a stable form either), in a broader sense it signals the dawn of the Enlightenment, an age whose greatest thinkers valued worldly truths in the form of demonstrable, material facts. And yet, despite her determined truth claims, and despite her practice of culling source material from contemporary history, Behn's narrative method is to escape into what modern readers generally recognize as her own imaginative invention. Or, her mode of storytelling alternates, often within the same text, between what modern readers would consider flights of romantic fancy and the convention of plausible reality that typifies the modern novel. While literary critics have sometimes deemed Behn's instability of form, as well as the discrepancy between her claim to reality and her unabashed practice of romance, to be a sign of artistic incompetence or inexperience, recent interest in seventeenth-century prose fiction has begun to teach readers to suspend judgments based on anachronistic aesthetic criteria. In other words, and in particular, it is a mistake to measure Behn's work against the full-fledged realist novel, whose standards are set in the eighteenth century.

A case in point is Behn's longest and first-published fictional work, *Love-Letters Between a Nobleman and His Sister*, whose three volumes appeared between 1684 and 1687. Behn takes as her source a real-life scandal of aristocratic proportions. In 1682, Ford, Lord Grey of Werke, who had married Mary, daughter of George, Lord Berkeley, eloped with Mary's sister Henrietta. When the *London Gazette* published a missing-person report for Henrietta, a scandal was born. As if this lurid family romance were not fodder enough for Behn's imagination, political machinations kindly complicated matters, doubtless to Behn's artistic satisfaction. Lord Grey was a stalwart Whig who, during the year immediately preceding his sensational romance, had supported the Exclusion Bill and who, the following year, would participate in the treasonable Rye House plot and again, two years later, in Monmouth's rebellion (Grey saved himself by informing on his confederates). Grey brazenly tangled the two threads of his notoriety when, in November 1682, he arrived at his own conspiracy trial with Henrietta in tow.

In Behn's version of the story, the names are changed not so much to protect the guilty but to obey the pastoral conventions of historical romance. Grey becomes Philander; Mary, Myrtilla; and Henrietta, Sylvia. Moreover, despite Behn's recent trouble with the *Romulus and Hersilia* epilogue, Monmouth makes a comparatively benign and peripheral appearance as Cesario, a rebellious Huguenot prince: the similarities between the real Protestant belligerent and Behn's fictional one are obvious. As would become her wont, Behn prefaces her unconventional conventional romance with truth claims. Since the story begins in epistolary form, but later develops into a narrative, the truth claim alters accordingly. First, by way of introducing the epistolary format of the first volume, we are told in "The Argument" (a standard prefatory synopsis borrowed from drama):

After their flight [that of Philander and Sylvia] these letters were found in their cabinets, at their house at St.

Denis, where they both lived together, for the space of a year; and they are as exactly as possible placed in the order they were sent, and were those supposed to be written towards the latter end of their amours.
(*Love-Letters*, 1987, p. 2)

Later, as the text moves away from the letter format toward a first-person narrative, the found-epistle pretext is succeeded by an eyewitness account that largely reads as a third-person narrative, since the narrative "I" intrudes only on occasion to validate the events of the story.

The curiosity of Behn's validating gestures is that while the Grey-Berkeley scandal may provide the nonfictional base for Behn's fiction, Behn seeks to authenticate the cover story of the rebellious Huguenot prince and the characters of the fictional French setting, rather than the genuine motivating events in current British politics and society that would be familiar to any contemporary reader. That is, instead of telling us she has altered real names and real places, Behn exalts the obvious fiction with her truth claim. If this patent breach of the consistency required for realism at first seems unaccountably daft, it ultimately indicates that Behn's authenticating practice, earnest as it may be, is nevertheless an established fictional convention. That the apparently contradictory customs of realism and romance overlap here recalls the fundamental instability of these categories in the period inaugurating the Enlightenment.

Similarly, the slow shift over the course of three volumes from an exclusive epistolary format to a narrative interspersed with a handful of letters may bespeak a lack of discipline or experience on Behn's part. This evolution, however, may also represent a willful experimentation with form—Behn's effort to find a medium that accommodates the integral elements of her story as well as her pretext of veracity. Although a number of later writers, Richardson chief among them, would manipulate the epistolary format with great success, Behn abandoned it, perhaps because the languishing tone and euphuistic style she employs for love letters make it difficult credibly to sustain detailed reports of narrative events. Richardson, of course, manages to introduce into the supposed private letters of both *Pamela* and *Clarissa* all sorts of narrative minutiae without straining credibility too far, but his characters' tones and styles, dramatic as they may be, are far less so than those of Behn's. (This having been said, it is worth noting points of resemblance between *Love-Letters*—which remained popular through much of the eighteenth century—and *Clarissa*, from the general theme of seduction-abduction to the various affinities between Behn's Philander and Richardson's Lovelace, each of whom, perhaps not coincidentally, refers to or addresses his beloved as "my charmer.")

If personal and political intrigue makes *Love-Letters* an attractive book, the element of incest suggested in the title gives it its unsettlingly seductive edge. Incest is, in fact, a recurring motif in Behn's work: it steers the plot in a short fiction called *The Dumb Virgin; or, The Force of Imagination* (1687) and forms an implicit subtext in *Oroonoko*. Here, the nobleman and his sister, Philander and Sylvia, are not, of course, consanguineous siblings. Philander is Sylvia's brother-in-law. Yet, as critic Ellen Pollak reminds us, "the English concept of marriage in the seventeenth century was based on the legal and religious doctrine of the unity of husband and wife," a tenet that renders the relationship between Philander and Sylvia worse than technically incestuous (Hutner, ed., pp. 153–154). Then again, notes Pollak, in reviewing the findings of Susan Staves, "an increasing dissociation of natural law theory from theology during the second half of the seventeenth century effectively established the conditions both for changes in the institutional treatment of moral crimes and for the emergence of a new brand of heroism in the imaginative literature of the age" (p. 153). Philander is the new hero who celebrates freedom from unnatural, not to mention stodgy, law and custom; as Pollak points out, he explicitly disputes the notion that relationships established through marital affinity constitute incest. Nevertheless, the very fact that Philander's behavior remains transgressive on some level—if not against his version of natural law, then against man-made law and custom—gives the plot its force and excitement: through Philander, Behn captures and capitalizes upon the seventeenth-century libertine zeitgeist.

Furthermore, in compromising the authority of Sylvia's father through the seduction of Sylvia, Philander gestures toward establishing his own Whiggish authority as a sovereign subject. The libertine is properly libertarian. *Love-Letters* thus joins current political and philosophical debates pitting individual freedom against patriarchal, and by extension monarchical, authority: Whigs are generally understood to champion the individual; Tories, the monarchy. Yet party ideology is finally too complex for such simple divisions. This complexity is underscored by the reader's awareness, first, that ideas of sexual and political freedom are embroiled in this book; and, second, that the Restoration tradition of libertinage, of sexual unrestraint, which the Whiggish Philander partly endorses, is customarily more a Tory than a Whig characteristic. It would be possible, therefore, and by way of example, to regard Willmore, the royalist hero of *The Rover*, and Philander as political foes yet brothers in morality, given that Philander's amorous hankerings eventually make him as much a rover as the Rover is a philanderer.

Sylvia, too, participates in what may or may not be read as an incestuous relationship, but her violation of social codes operates along lines that diverge from Philander's transgression, in part because women cannot securely occupy the role of libertine or, for that matter, of libertarian in the way that men do. Sylvia's role as rebel or, alternatively, as sexual pioneer is more complicated, since society regards women who experiment to be morally fallen. Yet Behn reveals an impulse to investigate and even celebrate women's autonomy and desire (including legally forbidden desire), for Sylvia, despite her impetuous exploits, tentatively remains the text's heroine. Then again, the narrator periodically, if perhaps half-heartedly, censures Sylvia's continued naughty behavior—Sylvia and other formerly virtuous women in the story (the not-so-distant prototypes for Defoe's wayward heroines Moll Flanders and Roxana) take multiple lovers and scheme to relieve lovestruck and otherwise incautious men of their money. The censure of Sylvia's behavior is, however, incommensurate with the virtual absence of criticism accorded the sexual exploits of male characters. Sylvia's difficulty thus resembles that of Hellena in *The Rover*, whose unrepentant exploration of desire may or may not be tempered by the text's ultimate recourse to conventional social paradigms. The difference is that Sylvia crosses legal and moral boundaries Hellena does not.

Heroines crossing legal and moral boundaries, especially those who appropriate the male prerogative of sexual inconstancy, appear in a good number of the more than a dozen works of short fiction Behn wrote between 1684 and her death in 1689. For instance, *The Fair Jilt* describes the altogether depraved escapades of the fatally beautiful Miranda, whose insidious flirtations lead to the death or near death and ruin of any man who catches her attention, and who enlists her enamored lackeys to attempt the murder of her more virtuous younger sister. Another story, *The History of the Nun; or, The Fair Vow-Breaker* (1689), relates the life of the lovely and cloistered Isabella, who at the outset breaks her holy vows for the love of a man. She ends up an unwitting bigamist who, thanks to a skewed set of moral scruples, murders both her husbands: she strangles the first and stealthily sews the sack containing his corpse to the coat of the second; as the second husband attempts to dispose of the first husband's body in a nearby river, he inadvertently disposes of himself as well and thereby fulfills Isabella's heinous plan. With the exception of a couple of fairly traditional romances, the stories that do not center on the activities of morally destitute women at least tend to depict women who are inadvertent social outcasts (unwed and pregnant) or physically disabled (blind, mute).

Utterly absent from these tales are the genuine sentiment and didacticism that would justify the popular eighteenth-century tales and novels of women in trouble. The fair jilt Miranda intermittently pays lip service to compunction but negates such moments through prompt and unchecked recidivism. At the story's close, Miranda, who inexplicably has been pardoned for her sins, appears to have mended her ways: "They say *Miranda* has been very penitent for her past life" (vol. 5, p. 124). Yet the eyewitness narrator's recourse to an indefinite third-person plural certification—"they say"—lends the statement the quality of an unsubstantiated rumor and, therefore, reinforces the reader's skepticism. Similarly, when the former nun Isabella, having confessed to the murder of her two husbands and eased her guilty conscience, stands upon the scaffold a seeming model of contrition, we expect our narrator to offer up a felicitous moral reflection on the harmony of divine and human justice. What we get instead verges on titillation: "Chearful as a Bride . . . [Isabella] set all Hearts a flaming." And, in the next and final paragraph: "she put off her Mourning Vail, and, without any thing over her Face, she kneel'd down, and the Executioner, at one Blow, sever'd her Beautiful Head from her Delicate Body, being then in her Seven and Twentieth Year. She was generally Lamented, and Honourably Bury'd" (vol. 5, p. 324). The story ends here, with no cautionary lesson on the exemplariness of Isabella's case in evidence. Sentimental and didactic these narratives resoundingly are not; they rather form a gripping and gratuitous series of exercises in sadomasochistic romance. But if Behn's bizarre, violent, and unsanitary stories seem anomalous precursors to the dominant traditions of prose fiction, their unwholesome features are, in fact, reproduced in unexpurgated versions of hugely successful minor genres, such as the eighteenth-century Oriental tale or the fairy tales popularized by the brothers Grimm in the nineteenth century.

The notion that the bulk of Behn's short fiction lacks sentiment and didactic intent will sound strange to those with a passing knowledge of Behn's most famous literary work, *Oroonoko; or, The Royal Slave,* and its critical reception. Behn's tale of an enslaved African prince is sometimes regarded as a centerpiece of didactic and sentimental British antislavery fiction, just as Behn herself is sometimes distinguished as a sympathetic abolitionist *avant la lettre*. Such beliefs are misleading, though, and risk obscuring both the complicated representations of race and slavery in the text as well as the text's actual relationship to British abolitionism.

What critics have considered sentimental in *Oroonoko* begins on the west coast of Africa when a slave-trading ship's captain, a man "better bred, and more engaging, than most of that sort of Men are" (vol. 5, p. 161) tricks the noble African hero into slavery; the reader's sympathy is enlisted through Oroonoko's and the white female "eyewitness" narrator's mutual sense of indignation at the injustice of the event. As Oroonoko and his loyal countrymen are transported to the South American colony of Surinam, and after their arrival there, the narrator revisits the feeling of indignation several times. Over and again, a succession of fools and knaves betrays Oroonoko: some are dastardly Europeans; others, the enslaved African compatriots who abandon him during a rebellion. Oroonoko's indignation and the reader's sympathy culminate in Oroonoko's sacrifice of his pregnant wife, Imoinda, and his stoic composure in the face of his own dismemberment and death. The death of Imoinda at the hands of Oroonoko is understood to be an act of dignity and mercy, for Oroonoko fears that if his enemies kill him while she yet lives, Imoinda, who already abides one fate worse than death—

slavery—may suffer the other: rape. Their unborn child, too, would doubtless be enslaved.

If the reader's sentiment appears bound up with a critique of slavery and its destruction of the nuclear family, it is not. The adaptations and revisionist readings of Behn's text that permit such a critique would appear a century later, when the British antislavery movement reached maturity and gathered widespread support. In fact, there is no coherent or consistent message in *Oroonoko* decrying the institution of slavery. Slavery per se is no injustice, according to the ethics of this text. Oroonoko himself, an unflinching model of civic virtue, owns and trades slaves before his ignominious capture and had once, in courting Imoinda, "presented her an hundred and fifty Slaves in Fetters" (p. 138). Indeed, when Oroonoko's fellow plantation slaves desert him during the rebellion—only the pregnant Imoinda and Tuscan, "a tall *Negroe* of some more quality than the rest," stand and fight—Oroonoko's righteous fury leads him to assert the fundamental, unbridgeable difference in quality between himself and those ignoble apostates. He tells Deputy-Governor Byam, via the narrator's indirect discourse: "he was ashamed of what he had done in endeavouring to make those free, who were by Nature Slaves, poor wretched Rogues to be used as Christian tools [Christians are on the whole a perfidious lot, from Oroonoko's perspective]; Dogs, treacherous and cowardly, fit for such Masters" (p. 196).

There is no inkling of pity here for the downtrodden masses. What, then, if not the sheer existence of slavery, breeds indignation? What enjoins the sympathy of reader and narrator alike? The violation of honor: a theme that harks back to Behn's earliest literary effort, *The Forc'd Marriage*, and that engages her ever after. Oroonoko's enslavement is dishonorable. It is dishonorable not by definition but because no worthy enemy has defeated this awesome hero in battle. In a speech designed to rouse the ire of his fellow captives in Surinam, those whom he subsequently regards as rabble, he demands, to an emphatic chorus of "Noes": "Have they vanquished us nobly in Fight? Have they won us in Honourable Battle? And are we by the Chance of War become their Slaves? This would not anger a noble Heart; this would not animate a Soldier's Soul" (p. 191). The idea that enslavement is legitimate when accomplished through honorable battle is not specific to Behn's fiction, but can be found in Restoration

neoclassical literature, as well as in seventeenth-century political philosophy. The exiled Whig philosopher John Locke, for one, incorporates what is known as the "just war" slavery argument into his watershed *Second Treatise of Government* (1689), which he was able to publish in the aftermath of the Glorious Revolution, a year after Behn published *Oroonoko*.

In addition to providing the narrative its crucial theme, honor directs the plot as well. The possibility that a seemingly respectable man—the slave-trading captain, for instance—can violate honor grants Europeans the chance to dupe Oroonoko time and again: these are the moments that shape Behn's tale of woe. What are we to make of Oroonoko's obtuseness? Surely, Oroonoko's initial failure to register the duplicity of others and his own seeming inability to resort to deception indicate his ingenuousness, yet they also bespeak his pristine nobility. No man of worth, according to Oroonoko's courtly precepts, would violate his sacred word of honor. It is not only unconscionable but unimaginable that they do so. As for himself: "I swear by my Honour; which to violate, would not only render me contemptible and despised by all brave and honest Men and so give my self perpetual Pain, but it would be eternally offending and displeasing all Mankind; harming, betraying, circumventing and outraging all Men" (p. 164).

The problem is that Oroonoko is a prince in a world of scoundrels. No unsullied court context exists for him, certainly not in Surinam, where profit dictates ethics. Nor is Coramantien, Oroonoko's African homeland (the setting of the seldom-discussed first half of the book), free of treachery despite its narrative distance from the slave-trading posts and despite its courtly—indeed its epic—backdrop. Oroonoko's aged and sexually impotent grandfather the king first confiscates Imoinda for himself, then sells her into slavery. Eventually realizing that he needs Oroonoko's strength to safeguard his throne, he determines, after a rather unkingly fashion, to beg Oroonoko's forgiveness. There are unmistakable Homeric traces here: Oroonoko, having lost Imoinda to his grandfather (a reenactment of Agamemnon's seizure of Briseis), plays the brooding Achilleus in his tent while his close companion Aboan makes a valiant, if futile, show in battle (unlike Patroklos, Aboan survives). But where the epic allows characters to indulge peevish moods while still maintaining grandeur, the part–historical romance, part–realist novel format of *Oroonoko* tends to undermine its own lofty pretensions by accentuating the plotting minds of its characters—which is not to suggest Behn fully explores character psychology as modern novelists do. This dual generic impulse thus renders petty and mean even the royal figure of the king. Honor and nobility are everywhere deflated. In fact, honorable names from classical antiquity are bathetically, if not ironically, conferred upon the hero and heroine as slave names. Oroonoko in slavery becomes Caesar, while Imoinda becomes Clemene. (If the latter sounds unfamiliar to modern readers, aside from suggesting clemency, it is actually a stock romance name, variants of which—Cleomena, Cemene—Behn employs elsewhere. What is more, Behn's colleagues Thomas Creech and Dryden were during this period in the process of making popular and accessible Plutarch's life of the Spartan king Cleomenes, a life that bears more than a few points of resemblance to that of Oroonoko.)

But another problem is that the narrator is a bit of a scoundrel herself, which circumstance necessarily calls into question the extent of her sympathy and her honor. That she deserves suspicion may come as a surprise, considering, first, that some critics make no distinction between the narrator and Aphra Behn. Second, the narrator is not only romantically sympathetic to Oroonoko's plight but serves him as self-appointed historiographer royal, despite her disingenuous and perfunctory habit of trivializing the fruits of her "Female Pen." And yet she tells us that when Oroonoko and Imoinda are in captivity in Surinam she "was obliged, by some Persons who fear'd a Mutiny" to monitor the activities of and to placate her hero, the potential incendiary, and his consort. To do so, the narrator

entertained them with the Loves of the *Romans,* and great Men, which charmed him to my Company; and her, with teaching her all the pretty Works that I was Mistress of, and telling her Stories of Nuns, and endeavouring to bring her to the Knowledge of the true God: But of all Discourses, *Caesar* likes that the worst, and would never be reconciled to our Notions of the Trinity.

(p. 175)

Under the guise of hospitality, the narrator carries out a missionary and pedagogical task—inculcating Christianity, European history, and domestic arts ("Works")—designed to tame Oroonoko's rebellious spirit and Imoinda's fierce loyalty, a loyalty that, perhaps due to her recent proximity to the Amazon River as well as her classical affect, develops into military prowess akin to that of the mythical Amazon women.

Of course, the narrator would not necessarily regard her own complicity with Oroonoko's captors to be inconsistent with her belief that Oroonoko deserves freedom and will eventually obtain it. Many of the most progressive British abolitionists of the late eighteenth century dreaded slave revolt, regarded it as unquestionably reprehensible, and in any case felt that even free black men and women required white paternalistic care. Nevertheless, the narrator's abrupt alternations among heartfelt sympathy, shrewd complicity, and detached journalistic sangfroid (the report of Oroonoko's death is so matter-of-fact as to cast an almost absurd pall across the would-be tragic climax) remain unsettling. They remain unsettling precisely because the reader of this tale—this tale whose cardinal motivation is the exploration of honor and trust—begins to suspect that the narrator's talent for participating in covert operations vis-à-vis Oroonoko may in fact make her capable of compromising the honorable contract between narrator and reader: the narrator who claims an unwavering attachment to "relating the Truth" (p. 129) may well be exercising undue control over the faithful reader by propagating "fiction." In evidence are plenty of instances—Oroonoko's epic man-to-tiger combat, let us say—where she oversteps the bounds of the plausible.

The narrator of *Oroonoko* could therefore turn out to be the moderate end to Behn's line of wily fictional heroines. At the very least, her divided allegiances complicate the tale's presumed didactic and sentimental impulses. We may wonder, then, how it is that *Oroonoko* came to be regarded as a model of didactic and sentimental antislavery fiction. We may wonder, too, how Behn-qua-narrator is deemed a proto-abolitionist. Although Behn's text went through several editions and remained popular throughout the eighteenth century, later writers also frequently adapted or translated it. More famous than Behn's narrative was Thomas Southerne's dramatic adaptation, *Oroonoko: A Tragedy* (1696), which incorporated material from Behn's other colonial play, the posthumously produced *The Widow Ranter* (1689), and which was first staged in November 1695. His tragic version was in turn bowdlerized into three subsequent adaptations that appeared in 1759 and 1760, one of which the notable midcentury writer John Hawkesworth penned, with the century's premier actor, David Garrick, performing the title role—unsuccessfully. Theater companies frequently produced versions of the play throughout the eighteenth century, while the following two centuries saw occasional performances: one nineteenth-century production featuring the black tragic actor Ira Aldridge gained attention, presumably because the play's African hero would normally have been played by a white actor. In the early part of this century, Sir Ralph Richardson acted the part.

The obvious irony here is that Behn, a major dramatist in her own right, chose to present as prose narrative a plot and cast of characters eminently suited to the drama. But by 1688, her proclivity for nondramatic genres, health problems that would have made it difficult to carry a play through production, and England's political turmoil most likely steered her toward narrative forms. It was Southerne's revision that rendered Behn's fictional work more appropriate for the antislavery movement, a movement that gained momentum and extensive support as the eighteenth century wore on. Southerne furnished the undiluted sentimental and tragic elements we tend to associate with the story and purged his version of Behn's realistic details. His decision to change the heroine Imoinda into a white European—an alteration that did not go unremarked by audiences—provided the tragic heft of the Othello-Desdemona plot. Even so, eighteenth-century abolitionists found it necessary to rewrite Southerne's play further in order to make it acceptable for their project. (Information on Southerne derives from Robert Jordan and Harold Love, eds., *The Works of Thomas Southerne*, vol. 2, Oxford, Eng., 1988, pp. 89–101.)

One longish point of qualification: Behn's failure to formulate a coherent critique of African-Caribbean slavery in *Oroonoko* does not mean race and ethnicity are bereft of meaning for her. To the contrary, race and ethnicity serve both as indices for organizing familiar philosophical concepts and as a cloak for Behn's political allegory. Philosophy: throughout the tale Behn juxtaposes the royal Africans to the native Surinamese so as to study the idealized customs and physical attributes of both groups and to contrast them to those of Europeans. Her stereotypical observations allow her to rehearse popular conceptions of the "noble savage" and the "state of nature" touted in philosophical literature from Montaigne

to Rousseau. What is especially interesting here for students of the novel is that Behn's realist fictional leanings invariably manage to intrude upon her investigation of these hypothetical categories. For example, by way of comparing the ideal state-of-nature to European civilization in order to illuminate the latter's advantages (progress) and disadvantages (corruption), Behn's narrator describes the "Natives" or "Indians" of Surinam in predictably childlike, prelapsarian terms—they are simple, harmless, naturally modest, easily befriended, and attracted to brightly colored baubles. Yet through occasional and apparently unguarded admissions of guileful colonial policy, the narrator twists philosophy's ideal collective type into a menacing group of individuals commonly found in realist novels and in traditional European histories of non-European cultures: "So that they being on all Occasions very useful to us, we find it absolutely necessary to caress 'em as Friends, and not to treat 'em as Slaves; nor dare we do otherwise, their Numbers so far surpassing ours in that Continent" (p. 133). Friends are in fact enemies, and nature's peace-loving children actually live in towns and slaughter Europeans. Serving two generic ends, Behn's racial and ethnic distinctions eventually end up a cluster of narrative incongruities she halfheartedly seeks to reconcile by attributing the Indians' newfound bad habits to the corrupting influence of Dutch colonists.

Politics: Behn published *Oroonoko* during the Glorious Revolution of 1688. Her beloved Stuarts were on the outs, and William of Orange, whom Behn regarded as a usurper and—for all practical purposes—a regicide, was soon to accede the throne of England. The story of the exiled and murdered African king maps fairly easily onto the current political upheaval and the ousting of James II, although it also clearly recalls the events of the Civil War and the execution of Charles I. So, too, Behn's persistent censure of what she regards as England's far too easy concession of Surinam to the Dutch during the 1660s becomes a warning against a bloodless surrender of an even more precious territory—England—to the Dutch Stadtholder William in the period 1688–1689. Oroonoko's curious combination of European and African racial features makes him perfectly suited to Behn's allegorical purpose. On the one hand, his facial features are not only European, but regal, and appeal to the narrator's refined

European aesthetic sensibilities (that Behn is racist or ethnocentric by today's standards is both obvious and beside the point): "His Nose was rising and *Roman*, instead of *African* and flat: His Mouth the finest shaped that could be seen; far from those great turn'd Lips, which are so natural to the rest of the Negroes" (p. 136). On the other hand, his skin is black, and this detail, along with the exotic setting, establishes allegory's necessary displacement of familiar people and politics.

Of particular importance to the narrative process of casting Oroonoko in blackface is the narrator's eagerness to make a fetish of skin color. She does so by distinguishing Oroonoko's color (and, in turn, Imoinda's) from that of the rest of his countrymen: "His Face was not of that brown rusty Black which most of that Nation are, but a perfect Ebony, or polished Jet" (p. 136). Oroonoko is a racial anomaly; he is one of a kind. Further still, his racial singularity is of a piece with his singularity of character and position: no one else in the text is as black or as honorable or as kingly as he. It is, of course, interesting that the narrator, who passionately argues for Oroonoko's individual freedom and against his enslavement, renders him the carnal object of her raffish racial fascination. What is more significant to Behn's royalist agenda, however, is that through the description of Oroonoko's racial uniqueness, she reproduces the still important political argument that a monarch is a monarch in body as well as in deportment and office. The race of kings—here "race" resumes its more familiar seventeenth-century meaning—is a rare breed for which there can be no substitution. Parliament cannot presume to replace a genuine Stuart with a Dutch pretender of its choosing. Genealogy is written on the body, and genealogy is crucial.

POETRY AND TRANSLATION

WHEN the theaters merged in 1682, Behn turned to fiction, but she also began to focus on poetry and translation. Poetry was not new to her. She had already published verse now and again, and she had the habit of scattering rhymed lyrics here and there in the drama: "Love Arm'd," the two stanzas of song that open *Abdelazer*, form what was until very recently Behn's most famous and best-respected poem. She wrote most of the verse pro-

logues and epilogues to her plays, too, despite the custom of farming out these poetic appendages to other authors who could properly eulogize the playwright's efforts. Behn used the occasions to peddle politics and aesthetic theory and to defend, if not praise, her dramatic achievements. In the 1680s she augmented her repertoire with attention to occasional poems, love poems, erotic poems, and philosophical poems—as well as a version of Aesop's fables—through translations, adaptations, and verse of her own invention. Behn published her poems either singly in broadsheet or in collections assembled by herself or others. Or, like many of her friends and colleagues, she circulated them privately among her coterie (publishing "privately" afforded some women poets the only viable option to disseminate their work while yet preserving a reputation for modesty). *Poems upon Several Occasions: With a Voyage to the Island of Love* (1684), Behn's major collection, is devoted exclusively to her own work, save the nine prefatory poems written in praise of her. Another collection, *A Miscellany of New Poems*, appeared in 1688. Often credited to Behn's editorial hand is a much earlier collection, *The Covent Garden Drolery* (1672), which introduces four of her poems alongside those of other writers.

The distinctions among original, adapted, and translated verse are complicated by the same issues that nettle the drama and fiction: seventeenth-century ideas of intellectual and artistic property differ substantially from our own. In addition, Behn's "original" work as a translator was, in her own estimation, thwarted by her ignorance or inadequate mastery of classical languages—no small source of frustration in a decade that treasured good translations. To produce her substantial segment of Abraham Cowley's *Of Plants* or her contribution to Dryden's collection of *Ovid's Epistles, Translated by Several Hands* (1680), she may well have adapted someone else's crude literal translation from Latin into English. She lamented in verse her lack of classical training, and her lament seems genuine: Behn hardly had the personality to hide a secret knowledge of Latin under a modest veil. Hence Dryden's commendatory disclaimer prefacing his publication of Behn's "Paraphrase on Oenone to Paris" may better reflect his scruples than hers: "I was desired to say that the author, who is of the fair sex, understood not Latin. But if she does not, I am afraid she has given us occasion to be ashamed who do" (quoted in Link, p. 116).

She writes boldly in her prefatory poem to Creech's highly acclaimed translation of Lucretius' *De rerum natura* (highly acclaimed in part because Lucretius' worldly philosophy was thought to authorize Restoration libertinage) that "Till now I curst my *Sex* and *Education*," which formerly prevented her from enjoying the classics. Creech's stellar performance, however,

> dost advance
> Our [women's] Knowledge from the State of Ignorance;
> And Equallst Us to Man!
>
> (pp. 26–27).[2]

Her identification of admission to the classics with gender equality is a familiar early feminist focal point: true equality would mean rigorous training for women in Latin and Greek.

Behn clearly knew French well and translated from it with gusto. Her 1684 collection includes *A Voyage to the Island of Love*, a lengthy translation of the Abbé Paul Tallemant's *Le Voyage de l'Isle d'Amour* (1663), which she followed in the 1688 collection with *Lycidus; or, The Lover in Fashion* (earlier spelled "Lycidas"), a translation of Tallemant's second "voyage." In the first voyage, Lysander describes to Lycidas his travels through a geography of moods and poses (the River of Pretension, the City of Discretion) toward his lover, Aminta. In the second voyage, Lycidus responds to Lysander's story of a lover's progress with his own rake's progress. The Tallemant translations are what Dryden, in his system of classification that distinguishes among "metaphrase" (literal), "paraphrase" (faithful), and "imitation" (liberal), might identify as lying somewhere between the latter two. Behn displays her skill in preserving the sense of the original, but she often indulges poetic interpolations of her own invention. Moreover, the second translation is hardly poetry at all: it consists of a prose narrative punctuated by stanzas of verse. The variation in form for this lengthy work undoubtedly reflects Behn's late preoccupation with prose. In fact, *Lycidus* bears several points of comparison to *Love-Letters*, another story that evolved during the same period and that Behn published in installments. *Love-Letters*, too, includes the intermittent verse, while each narrative relates the inconstancies of a heroine named Sylvia whose initially central adventures are pushed to the narrative margins by the escapades of a libertine male hero.

Other translation-adaptations of nonpoetic French works include some four hundred of La Rochefoucauld's maxims (1685), a mixed prose and lyric rendition of Balthasar de Bonnecorse's *La Montre; or, The Lover's Watch* (1686), and Mlle de Brillac's novella, *Agnes de Castro* (1688). Behn executed near-literal translations of B. Le Bovier de Fontenelle's French version of the Dutchman Antonious van Dale's Latin *The History of Oracles, and the Cheats of the Pagan Priests* (1688) and Fontenelle's own philosophical *A Discovery of New Worlds* (1688). Her verse rendition of *Aesop's Fables* (1687), for which Behn produced more than a hundred quatrains each succeeded by a "Moral" in couplet form, was commissioned by the artist Francis Barlow to accompany his celebrated engravings in a folio edition. Of interest here is Behn's inevitable introduction of Tory politics into several stanzas. It is difficult, for instance, not to read a reference to Monmouth's rebellion in the moral to "The Kite, Frog, and Mouse," a moral that is not terribly relevant to the fable: "The fond aspiring youth who empire sought / By dire ambition was to ruine brought" (p. 243).

Behn's original poetry addresses numerous topics and includes work without a precedent source, as well as work that departs sufficiently from a model to merit a label other than "imitation." Love is Behn's most frequent subject, the neoclassical pastoral love lyric in rhymed couplets or quatrains her most familiar form, although she sometimes counterfeits the Scottish ballad ("When *Jemmy*, first began to Love," p. 9). Typical in the love poems is a story of unrequited passion: the Maid runs headlong into amorous devotion, while the Swain basks in cruel indifference or slouches into dumb oblivion. Behn construes the pain of unrequited love and its debilitating power in graphic, physical terms, and she often figures love personified as conquering tyrant or wily traitor. Her acclaimed "Love Arm'd," for instance, opens thus in lurid splendor: "Love in Fantastique Triumph satt, / Whilst Bleeding Hearts a round him flow'd" (p. 53).

Ruthless love touches an autobiographical chord in the pastoral lyric "*The Dream. A Song.*" The maid Astrea spies a bound Cupid whimpering, "*Amyntas* stole my Bow away, / And Pinion'd

---

[2]All references to Behn's poetry are from vol. 1 of the Janet Todd edition.

both my Wings." Astrea, realizing that her lover has "wounded" her with Cupid's purloined "darts," cuts a deal with the distressed boy-god: she will free him, if he will launch a retaliatory strike against the heart of Amyntas. No sooner does Astrea untie Cupid's "Silken Fetters," however, than he blithely glides away, leaving her to wake in resignation from what has all the time been a dream, one "too true" (pp. 71–72). Astrea is Behn's pseudonym (the name has an immediate precedent in Honoré d'Urfé's epic romance *L'Astrée*, 1607–1627) and Amyntas that of her lover, John Hoyle, whom she sometimes also calls Lycidus. There is speculation but little certain knowledge about possible lovers Behn may have taken between William Scot and her death, but her affair with Hoyle was as public as it was agonizing. A consummate Restoration rake, Hoyle treated her badly; he demanded loyalty from her but balked at her suggestion that he return the favor. His widely publicized homosexuality (he was once indicted under harsh sodomy laws), if it represented more a genuine orientation than a casual Restoration libertinage, may also have complicated his relationship with Behn. Behn directed a number of love poems to and at Hoyle, poems full of sighs and reproaches and jealousies. Written in his honor, for example, is "On Mr. J. H. in a Fit of Sickness," in which the narrator begs the bedridden, or bower-ridden, Amyntas: "in pity to *Astrea* live," as though his illness were contrived to pain and spite her (p. 90). Hoyle resented the publicity, and Behn became an object of public scorn.

In Behn's poetry, women are not always the victims of a libertine's divided interests. Sometimes the gender roles are reversed. But unlike the fiction, where a strange breed of jilting women parade their peculiarly heartless disorder, the poetry presents an all-too-feeling woman as the victim tortured by her own indecision. In the lyric "On Her Loving Two Equally," the two male love interests, Alexis and Damon, unwittingly bring about the undecided woman's suffering: "if by chance they both are by, / For both alike I languish, sigh, and die" (p. 78). Of course, whether the woman is victim or perpetrator of inconstancy, we can attribute the exclusive attention to her anguish to the female poet's identification with her female character. Yet it is worth emphasizing that this identification is more keenly pronounced in Behn's poetry than in her fiction, where characters

of both genders are more likely to act than to feel, and where men usually feel more than women. It is as if the objective, journalistic pretense that Behn's female narrators affect in the prose steel them against the tempest of subjectivity so common to the verse.

On one or two occasions, men are almost wholly excluded from Behn's love lyrics. In "*To the fair* Clarinda, *who made Love to me, imagin'd more than Woman*," Behn's rare foray into lesbiana, the narrator describes her desire for another woman in a manner almost entirely free of the suffering and struggle that animate much of the heterosexual poetry. The same-sex relationship also has the advantage of being "innocent," since, at least within the narrator's poetic vision, lesbian desire lies beyond the purview of male-centered Restoration culture and law:

> In pity to our Sex sure thou wer't sent,
> That we might Love, and yet be Innocent:
> For sure no Crime with thee we can commit;
> Or if we shou'd—thy Form excuses it.
> (p. 288, ll. 12–15)

Here the narrator makes sure to emphasize the sexual possibilities of the relationship, lest the desire be understood solely to represent intense, but chaste, friendship of the sort described often in women's poetry of the time. One possible reading here is that innocence rests not upon celibacy, but upon society's failure to suspect or to trouble itself about sexual relations between women. Another is that the desired woman is so compelling that the narrator must be excused for taking leave of her senses. "Thy form" in the latter case would thus refer to the woman's perfection rather than her gender. That the love object is figured as androgynous or masculine further excuses the narrator's desire, at least according to heterosexual standards:

> Fair lovely Maid, or if that Title be
> Too weak, too Feminine for Nobler thee,
> Permit a Name that more Approaches Truth:
> And let me call thee, Lovely Charming Youth.
> This last will justifie my soft complaint.
> (p. 288, ll. 1–5)

Explicit lesbian subject matter in literature is more familiar to the Restoration than to later generations, although it was never a common theme. And one is more likely to come across it in political satires directed against powerful women (such as Queen Anne and her adviser-confidante Sarah Churchill, the Duchess of Marlborough) than elsewhere. Whether Behn herself had lesbian relationships is unknown, but developments in the nascent field of lesbian studies should give us a clearer sense of seventeenth-century lesbian culture and of the probability of Behn's bisexuality.

Several of the love lyrics suspend the pain of love in favor of eroticism, which Behn introduces either through high-flown euphemism ("His daring Hand that Altar seiz'd") or through simple, playful hints:

> A many kisses I did give,
> And she return'd the same
> Which made her willing to receive
> That which I dare not name.
> ("SONG," p. 6, ll. 13–16)

Janet Todd presents evidence that, in the name of decency, publishers may have suppressed more explicit lyrics, although the claim of indecency may represent an advertising ploy: then, as now, censorship was sometimes the best form of publicity (*Works*, vol. 1, p. 375, n. 2). Certainly, the Restoration saw the publication of much bawdy and some pornographic literature. But if the Earl of Rochester—whose language was coarser by far than Behn's—could produce such stuff with impunity, Behn, who was neither male nor aristocrat, could not. Her alternating boldness and suggestive coyness alike earned her the sting of her contemporaries' satirical pens and a more than two-hundred-year banishment from literary history.

Behn joins eroticism with a payback to men's numerous sexual satires against herself and against all womankind with "The Disappointment." The poem belongs to the genre of "imperfect enjoyment" verse, that is, poems about male sexual impotence or premature ejaculation. (This last may seem a nice distinction, but where Rochester's poem in this vein clearly describes the latter predicament, Behn's teasing indirection makes us wonder what, clinically speaking, has happened.) This pastoral romance in verse derives originally from Ovid, lately from French, and Behn's contribution to the genre is one among many English versions. Given the awkward subject matter of two young lovers foiled in their lovemaking enterprise by the curse of biology, the

rhetoric of romance and the pastoral conventions make for a humorous series of descriptions (such as: "the Insensible fell weeping in his Hand," p. 67, l. 90). But Behn impishly makes matters far more difficult for the male hero than some male poets would. When, for instance, the inflamed maiden Cloris discovers her lover Lysander's plight, she fulfills the stereotypically male paranoid fantasy by flying horrified from his arms in "both Disdain and Shame" (p. 68, l. 118). And again, where male poets inspire their heroes with a second wind and eventual triumph, Behn leaves her poor swain "Damn'd . . . to the *Hell* of Impotence." In a literary culture where women's sexuality endures an interminable barrage of crude verse, the satire on impotence is the lone response: Behn would take up the theme again in *Oroonoko* and *Love-Letters*.

A last love poem that bears mentioning, especially since it has been gaining more critical attention these days than almost any other, might be called Behn's philosophical love poem, insofar as it briefly touches upon neoclassical ideas circulating in philosophical texts of the period and inasmuch as it meditates upon the prelapsarian state of nature. "The Golden Age" (1684), a greatly expanded paraphrase on a French translation of Tasso, envisions a prefallen world of plenitude and freedom and untrammeled sexuality. Plenitude is, of course, a familiar condition in representations of the Edenic world, but where, say, the Adam and Eve of *Paradise Lost* (Milton was an ardent defender of Cromwell and therefore Behn's political opposite) toil in the garden, cultivating God's bounty, Behn's utopian vision banishes labor entirely. Behn's is a pastoral world, but not a georgic one; it is an egalitarian aristocratic world, too, a world with no monarchs, "Those Arbitrary Rulers over men" (p. 31, l. 52), and one where everyone consumes equally yet no one produces:

> The stubborn Plough had then,
> Made no rude Rapes upon the Virgin Earth;
> Who yeilded of her own accord her plentious Birth;
> Without the Aids of men;
> As if within her Teeming Womb,
> All Nature, and all Sexes lay,
> (p. 31, ll. 31–36)

The spontaneous, autochthonous, untiring generation and the earth's very hermaphrodite character obviate the cutting labor of plowshares and pregnancy alike. Meanwhile, free and easy maids and shepherds frolic in wanton innocence:

> The Nymphs were free, no nice, no coy disdain;
> Deny'd their Joyes, or gave the Lover pain;
> The yielding Maid but kind Resistance makes;
> (p. 32, ll. 97–99)

In fact, the poem concludes rather unexpectedly with a carpe diem theme by cautioning a theretofore unmentioned Sylvia against protesting her honor relentlessly: "But *Sylvia* when your Beauties fade, [. . .] / What will your duller honour signifie?" (p. 35, ll. 184 and 192). Honor, Behn's favorite motif, receives a summary dismissal in the poem: "Oh cursed Honour! thou who first didst damn, / A Woman to the Sin of shame" (p. 33, ll. 117–118). The principle so dear to Oroonoko is frowned upon here, since honor in this context is understood to signal man-made prudery and base artifice.

When Behn was not writing love poems or philosophical love poems, she was usually writing occasional poems. Some celebrated literary events, as did the commendatory verses affixed to the second edition (1683) of Creech's translation of Lucretius or those published with the second edition (1687) of Sir Francis Fane's tragic play *The Sacrifice*. Others lamented the death of artists in her circle: Behn produced an elegy to mourn the young but already famous portrait painter John Greenhill, who at the age of thirty-two stumbled drunkenly into a sewage gutter and promptly died; she also composed poems in heroic couplets to honor Rochester, who likewise died young and debauched at thirty-three, and the poet Edmund Waller, whom she admired greatly. Still others took a satirical turn: an attack on Dryden's conversion to Roman Catholicism has been credited to Behn, but this attribution warrants further investigation.

The rhymed couplets of the satirical "A Letter to a Brother of the Pen in Tribulation" gently chide the narrator's colleague, here given the pastoral name Damon, for having contracted a venereal disease that occasioned his temporary retirement to a remedial "Sweating-Tub." The real-life circumstance motivating Behn's verse epistle may have been that, upon suffering the affliction alluded to in the poem, the playwright Edward Ravenscroft failed to produce a prologue promised for Behn's play *The Dutch Lover*. Yet the narrator of the poem scolds Damon not for any personal inconvenience but on behalf of the close

group of wits and artists who want his company—the "whole Cabal" (an epithet Behn's circle ironically borrowed from the acronymic CABAL of five powerful men who administered Charles II's government). Janet Todd has observed the "man-to-man manner" between narrator and addressee and the poem's "identification with a male attitude towards prostitution" (*Works*, vol. 1, p. 395, n. 31). We may, of course, assume the narrator to be both female and a version of Behn herself: Behn's narrators usually are. But if the narrator's manly bluff does not give us pause, given the extraordinary role Behn forged for herself within a group of trendsetting male wits, then her identification with the rake rather than the prostitute does: "Now I could curse this Female, but I know, / She needs it not, that thus cou'd handle you" (p. 73, ll. 41–42). We are accustomed, at least in the drama, to Behn's siding with the prostitute, not the rake. That she does not do so here is a testament to her protean voice.

Behn also wrote poems on occasions of state, mostly in the ceremonial form of the Pindaric ode. In 1685, she composed two poems upon the death of Charles II, one of which she dedicated to Charles's Queen Catherine, and a third celebrating the coronation of James II. In 1687, Behn produced a Pindaric, noteworthy for its points of comparison to *Oroonoko*, on the occasion of the second Duke of Albemarle's appointment as governor of Jamaica. Then in 1688, before and during the Glorious Revolution (a revolution by no means glorious to Behn, who favored the Stuarts), she fashioned congratulatory odes to James's Catholic Queen Mary of Modena on her pregnancy and on the birth of the presumed Prince of Wales. At the same time, "To Poet Bavius" was published as Behn's scathing rejoinder to John Baber's disparaging verse on Behn's poetic account of the royal pregnancy, as well as on the pregnancy and birth themselves.

This birth of a Catholic prince to a Catholic queen was monumental. It precipitated the revolution, and the would-be James III, the "Old Pretender" to the throne, was passed over for the English monarchy in favor of his two Protestant elder half-sisters, first Mary (with her husband, William of Orange) and later Anne. Although Behn celebrated the Catholic royal family in verse, her own religious affiliation is disputed: despite the satire on Dryden's supposed conversion to Catholicism attributed to her, she herself variously defended Catholicism and Anglicanism, depending on whose company she was keeping. She was probably an Anglican with Catholic sympathies or background, at a time when anti-Catholic sentiment ran high in England; in any case, she was almost certainly not a Dissenting Protestant.

When it came to state occasions, Behn was not an opportunist in any simple sense. Although William and Mary's accession to the throne prompted a flurry of effusive responses from a number of poets, Behn, who could not bring herself to celebrate William of Orange, restricted her poetic commentary on the event to praise of the Stuart Mary. Even then, the gleeful tone that concludes a congratulatory poem on Mary's arrival in England is eclipsed by the narrator's plangent description in the opening stanzas of the Muses' solitary and dejected meditation on the ousted king. When Dr. Gilbert Burnet (a onetime intimate of the Stuarts who became a champion of William after 1684, and whom William rewarded with a bishopric in 1689) invited Behn to write a poem celebrating William's accession, she answered with "A Pindaric Poem to the Reverend Doctor Burnet." While Behn is effusive in her praise of Burnet and wonderfully eloquent in her response to him throughout, she ultimately declines his distinguished offer:

> But oh! if from your Praise I feel
>   A Joy that has no Parallel
> What must I suffer when I cannot pay
>   Your Goodness, your own generous way?
> And make my stubborn Muse your Just Commands
>   obey.
>   My Muse that would endeavour fain to glide
> With the fair prosperous Gale, and the full driving Tide
> But Loyalty Commands with Pious Force,
>   That stops me in the thriving Course.
>   (pp. 308–309, ll. 44–52)

Blaming her muse in order to detract attention from her own refusal, Behn tells Burnet, in her loftiest manner, thank you but no thank you. Angeline Goreau has pointed out that although Behn stood to be paid handsomely for a congratulatory poem to the new king, she was by this time too close to death—her health having steadily declined for some time—to think of worldly profits (pp. 291–292). But Behn claims loyalty to the exiled king, and one cannot help but wonder if writing a poem to William, under any circumstances, would have represented a form of prostitution that even Behn would find shameful.

CONCLUSION

"HERE lies a proof that wit can never be / Defence enough against mortality." Thus reads the couplet that serves as epitaph on the gravestone of Aphra Behn, who died on 16 April 1689. That the lapidary phrase summing up Behn's life should be a sneering or, perhaps, affectionate scrap of doggerel seems altogether as scandalous and appropriate as her burial site in the cloisters of Westminster Abbey. Behn did write indefatigably to the end, but not because she thought her wit could stave off the inevitable—she was keenly aware that her failing health would soon get the better of her. Rather, she seems to have known no other way of living. And, as always, she needed the money.

Any number of ailments may have troubled Behn toward the end of her life. In the icy winter of 1683–1684, apparently on her way to visit Creech, Behn took a bad spill in a carriage that left her "Scribling Fist . . . out of joynt, / And ev'ry Limb made great complaint" ("A Letter to Mr. Creech at Oxford"). There is speculation that she afterward suffered from arthritis. It seems she also contracted the common libertine affliction of syphilis. Goreau cites a rhymed attack on Behn, circa 1686, that, whether corresponding closely to reality or not, suggests signs of illness were in evidence: the verse refers rather nastily to assorted bodily emissions and expulsions as well as a painful, disfiguring condition (p. 261). Behn's late correspondence and poetry likewise mention a debilitating sickness. In a letter to Edmund Waller's daughter-in-law, she begs pardon for the quality of the commendatory verse that had been commissioned upon the poet's death in October 1687: "I am very ill and have been dying this twelve month" (Goreau, p. 291).

What is Behn's legacy? And what an apt eulogy? Here is Virginia Woolf, again in *A Room of One's Own*:

And with Mrs. Behn we turn a very important corner on the road. We leave behind, shut up in their parks among their folios, those solitary great ladies who wrote without audience or criticism, for their own delight alone. We come to town and rub shoulders with ordinary people in the streets. Mrs. Behn was a middle-class woman with all the plebeian virtues of humour, vitality and courage; a woman forced by the death of her husband and some unfortunate adventures of her own to make her living by her wits. She had to work on equal terms with men. She made, by working very hard, enough to live on. The importance of that fact outweighs anything that she actually wrote . . . for here begins the freedom of the mind, or rather the possibility that in the course of time the mind will be free to write what it likes. For now that Aphra Behn had done it, girls could go to their parents and say, You need not give me an allowance; I can make money by my pen. Of course the answer for many years to come was, Yes, by living the life of Aphra Behn! Death would be better! and the door was slammed faster than ever.

(1989 ed., pp. 63–64)

Of course, the answer for Woolf, if one were to cavil, is that she knows full well those solitary great ladies were, to put it blandly, not delighted. Woolf is famous for ironic simpers. Not so ironic, however, is her sense of Behn's art. Woolf's own elite sensibilities compel her to underrate Behn's oeuvre in favor of the independent life. Then, too, Woolf's single-minded vision allows her to dwell on the liberty of the libertine and to ignore the aristocratic worldview attending Behn's libertinage. But that, one supposes, is what comes of high-born romantic notions of mucking about in the lowbrow mud.

SELECTED BIBLIOGRAPHY

I. BIBLIOGRAPHY. Jack M. Armistead, *Four Restoration Playwrights: A Reference Guide to Thomas Shadwell, Aphra Behn, Nathaniel Lee, and Thomas Otway* (Boston, 1984); Mary Ann O'Donnell, *Aphra Behn: An Annotated Bibliography of Primary and Secondary Sources* (New York, 1986).

II. COLLECTED WORKS. Montague Summers, ed., *The Works of Aphra Behn*, 6 vols. (London, 1915; repr. New York, 1967); Maureen Duffy, ed., *Oroonoko and Other Stories* (London, 1986); Germaine Greer, ed., *The Uncollected Verse of Aphra Behn* (Essex, Eng., 1989); Janet Todd, ed., *Oroonoko, The Rover, and Other Works* (New York, 1992); Janet Todd, ed., *The Works of Aphra Behn*, 6 vols. (London, vols. 1–4, 1992–1995; vols. 5–6 forthcoming).

III. SEPARATE WORKS. *The Rover* (Lincoln, Nebr., 1967), ed. by Frederick Link; *Oroonoko; or, The Royal Slave* (New York, 1973), ed. by Lore Metzger; *The Lucky Chance; or, The Alderman's Bargain* (London, 1981), ed. by Fidelis Morgan; *Love-Letters Between a Nobleman and His Sister* (New York, 1987), ed. by Maureen Duffy; *The Rover* (Peterborough, Ont., 1994), ed. by Anne Russell.

IV. BIOGRAPHIES. Vita Sackville-West, *Aphra Behn: The Incomparable Astrea* (New York, 1928); George Woodcock, *The Incomparable Aphra* (New York, 1948); William J. Cameron, *New Light on Aphra Behn* (Auckland, N.Z., 1961); Frederick M. Link, *Aphra Behn* (New York, 1968); George Robert Guffy, *Two English Novelists: Aphra Behn and Anthony Trollope* (Los Angeles, 1975); Maureen Duffy, *The Passionate Shepherdess: Aphra Behn 1640–1689* (London, 1977); Angeline Goreau, *Reconstructing Aphra: A Social Biography of Aphra Behn* (New York, 1980); Sara H. Mendelson, *The Mental World of Stuart Women: Three Studies* (Brighton, Eng., and Amherst, Mass., 1987).

V. CRITICAL STUDIES. Ernest Bernbaum, "Mrs. Behn's Biography a Fiction," in *PMLA* 28 (1913); Edwin D. Johnson, "Aphra Behn's *Oroonoko*," in *Journal of Negro History* 10 (July 1925); Harrison G. Platt, "Astrea and Celadon: An Untouched Portrait of Aphra Behn," in *PMLA* 49 (1934); Wylie Sypher, "A Note on the Realism of Mrs. Behn's *Oroonoko*," in *Modern Language Quarterly* 3 (1942); Roland M. Hill, "Aphra Behn's Use of Setting," in *Modern Language Quarterly* 7 (1946); Edward D. Seeber, "Oroonoko and Crusoe's Man Friday," in *Modern Language Quarterly* 12 (1951); John A. Ramsaran, "'Oroonoko': A Study of the Factual Elements," in *Notes and Queries* 205 (1960); Henry A. Hargreaves, "A Case for Mr. Behn," in *Notes and Queries* 207 (1962); Robert Adams Day, "Aphra Behn's First Biography," in *Studies in Bibliography* 22, no. 5 (1969).

Maximillian E. Novak, "Some Notes Toward a History of Fictional Forms: From Aphra Behn to Daniel Defoe," in *Novel* 6 (winter 1973); Martine Watson Brownley, "The Narrator in *Oroonoko*," in *Essays in Literature* 4 (1977); Robert L. Root, Jr., "Aphra Behn, Arranged Marriage, and Restoration Comedy," in *Women and Literature* 5 (1977); J. F. Musser, Jr., "'Imposing Nought But Constancy in Love': Aphra Behn Snares *The Rover*," in *Restoration* 3 (1979).

Judith Kegan Gardiner, "Aphra Behn: Sexuality and Self-Respect," in *Women's Studies* 7 (1980); Gary Kelly, "'Intrigue' and 'Gallantry': The Seventeenth-Century French *Nouvelle* and the 'Novels' of Aphra Behn," in *Revue de Littérature Comparée* 55 (1981); Laura Brown, "The Romance of Empire: *Oroonoko* and the Trade in Slaves," in *The New Eighteenth Century: Theory, Politics, English Literature*, ed. by Felicity Nussbaum and Laura Brown (New York and London, 1987); Robert L. Chibka, "'Oh! Do Not Fear a Woman's Invention': Truth, Falsehood, and Fiction in Aphra Behn's *Oroonoko*," in *Texas Studies in Literature and Language* 30, no. 4 (winter 1988); Catherine Gallagher, "Who Was That Masked Woman? The Prostitute and the Playwright in the Comedies of Aphra Behn," in *Women's Studies* 15 (1988); Katharine M. Rogers, "Fact and Fiction in Aphra Behn's *Oroonoko*," in *Studies in the Novel* 20, no. 4 (spring 1988); Elin Diamond, "*Gestus* and Signature in Aphra Behn's *The Rover*," in *English Literary History* 56, no. 3 (fall 1989); Judith Kegan Gardiner, "The First English Novel: Aphra Behn's *Love Letters*, the Canon, and Women's Tastes," in *Tulsa Studies in Women's Literature* 8 (fall

1989); Mary Ann O'Donnell, "Tory Wit and Unconventional Woman: Aphra Behn," in *Women Writers of the Seventeenth Century,* ed. by Katharina M. Wilson and Frank J. Warnke (Athens, Ga., 1989); Rose Zimbardo, "Aphra Behn in Search of the Novel," in *Studies in Eighteenth-Century Culture,* ed. by Leslie Ellen Brown and Patricia Craddock (East Lansing, Mich., 1989).

Carol Barash, "The Political Possibilities of Desire: Teaching the Erotic Poems of Behn," in *Teaching Eighteenth-Century Poetry,* ed. by Christopher Fox (New York, 1990); Margaret W. Ferguson, "Juggling the Categories of Race, Class, and Gender: Aphra Behn's *Oroonoko,*" in *Women's Studies* 19 (1991); Deborah C. Payne, "'And Poets Shall by Patron-Princes Live':

Aphra Behn and Patronage," and Jessica Munns, "'I by a Double Right Thy Bounties Claim': Aphra Behn and Sexual Space," in *Curtain Calls: British and American Women and the Theater, 1660–1820,* ed. by Mary Anne Schofield and Cecilia Macheski (Athens, Ohio, 1991); Ros Ballaster, "New Hystericism: Aphra Behn's *Oroonoko:* The Body, the Text, and the Feminist Critic," in *New Feminist Discourses,* ed. by Isabel Armstrong (New York, 1992); Heidi Hutner, "Aphra Behn's *Oroonoko:* The Politics of Gender, Race, and Class," in *Living by the Pen: Early British Women Writers,* ed. by Dale Spender (New York, 1992); Heidi Hutner, ed., *Rereading Aphra Behn: History, Theory, and Criticism* (Charlottesville, Va., and London, 1993).

RUPERT BROOKE

(1887–1915)

Brooke Allen

RUPERT BROOKE'S SIGNIFICANCE to posterity lies more, perhaps, in his symbolic stature than in what he actually wrote. Though he produced a fairly substantial amount of poetry and journalism in his short life, most of that is now forgotten and he is frozen in the world's memory as the beautiful young soldier-poet of 1914, joyfully sacrificing his life for his country. He stands in the collective consciousness for the ideal type of young English manhood, a type that, it is said, was crushed by the tanks and mortar of the First World War. Winston Churchill, Henry James, Walter de la Mare, and the editor Edward Marsh were among those who boosted the Brooke myth.

The real Brooke was, of course, both more and less than that image. After his death in 1915, many of his friends stated their objection to such a depiction of his character and objected that the Rupert Brooke myth obscured a man who was in fact more interesting than the plaster god that had been erected. The great classical scholar Gilbert Murray recognized that the real, and imperfect, Brooke would soon be lost behind the mask; Virginia Woolf tried to defend Brooke's memory with a more measured look at his work, and there are many who believe that her character of Percival in *The Waves* was based on him.

As World War I progressed, any idealism that there had been about the war and England's great destiny in it was lost, and as a result Brooke and his poetry went quickly out of fashion. His war poetry was seen as naive, his prewar work lightweight. Intellectuals ceased to read Brooke much or to take him very seriously. But Brooke remained popular with the general public, continues to be popular in England, and attracts new enthusiasts with every generation. His poetry is accessible and conversational, laced with humor, unforced erudition, gentle irony, nostalgia, and a tremendous appreciation for beauty.

Among scholars, predictably, Brooke's life has attracted more attention than his work. Few critical studies on Brooke have appeared, yet he has been the subject of numerous biographies covering every aspect of his life. The definitive biography was written by Christopher Hassall (*Rupert Brooke, A Biography*, 1964), but several other works are of special interest: John Lehmann's *The Strange Destiny of Rupert Brooke* (1981) covers the intriguing subject of Brooke's sexuality; Michael Hastings' *The Handsomest Young Man in England* (1967) is a scathing critique of the Brooke myth that nevertheless provides a not unsympathetic assessment of Brooke as a poet; and Paul Delany's *The Neo-Pagans: Rupert Brooke and the Ordeal of Youth* (1987) provides a fascinating account of Brooke's own circle of bohemian youth.

Brooke was of central importance not only as a war poet but as one of the leading poets of the group labeled "Georgian." He collaborated in the editorship of the first two volumes of *Georgian Poetry* (1913 and 1915), and his poems were featured prominently in its pages. The Georgian poets, like Brooke himself, quickly faded in the wake of the far more vigorous modern movement. But out of fashion as the work of Brooke and the Georgians is, it nevertheless was important poetry in its day: the standards of *Georgian Poetry* were the standards of educated poetic taste in prewar England and deserve rather more attention than they now get.

Brooke himself remains a problematic figure. He is a better poet than his modern critics would have it, a worse one than his mythologizers insisted.

LIFE

RUPERT Chawner Brooke was born in Rugby on 3 August 1887, the second of the three sons of

William Parker Brooke and his wife Mary Ruth Cotterill. W. P. Brooke taught at Rugby School, a famous boys' school. At the time of Rupert's birth his father was a form master; he later became a housemaster. Rupert, along with his brothers Richard and Alfred, attended the nearby Hillbrow School as children, then entered their father's house at Rugby at the age of fourteen.

Rupert Brooke's school years were thus unusual in that he attended one of the great English public schools but, unlike his fellows, never left home: while most boys of the upper and upper-middle classes were separated from their families during their teenage years, he stayed with his. It was perhaps unfortunate that Rupert had to spend so much time under his mother's eye, for Mary Brooke was a formidable character who dominated her husband and sons, and Rupert was never entirely to escape her vigilance.

Brooke excelled at Rugby. He was popular, athletic, got on well with his peers, and achieved considerable academic success, though he was not outstandingly brilliant. He eventually became head of his father's house, School Field. It was during these years that he decided on a literary vocation. He applied himself diligently to this ambition, and he won school poetry prizes on set themes and experimented with the then-fashionable "decadent" style made popular by Algernon Charles Swinburne and Oscar Wilde.

In December 1905 Brooke went to Cambridge to sit for the university scholarship examinations. He was awarded a classical scholarship at King's College, and he began his studies there in the autumn of 1906.

Brooke's early life had centered on the small world of Rugby. At Cambridge he was to come into contact with a far wider circle. His Rugby friend, James Strachey, also went on to Cambridge, and it was through James that Brooke got to know his brother Lytton Strachey and other members of the "Bloomsbury set," a group he was to remain on the fringes of until his midtwenties. At the end of his first year he was initiated into the secret society of the Apostles, a discussion group that included many of the most brilliant minds in the university—though it has been suggested that Brooke was recruited into this largely homosexual group more for his stunning good looks than for his intellect. Through the Apostles he came in contact with the Stracheys, the economist John Maynard Keynes and

his brother Geoffrey (another Rugby friend), the young novelist E. M. Forster, Virginia and Leonard Woolf, and the philosopher G. E. Moore, whose theories had a powerful effect upon the group's thought and aesthetic.

Brooke began contributing poetry and essays to the *Cambridge Review* and joined the Marlowe Dramatic Society, a group dedicated to performing Elizabethan plays. Through the Marlowe Society he became friends with a group of young people, many of whom had attended Bedales School, a coeducational progressive school with ties to the socialist Fabian Society. Several were to become particular friends and form a tightly knit band that was to have great importance in Brooke's short life: Jacques Raverat, an artist; Raverat's future wife Gwen Darwin, also an artist and the granddaughter of Charles Darwin; her cousin Frances, a poet; Frances' future husband Francis Cornford, a classics don; Justin Brooke (no relation to Rupert), an avid amateur actor; Katherine ("Ka") Cox, a student at Newnham College, Cambridge; and the four beautiful Olivier sisters, daughters of Sir Sydney Olivier (later Lord Olivier), the socialist politician: Margery, Brynhild, Daphne, and Noel. Rupert was in love with Noel on and off for years.

At Cambridge, Brooke also became involved in the university branch of the Fabian Society. Under his mother's influence he had been active in liberal politics since childhood; at Cambridge, he moved further left and joined the Fabians, eventually becoming president of the Cambridge University Fabian Society.

In 1909 Brooke took his classical tripos and gained a second-class degree. In spite of this rather disappointing result, and of the fact that he was now devoting more and more time to poetry, he decided to apply for a Cambridge Fellowship, which would require that he first produce a significant work of scholarship. He left Cambridge and moved to the neighboring village of Grantchester, on the river Cam. He lived an informal, idyllic life in Grantchester, and many of his friends paid him extended visits. Their barefoot tea parties, nude swimming, and the easy mixing of the sexes caused Virginia Woolf to dub the group ironically the "Neo-Pagans."

Brooke's father died early in 1910, and he temporarily left his writing to take over his father's duties as housemaster. But he spent much of that year and the next in Grantchester, working on his poems and his fellowship dissertation on the Elizabethan playwright John Webster. (Though the final dissertation is not of particularly high quality, Brooke won the fellowship on his second try, though he never took up his place at the college.) In 1911 his first collection of poems was published by Sidgwick and Jackson, to generally favorable reviews.

Early in 1912 Brooke suffered a severe nervous breakdown, probably stemming from his conflicting feelings of love for both Noel Olivier and Katherine Cox, also from intense feelings of sexual frustration, for Brooke and his friends were by and large a chaste group. The doctors prescribed rest and feeding up, preferably abroad, so Brooke and his mother repaired to Cannes. After some weeks of mental torment he was able to break away from his mother and to persuade Ka to join him in Germany, but after his return to England he experienced a revulsion from the physical relations he had enjoyed with Ka and yearned again for the unattainable Noel. He spent a large part of this year in Germany, where, in spite of his misery, he wrote a good deal of poetry, including "The Old Vicarage, Grantchester," his most famous poem next to the war sonnets.

Toward the end of the year his spirits began to lift. He was approached by his friend Edward Marsh about contributing to a volume Marsh was editing called *Georgian Poets*. Though Marsh claimed that there were no aesthetic guidelines for inclusion in the collection ("Georgian" simply meant that the poetry was written during the reign of King George V), and indeed a very wide variety of poets are represented there, in fact a distinct Georgian tone did evolve: the movement's representative artists favored simplicity in language and meter, charm, and emotional directness. Brooke also contributed to Harold Monro's *Poetry Review* and to *Poetry and Drama*. He and his fellow Georgians Walter de la Mare, Lascelles Abercrombie, and Wilfrid Gibson also combined to create a new forum for their work, the periodical *New Numbers*, which was published throughout 1914.

Brooke's nervous breakdown had caused him to become rigid and intolerant where before he had been liberal and easygoing, conservative where before he had been socialist. He became nationalistic, anti-Semitic, antifeminist, and antierotic; he turned, in particular, against his former friends of the Bloomsbury group, who were passionately pacifist, left-wing, and internationalist. He classified them, disturbingly, as "dirty, hermaphrodites and eunuchs, Stracheys, moral vagabonds, pitiable scum . . ." (*The Letters of Rupert Brooke*, p. 573; cited hereafter as *Letters*).

Edward Marsh was private secretary to Winston Churchill, who was at that time First Sea Lord. Through Marsh, Brooke entered the inner circle of the Churchills and the Asquiths: Herbert Asquith was prime minister and had several lively children of Brooke's generation. It was a group concerned more with power politics than with the life of the mind, and among them, as had not been the case in Bloomsbury, Brooke was taken seriously as a thinker. During the last two years of his life Brooke was drawn into this group and away from his old friends. Cathleen Nesbitt, a rising young actress, became his principal romantic object.

In 1913 Brooke made a long trip to the United States, Canada, and the South Seas at the behest of the *Westminster Gazette*, which had commissioned him to write a series of articles on his travels. (These were published posthumously in book form in 1916 as *Letters from America*, with an introduction by Henry James, who had met and been smitten by the handsome young poet.) Brooke saw New York, Boston, Chicago (where his short play, *Lithuania*, was performed), Washington, California, and much of Canada; in the Pacific he visited Hawaii, Samoa, Fiji, New Zealand, and Tahiti. He stayed for some months in Tahiti, where he had a passionate affair with a beautiful islander girl named Taatamata—the only affair of his life, perhaps, in which his puritanical nature allowed him to experience sexual happiness.

He returned to England in the summer of 1914, only two months before war was declared on 4 August. His dilemma over what role he should play in the war effort—for a time he considered working as a newspaper correspondent—was solved by Marsh and Churchill, who obtained for him a commission in the Naval Division. Brooke and his battalion arrived on the Continent in time to witness devastation wreaked by the invading Germans during the fall of Antwerp. He was returned to England and later joined the Hood Battalion, along with Arthur Asquith and other of his friends. On 1 March 1915 the battalion set sail on the *Grantully Castle* for the Aegean, where Churchill had planned an offensive against the Turkish forces guarding the straits of the Dardanelles. When the ship reached Egypt, Brooke fell ill with sunstroke. They continued on to Trebuki Bay, off the Greek island of Skyros, waiting for the attack on Gallipoli to be called. There Brooke developed blood poisoning and died on 23 April.

Brooke's passionately patriotic war sonnets had recently been published in *New Numbers* and had, only days before his death, been read aloud by Dean Inge to the congregation at St. Paul's. With his death Brooke became an instant celebrity and an instant hero, and Churchill himself led the mythmaking campaign, aware that the shining example of a martyred soldier-poet would be of great help in drumming up conscriptions. Brooke's poetry, especially the five war sonnets of *1914*—published in 1915 and reissued and expanded the same year as *1914 and Other Poems*—was held up for far more veneration than it merited. The subsequent reaction against his work—and his perceived jingoism—was bitter. But the vagaries of Brooke's rising and falling literary reputation will be more fully discussed below.

BROOKE'S INTEREST IN CONTEMPORARY THOUGHT

RUPERT Brooke was very much a child of his time, and it is fruitless to approach his work without some knowledge of the political and social systems of thought with which the young man grappled. Though Brooke cultivated a carefree, nonconformist image, he was not in fact an unconventional man. His friend and first biographer, Edward Marsh, astutely observed that he "wished, of course, or rather wished to be thought to wish, to shock and astonish the respectable; but he did not in practice go very far in that direction" (*Rupert Brooke: A Memoir*, p. 16). And the fact that at the time of his death Brooke was the darling of the political establishment emphasizes that point. But the conservatism of his last two years should not, as has happened with the patriotic fervor of the *1914* sonnets, be taken as Brooke's characteristic or definitive pose. The many identities that he tried out during his life—decadent, Fabian, neo-pagan, eventually conservative nationalist—were all attitudes that genuinely attracted him, and for a time held him.

The Edwardian period (1901–1910) was the time in which Brooke came of age. It was a period of expanding imperialism abroad: the swift annexation of virtually uncharted areas of Africa, though designed to preempt England's competitors France and Germany, was also seen by large parts of the British population as an opportunity to bring the benefits of a specifically British civilization and Christianity to a savage part of the world. At home, the growing sense of social responsibility bequeathed by the great Victorian political thinkers was preparing the ground for a viable political left wing and the birth of the Labour party.

The Social Democratic Federation, founded in 1881 by Henry Hyndman, Karl Marx's translator, was unsuccessful, and in 1884 a group of intellectuals without political affiliations formed to found a socialist group they called the Fabian Society. The founding members included George Bernard Shaw, Beatrice and Sidney Webb (Sidney Webb, later Lord Passfield, was later to serve as secretary of state for Dominion affairs and the colonies), and Sydney Olivier, father of the four sisters who were Brooke's close friends.

The Fabians believed not in revolution but in the gradual permeation of British society by socialist ideas. The group was unwilling to ally itself with the growing trades-union movement, and therefore it lost any effective position it might have had within the newly born Labour party; from the time of the rise of Labour, the Fabians began their descent into passivity and, finally, obliteration. Nevertheless, the Fabians were during the first decade of the century an important force in liberal thought.

Education comprised a major element of the Fabian program of permeation, and the writings of Shaw, the Webbs, and H. G. Wells, who joined the society in 1903, influenced all of intellectual England. Brooke, who had been brought up by his mother to take an active interest in liberal politics, naturally became intrigued by the tenets of socialism. At Cambridge, inspired especially by Wells and the writings of the nineteenth-century socialist William Morris, Brooke became attracted by the Fabian notion of socialism without Marxism. He overcame his initial scruples, became a full member of the society, eventually became president of the university branch, and traveled and lectured to the populace along with other student Fabians such as Dudley Ward and Hugh Dalton. Membership also involved attendance, congenial to Brooke, at the Fabian summer schools: informal, outdoorsy gatherings where the young Fabians enjoyed hikes and dances, ate vegetarian food, and heard lectures by Shaw and other eminent Fabians. The sexes mixed freely at these schools, and here Brooke saw a great deal of the Olivier girls and other friends.

Brooke's Fabianism, while an important part of his life, had little visible effect upon his poetry. He wrote only one overtly socialist poem, "Second Best" (in *Poems*, 1911), a work that describes the soul's search for the place where, "behind the night, / Waits for the great unborn, somewhere afar, / Some white tremendous daybreak." The heaven the poet awaits is specifically a postrevolutionary circle of brotherhood, not a Christian heaven, for Brooke had in early youth become an atheist. Brooke's atheism was a position from which he never wavered, and while it is tempting to see it simply as a facet of his vigorous anti-Victorianism, it was in fact an instinctive and sincere conviction.

Brooke's poetry was influenced far more by the philosophical teachings of G. E. Moore than by the political ideas of the Fabians. His membership in the Society of the Apostles during the first decade of the century inevitably meant that he was thoroughly exposed to Moorist thought, which permeated that of the Apostles and of King's College, the most prestigious and advanced of the Cambridge colleges, with strong liberal and socialist leanings. Moore, then the leader of Cambridge philosophy, had written his famous *Principia Ethica* in 1905. In a nutshell, his thesis was that knowledge of anything outside of oneself was impossible. One could only know oneself, and therefore one had to pay the closest attention to one's self and one's senses and impressions. Experience appeared in a series of "states of mind"; consciousness was composed of a series of images and impressions.

The significance to aesthetic order that such a conception of experience implies is evident. It focuses artistic attention on the impressions of a moment, transient perceptions, the brief lulls in the flux of time. Moore's philosophy had a powerful effect on the work of several of the century's great artists. We can see it in the work of Virginia Woolf, closely allied with the King's College Apostles, with her formulation of life as an evanescent series of "luminous haloes"; in that of E. M. Forster, himself a former Apostle only eight years Brooke's senior, with his cult of personal re-

lations and his rejection of political exigencies and worldly "reality"; and in the work of younger writers who adopted Forster's aesthetic priorities, notably W. H. Auden.

Though Brooke did not actually read *Principia Ethica* until 1910, Moore's influence was nevertheless everywhere apparent in Brooke's work. A poem like "Dining-Room Tea," one of Brooke's better-known works, is characteristic. Here the poet, happily taking tea with his friends, looks across the table at his beloved and is able to freeze the very moment in contemplation:

> Till suddenly, and otherwhence,
> I looked upon your innocence
> · · ·
> I saw the immortal moment lie.
> One instant I, an instant, knew
> As God knows all.
> (in *Collected Poems*, 1915)

As with other of Brooke's love poems, the woman is the unknowing instrument of the poet's sudden vision: he sees her with new clarity, but she is unconscious of the moment she has allowed him.

Both Brooke's socialism and his Moorist cult of personal relations were fundamental to the style of life he adopted and stuck with for several years, the persona for which he is, perhaps, best remembered: that of the child of nature, the neo-pagan living a rural idyll at Grantchester. Shortly after Brooke's death Virginia Woolf wrote that he had been "consciously and defiantly pagan," an originator, "one of those leaders who spring up from time to time and show their power most clearly by subjugating their own generation. Under his influence the country near Cambridge was full of young men and women walking barefoot, sharing his passion for bathing and fish diet . . ." (cited in *Times Literary Supplement*, 8 August 1918). At Grantchester he gave up tobacco, alcohol, and meat, and wandered about barefoot and jacketless: Jacques Raverat wrote that Brooke "relished the romantic and Byronic impression given by his long hair and open-necked shirt" (Delany, p. 74). But while Brooke's pagan affectations could sometimes be ridiculous—Grantchester was only three miles from Cambridge, after all, and constantly full of Brooke's Cambridge and London friends—he was trying to live by standards that he found genuinely important.

Simple living, friendship, chaste love, nature:

all of these elements really mattered to a man who had inherited from his mother a crippling measure of puritanism yet rejected the Christian dogma in which it might have been focused.

Brooke's nervous breakdown in 1912 ended his close association with the progressive and liberal elements of prewar England. He moved away from the rarefied group of socialists and intellectuals who had been his closest friends. His relationship with Ka Cox, which had involved passionate desire, jealousy, and finally revulsion, had turned him away from the erotic side of life. From this time forward he perceived sex as dirty, and dirtiness was to be repressed at all costs. Feminism and homosexuality were as suspect as eroticism. At the same time he experienced a growing nationalism and conservatism: he was finally taking his place, it would seem, in the mainstream of middle-class English thought.

One of the first, and most telling, manifestations of Brooke's new attitudes was his hostility toward feminism. The feminist movement was at that time an explosive subject: in 1911 the suffragists, under their leader Emmeline Pankhurst, had begun demonstrations for female suffrage and the emancipation of women. He loathed feminists, he wrote Frances Cornford in 1914, but not, he assured her, women: "There *was* a period when I despised [women] a little, perceiving what fourthrate men they made. But lately I've cheered up, noticing what supreme women they make" (*Letters*, p. 592). Urging his new love, the actress Cathleen Nesbitt, not to go on tour to America, he finally admitted that in fact he did not approve of women performing on stage.

An insular nationalism, always the fatal flaw of the British, also began to pervade his writing in 1912. It is already noticeable in "The Old Vicarage, Grantchester" (1912), though that remains, perhaps, his most charming and enduring poem. Written at the Café des Westens in Berlin, it is a gentle, nostalgic piece about homesickness and spirit of place. "Not that I've really got much feeling for place," he wrote Frances Cornford, "but England = places + atmosphere + people I know" (*Letters*, p. 398). That is the secret of the poem's success: it is a very personal vision of one man's England, and it succeeds insofar as his readers share his vision.

> I only know that you may lie
> Day long and watch the Cambridge sky,

> And, flower-lulled in sleepy grass,
> Hear the cool lapse of hours pass,
> Until the centuries blend and blur
> In Grantchester, in Grantchester. . . .
>
> . . .
>
>   . . . oh! yet
> Stands the Church clock at ten to three?
> And is there honey still for tea?

This vision of a pastoral, timeless English village has always had a great attraction for English readers, and "Grantchester" has inspired later poets, notably John Betjeman. But Brooke's comparison of his dreamed village with the actuality of modern Germany, where "tulips bloom as they are told," displays what was quickly becoming an unpleasant xenophobia. The trauma of the 1930s and World War II was far in the future; nevertheless, lines like

> *Temperamentvoll* German Jews
> Drink beer around;—and *there* the dews
> Are soft beneath a morn of gold

have an unpleasant ring. Brooke's poetry, his prose (especially *Letters from America*), and his character were hardening into intolerance and into a mystical worship of England's past, much like that of Hilaire Belloc, a brilliant conservative writer whom Brooke much admired.

Brooke's close association with the Churchills and the Asquiths emphasized this new direction in his thinking. Brilliant as the group was, it was made up of those whose aim was power and who had interests in maintaining a social status quo and promoting a patriotic, insular attitude. Brooke, like many other prewar intellectuals, had always revered German philosophy and thought. His disillusion with Germany was made personal by the fact that much of his breakdown had occurred there, and his revulsion from that country was indicative of a general, and impoverishing, withdrawal from the entire Continent. Anti-German propaganda was rife throughout 1914, and in his own way Brooke contributed to it: "An Unusual Young Man," for instance, published in 1914 in the *New Statesman*, was clearly an autobiographical essay: "He was immensely surprised to perceive that the actual earth of England held for him a quality . . . which, if he'd ever been sentimental enough to use the word, he'd have called 'holiness'" (in *Letters From America*, p. 178). The implication is that the earth of Germany, unlike that of England, is not holy; and it was in writing like this that Brooke displayed the kind of sentimental jingoism that was the prevailing mood of the time but that later readers, sobered by the actuality of the war, have deplored.

POEMS, 1911

BROOKE wrote poetry steadily throughout his time at Rugby and his undergraduate years at Cambridge. At Rugby he won prizes for verse on set subjects: the pyramids and the Bastille. While at Rugby he became interested in the modish "decadent" school. The decadent movement had been brought to England in the late nineteenth century by the writings of Théophile Gautier and Charles Baudelaire and subsequently taken up in England by Walter Pater, who expounded a doctrine of "art for art's sake," by the poets Charles Algernon Swinburne and Arthur Symons, the artists James McNeill Whistler and Aubrey Beardsley, and most theatrically by the poet and dramatist Oscar Wilde. By the time of Rupert Brooke's school days, decadence had become virtually a convention. Brooke's efforts in the genre were encouraged by a young writer who lived in the vicinity of Rugby, St. John Welles Lucas-Lucas.

The young Brooke had also been impressed by the verse of Robert Browning, which he valued for its spontaneity and vigorous use of the vernacular and, despite his decadent pose, with the tough masculine poetry of Rudyard Kipling, W. E. Henley, Hilaire Belloc, and A. E. Housman. At Cambridge he developed a strong interest in the Elizabethans. Reading Elizabethan songs in 1910, he wrote, "I writhe with vain passion and with envy. How do they do it? . . . The lightness!" (*Letters*, p. 263). His fellowship dissertation, as mentioned, was on John Webster, and, like a slightly later poet, T. S. Eliot, he took an especial interest in the seventeenth-century Metaphysical poets John Donne and Andrew Marvell. The influence of Donne, in particular, was striking. In a review of *Poems* (1911), James Elroy Flecker called Brooke "our Donne Redivivus" (Hassall, p. 284). Brooke wrote that Donne was "the one English love poet who was not afraid to acknowledge that he was composed of body, soul, and mind; and who faithfully recorded all the pitched battles, alarms,

treaties, sieges, and fanfares of that extraordinary triangular warfare" (Hassall, p. 372)—a point that Eliot was also to make.

Though Brooke's first volume of poems (*Poems*, 1911) was published when he was twenty-four, some of the work dated as far back as his school days. He was vague about the dating on the individual poems: twenty were set aside in sections called "1905" and "Experiments," and while he thus implied that the other thirty were contemporary pieces, some of them in fact dated from much earlier. About one-fifth of the poems had been written during Brooke's undergraduate years, from 1906 to 1909. The volume as a whole is therefore uneven, the works of varying levels of maturity and skill; but the quality of the poetry was, and remains, pleasing and fresh.

Most of the poems in the 1911 volume deal with one of four themes: love, age, immortality, and death. The subject of love is hardly an unusual one for a young man to treat. But Brooke's love poems are nevertheless original, steeped, as they are, in metaphysical and platonic concepts. Brooke's virtual chastity as a young man almost certainly had something to do with this attitude toward love. He had a tendency to see women in two categories, either pure and unattainable or physical and slightly corrupt. As a result, he was somewhat uncomfortable with straightforward love poetry and often tended toward levity or somewhat derivative sublimity. Of the two, levity was for him the more effective, as with "The One Before the Last," where the poet wryly acknowledges that the woman who is so tormenting him will in a few years be as forgotten as the one who tormented him years ago:

> Oh! bitter thoughts I had in plenty.
> But here's the worst of it—
> I shall forget, in Nineteen-twenty,
> *You* ever hurt a bit!

In "The Hill," too, the poet mocks himself and his lover, though in a darker manner. The pair congratulate themselves upon the triumphant achievement of their love: "'We are Earth's best, that learnt her lesson here. / Life is our cry. We have kept the faith!' we said;" but at the last moment the girl "suddenly cried, and turned away." The simplicity of the poem marks an effective counterpoint to the inexplicable complexity of human relationships.

"Dining-Room Tea," discussed above, is another effective love poem from this volume, which again stresses the lack of communication between lovers; while one is experiencing an epiphany of love, the other's thoughts are elsewhere. "The Voice" carries the theme further yet. The narrator, ecstatic in his solitude, thinks of his beloved and of their mystical union:

> [. . .] slowly the holy three,
> The three that I loved, together grew
> One, in the hour of knowing,
> Night, and the woods, and you—

but the arrival of the actual beloved ruins the beauty of the woods.

> You came and quacked beside me in the wood.
> You said, "The view from here is very good!
>   . . .
> By God! I wish—I wish that you were dead!

All the love poems in the volume express a dissatisfaction with love, an inability to believe that it will last or satisfy. This feeling is probably allied with Brooke's distrust of physicality and in particular his horror of the aging process. Brooke was terrified of getting old. He wanted, like Browning's Waring, to disappear into the sunset as he hit middle age; the thought of no longer being young was intolerable to him. Several of his poems record his recoil from the idea of old age, some facetiously, like "Grantchester," where he suggests that perhaps the inhabitants of his half-mythical village shoot themselves when they begin to feel old; most with a fascinated wealth of hideous detail.

"Menelaus and Helen" provides a sort of flip side for Tennyson's "Ulysses," with the lovely Helen of Troy grown ancient and hideous. Menelaus wonders why he ever went to war for her; she "weeps, gummy-eyed and impotent; / Her dry shanks twitch at Paris' mumbled name," while Paris, well out of the marriage trap, sleeps on unconcerned. In "Jealousy," the poet watches the beloved with her new lover and consoles himself with thinking of how hideous the other man will be in old age, when "you, that loved young life and clean, must tend / A foul sick fumbling dribbling body and old." In "The Beginning," the poet posits a distant future in which he must seek and try to recognize the beloved, now grown old.

It is interesting to see the large proportion of these early poems that deal with death and immortality. At the outbreak of World War I, when Brooke came to write his *1914* sonnets, death and the longing for death had become his primary subjects, and these themes are understandable in light of the breakdown he had recently undergone. But in fact death had held a fascination for Brooke from early youth, and the 1911 poems linger on it almost lovingly, never as an evil to be feared but always as a sort of haven and achievement.

"Mummia" is one of the best poems in the 1911 volume and one of Brooke's better ones altogether. Two lovers lie on a bed, surrounded in spirit by centuries of dead lovers:

> Their blood is wine along our limbs;
>   Their whispering voices wreathe
> Savage forgotten drowsy hymns
>   Under the names we breathe.

The mummified lusts of centuries have gone to create that of the poet and his beloved;

> So I, from paint, stone, tale, and rhyme,
>   Stuffed love's infinity,
> And sucked all lovers of all time
>   To rarify ecstasy.

In "Dust," the poet suggests that the love and fire between himself and his beloved are so strong that even after their death, motes of their dust will seek each other out and achieve "such a light, and such a quiring, / And such a radiant ecstasy there," that other, ordinary lovers will be amazed.

These poems, both in theme and meter, owe a striking debt to the seventeenth-century Metaphysical works of Donne and Marvell. So does "Thoughts on the Shape of the Human Body," a platonic reverie in which the poet muses on the impossibility of ideal love when the bodies that house our souls are so very imperfect.

> Love's for completeness! No perfection grows
> 'Twixt leg, and arm, elbow, and ear, and nose,
> And joint, and socket; but unsatisfied
> Sprawling desires, shapeless, perverse, denied.

The achievement of the platonic ideal is always thwarted by our physical actuality, and the poet, like others before him, yearns for it: "Could we but fill to harmony, and dwell / Simple as our thought and as perfectible." It is tempting to see this poem, with its intellectualization of physical love, growing out of Brooke's new closeness to the Bloomsbury group; but the work is so obviously an exercise in Metaphysical stylistics that it is difficult to know how seriously its plaint is meant to be taken.

"The Fish" is another Metaphysical conceit taken close to the point of parody, but saved from being mere parody by its elegance and the strength of its imagery. Written in octosyllables, a form Brooke used more and more as time went on, it is a charming and beautifully drawn evocation of a fish living on a river bottom: the poet lavishes stately language on his unprepossessing subject, who lives, loves, and dies in his muddy home while unconscious humans conduct their frantic business above:

> O world of lips, O world of laughter,
> Where hope is fleet and thought flies after
> . . .
> You know the hands, the eyes of love!

The fish lives in a quieter, more secret world, cool and curving, and "ripples with dark ecstasies."

> His woven world drops back; and he,
> Sans providence, sans memory,
> Unconscious and directly driven,
> Fades to some dank sufficient heaven.

Two other interesting poems in the 1911 collection are "Wagner," a close description of a fat, sentimental man listening to music by that composer; and "Dawn," an evocative depiction of a train compartment between Bologna and Milan. Two works in *Poems*, both sonnets, were written with the rather deliberate intention to shock the middle-class reader. These were "A Channel Passage" and "Lust." The former describes a rough channel crossing, in which the seasick poet distracts himself by thinking of his beloved, a subject that sickens his soul. When he forgets her, "Retchings twist and tie me, / Old meat, good meals, brown gobbets, up I throw." When he thinks of her again, "Acrid return and slimy, / The sobs and slobber of a last year's woe." The latter poem is quite unexceptionable. Yet Brooke's publishers, Sidgwick and Jackson, insisted that he change its title from "Lust" to "Libido" and wished him to remove it from the collection altogether. He refused, saying,

"My own feeling is that to remove it would be to overbalance the book still more in the direction of unimportant prettiness. There's plenty of that sort of wash in the other pages for the readers who like it" (*Letters*, pp. 315–316). The critics disagreed; their disgust at the poems was so great as to overshadow their reactions, generally extremely favorable, to the rest of the work. Some of the reviewers were more astute, however: Robert Lynd in the *Daily News* (14 February 1912) wrote that Brooke's "ugliness" was really "an inverted reverence for beauty."

GEORGIAN POET AND JOURNALIST

TODAY the term "Georgian poetry" has a slightly negative ring. The word "Georgian" is often used to denote a sort of poetry that is taken to be sentimental, "pretty," naive, and above all nationalist. The fact that after the First World War center stage was taken over so swiftly and decisively by the superior vitality of the modernist movement took many of the notable prewar writers out of the mainstream and made them appear moribund. George Orwell called the Georgians the "beer and cricket school of English poetry," and the censure has stuck. The work of the poets now popularly associated with the Georgian movement—Brooke, Robert Graves, Walter de la Mare, Lascelles Abercrombie, John Drinkwater—appears pastoral, nostalgic, and diluted when compared with the sheer energy of the great moderns such as T. S. Eliot and Ezra Pound.

But it should be remembered that the term "Georgian" was never meant to apply to any particular "school" or style of poetry. The term was simply one of convenience, originally designed to draw the public's attention to a wide range of poets, mostly young, who were writing in 1913. It was invented by Edward Marsh, who edited the *Georgian Poetry* series (of which the volumes appeared in 1913, 1915, 1917, 1919, and 1922). Looking, today, at the list of contributors to the first volume, one is struck by the number of names that are not, now, considered "Georgian": Isaac Rosenberg, Siegfried Sassoon, and Edward Blunden we now see primarily as war poets, D. H. Lawrence and Robert Graves as modernists. Ezra Pound himself, the stage manager of the modern movement who called Abercrombie and Drinkwater "the stupidest set of blockheads to be found in any country" (Pearsall, p. 166)—though he admired Brooke—was almost a Georgian: he was scheduled to be published in the first volume of *Georgian Poetry* and only fell out through a difficulty with copyrights. Perhaps Brooke, had he lived beyond 1915, might have gone on to write a different sort of poetry, might, like Lawrence, Sassoon, and Graves, have outgrown the "Georgian" label. We will never know. In any case, as Robert H. Ross points out in his book *The Georgian Revolt, 1910–1922* (1967), the war and the modernist revolution together caused the term "Georgian" to shed its connotations of youth and energy and gain those of reaction and nostalgia.

The idea for *Georgian Poetry* began with Marsh, who contacted Brooke and relied heavily on his collaboration for the first volume. A meeting in 1912 between Marsh, Brooke, Harold Monro, proprietor of the Poetry Bookshop and the *Poetry Review,* and the poets John Drinkwater, Wilfrid Gibson, and Arundel del Re launched the project, and when he was on his American trip in 1913 Brooke was drawn into a parallel project: he, Abercrombie, Gibson, and de la Mare combined to publish their work jointly in a new magazine to be called *New Numbers.*

During the "Georgian" period of his life, the time between the publication of *Poems* and the *1914* sonnets, Brooke wrote his best poetry. His voice had achieved a certain maturity but had not yet reached the slightly hysterical pitch of the war sonnets. His voyage to the South Seas broadened his vision and presented him with a glorious view of a different world.

In 1912, not long after his breakdown, Brooke wrote "The Old Vicarage, Grantchester" in Berlin. As described above, the poem, one of Brooke's longest, is a nostalgic look at an idealized English village. It is half serious and half bantering; he is aware that he is idealizing the place, and jokingly compares it with other, less blessed, parts of Cambridgeshire:

> For Cambridge people rarely smile,
> Being urban, squat, and packed with guile;
> And Royston men in the far South
> Are black and fierce and strange of mouth
>   . . .
> Strong men have blanched, and shot their wives,
> Rather than send them to St. Ives;

whereas in Grantchester "The women there do all they ought, / The men observe the Rules of Thought." The poem combines the absurd with the learned; it allows itself to be frankly nostalgic by gently mocking its own nostalgia. It is an almost perfect poem of its kind and has done much to secure Brooke's reputation.

In spite of his interest in drama and his membership in the Marlowe Society, Brooke made only one attempt to write a play: the result was a one-act drama called *Lithuania,* written in 1912 and performed by the Chicago Little Theatre, under the direction of Brooke's friend Maurice Browne, in 1915. It was based on a story he had heard in Berlin, that of a young man of poor family who goes to America to seek his fortune. He returns, a rich man, after several years, determined to help his family. He spends the first night under their roof without revealing his identity, and the family rob and murder him. The story was not an original one, and the piece as a whole was slight, but the play was successful in Chicago. The circumstances of the crime, and the characters of the murderers, are reminiscent of Webster and the Jacobean dramatists in which Brooke was so well versed.

Brooke documented his voyage to North America and the South Seas in a series of essays for the *Westminster Gazette.* The essays were collected and published after his death as *Letters from America.* The book is in parts amusing and has a jaunty, adventurous tone; it can be seen as an early example of the sort of lighthearted travel books that the English would perfect in the 1930s, books by gentleman-travelers, determined to be amused and amusing, such as Robert Byron and Peter Fleming. But *Letters from America* does not show Brooke at his best. Though he had an original critical mind—some of his essays on literature are first-rate—to say that he was not a profound political or economic thinker is to put it mildly. Yet he had some pretensions to being a political thinker, and the *Westminster Gazette* determined to exploit that reputation.

The result is unfortunate: an innocent, even ignorant young man, full of ready-made opinions, at large in a part of the world he knew almost nothing about. Even Henry James, to whom everything Brooke did was perfect, sensed a problem: "We feel in a manner his sensibility wasted and would fain turn it on to the capture of deeper meanings" (*Letters from America*, p. xxxii). Brooke himself knew that he did not have enough knowledge to satisfy the *Gazette*'s expectations; but he tossed off the letters anyway, willy-nilly. In spite of the arrogance and even absurdity of much of the material, Brooke's natural sensitivity stood him in good stead: there are some wonderful passages about the American Indians, for example. And in the South Seas, Brooke, enchanted and seduced, was able to write with a lovely appreciation for the magic of the islands and the people.

The poetry Brooke wrote between "Grantchester" and the war sonnets, first collected in *1914 and Other Poems*, shows an ever-increasing assurance. "Mary and Gabriel" is uncharacteristic: relatively long, serious, it is Brooke's only poem on a biblical incident. It describes the Annunciation of Christ's birth by the angel Gabriel from the point of view of the young Mary. The moment of the conception is nicely depicted:

> Her hands crept up her breast. She did but know
> It was not hers. She felt a trembling stir
> Within her body, a will too strong for her

But the poem is artificial, very much an exercise in a certain genre, as was the case with so many of his poems. It is an accomplished piece of work, incorporating influences as diverse as Dante Gabriel Rossetti and William Butler Yeats, but as poetry it is rather lifeless.

Brooke, now in his mid-twenties, had still not experienced a love affair that was both physically and emotionally satisfactory. His view of love, always a bit cynical, was now becoming even more so. Two sonnets from this period are illustrative: "Love" and "Unfortunate," both of which appear in *1914 and Other Poems*. In the former there appear, in relation to love, the same words that were to reappear in the war sonnets as enemies to be defeated by a merciful death: "shame" and "agony." Even lovers who find requited passion and satisfaction are deceiving themselves, the poet suggests:

> . . . such are but taking
> Their own poor dreams within their arms, and lying
> Each in his lonely night, each with a ghost.

Even the best kind of love "grows false and dull." "Unfortunate" describes a certain kind of love af-fair, the kind Brooke had himself experienced with Katherine Cox. The distraught lover is cared for by a mothering beloved: "She'll give me all I ask, kiss me and hold me"—but, ultimately, "she will not care." In Brooke's poetry the two hearts, longing for love, seldom connect. "He Wonders Whether to Praise or to Blame Her" describes a dilemma very familiar to infatuated lovers: the poet wonders whether the beloved is worthless (in which case the lover is a fool) or perfect (in which case the doubting lover is still a fool).

"The Funeral of Youth: Threnody" is a fifty-eight-line poem in the form of a threnody, a lament for the dead. It is written in mock-Spenserian verse in imitation of a standard Renaissance genre. Youth is dead, and his friends have come to attend the funeral, friends who "laughed with him and sung with him and wasted, [. . .] / The days and nights and dawnings of the time / When *Youth* kept open house": Folly, Laughter, Pride, Joy, Lust, Ignorance, Fancy, and many more. But there is one missing guest, and we discover at the end that the reason Love is not present is that "*Love* had died long ago." The loss of Love, it is implied, has caused Youth's death.

In "Mutability," a sonnet, the octet presents the ideal of love, "Where Faith and Good, Wisdom and Truth abide," while the sestet denies that such an ideal exists; echoing Matthew Arnold's "Dover Beach," it asserts that we exist in solitude and are at best only able to snatch a few moments of solace from one another. "A Memory" is an affecting sonnet that laments the difficulty Brooke had in erasing the haunting memory of his affair with Katherine Cox.

But Brooke's journey to the South Seas went far toward healing the wounds of failed love. His sensuous response to the islands added a much-needed element of rhythmic physicality to his poetry, for his principal failing as a poet had always been overintellectualization. Already, in Hawaii, the beauty of the islands began to lead him away from his amorous and nervous preoccupations and to inspire his poetry with its magic. "Waikiki" marks the beginning of the new phase. In the darkness a ukulele "thrills and cries / And stabs with pain the night's brown savagery"; and the poet begins to forget the pain of past love.

The poems that Brooke wrote in Tahiti, collected in *1914 and Other Poems*, are his last prior to the war sonnets. "Fafaia," which appears in *Collected*

Poems, affirms the pessimistic Arnoldian message of "Mutability," in an elegant simplicity of meter and conceit. Brooke compares stars, which look so close together but are actually so distant from one another, with lovers: "Heart from heart is all as far, / Fafaia, as star from star."

"Tiare Tahiti" plays with the notion of a platonic, rather than a Christian heaven, then temporarily rejects such a heaven for the sensuous pleasure of love on earth. The poet addresses his Tahitian lover (Brooke's own lover, Taatamata): "Mamua, there waits a land / Hard for us to understand." "All are one in Paradise," he goes on, saying that he and his lover will be lost in the platonic idea of Love. "Instead of lovers, Love shall be; / For hearts, Immutability." Like Andrew Marvell in "To His Coy Mistress," and consciously echoing Marvell's phrasing, Brooke urges his beloved to enjoy their physical love while they still may: "And there's an end, I think, of kissing, / When our mouths are one with Mouth." The poem goes on to describe beautifully the lovers' island idyll, "Well this side of Paradise!"

"Retrospect" recalls the wistful memory of a woman once loved; the poet longs to be able to return to her as to a peaceful home and to find her, "as a pool unstirred," and sleep within her arms. The woman is a specific type, a lover who also acts as mother, who doles out unconditional love and acceptance and stills passion with her tenderness.

"Heaven" is a companion piece to Brooke's earlier poem "The Fish"; here Brooke uses the fish's point of view to examine, with humor, the Christian and the platonic view of the hereafter: the Fish has his own Fish-God, and his own Fish-Heaven. "The Great Lover" is a self-mocking yet also grandiose disquisition on the poet's capacity to love, not people, but things, sensations, beauty: it narrates a long list of beloved items, then describes the poet's grief at their inevitable loss.

Brooke left the South Seas to return to England, via the United States, in early 1914. Several months later, war was declared.

WAR POET

It is ironic that Rupert Brooke is known principally as a war poet—indeed one of the most famous poets of World War I. For in fact Brooke spent most of his short wartime service in England. The only action he saw was the five-day Allied retreat from Antwerp. He was dead before the Gallipoli campaign, of which he was to have been a part, had even begun. He survived only eight months into the war and died not in battle but in his bed, not from wounds but from blood poisoning contracted from a mosquito bite.

Yet in many ways Brooke defined a certain type of war poet, a heroic ideal derived from Sir Philip Sidney and Lord Byron. The ideal was an ancient, chivalric one, that of the gentleman warrior-poet willingly laying down his life in battle. In Brooke's case the image was exploited for political reasons, and it was helped by the fact of his dazzling good looks; photographs of Brooke, by S. Schell, virtually turned the young man into an icon.

Since his breakdown in 1912 Brooke had been turning away from Germany and the Continent in general. Upon the outbreak of war he wrote his real feelings to his friend Jacques Raverat: "*I want* Germany to smash Russia to fragments, and then France to break Germany. Instead of which I'm afraid Germany will badly smash France, and then be wiped out by Russia. France and England are the only countries that ought to have any power. Prussia is a devil. And Russia means the end of Europe and any decency" (*Letters,* p. 603). Brooke's short experience at Antwerp confirmed him in his opinion that Prussia was "a devil": the grim procession of civilians—women, old people, and children—routed by the Germans impressed him profoundly, and he became thoroughly anti-German.

And for personal reasons the war was not unwelcome to him. As we have seen in the discussion of Brooke's poetry, the idea of death had always held for him a powerful attraction. Combined with his idealistic conception of nation, and considering the way he had been emotionally adrift since 1912, the war provided a glorious opportunity for him to sacrifice the life he did not really know how to use. Death was "the worst friend and enemy," he wrote in one of his war sonnets ("Peace"), and in truth he greeted her more as friend than enemy. Before he set sail for Gallipoli in 1915 he wrote to Violet Asquith, "I've never been quite so happy in my life, I think. Not quite so *pervasively* happy; like a stream flowing entirely to one end" (*Letters,* p. 662). And it is clear that the happiness was not in anticipation of victory but of death: his sonnet sequence, *1914,* was, he emphasized, a "goodbye" (*Letters,* p. 678).

There were five sonnets in the *1914* sequence, as well as a sixth, "The Treasure," which Brooke had written before the others, in August 1914, shortly after the declaration of war. The other five were written toward the end of 1914, numbered I to V, and entitled "Peace," "Safety," "The Dead (part 1)," "The Dead (part 2)," and "The Soldier." These sonnets are traditional in form, Petrarchan sonnets with the octets grammatically and semantically separate from the sestets. "The Treasure," on the other hand, inverts the form and begins with the sestet.

All these sonnets are built around one unifying theme: that of sacrificial death. Death, England, honor, and sacrifice are the central ideas throughout; love, the subject that had formerly occupied so much of Brooke's thought and work, has become only a "little emptiness." The tone is set in the first sonnet of the five, "Peace."

"Now, God be thanked Who has matched us with His hour," goes the first line, and to those who knew Brooke and his work, there is already a paradox here, for Brooke did not believe in God, or at least not in a Christian God. The reference to God, along with the strong, ringing cadence, gives the poem the effect of a hymn (Brooke may have intended to echo "Now Thank We All Our God")—a martial hymn. This first line invokes God; the last line invokes another deity, Death ("And the worst friend and enemy is but Death"); the framing of the body of the sonnet within these two concepts brings God and Death together so that they are equated in the reader's mind. For the sonnets, in spite of Brooke's professed atheism, are full of Christian imagery and concepts, existing uncomfortably alongside the platonic ideas that Brooke had long used in his poetry.

"Peace" sets the tone for the ensuing sequence, a tone of joyful sacrifice. If one reads closely, it becomes evident that to Brooke death was perhaps no sacrifice but a longed-for goal, as D. H. Lawrence felt upon reading the poems, their "great inhalation of desire" for death (Delany, p. 209). With a knowledge of Brooke's personal history, the imagery of the poem and its theme are evident. The line "To turn, as swimmers into cleanness leaping" has offended many later readers who knew that cleanness was hardly the most appropriate adjective for the battlefields of World War I, but the word had a peculiar meaning for Brooke, who opposed it to the "dirtiness" of which he had had such a horror since his nervous break-

down. He was continually urging his friends, in particular Katherine Cox, to "be clean"; with the "cleanness" of sacrifice seen as an expiation for some perceived "dirtiness" in the life he had led in previous years, the poem comes to symbolize a very personal need and fear, not the cry of a generation that Brooke would have liked to make it, with his use of the first person plural.

Likewise his lines "And half-men, and their dirty songs and dreary, / And all the little emptiness of love!" "Half-men," or "hermaphrodites," were words he had used since his breakdown for the left-leaning, often homosexual intellectuals he had come to associate particularly with the Stracheys and the Bloomsbury group; as for the "little emptiness of love," the mystery of successful love—mutual, satisfying physical passion allied with friendship—had been one he had been trying throughout his life, unsuccessfully, to solve.

Seen in this light, "Peace" becomes an intensely personal statement: first, an admission of failure in ordinary life, or failure to find peace and honor in ordinary life; second, a leaping toward war as a solution to these otherwise insoluble problems, from "sick hearts," "half-men," "shame," and "grief."

The second sonnet, "Safety," found its inspiration in some lines of Donne's: "Who is so safe as we? where none can do / Treason to us, except one of us two" and plays with a notion of safety that might appear paradoxical to the reader. The poet addresses his beloved, asserts that they have found safety together, in love (like Donne and his beloved); then denies that war can threaten that safety, the safety being an emotional and spiritual rather than a physical condition. "We have gained a peace unshaken by pain for ever. / War knows no power." The poem is an answer to Donne, based, like so many of Donne's, upon a Metaphysical conceit, the conceit that safety can in fact consist in loss of safety, in death: "Safe though all safety's lost; safe where men fall; / And if these poor limbs die, safest of all." Again, the poet seeks death joyfully: for though he has enjoyed one form of safety with his beloved, the safety he will attain through death is greater still.

Brooke himself liked "The Dead" best of his war sonnets. The first of the two poems by that name presents a traditional, chivalric idea of war. The octet praises those already dead in battle, for having "poured out the red / Sweet wine of youth," and through their deaths "made us rarer gifts than gold." The gifts the dead have brought the living include Love, Pain, and "Holiness, lacked so long." Here, as elsewhere in the sonnets, Brooke implies that the period preceding the war has been corrupt and without honor. The dead, like Christ (though Brooke does not give a specifically Christian meaning to the sonnet), have sacrificed their selves and their sons, and now

> Honour has come back, as a king, to earth
> And paid his subjects with a royal wage;
> And Nobleness walks in our ways again;
> And we have come into our heritage.

"The Dead (part 1)," like the rest of the sequence, is purposely vague: in what way does the declaration of war with Germany constitute "honour"? The question seems unanswerable, but to Brooke war appeared to be a way for him to redeem honorably a life he felt had been dishonorably and "dirtily" spent.

"The Dead (part 2)" describes the simple fact that the dead were once living, that they had experienced joy, mirth, and care. Their lives have been stopped by Frost, that "with a gesture, stays the waves that dance." But Frost and Death, far from having their traditional attributes of cold barrenness, here produce a "white / Unbroken glory, a gathered radiance, / A width, a shining peace, under the night."

"The Soldier," the first of the sonnets to achieve fame, is still probably the most famous of the group, a poem that has become one of the standard pieces of patriotic rhetoric in English literature. "If I should die, think only this of me," it begins; the speaker will die, it is to be understood, and the poem goes on to describe what will become of this soldier after his death. The body of the soldier, whom "England bore, shaped, made aware," becomes dust, an English dust, enriching the foreign dust in which it is buried, so that "there's some corner of a foreign field / That is for ever England."

The poem is platonic rather than Christian, for the soldier's body does not await resurrection but becomes "A pulse in the eternal mind" that "Gives somewhere back the thoughts by England given." The thoughts of England that the poet gives the reader are deliberately vague; they do not evoke actual images of the country but a series of positive emotional states: "dreams happy as her day; / And laughter, learnt of friends; and gentleness." The vague prettiness of Brooke's depiction of En-

gland, in this poem as in earlier ones, was strenuously opposed by writers of the late 1920s and 1930s, who stressed the industrial grime of the country; indeed, Brooke's selective vision was one of the factors in his fall from fashion.

"The Treasure," which Brooke placed at the end of the sequence, is a simple poem; like "The Soldier," it deals with the beneficent power of memory. The poet likens himself to someone unlocking a case, a "scented store / Of song and flower and sky and face." He posits a tactile, physical quality to the memories and finally compares them with children playing under the eyes of their mother.

The poems appeared in *New Numbers* early in 1915. They created a considerable impression on the public, and more attention was drawn to them when Dean Inge read "The Soldier" aloud from the pulpit of St. Paul's Cathedral during the Easter service, comparing the poem with Isaiah 26:19—"The dead shall live, my dead bodies shall arise. Awake and sing, ye that dwell in the dust." Brooke, Inge believed, in spite of the platonic, non-Christian element in his work, would "take rank with our great poets—so potent was a time of trouble to evoke genius which must otherwise have slumbered" (cited in Hassall, p. 502). Of the poem itself, he said that "the enthusiasm of a pure and elevated patriotism had never found a nobler expression." The reviewer in the *Times Literary Supplement* agreed. "It is impossible to shred up this beauty for the purpose of criticism. . . . the very blood and youth of England seem to find expression in them" (11 March 1915).

The adulation had begun even before Brooke's death. With that event, it escalated rapidly. This praise was largely due to political expediency, of which Winston Churchill was a past master. The army was still a volunteer one in 1915, and the government needed to draw more and more young men in to reinforce the ranks following appalling casualties—more than 50 percent of the British Expeditionary Force in 1914. By apotheosizing Rupert Brooke as the ideal sacrificial hero, Churchill calculated that he could attract ever more volunteers. He was also interested in creating propaganda for his own Gallipoli campaign, which was designed to divert enemy forces from the stalemate at Flanders. With all this in mind, Churchill himself wrote an obituary for Brooke in the *Times*. Brooke, he wrote, "expected to die; he was willing to die for the dear England whose beauty and majesty he knew; and he advanced towards the brink in perfect serenity, with absolute conviction of the rightness of his country's cause, and a heart devoid of hatred for fellow-men." "Joyous, fearless, versatile, deeply instructed, with classic symmetry of mind and body, he was all that one would wish England's noblest sons to be in days when no sacrifice but the most precious is acceptable, and the most precious is that which is most freely proffered" (*Times*, 26 April 1915).

The circumstances of Brooke's death contributed to the mythology; except for the fact that he did not die in battle, it was the perfect laying to rest of the warrior-poet. He was buried on the island of Skyros, the very island where Achilles, the greatest warrior-hero of all, had lived. Like many crusaders before him and like Byron, he had died on a military mission to free Constantinople from Muslim rule. And he died on the anniversary of Shakespeare's birth and death, which was also the feast day of St. George, the patron saint of England.

Yet the reality of the war had already, by the time of Brooke's death, overtaken the romance that his military superiors were so desperately trying to keep akindle. The glamorous setting of Brooke's funeral immediately became a scene of hideous carnage as the Gallipoli offensive met its defeat with enormous casualties. And the vague, glimmering images in Brooke's sonnets were soon superseded by the granite-hard imagery of the poets fighting on the western front. Brooke epitomized the idealism of 1914, and some of his fellow poets, like W. N. Hodgson, shared it; but the rapid degeneration of the fighting into trench warfare, a grueling contest of attrition with machine gun and shells, made romance seem very far away and irrelevant. Shortly before he was killed in action, Isaac Rosenberg, one of the great poets whose work was inspired by the war, wrote memorably of "a man's brains splattered on / A stretcher-bearer's face" ("Dead Man's Dump," from *Poems*, 1922), and Siegfried Sassoon wrote of

> . . . a livid face
> Terribly glaring up, whose eyes yet wore
> Agony dying hard ten days before;
> And fists of fingers clutched a blackening wound.
> ("The Rear Guard," from *Collected Poems*, 1918)

These images became the ones by which the fighting in World War I is still evoked, and Brooke's assertion in "The Dead" that "Honour has come back, as a king, to earth," became more than faintly ridiculous.

But Brooke died before he really had any conception of what kind of war it was going to be. The question of what kind of writer Brooke would have become had he survived the war is unanswered, as it is with Rosenberg, Wilfred Owen, Charles Sorley, Julian and Billy Grenfell, and Edward Thomas. Would he have become disillusioned and disgusted by the war and written bitterly against it, as did Siegfried Sassoon, who became the leading poet of the latter part of the war, a sort of anti-Brooke? Or would he have continued on his conservative and nationalist course, becoming a poet like W. E. Henley, whom he had admired in his youth? Would he have found his ultimate vocation in poetry, like Robert Graves, or might he have gone into politics, as Virginia Woolf and E. M. Forster believed he eventually would? Brooke's biographer Christopher Hassall and his friend and the editor of his correspondence, Geoffrey Keynes, believed that the horror on the western front would eventually have ended Brooke's idealism as it had ended others'; other writers and poets felt that he was already too much a part of government circles to rebel.

CONCLUSION: BROOKE'S REPUTATION

WITH the progression of the war, the reaction against Brooke was as swift and devastating as his apotheosis had been sudden. This reaction was due not only to the grim realities of the war, as discussed above, but to the extreme fatuousness of much of the praise that he had received earlier. Brooke had been praised far above his actual abilities, and it was easy, and for many people irresistible, to puncture the balloon. Not only that, but the work for which he was being so extravagantly lauded was very far from being his best work, as his true supporters knew: E. J. Dent wrote in the *Cambridge Magazine*, "It is grotesquely tragic . . . that he should have died . . . just after a sudden and rather factitious celebrity had been obtained by a few poems which, beautiful as they are in technique and expression, represented him in a phase that could only have been temporary" (8 May 1915).

But the publicity went on. *Letters from America* was published in 1916 with an infatuated and foolish introduction by the elderly Henry James; Edward Marsh put out a volume of Brooke's collected poetry in 1918 and accompanied it with a fulsome and one-sided biographical sketch. Virginia Woolf wrote in her diary that Marsh's essay was "a disgraceful sloppy sentimental rhapsody, leaving Rupert rather tarnished" (Lehmann, p. 160) and subsequently wrote the truth about Brooke as she knew him in an unsigned essay in the *Times Literary Supplement.*

Woolf liked and admired Brooke, and tried to give a balanced vision of him in her essay. Others were less generous in their assessments, and with the advent of the modern movement Georgian poetry in general, and Brooke's in particular, came in for a large measure of ridicule. So modern during his life, Brooke soon after his death became impossibly old-fashioned. This attitude culminated in sneering contempt from the 1930s academic pundit F. R. Leavis, who was writing at a time when Brooke's upper-class attitudes and romantic idealism were particularly out of fashion: "He energized the Garden-Suburb ethos with a certain original talent and the vigour of a prolonged adolescence. His verse exhibits a genuine sensuousness rather like Keats' (though more energetic) and something that is rather like Keats' vulgarity with a Public School accent" (cited in Noel Stock, *The Life of Ezra Pound,* 1970, p. 182).

But to follow the vagaries of popular fashion in literature is not the best or even the most profitable way to evaluate an author. The jury is still out on Brooke: but let his fellow poets have the final say.

Ezra Pound, though he found the other *New Numbers* poets "blockheads," admired Brooke and thought him "infinitely better than his friends" (Pearsall, p. 166). D. H. Lawrence, another admirer, was devastated by Brooke's death. T. S. Eliot, the greatest of the modern poets, paid Brooke the flattery of imitation; Robert Graves, perhaps the best and most enduring poet to come out of the war, said of Brooke that "we all looked up to him as our older brother" (Pearsall, p. 123). Among a younger generation of poets, not only John Betjeman but W. H. Auden felt Brooke's influence, as he charmingly writes in "Letter to Lord Byron" (in *Letters from Iceland,* 1937): "For gasworks and dried tubers I forsook / The clock at Grantchester, the English rook." And Siegfried Sassoon, the poet of all poets whom posterity has set up as opposite to and superior to Brooke, was

himself an admirer: on Brooke, he wrote, "had been conferred all the invisible attributes of a poet. To this his radiant good looks seemed subsidiary. Here, I might well have thought—had my divinations been expressible—was a being singled out for some transplendent performance, some enshrined achievement" (Hassall, p. 451).

We should also examine the popular as well as the academic or intellectual opinion, and here Brooke fares better; for the fact is that throughout the century Brooke has continued to have many readers, and many editions of his collected poems have been printed. He possessed a grace and a charm which, though often frowned on as "facile," nevertheless have endeared him to readers. The overpraised war sonnets have unfortunately obscured his best work—"Grantchester," "The Fish," "Heaven," "Mummia," "Tiare Tahiti," and a few others—as Michael Hastings points out in his study of Brooke, *The Handsomest Young Man in England.* Christopher Hassall likens Brooke to the Cavalier poets, with his "lightness of touch graced by his metaphysical turn of wit" (Hassall, p. 530), and his touch of emotional reticence. And like the Cavalier poets, Brooke's appeal has endured, despite the large measure of critical disapproval he has incurred.

SELECTED BIBLIOGRAPHY

I. BIBLIOGRAPHIES. Geoffrey Keynes, *A Bibliography of Rupert Brooke* (London, 1954); John Schroder, *Catalogue of Books and Manuscripts by Rupert Brooke, Edward Marsh, and Christopher Hassall* (Cambridge, 1970); Timothy Rogers, appended to his *Rupert Brooke* (London, 1971); John Schroder, *Collecting Rupert Brooke* (Cambridge, 1992).

II. INDIVIDUAL WORKS. *Poems* (London, 1911); *1914 and Other Poems* (London, 1915); *John Webster and the Elizabethan Drama* (New York, 1916), Brooke's fellowship dissertation at Cambridge; *Letters from America* (London, 1916), travel essays, with an intro. by Henry James; *Democracy and the Arts* (London, 1946), posthumously published essays, with a preface by Geoffrey Keynes.

III. COLLECTED WORKS. George Edward Woodberry, ed., *The Collected Poems of Rupert Brooke* (New York, 1915); *The Collected Poems of Rupert Brooke* (London, 1918), with a memoir by Edward Marsh; Geoffrey Keynes, ed., *The Poetical Works of Rupert Brooke* (London, 1946; 2d ed. 1970); *Poems* (London, 1948); Christopher Hassall, ed., *The Prose of Rupert Brooke* (London, 1956); Timothy Rogers, ed., *Rupert Brooke: A Reappraisal and Selection from*

His Writings (London, 1971); Sandra Martin and Roger Hall, eds., *Rupert Brooke in Canada* (Toronto, 1978).

IV. THEATRICAL WORK. *Lithuania: A Drama in One Act* (Chicago, 1916).

V. LETTERS. Geoffrey Keynes, ed., *The Letters of Rupert Brooke* (London and New York, 1968); *Letters from Rupert Brooke to His Publisher, 1911–1914* (New York, 1975); Pippa Harris, ed., *Song of Love: The Letters of Rupert Brooke and Noel Olivier 1909–1915* (New York, 1991).

VI. RELATED WORKS. Edward Marsh, ed., *Georgian Poetry*, vol. 1 (London, 1913); Edward Marsh, ed., *Georgian Poetry*, vol. 2 (London, 1915); H. C. Foster, *At Antwerp and the Dardanelles* (London, 1918); E. B. Osborn, ed., *The Muse in Arms: A Collection of War Poems* (London, 1918); Jacqueline Trotter, ed., *Valour and Vision* (London, 1920; enl. ed. 1923); John Drinkwater, *The Muse in Council* (Boston and New York, 1925; Freeport, N.Y., 1970); H. W. Garrod, *The Profession of Poetry* (London, 1929; Freeport, N.Y., 1967); F. R. Leavis, *New Bearings in English Poetry: A Study of the Contemporary Situation* (London, 1932), criticism; Herbert Asquith, *Moments of Memory: Recollections and Impressions* (London, 1937), memoirs; Edward Marsh, *A Number of People: A Book of Reminiscences* (London, 1939); Robert Nichols, ed., *Anthology of War Poetry, 1914–1918* (London, 1943); David Garnett, *The Golden Echo* (London, 1953), memoirs; David Garnett, *The Flowers of the Forest* (London, 1956), memoirs.

Brian Gardner, ed., *Up the Line to Death: The War Poets 1914–1918* (London, 1964), on the Georgian period and the war years; Leonard Woolf, *Beginning Again: An Autobiography of the Years 1911–1918* (London, 1964); Joy Grant, *Harold Monro and the Poetry Bookshop* (Berkeley, Calif., 1967); Michael Holroyd, *Lytton Strachey*, vol. 1 (London, 1967); Colin Wilson, *Poetry and Mysticism* (London, 1970); Quentin Bell, *Virginia Woolf: A Biography* (London, 1972); Virginia Woolf, *The Letters of Virginia Woolf*, vol. 2, ed. by Nigel Nicholson and Joanne Trautmann (London, 1976); Cathleen Nesbitt, *A Little Love and Good Company* (Owings Mills, Md., 1977), autobiography; Virginia Woolf, *The Diary of Virginia Woolf*, ed. by Anne Olivier Bell (London, 1977–1984); Paul Levy, *Moore: G. E. Moore and the Cambridge Apostles* (London, 1979); Geoffrey Keynes, *The Gates of Memory* (Oxford, 1981), autobiography.

VII. BIOGRAPHICAL AND CRITICAL STUDIES. Edward Marsh, *Rupert Brooke: A Memoir,* published with *Collected Poems* (London, 1918), established the Brooke myth; Walter de la Mare, *Rupert Brooke and the Intellectual Imagination* (London, 1919); Stanley Casson, *Rupert Brooke and Skyros* (London, 1921); Maurice Brown, *Recollections of Rupert Brooke* (Chicago, 1927); Sibyl Pye, "Memoir of Rupert Brooke," in *Life and Letters,* May 1929; Klara Urmitzer, *Rupert Brooke* (Wurzburg, 1935), literary study; Arthur Stringer, *Red Wine of Youth* (New York, 1948), biography.

Christopher Hassall, *Rupert Brooke, A Biography* (London and New York, 1964), the most comprehensive life of Brooke; Michael Hastings, *The Handsomest Young Man in England* (London, 1967), a hostile appraisal; Robert H. Ross, *The Georgian Revolt, 1910–1922* (Carbondale, Ill., 1967); Robert Brainard Pearsall, *Rupert Brooke: The Man and Poet* (Amsterdam, 1974); John Lehmann, *Rupert Brooke: His Life and His Legend* (London, 1980); John Lehmann, *The Strange Destiny of Rupert Brooke* (New York, 1981); Paul Delany, *The Neo-Pagans: Rupert Brooke and the Ordeal of Youth* (New York, 1987), on Brooke and his circle; Mary Archer, *Rupert Brooke and the Old Vicarage, Grantchester* (Cambridge, 1989); William E. Laskowski, *Rupert Brooke* (New York, 1994).

FRANCES BURNEY

(1752–1840)

Margaret Anne Doody

THE SUBTITLE OF Frances Burney's best-known novel, *Evelina*, is *The History of a Young Lady's Entrance into the World.* It is easy to think of the author herself as standing in a doorway, looking with mixed anxiety, amusement, and quizzical satire at a threshold, or series of thresholds.

One can imagine her as she is portrayed in the paintings by a cousin, Edward Francesco Burney: a small woman with crisp features, light brown hair, deep hazel-blue eyes, and an inquiring look. She stands in the doorway of our imagination, perhaps hesitant, perhaps only observant. In her society, entering a room was a momentous social event, and a lady (or one who was passing for such) needed to know all the regulations about movement in the controlled social space of a room. In Burney's world and her fiction, rooms entered are almost always occupied by superiors in age, gender, and rank. She would immediately have understood Virginia Woolf's contentions in *A Room of One's Own*—she felt the need of a room of her own. In her arduous life at court, Burney tried to escape public spaces for the shelter of a private place. She lived in a society that set great store by the signals of thresholds and by public space. Escape to one's room was not always possible; there were too many doorways. At the court of Queen Charlotte in August 1786 she wrote:

I then passed on to my own room, which terminates the gallery. But I have since heard it is contrary to rule to pass even the door of an apartment in which any of the royal family happens to be, if it is open.

(*Diary and Letters*, vol. 3, p. 40)

There is a long way to go to achieve the safety of one's "own" room. To leave that room is always to enter the public space. As a girl, Frances shared a bedroom with her sister Susanna. Both girls were scolded by their father for leaving their journals elsewhere in the house, where they could be read. Even the home is largely public space. Most space belongs to other people and is full of prying eyes. It is easy to see why approaching a threshold can give a young woman pause. Burney dramatizes the moment at which one advances bravely over a threshold, through an open doorway, and into an enclosed and populous space.

We situate Burney on the threshold perhaps because her position in English literature has been liminal. She has never been quite in what we call "the canon"—yet she has never been quite out of it; even before the changes that began about 1965—since when writing by women figures more commonly in university study—Burney's first novel, at any rate, often turned up on reading lists. She was given some serious editorial attention in the nineteenth century. Her niece Charlotte Barrett, in editing her aunt's *Diary and Letters*, produced the journalist Burney, a female rival to James Boswell, a first-rate describer of people, manners, pastimes, and affairs of the eighteenth and early nineteenth centuries. Her diaries have been very valuable to historians, especially in reconstructing the court of George III. Burney the journalist was, however, in danger of shouldering aside Burney the novelist. Annie Raine Ellis edited Burney's *Cecilia* (an edition highjacked in 1986 by Virago Press, whose edition of *Cecilia* carries Ellis' notes, with no acknowledgment). Ellis' major production was her edition in 1889 of Burney's *Early Diary* with extensive notes. Burney was one of the first female authors to be given that kind of systematic historical attention.

Joyce Hemlow's biography of Burney (1958) built on the interest in Burney as a chronicler of her period. Hemlow headed the extremely ambitious Burney Project, which between 1972 and 1984 produced the *Journals and Letters*, in twelve volumes (covering Burney's life from the time she left Queen Charlotte to her death). Under Lars

Troide, the journals of Burney's earlier life are being edited starting with two volumes of the *Early Journals and Letters* (1988), a publication at last rendering Ellis' *Early Diary* obsolete.

It is useful at this point to trace the modern history of Burney criticism. The publication of so much diary material has seemed to turn Burney into a naive historian, a view emphasized by Hemlow. In the 1970s, however, a growing interest in women's fiction of the eighteenth century led to a reexamination of Burney the novelist. In Patricia Spacks's *Imagining a Self* (1976), Burney gets a chapter to herself that includes *Evelina* as well as her journal. Rose Marie Cutting (now Cutting-Gray) broke new ground in the same year by publishing an article entirely on *The Wanderer*, a novel disdained by Hemlow as much as by Thomas Babington Macaulay, and rarely read since the Regency period. Cutting also examined all of Burney's novels together in an important article in the following year. Susan Staves contributed an article on *Evelina* to *Modern Philology* in 1976, the same year that Edward Copeland's article on the role of money in Burney's novels appeared. The year 1976 may thus be regarded as a watershed in Burney studies, marking the reentry of her fictional works (and of manifold aspects of them) into public discussion.

The 1980s saw a further growth of interest in Burney, and more serious, sustained, and ambitious work on Burney as a novelist. Janet Todd considered *The Wanderer* as well as the other novels in a chapter on Burney in *Women's Friendship in Literature* in 1980. In the same year, J. N. Waddell wrote two articles on Burney's contributions to English vocabulary. Julia Epstein presented a radically new view of Burney the diarist and her connections with the novelist in her important article on Burney's mastectomy published in *Representations* in 1986. At that point, we began to deal with a different Burney, a writer of depth, with complex responses to cruelty and pain. Epstein followed this article with a major book, *The Iron Pen: Frances Burney and the Politics of Women's Writing* (1989). Two slim volumes, by Judy Simons and by David D. Devlin, appeared in 1987; these dealt with all the novels as well as the journals (though Devlin seems to wish to put Burney back in her place). Kristina Straub's book *Divided Fictions* also appeared in 1987. From articles or chapters on Burney, criticism had moved on to book-length studies.

The publication by Oxford University Press of all of Burney's novels in new annotated editions kept pace with the growing interest. *Evelina*, always the most popular of the novels, appeared in 1968 and *Camilla* in 1972; the annotated *Cecilia* came out in 1988 (preceded by a Virago issue in 1986), and these three were joined at last by the edited and annotated *Wanderer*, in 1991 (it had been preceded by a reprint of the novel in 1988 with an introduction by Margaret Drabble). My own literary biography of Frances Burney, which appeared in 1988, represents an attempt to synthesize the diarist and the novelist, and these with the writer of the (then) as yet unpublished plays, as well as to relate the woman who lived (insofar as she may be found) with the writer and what she wrote. My approach to the novels entailed taking the fables of the stories with some degree of seriousness instead of looking only for light humor, or finding entertainment only in those aspects of her writing where Burney most closely approaches Jane Austen (or what has been made of Austen). By the 1990s it became a standard approach to investigate seriously both the historicity of certain of Burney's character types (for example, Captain Mirvan) and the fables of identity and parentage within the novels. The essays in *Eighteenth-Century Fiction*'s special *Evelina* issue (July 1991) would not have been published twenty years earlier; all of these essays take it as a given that it is worth examining the convoluted and painful familial relationships in *Evelina*. We no longer have just the light comic novel comprised of funny Branghtons and outings to Vauxhall.

In the 1990s, Burney emerged as a fuller writer in every sense. "New" Burney writings—that is, works that have hitherto existed only in manuscript—continued to see the light of print. Katharine Rogers included *The Witlings* in an anthology of 1994. *The Complete Plays of Frances Burney*, edited by Peter Sabor with Geoffrey Sill and Stewart Cooke, came out in two volumes in 1995. Burney's comedy *A Busy Day*, edited by Tara Wallace, had appeared in 1984 and thus was available for production; it was produced by the Show of Strength Company in Bristol in 1993 and in London (at the King's Head Theatre, Islington) in the summer of 1994. *A Busy Day* is the first of Burney's comedies to reach the stage, but now that the others are available, there may soon be productions of *Love and Fashion* and *The Woman-Hater*, and the suppressed first comic play, *The Witlings*. Burney the dramatist has been an acceptable topic of discussion since the early 1990s; it is not unlikely that her life also may receive a dramatic treatment. The writer discussed in scholarly (and other) circles will be a writer with a much larger oeuvre than was available earlier in the twentieth century, or at any time in the past. A Burney anthology for students and general readers might include one or two of the author's plays, and even some of her verses, as well as portions of novels, some unfinished stories, and extracts from journals and letters. The founding of the Frances Burney Society in 1994 augurs a livelier fame in the future. Frances Burney may gain a more popular readership than she has had since the mid-nineteenth century.

The stature that Frances Burney had achieved by the high Victorian era might likewise be measured by the number of volumes then arranged on her shelf in the library. Annie Raine Ellis saw to it that Burney was given serious editing, a tribute rarely paid to female writers of her era. Yet, at the same time, the late-Victorian productions were creating the picture of a profuse but minor writer, an artless female character, a harmless inhabitant of drawing rooms.

Burney crossed the threshold—or was pushed—into another room, outside the House of Fiction, becoming an artless little female, the embroiderer of a fundamentally domesticated social existence. This personification of Burney became full-blown caricature with the publication of Austin Dobson's *Fanny Burney* in 1903. Ellis had called the novelist by her married name: Madame d'Arblay. But the diminution of Burney's identity was eagerly seized upon. She became "Fanny." She began to sound like a counterpart of Jane Austen's "creep-mouse" heroine in *Mansfield Park,* the shy little Fanny Price. She became one to whom it was safe to condescend. The Fanny-ing of Frances Burney was kept up until very recently (and in some quarters still continues). But this harmless little girl is not really the author whom we come to know in her published novels—nor, as they are emerging not only upon the page but also on the stage, her formerly unpublished and unperformed plays.

LIFE

FRANCES Burney was born on 13 June 1752 in King's Lynn, Norfolk, where her father, Charles Burney, a musician and music teacher, had taken the post of organist in St. Margaret's Church. The family maintained its associations with King's Lynn even after Charles Burney had returned to London, where his ambitions had always led him. Ill health and the threat of consumption had induced the move to the provinces. Charles was ready to tackle London again in the 1760s. It was his wife, the gentle Esther Burney (née Sleepe), who fell ill. Frances Burney lost her mother in September 1762, three months after her tenth birthday. The loss left a lifelong scar; Burney admitted in later life that she regularly prayed for her dead mother. The actual moment of loss was the more distressing because the younger children had been taken out of the house during Esther's last days and were living in Mrs. Sheeles's boarding school in Queen Square when the news was brought to them. A neighbor remembered Mrs. Sheeles's saying that Frances was the most afflicted child she had ever seen: "that you would take no Comfort—& was almost killed with Crying" (*Early Journals and Letters,* vol. 2, p. 104). Frances clung to her memories and a few precious relics, like her mother's sampler, still extant though faded, with a label by Frances: "Sampler of My own dearest Mother. Given to me by her precious Self, when I was 8 years of age."

Frances was the third of Charles and Esther Burney's six children; the eldest of these, Hester (or Esther) was in fact born before her parents were married, a fact always assiduously covered up by the family, leading to some confusions about dates. James, the elder son, later a famous sea captain and chronicler of Captain Cook's voyages, came next, followed by Frances, Susanna (born 1755), and Charles (born 1757). The last child of this marriage was the lively Charlotte, who seemed a baby to Frances, nine years her senior. Susanna and Charles were always Frances' closest friends within her own family, and with them she shared projects, games, jokes, and secrets. All the Burney children formed a kind of club, a complex phalanx against the rest of the world; during most of their lives they kept up with each other's thoughts as well as activities, even during long separations. The complexities of sibling relations are brought out most clearly in Burney's third novel, *Camilla; or, A Picture of Youth* (1796).

Burney's early bereavement seems to have been a catalyst for the first release of her powers as a writer. She herself dates her first great outpouring of writing to just after that time. To her father, and probably to other adults, the maturing child Frances seemed too serious, too solemn. Her father teasingly called her "the Old Lady." Other children saw a different side of her. A former playmate recollected the juvenile Frances: "*you* were always so merry, so gay, so droll, & had such imagination in making plays; always . . . some thing of your own contrivance" (*Journals and Letters*, vol. 6, p. 778). The child who was merry, who was witty, who made up games for all the children to play is certainly reflected in the comic novelist and dramatist.

The Burney children suffered a shock when their father remarried. In October 1767 Charles Burney eloped, in effect, with Mrs. Stephen Allen, a handsome widow of King's Lynn. The secret wedding seems to have been designed largely to circumvent the disapproval of Elizabeth Allen's family, who regarded Charles Burney, a lowly musician and burdened widower, as a fortune-hunting nobody. Contriving the affair thus also spared Charles the difficulties of breaking the news of his intentions to his dismayed children. They were faced with a fait accompli. James was already a midshipman on the high seas and had been absent when his mother died. The girls were particularly distressed by their father's remarriage, for they had to spend their time in the company of their new stepmother. Mrs. Allen had three children: Maria, the eldest (age sixteen at the time of her mother's remarriage), loved Charles Burney and became the enthusiastic and entertaining companion of his older daughters. She was a lifelong companion and "sister." Maria's energetic ways, amusing utterances, and difficult life undoubtedly provided material for Burney's novels. Stephen and Bessy Allen, however, seem never to have fitted in very well with the Burney children. The new marriage soon meant the arrival of more children, displacing earlier "youngests": Richard, the youngest son (later in disgrace and banished to India) and Sarah Harriet (who was to become a novelist like her older sister Frances). The combination of the three groups of children led to some unhappiness and jealousy. The children of Charles Burney's first marriage were not at all pleased with Mrs. Allen, and referred to her behind her back with insulting epithets: "Precious," "the *Lady*."

Their father's remarriage created a sense of displacement in the Burney children, even a sense of a new kind of orphanage. Mrs. Allen's money (though much of it had been lost through bad investments) assisted Charles in fulfilling his ambition to write a complete modern study of music and its history. He made long tours on the Continent, leaving his family behind. When he returned, he was usually either out of the house teaching or at work in his study, writing first the two volumes of his musical *Tours* (1771, 1773) and then his great *General History of Music*. The first volume of the *General History* came out in 1776; the rest followed in 1782 and 1789. This long labor of love and scholarship created a new form of knowledge, a new study: musicology. Charles Burney—*Doctor* Burney since receiving his Doctorate in Music from Oxford in 1769—had succeeded in proving that a lowly musician could be a scholar. Having raised his own status and that of his profession, he was received into the circles of the literati, most important the group at Streatham, of which Samuel Johnson was the major figure.

Her father's writing had its effects on Frances. Most immediately, it provided her with a responsible (if unpaid) occupation and an excuse to get away from her stepmother. She became her father's research assistant, secretary, and amanuensis (or copyist), and she learned about the publication of books (doubtless including the ways in which her anxious father rigged the reviewing of his publications). Her usefulness to her father meant she was in no serious danger of being married off against her inclination; when an unwanted suitor, Thomas Barlow, proposed to her in 1775, her father did not try to get her off his hands, as he otherwise might have done; Burney herself insisted at that time, "I have not a mind to be married."

The Burneys' social position was an anomalous one. Dr. Burney, as his biographer Roger Lonsdale has pointed out, was driven by a desire to prove that a musician could be a man of letters and a gentleman; in the end, he was successful. Yet Dr. Burney, a musician and music teacher, was not what the eighteenth century meant by "a gentleman." While the Burney children were growing up, the family was living, however respectably, among what would later be termed "the Bohemians." Burney entertained a number of musicians, opera singers, dancers, and actors. His house was populated by visitors speaking foreign languages. Such a company would have been considered highly dangerous and undesirable for impressionable young ladies among the truly genteel classes.

FRANCES BURNEY

Frances Burney was not quite a *lady* by birth. The position on a social cusp was of advantage to her, as she grew up knowing more about the larger world than most girls of her era could know, and she had the advantage of hearing about foreign countries, travel, books, ideas, and, of course, music.

Frances Burney dared to play the harpsichord only when nobody else was present—her musical talent was negligible compared with that of her father, her sister Esther, and her brother-in-law Charles Rousseau Burney. She responded strongly to music and to musical performances as she recounts them in her journals. In her novels, music always plays a part; she notices when fashionable or would-be fashionable members of an audience are attending to a performance, and when they are only pretending. We laugh at the Branghtons at the opera in *Evelina*, for they are blatant social climbers and musical illiterates. But in *Cecilia* (1782) it is the rich and wellborn who sin against music and show themselves unable to follow a performance. In her last novel, *The Wanderer* (1814), Burney depicts the life of a performer of great ability who must give music lessons to lazy or talentless rich folk. For this portrait she drew on the experience of her father, her sister Esther, and Esther's husband—all music teachers.

Family experience had long deepened her perception of what high society does to music—and other arts. At home, in her father's drawing room, people met to enjoy music itself. These actors and musicians, many of whom were considered exotic (such as the famous castrato "the divine Millico") received from many Englishmen the contempt (whether good- or ill-natured) allotted to most "foreigners." Frances, who had spent part of her childhood with her maternal grandmother, Frances Sleepe (née Dubois), a Frenchwoman, had reason to know that she was partly "foreign" herself. She would not speak French in public, but that may have resulted less from linguistic deficiency than from a reluctance to commit herself to a language that she might speak in an uneducated or "low" fashion. Her true knowledge of the language is demonstrated by an ability to record, in her diary accounts of conversations, other people's speeches in French—not as easy to do as it might seem. Her knowledge that on one side she came from immigrants, from people who were "foreign," raised Burney's awareness of the mistreatment of those who came from elsewhere.

Captain Mirvan, the rough sea captain in *Evelina*, feels it right to express an aversion to Madame Duval and Monsieur Du Bois on account of their Frenchness—an identity assumed by Madame Duval. Furthermore, Mirvan feels it a patriotic action to play cruel practical jokes on both Monsieur Du Bois and Madame Duval, on the ground that they are French. The brutality of such an attitude is examined more intently in *The Wanderer*, where a whole bourgeois society is indicted for its defensiveness against what we in the twentieth century have learned to call the "Other." As partly a member of the "Other," Burney learned early from her experience of the treatment meted out to her father's foreign friends and business associates what was in store for anyone whose foreignness was evident—or was found out.

Frances Burney's understanding of the position of those who were foreign made her a sympathetic servant to the German Queen Charlotte, although Burney undertook the post at Court as second Keeper of the Queen's Robes with the greatest reluctance. Her father was delighted with the honor, which he thought entailed bright prospects for the rest of the family, especially himself and his son James. Burney felt she was being sacrificed on 17 July 1786, when she entered the almost monastic seclusion of life at Windsor and Kew. The petty jealousies and general dreariness of a confined existence were overshadowed by the horror of the king's madness, which meant even closer confinement for the ladies about the queen. Burney's tragic plays were written in this unhappy period; one tragedy, *Edwy and Elgiva*, was later produced, in March 1795, but was a complete failure on stage. Burney at last left the queen's service, on the plea of ill health; the queen gave her a pension of one hundred pounds per annum, her first real income. That income made it possible for her to marry for love, despite her father's displeasure; on 28 July 1793 she married the émigré Alexandre D'Arblay, now exiled in England, a refugee from Revolutionary France.

Considering Frances Burney's early background, it is the less astonishing that at the age of forty-one she could amaze her friends and delight her detractors by marrying a penniless Frenchman—thus allying herself with the "Other." The difficulties under which D'Arblay was laboring perhaps roused in her what in a man we would call "chivalry"—a desire to protect and nourish that which is easily mistreated.

Frances Burney's marriage was undeniably a happy one, not least perhaps because at the beginning she was the active spirit, the provider. She literally put a roof over both their heads in writing *Camilla* (1796). The proceeds went into "Camilla Cottage." Her son, young Alex, was a joy to her, and he had a carefully bilingual upbringing. After the Peace of Amiens in 1802, D'Arblay went over to war-torn France to see what had become of both family and property. His wife and son followed him—and then were trapped in France when hostilities broke out again. It was in Paris that young Alex grew up and went to school, and in Paris that Burney had her agonizing operation, a mastectomy without anesthetic, in 1811. She contrived to go home to England in 1812 (in a somewhat clandestine fashion, on a ship ostensibly bound for America), and in England she completed her last novel, *The Wanderer* (1814). Her husband resumed his military career, fighting against Napoleon in 1815, and Frances Burney herself was in Brussels during the Battle of Waterloo; her account of the city on that occasion may have been an influence on Thackeray's *Vanity Fair.* General D'Arblay's exertions led to ill health; although the new French government appreciated him sufficiently to give him a title (Burney was now a "comtesse"), the couple would have appreciated more financial rewards. Frances wrote no new novels during her widowhood, but perhaps it was the death of her father (in 1814) that caused the flow of fiction to cease. Her last work was the *Memoirs of Doctor Burney* (1832), a biography (and hagiography) that allows her modestly to introduce some autobiography (not yet a suitable genre for a woman). Frances Burney died on 6 January 1840, having lived long enough to see the beginning of the reign of Queen Victoria. Unhappily, she had already survived her son, Alex, who died in 1837. Burney's marriage had brought her much joy, but also great sorrow.

ENGLISH OR "FOREIGN"?
NATIONALITY, CLASS, GENDER

IT is evident, not only in her marriage but in her early writings, that Burney felt an identification with "the Frenchies," "the frogs." "Hark you, Mrs. Frog," cries Captain Mirvan to Madame Duval, "you'd best hold your tongue . . . if you don't . . . I shall make no ceremony of tripping you out of the window, and there you may lie in the mud till some of your Monseers come to help you out of it" (*Evelina*, p. 57).

Burney was certainly not exaggerating the English suspicion and dislike of foreigners, which ran rampant in the time of the Gordon Riots (1780). During that uprising, all Roman Catholics (and those rumored to be such) or liberal sympathizers with the cause of Catholic emancipation were in danger. Hostility to foreigners, especially to the French, increased during the French Revolution and its aftermath. The émigré General D'Arblay, a man of proven valor, was disconcerted by English hostility and ignorance. He told Burney that a group of English soldiers refused to drink beer in the kitchen at Juniper Hall, where a party of French refugees from the Revolution were living, saying they were afraid that the French would put poison in their drink. "Vous jugez bien que si je désire rester en Angleterre, ce n'est pas pour cette sorte de gens" ("You can certainly judge that if I want to stay in England, it's not for that kind of people") (*Journals and Letters*, vol. 2, p. 40). Later experiences only confirmed Burney's youthful perception of the barriers erected against the "foreign," and of the cruelty that people are prepared to inflict on others. In her youth she had sufficient means of learning about this, and particularly of seeing to what spite and cruel taunts a foreign and defenseless woman could be subjected. The Italian soprano Lucrezia Agujari, called "La Bastardella," had suffered some kind of accident to her left side, a mishap the English thought fair game for mirth. Burney recorded the callous response in her journal:

you have doubtless heard the story of the Pig's Eating half her side, & of its being repaired by a silver kind of machine. You may be sure that she has not Escaped the Witticisms of our *Wags* upon this score: it is too fair a subject for Ridicule to have been suffered to pass untouched. Mr. Bromfield has given her the Nick name of *Argentine:* Mr. Foote has advised her, (or *threatened* to advise her) to go to the stamp office, to have her *side entered*, lest she should be prosecuted for secreting silver contrary to Law: & my Lord Sandwich has made a Catch, in Italian, & in Dialogue between her & the Pig beginning *Caro Mio Porco*—the Pig answers by a Grunt;—& it Ends by his exclaiming *ah che bel mangiare!* Lord S. has shewn it to my Father, but he says he will not have it set, till she is gone to Italy.

(*Early Journals*, vol. 2, pp. 98–99)

The modern editor of the *Early Journals*, Lars Troide, notes that Dr. Burney "had the good taste not to set it," but we may notice that Charles Burney is not in a position to object to the gross bad taste and ill nature of the would-be witty Lord Sandwich.

It has sometimes been asserted that in her novels Burney exaggerated the roughness of manners of those in the upper classes, but her own experience of those classes trained her observation. The fact that she was not a beautiful and protected young heiress brought out into society in a debut allowed her to see much more than such a lady would see; she had unusual opportunity to become aware of the cruel jokes, the ribaldry, the attitudes of real men—and women. It is unlikely that what Mary Poovey calls a "Proper Lady" would have included in her first published novel, which appeared while the author was in the maiden state, an example of a couple so dubiously connected as Madame Duval and Monsieur Du Bois, for the little Frenchman is clearly not a relative and not a mere friend of the heroine's grandmother. He is Madame Duval's gallant, her *cicisbeo*, and, we may assume, even her lover—which makes his turning his sexual attention to Evelina a complex problem for Madame Duval's granddaughter.

The girls in Dr. Burney's home were not sheltered, and they did observe a good deal of life. They also had their cruel jokes, indulging their violent sense of humor. Maria Allen, Frances' stepsister, in her first surviving letter to Frances (1768), joins in a game of imagining what might be done with men:

I like your Plan immensely of Extirpating that vile race of beings call^d man but I (who you know am clever (VÈRRÉE) clever) have thought of an improvement in the sistim [sic] suppose we were to Cut of [sic] their *prominent members*, and by that means render them Harmless innofencive [sic] Little Creatures; We might have such charming *vocal* Music Every house might be qualified to get up an opera and Piccinis Music would be still more in vogue than it is & we might make such usefull Animals of them in other Respects Consider Well this scheme.

(*Early Journal and Letters*, vol. 1, pp. 331–332)

That Frances was not offended—rather, she kept this Swiftian letter (written to her when she was sixteen and Maria was seventeen)—shows that they both had a wild, tough-hearted, even aggressive side. Both girls acknowledge that they live in a world where men can be castrated and women ruined only for someone's pleasure. The representation of Frances Burney as "Fanny" has made her too much a timid, sweet, "little thing." On that basis, critics have often ignored or censured what they regarded as irrelevant farce or strange fallings off from smooth genteel comedy. Austin Dobson in 1903 complained about the excess of "horseplay" in *Evelina*. Frances Burney was not Jane Austen and did not want to be. (Perhaps Jane Austen did not want to be, either—judging from her earliest works.) Burney found life violently funny, with an emphasis on the violence.

Satiric violence against the male is found in *Evelina*, deflected through Captain Mirvan, whose brutality makes him a most questionable satirist. Not content with sneering at the beau Mr. Lovel as a monkey, Captain Mirvan introduces the affected man-about-town to the animal emblem, his semblance and brother: "he hauled into the room a monkey! full dressed, and extravagantly *à-la-mode!*" (*Evelina*, p. 443). Mirvan continues to taunt foppish Lovel with the relationship; urging him to join in the game against himself: "just for the fun's sake, duff your coat and waistcoat, and swop with Monsieur *Grinagain* here, and I'll warrant you'll not know yourself which is which" (p. 444). Lovel, too frightened of the rough captain to engage in personal combat with him, "vented his passion by giving a furious blow to the monkey." The animal at once retaliates:

The creature, darting forwards, sprung instantly upon him, and clinging round his neck, fastened his teeth to one of his ears. . . .

It was impossible, now, to distinguish whose screams were loudest, those of Mr. Lovel, or of the terrified Lady Louisa . . . but the unrelenting Captain roared with joy. . . .

Poor Mr. Lovel, almost fainting with terror, sunk upon the floor, crying out, "Oh I shall die, I shall die!—Oh I'm bit to death!"

(p. 445)

The description gives immediate and close physical contact between monkey and man, and a momentary obliteration of the victim, whose "I shall die!" indicates his metaphorical social death, which occurs simultaneously with physical wounding. Embarrassment and humiliation create the theater that many of Burney's characters love to look upon. The comparison between man and monkey is a commonplace of seventeenth- and eighteenth-century literature, but the moral generalization had been sharpened by specific satiric comparisons of the specifically male human being to the monkey—as in the words of the lady to a monkey in the Earl of Rochester's "A Letter from Artemiza in the Town to Chloe in the Country": "Kisse mee thou curious Miniature of man;/How odde thou art? how pritty, how Japan" (ll. 143–144). In Susanna Centlivre's play *The Busy-Body* (1715), Miranda, hiding her lover, Sir George, in the fireplace behind the fireboard, pretends she has a monkey shut up there, a monkey that is yet to be tamed. Marplot's eager exclamation, "A monkey!" (act 4, l. 346) may be echoed in the exclamatory introduction of the animal in Burney's "he hauled into the room a monkey!" Centlivre's Miranda speaks in a series of double entendres, comparing her lover (and men in general) to the monkey, a feminist joke not understood by the men on the scene.

In Burney's novel Lovel has often tormented Evelina out of unceasing resentment of her refusal to dance with him at her first London ball. He has teased her about blushing, trying to make her blush with shame. Now he himself "blushes" with the blood streaming down his face, and the consolations suggested by his mischievous companions only add to the motif of humiliation: "it is but a slit of the ear: it only looks as if you had been in the pillory." Mrs. Selwyn adds, "It may acquire you the credit of being an anti-ministerial writer" (p. 446). To brutal Captain Mirvan, the original satirist of this scene, it would appear that only the fop is monkeylike. But Burney's broader joke takes in almost all those present (including even the sympathetic Mrs. Selwyn, who joins in loud laughter). They join, socially, in monkeylike imitation of each other, turning against the fallen member of their society. It is not just Lovel who is interrogated by the presence of the monkey, but the entire company.

Burney has some resemblance to Jonathan Swift in her appreciation of the yahooism of human beings. Her fiction often leads us through a fairly decorous or socially ornate and pretentious system of behaviors toward the point where there is some sort of breakdown. Accident itself may introduce literal breakdown, as Eliza's coach breaks, at the beginning of Burney's comic play *A Busy Day* (written around 1800), or as the heroine's conveyance breaks down on her urgent trip to London for her secret wedding in *Cecilia*. In real life, even an ordinary journey in the London streets could be hazardous. We find in Burney's *Early Journal* that a visit to the opera with her stepmother and sister in February 1773, to hear the castrato singer Giuseppe Millico, was attended by difficulty on the return; they at last succeeded in getting through the crowds and into their coach. They drove off, "but . . . there had been left a load of Gravel in the street . . . presently the Coach was entirely overturned, & we came side ways on the Ground." Frances was in some danger from flying glass, but was saved by the protection afforded by her "Bever Hat" (*Early Journal and Letters*, vol. 1, p. 239).

Such incidents are used to effect by Burney in her fiction. The danger that arrives unexpectedly from the external world of objects and accidents is not so important in itself as the fact that such a break in expected social routine offers an entrance for unplanned social brutality.

A surprising incident seems to offer a holiday from the strenuous routines of courtesy and other forms of social order. Hence, in *Evelina*, after the accident of a coach's breaking down, Madame Duval can be dropped in the mud by her would-be rescuer, Monsieur Du Bois, both of them probably pushed by the mischievous Captain Mirvan.

Some "accidents" are brought on by the malice of human will, or by the forms of selfishness that masquerade as mere carelessness. The vulgar Branghtons of *Evelina*, delighted at the prospect of riding in a "coronet coach," commandeer Lord Orville's coach for their party and then damage it. They run into a cart, and young Tom Branghton (unused to glass windows in vehicles) thrusts his head out of the window: "I never minded that the glass was up, and so I poked my head fairly through it. Only see, Miss, how I've cut my forehead!" (p. 276). Evelina, in her anguish over Lord Orville's loss of good opinion of her through the vulgarity of her relations, is not at all sympathetic about Tom's cut forehead: "A much worse accident to himself, would not . . . have given me any concern for him" (p. 276). All characters, even heroines, are capable of some hard-heartedness, and a certain degree of self-centeredness is universal.

In her tragic plays, written during the melancholic period of service at the court of Queen Charlotte, Burney tries to treat self-sacrifice as a good, but the results of sacrifice or docile obedience are uniformly disastrous; the death of the heroine is the consequence of heroic submission to duty and of self-abnegation. Even here, the self-abnegation is not achieved without struggle, what Burney called "conflict," meaning inner conflict. Adela in *The Siege of Pevensey*, Elgiva of *Edwy and Elgiva*, and Cerulia in *Hubert De Vere* have strong desires, even though the world around them acknowledges no right in them to their desires, and the young women try to conform to the judgment of the world by erasing themselves. In these distressing plays, Burney, who had been emotionally blackmailed by her father's wish for her to serve at Court into giving up all prospects of either marrying or writing, was struggling to justify a self-sacrifice she felt unjustifiable. In her published novels and the unpublished comic drama, the emotional tone and authorial judgments are very different.

A degree of "egotism" (a favorite word of Burney's) is found in her heroines and in all other central characters, virtuous as well as erring. Some of the favorite characters have a capacity for altruism, but in the four novels and in the dramatic comedies Burney is very suspicious of self-sacrifice. Even altruistic and reasonable characters have a strong center in self and are not to be swayed toward valuing the self-deficient sacrifice that yields everything up to others. Cecilia, the heroine of Burney's second novel, gives up a large part of her fortune to rescue her guardian, the spendthrift Mr. Harrel, from imminent ruin—but she knows she is being blackmailed into it. She does something against her self-interest but with her eyes open; she estimates exactly what she is doing, and what she can or should spare to help her former schoolfellow Priscilla, now Mrs. Harrel. Cecilia speaks very briskly to Priscilla's brother, Mr. Arnott, urging him not to sacrifice himself in bailing Harrel out again. Why should Harrel be saved from ruin—or from having to make a flight to the Continent?

"I am sorry," said Cecilia, "to speak with severity of one so nearly connected with you, yet, suffer me to ask, why should he be saved from it at all? and what is there he can at present do better? Has not he long been threatened with every evil that is now arrived? have we not both warned him . . . ? he has not submitted to the smallest change in his way of life. . . . Till the present storm, therefore, blows over, leave him to his fate."

(p. 378)

In an earlier draft, Burney made her heroine (at this point named Albina) even more strong-minded:

"I am sorry to speak with severity of one so nearly allied to you, but the too great ascendant which he has gained over yr. soft & compassionate mind, will end in yr. utter ruin . . . be steady, therefore, in refusing to part with even an Inch of Land, for if there you once Waver, depend upon it, you are undone!"

(draft of *Cecilia*, Berg MSS, act 3, fol. 92ʳ)

Of course a young woman was not supposed to speak in such a commanding and frank fashion to a male acquaintance, and Burney subsequently softened the heroine's speech—but she did not soften it very greatly. Cecilia is still clear-headed, determined, realistic. It is only Mrs. Harrel's danger, arousing Cecilia's fear of what Priscilla might suffer at the hands of an enraged and irrational husband, that makes Cecilia "waver," and she judges every concession as questionable.

When Cecilia says to Priscilla Harrel, "I know no longer what is kind or what is cruel, nor have I known for some time past right from wrong, nor good from evil!" (p. 396), she makes a statement that it would be astounding in the mouth of any character in eighteenth-century fiction—let alone a virtuous female character. Matters of right and wrong were customarily judged to be already decided. The "good" character has nothing to do but to act accordingly. Literary criticism in general emphasized that novels, read by women and young persons, should always be morally instructive. The mix of late Puritanism with seventeenth-century neoclassicism was cemented into supposed laws about fiction—its morality, its poetic justice, its duty to provide the exemplary character.

In *Evelina*, Burney covers her tracks by making the novel a light courtship comedy with an apparently perfect romantic hero in Lord Orville, and an apparently perfect paternal guardian in Mr. Villars. In the first part of the novel, Evelina herself is not an example of virtue, for she is too young, naive, and even (at moments) foolish. But readers can, if they wish, think of her as developing into grown-up niceness because of the good mentoring by her lover and her metaphorical "good daddy." Burney herself had an oddly complex and reliant attitude to her own father; the fashion of the time for representation of submissive obedience to fathers coincided in her half-orphaned case with a peculiar emotional need. Yet she had tacitly rebelled against her father by publishing *Evelina* anonymously and without his knowledge.

Her next work, the comic play *The Witlings* (not published until the 1990s), was so unpleasing to Dr. Charles Burney, and to his and Frances' elderly friend, the literary man Samuel Crisp, that Frances was in effect forbidden to put it on stage. Burney evidently had enough of "daddying" in her writing life. In *Cecilia*, there are no "good daddies," and the three guardians to whom Cecilia is entrusted during the short time between her uncle's death and her majority wreck her life—or nearly do so.

Cecilia, however, has learned the value of thinking for herself, and thinking for oneself is a theme of *Cecilia*. If one "thinks for oneself," of course, matters of morality become more complicated. For a young woman who thinks for herself, the disadvantages of self-sacrifice become readily apparent—and these disadvantages stretch beyond one's immediate circumstances to the unhealthiness of a society that expects docility and uncomplaining self-sacrifice from certain of its members—especially the poor, such as the family of the overworked carpenter Mr. Hill, as well as (in general) from women, particularly young women.

Burney is curiously modern in not endorsing any cult of self-sacrifice. She does not say it is wrong to sacrifice oneself—it may even be right. But it is right depending on the circumstances. An individual act of giving up one's own interest should never become habitual. In *Camilla* (1796), the heroine as a child readily falls in with her uncle's revision of his plan to make her his heiress. Feeling guilty over the harm he has done to Camilla's younger sister Eugenia, Sir Hugh plans to make the crippled girl, instead of his favorite niece, his heiress. To nine-year-old Camilla, this compensation makes perfect sense, and what she does in enthusiastically agreeing is not self-lacerating but pleasing to her. Cheerfully giving up one's own limited interests for the well-being—the *clear* well-being—of another or for the sake of justice is not the same, as Burney knows and shows, as the kind of self-sacrifice so often dinned into women. In the earlier draft of a third novel that was abandoned in favor of *Camilla*, a novel that I have termed "Clarinda," Burney shows a young woman making a distressing self-sacrifice: marrying a rich old man

she does not love. She does this (or nearly does it, rather, for her father saves her) out of guilt. But such a self-punishment is mistaken. Guilt leads to useless self-sacrifice, a self-wounding that is madly wrong.

GUILT IN BURNEY'S NOVELS

GUILT plays an important role throughout Burney's novels, yet it is an ironic role, because guilt does little good. It leads to a combination of self-wounding and disguise, and sets the scene for alienation from self and others. Guilt over his mistreatment of his dead wife, Evelina's mother, makes Sir John Belmont a fair target for an impostor; he accepts Polly Green as his own daughter because his guilt has fostered inertia. His guilt has prevented his looking in the right direction for the lost daughter; that would mean confronting Villars, his wife's friend, which would be too unpleasant. Belmont's poor detective work is the effect of a divided will and of melancholy.

In *Cecilia*, guilt combined with humiliation over the financial ruin he has consistently wrought drives Mr. Harrel to commit suicide after the weird party at Vauxhall. We do not associate champagne and self-destruction, so we (like the heroine) do not pick up the clues to Mr. Harrel's suicidal intention. We have set him down as a manipulator and poseur. Harrel labels his bills with the grandiose statement *"To be all paid to-night with a BULLET"* (p. 430). Of course, bullets do not pay debts, and his suicide does not much help his creditors. But Mr. Harrel does pay for his debts, even though he does not pay them. He sacrifices his life very stupidly to his guilt and to his lack of imagination (for he cannot imagine how to live other than as he has been living). Guilt is almost omnipresent in *Cecilia*. The heroine herself must feel guilty about Mr. Harrel's suicide, even though she knows rationally that she was not to blame. Mortimer Delvile, the "hero," is made to feel guilty for wanting to marry Cecilia at all, for it will ruin the family name. Mrs. Delvile, Mortimer's mother and Cecilia's friend, proves an expert manipulator and creator of guilt in both Cecilia and her son. Old Albany, the eccentric philanthropist, is working off his guilt for the harm caused by his ill treatment of a woman he had loved, a guilt that drove him into the madhouse.

In *Camilla*, Sir Hugh, another eccentric if benevolent man, likewise uses his guilt as a means to manipulate others.

It is not the least of the paradoxes of guilt, as Burney sees it, that it offers the guilty party an acceptable excuse for the exertion of unusual psychic force upon others. Both men and women in Burney's novels experience guilt, but the women can afford it rather less. Repentance and amendment are all very well, but these are matters that should be entered into rationally, with some ability to estimate to what extent one really did wrong, and to what extent others are only saying so. Guilt sustains a static condition in which neither analysis or progress is possible. Thus the creation of guilt in Camilla, the most lighthearted of the heroines, becomes a major crime in *Camilla*. It is bred chiefly of Dr. Marchmont's mad desire for perfection in others in combination with his resentful misogyny. Guilt is nourished by the "hero" Edgar Mandlebert, a character already wounded by self-doubt. Whenever Edgar feels guilty, he becomes resentful. Guilt apparently is not felt by those who (the reader feels) *ought* to feel it: the practical joker Lionel, who gets his sisters into trouble, or the sinister, judgmental Dr. Marchmont.

But if we look more closely, we can see in both of these characters the germs of melancholy nurtured by their own disbelief in themselves. Dr. Marchmont has never recovered from the fact that his second wife, his beautiful wife, did not love him. He thinks he is righteously indignant about her (mental) adultery, but he is actually piteous because, knowing that he forced her to marry him, he fears he is unlovable. Lionel's cocky facade conceals tremendous insecurity, as his sisters know very well. When he is caught both in an adulterous affair, for which he needs "hush money," and in his outrageous scheme to blackmail a relative, Lionel is not without some sort of repentance. Camilla is sickened by his light jests about his behavior, and wonders if he feels anything: "What have you done with your heart?" she cries (p. 739). But for Lionel any kind of conscious repentance becomes confused with self-abasement and even desire for self-annihilation:

"However, shall I tell you the truth? I hate myself! and so completely hate myself at this moment, that I dare not be grave! dare not suffer reflection to take hold of me, lest it should make life too odious for me to bear it. . . . What has bewitched me, I know no more than you, but I never meant to play this abominable part. And now, if I did not flog up my spirits to prevent their flagging, I suppose I should hang or drown."

(p. 739)

Lionel cannot even make a statement of love without a lust for self-inflicted suffering, a violent partial annihilation of being: "I would cut off my left arm for Lavinia and Eugenia, and for thee, Camilla, I would lop off my right!" (p. 739).

As the only son among his parents' four children, Lionel has had heavy burdens laid upon him. His guilt and nagging sense of inadequacy, a consistent sense of failure, have made it easy for him to associate pleasure with forgetting his family: "When some frolic or gambol comes into my way, I forget you all! clear out of my memory you all walk, as if I had never beheld you" (p. 739). The relieving absence of the family from Lionel's mind is treated as if it were an action on the part of the family itself. Whenever he remembers his family—his father, who is an Anglican minister, his mother with "her deuced severity"—Lionel is smitten by guilt. He can mock the family virtue (as he does when teasing his sisters) or try to anesthetize the guilt altogether. His father's thundering at him by letter about his wrongdoing and his deserving the penalties of the law is not nearly as helpful as a rigid moral code would lead us to think. The more Mr. Tyrold expatiates upon Lionel's guilt, the more readily we can understand Lionel's having entered into an affair with a married woman—whose husband, he claims, deserves it: "Such a tiresome quiz! . . . You never knew such a blockhead. The poor thing can't bear him, but she's fond of me to distraction" (p. 731).

All of the most interesting characters in *Camilla*, including eventually the heroine herself, suffer from the crippling sense that they are not loved—a sense that, far from inculcating virtuous discipline, drives these characters into strange and self-estranging forms of behavior. Getting another man's wife undermines the paterfamilias, and makes Lionel feel (momentarily) that he has succeeded, against the odds, in obtaining the love his mother will not give him. Burney hardly knows how to rescue Lionel from the plight into which she has brought him, for no eighteenth-century novelist, male or female, could let off too lightly a character who did what Lionel did—especially in a novel subtitled *A Picture of Youth* and dedicated by permission (and even by request) to Queen Charlotte. At the end of *Camilla*, the now gloomy Lionel can see no better way out than avoiding his family (now partially reconciled) as much as possible, by procuring "an appointment that carried him abroad," where "time aided adversity in forming him a new character" (p. 909). What Lionel must obtain to alleviate guilt is nothing less than "a new character"—there is no step-by-step retrieval of his old one; he could not psychologically endure that process. At the center of the novel, the chief guilt-inducer, Dr. Marchmont, whose moralizing has had a baleful effect on Edgar and Camilla, must recognize that he was wrong: "Dr. Marchmont . . . regretting the false light given by the spirit of comparison, in the hypothesis which he had formed . . . acknowledged its injustice, its narrowness and its arrogancy." That is the penultimate sentence of the novel. The last sentence is "What, at last, so diversified as man? what so little to be judged by his fellow?" (p. 913). It is the judgment of our "fellow" reflected on us that makes most of the disturbing self-doubt and the pointless guilt of human life.

The chief disturbers—the "villains," if you like—of Burney's novels are persons who love judging others, and who do not allow for the diversity within the diversified individual. The judgment of others is self-interested, although it can be ingeniously sophisticated. Guilt can be aroused in someone for loving or for not loving, for giving or for not giving. So diversified is the heart of the human being that the judge can coexist with the victim in the same person. Burney's two later novels in particular take a very close look at psychic self-tormenting. One of the other characters in *Camilla* calls Edgar Mandlebert a "self-tormenter." In *The Wanderer*, Elinor Joddrel, apostle of Revolution, is another self-tormentor. Excessively self-involved, Elinor tries to make Albert Harleigh feel guilty for not loving her. Once she has set her heart upon him, she feels that Juliet (presently known as "Ellis"), the refugee heroine, ought to feel guilty for attracting Albert. Yet Elinor reserves to herself her greatest capacity for inflicting injury. She is one of Burney's several suicides or would-be suicides—Elinor stabs herself at a concert where Juliet is about to perform. Her vivid and even witty sense of herself, thoroughly mixed with self-revulsion, coexists with an impossible demand for love. The demand becomes ever more insatiable with Elinor's developing belief that she is unworthy to be loved. She turns her judgmental eye on all around her but never spares herself. This self-attention renders her hopeless as a revolutionary—she has caught the suicidal aspect of Mary Wollstonecraft, while ignoring (or very largely ignoring) material reform, and the practical and ugly world that Juliet encounters when she tries to earn her living. Burney, in her experience of Queen Charlotte's household, at the loftiest possible level of "service," a position that aristocrats' daughters vied for, had gained an insight into the real difficulties faced by the woman who works for a living, and these "Female Difficulties" emerge in *The Wanderer; or, Female Difficulties*. Self-absorption like Elinor's keeps economic realities at bay.

Throughout Burney's novels there is a social vision that becomes increasingly visible even as the novels gain in complexity. An individual character may be very clearly in the wrong, but a "wrong" is usually something shared by the whole society, which creates roles that the individual may act out with more earnestness or more stupidity than average. Thus Mr. Harrel through his wild expenditure fulfills social laws as much as Compton Delvile does through his stiff and absurd pride in his family name. In a social world that is "guilty" in such a complex fashion, blaming the individual is an indulgence. Too much guilt is another, if perverse, form of self-indulgence, sparing one from seeing the whole picture, and thus from using one's mind. Burney is, certainly, an Enlightenment writer, though she is never simple or doctrinaire. She believes in the value of "thinking for oneself" and shows that it is sometimes very valuable to get away from the beaten path. She knows to what degree custom validates insanely stupid or unreasonably cruel behavior, and she shows us that the object of stupidity or cruelty is never merely an idea or a sign, but a real human being, placed in a perpetual pillory for the delectation of others.

In *Camilla*, the heroine's younger sister, Eugenia, contracts smallpox in early childhood through the carelessness of her uncle Sir Hugh and is dreadfully scarred by it, losing her beauty; after her recovery from the dread disease, she is crippled for life owing to an "accident" on the seesaw—even more directly the fault of Sir Hugh, who drops her from a height. Eugenia never realizes the extent of her misfortune until her late teens; her mournful enlightenment then comes through exposure to the public gaze. Lionel brings his sisters to the grounds of the retired wigshop owner Mr. Dubster, disregarding the girls' dislike of his vulgarity. When Dubster takes the party to the upper story of his unfinished summerhouse, Lionel mischievously takes away the ladder, leaving the unwilling host and the two young ladies to find what chance aid they can. When Eugenia tries to persuade the market women and a passing boy to get the ladder for them, her appearance elicits a barrage of jeers:

the boy exclaimed—"What were you put up there for, Miss? to frighten the crows?"

Eugenia, not understanding him . . . the first woman said—"I suppose you think we'll sarve you for looking at?—no need to be paid?"

"Yes, yes," cried the second, "Miss may go to market with her beauty; she'll not want for nothing if she'll shew her pretty face!"

"She need not be afeard of it, however," said the third, "for 'twill never be no worse. Only take care, Miss, you don't catch the small pox!" . . .

"Hoity, toity!" cried one of the women, as she moved off, "why, Miss, do you walk upon your knees?"

(p. 286)

In the earliest of her mature works (her juvenilia were sacrificed to the flames) Burney had treated scenes of pillorying more ambiguously. There might, after all, be some good in punishing *Evelina*'s egregiously offensive Mr. Lovel; "it only looks as if you had been in the pillory," says Mrs. Selwyn to him in insolent consolation when he has been bitten in the ear by the monkey. In *The Witlings*, Lady Smatter, the aunt of the heroine's fiancé, must be coerced into giving her blessing to the union; in the end this is achieved by the threat of a "lampoon." This lampoon is a cruel ballad, by the character named Censor, that mocks the lady's pretensions to learning; she "gulp'd such a Dose of incongrous matter/That Bedlam must soon hold the Carcase of Smatter" (Berg MSS, act 5).

In the later works there is little desire to resort for solutions to the joking and cruel disciplines of the "censors," whose modes of social discipline entail the creation of shame and guilt. In *Camilla* we focus on Eugenia's reactions to this pillorying, her exposure to public ridicule. Eugenia shrinks into herself, tries to retire to her room and hide herself from the light, expresses guilt and anger at her own bodily existence. Her anger at Sir Hugh for keeping the extent of her "deformity" from her (by ordering that no member of his household ever refer to it) is not unjustified. But the terrifying aspect of Eugenia's anger is its largely inward direction: "I will no more expose to the light a form and face so hideous:—I will retire from all mankind, and end my destined course in a solitude that no one shall discover" (p. 294). Her suffering is like that of the Inca princess in Mme de Graffigny's *Lettres d'une péruvienne* (1747), a novel alluded to in *Camilla*. Graffigny's Zilia, ashamed at her failure to commit suicide, feels guilty doubt about her right to occupy the earth: "Ensevelie sous le voile de la honte, je me tiens à l'écart; je crains que mon corps n'occupe trop de place" ("Shrouded by the veil of shame, I hold myself apart; I fear lest my body occupy too much space"; p. 42).

SELF-LOVE

To cross the threshold, to enter a room full of people, is to expose oneself, to risk sneers, jeers, offensiveness. Burney often focuses on the predatory nature of social intercourse—people make themselves strong by feeding on the reputations and self-love of weaker members. Shame is a socially created control. As Burney had learned from the lampoons and insults directed against "La Bastardella" and others, misfortunes and pain make easy fodder for ridicule. Vanity and conceit may easily be ridiculed, but we all have these qualities. In her later works Burney is more interested in examining the self-love that each individual must have in order to sustain existence.

The real "sin against the Holy Ghost," as it were, becomes robbing others of the self-love they need in order to exist. This is a national, not just an individual, sin. The heroine of *The Wanderer*, meditating on English rural scenes and economic life, sees "success without virtue; sickness without relief; oppression in the very face of liberty; labour without sustenance; and suffering without crime." Who can see this "and not feel that all call aloud for resurrection and retribution!" (pp. 701–702). Justice demands an eternal life because we need a place for a final judgment, a relief for those who have suffered unjustly in the long cruel centuries of the past as well as in the callous present.

The assault on the self of a poor person is represented everywhere in Burney's fiction, starting in *Evelina* with the race between the two old peasant women for the amusement of the young men in the fashionable watering place. The octogenarians may totter and stumble for the delectation of their mocking viewers. It is here that we may (if we are very perceptive) realize that Lord Orville, ostensibly so exemplary, falls short of the deeper moral vision. As Kristina Straub points out, he is concerned only with the wastefulness of the gambling involved, especially because one of the gamblers is his future brother-in-law; he sees none of the immorality of the exploitation of the women. Only one observer of the scene feels the cruelty of the situation, and that is Evelina; however, she has to submit to the authority of those who prevent her from helping one of the women. Nobody particularly wants the old women to survive, or to survive intact—except insofar as it helps the bet. Nobody (save Evelina) wishes the old women will survive with their dignity unwounded; fashionable women as well as men assist in mocking the female octogenarians. The "self" of the poor aged females is a joke on its own—they should be shown that they have no "self," no dignity. That is the deeper purpose of the men's apparently meaningless joke; it teaches women and the poor a valuable lesson.

In *Camilla*, the wealthy and fashionable hold public entertainments in honor of the Assizes—the courts that in a few days send many of the poor to the gallows. Burney thought of herself in that part of the novel as a public satirist and reformer; she tried to prevent her society from callously celebrating the infliction of a very partial human justice (or injustice) upon the poor. The figure of the poor man who is facing this "justice" for stealing a leg of mutton to feed himself and his starving family is the primary example. And although Camilla and her friends work to get this one offender off, the disjunctive cruelty still remains, along with the denial of the natural law that says the duty to oneself and to preserving one's life takes precedence over laws regarding property. Sir Hugh stumblingly realizes this:

God forbid, I should turn hard-hearted, because of their wanting a leg of mutton, in preference to being starved; though they might have no great right to it, according to the forms of law; which, however, is not much impediment to the calls of nature.

(p. 109)

In the 1790s it was not, however, considered in the social interest of England to think such thoughts. The death sentence waited as the ulti-

mate exposure, and the law tried to enforce guilt over stealing enough to live on. The desire to sustain one's own existence could be judged wrong and superfluous. Burney ironically shows this, chiefly through the figure of Eugenia—an easier personage to deal with than the poor thief. At the heart of these darker ironies is Burney's recognition of the true public view of women—fostered by her early knowledge of fashionable male jokes about female public entertainers. A female's self-love, even the humble and basic self-love entailed in a desire for continued survival, is itself an impertinence.

Lord Merton in *Evelina* says to the young heroine, "I don't know what the devil a woman lives for after thirty: she is only in other folks' way" (p. 305). Lord Merton is actually trying to ingratiate himself with Evelina when he passes this remark upon the older woman who temporarily stands in for the girl's guardian. It is a sober thought for a young woman who is just maturing that her ultimate maturity as a full adult being is not considered desirable. Her body, once it is no longer pretty, ought to erase itself from the scheme of things. Women ought to have a proper meekness emanating from their inner guilt at taking up any space at all. "I fear lest my body occupy too much space," cries Graffigny's unhappy Inca princess, Zilia, a deeply examined case of survivor guilt. Survivor guilt ought to be the common lot of women who have passed their youth. Before she reached the dangerous age of thirty, the author of *Evelina* knew about the deep assaults upon female self-confidence, the basic confidence that confers the sense of a right to exist.

In Burney's later novels, the works of her maturity written after she had married at the age of forty-one and had a child, she explores more openly the crudities of guilt-inducing mechanisms, the ironies of social organizations that apparently protect individual existence but also license attacks upon individuality—even upon the very being of others. There is thus a certain harshness to her writing. Burney's plots (including the stories of the two earlier novels) show us problems and dissonances that will not be mended by the mere union of hero and heroine. The courtship novel is, in Burney's hands, a useful formula that allows the exploration of many aspects of human living. By *The Wanderer*, we can no longer put much hope or confidence in the accomplishment of a marriage between Albert and

Juliet. Albert is well-meaning, and Juliet is genuinely heroic and compassionate, but their personal happiness will not re-create society, nor will it awaken England from its dull-eared lethargy.

The satiric qualities in Burney's writing have led to some harsh judgments of her in the past; she does not provide grace and charm in all her scenes, and her love stories are not fully satisfactory—because they are not meant to be. The emphasis of her aggressive comedy is on the analyses of violence and discord. These do not harmonize with our picture of the "ladylike," or with the endearingly diminutive and slightly antique "Fanny."

If Burney was sensitive to the threat of the threshold, it was because she recognized the large part that cruelty and pain play in society. She also recognized the power of learning, of recognition, but her Enlightenment sense of discovery was not purely optimistic. After *Evelina*, she becomes progressively less interested in the need for fiction to be reassuring. Her fiction plays about the threshold of the personal and the public, of the socially acceptable "self" and the inner desire; she looks for the interface of the articulate and the inchoate, the frontier where Lockean impressions meet Lockean reflection. The adjective "charming," formerly so frequently applied to Burney, becomes on consideration less and less applicable to a writer so capable of the complex and the grotesque, a novelist so little addicted to the saccharine.

SELECTED BIBLIOGRAPHY

I. DIARIES. *Diary and Letters of Madame D'Arblay*, ed. by Charlotte Barrett, 7 vols. (London, 1842–1846); *The Early Diary of Frances Burney, 1768–1778*, ed. by Annie Raine Ellis, 2 vols. (London, 1889; rev. ed. 1907); *The Journals and Letters of Fanny Burney (Madame d'Arblay), 1791–1840*, ed. by Joyce Hemlow et al., 12 vols. (Oxford, 1972–1984); *The Early Journals and Letters of Fanny Burney*, ed. by Lars Troide et al. (Oxford, 1988).

II. NOVELS. *Evelina; or, The History of a Young Lady's Entrance into the World* (originally published 1778; modern ed., London, 1994); *Cecilia; or, Memoirs of an Heiress* (1782), ed. by Peter Sabor and Margaret Anne Doody (Oxford, 1988); *Camilla; or, A Picture of Youth* (1796), ed. by Edward A. Bloom and Lillian D. Bloom (Oxford, 1972); *The Wanderer; or, Female Difficulties* (1814), ed. by Margaret Anne Doody, Robert Mack, and Peter Sabor (Oxford, 1991).

III. PLAYS. *Edwy and Elgiva*, ed. by Miriam J. Benkovitz (Saratoga Springs, N.Y., 1956); *A Busy Day*, ed. by Tara G. Wallace (New Brunswick, N.J., 1984); *The Witlings*, in *The Meridian Anthology of Restoration and Eighteenth-Century Plays by Women*, ed. by Katharine M. Rogers (New York, 1994); *The Complete Plays of Frances Burney*, ed. by Peter Sabor, Geoffrey Sill, and Stewart Cooke, 2 vols. (London, 1995).

IV. MANUSCRIPTS. "Clarinda," Barrett Collection, British Library, Egerton MS 3696, early draft of *Camilla*, now labeled "Draft of Camilla"; "The Witlings," Henry W. and Albert A. Berg Collection, Astor, Lenox, and Tilden Foundations of the New York Public Library.

V. CRITICAL AND BIOGRAPHICAL STUDIES. Thomas Babington Macaulay, "Madame D'Arblay," in *Edinburgh Review* 76 (1843), an unsigned review of *Diary and Letters of Madame D'Arblay*; Austin Dobson, *Fanny Burney* (London, 1903); Joyce Hemlow, *The History of Fanny Burney* (Oxford, 1958).

Edward W. Copeland, "Money in the Novels of Fanny Burney," in *Studies in the Novel* 8 (spring 1976); Rose Marie Cutting, "A Wreath for Fanny Burney's Last Novel: *The Wanderer*'s Contribution to Women's Studies," in *CLA Journal* 20 (September 1976); Patricia M. Spacks, "Dynamics of Fear: Fanny Burney," in her *Imagining a Self: Autobiography and the Novel in Eighteenth-Century England* (Cambridge, Mass., 1976); Susan Staves, "*Evelina; or, Female Difficulties*," in *Modern Philology* 73 (May 1976); Rose Marie Cutting, "Defiant Women: The Growth of Feminism in Fanny Burney's Novels," in *Studies in English Literature, 1500–1800* 17 (summer 1977).

Janet Todd, *Women's Friendship in Literature* (New York, 1980); J. N. Waddell, "Additions to *OED* from the Writings of Fanny Burney," in *Notes and Queries* 225 (1980), and "Fanny Burney's Contribution to English Vocabulary," in *Neuphilologische Mitteilungen* 81, no. 3 (1980); Mary Poovey, "Fathers and Daughters: The Trauma of Growing Up Female," in *Women and Literature* 2 (1982), and *The Proper Lady and the Woman Writer: Ideology as Style in the Works of Mary Wollstonecraft, Mary Shelley, and Jane Austen* (Chicago, 1984); Terry Castle, "Masquerade and Utopia I: Burney's *Cecilia*," in her *Masquerade and Civilization: The Carnivalesque in Eighteenth-Century English Culture and Fiction* (Stanford, Calif., 1986); Julia Epstein, "Fanny Burney's Epistolary Voices," in *The Eighteenth Century: Theory and Interpretation* 27 (spring 1986), and "Writing the Unspeakable: Fanny Burney's Mastectomy and the Fictive Body," in *Representations* 16 (fall 1986); David D. Devlin, *The Novels and Journals of Fanny Burney and the Feminine Strategy* (London, 1987); Judy Simons, *Fanny Burney* (Totowa, N.J., 1987); Kristina Straub, *Divided Fictions: Fanny Burney and the Feminine Strategy* (Athens, Ga., 1987); Margaret Anne Doody, *Frances Burney: The Life in the Works* (New Brunswick, N.J., 1988); Julia Epstein, *The Iron*

Pen: Frances Burney and the Politics of Women's Writing (Madison, Wis., 1989).

Margaret Anne Doody, "Beyond *Evelina:* The Individual Novel and the Community of Literature," in *Eighteenth-Century Fiction* 3 (July 1991); Julia Epstein, "Burney Criticism: Family Romance, Psychobiography, and Social History," in *Eighteenth-Century Fiction* 3 (July 1991); Susan C. Greenfield, "'Oh Dear Resemblance of Thy Murdered Mother': Female Authorship in *Evelina*," in *Eighteenth-Century Fiction* 3 (July 1991); Margaret Anne Doody, "Heliodorus Rewritten: Samuel Richardson's *Clarissa* and Frances Burney's *Wanderer*," in *The Search for the Ancient Novel*, ed. by James Tatum (Baltimore, 1994); John Hart, "Frances Burney's *Evelina:* Mirvan and Mezzotint," in *Eighteenth-Century Fiction* 7 (1994).

ANGELA CARTER

(1940–1992)

Michael Wood

"I LIKE ANYTHING that flickers," Angela Carter once said. She was thinking of old movies and the uncertain light of vaudeville; of the lost, stagy life to which her last two novels, *Nights at the Circus* (1984) and *Wise Children* (1991), are so lovingly dedicated. But she also uses the image in her first novel, *Shadow Dance* (1966)—"Henry Glass seemed to flicker as he walked, like a silent film, as if his continuity was awry" (p. 111)—so the liking itself is old, and the phrase says something about Carter's prose style, too. She writes as if stability were tantamount to death, her tone always flickering, aiming to unsettle, her diction always on the edge of parody (and of self-parody) because it is so delicately attuned to a world that feels it arrived too late at the party. Fashion, whether in literature or furniture or architecture or clothes or youth culture, is like an old film. This is where we came in; we have been here before. "The bar was a mock-up," the same novel begins, "a forgery, a fake; an ad-man's crazy dream of a Spanish patio" (p. 1). The bar is in a town that looks like Bristol, in the west country of England. A handsome Palladian mansion, now a mental hospital, strikes a character in Carter's novel *Love* (1971) "by the witty irrelevance of its grandeur to its purpose" (p. 67). The building isn't *trying* to be witty. Time and history have replaced what might have been pathos with an elegant joke: past pretensions turn not to dust but to the helpless ornaments of madness. "He could only say he was sorry," we learn of a character in *Shadow Dance*, "by pretending to be a sorry somebody else" (p. 121). One critic has suggested that the term "postmodern," if it did not exist, would have had to be coined for Carter's writing. But there's postmodern and then there's postmodern, and hers is demotic and bouncy, not depleted and cynical. She is full of energy and irreverence, yet is also an adept of the pleasures of high culture and committed to the project of rescuing human beings, where possible,

from their own bad dreams. They are our dreams, Carter insists, and no one else's. Perhaps we cannot end them, but we are our only chance.

LIFE AND REPUTATION

AT the time of her death Carter was highly regarded by literary critics and scholars and by fellow novelists like Salman Rushdie and Margaret Atwood. She was (and is) much read by the young, particularly in Great Britain, and she was a public personage, a lively performer of her own work, an editor of fairy tales. She wrote radio plays and children's stories; several pieces from her volume *The Bloody Chamber* (1979) were brought together to create Neil Jordan's successful film *The Company of Wolves* (1984). Carter had offended many men (and women) by her feminism, and had offended many feminists by her defense of the pleasures of sex and by her dislike of female victim stories of the kind associated with Elizabeth Smart (*By Grand Central Station I Sat Down and Wept*, 1945) and Jean Rhys (*Good Morning, Midnight*, 1938). *By Grand Central Station I Tore Off His Balls* was the title Carter said she had in mind. All was forgiven toward the end. In 1991 she was diagnosed as having lung cancer, and she died the following year, at the age of fifty-one. She became her admirers, as Auden said of Yeats on his death in 1939; her detractors had gone quiet, or had been converted.

All this fame and reconciliation is misleading, though—partly a matter of piety about the dead, partly the reflection of a strange cultural longing for the writer people thought Carter was: a female Salman Rushdie, an English Italo Calvino, proof that magical realism begins at home, that fairy tales did not die in France in the eighteenth century or in Germany in the nineteenth. But until her last years she was not repetitive or regular enough to match anyone's longing. Her very successes were full of interesting flaws, she liked those of her books that didn't quite work, and the most attractive feature of her writing is its restlessness, its distaste for repose and decorum. She began writing at a time when J. R. R. Tolkien had been and gone in British fiction, when Mervyn Peake had not yet been resurrected. A modest naturalism was the dominant mode, and Carter's work, which now seems tough and close to the nerves, then seemed flighty and whimsical. She kept remaking herself as a writer. She disconcerted all but the most agile of her readers, and she was not at all famous until very late in her career. Her vein was not magic realism but a fictional psychopathology of everyday life, pointing not to the fantastic nature of the real but to the persistent, lurid reality of so many fantasies. She liked tales, she said—"Gothic tales, cruel tales, tales of wonder, tales of terror"—because they can "deal directly with the imagery of the unconscious." "The tale does not log everyday experience as the short story does; it interprets everyday experience through a system of imagery derived from subterranean areas behind everyday experience" (afterword to *Fireworks*, pp. 132–133). In this sense all Carter's short works are tales, and her longer works are extended tales, or novels with a tale at their hearts.

Angela Carter was born Angela Olive Stalker on 7 May 1940 in Eastbourne, Sussex. She spent the years of World War II in Yorkshire with her maternal grandmother, a time she evokes lovingly in an essay in *Nothing Sacred*. She went to school in Balham, in South London, and on leaving school became a junior reporter on a local newspaper, the *Croydon Advertiser*. In 1960 she married Paul Carter, whom she was to divorce in 1972. From 1962 to 1965 she was a student at the University of Bristol, specializing in medieval literature, and the year after she graduated, she published her first novel, *Shadow Dance*. Her second novel, *The Magic Toyshop* (1967), won the John Llewellyn Rhys prize, and her third novel, *Several Perceptions* (1968), won the Somerset Maugham Award. Carter visited Japan in 1969, using the money she had received from this second prize, and then decided to live there. She returned to England in 1972. She was an Arts Council fellow in Sheffield and was visiting professor of creative writing at Brown University in Rhode Island and at Adelaide University, South Australia. She continued to publish novels, short stories, and a stream of brilliant and provocative articles, many of them for the English weekly *New Society*, whose editor and literary editor, Paul Barker and Tony Gould, are warmly thanked in *Nothing Sacred* as people "who, over a period of fifteen years or so, have never batted an eyelid and always corrected my spelling." From 1984 to 1987, Carter taught creative writing at the University of East Anglia, in a program that was already famous for the commercial and critical successes of its alumni, who include Kazuo Ishiguro, Ian McEwan, and Timothy Mo.

In 1982, Carter settled in Clapham, South London, with the potter Mark Pearce, and in 1983 their son Alexander was born. Lorna Sage suggests that Carter sometimes found it hard "to make up her life as she went along" (*Angela Carter*, p. 52), but that was Carter's principle, as a writer and as a person, and she managed somehow to be peripatetic *and* at home in her last years, a sort of gypsy who had a house to go to. Sage quotes a letter of 1989 in which Carter's enthusiasm and irreverence are beautifully in evidence, as she and Mark and Alexander explore the decaying wastelands of London:

the canals are wonderful. . . . You get this Ophelia-style view of the canal bank, huge juicy plants & flowers & grasses; and we saw herons, & a king-fisher, & it was that frail, chilly, early spring that is so English, & the East End—we went through mile after mile of abandoned factories returning to the wild. I kept thinking: "This dereliction produced the wealth that made London the richest city in the world." All gone. It was like Ozymandias.

(p. 57)

Carter was, she said, "the pure product of an advanced, industrialized, post-imperialist country in decline" (quoted in *Angela Carter*, p. 3). She was remembering William Carlos Williams' line about the pure products of America going crazy, but she was also smiling. She was as crazy as her country, no more, no less. Even if, especially if, her country was devoted to the idea that it wasn't crazy at all. "Anybody who had a stiff injection of Rimbaud at 18," she told Lorna Sage, "isn't going to be able to cope very well with Philip Larkin" (*Angela Carter*, p. 2)—where Rimbaud and Larkin are shorthand for extravagant revolt and modest expectations, respectively.

ANGELA CARTER

EARLY NOVELS

THE chief setting of Carter's early novels is an unnamed city that much resembles Bristol: large but provincial, a university town, handsome, slightly decaying. Her characters inhabit various fringes or interstices of city life, hanging out in pubs and cafés and desolate flats. They are tramps, prostitutes, unsuccessful painters and writers, would-be antique dealers; or they work in hospitals or offices or schools. The swinging England (which was mainly a swinging London and Liverpool) of the 1960s passes them by, except that they sometimes find themselves in music, and their motley styles of clothing and makeup look like an eerie prediction of punk. There are two early Carter novels that are not set in this city, but *The Magic Toyshop*, which takes place mainly in South London, scarcely moves its action out-of-doors, and *Heroes and Villains* (1969) is an apocalyptic future fiction that also seems to predict punk. "In 1969," Carter later said of a violent, near-psychotic character in *Love*, "Buzz was still waiting for his historic moment. . . . he was simply waiting for punk to happen" (afterword to *Love*, p. 116). Carter also wrote of what she came to feel was the "penetrating aroma of unhappiness" in this novel (p. 113), and this aroma, spliced strangely with a vivid and perky prose manner, an unmistakable happiness *in* the writing, defines all of her early work. Madness and death, damage and guilt, are its obsessive themes; but the writing seems to be dancing. The principal partners are the crazy girl and the alarmingly beautiful boy.

Shadow Dance (also published as *Honeybuzzard*) opens with the appearance of a once lovely, now hideously scarred girl in a pub, and it ends with her death in a sort of ritual game—as if the scar were only paint and death only a tableau. In between these moments, the various men who have slept with her skitter with guilt, a woman commits suicide, and various sturdier women find ways of getting on with their lives. Aloof from all this is the prince of this marginal kingdom, the alluring, sexually ambiguous, entirely amoral Honeybuzzard, who has cut the girl up in the first place and who kills her in the end. He has a way of frightening everyone and yet making everything seem all right, like a child whose charm hides his danger. Or perhaps his charm is his danger:

Honeybuzzard had the soft, squashy-nosed, full-lipped face one associates with angels blowing glad, delirious trumpets in early Florentine pictures of the Nativity; a nectarine face, bruisable and somehow juicy, covered with a close, golden fuzz that thickened into a soft, furry, animal down on his jaw but never actually coalesced into a beard. . . . He had a pair of perfectly pointed ears, such as fauns have and, curiously, these were also covered with down.

It was impossible to look at the full, rich lines of his dark red mouth without thinking: "This man eats meat."

(p. 57)

"They are all shadows," Honeybuzzard says to his nervous sidekick Morris, who says he feels sorry for their sad pub companions. "How can you be sorry for shadows?" (p. 87). Honeybuzzard's strength is his ability to see others as shadows; their weakness is their inability to insist that he is wrong. What proves him wrong is a series of flesh-and-blood risks and disasters, but when Morris vanishes "into the shadows" at the end of the novel, the moral situation remains uncertain. Morris is returning to Honeybuzzard and to the corpse of the girl Honeybuzzard has killed because it may be better to keep company with a murderer, to care for a murderer in need, than to call the police or return to a safer life. People are not shadows, however flickering their grip on life; but you may have to enter the world of real shadows to find this out.

Films and photographs are recurring images in Carter's early novels. "It was easier . . . to face the fact of Uncle Philip if she saw him as a character in a film, possibly played by Orson Welles" (*The Magic Toyshop*, pp. 74–75). "He wavered as he walked as if he were a piece of trick photography and might suddenly disappear altogether, so discreetly the air would not even be disturbed by his passage" (*Several Perceptions*, p. 152). Photographs are "frozen memories of the moment of sight" (*Love*, p. 25), and the following disturbing conversation takes place between a grieving young husband, describing the room as it appears from his position lying on the floor, and a hospital psychiatrist. The psychiatrist's implicit recognition of the visual world in question is almost eerier than the husband's anxious allusion.

"A kind of expressionist effect," he said.
"Pardon?"
"Everything is subtly out of alignment. Shadows fall awry and light no longer issues from expected sources."
"Do you go to the cinema often?"

(*Love*, p. 55)

What all this suggests is not only a culture saturated in movies and déjà vu, but a group of people who are afraid both of finding reality and of losing it. They are "connoisseurs of unreality," as Carter calls one couple (*Love*, p. 95). They wear their facial expressions like clothes: "Mentally he wandered through his wardrobe of smiles, wondering which one to wear to suit this ambiguous occasion" (p. 19), but they have trouble linking yesterday's self to anything in today's life: "There seemed no connecting logic between the various states of his life, as if each had been attained, not by organic growth but by a kind of convulsive leap from condition to condition" (pp. 26–27). One young woman lives so thoroughly by the mythic, magical assumptions of her fears that she has never "suspected that everyday, sensuous human practice might shape the real world. When she did discover that such a thing was possible, it proved the beginning of the end for her for how could she possess any notion of the ordinary?" (p. 4). To possess a notion of the ordinary would be to be able to leave the cinema if you wanted to, to see your Uncle Philip as if he weren't Orson Welles; or less psychologically, more pragmatically, to have an uncle you didn't have to turn mentally into Orson Welles.

Melanie, the heroine of *The Magic Toyshop*, is a fifteen-year-old whose parents have been killed in a plane crash. She and her brother and small sister go to live with their mysterious and tyrannical Uncle Philip, their mother's brother, known to Melanie only from a photograph where he looks like a villain in a Western, black suit, flat-topped hat, bootlace tie, walrus mustache, and emphatic absence of anything resembling a smile. He makes and sells toys and torments his wife and her brothers. His heart's delight is his puppet theater, and the climax of the novel has Melanie taking part in a performance of the myth of Leda and the swan, where the swan is a huge wood-and-rubber affair, but only, fortunately, "a grotesque parody of a swan; Edward Lear might have designed it," Melanie thinks. "It was nothing like the wild, phallic bird of her imaginings" (p. 157). This novel, like many of Carter's later tales, is about a young woman's growing up, and the element of parody, however threatening, is what helps the heroine to see through the mystery. Wicked uncles don't turn into nice guys—this one burns his house down in a rage—but it is possible to escape from them if you confront their actual power and weakness and do not lend them the omnipotence of your fears.

Joseph, the notional hero of *Several Perceptions*, has dreams like his biblical counterpart, but he doesn't dream of years of famine or harvest. He doesn't dream of years of anything.

Joseph dreamed he was a child walking home . . . down an ordinary street of privet hedges and clean milk bottles put out for the night under a fat, white moon but soon he realised a maniac with a knife was following him. The pace of the dream quickened; the child who was himself scurried and panted, quaking with terror, but the pursuer was relentless as the clock and gained on him; in and out of the shadows they went, in and out of moonlight. The blade of the knife flashed and Joseph saw the maniac's face was his own, himself. Mad for sanctuary, Joseph the child burst through a front gate and beat his fists on the nearest door. Which was immediately opened by himself again, smiling a long, narrow, wolfish smile as cruel as the knife he, also, carried.

(p. 5)

This is a pastiche of the bad dream, owing as much to Hitchcock as it does to Auden; but it is not a mockery. The fear and the self-distrust are vivid enough, all the more vivid, perhaps, because they take on the features of a well-worn movie. Joseph tries to commit suicide by simultaneously gassing himself and blowing himself up—his head is full of images of the war in Vietnam and protests against it. Unfortunately, the explosion merely smashes the windows of his drab room, and lets the air in. Joseph finds not death but a hospital and a profusion of bandages. The novel recounts his further picaresque encounters in the city, his slow and unwilling conversion to survival, to the principle that survival is as good as anything else. He is a literary fellow, although he gave up his studies some time ago. He thinks about William Blake and *Alice in Wonderland*, as Carter's characters often do. "We get so little sun in England," Joseph says, making conversation. "It's a weepy kind of country." "That's a fancy way of putting it," his companion comments (p. 75). But it is a weepy kind of country, and people are always crying, an act which brings out the purple best in Carter's prose. "She was an ugly weeper; the tears came reluctantly and her face screwed up in piteous, Gothic folds like weepers in medieval carvings and also became blotched and scarlet" (p. 100). Those "Gothic folds" are one kind of stylistic signature; another is the familiar idiom brushed up and put to new work. "I could take it or leave it," a young woman says of her love life, "and usually left it" (p. 130). "They struggled to entirely lose themselves in each other and make of each other's bodies a kind of home, since home is where the heart is and there is no place like it" (p. 16).

If *Shadow Dance* is the most striking of Carter's early novels in its sense of damage and danger, *Love* (1971) is the novel where the mood of the shadow city is most hauntingly caught. It is a "Surrealist poem for the forlorn daughter," Sue Roe says in an essay on Carter (*Flesh and the Mirror*, p. 62) "a poem which cannot take Annabel as its subject, except as *peinture-poésie*, photomontage, *cadavre exquis*, collage." Annabel is a suicidal young woman, who finally commits suicide. Before she does this, she marries Lee, or more precisely marries into the ménage of Lee and Buzz, two brothers so severely damaged by their mother's madness that they have made a homeland out of their relationship to each other and can scarcely connect to the world outside it. Lee is apparently well-adjusted, another of Carter's wonderful-looking men, Buzz is malign and violent; but both are sheltering from old fallout. They are pretty good at telling themselves stories, though:

When Lee attained the age of reason and acquired his aunt's pride, he was glad his mother had gone mad in style. There could be no mistaking her intention nor could her behaviour be explained in any other terms than the onset of a spectacular psychosis in the grand, traditional style of the old-fashioned Bedlamite. She progressed to unreason via no neurotic back alleyway nor let any slow night of silence and darkness descend upon her; she chose the high road, operatically stripping off her clothes and screaming to the morning: "I am the whore of Babylon."

(*Love*, p. 10)

Carter herself spoke of "the ornate formalism of the style" of this book, as well as of "its icy treatment of the mad girl" (afterword to *Love*, p. 113); but there is a sense in which everyone delights in style here: author, mad mother, remembering son, mad girl. Style is not an antidote to unhappiness, rather the reverse. But it is where almost everyone's energy comes from, as if the high road had all the virtues, even if it leads only to death and despair.

Annabel is destroyed not by her relationship with the brothers but by her attempt to escape from her solipsism into the world. Like Honeybuzzard, she sees everyone except herself as a shadow, but unlike him, she cannot manipulate others, cannot register them as real enough to be manipulated. When she demands that Lee have her name tattooed over his heart, he thinks she means to humiliate him, to take revenge for his infidelity to her. But this isn't so, couldn't be so, since she "was hardly capable of devising a revenge which required a knowledge of human feeling to perfect it" (p. 70). When she and Buzz make love, because Buzz inhabits her fantasy in a way that Lee doesn't, the event is a fiasco. "It is always a dangerous experiment to act out a fantasy; they had undertaken the experiment rashly and had failed but Annabel suffered the worst for she had been trying to convince herself she was alive." She is left to "wander off alone through the dark streets, a fragile, flimsy thing whose body had betrayed both their imaginations" (p. 95). Her suicide is her retreat from this body and this betrayal, and takes place in an atmosphere of distressing serenity, as if it were simply the accomplishment of the logic of her sense of her life:

She left no notes or messages. She felt no fear or pain for now she was content. She did not spare a thought or waste any pity on the people who loved her for she had never regarded them as anything more than facets of the self she was now about to obliterate so, in a sense, she took them with her to the grave and it was only natural they should now behave as if they had never known her.

(pp. 109–110)

There are moments in all of these early novels where the writing is too explicit, the result of an overflow of intelligence and an insufficiency of writing experience—Carter does not yet know how much she can trust the reader with. "He realized he could supply her only with a physiological answer while she would never be satisfied with less than an existential one" (p. 16). "She was cut to the heart for she did not realize they had only intersected by chance upon one another and exchanged spurious, self-contradictory falsehoods as if flashing lights in one another's faces" (p. 48). But then these instances are the measure of Carter's ambition, her desire to be as lucid and fantastic as she needs to be. And they are isolated instances, indications of how thoroughly Carter combines, the rest of the time, what she calls formalism with allusiveness and delicate indirection.

ANGELA CARTER

LOVE AMONG THE RUINS: FUTURE WORLDS

Heroes and Villains (1969), *The Infernal Desire Machines of Doctor Hoffman* (1972), and *The Passion of New Eve* (1977) make up a series of meditations on future worlds: after the end of our present civilization; after the invasion of the real by the rampant images of desire; after the onset of the literal wars between the races and between the sexes. These three novels are all about mutations, about the boundaries between the thinkable and the unthinkable, and about the violence of the imagination.

In *Heroes and Villains* an ultimate war has decimated the population of a country that looks like England. A social class called the Professors lives in steel and concrete towers which have survived "the blast." They are guarded by Soldiers, and no one sets foot outside the compound. Beyond are the Barbarians, and beyond them the mutant Out People. Very little remains of the old order and the old learning. Asked what the word "city" means, Marianne, the daughter of a Professor of History, can only hazard a guess: "Ruins?" Orphaned and bored with her life, Marianne takes off with a Barbarian called Jewel; she is raped and then married, saves her husband's life more than once, and holds him in her arms as he dies in a skirmish with the Soldiers. There is an element of class allegory about this whole story: Jewel the Barbarian represents the allure of the beautiful, disreputable lower orders, Marianne the prissy but courageous bourgeoisie. But there is no promise for the future, no lasting alliance or end to the class war. Here as in Carter's earlier novels, architecture carries much of the meaning, its haunting structures begging to be read. The Barbarians live, when Marianne first meets them, in a house that is a scrambled history of England, a monument and a mockery:

This house was a gigantic memory of rotten stone, a compilation of innumerable forgotten styles now given some green unity by the devouring web of creeper, fur of moss and fungoid growth of rot. Wholly abandoned to decay, baroque stonework of the late Jacobean period, Gothic turrets murmurous with birds and pathetic elegance of Palladian pillared façades weathered indiscriminately together towards irreducible rubble. The forest perched upon the tumbled rooves in the shapes of yellow and purple weeds rooted in gapped tiles, besides a few small trees and bushes. The windows gaped or sprouted internal foliage, as if the forest were as well already camped inside, there gathering strength for a green eruption which would one day burst the walls

sky high back to nature. A horse or two grazed upon a terrace built in some kind of florid English Renaissance style. Upon the balustrade of this terrace were many pocked and armless statues in robes, or nude and garlanded. These looked like the petrified survivors of a malign *fête-champêtre* ended long ago, in catastrophe.

(*Heroes and Villains*, pp. 31–32)

Marianne at one point calls Jewel an anachronism. "What's an anachronism," he asks, although he probably knows. "Teach me what an anachronism is." Marianne replies, "A pun in time" (p. 56). She's trying to be too clever for him but is caught in the landscape of her own definition. Puns in time are all the history that is available to her now, and the ruinous, many-styled house is a lesson in the detail of decay. The pathos concerns not people but styles. Behind those styles were people, of course, human creatures who thought their culture would save them, or at least express them, but they are now only the shadows of an idea. All the relics of their culture can express is the longing for expression, the desire to leave the trace of a difference.

There is a war in *The Infernal Desire Machines of Doctor Hoffman* too, but it is still being waged. It is called the Great War, and also the Reality War. Dr. Hoffman, a cross between Dr. Caligari, Dr. Mabuse, and any number of mad scientists out of Hollywood B movies, has begun a massive onslaught on what sensible people used to call reality. He is interested in the transgression of borderlines; he represents the "disciplined power of the utterly irrational" (p. 199) and is intent on rewriting history so that, for instance, Trotsky will have composed the *Eroica* Symphony, van Gogh will have written *Wuthering Heights,* and Milton will have painted the ceiling of the Sistine Chapel. His theory is that "everything it is possible to imagine can also exist," and that "the world exists only as a medium in which we execute our desires" (pp. 97, 35). He unleashes strange phantasms on the world:

Giant heads in the helmets of conquistadors sailed up like sad, painted kites over the giggling chimney pots. Hardly anything remained the same for more than one second and the city was no longer the conscious production of humanity; it had become the arbitrary realm of dream.

. . . And the very birds of the air seemed possessed by devils. Some grew to the size and acquired the temperament of winged jaguars. Fanged sparrows plucked out the eyes of little children. Snarling flocks of starlings swooped down upon some starving wretch picking over a mess of dreams and refuse in a gutter and tore what remained of his flesh from his bones. The pigeons lolloped from illusory pediment to window-ledge like volatile, feathered madmen, chattering vile rhymes and laughing in hoarse, throaty voices, or perched upon chimney stacks shouting quotations from Hegel.

(pp. 18–20)

The source of Dr. Hoffman's power, Carter says, is not only the suggestibility of the population, their eagerness to take their desires, or anyone's desires, for reality, but a literal factory of one hundred love slaves, endlessly copulating away to propel "the desire generators"—a splendid spoof both of the unlikely laboratories of so much science fiction and of the proposition that it is love that makes the world go 'round. Desiderio, our hero, now recounting his youthful adventures from the high perspective of old age, kills the doctor and his lovely daughter for the sake of reason, and because the doctor, as in all the best traditions of bogus liberation, is really a tyrant. He is a hypocrite, Desiderio thinks, a traitor to Blake's maxim that one should "sooner murder an infant in its cradle than nurse unacted desires." Dr. Hoffman uses desire against reality; he has, unforgivably, conscripted desire. "He penned desire in a cage and said: 'Look! I have liberated desire!'" (p. 208).

The setting of the novel is mostly South American, with a spectacular finale in the Andes—although the seaside resorts here look distinctly English, all piers and candy and buckets and spades. Desiderio, seeking the elusive Dr. Hoffman, finds a Debussy-playing young wraith, who later drowns herself; lives with the River People, and discovers their interest in cannibalism not a moment too soon; meets a sardonic, extravagant count, a composite of Dracula and the Marquis de Sade; encounters a herd of noble centaurs; and finally gets to the distant castle of Dr. Hoffman. Carter said that *The Passion of New Eve* was her favorite among her novels "because it is so ambitious, so serious and so helplessly flawed" (*Flesh and the Mirror*, p. 213), but *Heroes and Villains* creates a more intricate and haunting mood, and *The Infernal Desire Machines of Doctor Hoffman* is a good deal more spectacular and more thoroughly worked through. If *Love* is a surrealist poem, *Doctor Hoffman* is a surrealist epic, full of epigrams and illustrations of all that is lethal and irresistible

about the realm of desire. There are brilliant blasphemies here too. A little parable:

A man made a pact with the Devil. The condition was this: the man delivered up his soul as soon as Satan had assassinated God. "Nothing simpler," said Satan and put a revolver to his own temple.

(p. 38)

And a whirling image, a picture of the so-called acrobats of desire, a Moroccan circus act:

For perhaps thirty minutes they went through the staple repertory of all acrobats anywhere, though with incomparable grace and skill. And then Mohammed, the leader, took his head from his neck and they began to juggle with that until, one by one, all their heads came off and went into play, so that a fountain of heads rose and fell in the arena. Yet this was only the beginning.

After that, limb by limb, they dismembered themselves. Hands, feet, forearms, thighs and ultimately torsos went into a diagrammatic multi-man whose constituents were those of them all.

(pp. 113–114)

When Desiderio later sees the love slaves, he thinks "these were the true acrobats of desire, whom the Moroccans had only exemplified," but he has half missed the point. Love is a dismemberment, and Desiderio is intact, a reminiscing old man, because he refused its madness.

The Passion of New Eve (1977) certainly is ambitious thematically, a dystopian fiction which in many ways recalls Anthony Burgess' *A Clockwork Orange* (1962). Its theme is nothing less than human sexuality, a field so baffling that even Carter's brilliance keeps dipping into banality. "Masculine and feminine are correlatives which involve one another. I am sure of that—the quality and its negation are locked in necessity. But what the nature of masculine and the nature of feminine might be . . . that I do not know. Though I have been both man and woman, still I do not know the answer to these questions. Still they bewilder me" (pp. 149–150). The character's helplessness seems to be Carter's too, her inventive energies having gone into the plot of this novel rather than its language. The speaker here is Evelyn/Eve, whom we first see as a randy young Englishman, a sexual marauder in an apocalyptic New York, a place where the blacks and the women have taken to arms, where much of the city is a ruin:

The blacks had burned down Grand Central Station so there were few, if any, commuters. The inhabitants of the inner city had come into their own; Manhattan was an almost medieval city, for the gutters had become open sewers and the towers where the rich lived were as strongly fortified as castles. There were no lights in the street at night except those of burning buildings. Strikes reduced utilities to nil. The National Guard patrolled the banks; urban guerillas of many denominations added their bullets to the random bullets of the streets.

(pp. 32–33)

Escaping from this scene after his black girl-friend has had a horrendous abortion, Evelyn finds himself in a western desert and is soon kidnapped by a matriarchal sect that worships the Mother. Mother herself—the symbols are nothing if not literal here—performs an operation on the lovely Evelyn and turns him into the beautiful Eve. In a dizzying, narcissistic moment, the man he was actually fancies the woman he is. Eve escapes into various violent and picaresque adventures, involving Zero the one-eyed poet and a paramilitary group that has leapt straight out of the English idea of America, and culminating in an encounter and a relationship with the famed Tristessa, a Garbo-like movie star of haunting and tragic feminine allure who turns out to be a man. Thus both Eve and Tristessa are versions of Tiresias, men/women who have "foresuffered all," in T. S. Eliot's words, but have learned nothing. There is a deep anxiety here, but it concerns less the sexual roles it seems to invoke than what is pictured as the angry exitlessness of so many human situations. The only cheer here, the only terrain where Carter finds the verve which mitigates the despair in her other works, is characteristically located in the realm of cliché, in the sense that cliché cannot be parodied because cliché is always true. Mother raises her obsidian blade to perform the awful act on Evelyn, who writes " Oh, the dreadful symbolism of that knife! To be castrated with a phallic symbol!" and then adds, "But what else, says Mother, could do the trick?" (p. 70). Rilke is wrong, we are told in the opening pages of the novel, to believe that our symbols are inadequate. They are what we have, perfectly adequate to our inadequacy.

Our external symbols must always express the life within us with absolute precision; how could they do otherwise, since that life has generated them? Therefore we must not blame our poor symbols if they take forms that seem trivial to us, or absurd. . . . A critique of these symbols is a critique of our lives.

(p. 6)

Here Carter is parodying a certain sententious type of social commentary, and she would not herself be caught dead offering a critique of this kind. But her defense of the "poor symbols" is not a parody. It is an argument for popular culture.

NOTHING SACRED

THE essays Carter wrote between 1967 and 1981 and collected in *Nothing Sacred* (1982) constitute an informal autobiography. They evoke London and Yorkshire, Japan, and the elegant city of Bath, where Carter also lived for three years. Bath, she says with her habitual swift irony, "was built to be happy in, which accounts for its innocence and its ineradicable melancholy" (p. 74). She memorably compares the city to Marilyn Monroe, in a way which recalls her use of architecture as metaphor for retrospective sorrow in her novels:

Marvellous, hallucinatory Bath has almost the quality of concretised memory; its beauty has a curiously second-order quality, most beautiful when remembered, the wistfulness of all professional beauties, such as that of the unfortunate Marilyn Monroe whom nobody wanted for herself but everybody wanted to have slept with.

(p. 73)

There are essays on family, zoos, makeup, lingerie, *femmes fatales* ("This is the true source of the fatality of the *femme fatale;* that she lives her life in such a way her freedom reveals to others their lack of liberty," p. 123), movies, advertising, D. H. Lawrence ("It is impossible for any English writer in this century to evade the great fact of D. H. Lawrence, but taking him seriously as a novelist is one thing, and taking him seriously as a moralist is quite another," p. 165), and Colette (her Chéri novellas "transcend the notion of the battle between the sexes by concentrating on an exceptionally rigorous analysis of the rules of war," p. 178). There is a theory of the joke ("a joke need not be funny to give pleasure," p. 4), and a whole barrage of instances of jokes (many of them very funny, whether they need to be or not): "So we did not quite fit in, thank goodness; alienated is the only way to be, after all" (p. 16). "Maybe Yorkshire never really left the Third World" (p. 69). "At times, Bradford hardly seems an English city at all, since it is inhabited, in the main, by (to all appearances) extras from the Gorki trilogy, huddled in shapeless coats" (p. 61). "It won't be much *fun* after the Revolution, people say. (Yes; but it's not all that much fun, now)" (p. 111). Above all, we see here a writer fully engaged with her time, although never engulfed by it, fascinated by fashion, but never fashionable. "In the pursuit of magnificence," she says of Pete Townshend of The Who, "nothing is sacred," but her title also glances at the familiar, repressive idiom, "Is nothing sacred?" (p. 88). This is not a rhetorical question. Some things are sacred, and if you have provoked this angry or nagging response, you have no doubt just trampled on one of them. But for Carter absolutely nothing is sacred. This is not to say nothing is holy or worthy of respect; only that the sacred, in almost any given case, is the protected, and what it protects is privilege and mystification. Carter says similar things about myth and universals in *The Sadeian Woman:* "Myth deals in false universals, to dull the pain of particular circumstances" (p. 5); "The notion of a universality of human experience is a confidence trick and the notion of a universality of female experience is a clever confidence trick" (p. 12).

LATER WORKS

CARTER'S later work has many admirers, and *Nights at the Circus* represents a culmination of her writing practice in many ways. But to find the enduring heart of her work, one should look first at the two intimately connected works of polemic and fiction, which are *The Sadeian Woman: An Exercise in Cultural History* and *The Bloody Chamber and Other Stories*, both published in 1979. What we find in these extraordinary works is the full range of Carter's irreverence and intelligence, and the play of a considerable moral courage, which suggests that even our monsters, those figments of Goya's sleep of reason, will help us if we help ourselves. Carter's first move in this encounter with the monster is to distinguish between the oppressive, demeaning enterprise pornography currently is and the liberation that a "moral pornographer" might promote. This figure would not be any more re-

spectable, or any less violent and nasty, than the other kind of pornographer, but he would be "a terrorist of the imagination, a sexual guerilla," and would expose, by the sheer extremity of his inventions, the realities which underlie our sexual mythologies. (*The Sadeian Woman*, p. 21).

Sade became a terrorist of the imagination in this way, turning the unacknowledged truths of the encounters of sexuality into a cruel festival at which women are the prime sacrificial victims when they are not the ritual murderesses themselves.

The pornographer as terrorist may not think of himself as a friend of women; that may be the last thing on his mind. But he will always be our unconscious ally because he begins to approach some kind of emblematic truth.

(p. 22)

Does Carter believe this? Not quite. Her book on de Sade, she says, "is an exercise of the lateral imagination. Sade remains a monstrous and daunting cultural edifice; yet I would like to think that he put pornography in the service of women" (p. 37). What she shows is that pornography's mutilation and specialization of sex is the twin of respectability's denial of it, and that between the innocent Justine and the diabolical Juliette, de Sade's antithetical heroines, the one all sacrifice and the other all pleasure and will, we should always, if we have any respect for our bodies and our desire, choose Juliette. Justine is the grandmother of the bewildered and suffering Marilyn Monroe—"she cannot envisage a benign sexuality," she is "the persecuted maiden whose virginity is perpetually refreshed by rape" (p. 49), just as Monroe fails to realize that "her flesh is sacred because it is as good as money" (p. 66)—and her life, Carter says, "was doomed to disappointment before it began, like that of a woman who wishes for nothing better than a happy marriage" (p. 50). Juliette is the scary sexual predator, the "moral of [her] life suggests the paradox of the hangman—in a country where the hangman rules, only the hangman escapes punishment for his crimes" (p. 92). This is a way of saying, as Carter also says, that "a free woman in an unfree society will be a monster" (p. 27). And although she says she doesn't really want Juliette to renew her world, any more than she really thinks de Sade was on the side of women, it is important to see that the imaginary wreckage caused by Juliette, the real wreckage that could be caused by a woman who would resist hypocrisy in the way she does, will "have removed a repressive and authoritarian superstructure that has prevented a good deal of the work of renewal" (p. 111). Women (and men) need to understand the grammar of passivity—"To be the *object* of desire is to be defined in the passive case. To exist in the passive case is to die in the passive case—that is, to be killed" (pp. 76–77)—and to recognize that the pornographer, whether as terrorist or exploiter, is as frightened as we are, and of the same thing. In his fear we see our fear for what it is, the "perfect, immaculate terror" of love: "It is in this holy terror of love that we find, in both men and women themselves, the source of all opposition to the emancipation of women" (p. 150).

"If Little Red Riding Hood had laughed at the wolf and passed on, the wolf could never have eaten her," Colette says, and Carter literalizes precisely this argument in "The Company of Wolves," one of the ten dazzling fairy tales of *The Bloody Chamber*. "Since her fear did her no good," we read of the girl who is now alone with the wolf who has eaten her grandmother, "she ceased to be afraid" (p. 11). The wolf tries to act his oppressive part and responds in the proper way to the ritual comment on his teeth. "What big teeth you have!" "All the better to eat you with." But the girl just bursts out laughing: "she knew she was nobody's meat." She and the wolf get into bed together, and look to be set to live happily ever after. "See! sweet and sound she sleeps in granny's bed, between the paws of the tender wolf" (pp. 117–118). It remains true that the tender wolf has eaten grandma; but since when were fairy tales dedicated to kindness all 'round? "The tiger will never lie down with the lamb; he acknowledges no pact that is not reciprocal. The lamb must learn to run with the tigers" (p. 64). The imagery here recalls a wonderful Nietzschean joke in *The Sadeian Woman*: The lamb "is hampered by the natural ignorance of the herbivore, who does not even know it is possible to eat meat. The lamb could understand easily enough how mint sauce might be delicious but it does not have the mental apparatus to appreciate that its own hindquarters are also nourishing food if suitably cooked" (*The Sadeian Woman*, p. 139).

Of course Carter knows it's not so easy to give up your fear just because it doesn't do you any good; and she knows that the ferocity of male wolves, human and bestial, is not only a projection of female fear. To believe that would be to accept a sort of nursery-school version of Dr. Hoffman's theories of desire and the world. But

that is how Carter wants the fairy tale to work. It sketches out an idea of the possible—in this case the possible irrelevance of fear, the possibility that fear is the cause of the problem and not a reaction to it—and invites us to compare it with our own most cherished assumptions about reality. The fairy tale humanizes terror, just as pornography terrorizes humans, but its simplifications are so striking that the banished complications of the world cling to them like shadows. In a tale called "The Werewolf" Carter shows us how cruel these simplifications can be—de Sade begins to look positively friendly compared with this picture of folk culture. "It is a northern country," we read; "they have cold weather, they have cold hearts." Natural enough, the implication seems to be. These people have "a hard life"; "harsh, brief, poor lives" (p. 108). Are they superstitious? Of course. Wouldn't you be in their situation?

To these upland woodsmen, the Devil is as real as you or I. More so; they have not seen us nor even know that we exist, but the Devil they glimpse often in the graveyards. . . . At midnight, especially on Walpurgisnacht, the Devil holds picnics in the graveyards and invites the witches; then they dig up fresh corpses, and eat them. Anyone will tell you that.

(p. 108)

Except for the last sentence, where a hint of sarcasm seems to have crept in, this description remains sympathetic to the local beliefs—who are we to judge them; we are all anthropologists these days. Then we learn what these coldhearted folks do to the women they take to be witches—their cold hearts do not preclude a real enthusiasm for persecution.

When they discover a witch—some old woman whose cheeses ripen when her neighbours' do not, another old woman whose black cat, oh, sinister! *follows her about all the time*, they strip the crone, search for her marks, for the supernumerary nipple her familiar sucks. They soon find it. Then they stone her to death.

(p. 108)

The coolness of the writing here means the reader is likely to be startled by the conclusion of the paragraph, by the implicit outrage in the prose. "They soon find it" is like the writing of white anger. Not: they imagine they find it, they find something like it, or, even though they find nothing they still decide she is a witch. But: there is nothing there (of course), but they find it anyway, for the same reasons that they keep seeing the Devil. It is a hard life. Fairy tales are not liberating in themselves, although the reading of them may be.

Other tales in the volume recount the story of Beauty and the Beast—a lion turns into a man through the love of a beautiful girl, a girl turns into a tiger because she is able to love a beast—and of a melancholy Countess Dracula, the last of the Nosferatu line—"nothing can console her for the ghastliness of her condition" (p. 95)—who is also the Sleeping Beauty, killed by the kiss of the prince who should wake her. The wolves themselves "would love to be less beastly," and they howl as if they wish to express their "mourning for their own, irremediable appetites" (p. 112). Little girls and lambs are not in a position to exercise much sympathy, but monsters have their sorrows too, and the young woman in the title story, before she makes her dramatic escape from the aristocratic husband who is about to murder her, feels "a terrified pity" for him and thinks, "The atrocious loneliness of that monster!" (p. 35).

She is the heroine of the story of Bluebeard, the wife-killer who tempts his new bride by giving her the key to a room he says she must not open. From Carter's very earliest fiction onward, her young women characters think of themselves as caught in Bluebeard's castle, potentially willing victims of murderous men and of their own curiosity. "Bluebeard's castle, it was," Melanie thinks of Uncle Philip's house in *The Magic Toyshop* (p. 80). In *Shadow Dance*, one of Honeybuzzard's girlfriends casts herself in the same story:

"I found this key in one of his trouser pockets, see, and I thought, you know, of Bluebeard."
"Bluebeard?"
"Bluebeard. And the locked room."

(p. 105)

Bluebeard is the killer all husbands might be. He is the awe and danger of sex, what is objectively to be feared in men; and also an image of false fear, the nightmare form of fear itself. He is the wolf who devours and the toothless wolf turned into a terror by old wives' warnings and young girls' imaginings. In "The Bloody Chamber," he is also a connoisseur of torture, a relative of the sado-cinematic count young Desiderio meets in *The Infernal Desire Machines of Doctor Hoffman*. This

Bluebeard talks like a French novel, since much of his dialogue, and most of the furnishings of his world, have been lovingly borrowed from Colette, and he is also, like Uncle Philip, the puppet master cheated of the denouement of his grisly puppet play. The writing here, with its modulation from high camp to low proverb to striking double metaphor, shows Carter at her inventive, allusive, and irreverent best. "My virgin of the arpeggios, prepare yourself for martyrdom," the marquis has improbably said (*The Bloody Chamber*, p. 36)—the girl is an accomplished pianist. But then she escapes from the ax.

The Marquis stood transfixed, utterly dazed, at a loss. It must have been as if he had been watching his beloved *Tristan* for the twelfth, the thirteenth time and Tristan stirred, then leapt from his bier in the last act, announced in a jaunty aria interposed from Verdi that bygones were bygones, crying over spilt milk did nobody any good and, as for himself, he proposed to live happily ever after. The puppet master, open-mouthed, wide-eyed, impotent at the last, saw his dolls break free of their strings, abandon the rituals he had ordained for them since time began and start to live for themselves; the king, aghast, witnesses the revolt of his pawns.

(p. 39)

Nights at the Circus (1984) opens in raucous stage cockney, as if Eliza Doolittle had never met Professor Higgins: "'Lor' love you, sir!' Fevvers sang out in a voice that clanged like dustbin lids. 'As to my place of birth, why, I first saw light of day right here in smoky old London, didn't I! Not billed the "Cockney Venus" for nothing, sir'" (p. 7).

"Nobody talks like that," as Tony Curtis says in *Some Like It Hot*, during his memorable impersonation of Cary Grant, who did talk like that. Nobody outside of novels and movies, that is. Inside a novel or a movie, such open embraces of the expected produce a quality of unrepentant playfulness, a sense of the lurid avoidance of the tasteful avoidance of cliché. Fevvers' very name is a phonetic mauling of the word "feathers," a reference to the fact that, unlike most ordinary, unmythological women, she has wings, but also a sign of cockneyness so stereotyped it has to be a joke. Fevvers has all kinds of adventures, in a sprawling picaresque mode—this is Carter's longest work by far—and travels from London to Petersburg to Siberia with a "Grand Imperial Circus." She is brought up in a brothel run by a one-eyed madame called Ma Nelson, after the admiral who is supposed to have put his telescope to his blind eye in order not to see a signal he wished to ignore; she is assigned to Madame Schreck's museum of female monsters; teams up with and then escapes from a wealthy magus who has designs on her as a human sacrifice. In Russia she encounters bandits, shamans, revolutionaries.

But the most persistent adventure in the book is linguistic: Fevvers' and others' knockabout recounting of her life to the American journalist Jack Walser, who follows her across the world, lured by the enigma of her wings—are they real or not? Fevvers at the end seems to say they are not: "'To think I really fooled you!' she marvelled. 'It just goes to show there's nothing like confidence'" (p. 295). But she may be referring to her virginity rather than her wings, and reality in Carter's work is always a matter of faith and desire. Not that faith and desire can simply, directly, alter the literal world; only that the literal world is always already infiltrated by faith and desire, so that having real wings or not is not strictly a technical, biological, or aeronautical matter. The question is, Can you fly, or do people see you fly? Fevvers is a metaphor for the New Woman, or rather a blatant but sympathetic parody of the idea of the New Woman—the novel is set in the last months of the nineteenth century—and is described as "the pure child of the century that just now is waiting in the wings, the New Age in which no woman will be bound down to the ground" (p. 25). "'And once the old world has turned on its axle,' Fevvers says, 'so that the new dawn can dawn, then, ah, then! all the women will have wings, the same as I'" (p. 285). "Waiting in the wings" is an excruciating pun in the context, and Fevvers probably means "axis" rather than "axle." "Same as I" is Fevvers being posh, her little stab at being ladylike.

But then her language is like this, a patchwork of mismatched idioms and an emblem of Carter's dedication to the abolition of old stylistic decorums. Even the notion of parody doesn't quite catch what she and Fevvers are doing. "Like any young girl," Fevvers says, "I was much possessed with the marvellous blossoming of my until then reticent and undemanding flesh" (p. 23). But she also says, "Nobility of spirit hand in hand with absence of analysis, that's what's always buggered up the working class" (p. 232) and "This is some kind of heretical possibly Manichean version of neo-Platonic Rosicrucianism, thinks I to

myself" (p. 77). The last phrase comes out of old songs and music-hall routines; "much possessed" comes from T. S. Eliot's "Whispers of Immortality"; and the rest comes from various stations between Lukács, de Sade, and the local pub. The suggestion is not so much that language or culture does the writing, rather than the writer, as that all language is dialect, and the best a writer can do is understand the futility of all attempts at settled style.

The apparent (and often real) lack of control in Carter's writing is itself a political gesture; not an abandonment of responsibility or hard work, but an act of resistance to any coherence which can be felt as a coercion—as almost all coherences can, Carter would say. The uncertainty of her early characters, unable to keep track of their moral or psychological selves from day to day but wonderfully adept at inventing new stylistic selves by the minute, has become a principle. If you know who you are, you must be the wrong person, and there is no greater temptation for the writer, Carter is suggesting, than to award yourself the Olympian security your characters—and not only your characters, but you yourself, and everyone you know outside of fiction—so desperately lack. The narrative voices of this text, Lorna Sage says in *Angela Carter*, "are generously endowed with the kind of dubious plausibility that comes from the suspicion that they are making it up as they go along, *just like the author*" (p. 46). Carter's style, "sinuous and ramshackle" (as she describes the movements of one of her fictional young men), is a form of solidarity with the shaky but often hilarious world we have inherited and hope to change. It is a style which breeds laughter, and it is infectious:

Fevvers' laughter seeped through the gaps in the window-frame and cracks in the door-frames of all the houses in the village.

It seemed this laughter of the happy young woman rose up from the wilderness in a spiral and began to twist and shudder across Siberia.

The spiralling tornado of Fevvers' laughter began to twist and shudder across the entire globe, as if a spontaneous response to the giant comedy that endlessly unfolded beneath it, until everything that lived and breathed, everywhere, was laughing.

(*Nights at the Circus*, pp. 294–295)

Wise Children (1991) is an amiable, often very funny novel about the career and family of an imaginary legend of the Anglo-American theater—we remember Carter's fondness for such figures from her treatment of Tristessa in *The Passion of New Eve,* and a piece in her posthumous collection *American Ghosts and Old World Wonders* (1993) reworks the story of *Sunset Boulevard* one more time—but it lacks the anarchic energy of *Nights at the Circus.* Its very subversiveness is a little sedate, as if the Bohemian life were just the bourgeois life by another name. Dora and Nora Chance are twins, the illegitimate daughters of the Shakespearean ham Melchior Hazard, a man who has finally gone into advertising as his own grand self, a series of "old buffers in pipe tobacco, vintage port and miniature cigar commercials. You started to associate his face . . . with the music of Elgar" (*Wise Children*, p. 37).

The twins are old now, but very sprightly, and Dora is telling their story. "D'you know," she says at the end, "I sometimes wonder if we haven't been making him up all along. . . . If he isn't just a collection of our hopes and dreams and wishful thinking in the afternoons. Something to set our lives by, like the old clock in the hall, which is real enough, in itself, but which we've got to wind up to make it go." "Oh, very profound," her sister says. "Very deep" (p. 230). The title of the novel comes from the old saying that it's a wise child that knows its own father; wiser children, it seems, know that even real fathers are made up. Wise female children, that is. "If the child is father of the man," Nora muses, "then who is the mother of the woman?" (p. 224). The answer, in this novel, could only be some sort of affectionate fiction. What remains in the mind here is the dotty ordinariness of Dora and Nora, their ironic sense that survival itself is ridiculous but scarcely ever less than fun. At one point they make themselves up as the gaiety girls they used to be—"we painted the faces that we always used to have on to the faces we have now"—and then comment on their appearance. "It's every woman's tragedy," Nora says, "that, after a certain age, she looks like a female impersonator." Dora, who also knows her Wilde, quickly asks, "What's every man's tragedy, then?" "That *he* doesn't, Oscar," Nora replies (p. 192).

IN CONCLUSION: APES AND TIGERS

IN *Nights at the Circus* a group of chimps are seen practicing their act, a laughable simulation of chil-

dren in a classroom. There is a professor chimp with black suit, watch-chain, and mortarboard; there are twelve attentive, silent pupils, boys and girls, all in sailor suits, "each with a slate and slate pencil clutched in their leathery hands." "How irresistibly comic," Jack Walser thinks, watching them. But then he looks closer. Is that writing on the blackboard? Are the chimps perhaps asking real questions, actually learning, writing something down? When Walser stumbles and reveals his presence, the professor instantly wipes the blackboard clean, and the chimps start fooling around, gibbering and shooting ink pellets, doing their "apes at school" number. Walser's eyes meet those of the professor, and he never forgets "this first, intimate exchange with one of these beings whose life ran parallel to his, this inhabitant of the magic circle of difference, unreachable . . . but not unknowable" (pp. 107, 108).

Difference is Carter's great theme. We can know other creatures, including humans, but only if we know their difference. "I did not know his god," D. H. Lawrence says of a snake. Carter would say we probably wouldn't be any wiser if we did, but she shares Lawrence's sense of what otherness is like and how much our perception of it matters. That is why there are so many beasts, and images of beasts, in her fiction. The beast is absolutely other, what we are not. He is Blake's tiger, burning bright—Carter's work is littered with references to this extraordinary icon of ferocity and innocence. But he is not caged except by us, and beastliness is not a final, unshakable category, beyond transformation. Beasts are also what we could become, like Alice crossing into the world beyond the mirror to discover a place that is not a reflection of her own. And beasts can become human, as Carter's tales repeatedly show. So there are no monsters, there is only difference. The delicate, spiraling mystery of Carter's work lies in this complicated separation and interaction of kinds, men and women, young and old, human and other animal. Difference is total but not final; essential but not absolute. Parallel lives are unreachable (unless you cease to be yourself), but not unknowable.

The Princess of Abyssinia (born in Marseilles, of a West Indian mother and a Brazilian father) is a tiger-tamer who doesn't usually brood on the thoughts of her animal charges but always has a moment, as her act begins, when she remembers what these unreachable creatures might do: "Just for that moment, while she knew they wondered what on earth they were doing there, when her vulnerable back was turned towards them and her speaking eyes away from them, the Princess felt a little scared, and, perhaps, more fully human than she was used to feeling" (p. 149). "Perhaps" is very subtle; but the princess "knows" what the tigers are wondering. The tigers' own experience is evoked in this way:

The cats . . . leapt on to the semi-circle of pedestals placed ready for them and sat there on their haunches, panting, pleased with themselves for their obedience. And then it would come to them, always with a fresh surprise no matter how often they performed, that they did not obey in freedom but had exchanged one cage for a larger cage. Then, for just one unprotected minute, they pondered the mystery of their obedience and were astonished by it.

(p. 148)

Two later images in *Nights at the Circus* repeat this mood with an inflection of magical threat. When the circus train crashes in the steppes, "a great wonder" occurs. The tigers have become mirror tigers, and have broken when the mirrors broke.

They had frozen into their own reflections and been shattered, too . . . as if that burning energy you glimpsed between the bars of their pelts had convulsed in a great response to the energy released in fire around us and, in exploding, they scattered their appearances upon that glass in which they had been breeding sterile reduplications. On one broken fragment of mirror, a paw with the claws out; on another, a snarl. When I picked up a section of flank, the glass burned my fingers and I dropped it.

(p. 206)

A little later, another set of tigers appears, this time explicitly associated with Blake.

We saw the house was roofed with tigers. Authentic, fearfully symmetric tigers burning as brightly as those who had been lost. . . . They stretched out across the tiles like abandoned greatcoats, laid low by pleasure, and you could see how the tails that dropped down over the eaves like icicles of fur were throbbing with marvellous sympathy. Their eyes, gold as the background to a holy picture, had summoned up the sun that glazed their pelts until they looked unutterably precious.

(pp. 249–250)

The last phrase is a little feeble, as if Carter can't find all the words for the vision she wants us to see. But "like greatcoats" is wonderfully casual, military, and human; and "roofed with tigers" takes us into a world resembling that of Chagall. The mirror tigers make vividly metaphorical the implications of the mysterious acquiescence of their antecedents. They are beautiful, broken, and still dangerous. They are the magic of otherness, entirely unlike us. Except that we too, perhaps, in occasional unprotected moments, ponder the mystery of our obedience and are astonished by it.

Difference and obedience. We can take these apes and tigers in *Nights at the Circus* not only as summarizing continuing preoccupations in Angela Carter's work but also as evoking two essential features of her historical moment. Angela Carter's Britain—she remains a very English writer in spite of her cosmopolitan reading and her total lack of "English" reserve—is a multiracial, multicultural society that has great difficulty in recognizing and respecting its internal differences. The moral attraction of Carter's writing is that it thrives on difference—to a greater degree even than that of Salman Rushdie, since if he has a whole other culture behind him, she has behind her the full panoply of her unremitting eccentricity, her refusal to play safe or find anything sacred: difference as a kind of habitat.

The obedience of the tigers can be read as a metaphor for social submission, the readiness of wild creatures to accept the unreasonable routines of so-called civilization. The British, like the tigers, have long been "pleased with themselves for their obedience," regarding it as a cultural triumph—as if their remarkable circus performance were all they had ever wanted to achieve, and circus tigers were all they had ever been. Carter is not arguing that this submission is a mistake or that the tigers should go wild again at once. She is a radical, but not an anarchist, and like Joseph Conrad she admires the strange self-confidence of the country she needs also to criticize. But she sees the self-confidence cracking and thinks this is no cause at all for regret. She is saying that the tigers' obedience can't really be forced, was always a mystery, and could be revoked; that the human circus-masters of Great Britain should not be surprised if even the broken reflections of tigers burn their fingers.

ANGELA CARTER

SELECTED BIBLIOGRAPHY

I. NOVELS. *Shadow Dance* (London, 1966), also pub. as *Honeybuzzard* (New York, 1966); *The Magic Toyshop* (London, 1967; New York, 1968); *Several Perceptions* (London and New York, 1968); *Heroes and Villains* (London, 1969; New York, 1969, 1981); *Love* (London, 1971; with afterword, New York, 1988); *The Infernal Desire Machines of Doctor Hoffman* (London, 1972), also pub. as *The War of Dreams* (New York, 1977); *The Passion of New Eve* (London and New York, 1977); *Nights at the Circus* (London, 1984; New York, 1985); *Wise Children* (London, 1991; New York, 1992).

II. COLLECTIONS OF SHORT STORIES. *Fireworks* (London, 1974; New York, 1981; with afterword, New York, 1987); *The Bloody Chamber and Other Stories* (London, 1979; New York, 1980); *Black Venus* (London, 1985), also pub. as *Saints and Strangers* (New York, 1987); *American Ghosts and Old World Wonders* (London, 1993).

III. VOLUMES OF NONFICTION. *The Sadeian Woman: An Exercise in Cultural History* (London, 1979), also pub. as *The Sadeian Woman and the Ideology of Pornography* (New York, 1979); *Nothing Sacred: Selected Writings* (London, 1982); *Expletives Deleted: Selected Writings* (London, 1992).

IV. INTERVIEWS AND CRITICISM. John Haffenden, *Novelists in Interview* (London, 1985); David Punter, *The Hidden Script: Writing and the Unconscious* (London, 1985); Paulina Palmer, "From 'Coded Mannequin' to Bird Woman: Angela Carter's Magic Flight," in *Women Reading Women's Writing,* ed. by Sue Roe (Brighton, Eng., 1987); Elaine Jordan, "Enthrallment: Angela Carter's Speculative Fictions," in *Plotting Change: Contemporary Women's Fiction,* ed. by Linda Anderson (London, 1990); Lorna Sage, *Angela Carter* (Plymouth, Eng., 1994); Lorna Sage, ed., *Flesh and the Mirror: Essays on the Art of Angela Carter* (London, 1994); Marina Warner, *From the Beast to the Blonde* (London, 1994).

CYRIL CONNOLLY
(1903–1974)

Mason Cooley

EVEN THOUGH he never wrote the major work he longed to produce, Cyril Connolly has a place in the canon of English literature. Like that of Dr. Johnson, his reputation rests in part on the fascination he has exercised as a literary personality and as a center of the literary social life in the period 1920–1950. His journals and the quotations and anecdotes about him are an important part of his posthumous existence. He was one of the last English critics with a thoroughgoing classical education. He loved the Latin poets of the Age of Augustus and the Enlightenment culture of eighteenth-century France and England. He was unabashedly a highbrow critic, a proponent of great modernist writers such as William Butler Yeats, T. S. Eliot, Ezra Pound, Marcel Proust, and above all, James Joyce. Much of his writing is an intelligent, spirited elegy anticipating the death of humanistic high culture amid wars and the encroaching mass media. Like many of his distinguished contemporaries, he was on the cutting edge of tradition-shattering modernist literature and at the same time filled with an eloquent nostalgia for traditional culture.

He was also gregarious, witty, urbane, and hospitable. He was on friendly terms with most of the important British writers of his time, both as a friend and as the editor of the monthly literary journal *Horizon*. In many of his reviews, he makes remarks based on his personal knowledge of the writer, something few academic critics are in a position to do. Both in his conversation and in his writing, he was a maker of memorable sentences, many of which are still in circulation: he is quoted more than fifty times in *The Columbia Dictionary of Quotations* (1993).

Much of Connolly's literary journalism is still in print in book form—still fresh and provocative thirty to sixty years after its first appearance in a newspaper or a magazine. In a very general

sense, he can be thought of as the English equivalent of Edmund Wilson. Each was among the most influential literary figures of his time; each had a gift for writing brief journalistic essays that almost magically escape being ephemeral. Each had a restless, inquiring mind, an eye for illuminating detail, an ability to make quick and sure literary judgments, and a powerfully individual personality, all of which has kept their work alive. Wilson was the less personal of the two, the more productive and tenacious, and had a wider and deeper grasp of literature and history; he was a master of storytelling, both in wonderful summaries and in narrative history. Connolly was more witty and brilliantly aphoristic, more ironic. His self-portraiture, both seductive and occasionally exasperating, not his historical sense, is at the center of his writing.

EARLY LIFE

CYRIL Connolly was born on 10 September 1903 at Whitley, near Coventry in the English Midlands. But his place of birth had little significance for Connolly's life. The only child of an army officer, Matthew Connolly, and his wife, Muriel Maud Connolly, Cyril moved about from place to place like all army children. In February 1906 his father was posted to Gibraltar and then to South Africa, where he was joined later by Cyril and his mother. At Gibraltar and in the semitropical landscape around Cape Town, Cyril learned to love the Mediterranean type of landscape and weather, which inspired some of the most evocative passages in his travel writing. In *Enemies of Promise* (1938), he remembers "the walk to the sea through clumps of rushes and over white sand feathered with the tracks of lizard and all around me an indescribable irradiation of sun and wind and space and salt" (p. 145).

In 1910, Matthew Connolly was promoted to major and posted to Hong Kong. Fearful of the climate, his parents sent seven-year-old Cyril to live with relatives, first in Ireland and then in Bath. Cyril never quite forgave his mother for what he considered her rejection; for the rest of his life he had an irresistible desire to be loved and a fear of desertion. His parents' marriage was not a success. Maud had fallen in love with one of her husband's commanding officers, General Christopher Brook. Matthew and Maud never divorced, but she lived in her own flat in London during the 1920s and moved to South Africa with General Brook in the 1930s.

Though Cyril's parents were not rich, both came from well-to-do upper-class families. In *Cyril Connolly: Journal and Memoir*, David Pryce-Jones says, "The decorous and comfortably ordered Edwardian background into which Cyril had been born allowed him to make what he chose of it. On all branches of his family tree were large houses and private incomes" (p. 15). Cyril was enchanted by the wealth and the romantic houses of his Irish relations. The house that his Aunt Mab and Uncle Walter rented evoked "security and romance, fires and potato cakes, footmen, horses, and soft aquatinted Irish winter." Ireland meant "castles, holidays, riches, Upper Class" (*Journal and Memoir*, p. 19).

When Cyril was sent to Bath to stay with his paternal grandmother, he felt he was going to "Lodgings, School, Poverty, Middle Class" (p. 20). Cyril was determined to be indulged, and his grandmother was eager to indulge him. Later in life, Cyril decided that his character had begun to deteriorate at the age of seven. He blamed his grandmother's spoiling for the weaknesses of his character because she had taught him to believe that wishes should come true, and do. Pryce-Jones says, "Indecision, Ingratitude, Laziness, Impatience, Cruelty, and Giving Way to Moods had been cultivated in him, Cyril concluded, simply because small faults had been allowed to pay off" (p. 20). Taking advantage of the popular Freudianism of the era, Connolly often seemed to assume that, having assigned the blame for his failings to his grandmother, he had done all that could be expected of him.

To get Cyril away from what she regarded as the pernicious influence of his paternal grand-mother, his mother arranged for him to go to a well-known boarding school, St. Cyprian's, on the Channel coast south of London—on the other side of England from Bath. After a period of listlessness and homesickness, Cyril became involved in the life of the school. He made two lifelong friends: Cecil Beaton, the photographer, and Eric Blair, later to become famous under the pen name of George Orwell. Orwell's often-reprinted memoir of his years as a scholarship boy at St. Cyprian's, "Such, Such Were the Joys" (1953), gives an eloquent and bitter picture of the school and his largely wretched experience there. Paralleling Orwell's better-known work is the section of Connolly's *Enemies of Promise* entitled "A Georgian Boyhood." Cyril also suffered at St. Cyprian's and saw through its system of intimidation, beatings, emotional blackmail, and relentless inculcation of the character traits useful to the masters of a great empire. "Muscle-bound with character the alumni of St. Wulfric's would pass on to the best public schools, cleaning up all houses with a doubtful tone, reporting their best friends for homosexuality and seeing them expelled, winning athletic distinctions . . . and then find their vocation in India, Burma, Nigeria and the Sudan, administering with Roman justice those natives for whom the final profligate overflow of Wulfrician character was all the time predestined" (*Enemies of Promise*, p. 160).

Connolly is especially sardonic about the ups and downs of being in and out of favor in the capricious court of the headmaster's wife, nicknamed Flip. "I used to keep a favour chart in which, week by week, I would graph my position at her court. I remember my joy as the upward curve continued, and as I began to make friends, win prizes, enjoy riding and succeed again at trying to be funny. . . . On all the boys who went through this Elizabeth and Essex relationship she had a remarkable effect, hotting them up like little Alfa-Romeos for the Brooklands of life" (*Enemies of Promise*, p. 162). But he also enjoyed himself, learned a lot, and became popular with the other boys. He accommodated to the system, and it rewarded him. He paints the contrast between himself and Orwell thus: "I was a stage rebel, Orwell a true one. Tall, pale, with his flaccid cheeks, large spatulate fingers, and supercilious voice, he was one of those boys who seem born old. He was incapable of courtship and when his favour went it sank for ever" (*Enemies of Promise*, p. 163).

Cyril fell in love with a schoolmate, Terry Willson, the first of a series of schoolboy loves. In *Enemies of Promise,* Connolly wrote, "I came to see existence in terms of the couple; in whatever group I found myself I would inevitably end by sharing my life with one other" (p. 170). In *Journal and Memoir,* Pryce-Jones says, "There were four types to which he was susceptible in the search for his so-called Pair System, the Faun, the Redhead, the Extreme Blond and the Dark Friend, and all four had appeared by the time he was twelve. (What other types were left?)" (p. 31). This "falling in love" was emotionally powerful and complex, but apparently sexually innocent to an astonishing degree:

> To say I was in love again will vex the reader beyond endurance, but he must remember that being in love had a peculiar meaning for me. I had never even been kissed and love was an ideal based on the exhibitionism of the only-child. It meant a desire to lay my personality at someone's feet as a puppy deposits a slobbery ball; it meant a non-stop daydream, a planning of surprises, an exchange of confidences, a giving of presents, an agony of expectation, a delirium of impatience, ending with the premonition of boredom more drastic than the loneliness which it set out to cure.
>
> (*Enemies of Promise,* p. 190)

These youthful romances led Cyril mistakenly to expect that in adult life he would be homosexual. But such was not the case. By his early twenties he was fully involved with women. In his adult heterosexual love affairs he displayed the same extravagance, vulnerability, narcissism, and proneness to boredom and inconstancy that characterized his boyhood romances. A romantic hedonist, a permanent adolescent, as he himself said, and a skeptic in some ways very old, alternating between anxiety and fragile enjoyment, dependent but unfaithful, endlessly self-dramatizing—he presented his beloveds with a rich, exciting, seductive, frustrating, and finally impossible mixture of character traits.

Connolly had two periods of extraordinary growth and creative power in his life. The first began in the summer of 1918, when he was fourteen. He had obtained a King's scholarship to Eton College, the most prestigious public school in Britain. At fifteen he was, as he describes himself, "dirty, inky, miserable, untidy, a bad fag, a coward at games, lazy at work, unpopular with my masters and superiors, anxious to curry favour and yet to bully whom I dared" (*Enemies of Promise,* p. 187). Nevertheless, by the time he left to go to Oxford in 1922, he had achieved both social and intellectual success. By getting himself elected to Pop, the Eton Society, he was taken into the magic circle of the aristocratic and athletic elite of the college. The society included all the leading athletes of the school and also such young aristocrats as Antony Knebworth, the Earl of Lytton's son, and Alec Dunglass, later Sir Alec Douglas-Home, who became Conservative prime minister in 1963. Connolly made his way into these Olympian circles by becoming the school jester and by pretending to be a "brilliant idler," though studying long and hard in secret.

Through omnivorous reading, Connolly took in great tracts of history and literature during the Eton years. He knew "by heart something of the literature of five civilizations," especially French and Latin, in addition to English literature. At Eton he acquired his lifelong love of Latin poetry—especially that of Juvenal, Catullus, Martial, and Propertius; his favorite poets were not writers in the noble style like Virgil and Ovid. They were characterized by pessimism, skepticism, bitter satire, and a passionate, unhappy eroticism. As a teenager, Connolly discovered his preference for writers who combined melancholy and love longing with worldliness and sophistication—the Latin poets of the Empire and the dandies and decadents of England and France in the late nineteenth century—Baudelaire, Verlaine, Flaubert, Pater, and Wilde. They supplied the literary basis for his own most personal style: a disenchanted hedonism, sophisticated and often exuberant, but ringed about by sorrow and a sense of loss.

In 1922, Connolly went to Oxford with a Balliol scholarship in history. A friend at Eton had said, "Well, you've got a Balliol scholarship and you've got into Pop—you know, I shouldn't be at all surprised if you never did anything else the rest of your life" (*Enemies of Promise,* p. 252). Connolly was unable to shake the impression that this might well be true. Sixteen years later, he wrote that on leaving Eton, he felt "there was now nothing which could happen to me." As he summed up in what he called *The Theory of Permanent Adolescence,* "the experiences undergone by boys at the great public schools, their glories and disappointments, are so intense as to dominate their lives and to arrest their development" (*Enemies of Promise,* p. 253).

In fact, Connolly did waste his time at Oxford: he avoided his studies and spent his time partying with friends. He wound up with a third-class honors degree, to the great disappointment of his family and friends. He wrote brilliantly about Eton in *Enemies of Promise*, but had nothing to say in print about Oxford until one brief essay in 1973, at the end of his life, in which appears the famous sentence, "The only exercise we took was running up bills" (*The Evening Colonnade*, p. 10).

After Connolly graduated from Oxford in 1925, he spent five months as a private tutor in Jamaica and then became Logan Pearsall Smith's literary secretary. A wealthy American bachelor living in Chelsea, Smith became a minor celebrity with the publication of his aphorisms in the volumes *Trivia* (1918) and *More Trivia* (1922). Smith's parents had settled in London and were well connected in the London literary world. Gore Vidal sums up the family's position in his introduction to *All Trivia* (1984): "One daughter married Bertrand Russell; another married Bernard Berenson. One niece married Virginia Woolf's brother; another niece married Lytton Strachey's brother" (p. xi). Pearsall Smith himself was close to Henry James and knew George Bernard Shaw and the Bloomsbury group. Through Smith, Connolly gained access to the most distinguished London literary circles.

Being secretary to Smith was an undemanding job that brought him a modest income and left him free to pursue his own literary projects. Through Smith he met Desmond MacCarthy, the literary editor of the *New Statesman*, in the summer of 1926. That meeting led to a stint as a biweekly reviewer, which lasted until February 1929. Shortly thereafter he went to Spain, looking for a place to live cheaply while he worked on a novel. With him was an eighteen-year-old American girl, Jean Bakewell, whom he had met a year before. Well-read and self-assured, she was the daughter of a wealthy family. Within a year they married, and Jean's family gave her an allowance sufficient for them to live comfortably in Chelsea, near Smith's residence in fact, without either of them needing to work.

THE ROCK POOL

SUCH an easy situation was the perfect invitation for Connolly to procrastinate and be idle, much to his own chagrin. By 1934 he did manage to finish a brief novel, *The Rock Pool*, which he described as "very short, lyrical, and seedy," a work that came nowhere near living up to his conception of what a novel by Cyril Connolly should be. But as a novel, it was better by definition than his essays and reviews. He often seemed to feel that his journalistic works scarcely counted as positive achievement at all, though they are the basis of his literary reputation, and many of the sentences from his reviews have become part of our collective literary memory.

In part, Connolly's conviction that only a big novel would really establish him was an accurate reflection of the literary values of his modernist generation. That generation had seen the publication in the 1920s and 1930s of Joyce's *Ulysses* and *Finnegans Wake*, Proust's *Remembrance of Things Past*, and Thomas Mann's *The Magic Mountain*. These long novels had some of the scope and cultural authority of the classical epics from which they were descended, and like them were regarded as supreme productions of the human mind. From those heights it was a long way down to journalism and the literary essay. Had he lived in our own postmodern period, with its taste for short pieces, fragments, fast-paced brilliance, and a relaxed mixing of forms, Connolly might have been less dissatisfied with the natural bent of his talent toward the brief essay that mixed personal, literary, and political matters.

Not only Connolly found *The Rock Pool* lacking. It took him two years to find a publisher. English publishers turned the book down because of its awkward length and its "sordid" subject matter. They were undoubtedly put off by the first scene, in which two lesbians are dancing together in a French bar surrounded by bohemians. Connolly wrote to his friend Sylvia Beach of Shakespeare and Company in Paris, "Alas my little novel *The Rock Pool* is smut-bound . . . I think that I must try and have it done in America, or else it will have to appear in an under the counter way, like the Obelisks" (quoted in Shelden, p. 21). In fact, Scribners in New York and the Obelisk Press in Paris brought out the book in 1936, and it had to wait until 1947 to be published in London by Hamish Hamilton. There is nothing in the book that would strike a reader today as obscene, but at the time the love intrigues of a group of lesbian women and the unabashed womanizing of the protagonist were felt to be strong stuff.

In a letter to Peter Quennell that serves as the dedication and introduction to the novel, Connolly says, "I suddenly saw a story, the myth of Hylas perhaps, the young man flying from the Hercules of modern civilization, bending over the glassy pool of the Hamadryads, and being dragged down to the bottom" (p. xx). If the conception of the novel has roots in Theocritus' tale of Hylas, Connolly also confides to Quennell that it has even more important roots in the literature of the recent past:

Any first book is always in the nature of a tardy settlement of an account with the past, and in this case my debt is with the nineteen-twenties. It was a period when art was concerned with futility, when heroes were called Denis and Nigel and Stephen and had a tortured look. I wonder who remembers them now. In any case I think I may claim to have created a young man as futile as any. It also dates because the life it deals with has almost disappeared; the last lingering colonies of expatriates have now been mopped up, and if you were to pass by Trou-sur-Mer you would find no trace even of any of the characters in the *Rock Pool*. The bars are closed, the hotel is empty, the nymphs have departed.

(pp. xix–xx)

The "rock pool" of the title was an ancient hill town on the French Riviera. Before the Great Depression the place was an artists' colony. Since the crash of 1929 it has been in decline and is inhabited by a small group of impecunious artists, would-be artists, and drifters posing as bohemians. The protagonist, Naylor, decides to spend some time there. Now it is like a rock pool, "a microcosm cut off from the ocean by the retreating economic tide." Naylor conceives of himself as an anthropological observer. "Naylor was neither very intelligent nor especially likeable, and certainly not very successful, and from the image of looking down knowingly into his Rock Pool, poking it and observing the curious creatures he might stir up, he would derive a pleasant sense of power. Otherwise the only power he got was from his money" (p. 3).

Naylor is soon drawn into the life of the place by his vanity and by his attraction to a series of young women, mostly lesbian or bisexual. He commissions a portrait of himself by an impecunious artist, a Bessarabian Jew whose first words are, "Meet Rascasse—a pretty swell painter!" (p. 5). Naylor attempts to seduce various women, with little success beyond a couple of one-night stands. He is fascinated by two beautiful young lesbians, Toni and Sonia, with whom he develops a fragile friendship, which they exploit in an absentminded way. He is swindled, seduced, and cast aside by various women until his money is gone and he has a more or less continuous hangover.

By the end of the novel the season has ended and almost everyone has left; Naylor stays on, having settled into an extended drunk on Pernod. He has become one of the derelicts who remain through the winter. Ruby, who lives on alimony, has also stayed on. She is the only one of the women of the rock pool who, instead of treating him with contempt, comes to love Naylor. After his money and his credit run out, he moves in with her and they live on her alimony checks. She drinks as much Pernod as he does. He repays her love with drunken rages and occasional beatings. In the final scene, some tourists Naylor tries to pick up in a bar avoid his advances, and he overhears one say as they leave, "Just another bum, Jane" (p. 137). Naylor has liberated himself from his bourgeois snobberies and pettiness, but in the process has made a his life a shambles and landed himself deep in alcoholism and debt.

Connolly described the book as a study in "inverted snobbery," the snobbery of classless and often penniless bohemia proud of its sexual practices and unconventional manners. In his original conception the book was to be the centerpiece of a triptych, flanked by studies of English snobbery in London and among the country gentry, but that never developed. With a characteristic determination to attack his own work, Connolly told George Orwell that the novel was "lousy" and the best thing in it was the preface. The work attracted some favorable attention in the press, but most reviewers were more interested than impressed. Edmund Wilson gave the book a favorable mention in the *New Yorker*. V. S. Pritchett's judgment in the *Spectator* is a heavily qualified "yes, maybe," or perhaps almost a "no":

Sharing with Mr. Connolly an un-English preference for unpleasant characters in fiction and feeling often like busting up the whole simpering and mumbling tea party, I expected to find in *The Rock Pool* some scabrous abominations. They were not, however, so much abominable as futile; and being futile had nothing to say; and having nothing to say were boring. Under Mr. Connolly's direction, his collection of artists left behind in the Mediterranean after the slump, are dingy, the victims of Mr. Connolly's excessive intelligence.

(*Spectator* 157, 7 August 1936, p. 250)

That is, Connolly takes his characters apart with analysis and satire before he has put them together in his imagination.

Connolly's natural talents were as a journalist and an essayist, a writer of short pieces, not novels. He lacked powers of sustained construction: the characters in *The Rock Pool* are schematic representations of ideas for characters—more explanation than embodiment. He never is able to infuse the incidents of his story with genuine dramatic conflict. The hero's anger comes through as petulance, his amorousness as a kind of unfocused lustfulness. Connolly had a wonderful talent for description, analysis, reflection, comparison, and witty underlining of a point. When he attempted to narrate a story or dramatize rather than analyze a character, he went "off the boil," to use one of his favorite phrases. *The Rock Pool* is not successful, but it provided the hard experience of writing and publishing a novel that enabled Connolly to write one of his most successful works without much difficulty.

ENEMIES OF PROMISE

CONNOLLY'S next book, *Enemies of Promise* (1938), established him as an important critic, essayist, and autobiographical writer. His own struggles with the uncongenial novel form provided him with a lively sense of the internal and external threats to the development of a writer's talent. He set out to examine the forces that might prevent a writer from producing a book capable of lasting ten years. The results of this examination were far better received than his novel. Alfred Kazin wrote in his review, "Like all really good books of criticism, it reveals its author's mind as sharply as a good poem or novel; and without being systematic in the great tradition of criticism, it is a work of such resplendent intelligence as to be worth a dozen more pretentious histories or manuals of contemporary literature" (*Books*, 9 July 1939, p. 7). W. H. Auden wrote to Connolly shortly after the publication of *Enemies of Promise*: "I think *E. of P.* is the best English book of criticism since the war, and more than Eliot or [Edmund] Wilson you really write about writing in the only way which is interesting to anyone except academics, as a real occupation like banking or fucking with all its attendant egotism, boredom, excitement and terror" (quoted in Shelden, p. 23).

Enemies of Promise is divided into three parts. Part 1 examines the writing situation in Britain ten years earlier, in 1928. Part 2 examines the various influences that interfere with the development of the writer and circumvent his efforts to write a book that will endure for ten years or more. Part 3, entitled "A Georgian Boyhood," is an autobiographical memoir of the author's time at Eton, recounting Connolly's developing literary vocation.

Part 1, "Predicament," sets out to find the qualities that have enabled some books to last a decade—from 1928 to 1938. By this means, Connolly tries to discover what qualities might go into the writing of a book that would last for a decade *after* 1938. The "predicament" gives Connolly a frame and a set of questions to present a rapid, idea-filled sketch of modern British literature, chiefly the novel. Such theoretical strategies as Connolly uses have an air of being informal and ad hoc rather than carefully thought out; he always relies on intellectual inventiveness more than systematic development. Nevertheless he set up a distinction between vernacular style and the Mandarin style that has been much used in subsequent critical writing. Of the Mandarin style he says:

The Mandarin style at its best yields the richest and most complex expression of the English language. It is the diction of Donne, Browne, Addison, Johnson, Gibbon, de Quincey, Landor, Carlyle and Ruskin as opposed to that of Bunyan, Dryden, Locke, Defoe, Cowper, Cobbett, Hazlitt, Southey and Newman. It is characterised by long sentences with many dependent clauses, by the use of the subjunctive and the conditional, by exclamations and interjections, quotations, allusions, metaphors, long images, Latin terminology, subtlety and conceits. Its cardinal assumption is that neither the writer nor the reader is in a hurry, that both are in possession of a classical education and a private income. It is Ciceronian English.

(*Enemies of Promise*, pp. 17–18)

A figure closely associated with the Mandarin style but not strictly of it is the dandy, a type with whom Connolly himself has important affinities as a writer. His examples of the dandy are Ronald Firbank, T. S. Eliot, and Aldous Huxley. (Clearly, Connolly is thinking of the early Aldous Huxley of *Antic Hay* [1923] and the early T. S. Eliot of *Prufrock and Other Variations* [1917].) The hallmarks of the dandy are lyricism and wit. "As a wit he makes fun of seriousness, as a lyricist he exists to celebrate things as they are, not to change them" (*Enemies of Promise*, p. 33). Of Firbank he says, "When something bored him, he left it out," and, a little later, "Firbank is not epigrammatic, he is not easily quotable, his object is to cast a sheen of wit over his writing" (p. 34). The dandy is a perfectionist and a "utilitarian," alternating between gaiety and melancholy. Later, Connolly was to analyze Baudelaire as the greatest of all the dandies.

The vernacular style became more and more predominant as books became cheaper, the reading public grew larger, less well educated, and less leisurely in its attitude toward reading.

The struggle between literature and journalism began. . . . Prose, with the exception of Conrad who tried to pep up the grand style, began to imitate journalism and the result was the "modern movement"; a reformist but not a revolutionary attack on the Mandarin style which was to supply us with the idiom of our age. Shaw, Butler, and Wells attacked it from the journalistic side—George Moore, Gissing and Somerset Maugham, admirers of French realism, of the Goncourts, Zola, Maupassant, from the aesthetic.

(*Enemies of Promise*, pp. 18, 19)

Connolly sketches the history of the modern novel as an alternation between these two styles. The "new Mandarins"—Virginia Woolf, E. M. Forster, Lytton Strachey, André Gide, Marcel Proust, and the James Joyce of *Finnegans Wake*—did work of the highest distinction, but Connolly agreed with Edmund Wilson that they had carried "the cult of the individual . . . to such lengths as to exhaust it for a long time to come" (*Enemies of Promise*, p. 56).

The opposition to the Mandarins came from three quarters. The least important stylistically, in Connolly's view, came from English writers with the largest audience—John Galsworthy, George Bernard Shaw, H. G. Wells, and Rudyard Kipling. Somerset Maugham, somewhat separate from this group, returned to fiction after a long "excursion as a playwright" to champion "lucidity, euphony, simplicity, and the story with a beginning, a middle and an end" (*Enemies of Promise*, p. 58). From Paris, the second source of opposition, Gertrude Stein and James Joyce championed a more sophisticated and experimental use of the vernacular style. Finally, D. H. Lawrence and Wyndham Lewis championed a vigorous colloquialism against the artificiality and frequent falsity of the Mandarin style.

Moving toward a summing up of the situation in 1938, Connolly says: "At the moment the vernacular is triumphant. Damon Runyon sweeps the land. . . . Is there any hope? Is there a possibility of a new kind of prose developing out of a synthesis of Orlando and the Tough Guy? Will the strong writers of the colloquial school heighten the form of their work or can the Formalists deepen their content?" (*Enemies of Promise*, p. 78). In his concluding sentences for this first section of *Enemies of Promise*, Connolly moves beyond the war of the styles:

Our language is a sulky and inconstant beauty and at any given moment it is important to know what liberties she will permit. . . . Experiment and adventure are indicated, the boom of the twenties has been paid for by the slump of the thirties; let us try then to break the vicious circle by returning to a controlled expenditure, a balanced literary budget, a reasoned extravagance.

(*Enemies of Promise*, p. 92)

Part 2, "The Charlock's Shade," examines the forces that threaten the development of a writer's talent: outside jobs, journalism, politics, drink, conversation, religion, neurotic sloth, sex, religion, domesticity. And finally, "Of all the enemies of literature, success is the most insidious" (p. 117). Anything, in short, that deflects the writer from the primary task. With a fine sense of a writer's ups and downs in the actual doing of the work, Connolly weaves these themes together. In this passage his point of departure is sloth:

Sloth in writers is always a symptom of an acute inner conflict, especially that laziness which renders them incapable of doing the thing which they are most looking forward to. The conflict may or may not end in disaster, but their silence is better than the overproduction which must so end and slothful writers such as Johnson, Coleridge, Greville, in spite of the nodding poppies of conversation, morphia and horse-racing, have more to their credit than Macaulay, Trollope or Scott. To accuse writers of being idle is a mark of envy or stupidity—La Fontaine slept continually and scarcely ever opened his mouth; Baudelaire, according to Dr. Laforgue, feared to perfect his work because he feared the incest with his mother which was his perfect fulfilment. Perfectionists are notoriously lazy and all true artistic indolence is deeply neurotic; a pain not a pleasure.

(*Enemies of Promise*, p. 111)

Time and again Connolly's discussions of the writing life combine a familiar landscape and figures with a fresh and acute angle of vision—giving us both recognition and surprise. That may have been the quality V. S. Pritchett had in mind when he wrote, "As a critic, not only does he write with more spirit and wit and idiosyncrasy than anyone else living, but he has the virtue of being against the current, of not escaping from literary questions by calling them something else" (*New Statesman and Nation* 37, 11 June 1949, p. 616).

The self-portrait of Connolly found in part 3 of *Enemies of Promise*, "A Georgian Boyhood," is not primarily in the English tradition of reserve and moralism in depicting personal life, though Samuel Butler's *The Way of All Flesh* (1903) is a precursor. Its roots lie rather in French literature, beginning perhaps with Montaigne's seemingly impartial curiosity about himself and his accounts of his own peculiarities running through his *Essays*. It is also heavily indebted to Rousseau's *Confessions*, which give us a scrupulous account of all the author's flaws and foolishness, using lack of concealment and shame as a guarantee of authenticity.

Connolly almost tells us sometimes that he is drawing on Baudelaire's bitter and melancholy "Paris Spleen" as a source of inspiration. The strategy is the same as that in Yeats's "The Circus Animals' Desertion," in which he traces the sources of inspiration to their crude and debased origins. The "foul rag-and-bone shop of the heart" is the source of inspiration and creativity; from time to time the beleaguered ego surfaces to accomplish something lucid and energetic. This conflict is the often-repeated drama in Connolly's unflattering self-portraits. His depiction of himself in "A Georgian Boyhood" is the first of Connolly's failure-in-success, success-in-failure portrayals.

"A Georgian Boyhood" has been overshadowed by Orwell's parallel essay, "Such, Such Were the Joys," but once it is removed from that comparison, it can be seen not as just another depiction of the British public school, but as an acute and ironic self-creation through self-portraiture—Connolly's first major presentation of himself as a character in his writing. In *Enemies of Promise* he created a bildungsroman in the form of essays on the literary situation and a fragment of autobiography. His subject was not the family and love life of the writer, but the relation of the writer to writing itself in a cultural situation full of pitfalls.

THE FOUNDING OF HORIZON

FOR a number of years, Cyril and Jean had been on shaky ground in their marriage. Cyril had affairs with other women, more or less encouraged by Jean, in the hope that he would get womanizing out of his system. But by the summer of 1939, Jean had decided she would no longer live with Cyril until he was ready to do so with a real commitment. Without offering to change his ways, Connolly pleaded with her eloquently to return: "Without your help, advice, love, and enthusiasm I am a mutilated person, a genius without a cause—and with your active indifference, or opposition, I am a genius who is sick and miserable" (quoted in *Journal and Memoir*, p. 286). Jean declined to return and decided to go to America to visit her mother, who was in poor health. Both she and Connolly knew that if she went she was unlikely to return during wartime.

When the war began on 1 September 1939, Connolly was in Paris trying to convince Jean to return to London. He was also trying to persuade his wealthy friend Peter Watson to back a literary magazine with Connolly as editor. Both Jean and Watson had refused his proposals, but after the war broke out they both decided to return to England. Connolly was determined to find an occupation that would see him safely through the war, perhaps at the Ministry of Information or on a newspaper. He wrote, "I am determined to get something, as it will be intolerable to be only pink cannon fodder . . . if we're all back at school one must be a prefect" (quoted in Shelden, p. 30). In addition to all the other reasons Connolly had for wanting to found a magazine, the editorship of a literary review would provide just such a refuge. At a party given by novelist Elizabeth Bowen in the last week in September, Connolly again presented Peter Watson with the arguments in favor of beginning a new magazine, despite the war. This time Watson agreed. On 18 October, Watson signed an agreement as proprietor of the magazine to pay thirty-three pounds per month to subsidize one thousand copies of the magazine.

Peter was the youngest son of Sir William George Watson, one of the richest men in England. With a private income secured by a trust fund, he found an occupation in becoming a knowledgeable supporter of modern art. Connolly's mistress, known only as Diana in Shelden's biography of Connolly, noted about the beginning of the Watson-Connolly friendship: "They were almost in love with each other—very flirty. But early in the war Cyril began to complain that Peter was becoming too austere, that he didn't live like a rich man should, and that he ought to spend more lavishly on meals, hotels, clothes, car, etc." (quoted in Shelden, p. 41). Nevertheless, Watson was Connolly's closest male friend during the *Horizon* years and on up to the time of Watson's mysterious death by drowning in his own bathtub in May 1956. Watson was homosexual, and the great love of his life was an American southerner named Denham Fouts, whose various erotic entanglements, usually with juveniles, and drug addictions often made Peter miserable. Watson and Connolly were well matched in their propensity for finding unhappiness in love, though Watson was stoic and self-effacing in his suffering, and Connolly self-dramatizing and almost bombastic in his complaints and threats of suicide.

Watson was worried about his income being diminished by the war, and he was not sanguine about the prospects of *Horizon*. The magazine was beginning at what seemed a bad moment for any magazine, much less one committed to literary and artistic excellence and determined not to be swept up into politics and the war effort. In his first editorial, Connolly wrote, "Our standards are aesthetic, and our politics are in abeyance" (quoted in Shelden, p. 43), though later in the same piece he allowed for the possibility that a political position would emerge at some point. Watson was very fond of Connolly and admired his work. He knew Connolly could be a star editor. But he also knew that Connolly was wayward, easily bored, and prone to become distracted by his love affairs; as an editor, he would need an understudy. Consequently, Watson arranged for his friend Stephen Spender to become an associate editor of *Horizon*, though his name did not appear on the masthead because of another commitment to John Lehmann's *New Writing*. If Connolly strayed, Spender and Watson could take over.

With these precautions, the magazine was released on 15 December 1939. Virginia Woolf wrote in her diary the next day, "*Horizon* out; small, trivial, dull. So I think from not reading it" (quoted in Shelden, p. 41). Otherwise, the response was enthusiastic. There were favorable notices in the press. The first printing sold out in a few days, and so did the second printing. There was a lively demand for the magazine in the United States. Shortly after its beginning, the magazine had to clear another hurdle—a severe shortage of paper. The fall of Norway cut off Britain's leading supply of wood pulp, and after April 1940 no publication started after September 1939 had any claim to a paper supply. Only after negotiations through Harold Nicholson, a friend of Connolly's and parliamentary secretary at the Ministry of Information, was a rigidly rationed supply of paper given to *Horizon*. Thereafter *Horizon* survived gamely through the blitz, the shortages of food and paper, the deaths of promising young contributors, and even, most upsetting of all, the buzz bombs that fell at random during the last months of the war.

THE UNQUIET GRAVE

AT the same time he was guiding *Horizon* to its success, Connolly was working on the book most loved by his readers, *The Unquiet Grave: A Word Cycle by Palinurus*. Published in December 1944, it was written under the pseudonym Palinurus, the name of Aeneas' pilot who fell overboard and was murdered by a savage island tribe. He appeared to Aeneas on the latter's visit to Hades and begged for the burial of his corpse. Connolly had long meditated on the Palinurus legend and alluded to it in his earlier work. His rather eccentric reading of the Palinurus story was that the pilot had gone overboard, abandoning the voyage, out of a will to fail, an aversion to success just when it was in his grasp; the same pattern, of course, that he perceived in himself. Perhaps he adopted the rather thin disguise in an effort to establish a little distance between himself and the intensely personal book he was writing, though he immediately assimilated Palinurus to his own very recognizable literary personality.

The book had its emotional roots in his grief over his separation from his first wife, Jean, who had tolerated his brief affairs with other women, and even his serious affair with the very young woman known only as Diana in Connolly's biography. Jean had even put up with his periodic rebellions and accusations that the money and leisure she provided had brought out the worst flaws in his character and caused his talent to go "off the boil." Finally, in the spring of 1939 her patience was exhausted and she left Connolly.

Once she was gone, though he had done much to drive her away, Connolly was overcome by grief and exerted all his powers of persuasion to get her to return, threatening suicide but not saying that he was willing to give up Diana. When they met in Paris in the summer of 1939, Jean "told him that the possibility of her returning to him was slight, and that she was determined to live her life as freely as possible, without any definite plans for the future" (Shelden, p. 29). When she returned to New York she began a passionate affair with a young art critic, Clement Greenberg. When Connolly found out, he suffered from paroxysms of rage and grief. He wrote to her, "I think you deserted me in the most cruel and horrible way at a time when life was most intolerable and desertion hurt all the more." In 1943 he wrote, "Whatever I write or read or think about, if I persevere long enough, takes me back to the miseries of 1939; all ends in frustration, tears, and the sense of all-is-lost" (quoted in Shelden, p. 59). His memories of the death of his marriage were his "unquiet grave."

In 1943 Connolly turned forty, a birthday he took very hard, and which he later said added to the melancholy frame of mind in which he wrote *The Unquiet Grave*. In an article in *Horizon*, he wrote, "Sometime in that long year Middle-age angrily flung youth's last belongings out of the room . . . Locks of hair, teeth, kisses, memories and hopes; all perished during those slow months" (quoted in Shelden, p. 115).

In 1942 he began recording his thoughts both about Jean and about living and working in wartime London. In his introduction to the revised edition in 1950, Connolly writes of the pseudonymous author Palinurus:

the three notebooks filled up, while the personal sorrow came to a head and disappeared into a long false lull, like an illness. Working on the manuscript for another year, Palinurus began to see that there was a pattern to be brought out; in the diaries an art-form slumbered,— an initiation, a descent into hell, a purification and cure. The various themes could be given symphonic structure and be made to lead into and suggest each other.

(p. xii)

The biographical particulars out of which *The Unquiet Grave* grew are only vaguely felt in the book itself. The guilt is generalized, the source of the grief unspecific. The war is a distant rumble. Amid the violence of total war, Palinurus meditates on his private grief, claiming a space for the individual and his subjective life even in periods of mass destruction. He also tries with mixed results to "extricate himself from the war and to escape from his time and place into the bright empyrean of European thought" (p. xi). The first sentence of the book is, "The more books we read, the clearer it becomes that the true function of a writer is to produce a masterpiece and that no other task is of any consequence." A little later, "Writers engrossed in any literary task which is not an assault on perfection are their own dupes and, unless these self-flatterers are content to dismiss such activity as their contribution to the war effort, they might as well be peeling potatoes" (p. 1).

What follows is Connolly's one masterpiece, though he was hardly prepared to think so. He thought the masterpiece he should write would be big and powerful. The minor masterpiece he did in fact write is a collection of his and others' sentences and paragraphs circling around the themes of art, nature, pleasure, grief, and loss. Without a story, without a cast of characters, without a continuous line of argument, it is filled with aphoristic sentences, lyric flights of a paragraph or two, and gradually builds up an engrossing portrait of Palinurus himself. At least half of the text is quotation, most often from French writers. "He was determined to quote as many passages as he could from the French to show the affinity between their thought and ours, and to prove how near and necessary to us were the minds and culture of those across the channel who then seemed quite cut off from us, perhaps for ever" (p. xii). His own writing glows with the same quality of energy and imagination as the writings of the French and Latin masters he quotes so aptly. Two examples, a sentence and a paragraph:

My previous incarnations: a melon, a lobster, a lemur, a bottle of wine, Aristippus.

(p. 9)

Saint-Jean-de-Luz. Buying a melon in the morning market and eating it for breakfast in a café on the Bidassoa; pursuing a macintosh, a beret and a strand of wet curls round the sea-wall in the rain. Maize and pimento, light-footed Basques with round lean faces dancing Fandango and Arin-Arin, playing pelota against the church wall while a huge green sunset agonizes through the plate-glass windows.

(p. 85)

Contrary to Connolly's expectations, the book was a success. The conspicuously inconspicuous first printing by *Horizon* of one thousand copies was soon sold out. The subsequent trade edition was also successful. Even Evelyn Waugh, usually so cruel in his assessments of his lifelong friend Connolly, wrote of his descriptive passages that they were "as beautiful as any passages of English prose that I know" (quoted in Shelden, p. 114). The book got a lot of notice, mostly very favorable, in the American press. Edmund Wilson, writing in the *New Yorker,* defended Connolly's decision to stick to art and truth instead of trying to be patriotic: "People used to complain in London that Cyril Connolly was out of key with the wartime state of mind, but I think that we ought all to be grateful that one editor has resisted all pressures and followed his own tastes, and that one good writer has written not what was demanded by patriotism but a true natural history of his wartime morale" (27 October 1945, p. 88).

An unexpected admirer of *The Unquiet Grave* was Ernest Hemingway. After an unpromising meeting in Sylvia Beach's bookshop in Paris in the 1920s, the two men became friends in wartime London. Connolly was attracted to Hemingway as a man of action, and Hemingway was attracted to Connolly's melancholy, pleasure-loving sensibility. Hemingway wrote to Connolly, "I always get involved in wars but I admired the way that you did not. It would be wrong for me not to fight but it was many times righter for you to do exactly as you did. I am no good at saying this sort of thing but I wanted you to know how strongly I felt it and to tell you how much the Palinurus book meant to me" (quoted in Shelden, p. 121).

His wife Jean wrote a penetrating assessment of Connolly's source of inspiration: "I think you are one of the few people whom self-pity or unhappiness develops rather than shuts in. Only you mustn't stop there, let the next grave be a pyramid" (quoted in Shelden, p. 115). She was as unwise in counseling him to attempt a pyramid as she was wise in noting his ability to put his self-pity to creative use. His genius lay in dramatizing the fragmentations of his personality, not in feats of integration or transcendence.

THE ARTS SECTION OF HORIZON

THE success of *Horizon* was even more spectacular than that of *The Unquiet Grave.* From the beginning, its importance for the art and culture in the English-speaking world was recognized by its influential audience. For the next decade, it exhibited artistic energy, independence, and high spirits, qualities hard to find during the war and the grim years of austerity thereafter.

The services of *Horizon* to living painters and sculptors were as important as its services to living writers. Peter Watson served as art editor, a post for which he had the requisite taste and knowledge of contemporary British art. Lucian Freud's first drawing was published in *Horizon,* as was John Craxton's *Poet in Landscape.* Shortly after Henry Moore began his celebrated drawings of the London underground stations in wartime, two of them were reproduced in the magazine. Watson also collected Graham Sutherland's work and reproduced it in *Horizon.* Michael Shelden, Connolly's biographer, sums up as follows:

The list of artists whose work appeared in *Horizon* during the war years reads like a "Who's Who" of twentieth-century British painters, sculptors, and photographers. In addition to Moore, Sutherland, Craxton, Freud, Colquhoun and MacBryde, and the major painters of the Euston Road School, the magazine published works by Cecil Beaton, Bill Brandt, Cecil Collins, Naum Gabo, Barbara Hepworth, David Jones, Paul Nash, Ben Nicholson, John Piper, Ceri Richards, and Alfred Wallis (and after the war, Francis Bacon).

(p. 80)

"THE ANT-LION"

ON the literary side, Connolly was also finding the best contemporary work and writing some of it himself. The first issue of *Horizon* had articles by Stephen Spender and Geoffrey Grigson and poems by W. H. Auden, Louis MacNeice, John Betjeman, and Frederick Prokosch. It also had one of the best pieces Connolly ever wrote, "The Ant-Lion."

This short personal essay states more eloquently than any of his editorials his sense of the connections among nature, art, human social life, and writing. The narrator lies on a peaceful beach near the Maures mountains, meditating. "The woolly brain meddles with ethics. No more power, no aggression, no intolerance. All must be free" (reprinted in *The Condemned Playground,* p. 231). Then he hears a disturbance. An ant-lion is trapping an ant in a sandy funnel it has built; the narrator observes that there are funnels in the earth all around him. He seizes a horsefly and shoves it downward. "The fight proceeds like an atrocity of chemical warfare. The great fly threshes the soil with its wings, it buzzes and drones while the sand heaves round its propellers and the facets of its giant projectors glitter with light. But the clippers do not relax, and disappear tugging the fly beneath the surface." The combatants appear again, and again the ant-lion drags its prey under. "Legs beat the ground. A fainter wheeze and whirr, no hope now, the last wing-tip vanished, the air colder, the pines greener, the cone empty except for the trickle, the sifting and silting down the funnel of the grains of pearl-coloured sand" (p. 232).

The narrator finds a parallel to this contrast of idyllic peace and the violence within it in the bishop's palace at Albi and its environs, where "Art and Nature have formed one of the most harmonious scenes in Europe. The fortress cathedral, the Bishop's Palace with its hanging gardens, and the old bridge, all of ancient brick, blend into the tawny landscape" (p. 233). Within the cathedral are rooms exhibiting the works of Toulouse-Lautrec, placed there through the aggressive influence of his mother, the countess. After the undisturbing pastoral early work come the mature paintings where his bold stroke "hits off the brutality of his subjects, or the beauty of those young girls doomed to such an inevitable end. . . . The world of the hunchback Count is nocturnal, gas-lit, racy, depraved and vicious" (p. 233). The world outside seems beautiful and healthy, but there is something lacking

which only the unnatural world inside can supply. . . . And so the artist drags us in from the terrace because force and intelligence dominate that arrangement. And once back, we are back in his dream, in a hunchback's dream of the world; the sunlight seems tawdry, the red brick vulgar, the palace ornate; the crowd who stand in their tall hats gaping at the blossoming Can-Can dancers are in the only place worth being.

(pp. 234–235)

A meditation follows on the revolt against procreation by the Albigensian heretics of the region during the Middle Ages; like Toulouse-Lautrec, they kept nature at a distance through an extreme discipline—the Albigensians using asceticism, Toulouse-Lautrec using a joyless nocturnal round of pleasure. Each is granted its power and inter-

est and is still, like the ant-lion, inside nature. He concludes:

Much has happened since the summer. To-day the Maures are out of bounds, the Museum closed, and many generalizations based on incorrect assessment of the facts fallen to pieces, but (since the operations of the Ant-Lion have now been extended) it seems worth while to recall that the statements on the life of pleasure which Lautrec took from his witnesses at the Tabarin and the Moulin de la Galette, and which he so vigorously recorded on canvas, are still available to the traveller of the future, and assert their truth.

(p. 237)

This piece is a high point of Connolly's metaphorical and poetic powers, of his ability to condense his rapid thought into a series of compelling images. As the images mirror one another in their parallels, they also reveal the center of Connolly's sense of life, which never conceives of a melodramatic division into pure good and pure evil. Everything is necessary, and everything is justified—nature and the antinature of art, pastoral happiness and the relentless violence it contains. Evil is real and powerful and must be resisted, but it is an immortal part of the nature of things, mingled with nature and art and exerting its powers of attraction over us. With such a sense Connolly was incapable of demonizing the enemy and sanctifying the Allies. He believed the war against the Nazis had to be fought and won, but he did not believe that required descending into a single-minded patriotism or evaluating works of the mind according to their presumed usefulness in the war effort. "The Ant-Lion" is Connolly's most compelling, though oblique, statement of his reasons for continuing to live a personal life and exercise a personal taste in wartime—a decision on which the success of *Horizon* is in considerable measure based.

CONNOLLY AS EDITOR OF HORIZON

OF course, Connolly could only exercise his judgment on the manuscripts that were actually submitted to the magazine. Fortunately, he was on friendly terms with many of the most important English writers of his time and had a sharp eye for emerging talents and movements in France and the United States. Connolly liked to entertain, and during the war *Horizon* parties were famous. Connolly lived with Lys Lubbock for several years, and in addition to putting the *Horizon* office in order, she had the qualities that made the parties successful. She was a splendid cook and a good hostess and knew how to join with Connolly to create an atmosphere of gaiety and confidence even in blitzed and rationed wartime London.

Horizon was responsible for making the reputations of a number of new writers. Dylan Thomas often cadged money from Connolly and Peter Watson, but he more than repaid them by giving his best work of the war decade to *Horizon.* Among these poems were "There Was a Saviour," "Deaths and Entrances," "Vision and Prayer," "Fern Hill," "A Refusal to Mourn the Death, by Fire, of a Child in London," and "In Country Sleep." When Arthur Koestler came to London in 1942, Connolly befriended him and provided him with a place to stay. Koestler published three of his most important essays in the magazine: "The Yogi and the Commissar," "The Birth of a Myth," and "The Intelligentsia." Koestler wrote, "Cyril took me under his wing. . . . Instead of spending my time in loneliness and isolation like so many exiles, or confined to an emigré clique, I was welcomed into the *Horizon* crowd" (quoted in Shelden, p. 84). Connolly also was the first to publish Denton Welch, and he promoted his reputation in any way possible long after Welch's early death. Among writers already well established, Elizabeth Bowen, the Sitwells, T. S. Eliot, and W. H. Auden contributed regularly to *Horizon.*

One of the greatest prose writers Connolly found for his magazine was already nearby, for Eric Blair (George Orwell) had been a friend of Connolly's at St. Cyprian's. The first Orwell essay published by *Horizon* was "Boys' Weeklies"; it was hardly a promising subject for a highbrow magazine in the midst of a war, but the essay was brilliantly done and captured the fancy of *Horizon* readers. In 1946, *Horizon* published one of Orwell's most important essays, "Politics and the English Language." As a contributor and a friend of its editor, Orwell came to know Sonia Brownell, who was a mainstay of the office and a key member of the *Horizon* crowd. He fell in love with her and proposed marriage. She was at that point involved with the French philosopher Maurice Merleau-Ponty; later, however, she broke with Merleau-Ponty and accepted Orwell, marrying him a few months before his death from tuberculosis in January 1950.

Support for *Horizon* was by no means universal. It was not specifically named by the *Times* in its attacks on highbrows and escapist intellectuals, but was clearly near the center of the target. *Scrutiny* was the most influential journal of academic criticism of the time. Its critics, including Queenie D. Leavis, were outraged by the aestheticism and snobbery of Connolly, and vilified him and the magazine. The heavily moralized academic criticism they practiced and the lumbering prose that most of them wrote made them natural enemies of the glitzy Chelsea hedonists at *Horizon.* If the academic critics found *Horizon* lacking in moral earnestness, the Bloomsbury circle of Virginia and Leonard Woolf, Lytton Strachey, and E. M. Forster found them lacking in artistic earnestness and modernist austerity. Between *Horizon* and Bloomsbury, especially Virginia Woolf, there was antipathy imperfectly covered by a veil of politeness, the ostensible issues being the presumed frivolity and flamboyance of the *Horizon* group. Most writers and editors outside these two groups were enthusiastic about the magazine and accepted Connolly as a leading critical voice.

THE CONDEMNED PLAYGROUND

The Condemned Playground: Essays 1927–1944 (1945) is the first of four volumes of Connolly's essays collected during his lifetime. A fifth, *The Selected Essays of Cyril Connolly,* edited by Peter Quennell, appeared in 1984, ten years after Connolly's death. *The Condemned Playground* is Connolly's selection of his work from 1927, when he began publishing, up through 1944, four years into the editorship of *Horizon.* In the introduction, Connolly writes, "*The Condemned Playground* signifies for me the literary scene of the 1930's, the period of ebullience, mediocrity, frivolity and talent during which I wrote most of these essays and my first two books. I also chose the title to refer in a more limited sense to that leafy tranquil cultivated *spielraum* of Chelsea, where I worked and wandered" (p. vi). Connolly's choice of subjects in this early collection shows that his taste was already formed, his range of interests clearly defined. There are articles on James Joyce and André Gide, Jonathan Swift and Lord Chesterfield, Horace and Alexander Pope among others; there are parodies of English literary life; there are articles on the Spanish Civil War and the sinister rise of fascism; there are articles on French-English literary relations and on the writer and English society.

The first published piece Connolly wrote, "Distress of Plenty" (1927), was on the eighteenth-century novelist Laurence Sterne, the author of *Tristram Shandy* and *A Sentimental Journey*. Sterne has none of the powerful directness of Samuel Johnson, the virile energy of Henry Fielding, the enchantment with the feminine world of Samuel Richardson. Sterne is not part of the mainstream of Augustan common sense, classical balance, and forthright energy. He is meandering, perverse, a humorist, a trickster. For his own debut as an author, Connolly writes about the eccentric, the marginal, the endlessly digressive and often insincere Sterne—an oddity among mainstream British authors. By this move Connolly distances himself from gentlemanly earlier champions of the Augustan Age, such as George Saintsbury, with their fondness for harmony and moderation. Connolly is interested in the quirky and unexpected side of Enlightenment culture. He describes the experience of Sterne's readers as follows:

The reader indeed plunges into Sterne's work like a prince into an artificial and enchanted forest, . . . and in a moment the path narrows and the boughs thicken, and the sounds of the hunt recede as he struggles through thickets of dusty sycamore, lost in false metallic greenness, before he emerges angrily from the tangled breaks into one of Sterne's perfect sentences that opens before him like a moss-grown ride.
(*The Condemned Playground*, p. 26)

From the beginning, Connolly warned readers of his own work to expect surprises and shifts, thickets opening on greenswards, essays leaping brilliantly and at top speed through their argument, then loitering around a point. Connolly did not have to grow into his mature literary personality; he was completely himself from the beginning.

Connolly's 1929 article on James Joyce's Anna Livia Plurabelle section of *Finnegans Wake*, the first in English, helps place Connolly in the spectrum of British literary opinion. *Finnegans Wake* had not yet appeared in book form but was coming out in sections in the Paris-based *Transition*.

Joyce himself supplied Connolly with much of the material for his essay. Writing about *Finnegans Wake* announced Connolly as an advocate for the most advanced international modernism, a spokesman for the most scandalous and most difficult author of his time. Such a position was rarer and more isolated in England than it would have been in the United States, which gave an earlier and more enthusiastic welcome to modernism than England did. Indeed, the modernist canon never became as securely established in England as it did in the United States. As a defender of Joyce, Connolly also placed himself in direct opposition to Bloomsbury, for both E. M. Forster and Virginia Woolf had written hostile reviews of *Ulysses* and regarded Joyce with genteel disgust. To write in praise of Joyce was to raise the flag of rebellion against current English good taste, even in advanced literary circles.

Harry Levin in the *New Republic* found Connolly's book "gracefully diffident, self-consciously civilized and disappointingly slight." He felt it served notice that "England, long declining into a second-class power, has begun her decline into a second-class culture" (*New Republic* 115, 15 July 1946, p. 49). The other reviewers, who cared less about the absence of imperial pomp and self-assurance, were generally very favorable. Donald Stauffer wrote in the *New York Times*:

This book, then, pays off amply as social history, as esthetic autobiography, and as adult, penetrating literary criticism. It shows again that the English, even when they are Irish, do not lose their heads in war; and that between the wars they do not lose their heads irretrievably. And if for no other reason, it is worth its salt for its defense of the artist's way of life—"the path of what James called 'the lonely old artist man,' who is so easily destroyed and so quite irreplaceable."
(28 July 1946, section 7, p. 6)

CONNOLLY IN FRANCE AND THE UNITED STATES

FIVE months after the liberation of Paris in August 1944, Connolly received permission to visit France as a reporter for *Horizon*. The extent to which Connolly was securely inside British circles of privilege is indicated by his being invited by the Duff Coopers to stay at the British Embassy, an island of luxury in the war-torn city. The fruits of this visit for *Horizon* were impressive. Simone de

Beauvoir gave him a copy of Jean-Paul Sartre's manifesto for *Les Tempes modernes*, the key existentialist magazine Sartre and de Beauvoir were about to begin publishing. The manifesto appeared in *Horizon* before it appeared in Paris. The next year, *Horizon* published *Huis Clos* for the first time outside France.

During 1945, *Horizon* published so many articles on French culture that, as Michael Shelden wrote, "By the end of the year it must have seemed to many English readers that *Horizon*'s subtitle could more accurately be 'A Review of French Literature and Art'" (p. 125). Connolly was enthusiastic about postwar French cultural developments in themselves and also about doing what he could to combat the insularity of British taste by publicizing the intellectual ferment going on in Paris. From the beginning *Horizon* had a thoroughly international perspective, "international" in those days meaning Europe (primarily France), Great Britain, and the United States, with little thought of looking further afield. *Horizon* wanted to make its readers into "good Europeans" in Goethe's sense of an awareness of a common European culture more powerful and deeply civilized than any single national culture.

Connolly and Peter Watson sailed to New York together in the autumn of 1946. Once there, each went his own way. Watson spent much of his time with the painter Pavel Tchelitchew and two writers, Charles Henri Ford and Parker Tyler; these three gay men ran *View*, a magazine that published the avant-garde writers of the time and was particularly notable for the quality of its art contributors. It never equaled *Horizon* in range or quality but was in its function the American version of *Horizon*. Because of the popularity of *Horizon* and the success of *The Unquiet Grave*, which had been published in New York the preceding year, Connolly received full-scale celebrity treatment from the New York publishing world. He appeared on radio programs and was interviewed by the *New Yorker*. The director of the Metropolitan Museum gave a lunch for him and Peter Watson in addition to a special tour of the museum. More personally, Connolly had several engagements with E. E. Cummings, whose work he admired and collected.

Everything was very exhilarating, but after a few weeks Connolly was glad to escape from the flood of engagements and telephone calls and move on to California. He spent a couple of enjoy-able days at Big Sur with Henry Miller. He also visited the Huxleys and was much more at ease than he had been in 1930, when he and Jean had visited them in the south of France. Connolly returned to England with very few American submissions in hand, though he had invited many of the American writers he met to submit to the magazine. But he went back with a vivid impression of the electric energy of New York in contrast to the weariness and drabness of London.

FINAL YEARS OF HORIZON AND THEREAFTER

AFTER a highly successful run of ten years, *Horizon* ceased publication at Christmas 1949. In the preceding couple of years Connolly had spent less and less time on the magazine. He gave a party, it sometimes seemed, almost every week; he met more and more celebrities; he spent much of his time at the Gargoyle Club. He busied himself with the social aspects of running the magazine but left the actual operations to the office staff, chiefly Sonia Brownell, who took over when Connolly was away. Lys Lubbock handled the cooking and arranging for Connolly's social life. Though he still attended to *Horizon* business, Peter Watson had begun to distance himself after becoming a founding member of the Institute of Contemporary Arts, which was soon to be an influential part of British artistic life.

During the war, *Horizon* had the clear-cut mission of keeping literature and art moving forward in a time of crisis. In the dispirited and impoverished peace that followed, that focus was lost; no exciting new generation of writers presented themselves to *Horizon*. The magazine continued to sell well, particularly in the United States, but much of the original impetus was lost. Connolly also began to grow restless; he wanted to return to his "real" vocation as a writer. Peter Watson was willing to continue subsidizing the magazine for as long as Connolly wanted to edit it, but that was not enough to counterbalance the other considerations. At the end, Connolly wrote, "We closed the long windows over Bedford Square, the telephone was taken, the furniture stored, the back numbers went to their cellar, the files rotted in the dust. Only contributions continued to be delivered, like a suicide's milk" (quoted in Shelden, pp. 223–224).

After *Horizon* closed down Connolly hoped yet again to produce the great novel that would justify him as a writer. Though *Horizon* in its last couple of years did not take up a great deal of his time, Connolly complained that it was making it impossible for him to write seriously. After a year without *Horizon,* he had no completed writing to show. In the course of his adult life, Connolly's awareness that free time was not primarily what kept him from writing faded in and out of his consciousness. In a 1968 interview with Richard Kershaw, Connolly said, "I would say only myself has prevented me doing the writing I ought to have done. . . . A good writer rises above everything and it's an alibi to say: 'I can't write, I haven't got a room of my own . . .' 'I can't write, I haven't got a private income . . .' 'I can't write, I'm a journalist,' and so on. Those are all alibis" (*Contemporary Authors: Permanent Series,* vol. 2, p. 133). The truth of what Connolly said in 1968 was evident at any time during his life when he cleared away all other commitments in order to write a masterpiece, and nothing much happened.

During this first post-*Horizon* year Connolly married Barbara Skelton. The marriage was tempestuously unhappy. Without *Horizon,* Connolly was no longer at the center of London literary life, and there was no hope of reviving the magazine. He was also short of money. Without an income, without *Horizon* and the social position that went with it, without a masterpiece, with a disintegrating marriage, Connolly had come to the end of his most active and creative period. But his life, both literary and personal, was by no means over. Connolly exhibited remarkable powers of recovery. In 1956, Connolly divorced Barbara Skelton; three years later, he married Deirdre Craig, a young woman half his age. She bore him a son and a daughter, and Connolly, then in his fifties, became a family man for the first time. He and his family moved out of London, and in his last years they lived at Eastbourne, near St. Cyprian's, Connolly's old school. The glamour and excitement of the literary life were replaced by suburban domesticity and a regular job.

To get money, he went back to literary journalism, was offered a job by the *Sunday Times,* and wrote leading weekly reviews for the paper from 1951 until his death in 1974, producing hundreds of pieces. In the post-*Horizon* years he published three more books: *Ideas and Places* (1953), *Previous Convictions* (1963), and *The Evening Colonnade*

(1973). *Ideas and Places* is a collection of his writings for *Horizon,* including his editorials. *Previous Convictions* and *The Evening Colonnade* are made up of selections from his hundreds of pieces for the *Sunday Times.* His talent for writing with energy, style, and incisiveness about literature, travel, and nature had not decayed with the passage of time. Many of the essays in his last collections are as alive and compelling as those in his first, *The Condemned Playground.* Even the brief reviews have the unmistakable, idiosyncratic stamp of his literary personality. Connolly sometimes spoke of reviewing as hack work unworthy of his talents. But if there is anything of the hack about Connolly it shows more in the laborious artificiality of his fiction than in his reviewing. The bulk of his work published in book form is made up of journalistic articles, and they are the basis of his reputation.

In the introduction to *Previous Convictions,* Connolly asks, "Why a book?" His answer is in several parts. One is that the book may preserve his essays from oblivion for a few more years. A second is that the "book is so arranged that it builds up to a picture of the author; an ageing Narcissus complete with pool" (p. xi). At the end of the introduction (with what measure of irony?) he writes,

Secretly I am convinced that there is no happiness outside my prose and I want the world to know it. "In that case why not take more trouble?" "How can I take more trouble when I am still writing reviews all the time this is coming out?" "Well, couldn't you get another job?" "Such as?" "Oh, I don't know—teaching, lecturing, broadcasting—"

Vainglorious desiccation! No, writing for a Sunday paper has tempered my improvidence and widened my knowledge; it has respected my solitude and prevented *rigor mentis* from setting in. Without the weekly stint I might have written longer and better—or dissipated my powers in false starts and frustration.

Connolly may have been unable make his novels dramatic, but he can squeeze an astonishing amount of attention-getting drama out of the perpetual tug-of-war among ambivalences, ambitions, fears, avoidances, and alternations of pride and shame that characterized his career as a writer. Even toward the end of his career, when it might be thought that the battle was over, his subject is often his struggles and disappointments as a writer, which he makes exciting, fresh, and full of feeling, though in most hands the subject would certainly long since have turned stale.

In his last years, Connolly remained faithful to the favorite places and writers of his youth. Paris and the south of France were the most loved, then Venice and Florence; New York he found electrifying and brilliant. A newer love was for the great animal preserves and forests of Africa. Indeed, travel for him was a temporary cure for all unhappiness, and his travel writings reflect this joyousness. As for writers, Connolly's thoughts were never far from the Latin poets, especially Lucretius, Horace, Virgil, and Propertius; the English and French writers Donne, Dryden, Pope, Johnson, Voltaire, and Diderot of the seventeenth and eighteenth centuries; and the great modernists Eliot, Yeats, Pound, Joyce, and Proust. He continued to write about them whenever the opportunity offered, refining and extending his response, but never fundamentally changing it.

He also returned to the figure of the dandy whenever a book appeared that permitted him to do so. A wonderful passage in his review of Ellen Moers's *The Dandy* (1960) sums up his final judgment of the dandy as a social type. His judgment is complex and gives the stance its due as an aesthetic and moral position, one in which he himself participates.

Eternal inferiority of the dandy—that is my regretted conclusion; for, being committed to clothes and externals, he is committed to stupidity and physical ageing; spiritually opaque, he reigns for ten years and decays for forty more, while mind and body rust. The dandy is but the larval form of the bore.

(*The Evening Colonnade*, "The Dandy: 2")

The last essay in *The Evening Colonnade*, which came out shortly before Connolly's death, is titled "A Voice from the Dead?" Logan Pearsall Smith, who died in 1946, is telephoning from the beyond. He wants Connolly to find out which of his books is earning the biggest literary reputation. He has also, in the next life, written an essay: "Three Forgotten Aphorists: Joubert, Vauvenargues, Amiel." He wants Connolly to get the essay published. Unsure whether he is talking to a ghost or a figment of his own imagination, Connolly says, "Well, then, nobody reads you, all your books are equally dead. . . . Nor in this country is there any editor to print *Three Forgotten Aphorists,* and you'd better add a fourth one, yourself; you had a pretty good life between your library and the dividends

from the glass factory—what more do you want?" Logan Pearsall Smith takes his revenge by saying:

Writers die three times; first there is the bodily death which I will not go into, then the death of the personality as it becomes gradually distorted in the memory of the survivors, belittled by the littleness of the living, caricatured as you have caricatured me—then there is the death of their work as form and meaning evaporate like the frescoes on an Etruscan tomb. I'll give you a chime of words—*Qui nunc jacet horrida pulvis*—who's now reduced to filthy dust—first me and soon you—*qui nunc jacet horrida pulvis.*

I felt a chill wind of empty desolation. "It's not true!"

"All right. If it's not true, then you have offended an immortal spirit. You fell into my neat little trap to find out what you thought of me—and now I shall make you suffer—oh, in a hundred little ways. *Sunt aliquid manes:* A ghost is quite something."

The telephone rang. As far as I know it is still ringing.

This spiteful and mutually disappointing interchange between Connolly and his literary father is full of echoes of the last actual conversation between Connolly and Pearsall Smith. It was a telephone conversation that took place a day before the latter's death on 2 March 1946, at the age of eighty. Smith had just read *Animal Farm* and wanted to know all about Orwell. Connolly cut him off, saying he would tell about Orwell the next day. Before Connolly hung up, Pearsall Smith said that Orwell "beat the lot of you" (quoted in Shelden, p. 151). Connolly's farewell to Pearsall Smith, and to his readers, is a piece of dark comedy in which the writer, his ego battered but still enormous, insults his literary father and tries to fight off his prophecy of approaching oblivion. The last words are an oblique, despairing crying out for fame, while at the same time mocking that cry.

An unfinished novel of this period, *Shade Those Laurels,* was published in book form for the first time by Panthcon in New York in 1990, with an ending written by Peter Levi. The novel is written in the form of a murder mystery, but that is not its chief interest. In the *London Review of Books* Frank Kermode writes:

[Levi] notes that book's chief reason for existence was to accommodate a huge set-piece about a dinner party. . . . The table-talk is wonderfully *recherché* and mostly about French 19th-century literature. . . . Peter Levi has a good try at keeping up the tone—"High above my head the moon melted in *beurre blanc* among vestigial points of fire"—but it was certainly closing time in this particular garden of the West, and Levi's job was less a matter of tending the plants than of locking the gate.

(24 January 1991, pp. 20, 22)

This fragment of a novel shows no advance in construction or dramatic interest over *The Rock Pool*, written more than thirty years earlier. Connolly's talents had not grown more suited to the novel form with the passage of time. The marks of struggle and unfulfilled intentions are often evident, and the inference is strong that Connolly's sufferings as a writer were very real.

But his failure he also transmuted into success. As David Pryce-Jones, the editor of Connolly's *Journal and Memoir*, says, "The depiction of himself as some sort of royal failure was the foundation of his success." Speaking of Connolly's self-portraiture, he says, "This was surely a complicated parody of someone with the same name as himself whose brilliant new book each year set the whole world talking. Playing the leading part in this comedy of his own devising, he was imitating failure. . . . In the guises of dandy, dilettante, glutton, stoic, cynic, clown, Milord, he made himself a ringmaster personality, uniquely prominent and vulnerable" (*Journal and Memoir*, pp. 11–13). What he hid from view behind this persona were the craft, the scholarly thoroughness, and the tenacity that kept him going as a writer for forty years. Beneath the sparkling, theatrical "failure" was the hardworking, successful professional writer who met hundreds of deadlines on time with well-thought-out and polished work. Like the schoolboy he had been at St. Cyprian's, he pretended to be a brilliant idler and worked hard in secret.

CONCLUSION

CONNOLLY made much of his longing to create a great mirror of the world in the form of a big novel that would make him one of the artist-heroes of the twentieth century. That gift was denied him. Fortunately, he did not neglect to fabricate those small mirrors that catch sharp images here, there, and everywhere, giving to us a vivid picture of moments of direct experience or of excitement in reading—fresh, strong, and unexpected.

His best writing was deeply rooted in his personality. Connolly often said of himself that he lived only in discrete moments, rapidly alternating pleasure, guilt, anxiety, fantasy, boredom, or fascination; in these moments he was usually longing for other moments, or loves, or books, more perfect than the one he was in. The intensity of his moments formed the temperamental basis for the short pieces he did best; his longing always for elsewhere or some other to transcend the present moment has affinities with his longing to create the unifying architecture of a great novel that would tie all these intense moments together. This unfulfilled longing for unity endows his work with a poetic sheen of melancholy irony and rueful wit. He thought the discords of his temperament disabled him as a writer, but the reverse is actually the case. His intensity in the moment and his longing for an absent wholeness combined to create his unique combination of high spirits and despondency, romantic hedonism and ironic skepticism.

SELECTED BIBLIOGRAPHY

I. NOVELS AND ESSAYS. *The Rock Pool* (Paris and New York, 1936; rev. ed., London, 1947; Norfolk, Conn., 1948); *Enemies of Promise* (London, 1938; Boston, 1939; rev. ed., London, 1948; New York, 1949); *The Unquiet Grave: A Word Cycle by Palinurus* (London, 1944; rev. and enl. eds. New York and London, 1945, 1950); *The Condemned Playground: Essays 1927–1944* (London, 1945; New York, 1946); *Ideas and Places* (London and New York, 1953); *Les Pavillions: French Pavilions of the Eighteenth Century*, with Jerome Zerbe (London and New York, 1962); *Previous Convictions* (London and New York, 1963); *The Modern Movement: One Hundred Key Books from England, France, and America, 1880–1950* (London, 1965; New York, 1966); *The Evening Colonnade* (London, 1973; New York, 1975); *The Selected Essays of Cyril Connolly*, ed. by Peter Quennell (New York, 1984); *Shade Those Laurels*, concluded by Peter Levi (London and New York, 1990).

II. AUTOBIOGRAPHIES. *A Romantic Friendship: The Letters of Cyril Connolly to Noel Blakiston*, ed. by Noel Blakiston (London, 1975); *Cyril Connolly: Journal and Memoir*, ed. by David Pryce-Jones (London, 1983).

III. EDITED BY CONNOLLY. *Horizon Stories* (London, 1943; enl. ed., New York, 1946); *The Golden Horizon* (London, 1953; New York, 1955); *Great English Short Novels* (New York, 1953).

IV. CRITICAL STUDIES. Eric Bentley, ed., *The Importance of* Scrutiny (New York, 1948); Edmund Wilson,

Classics and Commercials: A Literary Chronicle of the Forties (New York, 1950); John Gross, *The Rise and Fall of the Man of Letters* (London, 1969); Robert Hewison, *Under Siege: Literary Life in London, 1939–1945* (London, 1977); Evelyn Waugh, "Present Discontents" and "Palinurus in Never-Never Land," in *A Little Order*, ed. by Donat Gallagher (London, 1977); Stephen Spender, *The Thirties and After: Poetry, Politics, People, 1939–1970* (New York, 1978); Cynthia Ozick, "Cyril Connolly and the Groans of Success," in *New Criterion* 2 (March 1984); J. M. Kertzer, "Cyril Connolly's *The Unquiet Grave:* The Pilot and the Noonday Devil," in *Mosaic* 20 (fall 1987); Barbara Skelton, *Tears Before Bedtime* (London, 1987); Michael Shelden, *Friends of Promise: Cyril Connolly and the World of Horizon* (London and New York, 1989).

CECIL DAY LEWIS
(1904–1972)

Tyrus H. Miller

IN HIS ALMOST fifty years as a poet, essayist, translator, and novelist, Cecil Day Lewis was driven by a powerful sense of responsibility to make the world around him cohere. Ironically, however, this impulse to unify led to conflicts within himself. In his restless search for a single perspective that could bring together poetry, politics, and personal happiness, Day Lewis made of his life a constant work of revision. In his late poem "St. Anthony's Shirt" (from *The Room and Other Poems*, 1965), he depicts the centrality of change in his life, and the self-abnegation that was often the agent and avatar of change in his work:

> A draught of memory whispers I was most
> Purely myself when I became another:
>
> Tending a sick child, groping my way into
> A woman's heart, lost in a poem, a cause,
> I touched the marrow of my being, unbared
> Through self-oblivion. Nothing remains so true
> As the outgoingness. This moving house
> Is home, and my home, only when it's shared.
>
> (p. 606)[1]

In poem after poem, Day Lewis sought to connect his writing to the constant changes in his own life and to the background of history in which that life was embedded.

Day Lewis came to understand the very mission of poetry as helping people live in and through a history that might otherwise prove debilitating to them. Thus, in his wartime poem "The Image" (in *Word over All*, 1943), he likened the poem to Perseus' shield, a mirror in which to view the Medusa's gaze of history, and thus paradoxically a means of preserving change against

---

[1] Unless otherwise noted, all poems quoted in this essay are from *The Complete Poems of C. Day Lewis* (London and Stanford, Calif., 1992).

change's own violence, a way to look upon history and not be turned to stone:

> Now, in a day of monsters, a desert of abject stone
> Whose outward terrors paralyse the will,
> Look to that gleaming circle until it have revealed you.
>
> The glare of death transmuted to your own
> Measure, scaled-down to a possible figure the sum of ill.
> Let the shield take that image, the image shield you.
>
> (p. 328)

As this poem suggests, Day Lewis derives his inspiration from the tension between a lyric poetry that can suspend change, fixing it in tropes and figures, and an ever-renewed mutability, which may at any moment blast through poetry's defensive shield. Language forms the arena of this struggle; individual words, its implements. In the poem, the poet momentarily forgets himself, throws himself into the fray, stakes himself on the danger of a glance at the historical monster or into his lover's eyes. To the poet who commits himself to words in the struggle to subdue history, the poem returns an image with a significance broader and more enduring than his limited personal life. Day Lewis portrays the poet as resisting history in his very engagement with it: facing history, as it were, by looking away. Language forms his shield, and his gaze is directed only at the poem's words, which stand between the poet and the outer world. The finished poem is a kind of stigma left behind by the poet's heroic resistance, a figure etched into the surface of language.

Looked at more closely, however, "The Image" also comments on its own indirection in facing the poet's dilemmas in the present age of historical "monsters." For as a poem describing the present task of poetry, it represents that task "poetically," through mythology. This poem appeared, significantly, in 1943, at the midpoint of Day Lewis' life and after his retreat from a serious engagement with communism. Its heroic tone retains the essence of his earlier conception of the poet, which likewise gave lyric poetry a decisive historical role to play. The difference lies, however, in Day Lewis' particular choice of the myth underlying the poet's heroism and the social content implied in this choice.

In his poetry of the 1930s, Day Lewis' animating myth was the hope for change and fulfillment embodied by such symbols as the newborn child and the "magnetic mountain." In communism, he saw the means by which these symbols might be made flesh and brought to reality in history. In "The Image," in contrast, he returns to classical myth, implicitly acknowledging that the ability to continue writing lyric poetry in his time would be paid for by a loss of actuality, a retreat into outmoded fiction. Yet Day Lewis' Perseus myth is not completely devoid of historical content. This content is, however, not to be found in Greece, but rather in the educational system of Great Britain: the classical humanist curriculum that formed a fundamental pillar of class distinction in Day Lewis' youth. In his retreat from commitment, Day Lewis recast poetic heroism in the nostalgic, politically conservative mold of British public school and Oxbridge culture. "The Image" may thus be understood as an early sign, later often confirmed, of Day Lewis' accommodation to a social system he had once revolted against.

In the course of his life, Day Lewis learned to derive his literary identity from the scars and setbacks incurred in the interminable agon of poetry and change. His career ran a wide gamut of roles, from the Oxford undergraduate romantic of the mid-1920s to the Audenesque political writer of the 1930s; to the chastened, aging poet-scholar of the postwar years; to the stately poet laureate of his final years. Intersecting with his often-abrupt changes of role are the diverse styles he employed in his writing. His stylistic mobility appears above all in his varying diction and betrays his evident debt to a number of literary predecessors and contemporaries: Donne, Marvell, Wordsworth, Keats, Clare, Yeats, Hardy, Frost, Eliot, Auden, and Thomas, among others.

Day Lewis' generosity in paying tribute to those who influenced him, and his many shifts in persona, have led some critics to dismiss his work as lacking authentic personality or "voice." While his weaker poems admit to the justice of this remark, Day Lewis' best works explicitly reflect on the poet's own divisions and indecisions in the face of a complex history. In them, the poet discovers in his very lack of "single-mindedness" the essential problem his poetry confronts.

LIFE

CECIL Day Lewis was born on 27 April 1904 at Ballintubbert, Queen's County, Ireland. Throughout his life he cherished his Anglo-Irish heritage and even devoted his last published book, *The Whispering Roots* (1970), to the landscape and history of his country of birth. His father, Frank Cecil Day Lewis, studied for holy orders at Trinity College, Dublin, and took a divinity degree in 1900, a year later becoming a priest in the Church of Ireland. His mother, Kathleen Squires, the daughter of a civil servant, died when Cecil was four. He was brought up by his father and his mother's sister Agnes Olive Squires, nicknamed "Knos."

This family circumstance played a crucial role in forming Cecil emotionally. As an only child, he developed an extraordinarily close, and later fraught, relationship with his father. In his 1960 autobiography, *The Buried Day*, Day Lewis describes how, after his mother's death, he became almost a surrogate mate for his father: "During the years immediately after my mother's death, he sought to be both father and mother to me, while I for my part was something more to him than his loved and only child. I was a receptacle for the love also which he had given my mother, the basket in which he would henceforth put all his eggs" (pp. 54–55). In his adolescence and young manhood, Day Lewis would resent his father's inconsistencies, weaknesses, and demanding dependence on the attentions of his son. His mother's absence, he claims, reinforced Day Lewis' natural reluctance to grow up, fixing him in a prolonged immaturity still evident in his political beliefs during the 1930s.

In 1909, Day Lewis' father transferred to a parish in central London, and Cecil entered Wilkie's prep school there in 1912. From age eight until his thirty-first year, when he retired from schoolmastering, academia would be his world. In 1917, at thirteen, he entered Sherborne School in Dorset. There he underwent a dizzying set of new experiences and influences: the classics, schoolboy sex (in his first year, he was considered a victim and not punished), rugby, and the often cruel social conventions of public-school life. In 1918 his father once again moved, to Edwinstowe in north Nottinghamshire, a country village on its way to becoming a mining town. Day Lewis spent his school holidays here, and continued to visit regularly during his university years and in the first several years of his marriage. It was here that Day Lewis developed a sense of division that would surface repeatedly in his poetry: "In more ways than one, I lived at Edwinstowe between two worlds. On the one hand there were the great houses . . . which I entered rarely and always with a sense of *de bas en haut:* on the other lay an equally inaccessible terrain—the world of the miners, farm labourers, railwaymen, small shop-keepers" (*The Buried Day,* p. 131).

In 1923, Day Lewis entered Wadham College, Oxford. There he met some of his closest friends, his fellow students Charles Fenby and Rex Warner, and his classics professor, Maurice Bowra. In 1925 he brought out his first book of poetry, *Beechen Vigil,* garnering some tempered praise from Robert Graves, who had read to Day Lewis' literary circle, The Jawbone (Samson slew the "Philistines" with the jawbone of an ass). It was also at Oxford that Day Lewis got his first taste of political activity. During the General Strike of May 1926, he enlisted to drive cars for the labor unions (while his friend Rex Warner gave aid to the strikebreakers in Hull and Charles Fenby stuck to his books in Oxford). In general, Day Lewis was more absorbed by poetry and intellectual friendships than with the rigors of academic studies, and he proved a lackluster student. He graduated with an undistinguished "third" from the already less prestigious Wadham College, an outcome that virtually ensured he would take up schoolmastering after university.

In his last year at Oxford, Day Lewis met the brilliant young W. H. Auden and received the mixed blessing of Auden's overbrimming personal vitality. Day Lewis and Auden jointly edited the *Oxford Poetry, 1927* anthology and coauthored the introduction, marked both by an abundance of novel ideas and an insufferable pomposity of style. They introduced here several themes that would become virtual leitmotivs for the "Auden generation" poets: a conception of the present public context as a "chaos"; the need to rediscover values and beliefs within a difficult environment; the necessity of struggle, effort, courage, and self-discipline. Auden's powerful personality and poetic style significantly influenced Day Lewis' early books, and a genial rivalry persisted between the two men throughout their lives.

In 1927, Day Lewis became a master at Summer Fields School, Oxford, then moved the following year to a new post at Larchfield School in Helensburgh, Scotland. He also brought out his second volume of poetry, *Country Comets,* and married Mary King, the daughter of a master at Sherborne School. Although in later years their marriage suffered increasing strain from Day Lewis' infidelities and Mary's emotional reticence, at this time it was a source of stability and maturing influence for him. In 1929, Day Lewis published what most critics (like the poet himself) have considered his first mature work: *Transitional Poem,* with a dedication to Rex Warner and tributes to Mary, W. H. Auden, and his psychologist friend Margaret Marshall.

With *Transitional Poem* and a new teaching position, beginning in 1930, at Cheltenham Junior School in Gloucestershire, Day Lewis entered into one of his most concentrated phases of literary work. In the next five years he would produce two more volumes of poetry, *From Feathers to Iron* (1931) and *The Magnetic Mountain* (1933), which with *Transitional Poem* constitute a kind of trilogy. He would also pen a critical apology for his work *A Hope for Poetry* (1934), which, as Stephen Spender has written, comes as close to a manifesto for the 1930s generation as can be found. He published his first novel, the boys' adventure story *Dick Willoughby,* in 1933. And, occasioning the poetic sequence *From Feathers to Iron,* his son and future biographer Sean Francis was born in 1931, followed two years later by a second son, Nicholas Charles.

A turning point in Day Lewis' career came in 1935, when he published the first of an eventual twenty detective novels under the pseudonym Nicholas Blake. *A Question of Proof* met with sufficient success to encourage Day Lewis to support his family as a full-time professional writer. He quit his teaching post at Cheltenham and, out of danger of losing his livelihood for his political beliefs, joined the Communist Party of Britain (he had been a fellow traveler for several years). In the next two years, the period of his active party membership, Day Lewis published the most politically hortatory of his poetic works, *A Time to Dance* (1935) and *Noah and the Waters* (1936); an earnest polemic against Aldous Huxley's pacifism entitled *We're Not Going to Do Nothing* (1936); and numerous political articles for the communist-leaning *Left Review*. In 1937 he edited a symposium volume on "socialism and the cultural revolution," *The Mind in Chains,* which included an introduction by Day Lewis and essays by Rex Warner, Edward Upward, Charles Madge, Anthony Blunt, and others. In 1938 he coedited *Anatomy of Oxford* with his friend Charles Fenby. The appearance of Day Lewis' first "straight" novel, *The Friendly Tree,* occurred in 1936, followed in 1937 by *Starting Point* and in 1939 by *Child of Misfortune*. In 1938, exhausted by political activity, Day Lewis left the Communist party by simply moving to Musbury in Devon (which had no party branch) and withdrawing from contact. While his last volume of poetry from the 1930s, *Overtures to Death* (1938), contains some "political poems" (notably, the Spanish Civil War poems "The Volunteer" and "The Nabara"), Day Lewis' poetry increasingly reflects his change of focus from politics to more traditionally "literary" themes.

Around the outbreak of World War II, Day Lewis' marriage with Mary King entered into what would prove an irreparable decline. Late in 1938, he began seeing the first of a series of lovers, Billie Currall, with whom he had a passionate affair that resulted in an illegitimate child. This relationship was followed a few years later by a nine-year liaison with Rosamond Lehmann, a successful novelist and sister of John Lehmann, the editor of *New Writing,* a left-wing literary journal with which Day Lewis had been closely associated. Day Lewis secured work with the Ministry of Information during the war and was thus able to spend much of his week in London with Rosamond, while traveling back to Musbury to spend weekends and holidays with Mary and the children. He dedicated his much-praised 1943 collection *Word over All* to Lehmann, while his 1953 volume *An Italian Visit* (mostly written in the late 1940s) recounts an idyllic Italian getaway with her.

World War II swept aside the political factionalism of the preceding years, and thereafter Day Lewis found wide acceptance as a major literary figure. In 1940 he published the first of three important translations from Virgil, the Roman poet's loving portrayals of rural life, *The Georgics*. He began reading for the publisher Chatto and Windus in 1946, a post he retained throughout his life (eventually, he became a partner in the firm). He was also tapped to deliver the 1946 Clark Lectures at Cambridge, a series of six talks published in 1947 as *The Poetic Image*. Finally, in 1948, he published his tenth volume of poetry, the compilation *Poems 1943–1947*.

In 1950, having shortly before met and fallen in love with the actress Jill Balcon, twenty-one years his junior, Day Lewis broke off his long relationship with Rosamond Lehmann and began proceedings to divorce Mary King. He and Balcon were married the following year. They had two children: in 1953 a daughter, Lydia Tasamin, now a documentary filmmaker, and in 1957 a son, Daniel Michael Blake, a renowned screen actor. In 1951, Day Lewis, in a narrow decision over the Christian apologist C. S. Lewis, was appointed professor of poetry at Oxford, obliging him to deliver three lectures per year for a five-year term. During the 1950s he brought out *An Italian Visit,* withdrawn from publication until 1953 on Rosamond Lehmann's request, as well as a new volume entitled *Pegasus* (1957). On a BBC commission, Day Lewis translated Virgil's *Aeneid* (1952), and he was active throughout the 1950s in a variety of literary organizations and committees. He also added six new titles to the Nicholas Blake corpus of detective novels.

By the 1960s, Day Lewis was a figurehead of the literary establishment, although his reputation as a poet had suffered decline among critics. He published two new volumes of poetry, *The Gate* (1962) and *The Room* (1965); a translation of Virgil's *Eclogues* (1963); and five new Nicholas Blake novels. In 1964 he delivered the prestigious Charles Eliot Norton Lectures at Harvard, which were published as *The Lyric Impulse* the following year. In 1965 he became a "companion of literature" in the Royal Society of Literature, and in 1968, after much wrangling, was named poet laureate of Great Britain. With the support of the poet and Hull librarian Philip Larkin, he became in 1968 the first Compton Lecturer in Poetry at Hull University and was awarded an honorary doctorate two years later.

In 1970, Day Lewis brought out the last volume of poetry to appear before his death, *The Whispering Roots*. Day Lewis' final years were marked by sharp contrasts of official honor, acrimonious criticism of his roles as poet laureate and arts council member, and progressively worsening illness. Although much weakened by inoperable pancreatic cancer, he remained active up to the end, filming "A Lasting Joy," a six-part BBC television series on poetry, at his Greenwich house only three months before his death. On 22 May 1972, at the age of sixty-eight, Cecil Day Lewis died in the north London home of Kingsley and Jane Amis.

LITERATURE AND POLITICS IN THE 1930S

ALTHOUGH his career was long and varied, Day Lewis' notoriety and influence were undoubtedly greatest in the 1930s. His name was then obligatorily linked with those of W. H. Auden and Stephen Spender, forming with them a trend-setting triumvirate of left-wing, university-educated poets. This unshakable association laid the ground for Roy Campbell's satire *Talking Bronco* (1946), which compounded Louis MacNeice with Spender, Auden, and Day Lewis to make up the pink poet-monster "MacSpaunday." The "group" character of these poets' work has no doubt been greatly overestimated by both friends and foes. In fact, the links were fairly loose, forged through mutual emulation and regular correspondence rather than through formal affiliation. Nevertheless, the poets themselves acted at times as if the group were a real and effective entity.

Day Lewis lent crucial impetus to the group myth with his 1934 apologia and manifesto, *A Hope for Poetry*. This book self-consciously sought to reveal group features in a small cluster of contemporary poets; to establish the canon of their most cherished forerunners; and to defend the poets' response to the historical situation in which they were living and writing. Day Lewis derives his literary tendency from the heroic "ancestors" Gerard Manley Hopkins, Wilfred Owen, and T. S. Eliot. More suprisingly, he claims its immediate point of departure to be the Scottish maverick poet Hugh MacDiarmid, who had set an example for young, radical poets with his 1931 poem "First Hymn to Lenin." Few critics have followed Day Lewis' account on this point (Samuel Hynes' authoritative study *The Auden Generation* does not even mention MacDiarmid), but his subsequent argument, depicting the 1930s as a "Red Decade" with Auden at its center, has become canonical.

Day Lewis mentions (somewhat stretching the truth) a series of anthologies and works influenced by or sympathetic to communism: "'New Signatures' (1932) showed the beginning of this trend; 'New Country' (1933) contained definitely Communist forms by Auden, Charles Madge, R. E. Warner and others: Spender's 'Poems' and my own 'Magnetic Mountain,' both published in 1933, continued the movement" (*Collected Poems 1929–1933, and A Hope for Poetry*, p. 224).

While fostering the myth of a group mentality, Day Lewis offers a number of acute observations about the poetry of his "generation." Most striking are his attempts to justify the obscurity of poetry written by the "postwar" poets. These poets, he argues, are uncertain of their tradition and their present reading public. To "reestablish communication with the past," the younger poets engage in "ancestor-worship," a "minor miracle of healing" best exemplified by Spender's paean to the heroes of literature, "I think continually of those who were truly great." In his discussion of audience, Day Lewis considers problems of politics, group identity, and collective action. The complexity of contemporary life, he claims, disorients the poet and leaves him on shaky ground. Forced to improvise his values and the community in which they may be effective, he inevitably directs his work to his closest friends and associates. From this starting point, however, the poet moves outward, learning to communicate his newly invented values to an ever broader circle of readers, and in the process, revolutionizes society. Exploitation and domination must be replaced by love (one hears echoes of both Freud and D. H. Lawrence in Day Lewis' romantic anticapitalism):

We shall not begin to understand post-war poetry until we realise that the poet is appealing above all for the creation of a society in which the real and living contact between man and man may again become possible. That is why, speaking from the living unit of himself and his friends, he appeals for the contraction of the social group to a size at which human contact may again be established and demands the destruction of all impediments to love.

(p. 206)

A Hope for Poetry and his later polemical and publicistic writing for the *Left Review* made Day Lewis a lightning rod for criticism, both from the literary Right and from fellow communists. By

1936 (as Samuel Hynes has suggested) Day Lewis had become the exemplary communist poet, representing the political aspirations and illusions of his generation more purely than the mischievous Auden or the incorrigibly liberal Spender. A brief look at three critiques of Day Lewis, written from radically different political perspectives, will help illustrate his centrality to the literary political debates of the 1930s, a pivotal role today too often underestimated.

Julian Bell, a moderate socialist and the son of the Bloomsbury couple Clive and Vanessa Bell, wrote a blistering open letter to Day Lewis on "The Proletariat and Poetry." Bell was disturbed by what he saw as the communist fellow traveler's abdication of his social responsibility to govern, in favor of an irrational noble savage myth of the working class. Taking Day Lewis as "the representative of a contemporary movement in politics and literature," and his writing as "the most important poetry, and the most honourable statement of a position, that your movement has yet produced" (Bell, p. 306), Bell goes on to attack him for his romantic view of the proletariat, his masochistic anti-intellectualism, and his failure to take seriously the real implications of communist ideology (ruthless, bloody civil war). As a counterprogram to communist affiliation, Bell recommends the conscious organization of intellectuals as a class, which may then make political alliances that truly foster its social interests and renew its fading commitment to reason and good sense.

The most serious criticism of Day Lewis from the Far Left appears in the concluding chapter of Christopher Caudwell's *Illusion and Reality*, published shortly after Caudwell's death in Spain in 1937. Caudwell writes perceptively about the troubled alliance a bourgeois artist like Day Lewis makes with the communist movement. In Caudwell's view, such a poet is put into an intolerably divided position:

All his proletarian aspirations gather at one pole, all his bourgeois art at the other. . . . His proletarian living bursts into his art in the form of crude and grotesque scraps of Marxist phraseology and the mechanical application of the living proletarian theory. . . . His bourgeois art bursts into his proletarian living in the form of extraordinary and quite unnecessary outbursts of bourgeois "independence" and indiscipline. . . . It leads to an unconscious dishonesty in his art—as of a man exploiting the revolution to his own ends.

(p. 285)

At the height of Day Lewis' public commitment to communism, Caudwell seems all but to predict the retreat from politics that would soon follow.

In 1939, finally, Day Lewis was battered in print by Harry Kemp and Laura Riding (with further strong-arms provided by Robert Graves and Alan Hodge) in their jointly authored blast *The Left Heresy in Literature and Life*. Although this work could properly be described as antipolitical, it expresses sympathy with conservatism, because, in the authors' view, conservatives do not universalize politics as leftists do. More important than the book's manifest political allegiances, however, is its unyielding defense of the autonomy of poetry and poetic thinking. In this respect, it represents an all-out, last-ditch resistance by hard-core modernists to a "heretical" invasion of poetry by politics. As their criticism of Day Lewis' poem "The Conflict" (in *A Time to Dance*, 1935) reveals, the crucial stake in this battle was the relation, if any, between the writer and the reading public. Day Lewis' relation to his readers, they claim, is pathological, paid on both sides by narrow-mindedness and coercion:

Day Lewis's poem is a threat passed on to others by one who has himself been bullied into Left politics. The poem is, as it were, a last poem by some one about to turn militant Left; and that should logically be the end of him as a poet. But, the sacrifice of the poet to political exigency must be repeated, because it is important to have some one constantly on the point of being converted—he may bring others with him. That should be the end of them as poem-readers. They are now equipped to bully poets into writing bullying battlecries.

(p. 99)

The only solution, the authors assert, is to step out of this vicious circle of writer and reader, in order to reaffirm one's commitment to poetry, untainted by political suasion. In fact, by the time *The Left Heresy* appeared, Day Lewis had already taken precisely this step, from politics toward pure poetry, of his own volition.

EARLY POETRY

DAY Lewis' first two books, *Beechen Vigil* (1925) and *Country Comets* (1928), could best be described as juvenilia, valuable only for their hints of later developments in his poetry. The first book is replete with nymphs, minstrelsy, veils, "hands rose-petal frail," quests, knights, lances, swords, "rose-lamped gardens," fountains, secret altars, and other such trappings of Romantic and Pre-Raphaelite medievalism. Only in a few places do portents of the later writing break through these mists of Avalon, as in "Beechen Vigil," the last lines of which anticipate Day Lewis' later use of landscapes as symbols of historical destiny:

> Shadow and sunset, leaf and fire
> Have sung together a rune miraculous
> To heal our doubts and blind desire.
>
> What though beyond a thousand years
> Stands the full pattern? It is enough that now
> Our purpose strides amid the stars.
>
> (p. 6)

Day Lewis evokes a future goal demanding present sacrifice, perhaps without perceptible reward in the present. Yet there is no question here of that goal's being political; there is only a vaguely intimated "purpose," someday to be fulfilled. Such passages suggest the political flexibility of Day Lewis' stock of poetic figures. Derived from romantic poetry, they draw out the political radicalism latent in Shelley's skyborne longing, Keats's aestheticized classicism, and Wordsworth's moral sense of landscape. Yet as Day Lewis' political interests waned, they could easily relax into a highly personal lyricism with little or no evident political content.

Country Comets, published three years later, offers ample evidence that by the mid-1920s Day Lewis had discovered the poetry of William Butler Yeats. Although the writing in this volume is no less derivative than that of *Beechen Vigil*, Yeats was a stringent and up-to-date master, brilliantly successful at mediating public and private concerns in poetry. Day Lewis' second book benefited greatly from his model's tonal range and forceful economy of diction. In "Retrospect: From a Street in Chelsea," one can hear the young poet skillfully mimicking the syntax of Yeats's ironic reversals:

> The child of fancy erring unreproved,
> Conceived in the hour when she and I almost
> Forgot we were not lovers, and almost loved.
>
> (p. 42)

Likewise, Yeats's "rag-and-bone shop" mode, with its mixture of stately and vulgar tones, offered its antidote to the fairy-wings of fancy marring Day Lewis' earliest poems:

> Disgruntled fools, you would think yourselves
> Fortunate, did you guess how soon
> Love, its Olympian discords vanished,
> Becomes a barrel-organ tune.
>
> (p. 43)

Yet *Country Comets* remains largely the siftings of a notebook, more the record of a poetic apprenticeship than a mature work. Day Lewis' most authentic emotions in this book appear to be self-doubt and the desire to emulate great poets. These impulses animate the best writing here, perhaps unwittingly. By contrast, the intentional "center" of the book, the perilous love of the poet for his lady, seems mawkish and contrived. Worst of all is when Day Lewis tries to imitate Yeats's Maud Gonne poems and render epic his troubles in love:

> Ravish divinity
> If you can, Actaeon.
> Never just play the spy.
>
> (p. 54)

Day Lewis concludes his book with a pompous quote from Dante's *Inferno*, canto 5, referring those in the know to the amorous readers Paolo and Francesca, who yielded to their passions and "read no more that day." Day Lewis' reader hardly knows how to respond to the poet's coy insinuation of "success" with his lady: whether like Dante, to swoon with chagrin, or like a schoolboy pal, to wink knowingly at this hesitant "ravisher of Artemis."

TRANSITIONAL POEM *AND THE 1930S*

Transitional Poem (1929) is Day Lewis' first major accomplishment and remains among his best books. While his emulation of other poets is still in evidence, the writing is more fluent and controlled than in the earlier work. Throughout he exhibits an intuitive, "figurative" sense of rhythm, as with the seventh poem's evocative use of three-stress lines with periodically appearing five-stress lines:

(So the antique balloon
Wobbles with no defence
Against the void but a grapnel that hops and ploughs
Through the landscape of sense.)

(p. 65)

More important, however, Day Lewis employed for the first time the sequential form that would characterize some of his best later work as well: *From Feathers to Iron* (1931), *The Magnetic Mountain* (1933), "Overtures to Death" (1938), "O Dreams, O Destinations" (in *Word over All*, 1943), and *An Italian Visit* (1953). The inspiration for this form was obviously the middle and later Yeats, Ezra Pound's *Hugh Selwyn Mauberley*, and above all, T. S. Eliot's *The Waste Land*. Like Eliot, Day Lewis equips his poem with notes to point out the allusions. And in keeping with the current symbolic interpretations of *The Waste Land*, Day Lewis provides a thematic summary of his own "quest" in *Transitional Poem*: "The central theme of this poem is the single mind. The poem is divided into four parts, which essentially represent four phases of personal experience in the pursuit of single-mindedness: it will be seen that a transition is intended from one part to the next such as implies a certain spiritual progress and a consequent shifting of aspect" (p. 99).

The individual sections, he goes on to explain, correspond to the metaphysical, ethical, and psychological aspects of the unified mind, followed by a final "attempt to relate the poetic impulse with the experience as a whole." The poems themselves do not clearly communicate this design, which asserts a stronger unity than the sequence really achieves. Still, the broad shifts of mood are apparent, and the sections cohere emotionally, even where there is no evident symbolic unity. The sequence is composed of thirty-four untitled, numbered poems, which are divided into four parts; each of the parts are prefaced with epigraphs (from Maximian, Whitman, Melville, and Auden, respectively). The first part opposes the ordering force of the mind against external chaos and change:

For the mind must cope with
All elements or none—
Bask in dust along with weevils
Or criticise the sun.

(p. 60)

Day Lewis asserts here the necessity of a radical and holistic vision against insect-like passivity and smallness (perhaps implying a narrowly liberal, empiricist, or domestic mentality). In the second part, in contrast, images of renunciation counter the forceful assertions of the previous section, as the poet turns from the sublime battle of the mind against chaos to the humble particulars to be found in nature and everyday life:

There's nothing but to recant
Ambition, and be content
Like the poor child at play
To find a holiday
In the sticks and mud
Of a familiar road.

(p. 69)

The poet's attempt to impose design on a recalcitrant world must necessarily fail. Yet so too founders the attempt to curb the mind's transcendence of the particular:

I am no English lawn
To build a smooth tradition
Out of Time's recession
And centuries of dew . . .

(p. 71)

The poet must strive to keep this opposition between particularity and transcendence in play, to see failure and loss not as defeat, but as the signs of an ungraspable yet worthy goal:

So I, perhaps,
Am neither mole nor mantis;
I see the constellations,
But by their gaps.

(p. 72)

The acceptance of discontinuity in experience, figured in the very gaps between the poems in sequence, allows a cosmic rhythm or "ideal tone" to emerge: "a Messiah sprig of certitude— / Promise of ground below the sprawling flood" (p. 73). In an attentive passivity akin to Keats's "negative capability," the poet opens himself to the dynamic, organic truth discernible in nature itself:

Why must I then unleash my brain
To sweat after some revelation
Behind the rose, heedless if truth maintain
On the rose-bloom her station?

(pp. 76–77)

122

The latter two parts of the poem grapple further with the problems of passivity and activity, submission and rebellion, set out in the first two parts. In a psychological acute passage, prophetic of his later political apostasy, Day Lewis reveals the paradox of his rebellion, which is motivated primarily by the void of authority he senses:

> Rebel alone because I
> Could not be slave enough.
>
> (p. 79)

Rebellion is for him an externally imposed state and would cease if legitimate authority could be found or instituted. At this moment, however, Day Lewis' rebellion is not so much political as moral, particularly in the realm of sexuality. He represents sensual life as more moral trial than physical pleasure: a kind of dark night of the body from which the soul may emerge purified on the other side. Sexual life is mortifying, but for that very reason, it throws a poetic light upon everything, the transfiguring light of death:

> Baring my skin to every bruise
> Love gives, I'll love the more; since they're but dues
>
> That flesh must pay to bone
> Till each is overthrown.
> There are going to be some changes made to-day.
>
> (p. 97)

In the last poem, Day Lewis closes his sequence on a restful note; the hawk's sublime flight shifts midpoem to the lark's descent by night into silence, which mirrors the action of the poet at the poem's end.

Day Lewis' next collection, *From Feathers to Iron* (1931), again employs the sequential form explored in *Transitional Poem*, while extending the range of diction into the lexicon of industry and science. This new sequence, composed of twenty-nine numbered poems plus an "Epilogue" in the form of a verse letter to W. H. Auden, records the poet's turbulent mood changes in the nine months before the birth of his first child. The restricted time frame helps to unify the sequence somewhat; a spare narrative involving man, wife, and unborn child can be obscurely glimpsed in many of the poems. Never-

theless, as in *Transitional Poem*, the unifying focus is the poet's emotional life, and the conflicts are lyrically transfigured rather than narratively recounted. This sequence is generally less effective than *Transitional Poem*, because Day Lewis seems uncertain how closely to refer to the concrete situation occasioning the poem. Many of the poems exhibit strong emotion, but in a kind of empty space, their gestures cut free of context. While this technique can be effective (one thinks of, for example, the evocatively sinister "situations" in Eliot's "Sweeney Among the Nightingales" and "Gerontion"), the lack of context renders *From Feathers to Iron* "Hamletish," histrionically self-absorbed.

In the first poem of *From Feathers to Iron*, Day Lewis characterizes his new sequence as an intensive development and exploitation of earlier "discoveries." In the language of technology and land reclamation, he announces his personal poetic vocation, which has emerged at the meeting point of pasture and machine:

> Now our research is done, measured the shadow,
> The plains mapped out, the hills a natural boundary.
> Such and such is our country. There remains to
> Plough up the meadowland, reclaim the marshes.
>
> (p. 106)

This passage typifies the rhetorical character of much of the poem, both in its appeal to some undetermined collective ("*our* research," "*our* country") and in its hortatory tone. Two major figurative patterns alternate from poem to poem. Most striking, and new to Day Lewis' writing, are hybrid nature/machine or body/machine images:

> Bodies we have, fabric and frame designed
> To take the stress of love,
> Buoyant on gust, multi-engined.
> Experiment's over . . .
>
> (p. 108)

The intermeshing of the organic and mechanic is redoubled by the clipped, compacted syntax, which mimics the angular movements of a machine. These self-announcedly "modernist" images yield at regular intervals, however, to the second major figurative pattern, the pastoral sententiae that could be taken as Day Lewis' poetic norm throughout his career:

> Speaking from the snow
> The crocus lets me know
> That there is life to come, and go.
> (p. 109)

Day Lewis' forced conjunction of mechanical and pastoral imagery represents a significant swerve from his poetic models and strikes out into new expressive terrain. In poem 14, thus, he provides a counterimage to the natural fertility evoked in Yeats's "Sailing to Byzantium." Day Lewis' version of Yeats's "no country for old men" is a hybrid world of technological, social, and natural productivity:

> Today crowds quicken in a street,
> The fish leaps in the flood:
> Look there, gasometer rises,
> And here bough swells to bud.
> (p. 115)

Similarly, Day Lewis takes up the inheritance of Eliot in historical and political, as well as personal, terms:

> This way the waste land turns
> To arable, and towns
> Are rid of drought.
> (p. 117)

In Marxian fashion, Day Lewis depicts Eliot's "wasteland" impasse as a blockage of human productive forces, which in turn also lays waste to nature. Yet in Day Lewis' poetic cosmos, a sign of natural generativity has appeared, his newborn child, which portends a release of dammed-up energies and a salutary convergence of natural and human powers.

In the latter poems of the sequence, the child becomes the focus of both the constructive and the destructive powers of modern technology. In poem 25, the poet wishes the child "luck," a grace conceived, significantly, as mechanical power:

> Lucky, will have also
> An outward grace to ease
> The axles of your world
> And keep the parts at peace:
>
> Not the waste random stuff
> That stops the gannet's wing;
> I mean, such oil ensures
> A turbine's smooth running.
> (p. 124)

One could restate Day Lewis' notion of "grace" as the ability to be truly at home in modernity. The child embodies Day Lewis' wistful admiration for the "technical" intellectual, organically part of the world of industrial labor and machines; it also occasions doubts about his own role as a "traditional" intellectual, who may at best aid the transition to a new world with no place for his type. In poem 27, Day Lewis presents the verso side of his technophilia, the threat of impersonal mass death by technological warfare:

> Is fighting on the frontier: little leaks through
> Of possible disaster, but one morning
> Shells begin to drop in the capital.
> (p. 126)

The poem ends, however, on a celebratory note. The airman reappears in poem 29, this time not as a bombardier but as the emblem of the poet in the age of modern technology, the skywriter:

> Now shall the airman vertically banking
> Out of the blue write a new sky-sign . . .
> (p. 128)

The message he writes is a joyous one, announcing the new birth (the son) and the birth of the new. As the concluding line of each of the five verses proclaims: "Take a whole holiday in honour of this" (pp. 127–128).

In 1933, Day Lewis published his most thematically and formally ambitious sequence, *The Magnetic Mountain*. Like *Transitional Poem*, it is divided into four sections, made up of individual numbered poems that present different perspectives. Interspersed within the second section appear four poems entitled "First [Second, Third, Fourth] Defendant Speaks"; the poems that follow these speeches respond to and comment on them. Day Lewis employs a similar design in the third section, except it is four "enemies" rather than four "defendants" who speak. In all, the sequence encompasses thirty-six loosely connected lyric poems.

The "magnetic mountain" is the poem's central image, intended to exercise an irresistible symbolic pull on the disparate elements of which the whole is composed. It symbolizes an indubitable source of authority, at present still undiscovered, which could renew both society and poetry after decades of decline. The provenance of this symbol is classical, although Day Lewis presents it in modern garb. Plato, in the *Ion*, had compared the poet's inspiration and the effect of poetry on his audience to a magnetism linking together rings of iron. Day Lewis' image suggests a similar force flowing through his poetry, but it gives Plato's analogy a contemporary political twist. Whereas Plato saw poetry as opposed to reason and therefore suspicious, Day Lewis accepts poetry's emotional force and likens it to the "magnetism" that will bond the masses and intellectuals in political struggle:

> Somewhere beyond the railheads
> Of reason, south or north,
> Lies a magnetic mountain
> Riveting sky to earth.
>
> (p. 136)

The political overtones are reinforced by the multiple resonances of "iron," which connotes modernity, industrial labor, large-scale construction, hardness, and durability. (It is also perhaps not irrelevant that the code name once adopted by a young Georgian communist, "Stalin," means the "man of iron.") Linked to the image of the magnetic mountain are two other central motifs: the poet's "kestrel joy," an up-to-date poetic aviator born of Shelley's and Hopkins' Romantic bird-spirits; and a dimly evoked narrative of journeying beyond known frontiers. These symbolic nodes—mountain, kestrel, and quest—struggle against the ever-threatening enemies of the future, "the temporal princes, fear and pain / Whose borders march with the ice-fields of death" (p. 136).

The second and third sections of the poem, which record the speeches of the "defendants" and "enemies," can be understood as staging a trial. Yet this "trial" is as much a test for those who listen (or read) as an indictment of the speakers: a steeling of the self against the temptations that might lead it astray from its quest for the magnetic mountain. It is necessary to stress the self-reflexive element of the speeches, since many critics have seen in these poems only a stereotyped leftist demonology. What they fail to remark is that these voices come from within the poet himself and represent politically conflictual elements of his own divided personality. Thus, for example, there is little difference between the first defendant's indecision and the romantic dilemmas Day Lewis explored in his earlier poems:

> . . . for I
> Must have life unconditional, or none.
> So, like a willow, all its wood curtailed,
> I stand by the last ditch of narrowing world,
> And stir not, though I see
> Pit-heads encroach or glacier crawl down.
>
> (p. 141)

Similarly, the second defendant is clearly a schoolmaster, Day Lewis' own profession at the time of his writing *The Magnetic Mountain*, and the target is the conformism he himself practices and preaches:

> Our methods are up to date; we teach
> Through head and not by heart,
> Language with gramophones and sex with charts,
> Prophecy by deduction, prayer by numbers.
>
> (p. 144)

Day Lewis' reorganization of poems, originally published in the 1932 anthology *New Signatures*, for publication in *The Magnetic Mountain* offers further evidence for the self-reflexivity of these speeches. Poems 7 and 14 appeared in *New Signatures* in a group of four poems under the title "Satirical Poems"; these two individual poems carried the titles "The Mother Speaks" and "The Wife Speaks," respectively. In *The Magnetic Mountain*, Day Lewis eliminated these titles and identified the speakers only as "first defendant" and "fourth defendant," thus incorporating them into the sequence less as satirical types than as personae in a many-sided psychological drama.

The enemies in the third part, admittedly, are cruder in tone and style, and the poet's attitude toward them more hostile. They are recognizable as social "enemies": perverters of sex, perverters of words (the press), perverters of God (the clergy), and perverters of art (aesthetes). Yet the problem with these poems is only superficially their stereotypical crudity. The more damaging problem is that Day Lewis peremptorily breaks off the psychological dialogue of the second section with an act of symbolic violence, a kind of silencing of all those aspects of himself that do not lead directly to decisive action. The temptation of sex, for example, leads to an almost hysterical act of defense:

> Hands off! The dykes are down.
> This is no time for play.
> Hammer is poised and sickle
> Sharpened. I cannot stay.
>
> (p. 153)

All that time spent tarrying in bedroom and backseat, the poet suggests, might have been spent more usefully distributing leaflets or writing polemical pamphlets. To the present-day reader, the hammer-and-sickle that looms up here seems less a political emblem than a grossly literal image of the castrating superego, a kind of political father figure who says "desist, or else!"

The latter poems of *The Magnetic Mountain* exhibit, above all, the psychological price of authoritarian politics. The poet attacks his own inner states—fear, pain, sexual desire, hesitation, despair—in a spirit of revenge and hatred. They are to be eliminated by violence, both social surgery and emotional lobotomy: "It is now or never, the hour of the knife" (p. 162). The new man is to cast aside everything that resists the attraction of "the magnetic mountain" and discover all value in action. If adhered to with sufficient single-mindedness, Day Lewis implies, action will make all contemplation and inner turmoil disappear like smoke, the mere vapor that it always was anyhow. The new self of action, purged of "bourgeois" emotions, appears with the clarity and power of heavy machinery:

> Out of that dark a new world flowers.
> There in the womb, in the rich veins
> Are tools, dynamos, bridges, towers,
> Your tractors and your travelling-cranes.
>
> (p. 165)

Yet as Day Lewis' one concrete attempt to envisage the future state reveals, this purified dynamo-self is little more than an imaginary resolution to a sexual problem (though not necessarily only Day Lewis' personal one):

Born haters will blast through debris or granite,
Willing work on the permanent ways,
And natural lovers repair the race.
As needle to north, as wheel in wheel turning,
Men shall know their masters and women their need,
Mating and submitting, not divided and defying,
Force shall fertilize, mass shall breed.

> (p. 166)

"Communism" represents here the fantasy of restored male potency, a social order in which all willingly submit to "their masters": women to their men and men to their state. Needless to say, little of Day Lewis' ideal vision would appeal to most readers today. Still worse, however, only a narrow divide separated Day Lewis' poetic utopia from fascist rhetoric of "mating and submitting," of "mass" and "force," of brawny male workers and fertile female "breeders."

The tensions between Day Lewis' politics, poetry, and personal concerns reach their acme in the next two collections, *A Time to Dance* (1935) and *Noah and the Waters* (1936). Both explore the intellectual's divided mind in the present historical situation; both argue that now more than ever, it is necessary to take courage and cast one's lot with the new world in the making. Perhaps the most personal statement of the intellectual's dilemma is found in the former volume, in the poems "The Conflict" and "In Me Two Worlds." These poems are clearly marked by the threat of war, which gives their psychological landscape the features of a World War I trench line:

> Move then with new desires,
> For where we used to build and love
> Is no man's land, and only ghosts can live
> Between two fires.
>
> (p. 184)

> The armies of the dead
> Are trenched within my bones,
> My blood's their semaphore, their wings
> Are watchers overhead.

> Their captains stand at ease
> As on familiar ground,
> The veteran longings of the heart
> Serve them for mercenaries.
>
> (p. 186)

The title poem of *A Time to Dance* is a long elegiac sequence for Day Lewis' friend and fellow schoolmaster, the cricket player L. P. Hedges. The central poem of the sequence narrates Hedges' flight, in a ramshackle airplane, from England to Australia after World War I. Into the memorial poem, Day Lewis successfully weaves a number of key motifs and concerns already introduced separately in earlier lyrics: the need to reinvent the hero in the present day, the analogy of flying and writing, the celebration of technology, and the necessity to decide in favor of the new and uncharted over the safe and traditional. Yet this collection also contains some of his most embarrassing attempts at political statement, as in his much-parodied poem "The Road These Times Must Take" (excised from later editions):

Yes, why do we all, seeing a communist, feel small?
   That small
Catspaw ruffles our calm—how comes it? That touch of
   storm
Brewing, shivers the torches even in this vault? And the
   shame
Unsettles a high esteem? Here it is. There fall
From him shadows of what he is building; bold and
   tall—
For his sun has barely mastered the misted horizon—
   they seem.
Indeed he casts a shadow, as among the dead will some
Living one. It is the future walking to meet us all.

Not only does Day Lewis' poem offer a highly dubious generalization about how "we all" react to the communist and the future he portends. It also reflects a certain masochism of the bourgeois intellectual within the communist movement, which browbeat its fellow travelers with inquiries into their class origins, their tendencies to petty-bourgeois deviationism, and their revisionist temptations. It is, perhaps, this fatal combination of political presumption and abjection that made this poem a magnetic hillock for hostile criticism.

Noah and the Waters did little to correct the impression that Day Lewis' poetry was suffering from his resolve to use it for single-minded political statement. The book, begun as the text for a choral ballet, eventually took on the form of an "everyman" play, dramatizing the need to decide in favor of the new world rather than go down clinging to the old one. Noah represents a Day Lewis–like intellectual, who must decide between the flood (the proletariat and the future) and the three Burgesses (the bourgeois world of the past). The poem suffers from at least two major flaws. The first is its hasty and rather incoherent allegory. In failing to think through the connotations of his symbols, Day Lewis left himself open to the cogent, if nasty, criticism of such opponents as Geoffrey Grigson. In his review of *Noah* in the June/July 1936 issue of *New Verse*, Grigson griped that "it is tactless . . . to make the proletariat an undifferentiated mass of H_2O, a substance which evaporates quickly, takes any shape and has only the force of gravity." Yet perhaps more immediately damaging than its allegorical infelicity is the silliness of much of the poem, which reaches its high-water mark when the flood, in good Marxian fashion, cries out, "Waters of the world, unite!" The poet has either simply lost control of his tone or has intentionally mixed in a schoolboyish

humor, robbing his message of its earnestness and urgency. It is doubtful whether Day Lewis won any new adherents to the cause with *Noah*; he almost certainly lost standing as a poet.

Day Lewis' last volume from the 1930s, *Overtures to Death* (1938), still includes a number of explicitly "political" poems: above all, the Spanish Civil War narrative poem "The Nabara." Nevertheless, this book sounds a more skeptical note than the previous three works, while a few poems allude to the poet's guilt about his retreat from political activity. The title sequence apostrophizes death as "Sir," thus employing, as did Auden in his 1929 poem "Sir, no man's enemy," a Hopkins-like address to a dark, potentially sinister deity. In this sequence, Day Lewis attempts to come to terms with death and to separate its "natural" and "unnatural" avatars:

You are in nature. These are most unnatural.
We shall desire your peace in our own time:
But with those, your free-lance and officious gunmen,
Our war is life itself and shall not fail.
              (p. 280)

As in the earlier works, Day Lewis employs seasonal motifs comparable to Shelley's "west wind" (a natural, renewing force of death and destruction) and brings historical and seasonal change in apposition. In "The Nabara," thus, he personifies freedom as a seasonally migrating bird:

She is bound to earth, yet she flies high as a passage
   bird
To home wherever man's heart with seasonal warmth
   is stirred
              (p. 290)

The antithesis of this soaring spirit is the enemy bomber, which appears in the poems "Bombers" and "Newsreel" to wreak havoc on a populace too long complacent in the face of fascism's advance:

Oh, look at the warplanes! Screaming hysteric treble
In the long power-drive, like gannets they fall steep.
But what are they to trouble—
These silver shadows to trouble your watery, womb-
   deep sleep?
              (p. 270)

Amid this black-and-white moral landscape, however, are the gray areas occupied by such poems as "Regency Houses" and "The Escapist."

In "Regency Houses," Day Lewis explores his suspicion that his generation's impulse to renewal and revolution has recently begun to wane:

> Are we living—we too
> Living extravagant farce
> In the finery of spent passions?
> Is all we do and shall do
> But the glib, habitual breathing
> Of clocks where time means nothing,
> In a condemned mansion?
>
> (p. 272)

"The Escapist" seems more personal in its focus, dealing with his own "escapes," from his Communist party ties and, increasingly, from his marriage to Mary King:

> Before their first reproach could reach his ears,
> He had set up a private court, accepted
> Full responsibility, and passed judgement.
> The man whom later they reviled because
> He would not face their music, was already
> Self-flayed and branded in his heart for ever.
>
> (p. 306)

The subtle interplay of political belief and personal doubt make *Overtures to Death* one of Day Lewis' most poignant books. It retains much of the moral urgency of his earlier works, but avoids their too frequent lapses into bluster and bathos.

THE 1940S

DAY Lewis published two collections in the 1940s, *Word over All* (1943) and *Poems 1943–1947* (1948). These volumes lack the heady enthusiasm of the 1930s collections, but they show Day Lewis at the height of his expressive powers. *Word over All* contains the nine-poem sonnet sequence, "O Dreams, O Destinations," which Day Lewis himself picked out as his finest work. Over the course of this meditation on aging and loss, the poet moves from infancy to maturity, ringing yet another change on his "kestrel joy" bird image:

> Alas, the bird flies blind,
> Hooded by a dark sense of destination:
> Her weight on the glass calm leaves no impression,

> Her home is soon a basketful of wind.
> Travellers, we're fabric of the road we go;
> We settle, but like feathers on time's flow.
>
> (p. 325)

The war poem "Watching Post" also provides an important indication of how the war affected Day Lewis' political outlook. Drawn from Day Lewis' experience as a troop leader in the Home Guard, this poem suggests that the poet had embraced an English patriotism rooted in the feeling for the local landscape and people and in England's long history of defense against foreign invasion. It is a sestina (minus the concluding three lines), and the repeating end words imply its range of themes: invaders, hope, night, valley, watch, countryside. The repetitions enforce the air of watchful attention, as well as the sense of historical continuity; they also imply the gradual turning of fear into reassurance and shared values. In their vigilance and care for their land and friends, the poet and the farmer share a common England:

> for both of us, hope
> Means a harvest from small beginnings, who this night
> While the moon sorts out into shadow and shape our
> valley
> A farmer and a poet, are keeping watch.
>
> (p. 332)

The second volume, *Poems 1943–1947*, collects a number of poems written in tribute to other writers: Emily Brontë, Thomas Hardy, Walter de la Mare, and Edmund Blunden. The remaining poems are self-absorbed meditations on aging, on the collapse of Day Lewis' marriage to Mary King, and the disappointments of commitment. The most shapely poems in this book are the two "portrait" poems, "Sketches for a Self-Portrait," which anticipates his autobiography, *The Buried Day*, and "The Sitting," occasioned by Laurence Gowing's portrait of the poet. The latter poem dramatizes, through the occasion of the portrait, the subtle interplay of imitation and invention in the labor of art:

> O man, O innocent artist
> Who paint me with green of your fields, with amber or
> yellow
> Of love's hair, red of the heart's blood, eyebright blue,
> Conjuring forms and rainbows out of an empty mist—
> Your hand is upon me, as even now you follow
> Along the immortal clue

Threading my veins of emerald, topaz, amethyst,
And know not it ends in you.

(p. 373)

Such moments of equanimity and balance are rare, however. The dark, brooding interiority of "The Neurotic" dominates much of the book:

> This man who turns a phrase and twiddles a glass
> Seems far from that pale muttering magician
> Pent in a vicious circle of dilemmas.
> But could you lift his blue, thick gaze and pass
> Behind, you would walk a stage where endlessly
> Phantoms rehearse unactable tragedy.
>
> . . .
>
> Death mask of a genius unborn:
> Tragic prince of a rejected play:
> Soul of suffering that bequeathed no myth:
> A dark tower and a never-sounded horn.—
> Call him what we will, words cannot ennoble
> This Atlas who fell down under a bubble.

(pp. 400–401)

This poem betrays Day Lewis' long-standing anxiety about his success as a poet, as well as reflecting his periodic bouts of clinical depression. For the neurotic of the poem, the imaginative faculty has run rampant and become artistically sterile. His melancholy thoughts shirk the discipline of words ("words cannot ennoble") and hence represent poetry's antithesis. Yet if the poem's persona can be interpreted as one aspect of Day Lewis' own personality, his skillful presentation of this unfortunate character wins an ironic distance from him. In this sense, the poem becomes the scene of a painful psychic drama: the poet's struggle to defeat the neurotic by a certain "ennobling" of him in words.

Day Lewis wrote most of his next volume, *An Italian Visit*, in 1948 and 1949, although he kept it from publication, on request of his lover Rosamond Lehmann, until 1953. For the first time since the 1930s, Day Lewis returns to the ambitious book-length sequence, in this case of seven parts framed by the poet's departure for and return from Italy. The opening and closing sections are dialogues between "Tom," "Dick," and "Harry," representing different aspects of the poet's personality. Tom is the sensualist, who wants new sensations and experiences; Dick is the classicist and historical enthusiast; Harry is, most nearly, the artist and constructor. Harry provides a kind of synthesis to the partial views of the other two:

> I find the whole in elusive fragments: let one be caught
> And profoundly known—that way, like a skeleton key, the part
> May unlock the intricate whole. What else is the work of art?

(p. 431)

Parts 2, 3, and 4 of the poem offer a mixture of travel commentary and meditations on the self occasioned by the experience of travel. The fifth part is composed of poems about Florentine artworks, written as parodies of Thomas Hardy, W. B. Yeats, Robert Frost, W. H. Auden, and Dylan Thomas. These brilliant pastiches reveal Day Lewis' gift for mimicry. Part 6 is the poignant "Elegy Before Death" for Rosamond Lehmann, one of Day Lewis' most beautiful poems:

> Oh, may my farewell word, may this your elegy
> Written in life blood from a condemned heart
> Be quick and haunting even beyond our day.

(p. 468)

Part 7, "The Homeward Prospect," returns to the inner dialogue of part 1, closing the sequence on a note of gentle self-mockery.

LATER AND POSTHUMOUS POETRY

THE last four volumes published during Day Lewis' lifetime, *Pegasus* (1957), *The Gate* (1962), *The Room* (1965), and *The Whispering Roots* (1970), all contain technically accomplished, though largely uninspired poems. The opening section of *Pegasus*, for example, employs the myths of Pegasus, Psyche, Baucis and Philemon, and Ariadne to explore themes that had occupied Day Lewis in earlier books: the necessity of both effort and failure, the difficulty of spontaneous love, the perils of self-reflection, the value of rootedness and simple virtue, and the need to forgive past wrongs. Yet precisely because these were Day Lewis' central concerns, the classical frame indicates all the more clearly his growing detachment, the routinization of his poetic impulse. If in the past these issues had led him to outstrip traditional means in his urgent search for adequate forms and symbols, his return to myth now suggests a mandarin leisure about his art. These books also bear witness to a creeping political conservatism, particularly in the elegies for Winston Churchill ("Who Goes Home?") and T. S. Eliot ("At East Coker"). The latter poem gives the orthodox, "Anglo-Catholic and monarchist" Eliot of *Four Quartets* the final word on "committed writing":

> Now, supplying
> Our loss with words of comfort, his kind ghost
> Says all that need to be said about committedness:
> Here in East Coker they have crossed
> My heart again—For us there is only the trying
> To learn to use words. The rest is not our business.
>   (p. 693)

These late books are not, however, without high points. *The Gate* contains the charming meditation on "pastoral" labors (both herding and poetry), "Sheepdog Trials in Hyde Park," which records an afternoon spent with Robert Frost. Among its virtues are Day Lewis' observational powers and depth of sympathy with the animals' perspective:

> An abstract game. What can the sheepdog make of such
> Simplified terrain?—no hills, dales, bogs, walls, tracks,
> Only a quarter-mile plain of grass, dumb crowds
> Like crowds on hoardings around it, and behind them
> Traffic or mounds of lovers and children playing.
> Well, the dog is no landscape-fancier; his whole concern
> Is with his master's whistle, and of course
> With the flock—sheep are sheep anywhere for him.
>   (p. 542)

Other distinguished poems from these late volumes include the dramatic monologues "The Disabused" and "Not Proven," and the song sequence "Requiem for the Living" (all from *The Gate*); "The Room," for the Greek poet and diplomat George Seferis; "On Not Saying Everything" (from *The Room*), a lyric distillation of Day Lewis' mature poetics; and the title poem of *The Whispering Roots.*

A volume of *Posthumous Poems* (1979) and a compilation of *Vers d'Occasion* for the 1992 *Complete Poems* have appeared since Day Lewis' death in 1972. The *Vers d'Occasion* provide, amid the poet laureate toss-offs, some unfortunate grotesquerie: the ex-communist's paean to the royal family, "For the Investiture of the Prince of Wales," and still worse, "Then and Now," a poem supporting the conservative *Daily Mail*'s "I'm Backing Britain" campaign, which sought to convince British employees to work extra hours without pay. The *Posthumous Poems* mostly offer paler variations on his already rather blanched late work. For the *Complete Poems*, however, the editors included with the posthumous works Day Lewis' moving deathbed poem "At Lemmons," which captures the poet's final peace at the home of his friends Kingsley and Jane Amis:

> Round me all is amenity, a bloom of
> Magnolia uttering its requiems,
> A climate of acceptance. Very well
> I accept my weakness with my friends'
> Good natures sweetening every day my sick room.
>   (p. 714)

With their unmistakable note of optimism and appreciation, the twenty lines of "At Lemmons" bring to a fitting close Day Lewis' uneven, but long and productive, life in poetry.

NOVELS AND DETECTIVE FICTION

WHILE Day Lewis is best known as a poet, he wrote three fairly well received novels in the late 1930s, as well as two adventure books for boys. In addition, between 1935 and 1968, he published twenty highly successful detective novels under the pseudonym Nicholas Blake.

His "serious" novels, *The Friendly Tree* (1936), *Starting Point* (1937), and *Child of Misfortune* (1939), all draw on autobiographical material to portray characters making crucial political and personal decisions in the historical situation of 1930s England and Ireland. *Starting Point,* which traces the intersecting paths of a group of Oxford friends from school up to the Spanish Civil War, best exhibits Day Lewis' strengths and faults as a novelist. Here, as in his detective novels, he is a skillful writer of dialogue, and the finely drawn conversations he stages in dorm rooms, at parties, and over dinner tables suggest with great economy the emotional subtleties of his characters. On the other hand, his plotting is weak and melodramatic (in a climactic scene, the snobbish yet tormented Theodore accidentally shoots his unloving mother, then himself). And between Day Lewis' political designs and the overbearing influence of D. H. Lawrence, the book is also full of moralizing oration, sometimes delivered to a group of characters and at other times to the private audience of the "speaker's" own thoughts. Presumably Day

Lewis did not intend for his characters to become mere puppets of a political argument (as did, for instance, Wyndham Lewis in his satirical novels of the 1930s), but in places they unwittingly tend toward this sort of abstraction. It is perhaps this latter fault that led Day Lewis later to reject his attempts at serious novel writing, on the grounds that it was not until some years later that he really "became interested in people."

His popular "Nicholas Blake" detective novels, in contrast, benefit greatly from their author's freedom from obligation to deliver a message to his readers. Day Lewis began writing them in the 1930s to allow himself to quit schoolmastering and devote himself to his political and literary labors. *A Question of Proof*, his first, appeared in 1935, and he wrote them steadily after that into his last years. These novels are, in fact, highly topical; Day Lewis weaves much historical, political, and autobiographical detail in among the stock generic features of the detective plot. The widely read communist journalist and theorist John Strachey went so far as to say that between Day Lewis and Nicholas Blake, the detective novelist was the better writer!

For many of these books, the secret of success was their delightful pairing of detectives, the irrepressible amateur sleuth Nigel Strangeways (a cross between Sherlock Holmes and the young W. H. Auden) with the grumbly, slow-moving but cunning Detective-Inspector Blount of Scotland Yard. Most interesting among these novels is, perhaps, *Minute for Murder* (1947), set in the Ministry of Information (where Day Lewis had served during World War II) just after the German surrender. In the course of their investigations of a murder, Strangeways and Blount take the reader on a revealing tour of the activities, personnel, and institutional politics of a modern propaganda agency. Even when saddled with ludicrous plots like that of *The Case of the Abominable Snowman* (1941), which has as its underlying premise a childhood "addiction" to marijuana, with its sexually corrupting property of inducing "erotic hallucinations," Day Lewis' quirky detectives keep these novels lively and entertaining.

CONCLUSION

DAY Lewis' literary reputation fluctuated a great deal during his lifetime and at present seems to be at an undeserved nadir. His regular exclusion from anthologies of British verse and from critical studies centered around W. H. Auden appears motivated as much by political aversion (whether for his communist associations or his role as poet laureate) as by any unbiased assessment of his historical and literary significance. One desirable outcome of the reassessment of 1930s writing now in progress among critics and historians might be to clear away the standing prejudice against Day Lewis' poetry, thus allowing a more impartial picture of his achievement to emerge.

Inevitably, Day Lewis' earlier poetry will be measured against that of Robert Graves, W. H. Auden, Stephen Spender, William Empson, Louis MacNeice, and Dylan Thomas. Considered in this setting, Day Lewis stands as one of the most ambitious, if not always the most consummately successful, of British poets in the 1930s and 1940s. His later work, admittedly, seems less central to the times and suffers by comparison to the poetry of younger traditional poets like Geoffrey Hill and Seamus Heaney, or to Basil Bunting, especially Bunting's late masterpiece, *Briggflats*. But Day Lewis negotiated with grace the passing of his visionary gleam, generously supporting younger peers and continuing to write distinguished verse into his last years. One might, in light of this, grant him that leniency he requested for all poets of his time. As he wrote in *The Lyric Impulse*: "Perhaps we go too far today in demanding that a poet should always be working at his top pressure—in dismissing such of his verse as is 'merely' graceful, accomplished, written from a relatively superficial level: but that is by the way" (p. 15).

SELECTED BIBLIOGRAPHY

I. BIBLIOGRAPHY. Geoffrey Handley-Taylor and Timothy D'Arch Smith, *C. Day Lewis: The Poet Laureate* (London and Chicago, 1968).

II. COLLECTED POEMS. *Collected Poems, 1929–1933* (London, 1935); *Collected Poems 1929–1933, and A Hope for Poetry* (New York, 1935); *Selected Poems* (London, 1940); *Collected Poems 1929–1936* (London, 1948); *Selected Poems* (Harmondsworth, Eng., 1951); *Collected Poems* (London, 1954); *Selections from His Poetry* (London, 1967); *Poems of C. Day Lewis, 1925–1972*, ed. by Ian Parsons (London, 1977); *The Complete Poems of C. Day Lewis* (London and Stanford, Calif., 1992).

III. SEPARATE WORKS. *Beechen Vigil and Other Poems* (London, 1925); *Country Comets* (London, 1928), poems; *Transitional Poem* (London, 1929).

From Feathers to Iron (London, 1931), poems; *Dick Willoughby* (Oxford, Eng., 1933), boys' adventure story; *The Magnetic Mountain* (London, 1933), poems; *A Time to Dance* (London, 1935), poems; *The Friendly Tree* (London, 1936), novel; *Noah and the Waters* (London, 1936), poems; *Starting Point* (London, 1937), novel; *Overtures to Death and Other Poems* (London, 1938); *Child of Misfortune* (London, 1939), novel.

Poems in Wartime (London, 1940); *Word over All* (London, 1943), poems; *The Otterbury Incident* (London, 1948), boys' adventure story; *Poems 1943–1947* (London, 1948).

An Italian Visit (London, 1953), poems; *Pegasus and Other Poems* (London, 1957); *The Buried Day* (London, 1960), autobiography; *The Gate and Other Poems* (London, 1962); *Requiem for the Living* (New York, 1964), poems; *The Room and Other Poems* (London, 1965); *The Whispering Roots* (London, 1970); *Posthumous Poems* (Andoversford, Eng., 1979).

IV. LITERARY CRITICISM AND NONFICTION. *A Hope for Poetry* (Oxford, Eng., 1934; postscript, 1936); *Revolution in Writing* (London, 1935); *Imagination and Thinking* (London, 1936); *We're Not Going to Do Nothing* (London, 1936); *Poetry for You* (London, 1944); *The Colloquial Element in English Poetry* (Newcastle upon Tyne, Eng., 1947); *Enjoying Poetry* (London, 1947); *The Poetic Image* (London, 1947); *The Poet's Task* (Oxford, Eng., 1951); *The Grand Manner* (Nottingham, Eng., 1952); *The Lyrical Poetry of Thomas Hardy* (London, 1953); *Notable Images of Virtue* (Toronto, 1954); *The Poet's Way of Knowledge* (Cambridge, Eng., 1957); *The Lyric Impulse* (London and Cambridge, Mass., 1965); *A Need for Poetry?* (Hull, Eng., 1968); *On Translating Poetry* (Abingdon-on-Thames, Eng., 1970).

V. WORKS EDITED OR TRANSLATED BY DAY LEWIS. *The Mind in Chains* (London, 1937), as editor; *Ralph Fox: A Writer in Arms* (London, 1937), as editor, with T. A. Jackson and John Lehmann; *Anatomy of Oxford* (London, 1938), as editor, with Charles Fenby; *The Georgics of Virgil* (London, 1940), as translator; *The Aeneid of Virgil* (London, 1952), as translator; *The Eclogues of Virgil* (London, 1963), as translator.

VI. DETECTIVE NOVELS (AS NICHOLAS BLAKE). *A Question of Proof* (London, 1935); *Thou Shell of Death* (London, 1936); *There's Trouble Brewing* (London, 1937); *The Beast Must Die* (London, 1938); *The Smiler with the Knife* (London, 1939); *Malice in Wonderland* (London, 1940); *The Case of the Abominable Snowman* (London, 1941); *Minute for Murder* (London, 1947); *Head of a Traveller* (London, 1949); *The Dreadful Hollow* (London, 1953); *The Whisper in the Gloom* (London, 1954); *A Tangled Web* (London, 1956); *End of Chapter* (London, 1957); *A Penknife in My Heart* (London, 1958); *The Widow's Cruise* (London, 1959); *The Worm of Death* (London, 1961); *The Deadly Joker* (London, 1963); *The Sad Variety* (London, 1964); *The Morning After Death* (London, 1966); *The Private Wound* (London, 1968).

VII. BIOGRAPHICAL AND CRITICAL STUDIES. Christopher Caudwell, *Illusion and Reality: A Study of the Sources of Poetry* (London, 1937); Julian Bell, "The Proletariat and Poetry: An Open Letter to C. Day Lewis," in *Essays, Poems and Letters*, ed. by Quentin Bell (London, 1938); Harry Kemp, Laura Riding, et al., *The Left Heresy in Literature and Life* (London, 1939); Clifford Dyment, *C. Day Lewis* (London, 1955); D. E. S. Maxwell, *Poets of the Thirties* (London, 1969); Derek Stanford, *Stephen Spender, Louis MacNeice, Cecil Day Lewis* (Grand Rapids, Mich., 1969); Katharine B. Hoskins, *Today the Struggle: Literature and Politics in England During the Spanish Civil War* (Austin, Tex., 1969); Joseph N. Riddel, *C. Day Lewis* (New York, 1971); Samuel L. Hynes, *The Auden Generation: Literature and Politics in England in the 1930s* (Princeton, N.J., 1972); J. A. Morris, *Writers and Politics in Modern Britain, 1880–1950* (London, 1977); Bernard Bergonzi, *Reading the Thirties: Texts and Contexts* (London, 1978); Sean Day-Lewis, *C. Day Lewis: An English Literary Life* (London, 1980); Adrian Caesar, *Dividing Lines: Poetry, Class, and Ideology in the 1930s* (Manchester, Eng., and New York, 1991); John Whitehead, *A Commentary on the Poetry of W. H. Auden, C. Day Lewis, Louis MacNeice, and Stephen Spender* (Lewiston, Maine, 1992); Albert Gelpi, *Living in Time: The Poetry of C. Day Lewis* (Oxford, Eng., and New York, forthcoming).

DAPHNE DU MAURIER

(1907–1989)

Nina Auerbach

THE NAME DAPHNE DU MAURIER is so euphonious that it seems created to charm us. The writer is equally appealing. When she began to publish fiction at the age of twenty-two her winsome beauty and famous family made her an ideal literary commodity; her vivid prose and artful plots did the rest. From the publication of her first novel in 1931 (which was enticingly if inaccurately called *The Loving Spirit*) to her last in 1972 (the abrasive *Rule Britannia*, in which England collapses under an American invasion), the name Daphne du Maurier was synonymous with atmospheric, feminine romance that was escapist rather than artistic.

But du Maurier was a controlled, tough-minded, sardonic artist who quickly became the victim of her own charm. An immediate commercial success, she was dismissed by the cultural establishment as too readable to be literary. No matter what she wrote, the label stuck. When she died in 1989, the famous author of seventeen novels, six biographies, four books of articles and memoirs, two plays, and nine collections of stories had attracted no sustained critical attention. The publication of Margaret Forster's biography in 1993 may turn the tide, but du Maurier died a curiosity: though her stories and characters were as well known as those of any other twentieth-century writer, she was a literary unmentionable.

Her near ostracism is due not only to her commercial success. Somehow, and it may be the lovely name itself, Daphne du Maurier has become identified with a femininity distasteful to misogynists and feminists alike, an ironic misconstruction of a woman who longed to be a man, whose proper marriage covered lesbian longings, who specialized in unsympathetic male narrators, and whose male characters—lovers, villains, or both—are etched in knowing, unromantic cynicism. "I would prefer to be a man. If I were, my novels would be more highly thought of," she told admirers in old age (Shallcross, p. 34). This perennial complaint of the woman writer seems, as it usually is, quite justified.

She was dismissed by traditional critics, yet du Maurier may be too traditional to appeal to feminists. Unlike her contemporary Virginia Woolf, she had no allegiance to woman writers or women's issues. Her love for Cornwall, which she celebrated in passionate prose, made her sound like a Brontë sister, but though she exploited this superficial affinity commercially, when she wrote a book about a Brontë it was not Emily, Charlotte, or Anne, but their dissolute, untalented brother, Branwell. In the same sardonic but deferential spirit, she ignored her own two daughters and pampered their little brother.

Politically, she was far from progressive. Privileged child of a theatrical aristocracy more admired than the real one, she complained about the "boredom of the General Strike" (quoted in Forster, p. 38), ignored the stock market crash, and preferred to any human being the decaying great houses that stood for a landed world of privilege whose leveling she deplored. She was an unabashed royalist; after her husband became comptroller to Princess Elizabeth in 1947, she abandoned her sequestered life whenever the royal family chose to be entertained. Her wealth (both inherited and earned); her dependence on servants; her appointment in 1969 as Dame Commander, Order of the British Empire; and her allegiance to an antidemocratic national tradition do not make her easily recuperable by feminists who favor female outsiders. Like Jane Austen, Daphne du Maurier is easy to patronize but difficult to pigeonhole. She attracts many stereotypes but accommodates herself to none.

Apart from the tenderly fantastic novels of her grandfather George du Maurier, with which she wrestled throughout her career, her declared literary influences were her early contemporaries Katherine Mansfield and Somerset Maugham, along with Guy de Maupassant and Mary Webb. Victorian novels, with their busy plots and complex, overbearing narrators, were her earliest reading and strongest allegiance. The ferociously vital, often unbalanced and murderous speakers in Robert Browning's dramatic monologues seem at times to tell Daphne du Maurier's stories as well.

But this seductive writer of apparent romances may be closest to a tradition of female horror narratives whose existence she never acknowledged. Like those less lovable writers, Isak Dinesen, Shirley Jackson, Angela Carter, and Joyce Carol Oates, Daphne du Maurier extracts fear from ordinary social transactions. Sometimes, especially in her tales, this fear is supernaturally tinged; it is hard to tell whether *Rebecca*, her most famous novel, is about demonic possession or conventional marriage; but her fear is inevitably, unsettlingly, contagious.

The source of du Maurier's particular horror is the stuff of romance: the relations between men and women. In an uncommonly self-effacing biography of her father, the renowned actor-manager Sir Gerald du Maurier, the author suddenly declares: "But no true harmony can exist between a man and a woman. They rub on each other's nerves. They do not work in tune" (*Gerald: A Portrait*, chap. 10).

This inharmonious rubbing is the core of her fiction. In her novels, men regularly murder the women they claim to love; the best known, *Rebecca* and *My Cousin Rachel*, are accounts of woman-killers. The tales, less polished and commercial, are more overtly violent. In "Kiss Me Again, Stranger" (1953), "Not After Midnight" (1971), and many others, women murder their men with scarcely motivated relish. The ferocity of du Maurier's work extends beyond domesticity; in her later works disharmony and doom are national, even cosmic, visitations; but her fundamental horror is the violence, dormant or active, between women and men.

THE MEN IN HER LIFE

DAPHNE du Maurier was the privileged heir of two generations of male artists, and she is a surprising beneficiary. Artistically, the men in her life were her famous grandfather and her father. George du Maurier (1834–1896), whom Daphne, born on 13 May 1907, never knew, affected her writing more than her father, Gerald, did. A popular illustrator and *Punch* cartoonist who mocked with endearing stuffiness the pretensions of social climbers and aesthetes, George became a famous author at the age of fifty-six with *Peter Ibbetson* (1891), the spectacularly successful *Trilby* (1894), and *The Martian* (1897). *Trilby*'s success on stage made "du Maurier" as potent a name in the theater as it already was in literature and journalism.

Trilby helped launch the career of his son Gerald (1873–1934), who played Dodor, a minor character based on his feckless Uncle Eugène. This familial enterprise was a springboard to fame. Epitome of the new, naturalistic school of actors, Gerald du Maurier was seductively relaxed on stage. He rejected the romantic heroism of the old Irving style, preferring instead, when he told an actress he loved her, to yawn, light a cigarette, and walk away. As Daphne described his oddly hostile anti-lovemaking: "He seldom kissed women on the stage, unless it was on the back of the neck or the top of the head, and then he would generally slap them on the face afterwards, and say, 'you old funny, with your ugly mug,' and walk away talking of something else as though he did not care" (*Gerald*, chap. 5).

Gerald specialized in gentleman-criminals: like their Victorian parents, Edwardian audiences loved actors in roles that emphasized doubleness and self-fabrication. For Daphne, however, he achieved true artistry only in the plays of J. M. Barrie, whose nostalgia for perpetual boyhood captured her father's heart. But the eternally boyish Gerald was the man of his age. In 1910, he became manager of Wyndham's Theatre. He was knighted in 1922, by which time he exuded the regal aura of the actor-managers who had dominated the theater since the 1880s. But Gerald was the last of a line extinguished by the commercialization—and, according to the clannish du Mauriers, the deplorable Americanization—of the English theater that followed the First World War.

Daphne absorbed her grandfather's conservative nostalgia and her father's noblesse oblige, but she also inherited the family curse: a melancholy awareness that "it had all been too easy." The facility that enervated her grandfather was her father's bane and her own as well. *Gerald: A Portrait* shrewdly re-creates her grandfather writing *Peter Ibbetson:* "And now that he had started he found it simple, almost too easy; he wrote, in fact, with dangerous facility, as somebody once put it. The words poured from his pen" (chap. 2). Within this gentlemanly ease lay the threat of artistic death.

Like her father, Daphne knew no struggle, resistance, or rejection. Though her autobiography, *Growing Pains: The Shaping of a Writer* (1977), depicts a hating child who blighted her two sisters' jolly family outings and games, she was never neglected. When the sullen seventeen-year-old chafed at her chic life, her parents sent her to a finishing school outside Paris. She loved her grandfather's native city and strained to relive the French childhood he romanticized in *Peter Ibbetson* and *Trilby;* she loved her glamorous teacher Fernande Yvon with an intensity that exceeded a schoolgirl crush, and long after Mlle Yvon was mysteriously dismissed from the school, her life and Daphne's remained enmeshed. The du Mauriers never considered sending the sophisticated young beauty to the new woman's colleges that were struggling for recognition in the 1920s, but her literary talent delighted them: Gerald proclaimed that she had inherited George's spirit and proudly marshaled his formidable contacts on her behalf. In 1929 her first story was published with great fanfare in her Uncle Willie's fashionable magazine, *The Bystander. Growing Pains* claims airily that her family was equally eager to set her up as a movie star: her dilemma was which career to choose! In the middle of an international depression, when even the most determined young women had to struggle to be heard, her royal name and inherited facility made love and work dangerously easy to win.

But being an heiress is harder than it looks. It was especially difficult for a volatile woman to inherit a style from such soft, lovable men. Her grandfather's famous Trilby hung over her. Trilby, jolly and boyish, is the darling of artists. British painters chivalrously adore and paint her, but the Jewish musician Svengali invades her grand body for sinister ends, mesmerizing her into expressing his own thwarted talent. As the acclaimed prima donna La Svengali, the seemingly triumphant Trilby is an empty puppet of twisted male artistry. For George du Maurier, a woman is glorified when she is painted but lost when she ascends the stage herself. Would Daphne's legacy turn her into Trilby, the mouthpiece of controlling men?

Daphne du Maurier said little about *Trilby;* following family tradition, she preferred the tenderer, more metaphysical *Peter Ibbetson;* but her writing is laced with *Trilby* twists. In *Trilby*, the true lover Little Billee immortalizes Trilby's grand foot by drawing it on a wall—a Cinderella-like tribute so romantic in the 1890s that it created a vogue for such foot-shaped commodities as ice cream, scarfpins, and even a "Trilby Sausage." But *Rebecca*'s Maxim de Winter makes his wife's foot his focus of hate. He murderously remembers "that foot of hers, swinging to and fro, that damned foot in its blue and white striped sandal" whose defiant motion leads him to kill her (chap. 20).

Trilby hats, another popular artifact of "Trilbymania" (though there are no such hats in the novel), bob through Daphne's tales like a sinister joke. They are always ominous. In "The Little Photographer" (in *Kiss Me Again, Stranger*, 1953), a spoiled Marquise takes as her lover the crippled photographer of the title. At first he is suitably deferential; it is only when he turns sinister that she notices his "cheap trilby hat." In "Ganymede" (in *The Breaking Point*, 1959), a jolly man in a trilby hat becomes the story's Satan. Mementos of her grandfather's loved book are Daphne du Maurier's messengers of doom.

No previous du Maurier woman had aspired even to be Trilby. The gracious wives who (with their servants) raised her were content to foster men's careers and fuss about their health. George du Maurier, who hated female sensation novelists (the genre Daphne perpetuated in the twentieth century), married a perfect womanly woman of whom Daphne wrote in *Gerald:* "Pem was like a hen clucking after her chicks, wrapping them up for fear of draughts and dosing everyone within sight, including Kicky [George], with cod-liver oil" (chap. 1). Her father married the same kind of woman. Her mother, Muriel, from whom Daphne felt unarticulated hostility, seemingly lived to worry about Gerald's "horrid colds." This exemplary ministering presence was as dampening as Trilby. As the spectral Rebecca, Muriel and other good wives hang in their perfection like succubi over the nameless, clumsy narrator.

But when she wrote about her grandfather, Daphne du Maurier was neither clumsy nor inhibited. Her acute family biographies cherish her role as legatee. *Gerald: A Portrait* (1934), her family saga *The Du Mauriers* (1937), and *The Young George du Maurier: A Selection of His Letters, 1860–1867*

(1951) depict with affection and wit the man she never met, the origin of the du Maurier fame. Her George du Maurier is no overbearing patriarch, but a melancholy, ambivalent dreamer torn between incompatible worlds: the France in which he grew up and the dreary England to which the family moved when he failed his *baccalauréat* examination (an ignominy he excises from his romantic self-portrait in *Peter Ibbetson*, which explains the move by killing the parents). "Half bourgeois, half Bohemian," as he called himself, he wavered between philistinism and aestheticism. He had aimed to be a great painter; his year as a Paris art student is romanticized in *Trilby*'s studio hijinks; but he suddenly lost his sight in one eye. He returned to England and the less demanding career of illustrator, in which he satirized the artists he had wanted to become. Until his late fame as a novelist, he lived happily in sequestered domesticity. His five children—of whom Gerald was the last and most pampered, his mother's "ewee lamb"—were, fortunately for them, beautiful enough to meet their father's exacting aesthetic demands.

Wavering, tender, an English paterfamilias suffocated by nostalgia for a romanticized France, he won love, as Daphne saw it, through his "irrational quality of tragedy." "There was something touching about his face, about his whole personality, that was impossible to explain. People longed to protect him for no reason" (*The Du Mauriers*, part 3). The homelessness of the hybrid, this "half bourgeois, half Bohemian" wavering between worlds and identities, was her own legacy as well. She concludes *The Du Mauriers* with a veiled self-revelation: "Kicky and Kicky's descendants hover in their characteristics between England and France, as do all hybrids who possess the blood of two countries in their veins" (part 6).

Daphne too tried to recapture her French roots, not only in her well-known novels *The Scapegoat* and *The Glass-Blowers*; but she was more radically hybrid, writing of herself during her futile, frenzied epistolary courtship of Ellen Doubleday as "a half-breed, . . . neither girl nor boy but disembodied spirit" (quoted in Forster, p. 222). Ensconced in happy domesticity like her grandfather, she dreamed like him of impossible meetings in lost countries.

Daphne shared many of George's dreams, but she pitilessly corrected others. He was her originary figure—the man who made the French name

a British public endowment—but George himself dreamed of his own origins among the nobility of medieval France. He was convinced that his grandfather, Mathurin-Robert Busson du Maurier, a gentleman glassblower, had been stripped of his estates and château by the French Revolution.

Daphne's superb research exposed Mathurin-Robert Busson as a liar: he was no dispossessed aristocrat, but a revolutionary sympathizer who emigrated to England in 1789 to escape a charge of fraud, stealing the name "du Maurier" from a local château. When he returned to France in 1802, he abandoned his wife and six children (one of whom was George du Maurier's father) in London. The magic name originated in swindle. Daphne revealed this hoax not only in her family chronicles and in *The Glass-Blowers* (1963), her stilted novel about her great-great-grandparents during the French Revolution, but also to Leonée Ormond, George's biographer. Ormond's *George Du Maurier* is a debunking account of a compromised life that relies heavily on Daphne's acerbic revelation of ancestral delusions and deceptions.

She swept away titles and châteaux, but she kept the glass as her own emblem of the family art. *The Glass-Blowers* is dedicated "to my forebears, the master glass-blowers"; its central symbol is a goblet engraved in 1769 for King Louis XV that becomes "a family symbol" and "a reminder of high craftsmanship through succeeding generations" (chap. 2). The faithful narrator Sophie Duval—one incarnation of dutiful family chronicler Daphne—accordingly preserves the goblet. Reexploring the French inheritance that fed her grandfather's dreams of glory, Daphne du Maurier found a fragile but useful talisman, one with none of the sinister potential of the *Trilby* artifacts.

She pillaged her grandfather's history, rejecting his faith but taking what she could use. Along with the glass goblet, she appropriated his maternal grandmother, Mary Anne Clarke. An English prostitute who became an infamous Regency courtesan, Mary Anne was for a few years the lover of the Duke of York, brother of George III. When the duke discarded her, she blackmailed him with old love letters. Only his generous annuity prevented her from publishing her memoirs; this annuity supported the entire next generation. When Mary Anne's sour daughter married Mathurin-Robert's unstable son, they lived on this embarrassing inheritance until their son George began to succeed.

George du Maurier beautified his parents; his *Peter Ibbetson* enthrones the musical young couple in a French garden. *The Du Mauriers* rewrites them as a wretched pair, but it recovers Mary Anne Clarke, banished from George's garden, as the source of the family vitality: "These fighting qualities were bequeathed to [George] by a woman, a woman without morals, without honour, without virtue, a woman who had known exactly what she wanted at fifteen years of age and, gutter born and gutter bred, treading on sensibility and courtesy with her exquisite feet, had achieved it laughing—her thumb to her nose" (chap. 7). Once again, Daphne embarrassed her grandfather's pretensions but found her own authorizing symbol—a woman the family was ashamed of, who lived before the great men and subsidized them. She could not write the ancestor she found; her novel *Mary Anne* (1954) is as lifeless as *The Glass-Blowers;* but her research into her French inheritance gave her a more urbane myth of origin than the *Peter Ibbetson* her grandfather had believed in so tenderly.

The novel the family loved, *Peter Ibbetson* is an exile's cry for return. His parents' deaths tear Peter from the idyllic garden of his Parisian childhood. He is trapped in England and the guardianship of his villainous uncle, a "Portuguese Jew, with a dash of colored blood in his veins besides" (part 2). He lives in limbo, longing for his past: "Oh, surely, surely, I cried to myself, we ought to find some means of possessing the past more fully and completely than we do. Life is not worth living for many of us if a want so desperate and yet so natural can never be satisfied" (part 3).

His Parisian playmate, now Mary, Duchess of Towers—wise, grand, and, like all George du Maurier's favored characters, exceptionally tall—returns and restores that past by teaching him the art of "dreaming true." Separated by circumstances (having killed his wicked uncle, Peter is in a hospital for the criminally insane), they live together in glorious shared dreams that allow them to return to their childhood at will, to furnish their home with the masterpieces of Western culture, and, eventually, to visit the deep past: having learned that they are relations, they meet their common great-great-grandmother at her glassworks, regressing back through French history to their primal ancestor, the first mammoth. The dreams cease when Mary dies, but this goddess-like ambassador returns with consoling messages about the afterlife.

This blend of faith and science fiction, occultism and nostalgia, is still passionately alive. Like Barrie's plays, which pervaded Daphne du Maurier's childhood, *Peter Ibbetson* is an anguished celebration of boyhood: it values no adult experience but regression and return. For a female descendant, *Peter Ibbetson* is a particularly difficult act to follow in that it posits a kind of genetic time traveling: Peter and Mary exchange minds with their great-great-grandmother, sharing her life and bringing her into their own time. In *The Martian,* which George du Maurier finished just before his death, the strapping hero is visited in dreams by a majestic extraterrestrial who instructs him in evolution, eugenics, and the progress of the race; she is reborn as his daughter. Was Daphne the saving female descendant her grandfather prophesied, sharing his consciousness and carrying him into the future?

She confronts this daunting prospect by threading through her works a mordant commentary on *Peter Ibbetson*'s cherished hope. Like her grandfather, she wrote about recovering the past, but her recovered past is horror. In *Peter Ibbetson,* the symbol of Mary's restorative capacity is an apple tree. "I shall soon be here again, by this apple-tree; I shall count the hours," she cries rapturously (part 5). Daphne's tale "The Apple Tree" (1952) is also a parable of a loving woman's restorative power. The sour widower who tells the story hated his sighing wife. He is horrified when a barren tree in his orchard miraculously flowers, producing bushels of inedible apples; he knows that his wife lives again through the tree. This resurrection tale, if it is one, escalates into a story of mutual murder.

The theme of the famous *Rebecca* is, similarly, the horror of restoration. The naive narrator begins with a *Peter Ibbetson*–like wish: "If only there could be an invention . . . that bottled up a memory, like scent. And it never faded, and it never got stale. And then, when one wanted it, the bottle could be uncorked, and it would be like living the moment all over again" (chap. 5). George du Maurier's Peter and Mary live that invention. As Peter rhapsodizes: "our greatest pleasure of all was to live our old life over again and again, and make Gogo and Mimsey [their childhood selves] and our parents and cousins and M. le Major go through their old paces once more" (part 5). In *Rebecca,* though, the old life returns to strangle, for the past is domestic murder. Rebecca, who like the wife in "The Apple Tree" refuses to die, is its

137

spirit. When Maxim's second wife wears a costume that resurrects both the ancestral de Winters and Rebecca herself, she uncorks only rage and disaster. For Daphne du Maurier, forgetting, not memory, is grace.

Her splendid, largely overlooked novel *The House on the Strand* (1969) is her darkest and most mordant revision of *Peter Ibbetson*. Like her grandfather's hero, the narrator is a time traveler who lives a double life; with the help of an equivocal male friend and an LSD-like drug, he escapes his dismal wife to visit the fourteenth century in visions. But though he tries to belong, the increasingly estranged Dick is a ghost in both the present and the past. Peter Ibbetson learned to touch the past and participate in it; Dick's touch makes his visions dissipate. As Dick decomposes, present and past become interchangeably violent and doom-ridden. Clinical rather than tender, Daphne du Maurier turns her grandfather's myth of redemption, and of noble medieval ancestors, into an account of madness, rage, and the impossibility of escape. The violence and terror within her gentle grandfather's backward yearning—and that of J. M. Barrie, who wrote such wonderful parts for her father—are, in *The House on the Strand*, ruthlessly exposed.

Like his daughter, Gerald du Maurier lived in George's melancholy shadow. The coddled family baby who became famous with no apparent effort, Gerald, as Daphne depicts him, suffered from enervating depression and cynicism. His father's motto, "à quoi bon?" ("what's the use?"), dimmed his energy. He fretted about the evanescence of performing; he fretted about the ephemeral plays he put on; but he turned away from bolder projects that might jeopardize his secure position. *Gerald* refuses to sentimentalize his compromise and discontent. "He was constantly at war with himself and his own beliefs . . . making him a creature of great promise, baffling, lovable, but for ever unfulfilled" (chap. 5).

His sense of belatedness and incompletion diluted his paternal authority. He played the first Captain Hook, "a tragic and rather ghastly creation who knew no peace, and whose soul was in torment," as Daphne described him (chap. 4); but essentially he was Peter Pan, a perpetual spoiled son for whom aging was death. Peter Pan was another outgrowth of George's garden; Barrie had named him for Gerald's nephew Peter Llewelyn Davies, who was himself named after Peter Ibbetson.

Clinging to a paternal dream of boyhood that colored his onstage life, Gerald was scarcely a traditional father. Tormented by the sudden sexuality of his three daughters, who were barely younger than his many mistresses, he murmured to Daphne: "I wish I was your brother instead of your father; we'd have such fun" (chap. 11). In a sense they had always been brothers. In 1952, her love affair with Gertrude Lawrence—who was, she wrote, "the last of Daddy's actress loves" (quoted in Forster, p. 422)—reaffirmed their fraternity.

Daphne du Maurier's feelings for her father are hard to gauge. She diagnosed herself with her generation's glib Freudianism: clearly, she was in love with him, thereby explaining not only her mother's dislike of her, but her own sexual attraction, at fourteen, to her flirtatious middle-aged cousin Geoffrey. *Gerald* coolly enumerates the great actresses who threw him over before he married her compliant mother. One of them was the volatile Ethel Barrymore, whom the biography slyly calls by her middle name, Daphne, emphasizing not only the brilliance of the author's namesake, but her forbidden sexual appeal.

Gerald was an enticing companion with whom Daphne identified, but he scarcely swept his cool daughter away. His importunate dependency frightened her. At ten, she found his Will Dearth in J. M. Barrie's *Dear Brutus* (1917) more terrifying than his Captain Hook: she relished the poisoning pirate, but the character of the loving father of a dream daughter sent her screaming out of the theater. The father-daughter scene in *Dear Brutus* is a midsummer illusion: the weak and profligate Dearth finds his imaginary daughter in a magic wood, but at the end of the scene he leaves her fading and crying: "Daddy, come back; I don't want to be a might-have-been." A murderous antifather like Captain Hook was fun; a father whose love was potent enough to make her materialize and evaporate was a menace (the du Maurier family's code word for sexual attraction). As a child, she resolved that neither Svengali nor Will Dearth would create her or make her their might-have-been.

She preserved herself by creating her father. When, in 1934, he died suddenly at sixty-one, she immediately began his biography; the astonishingly rounded and clear-eyed *Gerald: A Portrait* appeared the same year. As her father's biographer, Daphne has none of the rancorous indiscretion of a Christina Crawford or a Susan Cheever, but she gives no quarter. Gerald's glamour and charm are there, but so are his mistresses, his instability, his terror of aging, his grasping emotional demands. Her dry "too much latitude [has been] allowed to those unconscious tyrants who move in a world of their own moods and whims" (chap. 10) is frank about the strain of being part of a household of women that orbits around a spoiled father/child. Like Virginia Woolf's *To the Lighthouse* (1927), *Gerald: A Portrait* exposes the tension and inequities within an ideal Edwardian family headed by a childish great man.

Her fiction is less dispassionate. Her short story "The Menace" (in *The Breaking Point*, 1959) is a searing, surreal account of an infantile matinee idol fed by grotesque mothering who, to crown his menace, wears a trilby hat! *Gerald*'s distance is achieved by the omission of Daphne. It is dedicated "For Gerald and His Family"; there is no "me" or "us." No personal voice intrudes: she refers to herself in the third person. Perhaps the daughter's presence in the father's biography would have turned her, after all, into a might-have-been, swallowing her in her father's dreams. But her self-suppression taught her a craft for which she has been little recognized: she is a superb biographer of men. After *Gerald* came *The Du Mauriers* (1937), *The Infernal World of Branwell Brontë* (1960), *Golden Lads: Sir Francis Bacon, Anthony Bacon, and Their Friends* (1975), and *The Winding Stair: Francis Bacon, His Rise and Fall* (1976). Diligent researcher and astute portraitist, Daphne du Maurier studied the men in her life to great effect, producing brilliant biographical portraits as well as the more menacing male characters in her fiction.

Convinced that like a good Freudian daughter she harbored incestuous longings, Daphne du Maurier wove incest into her fiction. Characteristically though, that incest is most piquant when it precludes intimacy or even family. *The Parasites* (1949), her only novel that approaches family portraiture, involves the entanglements among the three children of the glamorous theatrical Delaneys. They are not true siblings; all come from different liaisons. Maria and Niall, beautiful, mercurial artists, are not technical relations, but they are the incestuous pair: dangerously lovable, they can love only each other. Celia, the legitimate child and good daughter, is a lumpish nurturer, as parasitic in her caretaking as Maria and Niall are in their careless artistry. Incest in *The Parasites* is more a transcendence of family than an extension of it.

Du Maurier's next novel, *My Cousin Rachel* (1951), is, as the title reminds us, technically about incest: after Ambrose marries his cousin Rachel and dies, Philip, another cousin and Ambrose's adopted heir, falls in love with her, is or is not poisoned by her, and finally murders her. But despite the familial title, Rachel is as foreign as she can be: not only was she raised in Italy, but she is a woman, "a race apart" to these ingrown men. In the same spirit, the ravenous father in *The Progress of Julius* (1933) murders his daughter because he does not understand and cannot possess her. Du Maurier's supposedly incestuous love stories have the look of family but the lure of distance. They resemble the familial nonfamily in *Peter Ibbetson,* whose lovers grow up together and discover a common ancestor in dreams though they are separated in their waking existence: their love story, like Maria and Niall's or Philip and Rachel's, springs from division. The du Maurier dream of incest is an escape from family life.

If, in Daphne du Maurier's fiction, distance haunts even incestuous men and women, potent affinity haunts her males. Her intent study of the men from whom she inherited her name, her career, and her material makes her a rarity among woman novelists: a creator of male characters who are not projections of female desire or resentment, but who exist on their own terms. Her well-known romances *Jamaica Inn* and *Rebecca* do feature cloudy emanations of the heroine's consciousness, but in *I'll Never Be Young Again* (1932), *The Progress of Julius* (1933), *My Cousin Rachel* (1951), *The Scapegoat* (1957), *The Flight of the Falcon* (1965), and *The House on the Strand* (1969), the men are as sharply etched and multidimensional as the Gerald of the biography. This male-centered group of novels owes much to Gerald, not because he resembled any of the protagonists, but because all recapitulate his theatrical identity. All are bound to a male double; all are implicated in the death of a woman.

The melodramatic *I'll Never Be Young Again*, du Maurier's second novel, defines this paradigm. Dick, du Maurier's first male narrator, is a bilious young man who moves from a passionate friendship with Jake to a sadistic love affair with Hesta. The friendship is all-embracing; the love affair is inchoate and tormented. In this novel the male double dies while the woman merely sinks into debauchery, but the book establishes du Maurier's central paradigm: intimacy between men, murderousness between men and women. Her third novel, *The Progress of Julius*, explores that paradigm and begins to control it.

Like George du Maurier, Julius Lévy is a French émigré who becomes wealthy in England, but Julius is an unsavory (and unpleasantly stereotyped) Jewish businessman, cruelly appetitive. During the siege of Paris, he sells rats to his starving countrymen, anticipating the later success of his cheap restaurant chains in England. He brings his gentle, musical father, Paul, to Algeria and learns to cheat at business. When Paul dies, Julius moves to England with an adoring prostitute; to save money, he lets her die of tuberculosis. The second half of the book, a moralized success story along the lines of *Citizen Kane*, traces his rise to prosperity, respectability, and insane loneliness.

But Julius' business success is less vivid than his violence against women. As a boy, he watches approvingly as the gentle Paul murders his adulterous mother. "It really served Mère right. She deserved to die after going with Jacques Tripet. He could understand why Père had killed her. He didn't want his thing to be spoilt. He would not allow anyone else to have it" (part 1). Here, in coarse form, is the motive that drives du Maurier's more genteel—and gentile—killers, Maxim de Winter and Philip Ashley.

The murder activates a startlingly lyrical, even erotic bond between father and son. In one of the most romantic passages Daphne du Maurier wrote, Paul envelops the boy in his naked body during the journey to Algeria. His legacy lives in the adult Julius, who is robustly sadistic to his prostitute mistress and his cultivated wife. When his fifteen-year-old daughter, whom he had previously ignored, plays Paul's flute, he becomes obsessed with her. To escape her father perhaps, she claims tauntingly that she is engaged; in a scene that anticipates Maxim's murder of the lying, laughing Rebecca, he drowns her.

This ugly story is far from the Daphne du Maurier of popular stereotype, but *The Progress of Julius* is the raw material of her more artful novels; her work becomes not less violent but more controlled. As with her grandfather's Svengali, the supposed primitivism of a Jewish protagonist may have allowed her to represent a possessive ferocity inhibited Englishmen masked. Though

Julius' tormented jealousy recalls the aging Gerald's infantile possessiveness, the ravenous immigrant is far from the coddled star. The tender union of father and son sealed in the murders of their women may nevertheless be Daphne du Maurier's private parable of her own artistic inheritance, one whose loving paternalism threatened to drown the dynamic daughter.

Her last male-centered novels—especially *My Cousin Rachel, The Scapegoat*, and *The House on the Strand*—are as subtle and chilling as anything she wrote. All question not only the bases of guilt and innocence, but the foundations of male identity; the narrators of all three lose the boundaries of their own being, so possessed are they by an engulfing male double. Nevertheless, these intricate novels take their pattern from the overwrought *The Progress of Julius*, for they too imbed a woman's murder in an indelible bond between men.

My Cousin Rachel is about its own puzzles. As with Thackeray's Becky Sharp in *Vanity Fair*, its unanswerable question is, "Was Rachel innocent or guilty?" (chap. 1). Trapped in Philip's obsessions, we are never certain whether she is murderer or murderee, perfect woman or perfect plotter, or all of these at once. We are given material for a Jamesian novel Rachel herself might write, that of a sophisticated foreigner enmeshed in the insane fantasies of two misogynist British landowners, but Rachel never writes her story: in the book we have, she is inscrutable. Its real marriage is between two inbred men, Ambrose and Philip, legator and legatee. When Ambrose dies, Philip inherits not only his estate, but his marriage, his fantasies, perhaps his being. At the end of his story, Philip wonders "whether his [Ambrose's] spirit left his body and came home here to mine, taking possession, so that he lived again in me, repeating his own mistakes, caught the disease once more and perished twice" (chap. 1). The authentic enigma is not Rachel's guilt or innocence, but the integrity of the man who insists on judging her.

The Scapegoat dwells on the possession that hovers in the background of *My Cousin Rachel*. A Victorian tale of doubling, like Dickens' *Tale of Two Cities* or Charles Reade's popular melodrama *The Courier of Lyons, The Scapegoat* deals with a disconnected Englishman who teaches French history. Alone in Paris, he suddenly meets his French double, Jean. Jean tricks John into an exchange of lives: the solitary Englishman suddenly finds himself lord of Jean's crumbling estate and wretched family. As unprepared to be a ruler as the narrator of *Rebecca* was to head Manderley, John implausibly becomes adept at love and power by living, for an interval, an alien life.

In many ways *The Scapegoat* is, like *My Cousin Rachel,* a novel about women's condition told from an oblique male perspective. As head of the family and estate, John is confronted with a pageant of female misery in Jean's mother, sister, mistresses, wife, and daughter. This newly fledged patriarch is stunned by the absoluteness of his power over their lives. Like the second wife in *Rebecca,* he initially blunders excruciatingly as he becomes enmeshed in Jean's past perfidies. Miraculously, though, the family is healed when his sour wife Françoise falls or jumps to her death. As is so often true in Daphne du Maurier's fiction, the wife is the authentic scapegoat. As her eerie daughter puts it: "since Maman died, everyone is getting what they want" (chap. 24). What these bitter, sniping women want is work, and at the end John has become lordly enough to give it to them.

Once again, the authentic, indissoluble marriage is between John and Jean. As in *My Cousin Rachel,* the legatee becomes his legacy. Appropriating for her own purposes that strange Victorian convention in which a man suddenly meets himself, Daphne du Maurier uses that convention to destroy the boundaries of male identity: to assume another's direction and acquire the trappings of another's life is to become another man. Daphne du Maurier's powerful male Trilbys are more easily extinguished than the women they destroy.

The Flight of the Falcon transposes this plot to Italy, always du Maurier's nightmare country. In this amalgam of fascist politics and sexual sadism, the narrator's consciousness is consumed by his charismatic brother, Aldo, a divine/demonic leader in a torpid Italian city. The more straightforward if equally nightmarish *The House on the Strand* returns to England, where a third man joins the union. Its time-traveling narrator, Dick, is plunged into the fourteenth century by a drug given to him by his Frankensteinian friend Magnus. In the past, he finds a new guide, the conjurer Roger, into whose visions he merges. When Magnus dies, Roger becomes Dick's controlling consciousness—and, we learn at the end, the murderer of Isolda, the woman they both love. *The House on the Strand* is a frayed novel

with no available redemption: in the fourteenth as well as the twentieth century, all guides lead to rot and doom. Its disillusionment, though, repeats the pattern that dominates Daphne du Maurier's male-centered novels: the mind of a powerful man is invaded by a controlling male double through whom a woman is directly or indirectly murdered.

This story of a theatrical woman-killer pervaded by his controlling double is not, of course, Gerald du Maurier's, but it does transmute into twentieth-century psychological horror the radiant Edwardian actor-manager who acted out his own father's compelling fantasies; who, to show off his virtuosity, played Mr. Darling as well as Captain Hook; whose gentleman-criminals made him a theatrical exemplar of a double life; who demanded so much mothering that he crammed his life with women. Daphne du Maurier's male-centered novels of inheritance give her magnanimous father his most torn and tragic roles.

THE BOY IN HER LIFE

THEY were roles for herself as well. Daphne du Maurier's male characters are her most distinctive achievement, but all are boys at heart—as she was. Her girlhood taught her the glamour of boys. George and Gerald clung to boyishness, leaving adulthood to the ancillary women who took care of them. Those twin hovering Peters, her grandfather's Ibbetson and Barrie's Pan, dominated not only her family but the masculine, nostalgia-drenched Edwardian cultural establishment. Though her father doted on his daughters, he gently pitied their femaleness. As a child, she reinvented herself as Eric Avon, rugby star and general paragon, a persona who, she said, evolved into her "undeveloped, inadequate" male narrators (*Growing Pains,* chap. 3). She never abandoned that boy-self, whom she called "the boy in the box," imagining that he, not Daphne, fell in love with women (quoted in Forster, p. 222). As a young mother, she clamored through two daughters for a boy, smothering Kits with love when he was finally born.

The heroine of her first novel, the family saga *The Loving Spirit* (1931), longs similarly for a male life. After settling into a proper but tepid marriage, Janet Coombe conceives her seafaring son as the incarnation of her passionate, adventuring self. Kits was not that son, but incredibly, Daphne du Maurier did marry a dashing military hero who was also Boy—Major Frederick Arthur Montague Browning, called "Tommy" by his family and "Boy" by his regiment. After a few lively but uncompelling love affairs, a husband named Boy who sported all the paraphernalia of successful military manhood seemed to fulfill all the requisite roles. She married Boy Browning when she was twenty-five.

Like a Victorian novel, her autobiography *Growing Pains* ends with her marriage. Introducing her future husband as "Boy" before listing his many other names, she assures her reader that marriage finished her: "Growing pains over, I was about to become mature" (1977 ed., p. 191). In the 1970s, though, she told Martyn Shallcross, "My childhood in London and Cornwall I think was interesting, but I feel I was boring after my marriage" (Shallcross, p. 15). Marriage made her neither mature nor boring, but it did, to some degree, force her to become the fussing, motherly woman she had always hated, for the boy in her manly husband was not the adventurous spirit J. M. Barrie taught her to believe in.

Like many men of his generation, Major Browning was an unexpected combination of imperial fortitude and nervous delicacy. The man she first saw looked like a romance hero. As Margaret Forster describes him, "He was tall—six foot—with dark hair and grey eyes, very alert and energetic, and with a confident but not arrogant bearing" (p. 87). He was awarded the DSO in 1917 for his bravery in World War I, despite the fact that in 1916 he had been invalided home for eight months with the evasive diagnosis, "nervous exhaustion." He relived the war in shattering nightmares. These flashbacks were common among veterans—even Lord Peter Wimsey, the omnipotent hero of Dorothy L. Sayers' detective novels, ends his series weeping in his wife's enfolding arms—but Daphne du Maurier had not thought she was marrying a man she would have to take care of. She wanted men to expand her life, not to enfold themselves in it.

Tommy—or Boy, or, as she began to call him, Moper—had always had incapacitating stomach pains. These and other nervous ailments intensified as he aged. His career as a public servant remained exemplary: he was knighted in 1946 for his service as brigade commander in World War II; he was comptroller and treasurer to the royal family until he retired in 1959 under a strain no one he worked with perceived. But he was crumbling under illness and alcoholism. In 1957 he had a breakdown, and du Maurier was shocked to learn of his mistress in London: despite her own affairs with men and women, and despite the publication of *The Scapegoat* in the same year, she had never thought her Moper was leading a double life. When he died in 1965, she mourned the man but seemed scarcely to miss a marriage in which she had never been comfortable. She lived on in Cornwall until she died on 19 April 1989 of stubborn self-starvation, a celebrated emanation of the landscape she had helped make famous.

Unsurprisingly in her generation, she hated being a wife. She loathed playing Mrs. Major Browning and listening to the other army wives, who seemed to her drearily oppressed. In 1937, during a miserable time when Tommy was stationed in Egypt and, as the major's wife, she was supposed to preside graciously over the regiment, she began *Rebecca*. *Rebecca*'s opening pages, where the drained couple live a suppressed existence in sunny, seedy exile, as well as the excruciating malaise with wifeliness at the heart of the book, owe their intensity to du Maurier's own exile, not only from England, but from her former resilient self—or, as she would have put it, her boy-self.

Marriage to a war hero rather than an artist had promised to preserve her from her own mother's caretaking role, but it didn't: Tommy's hidden invalidism made this confident model of a man as much an actor as her father. Unlike her mother, though, she was the breadwinner, the star, and the detached partner. Marriage seems to have left her self-communion undisturbed. Her grandfather and father are stronger presences in her fiction than her husband is, though Boy does surface in one of the more bizarre tales.

"The Old Man" (1952) features a devoted old couple who live by the sea. There is something ineffably sinister about this loving pair. Gradually, we learn of their three daughters and a great hulking son named Boy. Despite his majestic size, the narrator realizes that "Boy was just a great baby, and I have an idea he was simple" (*Kiss Me Again, Stranger*, p. 224). He doesn't understand that he interrupts his parents' devotion; when he persists in hulking around, his father murders him. "They were free to be together again, and there was no longer a third to divide them." Suddenly the story turns lyrical. In fairy-tale fashion, Boy's death transfigures his parents into swans. Emblems of beauty and freedom, they beat their powerful wings and "fly out to sea right into the face of the setting sun" (p. 230).

The beauty and power the swans embody are by definition dangerous. "The Birds," an apocalyptic tale in which the birds of the world mobilize mysteriously against humans, appeared in the same collection as "The Old Man." "The Old Man," however, deals with domestic, not global, attack; like a later tale, "The Chamois" (in *The Breaking Point,* 1959), in which a couple similarly solidifies their marriage by slaughtering a primitive and devoted creature, "The Old Man" exposes the murder on which marriage thrives. Loving couples devour outsiders as remorselessly as the artists of *The Parasites.*

But the name "Boy" as the murderee leads to personal ground. In 1951, when du Maurier was writing these tales, her own inner boy had sprung back. In 1947 she had fallen in love with Ellen Doubleday, wife of the publisher, to whom she wrote passionate, self-declaring letters. Always, she insisted, she wasn't "that unattractive word that begins with 'L'"; she was simply "a boy of eighteen all over again" (quoted in Forster, pp. 221–222). In the first half of the twentieth century, the clinical definition of lesbianism was as man-centered as Daphne du Maurier's view of the world: a lesbian was a man trapped in a woman's body. In du Maurier's role-playing, fragmented view of identity, this meant that the boy, not the woman, was in love; thus "that unattractive word" left the wife and mother untouched.

There was no possibility that Ellen Doubleday would respond: she was as womanly as the du Maurier wives. In a characteristically theatrical transference, the actress Gertrude Lawrence inherited Ellen's role by playing Stella Martyn—who was modeled on the perfect Ellen—in du Maurier's play *September Tide.* In *September Tide,* which was staged in London and New York in 1948, a lovely widow and her daughter's husband fall in love and, of course, renounce each other. The stiff love story is less interesting than the contrast between the traditional Stella, "positively World War One," who lives to love, and her modern daughter. The daughter is unromantic, undesirable, and generally pathetic; the retrograde Stella is the emotional interest. Left alone at the end of the play, Stella listens to Ethel Merman's voice blatting out, "Anything you can do, I can do better," her tenderness overwhelmed by strident modern womanhood.

But Gertrude Lawrence orchestrated a less conventional love story. "The last of Daddy's actress loves" and Daphne's "boy in the box" were lovers until the actress's sudden—and, for Daphne du Maurier, devastating—death in 1952. "The Old Man," written during their love affair, might be a parable of the murder of the Boy who was also the author. In this reading, Boy is killed by the snuggly insularity of heterosexual coupledom.

If Boy is Boy Browning, though, this story of transfiguration becomes a covert lesbian allegory in which, after murdering the needy husband/son, the devoted women metamorphose into ungendered birds. Daphne du Maurier told Ellen that her male incarnation was, like Peter Pan, essentially genderless, "neither girl nor boy but disembodied spirit" (Forster, p. 222). If "The Old Man" is a guarded account of her own romantic triangle in 1951, it imagines no resolution but murder and metamorphosis.

Daphne du Maurier writes fluently about male homoeroticism, but her treatment of female homosexuality is guarded and oblique. Even the evil Mrs. Danvers in *Rebecca* expresses her desire only vicariously: she goads the second wife into making love to the clothes of a ghost. "Here is her nightdress inside the case. You've been touching it, haven't you? This was the nightdress she was wearing for the last time, before she died. Would you like to touch it again?" (chap. 14). Compared to the intimacy with which her male characters share lives, du Maurier distills love between women into mediating symbols.

Her novella, *Monte Verità* (1952), published in the same collection as "The Apple Tree" and "The Old Man," is an allegorical and abstract account of lesbianism. Anna, an aspiring woman we see only through the eyes of two men who love her, abandons her husband to join a rarefied community of women on a mountaintop. This Shangri-la generates vague transformations that unnerved du Maurier's publisher Victor Gollancz, who wrote, "I don't understand the slight implication that there is something wrong with sex" (quoted in Forster, p. 257). In the spirit of transfiguration that governed "The Old Man," Anna was originally supposed to turn into a boy, but this upset Gollancz so much that Anna instead became a leper. Du Maurier's uncharacteristic compliance suggests that it scarcely mattered to her what Anna turned into. The 1950s had no appropriate image for the transforming experience she wanted to write about. Its most accessible idiom was the language of heterosexual romance she had already mastered so fluently.

THE ROMANCES

AT thirteen, Daphne du Maurier wrote crankily to her governess that she had nothing to read but a "soppy book" full of "romantic slush" (Forster, p. 16). She would hate her own romances to be similarly scorned by restless adolescents, but then hers are scarcely soppy. A consummate actress in prose, du Maurier suffused the romances in what she thought of as a female point of view, one vividly different from that of her defining males.

Du Maurier does sometimes drift into erotic escapism; in *Frenchman's Creek* (1941), which was inspired by her tantalizing wartime flirtation with the languid dilettante Christopher Puxley, a matron has an erotic interlude with a pirate in the spirit of J. M. Barrie's Wendy; the ever-willing Puxley also lent du Maurier tales of his colorful ancestors for her Irish saga, *Hungry Hill* (1943). In her best-known romances, though, menaced and solitary women are the quarry of gargantuan enigmas called men. Their stories are less about love than about browbeating and submission. But the very solitude of these women makes them strong: *Growing Pains* argues that while her male narrators all depend on older men, her female narrators depend "on no one but themselves" (p. 58). In Daphne du Maurier's world, to be a man is to be possessed; to be a woman is to be alone.

Three works from the 1930s—her first novel, *The Loving Spirit* (1931), her first best-seller, *Jamaica Inn* (1936), and her most famous novel, *Rebecca* (1938)—initiated the comparison with the Brontë sisters that dogs her to this day, but du Maurier's novels are grimmer and more confined than those of Charlotte and Emily Brontë. The Brontës' novels are a surge toward freedom; for du Maurier's protagonists, such elation is too remote to dream about. All learn, or always knew, the condition spunky Mary Yellan accepts near the end of *Jamaica Inn*: "She had no will of her own; they could make decisions for her. . . . Once more she knew the humility of being born a woman, when the breaking down of strength and spirit was taken as natural and unquestioned" (chap. 16).

The Loving Spirit is an ambitious family saga based on four generations of local shipbuilders whose history du Maurier studied with the same ardent intelligence she would soon apply to her own family. Janet Coombe, its presiding spirit, longs to go to sea but marries her stolid cousin instead. She lives through the generations as the regal figurehead on the family's prize ship; as the *Janet Coombe* deteriorates, the family declines until, in the 1920s, the fourth generation reverently restores its fortunes.

The novel is a tonal mess; Dickensian melodrama about a wicked capitalist uncle alternates with sardonic domestic satire and Lawrentian spiritual/erotic yearnings; but Janet Coombe's symbolic primacy unifies its disarray. Du Maurier makes Janet a more respectable version of her own great-great-grandmother Mary Anne Clarke, an invisible female force who controls the rivalries and posturing of men. Du Maurier's next two novels, *I'll Never Be Young Again* and *The Progress of Julius*, release her male alter ego, but the perspective of this first work is decorously female; moreover, du Maurier dubiously rewards Janet's rebelliousness by making her a matriarch. *The Loving Spirit* never lets us ask whether the sea-loving Janet is content to turn into an inspiring figurehead, or whether she would prefer to be an inspired sailor like Daphne du Maurier herself—or du Maurier's demonic alter ego, Rebecca de Winter.

The Loving Spirit courts comparison with *Wuthering Heights*. Its title comes from one of Emily Brontë's poems; other Brontë titles begin each of the four sections. But *The Loving Spirit* is a *Wuthering Heights* in which all the ferocious yearning to escape is channeled into a family stronger than any of its members. Early in the novel, Janet prophesies her own immortality: "I'll not bide in Heaven, nor rest here in my grave. My spirit will linger with the ones I love—an' when they're sorrowful I'll come to them; and God Himself won't keep me" (p. 18). Cathy in *Wuthering Heights* similarly cries in heaven for home, but not out of concern for loved ones: she cares only about what she loves. When, in an eerie reminder of *Peter Ibbetson*, Janet does return to comfort her devastated sailor son, she is an ineffectual ghost: Joseph, the most vigorous character in the novel, is no better for her brief visit; he remains blind, maddened, and broken. Immortality in *The Loving Spirit* is no more transcendent than the family that contains it.

Wuthering Heights is, like *The Loving Spirit*, a saga that produces a saving couple in the young generation, but Emily Brontë's Hareton and young Cathy are a progressive pair: they read and learn, they garden, they sweep away the tangled feuds of the Grange and abandon the Heights to its passionate ghosts. Daphne du Maurier's saving couple, John and Jennifer, renew the family by looking backward. These cousins fall in love reading, not improving books, but old family letters. John restores the family shipbuilding trade and Jennifer dispels Janet Coombe's resentful yearnings by announcing complacently: "people can say whatever they damn well please, about work, ambition, art, and beauty—all the funny little things that go to make up life—but nothing, nothing matters in the whole wide world but you and I loving one another, and Bill kicking his legs in the sun in the garden below" (p. 364). The family that in 1830 was too narrow to hold its best members has become, in 1930, the only sanctuary for the diminished young.

The Loving Spirit is a canny first novel. Its progressive structure masks a bleak sense of a world closing in; its evocation of Emily Brontë (who was not at all a loving spirit) dignifies du Maurier's material, but it obliterates the rage to improve, the faith in the future, that inform *Wuthering Heights* and even such post-Victorian family histories as Galsworthy's *Forsyte Saga*. In *The Loving Spirit*, the future, like Janet Coombe, has nowhere to go.

This dead end characterizes du Maurier's female-centered so-called romances. Superficially Victorian in their idiom, allusions, and sometimes their settings, they have none of the combativeness of actual Victorian novels. Daphne du Maurier raises the ghosts of Charlotte and Emily Brontë to dispel their hopes. *Jamaica Inn*, one of her most popular adventure stories, is set in the nineteenth century. Like so many Victorian heroes, Mary Yellan is an orphan. She travels from the cultivated south to live with her aunt in the rugged north. When, in Elizabeth Gaskell's *North and South* (1855), Margaret Hale makes a similar journey, her honor and courage (and some help from the plot) allow her to conquer every environment she enters, but Mary Yellan travels north only to be conquered.

Her terrifying uncle, Joss Merlyn, has turned her once-jolly aunt into a tremulous battered wife. The enormous, roaring Joss is an animalistic caricature of male violence, all drunken threats and broken teeth; Mary discovers that he is a smuggler and a shipwrecker as well. She is on some level drawn to this repulsive creature, eventually falling in love with his brother Jem, a younger and possibly tempered version of Joss, as Emily Brontë's Hareton was of Heathcliff. The only man Mary trusts, a gentle albino vicar, turns out to be the madman behind the wrecking operation. Jem saves her in the nick of time from entrapment in the vicar's grandiose religious fantasies. She and Jem go still farther north at the end, where they will live a vagabond, possibly brutal existence.

These three ravaging men dominate *Jamaica Inn*; Mary spends the novel bouncing from one to the other. Her progress is an increasing loss of control. Du Maurier's intense evocation of the Cornish moors recalls *Wuthering Heights*, but Brontë's Cathy belonged on the moors, while Mary is dragged about on them by one or another abductor. Only du Maurier's men—the giant Joss, the vagabond Jem, and the psychotic vicar, who imagines himself a Druid divinity, the spirit of a Tor—are allowed to emanate from the landscape.

A Brontë heroine would surely tame Jem Merlyn—who orders Mary around and talks gaily about wife beating—before marrying him; Mary meekly gets into his cart, not daring to correct him in anything. The Victorian veneer of *Jamaica Inn* is a dismal comment on the progress of romance. Written while the author was steeped in her paternal predecessors (it appeared between *Gerald* and *The Du Mauriers*), *Jamaica Inn* is dominated by insanely powerful men who claim its landscape. Women exist to be brutalized and carted around. Daphne du Maurier had written about—and as—too many men to see herself as one of those women, but in *Rebecca*, her next novel, she edged close enough to let them tell their story.

In *Rebecca*, du Maurier uses a female narrator for the first time, one who has no name but "Mrs. de Winter." And that name is scarcely hers, so besieged is she by her predecessor. For its author, *Rebecca* was no romance: she saw more hatred in it than love. Maxim de Winter, owner of Manderley, the estate that is more alive than any of the characters, is as brutal as the men of *Jamaica Inn*, but Maxim needs no huge body; his power is in his social class. When du Maurier transposed to a scion of the landed gentry the sadism of *Jamaica Inn*, choosing as her narrator a helpless girl who is more servant than wife, readers from 1936 to the present inexplicably proclaimed the novel a great love story in the manner of *Jane Eyre*.

Rebecca evokes Charlotte Brontë's *Jane Eyre* as deliberately as *The Loving Spirit* and *Jamaica Inn* evoke *Wuthering Heights*. As with her earlier novels, du Maurier resuscitates a Brontë sister to dash her hopes. *Jane Eyre* is, like *Rebecca*, a class romance, the first-person narrative of a poor working girl whose moody employer falls in love with her. Like Maxim, Brontë's Rochester is hagridden by a first wife, the secret of whose demonic existence he alone knows. Like Maxim's Manderley, Rochester's Thornfield burns down at the end, leaving its owner crippled and diminished, but a husband at last.

Jane Eyre, though, is about a reformer. Jane is a proud, self-affirming narrator; Mrs. de Winter is crushed and humble even when she is a wife. As a pauper, Jane refuses to accept her place; as lady of the manor, the fragile Mrs. de Winter cringes before the servants. Jane combats Rochester's sultanic pride even before she learns of his intended bigamy; Mrs. de Winter stands helplessly by as Maxim verbally cuffs her around, confesses, and falls. Subdued from beginning to end, she does nothing to tame a landowner far more dangerous than Rochester.

The marriage that ends *Jane Eyre* rewards Jane's integrity: only after making her own life (and, by the by, inheriting a fortune) does she return to Rochester, no longer a servant but "an independent woman." The marriage that ends *Jane Eyre* begins *Rebecca*. Rather than transcending servitude, it looks suspiciously like more of the same. Maxim's jocular proposal, "instead of being companion to Mrs. Van Hopper you become mine, and your duties will be almost exactly the same" (chap. 6), comes true in the course of the story. Creeping around Manderley in the shadow of its past and the servants who perpetuate that past, she is, as Maxim scathingly says, like a "between-maid" who doesn't know her duties. She ends as she began, escorting Max to oppressively sunny watering places, soothing him as she had Mrs. Van Hopper.

In *Jane Eyre*, a concluding marriage was an emblem of independence. *Rebecca* turns its focus to marriage itself and its stupefying dependence. Mrs. de Winter marries into the life from which

Jane Eyre saved herself. According to one critic, Jane Eyre cherishes her autonomy throughout her love story, while Mrs. de Winter tries only to dissolve into her husband's power: "Where the protagonist of *Rebecca* merges with Maxim as he narrates the murder of a vilified other woman, Jane cannot do so. The man she loves is in effect beating another woman: she neither calls it love nor justifies it through righteous hate; she can and does silently note it" (Massé, p. 228). A Victorian declaration of separateness becomes, in the twentieth century, a romance of submergence.

Rebecca disavows the progress and continuity inherent in even the most subversive Victorian novels. Like Evelyn Waugh's *Handful of Dust* (1934), it is a romance about England's last days. When Manderley burns, there is no smaller English house for the purified de Winters, but only foreign hotels. "There would be no resurrection," the narrator promises after dreaming that she, like Rebecca, is haunting a Manderley "gone native," choked with "nameless parasites" (chap. 1). Most of du Maurier's fans know that Manderley is modeled after Menabilly, the Cornish estate she discovered in 1928 and leased from 1943 to 1969: since the estate was entailed, she could not buy it. Du Maurier put as much energy into restoring Menabilly as she did into resurrecting the du Maurier family; she also restored it imaginatively as the setting of her historical novel, *The King's General* (1946); but her narrator does nothing with a Manderley no one can restore, for the England of *Rebecca* contains nothing to preserve.

Even in its flourishing time under Rebecca's management, Manderley was an empty showplace, besieged by the sea on the west and the overgrowth on the east. Mrs. Danvers reverently preserves the room Rebecca scarcely slept in: her true homes were the cottage by the bay and her London flat. Only Maxim was foolish enough to believe Manderley would have an heir, and out of fear that another man fathered that nonexistent heir, he killed Rebecca. Before either wife lived in it, Manderley was dead to the future. *Rebecca* is not only Daphne du Maurier's first novel with a female narrator; it is her first work about England's last days, a theme that suffused her writing after the Second World War.

Rebecca is so steeped in domestic claustrophobia that its great house scarcely seems associated with the rest of England. Moreover, Manderley strangles itself from within. After the war, du Maurier looked for external enemies. "The Birds" (1952) is as indisputable an invasion story as was her Uncle Guy's popular play, *An Englishman's Home*, in 1909. But *An Englishman's Home* had stirred war fever against the Germans; Daphne's birds are clearly following orders, but no one learns whose they are. Her last novel, *Rule Britannia* (1972), is less equivocal. The invading enemy is wealthy, paternalistic America, who plans to turn England into a theme park where cutely costumed natives will reenact the British past—no doubt at restored estates like Menabilly. A crusty old actress and her six adopted sons lead a resistance that expels the invaders, but the national future is bleak.

Rebecca is not so patriotic or politically explicit, but its domestic decay has national overtones du Maurier's later fiction will explore. The novel's awkward construction, whereby Rebecca, its governing spirit, mutates suddenly from oppressively good to oppressively evil, exposes the sham of Manderley itself, as well as the marriages Manderley breeds. *Rebecca* is not as well conceived as such later du Maurier works as the seamless *My Cousin Rachel* and *The House on the Strand*, but despite its self-division and essential despair, it has lasted longer than any of du Maurier's books.

Its popularity continues in part because Hollywood has implanted a softer *Rebecca* in the public memory. The 1940 Academy Award–winning film directed by du Maurier's countryman Alfred Hitchcock, in which Laurence Olivier and Joan Fontaine glamorize the central characters, tames the novel into being the tidy romance it isn't. Like the other actors who had been offered the part of Maxim, Olivier would not play a wife murderer, so Hitchcock makes Rebecca stumble and hit her head. The script demonstrates reassuringly that Olivier loves Joan Fontaine more than he does Manderley; the priorities of du Maurier's Maxim are less certain. A later BBC serialization with authentically creepy performances by Jeremy Brett and Joanna David is closer to du Maurier's novel, but Hitchcock's *Rebecca* was not the last film adaptation to turn fiction about hate into movies about love.

THE TALES AND THE MOVIES

DAPHNE du Maurier's nine collections of tales are less well known than her novels. Perhaps because she knew their audience would be smaller, their anger and despair are unrestrained. Some, like *Monte Verità* (1952) and "The Way of the Cross" (in *Not After Midnight and Other Stories*, 1971), are clotted with a murky religiosity that sits uncomfortably on a writer more at home with eeriness than reverence; some, like "The Chamois," are merely obscure; but most, in their intensifying mystery and danger, are as good as any tales of terror ever written. In these, the loved and patronized Daphne du Maurier does not perform on cue. It is tempting, though, to see the best tales as an extract of her vision, with no adulterating romance and adventure plots to distract from her mordant perceptions.

"The Blue Lenses" (1959), for example, is an extract of wifeliness as *Rebecca* defines it. *Rebecca* courts ghosts, but it stops short of the supernaturalism "The Blue Lenses" embraces. Convalescing from an eye operation, a once-contented wife sees with washed eyes her nurses, doctors, and husband: all wear the heads of predatory animals. When the lenses are removed, so are the animal heads—until she sees in the mirror that her eyes are "doe's eyes, wary before sacrifice, and the timid deer's head was meek, already bowed" (*The Breaking Point*, p. 86). The operation has allowed her to see her life too well.

In *Jamaica Inn*, Mary knew the kindly vicar was mad when she found his savage caricatures of his congregation as sheep and himself as a wolf. Daphne du Maurier's tales express a similar hidden bestiality; they expose the predation within the pieties. Such a vision is far from exceptional; since Ann Radcliffe became a best-seller in eighteenth-century England, woman writers have shared their sense of danger with avid female readers. Charlotte Perkins Gilman's novella *The Yellow Wallpaper* (1892), a maddened wife's view of her menacing sickroom, is only one possible precursor of "The Blue Lenses." Somehow, though, unlike those of the activist Gilman, Daphne du Maurier's dark visions looked escapist rather than seditious in their time.

Movies glamorized and in part obscured her. Just as George and Gerald were made for the theater, she seemed made for film, the medium her father hated. Strapped for money in his last unhappy years, Gerald had dragged himself through a few movies, including Alfred Hitchcock's *Lord Camber's Ladies* (1931), an experience he loathed. He urged his daughter to write plays, but when she did they were formulaic and conventional. Her novels and stories, however, seemed to transplant naturally to film, enhancing her popularity even when the movies were poor. But even the two best film adaptations—Alfred Hitchcock's *The Birds* (1963) and Nicolas Roeg's *Don't Look Now* (1973)—soften her tales of terror by adding alien love stories.

Du Maurier's "The Birds" is a bleakly impersonal account of the end of England, and perhaps of the world. Nat, the central character, is, unlike most of du Maurier's men, a mere function. He crams his family into smaller and smaller spaces, responding with futile practicality to the bird attacks on doors and windows. Guy du Maurier's 1909 invasion play, *An Englishman's Home,* had made audiences love his archetypal British family, Mr. and Mrs. Brown, but Daphne's Hockens are as characterless as her birds. The efficiency with which the birds attack, the characters respond, and the story is told generates terror without pity.

Hitchcock transplants the story from a cold, claustrophobic English winter to a northern California suffused with sun and space. Hitchcock's most frightening scenes are not claustrophobic, but panoramic: the birds come dive-bombing out of a huge sky, filling vast amounts of space. The focus is psychological, not, as it was in du Maurier's story, political: we hear about a few other California towns, but no one wonders about the rest of the world, nor does anyone speculate about which nation programmed the birds. Hitchcock's *Birds* plays on sexual rather than invasion fears. Its central character, the enigmatic blonde Melanie Daniels, may or may not have aroused the birds when square-jawed Mitch Brenner aroused her own sexuality. By the end of the movie, spoiled Melanie is tamed into near catatonia and, presumably, redeemed. Like her, the birds are at least quiescent at the end.

Hitchcock's love story makes one realize how loveless du Maurier's "The Birds" is. No one is tender; no one has memories; no one says gallant good-byes. None of du Maurier's characters has the power to cause the attack; they merely adjust to it. Hitchcock's *Birds* turns immobilized England into dynamic America and political paranoia into psychosexuality, but du Maurier's tale is larger than Hitchcock's movie because no one in it has time for a love story.

Du Maurier loved Nicolas Roeg's opulent *Don't Look Now,* but Roeg's movie is frightening in a different way from her own 1970 novella (in *Not After Midnight,* 1971). Both concern a bereaved couple traveling in Venice; they meet two spiritualist sisters who claim to have seen their dead daughter. The sisters assert that the child has come back from death to warn John, the husband, that he is in danger. Nevertheless, John obstinately remains in Venice, where he becomes increasingly drunk and lost. In his befuddlement, he follows a red-cloaked child up a flight of stairs. The child turns out to be a homicidal dwarf who murders him. In both the novella and the movie, the psychic husband has denied or misconstrued both his own visions and the women who understand them. His ignominious death is a failure of faith.

In du Maurier's novella, though, the emphasis is on the animosity between husband and wife. An occult community of women—the wife, the psychic sisters, the dead daughter—draws together against ill-tempered John. Lesbian undercurrents infuse this female alliance. "Venice" was du Maurier's code for "homosexual" (heterosexuals did "Cairo"); her earlier Venetian story, "Ganymede," adapts Thomas Mann's novella *Death in Venice* to trace the homosexual humiliation and criminal entanglement of a naive classical scholar. The psychic sisters in du Maurier's *Don't Look Now,* who, the wife jokes, are "male twins in drag," wear old-fashioned lesbian garb. In Roeg's movie, they are merely feeble and dithery and the psychic sister is blind; but in du Maurier's novella, they lure Laura beyond marriage into new, transforming perceptions as the mountain cult lured Anna in *Monte Verità.*

By contrast, Roeg's *Don't Look Now* is an uncommonly romantic celebration of married love. Nothing but accident and death can separate beautiful young Donald Sutherland and Julie Christie—who, as Pauline Kael points out, look alike "with matching curly hairdos" (*Reeling,* p. 320). Roeg inserts in the middle of the movie a lingering lovemaking sequence that flashes intermittently forward to the couple's dressing and dinner, suffusing these mundane actions with a tender erotic glow. Echoing John's psychic flashes into a tragic future, this famous sequence spreads its romantic warmth through the movie, overwhelming the hostility at the heart of du Maurier's *Don't Look Now.* Roeg's love scene gives the story emotional depth, making us care about the characters, but it is a love scene Daphne du Maurier would never have written.

Both Alfred Hitchcock and Nicolas Roeg soften the works they adapt by adding to du Maurier's stark vision love stories she never conceived. These gifted directors not only beautify du Maurier for the movies; they feminize her as well, turning her impersonal, almost inhuman tales into the romances her admirers want them to be.

CONCLUSION

DAPHNE du Maurier has been wrongly dismissed as a writer of escapist romances. She is an author of extraordinary range and frequent brilliance. Her need to come to terms with her du Maurier legacy was her primary literary training: her research into the lives of her grandfather and father helped her become a superb biographer and an acute portraitist of men. Her most sustained novels assume a male point of view, but even the familiar female-centered romances are darker and more probing than Hollywood adaptations have made them look. Like many woman writers, du Maurier has been sentimentalized by readers who refuse to see her anger, her insight into male madness, her sardonic analyses of social power and powerlessness, and her affiliation with a tradition of female horror fiction that began in the late eighteenth century and continues today.

SELECTED BIBLIOGRAPHY

I. NOVELS BY GEORGE DU MAURIER. *Peter Ibbetson* (New York, 1891; London, 1892); *Trilby* (New York, 1894); *The Martian* (New York, 1897).

II. BIOGRAPHY AND CRITICISM. Leonée Ormond, *George Du Maurier* (London, 1969); Pauline Kael, *Reeling* (Boston, 1976); Richard Kelly, *George Du Maurier* (Boston, 1983); Richard Kelly, *Daphne du Maurier* (Boston, 1987); James Harding, *Gerald du Maurier, the Last Actor-Manager* (London, 1989); Lillian Faderman, *Odd Girls and Twilight Lovers: A History of Lesbian Life in Twentieth-Century America* (New York, 1991); Martyn Shallcross, *The Private World of Daphne du Maurier* (London, 1991; New York, 1992); Michelle A. Massé, *In the Name of Love: Women, Masochism, and the Gothic* (Ithaca, N.Y., and London, 1992); Margaret Forster, *Daphne du Maurier: The Secret Life of the Renowned Storyteller* (London, 1993).

III. NOVELS BY DAPHNE DU MAURIER. *The Loving Spirit* (London and New York, 1931); *I'll Never Be Young Again* (London and New York, 1932); *The Progress of Julius* (London and New York, 1933); *Jamaica Inn* (London and New York, 1936); *Rebecca* (London and New York, 1938); *Frenchman's Creek* (London, 1941; New York, 1942); *Hungry Hill* (London and New York, 1943); *The King's General* (London and New York, 1946); *The Parasites* (London, 1949; New York, 1950); *My Cousin Rachel* (London, 1951; New York, 1952); *Mary Anne* (London and New York, 1954); *The Scapegoat* (London and New York, 1957); *Castle Dor*, with Arthur Quiller-Couch (London and New York, 1962); *The Glass-Blowers* (London and New York, 1963); *The Flight of The Falcon* (London and New York, 1965); *The House on the Strand* (London and New York, 1969); *Rule Britannia* (London, 1972; New York, 1973).

IV. BIOGRAPHIES AND MEMOIRS BY DAPHNE DU MAURIER. *Gerald: A Portrait* (London, 1934; New York, 1935); *The Du Mauriers* (London and New York, 1937); *The Young George du Maurier: A Selection of His Letters, 1860–1867* (London, 1951), as ed.; *The Infernal World of Branwell Brontë* (London, 1960; New York, 1961); *Vanishing Cornwall* (London and New York, 1967); *Golden Lads: Sir Francis Bacon, Anthony Bacon, and Their Friends* (New York, 1975); *The Winding Stair: Francis Bacon, His Rise and Fall* (London, 1976; New York, 1977); *Growing Pains: The Shaping of a Writer* (London, 1977), also pub. as *Myself When Young* (New York, 1977); *The Rebecca Notebook and Other Memories* (New York, 1980; London, 1981).

V. PLAYS BY DAPHNE DU MAURIER. *The Years Between* (London, 1945; New York, 1946); *September Tide* (London, 1949; New York, 1960).

VI. COLLECTIONS OF STORIES BY DAPHNE DU MAURIER. *Come Wind, Come Weather* (London, 1940; New York, 1941); *Happy Christmas* (New York, 1940); *The Apple Tree: A Short Novel and Some Stories* (London, 1952), repub. as *Kiss Me Again, Stranger: A Collection of Eight Stories, Long and Short* (New York, 1953); *Early Stories* (London, 1954); *The Breaking Point* (London and New York, 1959); *Not After Midnight and Other Stories* (London, 1971), also pub. as *Don't Look Now* (New York, 1971); *Echoes from the Macabre: Selected Stories* (London, 1976; New York, 1977); *The Rendezvous and Other Stories* (New York, 1980; London, 1981); *Daphne du Maurier's Classics from the Macabre* (Garden City, N.Y., 1987).

MARIA EDGEWORTH

(1768–1849)

Richard Braverman

MARIA EDGEWORTH is making a comeback. Although she was one of the most popular British novelists of the early nineteenth century, she fell out of favor in the 1830s and has lingered at the margins of literary history ever since. Whether she will secure a niche in the mainstream canon is hard to say, but given the current interest in women's fiction, Anglo-Irish relations, and colonialism, her reputation is on the mend. However, it is unlikely that she will again be revered as she was at the height of her popularity, the years between 1800 and 1815. Not only was she the best-known British novelist during that period, she was also the best paid, receiving £2,100 for her fifth novel, *Patronage,* in 1814. By comparison, Walter Scott was paid £700 for *Waverley* the same year. The disparity did not turn many heads at the time because Scott was still building a following, whereas Edgeworth's work guaranteed commercial success. The situation was soon to change, however. Following *Waverley,* Scott captured the fictional field that Edgeworth all but left after the death of her father in 1817. She continued to write but completed just one more novel, *Helen,* before her death in 1849, at the age of eighty-one. We can only speculate what else she might have contributed to English letters had she been as productive after 1817 as she was before. Even so, she left behind a formidable body of work that includes classics of children's literature and ground-breaking studies of Irish language and culture in addition to ten novels. Her modern biographer, Marilyn Butler, aptly sums up her achievement: "No Englishwoman had a comparable literary career before George Eliot."

Besides being a popular writer, Edgeworth was a major figure in early-nineteenth-century literary history. Her stories for children set the standard for juvenile literature well into the century; her novels of fashionable life did much to refocus fiction on social mores after the Gothic, sentimental, and philosophical trends of the 1790s; and her Irish tales established a subgenre, the regional novel. She was not an innovator by nature, however. Although she lived in the Romantic age, she was never caught up in the heady ideologies of the time; yet, wary as she was of the radical ideas that swept through England and France, she possessed liberal views on religion and class. Her instinctive Whiggism was grounded in an Enlightenment optimism about social reform. Convinced that society could be harnessed in the name of progress, she vigorously supported the socioeconomic rehabilitation of post-Union Ireland. But at the same time, as a member of the Anglo-Irish gentry, she held fast to the paternalistic assumption that social reform was contingent upon the stability of the landed gentry. That is, reform should proceed from the top down because it was the responsibility of the landed elite to create a more equitable Ireland.

Maria Edgeworth was born on 1 January 1768 at Black Bourton in Oxfordshire, the second surviving child of Anna Maria Elers and Richard Lovell Edgeworth. When Maria was five, her mother died in childbirth; just four months later her father married Honora Sneyd, whom he had come to know in the final years of his unhappy first marriage. His second was emotionally richer but less fertile; Honora bore two children before dying of tuberculosis in 1780. Less than eight months later he was married again, this time to Honora's sister, Elizabeth. The seventeen-year union produced nine children before Elizabeth's death in 1797. The following year Edgeworth married a fourth time; Frances Anne Beaufort, who outlived him, bore him six children. With the arrival of the last, Michael, in 1812, Edgeworth was a father for the twenty-second time.

Of the twenty-two children, eighteen survived infancy. The ever-growing family was the day-today focus of Edgeworth's life from her teens well into her forties. Not only did she serve as mother's helper and tutor to successive groups of half siblings but, as an unmarried woman, she seldom ventured far from the family seat in Ireland. Although it would have been unusual for an unmarried woman of her class to strike out on her own, there was another, more compelling reason why she remained at Edgeworthstown: she wanted to be near her father, who was the intellectual and emotional center of her life.

A man of enormous energy and diverse interests, Richard Edgeworth was very much a product of the Enlightenment. Although he read classics at Trinity College, Dublin, and at Oxford, he developed an interest in experimental science that led to his membership in the Lunar Society of Birmingham. But for all his involvement with men like Matthew Boulton and James Watt, who were at the forefront of the industrial revolution transforming English society, his most substantial contribution was to educational theory and practice. Fascinated by Rousseau, he applied the principles sketched out in *Emile* to the early training of his firstborn, Richard. The experiment was unsuccessful, but Edgeworth would not be deterred; he simply dropped Rousseau and pressed forward with a program based on ideas from John Locke and Joseph Priestley. Its academic core was the substitution of a modern curriculum for the classics, and its pedagogic foundation was the Lockean association of ideas: from the earliest age, learning should be experienced as a pleasurable activity.

Those were the precepts; what was lacking was instructional material to carry out the experiment. Anna Laetitia Barbauld's *Lessons for Children from Two to Three Years Old* (1778) was a start. But the dearth of available material written expressly for children led Edgeworth to tackle the problem himself. He had help from Honora, then from Elizabeth, and finally from Maria. Maria's contribution, by far the most important, resulted in two landmark collections, *The Parent's Assistant* (1796) and *Early Lessons* (1801), and a theoretical treatise, *Practical Education* (1798).

The years when Maria Edgeworth was developing into Britain's first classic writer for children were among her happiest. But they came after a long period of discontent caused by her only intermittent contact with her father before he moved the family from England to the ancestral estate in Ireland in 1782. Prior to that time she spent the better part of each year at boarding school, first at Mrs. Latuffiere's in Derby and later at the more upscale establishment run by Mrs. Devis in London. Maria did not thrive at either place. A shy girl with little confidence, she was self-conscious about her plain looks and diminutive stature. Although she was too withdrawn to make many friends, she was nevertheless admired for her skill as a storyteller. But that admiration did little to alleviate her sense of isolation because her parents paid little attention to her even during school vacations. That situation changed abruptly in the summer of 1781, when she was diagnosed with a severe eye disorder that threatened to blind her. Her father finally realized how much he had neglected a daughter desperate for his attention. The following year Maria accompanied the family to Edgeworthstown.

The Edgeworths had been landowners in County Longford for more than two centuries as the result of the post-Reformation policy that created a Protestant landowning class in Ireland. One of the by-products of the Protestant Ascendancy was a deep-seated contempt for the Catholic majority, a contempt that had not significantly abated by the later eighteenth century, despite stirrings of reform. The heart of the matter was religion, but it had deep economic ramifications. After William III's reconquest in the years 1689–1691, Ireland was burdened by a steady stream of restrictive laws aimed at eradicating the Catholic religion; the policy failed in the long run because most of the penal laws were repealed in the 1780s and 1790s. More successful was the economic yoke that held the nation in the grip of colonial subjection. While the English reaped profits from the Irish trade in woolens and cattle, the near-dictatorial role of Westminster bolstered the Anglo-Irish gentry, who owned the overwhelming majority of the country's land.

Responsibility did not necessarily go hand in hand with ownership, however. Many of the nation's approximately two thousand estate owners were lifelong residents, but the wealthier gentry migrated to Dublin for the winter and the largest landowners frequently lived outside of Ireland, rarely visiting their properties. Richard Edgeworth was an Irish absentee before he returned to County Longford in 1782, ostensibly to rescue an estate near bankruptcy. Before long, though, he had seized the opportunity to break with the pattern of his class by putting the principles of contemporary political economy to the test. Such a project was a formidable challenge, if the lament that one frustrated gentry improver, Edward Newenham, wrote in a letter to Benjamin Franklin (October 1784) is any indication:

I visited many of their wretched hovels, and endeavoured to convince them how easy it was to better their station. I explained the whole system of agriculture to them, and promised that their landlord would give them a long lease; I stated to them the comfort of warm clothing and comfortable houses; no answer, but that if such things had been possible, their father would have done so. The inhabitants of "Otaheiti" are intelligent beings and industrious people when compared to those wretches.

Progressive estate management was a crucial step toward reform but, as Edgeworth saw it, economic progress had to be accompanied by political justice for Catholics. Hoping to implement his ideas on a national level, he ran for a vacant seat in Parliament in 1796. But his bid failed when local gentry power brokers refused to support an advocate of Catholic emancipation.

It was not until after the Union with Britain in 1800 that the wounds from the abortive parliamentary bid healed sufficiently for the Edgeworths again to be welcome in local gentry society. In the meantime, Edgeworth ran his estate with a benevolent but firm hand, involving himself in the lives of his tenants without losing sight of their shortcomings. As Maria observed:

If the people had found or suspected him to be weak, or, as they call it, *easy*, there would have been an end of all hope of really doing them good. They would have cheated, loved, and despised a mere *easy* landlord; and his property would have gone to ruin, without either permanently bettering their interests or their morals. He, therefore, took especial care, that they should be convinced of his strictness in punishing, as well as of his desire to reward.

(*Memoirs of Richard Lovell Edgeworth*, p. 234)

Maria knew her father's business because she made it her own. Soon after the family's return to Ireland, she trained herself as his assistant, traveling with him when he first surveyed his properties in 1782 and serving as his amanuensis in the succeeding years. The experience proved to be invaluable for her studies of Irish culture and tales of Irish life. But those days were still some time

off, for her career as a writer began with her children's fiction.

Not until the second half of the eighteenth century did children have a literature of their own. Prior to that time, what was written for them was by and large the popular stuff of the chapbook variety. That changed in the 1780s, when booksellers discovered a market for quality literature for the children of the middle and upper classes. The field was soon crowded with authors. Sarah Trimmer, Eleanor Fenn, and Dorothy Kilner were among the best known when Edgeworth began writing for the children at Edgeworthstown, but it was not long before she surpassed them. She brought to juvenile literature something it had never had: an intuitive appreciation of the child's viewpoint. Stories like "The Purple Jar" and "Simple Susan" proved to be so popular because they had plots with which children could easily identify. While they pleased, the stories sought to instruct; as part of her father's pedagogic program, they were designed to build verbal skills incrementally. Their ultimate goal, however, was moral; their most familiar lesson was the value of self-discipline.

While she was developing as a writer for children, Edgeworth sought to establish a more independent voice in the fiction she began to write for a wider audience. Her first effort, *Letters for Literary Ladies* (1795), was a collection of short essays in the form of letters, exchanged between two educated women, on women's rights, marriage, and social conventions. *Letters for Literary Ladies* was in tune with the times because the "woman question" figured in the political discourse of the revolutionary 1790s. It was not the stuff of high politics, but it was an integral part of the debate in which conservatives like Edmund Burke reiterated "family values" against Jacobins at home and abroad. One of those home-grown Jacobins, Mary Wollstonecraft, opened the way for *Literary Ladies* with her treatise *A Vindication of the Rights of Woman* (1792). Unlike Wollstonecraft, Edgeworth was not a radical advocate of women's rights. Nevertheless, she firmly believed that women should be permitted greater latitude in thought and action than prevailing social conventions allowed. And she pursued that conviction in her novels of manners, taking issue with the routine presentation of women as emotional beings undone by their excessive sensibility.

The 1790s, a decade of revolution on the Continent, was also a tempestuous time in Ireland. After the defeat of imperial Britain in the American

Revolution, a vocal minority of Irishmen were inspired by patriotic sentiments that found political expression in the movement for national sovereignty. The movement brought the repeal of many of the religious restrictions on Catholics, but few Ascendancy Protestants were willing to share political power. Reform on that front was slow in coming until the Rebellion of 1798 demonstrated to Westminster that the situation in Ireland was an urgent political problem. The domestic threat was not the sole issue, for the Rebellion was quashed in a few weeks. What daunted the British was the participation of the French, which renewed long-standing fears that Ireland would be a staging ground for a full-scale invasion. That never happened, but because it was a distinct possibility in 1798, William Pitt the Younger pushed to bring Ireland into the United Kingdom. Two years later, it became part of Great Britain under the Act of Union.

The Union did not please Irish nationalists because it did little to further Catholic emancipation, but it was endorsed by the ruling elite as the best route to peaceful change. That view was shared by Richard Edgeworth, who revised his early Jacobinism after he was nearly lynched by a Catholic mob during the Rebellion of 1798. Although sympathetic to the Irish, Edgeworth favored gradual reform over radical change; he did not believe that the Irish were prepared for self-rule and therefore needed to be led by a committed gentry. That was the ideological context in which Maria wrote some of her most popular and enduring works, the novels of Anglo-Irish life that emphasized the obligations of the gentry both to their tenantry and to the nation. *Ennui* (1809), *The Absentee* (1812), and *Ormond* (1817) all turn on the central importance of the Union, which Maria, remarked Walter Scott in his preface to *Waverley*, "may be truly said to have done more towards completing . . . than perhaps all the legislative enactments by which it has been followed up." That is a big "perhaps," but in writing about provincial life, Edgeworth brought attention to Irish affairs in England as well as in Ireland in the quarter century preceding Catholic emancipation.

CASTLE RACKRENT *AND* IRISH BULLS

ALTHOUGH the Union with Great Britain was a significant subtext of the Irish novels Edgeworth wrote after 1800, that was not the case with *Castle Rackrent*, her first novel. It was published in 1800, though the idea for it first arose around 1795. Most of it was drafted that year and the next, with the section on the last Rackrent, Sir Condy, added sometime before the end of 1798. The title page says that the story is "An Hibernian Tale, Taken From Facts, And From The Manners of the Irish Squires, Before the Year 1782." Those "facts and manners" had their genesis in the Edgeworth past, for several of the Rackrent squires were drawn from Maria's research in the family archives. "Before the Year 1782" had a family subtext, too; that was the year Richard Edgeworth returned to Ireland to save the family estate. In *Castle Rackrent*, the mismanagement wrought by a slavish commitment to feudal custom is the root of an "Irish problem" that originates with the gentry and trickles down to the peasantry. The story is narrated by the old Irish servant Thady Quirk, who recounts the history of four generations of a gentry family of native Irish descent that had turned Protestant only recently. While Thady ostensibly reports on the Rackrent squires, he also provides the history of an estate that may very well pass from the Rackrents into the hands of his own son, Jason. That turnabout may mean nothing more than that the estate will no longer be abused by the Rackrents, but when all is said and done, the novel offers little solace to Ireland or the Irish.

As *Castle Rackrent* opens, Thady Quirk introduces himself as the venerable, if humble, caretaker of Rackrent history: "Having, out of friendship for the family, upon whose estate, praised be Heaven! I and mine have lived rent-free, time out of mind, voluntarily undertaken to publish the MEMOIRS of the RACKRENT FAMILY, I think it my duty to say a few words, in the first place, concerning myself" (4:1).[1] Although we learn little more than that he is called "honest Thady" by some and "old Thady" by others, what is implied is far more important: that we are about to view the gentry through the eyes of a servant. Thady has worked for all four Rackrents, and to set the record straight he starts with the first, Sir Patrick. A good-humored, besotted Irishman, Patrick is too generous for his own good, living beyond his means by having his house

---

[1] Unless otherwise noted, references in this essay to Edgeworth's work are from the 1967 ten-volume edition of her *Tales and Novels*. Citations are in volume:page format.

"from one year's end to another, as full of company as ever it could hold." Reputed to be the "inventor of raspberry whiskey," he not only lives by the bottle, he dies by it, too—right in the middle of a toast.

If Sir Patrick is too generous, the next Rackrent squire, Sir Murtagh, is just the opposite. A true rackrenter, he uses his knowledge of the law to prevent his tenants from taking advantage of him as they had Sir Patrick. His wife, Lady Murtagh, is no different. Thady suspects that "she had Scotch blood in her veins" because she constantly harasses tenants to see that they fulfill their feudal obligations. She gets under her husband's skin, too; he breaks a blood vessel and drops dead of apoplexy in the middle of a squabble over renewing a lease.

Next comes the rakish Sir Kit, who bleeds the estate to support his profligate ways. While he spends much time in Bath in the hope of snaring an heiress, he hires an unscrupulous agent who turns out old tenants, sells land, and rents farms below their value to produce cash. When nothing more can be squeezed from his holdings, he manages to salvage his lifestyle by the only option left: marriage. His wife, a rich Jew, brings a large dowry, but when she refuses to let him pawn her jewels, he is left with no choice but to mortgage the estate to Thady's son, Jason. Kit is killed in a duel soon after, and the last of the Rackrents, Sir Condy, is left with an estate on the brink of ruin.

Thady's favorite, Condy is a kindhearted Irishman who, like Sir Patrick, is too extravagant to manage his life or estate. He marries the daughter of a local landowner, but her father disapproves of the match and refuses to pay the dowry. Although he is short of money, Condy decides to stand for Parliament. He wins the election but loses his wife, who returns to her family as the creditors close in. Despondent, Sir Condy gorges himself until he is stricken with gout. When he dies following a drinking bout, the future of the Rackrent estate is uncertain. Some expect Jason to get it; others, Sir Condy's widow. But as Thady tells us, that is a matter for a court to decide.

When *Castle Rackrent* appeared anonymously in January 1800, Edgeworth had no reason to expect that it would be in its fifth edition by 1810 or that it would be admired by the likes of Walter Scott, William Pitt the Younger, and George III. The king reputedly remarked that the novel taught him something about his Irish subjects, yet like so many others he overestimated its social realism.

Thady's narrative is not about contemporary, but about feudal, Ireland, nor is it as disingenuous as the old servant claims at the end:

As for all I have here set down from memory and hearsay of the family, there's nothing but truth in it from beginning to end: that you may depend upon; for where's the use of telling lies about the things which every body knows as well as I do?

(4:63)

Although he is in general a devoted retainer, Thady does steal here and there from his masters; and at the end his own son sues for the estate. However, he is not an entirely reliable narrator. The conclusion conveys something of the Catholic resentment that pervaded the 1790s, but it is unlikely that many contemporary readers took the novel that way. What they found instead was a comic tale that brought Irish manners and characters to life in an unprecedented way. Their response indicated that they liked what they read.

If *Castle Rackrent* was meant to show English readers "a specimen of manners and characters which are perhaps unknown in England," the *Essay on Irish Bulls* (1802) took that intention a step further. Written by Maria in collaboration with her father, it revealed another dimension of Edgeworth's interest in Irish language and culture. Bulls are blunders that native Gaelic speakers make when using English. The ethnic jokes of their day, they were relished by the English as confirmation of Irish inferiority. Maria recorded and reproduced many of them verbatim in the essay, but she did so in an altruistic spirit. Fascinated by the idiosyncrasies of Irish speech from the time she first worked as her father's assistant, she recorded examples of usage and diction over the years; so did her father, who as an estate owner and local magistrate had numerous face-to-face encounters with the peasantry. Their collective research was the basis of *Irish Bulls*, which atoned for the unflattering image of Ireland in *Castle Rackrent*. There is some question whether the essay was exactly as advertised: "The examples we have cited are taken from real life, and given without alteration or embellishment" (4:84). But even if *Irish Bulls* veered toward the sentimental, it made a significant contribution to the study of Irish folk culture.

Because *Irish Bulls* finds linguistic blunders amusing, modern readers conditioned to look for signs of cultural patronization may miss its point. Edgeworth was not trying to convince the English that Irish Catholics were their equals; she merely aimed to suggest that they were worthy of something better than the cultural caricature that accompanied the nation's long, harsh subjection: "If in this slight essay we should succeed in diffusing a more just and enlarged idea of the Irish than has been generally entertained, we hope the English will deem it not an unacceptable service" (4:186). From the start, she insists that the Irish be understood on their own terms: "Many foreign pictures of Irishmen are as grotesque and absurd as the Chinese pictures of lions: having never seen that animal, the Chinese can paint him only from the descriptions of voyagers, which are sometimes ignorantly, sometimes wantonly, exaggerated" (4:185). But she is intelligent enough to avoid taking on the myth of Irish inferiority with an appeal to reason. Instead, she exploits Irish foibles to her argumentative advantage, converting weaknesses into strengths.

The strategy is similar to the one taken in the 1960s and 1970s when minorities were being assimilated into the American cultural mainstream through the medium of television. Comedy was the most conducive genre there, with the "sitcom" serving to ease fears about ethnic and racial "Others" by mixing newfound dignity with age-old vulnerability. Edgeworth does the same with the Irish, through focusing on their creative misuse of English. Although spoken bulls are the heart of the essay, she starts with written blunders, such as the official governmental proclamation describing the potato as "a species of grain." There are many others, but one of the best is the notice in a Cork newspaper for a plot of land, the inclusion of which in *Irish Bulls* demonstrates that "sporting" and "manure" were considered a mismatch even in the early days of advertising: "A few miles from Cork, in *a most sporting country*, bounded by an *uncommon fine* turf bog, on the verge of which there are a number of fine *lime kilns,* where that manure may be had on very moderate terms . . ." (4:93).

Found-humor aside, Edgeworth's main interest is the spoken idiom that she and her father observed and recorded. Her strategy here is to use folk culture to make the case for an Irish vernacular far more complex than it appeared to the English. The vernacular, she argues, is poetic, but it takes a trained ear to appreciate. Take, for example, the following description of an altercation between two Dublin bootblacks that her father heard in court:

Why, my lard, as I was going past the Royal Exchange I meets Billy. "Billy," says I, "will you sky a copper?" "Done," says he; "Done," says I; and done and done's enough between two jantlemen. With that I ranged them fair and even with my hook-em-snivey—up they go. "Music!" says he—"Skulls!" says I; and down they come, three brown mazards. "By the holy! you flesh'd 'em," says he. "You lie," says I. With that he ups with a lump of a two year old, and lets drive at me. I outs with my bread-earner, and gives it him up to Lamprey in the bread-basket.

(4:127)

Here is the translation: Two bootblacks were playing "heads and tails" when one threw a small paving stone at the other. The target of the stone drew out the knife (stamped near the hilt with the name of an eminent Dublin cutler, Lamprey) that he used to scrape shoes, and plunged it up to the hilt in the stone thrower's stomach. Edgeworth analyzes the passage as though it were a literary text, glossing words and phrases to show that the Irish routinely embellish their speech with figures and tropes. "To sky" for flip a coin, "copper" for a penny, "mazards" for heads—all are shown to make perfect sense. And what is more, they are not taken as vernacular oddities but as evidence of the Irish propensity for brilliantly evocative language, a propensity that led Edgeworth to find orators everywhere she stopped and listened:

The Irish nation, from the highest to the lowest, in daily conversation about the ordinary affairs of life, employ a superfluity of wit and metaphor which would be astonishing and unintelligible to a majority of the respectable body of English yeoman. Even the cutters of turf and drawers of whiskey are orators; even the *cottiers* and *gossoons* speak in trope and figure.

(4:141)

BELINDA

WITH *Castle Rackrent* and *Irish Bulls*, Edgeworth's interest in Irish life had just begun. Over the next decade and a half she would explore politics, class, and national identity in *Ennui, The Absentee,* and *Ormond.* However, the Irish novels were only a part of her story because she was equally renowned as a novelist of manners. When she arrived on the literary scene, women's fiction still had a rather low reputation; despite such practitioners as Fanny Burney and Elizabeth Inchbald, it was often dismissed as sentimental frivolity. Aiming to avoid that label, Edgeworth prefaced *Belinda* (1801), her first full-length novel, with a denial: "The following work is offered to the public as a Moral Tale—the author not wishing to acknowledge a Novel." But the work was very much a novel, even if one that was self-consciously aware of the pitfalls of sentimental fiction. Edgeworth was not alone there; Jane Austen objected to the prevailing forms of women's fiction in *Sense and Sensibility*, which had its origins in the 1790s. Like Austen, who took issue with the simplistic good girl–bad girl convention through two sisters, Marianne and Elinor, Edgeworth did much the same through Belinda's two mentors, Lady Delacour and Lady Percival. But Edgeworth does not quite carry it off because Belinda has too much sense and too little sensibility. As her friend and confidante Lady Delacour banters Belinda at the end of the novel:

Well, we have all of us seen *Pamela maritata*—let us now see *Belinda in love*, if that be possible. *If!* forgive me this last stroke, my dear—in spite of all my raillery, I do believe that the prudent Belinda is more capable of feeling real permanent passion than any of the dear sentimental young ladies, whose motto is "All for love, or the world well lost."

(3:456)

Belinda is not one of the "dear sentimental young ladies," yet she proves to be too rational because she chooses a man apparently incapable of a passionate attachment. Given her options, she makes the right choice, though it was not a choice that pleased Edgeworth. Some years later, she reflected in a letter to her cousin Sophy Ruxton: "I really was so provoked with the cold tameness of that stick or stone Belinda, that I could have torn the pages to pieces." But the public kept turning them; the novel was a hit.

The plot of *Belinda* was thoroughly familiar to contemporary readers. Like Fanny Burney's *Evelina*, it presents the story of a young lady's introduction to society and culminates in the choice of a marriage partner. As the novel opens, Belinda Portman's aunt, Mrs. Stanhope, uses her social connections to send her niece to London for the

season, in the hope that she will find a husband. She entrusts Belinda to Lady Delacour, a woman who knows how to negotiate London society as well as anyone. One of Edgeworth's most intriguing creations, Lady Delacour is fashionable to a tee. Yet she strains to keep up emotional appearances because her personal life has not been a happy one:

Abroad, and at home, Lady Delacour was two different persons. Abroad she appeared all life, spirit, and good humour—at home, listless, fretful, and melancholy; she seemed like a spoiled actress off the stage, over-stimulated by applause, and exhausted by the exertions of supporting a fictitious character.

(3:5)

She has taken to role-playing to compensate for a bad marriage, a predicament for which she blames herself: "I married my Lord Delacour, knowing him to be a fool, and believing that, for this reason, I should find no trouble in governing him. But what a fatal mistake!—a fool, of all animals in the creation, is the most difficult to govern" (3:31). To make matters worse, she fears she is suffering from breast cancer.

Belinda develops a strong rapport with this complex but tormented woman. Lady Delacour takes to Belinda, too, but as her troubles mount, she loses her equilibrium, eventually convincing herself that Belinda is no more than a schemer angling for her husband and his title after her death: "I am not so blind as you imagine—dupe as you think me, I have seen much in silence" (3:200). A stunned Belinda replies: "*You have suspected me long in silence!* Then I have mistaken your character—I can love you no longer. Farewell for ever. Find another—a better friend" (3:200). After the row, Belinda goes to live with the Percivals, who are a model of cheerful domesticity after the Delacours. She stays with them only a short time, however, then returns to see Lady Delacour through the treatment of her illness.

Between Lady Delacour and Lady Percival, Belinda gets more than enough advice about men. And she needs it because the marriage market provides her with three prospects: Sir Philip Baddely, who offers social status but is little more than a fop; Mr. Vincent, a more colorful character with a weakness for gambling; and Clarence Hervey, whose philosophical manner makes him a questionable candidate for a passionate attachment. In settling on Clarence Hervey, Belinda follows Lady Percival's sense rather than Lady Delacour's sensibility. Her unease with the choice comes across in her closing exchange with Lady Delacour, who proposes to conclude the novel as any respectable writer would: "'But I hope you will remember, dear Lady Delacour,' said Belinda, 'that there is nothing in which novelists are so apt to err as in hurrying things toward the conclusion: in not allowing *time* enough for that change of feeling, which change of situation cannot instantly produce'" (3:462). Lady Delacour volunteers to write five more volumes to give her the chance. But Belinda cannot hide the fact that she is not thrilled with the match. And Lady Delacour reminds her of it: "That's right, my dear Belinda; true to your principles to the last gasp. Fear nothing—you shall have *time* enough to become accustomed to Clarence" (3:462).

The year after *Belinda,* Edgeworth found herself in her heroine's situation: she received a marriage offer. The proposal came late in 1802, during a six-month stay in Paris with her father, stepmother, and sister Charlotte. Edgeworth was very attracted to Abraham Niclas Clewburg Edelcrantz, a reserved Swedish gentleman of forty-six who was private secretary to the king of Sweden. Her father, who had gone to Paris with the idea that Maria would have a better chance of finding a suitable husband there than in Ireland, favored the match. Maria, now thirty-four, was well aware that this might be her only opportunity for the husband and children she longed for. However, marriage to Edelcrantz meant leaving her home, family, and father; therefore she could not accept the offer.

Despite the disappointment, the trip to Paris was a success overall. Their work on education was known through French translation, so Maria and her father moved in the social circles of the intelligentsia. The brilliant salon life was a revelation to Maria, who must surely have recognized the deficiencies of the Irish gentry when she wrote to her brother Henry: "The title of philosopher or rather man of letters or science is the best possible title here. We see the French *scavans* mixing with most polite and elegant societies of both sexes not only without being considered heterogeneous beings, but as essential to the formation of *good* company" (*Maria Edgeworth in France and England,* p. 78). The visit came to an abrupt end after six months when Richard Edgeworth was summoned

to the British consulate. With the fragile peace between Britain and France about to end, the Edgeworths had to return to Ireland. Maria was not unhappy at the prospect, although for some time after, she could not get Edelcrantz out of her thoughts. She soon began a new novel, *Leonora,* hoping to please him with it. However, by the time it appeared in 1806, she once again was deeply involved with family life and literary projects. A spate of novels and tales appeared in the following years: *Manoeuvring* (1809), *Almeria* (1809), *Emilie de Coulanges* (1812), *Vivian* (1812), and *Patronage* (1814) are among the best. But the most significant works of these years were the Irish novels that were so admired by Scott, *Ennui* (1809) and *The Absentee* (1812).

ENNUI *AND* THE ABSENTEE

FIRST drafted in 1804, *Ennui* underwent extensive revision before it appeared in 1809. More ambitious than *Castle Rackrent* but less popular, it did not have a winning narrator like Thady Quirk and was not as nostalgic, being set in 1798 rather than "before 1782." Yet it was more political than *Castle Rackrent,* for 1798 was the year of the Irish Rebellion. Admittedly, the Rebellion plays only a marginal role in *Ennui;* however, it is a subtext throughout because the novel anticipates the Union that followed it. The Union, Ireland's best hope, is also the hope embodied by the work's hero, Lord Glenthorn, an Anglo-Irish absentee who suffers from the ennui of the title. A disease of the idle rich, ennui is also a disease of empire because it adversely affects Ireland through the neglect of expatriates like Glenthorn. To effect a cure, Glenthorn must return to the family estate and discover his Irish identity. His quest is at the same time political because his personal identity is bound up with Ireland's. As Edgeworth saw it, men like Glenthorn were needed to lead the nation into the post-Union future.

Ennui opens in London with Lord Glenthorn leading the life of a dissipated epicure. His parents died when he was young, and he has long since been confirmed "in the pride of helplessness" by being constantly reminded that he is "the only son and heir of the Earl of Glenthorn." With little incentive to apply himself, he drifts aimlessly through life, trying, with little success, to stave off boredom. He marries impulsively, and when that fails, he grows despondent. To combat his ennui, he decides to leave England for a respite and visit the family seat in Ireland.

On the first leg of the journey he travels to Dublin, where he reflects on the promise and shortcomings of pre-Union Ireland as he surveys the city: "In driving through the streets, I was, however, surprised to see buildings, which my prejudices could scarcely believe to be Irish. . . . I was struck with instances of grand beginnings and lamentable want of finish, with mixture of the magnificent and the paltry; of admirable and execrable taste" (4:242). He sees the squalor of the slums as well. Nevertheless, he leaves Dublin in high spirits, impatient to see his estate. On the four-day journey that follows, he gets his first taste of a peasant culture that is unlike anything he has ever experienced. In one unforgettable encounter, he comes face to face with Irish primitivism in the person of a coachman

dressed like a mad beggar, in half a hat and half a wig, both awry in opposite directions; a long tattered greatcoat, tied round his waist by a hay-rope: the jagged rents in the skirts of his coat showing his bare legs marbled of many colours; while something like stockings hung loose about his ankles. The noises he made, by way of threatening or encouraging his steeds, I pretend not to describe.

(4:243–244)

Glenthorn responds with the fascinated revulsion of an Irish lord who has spent his life in London, then presses on, anxious to reach the family seat.

The scene turns Gothic when he finally approaches Glenthorn Castle, which he glimpses by moonlight: "It seemed to rise from the sea, abrupt and insulated, in all the gloomy grandeur of ancient times, with turrets and battlements, and a huge gateway, the pointed arch of which receded in perspective between the projecting towers" (4:250). If he is taken by the mystery of the place, the place is certainly a mystery to him. After being greeted by joyous tenants, he soon finds out how he fits into their world. He is their benefactor, an almsgiver who attracts a steady flow of sturdy beggars:

The method of doing good, which seemed to require the least exertion, and which I, therefore, most willingly practised, was giving away money. I did not wait to inquire, much less to examine into the merits of the claimants; but, without selecting proper objects, I relieved myself from the uneasy feeling of pity, by indiscriminate donations to objects apparently the most miserable.

(4:263)

Glenthorn's impulse does not please his steward, M'Leod, a Scotsman who has been on the job for more than twenty years. A "hard-featured, strongbuilt, perpendicular man with a remarkable quietness of deportment," M'Leod resembles Edgeworth's own father in his kindly but sober view of the tenantry. He advises that they be given short leases that reward initiative, in order to make them rely on their own industry. Glenthorn ignores M'Leod at first, but later admits that the money he gave away was either

wasted at the dram-shop, or became the subject of family-quarrels; and those whom I had *relieved* returned to *my honour*, with fresh and insatiable expectations. All this time my industrious tenants grumbled, because no encouragement was given to them; and, looking upon me as a weak good-natured fool, they combined in a resolution to ask me for long leases, or reduction of rent.

(4:264)

Glenthorn offers bounties to his industrious tenants, but to little avail. He doesn't understand the Irish, and they do not trust him. Good intentions alone, he confesses, are not enough to reverse centuries of feudal practice: "In the impatience of my zeal for improvement, I expected to do the work of two hundred years in a few months: and because I could not accelerate the progress of refinement in this miraculous manner, I was out of humour with myself and with a whole nation" (4:276).

Meanwhile, Glenthorn makes the rounds of the local gentry. With the exception of Lady Geraldine, a beautiful, vivacious woman who is something of a mystery to him, they are not a particularly inviting lot. Glenthorn cannot determine whether she is English or Irish:

She did not speak with the Irish accent; but, when I listened maliciously, I detected certain Hibernian inflections; nothing of the vulgar Irish idiom, but something that was more interrogative, more exclamatory, and perhaps more rhetorical, than the common language of the English ladies, accompanied with much animation of countenance and demonstrative gesture.

(4:278)

Lady Geraldine is unlike any woman he has ever met. Possessed of a sharp tongue, she is a free spirit who speaks her mind: "She was not ill-natured, yet careless to whom she gave offence, provided she produced amusement; and in this she seldom failed; for, in her conversation, there was much of the raciness of Irish wit, and the oddity of Irish humour" (4:281). In her "raciness," Lady Geraldine is a symbol for the Ireland of 1798, struggling for a new identity. Her particular animus is the Anglophilia of the local gentry because, as an Irish patriot, she has no patience with an elite who refuse to acknowledge Ireland as their native land. Like other nations, Ireland had been figured as a woman before; what was different in this instance was her independent spirit. Because the nation had been under English subjection for so long, Ireland was more commonly represented as an old maid. That figure appears in *Ennui* in the person of the Irish servant, Ellinor. But because she is behind the reversal that changes Glenthorn's life, she is the image of Ireland past. Geraldine, in contrast, represents the future, but she does not become Glenthorn's wife, probably because for Edgeworth she was a bit too independent to represent post-Union Ireland.

Glenthorn, we soon discover, is not Lord Glenthorn at all but the son of Ellinor. He was switched at birth with the real Glenthorn heir, Christy O'Donoghue, whom Ellinor raised as her own son. When Glenthorn learns the truth, he surrenders his title and estate. The reversal is clumsy, but the fall from grace gives Glenthorn the chance to make himself over in the image of the post-Union gentry. He trains as a lawyer in preparation for his reascent, finally educating himself in the principles of political economy that Edgeworth held out as the surest path to reform. When Christy conveniently dies, Glenthorn marries Cecilia Delamere, the heir-at-law, and regains the estate. This time, however, he has earned it, having become an Irishman equipped to lead the nation into the post-Union future.

Edgeworth's next Irish novel, *The Absentee* (1812), had its origins in a play written and performed for the family at Edgeworthstown in 1811. Richard Edgeworth encouraged his daughter to write to Richard Brinsley Sheridan at Drury Lane about its possible London production. Less optimistic than her father, Maria was not surprised when Sheridan replied that Londoners were unlikely to be sympathetic to the Irish as she portrayed them. The verdict did not deter her, however. Confident that she had good material on her hands, she reworked the play as a novel. A year later, she sent *The Absentee* to her publisher.

The Absentee consists of three narrative sequences. The first presents Lord and Lady Clonbrony in fashionable London society; in the second, their son, Lord Colambre, travels incognito to Ireland to learn about the country and the family estate; and in the third, Colambre returns to England to rescue his father from a corrupt agent, then marries an heiress who accompanies him to Ireland. The novel has clear affinities with *Ennui:* like Glenthorn, Colambre is the heir of Anglo-Irish absentees, and his life is transformed when he returns to his native land. The account of his return is not as interesting as Glenthorn's, however; it comes off as a survey of political economy at times. Nevertheless, Edgeworth more than compensates for that deficiency with the scenes of London high life that open the novel, scenes that are among the best in all her writing.

A tour de force of social satire, the opening segment spotlights the social ambition of Lady Clonbrony. Lord Clonbrony is the antithesis of his wife; he befriends people who are socially beneath him while she plans the gala she expects to win her a place in London society. Even though she has lived most of her life in Ireland, Lady Clonbrony thinks of herself as English because she was born in Oxfordshire. But she is fearful of the Irish in her, lest a mispronounced word or a dubious expression give her away. Despite her efforts, she fails to impress the English quality:

"If you knew all she endures, to look, speak, move, breathe, like an Englishwoman, you would pity her," said Lady Langdale.

"Yes, and you *cawnt* conceive the *peens* she *teekes* to talk of the *teebles* and *cheers,* and to thank Q, and with so much *teeste* to speak pure English," said Mrs. Dareville.

"Pure cockney, you mean," said Lady Langdale.

(6:2)

At the ball the guests enjoy themselves but are careful to snipe afterward: "The company ate and drank—enjoyed themselves—went away—and laughed at their hostess" (6:39). We feel a bit sorry for Lady Clonbrony, though not for long; soon she is scheming to marry her son to the heiress Florence Broadhurst. Everyone seems to think the match will take place—except Colambre, who is interested in Grace Nugent. To sidestep the looming dilemma, he decides to leave for Ireland.

Like Glenthorn, Colambre journeys to the family estate, but along the way he sees evidence of the new, post-Union Ireland. Upon his arrival in Dublin, he meets an English officer, James Brooke, who tells him about the social transformation under way. Instead of a society dominated by the country elite, now, remarks Brooke:

You find a society in Dublin composed of a most agreeable and salutary mixture of birth and education, gentility and knowledge, manner and matter; and you see pervading the whole, new life and energy, new talent, new ambition, a desire and a determination to improve and be improved—a perception that higher distinction can now be obtained in almost all company, by genius and merit, than by airs and address.

(6:83)

That is true as well for the middle classes, who benefited the most from the new prosperity that followed the Union. Colambre meets a specimen of the new social order in the person of Mrs. Raffarty, a grocer's wife who invites him to a lavish dinner. Although she is sympathetic to middle-class diligence, Edgeworth balks when it comes to their social airs. Her country-house prejudices show through in her description of the obligatory house tour:

So she led the way to a little conservatory, and a little pinery, and a little grapery, and a little aviary, and a little pheasantry, and a little dairy for show, and a little cottage for ditto, with a grotto full of shells, and a little hermitage full of earwigs, and a little ruin full of looking-glass, "to enlarge and multiply the effect of the Gothic."

(6:88)

From the Raffartys, Colambre resumes his trek toward the family seat. As he travels, he penetrates further into the Irish past, meeting a succession of characters who introduce him to the feudal Ireland that still resists the changes initiated with the Union. At Killpatrick's-town, he sees the ruins of an estate mired in the feudal ways of Gaelic Ireland. But it is not the only specimen of Gaelic Ireland that he encounters; he soon meets Lord O'Halloran, an eccentric but noble aristocrat who understands how absenteeism has destroyed the fabric of Irish life. It is a view shared by Lady Oranmore, an Anglo-Irish aristocrat he meets next.

Finally, after a leisurely sojourn with the O'Hallorans, Colambre arrives at the family seat. In order to see how the estate has been run in his absence, he disguises himself as a mining engineer. He finds two overseers with sharply differing styles: the properties charged to Mr. Burke are a model of progressive methods, while those run by the Garraghty brothers have been milked for personal profit. Colambre reveals himself to give the Garraghtys their due, and when he does, he serves more than local justice; it is a gesture of national responsibility at the same time because, with it, Colambre accepts his place in Ireland. But first he must convince his parents, who are still in England. Colambre goes to London to save his father from his creditors, offering to take care of his debts on condition that the family return to Ireland. It takes some pleading, but he persuades them in the end.

The year after *The Absentee*, Edgeworth discovered just how well known a novelist she was during a six-week visit to London. The trip, her first prolonged stay in the capital, had been planned several years before. The visit was a great success, for Maria was a hit with the social set. She was befriended by Ladies Wellington, Landsdowne, and Whitbread, and even breakfasted with Lord Byron. All the while, she tried to keep her feet on the ground, as she wrote to her cousin Sophy Ruxton:

Pray do not think because I name these fine people and their civilities that my poor little head is turned or turning with them. Be assured that the whole panorama passes before me as a panorama. It amuses me but I no more would pass my *life* in this way than spend it looking at a panorama.

(*Maria Edgeworth: Letters from England*, p. 56)

But when she returned to Edgeworthstown she was eager for news of the "panorama." And she got that and more from the new set of correspondents who kept her in touch with London gossip for a long time after.

HARRINGTON

IT was, however, an unexpected correspondent who provided her with the motive for *Harrington* (1817). In August 1815, an American Jew, Rachel Mordecai, wrote to Edgeworth to complain of the numerous Jewish stereotypes that had appeared in her stories and novels:

Relying on the good sense and candour of Miss Edgeworth I would ask, how it can be that she, who on all other subjects shows such justice and liberality, should on one alone appear biased by prejudice: should even instill that prejudice into the minds of youth! Can my allusion be mistaken? It is to the species of character which wherever a *Jew* is introduced is invariably attached to him. Can it be believed that this race of men are by nature mean, avaricious, and unprincipled? Forbid it, mercy. Yet this is more than insinuated by the stigma usually affixed to the *name*.

(*Education of the Heart*, p. 6)

Duly chastened, Edgeworth replied with a gracious letter the following August:

Your polite, benevolent and touching letter has given me much pleasure, and much pain. As to the pain I hope you will sometime see that it has excited me to make all the atonement and reparation in my power for the past. It was impossible to remonstrate with more gentleness or in a more convincing as well as persuasive manner than you have done. Your own letter is the very best evidence that could have been offered of the truth of all you urge in favor of those of your own religious persuasion. And the candour and spirit of tolerance and benevolence you shew, you have a right to expect from others.

(*Education of the Heart*, p. 8)

Edgeworth took nearly a year to respond because in the meantime she had written *Harrington* to atone for the likes of Mr. Carat, the shady jeweler in "The Good Aunt"; Solomon, the swindler in *Belinda*; Rachub, the moneylender in "Murad the Unlucky"; and the host of unnamed Jewish characters that appear throughout her fiction. Such caricatures were not, of course, her own invention; they were part of a tradition that stretched back to the Middle Ages. Although Jews had been expelled from England in the thirteenth century, anti-Semitism continued to flourish even in their absence. A small number of converted Jews continued to live in England after the expulsion, but it was not until the Whitehall Conference in 1655 that readmission was permitted. Even so, relatively few settled in England, so that by the time of *Harrington* they numbered in the thousands in a country of some ten million. A handful were famous, like the financier Sir Solomon de Medina, who was knighted by William III, and the banker Samson Gideon, who married his daughter into a prominent gentry family. Nevertheless, most

Britons had little contact with Jews, who were still very much a people about whom much more was said than known.

Edgeworth herself said more about Jews than she knew. After Rachel Mordecai's letter, she realized that she was the product of a cultural tradition shaped by works like *The Jew of Malta* and *The Merchant of Venice*. The root of the problem, she recognized, was discursive; even though there were individuals sympathetic to Jews, Britons had no other way of speaking about them. That is the issue that *Harrington* confronts, and in addressing a young man's triumph over anti-Semitism it was the first British novel to present Jews in a wholly positive light.

Since the small Anglo-Jewish community could not possibly pose the threat ascribed to it, the hatred of Jews could only be located in the irrational. In *Harrington*, the irrational is first found in the innocent imagination of the hero, a young, impressionable boy of six who knows nothing whatsoever of Jews. In the vivid opening, Harrington, now an adult, recalls how on his first day in London many years before, he peered from the balcony of his father's house into the street below, watching with fascination as a lamplighter went about his business at dusk: "I saw him fix and mount his ladder with his little black pot swinging from his arm, and his red smoking torch waving with astonishing velocity, as he ran up and down the ladder" (9:1). After the lamplighter dismounts for good, his torch suddenly flares up again, unexpectedly illuminating

the face and figure of an old man with a long white beard and a dark visage, who, holding a great bag slung over one shoulder, walked slowly on, repeating in a low, abrupt, mysterious tone, the cry of "Old clothes! Old clothes! Old clothes!" I could not understand the words he said, but as he looked up at our balcony he saw me—smiled—and I remember thinking that he had a good-natured countenance. The maid nodded to him; he stood still, and at the same instant she seized upon me, exclaiming, "Time for you to come off to bed, Master Harrington."

(9:1–2)

But Harrington refuses, clinging to the rail. His resistance prompts a threat from his nurse: "If you don't come quietly this minute, Master Harrington, I'll call to Simon the Jew there, . . . and he shall come up and carry you away in his great bag"

(9:2). With that, an episode that started so innocently takes on a darker tone because Harrington cannot get the ragman's image out of his mind: "The old man's eyes were upon me; and to my fancy the look of his eyes and his whole face had changed in an instant" (9:2). "Struck with terror," he goes to bed full of fear, but it is only after his nurse terrifies him with "stories of Jews who had been known to steal poor children for the purpose of killing, crucifying, and sacrificing them at their secret feasts and midnight abominations" (9:2) that he begins to turn into the paranoid little Englishman for whom Jews are the root of all evil.

The process does not end there, because Harrington's parents do their best to reinforce his budding neurosis. Mr. Harrington, a Tory member of Parliament, takes his philosophy from the Shylock tradition: "It is certain that when a man once goes to the Jews, he soon goes to the devil. So, Harrington, my boy, I charge you at your peril, whatever else you do, keep out of the hands of the Jews" (9:3). The boy's parents are openly anti-Semitic in the company of guests, with his father encouraging him and his mother rewarding him when he tells an ethnic joke echoing his father's opposition to the Jewish Naturalization Act of 1753. A hit with the local gentry, the joke turns on the mistake that naturalization would be: "Why should not the Jews be naturalized? Why, ma'am, because the Jews are naturally an unnatural pack of people, and you can't naturalize what's naturally unnatural" (9:17).

From his precocious start Harrington proceeds to public school, where he falls in with a group of boys who harass a defenseless Jewish peddler. However, just when he seems to be in his element, he is inexplicably overcome with remorse. Why do we do this, he asks himself, since the peddler "was as unlike Shylock as it is possible to conceive." Despite his much too sudden conversion, Harrington still knows precious little about Jews. But that changes when he goes to Cambridge, where he comes into contact with a far different class of Jew than he knew before.

Shortly after his arrival in Cambridge, Harrington meets an eminent Jewish scholar, Israel Lyons. Lyons does not fit his preconceived notion of a Jewish rabbi—"a long-bearded old man in a black hat"—but he is a British stereotype all the same, the "saintly Jew." Through Lyons, Harrington meets another stereotypical Jew, the banker and philanthropist Mr. Montenero, a Sephardi from America. In England on business, Montenero is accompanied by his daughter, Berenice, who serves as the next test of Harrington's philo-Semitism. Although her religion does not pose a problem for Harrington, the same does not go for his father, who will surely disinherit his son if he marries the daughter of a Jew. When Mr. Montenero rescues Mr. Harrington from bankruptcy, it appears that he may relent. Yet while he is chastened, he cannot relinquish his deep-seated bias: "My prejudice against the Jews I give up—you have conquered them—all, all. But not the difference of religion between man and wife" (9:203). It was a bias many well-meaning Englishmen could not relinquish, since it was one thing to mix with Jews but quite another to marry one.

Edgeworth circumvents the problem when Montenero reveals that Berenice is not Jewish after all. Her mother was a Christian, and since she was raised in the Protestant faith, there is no further objection to the match. The reversal is a problem in another sense, however. In her reply to Rachel Mordecai, Edgeworth implied that *Harrington* was an act of atonement. But when all is said and done, the novel fails to bring down the social barrier that Mr. Harrington advocates. Edgeworth herself recognized that the ending was flawed: "It was an Irish blunder, which, with the best intentions, I could not avoid." Even so, the novel deserves to be recognized for what it was, a milestone in the portrayal of Anglo-Jewry.

ORMOND

EDGEWORTH wrote the last of her Irish novels, *Ormond,* under the stress of her father's final illness. Richard Edgeworth had been seriously ill with kidney and intestinal problems in 1814; when they recurred in early 1817, it was clear that the end was not far off. That, however, did not keep him from taking a keen interest in the novel that Maria was then writing. He made numerous suggestions for *Ormond* and even wrote several passages himself—one of them the funeral of the beloved Cornelius O'Shane—but did not live to see the book in print. When he died only a few days before it appeared in June, Maria was devastated. Her life would never be the same again.

Despite the unhappy circumstances surrounding its production, *Ormond* turned out to be the best of Edgeworth's Irish novels. Although it is superior to its predecessors in its formal economy, its success hinged on the creation of a hero with native Irish and Anglo-Irish roots. Harry Ormond's double identity is not the result of a natural inheritance, however. He comes into the novel an orphan, his mother having died "in an Irish cabin" soon after his father left for India to seek his fortune. But young Harry avoids the poorhouse; Edgeworth provides him with a pair of surrogate fathers in Sir Ulick O'Shane, a converted Catholic who has carved a niche for himself in the Protestant Ascendancy, and Sir Ulick's eccentric cousin, Cornelius, who heads an Irish clan in the Black Islands. Both make their mark on the boy, yet both come up short when it comes to preparing him for the world: Sir Ulick is too involved in his own political career to take an interest in Ormond's education, and Cornelius is too much the Irish primitive to teach Harry anything of practical value. Given the alternatives, the moral center of the novel lies elsewhere. We see little of Walter Annaly, but as the model of the Anglo-Irish landlord, he represents what Ormond aspires to. When Harry marries his daughter, Florence, he joins the ranks of the Protestant Ascendancy. However, Edgeworth shows us all along that Ormond has too much of the native Irish in him ever to forget his roots, making it clear that she intended him to be seen as the best of both cultural worlds—though with the Protestant in the ascendant, as usual.

Ormond opens during an evening's entertainment at Sir Ulick O'Shane's estate, Castle Hermitage. Having arrived boisterously as well as late, Sir Ulick snickers at the genteel ambience of the gathering: "What! no music, no dancing at Castle Hermitage to-night; and all the ladies sitting in a formal circle, petrifying into perfect statues?" (9:227). At first glimpse, Sir Ulick seems to be nothing more than the stereotypical free-spirited Irishman who drinks too much and has no head for business. Yet he is not that at all. Although he enters the party a "callous profligate," he is angling to marry his son, Marcus, to Florence Annaly, a young woman with "beauty, fortune, family connexions, every thing that the hearts of young and old desire" (9:233). Marcus aside, Florence is everything Sir Ulick desires because he foresees the political connections that an alliance

with a prominent Protestant family will bring. However, he soon comes to see that it is not Marcus but Ormond that Miss Annaly prefers. With that, he packs the nineteen-year-old Harry off to his cousin Cornelius O'Shane in the Black Islands.

In going off to live with his uncle, Ormond not only leaves Anglo-Irish society, he travels into the Irish past. The Black Islands symbolize the world of Gaelic culture, which, though inviting, poses the seductive danger of the proverbial "world we have lost." The focal point of life in the islands is Cornelius O'Shane, the beloved clan leader known to all as "King Corny." Although he heads a tight-knit community that functions as an extended family, the patriarchal structure only reinforces the dependent nature of the Black Islanders. They may be happy under Corny's rule, but they will always be poor because they hold to a tradition of self-sufficiency in the face of economic hardship. Ormond marvels when he observes how Corny makes his own boots, hat, and coat, yet such resourcefulness is merely quaint because it violates the first principle of political economy, the division of labor.

The sojourn in the Black Islands is not about political economy alone; it is about Ormond's education as well. Since he spends the better part of his stay hunting by day and drinking by night, he does not make up for a deficient formal education. Nevertheless, he makes time for reading after he discovers a cache of novels. One in particular captivates him "because he saw, or fancied that he saw [in it], a resemblance" to his own life there. The book is *Tom Jones*. Charmed by the "warm-hearted, generous imprudent young man, with little education, no literature, governed more by feeling than by principle, never upon any occasion reasoning, but keeping right and wrong by happy moral instincts," he resolves to "shine forth an Irish Tom Jones." However, his sentimental education is nipped in the bud when he learns that Dora, King Corny's daughter, was promised years before to White Connal, an Irish nobleman, to cover a debt. That is hardly the formula for a successful marriage, which is blissfully short because Connal soon dies in a hunting accident. But hardheaded Gaelic honor does not end there; by tradition Dora immediately passes to her late husband's twin brother, Black Connal. Connal promises to take Dora to Paris. Seduced by the prospect, she is only too happy to bid farewell to Ireland. But for betraying her Irish roots for continental sophistication, she will pay the price of an empty marriage.

With Dora gone and with Ormond still in need of a formal as well as sentimental education, Edgeworth gets her hero off the Black Islands and back into society with a second hunting accident. This time King Corny is the victim, his sudden death the reason for Ormond's return to Castle Hermitage. Another turn of events soon changes the prospects of the "Irish Tom Jones": with the news that he has come into a considerable legacy from his Indian stepmother, he is now a member of the Anglo-Irish elite. For the first time Ormond is on an equal footing with the gentry. But he is so repelled by their behavior that when a designing woman, aware of his fortune, tries to seduce him, he flees to the Irish countryside.

Edgeworth had earlier used the Irish tour as a narrative device in *The Absentee.* There, the Anglo-Irish landlord, Glenthorn, traveled through the countryside, viewing it with a proprietor's eye. Ormond's travels are different because, as the dual product of Anglo-Irish and Catholic-Irish culture, he sees the Irish from the inside. And what he sees is eye-opening: not only does he come to recognize the woeful ways of the Catholic peasantry, but he learns much about Sir Ulick, who has become the subject of popular tales because he lets his tenants have their way. The truth about Sir Ulick is the prelude to Ormond's ultimate destination, the Annaly estate; only there will he transcend the worlds of his fathers, Sir Ulick and King Corny. Having discovered his place in Anglo-Irish society at last, Ormond proposes to Florence Annaly. But when she hesitates, he assumes, incorrectly, that she does not want to marry him. He goes to Paris to visit Corny's daughter, Dora, but because he represents Ireland's future, he does not stay for long. Recalled by the news of Sir Ulick's death, he goes to the Annaly estate after the funeral. This time, Florence accepts him without hesitation. The "Irish Tom Jones" is a gentleman at last, and true to his dual patrimony he opts to settle in the Black Islands.

HELEN

AFTER the publication of *Harrington* and *Ormond* in 1817, Edgeworth did not complete another novel until *Helen,* in 1834. She had not given up writing in the interval, although it had become a much more difficult task than before. Her most important project in these years was the completion of her father's *Memoirs,* which appeared in 1820. In the years immediately following, she took the initiative in meeting some of the leading intellectual figures of the day, including David Ricardo, Robert Owen, and Walter Scott, who visited Edgeworthstown in 1826. Later that year, she took over the family estate from her brother Lovell, managing it until 1839. While that occupied a great deal of her time, she also tried her hand at several novels. But she was unable to complete any of them until *Helen.* The void left by her father's death was only part of the problem, though. Times had changed, and literary fashions had changed with them. The "silver fork" novelists—T. H. Lister, Edward Bulwer-Lytton, and Benjamin Disraeli—were in; Edgeworth's didacticism was out.

Helen was especially challenging because Edgeworth had to adapt her style to the times. What she produced was a work more focused on character and less crowded with incident than *Belinda,* *Vivian,* or *Patronage.* At the center of the novel is Helen Stanley, a young woman whose parents "both died when she was too young to know her loss." She was brought up by her uncle, Dean Stanley, "a man of genius, learning, and sincere piety, with the most affectionate heart, and a highly cultivated understanding"—but, unfortunately, little financial sense. Dean Stanley hoped that Helen would one day be an heiress, but when he dies unexpectedly, she sadly discovers that he had been too inattentive to money matters for that. As the novel opens, Helen is therefore not only an orphan for the second time but a poor one. Her fortunes take a turn for the better when she is invited to Clarendon Park, the country house where her childhood friend Cecilia lives with her husband, Lord Clarendon, and her mother, Lady Davenant. She is secure there for the time being, but without family or fortune she has limited prospects.

Edgeworth seems to have purposely designed Helen as a peripheral figure, an outsider whose social observations help to focus the first two volumes, which are largely devoted to the exposition of character. What we observe through her eyes is a cast of characters who are read shrewdly but not infallibly. General Clarendon is a sensible man whom Helen comes to like, but she is not so fond of his sister, Esther, who may be too outspoken for her own good, though she later helps Helen in her time of greatest need. Cecilia is attractive and intelligent, but she is dominated by her husband, just as she was by her mother, so she cannot be trusted in the crisis that nearly costs Helen her reputation.

The most intriguing character of all is Cecilia's mother, Lady Davenant. From her, Helen learns that people should not try too hard to conceal their flaws because that only makes them worse: "We must take people as they are; you may graft a rose upon an oak, but those who have tried the experiment tell us the graft will last but a short time, and the operation ends in the destruction of both" (10:51). She speaks from experience because she has failed at marriage and motherhood: while she tried unsuccessfully to "subdue her husband through power and provocation," that did not prevent her from making the same mistake with her daughter. "Differences," she now realizes, "must be solved through mutual tolerance, generosity, and forgiveness," but in the strange twists that take place in the third volume, those qualities are tested to the limit.

Although there is little action to speak of in the first two volumes, they establish the relationships that generate the taut action of the third. There the judgments that Helen first makes are subject to revision, for relations in the circumscribed world of Clarendon Park become far more nettled than she anticipates. A scandal brews when a packet of letters written by Cecilia years before arrives, addressed to her husband. Cecilia insists that Lord Clarendon was her first love, but the letters show that she was in fact in love with Colonel D'Aubigny. In a bind, Cecilia convinces Helen to confess that she was D'Aubigny's correspondent:

The letters are not signed with my real name, they are signed Emma—Henry and Emma!—Oh folly, folly! My dear, dear friend, save me but now, and I never will be guilty of the least deception again during my whole life; believe me, believe me! When once my mother is safely gone I will tell Clarendon all. Look at men, dear Helen, look at me and believe me.

(10:287)

Helen believes that Cecilia merely wants to keep her mother from hearing the news, since Lady Davenant is about to leave for the Continent in poor health. But as time passes, Cecilia does not make good on her promise. Meanwhile, rumors about Helen circulate beyond Clarendon Park. First, a local newspaper carries an account of the

affair, then word arrives that the correspondence is about to be published. General Clarendon uses his influence to suppress its publication, but the damage has been done. Seriously compromised, Helen leaves Clarendon Park. She finds shelter at the home of Lord Clarendon's sister, Esther, where she has a nervous breakdown. A few months later she recovers, but her reputation is still in jeopardy because Cecilia refuses to speak a word of the matter until her mother returns. When that happens, she finally confesses, permitting Helen to marry Granville Beauclerc. But with the revelation, her own marriage is in serious trouble. Lord Clarendon forgives her, but there is some doubt whether they will live happily ever after.

EDGEWORTH'S LATER YEARS

IN the decade and a half after *Helen*, Edgeworth spent her time as she had for much of her life, quietly involved in domestic matters. Several family members were still at Edgeworthstown, but the household had changed since the years when it was full of young children. Edgeworth had lost seven brothers and sisters by the 1830s, and as she entered her sixties, the ranks of her contemporaries were thinning as well. She made few new friends in these years but kept up a wide correspondence; she was particularly gracious in discussing her novels with the many admirers who wrote to her about them. However, her literary reputation had already begun to fade, even though her complete works were published in London (1832–1833) and New York (1832–1834). She toyed with the idea of writing another Irish novel, but it did not come off because her country-house view was out of step with the times. The nationalist movement led by Daniel O'Connell was fundamentally at odds with her gentry paternalism, leading her to suspect the man and his motives. As she wrote in a reproving letter of 1843 in response to a friend's sincere observation about O'Connell:

"But still—still has not he a real enthusiasm for his religion and his country?" I could only say that I did believe him to be a sincere bigotted Catholic—yet I could not say enthusiastic for I took a distinction between bigotry bred in a man and enthusiasm natural and genuine.

(*Maria Edgeworth: Letters from England*, p. 599)

His personal life aside, O'Connell was a far cry from the Irish-Protestant heroes of Edgeworth's fiction because he campaigned to repeal the Act of Union. The Union was the cornerstone of Maria's politics, as it was of her father's; but as a sign of the times it was under siege in the new Ireland that had begun to emerge after Catholic emancipation.

By the time of her death on 22 May 1849, Edgeworth had fallen out of literary favor. Her complete works were reissued in 1852, but few of her novels were reprinted after midcentury. Nevertheless, she continued to have her admirers. Ivan Turgenev, who knew her work in translation, acknowledged its importance to his own regional fiction; and John Ruskin claimed that he reread some of the tales and *Patronage* "oftener than any other books in the world, except the Bible." Few have been as enthusiastic since, although in 1950 the literary critic Percy Newby wrote, "Whereas Jane Austen was so much the better novelist Maria Edgeworth may be the more important" (p. 94). Although few would agree with him, critics are finally acknowledging Edgeworth's contribution to the development of the novel, particularly the social acuity of the Irish tales.

As Marilyn Butler writes: "Her really important innovation was to report Ireland as accurately as she could. . . . The result was a fresh lease of life for the novel, and a new fashion for social documentation" (p. 485). One of Edgeworth's greatest admirers, Walter Scott, claimed that he "owed his own successful career as a novelist about Scotland to her Irish example." In the 1990s, Edgeworth is still known largely as the author of *Castle Rackrent*. But that perception has begun to change, in no small part because the categories that once conferred marginal status on her—woman writer, regionalist, children's author—have been revised. And as that process of revision continues, she may at long last claim her place in the English canon.

SELECTED BIBLIOGRAPHY

I. COLLECTED WORKS. *Tales and Novels*, 18 vols. (London, 1832–1833; New York, 1832–1834), 10 vols. (London, 1893; New York, 1967).

II. SEPARATE WORKS. *Letters for Literary Ladies* (London, 1795); *The Parent's Assistant; or, Stories for Children*, 3 vols. (London, 1796); *Castle Rackrent: An Hibernian Tale* (London, 1800); *Early Lessons*, 5 vols. (London, 1801–1802); *Belinda*, 3 vols. (London, 1801); *Essay on Irish Bulls* (London, 1802); *Popular Tales*, 3 vols. (London, 1804); *The Modern Griselda: A Tale* (London, 1805); *Leonora*, 2 vols. (London, 1806); *Ennui* (London, 1809); *Almeria* (London, 1809); *Madame de Fleury* (London, 1809); *The Dunn* (London, 1809); *Manoeuvring* (London, 1809); *Vivian* (London, 1812); *Emilie de Coulanges* (London, 1812); *The Absentee* (London, 1812); *Patronage*, 4 vols. (London, 1814); *Comic Dramas in Three Acts* (London, 1817); *Harrington*, 3 vols. (London, 1817); *Ormond*, 3 vols. (London, 1817); *Memoirs of Richard Lovell Edgeworth, Esq.; Begun by Himself and Concluded by His Daughter, Maria Edgeworth*, 2 vols. (London, 1820); *Rosamond: A Sequel to Early Lessons*, 2 vols. (London, 1821); *Frank: A Sequel to Early Lessons*, 3 vols. (London, 1822); *Harry and Lucy Concluded: Being the Last Part of Early Lessons*, 4 vols. (London, 1825); "Thoughts on Bores," in *Janus; or, The Edinburgh Almanack* (Edinburgh, 1826); *Helen*, 3 vols. (London, 1834); *Orlandino* (Edinburgh, 1848).

III. LETTERS. Augustus J. C. Hare, ed., *The Life and Letters of Maria Edgeworth*, 2 vols. (London, 1894); Harold E. Butler and Harriet Jesse Butler, eds., *The Black Book of Edgeworthstown, 1585–1817* (London, 1927); Hans W. Hausermann, *The Genevese Background* (London, 1952); Christine Colvin, ed., *Maria Edgeworth: Letters from England 1813–1844* (Oxford, 1971); Edgar E. MacDonald, ed., *The Education of the Heart: The Correspondence of Rachel Mordecai Lazarus and Maria Edgeworth* (Chapel Hill, N.C., 1977); Christine Colvin, ed., *Maria Edgeworth in France and Switzerland: Selections from the Edgeworth Family Letters* (Oxford, 1979).

IV. BIOGRAPHICAL AND CRITICAL STUDIES. Isabel C. Clarke, *Maria Edgeworth, Her Family and Friends* (London, 1950); Percy H. Newby, *Maria Edgeworth* (Denver, 1950); Thomas Flanagan, *The Irish Novelists, 1800–1850* (New York, 1958); Elisabeth Inglis-Jones, *The Great Maria* (London, 1959).

James Newcomer, *Maria Edgeworth the Novelist, 1767–1849: A Bicentennial Study* (Fort Worth, Tex., 1967); Mark D. Hawthorne, *Doubt and Dogma in Maria Edgeworth* (Gainsville, Fla., 1967); Michael Hurst, *Maria Edgeworth and the Public Scene* (Coral Gables, Fla., 1969); A. Norman Jeffares, "Maria Edgeworth's *Ormond*," in *English* 18 (autumn 1969).

Oliver MacDonagh, *The Nineteenth Century Novel and Irish Social History: Some Aspects* (Dublin, 1970); Patrick Murray, *Maria Edgeworth: A Study of the Novelist* (Cork, 1971); O. Elizabeth M. Harden, *Maria Edgeworth's Art of Prose Fiction* (The Hague, 1971); Marilyn Butler, *Maria Edgeworth: A Literary Biography* (Oxford, 1972); Duane Edwards, "The Narrator of *Castle Rackrent*," in *South Atlantic Quarterly* 71 (1972); James Newcomer, *Maria Edgeworth* (Lewisburg, Pa., 1973); Vineta Colby, *Yesterday's Woman: Domestic Realism in the English Novel* (Princeton, N.J., 1974); Gerry H. Brookes, "The Didacticism of

Edgeworth's *Castle Rackrent*," in *Studies in English Literature, 1500–1900* 17 (1977); Patricia Voss-Clesly, *Tendencies of Character Depiction in the Domestic Novels of Burney, Edgeworth, and Austen: A Consideration of Subjective and Objective Worlds*, 3 vols. (Salzburg, 1979).

Roger McHugh and Maurice Harmon, *A Short History of Anglo-Irish Literature* (Totowa, N.J., 1982); Elizabeth Harden, *Maria Edgeworth* (Boston, 1984); Colin B. Atkinson and Jo Atkinson, "Maria Edgeworth, *Belinda*, and Women's Rights," in *Éire-Ireland: A Journal of Irish Studies* 19, no. 4 (1984); Tom Dunne, *Maria Edgeworth and the Colonial Mind* (Dublin, 1985); W. J. McCormack, *Ascendancy and Tradition in Irish Literary History from 1793 to 1939* (Oxford, 1985); Mary Anne Schofield and Cecilia Macheski, *Fetter'd or Free? British Women Novelists, 1670–1815* (Athens, Ohio, 1986); Coilin Owens, *Family Chronicles: Maria Edgeworth's* Castle Rackrent (Totowa, N.J., 1987); Beth Kowaleski-Wallace, "Home Economics: Domestic Ideology in Maria Edgeworth's *Belinda*," in *The Eighteenth Century* 29, no. 3 (1988); Michael Ragussis, "Representation, Conversion, and Literary Form: *Harrington* and the Novel of Jewish Identity," in *Critical Inquiry* 16 (1989); Mary-Elisabeth Fowkes Tobin, "'The Power of Example': Harry Ormond Reads *Tom Jones*," in *Reader* 19 (1988).

Martin Croghan, "Swift, Thomas Sheridan, Maria Edgeworth and the Evolution of Hiberno-English," in *Irish University Review* 20 (1990); Bege K. Bowers and Barbara Brothers, eds., *Reading and Writing Women's Lives: A Study of the Novel of Manners* (Ann Arbor, Mich., 1990); Kathryn J. Kirkpatrick, "'Gentlemen Have Horrors upon this Subject': West Indian Suitors in Maria Edgeworth's *Belinda*," in *Eighteenth-Century Fiction* 5, no. 4 (1993).

JAMES GEORGE FRAZER
(1854–1941)

Joseph Donahue

ON THE ENDPAPERS of his copy of *English Poems by Milton*, James Frazer, Trinity undergraduate, gathered into lists the poet's compound epithets: "snow-soft," "cold-kind," "yellow-skirted," "sable-stoled," "silver-buskined," "star-proof," "sin-worn," "vermeil-tinctured," and so forth. Perhaps Frazer found in these adjectives the glimmer of an earlier age, the era that shaped the Protestant culture that, in turn, shaped him. Frazer was collecting words as he would later collect legends. His literary taste was already settling in the eighteenth century, with the generations of writers who found their style amid the ruins of Milton's cadence. Frazer, of course, was a late Victorian. The bulk of his writing was published in the early part of the twentieth century and greatly influenced the writing of the modernist period. But to consider him in the act of sifting and sorting the vocabulary of John Milton is to be reminded of his deeper relation to the traditions of English writing.

Milton provided the example of how a writer might present an account of nothing less than the origin of the world. He gave literary form to what became such Frazerian obsessions as the relation between reason and belief, the true meaning of myths, and the death of kings. But most significant, Milton registered the discovery of the New World and the subsequent transformation of the European world. From the Elizabethans to the Victorians a stream of reports and analyses of newfound and "savage" cultures prompted a profound questioning of basic beliefs among European writers and intellectuals. Frazer, like many of his generation, was deeply involved in the continuation of this process. Frazer built upon a body of writing that included the reports of explorers, missionaries, diplomats, captives, and slaves, as well as the musings of philosophers, theologians, and psychologists. He was committed to forms of writing that could address the matter of custom and belief in a world that was furiously offering fresh evidence of things inexplicably ancient. A new field of study was evolving in Frazer's time that sought to understand the sudden wealth of cultures. Frazer was a founder of this field, anthropology, and to understand his masterpiece, *The Golden Bough*, requires us to have a sense of how the new discipline shaped his thought.

Anthropology gave Frazer his subject and showed him how to write about it: the comparative method. Without anthropology, Frazer would have been a renowned classicist and a minor poet, a don with a flair for literary pastiche and an occasional book reviewer, nothing like the cultural authority he became. His biographer described Frazer's encounter with anthropology as a conversion; once his course was set, he spent twelve to eighteen hours per day, most days of the year, gathering his data and writing his books. The floor of his apartment eventually sagged beneath the weight of his library. His correspondence with scholars and researchers around the world was massive. He did not teach; he had no children; his wife worked tirelessly as his research assistant, translator, and literary agent; he rarely traveled; and he had few personal friends. He gathered texts, collated texts, and produced texts largely about preliterate times and places. And while his books tell thousands of stories about the customs and beliefs of cultures around the world, they also tell a single story about one place and one time. That story concerns the life and death of Jesus Christ and the life and death of the Christian religion in post-Enlightenment Europe.

LIFE AND WORKS

BORN on 1 January 1854, James George Frazer was the first of four children of Daniel Frazer, a promi-

169

nent Glasgow pharmacist, and Katherine Frazer, who traced her lineage back to James I and II of Scotland and to Oliver Cromwell. Three previous children did not survive birth. If infant mortality were not a commonplace of nineteenth-century life one might be tempted to suppose a biographical origin for the obsession with the returning dead that governs Frazer's works. Daniel Frazer was also an author, producing various pamphlets and a work of local history as diversions from his thriving business. The family library contained volumes of Sir Walter Scott, John Calvin, Miguel de Cervantes, and *The Arabian Nights,* and in "Memories of My Parents," collected in *Creation and Evolution in Primitive Cosmogonies, and Other Pieces* (1935), James Frazer remembered reading Thomas Moore's *Lalla Rookh* "with youthful enthusiasm, reciting the verses aloud to the accompaniment of an old lute or guitar" (p. 134). Protestant piety suffused the Frazer household. A part of each day was given over to worship, through the reading of Scripture and prayer. Daniel Frazer was a member of the Free Church of Scotland, a dissenting faction of Scotch Protestants founded in 1843. Daniel Frazer's great uncle had played an important part in founding the Free Church; his actions in leading the dissenting clergy from the larger assembly had become a cherished part of family lore. James Frazer both continued this tradition of dissent and abolished it. His written works attack the conventions of religious belief while finding its essence everywhere. He lived his adult life in England, becoming a celebrated author and cultural authority there, and his Scottish past shaped his writing in crucial ways.

In 1869 Frazer matriculated at the University of Glasgow. He studied Greek, Latin, mathematics, physics, logic, metaphysics, moral philosophy, and English literature. At university he encountered William Thomson, a noted physical scientist, from whom he received "a conception of the physical universe as regulated by exact and absolutely unvarying laws of nature" (quoted in *Creation and Evolution,* pp. 123–124), as well as the sobering conviction that the sun would extinguish itself in but a few thousand years. As he wrote many years later at the close of his most famous work, *The Golden Bough:*

In the ages to come many may be able to predict, perhaps even to control, the wayward courses of the winds and clouds, but hardly will his puny hands have strength to speed afresh our slackening planet in its orbit or rekindle the dying fire of the sun. Yet the philosopher who trembles at the idea of such distant catastrophes may console himself by reflecting that these gloomy apprehensions, like the earth and the sun themselves, are only parts of that unsubstantial world which thought has conjured up out of the void, and that the phantoms which the subtle enchantress has evoked to-day she may ban to-morrow. They too, like so much that to common eyes seems solid, may melt into air, into thin air.

(abridged ed., p. 826)

In 1874 Frazer entered Trinity College at Cambridge to study classics. By his second year he had read all of Plato, Euripides, and Pindar, and far more widely in Latin authors than what was required of him. Sometime in the 1870s he encountered the work of Herbert Spencer. During this decade he established a deep affection for writers of the eighteenth century, especially the two often cited as the models for his prose style, Joseph Addison and Edward Gibbon. In Germany one summer he discovered the work of Heinrich Heine, who became his favorite poet. Heine's pungent mixture of pathos and irony as well as his careful juxtaposition of the classical and the modern world afford a glimpse into Frazer's evolving sensibility. In 1879 he won a fellowship for a dissertation on Plato. This gave him, at a time crucial to his intellectual development, six years of research unfettered by academic obligations or financial need. These six years marked his conversion from classics to anthropology. Not published in book form until 1930, *The Growth of Plato's Ideal Theory* spells out the ideas Frazer would spend a lifetime shaping into a vision of human history.

Frazer's dissertation contains the assertion that Plato committed a "splendid error" in his interpretation of Socrates, an error about the ontological status of the ideal. From the memories of particulars, Frazer summarizes, we develop a sense of similarity through the power of comparison. This leads us to the useful but limited command of generalizations. In a sentence that resonates for readers of Frazer's later work, he tells us, "Generalization is but the compendious and imperfect way in which a finite mind grasps the infinity of particulars" (p. 8). When one considers that the grasp of particulars is characteristic of, in Frazer's gloss upon Aristotle, the mind of God, one senses a deep and unarticulated poetics of accretion running throughout Frazer's works, which seems to have as its goal the creation of an "infinity of particulars" in the reader's mind. Plato confused logic with ontology, Frazer argues; he made of knowledge the definition of existence. Frazer contends that a similar mistake governs the mental life of all peoples at all time. The implications of this will be seen more fully in regard to Frazer's theories of magic.

During his fellowship Frazer read widely: classics, history, literature, and philosophy. For a brief while he considered becoming a philosopher. He traveled, sampled elements of contemporary European culture, saw Sarah Bernhardt perform in Paris, and observed religious rituals in Catholic Spain. In 1883 a traveling companion, the eminent psychologist James Ward, lent Frazer a book that would have a profound influence on him: Edward B. Tylor's *Primitive Culture* (1871). Frazer's encounter with Tylor was a significant step toward his embrace of the discipline of anthropology. From Tylor, Frazer took up the question of "survivals," ritual forms rendered obsolete by changes in a culture, which nevertheless continued to be practiced. The practitioners themselves often did not understand the meaning behind such rituals, but the analyst of culture could discern past history from present anomaly. Frazer never did actual fieldwork, and he traveled infrequently. The casual observation of Arabs in Spain is about the sum of his cross-cultural experience. He supplemented his own perceptions of Arab cultures with those provided in two early monuments of comparative anthropology, John Ferguson McLennan's *Primitive Marriage* (1865) and William Robertson Smith's *Religion of the Semites* (1889), which would soon deeply influence him. In January 1884 Frazer engaged a college dinner companion in a conversation about the Arabs he had seen the previous summer. That conversation—Frazer described it as an argument—changed Frazer's life. The companion was none other than Robertson Smith, who had recently arrived at Trinity, having spent two winters in Arabia under the name of Abdullah Effendi researching two subjects of tremendous interest to mid-nineteenth-century anthropologists, exogamy and totemism. He became Frazer's closest friend and most powerful single influence and set the terms on the inquiry Frazer pursued for more than forty years after Smith's death in 1894. Through Smith, Frazer wrote his first anthropological treatise. How he came to his subject underscores the Scottish intellectual traditions that shaped Frazer's work.

Robertson Smith came from the same religious culture that formed Frazer and his father. Raised in the Free Church, eight years older than Frazer, Smith studied Hebrew at the age of six, attended university at the age of fifteen, and began to prepare for the ministry at twenty. In 1869 he met the Edinburgh lawyer and anthropologist John Ferguson McLennan, who was twenty years his senior. He had entered the world of anthropological speculation by disputing Henry Maine's *Ancient Law* (1861). The fruit of that speculation, *Primitive Marriage,* was a major work of early anthropology. McLennan had found in the Bible the subject that Frazer would inherit, via Smith, and make the subject of a major scholarly undertaking: totemism.

It is quite possible that none of these men would be known to us today but for the *Encyclopaedia Britannica,* an Edinburgh publishing venture that transformed Victorian intellectual life. McLennan's book began as an article for the encyclopedia. Smith was invited to contribute to a later edition. His articles on the Bible led to public attacks in the press, a charge of heresy, and a dismissal from his academic chair. Smith had done no more than summarize German biblical scholarship, asserting little that he had not said before, but his career as a minister was over. Soon he was involved in selecting writers for the concluding volumes of the encyclopedia, and he assigned Frazer a number of articles, including one on totemism and one on taboo. And so Frazer the classicist left the established path for the wilds of anthropology. With the *Britannica* articles, Frazer's conversion to anthropology was complete. Frazer produced under Smith's supervision a book-length work, an excerpt of which appeared in the encyclopedia. The monograph published in 1887, *Totemism,* became a standard on the subject.

In this early theory of totemism Frazer posited that the totem—the animal, plant, or natural object that was taken as the sign of a clan or tribe—acted as a repository of individual souls. The soul was commonly believed to fly from the body on various occasions and therefore was subject to hazards. Because the totem was believed to be the guardian of the well-being of the group, Frazer asserted, members of the group were forbidden to hunt or kill it. The totem organized social relations and was the origin of religion, since over time the totem took on the character of a god.

In 1885, a year after meeting Smith, Frazer was not merely continuing his research into primitive cultures, he was participating in the rituals of the discipline, reading a paper at the annual meeting of the Anthropological Institute in London in the august presence of both Spencer and Tylor. This talk, "On Certain Burial Customs as Illustrative of the Primitive Theory of the Soul," set Frazer in an elite intellectual community. The topic of the lecture signals a principal preoccupation of Frazer's, one that sets him closer to some of his fin de siècle literary contemporaries: fear of the dead. Frazer posited this fear as the underlying motive for all religious belief in *The Golden Bough*. In his introduction to the one-volume abridgment (1922), Frazer attacked certain critics who he felt had misread his theory on the origin of religion:

I am so far from regarding the reverence for trees as of supreme importance for the evolution of religion that I consider it to have been altogether subordinate to other factors, and in particular to the fear of the human dead, which, on the whole, I believe to have been probably the most powerful force in the making of primitive religion.

(p. vii)

Frazer's lecture on burial customs was both a learned exposition and an entertainment. The lecture had colorful and recondite samplings of customs from around the world, abstract notions, wit, and pathos, and Frazer demonstrated complete command of the occasion. Collected in *Garnered Sheaves: Essays, Addresses, and Reviews* (1931), the lecture contains the fascinating information that Germans will not eat bread while there is a corpse in the house for fear that their teeth will fall out; that in Voightland, where it rains a great deal, the coffin is packed with umbrella and galoshes; or that in the case of the death of twins in Africa, a mother continued to fill a cup with breast milk each evening, "lest the spirits of the dead babes should torment her" (p. 16). The lecture reveals an aspect of Frazer that later works obscure: Frazer the showman, both erudite and popular, a researcher whose facts are always embedded in narrative. Further, in its choice of subject as well as its style, the lecture suggests a literary precursor in Sir Thomas Browne, who also addressed science, religion, and the afterlife.

By the late 1880s Frazer had amassed huge files of ethnographic data. Smith acknowledged the contributions of Frazer's researches to his magnum opus, *The Religion of the Semites*. Frazer, in the meantime, did not abandon his classical studies; the newest and the oldest of disciplines came together in Frazer's work. Like other great mythographers of the nineteenth century—Johann Hölderlin, Friedrich Nietzsche, Walter Pater—Frazer revitalized the classical world even as he undermined its privileged place as the pinnacle of rationalism. Greek thought may be riddled with savage assumptions, according to Frazer, but this gives it a renewed explanatory power. Greek gods no longer provide a key to Western culture but to world culture. Thus while Frazer was establishing himself as an authority in the world of anthropology, he was confirming his authority as a classicist. His deep involvement with classical literature imparted a cultural authority to his vision of prehistory. It is arguable to what extent Frazer would have accepted the notion that anthropology, philosophy, and classics were distinct fields of inquiry. *The Golden Bough*, after all, was a digression from another work, his commentary upon *The Description of Greece* by the second-century author Pausanias.

Pausanias was from Asia Minor, a doctor, a Roman citizen, a student of Greek culture, who traveled extensively and recorded his observations. His guidebook was an important source of information about the architecture, topography, and customs of classical Greece. *The Description of Greece* is a proto-anthropological work, showing the beliefs and customs of a vanished world. Frazer had initially intended merely to translate the text when he took it up in 1883. By the time of its publication in 1898, however, *Pausanias' Description of Greece* was composed of six volumes, translation, commentary, and maps. Pausanias turned out to be a strangely contemporary author. The wave of archaeological research following Heinrich Schliemann's discovery of Troy in the 1870s gave a new pertinence to the travels and observations of the ancient traveler. In the 1890s Frazer made two trips to Greece. He inspected archaeological sites and took scrupulous notes. His contact with other scholars fed his conviction that a new vision of the classical world was possible. There had been among intellectuals and artists of Frazer's time an intense interest in retrieving a numinous essence from the discarded icons of the past. Swinburne and Pater had brought an erotic fervor to the critique of Christianity, finding lewd divinities concealed in plaster saints.

It was a stroke of luck that Robertson Smith had interrupted Frazer's career as a classicist. The articles Frazer wrote for the *Britannica* delayed the completion of the Pausanias project. Had Frazer done the work in the middle 1880s rather than the early 1890s, as his biographer notes, his commentary would have been immediately outdated. Between 1885 and 1895, major excavations were carried out at Delphi, Corinth, Sparta, Thebes, and elsewhere. Schliemann's interest had been in the prehistorical period. These later archaeological projects, under the auspices of French, German, American, British, and Austrian classical schools established in Athens, focused on classical sites. The fervor of identification and corroboration surrounding even the most casual travelogue phrase suggested that the scroll of the earth was unraveling at last. Pausanias proved the talismanic power of a fact. Frazer returned to his classical origins throughout his writing, especially in his discussions of Dionysus and Demeter in *The Golden Bough.* Moreover, it was among classicists of the next generation that he found his truest heirs. Scholars who would come to be called the Cambridge Ritualists, Jane Harrison, A. B. Cook, Gilbert Murray, and F. M. Cornford, while differing from Frazer on such significant points as the primacy of ritual over myth, produced works that reflected the erudition, breadth, and anthropological concern of the Pausanias volumes and of *The Golden Bough.* Frazer knew some of these scholars personally, studying Hebrew informally in 1904 or 1905 in a group that included Harrison, Cornford, and Cook, who played a pivotal role in recasting the argument of the final volumes of the third edition.

In the world of classical studies Frazer found the central preoccupation of his anthropological research. The second book of Pausanias mentions a strange legend of Hippolytus shared by Greeks and Romans alike that he found carved on a tablet at a shrine near Corinth. Raised from the dead by Asclepios, the patron of medicine to whom the shrine was dedicated, Hippolytus was transported to Aricia in Italy. "There he reigned," Frazer translates Pausanias, "and there he dedicated to Artemis a precinct, where down to my time the priesthood of the goddess is the prize of victory in a single combat. The competition is not open to free men, but only to slaves who have run away from their masters" (vol. 1, pp. 112–113).

The single combat was, as other references in classical literature indicate, a fight to the death and was regarded by Strabo as a barbaric practice from an earlier age. For Frazer as well it was a ritual in which the classical world betrayed a primitive past. The priest tended a sacred grove and was called Rex Nemorensis, King of the Wood. To explain this grim ritual of assassination Frazer would chronicle the death of kings in all cultures in all times. His masterwork would be named in part for the branch the custom required the aspiring priest to break from a tree in the sacred grove before the battle could begin. Frazer had been gathering anthropological data throughout the 1880s. It was not until 1889, however, when Frazer read an eighteenth-century account of kings required to kill themselves at the end of a twelve-year reign that, according to Robert Fraser, *The Golden Bough* took shape. Frazer would write to the publisher George Macmillan before the year was out with a proposal for the first edition. The priest in the grove, readers would soon learn, was nothing less than a god. Frazer's ultimate preoccupation was and would be deicide. The first edition appeared in two volumes. Frazer then resumed his work on Pausanias. When the *Description of Greece* was completed in 1898, Frazer would immediately turn his indefatigable hand to a second edition of *The Golden Bough.*

Major developments in late-nineteenth-century anthropology also came to the assistance of the writer. During the 1890s researchers in Australia came upon aboriginal tribesmen, believed to be the most primitive of all the savage peoples yet documented by the West. Of extreme interest to Frazer in this new information was the report from the Australian anthropologist Baldwin Spencer about a tribe that ate its totem. The report shattered Frazer's earlier theory of the totem as a repository of the individual souls of the clan. Previously he had reasoned that eating the totem would constitute suicide by the clan. But with news of the *intichiuma* ritual, totemism would have to be rethought. That the Arunta tribesmen devoured their totem pointed directly to the principal sacramental act of Protestant and Catholic ritual, especially the latter, with its doctrine of transubstantiation. The Mass was a form of magic. The claim for the uniqueness of Christ's sacrifice was profoundly challenged by the practices of these most savage of communicants. Spencer became an invaluable correspondent of Frazer's, providing a steady stream of information. Through Spencer's reports, Frazer's library alcove opened onto the outback. Science confirmed Frazer's vision of the world, and with this confirmation came the large narrative arc that allowed Frazer's writing to infinitely expand. There was no detail that could not contribute to the telling of the tale. As ethnological reports from around the world found their way to Frazer, and archaeologists found fresh evidence of ancient things, Frazer could well believe that science and scholarship were in the process of revealing the truth about the past.

Published in 1900, the second edition of *The Golden Bough* introduces the central idea that provided a structure for Frazer's eventual expansion of the work from two volumes to twelve. The change in the subtitle from first to second editions is indicative: from *A Study in Comparative Religion* to *A Study in Magic and Religion.* All cultures go through three stages of development, Frazer argues, from magic to religion to science. This threefold progression has precedents deep in the eighteenth century as well as in the evolutionary arguments of the later nineteenth century. While the idea of stages gave Frazer a beginning, middle, and end for his epic story and offered a scientific basis for the skeptical but optimistic pose of the narrator, it is somewhat misleading. Magic certainly is documented in the book, but it is largely the operations of magic within the world of religion. Science is gestured toward, but Frazer has little interest in narrating its development. What animates the larger ostensible plot is the continual war between reason and superstition. The ontological error Frazer located at the heart of Plato is in *The Golden Bough* seen as endemic to human intelligence. The development of man from magician to scientist is not limited to historical time. Magic is everywhere, all the time, and so the speaker can leap cultures, can leap millennia, and not miss a beat in his chronicle.

In the second edition of *The Golden Bough* Frazer addresses the central enchantment of Western civilization, Christ. Frazer's shocking and speculative theories about the origins of Christianity provoked a controversy that made Frazer both famous and notorious. This speculation is at the heart of both the second and the third editions (where it was relegated to an appendix in the ninth volume, and not included in the single-volume 1922 edition). While Frazer clearly saw the first edition of *The Golden Bough* as a critique of Christian belief, he was content to have the reader *infer* the deconstruction of the Christian cosmos. As he wrote to his publisher, "The resemblance of many of the savage customs and ideas to the fundamental doctrines of Christianity is striking. But I make no reference to this parallelism, leaving my readers to draw their own conclusions, one way or the other" (quoted in Ackerman, p. 95). The discoveries of Baldwin Spencer led Frazer to speculate directly about the origins of Christianity, but his thinking about Calvary was illuminated by another source. In 1892 Frazer had read an article about an ancient tablet upon which a German scholar had discovered the name "Humman." The tablet had been carved by an ancient enemy of the Babylonians, the Elamites. Humman seemed to be their chief deity. The Babylonians, in conquering their enemy, had subsumed the alien mythology, recasting the enemy's god as a villain. This Babylonian story was in turn appropriated by the Jews during their captivity. What this would lead to was the theory that the Old Testament book of Esther was in fact originally a Babylonian tale. Humman became Haman.

This was one bit of evidence in a larger speculation that detected a source for the Jewish festival of Purim in the Babylonian celebration of Zagmuk. Frazer provoked a fury by contending that Christ was a common criminal ritually selected to play the role of Haman in a Purim rite, put to death at the end of the festival to assure a plentiful harvest. When attacking this assertion, critics pointed to what they saw as Frazer's historical imprecision and a certain lacuna in logic. Frazer's fiercest and most persistent critic was the Scottish poet and anthropologist Andrew Lang, whose book *Magic and Religion* (1901) was devoted to attacking Frazer and especially his theory of the origins of Christianity. In retrospect, what is striking is the effort Frazer made to come to a conclusion he could have made inevitable simply by the accretion of global evidence concerning ritual executions and god figures had he been content merely to imply that Christ was just another scapegoat in a virtually universal practice. It is indicative of Frazer's deep attachment to the personae of scholar and scientist that he took such pains in establishing what his Scottish Enlightenment forebears would have recognized as "conjectural history." This reclusive archivist of the archaic found himself, no doubt to his dismay, in the spirit of the 1890s, providing a historical basis for the magical thinking that he would dispel, wielding an argument that could easily have been a travesty of scholarship, a send-up of both traditional Christian belief and rationalism by a French decadent.

In the years following the publication of the second edition of *The Golden Bough*, Frazer considered a variety of projects, including a translation of Augustine's *Confessions*, a book on American Indians, and translations of French and Spanish exploration narratives. But he had already begun working on a third edition of his major work, composing a preface during a steambath in Wiesbaden in 1901, taking notes on a visit to Nemi, the site described in the opening of *The Golden Bough*. While in Italy he dined with William James, who suggested that the realm of psychic phenomena might hold clues to the mental life of the past. Everywhere around him new information about primitive cultures clamored for inclusion. His interest in the tribes of the New World, evident in unrealized projects proposed to his publisher, was matched by a heightened attention to ethnographic work done elsewhere. Between the publication of the second edition (1900) and the third (1911–1915) Frazer published a series of works that contributed to the reasoning and breadth of the third edition. *Lectures on the Early History of the Kingship* (1905) was the fruit of Frazer's friendship with the distinguished classicist A. B. Cook. Here Frazer complicates his understanding of kingship and suggests a notion that would be more fully articulated in his essay *Psyche's Task: A Discourse Concerning the Influence of Superstitions on the Growth of Institutions* (1909). In this work, Frazer reconsiders the role of superstition in human development. In coming to see superstition as something more than error or folly, Frazer clears the ground for a more nuanced characterization of the primitive and also deepens his understanding of atavism. Frazer sets four basic institutions of modern secular society in the context of primitive belief: government, private property, marriage, and respect for human life. While stipulating that no such institution could survive if founded solely on superstition, he then provides hundreds of examples of cultures in which the rationale for the existence of these institutions is illogical. Since the modern institutions are generally agreed to be beneficial, superstition is good to the degree that it helps to preserve these institutions. "It is better, far better, for the world that men should do right from wrong motives than that they should do wrong with the best intentions" (p. 83).

As the work of Bernard Spencer and his collaborator, Francis James Gillen, had come to Frazer at a critical time in his rethinking of the role of magic, so the reports of C. G. Seligmann from Africa affected the shape and argument of the third edition. Seligmann confirmed a central tenet of all Frazer's thought: there was a tribe in Africa that ritually executed its kings. The news seemed to prove a central link in Frazer's speculations about the origins of culture. And there was more: the king was believed to be the incarnation of an ancient hero. The first volume of what would become the third edition of *The Golden Bough* to appear was *Adonis, Attis, Osiris: Studies in the History of Oriental Religion* (1906). This volume itself went through several editions and expansions. Here Frazer persists in his attack on Christianity not by speculations about the exact origins of its central myth but by establishing a panorama of custom and belief from all the religions of the regions around the Holy Land. The abundance of parallels leads Frazer to the inescapable conclusion that no matter what the specific and perhaps forever lost origin of the story of Christ, he was a generic god, one of many amid the mystery cults of the East. The third edition was completed and published in a creative fury that had begun in 1910. Between 1911 and 1913, nine more volumes issued forth at a rapid rate. Frazer expanded the *Adonis, Attis, Osiris* section, publishing that in two volumes in April 1914. A year later he issued an index and a bibliography. The third edition, comprising twelve volumes, confirmed Frazer's place as the most famous living anthropologist, as a literary artist, and as a late manifestation of a Victorian sage. Frazer's ability to infuse the whole with a sense of drama, to sound a wide range of moods and tones, made of the work a grand adventure. His visual power, allusiveness, and poetic cadence and epic ambition provided a model for the novelists, poets, and dramatists who would transform literature in the early part of the twentieth century.

Frazer's fame and popularity were secure, but he was increasingly a man of letters. As a storyteller he was revered, but as an anthropologist he had long been an antiquated figurehead for the discipline that had defined him. Anthropologists made their name by repudiating him, both his theories and the examples he had gathered to support them. As has happened repeatedly throughout the history of anthropological writing, each new generation places its aging parent figure in the rest home called literature. Frazer continued working, editing the letters of one of his favorite poets,

William Cowper, and a volume of his favorite prose writer, Addison, and a new style of anthropological writing established itself. He published a series of Addison imitations, gathering them along with other literary essays in a volume titled *The Gorgon's Head and Other Literary Pieces* (1927). Frazer was knighted in 1914, and in 1918 his three-volume study *Folk-Lore in the Old Testament* appeared and sold well. Though generally regarded as a lesser work, it contained his favorite piece of his own writing, a retelling of the witch of Endor story. In 1913 he published the first volume of *The Belief in Immortality and the Worship of the Dead;* in 1922 he published the second volume, and in 1924 the third. The single-volume edition of *The Golden Bough* was published in 1922. This edition is the one most readers of Frazer have come to know. While it skillfully presents the arguments and main subjects of the larger edition, it affords a very different reading experience. Shorn of footnotes and the wilder stretches of cross-cultural association, the single volume omits much remarkable material, and the reader with a serious interest in Frazer will want to sample the third edition. In the 1920s Frazer returned to classics, the discipline he had been poised to master just before meeting Robertson Smith. Frazer's translation of and multivolume commentary on Ovid's *Fasti,* an epic fragment which in following the calendar of Roman feasts is a major source of information about Roman religious life, was the last major undertaking of his career. Published in 1931, it was called by Frazer's biographer "arguably the finest work he ever accomplished" (p. 300).

THE THEMES AND STRUCTURE OF THE GOLDEN BOUGH

THE third and final edition of *The Golden Bough* was published in twelve volumes, eleven of text and a bibliography. These eleven volumes comprise seven numbered parts, seven interrelated dissertations on the subject of magic and religion. Of these, five are devoted to the central theme of the dying god, while two, the first two, set out for the reader the historical evolution of the dying god myth. The first of the sections documents the place of magic in the religious life of primitive cultures and its contribution to our earliest notions of kingship, while the second focuses on a particular kind of magic, taboo, and details the relation of taboo to conceptions of the soul from around the world. Here are the seven parts as Frazer presents them:

   I. The Magic Art and the Evolution of Kings
   II. Taboo and the Perils of the Soul
   III. The Dying God
   IV. Adonis, Attis, Osiris
   V. Spirits of the Corn and of the Wild
   VI. The Scapegoat
   VII. Balder the Beautiful

Few discussions of Frazer avoid the opportunity to comment on the opening paragraphs of *The Golden Bough* and the story they tell. The story concerns a grove consecrated at Nemi, southeast of Rome, to the goddess Diana, and the grim contest that was ritually enacted there to decide who would be the priest. This story recurs throughout the many volumes and editions of *The Golden Bough* and provides a fixed point for the reader to plot his or her own progress. The scene in Frazer's description is mysterious, serenely tormented, and might strike the reader as an oddly indirect way for the writer to approach his topic. The legend of the contest is a minor one, but Nemi was a major site of religious practice in its time, mentioned by numerous ancient writers. Precisely what kinds of practice were considered should not be too narrowly construed: oracles, health cures, and recreational activities existed side by side. Nemi was so popular that the emperor Caligula attempted to shut it down, by sending in a thug to eliminate the King of the Wood. English and American archaeologists began exploring the site in the mid-1880s, and reports of their findings were published in *The Athenaeum,* where Frazer read about them. While the site was known through a variety of classical sources (Ovid, Strabo, Juvenal, and Statius all mention it), there was no archaeological evidence to support the legend of the bloody rite of succession. This is not to say Frazer ignored the findings of scientific researches, since the site was not widely excavated. Of particular significance was the discovery of the name of the goddess Diana in a script that predates all classical references to the site, going back possibly to the third century B.C., suggesting that the contest was a Tylorian "survival," a remnant of an earlier ritual, possibly from a people that predated the Romans.

The priests of Nemi afforded Frazer a dramatically charged tableau. There is acute psychological anguish—that of the priest and, perhaps, that of the author—at the center of the drama. The sleepless and solitary wait for a violent death and the obsessive attention to the state of one's body (since any illness or aging or exhaustion heightens one's vulnerability to attack) do not make the job seem especially desirable. The eerie absence of attention to the inner logic of the king lifts the figure out of the realm of historical evidence. He haunts the peripheries of all Frazer's discussions and seems to inhabit a very modern world, like a character in a postmodern drama, embodying a free-floating existential dread. Why would anyone want to be the King of the Wood? To understand the logic of this archaic practice—which in the modern world of political assassinations, mob rubouts, and slain religious potentates, seems quite contemporary—Frazer initiates us into the world of magic.

Magic gives shape and reason to human actions and institutions; only with an understanding of its fundamental laws can one proceed through the world that Frazer presents. We have seen the specific way in which magic became the center of the second and third editions of *The Golden Bough*. Magic was at the end of the nineteenth century of exceeding interest to a great many. Touching on an array of interrelated subjects, magic was a central concern of the nascent disciplines of psychology, anthropology, and comparative religion and was at the heart of symbolist aesthetics. Frazer, with his lifelong interest in the "splendid errors" of logic by which conjecture came to be taken as fact, was particularly taken by the clear demonstrations of magical thinking embodied in folk belief and lore. In this, too, Frazer was in step with his contemporaries. Ethnographers were reporting on magical thought and practice not only in obscure regions. W. B. Yeats and Lady Gregory canvassed the west of Ireland in the 1890s gathering Irish legends and superstitions. A generation of British folklorists was hard at work, gathering and scrutinizing, forming a society for the continued study of the fruits of native and naive genius. Americans had collected data from Native American cultures.

There were various motives for this interest in magic. One involved the question of what constituted a people. Were there unique legends that could be used to define a racial or ethnic essence? Yeats, for example, believed that the folk beliefs of the Irish could be used to create a vibrant new mythology that would rival that of Greece and Rome and lift the Irish race to prominence. Other researchers were looking for the origin of the races. In the century that debated the issue of slavery there was keen interest in establishing whether the peoples of the earth were the descendants of common ancestors, or whether the races had developed separately. Further, with the withering of Orthodox Christian religious practice in the light of Darwinian thinking and textually oriented biblical scholarship, there came a vogue of occultism throughout Victorian and Edwardian England. Mesmerists, psychics, and crystal gazers helped alleviate the nostalgia for invisible worlds.

Frazer stood at the midpoint between the fervent interest in the occult of the late 1890s and the skeptical stance toward the supernatural taken by modernist writers such as T. S. Eliot, Ezra Pound, and James Joyce. Frazer was no fellow traveler of occultists; his analysis was meant to demystify. But in robbing magic of one authority he gave it another, one with consequences for literature. His attention to magical thought gave anthropological validity to the most basic tool of poets and writers: metaphor. Frazer empowered modern writers to free themselves of nineteenth-century narrative conventions. If a literary work could utilize patterns of magical belief while retaining the cold eye for detail so privileged by realism, the atavistic impulse so pervasive in the new century could find an authentic form. The gods and heroes of ancient days could return. Frazer's contemporary Ferdinand de Saussure further validated the power of metaphor by arguing that language itself worked to establish meaning through laws not unlike those Frazer found to be characteristic of the primitive mind.

For his analysis of magic, Frazer returned to the Enlightenment, specifically to David Hume's *Treatise of Human Nature*. Frazer had studied this work in the 1860s at Glasgow, and he might have found a link between associationist psychology and magical thinking in the work of Tylor. At any rate, he evokes the association of ideas explicitly to discuss how magical thinking works, thereby anchoring his analysis of primitive cultures in the empiricist traditions of the Enlightenment. Hume had presented a scheme that explained how the mind came by its beliefs. According to Hume, belief began as impressions on the mind. For an impression to become an idea and then a belief, three conditions had to be met: contiguity, resemblance, and cause and effect.

Magic, for Frazer, requires a world devoid of the third of Hume's conditions. Cause and effect, Frazer argues, could not properly be understood until the advent of science. But what is important in Frazer's view is that the same mental laws govern men everywhere at all times. This belief attacks the mystique of the primitive and the occult that derived from the possibility that some wholly other kind of mental life was available. Frazer espoused rationalism, and one can see here the echo of his dissertation on Plato. The mistake that primitives made is that they confused the *way* they knew with *what* they knew, and so they believed that their thought could affect the larger world. Frazer defines two types of magic. The first he calls homeopathic, which proceeds from the belief that "like produces like": to bring about a desired event one has only to imitate it. The second type of magic assumes that things that have once been in contact remain so forever, and this type he calls "contagious magic." The idea of contagious magic accounts for the tremendous catalog of superstitions that Frazer sets before the reader as he explains why blood, nail parings, scraps of food, and articles of clothing could be charged with occult force. Both types of magic assume that a secret affinity unites all things; together, therefore, they are called sympathetic magic.

Frazer postulates that in the earliest stages of human evolution there was magic without what we have come to know as religion. An effective magician, one who could protect cattle from spells, crops from drought, and families from illness, accrued considerable prestige. He became, in effect, a king. Frazer does not say that all kings derived from magicians, but in his view, the magician and king were indissolubly linked. Kings drew upon an association with magic to preserve their reign and to a large degree their reign was itself governed by the laws of magic, especially with respect to taboos.

The age of pure magic was fleeting. While it hardly constituted what a religious culture would call an unfallen state, it shared certain assumptions with Christian belief, and it reflected debates ongoing when Frazer first began reading anthropology. One widely debated theory of origin held that men once enjoyed a more direct knowledge of religious truth, embodied in a lost language from which our modern tongues derived. Metaphor was a sign of the degeneracy of men. While this theory flourished among philologists and mythographers, it had an obvious appeal to Christian apologists. For Frazer, metaphor, or rather the principles that underlie metaphor, existed at the point of origin. His narrative of human history is not degenerative but progressive. At a certain point in human history, according to Frazer, a thought occurred, though that thought alone could not control the vast forces to which men and women were subject. Suddenly it became apparent that rain clouds did not instantly arise at the magician's whim, and religion was born. In the gap between an action and its efficacy poured gods, goddesses, demons, ghosts, and that most crucial of human constructions, the soul.

For Frazer, it is this second stage of mankind's slow progress that has dominated human history. The age of pure magic had a certain integrity. However mistaken the magician might have been, he shared with the modern scientist the belief in impersonal universal laws governing appearances. With religion there was a slight advance: the recognition of the mind's limits. While helpfully qualifying early man's belief in the omnipotence of thought, religion compounded the initial error, retaining sympathetic magic while adding a panorama of agents at work in any natural or human event. Thus there accrued to the earthly ruler not only the power of his predecessor but that of the priest. This world of religion founded in magic and suffused with a phantasmagoria of imagined forces was the world of the present as well as that of the distant past.

As discussed earlier, Frazer proposes a three-stage evolutionary process by which cultures move from magic to religion to science, and argues throughout *The Golden Bough* and elsewhere that all cultures conform to this model. In doing so he takes over earlier Enlightenment views of primitive culture, such as that proposed by Auguste Comte. However, by and large the world Frazer portrays is the world of religion. The first age, of pure magic, existed if at all in an inaccessible prehistory. The age of science is implied by Frazer but not dramatized. Again, the evolutionary narrative lends the monumental epic of human origins the benefit of an Aristotelian plot, a beginning, middle, and end, but there is scant example of the world of magic untainted by religion, and the world of science is represented in *The Golden Bough* largely by the perspective of the narrator and that of some of the authorities he cites.

The second preliminary discussion in the approach to the theme of the dying god derives from the first. Two concepts that Frazer contends are indispensable to the workings of a world that has lapsed into religious belief are introduced: taboo and the concept of the soul. The first of these terms Frazer defines as a form of magic, a negative form that did not bring about desired events but prevented fearsome ones from happening. Frazer found the origin of all religious thought in fear. Taboo was a form of magic that required a universe of spirits and ghosts and demons. Taboos formed a rigid pattern of belief in which the life of the community was invested in the life of the king. The king therefore was particularly subject to taboo, since his health and well-being were crucial to all. The evolution of kingship from magician to divinity went against the supposition of a greater personal liberty accruing to the king. He was the literal prisoner of the community's belief system. This is an important part of the interlocking grid of ideas in Frazer's world. It establishes a direct link between the mental life of the individual and the institutions that order his world. For Frazer the storyteller, it increases the possibilities of characterization. The king could be a hero or a fool, a terrified victim or the essence of calm nobility.

Taboos governed the social, political, religious, and sexual life of the primitive world. A key anxiety around which taboos formed had to do with interactions with strangers, since they were most likely to bring ills upon others. In addition to the king, there were other figures subject to stringent taboos, commonly those who had come into contact with common media of other spirits. These included hunters and warriors, since they were likely targets of retribution by the spirits of those they had slain; mourners, since they too were in commerce with the dead; women during childbirth; murderers; as well as a range of common objects, names (of gods, kings, the dead), and numerous common words. Anything that an ill-intentioned spirit might use against the living by means of contagious magic was closely regulated. This second discussion draws us closer toward Frazer's central subject, the dying god, by establishing a point of origin for our ethics and our inner lives.

By addressing the origin of humanity's central institutions, religion and the state, and giving hundreds of colorful examples of how the idea most integral to the biblical and classical past, the individual soul, was the fanciful result of a logical error, Frazer provides a context for the third and longest of his discussions. Kingship evolved to the extent that monarchs were routinely taken to be gods, but the cosmology that evolved along with the role of the king made of the king himself only the temporary vessel of the sovereign spirit. Therefore, taboo required the death of the king at the moment his vital powers started to wane. This raised an important question for the survival of primitive communities: the supply of kings. *The Dying God* discusses the belief that one person can take on the suffering and death of another, and begins with an immediate problem: how candidates for kingship were found, given that one requirement of kingship was the death of the king.

In a grim paradox, the king was killed in an effort to preserve his health. His regal power abided in his soul, and according to Frazer, the primitives were deathly afraid that the power of the kingship would deteriorate along with the physical health of the king. Frazer finds this model of kingship everywhere. There was even, he tells us, a tribe in Africa that killed its king at the end of each day; consequently, the throne stood vacant. The tremendous anxiety underlying this belief required that the failing king be put to death, since in addition to putting an immediate end to his deteriorating reign, murder afforded the best opportunity for the successor to capture the soul of the dying king as it tried to escape on the final breath. Kings were also killed according to fixed terms. This is important for the larger critique of Christian belief that *The Golden Bough* undertakes, since it means that ritual regicide was an integral part of the rhythm of primitive life, in essence, an act of sympathetic magic by which the culture renewed itself. The next and crucial step was the development of the idea of the substitute. Since it was believed that the sacrificial substitute for the king should share some of the king's attributes, sons were the first of the proxies. Frazer recounts the tale of a king who sacrificed eight of his nine sons to secure a long reign. Once the principle that one person could die in the place of another was accepted, the psychic economy of the primitive could entertain temporary kings: men, often criminals, allotted to be king for a brief period, to reign over a festival, at the end of which they were put to death so that the real king could be symbolically reborn and could resume his rule.

Frazer next takes up the Oriental religions from which Christianity emerged. This is the part of *The Golden Bough* best known to students of modern literature, since the two volumes that comprise this survey, *Adonis, Attis, Osiris,* are mentioned in footnotes to T. S. Eliot's *The Waste Land.* The vivid landscapes of these most descriptive of all the volumes can be felt throughout the last section of Eliot's poem, where a desiccated biblical landscape is so memorably evoked. In taking up the gods Adonis, Attis, and Osiris, and in subsequent volumes Dionysus and Demeter, Frazer anatomizes the components of the Christian myth. Having established that kings derive from magicians, and gods from kings, the discussion turns on the ritual practice surrounding certain gods, those gods who loom large in the foundation of Western spiritualism, and the relation of these gods to the agricultural life of early societies. Frazer himself points to the special attention lavished on landscape in *Adonis, Attis, Osiris:* "In studying afresh these three Oriental worships, akin to each other in character, I have paid more attention than formerly to the natural features of the countries in which they arose, because I am more than ever persuaded that religion, like all other institutions, has been profoundly influenced by physical environment" (part 4, vol. 1, p. v). His sudden interest in what amount to dithyrambic prose poems celebrating the desolation and sublimity of ancient sites serves a larger purpose, charting the physical dimensions of the worlds within which the gods moved. While all Frazer's gods turn out to be vegetation gods, the ecosystems are various and affect how each culture tells its stories of death and resurrection.

The Oriental deities Frazer discusses in this section resemble the worldly kings put to death at the height of their powers in order to preserve their powers. Although they are said by Frazer to be "akin of character," he treats each god quite differently, and the high pathos that attends the descriptions of Adonis is replaced by satiric irony in regard to Attis, until with Osiris there is scholarly curiosity with no affect. The coherence of the legends seems almost lost amid the evidence. Adonis entered the consciousness of the West from a dim Sumerian past, passing into Babylonian, Semitic, and Greek legend. A youth desired by both Persephone and Aphrodite, he was killed by a wild boar, and by decree of Zeus spent half a year below the earth and half a year above, thus honoring both the goddess of death and that of

life. His death and resurrection were commemorated yearly throughout the Mediterranean world, and in describing the ritual lament for Adonis, Frazer's prose captures the religious emotion that was associated with this god.

The god Attis brings together even more powerfully the concern with sexuality and violent death evident in the myth of Adonis, but calls upon himself the wrath of Frazer, whose description is a satire upon Roman Catholic ritual. Attis, a Phrygian god imported into the Roman empire during the Carthaginian wars and officially adopted by the Emperor Claudius, was often confused with Adonis. Both died in the service of a goddess; both were killed by a boar. However, Frazer's attention, given his interest in the origins of the Christian myth, is drawn to a more spectacularly violent tale about Attis. In this version, Attis castrates himself and subsequently bleeds to death beneath a tree. Attis was said to be the son of Cybele, the mother of the gods and an Eastern fertility goddess whose priests also castrated themselves on entering her service. The yearly celebration of Attis was wildly ecstatic, featuring music, processions, and brightly colored robes. Tourists who came to town to witness the spectacle of the dancing and singing eunuchs of the god would be swept up in the passion of the display, and reaching for a sword kept on hand for precisely this occasion would follow the lead of the god and his priests. The delirious converts would fling their severed body parts against the walls of any nearby residence, and those who lived there would be required to provide the novitiate eunuchs with girls' clothing. The description of the ritual is especially fulsome, mixing tones and elements that draw the reader ever onward, since the Attis ritual combines shocking violence, Roman pageantry and excess, and a peculiar humor—the center of the cult is now where the Vatican stands, Frazer tells us. A particularly important part of the myth is the proximity of the dying god to a tree. This clearly anticipates the story of Christ's crucifixion and also connects Attis to the legion of tree spirits endemic to the beliefs of primitive Europeans.

Turning to the Egyptian god Osiris, Frazer arrives at the traditional point of origin for Western religious thought. Building on the work of his contemporary Wallis Budge, Frazer finds a fully articulated afterworld, but also a confusion of beliefs and sources. Under the influence of Budge, Frazer leans in his interpretation toward a particular theory of the origin of myth called euhemerism, a theory that locates the origin of myths in the lives of actual men.

In turning at last to the two principal deities that shaped Christianity, Demeter and Dionysus, in the volume *Spirits of the Corn and of the Wild,* Frazer devotes increased attention to the vegetation that the deities are said to represent. The dominant myth of the West reveals itself to have a far more than symbolic relation to the bread and wine that constitute its principal ceremony. The deepest mysteries of the classical world, those practiced in the name of Demeter at Eleusis, and those practiced throughout Greece in the name of Dionysus, sprang from the material life of the primitive community. As a classicist of international reputation Frazer draws upon his considerable authority in placing these figures before us, then in surveying gods of grape and wine throughout the world, he undermines their special prestige in Western traditions by finding comparable figures throughout India, New Guinea, North America, and Northern Europe.

With the volume entitled *The Scapegoat,* Frazer returns to the phenomenon he has already documented in some detail, the substitution of temporary kings who are killed so that the reigning king in resuming his throne can appear to be reborn. But now he is ready to explore the ritual of scapegoating, which merged with agricultural rituals to create a proto-Christian drama. The practice of scapegoating had several crucial steps, the first being the transference of evil from person to object. A toothache, shooed from a sore jaw to a stone and buried at a crossroads, waits to enter the first unlucky traveler to tread on its grave. This act of transference is repeated with infinite variations. Animals and other people could be the recipients of ills. Demons as well as toothaches could be driven out, a society as well as an individual could seek to be rid of its pains. In *The Scapegoat,* Frazer offered the reader an anatomy of expiation.

A particularly vivid instance of such a custom occurred among the Aztecs. Frazer draws on a famous account of human sacrifice to present what amounts to a vision of Christianity stripped of sentiment. With their priestly orders, and their exaltation of blood, the Aztecs were Roman Catholic without knowing it. Their procession and stone edifices stand as the culmination of Frazer's survey of scapegoat rituals. In Greece and Rome a period of license accompanied the expulsion of evil. Slaves changed places with their masters, sexual liberties were allowed, and a mock king was chosen. Frazer shows how these saturnalias occurred throughout the world, often in conjunction with rituals of sowing. The ritual beating of scapegoats had a generative aspect. The true aim of the blows was not the hapless victim but the spirit of infertility that was believed to be inside him. In the hypnotic spectacle of ritual execution at the heart of Aztec ritual, the once benign accompaniments of vegetation rituals became horrific. The priest put on the flayed skin of the victim and joined the parade. Because Frazer banished his controversial speculation about the origins of Christian sacrifice to an appendix in the third edition of *The Golden Bough,* the Aztec ritual takes its place as the dramatic center of that edition:

The scene of the slaughter was the platform on the summit of the god Huitzilopochtli's temple. Some of the poor wretches fainted when they came to the foot of the steps and had to be dragged up the long staircase by the hair of their heads. Arrived at the summit they were slaughtered one by one on the sacrificial stone by the high priest, who cut open their breasts, tore out their hearts, and held them up to the sun, in order to feed the great luminary with these bleeding relics.

(vol. 6, pp. 297–298)

Frazer spent nine volumes in his attempt to "decompose the idea of the Divine Scapegoat" (vol. 9, p. v) and gathered up in his presentation some of the strangest and most shocking demonstrations of human nature ever recorded. Having completed the survey and discussion of the dying god with the most extreme emblems of incarnation, *The Golden Bough* draws to a close by returning to the great forest of northern Europe, to the Virgilian namesake and the grove at Nemi, and to the eerily beautiful and haunting fire festivals. In keeping with the larger theme of purification, the volumes open with portraits of abstinence: kings not allowed to touch the earth or see the sun, pubescent girls quarantined from village life. The incarnational fury that culminated in both Palestine and Mexico has abated, and as the documentary whirlwind begins, we find ourselves in a world calmly burning.

The last of the sacrificial gods in Frazer's pantheon, the Norse god Balder, presides over the sylvan world. It may seem somewhat peculiar to modern readers that Frazer concludes his survey of dying gods with Balder, a myth hardly of the stature of Adonis, Attis, Osiris, Dionysus, or Persephone, myths that have permeated the rituals and beliefs of Western culture. Yet Balder was there early on, in the first edition of *The Golden Bough*, and a consideration of his dramatic position as the presiding spirit of the concluding volumes illuminates other important precursors of Frazer's book and directs us to crucial suppositions of nineteenth-century mythography. Balder was a deity believed to be representative of an earlier Aryan religion that had once united all Europe. From Jakob Grimm and others Frazer knew that the central tenet of that religion was tree worship, and he believed that in primordial times all of Europe was one vast forest. The German ethnologist Wilhelm Mannhardt had exerted a powerful influence on the first edition of *The Golden Bough*, providing a wealth of European folk customs and evidence of tree devotions. Not only were Teutons and Celts and Saxons united by their common worship of the oak, but so too, Frazer inferred, were the Latins and Etruscans.

Balder was intimately connected to the grove at Nemi and to the King of the Wood, who was ritually slain at the hand of an aspirant king, whom ritual required to pick, before the regicidal violence could begin, a branch from a tree. Frazer had already assumed that the branch broken at Nemi was the golden bough described by Virgil in the *Aeneid*. He had come to this conclusion through a gloss in a fourth-century commentary by Servius. In the sixth book of the *Aeneid*, Aeneas is told by the Sibyl at Cumae that in order to go to the underworld to speak to his father he must break a branch off a great tree; Servius identified that branch with the one used in the ritual at Nemi. Frazer, following a lead of Grimm, further equated this branch with the mistletoe, the plant that in Norse legend had done in Balder the Beautiful. And the fire festivals celebrated throughout Europe were ritual reenactments of the funeral of Balder, whose body in legend had been set adrift on a burning boat.

In these concluding volumes one senses a Prospero-like renunciation of magic as Frazer returns to the Aryan landscape where his first investigations of myth and ritual had led him, and there is a poignancy in his revision of his theory of European fire festivals. Where he once—following the lead of Mannhardt—saw in the hilltop bonfires that seem to link all of Europe in a single con-flagration an act of sympathetic magic aimed at restoring sunlight to the earth, he now sees purgation of all things noxious, and more: the hint of human sacrifice, the witch burnings of the medieval past. After presenting such a vast and extravagant survey of human folly, *The Golden Bough* sounds a note of chastity and seclusion, telling of figures frozen between earth and sky, ritually protected from the contagion of life. The story of Balder itself seems stripped of the sexual violence and festive excesses of the other gods. The pages flow with a serenely apocalyptic ambience as the bonfires burn. As the festivals tend to highlight the pageantry of peasant life rather than its cruelty or stupidity, one senses as well a lament for the passing of European folk culture. Frazer was aware that urbanization and industrialization would soon render peasant and savage alike extinct. The fires were quaint survivals of the savage past, emblematic of a burning boat and the corpse of Balder the Beautiful, whose funeral pyre the lesser and later fires recall.

THE COMPARATIVE METHOD

FROM the mid-1880s on, Frazer dedicated himself to mastering the emerging science of anthropology. The field was new, rapidly developing, and there were possibilities beyond what the well-turned field of classical studies seemed to promise. Yet historians of anthropology take no vital interest in Frazer. Though his early articles for the *Britannica* and his address to the Anthropological Institute mark him as centrally involved in the emergence of the discipline, one prominent late-twentieth-century anthropologist has dismissed *The Golden Bough* as "The Gilded Twig" and suggested that Frazer's true fame should be found in the annals of Victorian pornography. But Frazer's writing is deeply enmeshed in the traditions of anthropological writing. *The Golden Bough* could not have taken shape without those traditions. At the heart of Frazer's conversion to anthropology, and of anthropology's refutation of him, is the comparative method. This method is not merely an exhibit in a museum of outdated ideas, it is how Frazer wrote his books, and an understanding of it is crucial to questions of style and structure, and to the larger question of authority, both Frazer's own and that of the generation of modernist writers who also made use of this method.

Virtually every page of Frazer's writing contains a demonstration of the comparative method. Cultural artifacts in one culture are explained by establishing them within a context of similar artifacts in other cultures. The author may move from Malaysia to Scotland to the coast of Alaska as he accrues instances of a certain ritual practice or superstition. In the massing of comparisons, a pattern emerges, and this pattern is the demonstration of the underlying universal laws of human development. For Frazer, the comparative method unites science and art in the act of writing. He refers to his method explicitly throughout *The Golden Bough*, both in prefaces and in the text. In an often quoted passage contained in the preface to the second edition, Frazer describes the comparative method as his weapon of choice:

It is indeed a melancholy and in some respects thankless task to strike at the foundations of beliefs in which, as in a strong tower, the hopes and aspirations of humanity through long ages have sought a refuge from the storms and stress of life. Yet sooner or later it is inevitable that the battery of the comparative method should breach these venerable walls, mantled over with the ivy and mosses and wildflowers of a thousand tender and sacred associations. At present we are only dragging the guns into position: they have hardly yet begun to speak.

(p. xxii)

One notes here the confrontational tone of the second edition, which is the edition that featured the description of Christ as a ritual victim in a Purim ritual, for which Frazer achieved a certain notoriety. In the depths of Frazer's research, however, the comparative method reveals itself in other metaphors, and we begin to suspect that Frazer believes the comparative method itself has magical properties. In the third edition volume titled *The Dying God,* the method appears as a light in the darkness: "I am fully sensible of the slipperiness and uncertainty of the ground I am treading, and it is with great diffidence that I submit these speculations to the judgment of my readers. The subject of ancient mythology is involved in dense mists which it is not always possible to penetrate and illumine even with the lamp of the Comparative Method" (p. 112).

The comparative method came to Frazer through his association with Robertson Smith. In his commemoration of Smith, Frazer outlined the descent of his method through the Scottish masters of early anthropology, McLennan and Smith, and took the opportunity to meditate on the comparative method. This method was already by the 1890s under attack by anthropologists such as Franz Boas and others who questioned its assumptions. Frazer, however, saw his entire project as dependent on this approach to facts and their meanings. For Frazer there was no anthropology, no writing, no real reasoning outside of the method. In the dramatization of the fate of the comparative method one readily senses Frazer's own anxiety about succession. After the death of his mentor and friend Smith, he saw himself as the sole keeper of the method, and rightfully brooded about its future. Few readers, even educated readers, he claimed, knew its principles, "its bearing on many profound practical problems which are pressing on us for solution now, and which loom still larger in the future" (*The Gorgon's Head*, p. 281). In his discussion, Frazer emphasizes the transformative power of the comparative method. It does not merely batter down institutions of superstition, or cast beams of intellection into the void, but it works upon what we know. Through the comparative method, it is not merely the juxtaposition of similar practices and beliefs that heightens our understanding. The explanation one culture gives of its practice can illumine the practice of another culture; there is no reason to believe that a given culture can adequately explain its own beliefs. The issue at stake for the modern reader is how to evaluate whether the beliefs and practices of any given culture are true and wise.

The comparative method points us to the disrelation between true beliefs and the arguments that defend them. How do we regard the outmoded customs and beliefs of contemporary society? While the comparative method promises to root out the savage origins of polite practices, thereby, we might presume, freeing us from them, it also bequeaths a certain indeterminacy upon custom and belief. As Frazer writes in *The Gorgon's Head,* "the proof that a belief is false or a practice foolish can never be complete or final, because it is always possible to allege that excellent reasons for it may exist which have hitherto eluded the scrutiny of our limited intelligence" (p. 283). To enter the practice of anthropology at the time Frazer did seemed largely a matter of choosing a topic for comparison. Further, the years from 1860 to 1890 comprised the reign of the comparative evolutionists. McLennan, Maine, Tylor, and Smith all used the comparative method to think anew about the oldest of institutions. The explosion of ethnological information made available by missionaries, colonial administrators, and adventurous travelers made comparisons to modern European life inevitable. The topics of anxious introspection entertained by mid- and late Victorians now underwent anthropological analysis. The anthropologists were quite aware of how attention to peoples in faraway places could cast a startling light on matters at home, even matters *in* the home. Through accounts of "savage" cultures as seen through the eyes of European travelers, a portrait of European culture as itself "savage" emerged. Anxieties about marriage rituals, property rights, religious truth, and the conceptualization of the family guided the inquiry into the collective past. Frazer shared the assumption of others of his generation that the peasants of Europe were as primitive as the tribes discovered at the farthermost ends of the Empire.

Historians of anthropological thought locate the origin of the comparative method in the period so crucial to Frazer's education and tastes: the eighteenth century. Though the art of comparing customs and mores of diverse peoples has a long pre-Enlightenment tradition stretching back to Herodotus, the combination of rationalism with the triumphs in such fields as zoology, botany, and anatomy, where the comparative method was used with unqualified success, and the increasing sense of cultural relativism brought about by the steady stream of information about other cultures, resulted in a call for a science of man. The comparative method stood validated by the scientific successes in other fields. Writers such as Montesquieu worked toward fitting the new data about human history into an overarching narrative of development. As we have seen, Frazer's roots in the eighteenth century were deeper than merely his taste for Addison, Gibbon, John Dryden, George Crabbe, and William Cowper. He was in many ways an inheritor of the Scottish Enlightenment, turning to Hume for the epistemology that underlies his world. Therefore it is hardly surprising that the very principles by which his imagination formed a vision of human origins should find precedent in his own cultural origins.

Powerful contributions to the still nascent science of man were made by Scottish writers. Adam Smith, Furguson, and Mackintosh took up the analysis of North American tribes for what light was to be thrown on the current state of European culture. Adam Smith and David Hume brought the comparative method to bear on the writing of what was called "conjectural history." The goal of such a history was to fill the gaps in the universal history of man, that project undertaken in various ways by a number of Enlightenment writers in order to account for the rapidly changing sense of chronology brought about by scientific advancement, and, importantly, by biblical scholarship that was calling into question the authority of the Bible. In the absence of hard facts, conjectural historians attempted to describe how an event might have happened. Their literary contemporaries, the realist novelists, similarly emphasized the high valuation of particulars and a secularized, scientific view of cause and effect in lending an air of authenticity to their narratives.

Archaeology further justified comparative approaches, especially in the nineteenth century. Frazer's research for his translation of Pausanias brought him into direct contact with archaeological excavations. The Pausanias annotations contain a major lesson. The past would eventually be palpably before us for examination. No history could yet contain it, but clearly a style of history writing had to be found that could accommodate current developments, principally, that the story of the ancient past was also the story of the present moment. One way of understanding the crammed foreground of Frazer's tableau is to see in it an attempt to fill the temporal void that the discovery of prehistory opened. Across Europe, archaeological research was lending a new immediacy to the eighteenth-century comparisons of modern Europeans with their "rude" equivalents on other continents. Digs in Denmark, in Ireland, and in Switzerland confirmed that Europeans themselves had once been savage, which in turn lent support to a major supposition of *The Golden Bough*, that savagery still existed in Europe in the form of peasants. The notion, popularized during debates over the issue of slavery that complicated the nineteenth-century inquiry into human origins, that the different races of the world resulted from separate acts of creation by God, thereby justifying racial hierarchies, was brought short by evidence of the European past. Whatever else it was, anthropological research was an act of self-knowing. The civilized could stand face to face with their fore-bears. Savages of the present existed in an almost timeless realm and could unlock the thoughts and beliefs of the savages of the past. The Australian outback, classical Greece, and the Scottish peas-antry were converging. One can easily imagine Frazer reading and collating in his study twelve to eighteen hours per day, believing that the world was doing his research for him and that it was his task merely to present it more memorably than the world itself had time to do.

Comparative linguistics also justified the com-parative method. We have seen in discussing the myth of Balder how the widespread European in-terest in an Aryan past lifted the Norse legends to a place alongside Egyptian, Greek, and Roman mythology. The object of this intense concern was the invention of philologists who in comparing similarities in European languages stipulated a common precursor language and along with the language a race to speak it. This so-called Aryan language (known also as Proto-Indo-European) fired fierce speculation about the vast prehistory of which it, of course, gave no direct evidence. Primordial migrations of the Aryan people from a variety of places were conjured by scholars. There was a serious attempt to derive a racial history from linguistic details. The prominence of Aryan mythology in *The Golden Bough* reflects these ear-lier controversies. Philology suggested that the name "Nemi" derived from a Latin cognate of the German word *Nimidas* for the sacred grove of the tree cults that Tacitus had observed in his remarks on the ancient Teutons, as Robert Fraser has noted. The history of words helped prove Balder and the King of the Wood at Nemi were one. Frazer had begun with languages, and he inherited from nineteenth-century philology an exalted sense of where the study of languages could lead. The research amassed by philologists searching for the homeland of this Aryan race proposed a model for the inquiry into primitive religion. In the quest for an Aryan homeland comparative historians did not confine them-selves to linguistic evidence but included rituals, folklore, anything that might help.

That similar events occurred in different cul-tures for similar reasons was a major assumption of the comparative method. This assumption rested on the doctrine of psychic unity: the belief that human minds everywhere and throughout history worked the same way. Other anthropolo-gists attacked Frazer on this point, arguing that the assumption was no more than that. Why should so much about human life evolve and thought remain the same? Was there, as some ar-gued, a "savage mind" forever closed off to us by evolution? Further, could one really assume that the minds of contemporary primitives were the equivalent of those of their primordial ancestors, when even preliterate societies have a history and have changed over time? The comparative meth-od might have died peacefully in its bed, an out-moded mental habit of our ancestors, had it not achieved a second life in twentieth-century imagi-native writing. The work of Eliot, Pound, and Joyce is inconceivable without it. Frazer lent an authority to the collection and arrangement of details that allow *The Waste Land*, *The Cantos*, and *Finnegans Wake* to speak about the origins and ends of culture. Moreover, interest in cross-cultural writing, in the incorporation of ethno-graphic materials in literary works, and the whole vexed question of the representation of difference suggest that the comparative method is more than just a survival of an archaic mode of representa-tion and make of *The Golden Bough* a crucial work in a tradition that links the eighteenth century with the present.

FRAZER'S METHOD

THE comparative method is not simply an analyti-cal tool with origins deep in the history of human reasoning about origins. It has a rich figural life within the world of Frazer's writing. What seems obvious to the modern reader of Frazer is that in his hands, the comparative method operates as a generative device, a way to breed texts from other texts. Fieldworkers and native informants ap-proach Frazer in his writing cell as do the talking deer that come to Yeats in his vision, saying "we come to bring you images." The obsessive search-ing for similitude among masses of heterogeneous materials has an occult aspect and sets Frazer's writing practice closer to those of his more ex-treme literary contemporaries than his eighteenth-century affectations might lead us to suspect. Frazer possessed, in the words of his biographer, a "mania for facts," and this mania charges his compilations with a psychic need that separates him from his Enlightenment forebears and social science contemporaries. Vast stretches of his prose would fit comfortably in an anthology of expressionist writing in English. Tempered and empowered by the grand if controversial tradition of the comparative method, Frazer nonetheless used it much more freely than did Tylor or Smith, challenging the very integrity of the method. The cascade of facts he presented was phantasmagoric. As James Joyce did in writing *Finnegans Wake,* we dream our way into the primordial past.

Frazer's extravagant deployment of the comparative method undermines its traditional usage, which relies on some preliminary assumption about the nature of the facts to be compared. Thus, for example, one criticism lodged against Frazer was that he leveled the distinction between his sources. The observation of a tourist was set against that of an experienced ethnographer or the account of a native informant. While this makes for poor science, it makes for great reading, since it increases the rhetorical possibilities. The narrator is free to strike different poses toward the facts he passes along. The sheer volume of detail sets the method against the subject it is supposed to illumine, obliterating the larger topic under discussion by the proliferation of examples. Frazer in the throes of comparison keeps the reader in a constant state of astonishment, and he presents us with the figure of an author who sounds like a rationalist skeptic but behaves like a compulsive fabulist, always on the verge of betraying his explicit conviction that religious consciousness is delusion and folly. While Frazer's "literaryness" is most often discussed in terms of his epic invocation and sense of grandeur, his scenic description, his borrowing of motifs and genres from literary sources, even his dithyrambic cadences, these things alone would not propel readers through eleven volumes of antiquated beliefs. The emotional life of Frazer's text resides in Frazer's adaptation of the comparative method. A culture may flicker before the mind's eye and vanish, a place name and an image out of *anima mundi*, in a quick sentence. Or the syntax may complicate itself, and an obscure region of the earth achieve dimension and depth. Or a sudden narrative unfold, holding us paragraph after paragraph, time enough for human figures to emerge, their pathos and folly, their rituals and gods.

The large theme of fecundity is mirrored in the seminal flow of comparisons. The anecdotal narratives that occasionally spring from them take on a significance incommensurate with the practice or belief they illustrate. The momentum affects the quality of the facts. The pace of the comparisons dare not falter lest an incidental illustration of some large theme begin to loom as large as the major deities evoked by *The Golden Bough.* In the cosmogonic ripple of details that carries the reader from volume to volume the comparative method becomes nothing less than the foundation of the world. Like a poet he studied early in his career, Hesiod, Frazer would speak of first things and the law of similitude (that is also a law of simultaneity) binding apparently heterogeneous materials together. But Frazer's irony and caution preserve him from the role of rhapsodist. The pose of the anthropologist was indispensable to his storytelling, as the prose of the storyteller was indispensable to his anthropology.

With the publication of Bronisław Malinowski's *Argonauts of the Western Pacific* (1922), a new model for the writing of anthropology was established. For Malinowski, who likened himself to Joseph Conrad, the authority of the writer resided in his experience with other cultures. The form most suited to such a conviction was the monograph. Malinowski had come to anthropology by reading *The Golden Bough,* and he acknowledged a debt to Frazer, especially in regard to the importance of description in portraying other cultures. With the advent of the fieldwork monograph, anthropological writing became narrower, more precise. Comparisons were between aspects of the single culture under analysis. The anthropologist became an adventurer, staking out an unknown tribe, living with it, participating in its rituals, and reporting one's findings to the world at large. Frazer represented the old era of library theorists, who sifted through the data of others, looking for universal laws. In *Patterns of Culture* (1934), Ruth Benedict epitomized the critique of Frazer's method:

Studies of culture like *The Golden Bough* and the usual comparative ethnological volumes are analytical discussions of traits and ignore all the aspects of cultural integration. Mating or death practices are illustrated by bits of behaviour selected indiscriminately from the most different cultures, and the discussion builds up a kind of mechanical Frankenstein's monster with a right eye from Fiji, a left from Europe, one leg from Tierra del Fuego, and one from Tahiti, and all the fingers and toes from still different regions.

(p. 49)

The monograph invalidated the comparative mode. The primacy of firsthand experience assured that no grand explanation could stand untested by fieldwork. The gain for anthropological writing was a greater accuracy in the information about other peoples and a greater appreciation of how primitive cultures worked. The loss was in the sense of what disparate cultures might have in common.

But as later critics pointed out, the fieldwork monograph is no less a literary composition. It relies on the rhetoric of experience. While appearing to transcribe experience directly in a style that does not call attention to itself, the new model of describing other people and other places reveals itself to be a concatenation of effects aimed at convincing the reader that the anthropologist has really been there. As anyone who has ever attempted a Hemingway pastiche can attest, it requires a great deal of cunning to create the illusion of reportage. Whatever the strategy of a particular piece of ethnographic writing, there is always an implied first-person narrator. The rhetorical power relies on the believability of the witness. One cannot take its claims for describing reality at face value. The need of the anthropologist to convince the reader that he has actually and authoritatively experienced tribal life will lead him to present his material in certain ways. The questions that arise when reading realistic fiction are inevitable: Who's speaking? Is he or she reliable? Who are these native informants? Are they quoted directly? Selectively? Are there aspects of the culture that the narrator's psychological limitations prevent him from describing? By comparison, some critics have argued, Frazer seems curiously authentic. His rhetorical gestures make no attempt to disguise themselves as naturalistic detail. His scrupulous footnoting allows the reader to check out the material for himself. Moreover, the masses of quotation that flood his pages have an effect much prized by critics anxious about the preservation of cultural differences within a written text. Frazer's writing can be seen as polyvocal, allowing for the possibility of points of view other than that of the author. At times one seems to be inside not a realistic account but an epistolary novel. We begin to check the footnotes to see whom we are hearing, to wonder what our commentator's life is like there in the outback or in Africa. (As Clifford Geertz observed: "What does an ethnologist do?—He writes.") And Frazer makes no attempt to conceal his presence in the inquiry, or its artfulness. His admission of shaping his material is made in plain view. The reader stands alerted if not warned, and thus can find in Frazer a rehearsal of the dilemma of anthropology's relation to writing.

According to Marc Manganaro, Frazer capitalized on the growing division between fieldworker and theorist in the late nineteenth and early twentieth centuries. By creating different "rhetorical identities," Frazer energized his massive work, freeing himself from a too rigidly defined authorial role. There were three James Frazers: the fact collector, the theorist, and the artist. The author defined himself differently at different times throughout his work, and in doing so he emphasized certain aspects of his writing. Here the reader who has only the 1922 abridged edition of *The Golden Bough* at hand is at a disadvantage, since many of Frazer's most intriguing descriptions of his intent are found in the prefaces to the individual volumes of the third edition. These three Frazers are hidden within the grain of the work and are called forth by different anxieties. The much noted humility that attends many of Frazer's statements, his willingness to change his mind, his concessions that future research may invalidate his conjectures, the gentlemanly deference shown to critics—this gracious pose allows him to define himself differently when needed, deflecting criticism. As a fact collector, the author banks his future on the usefulness of the facts he has assembled. (This aspect of Frazer too is less obvious without some familiarity either with the multivolumed *Golden Bough* or the other works, since the cascade of erudition thins to a stream under the pressure to cut down the amount of print.) After all, anthropology is in its earliest stages and must attend to the collection of data before savagery becomes extinct. A mere archivist of the archaic, Frazer can strike a tentative relation with his pet theories, claiming that his ideas may well be overthrown in time. What is important is the facts, upon which later generations will base their generalizations.

But Frazer held to his theories. His facts, after all, are evidence of his obsessive concern with the origin and meaning of Christianity. Despite his own suggestion about the provisionality of his findings, he continually asserted the role of theorist, particularly in regard to his sources. Enlightening in this regard is his relation to Baldwin

Spencer, the man whose account of totem feasts in Australia transformed *The Golden Bough*. In their correspondence, Frazer praised the directness of Spencer's prose. Spencer understood that the heart of anthropology is the presentation of facts. While works like his own, Frazer wrote, will be eclipsed by "better inductions based on fuller knowledge, books like yours, containing records of observation, will never be superseded." While Frazer was complimentary, he had a great deal at stake in maintaining a separation between the fieldworker and the theorist. As anthropology changed, the fieldworker had the authority to draw conclusions from his research. Soon only the writer in Spencer's position could theorize. Frazer crossed from one role to another. He preserved the facts that others gathered but, as Manganaro observed, his role as theorist permitted him to assign meaning to data. He readily overrode the conjectures of the witness with the truth as revealed by the comparative method. Frazer drew dramatic force from the rift between experience and meaning affecting both science and literature. Moreover, he maintained the rift, since it permitted a range of responses to any particular detail or account. His irony, pathos, and wit, directed as they were on epochal events, presumed a certain theorizing, since without a judgment on the meaning and worth of what passes, the inflections and comments that lead us through the material would be impossible. The last "rhetorical identity" survived not within anthropology, but within literary culture. As if cognizant of his ambivalent relationship to the discipline of anthropology, especially as it repudiated the beliefs that for him made art, science, and writing a single all-consuming activity, Frazer described himself as an artist within his work, thereby shifting the criteria by which he asked future readers to judge him.

CONCLUSION

JAMES Frazer helped define the literary climate of the first half of the twentieth century. His impact on writers such as Yeats, Eliot, Joyce, Pound, William Faulkner, D. H. Lawrence, Joseph Conrad, John M. Synge, Wyndham Lewis, and David Jones has been well documented, and if one considers those writers and artists touched less di-rectly by Frazerian themes, the calculation of his influence would be impossible. Frazer did not establish his preoccupations as the terms by which his culture took stock of itself simply through his own persistence. Many other forces were at work. One need only to consider, for example, the deep fascination with primitive art and its influence on modern painting, or the need of emerging national cultures to show examples of indigenous folk traditions, or the many other nineteenth-century investigations of syncretism and ritual forms to suggest that Frazer articulated larger trends in Western thought and writing. Given the complications of anthropology itself in the age of exploitation and empire, Frazer's work is implicated in political and cultural dilemmas that focus on the question of representation. The literate European bourgeois is clearly viewed as the evolutionary vanguard. But primitive beliefs are everywhere, a clear and present danger.

In 1931, in the middle of a banquet lecture, Frazer was struck blind. For several years afterward, assisted by secretaries, he continued to do research and publish, slowly weakening until dictating further works was beyond him. There are two versions of his final days. Both describe the same scene, but with a significant difference. In one version Frazer sat, blind, failing, and helpless but apparently enjoying his one pastime, hearing his own works read aloud by a paid secretary. In the other version he had requested to hear accounts of recent findings from fieldworkers around the world, but the secretary had been instructed by his wife not to read him anything except his own work, since the professional news tended to excite him, while his own words kept him calm. Frazer died on 7 May 1941 at his home in Cambridge.

SELECTED BIBLIOGRAPHY

I. BIBLIOGRAPHIES. Theodore Besterman, *A Bibliography of Sir James George Frazer* (London, 1934); Robert Ackerman, "Appendix I; Additions to Besterman's Bibliography," in *J. G. Frazer: His Life and Work* (Cambridge, Eng., and New York, 1987).

II. SELECTED WORKS. *Totemism* (Edinburgh, 1887); *The Golden Bough: A Study in Comparative Religion* (London and New York, 1890); *Pausanias, and Other Greek Sketches* (London and New York, 1900); *The Golden Bough: A Study in Magic and Religion*, 2d ed., rev. and enl. (London and New York, 1900); *Lectures on the Early History of the Kingship* (London and New York, 1905); *Adonis, Attis, Osiris: Studies in the History of Oriental Religion* (London and New York, 1906); *Adonis, Attis, Osiris,* 2d ed., rev. and enl. (London, 1907); *Psyche's Task: A Discourse Concerning the Influence of Superstitions on the Growth of Institutions* (London, 1909).

Totemism and Exogamy: A Treatise on Certain Early Forms of Superstition and Society (London, 1910); *The Magic Art and the Evolution of Kings* (London, 1911); *Taboo and the Perils of the Soul* (London, 1911); *The Dying God* (London, 1911); *Spirits of the Corn and of the Wild* (London, 1912); *The Belief in Immortality and the Worship of the Dead,* vol. 1 (London, 1913); *The Scapegoat* (London, 1913); *Psyche's Task,* 2d ed., rev. and enl., including "The Scope of Social Anthropology" (London, 1913); *Balder the Beautiful: The Fire-Festivals of Europe and the Doctrine of the External Soul* (London, 1913); *Adonis, Attis, Osiris,* 3d ed., rev. and enl., 2 vols. (London, 1914); *The Golden Bough,* 3d ed., rev. and enl., 12 vols. (London and New York, 1915); *Studies in Greek Scenery, Legend, and History* (London, 1917); *Folk Lore in the Old Testament: Studies in Comparative Religion, Legend, and Law* (London, 1918).

Sir Roger de Coverley and Other Literary Pieces (London, 1920); *The Magical Origin of Kings* (London, 1920); *The Belief in Immortality and the Worship of the Dead,* vol. 2 (London, 1922); *The Golden Bough: A Study in Magic and Religion,* abridged ed. (London, 1922); *Folk-Lore in the Old Testament,* abridged ed. (London, 1923); *The Belief in Immortality and the Worship of the Dead,* vol. 3 (London, 1924); *The Worship of Nature,* vol. 1 (London and New York, 1926); *The Gorgon's Head and Other Literary Pieces* (London, 1927); *Man, God, and Immortality: Thoughts on Human Progress* (London, 1927); *The Devil's Advocate: A Plea for Superstition* (London, 1927).

Myths of the Origin of Fire (London, 1930); *The Growth of Plato's Ideal Theory* (London, 1930); *Garnered Sheaves: Essays, Addresses, and Reviews* (London, 1931); *Condorcet on the Progress of the Human Mind* (Oxford, Eng., 1933); *The Fear of the Dead in Primitive Religion,* vol. 1 (London, 1933); *The Fear of the Dead in Primitive Religion,* vol. 2 (London, 1934); *Creation and Evolution in Primitive Cosmogonies, and Other Pieces* (London, 1935); *The Fear of the Dead in Primitive Religion,* vol. 3 (London, 1936); *Aftermath: A Supplement to* The Golden Bough (London and New York, 1936); *Totemica: A Supplement to* Totemism and Exogamy (London, 1937); *Anthologia Anthropologica,* vol. 1: *The Native Races of Africa and Madagascar* (London, 1938); *Anthologia Anthropologica,* vol. 2: *The Native Races of Australasia* (London, 1939); *Anthologia Anthropologica,* vol. 3: *The Native Races of Asia and Europe* (London, 1939); *Anthologia Anthropologica,* vol. 4: *The Native Races of America* (London, 1939), all edited by R. A. Downie.

III. SELECTED ARTICLES. "The Primitive Ghost and His Relations," in *Contemporary Review* (July 1885); "On Certain Burial Customs as Illustrative of the Primitive Theory of the Soul," in *Journal of the Anthropological Institute* (August 1885); "Penates," "Pericles," "Praeneste," "Praetor," "Priapus," "Proserpine," "Province," "Saturn," "Tabou," "Thesmophoria," and "Totemism," in *Encyclopaedia Britannica,* 9th ed. (Edinburgh, 1885–1888); "Witchcraft in Skye," in *Folk-Lore Journal* (September 1886); "The Legend of Narcissus," in *Journal of the Anthropological Institute* (February 1887); "Notes on Harvest Customs," in *Folk-Lore Journal* (March 1889); "A South African Red Riding-Hood," in *Folk-Lore Journal* (June 1889).

"Some Popular Superstitions of the Ancients," in *Folk-Lore* (June 1890); "Easter in Greece," in *Folk-Lore* (June 1890); "Highland Superstitions in Inverness-shire," in *Folk-Lore* (June 1890); "The Youth of Achilles," in *Classical Review* (July 1893); "William Robertson Smith," in *Fortnightly Review* (July 1894); "The Origin of Totemism," in *Fortnightly Review* (April–May 1899); "Observations on Central Australian Totemism," in *Journal of the Anthropological Institute* (1899).

"A Suggestion as to the Origin of Gender in Language," in *Fortnightly Review* (January 1900); "Men's Language and Women's Language," in *Man* (October 1901); "Purim," in *Encyclopaedia Biblica* (April 1902); "Artemis and Hippolytus," in *Fortnightly Review* (December 1904); "The Beginnings of Religion and Totemism Among the Australian Aborigines," in *Fortnightly Review* (July and September 1905); "The Origin of Circumcision," in *Independent Review* (November 1905); "Attis and Christ," in *Athenaeum* (4 January 1908); "Beliefs and Customs of the Australian Aborigines," in *Folk-Lore* (September 1909).

"Ritual Murder," in *The Times* (11 November 1913); "Ancient Stories of a Great Flood," in *Journal of the Royal Anthropological Institute* (1916); "Women Fertilized by Stones," in *Folk-Lore* (September 1918).

"The Mackie Ethnological Expedition to Central Africa," in *Man* (February, June, and December 1920); "The Scope and Method of Mental Anthropology," in *Science Progress* (April 1922); "The Mackie Expedition to Central Africa," in *The Times Literary Supplement* (24 May 1923); "Primitive Mentality," in *The Times Literary Supplement* (13 September 1923); "A Year Among the Maoris," in *The Times Literary Supplement* (8 January 1925); "Pygmies and Bushmen," in *The Times Literary Supplement* (15 January 1925); "Vanishing Tribes of Kenya," in *The Times Literary Supplement* (23 April 1925); "Old Faith and New Thought," in *The Times* (4 August 1926).

"Baldwin Spencer as Anthropologist," in *Spencer's Last Journey* (May 1931); "Gibbon at Lausanne," in *Mélanges Glotz* (1932); "Canon John Roscoe," in *Nature* (17 December 1932)

IV. EDITIONS AND TRANSLATIONS. *Passages of the Bible Chosen for Their Literary Beauty and Interest* (London,

1895; 2d ed. London, 1909); *Pausanias' Description of Greece* (London and New York, 1898); *Letters of William Cowper* (London, 1912); *Essays of Joseph Addison* (London, 1915); *Appollodorus: The Library*, 2 vols. (London and New York, 1921); *Ovid's Fasti* (London and New York, 1931).

V. BIOGRAPHICAL AND CRITICAL STUDIES. Bronisław Malinowski, "Sir James George Frazer: A Biographical Appreciation," in *A Scientific Theory of Culture, and Other Essays* (Chapel Hill, N.C., 1944); Stanley E. Hyman, *The Tangled Bank: Darwin, Marx, Frazer, and Freud as Imaginative Writers* (New York, 1962); R. Angus Downie, *Frazer and The Golden Bough* (London, 1970); J. B. Vickery, *The Literary Impact of The Golden Bough* (Princeton, N.J., 1973); Ludwig Wittgenstein, *Remarks on Frazer's Golden Bough*, trans. by A. C. Miles (Atlantic Highlands, N.J., 1979); Robert Ackerman, *J. G. Frazer: His Life and Work* (Cambridge, Eng., and New York, 1987); Robert Fraser, *The Making of The Golden Bough: The Origins and Growth of an Argument* (New York, 1990); Robert Fraser, ed., *Sir James Frazer and the Literary Imagination* (London, 1990); Marc Manganaro, *Myth, Rhetoric, and the Voice of Authority: A Critique of Frazer, Eliot, Frye, and Campbell* (New Haven, Conn., and London, 1992).

CHRISTOPHER FRY

(1907–   )

Glenn Loney

BY HIS OWN ADMISSION, Christopher Fry required a great deal of encouragement in finding and sustaining his creative voice. Almost all of the plays he wrote during his long career were commissioned, including his first published work, *The Boy with a Cart: Cuthman, Saint of Sussex* (1939). Had it not been for the strong belief some of Fry's literary and theatrical friends—including George Bernard Shaw and T. S. Eliot—had in his talents, Fry might never have gained the confidence to realize his potential as playwright.

A great part of Fry's frustration—the writer's block he experienced early on and at various stages in his career—was caused by his despair of finding, as one of the characters in his plays says, "words with the beat of the human pulse . . . the indwelling music that created us" (*One Thing More; or, Caedmon Construed*, p. 22). Fry has cited Teilhard de Chardin's concept of "the universe deposited in us" as the thing for which he wanted to find a language. This concept can be understood as the manifestation of the transcendent in human life and action. To convey it, Fry used the language of poetry. He wrote plays in verse because, as he explains in *Looking for a Language* (1992), poetry relays the concentricity of life, "a belief that all things express the same identity, one single creation, and are all contained in one discipline of revelation" (p. 16). Indeed, Fry saw language as a kind of music, heightening and enriching perceptions, intuitions, and emotions. Some of his plays, including the late comedy *A Yard of Sun*, seem conceived in terms of arias, duets, trios, and even choruses. This is not surprising, given Fry's musical ability; he is also a lyricist and composer.

Fry's dramas deal with philosophical issues, centering on the manifold paradoxes of life and death. Even those of his plays with overt religious themes contain layers of ambivalence, leading one critic to label Fry a "Christian agnostic." His comedies have been called dark comedies, what the critic Suzanne Langer has described as "averted tragedy."

Fry achieved widespread critical and popular attention as a dramatist after World War II, on both sides of the Atlantic. He appeared on the cover of *Time* magazine in 1950 and had four plays on view in New York in 1954. One of his chief artistic virtues in the eyes of his admirers was that he was writing in verse—that he, along with T. S. Eliot and others, was going to help restore poetry to the theater. He was also hailed as a new and vital force in religious drama. But Fry's star was on the descent almost as soon as it had risen, with the appearance in the mid-1950s of plays of gritty realism, a shocking contrast to conventional West End theater and especially to the comedies of Fry, with their heightened poetic language and mordant undertones. The antihero of John Osborne's play *Look Back in Anger* (1956) became the embodiment of the "angry young men" portrayed by the so-called kitchen-sink school of playwriting. The naturalistic plays of Osborne, Arnold Wesker, and Bernard Kops, themselves described as angry young men, achieved almost equal critical and commercial success on Broadway as in the West End. Clearly, this was not the time nor the place for the comedies of Christopher Fry.

At the close of the twentieth century, the viability of Fry's major plays in the commercial English-language theater was in doubt, not because of any inherent faults of theme, structure, character, or language, but rather because the economics of production discouraged dramas with large casts and impressive settings; intellectually engaged audiences had virtually vanished from Broadway theaters, if not yet from the West End, and the ravages of a steady diet of rapidly changing, colorful images on television had undermined most audiences' attention spans, eroding their capacity—or willingness—to grapple with the language and dilemmas of the dramatic stage. Fry's plays continued to be popular with professional regional theaters and college and amateur groups in performance, and they are still widely read and studied, for they are far more than merely interesting examples of a brief flowering of "poetic drama" after World War II.

It has been Fry's attempt throughout his career to reveal the complexities and ambiguities of character and human motivation, to convey the experience of the transcendent in ordinary life, and to find a redemptive, revelatory language sufficient to that attempt. He did not delude himself that he was providing answers to life's mysteries: in fact, he often criticized aspects of his plays that he thought fell short of his vision, and not infrequently revised works based on audience and critical response. But Fry did, ultimately, find the courage to present the mysteries, to give voice, at times brilliantly, to his own indwelling music.

LIFE

FRY was smitten by the magic of the theater from a young age. He traces the moment to a production of *Peter Pan* he saw when he was six years old, followed by the gift of a toy theater equipped with sets and characters from the James Barrie fantasy. The critic Emil Roy has singled out three major formative influences on Fry the playwright: a religious family, a good education in literature and the arts, and a love of nature. These are certainly echoed in Fry's works, if in transmuted forms.

Well before Fry was born, on 18 December 1907, in Bristol, England, his aunt Ada had kept a diary crammed with painfully honest—from her point of view, at least—comments on her life and that of her family. This diary proved a valuable resource for Fry when he set about uncovering the past on both sides of his family. The title of the book that resulted, *Can You Find Me: A Family History* (1978), was taken from a note his aunt had jotted on a postcard to Fry's mother, Emma Marguerite Hammond, showing Ada in the midst of sheepshearing. She used no question mark, nor does Fry, but it is suggestive that he considers himself present in the struggles and dreams, the passions and imperfections of his forebears and immediate relatives, some of whom were clearly of an artistic

bent. Much of the book is devoted to the people and events of a time before he was born, exploring the legacy of the Harris and Fry (his mother's side) family heritages. This is obviously a quest Fry had to complete, and it is dedicated to his elder brother, Charles Leslie Harris. Fry changed his surname from Harris to Fry by deed-poll at age eighteen. He has jested that he did it for the "euphony" of the name, but he was also much closer to his mother's side of the family, who encouraged him and whose Quaker beliefs he admired. Fry may well have written this book to dispel a sense of incompleteness in himself and to exorcise the ghosts of a somewhat deprived childhood.

For those interested in Fry's work, *Can You Find Me* is a revelatory text, more in what it hints at than in what it clearly states. But even if it did not concern Fry's early influences, it would still be of interest as a chronicle of English life in the late nineteenth and early twentieth centuries. A depressed British economy led Fry's young father and mother to Australia to seek their fortunes, as other adventurous family members had left England for Canada and New Zealand. Quite simply, there was little opportunity in Britain in those times.

The Harrises came back, defeated, to England after nineteen months in the antipodes. Charles and Christopher were born after their return. Fry's father, Charles John Harris, an architect and contractor with a dearth of commissions, became an activist lay preacher, involving himself in Christian work among the poor. Long hours and excessive drinking led to his death in 1911. Fry tried to "fix" the shadowy memory of his father in his mind; in *Can You Find Me*, he records an apparition he experienced after his father's death:

I woke to the feeling of an approach, of the darkness bringing something to me. I think the door was shut, and yet the place where the door was seemed very deep, like a tunnel, and it was bringing something to me with a kind of taut deliberation or slow emphasis. Then I saw my father standing beside the bed, faintly lit by the tiny paraffin lamp or night-light. I called out to my mother 'Daddy's here, daddy's here,' but my mother, barely awake, simply murmured to me to go back to sleep. . . . she wouldn't wake up properly and then the image was gone.

(p. 211)

Survival was difficult, even with financial assistance from her family, but Fry's mother was determined to maintain some standard of gentility. She and her sister Ada, the diarist, pooled their resources and moved to Bedford in 1913. Fry was enrolled in an advanced kindergarten attached to the Froebel Training College in Bedford. Called a "budding composer" at age two-and-a-half, Fry composed a "Pharaoh's March" on the piano. He also showed talent for drawing.

His imagination was extremely active. As a boy, Fry had the curious sensation that he had been born in India; he was convinced he could remember the buildings there. He also thought he had seen an elf, but such fantasies were soon discouraged. In 1914 he began to have strange sensations, as he described in *Can You Find Me:* "Suddenly I felt removed, as though I were only fractionally part of what was going on, or rather as though I were in the future looking far back to the present, a feeling I later got used to as nothing extraordinary, a physical quirk." At night, things got worse: "Space, time, sound, and bodily movement would all change their natures together." Fry remembered calling out for someone to talk to, to escape this "overcharged world" (pp. 235–236).

During World War I, Fry became increasingly aware of the horror of military conflict by the number of funeral processions that passed their tiny flat on the way to the nearby cemetery. Years later, the solemn beat of the funeral march would still recall this. To supplement their income, Fry's mother took in boarders; some of these were soldiers who later came back in coffins from the front in France. The Frys lived through zeppelin attacks and news of the German onslaught at Verdun, as well as shocking reports of the Easter Uprising in Dublin in 1916.

Though he did not excel in his studies, Fry was awakening to the possibilities of language: "I remember the morning when Miss Spence opened my ears to the life of words. . . . She gave each word so exactly its proper weight and meaning, yet so lightly, I felt I could hold the words like coloured stones in my hand." It would be years before Fry discovered his true talent for arranging the "stones" to give them meaning, but, as he noted, "such small things open windows in the mind" (p. 244).

Fry was given a walk-on part in a school pageant about the Burghers of Calais, and even wrote a play for the class, which he forgot about until a teacher reminded him of it much later in life. "Memory is a great eccentric, hoarding ran-

dom moments, trivial anxieties" (p. 245), he wrote in his family history. He was given private elocution lessons and got a press notice for dancing the hornpipe. An amateur performance by Fry and other neighborhood children raised six shillings for Dr. Barnardo's Homes, a charity for destitute children for which Fry would later work.

In 1916 he began writing verse. Longfellow's "Song of Hiawatha" and Tennyson's "Ode on the Death of the Duke of Wellington" opened his eyes and ears to the possibilities of poetry. Fry was fond of certain religious chants and musical settings, the Te Deum and the Nunc Dimittis among them. Although Fry was exposed to traditional religious services and pieties—no gossip or profanities were tolerated at home—his ideas about God were poetic rather than dogmatic: "I thought of Him in terms of space and light," he wrote in *Can You Find Me*, "and in certain sounds and words. I remember staring hypnotized at a frosty sky, vexing my mind with the thought of infinity; it seemed that where my imagination failed God began" (p. 255).

In 1918, as the war was coming to an end, he entered the respected Bedford Modern School as a "day boy." In the early 1920s, Fry began to experiment with drama, writing *Youth and the Peregrines.* Like Fry's uncles and his father, he began to long for an escape, to dream of getting away from home and Bedford, which he thought of only as the city of the Protestant moralist/fabulist John Bunyan, author of *The Pilgrim's Progress.* But he had persistent nightmares about escape. In 1923 he even wrote an Armageddon play, in which people fled the destruction of the metropolis to an island.

In *Can You Find Me*, Fry describes a defining moment of his boyhood:

The sun was setting. It glared through the chinks in lilac and hot-ember cloud, sent shafts of pure light in a fan shape above them, and catching a wisp of detached vapour turned it into gold so intense it could have contracted into a star. It was as though the doomed city had exploded into glory instead of horror. But because the glory was inexpressible and impossible to contain I felt stabs of almost physical pain in my chest and behind my eyes, a feeling of total inadequacy to deal with what I saw.

The experience left him with "a sense of cowardice," as though he had "sinned against the light," in trying to avoid discomfort. "I knew, or grew to know, a lack in myself, of confidence or determination, which made me turn aside from anything that threatened to demand a struggle, a too willing surrender to any feeling of insufficiency" (pp. 263–264).

Unable to attend university for want of funds, in 1926 Fry began teaching at the Froebel Kindergarten. He left that post in 1927 to work as an actor and assistant in a small company at the Citizen House Theatre in Bath. In 1928 he took a job at the Hazelwood Preparatory School in Limpsfield, Surrey, where he taught English, among other subjects. In 1929 he resumed his long and underpaid apprenticeship in the theater. In 1930 he provided the libretto for "Psalm in C," with score by Michael Tippett, who became one of Britain's most honored composers. But this was a time of great frustration and disappointment: Fry wanted to write but seemed unable to find his voice. In 1932 he spent the summer with the writer Robert Gittings. Almost twenty years later, in 1951, he dedicated his play *A Sleep of Prisoners* to Gittings. In a letter to Gittings that precedes the play, he gratefully recalled: "It is nineteen years this summer since you persuaded me to take a holiday from my full-time failure to make a living. . . . I had written almost nothing for five or six years, and I was to write almost nothing again for five years following." Gittings' constant encouragement and a sunny rectory as a study "increased in me the hope that one day the words would come. It was all very well that I should look obstinately forward to plays which I showed no sign of writing." For ten years, Fry remembered, Gittings had "loyally thought of me as a writer when clearly I wasn't." From 1932 to 1935 he was founding director of the semiprofessional Tunbridge Wells Repertory Players. He revised his school play *Youth and the Peregrines* as a curtain-raiser for the English premiere, in 1934, of George Bernard Shaw's *Village Wooing*, which Shaw had made available to the struggling troupe. In 1935 he received his first important commission: to write a fund-raising drama for Dr. Barnardo's Homes. Called *Open Door*, this toured England for two years. With Monte Crick and F. Eyton, Fry wrote songs for an André Charlot revue, *She Shall Have Music*, which ran at the Saville Theatre in the West End in 1935.

In 1936, Fry married Phyllis Hart, a British-born journalist who had earned her university degree in Canada. The two barely got by financially, subsisting for the most part on Hart's salary. Fry's first verse drama, *Siege*, remained unproduced and unpublished, but a modest breakthrough came in 1938 with the commission to write a play for the anniversary of a village church in Coleman's Hatch, Sussex. *The Boy with a Cart* was produced in the Sussex churchyard but much later mounted in London with the young Richard Burton as Cuthman, Saint of Sussex. Despite the humble circumstances of the initial production, it attracted some important spectators. There had long been a lively interest in religious drama in England, as well as in verse drama. The bishop of Chichester became a champion, and Fry was introduced to the Religious Drama Society, whose members were seeking exactly this kind of play. The stage director E. Martin Browne, who had helped T. S. Eliot bring his verse dramas to life, admired this simple but affecting play and encouraged Fry to build on the achievement. And, as Fry has gratefully recalled, Eliot himself was strong in urging him to forge ahead, even when Fry was full of doubts that the words would come.

Fry's collaboration with the composer Michael Tippett resumed with *Robert of Sicily: Opera for Children* (1938). In 1939 he wrote *Seven at a Stroke*, a play for children, and *Thursday's Child: A Pageant*, with music by Martin Shaw. This last was staged in London at the Albert Hall, with Queen Mary in attendance. Also in 1939 Fry received a commission from E. Martin Browne to write a play in celebration of the history of Tewkesbury Abbey for the Tewkesbury Festival. This commission resulted in *The Tower*.

Fry seemed, in 1939, on the verge of a creative breakthrough at last. As he wrote of one of his characters, the ex-fascist Luigi in *A Yard of Sun*, he was ready to "lurch" into success. He was appointed director of the prestigious Oxford Playhouse, but, with the outbreak of war in Europe, he was drafted in 1940. As a conscientious objector, he served for four years in a noncombatant role, clearing away bomb damage in Liverpool, among other grueling duties. Taken ill, he was sent to a military hospital in 1944. Upon his discharge from the army, he returned to the Oxford Playhouse.

Fry achieved sudden and wide recognition for his brief comedy of life against death, *A Phoenix Too Frequent*, in 1946. This was commissioned by E. Martin Browne for the intimate Mercury Theatre in London. Shown there in May, it was revived in November at the Arts Theatre, where Fry was director and resident playwright. The charm of the story and Fry's sparkling poetic dialogue, rich in imagery, made this play a great success with a wide range of audiences, and it remains one of Fry's most popular comedies.

In 1948, *The Firstborn* premiered at the new Edinburgh Festival. Fry had put aside this play, a drama of the epic clash between Moses and Pharaoh, to write *The Tower,* and did not complete it until 1945, as World War II was coming to a close. *Thor, with Angels,* commissioned for the Canterbury Festival, and *The Lady's Not for Burning,* shown initially at the Arts Theatre, were also produced in 1948. The latter play proved both a critical and popular success on both sides of the Atlantic. It was rapidly revived in the West End (1949), this time featuring Sir John Gielgud and Pamela Brown. It won the Shaw Prize in Britain and, in 1951, the New York Drama Critics' Circle Best Play Award, an honor also accorded Fry for *Venus Observed* and *Tiger at the Gates,* his translation from the French of a play by Jean Giraudoux. After years of poverty and obscurity, Fry was suddenly being praised for his dramatic and poetic gifts, financially rewarded, sought out for opinions and insights, and generally lionized.

Sir Laurence Olivier gave Fry his next commission, a verse comedy to launch Olivier's debut as actor-manager of the St. James's Theatre in the West End. The result, in 1950, was *Venus Observed,* which proved a triumph on Broadway with Rex Harrison in the leading role. Fry also adapted and translated Jean Anouilh's *L'Invitation au château* as *Ring Round the Moon.* Not only did he skillfully suggest the Gallic flavor of the original, but he was able to infuse the play with an aptly English wit as well. Produced by Peter Brook, *Ring Round the Moon* was highly praised at the time and has remained a favorite for stock and amateur productions. Also in 1950, *The Boy with a Cart* was given its first professional production, at the Lyric Theatre, in Hammersmith.

The following year, Brook invited Fry to provide music for his Stratford-upon-Avon production of Shakespeare's *A Winter's Tale.* Fry had also been commissioned to create a play for the 1951 Festival of Britain, to mark the nation's recovery from the devastations of World War II. *A Sleep of Prisoners,* designed to be performed in churches, was shown in London and on tour. Another festival year came in 1953 as the young queen, Elizabeth II, was crowned in Westminster Abbey. Fry

wrote the commentary for the official coronation film, *A Queen Is Crowned.* Fry and Denis Cannan collaborated on the screenplay for the film of John Gay's *The Beggar's Opera,* directed by Peter Brook and starring Olivier as Macheath.

For the actress Edith Evans, Fry wrote *The Dark Is Light Enough,* produced in London in 1954 and later seen on Broadway with Katharine Cornell in the leading role. The next year was devoted to translations from French originals, on which Fry left his distinctive stamp. Jean Anouilh's *L'Alouette* was produced as *The Lark;* Jean Giraudoux's *La Guerre de Troie n'aura pas lieu* was transformed into *Tiger at the Gates.* It was 1958 before Fry offered a new work, and this time it was again an adaptation-translation, Giraudoux's *Pour Lucrèce,* anglicized as *Duel of Angels.* Fry also provided the libretto for a Michael Tippett cantata, *Crown of the Year,* and wrote the screenplay for *Ben Hur,* which took Fry to Italy and introduced him to Siena and its colorful horse race, the Palio. Fry's sole history play, *Curtmantle,* premiered in Dutch at the city-theater in Tilburg, Holland, in 1961. A year later, it was staged in English in Edinburgh and in the West End.

It would be almost a decade before Fry offered another original play, *A Yard of Sun.* But he kept busy in theater and films: his translation of Giraudoux's *Judith* premiered in the West End in 1962, and he wrote the screenplay for *Barabbas* the same year. In 1964 he translated Colette's *The Boy and the Magic,* followed, in 1965, by a children's book, *The Boat That Mooed.* Fry himself has laughed at the suggestion that he might have been overreaching, in 1966, when he cowrote *The Bible,* the screenplay for a Dino di Laurentis film. Actually, the adapters had more than enough material in Genesis alone; the script is subtitled *In the Beginning.*

In 1968, Fry adapted Anne Brontë's *The Tenant of Wildfell Hall* for BBC-TV. By 1973 this had matured into a four-part TV series, *The Brontës of Haworth,* which was also published in two volumes in 1975. Other BBC scripts include *The Best of Enemies* (1976), *Sister Dora* (1977), and *Star over Bethlehem* (1981).

A Yard of Sun and his translation of Ibsen's *Peer Gynt* both had premieres in 1970. The latter was commissioned for the Chichester Festival, which followed this with a request for a translation of Edmond Rostand's *Cyrano de Bergerac* in 1975. As Fry approached the venerable age of eighty, he was asked by Chelmsford Cathedral and the BBC to create a new drama. In *One Thing More; or, Caedmon Construed*, he returned, in a sense, to the world of Cuthbert—to religious drama—with an episodic tale of God's grace to a simple, suffering man, a man with a song inside him but without the means to give it voice. As Fry told Naim Attallah: "In a curious way I was always aware that the plays were there, just waiting for me to catch up with them, to get to the point at which in fact I would write. That seemed like an imperative, but what it is I cannot say." In his own career, Christopher Fry may have considered himself a modern Caedmon.

RELIGIOUS DRAMAS

ALL of Fry's religious dramas were commissioned for religious festivals. They were intended to be performed—initially at least—in or around ecclesiastical structures, the action of the plays seemingly emanating from a rural English parish church, the austere majesty of Chichester or Canterbury Cathedral, or the ruined Gothic arches of the Abbey of Whitby, where Caedmon found his voice and finally sang his song. True, producing the plays in a church or gothicized stage environment certainly helps in creating atmosphere and establishing tone, but such settings are not required for production of the plays. In fact, the dramas can be very effective staged in a bare classroom or lecture hall. The simplicity of the setting works well with the structure of the plays themselves—with the exception of *The Firstborn*, which is divided into three acts, these are all seamless dramas, building by increments to their respective climaxes.

It is surprising that, in the eagerness of critics to detect influences on Fry of earlier eras or authors, none seems to have gone farther back than the Elizabethans, notably Shakespeare and Marlowe. But two of Fry's plays, *The Boy with a Cart* and *One Thing More*, obviously take as their model the medieval English mystery, miracle, and morality plays. These dramas dealt with biblical events, the lives of the saints, or moral issues and tended to be episodic; they often used narrative passages to bridge between specific short scenes, employing either a single speaker or a choral group; they included music and song to engage the audience and for emphasis; and they were rich in natural imagery. The plays were written mostly by anonymous clerical authors, and the diction was cast in heavy iambic syllables, with recurring rhymes, often couplets. Lines with a strong, regular rhythm and obvious, amusing end rhymes served the authors' purpose of inculcating moral precepts and clerical dogmas into a largely unschooled audience. A notable feature of the medieval English drama is its delight in alliteration. This special verbal skill is much in evidence in *The Boy with a Cart*.

In 1938 Fry was commissioned to write a play for the anniversary of a village church in Coleman's Hatch, Sussex. Fry constructed his drama from the story of a local saint, Cuthman, who founded a small church in Sussex. Cuthman is a simple Cornish shepherd boy, naive and untutored but clever, confident, and resourceful; he has reason to believe that God is watching over him—he describes his world as infused with the power of God, manifested in small but significant (even miraculous) ways. At the opening of the play, Cuthman is informed that his father has died; his mother and he are left destitute. Cuthman builds a cart, an inexplicable action to the chorus of villagers and neighbors who comment on events throughout the play; but Cuthman is responding to a higher power. He believes that the cart will enable him and his mother to "find our way in the world" (p. 13), that the hand of God is guiding them.

Cuthman sets off on his journey of faith, pulling his mother in the cart, which is attached to a rope around his shoulders. The trip yields evidence that Cuthman is indeed being watched over, and the mother and son come providentially to their destination, the town of Steyning, where Cuthman receives his vocation: he is to build a church. The church construction is obstructed by several members of the village who are promptly—and divinely—dispensed with, and Cuthman succeeds in his task, assisted at the end by Christ the carpenter. It is Cuthman's faith that blesses him, the intuition that it is not for men to understand God's ways but to joyfully submit to them. In this way, meaning can be found in life; as the chorus says at the end of *The Boy with a Cart*, "Between / Our birth and death we may touch understanding / As a moth brushes a window with its wing" (p. 40).

If Cuthman is the alpha in Fry's major works, then Caedmon may well prove to be the omega. Although *One Thing More; or, Caedmon Construed* appeared virtually in Fry's eightieth year, in 1986, it is closer to *The Boy with a Cart* than any play in between. This time a commission for Chelmsford Cathedral, the play was derived from a brief mention of Caedmon in the Venerable Bede's *Ecclesiastical History*. In providing a dramatic context for the divine inspiration that gave Caedmon a voice to sing of the world's creation, Fry made the famous cleric Bede, the canon of Jarrow, his Shakespearean chorus or Brechtian narrator.

As Bede introduces the tale, it is A.D. 664, just after the Synod of Whitby, which fixed, among other things, the date of Easter in the Christian calendar. Farmworkers on the lands of Whitby Abbey are mystified by a stranger they have seen lurking about, who is apparently interested only in hearing the nuns sing at religious services. One of the workers encounters the man, Caedmon, who is courteous but withdrawn. The overman (overseer) of the workers discovers he has been a mercenary soldier for thirty years, fighting most recently for the pagan king Penda. Disgusted with such wars, he returned to his village—which he left after his beloved wife died in childbirth—hoping to find his daughter. Believing she may have migrated to Whitby, he has come to seek her. Fry reveals these things—and the fact that Caedmon holds himself responsible for his wife's death—not in flashbacks, but via the medieval narrative frame, with Bede or the characters themselves recalling events of the past. Caedmon stutters; he finds speech difficult and singing impossible, partly from the great sense of guilt he harbors. He is engaged by the overman to work in the abbey stables.

Next we see Hilda, the abbess, meeting with a young novice who is troubled about her lost parents—Caedmon and his dead wife, it can be inferred. When the workers gather in celebration after a solar eclipse, Caedmon leaves feeling alienated after he is unable to sing with the group.

Bede, in a poetic passage, sets the stage for the visionary encounter that follows. In a long but eloquently simple scene, an angelic being explores Caedmon's life and his refusal to recognize the music that dwells in him. The angel demands that Caedmon wrestle with him, but this is a metaphor: Caedmon must make peace with his past. The image of his dead beloved, who strongly resembles the young nun of the previous scene, appears to absolve him. The angel then asks Caedmon to sing about "the beginning of created things." The voice of his lost love also urges him

on, and he begins, in language not unlike that of some medieval miracle plays: "I am ready to praise the measureless making / That in foreshadowing and seeking / Formed place and light, for all creation's sharing."

In the next scene, the overman is startled to hear Caedmon singing along with the monks and nuns outside the abbey walls. He arranges for Caedmon to tell the abbess of his remarkable vision. Bede describes this first encounter, and the abbess' setting of a test for Caedmon: Can he sing of the Israelites' flight out of Egypt? Before Caedmon appears for the test, the abbey's precentor remembers that he had once seen Caedmon in battle, throwing down his sword and going to the aid of the wounded on both sides, at great risk to his life. The abbess, the precentor, and the overman are deeply moved by Caedmon's song of the Exodus, hauntingly imagined by Fry: "The country promised—not Eden, but Eden forgiven . . ." (p. 38). Caedmon is invited to join the abbey's order of monks, and for sixteen years he remains there, singing daily with his daughter but never breaking his silence to her about his past. He dies a quiet, pious death, singing a last song to God.

Thor, with Angels is set in A.D. 596—nearly a century before *One Thing More* takes place—and it was written almost forty years before that drama, in 1948. Structurally, it is more complex than either *Boy with a Cart* or *One Thing More*. It also has a kind of chorus, in the person of the ancient magician Merlin, who appears, somewhat dazed after a long sleep, at midpoint in the play to comment on the events with the advantage of a legendary seer. Merlin remembers the distant time when Britain was Christian under King Arthur.

Thor's characters are Jutish settlers, invaders of Britain, still worshiping Woden and the bloodthirsty Germanic pantheon. When they are not hunting and farming, they are battling the Saxons for mastery of the territory. Christian worship, once established in the land, has been suppressed, the sacred altars destroyed. A few enslaved Britons remain, but most have forgotten their faith.

As the play opens, Cymen, a Jutish chief, returns to his farmstead—the setting of the play—with his two sons, Quichelm and Cheldric, and his wife's brothers, Osmer and Tadfrid, from a battle with the Saxons in which the Jutes have been defeated. Cymen is more than merely ashamed about the loss, he is profoundly troubled. In the midst of the fray, just when he was about to slay a British slave of the Saxons, his sword was mysteriously stayed. Baffled, he took the slave prisoner and has brought him home with him. The other men are eager to sacrifice the young man, named Hoel, to Woden. It was this slave, after all, who slew the great Earl of Eccha in the turning point of the battle. Cymen is intent on discovering what power the Briton has. Cymen's wife, Clodesuida, is fearful of angering the vengeful gods. She speaks of having gone to "early rite," a pun on the idea of early mass, and of having sacrificed half a goat for the men's success in battle. Cymen sarcastically suggests she must have used the wrong half of the goat. The household is completed by the daughter, Martina—who comes to love the boyishly innocent Hoel—and a pair of comic servants, Colgrin and his wife, Anna.

Fry's characters delight in medieval English alliteration and invective. Quichelm's opening lines include "Who's awake? Where's / The welcome of women for warfarers? / Where's my Woden-fearing mother?" (p. 1). Colgrin responds with an internal rhyme: "There's an infernal clatter. What's the matter?" In this play, Fry was careful to use words with Germanic origins, to evoke a time before Norman French and Church Latin influences entered the language. The play is rich in images of nature, nowhere more so than in Merlin's poetic meditations.

Cymen curses the failure of the promise that settling in Britain held out to the Jutes. Yielding to family pressure, he attempts to slay Hoel, but his sword nearly hits his son, another event that convinces him of Hoel's power. Hoel, an orphan, is torn between a desire for death and a passion for life. When Merlin enters the action, he greets Hoel in Celtic, a language Hoel only dimly remembers; his recall of the vanquished faith is also vague. Clodesuida is abrupt: "We should rid the country of these things which aren't ourselves" (p. 24). Cymen, however, is eager to learn from Merlin about the past, especially the Christian past, for the Germanic gods seem to be losing their power. Merlin, in a formulation worthy of the Hindu mystics, questions the nature, the validity, of victory and defeat: "Quest and conquest and quest again . . ." (p. 27). Irritated, Cymen emphasizes that he can rightfully kill both Merlin and Hoel, as conquered Britons, to which Merlin replies: "Death is what conquers the killer, not the killed" (p. 27).

When wolves attack the family's sheep, their very livelihood, the men, including Hoel, rush out to save the flock, a Christian symbol. Clodesuida describes Hoel's ferocious destruction of the most vicious wolf with his bare hands: "It was horror / And hope and terror and triumph to see it" (p. 34). Cymen's sons are now even more fearful of the power behind Hoel and demand his sacrifice. Cymen at first proposes an animal sacrifice—the story of Abraham and Isaac—but ends in destroying the pagan altar, to his family's horror. Cymen is then summoned by the king of Kent to meet St. Augustine, of whom Merlin says: "Sent by Gregory of Rome who on a market-day / Saw angels where we see our enemies" (p. 39). In his absence, Martina and Hoel have a brief, affecting interlude, discovering their love for each other, but Martina is unable to prevent Cymen's sons and brothers-in-law from seizing Hoel. They tie him cross-fashion to a tree and kill him with a spear thrust, "In Woden's way, the Woden death" (p. 50). Clodesuida, clinging to the only faith she knows, thinks Hoel's death is for the best to appease the gods. When Cymen returns, he describes how, upon learning of the Christian God, he "felt our lonely flesh / Welcome to creation" (p. 52). Cymen is appalled to learn of the death of Hoel and sorrowfully comments on man's cruelty to man, his seeming inability to live in love and peace. He sees the slain Hoel as a Christ-like sacrifice:

> We have still to learn to live.
> They say the sacrifice of God was brought about
> By the blind anger of men, and yet God made
> Their blindness their own saving and lonely flesh
> Welcome to creation. Briton, boy,
> Your God is here, waiting in this land again.
> Forgive me for the sorrow of this world.
>
> (p. 53)

Voices of St. Augustine's monks are heard in the background.

In writing *The Firstborn*, Fry was obsessed with the conflicts he imagined Moses must have experienced in demanding that the Israelites be freed from Egyptian bondage. Fry worked on the play during World War II, completing it in 1946, though it was not performed until 1948.

The Firstborn has a three-act structure, divided into three, two, and two scenes. The drama is unique among Fry's plays in that it begins with a tragic view and retains it. As Aristotle observed, the essential difference between tragedy and comedy is that the matter is *serious* in tragedy. The matter is certainly serious in *The Firstborn*. The drama takes place in 1200 B.C., not a good year for the Egyptians, as things turn out. The action alternates between the open terrace of the palace of Seti II—with pyramid construction under way in the background—and the stuffy enclosure of Miriam's tent among the enslaved Israelites; the settings themselves are symbolic of the status of the two peoples, and they atmospherically heighten the tensions and conflicts of the developing drama. Moses, once a great general for the Egyptians, has been in a self-imposed ten-year exile. Pharaoh's sister, Anath Bithiah, longs to see her adopted son again. The drama opens with a scream, which brings Anath and Teusret, Seti's daughter, out onto the terrace. They ask a guard what has happened. "Merely an Israelite," the guard tells them: a slave has fallen to his death from the steep pyramid. Anath tells Teusret about the conditions under which she had found and saved the infant Moses, "A tiny weeping Israel who had failed / To be exterminated" (p. 4). Seti appears then to ask if Anath knows where Moses can be found. He is in need of his services, as the country is menaced on the west by Libyans and on the south by Nubians. Young Ramses, Pharaoh's son and heir, makes his entrance, his excellent qualities and widespread popularity being duly and poetically noted. Ramses remarks that he saw two strange Jews while he was out that day, one who "seemed a man of authority" (p. 10). The men turn out to be, fortuitously, Moses and Aaron. But Moses has no interest in taking up his general's commission again. He wants his people freed from bondage and is adamant. Pharaoh sees the Israelites as having no purpose in life other than as laborers, even as Aaron tallies the list of the dead and oppressed. Moses challenges Seti's view of man's life and worth: worldly conquests and epic building projects, to him, have only put a crown on the skeleton.

It is the individual man
In his individual freedom who can mature
With his warm spirit the unripe world.
They are your likeness, these men, even to nightmares.
(p. 15)

Moses' later reunion with his sister, Miriam, in her tent is augmented by the arrival of Ramses, who seeks to make a friend of the man he thinks of as an uncle. He shows his eagerness to end the slavery of the Israelites, to become a just ruler. Moses says they should stay apart; their purposes are different: "We're not enemies so much / As creatures of division. You and I, / Ramses, like money in a purse, / Ring together only to be spent / For different reasons" (p. 26). Ramses prevents a group of Egyptian guards from seizing Miriam's son, Shendi, who was involved in a strike when the workers were told they had to gather their own straw to make bricks.

As act 2 opens, the plagues begin. Ramses succeeds in getting Shendi a commission with the Egyptians, a momentary hope of better times, but Shendi proves as oppressive to his own people as the worst of their Egyptian captors. In scene 2, Anath despairs over Seti's duplicity. Seti's empty promises to Moses have resulted in more plagues. Seti tells her he will bargain with Moses, which he does not intend to do. Ramses also urges him to free the Israelites, even though Egypt is under attack by her enemies. Fry suggests human reasons for Seti's intransigence, countering the biblical explanation that God had "hardened the heart of Pharaoh." Moses prepares his people for the Exodus and the final plague: the deaths of the firstborn of Egypt, man and beast. He is stricken when reminded that this will include the excellent, compassionate young Ramses:

Why had I not thought of him?—
When other boys were slaughtered I was spared for Israel.
Surely I who have been the go-between for God
Can keep one firstborn living now for Egypt?
(p. 74)

But God's ways are not man's, and Ramses dies. Shendi, refusing to stay inside Miriam's tent, where he is protected by the lamb's blood of Passover, also dies, to his mother's great despair. Even with the final freeing of the Israelites, Moses is still desolated and baffled by events: "Why was it I that had to be disaster to you? / I do not know why the necessity of God / Should feed on grief" (p. 86). As in many of Fry's plays, both life and death are mysteries to be pondered, as Moses says in farewell to Anath: "Until we meet in the meaning of the world."

The Religious Drama Society commissioned *A Sleep of Prisoners* for the 1951 Festival of Britain, at the instigation of E. Martin Browne. With its somber setting—a parish church converted into a military prison—and its small cast of deeply troubled soldiers, the play did not seem very festive. But it was nonetheless timely, for World War II was still a fresh and bitter memory, and the ensuing cold war held the menace of worldwide destruction. The festival was intended to stress Britain's postwar recovery and new material prosperity. Glenda Leeming has noted that Fry provided with this play "a small dissenting voice . . . suggesting that true progress lies in the improvement of values, not in technology" (1990, p. 115). At the time of its composition, Fry was living near Burford, where, in 1649, rebels from Cromwell's Parliamentary Army had been detained in a church; three of them were later shot.

As Fry wrote in the play's dedication: "Progress is the growth of vision: the increased perception of what makes for life and what makes for death." He described the play as "a complicated design where each of four men is seen through the sleeping thoughts of the others, and each, in his own dream, speaks as at heart he is, not as he believes himself to be."

The men, three privates and a corporal, are Peter Able, an easygoing, agreeable fellow "who doesn't know there's a war on"; David King, a bully with a very short temper; Tim Meadows, a retiring and apologetic (suggestive of Fry himself) widower who lied about his age to get into the war; and Joe Adams, accustomed to taking charge and maintaining discipline. As the play opens, the men are preparing straw pallets to sleep on. Peter's playing of the church organ annoys Dave, who demands he stop it. In fact, he almost strangles Peter in his rage, then regrets his actions. As the soldiers ready themselves for sleep, they voice their fears and uncertainties. In the course of the play they will act out in dreams four stories from the Old Testament. Meadows acts as a kind of chorus at times, calming the others, a voice of reason; in the first dream, which is his own, he is cast as the Deity: "No, no, no. I didn't ask to be God" (p. 11). But he is not required to do much, for the action concerns the strife between Cain, portrayed by David, and Abel, portrayed by Peter, with Joe Adams as their father, Adam. As in almost all of Fry's plays, images of nature abound; the dialogue here recalls medieval English versions of the story of Cain and Abel. Even after Cain has brutally murdered his brother, he still rages at God's injustice toward him in favoring Abel. This dream segues into David's dream of himself as King David, troubled by the rebellion of his beloved son Absalom, who is portrayed by Peter. Adams portrays King David's aide, Joab, who kills Absalom/Peter with a burst of tommy-gun bullets in this brief but powerful recreation of the biblical tale.

Obviously, this is not an easy drama to stage or to play, because of the dual roles of the actors and the fact that the church setting—whether real or constructed by design—does not always accommodate the suggestion of different locales and times. The third dream, Peter's, is that of the averted sacrifice of Isaac at the hands of his father, Abraham. Abraham, portrayed by Dave, is only—and sorrowfully—obeying God's demand for a human sacrifice, and Isaac, portrayed by Pete, is meek and accepting when he realizes the full horror of what is to occur. Adams, as the angel of God, comes timely to the rescue: "Hold your arm. / There are new instructions. The knife can drop" (p. 32). Meadows appears as a donkeyman, offering the greatly relieved Isaac/Peter a ride, recalling the Palm Sunday image of Jesus riding an ass into Jerusalem. The fourth dream is that of Corporal Adams: he is a bulwark for his two comrades, David and Peter, as the three endure the fiery furnace of Babylon's tyrannical Nebuchadnezzar. As Shadrac, Meshac, and Abednego, they are spiritually cleansed by this ordeal, observed by an unseen Nebuchadnezzar, who, in the biblical account, was so impressed with their bravery and their imperviousness to the flames that he released them. In Fry's dream-version, they are instead greeted by Meadows, who identifies himself as "Man," acting under God's commandment. If wars are viewed as an institutionalized extension of man's passions and urges to violence toward his fellowman, then the biblical dream-plays Fry enacts offer the counterpoint of transcendence both through divine initiative and the creative impulse.

COMEDIES

IN his comedies, Fry continues to explore the mysteries of human existence—though generally less seriously and intensely than in his religious dramas—and given the settings and themes of these plays, one could almost call them semi-secular comedies. As the critic Stanley Wiersma has insisted, with Fry's agreement, the plays are actually a comment on St. Paul's epistle to the Romans (6:23): "For the wages of sin is death, but the free gift of God is eternal life in Christ Jesus our Lord." In an essay titled "Comedy" published in *Adelphi* magazine in November 1950, Fry wrote:

When I set about writing a comedy the idea presents itself to me first of all as tragedy. The characters press on to the theme with all their divisions and perplexities heavy about them; they are already entered for the race to doom, and good and evil are an infernal tangle skinning the fingers that try to unravel them. . . . Somehow the characters have to unmortify themselves: to affirm life and assimilate death and persevere in joy.

For the critic Emil Roy, Fry's central characters are "fit for tragedy" but, dropped into a different world, they make their "narrow escape into faith" (p. 15). The effect, for Roy, is of tragedy transcended.

Fry's title *A Phoenix Too Frequent* comes from Robert Burton's translation from Martial: "To whom conferr'd a peacock's indecent, / A squirrel's harsh, a phoenix too frequent." And the story does indeed detail a symbolic rising from the dead, including a corpse saving the life of a doomed man. This may seem rather too serious to be presented as comic material. Yet Fry makes it work as comedy, even though the philosophical subtext is weighty if one chooses to excavate it. This exercise in the life force, as Shaw would call it, triumphing over the death wish, is found first in Petronius, but Fry discovered it in Jeremy Taylor's *The Rule and Exercises of Holy Dying*.

As the play opens, the body of a man is stretched out in the gloom of a family tomb, while a beautiful young woman, Dynamene, mourns him inconsolably. In the dim lamplight, she is preparing to starve herself to death—along with her devoted maidservant, Doto—and join her dead husband, Virilius, in the underworld. Starlight penetrates through an iron gate down the steps into the tomb, and aboveground, a row of trees can be seen, one of them a holly—traditionally the wood of Jesus' cross—on which six men have been hanged. The scene is in Asia Minor, near Ephesus, site of the great Temple of Diana. The temple doesn't figure in the plot, though as goddess of chastity, Diana might admire Dynamene's faithfulness to her husband, even in death.

Some of Fry's critics found the play lacking in action, being rather an ingenious exercise in colorful imagery and wordplay. Lack of action has been a frequent complaint against Fry, but usually by reviewers who have little understanding of the varied nature of drama. The action of *A Phoenix Too Frequent* is primarily in the hearts and minds of its three characters, and it is revealed through their discussions and arguments. Dynamene is a very dynamic young woman, not yet ready for death, but it is clear she fears life without the virility of her lost Virilius. He was, she says in effect, a coming man who didn't get to come, cut off before his promise was fulfilled. Dynamene's excess of grief is a comic extreme; she extols him: "You cut the glassy water with a diamond keel" (p. 2). But her own words suggest that Virilius was rather limited emotionally. Doto—who acts as Dynamene's confidante and a reverse image of her emotional state—has had a different experience of life and men and is not quite ready to give it all up. Into this gloomy little world comes Tegeus, a soldier charged with guarding the hanged men; the state does not want the bodies to be stolen and given burial. Doto and Tegeus share some wine and Doto becomes tipsy and bawdy. This wakes Dynamene, who mistakes Tegeus for a guardian from Hades, come to fetch her to her husband. Tegeus denies this, although he noted on his arrival at the tomb, "Death is a kind of love" (p. 8).

Trying to impress Dynamene with his honor, for he is falling in love with her, he swears an impressive oath on various gods. She chides him: "You needn't / Labour to prove your secondary education" (p. 16). *A Phoenix Too Frequent* abounds in witty comments, puns, and amusing similes and metaphors. There's even a virtual duel of images between Tegeus and Dynamene: "winter and warmth"; "moon and meadow"; "A cold bell sounding in a golden month"; "Crystal in harvest"; "a nightingale sobbing among the pears" (p. 19). She decides to rename him Chromis: "It has a breadlike sound. / I think of you as a crisp loaf" (p. 22). Their love ripens in bouts of poetic argument. She dismisses Doto; it was wrong of her to ask her servant to die as well. Tegeus leaves the tomb to check on the bodies, and returns in terror. One has been stolen, and he will surely hang in its place in the morning for being derelict in his duty. He proposes suicide before such dishonor. Dynamene will not hear of this: she does not want a dead body to come between them. She proposes that he substitute her dead husband's corpse for the missing body. He is shocked, but her answer is the core of the play: "I loved /

201

His life not his death. And now we can give his death / The power of life" (p. 43). This is, of course, a metaphor for Christ's sacrificial death, but Fry doesn't urge it. He doesn't need to.

The Lady's Not for Burning was the first of a seasonal cycle of plays Fry completed in 1970. In this cycle, a season of the year infuses and informs the action of the play and the movements of the characters: its atmosphere is gently pervasive. Fry has chosen to call these "comedies of mood": "It means that the scene, the season and the characters are bound together in one climate," he explained in a 1950 article in *Theatre Newsletter.* This is Fry's spring play, and the seasonal metaphor of rebirth after the death of winter is borne out in the saving of the heroine from certain death and the hero from his own death wish. In 1947 an English convict confessed falsely to a murder, explaining: "It was worth while being hung to be a hero, seeing that life was not really worth living." Fry uses this as the epigraph of his play text, suggesting a source of inspiration for his central character, Thomas Mendip, a bitterly disillusioned soldier who seeks to be rid of the world. His motive is different from that of Dynamene, but, by the end of the comedy, like her, he finds reason enough to go on living: he has fallen in love with Jennet Jourdemayne, a wealthy young village spinster accused of being a witch. While this name is resonant—it means "today, tomorrow"—it was, in fact, taken from a seventeenth-century Lancashire witchcraft trial record. Fry found the core of his plot in an old German short story, "Wooing the Gallows," by W. Heinrich von Riehl, whose hero, Jörg, seeks to be hanged for murders for which there is no evidence against him.

The year is 1400 in the English market town of Cool Clary, where the citizens are in full cry in the streets after Jennet, who is said to have bewitched an old rag-and-bone man, Matthew Skipps, into a dog. All three acts occur in a spacious chamber in the house of the mayor, Hebble Tyson. As the play opens, Thomas Mendip, in his late twenties, interrupts the work of Tyson's young clerk, Richard. He has come to see about being hanged. At this moment, the lovely Alizon Eliot enters: "Coming in from the light, I am all out at the eyes. I've an April blindness" (p. 6). She is to marry one of the mayor's two bumptious nephews, Humphrey. Humphrey's brother, Nicholas, who covets all Humphrey has, bursts onto the scene claiming to have killed Humphrey—they are a Cain and Abel

variation—just as Thomas insists he is also a murderer. Humphrey, it turns out, was only knocked unconscious, and contention between the brothers continues throughout the play. Tyson is too busy to bother with Thomas' claim to have killed the rag-and-bone man. With a witch-hunt outside his garden, he has much on his mind. Thomas decries the charge of witchcraft as superstition, but, when Jennet bursts into the room, seeking protection, it is clear most of the family are wary of her. She is beautiful, however, and despite what she has been accused of, Nicholas, Humphrey, and Thomas are smitten with her.

As the second act opens, Tyson and Tappercoom, the town's justice, are considering the results of their recent inquiry, by torture, of Thomas and Jennet. She insists she is innocent; he, that he is guilty and must be hanged. Since torture has not yielded incriminating information, Tyson decides to leave Thomas and Jennet alone in the chamber, while he and Tappercoom eavesdrop. Jennet has a passion for life, in contrast to Thomas, but his growing admiration and love for her is working changes. The two officials, after listening to Jennet articulate her despair, rush in, thinking they have heard a confession. Thomas, furious, knocks Humphrey down and threatens the mild-mannered house chaplain with his own viol. To bring Thomas to reason—and win him back to life—the chaplain suggests he and Jennet be invited to the bridal banquet of Alizon and Humphrey. In the final act, Humphrey tries to blackmail Jennet into bed as the price of helping her escape the town. She indignantly refuses. Richard, the clerk, and Alizon, having fallen in love, elope in all the confusion, but soon return to help free Jennet, having revealed old Skipps to be neither dead nor a dog. They slip away again, and Tappercoom decides to let Jennet and Thomas also leave the town under cover of night, as they declare their love for one another.

Venus Observed, the autumnal segment of Fry's seasonal cycle, conveys the sense of things ripening toward harvest and even to decay. The play is in three acts and opens with an explicit allusion to the mythical Judgment of Paris, as the fifty-year-old duke of Altair—a charming philanderer who now seeks to marry—asks his son Edgar to give a symbolic apple to one of three of the duke's former loves; in effect, to choose his own stepmother. The scene is the observatory in the duke's neglected, decaying mansion. The room was once a bedroom in which the duke entertained the three ladies, each in her time, before he devoted it to amateur astronomy. Edgar is an easygoing young man, primarily interested in the family stables and mounts. In contrast stands the straitlaced and priggish young Dominic, son of Herbert Reedbeck, the duke's estate agent. Dominic has discovered to his horror that his father has been systematically robbing the duke of revenues for years. He confronts Reedbeck, who denies any wrongdoing. The duke has invited his marriage prospects to witness an eclipse of the sun; the resultant gathering is something of a surprise to the guests, who were each under the impression that they would be meeting with the duke alone. The women are Rosabel Fleming, a lovely but insecure actress; Jessie Dill, a large, generous, contented lady; and Hilda Taylor-Snell, bored with her husband of years and possibly open to the duke's proposal. Once they are all assembled, Edgar somewhat impetuously awards the apple to Rosabel, but takes it away to give it to Jessie when Rosabel speaks out against the duke's behavior. Into this awkward contest enters Reedbeck's beautiful daughter, Perpetua, returned from a long residence in America. The duke is immediately attracted to her, but before he can offer her the apple, she shoots it with a pistol.

After lunch, Dominic and Perpetua meet in the estate's Temple of the Ancient Virtues, where he tells her of their father's crimes against the duke. His solution is to have her marry the duke so the matter will be concealed. Dismayed that she will not be free to make her own choice in love, she nevertheless assents. The duke arranges an assignation for that evening with Perpetua in the observatory. Later, Reedbeck is furious to learn of Dominic's plan. "To consider selling your sister? You, / Sprung from my loins, and so utterly / Unprincipled?" (p. 42). Edgar vies for the affections of Perpetua, and the duke becomes aware that a rivalry is developing between them. The scene ends with Rosabel making a threat to send the observatory "where Nero's Rome has gone" (p. 58). The duke woos Perpetua—who prefers Edgar—in the darkened observatory. He looks forward to their union, but she is appalled when she learns he knows of Reedbeck's embezzlement and, in fact, has taken steps to legalize it. Suddenly, they discover that the observatory is on fire. Perpetua clings to the duke in fear, not love, until they are rescued from the flames.

An hour later, the characters gather in the temple, where Rosabel, in tears, is hiding in the dark. She surrenders to the police after telling the duke it was she who set the fire. Characteristically, he dismisses this: he is glad to be free of the observatory and is touched by her motivation. She did it, she tells him, "to make you human, / To bring you down to be among the rest of us" (p. 80). The duke comments on the human condition: he is "amazed / That we can live in such a condition of mystery / And not be exasperated out of our flesh" (p. 81). He assures Reedbeck that all is well with the way he has been conducting the estate. Dominic expresses confusion: "Ethics are very difficult" (p. 94). And Perpetua tells Edgar she must be free; she is troubled that "no one is separate from another" (p. 95). The duke has come to the same conclusion: "It's all a unison of ageing" (p. 97). But he affirms the promise of rebirth the dying season holds—"An ancient love can blow again, like summer / Visiting St. Martin" (p. 99). At the play's end, he states his intention to marry Rosabel.

The Dark Is Light Enough is Fry's winter comedy, and it is a very dark comedy indeed. The title comes from a description by the French naturalist J. H. Fabre of the flight through darkness and storms of a butterfly that "arrives in a state of perfect freshness, its great wings intact. . . . The darkness is light enough." Fry cites this in an epigraph to the play text. In a jacket note to the published play he has commented:

There is an angle of experience where the dark is distilled into light: either here or hereafter, in or out of tune: where our tragic fate finds itself with perfect pitch, and goes straight to the key which creation was composed in. And comedy serves and reaches out to this experience. It says . . . groaning as we may be, we move in the figure of a dance, and so moving, we trace the outline of the mystery.

The action opens in the great hall of an Austrian country house presided over by the Countess Rosmarin Ostenburg. It is the winter of 1848–1849, in the closing days of the doomed Hungarian Revolution against the Austrians. Rosmarin's friends, Jakob and Belmann, and her personal physician, Kassel—who form a sort of chorus, commenting on the action and even interfering in it—are concerned about the well-being of the aged countess, who left alone on horseback in a snowstorm before dawn and was seen driving a sleigh in the direction of the advancing Hungarian troops. The countess' son, Stefan, has summoned his sister, Gelda, and Count Peter Zichy, Gelda's husband, to the house to assist in the crisis. Zichy is a Hungarian in the Austrian government, who has tried to improve his countrymen's freedoms diplomatically. Gelda arrives before Peter, just in time for the sudden appearance of Richard Gettner, her ex-husband, an obnoxious Austrian who has deserted from the Hungarian army, where he fancied himself a freedom fighter. Rosmarin, it turns out, has rescued him. A one-book author, Gettner is disliked by Rosmarin's friends, who are at a loss to explain her interest in him. During their encounter, and later, it is clear there are still surviving embers between Gettner and Gelda. Rosmarin's family and friends are concerned for her health and alarmed at the danger she faces in harboring Gettner, but she is serene. She calls them "uncertain people in an uncertain time" and throughout displays a strange sense of detachment. When Colonel Janik, the leader of the Hungarian forces, arrives to search the house for Gettner, Rosmarin refuses to cooperate, and Peter is taken hostage. Stefan urges his sister to persuade Gettner to surrender, to save her husband. She reminds Stefan that Gettner was also her husband once.

Gettner hides out in the stables, the scene of act 2. He has no intention of surrendering to spare Rosmarin or her family. The Hungarians—just beaten in a skirmish—have returned to occupy the house, and the family are forced out into the stables. Janik is baffled by Rosmarin's determination to protect Gettner, whom Fry has not depicted favorably. But Rosmarin explains, "Life has a hope of him / Or he would never have lived." And then, "Richard lives / In his own right, Colonel, not in yours / Or mine" (p. 54). Rosmarin offers other poetic formulations in the play, but implicit is her endorsement of the rabbinical concept that to save one man is to save the world. Saving Gettner, of course, is the mainspring of the play's conflicts, but Rosmarin's generous, forgiving attitude toward her family, friends, and even the invaders shows an encompassing benevolence. She remains unchanged in the play, but she helps others to change: she is a facilitator. Confrontations with her force all the main characters to reexamine their lives and beliefs. As the characters gather in the stable, a drunken Gettner comes out of hiding, only to be promptly captured by two soldiers. He kisses Gelda in front of her husband. Stefan is outraged and challenges him to a duel. Gettner brushes him off: the Hungarians will shoot him soon enough. To stall for time, Rosmarin urges the soldiers to perform a tavern song she has heard them sing. Stefan steals the soldiers' pistols while they are preoccupied with the song and insists that Gettner go outside with him. A shot is fired; Gettner has hit, but not killed, Stefan.

The rebellion has been quashed as act 3 opens, but the house shows the damage of occupation. Stefan is recuperating. Gettner has fled on one of Rosmarin's horses. Count Peter and Gelda reaffirm their commitment to each other, and Peter leaves for Vienna, to try to prevent the Austrian government from executing the rebels. Rosmarin is ill and nearing death. Janik, now considered a traitor, arrives at the house, and Rosmarin gives him sanctuary. To everyone's surprise, Gettner returns, despite the danger to himself of apprehension. He has heard that Rosmarin is dying. Misreading all her past efforts on his behalf, he asks her to marry him. But Rosmarin has never loved Gettner; she does not even like him much. "We're elected into love," she says (p. 99); there is no free will or choice in the matter. He is stunned by her admission, but she gives him a strange kind of hope as she dies: "I'll not / Leave you until I can love you, Richard." She adds, though, "I don't mean / Necessarily here" (p. 101). A fierce pounding is then heard at the door; the avenging Austrians are seeking Janik. It is Gettner's instinct to flee, but he changes his mind and stands his ground beside the dead Rosmarin. He has found his courage; in her death, he has been reborn. And Rosmarin has, perhaps like Fabre's butterfly, come through the darkness and the storms into a realm of light.

The same collection of German stories that gave Fry the inspiration for *The Lady's Not for Burning* offered him an idea for *A Yard of Sun*, which concluded his seasonal cycle. In elemental outline, it is the fable of "the man who had three sons," each with a different nature.

This is Fry's summer play, and the title refers to the sunny courtyard of the long untenanted Palazzo Traguardo, seen on the morning of the day the eagerly anticipated horse race, the Palio, is to be run. Angelino Bruno is the caretaker of the palazzo. He runs a tavern on the ground floor, adjacent to an apartment occupied by a woman named Giosetta and her lovely daughter, Grazia.

Giosetta's lover, Cesare, who is Grazia's father, deserted from the Italian army and was denounced to the Nazis. Nothing has been heard of him for three years, and Grazia privately broods that a chance remark of hers to a neighbor might have given her father away. Angelino is anticipating the arrival of the new owners of the palazzo and is looking forward to a victory in the Palio; Italy's best jockey is riding for the parish. It will be the first running of the race since the disastrous world war, which has left Italy strongly divided politically and in economic difficulties. Angelino's two sons—mention of the absent third, Edmondo, is forbidden by the father—are constantly wrangling. The amiable, trivial, but ambitious Luigi has disgraced himself by having been a follower of Mussolini, but he wants to make a new start. His angry bother, Roberto, a doctor, was a member of the opposition and cannot forgive Luigi his actions and his politics. He treats only the poor and is fiercely proud of his activist communism. At one point in the first act, Roberto nearly strangles Luigi, recalling Fry's Cain and Abel motif in *A Sleep of Prisoners* and *The Lady's Not for Burning*. A young man introducing himself as Alfio Scapare arrives at the palazzo, seeking his father. Roberto and Luigi dismiss him abruptly when they learn he is a jockey for a rival parish. The new owner of the palazzo turns out to be the third son, Edmondo, now a venture capitalist who has made a fortune sitting out the war in Portugal. He arrives with his wife, the beautiful, charming, patrician Ana-Clara. Roberto despises what Edmondo stands for; Edmondo left Siena with money he blackmailed from a neighbor. But Angelino and Luigi are delighted with his success—not only is Edmondo rich, but he will give the family new status as owners of the palazzo. In fact, it was Edmondo who arranged for Italy's best jockey to ride in the Palio for the parish. Roberto has a brief romance with Ana-Clara, who accompanies him on his rounds—he wants to shame her with the misery he can show her, but this backfires on Roberto when Ana-Clara reveals that she is herself a child of the Lisbon slums. Edmondo's plans to be the family's savior begin to unravel when the rider he hired to run the Palio withdraws from the race. Luigi volunteers to ride, though he's no horseman. He thinks the exposure may improve his image politically. News arrives that Cesare has been spotted in the vicinity; and just as he appears in the archway of the courtyard, a gunshot announces the start of the great race. Although Edmondo's attempts to fix the race failed, the parish is victorious anyway when Luigi falls off his mount, which goes on to win the Palio. Luigi is embraced by the Sienese as something of a hero. Cesare, with Giosetta's acquiescence, decides to return with his son Alfio to his dying wife in Naples to make his peace. Edmondo, whose acts of self-gratification have not had their intended effect, departs with Ana-Clara to resume their former life.

Again in this play, little of the action is of a visual or physical nature. In fact, the race is suggested in the rippling of banners above the set. Rather, the action is revealed in the various conflicts and complications of the unfolding plot, most of which are manifested, intellectually and emotionally, through language. And Fry does indeed seem to be commenting on the limits of human action, with the suggestion that volition is not the only thing at play in the unfolding of events.

There is something appealing about Luigi's observations on what he sees as "the first day of a better world." He explains to the sullen Roberto:

> I remembered it as soon as it was light.
> I swallowed the last black morsel of what I was
>   dreaming
> And said Here it is, we're all new men
> In a new world. I stood at the window, like Adam
> Looking out on the first garden.
>
> (p. 5)

Roberto responds, "You seem to think that every change of wind / That crosses your mind is a kind of baptism" (p. 12). And late in the play, Ana-Clara comments on a redemptive, transcendent light that infused the running of the Palio:

> It's a great slow love-making, anyway,
> And left me vibrating like an instrument.
> So nearly the city had no need of the sun
> Or the moon to shine on it. I could almost see
> By the light that streamed from the trumpets
> And shimmered from the bell. The courting sun-birds,
> The birds of paradise, so nearly sang
> The indwelling music which created us.
>
> (p. 107)

Caedmon would have recognized that perception!

HISTORY AS MEMORY: CURTMANTLE

FRY'S play about Henry II was well received in London in 1962, but it was never produced on Broadway, and it remains little known in North America. Fry had long been fascinated by this English king whose historical nickname derives from the short coat he customarily wore. Henry was also a great power in France, from which his Angevin (Anjou) Plantagenet family came: the "devil's brood" they were called. Henry had won his queen, the legendary Eleanor of Aquitaine, from the pious, weak Louis VII of France, after she had borne that monarch a series of daughters but no male heirs. With Henry, however, she had four sons: Geoffrey, King Henry (crowned while his father was still in his prime), King John, and King Richard, called the Lionhearted.

In his foreword, Fry explains his fascination with Henry (1133–1189), king at twenty-one and the richest monarch in Europe. His father, Geoffrey Plantagenet, was Count of Anjou; his mother, Matilda, was daughter of Henry I, his claim to the throne. Henry's great crusade—and his enduring legacy to Britain—was his attempt to lay the basis for English common law. Fry notes that in Henry's turbulent thirty-five years' reign are "all that we need for a lifetime's study and contemplation of mankind." His problem as a playwright was, since he did not want to distort history, what events to select to give spectators an idea of Henry—"Where is the King?" is something of a refrain in the play—and what he did. This, Fry said then, is "putting a shape on almost limitless complexity." Nevertheless, there is a necessity to shape: "'making a play of it' . . . is inherent in us, because pattern and balance are pervading facts of the universe." Fry presents the dramatized events in chronological order, but he has insisted *Curtmantle* is not a chronicle play. In order to encompass so much, "I have tried to do away with time and place, and convey thirty years in one almost uninterrupted action." To achieve this, he has the play effectually take place in the memory of William Marshal, Earl of Pembroke, similar to Bolt's and Shaffer's solutions in *A Man for All Seasons* and *The Royal Hunt of the Sun*.

In a prologue and two acts, Fry explores the reality of the king and a second theme: "Law, or rather the interplay of different laws: civil, canon, moral, aesthetic, and the laws of God; and how they belong and do not belong to each other." In the prologue, which suggests Brecht's *Mother Courage*, court followers complain bitterly one rainy night about the king's endless and sudden moves about the kingdom, to catch local justices out in wrongdoing. Here Blae is introduced, a prostitute who will soon bear the king's illegitimate son, later to be the only true son, who is faithful to the king till the end. In act 1 Thomas à Becket, the king's chancellor, has just returned from France with a handsome dowry for young Prince Henry's child-bride, daughter of King Louis. Henry comments on the brilliant spectacle Becket made in France with his train: "Hawks, and dogs; and longtailed apes / Up on the backs of the horses: all his gold plate / And his private chapel, a holy menagerie / Of opulence and power." Henry questions: "What are you, Becket? / Force, craft, or the holy apprentice?" (p. 13). Offhandedly, he makes Becket archbishop of Canterbury, thinking to have his chancellor compel the church to civil law. Becket warns: "Whoever is made Archbishop will very soon / Offend either you, Henry, or his God" (p. 21). Becket takes on the duties of archbishop reluctantly; he and Henry have different ideas about what he calls the "true and living / Dialectic between the Church and the state" (p. 21). Eleanor warns Becket that they, with the children, "the nest of young eagles," are not free spirits, having "our future state only in a world of Henry" (p. 24). Henry is furious when Becket resigns as chancellor to dedicate himself to his duties as archbishop. Henry accuses Becket of avoiding him to strengthen "a spiritual authority you know you're weak in" (p. 31). They contend furiously about the claims of secular and spiritual law and power. In act 2, the contentions have powerful consequences. Henry's unquiet sons are seen for the first time. Henry is angry with Becket for excommunicating ministers of state and for departing from England without his permission. He rages, abolishes clerical immunity, and threatens death to opponents. Becket rejects the document of common law. A fearful Eleanor temporizes: "Consider complexity, delight in difference. / Fear, for God's sake, your exact words. / Do you think you can draw lines on the living water?" (p. 47). Becket rejects the judgment of a secular court that he is a traitor and flees to France. He has already become almost a saint to many common people. The queen returns to France with her son Richard, who will oppose his father. Louis has an heir to the throne at last. A worried Henry crowns his son, a second

King Henry, but without the necessary benediction of Becket as archbishop, who, on his return to England, excommunicates all who took part in the coronation. Furious, Henry muses, "Who will get rid of this turbulent priest for me?" (p. 71). Some of the king's agents act on this statement. When Henry hears of Becket's martyrdom, he is eloquent in his regret.

Act 3 begins with Henry's contrition. His ritual beating at Becket's tomb is spoken of, not shown. His people, he knows, hate him for what was done to Becket. The scene shifts, in William Marshal's mind, to Eleanor's court in Poitou, where Richard, Geoffrey, and even young Henry and their wives are in attendance. They speak of forging an alliance against Henry with young Philip of France, when Henry enters and arrests Eleanor. Eleanor warns him about his actions, that he will be the real prisoner at last. At the close, Henry is dying on an old woman's goose-feather mattress, cursed by the people of Le Mans for firing their city. Philip forces Henry to surrender all he has in France, plus an indemnity. Monks come from Canterbury with a petition, which Henry rejects. A departing monk curses him. Contrite and fearful, Henry calls the monk back to be forgiven. But by then, it is too late.

THE CRITICAL RESPONSE

AT the height of Fry's celebrity in the commercial theater, even those reviewers who professed themselves puzzled by the import of the plays tended to confess themselves dazzled by their verbal conceits: "Christopher Fry has brought back into the theatre all the wealth of our literary heritage," *The Stage* reported. Fry was called "one of the brightest hopes of the British theatre. A poet and a wit . . . a man of rich and abundant fancy with an ironic sense of humor." Of *Venus Observed*, Harold Hobson, of the *London Sunday Times* and the *Christian Science Monitor*, observed, "Over these delicate emotions, Mr. Fry performs a breath-taking verbal dance." Writing about *The Firstborn*, in 1952, the *Times* of London's reviewer said, "In no other play more effectively . . . has Mr. Fry expressed his sense of the mystery of existence."

Fry had, however, severe critics among the reviewers, even before his plays were eclipsed by the social and political theater of the mid-1950s. In a 1954 essay, "Prose and the Playwright," Kenneth Tynan attacked "the post-war vogue of T. S. Eliot and Christopher Fry," decrying the idea that "the upper reaches of dramatic experience are the exclusive province of the poet." "Everyone agrees that formal poetic diction is dead," Tynan insisted dismissively. He quibbled with a bathetic—as he saw it—use of imagery in *The Firstborn*, but did allow that "poetry in the theatre should be confined to comedy, where its potency still lingers." Admitting "some fine set pieces of rhetoric" in *The Dark Is Light Enough*, Tynan argued that even these embodied "the germ of poetry's weakness: it describes in repose rather than illustrates in action." Of Fry's characters, he noted, "They *tell* us, with ruthless fluency, what kind of people they are, instead of letting us find out for ourselves." Regarding the poetry in the plays, he said: "Fry gilds where Eliot anoints; in neither procedure are there seeds of real dramatic vitality" (pp. 68–74).

For the critic Harold Clurman, the theater had not for a long time heard "so dazzling an arrangement of words." Clurman's early judgment seems still valid: "Fry will ultimately have to stand by what he means as well as by his manner of speech, although, it is true, the style of Fry's statement is as much part of what he means as any abstract formulation of his meaning can be." Writing of *Venus Observed* and *Ring Round the Moon* in London, Clurman preferred Fry to Eliot: Fry was "spinning a dry wisdom," but Eliot was just spinning. Clurman suggested that the less serious one was about Fry's work, the more it seemed to improve. He also felt most directors missed Fry's meanings, content to emphasize the language. Clurman contrasted Fry's "placid and passive" plays with the more activist existentialists, whom he did not favor. "Fry's plays," he said, "are poems of resignation in which tragic substance is flattened into lovely ornament" (pp. 192–193). In another essay, he admitted having changed his opinion of Fry several times and did "not intend to come to a *conclusion* about him for, I hope, a long time" (p. 273).

In Emil Roy's intriguing analyses of Fry's plays, Roy is quick to point out shortcomings. On the other hand, notably in comparisons with those whom Roy sees as influences, he often finds occasion to praise. In Fry, there is, for example, "a keener sense of evil and sin lying at the base of man's soul" than in Shaw or Wilde (p. 154). David

Daiches had serious reservations about Fry: his poetic imagery was "too indiscriminate, too loose, too much the same in different dramatic circumstances, to be the full and profound expression of completely realized drama. . . . One feels that a brilliant but lax imagination, going hand in hand with a sense of the humor and wonder of man and nature, is letting itself go. . . . It is not mature art, and we can only wonder whether it will develop until it becomes so" (pp. 166–167). James Woodfield has observed that the plays "concentrate on a group of closely related themes: the redemptive power of love, both *eros* and *agapé*; the wonder, paradoxes and unity of existence; the cycle of life, death and renewal; the operation of necessity and the nature of individuality; and man's relationship with the universe and with God." In his generally admiring analysis of *Curtmantle*, Woodfield notes: "because Fry succeeds in subordinating time, place and specific issues to the tragic pattern and to the timeless quest for identity, law, order, truth and meaning, and because the elements of language, action and character are so integrally structured, he succeeds in eloquently expressing his own sense of this mystery" (pp. 307, 317).

J. A. Collins has insisted: "Unfortunately (and unjustly as well) the name of Christopher Fry has been linked with that nebulous monster, The Establishment. And since the mid-fifties responsible theatre in England, as elsewhere, has been out to get the Establishment. Fry, in my opinion, deserves more than a summary dismissal, a dismissal (for some) decided on by applying the criterion of guilt-by-association" (p. 62). For some, Fry's focus on the aristocracy in *Venus Observed* and *The Dark Is Light Enough* was sufficient proof of his establishment leanings: for others, his preoccupation with verse, however free, was an indictment. It is true that Fry did not join John Osborne and Arnold Wesker and other playwrights then in vogue in exposing the evils of modern society. Fry was interested in quite a different kind of reform, that of the human heart in its relations with other human beings and with God. Stanley Wiersma has made this impressively clear in *More Than the Ear Discovers*. In his summation, he notes a relationship between Fry's plot structure and his poetic one, and it is in this latter structure that Fry makes "some statement about humankind's evolving idea of God. . . . The poetic structure suggested by the dramatic structure is sometimes more than the ear discovers listening to the plays. The poetic structure is first of all intuited and enjoyed, not analyzed, but analysis helps us discover what was intuited and enjoyed. The plays exist to liberate God from the liberal-conservative straitjacket" (p. 285).

Glenda Leeming, without advancing Wiersma's theological agenda, has suggested that the aristocratic milieus of *Venus Observed* and *The Dark Is Light Enough*, which once made them anathema to the socially aware, can now be seen as a "factor of their period of writing." Her summation: "Fry's plays have passed through the common cycle of great popularity followed by neglect but are now accepted as valid products of their time" (p. 168).

Whether Fry's plays prove to be, as Wiersma insists, more than merely "products of their time," remains to be seen. As texts—without the vitalizing effects of life performance and the enhancements of full-stage production—most plays seem incomplete. That is not quite the case with Fry's dramas: each is its own little world, with a form and language peculiarly appropriate and situations and characters that engage interest and thought. The richness of Fry's imagery and the elegance of his philosophical formulations, however, present formidable challenges to those who would produce his plays—even those most like medieval mysteries—in terms of finding actors who can articulate Fry's emotions and ideas, designers who can interpret his imagery, and audiences with attention spans long enough to respond to the dramas. Fry's vogue may in fact be long past, but the plays remain as textual tributes to a visionary talent always a bit unsure of himself.

SELECTED BIBLIOGRAPHY

I. BIBLIOGRAPHY. Bernice L. Schear and Eugene G. Prater, "A Bibliography on Christopher Fry," in *Tulane Drama Review* 4 (March 1960).

II. COLLECTED WORKS. A number of Fry's original manuscripts are housed at the Harvard University Theatre Collection.

Three Plays (London, 1960), includes *The Firstborn, Thor, with Angels,* and *A Sleep of Prisoners; Plays* (London, 1969), contains *Thor, with Angels* and *The Lady's Not for Burning; Plays* (London and New York, 1970), includes *The Boy with a Cart, The Firstborn,* and *Venus Observed; Plays* (London and New York, 1971), includes *A Sleep of Prisoners, The Dark Is Light Enough,* and *Curtmantle; Se-*

lected Plays (Oxford, Eng., and New York, 1985), includes *The Boy with a Cart, A Phoenix Too Frequent, The Lady's Not for Burning, A Sleep of Prisoners,* and *Curtmantle.*

III. SELECTED WORKS. *The Boy with a Cart: Cuthman, Saint of Sussex* (London, 1939; 2d ed. 1945); *Thursday's Child: A Pageant* (London, 1939); *A Phoenix Too Frequent* (London, 1946); *The Firstborn* (Cambridge, Eng., 1946; 3d ed., London and New York, 1958); *The Lady's Not for Burning* (London, 1949; rev. ed. 1950); *Thor, with Angels* (London and New York, 1949); *Venus Observed* (London and New York, 1950); *A Sleep of Prisoners* (London and New York, 1951; 2d ed. 1965); *An Experience of Critics,* pub. with W. A. Darlington et al., *The Approach to Dramatic Criticism,* ed. by Kaye Webb (London, 1952); *The Dark Is Light Enough* (London and New York, 1954); *Curtmantle: A Play* (London and New York, 1961); *The Boat That Mooed* (London and New York, 1965); *The Modern Theatre,* ed. by Robert Corrigan (New York, 1965), with a contribution by Fry; *Representative Modern Plays,* ed. by Robert Warnock (Chicago, 1965), with a contribution by Fry; *The Drama Bedside Book,* ed. by H. F. Rubinstein and J. C. Trewin (New York, 1966), with a contribution by Fry; *A Yard of Sun: A Summer Comedy* (London and New York, 1970); *The Brontës of Haworth,* 2 vols. (London, 1975); *Can You Find Me: A Family History* (Oxford, Eng., and New York, 1978); *Death Is a Kind of Love* (London, 1979); *Charlie Hammond's Sketchbook* (London, 1980); *One Thing More; or, Caedmon Construed* (London, 1985); *Genius, Talent, and Failure* (London, 1987); *Looking for a Language* (London, 1992).

IV. ESSAYS. "Comedy," in *Adelphi* 27 (November 1950); "Poetry and the Theatre," in *Adam* 19 (1951); "How Lost, How Amazed, How Miraculous We Are," in *Theatre Arts* 36 (August 1952); "Why Verse?" in *World Theatre* 4, no. 4 (1955); "Comedy," in *Tulane Drama Review* 4, no. 3 (1960); "Talking of Henry," in *Twentieth Century* (February 1969); "Theatre and History," in *Essays and Studies* 30 (1977); "Looking for a Language," in *Adam* (1980).

V. SCREENPLAYS AND TELEPLAYS. *The Canary* (London, 1950); *The Beggar's Opera,* with Denis Cannan (London, 1953); *The Queen Is Crowned* (London, 1953); *Ben Hur* (Rome, 1959); *Barabbas* (New York, 1961); *The Bible: In the Beginning,* with Jonathan Griffin (New York, 1966); *The Tenant of Wildfell Hall* (London, 1968); *The Brontës of Haworth,* in 4 parts (London, 1973); *The Best of Enemies* (London, 1976); *Sister Dora* (London, 1977); *Star over Bethlehem* (London, 1981).

VI. TRANSLATIONS. Jean Anouilh, *L'Invitation au château,* trans. as *Ring Round the Moon: A Charade with Music* (London and New York, 1950); Jean Anouilh, *L'Alouette,* trans. as *The Lark* (London, 1955); Jean Giraudoux, *La Guerre de Troie n'aura pas lieu,* trans. as *Tiger at the Gates* (London and New York, 1956; 2d ed. 1961) and as *The Trojan War Will Not Take Place* (London, 1983); Jean Giraudoux, *Pour Lucrèce,* trans. as *Duel of Angels* (London and New York, 1958); *Judith* (London, 1962),

adapted from Jean Giraudoux; Jean Giraudoux, *Plays* (London and New York, 1963), includes *Judith, Tiger at the Gates,* and *Duel of Angels; The Boy and the Magic* (London, 1964), adapted from Colette; *Peer Gynt* (London and New York, 1970; rev. ed. 1989), adapted from Henrik Ibsen; *Cyrano de Bergerac* (London and New York, 1975), adapted from Edmond Rostand; *Jean Anouilh: Five Plays,* with Timberlake Wertenbaker (London, 1986).

VII. INTERVIEWS. William B. Wahl, "A Visit to the Toft: Interview with Christopher Fry," in *Salzburg Studies in Literature* (1977); Naim Attallah, "The Oldie Interview: Christopher Fry," *The Oldie,* 29 October 1993.

VIII. BIOGRAPHICAL AND CRITICAL STUDIES. B. W. Anderson, "The Poetry of Mr. Fry," in *Spectator* (31 March 1950); William Arrowsmith, "Notes on English Verse Drama: Christopher Fry," in *Hudson Review* 3 (summer 1950); Stephen Spender, "Christopher Fry," in *Spectator* 184 (1950); Monroe K. Spears, "Christopher Fry and the Redemption of Joy," in *Poetry* 78 (April 1951); Marius Bewley, "The Verse of Christopher Fry," in *Scrutiny* 18 (June 1951); Derek Stanford, *Christopher Fry: An Appreciation* (London and New York, 1951); J. C. Trewin, *The Theatre Since 1900* (London, 1951); Audrey Williamson, *Theatre of Two Decades* (London, 1951); Harold Hobson, *The Theatre Now* (London and New York, 1953); Richard Findlater, "The Two Countesses," in *Twentieth Century* 156 (August 1954); Bonamy Dobrée, "Some London Plays, in *Sewanee Review* 63 (spring 1955); John Alexander, "Christopher Fry and Religious Comedy," in *Meanjin* 15 (autumn 1956); Harold Clurman, "Christopher Fry," in his *Lies Like Truth* (New York, 1958); David Daiches, *The Present Age in British Literature* (Bloomington, Ind., 1958); Kenneth Pickering, *Drama in the Cathedral: The Canterbury Festival Plays, 1928–1948* (London, 1958); Jacob H. Adler, "Shakespeare and Christopher Fry," in *Educational Theatre Journal* 11 (May 1959); Denis Donoghue, *The Third Voice: Modern British and American Verse Drama* (Princeton, N.J., 1959).

Eleazer Lecky, "Mystery in the Plays of Christopher Fry," in *Tulane Drama Review* 4 (March 1960); Kenneth Tynan, "Prose and the Playwright," in his *Curtains* (New York, 1961); Gerald Weales, *Religion in Modern English Drama* (Philadelphia, 1961); Geoffrey Bullough, "Christopher Fry and the 'Revolt' Against Eliot," in *Experimental Drama,* ed. by William A. Armstrong (London, 1963); Walter Kerr, "Christopher Fry," in *Essays in the Modern Drama,* ed. by Morris Freedman (Boston, 1964); John Ferguson, "*The Boy with a Cart,*" in *Modern Drama* 8 (December 1965); W. Moelwyn Merchant, *Creed and Drama: An Essay in Religious Drama* (London, 1965); Nelvin Vos, *The Drama of Comedy: Victim and Victor* (Richmond, Va., 1966); William V. Spanos, *The Christian Tradition in Modern British Verse Drama* (New Brunswick, N.J., 1967); Emil Roy, *Christopher Fry* (Carbondale, Ill., 1968).

J. A. Collins, "Poet of Paradox: The Dramas of Christopher Fry," in *Literary Half-Yearly* 12, no. 2 (July

1971); James Woodfield, "Christopher Fry's *Curtmantle: The Form of Unity*," in *Modern Drama* 17 (September 1974); Gareth L. Evans, *The Language of Modern Drama* (London and Totowa, N.J., 1977); Arnold Hinchcliffe, *Modern Verse Drama* (London, 1977); Diane Filby Gillespie, "Language and Life: Christopher Fry's Early Plays," in *Modern Drama* 21 (1978); Robert Gittings, "The Smell of Sulphur," in *Encounter* 50 (January 1978);

James Woodfield, "'The Figure of a Dance': Christopher Fry's *A Phoenix Too Frequent*," in *Ariel* 9 (July 1978).

E. Martin Browne, *Two in One* (Cambridge, Eng., and New York, 1981); Stanley M. Wiersma, *More Than the Ear Discovers: God in the Plays of Christopher Fry* (Chicago, 1983); Glenda Leeming, *Poetic Drama* (London and New York, 1989); Glenda Leeming, *Christopher Fry* (Boston, 1990).

H. RIDER HAGGARD
(1856–1925)

John L. Tucker

THERE IS SOME disagreement as to what kind of bad books Rider Haggard wrote. C. S. Lewis fondly remembered them as "good" bad ones, by which he meant adventure stories of limited skill but archetypal significance, "myths" with "roots far below the surface of the mind" (1939, p. 100; 1961, pp. 48–49). A more recent critic, Wendy Katz, sees Haggard's whole career as a defense of the British Empire, and his stories, "only superficially innocuous," as insidious agents of imperialist repression. Haggard has always belonged in the "bad book" category for those who object to popular literature. He was the best-selling writer of his day, author of thirteen nonfiction works and fifty-five novels. A factor in his success was the new high-speed printing technology, which was just beginning to open up the working-class market for cheap one-volume editions. Hostile reviews of the period show how much the establishment feared that audience: Haggard was accused of contributing to "the literature of gross excitements and vulgar display," of pandering to a "craving for coarse and violent intoxicants" (quoted in Higgins, 1981, pp. 126–127). Not all of Haggard's books are overtly lurid. He wrote several kinds of fiction, including domestic melodramas, studies of social problems, speculative fantasies, and historical romances, but he owes his fame to the African adventures of his most productive period, the years 1885–1890. Two of these have never gone out of print, and today they are Haggard's best-known books, the primary focus of this essay: *King Solomon's Mines* (1885) and *She* (1887). These novels have an independent life as entertainment for adolescents, abetted by movie adaptations and "Indiana Jones" spin-offs, but they also continue to attract serious readers. Though inferior in plot, character, and style to comparable works of the period by Robert Louis Stevenson and Rudyard Kipling, they offer disturbing insights into the po-litical and psychological anxieties of late Victorian culture.

Separating literary from documentary value in Haggard's work is not always easy. V. S. Pritchett gave an acid summary of the problem in 1960, when he noted that "Mr. E. M. Forster once spoke of the novelist sending down a bucket into the unconscious; the author of *She* installed a suction pump. He drained the whole reservoir of the people's secret desires" (pp. 277–278). Pritchett puts the best-seller in its place, but he also wants to see what the pump brought up: perhaps the vulgar machine will reveal truths that a more genteel technique cannot or will not approach. It is a feeling shared by critics of various persuasions, from Haggard's day to ours. What distinguishes Pritchett's remark is its implication that Haggard knew what he was doing. A more common assumption has been that naïveté gave Haggard access to the unconscious or, as the more recent studies have it, to the skeletons in the imperialist closet.

To a certain extent Haggard collaborated with this assumption. Imperfectly educated and unsure of his standing in the literary world, he wrote fast, revised little, and made a merit of necessity by claiming that because his brand of "romance" emerged from visionary intuition it was morally superior to realism. That infuriated the literary pundits of his own day, but it has gratified Haggard's psychologically oriented readers, who use him as a window to whatever they believe Victorian culture suppressed. Norman Etherington has collected some of their findings (1984, pp. 37–38). Henry Miller, not surprisingly, saw a surface of respectability, and beneath it "a hidden nature, a hidden being" that Haggard reached by a kind of automatic writing, "hardly stopping to think, so to speak." Carl Jung thought Haggard's "exciting" (that is, unself-conscious) narrative permitted the analyst to see "a background of unspoken psychological assumptions." Sigmund Freud recommended *She* to a patient as "a strange book, but full of hidden meaning" about "the eternal feminine, the immortality of our emotions." Politically oriented interpreters have been harsher; in their view, Haggard just could not help saying out loud what more sophisticated imperialists, racists, and antifeminists secretly thought.

LIFE

HENRY Rider Haggard was born on 22 June 1856, the eighth child of a well-to-do Norfolk family, the sixth of seven sons. His father, William Haggard, was the third squire of Bradenham, a country estate of several hundred acres; the family claimed descent from a fifteenth-century Danish knight. Rider's grandfather entered a banking house in St. Petersburg, where he met and married Elizabeth Meybohm (Rider always avoided reference to her German-Jewish ancestry). Another strain of disreputable exoticism came into the family through Rider's mother, Ella Doveton, born and partly raised in India; her maternal grandmother, who deserted her husband, was half-Indian. Sickly in early childhood, Haggard had morbid fears of death from an early age; as a small boy he was terrified of an ugly rag doll that he called "She-Who-Must-Be-Obeyed," the name he later gave to one of his most famous characters. His family thought him stupid and denied him the upper-class education that his brothers received. At age seventeen he failed the army entrance examinations and was sent to London to be tutored for the Foreign Office. He spent two years in London, frequenting an upper-class spiritualist circle and attending séances, one of which in particular was so disturbing that he never repeated the experiment. At a ball, he fell in love with a Yorkshire heiress but put off proposing to her as he had no money of his own, and no career.

The expanding empire gave Haggard a direction that shaped his character and, later, his fiction. In 1875 his father arranged a post for him as unofficial aide on the staff of the newly appointed lieutenant governor of Natal, Sir Henry Bulwer (a nephew of the novelist Edward Bulwer-Lytton), and he spent four years in southern Africa. Haggard heard frontier tales that fascinated him, and he volunteered for diplomatic visits to the interior, where he learned at first hand the language, history, and customs of the Zulu people, whom he admired. He became a protégé of Theophilus Shepstone, the secretary for native affairs, who was helping to engineer the expansion of British mercantile interests in southern Africa. In December 1876 Haggard made the 400-mile trek to Pretoria with Shepstone, whose secret mission was to annex the Transvaal for Great Britain. During negotiations with the Boer government, Haggard was one of a small committee sent to visit the Bapedi chief Secocoeni; he narrowly escaped ambush during the return journey.

On 24 May 1877, Haggard helped to raise the British flag at Pretoria, and in June he was appointed as English clerk to the colonial secretary. Despite his youth and lack of legal training he was chosen master and registrar of the new High Court of the Transvaal, for which he periodically rode a circuit of towns by ox-drawn wagon. By the end of 1877, Boers opposed to British rule were threatening Shepstone's government from within, while on the outside, native resistance to European encroachment was gathering under the powerful Zulu king, Cetshwayo. Haggard enlisted in the cavalry; he was kept in Pretoria, but many of his friends were killed when Cetshwayo's disciplined army wiped out an invading British regiment at Isandhlwana on 22 January 1879, a disaster that echoes and reechoes in Haggard's African tales. Cetshwayo's advantage was only temporary; a superior force under Sir Garnet Wolseley overwhelmed the Zulus at Ulundi, capturing Cetshwayo and burning his capital. Cetshwayo was banished, and Wolseley divided the territory into thirteen petty kingdoms, encouraging intratribal warfare. Shepstone was recalled.

Haggard was disillusioned with what he regarded as England's inept and immoral policy in southern Africa. "When we conquered the Zulu nation and sent away the Zulu king," he later wrote, "we undertook, morally at any rate, to provide for the future good government of the country: otherwise the Zulu war was unjust indeed. If we continue to fail . . . to carry out our responsibilities as a humane and Christian nation ought to do, our lapse from what is right will certainly recoil upon our own heads" (*Cetywayo and His White Neighbours*, p. 52). Meanwhile, Haggard's private plans had also collapsed. In 1877 he had obtained leave to go home to propose to his intended, but he canceled the trip when an angry letter from his father arrived telling him to stick to his work (at that point, he still had no official appointment, and no salary). The following year, Haggard's fiancée wrote that she was going to marry another man. Haggard was crushed and blamed himself for having given in to his father. Now Haggard decided on a new career; he and a friend, Arthur Cochrane, bought a farm in Natal where they planned to raise ostriches. Haggard resigned his government post in May 1879 and returned to England, hoping his father would invest in the new venture.

Haggard's father refused. Then Haggard met and proposed to Louisa Margitson, an orphan with a substantial estate in trust. Her guardian opposed the marriage, but this time Haggard had his father's support, and after winning an expensive legal battle, Rider and "Louie" were married in the summer of 1880. In November they sailed for Africa, arriving on the eve of the first Boer War. Their farm was near the Transvaal border, and for several months they were in considerable danger. The decisive Boer victory took place at nearby Majuba Hill on 27 February 1881, and the retrocession of the Transvaal to home rule was negotiated at the Haggards' house. Their first child, Arthur, known as Jock, was born in May. Convinced that the English position in southern Africa was deteriorating, the Haggards and Cochrane decided to return home, leaving a third partner to manage the farm; Haggard didn't see it again until the eve of the First World War, when he visited South Africa as a member of the Dominions Commission.

Back in England, Haggard moved his family to a London suburb and began reading for the bar. He wrote articles on South African affairs for newspapers and periodicals; his first book, *Cetywayo and His White Neighbours*, a critique of British policy in the Transvaal, was published at his own expense in 1882. Meanwhile, he had also begun a melodramatic first novel. John Cordy Jeaffreson, a novelist, biographer, and critic, read the manuscript and convinced Haggard to rewrite it, something he rarely did thereafter. On Jeaffreson's recommendation, *Dawn* was published by Hurst and Blackett in 1884. The following year, the same firm published *The Witch's Head*, which included some episodes with an African setting. Several reviewers preferred the African sections and thereby influenced, perhaps, the direction of Haggard's next efforts.

Haggard was called to the bar in January 1885. Then one of his brothers challenged him to write an adventure story to match Robert Louis Stevenson's *Treasure Island* (1883), and in six weeks Haggard wrote *King Solomon's Mines*. The manuscript was praised by the poets William Henley and Andrew Lang, who helped Haggard land his first moneymaking contract. Cassell's published the book in September 1885 after papering London with handbills advertising "the most amazing story ever written." It was an immediate success, drawing enthusiastic reviews on all sides and selling 31,000 copies in its first year. Haggard had found the mother lode, and he proceeded to mine it diligently; within a year he finished *Jess*, a realistic novel about Africa, and two more African adventure stories, *Allan Quatermain* and *She*. He changed publishers and adopted the common Victorian strategy of serialization: *Jess* began its run in the *Cornhill* magazine in May 1886, *She* in the *Graphic* in October, and *Allan Quatermain* in *Longman's* early the next year. All three titles appeared in book form in 1887, the year Haggard was elected to the Savile, a literary club at which he would make the acquaintance of prominent writers, including Walter Besant, Edmund Gosse, Arthur Conan Doyle, Henry James, H. G. Wells, and Rudyard Kipling, who became a lifelong friend.

She was an immense success, outselling *King Solomon's Mines*. Haggard stepped up production, publishing *Maiwa's Revenge, Mr. Meeson's Will,* and *Colonel Quaritch, V.C.* in 1888, and beginning *Beatrice* (1890) and *The World's Desire* (1890, cowritten with Andrew Lang). He gave up his legal practice, and early in 1887 he was able to realize his long-standing dream of visiting Egypt, where he gathered material for *Cleopatra* (1889). Haggard was selling well, but his critical reputation had begun to suffer. Stung, perhaps, by a grandiose and self-promoting article Haggard wrote for the *Contemporary Review* ("About Fiction," February 1887), critics and writers began to attack his work as vulgar and poorly crafted; several accused him of plagiarism. The latter charge had an accidental basis in fact: he had included in the first edition of *Jess* some verses sent to him by a correspondent, not knowing that they were by a third hand and already in print. Beyond that incident, the charge of plagiarism appears unfounded, although Haggard's plots and characters do reflect various influences. But the language used against him by his critics was more often that of chastisement for a social transgression: to some extent he was being blamed for encouraging working-class readership. Embittered by the controversy, he stopped reading reviews, but also in a sense accepted the critical verdict, for he came increasingly to think of his writing as a moneymaking formula.

In the summer of 1888, Haggard went to Iceland to gather material for a Viking saga, *Eric Brighteyes* (1891); the return voyage ended in a near disaster when the vessel stranded and all aboard had to be taken off in small boats. At the end of 1889 his mother died; he dedicated to her the last work of his peak period, a Zulu tale called *Nada the Lily* (1892). In the winter of 1891, Haggard's nine-year-old son Jock died, apparently of meningitis. The news reached Rider and Louie in Mexico City, where they had gone to visit friends. Haggard was so distracted with grief and guilt that even years later the family were forbidden to mention the lost child; an atmosphere of guilt and doom pervades the Mexican novel he wrote that year, *Montezuma's Daughter* (published in 1893).

After Jock's death, Haggard went into retirement in Norfolk for almost two years, writing and avoiding company. He began to rally with the birth of his daughter Lilias in December 1892 but declined a Tory invitation to stand for Parliament. Then in 1894 he was invited again to stand, this time as a Conservative candidate in East Norfolk. Espousing a program of protection for local agriculture, he campaigned hard through the first half of 1895 and was narrowly defeated in an election marked by vilification and stone throwing. Though deeply disappointed, he began turning his attention more and more to public affairs. With an income of more than £3,000 a year from his stories, he could afford to farm his expanding Norfolk estate even in a period of recession, and this interest led to a new, practical kind of writing: *A Farmer's Year* appeared in 1899, *A Gardener's Year* in 1905. He wrote and spoke in support of the garden-suburb movement in city planning. He purchased a vacation home on the Suffolk coast and experimented with plantings to prevent erosion; his efforts were nationally recognized in 1906, when he was named to a royal commission studying the problem. The public interest also prompted his 1898 novel *Doctor Therne*, a defense of smallpox vaccination, a practice unpopular at the time and opposed by the government. When the second Boer War broke out in 1899, Haggard's South African expertise was again in demand, and *Cetywayo* was reissued.

Travel always stimulated Haggard's writing. In 1900 he took his family to Florence and went on with his nephew to Rome, Naples, Cyprus, and Palestine, where he gathered material for two historical novels, *Pearl-Maiden* (1903) and *The Brethren* (1904), and a travel memoir, *A Winter Pilgrimage* (1901). In 1904 Haggard visited Egypt again, where he met the archaeologist Howard Carter, who was to discover the tomb of Tutankhamen in 1922. Haggard went back to Egypt in 1912 and again in 1924. His Egyptian research contributed to *The Way of the Spirit* (1906), *Morning Star* and *Queen Sheba's Ring* (1910), and *Smith and the Pharaohs and Other Tales* (1920); his return through Spain inspired *Fair Margaret* (1907). Psychic phenomena remained a preoccupation of Haggard's. He wrote up an account of a prescient dream for the *Journal of the Society of Psychical Research* and corresponded with Sir Oliver Lodge, a radio-wave researcher who believed in life after death and telepathy. Haggard continued to turn out fiction that imitated his early manner, including a long-delayed sequel called *Ayesha: The Return of She* (1905), and a fictionalized history of the Zulu tribes in three volumes: *Marie* (1912), *Child of Storm* (1913), and *Finished* (1917), but sales were dropping; he no longer dominated the market.

Increasingly, Haggard wanted to make practical contributions to public life. Worried by the loss of farm labor to urban manufacturing, he toured the English agricultural counties with his old friend Arthur Cochrane and wrote a series of anecdotal reports for the *Daily Express*, published in 1902 under the title *Rural England*. Haggard's message was similar to his campaign platform of 1895: revive the smallholding yeoman class with affordable loans, lower taxes, tariffs on agricultural imports, and cheap rail transport. *Rural England* won good reviews and mention in Parliament, but the government had other concerns during the financial retrenchment that followed the Boer War and took no substantial action until the proposal of a development bill in 1910. Eventually, Haggard looked abroad for inspiration; he published *Rural Denmark*, a study of Danish farm collectives, in 1911. In 1905, Haggard was appointed by the Rhodes Trust to study ways of encouraging British emigration to the dominions. In particular, he was to investigate as a possible model the Salvation Army's "labor colonies," which were established in England and the United States to retrain the urban poor for agricultural life and work.

Haggard became a friend of the Salvation Army's founder, William Booth; he visited a colony in Essex and then sailed for the United States. In Washington he met the newly elected president, Theodore Roosevelt, who knew and admired Haggard's book *Rural England;* a friendship sprang up that was to last until Roosevelt's death in 1919. Traveling by train, Haggard visited Ohio, Colorado, Salt Lake City, and California, then went on to Toronto and Ottawa. Published in 1905 as a government blue book and then commercially reprinted as *Report on the Salvation Army Colonies* (1905), Haggard's report received universal praise. His resettlement program was debated in Parliament, but it was shelved as too expensive. Disappointed, Haggard accepted a commission from William Booth to write *Regeneration* (1910), an account of Salvation Army work in the English slums. In 1912, Haggard's public spirit was acknowledged with a knighthood and membership in a royal commission to study economic and social conditions in the dominions. That mission kept him traveling for two years—first to India, Ceylon, and Australia, returning to England via San Francisco and New York; then to South Africa and Rhodesia; finally to Newfoundland and Nova Scotia on the brink of the First World War.

Haggard's nephew, Mark Haggard, was killed in action in September 1914. His friends the Kiplings lost their son John the following autumn. Bombs dropped in zeppelin raids shook the windows of Haggard's Norfolk house and cratered the fields. Haggard drilled with local militia and made recruiting speeches. He went back on tour in 1916 to gather information for a plan to resettle soldiers after the war, visiting South Africa, Australia, New Zealand, and Vancouver, then crossing Canada to sail home from New York. A scaled-down version of his plan became the Empire Settlement Bill of 1922. He continued to write fiction throughout the war; reluctantly, he gave up farming in 1917.

Signs of discouragement and disorientation can be seen in Haggard's postwar years. Along with Kipling he joined the anti-Bolshevik Liberty League, which was disbanded following an embezzlement scandal; he became increasingly anti-Semitic and recanted his earlier support for the Zionist movement. He released eleven more nov-

els, but his sale of film rights now made him more money than did publication. Like Kipling, he saw the King Tut fever that followed Howard Carter's sensational discovery of 1922 as the kind of superstition "which always presaged the downfall of great civilisations" (quoted in Pocock, p. 230). He left Egypt for the last time in 1924, having seen "the ancient land . . . degraded with tourists, harlots and brass bands" (quoted in Pocock, p. 234). That fall he developed a bladder infection, and his illness accelerated during the winter. He died in a London nursing home on 14 May 1925, at the age of sixty-eight.

KING SOLOMON'S MINES *AND OTHER AFRICAN ADVENTURE STORIES*

HAGGARD'S famous narrator, Allan Quatermain, is often said to be loosely based on a well-known hunter of the late nineteenth century, Frederick Selous. Quatermain's age was revised in later tales to make a more credible sequence, but in *King Solomon's Mines,* his first outing, he is about fifty-five years old, a widower with a grown son in England, misogynistic, practical, and not well educated. Two young Englishmen, Sir Henry Curtis and Captain John Good, RN, enlist Quatermain to help locate Curtis' younger brother George, who has gone in search of Solomon's legendary diamond mines. Quatermain knows where to look, for he has in his possession a treasure map, the gift of a dying Portuguese adventurer whose sixteenth-century ancestor had drawn it with his own blood. The travelers hire three African servants, among them a former comrade of Quatermain's from the battle of Isandhlwana, a handsome, mysterious warrior called Umbopa, who wishes to return to the land of his birth somewhere in the north.

It takes fourteen weeks to reach the last outpost on the map. After that comes desert, then a climb over one of the mountains called Sheba's Breasts, during which one of the Africans dies of exposure. On the far side lies "an earthly paradise," traversed by a great road, laid out, Quatermain assumes, by an "Old World engineer" (chap. 7). They fall in with a party of Kukuana soldiers, led by an "old gentleman" called Infadoos, son of the former king, and Scragga, son of Twala, the current king. The English represent themselves to the "astonished aborigines" as immortals from another world. Unfortunately for the fastidious Captain Good, he is half-shaved and trouserless when the natives first catch sight of him, and they so admire his (to them) other-worldly appearance that he has to maintain it throughout the expedition. At Loo, the Kukuana capital, the travelers meet Twala and his witch-finder, Gagool, a "wizened, monkey-like" crone. She foresees white people coming again to the land, drawn by the "bright stones," bringing "rivers of blood" (chap. 9). That night, Umbopa reveals himself to Infadoos and the Englishmen as Ignosi, the rightful heir to the Kukuana throne, and enlists their aid in an insurrection against Twala. Good, who happens to have an almanac, suggests using a forthcoming solar eclipse to awe the wavering Kukuana chiefs. The day turns out to be scheduled for an annual ceremony in which the most beautiful maiden of the tribe is put to death. Foulata, the victim, throws herself on Good's mercy, clasping his "beautiful white legs"; at that moment the eclipse begins (chap. 11). Scragga tries to spear Curtis, who kills him, signaling panic; the rebels withdraw under cover of dark to a hilltop camp prepared by Infadoos.

Greatly outnumbered, Ignosi has the advantages of high ground, a disciplined army of veteran troops, and his English friends, especially the giant Curtis, who arrays himself in native battle dress and fights with the savagery of his Viking ancestors. Ignosi's army repels three enemy assaults, taking terrible losses, and wins the field. Curtis kills Twala in single combat, and Ignosi is proclaimed king. Under compulsion, Gagool then shows the way to the mines, located in a vast pit at the junction of three mountains, the doorway flanked by colossal sculptures. The travelers pass through a chamber where the bodies of former kings are seated at a stone table, slowly being turned into stalactites by dripping silica. Gagool presses a hidden lever and a stone door rises, revealing Solomon's treasure chamber, filled with ivory, gold, and uncut diamonds. Gagool tries to trap them in the chamber and stabs Foulata; the stone door falls, crushing Gagool. Buried alive, the three Englishmen prepare to die, but a draft of fresh air reveals a trapdoor. Quatermain fills his pockets with diamonds, and the Englishmen make their way through underground passages, finally emerging through a jackal hole near the bottom of the mine pit. Ignosi bids his friends

farewell but announces that the borders will henceforth be closed to white men. Recrossing the desert, they come upon Curtis's brother George at an oasis where he has been recuperating from a rock fall. The novel ends with a letter to Quatermain from Curtis detailing the sale of the diamonds; Quatermain decides to sail to England to get the "history" printed.

King Solomon's Mines can be read simply as an escapist adventure tale for young readers. But the novel's African setting is neither casual nor trivial; it invites us to consider the book as both belonging to and reflecting the history of British imperialism. It is useful to recall that when Haggard went out to Africa in 1875 the heroic phase of European exploration was already over, and large-scale economic exploitation was beginning. The year of Haggard's birth had seen the conclusion of David Livingstone's second expedition, during which he crossed Africa and discovered Victoria Falls; Richard Burton and John Speke had located Lake Tanganyika shortly thereafter. The British had been in South Africa since 1795, using Cape Colony as a supply base for their East India transports. They were not the only Europeans in South Africa: England had recognized the Boer republics (founded by Dutch settlers) in the 1850s. Having subjugated the coastal tribes, England could afford to ignore the interior; the first diamond strike even occurred on the coast, in Cape Colony. But the Kimberley diamond field, discovered in 1870 in what was then called Griqualand West, called for a new policy: the territory was annexed the following year, creating vast new fortunes for entrepreneurs like Cecil Rhodes and setting in motion the forces that led to the costly and humiliating Boer wars. The Transvaal gold rush of 1886 accelerated the process. Along the way, the competing powers wiped out the remnants of the Zulu and Ndebele empires and an ancient way of life.

King Solomon's Mines both evades and reflects the violence of this transition. "Kukuanaland" is an African Shangri-la, protected by deserts and an impassable mountain range. Haggard is careful not to locate the land too precisely; actual place-names give us a general orientation north and west of the Transvaal, but the names become fictitious as we move into the territory: rivers and towns no longer correspond to the map. As Haggard wrote in *Cetywayo and His White Neighbours*, "The Transvaal is a country without a history. Its very existence was hardly known of until about fifty years ago. Of its past we know nothing. The generation who peopled its great plains have passed utterly out of the memory and even the tradition of man, leaving no monument to mark that they have existed, not even a tomb" (p. 87). The most remote outpost is identified as subject to Lobengula, one of the last Ndebele chiefs to hold out against European imperialism; Quatermain calls him "a very great scoundrel" (*King Solomon's Mines,* chap. 4). The portrait of Twala probably owes something to Lobengula, who was nearly six feet tall, weighed over twenty stone, and was celebrated for unpredictable cruelty. Lobengula had one of his advisers "smelt out" as a witch and murdered, an event that may have suggested Gagool's witch-hunts in the novel. Another territorial indicator is the fact that the Kukuanas are not the original inhabitants; all around are relics of an earlier civilization: a wondrous road, remarkable reliefs and inscriptions of an apparently "Semitic" or "Phoenician" type, and the mines themselves. Contemporary observers like Sir Harry Johnston described Zimbabwe as "dotted" with stonework villages, towns, and forts of a type that no indigenous race was known to have built in Africa; Johnston theorized that they had been built by pre-Islamic Arabs. At the time, Zimbabwe was widely thought to be the biblical Ophir, site of King Solomon's fabled mines. In the sixteenth century, the Portuguese had found the Zimbabwe works already in decay; they were thought to have been taken over by a mysterious African kingdom that had also disappeared.

All this must have been in Haggard's mind when he drew his picture of Kukuanaland. Interestingly, Haggard's novel seems to discourage commercial exploitation; his Englishmen get in and get out with their private fortunes, but they approve of Ignosi's decision to close the borders. *Allan Quatermain* (1887) has a similar ending: the land of Zu-Vendis, where Curtis elects to settle, is closed to outsiders. The pattern is not as anti-imperialist as it looks. It belongs to a classic imperial fantasy, along with the notion of a preexisting white culture and the outsider's frame tale. Kipling used the same three elements for his story "The Man Who Would Be King" (1888). Like Robert Louis Stevenson's *Treasure Island* or the submarine world of Jules Verne's *Twenty Thousand Leagues Under the Sea* (1870), Kukuanaland has to be kept from becoming just another plundered re-source, which would expose the rapacity of invasion, as the devastated trading stations do in Joseph Conrad's *Heart of Darkness* (1902). In Stevenson, Verne, and Haggard, closure is deceptive, for there are no consequences in romance. Sometimes, as Arthur Conan Doyle discovered when he tried to kill off Sherlock Holmes, the public will not let the story end. If Quatermain never returns to Kukuanaland, it is because history annexed the territory so successfully. In 1889, Cecil Rhodes's British South Africa Company got its charter; in 1896, the Ndebele were driven into exile. Their territory was eventually renamed Rhodesia.

In *King Solomon's Mines,* the history of imperialism intersects with the history of a literary genre. When Haggard identified his African tales as "romances," he was deliberately taking sides in a well-publicized controversy about the nature and purpose of fiction. At one extreme stood Robert Louis Stevenson, who maintained in "A Humble Remonstrance" (1884) that fiction could not hope to imitate reality, and ought not to try. Henry James disagreed, arguing first, in "The Art of Fiction" (1884, rev. ed. 1888), that genre labels mattered less than sincerity of performance, and later, in the preface to *The American* (1907), that a novel need not be exotic to be essentially a romance. "The real," James suggested, meant "the things we cannot possibly *not* know, sooner or later," while "the romantic" stood for everything "we never *can* directly know; the things that can reach us only through the beautiful circuit and subterfuge of our thought and desire" (quoted in *The Art of Criticism: Henry James on the Theory and the Practice of Fiction,* ed. by William Veeder and Susan M. Griffin, 1986, p. 279). Ironically, James's early stories share a theme with Haggard's romances: both are haunted by a sense of potential violence beneath the veneer of civilized life. "Civilization is only savagery silver-gilt," Haggard wrote in the introduction to *Allan Quatermain,* a feeling that can be traced back to Alfred, Lord Tennyson's bleak vision of "nature red in tooth and claw" (*In Memoriam,* 1850), and the impact of Charles Darwin's *On the Origin of Species* (1859) and *The Descent of Man* (1871). Anthropological variants of the same idea occur in the work of Haggard's friend and mentor Andrew Lang, who in *Custom and Myth* (1884) studied modern survivals of ancient heroic ideals; it was Haggard's admiration for Zulu warriors and Vikings that recommended him to Lang.

King Solomon's Mines offers its English heroes a chance to recover that warrior ethos. Curtis, the Viking throwback, is the story's fighting ideal; Captain Good, with his fussy monocle, is the hero's comic foil. In chapter 4, Good's obsession with punctilio nearly gets him killed by a wounded elephant: "A dreadful thing happened: Good fell a victim to his passion for civilized dress. Had he consented to discard his trousers and gaiters as we had . . . it would have been all right, but as it was his trousers cumbered him in that desperate race." Good's trousers are denied him throughout his stay in Kukuanaland. By contrast, when Curtis arms for battle in full native costume he unites the Viking romance of England's past with the African romance of its imperial present. Curtis does not have to "go native," he *is* native; he needs the war to reveal his true nature, which he cannot experience in England.

The battle scenes are perhaps the book's main reason for being: they showcase one of the most important trophies Haggard brought back from Africa, namely, his knowledge of Zulu military genius. It is interesting to speculate on Haggard's attraction to those who inflicted such a humiliation on the English at Isandhlwana in 1879. The Zulu warrior world is an army of bachelors, for one thing (Haggard is silent on the homosexual behavior noted by other travelers), perfect in its feudal discipline (Haggard frequently compares the Zulu war machine to Bismarck's), and expansionist in its direction and aims. Haggard's admiration is partly fueled by nostalgia, for the modern army has eradicated heroism. Just before the battle, Good groans, "'Oh, for a gatling! . . . I would clear the plain in twenty minutes'" (chap. 13). Some of Haggard's readers were probably happy to recollect that the Gatling gun helped to scatter Cetshwayo's forces and end the real Zulu War of 1879. As he would later do in *She*, Haggard expresses his contradictory feelings by dispersing them among several characters: Curtis gets to play Zulu, while Quatermain remembers Isandhlwana.

Ignosi's Grays are instructed to draw Twala's forces to a "last stand" in the center while the wings slip around behind—this tactic is always described as the Zulu style of battle, used by Chaka in his generation and by Cetshwayo in his. Quatermain admires the stoic discipline of the Grays, "foredoomed to die" by a strategy of "wise recklessness of human life": "Never before had I seen such an absolute devotion to the idea of duty, and such a complete indifference to its bitter fruits" (chap. 14). The scene is deliberately classical, echoing Thomas Macaulay's *Lays of Ancient Rome* (1842): the Grays are set to hold a narrow gorge "as the three Romans once held the bridge against thousands" (chap. 14). The battle seesaws, heightening the tension. Then comes one of Haggard's most vivid passages:

> Suddenly, like puffs of smoke from the mouth of a cannon, the attacking regiment broke away in flying groups, their white head-dresses streaming behind them in the wind, and left their opponents victors, indeed, but, alas! no more a regiment. Of the gallant triple-line, which, forty minutes before had gone into action three thousand strong, there remained at most some six hundred blood-bespattered men; the rest were under foot. And yet they cheered and waved their spears in triumph, and then, instead of falling back upon us as we expected, they ran forward, for a hundred yards or so, after the flying groups of foemen, took possession of a gently rising knoll of ground, and, resuming the old triple formation, formed a threefold ring around it. And then, thanks be to God, standing on the top of a mound for a minute, I saw Sir Henry, apparently unharmed, and with him our old friend Infadoos. Then Twala's regiments rolled down upon the doomed band, and once more the battle closed in.
>
> (chap. 14)

Haggard's prose rhythms gain confidence as he warms to his real subject. Just at this moment Quatermain starts to interject one of his customary antiwar remarks, but he finds himself stirred for the first time:

> I am, to be honest, a bit of a coward, and certainly in no way given to fighting, though, somehow, it has often been my lot to get into unpleasant positions, and to be obliged to shed man's blood. But I have always hated it. . . . At this moment, however, for the first time in my life, I felt my bosom burn with martial ardor. Warlike fragments from the "Ingoldsby Legends," together with numbers of sanguinary verses from the Old Testament, sprang up in my brain like mushrooms in the dark; my blood, which hitherto had been half-frozen with horror, went beating through my veins, and there came upon me a savage desire to kill and spare not.
>
> (chap. 14)

So the "quarter-man" gets swept up along with the Dane. "Bit of a coward" is partly just trick characterization, but it's also an index of tension. We have been invited to see Quatermain as the quintessential modest British hero; Curtis reads him that way, but Curtis never knows him as intimately as we do in the battle scene. "Cowardice" is the only word available to code-bound males for resistance to this abnormal situation, where the civilized man turns savage.

Haggard's version of imperialist romance makes use of both racial and sexual fantasies. Haggard's portrait of Twala is obviously racist: "an enormous man with the most entirely repulsive countenance we had ever beheld. The lips were as thick as a negro's, the nose was flat, it had but one gleaming black eye (for the other was represented by a hollow in the face), and its whole expression was cruel and sensual to a degree" (chap. 9). Interestingly, Haggard treats no other African this way; the Kukuanas are generally handsome and dignified. But Twala is Curtis' mythic antagonist; their single combat is inevitable. Haggard invokes a "native law" that forbids Ignosi from championing his own cause, but it is obviously a piece of stage management in order to create the scene Haggard and his audience wanted to see: the blond berserker against the huge, black, one-eyed monster. It's a gladiatorial fantasy right out of the penny dreadfuls, rendered in the appropriate prose style: "The ex-king laughed savagely, and stepped forward and faced Curtis. . . . They were a well-matched pair" (chap. 14).

Plot is equally irrelevant to that hoary old trick, the white man's display of "magic" timed to coincide with an eclipse. (Mark Twain parodied this scene in *A Connecticut Yankee at King Arthur's Court* [1889], turning the tables on Haggard by depicting British savages.) Haggard's version links fraudulent power and deception with sexual fantasy. He stages the eclipse on the occasion of a girls' dance (chap. 11), at which Twala invites the Englishmen to choose the most beautiful. Quatermain picks Foulata, "unthinkingly," for the prize is death. In terms of plot, the moment is absurd: why would Quatermain let Twala use him this way? To the modern eye, of course, the answer is that Quatermain *wants* to kill beautiful women: he has already said that "women bring trouble as surely as the night follows the day" (chap. 11), and all along his comments on the native beauties have a ring of falseness. "Unthinkingly," indeed—unconsciously, Quatermain *is* Twala; he predicts Twala's death in chapter 13, and after the battle, finding the king abandoned by his army, Quatermain says, "notwithstanding his cruelties and

misdeeds, a pang of compassion shot through me as I saw him thus 'fallen from his high estate.' . . . Poor savage! he was learning the lesson that fate teaches to most who live long enough, . . . that he who is defenceless and fallen finds few friends and little mercy. Nor, indeed, in this case did he deserve any" (chap. 14). There is a pattern of approach and avoidance in this passage, with its quotation from John Dryden (*Alexander's Feast*, 1697) leading to sudden reversal and revulsion.

Haggard seems to have been unconscious of these ambiguities; he was protected perhaps by the conventions of romance. The eclipse trick is simply felt to be inseparable from the rescue-the-maiden-from-the-savage-sacrifice scene, which then gets linked to the white-hero-nursed-back-to-health-by-adoring-dusky-maiden gimmick (otherwise known as the Pocahontas myth), which turns the focus of attention back to Good, the susceptible sailor. The triplet of Quatermain-Good-Curtis displays three faces of one adventurer. If we reconstructed his career, we would have a myth representing some of the contradictory motives behind the imperialist enterprise. Haggard may not have been aware of how disturbing such a revelation might be. In any case, the effect of his narrative strategy here and in *She* is to keep the whole potentially disturbing myth in view, simply segregating its most volatile elements. Thus, Quatermain looks on disapprovingly while Good acts out the sexual fantasy, only possible in a state of weakness; he must have "rescued" the maiden for this to occur. Quatermain admits that Foulata is lovely and true, but, he tells Twala, "we white men wed only with white women like ourselves." Significantly, Twala is given the tolerant line, "Women's eyes are always bright, whatever the color." Putting this sentiment in Twala's mouth turns colorblindness into cynicism, making prejudice seem moral and wise by comparison. Quatermain says that it is women in general he distrusts; he is meant to seem not so much racist as misogynist, but as we will see even more clearly in *She*, these two antagonisms often overlap.

SHE

THE story is told by L. Horace Holly, a Cambridge mathematician in his forties. Twenty years before the main events of the story, Holly's friend Vincey, fatally ill, begs him to become the guardian of his five-year-old son, Leo. Vincey claims to be the sixty-fifth descendant of one Kallikrates, a Greek priest of Isis, who in 339 B.C. broke his vows and fled with an Egyptian princess, Amenartas, down the east coast of Africa, where they were shipwrecked and taken in by the white queen of a savage people. The queen, Ayesha, murdered Kallikrates; his Egyptian wife escaped to Athens. Amenartas' descendants moved to Rome, Lombardy, Brittany, and finally England, where they rose to power and wealth. Vincey settles half his income on Holly, the other half to be saved for Leo, and entrusts Holly with a mysterious chest to be opened on Leo's twenty-fifth birthday.

Leo grows up with Holly and a servant named Job. On the appointed day, Leo and Holly open the chest and find an ancient sherd inscribed with writing in several languages. The main text is by the princess Amenartas; it describes her flight with Kallikrates, shipwreck, and journey inland to a queen who lives in a "hollow mountain." Amenartas tells how the queen took them to a "great pit" where she stood in the flames of a "rolling Pillar of Life that dies not," from which she emerged "unharmed, and yet more beautiful." She offered to make Kallikrates immortal if he would kill his wife and marry her, but he refused; she slew him and sent her rival away. Amenartas gave birth aboard ship and came to Athens. Her inscription records her command to her son to "seek out the woman, and learn the secret of Life" so that he may avenge his father; should he "fear or fail," he must pass on the mission to his descendants (chap. 3).[1]

Leo, Holly, and Job undertake the quest. Shipwrecked on the east coast of Africa with their Arab steersman, they find the river mentioned by Amenartas and follow it into the interior. At the point of exhaustion, they are taken by a party of Amahagger, a cannibal tribe speaking an Arabic dialect. Their leader, a courtly old man named Billali, has been sent to escort them to Kôr, the hidden city of their queen, whom they call "She-Who-Must-Be-Obeyed," or more briefly, "She." Ustane, a young Amahagger woman, falls in love with Leo. Job repulses another woman of the tribe, and in revenge she incites the band to eat the Arab sailor, Mahomed. A fight breaks out, in which Leo is seri-

ously wounded. Billali intervenes, and the journey continues, with Ustane going along to care for Leo. Reaching a great volcanic mountain, they are blindfolded and taken through a tunnel up into a "huge rock-surrounded cup" with colossal ruins in the distance. Dug into the volcano wall are extensive catacombs where She and her retinue of mutes live among the embalmed dead of an ancient civilization.

Leo becomes gravely ill. Leaving Job and Ustane to care for him, Billali and Holly wait on the queen, who appears shrouded in gauze like "a corpse in its grave-clothes" (chap. 12). Inviting Holly into her "boudoir," she tells him her name, Ayesha, and something of her story; the astonished Holly begins to have an inkling of her great age. She believes in reincarnation, mentions that she is waiting for the rebirth of her lost beloved, and hints at having discovered the secret of prolonging life. Holly asks to see her face, but when she unveils, he shrinks back, "blinded and amazed" by an "awful loveliness and purity" that also strikes him as somehow evil (chap. 13). That night, Holly discovers the cavern where for two thousand years Ayesha has kept the preserved body of Kallikrates. The next day, Ayesha recognizes Leo as a reincarnation of Kallikrates and gives him a medicine that saves his life. Ustane proclaims her love, but Ayesha frightens her away. She comes back in secret, but Ayesha kills her with "some mysterious electric agency or overwhelming will-force," and over Ustane's body Ayesha bewitches Leo with her beauty (chap. 20). She uncovers the body of Kallikrates, revealing features exactly like Leo's, and then destroys the corpse. Leo weeps for Ustane, but confesses himself, like Holly, in love with Ayesha.

Ayesha plans to take Leo to the Fire of Life, marry him, and then make him ruler of England, a prospect that fascinates and horrifies the Englishmen. Across the volcano, they enter a natural cave and come to a chasm, which they bridge with a plank, resting the far end on a huge "rocking-stone." They cross safely but lose the plank; then they descend into the "dead heart" of the volcano. They proceed through passages and caves to a cavern where they witness the periodic appearance of "an awful cloud or pillar of fire," which Ayesha says is "the substance from which all things draw their energy, the bright Spirit of this Globe" (chap. 25). Leo is afraid to enter, so Ayesha goes first. She removes her clothes, kisses

---

[1] Quotations from *She* are taken from the 1888 version, reprinted in Etherington, *The Annotated She.*

Leo, and stands in the fire. First she looks glorious; then she ages hideously, shrinking until she is "no larger than a monkey" (chap. 26). With her last words she promises to come again and regain her beauty. Job dies of shock. Leo's hair turns white; neither he nor Holly wants to live forever now. They each take a lock of Ayesha's hair and dedicate themselves to her memory. Returning with no plank, they have to jump the chasm; the rock tips back, sealing the passage to the Place of Life. They struggle out and find Billali, who helps them over the volcano wall and through the swamp. After "incredible hardships and privations," they reach the coast, take ship, and arrive in England two years to the day from their first departure. The story ends with Holly dreaming of meeting Ayesha again in "the next act" of "the great drama."

The plot of *She* offers two distinct perspectives, male and female, yielding different constructions of the same events. From Leo and Holly's standpoint the story is a phallic nightmare: progressive unveiling and penetration culminate in death and crippling; from Ayesha's standpoint the story is a cyclical reenactment of frustrated desire. From either perspective the plot describes pathology. Ayesha murders her beloved, sleeps by his corpse until he is reincarnated, then dies on their wedding day. Seeking to verify his identity, Leo takes the sexual place of his father and becomes both lover and killer of the woman who has murdered him.

Like several of Haggard's novels, *She* is told by a middle-aged misogynist, not handsome, an experienced outdoorsman, adept at dealing with natives; in short, Allan Quatermain again. Haggard's narrators of this type leave looks and love to another man who usually gets the girl and most of the glory. In *She,* however, Leo, the ostensible hero, plays a significantly diminished role. He is unconscious when the whaleboat shoots the breakers, asleep when the party is surprised by the Amahagger, delirious on the journey to Kôr, and barely alive at the first encounter with Ayesha—he does not even see her until after she saves him from death. He cannot protect Ustane from being marked, banished, and killed. After submitting to Ayesha's erotic power he does little but stand around in attitudes of horror or joy, and finally hangs back from the Fire of Life, with fatal consequences. All this passivity bothered Andrew Lang. "There is a difficulty about Leo," he wrote to Hag-

gard. "He is not made a very interesting person. Probably he was only a fine animal" (quoted in Etherington, 1991, p. 212). Lang evidently missed the point. To make it clearer, Haggard wrote a satirical postscript for the introduction, putting Lang's objection in the mouth of the supposed editor: What, he wonders, would draw an "intellect" like Ayesha's to a "not . . . particularly interesting" man, when a mind like Holly's was available? Anyone who would ask such a question, Haggard implies, does not know much about sex. But the joke backfires. By insisting on disconnection between sex and mind, it spotlights the fear of sex that permeates the story.

As in *King Solomon's Mines,* Haggard sends the heroes of *She* into a psychologized landscape resembling the female body. After a journey upriver to a barrier swamp, they are carried by litter to "cup-shaped" volcanic hills where there are caves deep in "the living rock." Kôr lies on the bed of a drained lake, accessible, like Ayesha's boudoir and the Place of Life, only through tunnels. Haggard's symbolism is never subtle. In chapter 24, for example, the travelers work their way out to "the very tip of the spur . . . that throbbed and jumped . . . like a living thing." This phallic bridge gives access, in the next chapter, to "bottomless deeps," a "cleft" going down "to the very womb of the world," which they eventually reach by passing through an "inverted cone or tunnel" and a cavern with "rent and jagged walls . . . torn in the bowels of the rock." Haggard's erotic scenery might be amusing if it weren't so persistently associated with death: the womblike caves are filled with corpses. In chapter 16, Holly lifts graveclothes to see the bodies of a woman with a baby at her breast and her husband lying opposite; another pair are found embraced, each with a dagger wound over the heart, under the inscription "Wedded in Death."

Such necrophiliac images are variants of the novel's central motif, the mummy, repeated and elaborated throughout the story as a focus of sexual, political, and aesthetic fears. The mummy transcends time: it contains and signifies a history, as writing does. In this respect, *She* has affinities with another archaeologically inspired work, John Keats's "Ode on a Grecian Urn" (1820), but the mummy is an older and more alien artifact, a claustrophobically literal container. Keats's urn remains a "still unravish'd bride," but the mummified body is twice violated—the first time, ironically, in order to prevent the second. Of course, the more elaborate the defenses, the more they invite penetration. Inscriptions are deciphered, labyrinths explored. Grave robbing is both the structural principle and the theme of Haggard's novel. At the center of the book is an outraged body, terrible and alluring, wrapped in narrative. The reader who uncovers it becomes an archaeologist, tomb robber, colonial freebooter, and rapist.

In the first edition, *She* begins its striptease even before the title page, with colored facsimiles offering front and back views of the "Sherd of Amenartas." Behind this flat illusion lay a three-dimensional forgery, an actual artifact that Haggard "compounded," as he put it in his autobiography, with the help of his secretary, Agnes Barber (later his sister-in-law). The meaning of the sherd remains hidden until chapter 3, when Holly and Leo open a series of nested boxes, the innermost a "casket" (in later editions, "coffer") of Egyptian silver. The writings inscribed on the sherd require ten pages of transcription—the nested-box motif again in linguistic form. We get the "original" Greek supposedly written by Amenartas, then a more readable cursive version, a 1495 translation into black-letter Latin, Holly's "Expanded Version of the Above Medieval Latin Translation," Vincey's "accurate and elegant" English version, a black-letter Latin inscription dated 1445 (for which Holly provides "Expanded," "Old English Black-Letter," and "Modernised" equivalents), an Elizabethan-style entry dated 1564, and an eighteenth-century misquotation of *Hamlet* with a learned footnote tracing the error to an acting copy circa 1740! Haggard obviously had fun concocting all this apparatus, but it was a game he took seriously. The map and geographical clues in *King Solomon's Mines* had fooled some readers to the point of actually planning mining expeditions. This time Haggard aimed to put one over on the dons. He hired scholars to produce the Greek and Latin texts he needed and rewrote his manuscript to match the results. The sherd itself, he insisted, was "good enough to fool experts" (quoted in Etherington, 1991, pp. 213–214, nn. 6–8). All this was partly defensive cover for his own incomplete education and partly satire (in the course of the story, Holly takes several swipes at university stuffed shirts). But the sherd and its texts are also mummy wrappings, a teasing invitation to lay bare the hidden body, and the effort Haggard put into making them seem real suggests that he took the inner story seriously, too.

This inner story seems to have been one that Haggard could not directly avow. The text, however, is full of hints. In chapter 23, when the travelers camp among the ruins of Kôr, Ayesha lights a lamp with tinder made from "broken fragments of mummy carefully damped." Haggard's "editor" adds a footnote: "After all we are not much in advance of the Amahagger in these matters. 'Mummy,' that is pounded ancient Egyptian, is I believe, a pigment much used by artists, and especially by those of them who direct their talents to the reproduction of the works of the old masters." This could be a poker-faced crack at Haggard's competition, mere copyists, recycling the dead for profit. It could also be an uneasy self-portrait, suggesting Oedipal anxieties: to "reproduce" like an "old master," the artist must make use of a dead "mummy." Haggard wanted to think of himself as an "artist," and he had already begun to use Egyptian "pigment." As a teenager, he had been fascinated by Egyptian antiquities in the Amherst family museum at Didlington, Norfolk, which seems to have provided his fiction with a recurring motif: in his first novel, *Dawn* (1884), one of the leading men falls for a widow who has a private Egyptian collection; in *The Ancient Allan* (1920), a drug taken in a private museum sends Quatermain into the past for a rendezvous with an Egyptian priestess.

In 1886, when Haggard wrote *She*, he was planning the first of several trips to Egypt; these would eventually contribute to *Cleopatra* (1889), *The World's Desire* (1890), *Ayesha: The Return of She* (1905), *The Way of the Spirit* (1906), *Smith and the Pharaohs* (1920), and *Queen of the Dawn* (1925). Egyptian romance was good business, partly, no doubt, because it helped to allay the discomfort of England's actual experience in Africa and the Levant. But Haggard wasn't just getting up local color. He was an amateur of anthropology and archaeology, with a library of learned works; he became a friend of E. Wallis Budge, whose translation of *The Book of the Dead* he studied and admired, and later of the archaeologist Howard Carter, who discovered the tomb of Tutankhamen in 1922. Haggard visited digs on several occasions and once brought home two mummy teeth for his wife's birthday. There is even a story that in 1886, Haggard's brother Andrew, serving in Egypt, sent him a mummy; he kept it overnight in his study, and it apparently gave him an experience so disturbing that he donated it the next day to the Castle Museum at Norwich.

In *She* the mummy often burns, an ironic counterpoint to the Fire of Life. En route to Kôr in chapter 10, Holly sees "corpse-candles," flickering balls of marsh gas, which represent to him the spirit clogged with flesh. In chapter 9, Billali tells how as a boy he fell in love with "the body of a fair woman." His mother, "a watchful woman," intervened, "half in dread, and half in anger," and fired the corpse by the hair, burning it down to the feet. Billali shows Holly a relic of the beloved, "a beautifully shaped and almost white woman's foot, looking as fresh and firm as though it had but now been placed there." Holly imagines its history as a series of disembodied acts: the foot stealing to a lover's side, or set on "the proud neck of a conqueror bent at last to woman's beauty," with "the lips of nobles and of kings . . . pressed upon its jewelled whiteness." In imaginatively appropriating the foot, Holly identifies himself with Billali, his surrogate father. Holly admires Billali's long white beard, addresses him in Arabic as "my father" and always speaks of "the old gentleman" with affectionate respect. "Billali" can also be read as an echo of William, Haggard's father's name. Here again, the mummy motif hints at repressed psychosexual conflict, an inner story of mutilation and self-abasement alternating with grandiosity, where flesh is displaced—fresh not as it was when alive, but as it was when the boy hid it—and doubled: preserved, but wrapped "in the remains of a rotting rag."

Billali's story prefigures Holly's obsession with Ayesha, in whom desire and death are also conjoined. Haggard approaches her with a tone that veers between horror, prurience, music-hall comedy, and wooden objectivity. Partly just a failure of technique, these shifts may also indicate the extent to which Haggard's materials disturbed him. Like many of her literary kind, Keats's "Lamia," for instance (1820), and the mysterious Geraldine who seduces the title character in Samuel Taylor Coleridge's "Christabel" (1816), Ayesha has snakelike qualities; "a certain serpent-like grace that was more than human," says Holly. Every description of her combines evil and purity: her beauty is a dark sublimity, a glory "not all of heaven" (chap. 13). Her very "diablerie" attracts, a common theme

in late-nineteenth-century literature, as Etherington observes, citing "the fascination of the abomination" in Joseph Conrad's *Heart of Darkness* and Bram Stoker's *Dracula* (Etherington, 1991, p. 228, n. 1). Ayesha is Byronically sad, like a female Manfred, with "a look of unutterable experience and of deep acquaintance with grief and passion." Above all, she makes sexuality dangerous. When Holly asks to see her face, she teases him with the story of Actaeon, who was turned into a stag and torn to pieces by his own hounds for having spied on the goddess Diana bathing. To see Ayesha is to become a voyeur and blasphemer, risking madness, bestiality, and death.

The beautiful-but-fatal enchantress is found, of course, in ancient religions around the world; in Western culture, images of her were transmitted in ballads and folktales, and via medieval representations of the dance of death. Haggard may have been familiar with this tradition in a general way, though he was, as he admitted, "no great reader." Ayesha's name and some of her characteristics could have been suggested by Bulwer-Lytton's *A Strange Story* (1862), which has several thematic parallels to *She*. Various mythical and historical sources have also been suggested, including white queens rumored to exist in the Africa of Haggard's day. Ayesha first appears to Holly in a dream as "a veiled form . . . which, from time to time, seemed to draw the coverings from its body, revealing now the perfect shape of a lovely blooming woman, and now again the white bones of a grinning skeleton" (chap. 9). Haggard was accused of plagiarizing this image from Thomas Moore's *The Epicurean* (1827), but it has many nineteenth-century avatars: Keats's "La Belle Dame sans merci," first published in 1820, for example, and Coleridge's "Rime of the Ancient Mariner" (1798), whose picture of the deadly female Haggard's readers might well have recalled:

> Her lips were red, her looks were free,
> Her locks were yellow as gold:
> Her skin was as white as leprosy,
> The Night-mare Life-in-Death was she,
> Who thicks man's blood with cold.
> (ll. 190–194)

In chapter 12 Ayesha makes her entrance like "a corpse in its grave-clothes." Again it is a tease: "the wrappings were so thin that one could distinctly see the gleam of the pink flesh beneath them." The language anticipates further voyeuristic scenes: chapter 14, where Holly spies on her in the tomb of Kallikrates and sees her "letting loose her passion on the dead," and chapter 26, appropriately titled "What We Saw," when Ayesha disrobes to stand in the Fire of Life. In that ultimate unveiling, nakedness is only the last disguise, a scant costume for death and decay. The final revelations read like a Puritan indictment of women: Ayesha's white skin turns "dirty brown and yellow, like an old piece of withered parchment," her hand becomes "a claw . . . a human talon like that of a badly-preserved Egyptian mummy." She shrinks into another Gagool, "no larger than a monkey" with a "shapeless" face the size of an infant's—a sight to make men mad. Holly keeps a grip on his own sanity by interpreting the change as a "shocking epitome of human beauty and human life":

She who, but two minutes before had gazed upon us the loveliest, noblest, most splendid woman the world has ever seen, she lay still before us, near the masses of her own dark hair, no larger than a big monkey, and hideous—ah, too hideous for words. And yet, think of this—at that very moment I thought of it—it was the *same* woman!

Holly's moralizing is a revenge; even in his horror there is a sense of satisfaction at having known that Ayesha was a burning mummy all along.

In *She*, psychosexual anxieties are closely connected with racial and political ambiguities. Some of these are summed up in Haggard's treatment of the Amahagger. Holly describes the tribe in chapter 6; he admires them for their Caucasian appearance, noting a wide range of skin color and hair "not frizzed up. . . . not crisped like a negro's." Tall, with features "aquiline, and in many cases exceedingly handsome," the Amahagger wear leopard skins and the warriors carry spears. Their name is formed on a Bantu model, like the word "Amazulu" Amahagger supposedly means "People of the Rocks," but it seems to invoke Hagar, the outcast mother of the Ishmaelites and also Haggard's own name, perhaps a hidden reference to the paternal grandmother whose Jewish origin Haggard's family tended to conceal. At first glance the Amahagger look like another of Haggard's many variations on the Zulu type, reminiscent of the Kukuanas of *King Solomon's Mines*. On the other hand, no admiration is expressed for the Amahagger's bearing or discipline. They are cannibals, handsome but unsmiling, and their faces, says Holly, had "an aspect of cold and sullen cruelty stamped upon them that revolted me." Holly cannot place them linguistically or racially; they speak "bastard Arabic, and yet they were not Arabs. . . . too dark, or rather yellow." A degenerate offshoot of the ancient people of Kôr, adulterated through contact with either Arabs or black Africans, they have no written laws, only customs, and these too are ambiguous. For example, the men do all the agricultural labor, which prompts Holly's remark that "contrary to the habits of most savage races . . . among the Amahagger the weaker sex has established its rights" (chap. 7). It turns out, however, that those rights are only temporary. In fact, the Amahagger have a violently bipolar attitude toward women, as Billali explains to Holly in chapter 10:

"We worship them, and give them their way, because without them the world could not go on; they are the source of life."
"Ah," I said, the matter never having struck me quite in that light before.
"We worship them," he went on, "up to a point, till at last they get unbearable, which," he added, "they do about every second generation."
"And then what do you do?" I asked, with curiosity.
"Then," he answered, with a faint smile, "we rise, and kill the old ones as an example to the young ones, and to show them that we are the strongest."

Here the Amahagger seem to function as a projection of Holly's own misogyny, a theme announced and underscored in the opening of the novel, where Holly is introduced as a version of Allan Quatermain, opposed to his male companions' involvements with women. Haggard employs a variant of this type in many of his romances, a constant reminder of the mode from which they originated: boys' adventure fantasy, which is traditionally misogynistic to some degree. Haggard is not entirely naive in his use of this mode; he appreciates its comic possibilities (as, for instance, in Holly's observation that the idea of women as the "source of life" had never "struck" him "quite in that light before"). But misogyny is also an expression of Haggard's politics; the Amahagger gender war anticipates the novel's central allegory, which is both psychosexual and political: when Ayesha tries to use the "source of life" as an avenue to world power, it destroys her.

As in many of Haggard's adventure novels, the plot of *She* explores an imperialist fantasy. Compared to diamonds, the Fire of Life may seem like an ethereal goal, but its ultimate gift is power. Haggard sounds this theme at the outset, when Vincey's letter to Leo suggests that with the secret of life he could end up ruling the world "by the pure force of accumulated experience" (chap. 3). Holly and Leo find this idea both compelling and terrifying. Ayesha's plan of going to England makes Holly "shudder to think what would be the result," for she would no doubt "assume absolute rule over the British dominions, and probably over the whole earth" (chap. 22). Holly thinks this would "make ours the most glorious and prosperous empire that the world has ever seen," but he and Leo cannot approve of Ayesha's plan to dispose of queen and parliament. Despite his misgivings, however, Holly's thoughts about the plan betray excitement: "The whole thing sounded like a dream or some extraordinary invention of a speculative brain. . . . This marvellous creature . . . was now about to be used by Providence as a means to change the order of the world, and possibly, by the building up of a power that could no more be rebelled against or questioned than the decrees of Fate, to change it materially for the better."

Ayesha introduces the unthinkable; her power allows Holly (and Haggard) to toy with totalitarian means, if not ends. This seemingly protofascist theme is at least partly satiric. Holly warns Ayesha against meddling in the affairs of a country where "real power . . . rested in the hands of the people," and then adds that England is "in fact ruled by the votes of the lower and least educated classes of the community." Haggard is reaching here for Swiftian irony, but he is not sure enough of his own motives to be an effective satirist. His underlying difficulties are easier to see in the manuscript version of the text—there he explicitly targeted liberalism and Home Rule—he made Ayesha plan to kill Herbert Gladstone and wipe out the Irish. In that version Haggard tried to manage his contradictory political views by splitting them up between characters: Leo was allowed to grin at the prospect of replacing Gladstone (whom Haggard detested), while Holly provided the tut-tutting liberal superego. But in the manuscript even Holly's reaction to Ayesha's policy is curiously mixed. As a liberal, Holly ought to be in favor of broadening the franchise,

but he talks with condescension and fear about "the people in their masses," and he seems to enjoy thinking about what Ayesha, as "a kind of glorified Bismarck," could do to the social and political establishment (quoted in Etherington, 1991, pp. 233–234, nn. 19–22). Haggard muted these complexities in the published version of the novel: there was no point in antagonizing liberal readers, and anyway, Gladstone was out of office. But Haggard never liked to revise; when he did it at all he was apt to be careless. In this case, traces of his original intent remain in the final version to hint at the totalitarian fantasy behind Holly's liberal facade.

Another kind of political trace appears in chapter 3, as a prelude to the unveiling of the Sherd of Amenartas. Describing their nervous breakfast that fateful morning, Holly says that Job, "to whom the contagion of excitement had, of course, spread, managed to break the handle off my Sèvres china tea-cup, the identical one, I believe, that Marat had been drinking from just before he was stabbed in his bath." The teacup is wonderfully and absurdly overdetermined: a piece of Louis XV's royal porcelain in the hands of the revolutionary Jean-Paul Marat, ironic witness to his assassination by Charlotte Corday in 1793. Haggard deploys this impossible cup partly to allay political fear, saying that revolutionaries merely appropriate the old symbols of power, which then infect and destroy the revolution. Marat becomes a piece of china, feminized and fragile; two generations later, the cup is no more than a curiosity, and when it falls victim to a "contagion" that has "of course, spread" to the servant class, it is only a teacup revolution (chap. 3). Furthermore, when Job, the "male attendant," breaks off Marat's "handle," he domesticates the castration fear implicit in Corday's Clytemnestra-like attack. On the other hand, the teacup's very unlikeliness calls attention to what it seeks to suppress, a connection between sexual and political paranoia. Like the Sherd of Amenartas it introduces, the teacup is a forged artifact, but of an opposite kind, haunting the world of fantasy with recollections of real terror.

Haggard's view of imperialism is more complicated than his obvious fear of radicalism might suggest. For example, Ayesha, who rules less by force than by innate superiority of mind, is often thought to represent Shepstone's South African policy of "indirect rule," in which he maintained control by avoiding interference in tribal matters.

Haggard admired Shepstone, his friend and mentor in South Africa, and defended his administration. But if *She* is a portrait of colonialism, it is a sinister one. Ayesha asserts the rationality of her rule and insists that her emotions are not involved, but in chapter 15 Holly remains uncomfortably aware of the prostrate "corpselike" Amahagger arraigned before her, and the "cave of torture" that awaits the convicted just offstage. This is not an allegory of imperial progress so much as an apocalyptic vision of a civilization in love with death. Neither the Amahagger nor their queen wish to reinhabit the cities left by the people of Kôr; instead they live in catacombs, sleeping on stone benches made to receive corpses, eating from tables designed for use in the embalming process, wearing clothes made from ancient tomb linen. Ayesha's palace is a necropolis, described in terms reminiscent of London: the lamps in the caves recall London streetlights, and the "vast charnel-house" under Ayesha's council chamber looks like "the space beneath the dome of St. Paul's" (chap. 16). The city of death, with a long tradition in literature and art as a religious emblem, became associated in eighteenth-century England with political and moral satire, as in the prospect of London in Alexander Pope's *Windsor Forest* (1713), and was later developed by, among others, William Blake, Percy Bysshe Shelley, Lord Byron, and the painter John Martin into a focus of nineteenth-century anxieties about industrialization and class conflict. Haggard rejected radicalism, but he shared in the widespread alarm at urban decay and what he called the "glutted, foul, menacing cities" in a letter to Theodore Roosevelt (quoted in Pocock, p. 166).

The mummy motif combines Haggard's political anxieties with the sexual themes discussed above. The most vivid example occurs in chapter 19, when Ayesha invites the travelers to a savage dance illuminated by flaming corpses. Holly declares himself "thoroughly disgusted with the grotesque weirdness of the spectacle," but he is plainly fascinated as well as repelled. He tries to distance the scene as an example of Gothic sublime—"the awful and hideous grandeur of the spectacle thus presented to us is . . . so absolutely beyond my poor powers that I scarcely dare attempt it"—but it is too familiar: the human torches remind Holly that Nero once burned Christians to illuminate his gardens. As the Amahagger do not use live bodies (Holly makes a

point of this), the suggestion of sadism seems to arise as much from Holly's own mind and culture as from theirs. Holly tries to take Hamlet's view: "Caesar's dust—or is it Alexander's?—may stop a bunghole," but this line of thought also leads home, to the prospect of a degenerate Europe savagely desecrating its ancestors: "To such base uses may we come, of so little account may we be in the minds of the eager multitudes that we shall breed, many of whom, so far from revering our memory, will live to curse us for begetting them into such a world of woe." The eugenic theme in Holly's language suggests a close relationship between antidemocratic politics and Puritan guilt: Holly fears the "eager multitudes" to come, but he also hates his own generation for weakly breeding and begetting them. "Savagery is only a question of degree," Haggard wrote in *Cetywayo* (p. liv), doubting "whether the civilised man, with his gin, his greed, and his dynamite, is really so very superior to the savage." In 1911 he wrote to Theodore Roosevelt that he expected "the practical destruction of the white peoples" within "two or three centuries," partly because, he thought, "the Almighty has had enough of the white races and is bringing about their ruin through their own failings as in past days He brought about the ruin of Rome" (quoted in Pocock, p. 159).

At the end of the novel, Holly regrets never having received from Ayesha a full explanation of her "philosophy." Haggard probably could not have supplied it—the omission represents an absence in his own thought. He was always attracted to spiritualist notions (he liked to think of himself as a reborn Viking or Egyptian) but he had been disturbed by the séances he attended in London, and he never completely broke away from his Church of England upbringing. *She* reflects no clear school of thought, but rather confusion and longing; it is bad philosophy, but an accurate sample of the spiritual ambivalence shared by many of Haggard's contemporaries. Holly's language often has a Puritan ring, as, for example, when he refuses the Fire of Life in chapter 22: "For I do hope for an immortality to which the little span that perchance thou canst confer will be but as a finger's length." Ayesha on the other hand discounts all religions:

Ah! if man would but see that hope is from within and not from without—that he himself must work out his own salvation! He is there, and within him is the breath of life and a knowledge of good and evil as good and evil is to him. Thereon let him build and stand erect, and not cast himself before the image of some unknown God, modelled like his poor self.

(chap. 17)

Holly thinks "that her argument sounded very like some that I have heard in the nineteenth century . . . with which, by the way, I totally disagree." In terms that would have seemed familiar to embattled Christians in late-Victorian England, he likens Ayesha to a "materialist, who hurls statistics and whole strata of geological facts at your head, whilst you can only buffet him with deductions and instincts and the snowflakes of faith." Holly often takes the antiscientific line: "For what is the first result of man's increased knowledge interpreted from Nature's book by the persistent effort of his purblind observation? Is it not but too often to make him question the existence of his Maker, or indeed of any intelligent purpose beyond his own?" (chap. 10). But he has little or no theology, and his private thoughts are filled with doubt. He may begin with pious references to "the Almighty" and "His works," but his meditations soon take an agnostic turn: "Without Hope we should suffer moral death, and by the help of Hope we yet may climb to Heaven, or at the worst, if she also prove but a kindly mockery given to hold us from despair, be gently lowered into the abysses of eternal sleep." Falling into depression, he can sound nihilistic: "What is the purpose of our feeble crying in the awful silences of space? Can our dim intelligence read the secrets of that star-strewn sky? Does any answer come out of it? Never any at all, nothing but echoes and fantastic visions!" His highest hope is that humanity might someday achieve a nonphysical existence.

Combining Puritan typological thinking, Victorian progressivism, and spiritualism, Holly sees in the distant kinship between stars and balls of swamp gas "a type and image of what man is, and what perchance man may one day be, if the living Force who ordained him and them should so ordain this also." Despite Holly's distrust of science, the impact of Darwinism can be seen in his reduction of God to a "living Force." Illogically enough, Holly's frame of mind also has Romantic origins: alluding to Keats, Holly wants to "shake loose the prisoned pinions of the soul and soar to that superior point, whence, like to some traveller looking

out through space from Darien's giddiest peak, we might gaze with the spiritual eyes deep into Infinity!" Holly's is a Faustian desire, doomed partly because it springs from a disgust at the flesh that is itself a tormented sexuality, a desire "to cast off this earthy robe, to have done for ever with these earthy thoughts and miserable desires; no longer, like those corpse candles, to be tossed this way and that, by forces beyond our control . . . to have done with the foul and thorny places of the world." Holly's often inconsistent struggles can be compared to pessimism and doubt in Byron ("Darkness," 1817), Tennyson (*In Memoriam*, 1850), Edward FitzGerald's translation of *The Rubáiyát of Omar Khayyám* (1859), and Matthew Arnold ("Dover Beach," 1867).

CONCLUSION

King Solomon's Mines and *She* explore similar themes in different modes. The earlier novel begins with a tongue-in-cheek attitude, with Haggard enjoying the boys' adventure style that it consciously sets out to imitate. That mode barely controls the racial and sexual fantasies to which it gives access. Echoes of adult military and economic history complicate the tone; the real Zulu wars are visible through the smoke of fictional battle. Haggard's initial comic manner almost disappears in *She*; the result is psychologically daring, but disappointingly humorless. To grasp the whole significance of Haggard's mythmaking, one needs to keep both novels in mind. There will always be those for whom Rider Haggard is "the Great Storyteller," without apology or qualification, but the day has passed when serious readers can say with Graham Greene that Haggard was "the greatest of all who enchanted us when we were young."

SELECTED BIBLIOGRAPHY

I. BIBLIOGRAPHIES. James E. Scott, *A Bibliography of the Works of Sir Henry Rider Haggard: 1856–1925* (London, 1947); Roger T. Allen, *The Haggard Guide* (Peoria, Ill., 1987); Denys C. Whatmore, *H. Rider Haggard: A Bibliography* (London and Westport, Conn., 1987); Lloyd Siemens, *The Critical Reception of Sir Henry Rider Haggard: An Annotated Bibliography, 1882–1991, English Literature in Transition: 1880–1920* special ser., no. 5 (Greensboro, N.C., 1991); see also bibliographies in Etherington (1984) and Katz.

II. SEPARATE WORKS: FICTION. *Dawn* (London, 1884); *The Witch's Head* (London, 1885); *King Solomon's Mines* (London, 1885); *She* (London, 1887; rev. eds. New York, 1888 and 1891); *Jess* (London, 1887); *Allan Quatermain* (London, 1887); *Maiwa's Revenge* (London, 1888); *Mr. Meeson's Will* (London, 1888); *Colonel Quaritch, V.C.* (London, 1888); *Cleopatra* (London, 1889).

Beatrice (London, 1890); *The World's Desire*, with Andrew Lang (London, 1890); *Eric Brighteyes* (London, 1891); *Nada the Lily* (London, 1892); *Montezuma's Daughter* (London, 1893); *The People of the Mist* (London, 1894); *Joan Haste* (London, 1895); *Heart of the World* (New York, 1895); *The Wizard* (Bristol and London, 1896); *Dr. Therne* (London, 1898); *Swallow* (London, 1899).

Lysbeth (London, 1901); *Pearl-Maiden* (London, 1903); *Stella Fregelius* (New York, 1903); *The Brethren* (London, 1904); *Ayesha: The Return of She* (London, 1905); *The Way of the Spirit* (London, 1906); *Benita* (London, 1906); *Fair Margaret* (London, 1907); *The Ghost Kings* (London, 1908); *The Yellow God* (New York, 1908); *The Lady of Blossholme* (London, 1909).

Morning Star (London, 1910); *Queen Sheba's Ring* (London, 1910); *Red Eve* (London, 1911); *The Mahatma and the Hare* (London, 1911); *Marie* (London, 1912); *Child of Storm* (London, 1913); *The Wanderer's Necklace* (London, 1914); *The Holy Flower* (London, 1915); *The Ivory Child* (London, 1916); *Finished* (London, 1917); *Love Eternal* (London, 1918); *Moon of Israel* (London, 1918); *When the World Shook* (London, 1919).

The Ancient Allan (London, 1920); *She and Allan* (London, 1921); *The Virgin of the Sun* (London, 1922); *Wisdom's Daughter* (London, 1923); *Heu-Heu* (London, 1924); *Queen of the Dawn* (London, 1925); *The Treasure of the Lake* (London, 1926); *Allan and the Ice-Gods* (London, 1927); *Mary of Marion Isle* (London, 1929); *Belshazzar* (London, 1930).

III. SEPARATE WORKS: NONFICTION. *Cetywayo and His White Neighbours* (London, 1882; 2d ed., with new material, London, 1888); *A Farmer's Year* (London, 1899); *The Last Boer War* (London, 1899); *A Winter Pilgrimage* (London, 1901); *Rural England* (London, 1902); *A Gardener's Year* (London, 1905); *Report on the Salvation Army Colonies* (London, 1905); *The Poor and the Land* (London, 1905); *Regeneration* (London, 1910); *Rural Denmark* (London, 1911); *The After-War Settlement and Employment of Ex-Servicemen* (London, 1916); *The Days of My Life* (London, 1926); *A Note on Religion* (London, 1927).

IV. COLLECTED SHORT FICTION. *Allan's Wife and Other Tales* (London, 1889); *Black Heart and White Heart and Other Stories* (London, 1900); *Smith and the Pharaohs and Other Tales* (Bristol and London, 1920).

V. FILMS, PLAYS, RADIO BROADCASTS. See the bibliographies by Siemens and Whatmore.

VI. PAMPHLETS AND REPORTS. *An Heroic Effort* (London, 1893); *Church and State* (London, 1895); *The Real Wealth of England* (London, 1908); *Reports of the Royal Commission of Coast Erosion* (1907–1911); *Reports of the Dominions Royal Commission* (London, 1912–1917). For Haggard's numerous uncollected nonfiction articles, reviews, letters to periodicals and newspapers, and speeches, see Whatmore, pp. 103–129.

VII. DIARIES. *The Private Diaries of Sir H. Rider Haggard 1914–1925*, ed. by D. S. Higgins (London, 1980).

VIII. BIOGRAPHICAL AND CRITICAL STUDIES. Lilias Rider Haggard, *The Cloak That I Left: A Biography of Rider Haggard* (London, 1951); Morton Cohen, *Rider Haggard, His Life and Works* (London, 1960; 2d ed., London, 1968); Morton Cohen, ed., *Rudyard Kipling to Rider Haggard: The Record of a Friendship* (London, 1965); Alan Sandison, *The Wheel of Empire* (London and New York, 1967); Peter Berresford Ellis, *H. Rider Haggard: A Voice from the Infinite* (London, 1978); D. S. Higgins, *Rider Haggard: The Great Storyteller* (London, 1981); Norman Etherington, *Rider Haggard* (Boston, 1984); Wendy R. Katz, *Rider Haggard and the Fiction of Empire: A Critical Study of British Imperial Fiction* (Cambridge, 1987); Norman Etherington, ed., *The Annotated She: A Critical Edition* (Bloomington, Ind., 1991); Tom Pocock, *Rider Haggard and the Lost Empire* (London, 1993).

IX. SELECTED SHORTER CRITICISM. C. S. Lewis, "Haggard Rides Again," in *Time and Tide* 41 (3 September 1960), repr. as "The Mythopoeic Gift of Rider Haggard," in *Of This and Other Worlds*, ed. by Walter Hooper (London, 1982); V. S. Pritchett, "Haggard Still Riding," in *New Statesman* 60 (27 August 1960); Evelyn J. Hinz, "Rider Haggard's *She:* An Archetypal History of Adventure," in *Studies in the Novel* 4 (1972); Laura Chrisman, "The Imperial Unconscious? Representation of Imperial Discourse," in *Critical Quarterly* 32, no. 3 (fall 1990); William J. Scheick, "Adolescent Pornography and Imperialism in Haggard's *King Solomon's Mines*," in *English Literature in Transition* 34, no. 1 (1991).

X. COMMENTS IN PASSING. Graham Greene, *Journey Without Maps* (London, 1936), and *The Lost Childhood and Other Essays* (London, 1954); C. S. Lewis, *Rehabilitations and Other Essays* (London, 1939), *Essays Presented to Charles Williams* (London, 1947), and *An Experiment in Criticism* (Cambridge, Eng., 1961); Susan Howe, *Novels of Empire* (New York, 1949); Nandor Fodor, *The Search for the Beloved* (New York, 1949), and *New Approaches to Dream Interpretation* (New York, 1951); Henry Miller, *The Books in My Life* (London, 1952); Sigmund Freud, *The Interpretation of Dreams*, trans. by James Strachey (London, 1954); Carl G. Jung, *Collected Works*, vols. 7, 9, and 10, trans. by R. F. C. Hull (London, 1954–1966); Nina Auerbach, *Woman and the Demon: The Life of a Victorian Myth* (Cambridge, Mass., 1982); Margery Fisher, *The Bright Face of Danger: An Exploration of the Adventure Story* (London, 1986); Sandra M. Gilbert and Susan Gubar, *Sexchanges*, vol. 2 of *No Man's Land: The Place of the Woman Writer in the Twentieth Century* (New Haven, Conn., 1989).

DAVID HUME
(1711–1776)

John Richetti

ALONG WITH THE GREAT Enlightenment thinkers Jean-Jacques Rousseau and Immanuel Kant, David Hume is recognized as one of the founders of modern thought. His writings about crucial philosophical problems, especially the elusive nature of personal identity and human knowledge of causation, have been at the center of intense philosophical debate since the eighteenth century. Academic philosophers consider Hume's *A Treatise of Human Nature* (1739–1740) nothing less than one of the foundational works of modern philosophy, although many of his ideas have been rejected or substantially refined by subsequent thinkers. From the start, Hume's philosophy was controversial, and some critics reacted aggressively and even angrily to his skepticism, which was often seen as hostile to the Christian religion and traditional morality. But for many serious thinkers Hume was profoundly important, and his intellectual system provoked important responses. Kant once remarked that Hume had awakened him from a "dogmatic slumber" and had given his "investigations in the field of speculative philosophy quite a new direction."

Such intellectual fame as posterity has granted him was not quite what Hume sought for himself. He embarked when still a youth upon a career in philosophy at a time well before the academic disciplines were organized into mutually exclusive specializations, and from the beginning of his career Hume saw his intellectual role in the world not as a philosopher speaking only to other philosophers but as a writer of "literature" for a wider reading public, mainly as an essayist and historian. Indeed, it was as the author of the six-volume *History of England* (1754–1762) that he achieved fame (in Europe as well as in Britain) and considerable fortune. Hume was, in fact, the first British man of letters to acquire substantial wealth exclusively from the sale of his books, quite independent of support from aristocratic patrons or of reader subscriptions.

Born on 26 April 1711 into a moderately prosperous branch of a distinguished Scottish family, Hume was one of three children of Joseph Hume, a small landowner and lawyer, and Katherine Falconer. The family lived in Ninewells, in the southeastern part of Scotland, Berwickshire. All his life Hume retained what contemporaries tell us was a broad Scottish accent. At fifteen, after three years of study at the University of Edinburgh, Hume returned without a degree (a common enough educational sequence in those days in Scotland) to the family home at Ninewells. Pushed by his family to study law, as he explained in "My Own Life," a short autobiographical essay published after his death, Hume as an eager young student was drawn not to the writings of those legal theorists who would prepare him for a career at the bar but to authors such as Cicero and Virgil and to the pursuit of what he called "philosophy and general learning." From his student days, Hume aspired to cultivate his talents in "literature, which has been the ruling passion of my life, and the great source of my enjoyments." ("My Own Life" is included in the 1993 edition of Hume's *Dialogues Concerning Natural Religion; and The Natural History of Religion,* edited by J. C. A. Gaskin, pp. 3–10.) In the eighteenth century, the word "literature" had a far wider and more comprehensive sense than it does now, taking in much more than poetry, prose fiction, and drama, and including writing in philosophy, theology, politics, history, and just about all intellectual topics.

As a young student in Edinburgh, Hume studied diligently and was, by his own account, filled with the grandest, most exalted intellectual ambitions. When he returned home to Ninewells, he began in an extended period of intense study and solitary speculation to lay the groundwork for his future as a philosopher. Hume sought nothing less than to revolutionize what he called in his first book, *A Treatise of Human Nature*, "the science of man." As he wrote to Dr. George Cheyne in 1734, he was eighteen years old when his studies fell into place: "There seem'd to be open'd up to me a new scene of thought, which transport'd me beyond measure, & made me, with an ardor natural to young men, throw up every other pleasure or business to apply entirely to it. The Law, which was the business I design'd to follow, appear'd nauseous to me, & I could think of no other way of pushing my fortune in the world, but that of a scholar & philosopher" (quoted in Greig, ed., *Letters*, vol. 1, p. 13). But as Hume went on to tell Cheyne (famous in his day for treating what we would call depression), one unfortunate result of his intense studies was a disorienting psychological episode that seems to have been something like a nervous breakdown. Seeking relief from stress and anxiety, apparently caused by an "ardent application" to his grand intellectual ambitions, Hume decided to give up his studies, and in 1734 he went to work as a clerk for a Bristol merchant. After only a few months, he left commerce behind and resumed his philosophical quest. Supporting himself on a small private income inherited from his father, he went to France (where he could live inexpensively). After a short stay in Paris, he spent a year at Reims and then lived for two more in the small town of La Flèche in Anjou, where at the precocious age of twenty-six he finished writing his first great philosophical work, *A Treatise of Human Nature: Being an Attempt to Introduce the Experimental Method of Reasoning into Moral Subjects*.

As Hume remarked in "My Own Life," to his chagrin the *Treatise* "fell *dead-born from the press*, without reaching such distinction, as even to excite a murmur among the zealots." In fact, Hume's *Treatise* was noticed to some extent by the learned world, even if it was totally ignored by the larger public. Several long reviews of the book appeared, although these were uniformly hostile to his work. Hume attempted to make his ideas clearer by publishing (anonymously) in 1740 a pamphlet summary of the text: *An Abstract of a Book Lately Published; Entitled, A Treatise of Human Nature, &c. Wherein the Chief Argument of That Book Is Farther Illustrated and Explained*. Remarkable for its naive and grandiose self-promotion, this pam-

phlet summarized what would be the most controversial aspect of Hume's thought, his theory of the knowledge of causation, but it also dramatized more plainly than the *Treatise* the young Hume's revolutionary philosophical ambitions as he aligned his book with what he saw as the great tradition of British empirical thought that began with Francis Bacon.

Speaking of himself in the third person, Hume noted that the author of the *Treatise* "promises to draw no conclusions but where he is authorized by experience" (quoted in L. A. Selby-Bigge, ed., *A Treatise of Human Nature*, p. 646). To pursue what he here called "the science of human nature" is to follow the model of the experimental sciences, and in forswearing mere hypotheses to follow the lead of "Mr. Locke, my Lord Shaftesbury, Dr. Mandeville, Mr. Hutchison, Dr. Butler, who, tho' they differ in many points among themselves, seem all to agree in founding their accurate disquisitions of human nature intirely upon experience" (p. 646). In thus presenting himself as above all an empiricist, Hume called himself a skeptic but also pointed to his resistance to the sort of disabling philosophical doubt that his age called "Pyrrhonism." "The reader will easily perceive," he remarked near the end of the *Abstract*, "that the philosophy contain'd in this book is very sceptical, and tends to give us a notion of the imperfections and narrow limits of human understanding" (p. 657). Sketching his startling and subversive notion, treated at great length in the *Treatise*, that the belief we have in the validity of our experiences is "nothing but a peculiar sentiment, or lively conception produced by habit," and noting that human belief in the stable existence of external things is also merely a sentiment, Hume concluded "that we assent to our faculties, and employ our reason only because we cannot help it. Philosophy wou'd render us entirely *Pyrrhonian* were not nature too strong for it" (p. 657).

The *Abstract* balances the devastating skeptical conclusions reached by Hume's philosophy with Hume's quick affirmation of the irrelevance of those conclusions with respect to daily action. In his summary of the *Treatise*, Hume outlined the ironic and deeply moral shape of his thought and adumbrated a theme to which he would return over and over again in the years to come. As one of his major twentieth-century commentators, Norman Kemp Smith, pointed out, Hume's philosophy essentially proved that commonsense notions such as the existence of bodies and of a personal self, and our belief in causation, are not accounted for logically by the systems of his great immediate predecessors, John Locke and George Berkeley. As Kemp Smith puts it, for Hume the paradoxical truth is that such notions simply cannot be proved but must nevertheless be believed. Hume was aware of this paradox from the first. "Nothing," Hume insisted, "is ever really present to the mind, besides its own perceptions" (p. 197). We infer the steady existence of the objects of sense "from their coherence, and the frequency of their union," and we thereby construct a stable world from what Hume calls "custom," that is from the recurrence and repetitions of our perceptions. Our senses (what Hume sometimes calls our "imagination") construct a world of continuing existences and steady objects, but our philosophically informed reason indicates that our perceptions are "interrupted and different" (p. 215). Which account of the world is valid? Hume says that our feeling at different times that each is valid makes skepticism inevitable and ineradicable:

This sceptical doubt, both with respect to reason and the senses, is a malady, which can never be radically cur'd, but must return upon us every moment, however we may chace it away, and sometimes may seem entirely free from it. 'Tis impossible upon any system to defend either our understanding or our senses; and we but expose them farther when we endeavor to justify them in that manner. As the sceptical doubt arises naturally from a profound and intense reflection on those subjects, it always encreases, the farther we carry our reflections, whether in opposition or conformity to it. Carelessness and in-attention alone can afford us any remedy.

(p. 218)

The history of the publication of the *Treatise* is the key to Hume's life as an eighteenth-century man of letters (or, in modern parlance, an intellectual) and to the special qualities he learned to cultivate in his writing in order to play that role. The spectacular failure as he saw it of the *Treatise* confirmed Hume in the notion that he needed to refine his style and to move toward an elegance and ease in his writing that would gain him the wide audience he sought. "I had always entertained a notion, that my want of success in publishing the Treatise of Human Nature," he wrote in "My Own Life" just before he died, "had proceeded more from the manner than the matter, and that I had

been guilty of a very usual indiscretion, in going to the press too early." Much of the subsequent philosophical writing that Hume accomplished constituted a reworking of material from the *Treatise* to make his ideas clearer, simpler, and more accessible to a wider audience. Specifically, he recast a good deal of his enormous first book into three separate and much shorter works: the *Enquiry Concerning Human Understanding* (1748), the *Enquiry Concerning the Principles of Morals* (1751), and *Four Dissertations* (1757), which contained "The Natural History of Religion," "Of Tragedy," "Of the Passions" (a brief version of book 2 of the *Treatise*), and "Some Considerations Previous to Geometry and Natural Philosophy" (a reworking of book 1, part 2 of the *Treatise*). In rewriting his youthful summa, Hume sought to cultivate an elegant ease, a clarity and economy of expression that became his literary signature as an essayist and historian, but he also exemplified in those revisions what he saw as the public mission of the man of learning or the intellectual, whose responsibility it was to bridge the gap between the world of ordinary affairs and the world of philosophy.

In "Of Essay-Writing," which appeared as part of a two-volume collection called *Essays, Moral and Political* published anonymously in 1741 and 1742, Hume divided the "elegant part of mankind, who are not immers'd in the animal life, but employ themselves in the operations of the mind" into two parts, the "learned" and the "conversible." By the latter he had in mind the more or less educated public, the leisured classes who occasionally took an interest in ideas and turned their conversation from gossip to serious matters. Looking back to the "last age" (meaning the period from the Restoration through the reign of Queen Anne, 1660 to 1714), Hume saw the separation of the learned and conversible worlds as its great cultural defect, wherein social discourse had been trivialized and degraded and learning had become secluded and awkward. "By that means every thing of what we call *Belles Lettres* became totally barbarous, being cultivated by men without any taste of life or manners, and without that liberty and facility of thought and expression, which can only be acquir'd by conversation." And even philosophy, Hume continues, was made "unintelligible in her Stile and Manner" by its isolation from the experience of "common life and conversation." Hume was gratified to see that there was now much more commerce between these worlds, and he styled himself an "ambassador from the dominions of learning to those of conversation."

Although "Of Essay-Writing" is in part a puff for the volume of essays in which it appears, the notions that Hume articulated here are crucial for understanding the rest of his career. Hume aspired to purge his early writing of abstruseness and to bridge the gap between the profoundly subversive nature of his early philosophical investigations and the values of the leisured and polite society to which he himself came to belong and hoped to serve. To be sure, Hume's mature philosophical writing is not a repudiation of the insights of his first book, but rather an adaptation of them for a wider and what he would have called a more "polite" audience. And in fact even as he contemplated writing the *Treatise*, as he explained in the previously mentioned letter to Dr. Cheyne, he agonized about the difficulty of making himself clear to his audience: "I had no hopes of delivering my opinions with such elegance & neatness, as to draw to me the attention of the world, & I wou'd rather live & dye in obscurity than produce them maim'd & imperfect" (*Letters*, vol. 1, p. 17).

But *A Treatise of Human Nature* is much more than the literary failure Hume took it to be. Although it is a complex philosophical treatise, it is also a rich and varied rhetorical performance that deserves reading (at least in part), and not just by academic philosophers and students of the history of ideas. What it presents and what (paradoxically enough) Hume took great pains to remove as he excavated and revised it in later years is the dramatic contradiction between its author's astonishingly self-confident ambitions to revolutionize our philosophical understanding of our experience and his sometimes anguished admissions of difficulty and even defeat as he proceeds toward that end.

THE TREATISE

DIVIDED into three books, "Of the Understanding," "Of the Passions," and "Of Morals," *A Treatise of Human Nature* defies adequate summary; it is an encyclopedic (and not always consistent) consideration of the major philosophical problems of the day and a deliberately outrageous and iconoclastic revision of the idea of philosophy itself. Brash and daring, the young Hume de-

clared in his introduction to the *Treatise* that "'tis easy for one of judgment and learning, to perceive the weak foundation even of those systems, which have obtained the greatest credit, and have carried their pretensions highest to accurate and profound reasoning." The systems, he continues, "of the most eminent philosophers" are incoherent and founded upon unproved assumptions; indeed, they "have drawn disgrace upon philosophy itself" (p. xiii). Hume's bravado was intentional. He wrote to his friend Henry Home two weeks after the publication of the *Treatise* that his principles were "so remote from all the vulgar sentiments on the subject, that were they to take place, they would produce almost a total alteration in philosophy" (*Letters*, vol. 1, p. 26).

And yet for all his youthful confidence in the explosive originality of his thought, Hume from the very beginning of the *Treatise* presents the reader with a complicated philosophical scene in which self-doubt and uncertainty play an important and recurrent role. Along with the triumphant scientism of his study of man is a moralizing irony and skepticism that compromises his own thinking and prevents (or even satirizes) absolute certainty and self-satisfaction. Thus at the end of the introduction to the *Treatise*, Hume concedes that his science cannot explain "ultimate principles," and his "moral philosophy" suffers from a special disability not found in the natural sciences:

When I am at a loss to know the effects of one body upon another in any situation, I need only put them in that situation, and observe what results from it. But should I endeavour to clear up after the same manner any doubt in moral philosophy, by placing myself in the same case with that which I consider, 'tis evident this reflection and premeditation would so disturb the operation of my natural principles, as must render it impossible to form any just conclusion from this phenomenon. We must therefore glean up our experiments in this science from a cautious observation of human life, and take them as they appear in the common course of the world, by men's behaviour in company, in affairs, and in their pleasures.

(p. xix)

Hume insisted on the local rather than the generalizing and the systematic; his writing, like his philosophic method, favored particularized and vivid narrative: "To explain the ultimate causes of our mental actions is impossible," he wrote in part 1 of book 1. "'Tis sufficient, if we can give any satisfactory account of them from experience and analogy" (p. 22). Hume's ambition for his thought was that it return to experience and that it recognize the role of approximate rather than definitive representations of that experience.

Compare this ambition with other philosophers' perspectives in the act of philosophizing—René Descartes's observation of his own mental states in the *Meditations*, John Locke's pondering in *An Essay Concerning Human Understanding* of the ways particular and isolated individuals encounter the world, and Bishop Berkeley's evocation in the *Principles of Human Knowledge* of a solitary mind whose perceptions sustain so-called objective existence, for example—and Hume's mistrust of his own distorting subjectivity and his emphasis on the necessity of observing human knowledge (including his own) as it occurs in social interactions are striking and characteristically revealing of his philosophical preferences and of the turn of his thinking throughout his career. Like the eighteenth-century novelists with whom he shared the wider literary stage, Hume proposed to look not simply inward at his own psychological and logical processes but always at the same time outward at the human and the moral scene, and to describe how that social scene intersected with this solitary reasoning. In the contemplative solitude of a foreign city, Hume kept his eye fixed on life as it was lived in the world beyond the philosopher's study. Young as he was, Hume was even then not a reclusive system-builder but a moral and social writer whose isolated bookishness was balanced by an intense awareness of social interaction.

The attention Hume promised to pay to social reality is crucial, since much of the *Treatise* involves intense scrutiny of the reliability of the isolated and experiencing individual, whom the empiricist tradition made the center and test of reality. Indeed, the book begins with an examination of the psychology of individual perception, and the opening chapter introduces a distinction between impressions and ideas. As Hume noted in a footnote, Locke had used the term "ideas" to refer to all perceptions. For Locke in *An Essay Concerning Human Understanding* (1690), an individual registers as "ideas" his sense experience of an external world, and Locke divided those ideas into two types, simple, or primary, and secondary ideas. By the former, Locke referred to sense experience of qualities, such as solidity, shape, and extension, that seem actually to be in objects; whereas secondary qualities, such as taste and color, are not inherent in objects but vary according to human sensory abilities and dispositions. As Locke put it, there is a power in objects to provoke sensory responses, but that power is not of the essence of those objects. For Hume, the emphasis fell much more strongly on the individual perceiver, and the reality or external integrity of objects tended to be much less of an issue. Perceptions, Hume believed, differ in a significant degree according to the "force and liveliness, with which they strike upon the mind." The emphasis shifts from Locke's defense of the adequacy of human sensory experience of the external world to Hume's bold endorsement of those experiences as constituting all we know and indeed all that we need to know. Perceptions, for Hume, took two forms:

Those perceptions, which enter with most force and violence, we may name *impressions;* and under this name I comprehend all our sensations, passions and emotions, as they make their first appearance in the soul. By *ideas* I mean the faint images of these in thinking and reasoning; such as, for instance, are all the perceptions excited by the present discourse, excepting only, those which arise from the sight and touch, and excepting the immediate pleasure or uneasiness it may occasion.

(p. 1)

As he proceeds, Hume will generally seek to disparage the integrity of "ideas" by showing that they are diminished or less intense and immediate versions of original impressions, and in due course he will give the primacy in human epistemology to the passions or emotions over the rational or logical faculties. At first sight, this looks like a reduction of human powers, a potentially solipsistic limitation of knowledge to that of ourselves and our own psychological processes. Book 1 of the *Treatise*, "Of the Understanding," is an analysis of what we know and how we seem to know it. The conclusion of part 2 ("Of the ideas of space and time") warns about the necessary human limits of these investigations: "Now since nothing is ever present to the mind but perceptions, and since all ideas are deriv'd from something antecedently present to the mind; it follows, that 'tis impossible for us so much as to conceive or form an idea of any thing specifically different from ideas and impressions." And as if such a bleak assertion were not enough, Hume rises to a moralizing warning:

Let us fix our attention out of ourselves as much as possible: let us chace our imagination to the heavens, or to the utmost limits of the universe; we never really advance a step beyond ourselves, nor can conceive any kind of existence, but those perceptions, which have appear'd in that narrow compass. This is the universe of the imagination, nor have we any idea but what is there produc'd.

(pp. 67–68)

As it turns out, the "universe of the imagination" is in Hume's rendering an exceedingly rich and diverse locale, and the *Treatise* must be a very thick volume to trace its many and complicated ways. "Know then thyself, presume not God to scan," Alexander Pope wrote in *An Essay on Man* (1733), "The proper study of Mankind is Man." Hume's system is in general a subversive response to Pope's aphorism and very much a refutation of the sweeping optimism of Pope's poem and the worldview that it represents. But the *Treatise* is never a gloomy or cynical correction of Enlightenment cheerfulness about the state of the universe; inventive and ingenuous in its introspective moments, Hume's book explores the sometimes comic gaps between its narrator's experience of the world and his philosophical transformations of that experience as he ponders its nature and its origins. For example, at the very beginning of book 1, as he contemplates the difference between impressions and ideas, Hume at first thinks that the two are identical, for when he closes his eyes and thinks of the room in which he is writing, "the ideas I form are exact representations of the impressions I felt," and in "running over my other perceptions, I find still the same resemblance and representation." But Hume dramatizes in the following paragraph just how his own naive and local certainty is complicated by further reflection specifically grounded in a larger public world:

Upon a more accurate survey I find I have been carried away too far by the first appearance, and that I must make use of the distinction of perceptions into *simple and complex*, to limit this general decision, *that all our ideas and impressions are resembling.* I observe, that many of our complex ideas never had impressions, that corresponded to them, and that many of our complex impressions never are exactly copied in ideas. I can imagine to myself such a city as the *New Jerusalem,* whose pavement is gold and walls are rubies, tho' I never saw any such. I have seen *Paris;* but shall I affirm I can form such an idea of that city, as will perfectly represent all its streets and houses in their real and just proportions?

(p. 3)

Book 1 of the *Treatise,* "Of the Understanding," is divided into four parts, and the first three relentlessly expose many commonsense notions as fallacious and untenable. The most shocking of Hume's conclusions is that relationships between objects and events, the existence of which we depend on to organize our world, cannot be described as cause and effect. Rather, he insists, we must speak of more literal connections between things such as succession and contiguity, which are what we actually experience. He offers two principles: *"There is nothing in any object, consider'd in itself, which can afford us a reason for drawing a conclusion beyond it;* and, *That even after the observation of the frequent or constant conjunction of objects, we have no reason to draw any inference concerning any object beyond those of which we have had experience"* (p. 139, emphasis in original).

Strict speaking, then, is what Hume insists upon. There are no logical or rational connections between events, he argues, and the belief in an orderly world of cause and effect is entirely a matter of custom. Hume illustrated this situation in his abstract to the *Treatise:* "[When] I see a billiard-ball moving towards another, my mind is immediately carry'd by habit to the usual effect, and anticipates my sight by conceiving the second ball in motion." But no matter how many times he witnesses this relationship between the billiard balls, "there is no argument, which determines me to suppose, that the effect will be conformable to past experience." Hume's skeptical question is just this: How do we know the same thing will occur, that our experience of regularity is valid and meaningful? "The powers by which bodies operate, are entirely unknown. We perceive only their sensible qualities: and what *reason* have we to think that the same powers will always be conjoined with the same sensible qualities?" (p. 652).

Hume in the *Treatise* conducts two implicit dialogues: one with a lay audience, with whom Hume is sympathetic, and one with philosophic rivals, in which Hume takes the side of the ordinary person: "Whatever has the air of a paradox, and is contrary to the first and most unprejudiced notions of mankind is often greedily embraced by philosophers, as showing the superiority of their science, which could discover opinions so remote from vulgar conception" (p. 26). Hume uses his own persona as earnest inquirer to stage, as it were, the recurring discovery of his own uncertainty, which continually undermines the superiority philosophy claims over ordinary perception. Hume's philosophy exposes the ulterior motives of those with whom he disagrees and presents his own unswerving allegiance to a clarity and truth that are defined in universal terms rather than in the professionalized jargon of philosophy. Thus in rejecting the notion that it was possible to have an idea of a thing without thinking of any particular instance of it, Hume asserted that philosophers who put forward such statements are out to mystify: "'Tis easy to see, why philosophers are so fond of this notion of some spiritual and refin'd perceptions; since by that means they cover many of their absurdities, and may refuse to submit to the decisions of clear ideas, by appealing to such as are obscure and uncertain" (p. 72).

So Hume's account of the understanding is both profoundly destructive of commonsense notions of a stable external world and emphatically affirming about the validity and reliability of human knowledge. On the one hand, Hume reduced human knowledge to instincts not all that different from the impulses that guide animals. Just as beasts infer connections between objects by experience, so too human "reason is nothing but a wonderful and unintelligible instinct in our souls, which carries us along a certain train of ideas, and endows them with particular qualities, according to their particular situations and relations" (p. 179). On the other hand, as he begins the last section of book 1 of the *Treatise*, "Of the Sceptical and Other Systems of Philosophy," Hume can be seen as making up for this somewhat malicious equation of human reason and animal instinct as he redefines both reason and truth by exchanging knowledge for probability:

In all demonstrative sciences the rules are certain and infallible; but when we apply them, our fallible and uncertain faculties are very apt to depart from them, and fall into error. We must, therefore, in every reasoning form a new judgment . . . and must enlarge our view to comprehend a kind of history of all the instances, wherein our understanding has deceiv'd us, compar'd with those, wherein its testimony was just and true. Our reason must be consider'd as a kind of cause, of which truth is the natural effect; but such-a-one as by the irruption of other causes, and by the inconstancy of our mental powers, may frequently be prevented. By this means all knowledge degenerates into probability; and this probability is greater or less, according to our experience of the veracity or deceitfulness of our understanding, and according to the simplicity or intricacy of the question.

(p. 180)

This is as much a short moral essay as it is a philosophical statement, and Hume's vocabulary— "deceive," "just," "inconstancy," "degenerates"— evokes a regulatory moral order next to the epistemological confusion he outlines. Hume's analysis of the shortcomings of human reason has an elegiacal and monitory quality as he warns that knowledge is really mere probability and that truth must be understood as the effect of human exertion rather than some sort of absolute and external entity. There is a control in Hume's writing not only of the philosophical issues being treated but to a greater extent of their moral and psychological implications, which are, after all, the sorts of things that respond to human ordering. Such control is a defining feature of the *Treatise* and of Hume's philosophical writing in general, but it seems to falter in the last two sections of book 1, "Of Personal Identity" and the book's conclusion.

In the former section Hume applies his notions about impressions to the idea of selfhood. This is risky, since it casts doubt on Hume himself as the author of (and the self behind) the *Treatise*. But Hume pursues the ultimate implications of his theory. If the self is to be stable and continuous, the impression that gives rise to the idea of the self "must continue invariably the same, thro' the whole course of our lives; since self is suppos'd to exist after that manner." And in the most daringly personal moment thus far in the *Treatise*, Hume subjects his own self to his analytic gaze:

For my part, when I enter most intimately into what I call *myself*, I always stumble on some particular perception or other, of heat or cold, light or shade, love or hatred, pain or pleasure. I never can catch *myself* at any time without a perception, and never can observe any thing but the perception. . . . If any one upon serious and unprejudic'd reflexion, thinks he has a different notion of *himself*, I must confess I can reason no longer with him.

(p. 252)

Cool as well as consistent, Hume dissolves personal identity into an entity produced by perceptions or an arrangement composed out of them and as such unstable and even alien. In the end he says that personal identity is a convenient and inevitable fiction, a grammatical rather than philosophical notion. And yet in the conclusion to book 1 that follows, it is precisely this fictionalized selfhood that takes center stage, and in spite of the philosophic control he has exercised, Hume is not immune to the moral and psychological stress such control involves. The difficulty in pinning down personal identity is both painful and confusing: "But before I launch out into those immense depths of philosophy, which lie before me, I find myself inclin'd to stop a moment in my present station, and to ponder that voyage, which I have undertaken." Overcome, he writes, with the "forlorn solitude" of philosophizing, Hume fancies himself "some strange uncouth monster, who not being able to mingle and unite in society, has been expell'd all human commerce, and left utterly abandon'd and disconsolate" (pp. 263–264). How seriously is a reader to take this? Do we believe Hume when he says that as he looks "inward, I find nothing but doubt and ignorance"? To some extent this part of Hume's conclusion is general and rhetorical, designed not so much to reveal what the young philosopher may actually have felt as to dramatize the eventual solution to the book's radical recasting of philosophy. For as Hume admits a bit later on, his reflections do have an emotional effect, in spite of everything he has told us, and "the *intense* view of these manifold contradictions and imperfections in human reason has so wrought upon me, and heated my brain, that I am ready to reject all belief and reasoning, and can look upon no opinion even as more probable or likely than another." Philosophical vertigo and intellectual disorientation ensue: "Where am I, or what? From what causes do I derive my existence, and to what condition shall I return? . . . I am confounded with all these questions, and begin to fancy myself in the most deplorable condition imaginable, inviron'd with the deepest darkness, and utterly depriv'd of the use of every member and faculty" (pp. 268–269).

On the rhetorical level, Hume's return from these depths is a matter of exchanging the soliloquizing monologue of philosophical discourse for the comforting dialogue of social life, and this scene predicts the direction his writing will shortly take. In part, as well, these personal interjections guard against the systematic impersonality of philosophy that Hume resisted, since for him philosophizing was inseparable from an antiphilosophical rhetorical stance that rejected past systems, with their superiority to ordinary experience. Thinking for him always takes place in a dramatic scene in which tension and uncertainty surrounds the whole enterprise of philosophy. Hume is rescued from the failure of "reason" to "[dispel] these

clouds" by the return of what he calls "nature," which cures him of "this philosophical melancholy and delerium": "I dine, I play a game of back-gammon, I converse, and am merry with my friends; and when after three or four hour's amusement, I wou'd return to these speculations, they appear so cold, and strain'd, and ridiculous, that I cannot find in my heart to enter into them any farther" (p. 269). Perhaps the most resonant philosophical notion of Hume's time, signifying a self-conscious exercise of the individual's cognitive faculties such as the *Treatise* has both exemplified and radically redefined, reason is placed throughout Hume's writing in tension with nature, with social interaction and deliberately thoughtless refreshment by social activities.

In the next two long books of the *Treatise*, "Of the Passions" and "Of Morals," Hume employed his revised account of the workings of human understanding to examine social activities. In the third book he replays the organizing opposition between reason and natural beliefs, the resistance of the mind to the abstract proofs of philosophy: "When we leave our closet, and engage in the common affairs of life, its conclusions seem to vanish, like the phantoms of the night on the appearance of the morning; and 'tis difficult for us to retain even that conviction, which we had attain'd with difficulty" (p. 455). But in fact the drift of this book if a reader follows it is precisely to break down this strict opposition between nature and reason. Morals come last in his long sequence because they have been effectively redefined in the first two books; morals can no longer be understood as the struggle between the understanding and the passions, since both are derived from those impressions that constitute experience. Indeed, in a famous chapter in book 2 entitled "Of the Influencing Motives of the Will," Hume quite specifically rejected the idea that passion and reason are opposed. Reason (the "understanding") has to do with strictly intellectual activities: "it judges from demonstration or probability [and] regards the abstract relations of our ideas, or those relations of objects, of which experience only gives us information" (p. 413). Experience may, Hume continues, offer us pleasure or pain, and reason will help us to understand how this happens. "'Tis from the prospect of pain or pleasure that the aversion or propensity arises towards any object," and "as reason is nothing but the discovery of this connexion, it cannot be by its means that the objects are able to affect us" (p. 414). Reason as the opponent of passion is not, properly speaking, a rational act but is rather just another and contrary passion or impulse. "Thus it appears, that the principle, which opposes our passion, cannot be the same with reason, and is only call'd so in an improper sense. . . . Reason is, and ought only to be the slave of the passions, and can never pretend to any other office than to serve and obey them" (p. 415). Passions, in fact, can never be called unreasonable except when they are based on false information, and then it is the understanding that is unreasonable. These notorious sentences reject the pieties of a tradition of moral representation stretching back to the Stoic philosophy of antiquity, and Hume knew that he was being outrageous when he made this argument.

Equally provocative is his contention at the beginning of book 3, "Of Morals," that vice and virtue are not objects that reason can comprehend. What the study of morals reveals is that there are "certain passions, motives, volitions and thoughts" (p. 468). There is in such phenomena for Hume no "matter of fact" until an individual examines his own sentiments toward them. Vice and virtue are the feelings we have for these actions; they are like the perceptions we have of the physical world, and they "may be compar'd to sounds, colours, heat and cold, which, according to modern philosophy, are not qualities in objects, but perceptions in the mind." Moralists, Hume concludes, rising to his most overtly provocative, have a way of sliding from the descriptive to the prescriptive:

In every system of morality, which I have hitherto met with, I have always remark'd, that the author proceeds for some time in the ordinary way of reasoning . . . when of a sudden I am surpriz'd to find, that instead of the usual copulations of propositions, is, and is not, I meet with no proposition that is not connected with an ought, or an ought not. This change is imperceptible; but is, however, of the last consequence. For as this ought, or ought not, expresses some new relation or affirmation, 'tis necessary that it shou'd be observ'd and explain'd; and at the same time that a reason should be given, for what seems altogether inconceivable, how this new relation can be a deduction from others, which are entirely different from it.

(p. 469)

This kind of ironic, insinuating, almost disingenuous passage, with its understatement and transparently false modesty as it delivers its subversive ideas, occurs fairly often in the *Treatise*, and smoother versions of such tonalities and rhetorical strategies mark Hume's mature philosophical style in the two *Enquiries*. But in the next couple of years Hume turned away from philosophy, cultivating the essay and writing extensively on a wide range of topics including morality, politics, economics, literary criticism, and religion. Indeed, Hume was from the start essentially an essayist. The *Treatise*'s various sections are themselves essayistic in appearance, and the book is a series of discussions of topics that are linked by Hume's philosophical project of bringing together his three great subjects of inquiry, the understanding, the passions, and morals.

ESSAYIST AND DIPLOMAT

As an essayist, Hume produced thoughtful and elegant writing, more elaborate and extended than the periodical pieces that are associated with Joseph Addison, Richard Steele, and Samuel Johnson. *Essays, Moral and Political*, published in two separate volumes in 1741 and 1742 in Edinburgh, comprise twenty-seven essays in all, and those dealing with political subjects seem to have made the greatest impression on the public. Hume was in these years seeking employment and presented himself at the suggestion of friends as a candidate for the professorship of ethics and pneumatical philosophy at the University of Edinburgh. But as he wrote to a friend in 1744, a clamor was raised against him in Edinburgh "on account of scepticism, heterodoxy and other hard names, which confound the ignorant, that my friends find some difficulty, in working out the point of my Professorship, which once appear'd so easy" (*Letters*, vol. 1, p. 59). So in 1745 Hume accepted a job as tutor to the young marquess of Annandale, a Scottish nobleman living in London. This young man proved to be deeply unstable and eccentric in his behavior (he was declared insane a few years later), and Hume was dismissed in 1746 with part of his salary unpaid. A new opportunity presented itself almost immediately when a distant relation, Lieutenant-General James St. Clair, offered Hume a post as his secretary. He wanted Hume to accompany him on a projected expedition to drive the French out of Canada. Mismanagement and uncooperative weather kept the naval expedition from ever reaching Canada, and the adventure ended disastrously with an ill-conceived attack on the port of Lorient in Brittany. The British fleet turned back, it seems, just at the moment when the French garrison had decided to surrender. But Hume profited from his time as the general's secretary, and in 1747 and 1748 he served as one of St. Clair's aides-de-camp in Vienna and Turin, where the general was sent to confer with the British allies against France in the War of the Austrian Succession. During these years Hume, always a large man, grew enormously fat as he enjoyed the intense socializing of life as a diplomat. As a young man who saw him in those years remembered, "his face was broad and fat, his mouth wide, and without any other expression than that of imbecility. His eyes vacant and spiritless, and the corpulence of his whole person was far better fitted to communicate the idea of a turtle-eating alderman than of a refined philosopher" (Mossner, p. 213).

But even as he launched this new career as a diplomat, Hume was advancing his reputation as a writer and thinker. He revised the first book of the *Treatise* into *Philosophical Essays Concerning Human Understanding*, published in 1748 and later retitled *An Enquiry Concerning Human Understanding*. That same year he also published a volume called *Three Essays, Moral and Political*. By 1751 he had finished revising and also augmenting that part of the *Treatise* dealing with morals, which he published as *An Enquiry Concerning the Principles of Morals*. Of all his writings, "historical, philosophical, or literary," Hume considered this one "incomparably the best." In 1753 and 1754 Hume published *Essays and Treatises on Several Subjects*, a collection in four volumes of his essays and the *Enquiries*. In the years to come until his death in 1776, these volumes in different combinations were reprinted a number of times and made Hume famous, not only in Britain but in Europe and in America. About this time, as well, Hume began to do research for his projected *History of England*, which occupied him for most of the 1750s, with the first two volumes on the Stuarts, dealing with the reigns of James I, Charles I, and James II, appearing in 1754 and 1756. The subsequent four volumes, which worked back to the invasion of Britain by Julius Caesar, appeared in 1759 and 1762, and in 1763 the entire *History* was published in eight volumes. In addition to this monumental history Hume also published in 1757

a volume of essays entitled *Four Dissertations*, part of which ("Of the Passions") was a condensed version of book 2 of the *Treatise*, and another part of which was "The Natural History of Religion."

Although the *History* was controversial at first, with critics accusing Hume after the publication of the opening volume of having a Tory bias in favor of the deposed Stuart dynasty, the complete *History of England* within a decade was a standard and popular work that made its author both rich and famous. As he explained in a letter to the French historian Jean-Bernard Le Blanc, he set out in the first volume of the *History* to deliver a crisp and fast-paced narrative of events, modeled on the manner of ancient historians rather than on the slow style of modern authors:

If you consider the vast variety of events, with which these two reigns [James I and Charles I], particularly the last, are crowded, you will conclude that my narration is rapid, and that I have more propos'd as my model the concise manner of the antient historians, than the prolix, tedious style of modern compilers. I have inserted no original papers, and enter'd into no detail of minute, uninteresting facts. The philosophical spirit, which I have so much indulg'd in all my writings, finds here ample materials to work upon.

(*Letters*, vol. 1, p. 193)

Hume's *History* is little read today, mostly because of his accomplishments as a philosopher, and critics sometimes see his transformation into a popular historian as an easy way for him to achieve the literary fame he sought. But as he explained to Le Blanc, Hume's *History* was a continuation of the spirit of his philosophical writings, a further contribution to the empirical science of man that he had described in the opening pages of the *Treatise*. And just as Hume offered his philosophy as a reformation of an irrelevant and abstruse metaphysics, so, too, his history was conceived as a revival of the great tradition of history writing as it was practiced by the ancient historians such as Thucydides and Tacitus.

Hume was a "philosophical" historian in two senses. First and especially in his rendition of the turbulent history of seventeenth-century England from James I through to Charles I and the English Civil War, the Restoration of the Stuarts in 1660, and the end of the dynasty with the forced abdication of James II and the arrival as monarch of William III, Hume provided for mid-eighteenth-century British readers a narrative that illustrated the political necessity of balancing parliamentary liberty with sufficient royal authority to avoid violent change in the future. Hume's thesis in his narrative of the previous century of English history is essentially that violent revolution is not worth the price and that England needs to strike a balance between parliamentary and regal power:

Under color of advice [Parliaments] may give disguised orders; and in complaining of grievances, they may draw to themselves every power of government. Whatever measure is embraced, without consulting them, may be pronounced an oppression of the people; and till corrected, they may refuse the most necessary supplies to their indigent sovereign. From the very nature of this parliamentary liberty, 'tis evident, that it must be left unbounded by law: For who can foretell, how frequently grievances may occur, or what part of administration may be affected by them? From the nature too of the human frame, it may be expected, that this liberty would be exerted in its full extent, and no branch of authority be allowed to remain unmolested in the hands of the prince: For, will the weak limitations of respect and decorum be sufficient to restrain human ambition, which so frequently breaks thro' all the prescriptions of law and justice?

(Forbes, ed., *History*, pp. 388–389)

For Hume as for other philosophical historians of the Enlightenment, history also yields general lessons about human nature, which underneath the variety and multiple particularity of the past is a constant and recurring factor in human dealings. So when his history turns to particulars, Hume will often enough remark that the lesson in these events is a general one: "Such circumstances, tho' minute, it may not be improper to transmit to posterity; that those, who are curious of tracing the history of the human mind, may remark, how far its several extravagancies and singularities concur in different ages" (p. 348). Hume wrote his *History* from the same perspective as his philosophical works: he is an urbane and detached observer, looking at the past with the superior wisdom of the enlightened present, free of illusions and secure in a totally secular understanding of human psychology and history. Thus much of the controversy surrounding the first volume of the *History* came from the cool skepticism with which Hume surveyed the religious passions and controversies at the center of the English Civil War:

The great courage and conduct, displayed by many of the popular leaders, have commonly inclined men to do them, in one respect, more honor than they deserve, and to suppose, that, like able politicians, they employed pretexts, which they secretly despised, in order to serve their selfish purposes. 'Tis however probable, if not certain, that they were, generally speaking, the dupes of their own zeal. Hypocrisy, quite pure and free from fanaticism, is perhaps as rare, as fanaticism intirely purged from all mixture of hypocrisy. So congenial to the human mind are religious sentiments, that, where the temper is not guarded by a philosophical scepticism, the most cool and determined, it is impossible to counterfeit long these holy fervors, without feeling some share of the assumed warmth.

(pp. 502–503)

Throughout his *History* and especially in its opening volume, Hume sought to make British history intelligible, to find pattern, recurrence, and moral and political inevitability in the past, thereby showing his readers "that those events, which they impute to their adversaries as the deepest crimes, were the natural, if not the necessary result of the situation, in which the nation was placed, during any period" (p. 391). His "philosophy of government," as he called it here, rendered history "more intelligible as well as instructive." Such establishment of order and moral utility is the goal of all of Hume's writing, and the *History* was his most successful effort to achieve his ends as a writer.

Although he lived in Edinburgh with his sister during the 1750s, Hume made a number of trips to London to see his *History* through the press, and he was attracted to the capital's cosmopolitan charms and thought of moving there. By the early 1760s his fame in Britain and in Europe was complete, and he was especially celebrated in France, where his writings had drawn the praise of the great French intellectuals of the time, such as Montesquieu, Mirabeau, Voltaire, the Abbé Prévost, Diderot, and d'Alembert. In 1763 Hume was asked by Lord Hertford, the new ambassador to France, to accompany him as his personal secretary, and when he arrived in Paris that same year he was lionized, celebrated, and caressed in the salons and aristocratic ballrooms as *le bon David*. Hume enjoyed the attention. He made friendships among the *philosophes*, especially with Diderot and d'Alembert, and he received the admiration of many women, including the Countess de Boufflers, who fell in love with him. The only sour note in his Parisian adventure of these years was his relationship with Rousseau, who had been exiled from his native Geneva for his unorthodox religious opinions. When Hume returned to England in 1766 he arranged for Rousseau to follow him. He found him a house in the country to live in for a nominal rent and arranged for the great man to receive a pension from the king of two hundred pounds per year. But Rousseau had paranoid fantasies and was convinced that Hume was out to embarrass him. He returned to France in 1767 after quarreling with Hume and several of his other friends in England.

Hume had proved a capable diplomat in Paris, and Lord Hertford offered to take him to Ireland in 1765, where he had been appointed lord lieutenant. Instead, Hume in 1767 accepted a post in London as undersecretary of state for the Northern Department (which handled relationships with Scotland but also with European states to the north of France), and for two years he carried out the duties of this post with some efficiency. At this point in his life, Hume moved in exalted social and intellectual circles, and his friends and acquaintances in London as in Paris included the most eminent persons in politics, the arts, and literature. Hume was also at the center of a circle of Scottish writers and thinkers who lived in London or visited there often, such as James Macpherson, Gilbert Elliot, Adam Ferguson, John Home, William Robertson, and Hugh Blair. In 1769 Hume returned to Edinburgh, where he built a new house and spent the rest of his life in ease and comfort, enjoying as he boasted to friends an annual income exceeding £1,000. Although he continued to revise and refine his works for new editions, Hume published almost nothing new during these years, but he did busy himself during the last few months of his life revising his *Dialogues Concerning Natural Religion*, which had been first composed in 1750 and 1751 and had been read by friends in manuscript. Hume died in Edinburgh on 25 August 1776. He left directions in his will for the posthumous publication of the *Dialogues* by his young nephew, and it appeared in 1779.

RELIGIOUS SKEPTIC

DURING his lifetime Hume had become notorious for many eighteenth-century believers as a religious skeptic and even what the age called an "infidel," an unbeliever or atheist. Brought up as a Scottish Presbyterian, he always denied that he was a deist or an atheist, although his writings are consistently skeptical about any knowledge it is possible to have of the existence or nonexistence of God. *The Natural History of Religion* (1757) offers a psychological-anthropological narrative of the origins of belief; Hume traces in this treatise the primal religious impulse in a polytheism founded on primitive man's fear and confusion: "A monstrous birth excites his curiosity, and is deemed a prodigy. It alarms him from its novelty; and immediately sets him a trembling, and sacrificing, and praying" (p. 136). But here as elsewhere Hume was no simple village atheist, and his analysis of religion includes an attack on special philosophical-theological understanding. Indeed, in his representations of the universe projected by monotheism and polytheism, Hume finds in the latter the more natural and even attractive response to nature:

There is an universal tendency among mankind to conceive all beings like themselves, and to transfer to every object, those qualities, with which they are familiarly acquainted, and of which they are intimately conscious. We find human faces in the moon, armies in the clouds; and by a natural propensity, if not corrected by experience and reflection, ascribe malice or good-will to every thing, that hurts or pleases us. Hence the frequency and beauty of the *prosopopoeia* in poetry; where trees, mountains and streams are personified, and the inanimate parts of nature acquire sentiment and passion. And though these poetical figures and expressions gain not on the belief, they may serve, at least, to prove a certain tendency in the imagination, without which they could neither be beautiful nor natural. Nor is a river-god or hamadryad always taken for a mere poetical or imaginary personage; but may sometimes enter into the real creed of the ignorant vulgar; while each grove or field is represented as possessed of a particular *genius* or invisible power, which inhabits and protects it. Nay, philosophers cannot entirely exempt themselves from this natural frailty; but have oft ascribed it to inanimate matter the horror of a *vacuum,* sympathies, antipathies, and other affections of human nature.

(p. 141)

Personification (*prosopopoeia*), or more generally any "transfer" of meaning, Hume notes, is a "universal tendency among mankind." Knowledge consists of a transit from the vivid and immediate to the unknown or distant. In the telling or expression, certain perceptions are never literal or direct but always shifted; they operate like tropes or metaphors, for something is always described in terms of something else. Even the argument from design for the existence of God, whereby the deity is manifest in the intricacy and purposefulness we observe in the natural world, Hume notes, operates by means of a trope-like transfer from effects to divine cause. Of course, Hume claims to speak for a latter-day, more sophisticated stage of knowledge, where such natural propensities are "corrected by experience and reflection." Poetic personifications, however charming, must be held at arm's length and "gain not on the belief." And yet even philosophers, presumably capable of experience and reflection, find their notions infected by this sort of natural transfer of the "affections of human nature."

In *The Natural History of Religion*, Hume wavers in his divisions and exclusions; he speaks of "universal" human tendencies, of mankind in general but also of the "ignorant vulgar" and of "philosophers." The drift of his exposition cancels anyone's exemption from the inevitable pattern or immunity from the transfer of meaning that makes the unknown intelligible. He moves from a history or anthropology of religion to a psychology of religion that is more or less visible in everyone's experience or at least appeals to anyone's reconstruction of possible experience. That sort of ironic contemplation of necessary involvement is where Hume himself stands, moved not so much by the varied images that provoke religious belief as by the spectacle of a uniformly responsive human nature. Hume describes the history of religion as a series of inevitable representations of the deity. The "flux and reflux of polytheism and theism" (p. 158) is caused by the success or failure of such representations, by their rhetorical transformation from one kind of image to another. Initial notions of the deity are altered by "men's exaggerated praises and compliments," and monotheism is a textual invention, as an accumulation of such praise of the gods leads to "the attributes of unity and infinity, simplicity and spirituality" (p. 159). But such ideas are difficult to sustain, and idolatrous conceptions reappear, only to destroy themselves again, this time "by the vile representations, which they form of their deities" (p. 160). A species of aesthetic good taste returns men to monotheism but an inevitable reassertion of ordinary needs leads back to the easy and human images of polytheism.

Religious man for Hume lacks steady or consistent discrimination, since he is moved to belief and worship by various representations, "from the statue or material image to the invisible power; and from the invisible power to an infinitely perfect deity, the creator and sovereign of the universe" (p. 160). Hume and his ideal audience represent a rhetorical and psychological sophistication, the basis of an unwavering good taste whose presence is signified in Hume's writing by the avoidance of rhetorical extravagance. Such superiority consists precisely in recognizing the appeal of rhetorical extravagance in these representations of the deity and thereby avoiding that cycle of persuasive representations which is the history of religion. But in their understanding of the causes and origins of such representations, Hume and his ideal readers testify to their inevitability. The only escape is a comic retreat into speculation:

The whole is a riddle, an enigma, an inexplicable mystery, Doubt, uncertainty, suspence of judgment appear the only result of our most accurate scrutiny, concerning this subject. But such is the frailty of human reason and such the irresistible contagion of opinion, that even this deliberate doubt could scarcely be upheld; did we not enlarge our view, and opposing one species of superstition to another, set them a quarrelling; while we ourselves, during their fury and contention, happily make our escape into the calm, though obscure, regions of philosophy.

(p. 185)

For writing like this, Hume and his works were attacked with some regularity by pious polemicists. He took all this criticism with ironic good humor and never replied to such attacks. But he saw his critics as roadblocks to a civilized and progressive enlightenment in which he believed profoundly. He wrote to Edward Gibbon upon the publication of the first two volumes of *The Decline and Fall of the Roman Empire* in 1776 to warn him that a clamor was sure to arise about Gibbon's treatment of Christianity in his history: "Among many other marks of decline, the prevalence of superstition in England, prognosticates the fall of philosophy and decay of taste; and though no body be more capable than you to revive them, you will probably find a struggle in your first advances" (*Letters*, vol. 2, p. 310). One needs to keep Hume's strong sense of intellectual and cultural mission in mind to read his mature writing, which attempts to balance his ridicule of religious superstition (along with other less specific kinds of ignorance and misapprehension) with a revised understanding of the limits of philosophy. Hume was a paradoxical Enlightenment figure, distinct from his *philosophe* French friends, in that he attacked ignorance and superstition even as he dramatized the limitations of rationality and championed traditional social and moral arrangements. He was a radical thinker who espoused conservative or at least traditional moral, social, and political values. And as the posthumously published *Dialogues Concerning Natural Religion* dramatize, he was above all an elusive and skeptical thinker who refused to be pinned down and whose greatest respect was for the intellectual sociability of the dialogue form. Value and truth for Hume were not absolutes but resided in the active life of the mind, in the process of philosophical activity rather than in any particular set of conclusions. His great hero from antiquity was Cicero, who articulated in his *Academica* a moderate skepticism whereby philosophical dogma is rejected and probable knowledge is accepted as a necessity for the practical business of life.

In 1753, for example, Hume wrote to James Balfour, the author of several attempts to refute Hume's philosophy, to offer friendship in spite of their differences: "Let us revive the happy times, when Atticus and Cassius the Epicureans, Cicero the Academic, and Brutus the Stoic, could, all of them, live in unreserved friendship together, and were insensible to all those distinctions, except so far as they furnished agreeable matter to discourse and conversation" (*Letters,* vol. 1, p. 173). And when he wrote to Gilbert Elliot in 1751 to ask his opinion of the sample he had sent him of an early version of the *Dialogues Concerning Natural Religion,* Hume articulated his ideal for composing a philosophical dialogue: "The best way of composing a dialogue, wou'd be for two persons that are of different opinions about any question of importance, to write alternately the different parts of the discourse, & reply to each other. By this means, that vulgar error wou'd be avoided, of putting nothing but nonsense into the mouth of the adversary" (*Letters,* vol. 1, p. 154). The *Dialogues* is a debate among Demea, an orthodox and somewhat intolerant religionist, Cleanthes, a deist or philosophical theist, and Philo, a careless skeptic (as characterized by the fictional narrator, Pamphilus, who reconstructs the dialogues for a young friend, Hermippus). Hume noted in his letter to Elliot that he made Cleanthes, a philosophi-

cal theist, the "hero of the dialogue." Readers of the *Dialogues* have indeed wondered where Hume himself stands. His sympathies seem clearly to lie with the skeptical Philo, but he allows Cleanthes considerable and persuasive eloquence in the dialogues and in the end has even the skeptical Philo concede that there is a divine being who "discovers himself to reason, in the inexplicable contrivance and artifice of nature" (a position that he elsewhere in the *Dialogues* effectively refutes).

At one point Cleanthes urges in these eloquent terms the so-called argument from design (or *a posteriori,* derived by reasoning from observed facts):

Look round the world: Contemplate the whole and every part of it: You will find it to be nothing but one great machine, subdivided into an infinite number of lesser machines, which again admit of subdivisions, to a degree beyond what human senses and faculties can trace and explain. . . . Since therefore the effects resemble each other, we are led to infer, by all the rules of analogy, that the causes also resemble; and that the Author of nature is somewhat similar to the mind of man; though possessed of much larger faculties, proportioned to the grandeur of the work, which he has executed. By this argument *a posteriori,* and by this argument alone, do we prove at once the existence of a Deity, and his similarity to human mind and intelligence.

(p. 45)

Demea is outraged. "What! No demonstration of the being of a God! No abstract arguments! No proofs *a priori* [that is, without reference to experience]! Are these, which have hitherto been so much insisted on by philosophers, all fallacy, all sophism?" Demea is a believer, of course, but he is also an ordinary and unreflective man who says that "each man feels, in a manner, the truth of religion within his own breast; and from a consciousness of his imbecility and misery, rather than from any reasoning" (p. 95). He is caught between the elegant reasonings of Cleanthes and the subversive theories of Philo, and in part 11 he departs in a huff after Philo argues that the presence of evil in the world argues for a deity who is not the moral God of Christianity. In a passage that Hume added in his final revisions, Philo articulates a negative and satiric revision of the affirmations of the design argument:

Look round this universe. What an immense profusion of beings, animated and organized, sensible and active! You admire this prodigious variety and fecundity. But

242

inspect a little more narrowly these living existences, the only beings worth regarding. How hostile and destructive to each other! How insufficient all of them for their own happiness! How contemptible or odious to the spectator! The whole presents nothing but the idea of a blind nature, impregnated by a great vivifying principle, and pouring forth from her lap, without discernment or parental care, her maimed and abortive children.

(p. 113)

Demea discovers in this part that Philo has not after all been agreeing with him about the "incomprehensible nature of the divine Being," but is in fact a greater enemy to religion than Cleanthes. Philo, as Cleanthes remarks to Demea, has "been amusing himself at both our expence; and it must be confessed, that the injudicious reasoning of our vulgar theology has given him but too just a handle of ridicule" (p. 115). In the end, Philo and Cleanthes are united not in their beliefs but in their common commitment to rational examination and their mutual enjoyment of each other's intelligence and coherence, just the sort of appreciation of intellectual style that Demea lacks.

THE ENQUIRIES

Dialogues Concerning Natural Religion is fully and frankly skeptical, no matter where one decides Hume actually stands, and it is not surprising that Hume did not publish it during his lifetime. But he achieved notoriety with his views on religion in his other works. In *An Enquiry Concerning Human Understanding*, for instance, Hume included two notorious chapters challenging belief in miracles and in Providence and a future state. He develops in this *Enquiry* a view of "accurate and just reasoning" as a liberation from what he calls "abstruse philosophy and metaphysical jargon," as well as from popular superstitions, which "lie in wait to break in upon every unguarded avenue of the mind, and overwhelm it with religious fears and prejudices" (p. 11). He makes clear at the outset of this *Enquiry* his belief that abstruse philosophy and popular superstition are two sides of the same coin, feeding upon one another and excluding the clarity and reason that come from attending to what experience teaches those who are willing to listen and look. Philosophy, he writes, is of two kinds, the easy and obvious such as practiced by the elegant moralists Cicero and Addison, and the abstruse and difficult as exemplified by Aristotle and Locke. The trick is to balance the two kinds by listening to nature, here personified and eloquent:

Indulge your passion for science, says she, but let your science be human, and such as may have a direct reference to action and society. Abstruse thought and profound researches I prohibit, and will severely punish, by the pensive melancholy which they introduce, by the endless uncertainty in which they involve you, and by the cold reception which your pretended discoveries shall meet with, when communicated. Be a philosopher; but, amidst all your philosophy, be still a man.

(p. 9)

What, we may ask, does it mean to be a man? To be properly human means, as Hume explains it here and elsewhere, admitting that we are limited to what our experience teaches, recognizing that our reasoning philosophically about those experiences reveals that we cannot go beyond our perceptions. Hume defines his task as a philosopher, then, essentially in rhetorical terms, a matter of merging Locke and Addison, of "reconciling profound enquiry with clearness, and truth with novelty!" (p. 16). In this opening section of the *Enquiry*, Hume answers nature and tries to defend rigorous philosophy. He calls, especially, for an end to "that abstruse philosophy and metaphysical jargon, which being mixed up with popular superstition, renders it in a manner impenetrable to careless reasoners, and gives it the air of science and wisdom" (pp. 12–13). Philosophy can avoid the trap of obscurity and irrelevance by serious inquiry into "the nature of human understanding," which will be difficult and rigorous but will have as its goal securing human comfort and clarity by driving out false metaphysics: "We must submit to this fatigue, in order to live at ease ever after: And must cultivate true metaphysics with some care, in order to destroy the false and adulterate" (p. 12). Always in Hume's rendition of the scene of thinking there is an implicitly comic insistence on the narrow and self-enclosed limits of human knowledge, and especially of the knowledge available to us as individuals. "The mind has never anything present to it but the perceptions, and cannot possibly reach any experience of their connexion with objects" is a sentiment to which Hume always returns. We must not, he concludes the *Enquiry* by affirming, "be tempted to go beyond common life" or to reason concerning anything except "quantity and number" (p. 153). Humean empiricism is a moral warning; the *Enquiry* ends with a bonfire of the accumulated errors of the past. Look through your library, he says, and if you find a volume of, say, divinity or scholastic metaphysics, scrutinize it carefully: "*Does it contain any abstract reasoning concerning quantity or number? No. Does it contain any experimental reasoning concerning matter of fact and existence? No.* Commit it then to the flames: for it can contain nothing but sophistry and illusion" (p. 165).

The *Enquiry Concerning the Principles of Morals* is also in one sense a collection of moral essays about the problems of thinking accurately and dispassionately. To some extent, these revisions of the *Treatise* are a repudiation of that work's dogmatism and youthful self-assertiveness, and this *Enquiry* begins by attacking errors just such as those the younger Hume might well have been accused of embodying: "Disputes with men, pertinaciously obstinate in their principles, are, of all others, the most irksome; except, perhaps, those with persons, entirely disingenuous, who really do not believe the opinions they defend, but engage in the controversy, from affectation, from a spirit of opposition, or from a desire of showing wit and ingenuity, superior to the rest of mankind" (p. 169). This polite and public-spirited persona is a far cry from the brash and assertive analyst of the *Treatise*. Hume is now out to serve rather than to shock mankind, and as he remarks in section 3, "Of Justice," "in order to establish laws for the regulation of property, we must be acquainted with the nature and situation of man; must reject appearances, which may be false, though specious; and must search for those rules, which are, on the whole, most *useful* and *beneficial.* Vulgar sense and slight experience are sufficient for this purpose; where men give not way to too selfish avidity, or too extensive enthusiasm" (pp. 194–195).

Both of the *Enquiries* project an implicit dialogue, and Hume's persona is an urbane, philosophically informed spectator who warns against the dangers of taking rationalistic conclusions too far and disrupting necessary human order. Thus in the *Enquiry Concerning the Principles of Morals,* a long consideration demolishes the idea that justice is a natural instinct, but recommends it nonetheless as a human necessity. Hume's mature irony as a thinker lies exactly in this strategy of taking things apart and reconstructing or reauthorizing them for social and political reasons. "Have we original innate ideas of praetors and chancellors and juries? Who sees not, that all these institutions arise merely from the necessities of human society?" Birds from every age and country follow instinct in building their nests alike; men by virtue of reason and custom frame their houses differently depending on the age and place: "A like inference may be drawn from comparing the instinct of generation and the institution of property" (p. 202). Hume's examples and instances (he was, after all, a historian, and his philosophy appeals to a sense of reality, not of theory) compel him to argue against the "theory, which accounts for every moral sentiment by the principle of self-love. We must adopt a more public affection, and allow, that the interests of society are not, even on their own account, entirely indifferent to us." Justice and indeed other moral sentiments are produced by their usefulness, Hume believed, and utility seems to account "in great part, for the origin of morality: And what need we seek for abstruse and remote systems, when occurs one so obvious and natural?" (p. 219).

An Enquiry Concerning the Principles of Morals, Hume's favorite philosophical work, concludes with what can be taken as his summarizing thoughts on philosophy, which, as it turns out, according to Hume, can only record what men in practice already know. To be sure, they don't really know it; they have to be reminded that common practice enshrines truth, and it requires the special perspective of the philosopher to validate the ordinary and the commonplace via a rigorous reflection and examination of experience. In the moral world, "if we observe men, in every intercourse of business or pleasure, in every discourse and conversation, we shall find them nowhere, except in the schools, at any loss upon this subject." Our "natural understanding," writes Hume, has been perverted by "systems and hypotheses." Truth for Hume must recommend itself to what mankind wants and will accept, and the *Enquiry* concludes by suggesting two related propositions in one compact and witty sentence: "Truths which are *pernicious* to society, if any such there be, will yield to errors which are salutary and *advantageous*" (p. 279). Hume's clear implication is that there are in fact no truths that are not salutary to society, since truth is nothing less than that which society finds useful. Hume's thought and writing are always in this sense deeply ironic, an affirmation of truth but a denial of the existence of truth in any absolute sense, an affirmation of what humans know and think but a rejection of conventional ideas about why they do so.

SELECTED BIBLIOGRAPHY

I. BIBLIOGRAPHIES. T. E. Jessop, *A Bibliography of David Hume and of Scottish Philosophy from Francis Hutcheson to Lord Balfour* (London, 1938); Roland Hall, *Fifty Years of Hume Scholarship: A Bibliographic Guide* (Edinburgh, 1978).

II. MODERN EDITIONS OF INDIVIDUAL WORKS. *An Abstract of a Treatise of Human Nature*, ed. by J. M. Keynes and P. Sraffa (Cambridge, 1938); *The History of Great Britain: The Reigns of James I and Charles I*, ed. by Duncan Forbes (Harmondsworth, Eng., 1970); *Enquiries Concerning Human Understanding and Concerning the Principles of Morals*, 3d ed., ed. by L. A. Selby-Bigge, rev. and annot. by P. H. Nidditch (Oxford, 1975); *A Treatise of Human Nature*, ed. by L. A. Selby-Bigge, 2d ed. rev. and annot. by P. H. Nidditch (Oxford and New York, 1978); *The History of England: From the Invasion of Julius Caesar to the Revolution in 1688*, 6 vols. (Indianapolis, Ind., 1983); *Essays, Moral, Political, and Literary*, ed. by Eugene F. Miller (Indianapolis, Ind., 1985); *Dialogues Concerning Natural Religion; and, The Natural History of Religion*, ed. by J. C. A. Gaskin (Oxford, 1993).

III. CORRESPONDENCE. *The Letters of David Hume*, 2 vols., ed. by J. Y. T. Greig (Oxford, 1932); *New Letters of David Hume*, ed. by Raymond Klibansky and Ernest C. Mossner (Oxford, 1969).

IV. BIOGRAPHICAL AND CRITICAL STUDIES. H. H. Price, *Hume's Theory of the External World* (Oxford, 1940); Norman Kemp Smith, *The Philosophy of David Hume: A Critical Study of Its Origins and Central Doctrines* (London, 1941); A. H. Basson, *David Hume* (Harmondsworth, Eng., 1958).

Antony Flew, *Hume's Philosophy of Belief: A Study of His First Inquiry* (London, 1961); Charles W. Hendel, *Studies in the Philosophy of David Hume* (Indianapolis, Ind., 1963); John B. Stewart, *The Moral and Political Philosophy of David Hume* (New York, 1963); Laurence L. Bongie, *David Hume: Prophet of the Counter-revolution* (Oxford, 1965); John Valdimir Price, *The Ironic Hume* (Austin, Tex., 1965); D. G. C. McNabb, *David Hume: His Theory of Knowledge and Morality*, 2d ed. (Hamden, Conn., 1966); V. C. Chappel, ed., *Hume: A Collection of Critical Essays* (Notre Dame, Ind., 1968).

Jonathan Bennett, *Locke, Berkeley, Hume: Central Themes* (Oxford, 1971); James Noxon, *Hume's Philosophical Development: A Study of His Methods* (Oxford, 1973); Duncan Forbes, *Hume's Philosophical Politics* (Cambridge and New York, 1975); Anand Chitnis, *The Scottish Enlightenment: A Social History* (Totowa, N.J., 1976); Barry Stroud, *Hume* (London and Boston, 1977).

Ernest C. Mossner, *The Life of David Hume*, 2d ed. (London, 1980); John Passmore, *Hume's Intentions*, 3d ed. (London, 1980); David Miller, *Philosophy and Ideology in Hume's Political Thought* (Oxford and New York, 1981); Peter Jones, *Hume's Sentiments: Their Ciceronian and French Context* (Edinburgh, 1982); David Fate Norton, *David Hume: Common Sense Moralist, Sceptical Metaphysician* (Princeton, N.J., 1982); John J. Richetti, *Philosophical Writing: Locke, Berkeley, Hume* (Cambridge, Mass., 1983); Donald W. Livingston, *Hume's Philosophy of Common Life* (Chicago, 1984); Jerome Christensen, *Practicing Enlightenment: Hume and the Formation of a Literary Career* (Madison, Wis., 1987); V. M. Hope, *Virtue by Consensus: The Moral Philosophy of Hutcheson, Hume, and Adam Smith* (Oxford, 1989).

M. A. Box, *The Suasive Art of David Hume* (Princeton, N.J., 1990); Leo Damrosch, *Fictions of Reality in the Age of Hume and Johnson* (Madison, Wis., 1990); Donald T. Siebert, *The Moral Animus of David Hume* (Newark, Del., 1990); Keith E. Yandell, *Hume's "Inexplicable Mystery": His Views on Religion* (Philadelphia, 1990); Annette Baier, *A Progress of Sentiments: Reflections on Hume's "Treatise"* (Cambridge, Mass., 1991); Adam Potkay, *The Fate of Eloquence in the Age of Hume* (Ithaca, N.Y., and London, 1994).

C. S. LEWIS

(1898–1963)

Sanford Schwartz

AN OXFORD DON AND author of several distinguished books on English literature, C. S. Lewis is best known for his literary fantasies and for the apologetic tracts he composed in defense of traditional Christian doctrine. Lewis began to gain public recognition during the 1930s, but he became an overnight celebrity in 1941, when a series of BBC radio broadcasts made him a household name in England. During and after World War II he also published a highly applauded series of books, including his celebrated cycle of children's stories, *The Chronicles of Narnia* (1950–1956), which established his reputation throughout the English-speaking world. Altogether he published some forty books in his lifetime, and, as a consequence of his enduring popular appeal, more than twenty volumes of stories, poems, essays, and letters have appeared since his death in 1963. With his gift for spiritual fable and for finding the illuminating image, Lewis has not only survived his midcentury vogue but is now generally regarded as one of the most influential Christian apologists of the twentieth century.

LIFE

CLIVE Staples ("Jack") Lewis was born in Belfast on 29 November 1898. His father, Albert, was a solicitor descended from Welsh immigrants who prospered in Belfast's shipbuilding industry. His mother, Florence Hamilton Lewis, was the daughter of a minister from an established Protestant family. The first of their two children, Warren ("Warnie"), was born a year after their marriage in 1894. He was Jack's best childhood friend, and after 1930 his permanent companion.

The most vivid portrait of Lewis' early life is his own autobiography, *Surprised by Joy* (1955). Lewis depicts the life of a flourishing middle-class family in the suburbs of Belfast, a dirty but thriving city still unravaged by sectarian strife. Warnie and Jack (his lifelong nickname) constructed their own playland in the attics and crawl spaces of their large, rambling house. Anticipating things to come, they created a sprawling imaginary kingdom, "Boxen," populated with human and animal figures derived from the rich world of Edwardian children's fiction. This blissful existence, as Lewis describes it, came to a sudden end with the death of their mother in 1908. Soon afterward, the grieving widower sent his children to various boarding schools, the first of which was tyrannized by a headmaster whose meanness (actually incipient madness) reached Dickensian proportions. (Conditions were better elsewhere, but in later life Lewis never missed an opportunity to witness to the horrors of the British public school system.) Finally, in 1914, Lewis was sent to his father's former teacher, William T. Kirkpatrick ("Kirk"), in whose home he spent two happy years learning the languages and literature that provided the basis for his later career.

Lewis' entrance to university was delayed by enlistment in the army. During military training Lewis was introduced to Janie Moore, the mother of a fellow recruit, E. F. C. ("Paddy") Moore, and a divorcée in her forties. Lewis and Mrs. Moore quickly took to one another, and after Paddy's death in France they remained together for more than thirty years. No one—including Lewis' brother, who purchased a house with them in 1930—knew the precise nature of their relationship. In *Surprised by Joy*, Lewis restricts himself to the remark that "one huge and complex episode will be omitted. . . . All I can or need say is that my earlier hostility to the emotions was very fully . . . avenged" (p. 198).

In January 1919 Lewis finally entered Oxford, where he read classical philosophy, history, and literature ("Greats") for three years and then spent an additional year studying English literature. After another two years of uncertainty over his future, he received an offer of employment as a tutor in English from Magdalen College, Oxford, where he remained for the next three decades. During his early years at Oxford, Lewis established a number of significant friendships: with Owen Barfield, who gained an early reputation with *History in English Words* (1926) and *Poetic Diction* (1928); Nevill Coghill, a promising scholar of medieval literature; Hugo Dyson, an Oxford wit and later lecturer at Reading University; and J. R. R. Tolkien, another rising medievalist, who was transforming his knowledge of Celtic, Germanic, and Norse mythology into an ample fictional world of his own. Together with the London-based Charles Williams (whom Lewis met in 1936), they eventually formed the nucleus of the now-celebrated circle known as the Inklings, which gathered each week to listen to its members' work in progress. Dyson and Tolkien were particularly instrumental in the final stage of Lewis' conversion to Christianity. In *Surprised by Joy*, Lewis recalls that his long trek through agnosticism, philosophical idealism, pantheism, and abstract theism came to an end as the result of a late-night walk in September 1931, when his two companions overcame his last reservations to Christian belief.

Lewis examined his spiritual awakening in *The Pilgrim's Regress* (1933), an allegory of his own journey to faith. Three years later he published his classic study *The Allegory of Love: A Study in Medieval Tradition* (1936), which secured him a solid reputation as a literary scholar. In the ensuing years he published several additional books, and by the end of World War II he was regarded as one of the most distinguished literary scholars in England. In the later 1930s Lewis had also returned to fiction, and over the next half decade or so he composed a trilogy of science-fiction novels: *Out of the Silent Planet* (1938), *Perelandra* (1943; reissued as *Voyage to Venus* in 1953), and *That Hideous Strength* (1945). In 1939 he was invited to contribute to a series of religious books, Christian Challenge, and wrote *The Problem of Pain* (1940), which launched his career as an apologist for Christianity. The book caught the attention of the director of religious broadcasting for the BBC, James Welch, who asked Lewis to consider a set of radio talks to a national audience. *Right and Wrong: A Clue to the Meaning of the Universe?* was broadcast in fifteen-minute segments each Wednesday evening in August 1941. Delivered during the darkest hours of World War II, these broadcasts proved so popular that Lewis was asked to continue. He disliked the medium of radio, but his spectacular success resulted in three sequels: *What Christians Believe*, which aired in January and February 1942 (published with the first series as *Broadcast Talks*, 1942; in the United States as *The Case for Christianity*); *Christian Behaviour*, which aired September through November 1942 (published in 1943); and *Beyond Personality*, which ran February through April 1944 (published in 1944). (The entire collection now circulates in a revised four-part edition, *Mere Christianity*, published in 1952.) As a result of these broadcasts, Lewis became a major celebrity. His reputation was compounded by the appearance of other works of apologetics—*The Screwtape Letters* (1942), *The Abolition of Man* (1943), *The Great Divorce* (1945), and *Miracles* (1947)—and by the end of the decade Lewis enjoyed a major following in Christian circles throughout the English-speaking world.

In 1948, Lewis began to compose the celebrated cycle of children's stories, *The Chronicles of Narnia*, which appeared over a seven-year period: *The Lion, the Witch, and the Wardrobe* (1950); *Prince Caspian* (1951); *The Voyage of the Dawn Treader* (1952); *The Silver Chair* (1953); *The Horse and His Boy* (1954); *The Magician's Nephew* (1955); and *The Last Battle* (1956). Around the same time he wrote his autobiography, *Surprised by Joy: The Shape of My Early Life* (1955), and his most intriguing though least appreciated work of fiction, *Till We Have Faces* (1956). Lewis' private life also changed during these years. In the late 1940s Mrs. Moore became increasingly infirm; she died in 1951 at the age of seventy-nine. In the following year Lewis was visited by one of his many American admirers, Helen Joy Gresham (née Davidman), a writer and a Jewish convert to Christianity, who was at the time estranged from her husband, the author William Lindsay ("Bill") Gresham. Lewis eventually married Joy Davidman in a civil ceremony in 1956, and after she was diagnosed with cancer, they were wed in a religious ceremony in 1957. The story of their later relationship—the sudden remission of the disease, their three happy years as husband and wife, and the pathos surrounding her death in 1960—has been dramatized in William Nicholson's BBC teleplay *Shadowlands*

(1985) and the stage and film versions based upon it. Lewis registered his own sense of loss in a book of anguished meditations, *A Grief Observed* (published in 1961 under the pseudonym N. W. Clerk), which departs dramatically from the buoyant tone of his other religious writings.

The other major change of this period was his departure from Oxford. After several unsuccessful bids for a professorship, Lewis accepted a new chair of Medieval and Renaissance English at Magdalene College, Cambridge, in 1954. From then on he commuted between the two university towns, returning home to Oxford each weekend. The move to Cambridge was also accompanied by a new flurry of scholarly work. His monumental *English Literature in the Sixteenth Century, Excluding Drama*, volume 3 of the *Oxford History of English Literature* (or *OHEL*, as he called it), appeared in 1954, followed by *Studies in Words* (1960), *An Experiment in Criticism* (1961), and *The Discarded Image: An Introduction to Medieval and Renaissance Literature* (1964). At the same time Lewis composed a new set of religious writings: *Reflections on the Psalms* (1958); *The Four Loves* (1960); *A Grief Observed* (1961); and *Letters to Malcolm: Chiefly on Prayer* (1964). But soon after Joy's death, Lewis' own health began to deteriorate. After a long struggle with complications from a prostate condition, he died on 22 November 1963, one week before his sixty-fifth birthday.

SCHOLAR AND CRITIC

THE foundations for Lewis' achievement were laid in the long years of study prior to his religious conversion. His early letters, especially the correspondence with his lifelong friend Arthur Greeves (1895–1966), indicate the breadth and focus of his reading: his attraction to epic tradition from Homer to Wagner; the discovery of George Macdonald's *Phantastes* (1858), William Morris' *The Well at the World's End* (1896), and other fantasy narratives; the metaphysical questions provoked by his extensive reading in philosophy; and the fortunes of his various poetic projects. By comparison to Barfield and Tolkien his scholarly career began slowly, but by the early 1930s Lewis was publishing the articles that would culminate in *The Allegory of Love: A Study in Medieval Tradition* (1936), still his most influential work of scholarship. Several other books appeared over the next few years: *Rehabilitations* (1939), a collection of essays on a variety of literary subjects; *The Personal Heresy: A Controversy* (1939), a debate with a well-known scholar, E. M. W. Tillyard, over the role of the author's "personality" in the construction and interpretation of a text; and *A Preface to* Paradise Lost (1942), which was instrumental in resituating Milton's poem in the traditions of classical epic and Christian theology. By the early 1940s Lewis was widely regarded as Oxford's most popular lecturer and one of England's most renowned literary critics.

Lewis' major scholarly achievement of this period was *The Allegory of Love*, which also sheds light on his fiction and apologetics. It is a book of broad historical scope, extending from the birth of allegory in late antiquity to its flowering in the Middle Ages and the Renaissance. Lewis begins with the death of the pagan gods and the concomitant birth of a new sense of interior consciousness, common to both pagan and Christian authors, in the late Roman Empire. The revolutionary nature of this development is epitomized by Saint Augustine's amazement at the sight of Bishop Ambrose reading without stirring his lips (*Confessions*, book 6). According to Lewis, allegory emerges when poets begin to use the obsolete pantheon of pagan gods to personify internal conflicts within the newly discovered "soul." But it is not until the advent of a second spiritual revolution—the birth of "romantic" love in eleventh- and twelfth-century France—that allegory develops into a sophisticated means of exploring a new domain of sensibility. This literature often oscillates between a new worldliness and the traditional demand for sensual renunciation, but Lewis is most drawn to authors who envision "a *tertium quid* between the courtly and the religious conceptions of the good life" (p. 102). He finds this reconciliation in the twelfth-century Platonism of the School of Chartres and in the literary development of "the 'other world' not of religion, but of imagination; the land of longing, the Earthly Paradise, the garden east of the sun and west of the moon" (pp. 75–76). Lewis traces the allegorical elaboration of this "third world of myth and fancy" (p. 82) from the *Romance of the Rose* in the thirteenth century to its final flowering in Edmund Spenser's *The Faerie Queene* at the end of the sixteenth. By that point the worldview supporting such a phenomenon was already yielding to currents that would alter the character of European literature.

The Allegory of Love breaks off abruptly after Spenser, but Lewis has already informed us that several centuries after the demise of allegory as a dominant mode, "that free creation of the marvellous which first slips in under the cloak of allegory" (p. 82) would be reconstituted by the Romantics under the aegis of symbolism. Thus the Romantics perpetuate the "third world of myth and fancy," but with a significant difference: whereas allegory is merely a poetic device for expressing passions by means of fictional personifications, symbolism—or "sacramentalism" (p. 45)—is a mode of thought implying the presence of a higher reality:

The difference between the two can hardly be exaggerated. The allegorist leaves the given—his own passions—to talk of that which is confessedly less real, which is a fiction. The symbolist leaves the given to find that which is more real. . . . There is nothing "mystical" or mysterious about medieval allegory; the poets know quite clearly what they are about and are well aware that the figures which they present to us are fictions. . . . Symbolism comes to us from Greece. It makes its first effective appearance in European thought with the dialogues of Plato. The Sun is the copy of the Good. Time is the moving image of eternity. All visible things exist just in so far as they succeed in imitating the Forms. . . . But of course the poetry of symbolism does not find its greatest expression in the Middle Ages at all, but rather in the time of the romantics.

(pp. 45–48)

This convergence of symbolism, sacramentalism, and Platonism is crucial to all of Lewis' works. From his conversion until his death, Lewis held to a form of Christian Platonism that had as its central tenet a belief "in an 'other' world . . . that Nature, the totality of phenomena in space and time, is not the only thing that exists" (*Studies in Medieval and Renaissance Literature*, p. 144). Christianity and Platonism, in common with the particular conception of romanticism he was prepared to defend, point to a higher reality of which the natural world is merely the confused and partially spoiled copy.

THE PILGRIM'S REGRESS

PRIOR to his conversion, Lewis' literary publications were confined to two slender volumes of verse: *Spirits in Bondage* (1919), an assemblage of forty loosely related lyrics, and *Dymer* (1926), a long mythical narrative. Out of step with the innovative techniques of modernist poetry, Lewis' verse was ignored at the time, and even now its interest lies primarily in the anticipation of his later work. Both volumes focus on "immortal longings" for a higher reality that transcends mundane existence. This desire (or *Sehnsucht*, as he called it) is awakened by a brief vision of "wondrous islands" or a "Hidden Country" (prologue, *Spirits in Bondage*), which imbues the soul with a permanent longing to retrieve and retain its fleeting state of joy. The pre-Christian Lewis is haunted by the specter that these flashes of transcendence are empty illusions, and that Divinity, if it exists, is indifferent or even hostile to our aspirations. *Spirits in Bondage* struggles toward a timid affirmation of the "Country of Dreams" (p. 75), while *Dymer* passes through the most frightful earthly calamities, produced ironically by the very quest for the "sacred shiver / Of joy" (*Narrative Poems*, p. 24), to achieve a final slim ray of hope. The Christian Lewis would close this gap between aspiration and reality. But he retained the notion of *Sehnsucht*, elaborating this romantic longing into the more complex "dialect of Desire" (preface, *The Pilgrim's Regress*, 3d ed.) that informs his subsequent writings.

This new development appears in Lewis' first work of prose fiction, *The Pilgrim's Regress: An Allegorical Apology for Christianity, Reason, and Romanticism* (1933), written in the manner of John Bunyan's *The Pilgrim's Progress* (1678) soon after Lewis' conversion. The pilgrim personifies the spiritual condition of Everyman, but in fact his particular trials follow Lewis' own journey to faith. The story begins in Puritania, a thinly veiled Ulster administered by the Steward on behalf of the stern absentee Landlord. John, the pilgrim, knows that the Landlord's Castle lies in the nearby mountains to the east, but his focus is directed to the distant west where he briefly glimpses a beautiful island and feels "a sweetness and a pang so piercing that instantly he forgot his father's house, and his mother, and the fear of the Landlord, and the burden of the rules" (book 1, chap. 2). Smitten by *Sehnsucht*, John leaves home in quest of the island, even though he recognizes "with one part of his mind . . . that what had befallen him was not seeing at all. . . . that it was not entirely true" (book 1, chap. 2). His subsequent adventures allegorize the propensity of the soul to wander from its true objective by settling on lesser objects (idolatry), by trying to reproduce the emotion in the absence of its correlative object (some versions of romanticism), or by abandoning the quest altogether (the way of modern naturalism). Only at the end of his pilgrimage does he discover that the island in the west is in reality the other side of the mountains to the east, and to reach his true destination, the Landlord's Castle, he must journey back the way he came. It turns out that spiritual progress is also a regress—a circle perhaps, though not a vicious one, since it is only by means of the journey that the soul discovers the reality it has left behind.

Between the beginning and the end of his travels, Lewis' pilgrim encounters allegorical figures personifying modern forms of intellectual seduction. He reckons with the seemingly antithetical temptations of the Enlightenment and romanticism—the former personified by Mr. Vertue's commitment to morality without God, the latter by harp-playing Mr. Halfways, who dissolves the supernatural into a mere state of mind: "the Landlord they dreamed to find, we find in our hearts: the Island you seek for, you already inhabit. . . . it is an Island of the Soul" (book 2, chap. 5). Geographically, Enlightenment and romanticism lie on either side of the Main Road that divides this fictional world into northern and southern zones. In the north dwell the excesses of intellection, in the south the lures of emotional satisfaction. The Main Road represents a desirable middle way, since "we were made to be neither cerebral men nor visceral men, but Men. Not beasts nor angels but Men—things at once rational and animal" (preface, 3d ed.). The pilgrim errs in both directions, but Lewis regarded the ascetic north as the characteristic terrain of his own disillusioned age and devotes much of the book to contemporary sins of the intellect: cynical postwar poets who scorn the "immortal longings" of their predecessors; disciples of Freud who reduce the soul to elemental mechanisms of desire— "the Island was the pretence that you put up to conceal your own lusts from yourself" (book 3, chap. 6); and, perhaps surprisingly, various modern conservatives—neoscholastics, neohumanists, and neoclassicists—who trample on human emotion by formulating hyper-rational defenses of traditional religious values. The hostility directed at the neoconservatives is significant in pinpointing Lewis' own position. If Mr. Halfways' romanticism

offers emotional satisfaction without objective foundation, Lewis found the antiromanticism of moderns such as T. S. Eliot far more dangerous. Properly understood, romanticism expresses our natural longing for the reality beyond the material realm. Lewis could agree with certain articles of the neoconservative creed, but he saw the solution not in the renunciation of emotions but in the recovery of their transcendent object.

As his sojourn continues, John learns of trouble stirring to the far north, where multitudes of angry "revolutionary sub-men" (book 6, chap. 6), at once the victims of the modern malady and its most aggravated symptom, are assembling for a great invasion. But Lewis is concerned less with fascism and communism than with his own pilgrimage to faith, and he sends his pilgrim south to encounter less harsh dispositions of the soul. The story of John's adventures now follows Lewis' own passage through a variety of philosophical and spiritual allegiances until his final acceptance of Christianity. As Lewis marches his pilgrim through some rarefied academic debate, many readers find themselves in the dark, struggling to decode an allegory based on the concerns of a few Oxford intellectuals in the 1920s. But in a certain respect this is the most profound section of the book. Lewis discriminates among some deceptively similar philosophies, identifying seemingly small but crucial differences in their ontological commitments. As a result of this process, John arrives at Christianity not by a sudden lurch into faith but through a carefully measured progress of the mind toward the reception of what would otherwise seem the most improbable of doctrines.

Having discovered that his true goal lies to the east, the converted pilgrim quickly begins his "regress" home. The surprise is that the same terrain looks so different on the return journey. Ideas that once loomed large in his thinking have shriveled into insignificance. "Your eyes are altered. You see nothing now but realities" (book 10, chap. 2), John learns from a reliable guide. The finale takes place in Puritania, where the pilgrim is instructed to prepare for death. Believing he had transcended his attachment to worldly things, John is surprised to find himself weeping over his imminent departure from this world and over the news that many of his family and friends have died. Lewis' point is that we are at once cursed and blessed by "the tether and pang of the particular." He modulates into verse to express the mingling of sorrow and joy that not only "turns all / Spirit's sweet water to astringent soul," but also draws us closer to the divine suffering so that we may

> . . . not reflect merely,
> As lunar angel, back to thee, cold flame.
> Gods we are, Thou hast said: and we pay dearly.
> (book 10, chap. 10)

The author's poetic gifts are limited, but the tension between irrecoverable loss and redemptive hope at the end of *The Pilgrim's Regress* achieves an emotional depth equal to anything in his more mature works.

The Pilgrim's Regress made considerable demands on its audience. The book sold reasonably well, though the archaic style, allegorical form, and philosophical exposition limited its appeal. Lewis addressed these difficulties in the 1943 edition, to which he appended an illuminating preface and explanatory headlines for each chapter (absent from some later editions). At the same time he acknowledged the irreparable difficulties of a book that required such ancillary apparatus. *The Pilgrim's Regress* remains an oddity in the Lewis canon, but it also anticipates the structure and thematics of the major fiction. Most of Lewis' later stories are journeys of the soul toward the recognition of a transcendent reality. Like *The Pilgrim's Regress*, they are voyages through imaginary landscapes that reveal the shortcomings and expand the horizons of their protagonists, culminating in their spiritual transformation. For Lewis the imagination is a means of awakening the mind to new possibilities of thought, feeling, and action. In this respect the literary voyages to the alternative worlds of Puritania, Mars, or Narnia are designed to detach us from habitual patterns of thought and allow us "to see with other eyes, to imagine with other imaginations, to feel with other hearts, as well as with our own" (*An Experiment in Criticism*, p. 137).

SPACE TRILOGY

AFTER completing *The Pilgrim's Regress*, Lewis devoted himself primarily to scholarly activities, but in the late 1930s and early 1940s he returned to fiction and composed a series of novels—*Out of the Silent Planet* (1938), *Perelandra* (1943), and *That Hideous Strength* (1945)—that are now well established classics of science fiction. The new venture was influenced by the popular scientific romances of H. G. Wells and Olaf Stapledon, but its principal source of inspiration was David Lindsay's *Voyage to Arcturus* (1920), which used interplanetary travel as a means for exploring spiritual issues. Lewis' unlikely protagonist, Elwin Ransom, is a Cambridge philologist who becomes entangled in spiritual warfare on Mars, Venus, and finally Earth. Ransom is a Christian from the outset, but until his departure from Earth he is only dimly aware of the true glory of creation and the terrible plight of our own "silent planet." Over the course of the trilogy Ransom develops from a perplexed spectator to an anointed agent of divine redemption, confronting the demonic powers that threaten the beneficent order of the universe, which is overseen by a loving God (Maleldil) and his angelic ministers (*eldila*) but imperiled by the abuse of the very freedom that consummates the creation.

Out of the Silent Planet is the story of Ransom's adventure on Mars. It pits the hero against two villains—Weston, a brilliant physicist, and Devine, a rapacious businessman—who are preparing to conquer the red planet, the former out of a twisted view of human destiny, the latter out of sheer lust for power. The two schemers kidnap Ransom in the mistaken belief that the Martians, whom they equate with primitive tribesmen, have demanded an earthling as a sacrificial victim. As a prisoner on their spaceship, Ransom experiences the first of many surprises. The vast regions beyond our world are not the dark, alien void envisioned by popularizations of modern physical theory, but an ocean of radiant light:

A nightmare, long engendered in the modern mind by the mythology that follows in the wake of science, was falling off him. He had read of "Space": at the back of his thinking for years had lurked the dismal fancy of the black, cold vacuity, the utter deadness, which was supposed to separate the worlds. He had not known how much it affected him till now—now that the very name "Space" seemed a blasphemous libel for this empyrean ocean of radiance in which they swam. . . . No: Space was the wrong name. Older thinkers had been wiser when they named it simply the heavens—the heavens which declared the glory.

(p. 32)

The planets, as Ransom now sees them, are "mere holes or gaps in the living heaven . . . formed not by addition to, but by subtraction from, the surrounding brightness," and perhaps "visible light is also a hole or gap, a mere diminution of something else. Something that is to bright unchanging heaven as heaven is to the dark, heavy earths" (p. 40).

After landing on Malacandra, Ransom experiences a second reversal of expectations. Influenced by H. G. Wells, he had imagined Mars as a desolate expanse or a labyrinth of monstrosities. Instead he discovers a world of great beauty populated by initially odd-looking but peaceful and rational beings. Escaping from his captors, Ransom learns from the planet's inhabitants that Malacandra possesses three species of rational beings. Thematically, the crucial point about Martian society is that for all their differences in appearance, custom, and skill, none of these species seeks to exercise control over the others. Unlike their counterparts on Earth, who enslave other members of their own species, or even define them as members of a lesser species, the three types of Martian humanity dwell separately but harmoniously in the same world. Dreams of colonial conquest never cross their minds. All three species pay homage to another type of being, the angel-like *eldila*, who are plainly visible to the Martians though at first barely discernible to Ransom.

The rest of the plot is simple. Ransom is summoned before the chief *eldil*, or Oyarsa, who rules Malacandra on behalf of Maleldil the Young (analogous to the second person of the Christian Trinity). Here Ransom is instructed in cosmic history—how the once magnificent Oyarsa of Earth rebelled against Maleldil; how his attempt to ruin Mars damaged the surface of the planet and forced the construction of the canals visible from Earth; and how he was eventually driven back to his own planet, where "he lies to this hour, and we know no more of that planet: it is silent" (p. 121). At this point Weston and Devine are led in with the bodies of several Martians whom they have killed. Still regarding Oyarsa as little more than a savage chieftain, they are sent back to Earth, punished by the fear that they will perish on the voyage. Ransom, offered the opportunity to remain on Mars, elects to return home, and enters the spaceship protected by the "unseen presences" (p. 146) that fill the heavens.

The cosmic struggle continues in *Perelandra*, where the scene shifts from the aging civilization of Mars to the newly created world of Venus. In the first novel, Ransom's involvement seems accidental; in the second, he sets out on a divinely appointed though unspecified mission. When he reaches Venus he finds himself in the midst of a pleasurable flux:

It looked exactly as though you were in a well-wooded valley with a river at the bottom of it. But while you watched, that seeming river did the impossible. It thrust itself up so that the land on either side sloped downwards from it; and then up farther still and shouldered half the landscape out of sight beyond its ridge; and became a huge greeny-gold hog's back of water hanging in the sky and threatening to engulf your own land, which was now concave and reeled backwards to the next roller, and rushing upwards, became convex again.

(p. 51)

These vertiginous descriptions are not simply a display of their author's visionary gifts. In part Lewis is attempting to counter the common view of paradise as an intolerably static condition of being. But more important, his portrayal of the unfallen world as a ceaseless flux is a means of examining the human predicament in our own fallen world, where temporal progression is distorted by insecurity and the specter of death.

This theme moves to the foreground when Ransom notices his desire to freeze the perpetual movement around him. The impulse appears initially as a temptation to repeat a pleasant experience:

This itch to have things over again, as if life were a film that could be unrolled twice or even made to work backwards . . . was it possibly the root of all evil? No: of course the love of money was called that. But money itself—perhaps one valued it chiefly as a defence against chance, a security for being able to have things over again, a means of arresting the unrolling of the film.

(p. 48)

In other words, our attempt to deny the temporal conditions of our existence and control our own destiny is the very basis of our fallen state. Lewis underscores this point when Ransom meets the Green Lady—the Eve of this new Eden—who simply accepts the "unrolling of the film" and never imagines that the stream of life could be anything other than it is. The one prohibition in her fluid world—its Tree of the Knowledge of Good and Evil—is that she must not settle on the Fixed Land.

253

Perelandran paradise is soon disturbed by the arrival of Weston, or as Ransom comes to realize, the diabolical Un-man who is taking possession of Weston's body. The physicist is now espousing a theory of creative evolution—the postulate of an immanent Life-Force (Bergson's *élan vital*) that impels creation to ever-higher forms of development—and declares himself the instrument through which this vital impulse will take its next leap forward. Lewis sees major dangers in this theory. By placing humanity at the forefront of cosmic development, the idea of creative evolution can turn into a means of rationalizing our worst impulses. In Weston's hands it is a mere excuse for interplanetary conquest, but closer to home it gets twisted into a pseudotheory that justifies the domination of one sector of humanity over another. From this perspective, the theory of creative evolution is simply another expression of our desire to usurp control over the conditions of our existence. It is a parody of true temporality, a theory of flux that paradoxically reveals our inability to accept the natural flow of time.

The real aim of the Un-man's mission is to extend the dominion of evil. In a reprise of the biblical story, the Un-man urges the Green Lady to inhabit the Fixed Land. (Lewis published *A Preface to* Paradise Lost a year before *Perelandra,* and the Un-man's arguments derive much of their ingenuity from the tempter in Milton's poem.) Ransom tries to assist the Lady, who in her innocence proves nearly as shrewd as her adversary. But fearful that they are no match for the Un-man's tireless casuistry, Ransom despairs of reasoning and resorts to physical combat. The Un-man turns out to have no more physical strength than the body he inhabits, and in extended combat Ransom succeeds in destroying it.

Perelandra concludes with a celebration of Deep Heaven, though for many readers the finale fails to dispel the bad odor left by the recourse to physical violence. Lewis had his reasons for this resolution. Like many of his compatriots, he looked back on his nation's reluctance to use force against Nazi Germany as the fatal error of the 1930s. He had little patience for Christian pacificism and wished to remind his contemporaries that some of the Lord's work might require the virtues of Saint George. The problem of *Perelandra,* however, is not physical combat per se, but the fact that the violence is initiated by Ransom out of despair over the impotence of dis-

course. Lewis had his reasons for this as well, but it left him with a morally problematic and artistically unsatisfying resolution.

The conflict returns to Earth in *That Hideous Strength,* the final and by far the longest volume of the trilogy. The plot revolves around a callow young couple—Mark Studdock, a fellow in sociology at a small provincial university, and his wife, Jane—who drift into opposite sides of a monumental conflict. Mark, a member of his college's "progressive" faction, is lured into a powerful organization—the National Institute of Co-ordinated Experiments (N.I.C.E.)—whose real aim is control of the planet, while Jane is drawn into the small spiritual remnant left to combat the seemingly irresistible force of the enemy.

N.I.C.E. first appears as a vaguely benign research center, but it soon consolidates its hold on the region by employing techniques of violence and fraud reminiscent of the Nazi rise to power. N.I.C.E.'s scientists are attempting to resurrect the dead: their aim is to conquer the basic conditions of life and replace humanity with "the New Man, the man who will not die, the artificial man, free from Nature" (p. 177). They seek to locate and revive the corpse of the ancient magician Merlin in the hope of combining the lost art of magic with the power of modern science. And peering beyond the limits of scientific rationalism, the N.I.C.E. elite has intimations of superhuman intelligences (*macrobes*) that may be harnessed to consolidate the reign of evil. In a scientistic manner they are groping toward their true masters—the *eldila* that have turned Thulcandra into "the silent planet." This macabre stew of scientism and demonism is the "hideous strength" poised for final conquest of humanity.

Opposed to N.I.C.E. is a motley assemblage of Christians centered in a nearby village. When certain members of this group discover that the initially non-Christian Jane is having dream visions of the impending struggle, they introduce her to their director, Elwin Ransom, now Pendragon of Logres, anointed by Maleldil to battle the power of N.I.C.E. The office of Pendragon descends in a kind of apostolic succession from King Arthur; it serves the secret kingdom of Logres that has kept the spirit of Maleldil alive in Britain for many dark centuries. Merlin, Ransom tells us, was "the last vestige of an older order in which matter and spirit were, from our modern point of view, confused. . . . After him came the modern man to whom Nature is something dead—a machine to be worked, and taken to bits if it won't work the way he pleases. . . . In a sense Merlin represents what we've got to get back to in some different way" (pp. 285–286). Ransom's immediate goal is to find Merlin's body before it falls into the hands of the enemy. The ultimate goal is to refashion the way modern humanity conceives itself and the world around it.

Once the various elements of main conflict are in place, the resolution is vigorous if distressingly clumsy. Merlin is recovered, and the Christian remnant, inspired by an impressive display of cosmic pageantry, marches to a lopsided victory over N.I.C.E. Lewis ties this reunion of Heaven and Earth to the restitution of right relations between the sexes. Mark's eleventh-hour rejection of his demonic masters exempts him from their fate, and the chastened couple look forward to the real beginning of their marriage.

By 1945, Lewis had a large and receptive audience, but many readers considered *That Hideous Strength* a flawed book and a disappointing conclusion to the trilogy. The shift in locale from imaginary worlds to our own is accompanied by an irreparable loss in inventiveness. The development of the plot is painfully slow and aggravated by constant shuffling from place to place within each chapter. The strains of integrating Arthurian legend, along with the jumble of ideologies fused together in the army of evil, make the final showdown something of a hash. Moreover, Lewis' message was an offense to a portion of his audience. From his perspective the novel is an attempt to depict the ultimate consequences of Enlightenment rationality, which has despiritualized the natural order and given us the arrogance to believe that we can refashion the world to our liking. In this respect, the apparent benevolence of social engineering is only one step away from the open coercion of fascism. Composed as the tide began to turn against the Axis powers, *That Hideous Strength* is a warning that the threat posed by modern naturalism will not disappear with victory over Germany. But many readers did not take kindly to this near equation between a progressivist social agenda and fascism. Even under ordinary circumstances the book would have met considerable resistance; but appearing at the very moment when Britain was mobilizing for its own ambitious experiment in social reform, Lewis' novel was dramatically out of step with the times.

APOLOGETICS

For nearly thirty years Lewis bore witness to Christianity in a stream of books, essays, sermons, poems, and letters. But the period around World War II may be distinguished for his commitment to apologetics—the reasoned defense of Christianity designed to answer objections, dispel doubts, and win the assent of a general audience. In addition to his radio broadcasts and the openly apologetical elements of his space trilogy, Lewis published *The Problem of Pain* (1940), *The Screwtape Letters* (1942), *The Abolition of Man* (1943), *The Great Divorce* (1945), and *Miracles* (1947). His wartime audience was struck by the vitality of his prose, the cogency of his reasoning, and the images, metaphors, and analogies he relied on to clinch an argument. His paragraphs flowed with such ease that readers missed, or were prepared to forgive, the missteps in argumentation: the miscasting and trivializing of objections, the use of an unproven conclusion from one argument as the premise for the next, the reduction of complex issues to either/or alternatives equally embarrassing to the opposing side, or the slippery equation between Christianity's case against naturalism and Britain's struggle against fascism. But to Christians eager for a spirited defense of the faith, and an embattled populace receptive to moral justifications of its cause, Lewis possessed an immense appeal.

His first effort at apologetics, *The Problem of Pain,* is one of his most controversial. The Judeo-Christian tradition has long struggled with the problem of reconciling the goodness of an omnipotent creator with the suffering of the innocent and just in this world. From Job to the present, the integrity of this tradition has depended in part on the reluctance to brush away the scandal of human suffering. Lewis opens safely enough by claiming that pain ("suffering" would have been the more appropriate term) is a scandal only because we possess the notion of originary goodness and therefore regard affliction as an aberrant state of being. While naturalism dismisses religion as a defensive reaction to the terrors of insecurity, suffering, and death in this world, Lewis contends that these terrors are not so much the cause as the effect of our apprehension of the supernatural. In other words, the supernatural "creates, rather than solves, the problem of pain, for pain would be no problem unless, side by side with our daily experience of this painful world, we had received what we think a good assurance that ultimate reality is righteous and loving" (p. 24). To explain the rift between ultimate reality and our existing condition, Lewis adopts the Augustinian view that attributes evil to mankind's misuse of free agency, a willful defection that has produced "a radical alteration of his constitution, a disturbance of the relation between his component parts, and an internal perversion of one of them" (p. 84).

The argument begins to creak, however, when Lewis jumps from this traditional explanation to the conclusion that God sanctions pain for our own benefit. At the point where a Christian might have expected him to turn to the redemptive act of divine suffering, Lewis dwells instead on the divine use of human suffering. Pain is the means by which God "shatters the illusion that all is well" (p. 95), disrupting our slide into complacency with the world we have arranged for ourselves. At this stage Lewis is on the verge of transgressing the limits of Christian doctrine by positing a "tribulational system" (p. 105) in which suffering becomes the "sterilised or disinfected evil" (p. 116) through which God summons his wayward creatures back to himself. It is no accident that even sympathetic readers prefer the tormented sufferer of *A Grief Observed*. (Nor is it an accident that William Nicholson begins his play *Shadowlands* with a self-assured Lewis paraphrasing *The Problem of Pain* before he tastes the bitter cup of grief.) The original audience found much to praise in the book, but the metaphors were misleading, the prose too glib for so sensitive an issue, and the notion of a beneficent "tribulational system" bore spiritual and social implications that Lewis himself would have deplored.

No such problems beset the fictional *Screwtape Letters*, where the agency of tribulation shifts from a real heaven to an imaginary hell. The book comprises epistles from a senior devil to his nephew Wormwood, an apprentice in the art of temptation who is cutting his teeth on a new convert to Christianity. Screwtape has a nose for human folly and a knack for exploiting the favorable conditions of modernity. He advises Wormwood to capitalize on the novice's petty foibles and secret pride:

Work hard, then, on the disappointment or anticlimax which is certainly coming to the patient during his first few weeks as a churchman. . . . What he says, even on his knees, about his own sinfulness is all parrot talk. At bottom, he still believes he has run up a very favourable credit-balance in the Enemy's ledger by allowing himself to be converted, and thinks that he is showing great humility and condescension in going to church with these "smug," commonplace neighbours at all. Keep him in that state of mind as long as you can.

(pp. 13–14)

Although the young man's faith survives these early trials, Screwtape knows that every stage of spiritual growth offers fresh opportunities for seduction. If the patient shows signs of true humility, tempt him to become proud of it; if he begins to amend his life, "let the reflection 'My feelings are now growing more devout, or more charitable' so fix his attention inward that he no longer looks beyond himself to see our Enemy or his own neighbours" (p. 30). The trick at any stage is to attenuate our focus on the reality external to ourselves—"the taste for the *other*" (*The Problem of Pain*, p. 123)—and elevate the self into the principal object of its own attention.

Self-glorification, according to Screwtape, is the very essence of the infernal "Lowerarchy":

The whole philosophy of Hell rests on the recognition of the axiom that one thing is not another thing, and, specially, that one self is not another self. My good is my good and your good is yours. What one gains another loses. . . . for us, it means the sucking of will and freedom out of a weaker self into a stronger. "To be" *means* "to be in competition."

(p. 81)

The self-giving nature of divine love is beyond demonic comprehension, though Screwtape is confident that infernal science (another slap at naturalism) will one day penetrate the mystery: "If we could only find out what He is *really* up to! Hypothesis after hypothesis has been tried, and still we can't find out. Yet we must never lose hope; more and more complicated theories, fuller and fuller collections of data, richer rewards for researchers who make progress, more and more terrible punishments for those who fail" (p. 87). Unable to fathom or contain the Enemy, Screwtape grows short-tempered with his nephew as the new Christian repeatedly slips out of his net. By the time the young man dies in a bombing raid, he is beyond the grasp of his tempters, who in accord with their own nature have also turned on one another.

Christian tradition has generally pitched itself between privative and positive conceptions of evil. On one side is the Augustinian view that evil is ontologically void, and therefore nothing other than a defection of the will from God. On the other side is the dualist view that evil has the kind of substantial being implied by figures such as Satan and his brood. Each of these conceptions entails certain consequences, and each has been used at times to offset the excesses of the other. Lewis himself was an Augustinian and knew that the pragmatic advantage of the privative notion is that it checks the temptation to displace evil onto forces external to ourselves. In *The Screwtape Letters* he takes an imaginary excursion in the opposite direction to make playful use of the dualist element in Christian doctrine. By objectifying evil as an external power we can treat our own frailties as the effect of a power alien to our essential nature and better mobilize ourselves against them. The key to Lewis' success is that the objectifying mirror provokes much laughter and a little sympathy for our fragile condition.

In *The Abolition of Man* (1943), Lewis continues to reflect on suffering and evil in the modern world. Roughly contemporaneous with *That Hideous Strength*, the book situates the horrors of totalitarianism in the context of the more fundamental change associated with naturalism. In *The Abolition of Man*, Lewis attributes this change to the modern dissociation between mind and nature, emotion and object, values and facts—which has drained morality of its objective foundations and transformed external reality into a measurable and purely material domain. In line with contemporaneous critiques from the other end of the ideological spectrum, such as Theodor Adorno and Max Horkheimer's *Dialectic of Enlightenment* (1947), Lewis claims that in the modern era, rationality has been reduced to an instrumental mechanism for the conquest of Nature. Paradoxically, this rationality becomes a monstrous irrationality when it turns its gaze on humanity itself:

We reduce things to mere Nature *in order that* we may "conquer" them. . . . But as soon as we take the final step of reducing our own species to the level of mere Nature . . . the being who stood to gain and the being who has been sacrificed are one and the same. . . . It is the magician's bargain: give up our soul, get power in return. But once our souls, that is, our selves, have

been given up, the power thus conferred will not belong to us. We shall in fact be the slaves and puppets of that to which we have given our souls. It is in Man's power to treat himself as a mere "natural object" and his own judgements of values as raw material. . . . not raw material to be manipulated, as he fondly imagined, by himself, but by mere appetite, that is, mere Nature, in the person of his dehumanized Conditioners.

(pp. 82–84)

Humanity's conquest of Nature has turned into Nature's reconquest of humanity, and the very agency of humanity's emancipation has become the instrument of its re-enslavement. The political implications of this process are as frightening as they are obvious: "the power of Man to make himself what he pleases means . . . the power of some men to make other men what *they* please" (p. 72).

Against this self-destructive rationality Lewis marshals the perennial wisdom of the ages. Reversing the modern tendency to subjectivize values, Lewis draws on the sages of various traditions, pagan and Christian, Western and non-Western, to demonstrate the universality of moral law—"the doctrine of objective value, the belief that certain attitudes are really true, and others really false, to the kind of thing the universe is and the kind of things we are" (p. 29). Lewis is enough of a philosopher to know that mere agreement on certain principles does not demonstrate their inherent validity. Nevertheless, by gathering diverse testimonials as evidence of common rationality based on principles of justice, kindness, loyalty, and courage, he portrays modern rationality as a grisly aberration from the human norm. A demonstrable proof may be beyond our grasp, but as Lewis sets up the alternatives, the consequence of denying the moral law will be the "abolition of man" as envisioned in the inner sanctum of N.I.C.E.

In *The Great Divorce* (1945), Lewis returns to the fictional mode of *The Screwtape Letters* and lays out his Augustinian view of evil. The book is a dream vision based on the medieval idea of the *Refrigerium* (p. 66)—the speculative notion that God continues to woo the damned in Hell by offering them periodic glimpses of Heaven. At the outset an unnamed narrator finds himself boarding a bus with some inhabitants of a dull sprawling town. Before long he realizes from their incessant griping that his fellow riders belong to the infernal regions, and when their bus arrives at the outer precincts of Heaven, he notices that they appear insubstantial by comparison to the bright solid people they encounter. In a series of exchanges with former colleagues, friends, and relatives, most of the visitors reaffirm the choice they have already made: a former bishop maintains his conviction that "to travel hopefully is better than to arrive" (p. 43); a hard-bitten cynic asserts that Heaven and Hell are run by the same Combine; a woman fixated on the child she has lost remains indifferent or hostile to God.

At the center of the book the narrator meets his venerable mentor, George Macdonald, who unravels the meaning of the dream vision. Heaven is the only Reality, Macdonald explains, while Hell is a but a "state of mind." The damned are those who have chosen to reject or ignore God, and "without that self-choice there could be no Hell" (p. 72). The freedom to decide remains open to them even beyond the grave, and nothing but their own will prevents them from staying forever in the company of the blessed. The consequences of choice, according to Macdonald, transcend mortal conceptions of time and space. For the individual who turns to God, the past itself "begins to change so that his forgiven sins and remembered sorrows take on the quality of Heaven" (p. 68). At the same time, Hell dissolves into nothing so that "the Blessed will say, 'We have never lived anywhere except in Heaven'" (p. 68). By the end of the book the privative conception of evil has been pushed so far that the infernal dominion has dwindled into a minute crack in Deep Heaven, and Macdonald declares that the tiniest element in the Real World is more substantial than Hell in its entirety. In language ascending to an almost mystical plane, Macdonald affirms the eternal significance of freedom— "the gift whereby ye most resemble your Maker" (p. 125)—and in suggesting that true freedom may transcend our mortal understanding of choice he hints at the universalist position that ultimately every soul will be redeemed. Nevertheless, he reminds the narrator that Hell is real enough for those who continue to choose it. Or as Lewis puts it in the preface: Hell may be ontologically void, but we should resist the "false and disastrous" conclusion "that everything is good and everywhere is Heaven" (p. 7).

In his last major work of apologetics, *Miracles* (1947), Lewis abandons the more conversational manner of previous books and attempts a sustained philosophical treatise to demonstrate "the possibility or probability of the miraculous" (p. 4). His initial assault on naturalism runs into trouble, however, and in the view of some readers, he never quite recovers. In *The Abolition of Man*, Lewis considered the dualistic element of naturalism and successfully picked apart its dissociation between value and fact, mind and matter. In *Miracles* he approaches naturalism as a monistic system that reduces everything to matter governed by deterministic laws. Few would quarrel with this formulation, but Lewis goes on to argue that naturalism is caught in a vicious circle, since it calls into question the integrity of the rational processes upon which it (or any conceptual system) depends. By employing this argument Lewis walks into the midst of a long and complex debate over the relationship between mind and reality, a debate involving a host of issues that he never bothers to address.

Lewis has better success in later sections of the book, where he offers a vivid if not entirely original reconception of miracles as the fulfillment rather than the disruption, or "invasion," of the natural order: "Our whole picture of Nature being 'invaded' (as if by a foreign enemy) was wrong. When we actually examine one of these invasions it looks much more like the arrival of a king among his own subjects" (p. 32). In other words, Lewis naturalizes the miraculous not by eliminating the supernatural but by subsuming the natural into a more inclusive reality in which the common distinction between natural and supernatural no longer holds. But as compelling as this vision may be, the argument of *Miracles* is hobbled throughout by the casual use of problematic terms, inferences, and analogies. Lewis himself was dissatisfied with the book, particularly after it received a drubbing from the philosopher G. E. M. (Elizabeth) Anscombe during a now-legendary Oxford debate in February 1948 (chapter 3, the main target of her attack, was revised for the 1960 edition). It is difficult to say whether this incident affected the subsequent course of Lewis' career, but never again did he attempt a treatise on the order of *Miracles*, and it was nearly a decade before he returned in a serious way to religious exposition of any sort. When *Reflections on the Psalms* appeared in 1958, Lewis made it clear from the start that he had left behind apologetics for a more intimate mode of spiritual reflection.

C. S. LEWIS

THE CHRONICLES OF NARNIA

LEWIS may have been disappointed by *Miracles* and its reception, but part of the ill-fated book proved fertile for his next venture into fiction. At one point in *Miracles,* Lewis speculates on the possibility of natural systems other than our own. For the modern naturalist, he claims, the system of nature as we know it is the only existent reality; for the supernaturalist, however, there is a higher reality transcending nature, and the latter "may, or may not, be the only reality which the one Primary Thing has produced" (p. 9). Lewis goes on to imagine that God might bring two natures into partial contact at some point, and "if this occurred each of the two Natures would be 'supernatural' in relation to the other. . . . It would be one kind of Miracle" (p. 10). For Lewis, this notion of alternative worlds serves several ends: first, it establishes the point that our spatiotemporal system is a derived, contingent, and relative arrangement; second, it suggests that we may live in a created universe far richer than we ordinarily assume; and finally, it holds out the possibility that our own nature may be influenced by other natures, or, as Lewis indicates elsewhere, by the power of imagination to disrupt and transform the "natural" order of things.

These ideas came to fruition in *The Chronicles of Narnia,* begun in 1948 and published in seven installments between 1950 and 1956. They relate the stories of several English children who find themselves transported periodically to the world of Narnia. The children become leaders and agents of redemption at crucial points in Narnian history, and in this respect their exploits are a kind of miraculous intervention in the affairs of a different natural order. At the same time the sudden translation to another world is a kind of miracle in the lives of the children, who return home tested and transformed by their adventures. The fact that these journeys take up no earthly time—the children return to the same place at the same time they departed—underscores their "miraculous" character.

Narnia is at once the name of the world and of a particular kingdom within it. The latter is inhabited by the Talking Beasts, the Waking Trees, and a variety of other creatures such as the Fauns, Naiads, Satyrs, and Centaurs. Like the Malacandrans of *Out of the Silent Planet,* the various inhabitants of Narnia possess rational intelligence. Once

again, Lewis is imagining what it would be like to dwell in a world where rationality is not confined to a single species but permeates the entire creation. The Waking Trees play a minor role in Narnian affairs, but they illustrate the mingling of consciousness and matter associated with Merlin in *That Hideous Strength* and presumably lost to nature as we now conceive it. The Fauns and other mythological beings exemplify Lewis' hypothesis that the myths of one world may be the realities of another, as if to say that the mythopoeic imagination has an objective foundation in the cosmic order. Together these creatures constitute a natural system that is corrupted not by willful rebellion from within, as is our world, but by external intervention from beyond. Throughout its history Narnia has kings and queens imported primarily from our world, and while the virtuous monarchs reign on behalf of the lion Aslan—creator and sovereign of this alternative world—others exercise tyrannical control, muting the Talking Beasts and polluting the Narnian landscape. (Late in the cycle Lewis introduces another source of evil in the mighty, despotic empire of Calormen, inhabited by humans of unexplained origins and alien customs, to the south of the Kingdom of Narnia. Unfortunately, Lewis depicts the difference between free and imperial societies in terms of a transparent contrast between fair-skinned, northern followers of Aslan and dark-skinned, desert dwellers who worship the bloodthirsty Tash.) Aslan himself appears periodically in Narnian history, and though he may disappear for centuries at a time, he returns at the end as judge and redeemer.

In *Miracles,* Lewis speculates that "other Natures might not be spatio-temporal at all" (p. 9). Narnia is a spatiotemporal world, but it is governed by natural laws different from our own. Physical conditions are similar, but the sudden metamorphoses confined to mythology in our world are literal in Narnia: witches transform living beings into stone; a greedy child turns temporarily into a dragon; Aslan turns a stiff-necked prince into a braying donkey. Narnian time is also slightly different. Altogether *The Chronicles* span a half century of Earth time—approximately 1900 to 1950—corresponding to roughly twenty-five hundred years Narnian years. But compared to our world, Narnian time runs not only faster but also at an uneven rate: one year on Earth may correspond to a Narnian millennium, another year to a Narnian decade, and whenever the children are in Narnia no time transpires in our world. By relating the two temporalities in this asymmetrical manner, Lewis attempts to disrupt our ordinary sense of time and hints at the possibility of unexpected disruptions in the rhythm of temporal progression. The sense of the uncanny is highlighted by the fact that the children cannot enter Narnia at will. They are translated by Aslan without warning and have no foreknowledge of the span of Narnian time that has transpired since their previous visit.

The plots of the first five books are relatively simple: overcoming the tyranny of a wicked witch (*The Lion, the Witch, and the Wardrobe*); delivering Narnia from foreign overlords (*Prince Caspian*); journeying to the End of the World (*The Voyage of the Dawn Treader*); recovering a lost prince (*The Silver Chair*); and alerting the kingdom to a surprise invasion (*The Horse and His Boy*). The first story is Christological—an archetypal tale of redemption and sacrifice resembling the story of the crucifixion and resurrection of Christ. The next four stories focus on issues of moral development: trust, loyalty, and steadfastness in *Prince Caspian*; temptations of flesh and spirit in *The Voyage of the Dawn Treader*; wisdom and discernment in *The Silver Chair*; and confidence and humility in *The Horse and His Boy*. The last two books—*The Magician's Nephew* and *The Last Battle*—provide a mythic frame for the cycle by telling the story of Narnia's creation, destruction, and final transfiguration.

Lewis' Christian Platonism underlies the entire sequence. Christian myth is at the center of the first tale; Platonism is introduced in the fourth tale, and synthesized with Christianity in the finale. In *The Lion, the Witch, and the Wardrobe*, four children enter Narnia to find a land tyrannized by the White Witch, who has "made it always winter and never Christmas" (p. 102). The Witch quickly seduces the boy Edmund into betraying his siblings, but the other three children are drawn to the figure of Aslan, who has returned to restore his kingdom. In her climactic encounter with the Lion, the Witch lays claim to Edmund, invoking the Deep Magic by which "every traitor belongs to me as my lawful prey" (p. 139). Offering his own life in exchange for the boy, Aslan is bound to the Stone Table, muzzled, and killed by the exultant Witch and her crew. Lewis' depiction of the children's grief over Aslan's death, and their joy over his reappearance, is skillful enough to offset the element of predictability

and recapture some of the wonder of the original resurrection story. As the Lion explains, the Deep Magic of the law has been superseded by the Deeper Magic of grace: "It means," said Aslan, "that though the Witch knew the Deep Magic, there is a magic deeper still which she did not know. . . . when a willing victim who had committed no treachery was killed in a traitor's stead, the Table would crack and Death itself would start working backwards" (pp. 159–160). The Narnianism of death "working backwards" conveys the sense of the miraculous but in the concrete terms of a natural process in reverse. Once the point is made, Lewis provides the satisfaction of watching Aslan rout his adversaries and install the children as monarchs of the realm.

The Silver Chair introduces the Platonic elements that loom large at the end of *The Chronicles*. Two children are assigned to recover the lost Prince Rilian, who was ensnared by a beautiful witch ten years earlier. Armed with instructions from Aslan and a shrewd, skeptical guide, the children are compelled at every turn to exercise vigilance and remain attentive to the signs that will lead them to their destination. Eventually they descend into the gloomy, subterranean Underland where they find the enchanted Prince. Unaware of his own identity, Rilian believes that the Witch protects him from a curse that sends him into a frenzy once each night. In fact, it is during his nocturnal fits, when he is bound to a silver chair, ostensibly to keep him from harming others, that Rilian briefly recovers his true identity and demands his release. Echoing Plato's allegory of the cave (*Republic*, book 7), the Witch uses her powers of enchantment to lull her new adversaries into believing that the world outside her kingdom is only a dream. Employing the logic of naturalism, she explains away their appeal to the "sun" and other elements of the Overworld:

When you try to think out clearly what this *sun* must be, you cannot tell me. You can only tell me it is like the lamp. Your *sun* is a dream; and there is nothing in that dream that was not copied from the lamp. The lamp is the real thing; the *sun* is but a tale, a children's story. . . . There is no Narnia, no Overworld, no sky, no sun, no Aslan.

(pp. 155–157)

The Witch reverses image and archetype, copy and original, claiming that the Underland is the reality and the Overland an illusory extrapolation.

It is the children's guide, skeptical as always, who summons his last ounce of strength and breaks the metaphysical spell:

Suppose we *have* only dreamed, or made up, all those things—trees and grass and sun and moon and stars and Aslan himself. Suppose we have. Then all I can say is that, in that case, the made-up things seem a good deal more important than the real ones. . . . I'm on Aslan's side even if there isn't any Aslan to lead it. I'm going to live as like a Narnian as I can even if there isn't any Narnia.

(p. 159)

This response is more the tentative reasoning of William James's "The Will to Believe" (1896) than the credo of an assured believer. But for Lewis the guide is expressing an intuitive apprehension of a true homeland beyond the confines of the natural world. His gesture proves potent enough to overcome the enchantment, since the Witch instantly turns into a serpent and is put to death. Lewis reiterates the Platonic theme when the triumphant company returns to the Narnian Overland. The old Narnian king dies in the midst of the reunion with his son, but anticipating the miraculous conclusion of the final book, the children are briefly transported to Aslan's country to witness the king's awakening, or as Lewis would put it at the end of *The Chronicles*, "the beginning of the real story" (*The Last Battle*, p. 184).

Christian eschatology and Platonic metaphysics come together in *The Last Battle*. For readers of the first six stories, the tale of Narnia's downfall is a particularly grim affair. External enemies overrun the kingdom, while moral confusion erodes it from within, as an insidious ape dupes a gullible donkey into posing as Aslan and holding court inside in a stable. The always skeptical Narnian Dwarfs become more suspicious than ever in this deceitful atmosphere and finally desert their countrymen. For the first time the arrival of children from our world fails to rescue Narnia. Moreover, in the midst of this consuming chaos the children begin to recall that on earth their train was crashing at the moment they were translated to Narnia, and they gradually realize that their own lives are coming to an end. Lewis is drawing together his two worlds.

Just as all hope of temporal deliverance vanishes, the scene of the final battle turns into the site of redemption. The stable of the false Aslan becomes the judgment seat of the true Aslan, and its

door the gateway to eternity. In a vivid account of cosmic devolution the stars fall from the sky, the last living things are gathered into the stable, and the land, the sea, and the sun dissolve into darkness. But following the de-creation of Narnia comes its final transfiguration. It begins with some signs of Aslan's mercy—the salvation of a virtuous worshiper of Tash and the poor donkey who posed as Aslan. The intensity rises steadily in anticipation of the discovery that the Narnia left behind "was only a shadow or copy," and the world beyond death is "the real Narnia, which has always been here and always will be here" (p. 169). "It's all in Plato" (p. 170), we are reassured, as Lewis tries to capture his characters' mixture of astonishment and recognition upon arrival in the "deeper country": "I have come home at last! This is my real country! I belong here. . . . The reason why we loved the old Narnia is that it sometimes looked a little like this" (p. 171). In the final chapter, "Farewell to Shadow-Lands," the limitations of space and time are suspended as the newcomers swim up the face of a waterfall, and their pace continues to quicken "till it was more like flying than running" (p. 175). The children are reunited with old Narnian and earthly friends, and catching a glimpse of "the real England" they learn from Aslan that indeed they have all died in a railway accident. But the Lion quickly puts it in the right light, welcoming them to their true home beyond the contingencies of the natural order: "'The term is over: the holidays have begun. The dream is ended: this is the morning.' . . . the beginning of the real story" (pp. 183–184).

On the basis of the lukewarm early reviews, it would have been difficult to predict the remarkable response to the Narnia tales. *The Chronicles* are among the most celebrated children's stories in circulation, and the attraction seems to extend well beyond childhood. Since they have achieved classic status, it has become common either to expect too much from them or to fall prey to the suspicion such popularity breeds. Lewis himself never took these stories as seriously as either his followers or his disappointed detractors. But if the Narnia stories are no foundation for a degree in theology, they are wise and edifying. If they fail to rise to the level of the most distinguished modern fiction, they are still masterpieces of a more limited kind, and in their moments of highest mythopoeic intensity they far transcend the limitations of their genre.

C. S. LEWIS

TILL WE HAVE FACES

FOR many years Lewis had dreamed of refashioning the tale of Cupid and Psyche as it appears in Apuleius' second-century romance, *The Golden Ass*. The story had obvious appeal as an allegory of the soul's search for love, but in Lewis' reworking (*Till We Have Faces*, published in 1956) it becomes a portrait of the corruption of love and the ease with which love can turn into its own opposite. The narrator and main protagonist is not Psyche but her sister Orual, a minor figure in Apuleius. Her narrative is divided into two sections. In part 1 she tells the story of her life in the form of a complaint against the gods, who have left her embittered in old age. In the brief part 2, written as she approaches death, Orual relates the eleventh-hour transformation of soul that compels her to reinterpret her life and reconciles her to the mysterious ways of the divine. Whether or not Lewis intended it, the relation between the telling and the retelling of her story is not simply a matter of error and correction of error. Orual's initial self-portrait is sufficiently persuasive, and her complaint against the gods sufficiently cogent, to make this work of fiction the most complex in the Lewis canon.

The novel takes place in the pagan kingdom of Glome, "a little barbarous state," as Lewis later described it, "on the borders of the Hellenistic world with Greek culture just beginning to affect it" (*Letters of C. S. Lewis*, 1993 ed., p. 462). Orual describes her upbringing as a physically unattractive but intelligent princess who is tutored by a wise Greek—the Fox—with clear ties to Stoic philosophy. Orual's principal attachment, however, is to her beautiful younger stepsister, Psyche, whose mother died while giving birth to her. Psyche's beauty is "'according to nature'; what every woman, or even every thing, ought to have been and meant to be, but had missed by some trip of chance. Indeed, when you looked at her you believed, for a moment, that they had not missed it. She made beauty all around her" (p. 22). The relationship between the two sisters changes dramatically when a ruinous plague afflicts the kingdom. The priest of the goddess Ungit (Lewis avoids the name Aphrodite) descends from the sacred mountain and demands the sacrifice of royal blood to the mysterious shadow known as the Brute. When the Fox argues that the demand for human sacrifice is irrational and barbaric, the Priest responds with a chilling but prophetic statement:

We are hearing much Greek wisdom this morning. . . . but it brings no rain and grows no corn; sacrifice does both. . . . They demand to see such things clearly, as if the gods were no more than letters written in a book. I, King, have dealt with the gods for three generations of men, and I know that they dazzle our eyes and flow in and out of one another like eddies on a river, and nothing that is said clearly can be said truly about them. Holy places are dark places. It is life and strength, not knowledge and words, that we get in them. Holy wisdom is not clear and thin like water, but thick and dark like blood.

(p. 50)

At this point it is tempting to identify with the humane position of the Fox, who resists the pagan demand for human sacrifice, and after the lot falls on Psyche we also identify with the plight of Orual, who is threatened with the loss of her sister. But to Orual's dismay Psyche seems to welcome her fate:

I have always—at least, ever since I can remember—had a kind of longing for death. . . . The sweetest thing in all my life has been the longing—to reach the Mountain, to find the place where all the beauty came from. . . . All my life the god of the Mountain has been wooing me.

(pp. 74–76)

This is vintage *Sehnsucht*, and Orual's response—"I only see that you have never loved me" (p. 76)—takes us to the thematic crux of the book. If the exchange between the Fox and the Priest defines the conflict between natural and supernatural points of view, the encounter between Orual and Psyche establishes a parallel but more problematic opposition between human and divine love. Orual's control over the narrative keeps the reader sympathetic to her and to the Fox, but the course of subsequent events will reveal the shortcomings of her passionate attachment to Psyche and confirm the sacred wisdom of the Priest.

After Psyche is led away to sacrifice, Orual journeys to the Mountain to give her a proper burial. She is shocked to find her sister alive and is perplexed by Psyche's report that she is now dwelling in a palace with an unnamed god whose face she is forbidden to see. In her account of the situation, Orual recalls her own uncertainty over her sighting of the palace:

It might have been a true seeing; the cloud over my mortal eyes may have been lifted for a moment. It might not. . . . Either way, there's divine mockery in it. They set the riddle and then allow a seeming that can't be tested and can only quicken and thicken the tormenting whirlpool of your guess-work. If they had an honest intention to guide us, why is their guidance not plain?

(pp. 133–134)

After consulting the Fox, who shares her suspicions, Orual returns to her sister and threatens to take her own life unless Psyche will "set all our doubts at rest" (p. 162) by looking at the face of her lover. Out of love for her sister Psyche reluctantly agrees, lamenting "that I am betraying the best of lovers" (p. 166). Soon afterward Orual has a fleeting recognition that "from the beginning, I had known that Psyche's lover was a god," and hears a voice tell her, "Now Psyche goes out in exile. . . . You also shall be Psyche" (pp. 173–174). She then returns home, and hiding her face with a veil—symbolic of the suppression of her wounded soul—she commits herself to serving the kingdom.

Part 1 ends many years later when the aging Orual, after a long and successful reign as queen of Glome, travels abroad and hears a priest relate a distorted version of Psyche's story. In this account (essentially Apuleius'), Orual's decision to compel Psyche to gaze on her lover's face is motivated by sheer envy:

It was as if the gods themselves had first laughed, and then spat, in my face. . . . For if the true story had been like their story, no riddle would have been set me; there would have been no guessing and no guessing wrong. More than that, it's a story belonging to a different world, a world in which the gods show themselves clearly and don't torment men with glimpses, nor unveil to one what they hide from another. . . . In such a world (is there such? it's not ours, for certain) I would have walked aright. The gods themselves would have been able to find no fault in me. And now to tell my story as if I had had the very sight they had denied me.

(pp. 243–244)

Orual returns home to write her indictment of the gods, who will neither leave us alone nor "show themselves openly . . . what is all this but cat-and-mouse play, blindman's buff, and mere jugglery? Why must holy places be dark places?" (p. 249). Her narrative ends with a demand for a response from the gods in the expectation that "they have no answer" (p. 250).

In part 2, the dying Orual relates the events that transform her life and bring about a recantation of her earlier narrative. "The gods' surgery" (pp. 253–254) begins with the memories awakened by the very act of composing part 1, proceeds to the recognition of her past insensitivities to family and friends, and culminates in two significant dream visions. In the first, Orual looks into a mirror and beholds the loathsome face of Ungit. Tearing the veil from her own face, she confronts the spiritual ugliness that she has concealed for so long. In the second, Orual is led into a divine courtroom and instructed to read her complaint against the gods. In the course of this testimonial she becomes aware of the true beauty of the gods, though it merely fuels her resentment and betrays the selfish nature of her love for Psyche:

Do you think we mortals will find you gods easier to bear if you're beautiful? I tell you that if that's true we'll find you a thousand times worse. For then (I know what beauty does) you'll lure and entice. You'll leave us nothing. . . . The girl was mine. What right had you to steal her away into your dreadful heights? . . . Oh, you'll say you took her away into bliss and joy such as I could never have given her, and I ought to have been glad of it for her sake. Why? What should I care for some horrible, new happiness which I hadn't given her and which separated her from me? Do you think I wanted her to be happy, that way? It would have been better if I'd seen the Brute tear her in pieces before my eyes. . . . She was mine. *Mine.*

(pp. 290–292)

Orual does not need the judge to pronounce the verdict. Condemned by her own selfishness, she knows that "the complaint was the answer. To have heard myself making it was to be answered" (p. 294). She now understands that the failure to understand the divine is closely tied to the failure to know ourselves: "I saw well why the gods do not speak to us openly, nor let us answer. Till that word [the truth at the center of our being] can be dug out of us, why should they hear the babble that we think we mean? How can they meet us face to face till we have faces?" (p. 294).

Exposed to the depths of her own soul, Orual hears the voice of the Fox, who instructs her in divine wisdom and leads her to the threshold of Psyche's palace. Hand in hand with her sister she is prepared to come before the presence of the sacred:

The air was growing brighter and brighter about us; as if something had set it on fire. Each breath I drew let into me new terror, joy, overpowering sweetness. I was pierced through and through with the arrows of it. I was being unmade. . . . The most dreadful, the most beautiful, the only dread and beauty there is, was coming. The pillars on the far side of the pool flushed with his approach. I cast down my eyes.

(p. 307)

After the voice of the god fulfills the old prophecy by declaring, "You also are Psyche" (p. 308), the vision fades and Orual prepares for death. Her narrative breaks off in the midst of a final prayer that replaces the divine silence at the end of part 1 with the recognition, echoing the conclusion of the Book of Job, that "You are yourself the answer. Before your face questions die away" (p. 308).

Till We Have Faces met a confused and rather cool reception. Lewis himself could not understand his readers' difficulties. In his view Orual presented a case of "human affection in its natural condition: true, tender, suffering, but in the long run, tyrannically possessive and ready to turn to hatred when the beloved ceases to be its possession. What such love particularly cannot stand is to see the beloved passing into a sphere where it cannot follow" (*Letters of C. S. Lewis*, 1993 ed., p. 462). Lewis provides a sufficiently accurate gloss, but it fails to take into account the uncharacteristically sharp opposition between reason and faith, human and divine knowledge, that cuts through this text. Nor does it acknowledge the tricky and sometimes equivocal relations between the meaning and the vehicle used to convey it. Consider, for example, Orual's physical appearance. The use of facial ugliness to signify a spiritual condition may be an acceptable convention in certain genres, but in this work of mixed and almost indefinable genre Orual's unsightly face—a brute fact of her existence—is a misleading figure for spiritual "ugliness," which implies a disposition of the will and therefore a condition for which we are ultimately responsible. Similar difficulties arise in the relationship between the pagan setting and the Christian meaning. Given the initial contrast between the humane rationality of the Fox and the barbaric rituals of Glomian religion, it should come as no surprise that readers identify with Orual's complaint against the gods, or that they sense something monstrous in the Priest's call for human sacrifice and in his victim's eagerness to offer herself. In other words, it is not just a lack of discernment that prompts certain readers to prefer Orual's love for Psyche to Psyche's love of death, and to feel a bit deceived or even cheated when the former is declared tyrannically possessive and the latter divinely inspired. At the end of *The Pilgrim's Regress*, Lewis carefully mediated between otherworldly *Sehnsucht* and the recognition that human beings do not possess the "angelic indifference" to detach themselves entirely from "the tether and pang of the particular." Perhaps those readers who are troubled by the austere detachment of the Priest, and Psyche's all-too-angelic compliance with his demand, are defending Lewis' own deeper sense of the doubleness of the human condition.

LATER WORKS

LEWIS remained a prolific writer until his death, despite the wearing effects of illness in his final years. In his last decade he published four scholarly works: His classic survey, *English Literature in the Sixteenth Century, Excluding Drama* (1954); *Studies in Words* (1960), an analysis of axial terms such as "nature," "sense," and "conscience" (and their cognates in other languages) from the Greeks to the present; *An Experiment in Criticism* (1961), an essay on the practice of reading; and *The Discarded Image* (1964), an introduction to medieval cosmology. The last, designed as a practical guide for students, is characteristic of the workmanlike, almost offhand style of his later prose. Occasionally mistaken for fatigue or laziness, the new style proceeds from an attempt to adopt a less declamatory and more companionable voice.

This stylistic change is also evident in the religious writings to which Lewis returned after nearly a decade—*Reflections on the Psalms* (1958), *The Four Loves* (1960), *A Grief Observed* (1961), and *Letters to Malcolm: Chiefly on Prayer* (1964)—which depart from the platform manner of the 1940s. The very choice of topics indicates the new direction. Lewis is no longer the public orator demonstrating the truth of Christianity to a general audience. As he states in the opening of *Reflections on the Psalms*, "A man can't be always defending the truth; there must be a time to feed on it" (p. 7). His voice becomes warmer and more personal. The genial *Four Loves*, originally commissioned for broadcast on American radio, reflects candidly on the pleasures of natural affection, friendship, and sex (for which it ran into trouble). *A Grief Observed* is openly confessional, and *Letters to Malcolm* (an imaginary friend) has the ambling manner of "two people on the foothills comparing notes in private" (p. 63). Whether or not it is attributable to the intimacies of his relationship with Joy Davidman, a new recognition of the more personal recesses of faith, already apparent in *Till We Have Faces*, underlies the style and substance of these works. Never far from view is a concern with the images, fictions, and illusions that mask us from our own selves and from the divine reality beyond us. Echoing Orual's realization of the difficulty of meeting God "face to face" (*Till We Have Faces*, p. 294), Lewis tells Malcolm in his final book that "the prayer preceding all prayers is 'May it be the real I who speaks. May it be the real Thou that I speak to'" (*Letters to Malcolm*, p. 82).

A Grief Observed is the most intimate and rhetorically complex of these religious writings. Originally published under a pseudonym, it comprises several notebooks expressing the author's anguish after the death of his wife. The risk of such a book is that it courts the inauthentic at every turn. The problem is apparent in the double meaning of the title: the experience or "observance" of mourning is threatened by the very act of observing it. The reader is alert to any hint that the writer is glancing over his shoulder at a prospective audience or, worse still, using the situation as another occasion for writing. Lewis confronts these difficulties by representing the process of mourning as a ceaseless struggle against the very temptation to lapse into the counterfeit. He expresses disgust with his own efforts to dramatize his grief, to reduce it to something less painful or to produce more self-satisfying images of his wife:

Slowly, quietly, like snow-flakes—like the small flakes that come when it is going to snow all night—little flakes of me, my impressions, my selections, are settling down on the image of her. The real shape will be quite hidden in the end. . . . The rough, sharp, cleansing tang of her otherness is gone. . . . As if I wanted to fall in love with my memory of her, an image in my own mind! It would be a sort of incest.

(pp. 21–22)

As he grows more concerned with the fictions that cloud his relations to other persons and to God, the cross becomes the image for the shattering of images: "Images of the Holy easily become holy images—sacrosanct. My idea of God is not a divine idea. It has to be shattered time after time. He shatters it Himself. He is the great iconoclast. Could we not almost say that this shattering is one of the marks of His presence?" (p. 76). A similar gesture leads to the final recognition that in the process of nullifying our efforts to explain its mysteries, "Heaven will solve our problems, but not, I think, by showing us subtle reconciliations between all our apparently contradictory notions. The notions will all be knocked from under our feet. We shall see that there never was any problem" (p. 83). Paradoxically, it is this iconoclastic demand for the real that allows Lewis to portray his grief, and project a vision of the afterlife, without seeming to fictionalize them in the process.

LEGACY

SEVERAL decades after Lewis' death it is still difficult to assess the significance of his achievement. From one perspective he seems a relatively minor figure in twentieth-century letters: his scholarly works are still read but are no longer in vogue; his fiction receives scant attention in mainstream literary histories; and his religious writings cater primarily to sectarian interests. But this assessment ignores the fact that Lewis retains a huge following that has shown no sign of slackening. In particular it overlooks the extraordinary and enduring appeal of the Narnia tales, and the esteem in which his religious writings are held in many Christian churches. In other words, Lewis has left a divided legacy that reflects more basic divisions within our culture.

Lewis' influence as a scholar and critic has lasted several generations. *The Allegory of Love* restored appreciation for a literature alien to twentieth-century ears, and though its main premises have been successfully challenged, the book remains the *locus classicus* of a still-influential view of medieval literature. Lewis' second major study, *English Literature in the Sixteenth Century*, is a standard work in the field and an indispensable guide to the less-celebrated authors of the period. These books, supported by *A Preface to* Paradise Lost, *Studies in Words*, *The Discarded Image*, and any number of influential articles, constitute one of the century's most imposing interpretations of medieval and Renaissance literature.

As a writer of fiction, Lewis stood apart from the literary realism that was still dominant in the first half of the century, and to a degree he has suffered from his allegiance to narrative modes that are only now securing their share of cultural prestige. In 1947 (the year prior to the birth of Narnia) Lewis expressed a forlorn hope for "a better school of prose story in England: of story that can mediate imaginative life to the masses while not being contemptible to the few" ("On Stories," in *Of This and Other Worlds*, p. 42). As a member of the Inklings, he was struggling to create the taste for an alternative fictional tradition that looks back to Macdonald and Morris and within a few years would include Tolkien's *The Lord of the Rings* and his own *Chronicles of Narnia*. At that point it would have been difficult to envision the spectacular success of his enterprise. But it is also hard to imagine that he would have relished the mutation of his "better school of prose story" into a major popular industry with Tolkien as high priest and Lewis as his prophet.

In the realm of popular Christian apologetics, Lewis seems to have no peer. His books are steeped in the ethos of a bygone era, but the audience first stirred by his wartime books and broadcasts now makes up only a tiny portion of his vast readership. His extraordinary popularity in the United States, especially among evangelical Protestants, has given rise to a substantial industry (see the bibliography) sustained by Christian publishing houses, enterprising author societies, and the establishment of a major archive in Wheaton, Illinois. Such lionization produces its own frictions, but it should not obscure the fact that the Lewis mystique transcends many of the prevailing divisions within contemporary Christendom. To many who are unfamiliar or unmoved by the discourse of modern theology, he holds out the prospect of a rationally sustainable Christianity in an age when it can no longer rely on its traditional metaphysical supports. Although his defense of Christian doctrine skirts some of the difficult questions raised by modernity, his appeal to the mind through the imagination has made him the most influential apologist of our time.

SELECTED BIBLIOGRAPHY

I. Bibliographies. Joe R. Christopher and Joan K. Ostling, *C. S. Lewis: An Annotated Checklist of Writings About Him and His Works* (Kent, Ohio, 1974); Walter Hooper, "A Bibliography of the Writings of C. S. Lewis: Revised and Enlarged," in *C. S. Lewis at the Breakfast Table and Other Reminiscences*, ed. by James T. Como (New York, 1979; London, 1980); Susan Lowenberg, *C. S. Lewis: A Reference Guide, 1972–1988* (New York, 1993).

II. Separate Works. *Spirits in Bondage: A Cycle of Lyrics* (London, 1919), pub. under pseudonym Clive Hamilton; *Dymer* (London, 1926), poem pub. under pseudonym Clive Hamilton; *The Pilgrim's Regress: An Allegorical Apology for Christianity, Reason, and Romanticism* (London, 1933; 3d ed. 1943); *The Allegory of Love: A Study in Medieval Tradition* (Oxford, 1936); *Out of the Silent Planet* (London, 1938); *The Personal Heresy: A Controversy*, with E. M. W. Tillyard (London, 1939); *Rehabilitations and Other Essays* (London, 1939).

The Problem of Pain (London, 1940); *Broadcast Talks* (London, 1942; pub. as *The Case for Christianity*, New York, 1943); *A Preface to Paradise Lost* (London, 1942); *The Screwtape Letters* (London, 1942; New York, 1943; repr. with additional letter in *The Screwtape Letters and Screwtape Proposes a Toast*, London, 1961; New York, 1962); *The Abolition of Man; or, Reflections on Education with Special Reference to the Teaching of English in the Upper Forms of Schools* (London, 1943); *Christian Behaviour: A Further Series of Broadcast Talks* (London and New York, 1943); *Perelandra* (London, 1943; New York, 1944; repub. as *Voyage to Venus*, London, 1953); *Beyond Personality: The Christian Idea of God* (London, 1944; New York, 1945); *The Great Divorce: A Dream* (London, 1945; New York, 1946); *That Hideous Strength: A Modern Fairy-Tale for Grown-Ups* (London, 1945; abridged as *The Tortured Planet [That Hideous Strength]*, New York, 1946); *Miracles: A Preliminary Study* (London and New York, 1947; repr. with revised chapter 3, London, 1960); *The Arthurian Torso: Containing the Posthumous Fragment of "The Figure of Arthur" by Charles Williams and "A Commentary on the Arthurian Poems of Charles Williams" by C. S. Lewis* (London, 1948); *Transposition and Other Addresses* (London, 1949; pub. as *The Weight of Glory and Other Addresses*, New York, 1949; rev. and exp., 1980).

The Lion, the Witch, and the Wardrobe: A Story for Children (London and New York, 1950), book 1 of *The Chronicles of Narnia*; *Prince Caspian: The Return to Narnia* (London and New York, 1951), book 2 of *The Chronicles of Narnia*; *Mere Christianity* (London and New York, 1952; repr. with some original broadcast material, New York, 1981), a revised and amplified edition, with a new introduction, of *Broadcast Talks* (1942), *Christian Behaviour* (1943), and *Beyond Personality* (1944); *The Voyage of the Dawn Treader* (London and New York, 1952), book 3 of *The Chronicles of Narnia*; *The Silver Chair* (London and New York, 1953), book 4 of *The Chronicles of Narnia*; *English Literature in the Sixteenth Century, Excluding Drama* (Oxford, 1954), *Oxford History of English Literature*, vol. 3; *The Horse and His Boy* (London and New York, 1954), book 5 of *The Chronicles of Narnia*; *The Magi-*

cian's Nephew (London and New York, 1955), book 6 of The Chronicles of Narnia; Surprised by Joy: The Shape of My Early Life (London, 1955; New York, 1956); The Last Battle: A Story for Children (London and New York, 1956), book 7 of The Chronicles of Narnia; Till We Have Faces: A Myth Retold (London, 1956); Reflections on the Psalms (London and New York, 1958).

The Four Loves (London and New York, 1960); Studies in Words (Cambridge, Eng., 1960); The World's Last Night and Other Essays (New York, 1960); An Experiment in Criticism (Cambridge, Eng., 1961); A Grief Observed (London, 1961), pub. under pseudonym N. W. Clerk; They Asked for a Paper: Papers and Addresses (London, 1962); The Discarded Image: An Introduction to Medieval and Renaissance Literature (Cambridge, Eng., 1964); Letters to Malcolm: Chiefly on Prayer (London, 1964), first appeared as Beyond the Bright Blur (New York, 1963), a limited edition of chaps. 15–17.

III. POSTHUMOUS COLLECTIONS. (All collections edited by Walter Hooper unless otherwise noted.)

Poems (London, 1964); Screwtape Proposes a Toast and Other Pieces (London, 1965); Of Other Worlds: Essays and Stories (London, 1966); Studies in Medieval and Renaissance Literature (Cambridge, Eng., 1966); Christian Reflections (London and Grand Rapids, Mich., 1967); Spenser's Images of Life, ed. by Alastair Fowler (Cambridge, Eng., 1967); A Mind Awake: An Anthology of C. S. Lewis, ed. by Clyde S. Kilby (London, 1968); Narrative Poems (London, 1969); Selected Literary Essays (Cambridge, Eng., 1969).

God in the Dock: Essays on Theology and Ethics (Grand Rapids, Mich., 1970), pub. as Undeceptions: Essays on Theology and Ethics (London, 1971); Fern-Seed and Elephants, and Other Essays on Christianity (London, 1975); The Dark Tower and Other Stories (London and New York, 1977); The Joyful Christian: 127 Readings from C. S. Lewis, with a foreword by H. W. Griffin (New York, 1977).

The Visionary Christian: 131 Readings from C. S. Lewis, ed. by Chad Walsh (New York, 1981); Of This and Other Worlds (London, 1982), pub. as On Stories, and Other Essays on Literature (New York, 1982); The Business of Heaven: Daily Readings from C. S. Lewis (London and San Diego, 1984); Boxen: The Imaginary World of the Young C. S. Lewis (London and San Diego, 1985); First and Second Things: Essays on Theology and Ethics (London, 1985); Present Concerns (London and San Diego, 1986); Timeless at Heart: Essays on Theology (London, 1987); The Essential C. S. Lewis, ed. by Lyle W. Dorsett (New York, 1988); The Quotable Lewis, ed. by Wayne Martindale and Jerry Root (Wheaton, Ill., 1989).

Christian Reunion and Other Essays (London, 1990); Daily Readings with C. S. Lewis (London, 1991).

IV. LETTERS AND DIARIES. Letters of C. S. Lewis, ed. with a memoir by W. H. Lewis (London and New York, 1966; rev. and enlarged edition, ed. by Walter Hooper, San Diego, 1993); Letters to an American Lady, ed. by Clyde S. Kilby (Grand Rapids, Mich., 1967), to Mary Willis Shelburne; They Stand Together: The Letters of C. S. Lewis to Arthur Greeves, 1914–1963, ed. by Walter Hooper (London and New York, 1979); Letters to Children, ed. by Lyle W. Dorsett and Marjorie Lamp Mead (London and New York, 1985); Letters—C. S. Lewis and Don Giovanni Calabria: A Study in Friendship, trans. and ed. by Martin Moynihan (Ann Arbor, Mich., and London, 1988); All My Road Before Me: The Diary of C. S. Lewis, 1922–1927, ed. by Walter Hooper (London and San Diego, 1991).

V. BIOGRAPHICAL STUDIES. Carolyn Keefe, ed., C. S. Lewis: Speaker and Teacher (Grand Rapids, Mich., 1971); Roger Lancelyn Green and Walter Hooper, C. S. Lewis: A Biography (London and New York, 1974); Sheldon Vanauken, A Severe Mercy: C. S. Lewis and a Pagan Love Invaded by Christ, Told by One of the Lovers (London and San Francisco, 1977); Humphrey Carpenter, The Inklings: C. S. Lewis, J. R. R. Tolkien, Charles Williams, and Their Friends (London and Boston, 1978); C. S. Lewis at the Breakfast Table and Other Reminiscences, ed. by James T. Como (New York, 1979); Walter Hooper, Through Joy and Beyond: A Pictorial Biography of C. S. Lewis (London and New York, 1982); W. H. Lewis, Brothers and Friends: The Diaries of Major Warren Hamilton Lewis, ed. by Clyde S. Kilby and Marjorie Lamp Mead (London and San Francisco, 1982); Lyle W. Dorsett, And God Came In: The Extraordinary Story of Joy Davidman, Her Life and Marriage to C. S. Lewis (New York, 1983); Brian Sibley, Shadowlands: The Story of C. S. Lewis and Joy Davidman (London, 1985); William Griffin, Clive Staples Lewis: A Dramatic Life (San Francisco, 1986); Lyle W. Dorsett, Joy and C. S. Lewis (London, 1988); Douglas H. Gresham, Lenten Lands: My Childhood with Joy Davidman and C. S. Lewis (New York, 1988); George Sayer, Jack: C. S. Lewis and His Times (London and San Francisco, 1988); Owen Barfield, Owen Barfield on C. S. Lewis, ed. by G. B. Tennyson (Middletown, Conn., 1989); A. N. Wilson, C. S. Lewis: A Biography (London and New York, 1990).

VI. CRITICAL STUDIES. Chad Walsh, C. S. Lewis: Apostle to the Skeptics (New York, 1949); Clyde S. Kilby, The Christian World of C. S. Lewis (Grand Rapids, Mich., 1964); Jocelyn Gibb, ed., Light on C. S. Lewis (London, 1965); Peter T. Kreeft, C. S. Lewis: A Critical Essay (Grand Rapids, Mich., 1969).

Kathryn Ann Lindskoog, C. S. Lewis: Mere Christian (Glendale, Calif., 1973; rev. ed., Downers Grove, Ill., 1981; rev. ed., Wheaton, Ill., 1987); Corbin S. Carnell, Bright Shadow of Reality: C. S. Lewis and the Feeling Intellect (Grand Rapids, Mich., 1974); Peter J. Schakel, ed., The Longing for a Form: Essays on the Fiction of C. S. Lewis (Kent, Ohio, 1977); Lionel Adey, C. S. Lewis's "Great War" with Owen Barfield, English Literary Studies monograph series no. 14 (Victoria, B.C., 1978); Gilbert Meilaender, The Taste for the Other: The Social and Ethical Thought of C. S. Lewis (Grand Rapids, Mich., 1978); Peter J. Schakel, Reading with the Heart: The Way into Narnia (Grand Rapids, Mich., 1979).

Paul F. Ford, *Companion to Narnia* (San Francisco, 1980); Evan K. Gibson, *C. S. Lewis, Spinner of Tales: A Guide to His Fiction* (Grand Rapids, Mich., and Washington, D.C., 1980); Martha C. Sammons, *A Guide Through C. S. Lewis' Space Trilogy* (Westchester, Ill., 1980); Donald E. Glover, *C. S. Lewis: The Art of Enchantment* (Athens, Ohio, 1981); Margaret P. Hannay, *C. S. Lewis* (New York, 1981); Robert H. Smith, *Patches of Godlight: The Pattern of Thought of C. S. Lewis* (Athens, Ga., 1981); Stephen Schofield, ed., *In Search of C. S. Lewis: Interviews with Kenneth Tynan, A. J. P. Taylor, Malcolm Muggeridge, and Others Who Knew Lewis* (South Plainfield, N.J., 1983); Dabney Adams Hart, *Through the Open Door: A New Look at C. S. Lewis* (University, Ala., 1984); Peter J. Schakel, *Reason and Imagination in C. S. Lewis: A Study of* Till We Have Faces (Grand Rapids, Mich., 1984); John Beversluis, *C. S. Lewis and the Search for Rational Religion* (Grand Rapids, Mich., 1985); James Patrick, *The Magdalen Metaphysicals: Idealism and Orthodoxy at Oxford, 1901–1945* (Macon, Ga., 1985); Joe R. Christopher, *C. S. Lewis* (Boston, 1987); Thomas Howard, *C. S. Lewis, Man of Letters: A Reading of His Fiction* (Worthing, Eng., 1987); Colin N. Manlove, *C. S. Lewis: His Literary Achievement* (Basingstoke, Eng., and New York, 1987); Bruce L. Edwards, ed., *The Taste of the Pineapple: Essays on C. S. Lewis as Reader, Critic, and Imaginative Writer* (Bowling Green, Ohio, 1988).

Colin Duriez, *The C. S. Lewis Handbook: A Comprehensive Guide to His Life, Thought, and Writings* (Eastbourne, Eng., and Grand Rapids, Mich., 1990); Peter J. Schakel and Charles A. Huttar, eds., *Word and Story in C. S. Lewis* (Columbia, Mo., and London, 1991); David C. Downing, *Planets in Peril: A Critical Study of C. S. Lewis's Ransom Trilogy* (Amherst, Mass., 1992); Kath Filmer, *The Fiction of C. S. Lewis: Mask and Mirror* (Basingstoke, Eng., and New York, 1993); Colin N. Manlove, The Chronicles of Narnia: *The Patterning of a Fantastic World* (New York and Toronto, 1993); Doris T. Myers, *C. S. Lewis in Context* (Kent, Ohio, 1994).

VII. ARCHIVES The Marion E. Wade Center at Wheaton College, Wheaton, Ill., holds the papers and letters of Lewis' brother, Major Warren Lewis, including his vast compilation of family history entitled *Lewis Papers*. The collection also includes manuscripts, first editions, a major collection of letters, and other Lewis memorabilia. The Department of Western Manuscripts at the Bodleian Library, Oxford, Eng., has an extensive collection of Lewis' books and articles, plus some manuscripts and letters. Each of the two centers has photocopies of the unique manuscripts in the possession of the other.

NOTE: Several C. S. Lewis societies publish journals: *CSL: The Bulletin of the New York C. S. Lewis Society* (1969–); *Chronicle of the Portland C. S. Lewis Society* (1972–1984); *The Lamp-Post of the Southern California C. S. Lewis Society* (1977–); and *The Canadian C. S. Lewis Journal* (1979–). Other journals devoted to Lewis and friends: *Mythlore: A Journal of J. R. R. Tolkien, C. S. Lewis, Charles Williams, General Fantasy, and Mythic Studies* (1969–); *Seven: An Anglo-American Literary Review* (1980–); and *Inklings: Gesellschaft für Literatur und Asthetik* (1983–).

MALCOLM LOWRY

(1909–1957)

David Galef

MALCOLM LOWRY TURNED a tortured life into complex art, surviving the extremes of existence to record their grim specifics. Practically everything he wrote can be traced to an incident he experienced, a personal relationship, a drunken binge, or a journey he undertook. At the same time, Lowry also belongs to a long line of sodden writers who sought to escape the world through a haze of alcohol, who postured in public and wrote in private. His greatest work is unquestionably *Under the Volcano,* a densely allusive, half-neglected masterpiece. Since his death in 1957, however, a series of books, both Lowry's posthumous work and the critics' belated appraisals, have done much to augment his reputation.

Aligning Lowry's temperament with a specific era and style is difficult: a romantic in his early search for adventure, he worked belatedly in the high modernist mode twenty-five years after James Joyce's *Ulysses.* He followed T. S. Eliot's style of imagery but not his theory of impersonality, according to which the artist must keep outside his work. Lowry's subject was always Lowry himself, the beleaguered artist, albeit in several guises and from varying angles. Yet, as with Dylan Thomas and Brendan Behan, the person and the persona became indissolubly wed. As Gordon Bowker once wrote: "Lowry was a contriver of fictions and one of his finest fictional contrivances, it sometimes seems, was his own life" (*Malcolm Lowry Remembered,* p. 9).

EARLY LIFE AND INFLUENCES

THE uncontrived facts are these: Clarence Malcolm Lowry was born in Liscard, Cheshire, on 28 July 1909. The family was upper middle class, the father a cotton broker who stressed the impor-

tance of diligence and whose autocratic manner cast a long shadow over Lowry's boyhood. Soon after Lowry was born, the family moved to the Wirral peninsula, bordered by the Mersey and Dee rivers, as well as the Irish Sea. Lowry conceived an early fascination for the sea and eventually used it as a means to escape his social milieu. In fact, much of Lowry's background undergoes a sea change in his writing: his maternal grandfather, for instance, a Liverpool shipbuilder, metamorphoses into a crusty Norwegian captain in one of Lowry's late-career novellas, *Through the Panama.*

Lowry himself was fat and clumsy. The youngest of four sons, he felt inferior to his more athletic brothers and was taken care of by a nanny. That he was somewhat coddled did little to settle his resentment. When he was nine he developed an eye infection, which resulted in corneal ulcers so severe that he eventually had to go to a London specialist to have his eyeballs scraped. This incident became aggrandized as Lowry retold it later, transformed into years of half-blindness and neglect, as well as a symbolic affiliation with Joyce and his many eye operations. Lowry was also ashamed of his small hands, a physical attribute he gave to many of his protagonists. When Dana Hilliot, in Lowry's first novel, *Ultramarine,* thinks of "my all-abiding sense of guilt about my hands" (p. 117), or when Bill Plantagenet of *Lunar Caustic* holds out his hands and complains, "They're not big enough for a real pianist" (p. 19), Lowry is expressing his own feelings of inadequacy, tied in part to the 1930s socialist idea that a real man is a workingman. (Henry Green, another writer from a well-off business family, felt similarly ashamed of his "podgy" hands, unfit for real work.) In Lowry's fiction, this stigma is further extended to an ambivalence about the artistic life, removed from the bracing experience of physical labor.

Lowry overcompensated for these feelings. At The Leys, a public school in Cambridge, he practiced his golf, eventually winning the school championship, and started a course of weight lifting that eventually made him barrel-chested and muscle-bound. He took up the ukulele and in his last year at The Leys collaborated with another student to put out several songs in sheet music. Nothing ever came of the venture, which he retold in *Under the Volcano*, but for the rest of his life Lowry was a passionate jazz fan and even created a few protagonists—including Bill Plantagenet in *Lunar Caustic*, and the I-narrator of "The Forest Path to the Spring"—whose art is primarily musical.

Around this time, he also began drinking, a habit central to both his life and fiction. Lowry's critics have explained his alcoholism in a variety of ways, from rebellion against authority to an oral fixation, but, as his friends have noted in reminiscences, Lowry also needed to drink as a release—from his own expectations, perhaps, as well as others'. What was expected of Lowry was clear: follow his brothers by attending Cambridge and joining the family business. But Lowry had begun to write at The Leys, first a story in *The Leys Fortnightly* that won the prize for the year's best, followed by some comic verse and sportswriting. Two early stories, "A Rainy Night," in which a sailor dies of starvation on a train of well-fed travelers, and "Satan in a Barrel," which ends "Nineteen clocks chimed eight unevenly" (in Bradbrook, p. 150), show a preoccupation with language and irony that marks the development of Lowry's mature style.

As a teenager, Lowry also fed on Jack London and Joseph Conrad, and before going on to Cambridge he insisted on a chance to prove himself at sea. In May 1927, Lowry shipped out on the SS *Pyrrhus*, unaware that his workmates might resent both his education and income level. The voyage began badly at the docks, where Lowry's father had him chauffeur-driven to the ship. Regarded as a toff who had deprived a needier boy of a job, Lowry was assigned to be a deckhand, scraping the barnacles off bulkheads. His romantic view of seafaring soon gave way to a more experienced appraisal: as Dana Hilliot remarks in *Ultramarine*, "For this is what sea life is like now—a domestic servant on a treadmill in hell!" (p. 49). Though he eventually made peace with his mates and visited ports as far off as Singapore and Japan, he found

little occasion for riotous living. His lifelong fear of syphilis kept him from much contact with the opposite sex, and he seems largely to have compensated through alcohol, with a voracity that shocked even his shipmates. As one of the sailors in *Ultramarine* tells young Hilliot, "You drink enough to put out the bloody fires of the ship. It's not natural at your age—that's what we all says" (p. 65).

In any event, five months at sea was enough for Lowry, who returned to Liverpool in time to miss the cutoff for Cambridge that year. In the interim, he persuaded his father to let him study German in Bonn, where he followed his practice of picking up foreign atmosphere and interesting phrases rather than the rules of the language. He was never much of a linguist, despite his boasts, but rather was adept in fashioning the modernist bricolage of signs and symbols that approximates a world.

After Germany, he moved to London on his father's allowance and began taking down notes for a book on his experience at sea. At a loss for a model, he stumbled upon Conrad Aiken's *Blue Voyage* and was so inspired that he wrote the author a letter. "I have lived only nineteen years and all of them more or less badly" (*Letters*, p. 3), he began, and when Aiken replied sympathetically, Lowry proposed in a second letter that he be allowed to study under the master. Aiken tentatively agreed (a stipend from Lowry's father clinched the deal), and, as Aiken had since left Sussex for Cambridge, Massachusetts, Lowry sailed over that summer.

Lowry's apprenticeship was based on a firm friendship with Aiken, which lasted over the years even as the pupil outstripped the teacher. That summer, as Lowry worked on his first novel, Aiken instructed him in the modernist techniques of achronology, psychological association, and the use of naturalistic symbols. By the time Lowry was ready to matriculate back in Cambridge, England, he had developed a definite, if somewhat derivative style, compounded of Melville and Joyce, cemented by Aiken and Eugene O'Neill.

Few if any of the students at Cambridge had knocked around the way Lowry had, and he never fit into undergraduate life—in part deliberately so. Living in a seedy rented room filled with old books and phonograph records, he desultorily attended classes as he worked on his first novel. Lowry's own program of reading became, as it remained for the rest of his life, extremely eclectic.

Bits of August Strindberg, Dante, Thomas Mann, Knut Hamsun, T. S. Eliot, Herman Bang, and Joyce filtered through Lowry's consciousness and into the minds of his protagonists. He was particularly taken with the Norwegian author Nordahl Grieg, whose work *The Ship Sails On* provided another model besides Aiken's for a coming-of-age novel set at sea. In characteristic style, Lowry during his last college summer vacation journeyed all the way to Oslo to visit Grieg. Like all the incidents in Lowry's life, the journey itself took on symbolic proportions and eventually became the cornerstone for a huge, sprawling, unfinished novel entitled *In Ballast to the White Sea*.

Lowry graduated with a third-class degree from Cambridge in 1932, the draft of his first novel *Ultramarine* submitted as his senior thesis. He moved to London on an allowance from his father and became known around town as a drunken artistic genius, a label that countless reminiscences about Lowry seem to support. The novel manuscript was accepted—and lost—by an editor at the publishing house Chatto and Windus. After painfully recreating it from an earlier draft and resubmitting it, Lowry began to suspect that the publisher was not particularly committed to his work. Requesting his manuscript back, Lowry sent it to Jonathan Cape, who came out with the book in 1933.

ULTRAMARINE

Ultramarine is a curious work, though in some ways typical of a promising first novel: derivative yet original, adolescent yet wise, awkward and graceful. Borrowing heavily from Joyce, the language-play throughout the novel starts in the title. "Ultramarine" is not just a gem and a color, but also a form of the blues as sung by the protagonist Dana Hilliot, who as a novice seaman is far from being an "ultra-marine." Hilliot is the same improbable mix that Lowry was, a deckhand who went about his duties while thinking in tags from John Keats, Aeschylus, and Beatrix Potter. The ship itself, with its fiery furnaces below, is evocative of Dante's *Inferno*. The sailors emerge as fiends who torment Hilliot, though he also suffers guilt from abandoning his family and their expectations. Hilliot's "Misericorde" (p. 54) parallels the agenbite or stab of remorse that Joyce gives Stephen Dedalus.

The style of the novel vacillates between an impressionistic stream of consciousness and mimetic realism. The main source of action is the struggle between Hilliot and the rest of the crew, which is in essence a class conflict. As one sailor explains his calling Hilliot a toff: "No, but what I mean to say is, you know, you've got the position, like. We all know that you got eddication and we ain't" (p. 63). Slowly, Hilliot manages to convince them that he has few pretensions, and he even makes friends with a few of the men. The bosun, an overbearing man named Andy, particularly has it in for Hilliot, but even he eventually makes his peace with Hilliot through the all-purpose lubricant in the novel, alcohol.

In the background is Hilliot's troubled relationship with Janet, the girl he left behind. Many of his mental dialogues are aimed at her, and he replays certain cherished scenes from back in England. Yet, enacting the modernist shift from romance to irony, even as he wishes she were more punctual in writing to him, he plans to cheat on her when the boat pulls into Nagasaki. Part of his yearning has little to do with Janet or even women per se, but with a lust for experiences prevented by his cloistered upbringing. A sailor's pet pigeon escaping its cage is a fitting analogy to Hilliot's condition, prefigured by one of the novel's epigraphs, an excerpt from Geoffrey Chaucer's "Manciple's Tale" on how birds in gilded cages prefer the wilds. This may be the start of Lowry's literary fascination with birds, not just because Lowry became a keen naturalist but also because birds are often a symbol of the soul in flight. That the sailor's pet pigeon soon drowns overboard in the ship's wake is an ominous sign, but a fate that Hilliot avoids.

Though large parts of the novel stylistically resemble Aiken's and Grieg's accounts of seagoing apprenticeship, the book is remarkable for the accuracy of Lowry's ear, especially in the passages of sailors' talk that form whole sections of the novel: "a selection of the real language of men" (p. 66), Hilliot thinks, in an echo of William Wordsworth. Yet he also begins to yearn for intellectual conversation, as much a part of life as manual labor. When a German sailor from another ship proves agreeable, Hilliot engages him in discussion that ranges from cultural matters to falling in love. But when he suggests that Hilliot write a book about his experiences, Hilliot hedges, expatiating instead upon his theory of writing:

the desire to write is a disease like any other disease; and what one writes, if one is to be any good, must be rooted firmly in some sort of autochthony. And there I abdicate. I can no more create than fly. What I could achieve would be that usual self-conscious first novel, to be reviewed in the mortuary of *The Times Literary Supplement,* a "crude and unpleasant work," something of that nature, of which the principle character would be no more and no less, whether in liquor or in love, than the abominable author himself. I fear, also, that the disease is a childish one, diarrhoea scribendi simply.

(p. 96)

The passage, a remarkable piece of self-dissection, exposes not only Dana Hilliot's–cum–Lowry's flaws as a fledgling writer but also the genesis of inspiration and the all-too-common substitute impulse, to empty oneself in a flow of words. The set speech itself displays the very sins it decries, adding a note of irony. It illustrates the direction of Lowry's future greatness—the merciless analysis, the multivalent references—as well as the potential pitfalls in such a style—self-pity and posturing. All in all, it is rather startling from a nineteen-year-old upstart sailor.

It is precisely this kind of thinking, however, that convinces Hilliot not to remain a sailor much longer, not even a sailor-writer, though he feels that all writers should learn a trade to give them some perspective on life. In his case, achieving competence as a seaman has given him the confidence to move away from it. Similarly, Janet's pledged love makes him realize only that he has changed, and the end of the novel is his protracted letter to her, interspersed with the sailors' voices around him. "I don't know a damn thing yet" (p. 186), he concludes, regretting the years he has so far spent in ignorance.

The critical reception of *Ultramarine* was mixed but not ungenerous. Discerning critics saw patches of virtuoso talent, though most saw it equally as derivative, a charge that would be attached to Lowry's work all his life. By the time it was reviewed, Lowry had moved on again, first to Paris, having told his father that he intended to study at the Sorbonne, and then to Spain with the Aikens. In Granada he met Jan Gabrial, a young American writer; they met again in London and married four months later in Paris. The relationship was marked from the start by Lowry's drunkenness and sexual impotence, as well as Jan's infidelities, in a vicious circle of cause and effect.

For a while, Lowry worked on short stories,

some later expanded into longer works; others not published until the end of his career or posthumously. In 1934, however, *Story* magazine came out with "Hotel Room in Chartres," which described all too aptly the state of Lowry's marriage: a young couple in Paris, the wife discontent, the ex-sailor husband wishing he were back at sea. Brief as it is, the story is filled with the kind of sensitive, regretful observation for which Lowry was developing a real flair. Continually, the husband wishes to make amends—"But he could not merely be kind to her at that moment, his conflict was buried too deeply, and he loved her too much to insult her with sympathy" (in *Malcolm Lowry: Psalms and Songs,* p. 21). After several miscues, they end up traveling to Chartres, where they achieve a private if transitory happiness at their hotel, "up in the only room in the world" (p. 24). The couple and the fragile Eden they re-create are reminiscent of the lovers in John Donne's "The Good-Morrow," whose love "makes one little room an everywhere." Lowry himself was to follow this pattern later in Canada, where he could love and work best while living on a modest scale in comparative isolation. Everyday life provided a sufficiency of small details to be developed into art. As Lowry observes in "Hotel Room," paraphrasing Charles Baudelaire, "See how the world is a forest of symbols" (p. 22).

For Lowry in France in 1934, however, life was stormy. Jan soon left him to go to New York, and Lowry, hoping to salvage the relationship, followed her. The next two years were a chaos of cheap addresses and weeklong benders. Jan openly took on other lovers (the theme of infidelity in Lowry's work is recurrent), and by the fall of 1935 the two of them were living mostly apart. Ostensibly, Lowry was working on *In Ballast to the White Sea,* but finally his alcoholism became so severe that he checked into Bellevue Hospital. From this experience emerged a short story, "The Last Address," built into a novella first called *Swinging the Maelstrom,* then *Lunar Caustic.* Lowry worked on it sporadically for years, but, as with many of his works, it was published posthumously.

LUNAR CAUSTIC

Lunar Caustic opens with the seaman Bill Plantagenet leaving a bar and ending up in a psychiatric ward. He enters the hospital almost unintention-ally, but once inside he discovers a microcosm of patients and caretakers, among them old Mr. Kalowsky, also known as the Wandering Jew; a lit-tle boy named Garry, who once cut a girl's throat; a nameless nurse; and the presiding Doctor Clag-gart, who talks with Plantagenet after his bout of delirium. Plantagenet's problem, Claggart reveals unsurprisingly, is alcohol, though the roots are patently Freudian:

The doctor smiled slightly. "You said, 'Hullo, father, return to the presexual revives the necessity for nutri-tion.' Sounds as though you once read a little book."
"Oh Christ! Oh God! Oh Jesus!"
"You made some fine giveaways."

(p. 18)

Plantagenet's giveaways, made under the influ-ence, involve fear of his father and castration, with refuge in a pre-Oedipal oral fixation and a flight from authority. Linked by association to all this is Ruth, a woman he left behind, reminiscent of Jan; and the Seven Hot Cantabs, a jazz band he led for a while. Performing music and performing sexually seem to be sources of anxiety for him, both symbolized by his small hands. He boasts about his weight lifting but ends with another giveaway: "matter of fact, the only weight I can't lift—" (p. 20), a veiled reference to impotence.

Having made his confession, Plantagenet en-dures a stay in the ward. (The confession is one in-stance of the way Lowry's fiction embraces a range of faiths, from Catholicism to Buddhism, despite his Methodist upbringing.) He learns more about the other patients, including a black sailor named Battle with an inexhaustible supply of sea chanties, and he even condescends to play a little piano. But he clearly regards his invalid sta-tus as temporary. As he tells Claggart, ". . . Sorry. I'm only a passenger on the ship. With these peo-ple, with Garry and Mr. Kalowsky, it's deadly se-rious. They're the crew" (p. 55). The maritime metaphor is fitting not only because Plantagenet has been a seaman of sorts, but also because Lowry is tapping into Conradian images of sailors and their tales of unrest. In a sense, Plantagenet is Conrad's Marlow in Manhattan, a witness to the horrors of the inner ward. As in *Heart of Darkness*, however, the true terrors reside in so-called civi-lization, as Plantagenet realizes when he looks out

at the cityscape and remarks, "The horrors. . . . Well—do you see New York? That's where they are" (p. 51).

No real escape is possible in either Conrad or Lowry since the horrors are internalized. Though Plantagenet eventually leaves the hospital as abruptly as he entered it, he soon returns to his drinking, this time in a church. The bars that he has frequented have become bars across his mind, an imprisoning force. He hallucinates that he sees Ruth and that inanimate objects are feeding him messages: "In the subway, the roar of the train seemed to be trying to communicate with him. First it said 'womb,' then 'tomb'" (p. 74). Only the craving for oblivion at either end of life drives him onward. Predictably, he ends up in a saloon, "where, curled up like an embryo, he could not be seen at all" (p. 76).

In real life, Lowry was more resilient. After re-uniting with Jan, he left New York in the fall of 1936 to try his hand at Hollywood scriptwriting. With no ready job and his paternal allowance running out, however, Lowry and Jan decided to try their luck in Mexico. Traveling by boat from San Diego, they arrived in Acapulco on 2 Novem-ber, the traditional Day of the Dead. Lowry was entranced by the foreign culture, not to mention the exotic variety of alcoholic beverages, and by Christmas they were living in Cuernavaca.

If there were no Mexico, it would have been necessary for Lowry to invent it. From the lush gardens to the cracked swimming pools, from the ubiquitous cantinas and the comical, tortured English spoken to the hellish bus rides and polit-ical corruption, Mexico was a perfect literary mine for an expatriate. For a while, Lowry found the time to record all the new sights and sounds. He lived within sight of two inspiring yet frightening volcanoes, as well as the *barranca*, or ravine, that traverses the town. Working on an ever-lengthening manuscript, *In Ballast to the White Sea*, he also embarked on a short story about a Mexican bus ride to disaster, which eventually became a pivotal chapter in *Under the Volcano*.

But the vicious circle of Lowry's life began to re-volve around him again. His continual drinking provoked Jan to desert him for other men, which in turn led him to drink more. When Jan finally left him a year later, Lowry began to deteriorate rapidly. At one point, he even spent time in jail for drunkenness and creating a public nuisance, as

273

well as for passport difficulties. Later, in typical Lowry fashion, possibly with a grain of truth, he would claim he was arrested for suspected espionage. He even wrote a poem called "In the Oaxaca Jail," describing the dark passage of an incarcerated soul, "the night when hope's last seed is flown . . . And I crucified between two continents" (*Selected Poems*, p. 28).

Lowry did strike up one enduring friendship in Mexico, with Juan Fernando Márquez, a tall, cultured Zapotecan man who inspired *Dark As the Grave Wherein My Friend Is Laid* and who contributed to the characterization of Dr. Vigil and Juan Cerillo in *Under the Volcano*. Márquez, who rode horseback as a bank courier, was for a time Lowry's drinking partner and adviser, providing the kind of fatherly counsel that Aiken had dispensed. But by 1938, Mexico had grown distinctly uncomfortable for Lowry; it was not merely a private hell but also a country rife with fascist informers and paramilitary groups. In addition, Mexico had severed diplomatic relations with Great Britain in April, ostensibly over a dispute about oil companies.

Lowry was not deported as an undesirable alien, as he indicated in some of his correspondence, but he did leave in debt, bailed out as usual by his father's long fiscal reach. He ended up alone in Los Angeles, ensconced in a hotel, with a first draft of what was to become after many revisions *Under the Volcano*. Like most of Lowry's work, and like Joyce's high-modernist style, the manuscript was to accrete and accumulate layers before its final form. It also required the help of someone who could be an amanuensis, a spiritual solace, a caretaker, and a good editor. Lowry was lucky enough to find all these in Margerie Bonner, a former starlet whom he met through a friend.

At the time, Lowry had been living on a diminished paternal stipend while working on poems, stories, and *Under the Volcano*. The attraction between Lowry and Margerie was both mutual and instantaneous. Having just paid off Jan's alimony claims, however, Lowry's father was anxious to have Lowry leave the area entirely. Through the offices of the family lawyers, he insisted that his son travel to Vancouver, British Columbia, where Lowry lived in equally straitened circumstances and spent much of his time trying to contact Margerie back in Los Angeles. When a drunken bus trip to see her ended with detention at the border—breeding a long-standing fear of customs officials—he called Margerie to come to him instead. She joined him in Vancouver, rescued him from the usual difficulties (Lowry had a habit of trusting unscrupulous types), and lived with him in an attic rental during the long winter, as Lowry worked on the first full-length draft of *Under the Volcano*. Vancouver, which Lowry once termed "the most hopeless of all cities of the lost" (*Letters*, p. 20), proved increasingly uncomfortable, especially on the limited income allowed him by his father. After some moving around, he and Margerie managed to locate a squatter's shack on Dollarton Beach, where they were to live in comparative isolation until 1954. A few months after they took up residence there, Lowry's divorce came through, and he was able to marry Margerie. Living a bit like Thoreau with a wife, or a modern Wordsworth in a newfound Lake District, Lowry worked for the next four years on his stories, some poetry, and a grab bag of unfinished manuscripts, but mainly on the novel growing ever closer to completion.

UNDER THE VOLCANO

LIKE Joyce's *Ulysses*, to which it is all too often compared, *Under the Volcano* is a many-tiered, self-referential work, ruled by polysemous overdetermination. Yet it is also an intensely personal document, a prolonged meditation on private hells, one-upping earlier modernist streams of consciousness by tracing the currents of a highly intelligent but inebriated mind. In its showcase of horrors, from delirium tremens to sordid death, it resembles the work of Conrad, even to the labyrinthine syntax in which its visions are expressed. Its private confessional mode is also reminiscent of Graham Greene, whose own novel of whiskey and faith in Mexico, *The Power and the Glory*, came out seven years prior to Lowry's. But one should be wary of tracing influences on a book that took so long to publish. Charles Jackson's famous alcoholic novel *The Lost Weekend*, for instance, came out three years before *Under the Volcano*, leading people to think that Lowry had copied Jackson's idea, though he had just about finished the last of his many drafts right before the publication of Jackson's book. Lowry chronicles his mortification in *Dark As the Grave Wherein*

My Friend Is Laid, in which the protagonist-author Sigbjørn Wilderness has written *The Valley of the Shadow of Death* (the original title of *Under the Volcano*). *The Lost Weekend*, made into a successful film that continues to haunt Wilderness, is called *Drunkard's Rigadoon* in this novel.

Beyond the concept of an alcoholic trying to come to terms with himself and his surroundings, the two books by Lowry and Jackson have little in common. *Under the Volcano* is a baroque masterpiece, sui generis, its plot engaged in the same convolutions and weavings that possess the characterization and imagery. The novel opens with a discussion between Dr. Arturo Díaz Vigil and the French film director Jacques Laruelle in Quauhnahuac on the Day of the Dead. Exactly one year after the death of the Consul, Geoffrey Firmin, the two men are reminiscing over their lost friend. Given the Consul's rampant alcoholism and self-destructive behavior, his end was perhaps inevitable, but one aspect still puzzles them: Why did he die just when his estranged wife Yvonne had returned and his half brother Hugh had come to visit? After bidding good-bye to Dr. Vigil, Laruelle ends up at a cantina next to the local cinema, where the barman gives him a book left by the Consul. The book has an unsent letter from the Consul to Yvonne inserted between its pages, providing some background on his despair and provoking Laruelle to further memories. As Dr. Vigil has earlier remarked of the dead man: "Sickness is not only in body, but in that part used to be call: soul. Poor your friend, he spend his money on earth in such continuous tragedies" (p. 5). Over the course of the novel, the Consul achieves the status of a modern-day martyr.

The subsequent chapters backtrack a year earlier to the Consul's last days, involving Hugh, Yvonne, and Laruelle. Alone in Quauhnahuac after Yvonne left him, the Consul has fallen into a drunken acedia, though his half brother Hugh is now staying with him and he maintains a tenuous friendship with Laruelle. When Yvonne returns for an attempted reconciliation, their old relationship soon reasserts itself: the Consul is drunk and impotent, and Yvonne has started to approach other men. Much of the interim action, from the Consul's trying to shave with the shakes to surviving a nightmarish Ferris-wheel ride, is concerned with his continual drinking, despite his repeated attempts at restraint. Adding to the Consul's problems are the encroaching fascist agents in Mexico who have begun to oversee the Consul's movements.

The final events in the Consul's life are filled with misunderstanding and casual terror. On a bus ride that he, Hugh, and Yvonne take to Tomalín to see the bull-throwing, they encounter an Indian by the roadside who has been attacked and left to die. Unable to act as Good Samaritans, they proceed to Tomalín. Hugh joins in the bull-throwing, after which they have dinner at a local restaurant. The Consul, who has been soaking up mescal and other alcoholic drinks all day, finally works up enough indignation to accuse his wife of adultery with Hugh—and many others. He then flees into the growing storm, ending up at the Farolito, a lighthouse that doubles as a cantina.

Hugh and Yvonne try to track him down, first tracing him to a cheap hotel, where only his drinking bill remains. They are on their way to the Farolito when the storm suddenly worsens, separating Yvonne from Hugh. Meanwhile, the Consul absorbs some more alcohol at the Farolito and wanders into bed with a young prostitute. He emerges to face a range of accusations, from the pimp who wants money to the policemen who think the Consul is a foreign spy. Suspecting the hand of fascism behind all this, the Consul charges them with killing the Indian along the roadside. The arguments escalate until he is hauled outside and shot by the chief of police. His last act, ironically, is to free a tethered horse that in its runaway course tramples Yvonne to death. The Consul himself dies in a ditch.

Such, at least, is the broad outline of events in the novel. The abundant details, from the minatory ravine to the ruined garden, from the Peter Lorre film at the local cinema to the snatches of poetry that flit through the Consul's mind, form a matrix of symbolism with many levels and slants. Politics, culture, and history intersect with art, religion, and myth; the quotidian reaches toward the extraordinary; and the private realm merges with the public arena. A day in a man's life comes to represent the existence of a tortured martyr for all time. Douglas Day, Lowry's biographer, provides a fivefold analysis of the novel's structure: chthonic, human, political, magical, and religious. The Lowry critic Dale Edmonds offers a breakdown based on the past, the present, doom, drink, and love. As Lowry himself explained when defending the book to Jonathan Cape, its prospective publisher: "For the book was so designed, counterdesigned and interwelded that it could be read an indefinite number of times and still not have yielded all its meanings or its drama or its poetry" (*Letters*, p. 88). This is not mere salesmanship: the novel's material and patterns are seemingly inexhaustible, from a tiny biographical incident to the overarching mysteries of the cabbala.

Lowry is particularly adept at combining naturalism and symbolism to yield additional layers of significance. Since the Consul's plight represents hell, allusions to Dante reverberate throughout the novel. Brooding on his thirtieth year, Hugh confusedly recalls the famous first three lines of the *Inferno*.

> *Nel mezzo del cammin di nostra vita*
> *mi ritrovai per una selva oscura,*
> *che la diritta via era smarrita.*

> (In the middle of the road of our life,
> I found myself in a dark wood,
> for the right way was lost.)

The same words run through the Consul's mind when he goes for a drink after his Ferris-wheel ride: "The Terminal Cantina El Bosque, however, seemed so dark that even with his glasses off he had to stop dead . . . Mi ritrovai per una bosca oscura—or selva? No matter. The Cantina was well named, 'The Boskage'" (p. 225). The collecting associations of "Terminal," "El Bosque," "dark," and "dead" all point to Dante's dark wood. Yvonne also loses her way and her life when traipsing through a darkening forest. Even the Hotel Casino de la Selva, where Vigil and Laruelle meet to discuss the Consul, is evocative of a *selva* or wood, and Quauhnahuac, the original Nahuatl name for Cuernavaca, means "near the wood." From underground, the twin volcanoes threaten subterranean fire as does Dante's Mount Purgatory, and the local ravine is labeled Malebolge (p. 100), the "evil ditch" or eighth circle in the *Inferno*. Vigil himself functions as a version of Dante's Virgilian guide, though he cannot save the Consul from his death in the ditch.

In his damnation, Firmin is a curious blend of passivity and valor. Like T. S. Eliot's Prufrock, he dreams of escaping mundane reality but is confined by his own hopes and fears. As Eliot's character Edward remarks in *The Cocktail Party*, echoing Milton, "Hell is oneself" (*The Complete Poems and Plays, 1909–1950* [1971], p. 342). At the same time, in his ambition to do more than an ordinary mortal, the Consul evokes the figure of Faust, from Christopher Marlowe to William Blake and Goethe. In fact, the Consul's book that Laruelle picks up at the cantina is a collection of Elizabethan plays containing Marlowe's *Tragedy of Dr. Faustus*, which Laruelle hopes to turn into a film. Yet, in Lowry's vision, Faust is not merely a model for sinful overextension. Of the three epigraphs to the novel, the first is from Sophocles' *Antigone* and exclaims over the wonder that is man, the second from John Bunyan's *Grace Abounding for the Chief of Sinners*, and the third from Goethe's *Faust*, holding out the possibility of salvation for he who strives upward. Like Dante's progression from hell to purgatory to paradise, Lowry's plan was to connect all his works in a giant narrative entitled *The Voyage That Never Ends*, which would end in redemption. Sadly, in his life as well as in his art, the plan was only partially accomplished, though *Under the Volcano* is indicative of the grandeur of the promised whole.

In its movement from what once was to what might have been, the novel becomes a grand allegory of man's fall. The marks of a ruined Eden are painfully visible to the Consul:

The tragedy, proclaimed, as they made their way up the crescent of the drive, no less by the gaping potholes in it than by the tall exotic plants, livid and crepuscular through his dark glasses, perishing on every hand of unnecessary thirst, staggering, it almost appeared, against one another, yet struggling like dying voluptuaries in a vision to maintain some final attitude of potency.

(p. 65)

This Lowryesque catachresis links external desolation to the Consul's plight: his unquenchable physical and spiritual thirst, the unattainable wholeness that once was his, the present situation further worsened through his darksome vision. Yet this is no mere solipsism: as Yvonne remarks, gazing at a ruined flower bed outside the house, "My God, this used to be a beautiful garden. It was like Paradise" (p. 98). The invading corruption is further emphasized when the Consul, suffering from a severe hangover, runs into a snake on his property. Yvonne later dreams of a cottage with an unspoiled garden between the forest and the sea, an image of the Lowrys' own shack in Vancouver, but such a return to innocence proves impossible. The harsh postlapsarian reality is to be found in the notices in the public gardens of the city:

¿LE GUSTA ESTE JARDÍN?
¿QUE ES SUYO?
¡EVITE QUE SUS HIJOS LO DESTRUYAN!
(p. 128)

The Consul's mistaken translation says a great deal about his feelings of guilt: "You like this garden? Why is it yours? We evict those who destroy!" (p. 128). Only later does the Consul learn the correct meaning from another of these signs: "Do you like this garden, the notice said, that is yours? See to it that your children do not destroy it!" (p. 232). But the only occupant of this garden is a man on a bench who looks like the devil. Evil is loose in the world.

The extension of the fall from private sin to public corruption moves the novel into the sphere of politics. Fructuoso Sanabria, the chief gardener of Quauhnahuac, who has put up the warning notices in all the public gardens, turns out to be a Castilian aiding the right-wing infiltration of the country. In 1938, Mexico was a seedbed for fascism, as Franco's agents and Nazi feelers dug in like weeds. The Mexican president Cárdenas, though no doctrinaire communist, had socialist affiliations and faced the threat of overthrow by right-wing forces. Whether Firmin, desolate after Yvonne left him, has actually been spying against the fascists is a moot point; still, he does seem to have been keeping an eye out for intrigue since Britain broke relations with Mexico and pulled all its consuls from the country. His record against the Germans in the Great War showed an uncompromising attitude akin to bravery, though the ill-considered zealotry of others during the capture of a German U-boat led to German deaths and a court-martial for him.

The Consul's free-floating paranoia does have some grounds. Mexico has suffered a history of invasion ever since the conquistadors, and the political scene during the 1930s made the country ripe for another takeover. The question was which group would make more headway, and with what motives. Like many other writers of the period, Lowry flirted with socialism but emerged suspicious of all mass movements. The Consul is similarly wary, especially in such a place and era: "Quauhnahuac was like the times in this respect,

wherever you turned the abyss was waiting for you round the corner" (p. 15). Thus, not only must Firmin watch out for fascists like the American Weber, but he must also steer clear of a "professional indoor Marxman" (p. 8) like Hugh, whose convictions consist largely of empty rhetoric. *Under the Volcano* emerges as a prophetic novel, depicting man's guilty hand in the coming atrocities of war. Proleptic casualties show up everywhere, from the bloody hands in the Peter Lorre movie poster to the Indian murdered by the roadside. The inevitability of history is based on the depravity of man's character and so affects all human realms.

Yet for all the novel's slow, encompassing movement of time, the scenes glide and jump-cut with cinematic grace, from tight close-ups to wide-angle panoramas. Lowry was an inveterate movie-goer; references to actors, directors, and films unreel on his characters' screens of consciousness. Just as many of Lowry's protagonists are writers, adding a metafictional aspect to the plot, *Under the Volcano* provides a metacinematic level: Yvonne was once an adolescent film star, and Laruelle is a director still hoping to change the world by making a great film. Films exist in the novel—*The Hands of Orlac*, for example, or *The Student of Prague* (a German Expressionist film about a man losing his soul)—but so does the novel exist in the dimension of film: when the luminous Ferris wheel turns backwards, it represents not only the wheel of karma but also a movie reel, replaying the events of a year ago. When the Consul rides the Ferris wheel or *máquina infernal*, it is a physical representation of Jean Cocteau's *La Machine infernale*, a metaphor for the sinister ordering of the universe. Events themselves acquire significance through Sergi Eisenstein's technique of montage, in which meaning is created through visual juxtaposition. And when the storm makes the lights in the local cinema flicker out, the screen is plunged into darkness, and by extension, so are this place and time.

These juxtapositions and coincidences are more than mere cinematic tricks, however. Lowry was a great believer in mysticism and the cabbala, and in *Under the Volcano* they impose pattern on the most casual aspects of life. In fact, the Consul has amassed an occult library and is no stranger to these patterns. In line with the Faust legend, he functions as a corrupted sorcerer: having violated the laws of purity, he moves inexorably toward damnation. As many Lowry critics have noted, for instance, numerology in the novel establishes not only symbolism but fate. One can see such an effect in the address "666, Cafeaspirina" (p. 208) that the Consul finds in a phone book, a random finding—yet 666 is the number of the beast in the book of Revelation. Similarly, the number 7 branded on the runaway horse's rump is the Old Testament symbol of sacrifice, as well as the morning hour at which Yvonne arrives back in town and the evening hour in which both the Consul and Yvonne die. It is no exaggeration to say that nearly every incident in the novel is a portent for another event. Nature itself seems a partner in collusion, from the rumbling elements of earth, air, fire, and water to the predatory *xopilotes,* or vultures, that hover over the landscape. Even ghostly memories return: on the Day of the Dead, spirits communicate with the living.

The supernatural also extends into the mythic dimension, as David Markson, an early champion of Lowry, noted as early as 1952. Homeric visions of Hades infest the hellish existence of the Consul, who seeks numbness in mescal, making him the modern-day counterpart of a lotus-eater. Yvonne, for her part, is a kind of Circe, turning men into swine. Hugh's bull-throwing feat is reminiscent of Heracles' conquering the Cretan bull. From the East, Lowry also brings in the Hindu epic *Mahabharata:* the Consul as the last surviving hero, making a pilgrimage to a holy mountain accompanied by a dog. But the overwhelming myth behind the novel is that of Tantalus, whose thirst is forever unabated. Christianity offers a similar parable: in a twist on the Fisher King of the Grail legends, who seeks water to dispel spiritual aridity, Firmin must have alcohol, not merely to assuage his soul, but also to satisfy a physical craving.

Much of the overriding tension in the novel stems from the urgency of addiction, at times romanticized, at other times depicted in gutter realism. No scene is more comically poignant than when Hugh helps his half brother shave because the d.t.'s make the Consul's hand too unsteady to hold a razor. Firmin's desperation is such that, halfway through the ordeal, he swigs from a bottle of bay rum—and promptly throws it up. Like so many addictive substances, alcohol brings blessed relief to the Consul while also hastening his demise. In one drunken hallucination, he feels that the very clouds in the sky approve: "Drink all morning, they said to him, drink all day. This is life!" (p. 93). In fact, the appeal of inebriation goes beyond the mere guzzling of alcohol. As he wishes to tell Yvonne but never quite says:

you misunderstand me if you think it is altogether darkness I see, and if you insist on thinking so, how can I tell you why I do it? But if you look at that sunlight there, ah, then perhaps you'll get the answer, see, look at the way it falls through the window: what beauty can compare to that of a cantina in the early morning? . . . All mystery, all hope, all disappointment, yes, all disaster, is here, beyond those swinging doors.

(p. 50)

Tracing the cause of addiction is a tentative business at best, but Lowry does provide a model in his portrait of the hard-drinking Taskerson family, at whose house both Firmin and Laruelle stayed in adolescence. As Laruelle recalls, the Taskerson boys were all capable of downing six pints and walking a good twenty-five miles during the day; the parents imbibed quantities in the evening. The Taskersons' facade was near perfect, with only a "wibberlee wobberlee" feeling in place of a hangover. The blustery family helped Firmin to overcome his shyness. But their common history does not explain why Laruelle emerges unscathed whereas Firmin becomes a lush, nor does it reveal the real reasons for the Consul's despair, which is abetted by a combination of self-destructive behaviors. His alcoholism is more a symptom than a cause, a gross means to treat an underlying sense of failure.

On the deepest level, *Under the Volcano* is a story of love and betrayal. In the realm of personal relations, the Consul is a much-abused and abusing figure, tender yet narcissistic. As with Lowry, Firmin's wit and feeling make him extraordinarily good company, a genuinely lovable figure. At the same time, his self-absorption and tendency to retreat make him impossible to be with. For all his grand martyrdom, there is something personally offensive in his self-destruction. As the ghost-voice of Yvonne quarreling with Firmin resonates in Laruelle's head: "No, you loved yourself, you loved your misery more than I" (pp. 14–15). Moreover, the destructive impulse pulls in others as well, as Hugh cautions Yvonne. When a little girl wishes to sell her an armadillo as a pet, he warns her about trying to domesticate it: "It'll not only never come back, Yvonne, but if you try to stop it it will do its damndest to pull you down the hole too" (p. 113). In the process, both Hugh and Yvonne get dragged under with Firmin.

Despite Lowry's layers of allegory and symbolism, this is an all-too-human drama filled with questionable behavior and motives. Yvonne herself is no paragon of virtue; neither is Hugh, with whom she has had an affair; nor is Laruelle, whose house of adultery is entirely too close to the Consul's home. The inscription on one of the panels of Laruelle's house presents a magnificent irony: "*No se puede vivir sin amar*" (p. 209), "One cannot live without love." On the crudest level, this truth is borne out by the cycle of addiction and infidelity into which the Consul and Yvonne fall, to the point where Yvonne leaves. In his continual state of intoxication, the Consul cannot even perform sexually, though as Lowry explained to his publisher, "meanings of the Consul's impotence are practically inexhaustible" (*Letters*, p. 73). At base, it is an inability to connect. That Yvonne has returned seems a miracle, but it is simply another proof that one cannot live without love. Commitment, of course, presents its own problems. The various bonds of affection in the novel, between husband and wife, between friends, and among family members, all strain and tear against the weight of quotidian reality. Eros is forced into a marital straitjacket, and agape faces a spiritual void.

The two volcanoes, Popocatepetl and Ixtaccihuatl, whose brooding presence and fiery intimations dominate the landscape of the novel, are symbolic of everything from the numinous to damnation and sex. These meanings are not all disjunctive, however, just as quotidian love can ascend to Love. As Stephen Spender suggests in the standard preface to the novel, the characters and events enact the progress of the soul. Alienation and loneliness are the real crippling forces. In the background is Dr. Vigil, praying "for those who have nobody with" (p. 6), a locution and sentiment that Lowry takes up again in *Dark As the Grave Wherein My Friend Is Laid*. The power of love to unify and connect is something the Consul learns only too late, after he has fled from Yvonne to the drunken squalor of the Farolito. Regretting how his flight into alcohol has separated him from others, he realizes that the same impulses could have been turned outward: "Here would have been no devolving through failing unreal voices and forms of dissolution that became more and more like one voice to a death more dead than

death itself, but an infinite widening, an infinite evolving and extension of boundaries, in which the spirit was an entity, perfect and whole" (p. 361). This is Lowry's novelistic achievement, an individual affliction enlarged to a tragedy that resonates on all levels.

LATER LIFE

LOWRY finished the third draft of *Under the Volcano* in mid-1940 but could not interest a publisher in the manuscript. The next four years were spent revising and enlarging the novel, a labor evident in the dense thematic interweaving that became a Lowry trademark. During this period, he and Margerie also worked on other projects. Margerie proved to have a facility for writing mystery novels, and Lowry worked on poems, stories, and the longer and longer novel *In Ballast to the White Sea*. In June 1944, catastrophe occurred: a fire leveled the Lowrys' shack, taking with it the manuscript of *In Ballast*. Though the Lowrys soon rebuilt their home, the unfinished novel was unrecoverable, and the sense of loss pervades much of Lowry's fiction from then on. Compounding their problems, the Vancouver Harbour Board started eviction proceedings against the squatters in Dollarton, meaning that the Lowrys would eventually have to move. By this time, however, Lowry had finished the final version of *Under the Volcano* and sent it off to his agent for submission. Perhaps because he could now view the material more calmly, or perhaps because the death of Lowry's father had made Lowry financially stable for the first time, he and Margerie decided to travel to Mexico, the country that had given rise to the dark vision of his novel.

In Mexico, life began to imitate art with frightening rapidity. Cuernavaca possessed a string of cantinas entirely of a piece with those described in *Under the Volcano*, the *barranca* running through the town like a trace of hell. Both Lowry and Margerie began drinking rather heavily, in part to escape the ghosts evoked by the book, but also to dispel the tension of waiting for a verdict on the finished opus. On New Year's Day, Lowry at last received a letter from Cape. The readers' reports criticized the rambling length first and foremost, harping on the "eccentric word-spinning and . . . stream-of-consciousness stuff" (cited in Day, p. 317), and suggesting massive cuts. Cape did not go so far as to reject the novel as it was, but in general concurred with his readers. Lowry's considered reply, thirty-one pages long and written over the course of two weeks, is not only a brilliant polemic for modernist aesthetics but also an eloquent exposition and artistic defense in its own right. In it, Lowry explained and justified nearly every pattern and event in the novel. In the face of such argument, Cape capitulated and accepted the novel. The American publisher Reynal and Hitchcock was also to accept the manuscript—but Lowry could not know either decision for some time, and in the interim he waited miserably in Mexico. His good friend Juan Fernando Márquez, he learned in Acapulco, had been shot dead in a cantina. Back on mescal, at one point Lowry even attempted suicide. Eventually, he ran into some minor trouble with the police, a problem that could easily have been fixed with a bribe. Instead, attempting to fight the charge but faced with a police dossier of his drunken misconduct in 1938, he only worsened his situation. After payment of a large fine, he and Margerie were unceremoniously deported.

Back in Vancouver, he began the trying task of moving from accepted manuscript to page proofs. When he finished in December 1946, he and Margerie sailed for Haiti. Haiti's aura of voodoo and mysticism further spurred Lowry's interest in the occult, which in his later works becomes more of a controlling and less of a coincidental force. He and Margerie arrived in New York for the publication of *Under the Volcano* in February 1947. Though some reviews pointed out the heavy debt Lowry owed to the earlier modernists, most were adulatory, and Lowry enjoyed—or endured—a brief spell as a celebrity. Social situations made him nervous, and his lack of self-confidence drove him to constant inebriation. Returning to his shack in Vancouver, he found his former isolation challenged by the press. Suddenly he was a known presence. His friend Gerald Noxon did a radio drama of *Under the Volcano*, and Lowry heard that Hollywood might be interested in producing a movie of the novel. (John Huston eventually came out with a film version of the novel, but not until twenty-seven years after Lowry's death.)

As the book slowly became more popular, Lowry worked hard on *La Mordida* and *Dark As the Grave Wherein My Friend Is Laid*, based on the notes of the Lowrys' journey to Mexico. Late in 1947, they sailed to Europe through the Panama Canal, a journey that Lowry was to turn into the novella *Through the Panama*; other tales were based on his stays in Paris, Rome, and Pompeii. But the time abroad was marred by increasingly violent binges, which the return to Dollarton alleviated only for a while.

Plagued now by varicose veins and eczema in addition to his alcoholism, Lowry struggled forward with various drafts of novels and stories. In 1949, captivated by F. Scott Fitzgerald's *Tender Is the Night*, he and Margerie collaborated on a screenplay of the novel. The resulting work, detailed and drawn out in typically Lowryesque manner, was highly praised by Hollywood but finally deemed unfilmable. Meanwhile, Lowry's relationship with his editors was growing increasingly strained, based on promises and plans rather than completed manuscripts. But as Lowry worked on stories that kept turning into novel manuscripts, he became more and more interested in a grand fictional design to encompass his life's work. In 1951 he drew up a document entitled *Work in Progress*, which included a schema that consolidated all his work to date as well as plans for future material. The proposed title, fittingly enough, was *The Voyage That Never Ends*. The voyage was to be bracketed fore and aft by *The Ordeal of Sigbjørn Wilderness*, comprising the stories Lowry was then working on. Following the first part of *Sigbjørn Wilderness* was *Untitled Sea Novel*, a much-reworked version of *Ultramarine*; then *Lunar Caustic*, which Lowry was also still revising. *Under the Volcano* was to be the centerpiece of the oeuvre, followed by an intended trilogy: *Dark As the Grave Wherein My Friend Is Laid*, *Eridanus* (a paean to Dollarton), and *La Mordida* ("The Bite," an account of Lowry's troubles with the Mexican police). Death intervened before Lowry finished—if indeed he ever would have—but Lowry was such a linking, self-referential writer that these rough manuscripts, many pieced together and published posthumously, exhibit a high degree of coherence, as in the connective work he must have envisaged.

For a while, Lowry worked on his short stories, but upon receiving a contract for two novels and a collection from Random House, he turned his attention back to lengthier narratives. Longer works-in-progress were to occupy him for some time, though a couple of his stories were soon published in *Partisan Review* and *New World Writing*. Meanwhile, the Lowrys' isolation in Dollarton was increasingly threatened by the Vancouver authorities' plans for eviction of all squatters on the shorefront. As early as 1946, the Lowrys had contemplated moving to Gabriola Island off the coast of British Columbia, but now they thought seriously of leaving for Europe. Lowry's literary project at the time began as a story about traveling to Gabriola but gradually assumed the monumental proportions of another magnum opus. But the project did not find favor at Random House, and Lowry grew despondent. Poor health and a broken leg forced Lowry to move with Margerie to a Vancouver apartment during the winter of 1953. The departure from paradise, so keenly described by Lowry in all his major works, was imminent. In January 1954, Random House severed its connection with Lowry. Later that year the Lowrys embarked for Europe, starting in Italy. This time, they left Dollarton for good—or ill, as it turned out.

Their stay in Sicily was not a success: Lowry's alcoholism had grown into a constant torment, both to himself and to those around him. In London, his debilitation became so severe that he was hospitalized, as much for psychiatric observation as for physical recuperation. The Lowrys ended up in the Sussex town of Ripe, where Lowry worked on revising the stories for his collection and adding to the growing manuscripts of his novels. It even seemed for a while that he had found another haven in which he could write, but his depression and urge for oblivion inevitably creeped back. His excesses were followed by self-recriminations, which deepened his feelings of guilt and led to further abuse. In June 1957, after a particularly violent quarrel with Margerie, Lowry, already drunk, swallowed a bottleful of sleeping pills. Partly to protect people's feelings, and given Lowry's propensity to act in haste, the coroner ruled it "death by misadventure." He was buried in Ripe.

HEAR US O LORD FROM HEAVEN THY DWELLING PLACE

THE literary estate Lowry left behind included not merely a growing reputation but also hundreds of pages of manuscripts. Through his wife's careful stewardship and editing, Lowry's output broadened considerably in a body of posthumously published work. Stories continued to appear from time to time in magazines, and in 1961 emerged the long-awaited collection *Hear Us O Lord from Heaven Thy Dwelling Place*. It contained seven stories, some of which Lowry had been working on until just before his death.

The title of the book comes from a Manx fishermen's hymn; it echoes the sea themes and the appeals to some higher force that run through the collection. In "The Bravest Boat," for example, Astrid and Sigurd Storlesen's relationship is compared to the boat Sigurd set adrift with a message in it, when he was ten years old. That Astrid found the boat is a testament to the enduring quality of love, capable of weathering all storms. The image of a message sent into the void and finally reaching an admiring reader is also a symbol of art and, specifically, of Lowry's own difficulties in finding an audience.

Other stories in the collection are more self-centered, having to do with a writer, his travels and travails. A typical example is "Strange Comfort Afforded by the Profession," in which Sigbjørn Wilderness, in Rome on a Guggenheim Fellowship, tries to find Keats's final residence and meditates on literary posterity. "Elephant and Colosseum" casts light on a similar but differently named writer, Kennish Drumgold Cosnahan, also in Rome, who has produced a best-seller entitled *Ark from Singapore*. Like Wilderness, he is an alcoholic trying to fight his addiction, though another insidious problem is his growing reputation. Reminded of Edward Gibbon, he notes: "How right was that historian he must one day read: success invites self-neglect; by means of self-indulgence" (p. 139). This is typical of Lowry, to compare his own decay with Gibbon's concern, the collapse of the Roman empire, but the main flaw of these stories is that they have too little scope to contain the grandeur they envision. Cosnahan does have an errand, to see his Italian translator, but instead he is preoccupied by elephants, from the memory of a menagerie aboard a ship to a caged beast at the zoo. Unfortunately, the symbolism remains as gray and voluminous as the elephant itself, the pattern of imagery simultaneously too solipsistic and peripatetic. "Present Estate of Pompeii" ostensibly concerns a friend of Wilderness, Roderick McGregor Fairhaven, who is sightseeing among the ruins of Pompeii with his wife and musing on art and loss. Like Popocatepetl and Ixtaccihuatl in *Under the Volcano*, Vesuvius possesses an awe-inspiring destructive force, and, as with any natural disaster, the question of when a volcanic eruption will recur arises. The fire that ravaged Lowry's shack in Dollarton, never far from recall, appears here as Fairhaven's memory of a refinery blaze in Eridanus.

By far the longest piece in the collection is *Through the Panama*, billed as Sigbjørn Wilderness' journal excerpts as he voyages on the SS *Diderot* along with his wife, Primrose. As in much of Lowry's fiction, the story is more a voyage of the mind than any physical journey. Its coherence is created through self-consciousness, modernist associationism, and literary points of reference. Allusions to W. B. Yeats, Joyce, Samuel Taylor Coleridge, D. H. Lawrence, Robert Penn Warren, Henry Miller, and many others dot the pages. Sigbjørn himself is trying to write a novel and complicates the metafictional references by observing, "The further point is that the novel is about a character who becomes enmeshed in the plot of the novel he has written, as I did in Mexico" (p. 30). The reference to Mexico and Lowry's own past involves the author in his work in a manner calculated to rebuff the New Critics, for whom a piece of art was meant to be sufficient unto itself. Lowry's fiction was always intensely, inescapably personal.

But instead of moving ahead on his novel, Sigbjørn continues to struggle with his journal, sometimes too hard. Rounding Cape Flattery, Sigbjørn describes the "finny phallic furious face of Flattery" (p. 30). Majestic marginal notations begin to creep in, resembling those in Coleridge's *Rime of the Ancient Mariner*, or in Hart Crane's *The Bridge*. The puns and allusions multiply—"Alcoholics Hieronymous" (p. 72), "delirium Clemens" (p. 73)—but Sigbjørn is all too aware of his posturing—"Joyced in his own petard" (p. 41), as he puts it. In the end, Lowry moves past modernist appropriation into the realm of mere collage.

The last two stories, however, show Lowry's talent for sustained descriptions of nature. "Gin and Goldenrod" portrays a somewhat altered Sigbjørn and Primrose back in Eridanus, heading through the forest to the local bootlegger to buy alcohol on a Sunday. The journey is fraught with the urgency of their errand, contrasted with the gorgeous profusion of flora along the way. Cynically, the sense of hope at the end may have more to do with the bottle of gin that Primrose has squirreled away than with the beauty of the woods. But an answer to this story occurs in "The Forest Path to the Spring," regarded by many as Lowry's best short fiction. Here, Eridanus again comes across as Eden, but this time infused with an immanent joy from living in harmony with nature, a joy that appears more Taoist than Christian. The footpath that leads to the spring is the Way, rather than the confusing trail through the woods in "Gin and Goldenrod." And whereas that story ends with the promise of a cocktail, "The Forest Path to the Spring" culminates with a drink from a pure stream.

POETRY

IN 1962, *Selected Poems of Malcolm Lowry* came out, edited, with Margerie's assistance, by Earle Birney, an early Lowry scholar and Vancouver friend. Divided into seven sections, from "The Roar of the Sea and the Darkness" to "Thunder Beyond Popocatepetl," the structure of the collection is more the idea of Birney than of Lowry, who had at one time envisioned a volume entitled *The Lighthouse Invites the Storm*. Here, the poems are organized roughly thematically: nautical, Mexican, alcoholic, love-inspired, and so on. Given Lowry's propensity to transmute and recycle, it is not surprising to see many phrases and images as outtakes from the fiction. "The Lighthouse Invites the Storm," for instance, a poem title, is a phrase the Consul entertains, the image of a self-destructive beacon that applies to him. "For *Under the Volcano*" unscrolls the bloody tapestry of Mexico, including "a tilted turtle dying slowly on the stoop, / of the sea-food restaurant" in "this ghastly land of the half-buried man" (*Selected Poems*, p. 23). Like so many of Lowry's visions, these are based on real sightings. Those that are not darksome visions are often the opposite, beatific scenes of nature from Dollarton.

The level of craft that some of the poems display is surprising, from villanelles and sonnets to the intricate "Sestina in a Cantina." In the course of his apprenticeship under Aiken, Lowry had learned his lessons in prosody. In fact, certain of the more involved passages of *Under the Volcano* were apparently first written in verse. And though Lowry was thought to have started *The Lighthouse Invites the Storm* in New York and largely finished the collection in Mexico, he wrote poetry for most of his life, as *The Collected Poetry of Malcolm Lowry* proved when it came out in 1992. Moreover, he was the kind of correspondent whose letter to a friend might turn into a poem (as the posthumous *Selected Letters of Malcolm Lowry* shows), and much of his verse is occasional. Yet the combination of casual reflection and deeply felt pain can strike hard, as in "Men with Coats Thrashing":

> Our lives we do not weep
> Are like wild cigarettes
> That on a stormy day
> Men light against the wind
> With cupped and practised hand
> Then burn themselves as deep
> As debts we cannot pay
> And smoke themselves so fast
> One scarce gives time to light
> A second life that might
> Flake smoother than the first
> And have no taste at last
> And most are thrown away.
> (*Collected Poems*, pp. 141–142)

The image of self-consuming man occurs in practically everything Lowry ever wrote, a subject as personal as it is universal.

DARK AS THE GRAVE
WHEREIN MY FRIEND IS LAID

IN 1962, Lowry's revised version of *Ultramarine* came out, incorporating a list of minor alterations accumulated since the first publication of the novel. *Lunar Caustic* was finally published in *Paris Review* the following year and printed as a book five years later. Meanwhile, Lowry's poems and stories kept appearing in various journals, adding to his posthumous reputation. And in 1968, Margeric, with Douglas Day, who was to write Lowry's most extensive biography to date, produced an edited version of a Lowry novel that had heretofore existed only in manuscript form, *Dark As the Grave Wherein My Friend Is Laid*.

Once titled *The Valley of the Shadow of Death*, and cobbled together in part from Lowry's unfinished *La Mordida*, *Dark As the Grave* is another journey narrative. Opening with a minutely described airplane trip, the narrative is a version of Lowry's return to Mexico to search for his friend Márquez, a quest as strewn with obstacles as a modern-day *Pilgrim's Progress*, or a dark unwinding not unlike the search Conrad's Marlow makes for Kurtz. The characters are again Sigbjørn and Primrose Wilderness; the scene is the Mexico of so many drunken nights and days, when Sigbjørn lived there with his former wife, Ruth. As in *Under the Volcano*, there is a Ferris wheel, a warning notice in all the gardens, and a *farolito* whose sign has been painted out. For all the pride he takes in being his wife's guide, Sigbjørn worries about the return of the repressed, "the agony of repeating experiences" as Sigbjørn puts it in *Through the Panama* (p. 50). Even the scents are reminiscences: in Mexico City, he whiffs "the familiar smell, to him, of gasoline, excrement, and oranges" (p. 99).

Yet the tortured beauty inherent in the very landscape brings back Lowry's descriptive powers at their height. "Sunken waterholes in the desert, far rock formations like Inca cities, pools of alkali like frozen rivers, wrinkled rhinoceros hide of the foothills, like pyramids too, tender blue sky with one long motionless still white cloud a benign unwinking swordfish . . ." (p. 56). The people are equally picturesque, a peasant mixture of piety and corruption, readily co-opted as symbols before Sigbjørn's observant gaze. Setting up house in Cuernavaca, he and Primrose briefly attain a prelapsarian mood in the ruined garden estate, but conditions have altered irrevocably. Among the changes is the transformation of Sigbjørn's own status, from a drunk with a failed marriage, to a more temperate man in a far happier second marriage, though no return to innocence is possible. Equally significant is that Sigbjørn, once a drunken scribbler with few prospects, has become an author with a reputation to consider, who worries about the critics and their reviews.

Indeed, the entire book is permeated by Sigbjørn's anxieties, less urgent than the Consul's in *Under the Volcano*, but with the additional perspective of hindsight. Ghostly memories pervade every stopping point, as continual references to Edgar Allan Poe's "The Fall of the House of Usher" suggest. Contending with the ghost of his earlier self, he also pursues another spirit: his friend Juan Fernando Martinez, killed in a barroom, though Sigbjørn does not yet know this. In the interim, he meets Eduardo Kent, "reputed to be a murderer, five times married, and a crook" (p. 137), with whom he shares his views on life and art. This scene represents both the potential intricacy and shortcoming of the novel: as a modernist writer pursuing the hyperconsciousness of reality, Sigbjørn is trying to live and write simultaneously. The result, when it works, is a bracing immediacy, but at other times it smacks of artistic appropriation, as Sigbjørn himself recognizes: "He had no sooner made an interesting friend than he began to think of that person as a character" (p. 198).

Half real, half character himself, Sigbjørn is possessed by the memory of his house in Eridanus burning with all his creations—his manuscripts—still inside. Thus, he brings his own torment wherever he goes, comparing himself to the Greek mythical image of the doomed prophet: "Every man his own Laocoön!" (p. 43). In Oaxaca, learning of Martinez's death, he attempts to find his friend's grave but wanders hopelessly around the churchyard graves, eventually returning with Primrose to his hotel. Finally, in the early dawn hours, he arises alone to take a walk, and in the vision of the awakening streets he receives the illumination of a new beginning. The financial institution for which Martinez worked has funded agrarian reform, a political move that Sigbjørn imbues with quasi-religious significance: "The Banco Ejidal had become a garden" (p. 255). In parallel, the flames of the burning house in Eridanus become the votary candle for the dead, offering the hope of the phoenix, a resurrection from the ashes.

The labor that went into editing *Dark As the Grave* was massive; different notebooks were basted together, repetitive scenes were cut, all while trying to preserve Lowry's thematic unity. Inarguably, the best person to do the work was Lowry himself, though Margerie had served as both typist and editor during the greater part of her husband's writing career. If the material in the novel occasionally resembles an undigested bolus (Lowry's term), this is in part due to scholarly reticence: no one could interweave disparate elements like Lowry, and at this stage no one else would even attempt it. Lowry's words, in whatever order, had acquired canonical status. The bulk of his manuscripts were now objects of research, stored at the University of British Columbia in Vancouver.

OCTOBER FERRY TO GABRIOLA

STILL, there was enough material for one more novel: *October Ferry to Gabriola*, which was published in 1970. As in his earlier books, the genesis of the narrative is a journey, in this instance the trip that Lowry and Margerie made to Gabriola Island in 1946. Convinced that the Harbour Authority was finally going to evict them from Dollarton, they were searching for another paradise, and this, with a great deal of elaboration, is the motive behind the novel. For the first time, the protagonist is not the writer-as-lush but a Canadian lawyer named Ethan Llewelyn, in semi-retirement with his wife Jacqueline after a gruesome case, in which he fought to exonerate a client who turned out to be a murderer. Other familiar Lowry fixations are there, however, from a passion for film to an obsession with the occult. In fact, the entire novel follows a reading and misreading of strange signs, from advertisements to visitations.

Just as *Dark As the Grave* begins with an airplane trip, *October Ferry* starts with a bus ride to Nanaimo, the middle leg of the Llewelyns' journey to Gabriola. The act of leave-taking sets the mood, since the Llewelyns are searching for a new home after being threatened with eviction from Eridanus. Philistine Canada is to blame, with its emphasis on materialism and morality. Billboards assault their view, and the Llewelyns feel half smug, half desperate, as they travel toward what they hope will be another unspoiled spot. Meanwhile, social restrictions extend to everything from alcohol to sexual license. For all that Canada embraced its famous adopted son after his death, Lowry's sum-up, as Llewelyn enters the men's side of a pub, is damning: "What a country of fatuous prohibitions!" (p. 39).

In the back of Llewelyn's mind is the Lowryesque memory of one's home burning down, in Llewelyn's case caused by a freak lightning bolt that sparked the fire. Though Llewelyn tries not to dwell on the incident, it becomes an overarching symbol, a weltanschauung: "Well, their house was dead. And the world still burned on" (p. 90). As with so many of Lowry's symbols, however, this one contains its opposite: the fire of destruction may also be the purifying fire of renewal, as it becomes in a vision of a man burning tree stumps on Gabriola.

In addition to natural cycles, the supernatural orders many of the events and pseudo-events in the novel. Some of the observations seem coincidental, as in a man getting off the bus carrying a suitcase monogrammed R.I.P., or the sign at-

MALCOLM LOWRY

tached below the license plate of an old sedan "SAFESIDE-SUICIDE" (to indicate the proper lane to pass). Others, such as the remarkable incidence of fireballs and mystical mayhem in Vancouver, begin to move beyond a mere pattern to suggest a force of some kind. Jacqueline's Scottish father, Angus McCandless, it turns out, is an adept in the cabbala, and Llewelyn's ruminations about this fact provide a great deal of exposition on unseen forces. As the narration notes: "Ethan's method of thinking—that is the way he had been thinking, or thought he had been thinking, this morning up to this point—involved a process akin to composition" (p. 210). The general effect, unfortunately, is to smother the inexplicable under too many layers of measured musing.

Predictably, much of the material is ransacked from Lowry's own past, including a childhood eye injury and a lingering remorse over the death of Paul Fitte (Peter Cordwainer in the novel), a suicide at college that Lowry perhaps could have prevented. Also, Lowry's (and Llewelyn's) interest in film provides the same cinematic dimension as it does in *Under the Volcano*. At one point, Llewelyn even imagines his life as a movie, *The Ordeal of Ethan Llewelyn* (p. 27). And it is here that messages from one medium segue into those of another. The Llewelyns first meet in a Toronto cinema showing *Outward Bound*, a title that will come to characterize the Llewelyns' journey. A piece of dialogue from the film, along with Lowry's annotation, further illustrates their condition:

"—but are we going to heaven, or hell?" the great voice of one of the characters in the show boomed through into the foyer. . . . "*Ah*," came back the answer, "*But they are the same place, you see.*" Had the voice been that of the Inspector, who was supposed to be God, who had come aboard that ship of the dead to judge the passengers? Or was it Scrubby the barman speaking, the "halfway," destined because of his suicide to commute eternally on that spectral ferry between earth and the unbeholden land?

(p. 13)

The reverberations from these grand themes echo throughout the story, and when the Llewelyns finally board the ferry to Gabriola, they are poised at exactly this halfway point. Only the pastoral vision of the island indicates that they will somehow move beyond.

MALCOLM LOWRY: PSALMS AND SONGS

A final roundup of Lowry's short pieces appeared in 1975, entitled *Malcolm Lowry: Psalms and Songs*. Some of these are outtakes from the novels, including "Seductio ad Absurdam" and "On Board the *West Hardaway*" from *Ultramarine*, as well as the story that became chapter 8 of *Under the Volcano*. Other pieces, such as "Kristbjorg's Story: In the Black Hills," are sketches that Lowry never fully developed. "Enter One in Sumptuous Armour," about a prep-school experience, is clearly juvenilia, though it displays Lowry's growing interest in interiority, as well as literary reference. The title itself is borrowed from Shakespeare's stage direction in *Troilus and Cressida*, in which a walking suit of glittering armor eerily contains a putrefied corpse; in the story, it obliquely refers to a boy in a padded goalkeeper's uniform. Even "Ghostkeeper," preserved as a draft about a couple walking around Stanley Park in Vancouver, has some polished Lowryesque turns. As the man remarks to the woman, "This is like a nightmare, but it is also extremely pleasant" (p. 203). In a metafictional aside, Lowry also remarks on his method of composition as accretion and insertion: "not merely the wheels within wheels, but the wheels within wheels within wheels" (p. 227).

Perhaps the finest story in the collection is "June the 30th, 1934," a previously unpublished account of two men on a train bound for Boulogne. When one of the men, Firmin, reminisces about the Great War, the main character Bill Goodyear feels ashamed of having been too young to fight in it and so lies about his past. Interspersed among the talk and travel are contemporary advertisements and ominous signs of the upcoming war, as personal history merges with larger social forces. The story ends symbolically with both characters "fast asleep under the lamp as the express screamed on like a shell, through a metal world" (p. 48).

Psalms and Songs also contains a reprint of *Lunar Caustic*, as well as a section called "Malcolm Lowry Remembered," penned by various hands, and a section by A. C. Nyland on the evolution of Lowry's style. The Lowry archives still reside at the University of British Columbia and may yet yield up more material. The Lowrys' screenplay of *Tender Is the Night*, for example, was published in a scholarly edition in 1990. Writings from Lowry's days at The Leys School have also emerged in print. Given Lowry's sometimes

285

ghoulish sense of humor, as well as his interest in the occult, the spate of posthumous publication would probably amuse him.

It is poignant, however, that so much fame has accumulated around an author so tortured by feelings of inadequacy during his lifetime. The suffering is visible in so much of Lowry's work. As John Berryman once said: "The artist is extremely lucky who is presented with the worst possible ordeal which will not actually kill him" ("John Berryman: The Art of Poetry," *Paris Review* 53 [winter 1972], p. 207). On the other hand, Lowry had a knack for coming up with his own ordeals, just as "the lighthouse invites the storm." Self-battering and self-consciousness conspired to produce a brilliantly bruised art. Throughout the work, one can also see an alternate current of cheeriness—and both are Lowry. In his poem "Conversations with Goethe," he reveals: "I have two selves and one lives free in hell, / The other down a well in Paradise" (*Collected Poems*, p. 167). The reference to Faust is clear enough. These are the internal divisions that make for greatness at a price.

SELECTED BIBLIOGRAPHY

I. BIBLIOGRAPHIES. Earle Birney and Margerie Lowry, "Malcolm Lowry: A Bibliography," in *Canadian Literature* 8 (1961) and 9 (1961), with supplements in 11 (1962) and 19 (1964), the first attempt at a comprehensive bibliography; William H. New, *Malcolm Lowry: A Reference Guide* (Boston, 1978); J. Howard Woolmer, *Malcolm Lowry: A Bibliography* (Revere, Pa., 1983), offers the most complete listing.

II. COLLECTED WORKS. *Hear Us O Lord from Heaven Thy Dwelling Place* (New York, 1961); *Selected Poems of Malcolm Lowry*, ed. by Earle Birney (San Francisco, 1962); *Malcolm Lowry: Psalms and Songs*, ed. by Margerie Lowry (New York, 1975), stories, including a reprint of *Lunar Caustic*, reminiscences of Lowry by others, and a study of Lowry's style; *The Collected Poetry of Malcolm Lowry*, ed. by Kathleen Scherf (Vancouver, B.C., 1992).

III. SELECTED WORKS. *Under the Volcano* (New York, 1947); *Ultramarine* (New York, 1962), the standard version, though it is a revision of the 1933 Jonathan Cape edition; *Selected Letters of Malcolm Lowry*, ed. by Harvey Breit and Margerie Lowry (New York, 1965); *Dark As the Grave Wherein My Friend Is Laid*, ed. by Douglas Day and Margerie Lowry (New York, 1968); *Lunar Caustic*, ed. by Earle Birney and Margerie Lowry (London, 1968), a reprint of the *Paris Review* 29 (1963) manuscript; *October Ferry to Gabriola*, ed. by Margerie Lowry (New York, 1970); *The Cinema of Malcolm Lowry: A Scholarly Edition of Lowry's* Tender Is the Night, ed. by Miguel Mota and Paul Tiessen (Vancouver, B.C., 1990); for stories still uncollected, such as "Bulls of the Resurrection" (*Prism International* 5, no. 1 [summer 1965]), or collected elsewhere, see M. C. Bradbrook's *Malcolm Lowry: His Art and Early Life*, listed here under "Biographical and Critical Studies"; see also Woolmer bibliography.

IV. BIOGRAPHICAL AND CRITICAL STUDIES. Dale Edmonds, "*Under the Volcano*: A Reading of the Immediate Level," in *Tulane Studies in English* 16 (1968); Perle S. Epstein, *The Private Labyrinth of Malcolm Lowry*: Under the Volcano *and the Cabbala* (New York, 1969); Daniel B. Dodson, *Malcolm Lowry* (New York, 1970); George Woodcock, ed., *Malcolm Lowry: The Man and His Work* (Vancouver, B.C., 1971), includes Lowry's "Preface to a Novel," the introduction to the French edition of *Under the Volcano*, a brief selection of poems, and a variety of short essays on Lowry; Richard Hauer Costa, *Malcolm Lowry* (New York, 1972); Douglas Day, *Malcolm Lowry: A Biography* (New York, 1973); M. C. Bradbrook, *Malcolm Lowry: His Art and Early Life; A Study in Transformation* (London, 1974), includes three early stories: "Ghostkeeper" (reprinted in *Psalms and Songs*), "A Rainy Night," and "Satan in a Barrel"; David Markson, *Malcolm Lowry's* Volcano: *Myth, Symbol, Meaning* (New York, 1978); Anne Smith, ed., *The Art of Malcolm Lowry* (New York, 1978), includes a reminiscence by Lowry's brother Russell.

Richard K. Cross, *Malcolm Lowry: A Preface to His Fiction* (Chicago, 1980); Sherrill E. Grace, *The Voyage That Never Ends: Malcolm Lowry's Fiction* (Vancouver, B.C., 1982); Chris Ackerley and Lawrence J. Clipper, *A Companion to* Under the Volcano (Vancouver, B.C., 1984); Ronald Binns, *Malcolm Lowry* (New York, 1984); Gordon Bowker, ed., *Malcolm Lowry Remembered* (London, 1985), reminiscences, including material from Jan Gabrial, Lowry's first wife; Sheryl Salloum, ed., *Malcolm Lowry: Vancouver Days* (Madeira Park, B.C., 1987), further reminiscences; Tony Bareham, *Malcolm Lowry* (New York, 1989).

See also *The Malcolm Lowry Newsletter* (Waterloo, Ont., 1977–1984; subsequently *The Malcolm Lowry Review*).

BEATRIX POTTER

(1866–1943)

Lisa Hermine Makman

ALMOST A CENTURY after Beatrix Potter published *The Tale of Peter Rabbit* in 1902, initiating her series of beloved fables and inaugurating her life as a writer, her stories remain favorites; translated into more than a dozen languages, they have become the common property of children all over the world. Their eminence attests to Potter's gifts as a writer and illustrator and expresses an ongoing predilection for the brand of fantasy depicted in them. Contemporary admirers of the Peter Rabbit stories have inherited a legacy from Potter's culture, a set of ideas about childhood and about the spaces associated with children that have remained resonant for nearly one hundred years.

Since their original publication in the first third of the twentieth century, Potter's books have been grouped with the "classics" of British children's literature, a canon that has included the writings of Lewis Carroll, George Macdonald, and Kate Greenaway, who preceded Potter; works of her contemporaries Frances Hodgson Burnett, J. M. Barrie, Rudyard Kipling, Kenneth Grahame, and Edith Nesbit; and the stories of those who followed Potter, such as A. A. Milne, C. S. Lewis, and J. R. R. Tolkien. For the most part, the canon comprises works written between the 1850s and the 1950s. Over the course of this period, with increasing frequency, writers describe childhood in spatial terms, as a protected place, distant from yet ever threatened by the grown-up arena of politics, sexuality, commerce, and work. The universe Potter imagines, inhabited principally by anthropomorphic animals, resembles such a sheltered childhood realm. Though the Peter Rabbit books have commonly been associated with the Victorian society into which Potter was born on 28 July 1866, the vision of childhood within them differs from the more traditional Victorian childhood spaces: rural paradises in which cheerfully obedient children freely romp. Something ominous lurks within the Arcadian landscapes Potter paints.

Although in many ways Potter experienced a prototypically Victorian childhood, she wrote for an audience she called "the modern child." Moreover, she came of age and wrote her most lauded work during the period of literary modernism, which, roughly speaking, spanned the last two decades of the nineteenth century and the first three decades of the twentieth. In her style of language and in the motifs she develops in her writings, Potter is much more a modernist than a Victorian. Her prose—wry, clipped, and to the point—links her work stylistically to modernist writing and offers a striking contrast to the Victorian idiom, which typically is tortuous and wordy. It works in counterpoint with her dreamy, often romantic—quite Victorian—illustrations. The disclosure of mythic and sinister aspects of everyday life in her tales links her work thematically to modernist writing, bringing her close to luminaries of modern adult fiction such as Virginia Woolf. Critics have noted the influence of her work on modernist writers, such as Graham Greene, W. H. Auden, Christopher Isherwood, and George Orwell, all of whom read and admired her tales.

Potter's attitude toward the "modern child," the child to whom she addressed her stories, was equivocal. In letters she complained about this entity, whom she believed to be spoiled and greedy—endowed with too many possessions. As a child, Potter herself possessed few consumer items—several books and almost no toys. She maintained that this seemingly scanty supply of goods was fuel enough for her imagination. Though Potter claimed to frown upon children's activity as consumers, however, she profited from it as well. Her books themselves are consumer goods, carefully crafted to solicit children's desires; but Potter did not limit her sales to books.

She was constantly dreaming up new schemes to create merchandise that capitalized on her characters and their stories. These ventures, which she named her "sideshows," have, like her tales, been an enormous success since they first began to appear. Potter's characters have been reproduced as porcelain figurines and as dolls; they have appeared on myriad items for children—dishes, stationery, bookmarks, hankies, wallpaper, tea sets, calendars, game boards, puzzles, slippers, and more. Potter, who began to design such items shortly after she published her first tale, was the first writer of children's books to explore the lucrative market of child consumers so effectively.

Potter not only viewed children's role as consumers with disfavor; she also took exception to children's position as workers—her tales undermine the Victorian "busy bee" paradigm of child behavior, which Lewis Carroll parodies in *Alice in Wonderland*. Unlike many earlier writers of animal tales for children, Potter never exhorts children to work. On the contrary, in many of her stories she promotes play as an aim for young creatures. In play, the "child" protagonists of her early stories question and subvert authority. Peter Rabbit, certainly *not* a good little bunny, chooses a less conventional, more adventuresome path than his obedient and industrious sisters when, instead of methodically picking and saving berries as do the girls, he dives into the proscribed garden of Mr. McGregor and gorges himself with its forbidden fruits. Though *Peter Rabbit* has been interpreted by many readers as a cautionary tale—a warning against defiance of authority and lack of diligence—Peter is never punished by his mother for his transgressive garden frolic. In fact, he suffers no worse than a stomachache for his sins; and, instead of inflicting the anticipated castigation, his mother gently nurses him with chamomile tea to soothe his sore belly.

Potter celebrates the unproductive ethic of Squirrel Nutkin, the hero of her third tale, just as she toasts that of Peter. In *The Tale of Squirrel Nutkin* (1903), a group of young squirrels make elegant daily offerings of food to Old Mr. Brown, a drowsy but daunting owl, in exchange for permission to partake of the nuts that abound on his island. The industrious creatures rise early each morning to prepare their gifts for the owl and then spend the rest of the day laboring—gathering nuts. Though Nutkin accompanies his comrades on their visits to Owl Island, he chooses not to participate in their barter. Instead, he whiles away time engaged in two wasteful activities—jubilant solitary games and playful provocation of Old Brown. For a number of days, Brown sits on his stoop, ignoring Nutkin's vexatious behavior, silently receiving the series of thoughtful and neatly packaged gifts brought to him by his assailant's companions. Though Nutkin ultimately comes close to losing his life under Brown's claw, he miraculously escapes, saving his skin, but, in the process, losing most of his tail. Though Nutkin does suffer a great loss—this is one of the most severe punishments that occur in Potter's oeuvre—Potter's tone at the end of the tale is hardly moralizing. She writes that even now, if one asks Nutkin a riddle, his response is to shout and throw sticks. In other words, though he develops a distaste for riddles, his behavior has not improved.

In Potter's tales, animal children who are sent off to work face fates at least as grisly as that which menaces the slothful Nutkin. They do not reap rewards as they should, according to the morality promulgated by many of the books that Potter read as a child—the works of Maria Edgeworth and Sarah Trimmer, for example. Instead, guardians in Potter's tales who send their children off to work send them into danger or to their graves. The heroes of Potter's porcine stories—*The Tale of Pigling Bland* (1913) and *The Tale of Little Pig Robinson* (1930)—placidly submit to their caretakers' injunctions that they work. Pigling Bland and his siblings are sent away from the farm where they live and out into the world because at home they consume too much and produce nothing. At the beginning of *Pigling Bland*, the keepers of the pig protagonist—his mother, called Aunt Pettitoes, and the farmer narrator of the tale—send their young ward off to market to seek his fortune. With his brother Alexander, Pigling leaves home for a hiring fair, to be pinched and poked and ultimately selected by farmers for an unspoken purpose.

Whether Pigling will be hired as a laborer or purchased for slaughter remains unclear, but the piglet's evident fear of the market suggests that ultimately his "end [will be] bacon" (p. 347).[1] Child labor in Potter's stories is closely associated with the child's death and metamorphosis into

[1]Citations from all of Potter's tales except *The Fairy Caravan* and *Sister Anne* refer to *The Complete Tales of Beatrix Potter*.

someone else's meal. In *Little Pig Robinson*, as in *Pigling Bland*, a young pig is shunted off to a perilous marketplace. When Robinson's aunts send him to sell and buy goods at the Stymouth market, he meets many creatures (including a fatherly human) on his journey who are disturbed to see a young pig alone and at work. It seems their fears are justified. Soon after the credulous Robinson arrives at the market town, a ship's cook kidnaps him by luring him onto the boat with the promise of a tour. The cook furtively plans to flatter and fatten the piglet in order to serve him as ham for the crew.

Many of Potter's contemporaries shared her ambivalent attitude toward child consumers and child workers. During the course of Potter's life, as protracted struggles over child-labor legislation took place, children gradually ceased to be seen as having economic value: no longer active as producers, they were viewed as objects for whom to buy. Yet at the same time, in an increasingly commercialized society, children were commonly represented as belonging to a separate noncommercial world, a world threatened by a corrupting economic market. The many attempts to protect children and to preserve childhood that were initiated during this period were at least in part motivated by a will to distance children from the world of commerce—the world of production, which rendered children commodified objects, and the world of consumption, which rendered children desiring subjects. While national public schools, nurseries, clubs, and parks were believed to protect children, they were also thought to function as preserves, in which children could be contained and, it was hoped, controlled. This idea of "preservation" expresses a paradoxical view of childhood. Children are a hazard to society and at hazard in society: thus they must be both restrained and protected. Potter expresses these divergent views of childhood and roles for children both in her tales for children and in her life history.

LIFE AND WORKS

HELEN Beatrix Potter spent her entire childhood and a considerable stretch of her adult life sequestered in the upstairs nursery of her parents' South Kensington home. In fact, for Potter this cloister served not only as a playroom, but as a classroom and ultimately as an art studio, until finally, at the age of forty-seven, she married and left her family home to settle permanently in the Lake District. In the Potter's London abode, as in a multitude of affluent Victorian homes, the organization of domestic space reflected changing attitudes toward children and toward the span of years labeled "childhood." The nursery, the sole place designated for children, was isolated from the rest of the house. This spatial arrangement made manifest the view that children should be excluded from the lives of their parents and segregated in a place that could accommodate childish misbehavior—a place where they could be needy, noisy, and fractious, and then be presented in good form to parents after tantrums had passed. And yet the idea of the nursery also implied a perceived need to shield children from malignant influences by limiting their world to a hermetic, supervised sphere.

However necessary the British nursery seemed to some, it was not a universal institution; dependent on the possession of space enough to provide children with a private room of their own, it was a luxury available only to the affluent. Helen Leech Potter and Rupert Potter, parents of Beatrix, belonged to families that had profited from the Industrial Revolution. After accumulating wealth in the Lancashire cotton trade, both clans joined the growing ranks of the self-made wealthy. Each possessing a formidable inheritance, Potter's parents could easily afford a well-staffed nursery. Their lifestyle typified that of a class for whom idleness represented an ideal way of life. Potter's father was a barrister by vocation, yet he had never practiced, and spent much of his time quietly with friends at the Reform Club or engaging in his avocation—photography. Often he socialized with his close companion, the painter John Everett Millais, whom he helped by photographing sitters and backgrounds for use in portraits. Potter's mother, an austere woman, inveterately dressed in black, adhered religiously to a rigid schedule of daily events, including a silent breakfast and a drive in the family carriage to make social calls. Only on rare occasions did she visit the nursery, where nannies and governesses reigned.

Though perhaps a lonely place at times, the insular nursery that Potter shared with her only sibling, Bertram, provided refuge from intrusive parental scrutiny. Bertram, born when his sister was almost six, encouraged her scientific and artistic endeavors, and she, in turn, inspired his. Together they planned to elicit parental interest in Potter's artwork, with the hope that the adults might help her to begin a professional life as an artist. In her journal, she writes of their attempts: "We work a mutual admiration society and go *in moaning* together over the apathy of the rest of the family. We decided that I should make a grand effort in the way of Christmas Cards, and if they fell flat, as usual, we would take the matter into our own hands" (May 1890, p. 212).[2]

Indeed, they took matters into their own hands, and the result was that Potter, at age twenty-four, made her first sale. Bertram sent his sister's drawings to the firm of Hildesheimer and Faulkner, and they were purchased for use as holiday cards and as illustrations for a small book of verse called *A Happy Pair*. Soon after this, a German firm of fine art printers, Ernest Nister, also bought some of Potter's artwork. The inmates of the nursery had produced marketable goods and had started to raise funds that could facilitate their escape from dependence and seclusion. However, Beatrix Potter would have to wait more than ten years before she would launch her profitable career as an author.

Altogether, over the course of her life, Potter published twenty-nine books: four for very small children, two of which are books of nursery rhymes, and twenty-five longer tales. Five more of her stories were published posthumously. The nineteen tales that represent her best work appeared during the brief period between her private publication of *Peter Rabbit* in 1901 and her marriage to William Heelis in 1913. Potter's life as a writer of children's stories can be divided roughly into three stages. The initial period spans the years during which she worked closely with her first editor, Norman Warne. During this time, at a brisk clip, she wrote some of her most well known stories: *The Tale of Peter Rabbit* (1902), *The Tale of Squirrel Nutkin* (1903), *The Tailor of Gloucester* (1903), *The Tale of Benjamin Bunny* (1904), *The Tale of Two Bad Mice* (1904), *The Tale of Mrs. Tiggy-Winkle* (1905), and *The Tale of the Pie and the Patty-Pan* (1905). In her dealings with Frederick Warne and Company, her publisher, Potter corresponded primarily with Norman, the youngest son of the

company's founder. After they had enjoyed many pleasant meetings and exchanged dozens of increasingly intimate letters, Warne proposed to her early in the summer of 1905, although, according to Warne family lore, the pair had never been alone together.

In the tales written during the period of her collaboration with Norman Warne, Potter introduces themes that deal with social behavior, appearances, and clothing, which recur in much of her work. In four of the seven tales written during this time, clothing plays a pivotal role: *Peter Rabbit, The Tailor of Gloucester, Benjamin Bunny,* and *Mrs. Tiggy-Winkle*. In the other three tales, social "clothing"—rules of etiquette—is of central importance. In these stories, codes of polite behavior are teased apart and discarded. Potter herself was guilty of unseemliness during this period. When Norman Warne proposed, Helen and Rupert Potter did everything they could to prevent the union, but their usually dutiful daughter was obstinate. She was thirty-eight—almost thirty-nine—and accepted Warne's offer despite her parents' opposition. Never before had Potter been so close to an escape from her parental home. However, soon after the engagement, Norman Warne, who was thirty-seven years old, became seriously ill, and in August 1905 he died of pernicious anemia.

At about the same time Potter became engaged to Norman Warne, she became a landowner. Using all of her savings and a small legacy from an aunt, she purchased a working farm in the Lake District: Hill Top Farm in Near Sawrey. Potter had first seen Hill Top when she stayed with her parents in Sawrey during summer holidays in 1896. During the years before her marriage to William Heelis, though she was very much caught up with the affairs of the farm, she was not able to spend more than one month of the year there, as a result of her parents' insistence that she attend to them. Nevertheless, many of the stories of Potter's middle period—from the time of Norman Warne's death until she became Mrs. Heelis just before the First World War—are set at Hill Top Farm, in the town of Sawrey, or in the surrounding woods and countryside: *The Tale of the Pie and the Patty-Pan* (1905), *The Tale of Tom Kitten* (1907), *The Tale of Jemima Puddle-Duck* (1908), *The Tale of Samuel Whiskers* (1908), *The Tale of Ginger and Pickles* (1909), *The Tale of Timmy Tiptoes* (1911), *The Tale of Mr. Tod* (1912), and *The Tale of Pigling Bland* (1913). The stories of this period tend to be longer and

---

[2]Citations from Potter's journal refer to *The Journal of Beatrix Potter*, 1989 ed.

more involved than those of the first period. They also tend to be somewhat more ominous, the threats they present more vivid.

The last period of Potter's writing life begins in October 1913, the month she married William Heelis—a timid solicitor who had helped her to acquire Lake District property—and achieved independence from her parents, and the month she published *The Tale of Pigling Bland*, a story of escape from bondage. This marks a new stage in her life, no longer dominated by writing. Critics have agreed that when she married, she rapidly lost interest in her little books and her writing declined in quality. Struggling to meet Warne's demand for new titles, she announced to her editor that she continued to write only for the sake of the old firm, that is, for the sake of Frederick Warne and Company. During the First World War, Potter barely worked on her books. Between *Pigling Bland*, published in 1913, and *Appley Dapply's Nursery Rhymes*, published in 1917, she wrote nothing. Moreover, *Appley Dapply* contained no new writing or pictures—it was a compilation of work she had accomplished at various times earlier in her book-writing career. Most of her late tales were old ideas that she had reworked or offshoots of *The Fairy Caravan* (1929), a collection of stories loosely woven together. The *Fairy Caravan* stories vividly express the theme that predominates in the works of this last period of writing—escape. Though the world Potter creates for her child readers in all of her books provides an escape from the prosaic adult world, most of the stories she composed in the last decades of her life deal explicitly with this theme.

Not only in her tales, but in her journal entries and letters, Potter intimates her longing for escape from the confining home of her parents and implies that she found some respite in artistic and scientific endeavors, both of which provided her with excuses to wander alone for hours outdoors. Potter studied the fossils, flora, and fauna that she came upon while wandering through the British countryside, and she meticulously painted what she discovered. She found solace in creative representation—in writing, photography, and painting, and these activities granted her a language with which she could communicate to those outside the Potter household. However, before Potter cultivated these means to express herself publicly, she had developed her abilities as a writer in private, in her diary.

THE JOURNAL

IN the early 1950s, a mystery was uncovered at Castle Cottage—the farmhouse where Beatrix Potter had lived with her husband for thirty years, from the time of her marriage in 1913 until her death on 22 December 1943. The daughter of one of her cousins discovered an enigmatic sheaf of loose sheets and exercise books inscribed with minute writing in an inscrutable code. Leslie Linder, a devoted Potter scholar, was shown these documents and tried to decipher the writing, making numerous attempts over the course of many years. Finally, in 1958, he cracked the code. He discovered that between 1880 and 1897, from about age thirteen until age thirty, Potter had kept a secret journal using a code of her own invention. Ever since it was unearthed, the diary has greatly facilitated Potter scholarship.

Although the extant journal begins in 1880, scholars speculate that Potter discarded prior entries when, at the age of twenty, she reviewed her writings and purged all that she disliked; according to her own record, she preserved only the early fragments that pleased and amused her. The size and incomprehensibility of the ciphers indicate that journal writing for Potter was an intensely private act. She believed she wrote for herself alone, proclaiming with confidence in a journal entry that no one would read what she wrote. On only one documented occasion during her lifetime did Potter refer to the journal. About a month before she died, in a letter written to a cousin, she noted that she had kept a journal in code, but that she could at that time neither make out the tiny letters nor decode the ciphers.

In sections of the journal her writing was so tiny as to be almost illegible. Between the years 1882 and 1887, the characters were in places so small that she could cram more than 1,500 words onto one side of a 6.5-by-8-inch page. In the tales she later composed, the concern for secrecy that the form of her diary expresses is conveyed through recurrent themes of hiddenness and masquerade. Despite Potter's assiduous attempt to conceal the contents of her journal, in it she reveals remarkably little of her inner life. Although journal writing may have offered Potter a temporary escape from her family's cramped circumstances in London and from her mother's demands, she rarely gave ire and frustration free rein.

Like the nursery, the journal functioned for Potter as a "preserve," confining her mutinous ideas and impulses in a private zone, while at the same time giving her a place in which she was entirely free from the pressures of Victorian-style propriety. The diary reveals Potter's unheard and unseen rebellion against norms dictated by her parents and by her culture. Like the tales she later composed, it contains astute criticisms of Victorian bourgeois values, values her parents held and promoted. With irony, she pokes fun at the absurdities of Victorian imperatives—social decorum, the class system, and various manifestations of religious piety. However, Potter rarely glares directly at her parents with her satirical eye; usually she gently or indirectly criticizes her parents' behavior and opinions. She writes of one brief escape from her home in the family's carriage, "I had a delightful drive, defying the enemy, and after all got home in time for lunch" (*Journal*, p. 346).

The unnamed adversary, Potter's mother, was always "difficult" and rarely gave Beatrix the opportunity to leave the house alone, always seeking excuses to keep her daughter at home. While on several occasions Potter refers to her mother's refractory nature and sundry health woes, overall there is a marked silence in the diary about her parental foe. Helen Potter's most prominent role in the journal is as an impediment in her daughter's life—her habits imposed strict limitations on those of Beatrix, who was permitted to visit friends only on the rare occasions when her mother was absolutely certain she would not need the family's carriage. If the carriage was free, there were other excuses to keep Beatrix at home, such as her mother's somewhat fragile health and Beatrix's delicacy.

According to reports in the journal, Potter's father played a more active and more positive role in his daughter's life than did his wife. Potter and her father shared many interests, including art, photography, and the British countryside. In London, they visited many exhibitions, and Potter documents them in her journal in great detail. Whenever the Potter family sojourned outside of London, Potter, who busily trained herself as a naturalist, and her father, who like her was an amateur photographer, together explored fields, woods, and villages, with heavy cameras in tow. Though sometimes in records of these travels Potter complains of her father's contrariness, overall the trips revived Potter. They liberated her from the routine of the Kensington homestead and introduced her to another world, a world filled with animals, plants, insects, fossils, and fungi, all of which she fervidly drew, photographed, and painted.

Over the course of the 1890s, Potter's investigations of nature grew increasingly rigorous. Though she examined and copied myriad flora and fauna, she concentrated her studies on fungi and made innovative discoveries about lichen, in addition to making hundreds of aesthetic and accurate drawings of rare fungi. The journal ends suddenly early in 1897, just before Potter submitted a paper to the Linnean Society of London, "On the Germination of the Spores of *Agaricineae*," in which she presented an innovative way to grow lichen spores. Potter could not participate in the society's meeting at which her paper was read in April 1897 because women were not permitted to attend these gatherings.

Ironically, George Massee, a principal assistant at the Royal Botanic Gardens at Kew, who had refused to take Potter seriously, proudly presented her paper to the society. Not long after her paper was presented, she withdrew it from the society, so that it was never published. At this point in her life, it seems, she perceived that she would not be well received by professional scientists. Hostility directed at her by competitive professionals at Kew, where she had been granted permission to conduct research, highlighted the limitations imposed on her because of her lack of conventional training and, even more, because of her gender. She notes to herself in her journal that the director of Kew "may be something of a misogynist" (p. 442). In her journal she writes, somewhat enigmatically, "if I was a boy and had courage" (p. 120), not stating directly what precisely boyhood might permit.

The diverse trajectories taken by Potter and by her younger brother suggest the degree to which the strictures inflicted on middle-class girls of Potter's era limited their lives. Whereas Beatrix was destined to stay at home until she married someone whom her parents chose or approved, Bertram left home for school at age eleven and later, after studying briefly at Oxford, decided to become a professional painter. During his youth, he was permitted to journey independently and made frequent trips to the north of England and to Scotland to sketch and paint. Eventually, on one such trip, he fell in love with Mary Scott, a woman employed in a house where he lodged. He married her in secret and settled permanently in Scotland, running a farm and seldom venturing south to visit his family. He lived thus for seven years before he informed his parents of his marriage, and he did so at that time only to aid his sister, who was then experiencing difficulty gaining parental approval for her engagement to William Heelis.

Though Potter was not free to travel independently like her brother, she had frequent opportunities to make trips away from London. In addition to traveling to visit relatives in the countryside of England and Wales, the Potters left London to vacation twice a year. During the almost five decades Potter lived in her family home, she accompanied her parents on these trips. At Easter they traveled to the seaside, and each summer they resided in Scotland for three months. The Scottish countryside was the enchanted landscape of Potter's childhood. Nurse Mackenzie, who presided over the Potter nursery for many years, hailed from the Highlands of Scotland, where the Potters spent ten summers. Beginning in 1882, the year Beatrix turned sixteen, her family began to spend summers in the Lake District.

Scotland and the Lake District remained sites associated with childhood freedom throughout Potter's life. Her experiences of these places as a child influenced her representations of nature in the tales she later wrote. In her diary, she avowed that the fantastical world generated by her childish fancy in these bucolic landscapes was more a "home" for her than was her parents' house in Kensington. When she was a child at Dalguise House, the estate her parents rented in Scotland, she inhabited a self-contained, timeless realm: "seeing my own fancies so clearly that they became true to me, I lived in a separate world." In this magical fantasy world, the past was vividly present: "Everything was romantic in my imagination. The woods were peopled by the mysterious good folk. The Lords and Ladies of the last century walked with me along the overgrown paths" (*Journal*, p. 85).

In the summer of 1892, after more than a decade of vacationing away from Scotland, the Potters once again rented a house near Dunkeld, the site of Dalguise House. Though the prospect of a trip to Edinburgh excited Potter, the possibility of visiting her old "home" unsettled her: "Dunkeld, O Home, I cannot bear to see it again. How times

and I have changed!" (*Journal*, p. 87). Dramatically, she declares that great shifts have taken place in herself since she last saw Dunkeld: "What has not happened since we left? What may happen before I see it again if I ever do." In Dunkeld, she finds that, though people and their creations pass away, nature remains, unchanging; she writes, "Man may spoil a great deal, but he cannot change the everlasting hills, or the mighty river, whose golden waters still flow on at the same measured pace, mysterious, irresistible" (*Journal*, p. 89). Nature offers respite from change: the changes people effect and the changes they themselves endure. Changeless nature retrieves the past; the smell of the river brings pleasant memories back to Potter. Soon after this disturbing return to her home, Potter began to produce the stories she later published.

In her small books she fabricates her own version of the unchanging nature she rediscovered in Scotland. She contrives in her tales a self-sufficient world set apart from the difficulties and disappointments of the world in which she lived; she forges a world of her own, a universe in which she can feel at home.

At the end of her life, Beatrix Potter understood the perennial success of her stories about Peter Rabbit and his cohorts as a function of her characters' remoteness from the human world; in a letter, she describes how these creatures, immune to transient human history, live their predictable lives in an unshifting environment: according to Potter's fantasy, they "keep on their way, busily absorbed with their own doings . . . always independent" (*Letters*, p. 422).[3] Toward the beginning of the Second World War, four years before Potter died, she described this changeless world of her books as she tried to recall the origins of her first tale, *Peter Rabbit*:

It seems a long time ago; and in another world. Though after all the world does not change much in the country, where the seasons follow their accustomed course—the green leaf and the sere. . . .

In towns there is change. People begin to burrow underground like rabbits. The lame boy for whom Peter was invented more than forty years ago is now an air warden in a bombed London parish.

(p. 442)

[3]This and further citations from letters refer to *Beatrix Potter's Letters*.

293

When Potter cites "another world," she seems to refer both to the timeless fantasy world her tales depict and to actual rustic life before World War I. She conflates a mythic place—a rustic realm untouched by change, and a mythic time—an immaculate prewar past; and she contrasts this mythic time-space with towns: places where a "lame boy" can metamorphose irrevocably into an "air warden."

The "preserve" she depicts in her books, however, is not free of problems. Though Potter stresses the spatial and temporal distance between the world belonging to "nature" and more urban worlds, by comparing wartime activity with the burrowing of rabbits, she implies that her fictive Arcadia indeed meets the world in which wars occur. When war intervenes in human lives, the difference between people and other sorts of creatures collapses; people behave like beasts: like beasts, they prey and are preyed upon. Potter's conflicting impulses—to represent the proximity of beast world and human world and to proclaim their separation—mark all of her writing.

Despite Potter's idyllic portrayal of the period during which she wrote *Peter Rabbit*, at this time political turmoil was not absent. The political climate in Britain during the decades before 1914 provided another impetus in Potter's search for a safe and stable haven, a "preserve." Like Matthew Arnold, in whose writings she found consolation, she believed that anarchy raged beneath the surface of polite society—that social codes only masked dangerous irrationality. Although Potter was born during a relatively peaceful period in England, she came of age in the 1880s—a time of increasing political turbulence. Many journal entries, especially those written between 1886 and 1887, convey Potter's deep fears of social disorder, which are for the most part provoked by agitations for home rule and by threats of working-class revolt.

Potter viewed home rulers and protesting workers with hostility and condemned their activities as criminal. In her journal she writes, "How anyone can really talk of the Home Rulers as anything but a band of self-interested assassins passes my comprehension" (p. 172). She decries the disruptive behavior of "the working men" (p. 180), complaining that the socialists H. M. Hyndman, H. H. Champion, and John Burns, members of the Social Democratic Federation, were being treated with too much civility. Encouraging the violence she claims to disdain, she argues, "Why, they ought to be hung at once like dogs. I consider they are the most dangerous kind of criminals in existence. A murder affects but a small circle, they, if unchecked, will cause wholesale slaughter, and ruin society" (p. 183).

In her journal, Potter records internal tumult as well as turbulence in the outer world. Margaret Lane's 1946 biography, published before the discovery of the journal, depicts Potter as shy and withdrawn, and describes her first thirty years as dull and uneventful. Yet from the first entries, the journal shows Potter's exuberant interest in the people and events that influence her life and reveals her as a formidable, stormy character, with strong tastes and opinions. While Lane claims that Potter's life was vacant before she began to write her books, the journal contradicts this proclamation. In fact, even before she reached twenty, Potter felt that too much had occurred in her life—too much loss compressed into too few years. "I, seventeen. I have heard it called 'sweet seventeen,' no indeed, what a time we are, have been having, and shall have" (*Journal*, p. 49). And the following year she writes, "I am eighteen today. How time does go. I feel as if I had been going on such a time" (p. 104). The time that passes, densely filled with events and sensations, becomes a focus of attention in the diary.

Potter's journal evinces a turbid preoccupation with the passing of time, with change, with loss and death, and a concomitant longing for a repose and stability associated with childhood. An urge to preserve the past, to make permanent the memories it comprises before they slip from her grasp, seems to compel her to write. Just as her abundant drawings and photographs preserve what she sees, her writing preserves her overall perceptions, her thoughts and feelings. Many passages of her diary disclose her fixation on the nature of time's flux—on irrevocable loss. During her late teens in particular Potter expresses pessimism about the future. Periodically, she refers bleakly to the ineluctable passing of time and to the loss of old friends. After her maternal grandmother dies, she writes, "There will be no one soon" (*Journal*, p. 62), and this phrase echoes several times in the diary as elderly friends and family members fall ill or pass away. She writes, "There will be none of the old faces left soon. Time goes so fast I cannot keep up with it" (p. 55). The years take people with them: "If the next year takes away as many dear faces it will bring death very near home" (p. 109). Time threatens Potter, who in her youth declares that she fears the future; it is "a great moving creeping something closing over one object after another like rising water" (p. 109); elusively, it passes "into space never to return" (p. 168).

Potter equates the loss of those with whom she shared her childhood with the loss of her childhood and child self. Upon the death of Mr. Gaskell, a Unitarian minister and spouse of the well-known novelist, she writes, "Another old friend gone to rest. How few are left" (p. 93). Meditating on his life, she remembers herself as a child, presenting him with flowers: "He is gone with almost every other, home is gone for me, the little girl does not bound about now, and live in fairyland, and occasionally wonder in a curious, carefree manner, as of something not concerning her nature, what life means, and whether she shall ever feel sorrow. It is all gone, and he is resting quietly with our fathers. I have begun the dark journey of life" (p. 94). What exactly has Potter lost as she embarks on this "dark journey"? In her imagination, the world of her childhood is closely tied to the world of a generation becoming lost: she loses the two simultaneously.

She conflates her personal lost time with historical lost time. Like her contemporary J. M. Barrie, who claimed to evoke in his writings his mother's childhood in preindustrial Scotland, Potter strives not only to keep alive the pristine rural world she associates with her own childhood, but to resuscitate that which she associates with those who lived in the last century. In passages throughout the journal she discloses a deep desire to preserve a record of the life of her paternal grandmother. In her 1946 biography, Lane describes how Potter recorded bits of her grandmother's conversation verbatim, mimicking both content and dialect.

Potter's memory of her grandmother was bound to her memory of "the place I love best in the world," Camfield Place, an immense estate Rupert Potter's father purchased in 1866, the year that Beatrix was born. Potter writes that her memory of this place, a mix of "fact and fancy," comprises a "perfect whole" (p. 444). The realm of childhood memories constitutes an intact and complete sphere that resembles the world of her animal characters as she imagines it. Following the death of Grandma Potter, whom Beatrix asserted in her journal was as near perfect as a person could be, the family was forced to countenance the necessary sale of Camfield Place. At this difficult time, in the spring of 1892, Potter wrote her earliest known illustrated letter to the eldest child of her friend Annie Moore, a woman only three years older than she, who had for a short time been employed as her governess. These letters she later rewrote as stories—her famous tales.

Potter's at times fervent journal writing seems to have served a function for her analogous to that which her letter writing and fiction writing eventually served. In these forums writing seemed to be a response to loss, an act of re-creation. She turned her attention fully toward writing fiction only after she abruptly stopped writing in her journal in 1897, shortly after her failure to be taken seriously as a scientist. Her activities from this time were directed toward tale writing and illustration. Within five years of her last journal entry in 1897, she had published a best-seller, *The Tale of Peter Rabbit*.

THE FIRST TALE

ACCORDING to Potter, *Peter Rabbit* succeeded not only because of its content but because of its audience: it was addressed to an individual child and not "made to order." Like *Peter Rabbit*, most of Potter's works were written for specific children. She derived her early stories from illustrated letters she had written to the plentiful offspring of her friend and former governess, Annie Moore. In 1893 she sent the tale that was to become *Peter Rabbit* to Moore's four-year-old invalid son Noel in the form of a picture-letter. Eight years later, encouraged by Annie Moore and by Canon Hardwicke Rawnsley, a close family friend who was familiar with the juvenile publishing trade, she borrowed the original letter, and, lengthening it, transformed it into a book.

All of the publishers she initially approached rejected the manuscript. They wanted large books with color illustrations, but Potter envisioned her project differently. She conceived of a book that would attract a child and not a parent; she considered the size of a child's hands and the size of a child's purse when she determined her book's format and price. She believed that by refusing to use color, and by insisting on small volumes, she could keep the cost of her book down so that children could afford to buy it themselves. In a letter to Noel's sister Marjorie, she explained that she could not comply with the wishes of the publishers with whom she dealt because "she [thought] little rabbits [could] not afford to spend 6 shillings on one book and would never buy it" (*Letters,* p. 53). Eventually, the cost of her books would be fixed at one shilling.

Keen to see her vision realized, she determined to publish the story privately, as Lewis Carroll had done with *Alice in Wonderland* several decades earlier, and, in December 1901, she had 250 copies printed. Within two months, however, because of the book's popularity, she was compelled to print 200 more copies. Motivated by her success, she sent the book to Frederick Warne and Company, a publisher that had expressed interest in her drawings ten years earlier; but while Warne agreed to keep the small format, they too insisted on color illustrations. After some negotiations Potter agreed to make the required color paintings, and so, in October 1902, Warne printed 8,000 copies of a slightly modified version of the tale. Within a year, there had been six additional printings and more than 50,000 books sold: from the start, *Peter Rabbit* was a best-seller.

Potter's ideas about the format of children's books clashed with contemporary trends in the publishing trade. The small, inexpensive volume she had privately printed lacked the glamour and ostentation that sold books at the time: its simple cover was a drab gray-green, and, except for a small, solitary color frontispiece, the drawings were all black and white. But clearly there was a market for such a humble item. After compulsory education was authorized in England by the acts of 1870 and 1876, the market for children's books shifted dramatically; the number of literate children increased, and subsequently the demand for inexpensive children's books multiplied. Mandatory public schooling and the juvenile publishing industry evolved together, conditioned by emergent ideas about childhood. Late Victorian conceptions included the ideal of a peaceful, secure, preferably nonurban childhood for children of all classes.

Potter's strong ideas about the design and price of children's books, evident especially in her privately printed volumes, expressed her desire to create a world accessible to all children, and a world belonging only to children. The small books she imagined seemed to belong to the miniature world the *Peter Rabbit* tale depicted—a child's world of the imagination that excluded and sometimes even antagonized adults. Her child-centered conception of the picture book contrasted sharply with the more lavish and extravagent visions of her contemporaries. Expensive, ornate gift books were popular from the start of the twentieth century until the end of World War I. These elegant items were treated as drawing-room volumes, designed not only for children, but for the entire family. Although, like Potter's tales, they were typically published at Christmastime—supposedly as gifts for children—once unwrapped, the heavy volumes were likely to be entombed in cabinets, locked away from the younger members of the household.

In the late nineteenth century, educators had encouraged the growing trend toward increasingly elaborate children's-book illustration by emphasizing the importance of visual stimulation to children's development. Large-format color picture books had been the fashion since the latter half of the nineteenth century. They came into vogue with the success of Heinrich Hoffmann's grand-sized nonsense book for children, *Struwwelpeter* (1845), which achieved immediate fame in England after being imported from Germany in 1848. The illustrations in Hoffmann's book, which impressed British readers, were lithographed and hand colored; but these methods of reproduction were soon outmoded by novel technologies. Three-color and four-color printing, in which separate blocks are used to reproduce distinct colors, came into common use in the first years of the twentieth century. This new medium was a far superior alternative to lithography for the reproduction of watercolor paintings. Although Potter's goal was to make children's books smaller and less ornate, she made use of the most innovative printing techniques to reproduce her paintings. Even in her first privately printed edition of *Peter Rabbit* she employed the three-color process for her solitary color illustration.

The newly available methods of printing were often used for more elaborate illustrated books, like those of the popular artists Edmund Dulac and Arthur Rackham, whose lives spanned approximately the same decades as Potter's. Influenced by Persian and Indian miniatures, Dulac creates an exotic Orient in his paintings and, for some works, he produces orientalized images of Europe. Rackham, born a year after Potter, imagines European landscapes as mysterious places inhabited by goblins, fairies, and anthropomorphic trees. His vision resembles that of J. M. Barrie, for whom he provided the first illustrations for the earliest version of the Peter Pan story, *Peter Pan in Kensington Gardens* (1906).

Potter's illustrations and stories offer a stark contrast to those of her peers. She represents the apparently mundane, the everyday; in her tales no adventurers voyage into wonderland, as they do in the works of many of her successful colleagues, such as Barrie, Edith Nesbit, George Macdonald, and Lewis Carroll; no otherworldly excitement transpires beyond the pale of familiar British villages, gardens, and homes. Only in a single late tale does she venture far from the familiar turf of Britain to the "hot countries": in her robinsonade, *The Tale of Little Pig Robinson* (1930), the intrepid pig protagonist makes his way from a farm near "Stymouth" (really Sidmouth, in Devon) to "the land where the Bong tree grows." And yet even in this fable Potter does not dare to carry her characters beyond the pale of Britannia. Instead of leaving the safety of familiar shores, her Robinson simply sails to another English text: Edward Lear's poem "The Owl and the Pussycat," from which Potter borrows not only the idea of the Bong tree island but a number of characters and textual details.

Although Potter's fictive world includes no further fanciful islands, it consistently represents a fantastic and insular Britain. Potter depicts the British countryside as a quasi-magical place, a place where the real and the imaginary collide. Though her representations of homes and gardens mix mundane and magical elements, they most frequently depict "real" places. In her diary, Potter claimed she did not believe in imagination—there is only collage, no originality; and often the scenes she paints comprise a pastiche of actual places.

Although the settings for Potter's tales are never unreal, or at least never exotic, in her works everyday terrain, familiar landscapes and interiors, reveal unfamiliar aspects. Instead of creating a mysterious Orient, as does Dulac, she concocts an enigmatic Occident. The "magic" she depicts often emanates from ordinary occurrences and objects, like old tea kettles, cupboards, and mice. Potter's depictions of unfamiliar turf within familiar homes follow a paradigm not uncommon in canonical modernist children's fiction; one can discern it in works of Carroll, Nesbit, Macdonald, and Frances Burnett. In several of Potter's stories,

homes open up into great unknown expanses. In *The Tale of Samuel Whiskers*, Tom Kitten, who has climbed up the chimney of his mother's house, crawls through a labyrinth of flues, and then falls down a hole to find "himself in a place that he had never seen before, although he had lived all his life in the house" (p. 186). Homes in Potter's tales can conceal regions and occupants unknown to their licit residents. In the stuffy "room" into which poor Tom has fallen, he encounters Samuel Whiskers, a voluminous rat, and his wiry but robust wife, Anna Maria, who in a blink has unclothed Tom and tied him up with string. These alarmingly uncanny creatures use a haughty archaic English that makes them seem all the more ominous.

To a certain extent, all of Potter's anthropomorphic creatures share some of these rats' abundant uncanniness. Because Potter freely intermixes human and animal traits in her beasts' language and actions, her animals, like the interiors she represents, are at the same time familiar and unfamiliar: in the case of the rats, they are both eloquent interlocutors and vicious vermin. When Potter juxtaposes animal and human worlds, she examines the bourgeois world of her parents. Strategically, she displays the humanoid behavior of animals in order to highlight the beastlike behavior of humans.

ANTHROPOMORPHISM

ALMOST all of Potter's tales concentrate principally on the activities of humanized animals. Like Aesop, the master of animal fables from whom she borrowed material and to whom she dedicated one of her books—*The Tale of Johnny Town-Mouse* (1918)—she disguises people's foibles behind animal masks; yet unlike Aesop she names her animal characters and grants them individual personalities. It has been claimed that Potter participates in the tradition of British anthropomorphic animal stories that began in the eighteenth century. Unlike conventional English fables, however, her stories do not exhort children to be compliant, docile subjects. Many of Potter's animals behave like untrained small children, whose needs are expressed in raw, unmediated form. They are rambunctious, impulsive, and rude.

Like the American yarn-spinner Joel Chandler Harris, whose Uncle Remus stories she read as an adolescent, Potter depicts animals' struggles for survival and encourages subversive rather than moral action. Following Harris, she filches traditional folktale motifs, such as the theme of a weak creature's triumph over a powerful foe: often in her tales, small, quick-thinking creatures outwit or at least outrun dumb, lumbering McGregors. Other late-nineteenth- and early-twentieth-century children's writers like Rudyard Kipling and Kenneth Grahame also told animal stories that diverged from the tradition of moral English animal tales; however, Potter claimed to be influenced not by other writers, but by other artists. She emulated Walter Crane, a devotee of the Pre-Raphaelites, who had created some of the first successful children's books printed in color, books Potter had owned and loved as a child; and since childhood she had revered the creations of Randolph Caldecott, whose original works her father collected. Caldecott's *A Frog He Would A-Wooing Go* (1883) inspired her first to make a series of sketches in 1894, which she submitted to the firm Ernest Nister in a booklet called *A Frog He Would A-Fishing Go*, and then to write her well-known frog story, *The Tale of Mr. Jeremy Fisher*, published in 1906.

Though Potter's work was affected by that of her predecessors, she spawned a new breed of beast tale that has influenced later twentieth-century storytellers. Peter Rabbit and Hunca Munca more resemble Bugs Bunny and Mickey Mouse than they do the animal characters that populate children's fiction prior to the turn of the twentieth century. One still finds echoes of Potter in the now-familiar anthropomorphism of Walt Disney and his emulators: in full-length animated films, in Saturday morning cartoons, and in nature shows that feature live animals. In ways that recall the works of Potter, these entertainments for children mix images of wildness with images of domesticity; they combine the familiar and the unfamiliar. Like Potter's stories, they are often tales of danger, of risk—of close calls. They are not usually stories that encourage traditional moral thinking. Sometimes they advance a survival ethic that seems to borrow from Charles Darwin. In the late nineteenth century, Darwin's scientific evidence of the proximity of people and animals had cast a new light on popular animal stories. During Potter's childhood and youth, public interest in Darwin's theories of evolution surged. Most of Potter's tales create a universe of predators and prey in which each animal's position and fate is uncertain.

Potter's interest in the animal world began early in her life. Though Helen and Rupert Potter strictly limited their daughter's interaction with other humans, thus encouraging her reclusive tendencies, they were permissive about her contact with animals. Throughout her childhood and well into adulthood, Potter sheltered a menagerie of creatures in the nursery she shared with her brother. While Beatrix and Bertram were fond of their pets, their attitude toward them, never sentimental, was at times somewhat detached and scientific. When pets died, or when the siblings found dead animals, they would often boil the carcasses and reconstruct the skeletons for study. Nevertheless, Potter's animals were treasured companions, whom she avidly sketched and with whom she could spend endless hours playing. Potter's scientific studies of animals and her games with pets not only provided her with an escape from the suffocating human world in which she lived in London, but furnished her with a medium for its critique.

Potter customarily cast her own pets as the heroes and heroines of her stories; Benjamin Bunny, Peter Rabbit, Hunca Munca, Pig-Wig, and Mrs. Tiggy-Winkle, among many others, were actual creatures that Potter, who claimed she could tame any sort of animal, had domesticated. Potter's menagerie included, at various times, bats, lizards, snakes, rabbits, squirrels, newts, rats, mice, snails, hedgehogs, toads, and other sorts of creeping beings humans usually consider to be a nuisance. Before her life as a farmer began, her selection of animals to humanize for tales was somewhat subversive. From the time she wrote her first picture-letters and stories for children, she showed a predilection for animals that her society and even she determined to be vermin. One of her publishers, Harold Warne, quarreled with Potter about her inclusion of insects he considered to be offensive in *The Tale of Mrs. Tittlemouse* (1910): an earwig and wood lice. Even Norman, Potter's sympathizer at Frederick Warne, lacked interest in her ideas for a frog book, because he believed frogs were unappealing creatures that would not endear themselves to children (the book was eventually completed and published after Norman Warne's death as *The Tale of Mr. Jeremy Fisher*).

Potter's focus on animals enables her to dwell on and to celebrate sensory experience. Her characters enjoy physical pleasures that were taboo for a middle-class girl like Beatrix. This animal experience of satisfaction is akin to her own childhood experience. In her journal, she associates Camfield Place, the estate of her grandparents, with culinary ecstasy; she describes a bliss reminiscent of animals' food-induced euphoria, inspired by the consumption of fresh milk and fresh eggs. Many of her heroes and heroines relish food, eating greedily when they can. Peter eats a feast's worth of vegetables; the Flopsy bunnies gorge themselves with soporific lettuces; and Jemima Puddle-Duck is tempted with the promise of a delectable omelette. In Potter's stories, as in Carroll's *Alice in Wonderland*, eating can rapidly invert into being eaten. Many of Potter's books express the fear of being made into an edible thing. Pig Robinson, in town on his errand, is called a pork pie by rude men in a bakery (p. 366); Tom Kitten is called "this pudding" (p. 191) by the rats who want to eat him.

Such trepidatious representations of desire, especially female desire, were common in Victorian culture. Christina Rossetti's narrative poem for children, "The Goblin Market," typifies this phenomenon. In Rossetti's harsh cautionary tale, published four years before Potter was born, illness, madness, sexuality, and early death are all linked with two sorts of consumption—buying and eating. In Potter's *The Tale of Ginger and Pickles*, the cat and dog proprietors of a general store patronized by assorted rodents must control their appetites in order to preserve their customers and thus their business. They perceive the small customers, who both buy and eat the goods of their shop, as possible prey. Not only do they defer the satisfaction of their hunger, but the cat and dog endlessly defer the receipt of payment for the merchandise they sell—endlessly they accept credit instead of cash, and this leads to the demise of their business. When ultimately the well-meaning carnivores are forced to abandon their store, they revert to their natural behavior and chase after those creatures whom they once served. The cat, Ginger, we are told, can be found in the warren; the dog, Pickles, makes a living as a gamekeeper.

Potter's depictions of animal antics indicate ways in which social customs mask animal nature. For instance, in *The Pie and the Patty-Pan*, animal impulses upset the niceties of class ritual. The genteel dog Duchess, who visits her feline friend Ribby for an elegant tea, balances sugar on her nose at the table in an unseemly manner, and when the lump falls, she ducks under the table to fetch it. Even worse, she sneaks into Ribby's house before teatime, while the mistress is out, in order to replace a pie made of mouse—repugnant to her—with a veal and ham pie she has made herself. She could not bring herself to breach the laws of etiquette and tell her friend directly that she dislikes mouse.

Because Potter represents animals instead of people, she is able to show her protagonists engaging in outrageously foul behavior—her creatures conduct themselves in beastly ways that would be unacceptable if perpetrated by humans. Although Potter does condemn certain forms of "bad" behavior, she celebrates most modes of disobedience that occur in her stories, especially those that conform to her ideas about animal character. Her animals tend to break or bend human laws and rules, so as to obey the laws of their own animal nature. When they violate codes of conduct, they illuminate the inanity of human social conventions.

The denouements of Potter's tales—the escapes of Squirrel Nutkin and Peter Rabbit, for example—seem to affirm rebellious action. Only on rare occasions do Potter's lawless heroes receive harsh punishment. In all of Potter's oeuvre, the only corporal punishments that young creatures suffer occur in *Benjamin Bunny* and *Tom Kitten*; but neither of these beatings remains unavenged. In *The Tale of Benjamin Bunny* (1904), Benjamin's father whips his disobedient son and his nephew Peter after he saves them from a cat they encounter during a risky foray onto Mr. McGregor's property; the youngsters had invaded McGregor's garden to reclaim Peter's garments, lost during the adventure recounted in *Peter Rabbit*. A few years later, in the *The Tale of Mr. Tod* (1912), Potter seems to retaliate on behalf of the bruised young bunnies.

Old Mr. Bouncer, who now lives with the family of his grown-up son Benjamin, is left at home to care for a group of newly born bunnies. The newborns lie in a hole separate from the main burrow—a nursery of sorts—forgotten by their guardian. Failing to mind the children, old Mr. Bouncer invites a hungry badger, Tommy Brock, into the house to smoke a cigar and drink some wine. When the old rabbit drifts off to sleep, the badger slips away with the babes, intending to cook them for his dinner. Soon Bouncer's daughter-in-law, Flopsy, returns home and discovers what has transpired. She madly slaps the old rabbit and then condemns him to crouch, humiliated, in a corner, huddled behind a chair. To mortify him further, she snatches his pipe from him and hides his rabbit tobacco. He remains thus shamed until the next day, when the babies are retrieved and he is forgiven. In this way Potter castigates her most distinguished punishing character.

In a great number of Potter's tales, the negligence of parents or other authority figures endangers the lives of the young creatures in their care. In the universe of Potter's stories, authority is tested, and helpless creatures are kidnapped or otherwise endangered because those in positions of power have failed them. While Potter's father has a much more prominent position than his wife in Potter's journal, in the stories, few fathers appear. Old Mr. Bouncer and his son Benjamin are among the few. Most often, the irresponsible elders in Potter's stories are mother figures.

In *The Tale of Tom Kitten,* Tom's punishing mother, like Benjamin's switch-wielding father, is the object of vengeance. During a series of misadventures, Tom Kitten and his sisters manage to lose the elegant tea-party clothes in which their fastidious mother, Tabitha Twitchit, has so carefully encased them. Just before the tea guests are to arrive, Tabitha discovers her unclothed kittens, and subsequently smacks them, confining them in their room. At the end of the story, the reader finds a surprising lesson. The moralistic narrator of *Tom Kitten* reprimands mother Tabitha and not her unsubmissive kittens. The narrator scolds Tabitha for lying to her feline tea guests—she tells them that her children are in bed with the measles—and rewards the "naughty" kittens for their delinquency: they enjoy themselves in their nursery retreat, avoiding a stuffy adult meal, liberated from both clothing and social duties.

Potter wrote one of her most direct attacks on conventional behavior, *The Tale of Two Bad Mice* (1904), when she herself was behaving like a bad mouse, questioning the authority of her parents. In this story, she blurs the borders between the human and the animal in order to criticize Victorian mores. *Two Bad Mice* was written in the period during which Potter was becoming increasingly close to her editor, Norman Warne, and was forced to contend with her parents' objections to the developing friendship. Potter's mother in particular opposed her daughter's close association with Warne and with his family. The prob-

lem, put simply, was that the Warnes were "in trade"; the Potters were not. The Potters had not labored for several generations and now were firmly ensconced in a station well above that of textile workers and publishers alike. The tale, perhaps in response to the conflict between Potter and her parents, emphasizes the emptiness of class distinctions.

In the story, two "bad" mice, Hunca Munca and Tom Thumb, raid a dollhouse that belongs to a duo of dolls, Jane, who is the cook, and her mistress, Lucinda. Though the narrator delineates the class difference between the servant and her mistress, she undermines this distinction throughout the tale. Jane may be a cook, but the reader soon learns that she never sets foot in the kitchen; the dolls have beautiful ready-made food that has come to them in a box: food that is not real. In fact, as we later learn, it is made from plaster. In this story Potter plays with the idea of what is real. Class distinctions and other matters of Victorian convention are determined to be unreal.

Although the intact dollhouse prior to the mouse attack seems to present a picture-perfect vision of middle-class English domestic comfort, the mice dispel this image. After the dolls go out in their carriage, the mice arrive in the dollhouse and find a table laid with exquisite dishes. But the meat cannot be cut; the fish cannot be gnawed. Upon discovering that the meal is made of plaster, they wax violent, incensed because their appetites are thwarted. Soon they discover that nothing in the dollhouse is real: the fire is made of paper; the rice in the canister is merely beads. The rampage that follows these revelations is inspired by anger at the useless things that fill the house, which resemble the superfluous objects that cluttered many Victorian homes. Potter, who lived in one such house, revels in the mischief perpetrated by the mice against the useless items. The mice are like children let loose in the sort of household in which everything is for show only—nothing may be tasted, smelled, or felt.

The ravages on the house and its contents come to an abrupt halt when the mice realize that some of the functionless things they destroy might in fact be of some use to them—they then pilfer as much as they can, and their spoils include a feather bed, a birdcage, a cradle, "useful" pots and pans, which clearly were of no use to the two dolls, and more. They even plunder Lucinda's wardrobe, though neither mouse has worn clothes before. Over the course of the story, Potter displays an ironic transmutation of Hunca Munca from thief to bourgeois housewife. After the raid, we see Hunca Munca neatly enrobed in Lucinda's clothes, which fit her spectacularly well. The filched cradle, which has lain vacant in the dolls' house, is now filled with mouse babies. The brimming bed makes evident a stark difference between the sterile doll household and the almost comically fertile home of the mice. The dolls and their luxurious world are revealed to be empty entities, useless things; in contrast, the mice are shown to be lively, determined creatures, much more "human" than the dolls.

The narrator clearly sides with the mice who, as repayment for all they have taken, leave a sixpence in the dolls' stocking at Christmas; as an additional recompense, the now-domesticated Hunca Munca comes to sweep every morning before the dolls awaken. But there are other residents of the nursery who are not appeased by such conciliatory gestures: "The little girl that the doll's-house belonged to, said,—'I will get a doll dressed like a policeman!' But the nurse said,—'I will set a mouse-trap!'" (pp. 82–83). The little girl's statement highlights the unreality of the dolls, their lack of animation, of life. The girl can act; the dolls cannot. In turn, the nurse's statement puts into perspective the child's world of make-believe in which the reader has invested belief—a policeman doll will be as ineffectual as the original dolls in ridding the house of rodents. By suddenly calling attention to living human characters, Potter underlines the location of the action—a nursery—and the artificial nature of the dolls, their impotence and the superficiality of their beauty: like the objects in the house they inhabit, they are empty shells—attractive but vacuous imitations.

Several other Potter tales feature domestic invasions. While *The Tale of Mrs. Tittlemouse* (1910) tells the story of repeated raids of a mouse's house by insidious insects and other "vermin," *The Tale of Samuel Whiskers* (1908), like *Two Bad Mice*, features rodent interlopers. Once again, the vermin are the most engaging characters in the story. In *Samuel Whiskers*, as in *Two Bad Mice*, a beautiful surface hides a unsettling interior; but *Samuel Whiskers* is a more forboding dissection of that interior. The polished surfaces in Tabitha Twitchit's house are deceptive; behind the walls of the cat's cozy home lies an unseen underworld strewn with bones. Potter's endearing animals, like the homes in which they live, cover over human truths that are not so dear.

CLOTHING

IF Potter's anthropomorphism is a sort of clothing over human antics, this clothing, like the actual garments donned by Potter's characters, is likely to fall off or be lost, revealing the human beneath. Potter dresses animals—and dresses humans as animals—in order to investigate the relationship between clothing and inner nature and the relationship between clothing and bodies. Does clothing hide or express what someone is? Does it constrain bodies or protect them? To answer these questions, it is necessary to determine what precisely constitutes "clothing" in Potter's works. Why does Old Brown, the austere owl in *The Tale of Squirrel Nutkin*, possess a "waistcoat pocket" even though he wears no waistcoat? The laundry pile that makes an appearance in *The Tale of Mrs. Tiggy-Winkle* provides some clues. In the hedgehog's basket, an assortment of articles is heaped together and called wash: human-type clothing, like Peter Rabbit's little jacket and a little girl's "pinny," are mixed in with parts of animals bodies that usually cannot be removed—like the wooly coats of lambs and the "scarlet waist-coat" of Cock Robin. When Potter stretches the meaning of clothing in her books, she draws attention to the subject of dress; dress is the central motif in many of her stories, especially those she wrote during her collaboration with Norman Warne.

Although most of Potter's stories implicitly deal with the relationship between animals and people or, rather, animal qualities and human qualities, only rarely do they focus explicitly on the relationships between beasts and humans. There are a few notable examples, the foremost being two early tales that take clothing as their central theme: Potter's story about her pet hedgehog, *Mrs. Tiggy-Winkle*, and her second tale, a book she claimed was her personal favorite, *The Tailor of Gloucester*. The tailor and Mrs. Tiggy-Winkle share many traits: they both live, not in homes, but in cozy, rustic kitchens; in fact the tailor, allegedly penniless, lives in a neatly arranged and amply decorated kitchen, which looks like it might belong in Potter's home. Yet the tailor, like Mrs. Tiggy-Winkle, is lowly and modest; they both work in the service of others, and their work revolves around clothes.

In both stories, magical animals perform redemptive tasks for people. In *The Tailor of Gloucester*, as in the Grimms' fairy tale "The Elves and the Shoemaker," fantastical creatures help to complete work overnight for a good soul in trouble. *Mrs. Tiggy-Winkle* also follows a traditional fairy-tale pattern, wherein something lost is found with supernatural aid. Like *The Tale of Benjamin Bunny*, *Mrs. Tiggy-Winkle* begins with the search for lost clothing. A small child named Lucie, one of Potter's rare human protagonists and one of her few heroines (her human characters, when they make their rare appearances, are generally male), sets off into the countryside to find her lost pinafores and hankies. She discovers a tiny door on a hillside, which she opens, startling a small washerwoman who seems to be living comfortably within. Lucie explains her predicament as the washerwoman sorts her laundry, which, of course, includes the girl's lost items.

Instead of uncovering a wild, unfamiliar place inside a house, as Tom does in *Samuel Whiskers*, Lucie discovers a homey place beneath the grassy ground outside. Even the strange articles of clothing in Mrs. Tiggy-Winkle's basket are not unknown to the child reader of Potter's books: recognizable from earlier stories, they stand in for familiar characters. At the end of the story, Mrs. Tiggy-Winkle makes an abrupt exit that illustrates the significance of clothing: as Lucie turns to wave farewell to her new friend, she sees that Mrs. Tiggy-Winkle's clothes have suddenly disappeared. Without the clothing that has marked her as a laboring woman, she is "nothing but a HEDGEHOG!" (p. 100).

In Potter's favorite tale, an amiable tailor and his mouse cohorts exchange "gifts" of clothing. The gentle mice who appear in the story, clearly upper-class creatures, accept tippets of cloth as gifts from the old impoverished tailor who also grants them their lives, liberating them from the teacups in which his cat Simpkin has imprisoned them. In return for his magnanimity, the mice rush to his aid when he falls ill, sewing a jacket just in time for the Mayor's wedding. Thus they save his livelihood and his life.

The Tailor of Gloucester differs from Potter's other tales in several key ways. First of all, it is the only one that does not employ the ahistorical once-upon-a-time mode of traditional tales. It is firmly located in a specific era; it begins, "In the time of swords and periwigs and full-skirted coats with flowered lappets—when gentlemen wore ruffles, and gold-laced waistcoats of paduasoy and taffeta" (p. 39). It is a tale of the bygone era Potter associates with her beloved grandmother, Jessy Crompton Potter, and, as she makes clear in this initial sentence, it is a celebration of elegant clothes. Elaborately ornamented costumes appear in the tale—the Mayor's embroidered wedding jacket and the impeccable outfits that the mice have sewn for themselves from the "tippets" given them by the generous tailor.

Clothing in *The Tailor of Gloucester* is lovingly made by the human hero and his mouse helpers and lovingly painted by Potter. To complete the illustrations for this story, Potter carefully copied eighteenth-century clothing at the South Kensington Museum. Excitedly, she wrote to Norman Warne that the museum authorities had allowed her to remove the clothing from the glass cases in which it was displayed in order to draw it. The clothing in the story is far from the practical garments Potter wore as a child. Potter contended that her childhood costume was stiff and uncomfortable. In a letter, Potter describes how each day, Nurse Mackenzie, a strict Calvinist, would pull Beatrix's hair back tightly with a somber black or brown band that fastened painfully behind her ears. Like the young Beatrix, animal children in Potter's world must behave "unnaturally," wear uncomfortable clothes, walk on their hind legs, and mind their manners.

Anthropomorphism provided Potter with an escape from a variety of Victorian rules. It not only freed Potter to depict creaturely delight in eating and destruction, but it authorized her to unclothe her characters. Because she represented animals and not people, she believed she need not worry about the squeamishness of her peers with regard to naked bodies. Despite her confidence, she did manage to scandalize her publisher on one occasion. Harold Warne strongly objected when *all* of Tom Kitten's clothing tore off in *The Tale of Tom Kitten*, but Potter refused to alter the story and illustrations to suit his prudery. Potter herself found neither paintings of naked animals nor paintings of naked people the least bit offensive. In her journal, she writes, "I do not see the slightest objection to nude pictures as a class, nor are they necessarily in the least more indecent than clothed ones" (p. 149). In the journal, a discussion of Potter's own clothing woes precedes this pronouncement. She relates an anecdote about her father's response to her partial disrobing in public.

It seems that Beatrix herself was a bit of a naughty little rabbit; she describes an incident at an exhibition in London that she attended with her father in 1885, prefacing the anecdote with an ironic confession: "I always thought I was born to be a discredit to my parents." Her crime is this: the wind whisks her hat to an inaccessible fountain, horrifying and humiliating her father, and amusing others, including Beatrix herself. Like the parents of Tom Kitten and Peter Rabbit, Potter's father becomes exasperated when his daughter's clothing will not stay put. His shame is enhanced because, owing to a recent illness, Potter has recently had her hair cropped short, so that—hatless and hairless—she is doubly naked, doubly exposed. And yet, despite her father's chagrin, she revels in the adventure: "It is one of the peculiarities of my nature that when there *is* anything to be shy about, I don't care in the least, and I caused a good deal of harmless amusement." Her only complaint is that in the future her father will be more reluctant to take her out: "If only I had not been with papa, he does not often take me out, and I doubt he will do it again for a time" (p. 149). Like Tom Kitten and his sisters, she will be confined, and like them she will make the most of it.

Frequently in the tales it seems "natural" and amusing to lose one's clothing, as it seems natural and amusing for Potter to lose her hat in the wind. Often Potter draws attention to or mocks the dress of her animal characters, disclosing the unnatural nature of clothes. In the tales, Tom Kitten and his sisters lose their elegant tea-party garments because clothing will not stay on playful kittens, just as it will not stay put on the Puddle-Ducks, who dress in the clothes the kittens shed, only to lose them while ducking in the water. But clothing is not always only foolish and cumbersome.

Clothing serves multiple functions; like British nurseries, garments both constrict and preserve youngsters. The brass buttons on Peter's jacket, which catch in a gooseberry net, almost effect the rabbit's fatal capture; luckily, because Peter manages to slip out of his constraining clothing during his frenzied flight from Mr. McGregor, he escapes. In contrast, clothing ensures the safety of the staunch frog Jeremy Fisher. His apparently unsavory raincoat saves his life when a hungry trout gulps him up, then spits him out because it dislikes the flavor of his macintosh. Animals' dress can protect them from being eaten alive, or it can be a preparation for being eaten. Tom Kitten is undressed and then "dressed" again—this time in dough—to be eaten by the rats who have kidnapped him.

Jemima Puddle-Duck almost meets with the fate Tom barely escapes. Critics have pointed out the absurdity of Jemima Puddle-Duck's costume at the beginning of her tale, when she leaves the farm where she resides. She abandons her barnyard home because on the farm duck eggs are given to hens to hatch because ducks are known to be poor sitters. The rebellious Jemima wants to hatch her own family. Her dress when she leaves the farm—an unfashionable shawl and bonnet—points to her class and character. She belongs to a certain type—the naive farmgirl. Clothing here seems to indicate social position, which, Potter intimates, can be a senseless construct, a false signal of what lies beneath. The wily fox's elegant suit seems to mark him as a member of a certain class, but it masks predatory intentions. To eliminate clothing is to eliminate deceptive class markers, and this is just what Potter does. In an illustration, she paints the fox greedily pawing Jemima's eggs, wearing no clothing at all, exposing his foxy nature. After the suave fox fools the duck with his gentlemanly manners and dress (manners, in this context, are also a form of dress), he convinces her to lay her eggs in his ramshackle shed. Compliant Jemima builds her nest from feathers she finds in the shed, failing to recognize them as the natural garments of her host's previous victims. When she has finished laying her eggs, he entices her to join him for a dinner party featuring a "savoury omelette," which she fails to recognize as a threat to her own eggs, and requests that she gather herbs and onions from the farm garden for their meal. Thus, cunningly, he compels her to collect the ingredients for her own "dressing"—stuffing for roast duck.

In Potter's later works, dress loses some of its ominous connotations. In *The Fairy Caravan* (1929), costume has a liberating function. The characters perform a circus show in which they masquerade as exotic creatures: the guinea pig protagonist costumes himself as a sultan; a pig represents a pygmy elephant; a dormouse poses as a princess; a toothless old ferret plays a dangerous carnivore. The circus frees the animals from their conventional roles and behaviors. Instead of hiding the body, the attire in which the caravan characters deck themselves transfigures them: it reshapes them as art to be displayed.

ESCAPE

In several journal entries Potter mentions her affinity for the circus; she writes, "I would go any distance to see a Caravan . . . it is the only species of entertainment I care for" (p. 397). Several qualities of the caravan must have appealed to Potter—the liberated, itinerant life of the performers, the mix of humans and animals, the elaborate costumes, and the unabashed display of scantily clad bodies. *The Fairy Caravan*, which Potter claimed was the most autobiographical of her works, is more than just a tribute to her favorite form of entertainment. The book comprises not only one tale, but a series of stories told by different animal narrators. To a certain extent, it is a story about storytelling, narration as a form of escape, for when Tuppenny leaves his home and cruel wife, he meets a gentle, storytelling dormouse, Xarifa, a caravan member who becomes his principal companion. For Potter, the composition of *The Fairy Caravan* was an ongoing project that she continued even after the book was published. In her preface to the work she writes, "Through many changing seasons these tales have walked and talked with me." They are tales told to herself when alone. The stories are Potter's companions in the same way that her tamed animals are companions: they facilitate her escape from the world of her parents.

The *Caravan* project presents the most elaborate articulation of the fantasy of escape that Potter developed in the books of her final period of writing. In these last three decades of her life, Potter published only five books in which she used new material: *The Tale of Pigling Bland* (1913), *The Tale of Johnny Town-Mouse* (1918), *The Fairy Caravan* (1929), *The Tale of Little Pig Robinson* (1930), and *Sister Anne* (1932), an offshoot of *The Fairy Caravan*. All of these stories, in which escapes dominate the action, include visions of possible places to which one might wish to escape.

The protagonists of the pig tales escape from life-threatening predicaments to the land of happy endings. Their stories hint at what "escape" signifies for Potter. She composed *The Tale of Pigling Bland*, her only romance, while she was being courted by William Heelis and as the couple made plans to marry. Shunted off to a hiring fair, Pigling, shy, polite, and mature for his years, has only one desire: "I wish I could have a little garden and grow potatoes" (p. 291). By the end of the story, it looks as though his wish, which echoes Potter's own desire for independence and for a farmer's life, may be fulfilled. Between market and home, Pigling loses his way and falls into the clutches of the notorious pig thief Mr. Piperson, a rude crook who traps our hero in a hamper, and, after feeding the frightened piglet, pinches his ribs to check if he is ready for slaughter. In Piperson's grim home Pigling meets his lady-love, a girl pig named Pig-Wig, who has been stolen and locked into a cabinet to be made into "Bacon, hams" (p. 299), as she says with a smile. Pigling then proceeds not only to save himself but valiantly to rescue Pig-Wig.

The environs of Piperson's abode, through which the runaway pigs must skulk, express the thief's inner nature. The grounds around his home are untidy and scratched up by fowl. Significantly, his house has no garden. This is a tale in which class matters, and to have no garden surely is a sign that one lacks breeding. Notably, the antiparadise of the Piperson yard resonates in Potter's later work *Sister Anne*, in the barren sweep of unfenced land belonging to the brutal Baron Bluebeard, who, though he is an aristocrat, is ill-mannered and horrifyingly exotic. Potter's descriptions of Bluebeard resemble descriptions of malignant despots of the Orient in British imperialist texts. In Potter's era, colonized subjects were often described in terms similar to those used to describe the domestic poor.

The place to which Pigling and Pig-Wig flee in *Pigling Bland* functions as an antidote to the dreary landscape of Piperson's yard, which is as barren as the desert domain ruled by Bluebeard. The reader supposes that the pigs will indeed grow their own potatoes on a small plot of land once they cross the county border. Describing the land of freedom beyond the county line at the end of the story, Potter soars into verse: "They came to the river, they came to the bridge—they crossed it hand in hand—then over the hills and far away she danced with Pigling Bland!" (p. 308).

The wish-fulfillment ending of *The Tale of Little Pig Robinson*, like the ecstatic finish of *Pigling*

Bland, gestures at Potter's vision of an ideal escape. When Robinson flees the ravenous crew of the ship on which he is trapped, the *Pound of Candles,* he lands on the Edenic isle of the Bong tree, a place where he can eat as much as he wants, free of the fear of being eaten. Like Pigling, who longs for his own tract of land on which to grow food, Robinson lives "perfectly contented" on his island refuge, where delicacies sprout already prepared from the earth, and where he "grew fatter and fatter and more fatterer; and the ship's cook never found him" (p. 383).

Tuppenny, the guinea pig hero of *The Fairy Caravan,* also escapes from his cheerless life to a place where he can experience the pleasures of the body. He runs away from a domestic life dominated by his imperious, uncaring wife and a public life in which class distinctions matter too much; he leaves behind illness and physical discomfort, as well. Tuppenny re-creates himself in a new world, with the assistance of his newfound family, the creatures of the caravan. Caravan life is an escape for the guinea pig in several ways. First of all, the pig escapes suffering and can enjoy sensory pleasure—the taste of food and the feeling of his hair being brushed. Also, he carries magical fern seed, as do all the members of the circus: fern seed renders him a "fairy" creature, visible only to small children and animals. Finally, though he remains hidden from most beings, he becomes a spectacular object, a public performer.

At the beginning of the story, Tuppenny differs from his companions in the town of Marmalade. His coat is shabby; his hair grows only in patches; he is always ill. His pals use him as a "guinea pig" to test a new hair tonic, and the results are impressive. His hair grows and grows, but unfortunately, it will not stop growing. Mrs. Tuppenny soon becomes frustrated with constantly cutting her husband's hair, so she tries a new technique—pulling his hair out. When the long-haired pig runs away and joins a circus, his bounteous hair, which had been a liability at home, is celebrated jubilantly. He is transformed into "The Sultan of Zanzibar," who parades across the stage on a "pygmy elephant" with the princess Xarifa at his side.

Sister Anne resembles Potter's earlier stories that feature humans as central characters. Feelings of isolation and anxiety predominate; animals rescue people—a dog protects the girl protagonists from a villain's attack, and ultimately pigeons convey a message of distress to heroic young res-

cuers. Though *Sister Anne* sheds light on Potter's more popular fiction, the story has virtually been ignored by biographers and critics, perhaps because it differs substantially from her other work. First of all, as even Potter agreed, it is not a work for children, though it still can be found in the juvenile section of libraries. Also, the story is much longer than any of Potter's earlier books, and it is much longer than her source for the story, Charles Perrault's retelling of the Bluebeard legend in his *Histories and Tales of Long Ago* (1697). In *Sister Anne,* Potter develops Perrault's seven-page tale into a lengthy novella. Though no talking animals appear in the story, a mouse replaces Potter's usual human narrator. In the awkward frame tale, a vestige from *The Fairy Caravan,* three mice spin, and two ask a third for a story to pass the time, one requesting a story about a cupboard, and the other requesting a story about cats. From the perspective of mice, cupboards and cats signify entrapment and predators. *Sister Anne* is the legend recounted by the third mouse, the tale of an escape from both of these threats.

Instead of a story of humanized animals, *Sister Anne* is a narrative of animalized humans. Bluebeard, with his hawk's nose and bestial behavior, is constantly being compared with predatory beasts. Like Samuel Whiskers and his wife Anna Maria, the rats in *The Tale of Samuel Whiskers,* Bluebeard combines genteel and brutelike behavior in an uncanny manner. Anne and her sister Fatima, on the other hand, are represented as quarry. Throughout the tale, they are compared with preyed-upon animals, especially pigeons. Screaming as Bluebeard attacks them, the sisters are mistaken for pigs being slaughtered. Most of the women who appear in this story risk being killed or devoured. Bluebeard calls the wealthy, redheaded widow he pursues and aspires to marry after he has done away with Fatima his "carrot."

Sister Anne traces the escape of the unlucky Fatima from marriage and from her predatory spouse. In the tale, Potter contrasts the idyllic farm life Anne and her sister lead prior to Fatima's marriage to Bluebeard with a domestic horror, a horror of married life. Fatima's bucolic experience before marriage bears some resemblance to Potter's married life at Castle Cottage; the entrapment from which the heroines of Potter's story must escape echoes Potter's experience of life with her parents in London. Like Potter, who spent the better part of the years before her marriage cloistered in the upstairs nursery at Bolton Gardens, Fatima lives an isolated existence in the lofty chambers of her husband's castle, forbidden—for her own safety, her husband tells her—to descend to the lower floors and courtyard. Lupine Wolfram, Bluebeard's one-eyed porter, exemplifies the devouring masculine threat that awaits "below." Whenever Fatima and her sister stray into some forbidden segment of the palace, they hear Wolfram burst into song below them; he sings a sinister ballad that tells of the dismemberment of a woman's body and the reorganization of her parts into a musical instrument. The ditty begins, "What did he do with her breast bone . . . He made him a fiddle to play thereon" (*Sister Anne*, p. 45). The fate that awaits this unlucky bride and the sensible sister who has come to her rescue resembles the destinies of many of Potter's preyed-upon animal characters: she will become an object.

In Potter's fable, the horror of being an object is closely related to the horror of being the object of a gaze. Fatima's predicament reflects Potter's position in the nursery—she is at the same time hidden and watched. The fear of being seen that permeates *The Fairy Caravan* is even more pervasive in *Sister Anne*. A brand of paranoia that belongs to the genre of Gothic horror infuses Potter's last book. Inanimate objects seem to glare, and the "eyes" of objects do not gaze benignly; arrows fly from the eye slits of the castle. The gaze, here the gaze of a house, possesses a destructive power. This power to look is aggressively denied to women in Potter's tale. Fatima's position, like that of the vulnerable Victorian child, is defined by her ignorance: she is not permitted to look, to see outside her closely watched world. As long as she remains ignorant of the contents of her husband's secret cabinet, she remains safe. As soon as she looks, her life is endangered. But blindness and ignorance have endangered her in the first place.

Fatima has fallen into Bluebeard's clutches because her mother has turned a blind eye. In marrying Bluebeard, Fatima has taken the place of her widowed mother, whose hand Bluebeard initially requested. Fatima's mother offers her favorite daughter in her stead, pronouncing herself both too old to remarry and too content managing her farm to budge. In giving her daughter to the baron, she joins the other negligent parents in Potter's stories. Anne, the most sensible character in the tale, observes that her mother has been incau-

tious and has launched her young daughter into a marriage with a fiend. The girls' mother has been seduced by Bluebeard's title, behind which hides a monster. The land over which he reigns, like the seven wives he has killed, is dead, a desert of empty waste; like his murdered wives, the land is barren. Bluebeard's land lacks fruit; he himself lacks an heir.

The unsung hero of *Sister Anne*, Fatima's faithful admirer Lancelot Lackland, rushes to the aid of his lady in the last few pages of the novel. To his romantic first name, evocative of the age of chivalry, Potter tacks a thudding family name: a literal description of his position as the younger son of a local nobleman. Alas, Lancelot, unlike Bluebeard, lacks land, and thus might be deemed unworthy of a wealthy middle-class lass such as Fatima. And yet, in the context of *Sister Anne*, a landless man is a safe bet—he is a man without destructive power.

PRESERVING CHILDHOOD

POTTER herself did not lack land. After Norman Warne's death, she made herself even more of an anomaly than she already had been—as a middle-aged spinster who wrote stories—by buying property for herself instead of marrying and bearing children. Even though she could not spend more than a month of every year at Hill Top before her marriage because of her parents' demands, land for her was an emblem of economic and emotional independence. At the farm, her actions were not watched and controlled by her parents, who disliked and avoided visits to Hill Top. Potter had longed not for a mere room of her own—she had that in her London nursery—but for a grander stretch of property: a field, a farm, two farms, even more. Like the infamous fisherman's wife in the Grimms' story, Potter wanted more and more and more turf to control. She accumulated land throughout most of her life as a writer, so that, in her will, she was able to bequeath 4,000 acres to the National Trust, having already bought much acreage on behalf of the trust, some of which she had managed herself.

Land acquisition and preservation became a major concern to Potter, especially during the last decades of her life. Her expanses of land, which constituted a private haven, had great symbolic significance. The purchase of land was for her a way to preserve the past—the landscape of her childhood; it was a form of self-preservation. However, for Potter the accumulation of property was not just a personal venture, but a nationalist enterprise. In part, Potter shared the motivation of the brothers Grimm, who gathered what they deemed to be German fairy tales to preserve German folk culture. Potter acquired land and wrote tales in order to preserve a British natural and cultural heritage she perceived to be disappearing.

Since the mid-nineteenth century, complaints had been made that the development of the railways would ultimately destroy the English countryside. Potter increasingly did her part to preserve the Lake District, inspired by the work of her close friend Canon Hardwicke Rawnsley. Rawnsley had been the Vicar of Wray, where the Potters rented a house for the summer when Beatrix was sixteen. He introduced teenaged Beatrix to ideas about the protection of land and the conservation of ancient ways of life. In addition to being a prolific writer, Rawnsley had started a school of industrial arts to promote the continued production of handcrafted items; and he had formed the Lake District Defence Society, a precursor of the National Trust, which was established to combat industry and tourism in the Lake District.

In 1906, influenced by Rawnsley, Potter bought a small flock of Herdwick sheep, a tough breed, native to the fells of the Lake District, whose strong and waterproof wool had customarily been used for carpets, but was now failing to sell as a result of the increasing use of linoleum to cover floors. Because of this decline in sales, farmers rapidly ceased to raise the sheep, replacing their Herdwicks with other breeds not native to the fells. Rawnsley, who campaigned to reestablish the old breed, in 1899 founded the Herdwick Sheepbreeders' Association, a group dedicated to bringing back the Herdwicks. In 1930, Potter, by then an expert sheepbreeder, became the first female president of the association.

In *The Fairy Caravan*, Herdwicks make a memorable appearance. As a Herdwick sheep belonging to Mrs. Heelis tells a tale, suddenly a peculiar shift occurs in its narrating voice: the sheep begins to speak as a colossal "we." In this collective voice, it explains that the breed has been on the fells for millennia, during which time countless human invasions and battles have taken place; people come

and go but these sheep remain "unbeaten," passing on their tough character as a legacy. The sheep narrator's description of its lineage resembles Potter's representations of her paternal grandmother's Crompton heritage—ancient, obstinate, and closely tied to the Lake District. The land belongs to the sheep and is a part of them, as it belongs to Potter and is a part of her.

CONCLUSION—GROWING UP

IN most of Potter's late works, characters escape entrapment and dependence to lead self-determined lives on their own plots of land. The hero of *The Tale of Johnny Town-Mouse* (1918), Timmy Willie (whose second name conjures Potter's husband, who was called Willie), is trapped in a hamper and accidentally transported from his idyllic country home to a nearby town. Once there, he becomes the reluctant guest of the urban town-mouse, Johnny, who was born in a cupboard and lives parasitically by "borrowing" the goods of humans. Once Timmy Willie has eluded assorted urban dangers, with great relief he returns to his happy, self-sufficient life in the country. This conclusion to the mouse's town adventure echoes Potter's return to the countryside of the Lake District: her return to childhood.

Potter, who claimed to be an eternal child, could conceive of no heaven more vivid than a childhood that persists. On a visit to Sawrey just after she turned thirty she writes in her diary:

I remember I used to half believe and wholly play with fairies when I was a child. What heaven can be more real than to retain the spirit-world of childhood, tempered and balanced by knowledge and common-sense, to fear no longer the terror that flieth by night, yet to feel truly and to understand a little, a very little, of the story of life

(*Journal*, p. 435)

The "spirit-world of childhood" suffuses Potter's stories. Potter's animals, like Grahame's beasts and Barrie's Peter Pan, are eternal children, closely linked to nature and to the supernatural world of fairies. Though life for these animals often is fraught with fear, a utopian vision opens up in their stories that seems to look both forward and back. The animals Potter depicts are children as they were imagined by many of her contemporaries—they engage in a life of fun but are chronically at risk. However, Potter defined not only childhood as play in a perilous garden; she defined adult life in the same way. The "preserve" of the stories her characters inhabit became, to a certain extent, a reality for Potter after her marriage.

Then did Potter grow up, or did she, as she claimed, remain a child? Certainly, Potter did not mature in any way prescribed by her culture. She rejected versions of womanhood propagated by her parents and their peers: she refused to consider entering into a marriage that would maintain the roles of domination and subordination played out in her relationship with her parents. When women of her era and class did marry, it was commonly believed that they were not adults, as were their husbands; no woman could achieve male adult status. Though Potter did not behave in a passive, subordinate, or childlike manner, as was often expected of women in her class, she chose to create the Victorian fantasy of childhood for herself as a reality of adulthood. But first, for almost five decades, Potter suffered a fate similar to that of many middle-class women of her time: after a restricted childhood, her independent adult life was undermined. Unlike many of her peers, her talents and wealth helped her to escape from her domineering parents, and marriage ultimately freed her from their power.

Although Potter longs for childhood, she does not condone dreams of a return to childhood. When she was in her teens, she articulated the impossibility and undesirability of such a return in her journal: "Then as we struggle on, the thoughts of that peaceful past time of childhood comes to us like soft music and a blissful vision through the snow. We do not wish we were back in it" (p. 85). Potter revises the childhood-as-garden cliché. In her fictional world, childhood more resembles Mr. McGregor's garden than Frances Hodgson Burnett's secret garden. She amends the Victorian ideal in a way that suits the tenor of her time and ours.

Interest in Potter has blossomed since the 1970s. Documentaries about her life and filmed versions of her tales have been produced; exhibitions of her work have taken place with great success; her writings have been published in new forms. Potter scholarship has increased dramatically, and she has become a cult figure in Japan. As ideas about childhood engendered in Potter's time have revived, interest in Potter and her work has grown. In Anglo-American culture, childhood has been represented increasingly and with growing fervor as a precious but threatened preserve. This renewed interest in childhood has coincided with a new wave of concern about children: a growing conviction that childhood "disappears." Potter too believed that childhood as she had known it dwindled, and yet she firmly believed that in her writing she could preserve it.

SELECTED BIBLIOGRAPHY

I. BIBLIOGRAPHY. Jane Quinby, *Beatrix Potter: A Bibliographical Checklist* (New York, 1954).

II. COLLECTED WORKS. *The Complete Tales of Beatrix Potter* (London, 1989).

III. SEPARATE WORKS. *The Tale of Peter Rabbit* (privately printed, 1901; rev. ed., London, 1902); *The Tailor of Gloucester* (privately printed, 1902; rev. ed., London, 1903); *The Tale of Squirrel Nutkin* (London, 1903); *The Tale of Benjamin Bunny* (London, 1904); *The Tale of Two Bad Mice* (London, 1904); *The Tale of Mrs. Tiggy-Winkle* (London, 1905); *The Tale of the Pie and the Patty-Pan* (London, 1905); *The Story of a Fierce Bad Rabbit* (London, 1906); *The Story of Miss Moppet* (London, 1906); *The Tale of Mr. Jeremy Fisher* (London, 1906); *The Tale of Tom Kitten* (London, 1907); *The Roly-Poly Pudding*, later renamed *The Tale of Samuel Whiskers* (London, 1908); *The Tale of Jemima Puddle-Duck* (London, 1908); *The Tale of the Flopsy Bunnies* (London, 1909); *The Tale of Ginger and Pickles* (London, 1909).

The Tale of Mrs. Tittlemouse (London, 1910); *Peter Rabbit's Painting Book* (London, 1911); *The Tale of Timmy Tiptoes* (London, 1911); *The Tale of Mr. Tod* (London, 1912); *The Tale of Pigling Bland* (London, 1913); *Appley Dapply's Nursery Rhymes* (London, 1917); *Tom Kitten's Painting Book* (London, 1917); *The Tale of Johnny Town-Mouse* (London, 1918).

Cecily Parsley's Nursery Rhymes (London, 1922); *Jemima Puddle-Duck's Painting Book* (London, 1925); *Peter Rabbit's Almanac for 1929* (London, 1928); *The Fairy Caravan* (privately printed, 1929; Philadelphia, 1929; London, 1952); *The Tale of Little Pig Robinson* (Philadelphia and London, 1930); *Sister Anne* (Philadelphia, 1932).

IV. WORKS PUBLISHED POSTHUMOUSLY. *Wag-by-Wall* (London and Boston, 1944); *The Tale of the Faithful Dove* (London, 1955); *The Sly Old Cat* (London, 1971); *The Tale of Tuppenny* (London, 1973); *Country Tales* (London, 1987).

V. LETTERS. *Dear Ivy, Dear June: Letters from Beatrix Potter*, ed. by Margaret Crawford Maloney (Toronto, 1977); *Beatrix Potter's Americans: Selected Letters*, ed. by Jane Crowell Morse (Boston, 1982); *Beatrix Potter's Letters*, ed. by Judy Taylor (London, 1989).

VI. JOURNAL. *The Journal of Beatrix Potter from 1881 to 1897*, ed. by Leslie Linder (abridged ed., London, 1966; unabridged ed., London, 1989); *Beatrix Potter's Journal* (abridged), ed. by Glen Cavaliero (Harmondsworth, Eng., 1986).

VII. COLLECTIONS OF ARTWORK. Joyce I. Whalley and Wynne K. Bartlett, *The Derwentwater Sketchbook* (London, 1984); Joyce I. Whalley and Anne S. Hobbs, *Beatrix Potter: The V & A Collection* (London, 1985).

VIII. BIOGRAPHICAL AND CRITICAL STUDIES. Margaret Lane, *The Tale of Beatrix Potter* (London, 1946; rev. ed., London, 1985); Leslie Linder, *The Art of Beatrix Potter* (London, 1955); Marcus Crouch, *Beatrix Potter* (London, 1960); Leslie Linder, *Beatrix Potter, 1866–1943: A Centenary Catalogue* (London, 1966); Grahame Green, "Beatrix Potter," in his *Collected Essays* (London and New York, 1969).

Rumer Godden, *The Tale of the Tales: The Beatrix Potter Ballet* (London and New York, 1971); Leslie Linder, *A History of the Writings of Beatrix Potter, Including Unpublished Works* (London, 1971), and *The History of the Tale of Peter Rabbit* (London, 1976); Gordon N. Ray, *The Illustrator and the Book in England from 1790 to 1914* (New York, 1976); Margaret Lane, *The Magic Years of Beatrix Potter* (London, 1978).

Ulla Hyde Parker, *Cousin Beatie: A Memory of Beatrix Potter* (London, 1981); Susan E. Meyer, *A Treasury of the Great Children's Book Illustrators* (New York, 1983); Humphrey Carpenter, *Secret Gardens: A Study of the Golden Age of Children's Literature* (Boston, 1985); Elizabeth Battrick, *The Real World of Beatrix Potter* (Norwich, Eng., 1986); Ruth Macdonald, *Beatrix Potter* (Boston, 1986); Judy Taylor, *Beatrix Potter: Artist, Storyteller, and Countrywoman* (London, 1986); William R. Mitchell, *Beatrix Potter Remembered* (Clapham, Lancaster, 1987); Judy Taylor, *That Naughty Rabbit: Beatrix Potter and Peter Rabbit* (London, 1987); Joyce I. Whalley and Tessa R. Chester, *A History of Children's Book Illustration* (London, 1988); Humphrey Carpenter, "Excessively Impertinent Bunnies: The Subversive Element in Beatrix Potter," in Gillian Avery and Julia Briggs, *Children and Their Books* (Oxford, 1989); Ruth Macdonald, "Narrative Voice and Narrative View in Beatrix Potter's Books," in Charlotte F. Otten and Gary D. Schmidt, eds., *The Voice of the Narrator in Children's Literature* (London, 1989).

Richard Dalby, *The Golden Age of Children's Book Illustrations* (London, 1991); W. Nikola-Lisa, "The Cult of Peter Rabbit: A Barthesian Analysis," in *The Lion and the Unicorn* 15 (December 1991); Carole Scott, "Between Me and the World: Clothes as Mediator Between Self and Society in the Work of Beatrix Potter," in *The Lion and the Unicorn* 16 (December 1992).

V. S. PRITCHETT

(1900–)

Robert Squillace

V. S. PRITCHETT HAS LONG held a reputation as a writer's writer. That he has not entirely been a reader's writer is largely due to his chosen medium, the short story. Of traditional literary genres, only the novel has retained a large enough readership in the post–Second World War era to allow a writer to claim critical attention by first making a splash with the public. It has also been virtually the only way a creative writer could support him- or herself strictly by writing literature. Yet Pritchett is so convinced that his gift operates strictly within the boundaries of short fiction that he has twice abandoned the novel for extended periods: fourteen years between his fourth novel, *Dead Man Leading* (1937), and his fifth, *Mr. Beluncle* (1951), and more than forty years since *Mr. Beluncle.* It seems reasonable to begin an assessment of Pritchett's career with a consideration of his self-imposed identity as a short-story writer.

Pritchett seems to have chosen a highly circumscribed form in consonance with his own highly particular ambitions as a writer of fiction. His complex response to the phenomenon of modernism, a style of almost boundless ambition, is especially instructive in this regard. Modernist literature in English was reaching its artistic peak in the 1920s, just as Pritchett began his career as an author (his first story was published in 1926). Its tenets clearly left some mark on Pritchett; throughout his life, he has made the familiar modernist claims about the artist's necessary exile and the primacy of the word—the identification of painstaking verbal craft with artistic distinction that runs back through Ezra Pound and Ford Madox Ford to one of modernism's favorite ancestors, Gustave Flaubert. Pritchett concludes the first volume of his memoirs, *A Cab at the Door* (1968), with the Joycean pronouncement that "for myself that is what a writer is—a man living on the other side of a frontier" (p. 244); in the charming account of

turning eighty that he wrote for the *New York Times Magazine,* later published in book form as *The Turn of the Years* (1981), he describes the "ant's colony of corrections" he imposes on each draft page and calls writing itself "[falling] under the spell of language which has ruled me since I was ten."

And yet, Pritchett's own style shows virtually no trace of modernist influence; he employs none of the dislocations of ordinary language that for the modernists are at once the mark and logical consequence of their exile. Significantly, Pritchett's three book-length critical and biographical studies all deal with nineteenth-century continental realists: Balzac, Chekhov, Turgenev. This trio seem more likely influences for a novelist of Pritchett's Edwardian boyhood than for a writer whose best work comes after midcentury. That they are all continental realists, however, offers a clue to the dimensions of Pritchett's belief in the necessity of the writer's alienation. He shares the realist regard for the revelation of character; his fiction is consistently domestic, not in limiting its interest to personal relationships, but in giving precedence to the theme of Englishness. Indeed, V. S. Pritchett is one of the greatest chroniclers of the transformations of English character over the course of the twentieth century. His brand of alienation answers this need; to perceive Englishness, he must in some respect stand outside it. But at the same time, Pritchett seems to want the weight of centuries of English prose style behind him; those traditions are not a restraint to him, but a way of deepening the texture of his depiction of English character. He shows no interest in repeating the journey that took James Joyce from the sketches of Irish character one finds in *Dubliners* (1914) to the progressively more word-centered novels *Portrait of the Artist as a Young Man* (1916), *Ulysses* (1922), and *Finnegans Wake* (1939). Pritchett does not, in fact, display the alienation from the English language, perhaps from language itself, that the modernists felt. Indeed, he freely assumes the ability to report his characters' true feelings and thoughts, even when they are unknown to the characters themselves; often, he shifts seamlessly between the voices of his characters and his own narrative voice. It is precisely this method of psychologizing his characters by direct authorial report that makes Pritchett's novels less successful than his short stories. Long fiction, at least for twentieth-century readers, has required a multiplicity of voices, of perspectives, of points of observation—indeed, the prototypical conflict of the modern novel is a conflict between points of view. Pritchett's novels lack such conflict; while perhaps it is true of all fiction that we in effect always hear the voice of the author, Pritchett does not divide that voice into conflicting parts. Significantly, Pritchett's version of the familiar story of the European explorer breaking apart in uncharted lands, *Dead Man Leading*, a clear response to Joseph Conrad's *Heart of Darkness* (1902), employs an omniscient third-person narrator rather than a character like Marlow, whose deep implication in the tale he tells produces so much of *Heart of Darkness*'s interest.

Even when Pritchett does employ a dramatized narrator, as he does in "The Scapegoat," "When My Girl Comes Home," and "The Camberwell Beauty," that narrator tends to act as spokesperson for a group whose psychology he knows intimately. Of course, the great novels of Pritchett's nineteenth-century favorites follow the convention of authorial infallibility in reporting psychology as well—and characters are, after all, constructed in accordance with literary conventions; they are not beings with interiors that one must read from exterior clues. But the novels of Balzac and Turgenev observe conventions of plot that externalize the same sort of conflicts of perspective that most modern novels develop from within. Pritchett is too much a twentieth-century author to reproduce that sort of plot, nor has he quite found another mode of constructing a novel that belongs neither to modernist nor realist practice.

The very methods of explaining the essence of Englishness that undermine Pritchett's novels contribute to his mastery of the short story. The brilliance of Pritchett's authorial perception lends his tales a compression, a density of suggestion, paralleled by few others. While one gets the impression in reading Pritchett's novels that his characters have been pinned and dissected rather than allowed to live and speak, the same sort of directly reported psychological insights over the shorter haul strike with the force of revelations. The same intensity of light that can only blind on prolonged exposure illuminates in the form of lightning. Further, the genre of short fiction creates a sense of confinement, of limited space, that mimics both the particularity of Pritchett's thematic interest and the limitations of the peculiarly English space within which his characters move. To read the eighty-two pieces he has seen fit to preserve in his *Complete Collected Stories* (1991) is to feel the texture of English life over the last sixty years and see how men and women have responded to its changes. The sense of how it felt to live and move within the social framework of a certain place and time, something that (as Pritchett recognized) readers once looked chiefly to novels to provide, Pritchett gives more fully in his short stories than perhaps any novelist of his time.

LIFE

VICTOR Sawdon Pritchett missed being born in the first year of the twentieth century by only fifteen days, arriving in the world—or, to be more precise, in Ipswich, Suffolk—on 16 December 1900. Although he spent barely a fortnight in the nineteenth century, it is appropriate that he was born at its end, as so much of his fiction chronicles the slow dissolution of that century's habits of thought. That Pritchett himself managed not only to escape those concepts but to make himself a writer who could view them from afar borders on the miraculous. His memoirs, *A Cab at the Door* and *Midnight Oil* (1971), amply detail the formidable obstacles he needed to overcome to be a writer. The first obstacle took the unfortunate form of his father. Victor Sawdon was the first of Walter and Beatrice Pritchett's four children. Walter was a merchant in various trades and master of none; his impecunities and his tendency to vanish into his work for long periods kept the family on the move in a way that seriously jeopardized Victor's success in education. A Christian Scientist who absorbed all the family's resources without seeming to notice the straits in which he thus left them—the body, after all, being a mere illusion—Walter removed his eldest son from school before he had reached sixteen and apprenticed him to the leather trade.

After five years in the tannery, Pritchett took his generation's archetypal step toward a writer's life—he went to Paris. After two years in a company that sold photographic supplies, he found his first literary work. Not surprisingly, it was as a correspondent for the *Christian Science Monitor;* the sect that stressed the unreality of the body at least helped keep it attached to Pritchett's soul for the next four years. Assigned to Dublin, Pritchett met and married his first wife, Evelyn Maude Vigors, in 1924. Although the marriage endured until 1936, it seems never to have been very successful; indeed, Pritchett implies in *Midnight Oil* that the couple married in part because of the opportunity it afforded to flout parental advice. Divorce was followed in extremely short order by remarriage: to Dorothy Roberts, to whom, despite some very difficult times in the mid-1950s, Pritchett has remained married ever since. In the dozen years between his first and second weddings, Pritchett undertook the hard spadework of founding a reputation. Fired by the *Monitor* in 1927, over the next nine years he published three novels, his first collection of short stories (which he has since repudiated, though it sold about five times the number of copies anyone expected), and his first travel book. Pritchett himself looks on this period as an extended apprenticeship, the end of which was marked by the publication of Pritchett's fourth novel, *Dead Man Leading,* in 1937. The first fruit of his revitalizing new and lifelong love for Dorothy, the novel was, Pritchett believes, a casualty of the war. But the appearance throughout the 1930s of the stories later included in his second collection, *You Make Your Own Life* (1938), established Pritchett's identity as a writer for both his reading public and for Pritchett himself. While he would make one more full-scale assault on the novel in *Mr. Beluncle,* he would increasingly be identified as, and identify himself as, a writer of short stories.

Subjects other than the art of short fiction continued to occupy Pritchett, however. His first volume of collected critical essays, *In My Good Books,* appeared in 1942; over the next fifty years he was to publish many more (now gathered together as *Complete Collected Essays,* 1991), as well as writing critical and biographical studies of Turgenev, Chekhov, and Balzac. He also enjoyed a long and fruitful association with the *New Statesman,* beginning as its fiction critic in 1937, serving as literary editor from 1945 to 1949, then returning as director

from 1951 to 1978. But it was not until the 1970s—and so his own seventies—that Pritchett finally attained a measure of security commensurate with the reputation he had long, if somewhat quietly, enjoyed. The precipitous decline in the popularity of magazine fiction after the Second World War caused a number of stories Pritchett wrote in the 1950s to be rejected by the first periodicals to which he submitted them. Fewer outlets for the short story also meant ever smaller checks for acceptance. Only the publication of his three greatest collections of tales—*When My Girl Comes Home* (1961), *Blind Love and Other Stories* (1969), and *The Camberwell Beauty and Other Stories* (1974)—secured Pritchett the honors that ensure a contemporary writer remains in print. Many of the most significant of these honors came from his fellow authors. Pritchett was elected president of the English branch of PEN (Poets, Playwrights, Editors, Essayists, and Novelists) in 1971 and then was elected to a two-year term as president of the international organization in 1974. Knighted in 1975, Pritchett had to wait only a year after his PEN presidency ended to garner another significant honor: presidency of the Society of Authors. Throughout his eighties, Pritchett steadily continued to write fiction and criticism. The publication of his *Complete Short Stories* in 1990 and *Complete Collected Essays* in 1991 suggests that V. S. Pritchett has retired from the difficult art of the word. Few have demonstrated a longer or more ardent devotion to that art.

NOVELS

PRITCHETT managed five novels before concluding that his metier was the short story. The first three of these belong to his period of apprenticeship. *Clare Drummer,* which appeared in 1929, concerns a former Black and Tan living on in Ireland after the civil war. The year 1932 saw the publication of *Shirley Sanz* (titled *Elopement into Exile* in the United States), which follows the relationships of a quartet of English expatriates—two men and two women—in Spain. *Nothing Like Leather* (1935) follows the career of Mathew Burkle, a merchant in the tanning trade, as his growing obsession with financial success leads him first to the summit of power in the local tanning industry, and then to that trade's nadir—he accidentally falls into a tanning vat and dies. The style of symbolism apparent in this incident—demonstrating how absorption in his work may destroy a man by having him literally drown in it—suggests the difference between this trio of early novels and the subtlety of presentation Pritchett would later achieve.

While his ultimate dissatisfaction with his last two novels, *Dead Man Leading* and *Mr. Beluncle*, convinced Pritchett to abandon the form, he also considered them to represent his most mature attempt at the novel—he felt sure he had done his best in the genre. Both these works shed a great deal of light on the nature of Pritchett's gift and are worthwhile texts in their own right. Paradoxically, one can perhaps most clearly perceive the tendencies that suited Pritchett so well for short fiction in his most ambitious novel, *Dead Man Leading*. The book concerns an Amazonian expedition conducted by a pair of Englishmen, Gilbert Phillips and Harry Johnson, that grows increasingly confused in both direction and object after the accidental death of the group's leader, Charles Wright, with whose stepdaughter, Lucy Mommbrekke, both men have had affairs. Much of the work is devoted to investigating the somewhat unusual theme of Protestant guilt. Harry Johnson, a masochist in physical, psychic, and sexual matters, almost unconsciously turns the expedition into a search for his father, a missionary who had disappeared in the same area seventeen years earlier. Often entertaining the impossible notion that his father might yet be alive among the Indians of the rain forest, he ultimately vanishes in the same jungle, symbolically becoming his father rather than finding him. The search, which is frequently glossed by references to Hamlet (as is Stephen Dedalus' struggle with the question of his origin in James Joyce's *Ulysses*), is inspired less by guilt at having fallen away from the father's religion than by guilt for having been born; Harry needs to confront the party responsible for his own being. Individual responsibility, after all, is the feature by which Protestantism often seeks to define itself. Harry's overwhelming fear when he finally sleeps with Lucy after years of independent chastity is that he might himself become a father, responsible for the existence of another being. For Harry Johnson, vanishing into the shadow of his father lets him retract his own birth.

The section of the novel that deals with Phillips and Johnson in the jungle would have made an ex-

cellent short story; Harry Johnson is the sort of character who continues to live in one's mind after the story is over. But as a novel the work seems simultaneously incomplete and too restricted. It lacks the free play of perspective consonant with the ambiguity of the events it depicts—as Dean Baldwin has pointed out in his *V. S. Pritchett* (1987), Pritchett refers to the fact that many different characters' versions of what happened on the expedition exist, yet he directly reports the true events, both physical and psychological, in his own third-person authorial voice. He seems largely uninterested in exploiting the potential ambiguity of interpretation his own story provides. Pritchett especially reveals himself in the artist figure he offers in this novel, a Portuguese man named Silva, who exposes the hidden desires of the English characters through artfully improvised séances in which he imitates their dead—it is he who introduces the ghost of Hamlet into events. Silva brings the sort of foreign perspective to the English characters that Pritchett considered the artist's necessary position, but, like Pritchett himself, Silva brings his perspective to bear wholly on the question of Englishness; he is obsessed with the English; his voice is more fully possessed of the traditions of English style than any other voice in the novel. One would not wish Pritchett to reproduce the Conradian play of voices one finds in *Heart of Darkness*, but he seems not to have found an adequate way to revise it. While Conrad compresses into a novella a tale that concerns the whole European spirit of colonialism—Kurtz belongs to many nations—Pritchett stretches a tale of a peculiarly English guilt, a tale that reveals no more than many of his short stories, onto the frame of a novel.

Mr. Beluncle is an entirely different case. While *Dead Man Leading* takes up the themes of Conrad and Joyce, *Mr. Beluncle* revisits territories that were first opened by Dickens and H. G. Wells. It is a fictionalized version of Pritchett's own experience of growing up under a father whose professed faith in the sole reality of Mind served to impoverish every family member's body and spirit save his own. Here Pritchett handles the primal father-son conflict comically, rather than in the agonized fashion of his previous novel. Not only does the narrator concentrate on puncturing the absurd pretensions of an extremely present, rather than absent, father, he decentralizes and thus deintensifies the central struggle by including the rest of the Beluncle family. Indeed, the novel identifies the male world as fiction's proper subject to a much lesser extent than the earlier novel (though Pritchett does manage to omit his sister from the family circle). Often extremely funny, the book does not treat familial conflict itself farcically; it does not offer a comic resolution. Rather, it contains moments of great sadness arising out of the awful spectacle of the frustration of practically everyone's desires by the title character. One wonders, however, how vital its identity as a novel is to its success. *Mr. Beluncle,* in fact, reworks several of Pritchett's earlier short stories; incidents from "The Saint," "It May Never Happen," and "The Collection"[1] all find their way into the novel. Pritchett does not seem to make any great use of the novel genre itself in *Mr. Beluncle;* he does not seem, that is, to offer any implicit comment on the genre's conventions, or to use the conventions of the genre to illuminate his material. His subsequent and permanent return to the short story is not surprising.

CRITICISM

LIKE many writers who truly live by the pen, V. S. Pritchett found that forms other than the traditional literary genres often provide handsomer remuneration. Unlike the similar work of many of his peers, however, Pritchett's nonfiction repays readers at least as well as it has paid him. Given the volume of his writing in these fields, the fortune is munificent: seven books detailing his travels, including works on London, New York, and Dublin, and twice as many books of criticism (eight of which are preserved in his *Complete Collected Essays*), including full-length biographical studies of Balzac, Chekhov, and Turgenev.

All these pieces show the unmistakable mark of Pritchett: in his travel writing and his criticism, as in his short fiction, Pritchett is an extraordinarily perspicacious observer. Indeed, observation is enshrined as the chief principle of his criticism (which usually concerns prose fiction)— not merely observation of the patterns apparent in the works themselves, but of the character of his own reaction to them. His unit of inquiry is generally the individual novelist—there are very

few thematically organized essays. Pritchett's literary criticism often represents an attempt to put into words his informed experience of, and response to, the implied person of the author he reads. Unlike many academic critics, Pritchett has no fear of self-exposure; he is quite willing—even eager—to judge the degree of success of the author under consideration. He strikingly observes of Hardy, for instance, that "he seems to be the only English novelist to have read his Darwin and . . . to have had his imagination enlarged, not by the moral conflicts which Darwinism started among English writers, but by the most striking material contribution of Darwinism to our minds: its enormous widening of our conception of time" (*Complete Collected Essays*, p. 74). Pritchett responds here not to the content of Hardy's novels but to their atmosphere—to the Hardy that the rhetoric of the novels implies, the image the novels themselves create of the mind that created them. That his long critical studies were essentially biographical is not surprising.

The use of the pronoun "our" in the preceding reference to Hardy is especially illuminating; Pritchett invariably writes his criticism from the perspective of one who is in possession of the traditions of English fiction. This sense of writing from the inside has both advantages and drawbacks. At its worst, it suggests a refusal to examine or even fully articulate bases of judgment. When Pritchett declares (as other critics have) that "Conrad exists in English literature, but he is a harsh exotic who can never quite be assimilated to our modes" (*Complete Collected Essays*, p. 721), one wonders precisely who is meant by "us" and why only certain modes are proper to that group. Pritchett again betrays his saturation in the question of Englishness; he cannot resist dividing the English from the foreign even when such terms raise more questions than they answer. At the same time, Pritchett's lack of an overriding theory allows him to respond to the features peculiar to each author he considers; one never has the sense that he is imposing a theory on his own reactions and so substituting what he thinks his reaction ought to be for what it actually has been.

TRAVEL WRITING

PRITCHETT'S remarkable ability to capture moments, displayed repeatedly in his short stories,

---

[1] All of the short stories discussed in this article can be found in *Complete Collected Stories* (New York, 1991); page numbers refer to that edition.

does not desert him in his travel writing. And while travel writing may purport to concern space, it is always in fact about time; the place the writer visits has begun to cease to exist before the book or essay has even journeyed through the process of publication. The most troubling aspect of Pritchett's travel writing is, again, its tenacious pursuit of national character. One is reminded that, despite all his journeys abroad, Pritchett wrote very few stories that contain foreigners who were more than foils to the English protagonists. He continually makes startlingly astute observations—noticing, for instance, in "The Americans in My Mind" (1963, repr. in *At Home and Abroad*, 1989), that the European country most resembling the United States is the Soviet Union—but he has only one generalization to move toward: a statement of the fundamental identity of the people under consideration. While he never generalizes grossly, while he always takes many types into account—his books on America carefully avoid privileging a single ethnicity—the idea of "type" seems always implicit to his perspective.

EARLY SHORT STORIES

THE central subject of Pritchett's short stories, sometimes openly, sometimes subliminally, is English character. His tales certainly have an interest and a significance that goes beyond both the English audience and even the audience interested in England; in investigating Englishness, Pritchett examines much broader human conditions. But his investigation is both bounded and inspired by the peculiar situation of England. In "The Americans in My Mind," Pritchett notes that "we [the British] live intensely, privately" (*At Home and Abroad*, p. 204); he attributes this preoccupation with the private self to the severe limitations of English space. Virtually all of Pritchett's habitual themes, however great their relevance to other lands and other peoples, grow from the conflict between the impinging public eye and the invaded private self. He focuses primarily on how the inescapable public presence goads the individual into a self-protective posture that is itself ultimately destructive; his favorite tension on which to build a story is that between disguise and exposure. Indeed, his tales question whether true human contact is possible in such an atmosphere.

Often, his tales live on the boundary between public and private, being replete with characters who encounter themselves from the outside, or refuse to, or imagine that they do: the double and the other are key figures in Pritchett's fiction. Recognition or its failure is thus frequently the defining moment of the story. Pritchett often employs a dramatized narrator who walks the border between insider and outsider, a narrator who perceives his or her fellow characters from a certain distance, but who fails to see his or her own resemblance to them, who mistakes the double for the other. The ambiguous exile of Pritchett's narrators, who are both raised above their communities and more on a level with them than they ever comprehend, means that his stories simultaneously concern both a physical and a psychological landscape. But in treating these dual environments, Pritchett distinguishes himself from many twentieth-century writers by not yielding the psychological world pride of place. Not only does he begin from the assumption that the material facts of English geography produce the intense privacy of the English self, he often examines how the particular material context in which a character or set of characters must obtain the necessities of shelter, food, and security determines their behavior. His work also admits a historical component, as Pritchett clearly sees the pressures on the private English self waxing with the progress of the twentieth century. Over the course of his career, Pritchett's interest shifted more and more decisively to the interior Englishperson, but the sociocultural context in which he or she moves always remains a half-hidden influence.

"Main Road" is one of the most compressed of Pritchett's early exercises in delineating the psychic effects of the struggle to secure the material necessities of life. The tale appears in *You Make Your Own Life*, Pritchett's second collection of short stories and the first that he has consistently seen fit to reprint—he prefers that the tales from his period of apprenticeship, which appeared in his first collection, *The Spanish Virgin and Other Stories* (1930), remain obscure. Set in the great economic slump of the early 1930s, "Main Road" concerns two tramps, a young man and an old, who assault and rob a country lad after three days of fruitless wandering in search of rumored work in a town they never reach. Pritchett lends an air of inexorability to the tramps' progress toward the crime. Early in the tale, the younger tramp, disgusted both by his partner's fondness for begging and his spectacular lack of success at it, grumbles to himself that he would "sooner sock a man in the jaw than beg" (p. 25). Angry when the old man turns off the main road they have finally reached in order to beg unsuccessfully once more, the young man raises his fists. His blow falls, not on the old man, but on the old man's "prey," the country youth. The old tramp's transformation into a predator is equally inevitable. Jesting continually of food, he descends from "tinned salmon, cabbage, suet pudding and cheese" to "grass and rubbish heaps, dogs and cats. . . . In imagination he was grazing off everything he saw" (p. 26). Even the occupants of a passing bus come to resemble "meat in a shop" to the two tramps (p. 27). They have planned nothing; the roads themselves have simply led them to their crime, "as if silently under all their talk and in all their silence they had been rehearsing this all day, working out every detail to perfection" (p. 29).

The main road of the title, however, represents more than the inevitable track from poverty and isolation to lawlessness; it suggests a dehumanization in the progress of the century itself. The old tramp favors country lanes, begging, and speech; he preserves a sense that common humanity binds others to him, obliges them to render him aid. When the tramps achieve the safety of a bus with their booty, he relaxes into smiles that set the other passengers smiling. "He loved the world" (p. 30). The young tramp, desperate to reach the main road, favors silence and sees too little evidence of human community to beg. The future is his; he shuts up the older man's stream of chatter with the reminder that "you're not a boy now" (p. 27). The older man's world of country lanes is yielding to the "appalling inhuman vacancy" of the main road, which "the younger one understood" (p. 27). When he accuses the youth they rob of being a thief, the younger tramp expresses a fundamental vision of what human life has become—a bitter struggle in which to live is to take the sustenance from others. In the bus, he pursues this implicit line of thought: "There goes the bloody butcher, the bloody baker, money streaming down the world in petrol" (p. 30). Food does not palliate his hunger, as it does for the old tramp whose sense of humor is intact: "What he wanted, his tortured hating soul cried out within him, was not food" (p. 30).

A more ambitious story from *You Make Your Own Life* is "The Scapegoat," the first major instance in Pritchett's fiction of the disturbing tendency of the double and the other to change into each other. In "The Scapegoat," the theme works itself out in terms of social, rather than personal, psychology. Pritchett creates a scapegoat whose crime is smothered by its victims in a frenzy of appreciation for imaginary virtues. The title character, widower Art Edwards, is chosen as the most trustworthy candidate in Terence Street—where "we trust each other. There is not a man in Terence Street you cannot trust" (p. 107)—to hold the money collected for the celebration of George V's Jubilee. The inhabitants of Terence Street see the occasion of the Jubilee as another battle in their endless, motiveless war against their "best enemies [who] are the ones nearest home" (p. 105), their neighbors on Earl Street. At the height of the struggle to raise the most money, Edwards falls under the spell of Harry Law, a man who has "had his ups and downs" (p. 113) in finance; besotted by Harry's grandiose tales of "investment," Edwards loses the entire collection at the dog track and hangs himself. Initially vilified by those who trusted their money to him, Edwards becomes "ourselves, our hero, our god" when Earl Street jeers him, his funeral replacing the Jubilee—"Art Edwards our king" (p. 119)—as an implement of war in the great rivalry.

The apotheosis of Edwards is a means by which the community staves off recognition of uncomfortable truths about itself, particularly the fallacy of its status as a community. The narrator avers that the whole street inwardly knows the thoughts that impel Edwards to the Wembley track: "It came to him that he had never felt anything for years. He had just gone on standing in the High Street by the stall. He had never taken a holiday. He had never bought himself anything he wanted. He had never done anything" (p. 113). Edwards bears the sins of Terence Street in that he attempts the escape they all secretly desire; he earns its gratitude by removing that temptation (in the form of the money) from them. Harry Law completes Edwards' transformation into a hero when he declares that Edwards had only wished to increase the collection by investing it. The community's hope that responsibility for the collection will help the widower out of his shell is ironically realized not in the expected remarriage but in his escape and death. The enormous funeral, reports the narrator, "looked like a wedding" (p. 119).

The scapegoat, then, is at once the true double of the community and the false other onto whom it projects its own desires in order to distance them. Edwards thus fulfills the same role as the enemy, also a putative other, in maintaining an illusion of community identity. Such an identity depends on arbitrary exclusions; being a Jew, Lupinsky, the prime mover of all community action in Terence Street, is never fully acknowledged as one of its members. The narrator reports that "they had another Jew in Earl Street doing the same" (p. 107); indeed, "one street seemed to blend into the other" (p. 106), so that only the active ministrations of the inhabitants of the two streets themselves introduce any difference. Given the story's appearance in 1938, it is tempting to perceive some allusion to Nazi scapegoating, but such a parallel is at best inexact. Pritchett's scapegoat, after all, is acclaimed a hero.

IT MAY NEVER HAPPEN

By the time of *It May Never Happen and Other Stories* (1945), Pritchett was ready to give his characteristic theme of double and other a more solely psychological context, as he does in the brilliant tale of fat men titled "Pocock Passes." Rogers, an obese ruin of a country squire who has secretly begun to live off his capital, encounters his improbable image in Pocock, an enormous failed artist from London who has also dipped into his capital. The Falstaffian size of the men indicates a need to nullify the prying world by absorbing it. Narrated in indirect third-person discourse, the tale records Rogers' vacillation between recognition of a fellow spirit in Pocock and denial of their identity. Rogers particularly attempts to distance himself from Pocock's singleness and takes refuge in his absurd vision of himself as a family man, despite the fact that living on his capital means consuming his children's livelihood. Even here, though, Rogers unwittingly confirms the sameness of the two men; in considering his family "his own picture . . . that private masterpiece of his" (p. 231), he both borrows the language of Pocock's profession and reveals an inability to acknowledge his family's independent existence—a painting, after all, is an object—thus giving the lie to the central point by which he differentiates himself from Pocock.

The tale slowly works itself into a tension between exposure and disguise. Exposure horrifies Rogers; he is appalled by a woman's nude portrait he sees in Pocock's rooms, not simply because the subject is naked, but because the painting depicts exposure itself: "Not lascivious, not beautiful, not enticing, just naked and seeming to say, 'It don't feel natural, I mean having nothing on'" (p. 233). After Pocock's death the painting comes to symbolize "the incomprehensibility of the existence of other people . . . the picture [was] the man he did not know at all" (p. 236). Through this self-protective interpretation, Rogers escapes ever knowing Pocock and himself. He conveniently twists a knee to avoid Pocock's funeral and eventually refrains from mentioning or thinking of him.

The story might well have ended on that note of protective unknowing, but Pritchett works a brilliant reversal that throws Rogers' dilemma back at the reader of the story. Two years after Pocock's death, Rogers encounters his friend again, playing a sleeping man in a hilarious two minutes of a four-year-old film that has finally reached the provinces. After seeing the scene six times, pursuing the film from one town to the next, Rogers at last wishes he could see Pocock alive again. The scene convinces him that "life was incomprehensible no more. Something had been settled" (p. 237). He subsequently burns the nude, feeling he has totally cleansed Pocock's "stain." What has been settled is open to question. Rogers has achieved no greater recognition of Pocock but has accepted him, has opted to affirm the reality of the disguise. Pocock, inert and unreachable, doing "nothing at all" (p. 237), recovers the "sacred and innocent" look that Rogers had noted the first time he had seen him "remote in sleep" (p. 234) in his rooms. Readers thus face the same issue of disguise and exposure that Rogers does; they may empathize with Rogers' regained acceptance of his friend, thus refraining from looking into Rogers as Rogers refrains from looking into Pocock, or they may question Rogers' inability to know a man who is so much himself—they may look beneath the surface and condemn.

Another instance of Pritchett's increasing tendency to favor the problems of the inner life over the social circumstances with which he nevertheless recognized they were intimately connected comes in "The Saint," which also appears in *It May Never Happen*. The tale, narrated in the first person by a man recollecting his loss of religion at the age of seventeen, begins as a satire of the Christian Science faith in which Pritchett had been raised, here as elsewhere in his works christened the "Church of the Last Purification." The church's doctrine that all material affliction is an illusion arising from the deficient faith or understanding of the human mind ironically wins it a congregation concerned primarily with material success. Attracted by the promise of mental control over the very matter the church repudiates as an illusion, such adherents as the narrator's uncle are converted by the willingness of a wealthy member to invest in their businesses; they meet "in a room at the Corn Exchange" (p. 187). When Mr. Hubert Timberlake, a leader of the church, arrives in town, his alleged raising of the dead (twice) causes less stir among the parishioners than the fact of his having spent time in Toronto, the point of the church's inception and its headquarters. The narrator's uncle is especially impressed at Mr. Timberlake's feat of raising his already considerable yearly income by 50 percent after only two years as a church leader.

The Timberlake episode of the story introduces a set of concerns that move the import beyond satire. Apprised of the narrator's doubts about the origin of the supposedly illusory evil—"even illusions have an origin" (p. 188)—Timberlake goes on the river in a punt with the youth in order to speak with him alone. By taking the nephew's side against the uncle in a minor exchange of witticisms, Timberlake has already won his faith; what occurs on the river entirely loses it. Timberlake attempts to push a willow branch away while punting, then winds up grasping it, suspended over the river, while the punt glides from under his feet, and finally splits a seam of his shirt as he slips into the water. Convinced by this catastrophe that "the final revelation about man and society on earth had come to nobody and that Mr. Timberlake knew nothing at all about the origin of evil" (p. 195), the youth begins to notice how Timberlake's very rejection of the reality of material evil renders him unable to perceive material beauty either; he negates the reality of his own existence by denying what his senses tell him: "I understood that Mr. Timberlake was formally acknowledging a world he did not live in. It was too interesting, too eventful a world. His spirit, inert and preoccupied, was elsewhere in an eventless and immaterial habitation" (p. 197). After

lying indifferently in a field of buttercups (whose name he does not know), Timberlake arises covered with pollen that he makes no attempt to remove, a saint "golden and bored" (p. 198).

Mr. Timberlake's death both provides the narrator with an occasion for telling the story of his loss of faith and augments his understanding of that faith's nature. The reason Timberlake had not engaged him on the question of the origin of evil, the narrator at last recognizes, was that he was tormented by it. On that day on the river, the narrator understands, doubt that "merely followed me was already inside Mr. Timberlake eating out his heart" (p. 199). In a flash, one recognizes that the effort of the faith is not to repress evil (or "error") itself, but to repress the question of its origin; denying the reality of hardship does little to ease the hardship but avoids the problem of its existence. Such repression has a high price; the doctor who examines Timberlake's body identifies the cause of death as heart disease and declares, in an inadvertent, ironic echo of the faith's rhetoric, "It was a miracle . . . that he had lived as long" (p. 199).

"THE SNIFF" AND "THE SATISFACTORY"

"The Sniff" and "The Satisfactory," a pair of stories that appeared in volume form for the first time in *Collected Stories* (1956), show Pritchett in his most cynical period regarding the value of human contact, at least among the English; the apparent demise of his second marriage (subsequently restored to twice its original strength) may have encouraged this attitude, but in any case Pritchett did not publish a single story that ended with a vision of happiness until he was nearly seventy. "The Satisfactory" concentrates such a variety of oppressions into a single relationship that its import might best be described by the Upanishadic observation that "All the world is eater and eaten." The tale relates the deprivations suffered in the Second World War and the postwar rationing period by an antique dealer named Mr. Plymbell. His trade in old furniture, however, consists mainly in housing the contents of the abandoned London house of Lady Hackthorpe, Plymbell's idol, who has fled to America, presumably to escape the blitz. Plymbell, in fact, functions as "The Satisfactory"'s caretaker of English, perhaps Western, civilization; the first words of the story quote Plymbell to the effect that "what one is still inclined to call civilisation is passing through a crisis" (p. 364).

The civilization he represents, though, is the organization of the world into master and slave; when he contemplates following Lady Hackthorpe's line on servants by treating his secretary-cum-housekeeper offensively in order to retain her, the narrator remarks that "two thousand years of civilisation lay in those remarks" (p. 376). The secretary, Miss Tell, places herself in thrall to Mr. Plymbell in order to obtain "the satisfactory." The role that fulfills Tell seems grotesque—she starves herself in order to spend her ration book (and those of her dead parents) on feeding the ever-hungry Plymbell; she obtains such dainties as are available for him on the black market; she daily feeds him her own lunch at a local restaurant so that he may have two. But Tell's choice of satisfactions merely exaggerates the two roles for which Plymbell's, and Lady Hackthorpe's, civilization has marked her in accordance with her class and gender: self-effacing servant and self-effacing nurturer. In her feeding of Plymbell, she acts the part of the nurturing woman to a sort of perfection. "It's wrong, Mr. Plymbell," she announces. "The government ought to give men more rations. A man needs food. Myself, it never worries me. I never eat" (p. 371). The narrator reports that "her small bosom" was "ribbed like a wicker basket" (p. 371)—the area of the body most closely associated with feeding is thus conflated with the basket into which she drops her lunchtime bread each day to save it for her employer.

The process by which Tell and Plymbell strike their peculiar deal involves not the slightest touch of human contact, although they consummate the bargain by what in other circumstances would be called making love. Plymbell pictures every emotion in a single way—"It was a hunger" (p. 369). Such was his reaction to his grief over his mother's death: after she died, he "ate one of the largest meals of his life" (p. 369); so also the desire he musters for Miss Tell when he believes he must do so to retain her culinary favors: "he had discovered how close to eating kissing is, and as he allowed his arm to rest on Miss Tell's lower-class waist, he had the inadvertent impression of picking up a cutlet in his fingers" (p. 375). Pritchett hints broadly that Mr. Plymbell is either homosexual or asexual; like many heterosexual writers, he seems to have been content to wield homosexuality as a symbol of refused "natural" desires with

little regard to actual gay and lesbian experience. Only the perception of Miss Tell as a source of nourishment arouses Plymbell; after all, his credo is "a human being was a creature who fed one" (p. 370). Miss Tell has no more genuine a desire for Mr. Plymbell. She begins feeding him because her cat Tiger, to whom she would prefer donating her own food, has been lost in an air raid (as have her parents, for whom Tiger may serve as a surrogate). Their one potential moment of contact—and also Mr. Plymbell's first sexual encounter, at the age of fifty—is undermined both by being passed over in narrative silence and by serving as the occasion for the introduction of Miss Tell's scheme to obtain double rations for her lover. At the same time, Miss Tell has little chance to rise from her class status except through identification with Mr. Plymbell. She has neither the training nor the inclination to share her employer's epicurean delight in fine old furniture or fine fresh food; it is Plymbell's general refinement, his air of class superiority, she covets. As the narrator reports, "Miss Tell lived by what she did not understand. It was an appetite" (p. 366). Indeed, Tell can only phrase her aspirations in the language of her oppressor; not only does her characteristic term for the disappointments of her life (her situation is invariably "unsatisfactory") seem an adopted locution from a higher class, she adopts Mr. Plymbell's voice when addressing her family about him, noting that "I don't *query* his private life" (p. 367) and employing his signature pronoun, "one." As her mother puts it, "To hear you talk he might be the Fairy Prince or Lord Muck himself" (p. 367). The story ends with a crushing irony. Miss Tell's achievement of her impoverished version of the satisfactory is not destined to outlast rationing: "But now, of course, French cookery has come back" (p. 380). Even the minimal equalization of the classes that the war brings about is temporary.

The vision of human relations presented in "The Sniff" is in a sense even more disturbing than that of "The Satisfactory," as its troubled couple are far more attractive figures than Mr. Plymbell and Miss Tell. They are fully aware of their growing disconnection from each other and show no desire to profit from each other's pain. Like "The Satisfactory," though, "The Sniff" establishes in its opening sentence that it concerns more than the particular difficulties of a particular couple. "It is hard to say what the present situation is," Pritchett writes, "whether it is improving or whether it is becoming one of those everlasting situations that mark the characters and memories of children" (p. 391). The immediate situation in question is the mingled fear and fascination with which Mrs. N. (significantly, no particular name is ever attached to the initial) regards the sudden reversion of her husband, a war veteran who now works in a shop, to his old hobby of painting. The larger situation, however, is much darker—in considering the relationship of Mr. and Mrs. N., the tale recounts an apparently irreparable rift between love and art that diminishes the ultimate worth of either. The war has allowed Mr. N. to encounter a world left unorganized by work; as his wife recalls, "The hateful thing about the war was that neither she nor the shop ruled him, and what he would be like then she could not imagine" (p. 392). The one lesson Mr. N. draws from his profound wartime experience of unstructured time—boredom is one of the most common afflictions of soldiers—reawakens his need to paint: "Time drags, you've got to do something" (p. 395). Mr. N.'s art, however, does not communicate a compensatory vision of order; it merely removes him from life. Challenged by his wife to affirm that he is a real artist, he can only answer that he is not, "out of a frozen, obdurate, empty desolation" (p. 398).

Pritchett insistently opposes Mr. N.'s art to Mrs. N.'s sexuality in the tale. Not only had Mr. N. "stopped drawing altogether when he was in love with her" (p. 395), but Mrs. N. gradually perceives that "this painting was an infidelity. It was like another woman" (p. 399), and she attempts to win back her husband by posing nude for him, hoping to overwhelm the painter's distance in desire. Her warning after she has undressed that "this is not to be an excuse. The children will be back soon" (p. 398) seems rather an invitation than a discouragement, as Mr. N. has shown no inclination to seduce. He merely replies that "a painter doesn't think like that." Pritchett may to some extent be reiterating a facile, harmful equation: art is male creation as birth is female creation, and the boundary between the two ought not to be passed in either direction. But "The Sniff" also hints strongly that the boundary is precisely the problem. Even as Mr. N.'s art distances him from his wife, it allows him to perceive the narrow limits of her world. As he paints her, he momentarily escapes his chronic inarticulateness to say: "You have a hard life . . . shut up with three children, al-ways at the stove or at the sink. You don't have a chance. I often think . . . you never have a life, not to call it life" (p. 398). Mrs. N.'s heart may be caged by the smell of the paintings, she may affirm that "a woman's life is a man, a child, another person. If I had had a life of my own it wouldn't be you" (p. 399), but the tale ends with her sniff for paint balancing equally between suspicion and anticipation. She and Mr. N. are both held in thrall to an as yet unrealized vision. Mr. N.'s paintings are "living, chopped-off little pictures, unbearably new . . . like small joints of meat" (p. 396), while in the meantime the very art that allows Mr. N. to see his wife separates him from her. "The present situation," while it may allow Mr. N. a private self, allows no human contact whatsoever—at least, as long as Mrs. N. has no parallel private self.

WHEN MY GIRL COMES HOME

THE title story of the 1961 collection *When My Girl Comes Home* is the crowning achievement in Pritchett's investigation into the psychological consequences of what he sees as the peculiarly English tension between privacy and publicity. Pritchett has called "When My Girl Comes Home" his best story; critics have tended to label it complex or problematic, often with at least a faintly pejorative implication. The pleasure its author takes in it originates in the technical difficulties of its execution, of affording almost a dozen characters sufficient attention to give each an individual interest within the limited compass of a short story. But more dazzling is Pritchett's interconnection of several major themes—the war on the English home front, the domestic legacy of colonialism, the fragmentation of the modern self, the erotic fantasies that underlie the phenomenon of celebrity—in the course of only 20,000 words. Critics who have found the tale obscure have perhaps looked in vain for the singleness of effect one normally associates with the short story, the central moment from which all significance radiates. "When My Girl Comes Home" contains no such hub of light, but it delineates the relation between its several themes with a lucidity uncommon even to works of considerably greater length. Its title character, Hilda, particularly functions as a multivalent symbol, evading any unitary reading of her significance.

The story focuses on the members of a family who live in Hincham Street, which is simultaneously in London and nowhere, being "less a street than an interval" (p. 444) by which trolley buses make their connections between one segment of the main road and another. Mrs. Johnson and Mrs. Draper, two elderly sisters, share a house with Constance Draper, a schoolteacher who is one of Mrs. Draper's daughters. Constance, to everyone's mingled amusement and embarrassment, is carrying on with Bill Williams, a survivor of a Japanese prisoner of war camp who, unable to hold any job for very long, has taken work driving a company van, from the back of which he conducts frequent shady deals. Mrs. Draper, generally referred to as "old Mrs. Draper" or Gran, has a married son, Jack, whose wife is "young Mrs. Draper," and a second daughter, who is married to Ted Fulmino. The Fulminos' daughter, Iris, has been dating Harry Fraser, the narrator of the tale, for several weeks before the point at which "When My Girl Comes Home" begins. The girl of the title is Hilda, Mrs. Johnson's daughter, whose return from Japan, engineered with great effort by Mr. Fulmino and Harry, initiates the narrative. It turns out that Hilda, who had left England for Bombay as the wife of a Mr. Singh thirteen years earlier, has not been interred in a Japanese labor camp, as everyone assumed, but had married a Japanese soldier, Shinji Kobayashi, after the death of her first husband and just before the outbreak of the war. She has instead spent time in an American detention center. Returning to England flush with health and money—or, at least, expensive gifts from a shipboard romance or two—she spends heavily while waiting for either a Mr. Faulkner or a Mr. Gloster, or perhaps both, to come for her. Eventually, the death of Hilda's mother forces her to find work. Obtaining a job through Bill Williams, she is eventually menaced and burglarized by him, after which she departs again, embittered by the humiliating charities of Hincham Street.

Without in any way being an allegory for colonial occupation, Hincham Street's reclamation of Hilda Johnson Singh Kobayashi nevertheless illuminates the damage centuries of colonial power have done to the English psyche, even as the power itself irretrievably wanes. Mr. Fulmino, the prime mover of Hilda's "liberation," possesses a "gift for colonising" (p. 449) that allows him to achieve his "deeply British miracle" (p. 444). Ful-

mino's need to annex others reflects both his isolated neighborhood and his island nation—he becomes "a genuine official" in the course of the story and is clearly "heading for politics" (p. 478). As with all the other members of the Draper family, Mr. Fulmino's desire to reclaim Hilda involves considerable self-delusion; he (and Harry Fraser) somehow miss in their correspondence with government officials the fact that Hilda is identified both as Mrs. Singh and Mrs. Shinji Kobayashi, Mr. Fulmino feebly explaining to his wife that Kobayashi is "the family or Christian name of Singh," and that "some Indians write Singh, some Shinji" (p. 454). The Drapers do not merely project onto the title character their own desires to escape their narrow existence into the foreign, exotic, and free, as the residents of Terence Street did in "The Scapegoat"; they rather need to make her an object of pity, and so to subdue what is independent to their own group solidarity—to affirm the public self. Mr. Fulmino will be satisfied only by a colonized Hilda, a Hilda who requires his paternal aid, and he and the rest of Hincham Street do their best to transform the Hilda with whom they are initially faced to a proper state of dependency. An empire makes itself central, real, and authoritative by consigning someone else to the margin.

The Drapers assert the necessary dominance of connection so strongly because they are in fact flying apart (rather as the British Empire did after the Second World War); the public self is losing its meaning because there is no meaningful public entity in which it may exist. Significantly, terms of family relation—cousin, sister, aunt—are rarely employed in this tale, particularly for the younger generation; it takes one quite a while to work out the fact that Constance is Mrs. Fulmino's sister and both are Hilda's first cousins. The death of Mrs. Johnson draws an unexpected response from the community (mainly from people who barely knew her): "[it was] because she was a fragment in their minds, that her death affected them. They recognised that they themselves were not people but fragments" (p. 475). Her death even reduces Mr. Fulmino to a moment of helpless tears, whereupon "he looked at us with panic, astonished by this discovery of an unknown self" (p. 476)—the unacknowledged private man. The war having exploded Hincham Street's illusion of importance—"living in a period when events [had] reduced us to beings so trivial that we had no strong feeling of our own existence in relation to the world around us" (p. 468)—it curls all the more firmly upon itself. Rather than feel any anger at the newspaper stories that (relying on Mr. Fulmino's speculations) falsely report Hilda's ordeal at the hands of her Japanese captors, the neighborhood simply pretends that they always suspected that the news was mainly invention. Hilda alone seems to accept this depersonalization without delusion; her face is "eventless," "smooth and blank," "dead" (pp. 450, 482); "by the smallest twitch of a muscle, it became nothing" (p. 482). That she leaves Mrs. Draper's cramped, uncomfortable home after her mother's death disturbs the Drapers, for "grief ought to hold people together and it seemed too brisk to have started a new life so soon" (p. 476). Her freedom is consequently almost intolerable to the Drapers.

For the Drapers, for Mr. Fulmino in particular, nothing provides the security of a recognized, public self like a pension. Indeed, the pension that Harry's job as a librarian secures is a prerequisite to his being allowed to date Iris Fulmino. A pension, of course, provides more than a monetary security, as the neighborhood reaction—"The phrase 'the old pensioner' was one of envy, abuse and admiration" (p. 458)—testifies. To draw a pension is to have an officially recognized existence, to be connected to the great machinery of the state—to be someone. Mr. Fulmino's promotion assures him of one; Hilda has none (the Drapers inquire whether the Japanese government owes her one, given Shinji's status as a soldier). Indeed, Iris Fulmino equates the insecurity and freedom of pensionlessness with allegiance to Hilda—when Harry talks of abandoning his librarian's job to visit foreign places, she charges, "You're potty on that woman too. You all are" (p. 471).

The freedom Hilda represents (without herself ever actually possessing) is fundamentally sexual, as Iris' words imply. Her sexuality, like that of a celebrity or a fallen woman, is thoroughly objectified by the other characters as a repository for the secret desires they cannot themselves openly declare, as they barely acknowledge the private self. Hilda is invariably transformed, particularly by the narrator, Harry Fraser, into a veritable metaphor of objectified sexuality. Mrs. Fulmino, who becomes "demented"—"In bed," Mr. Fulmino cryptically says (p. 449)—imagines "above all" (p. 455) Hilda's unbearable sexual contact

with the nonwhite Mr. Singh and envisions her in Japan "captured, raped, tortured, murdered in front of her eyes" (p. 455); at her wedding, Hilda appears with "all the sexuality of an open flower" (p. 455); the narrator's brother used to whisper to his friends about his encounters with Hilda; the narrator himself notes that "if Hilda's face was eventless, it was the event itself, it was the dance" (p. 482), describes her as "the dream" (p. 475), and "a picture . . . that makes you feel sad because it is painted" (p. 462).

For Hilda herself, sexuality is no empowering freedom; she simply "takes care of herself" and does not conceal that she is doing so. She is not made cosmopolitan by travel either; she summarizes her reaction to the foreign lands in which she has lived by saying "I didn't see anything to them" (p. 491). This incomprehension, however, at least means she does not deceive herself by projecting her own desires on other nations. She alone does not make herself central by indulging in the fantasy of other nations as marginal. While the exigencies of the war have left "a closed door in everybody's conscience" (p. 469), Hilda is entirely open, explaining her past with the simple declaration "I had to eat" (p. 484). She informs the Drapers of her true war history as soon as she is aware that they have misconceived it, though she could self-servingly dissemble merely by accepting in silence the tale Mr. Fulmino has contrived. Constance, the old-style Marxist, is Hilda's most direct inverse. She is nothing but disguise, maintaining the pretense of acting solely on principle, rather than on private desires, by insisting that her unsavory lover, Bill Williams, is "politically educated." "Not his hands aren't," Hilda replies (p. 477). But even Harry Fraser, distant enough from the Drapers to recognize some of the dynamics behind their treatment of her, imputes a "strangeness" to Hilda that "had concealed [her] from us" (p. 484). Hilda is concealed only by the self-deception in the gaze of Hincham Street; the mask she wears is the mask they have fixed on her.

The Drapers, indeed, have always needed to make Hilda a fallen woman or a distant dream to avoid seeing themselves. When Hilda remarks on the attractiveness of one of the newspapermen at the beginning of the tale, Mr. Fulmino exclaims, "We've got the old Hilda back!" (p. 448), apparently referring to a prewar affair between Hilda and Harry's older brother that began Hilda's inadvertent career as a receptacle for other people's

323

fantasies. At the end of the tale, the Drapers seem to have at last reduced Hilda, whose flat has been robbed by Bill Williams, to their initial image of the pitiable fallen woman: "we had at last got her with us as we had, months before, expected her to be." But when Hilda at last returns their gaze, "seeing us for the first time," she perceives an old allegiance to public convention that has long provided Hincham Street with its illusion of importance and selfhood. "you're a mean lot, a mean respectable lot. . . . I remember you" (p. 489), she declares, and scoffs at the Fulmino suggestion to call in the police at once, for "you've got one in every house in this country" (p. 490). The story ends with a pronounced irony. The Mr. Gloster Hilda had announced was going to take her away and write about her "experiences" at last does so: "But Mr. Gloster's book came out. Oh yes. It wasn't about Japan or India or anything like that. It was about us" (p. 491). Hilda's experience has not been torture at the hands of Japan but at the hands of Hincham Street.

Indeed, the Japan and India about which the Drapers and Harry Fraser presume the book will be written are themselves the product of Hincham Street's desperate need to assert its own solidity; it defines its reality and centrality in reference to such fictional elsewheres. Mrs. Fulmino's fantasy of Hilda's being murdered "in front of her eyes" (p. 455) threatens to occur as reality in Hincham Street. Rather than being the inquiring subjects who judge Hilda as an object, the Drapers are transformed into the objects themselves. Having waited for Mr. Gloster as they once waited for Hilda, the Drapers never suspect that they will be the objects of his scrutiny. Hincham Street can no longer pretend that it is the standard of normality against which others are judged; it is itself measured on some foreign scale (Mr. Gloster is an American). Readers who believe themselves to have been reading a story about Hilda are jolted into recognizing that they have actually been reading the story of her interlocutors. Hincham Street's close reading of Hilda has revealed virtually nothing about Hilda herself—she is all on the surface anyway—but has instead uncovered the corruption of its own depths, the self-deceptions, distortions, and misinterpretations by which it maintains the very English illusion that it holds some sort of empowering position of judgment in a world of such size, variety, and incomprehensibility that no such position in fact exists.

THE KEY TO MY HEART

PRITCHETT'S most extended performance in the medium of the short story is the trilogy of tales published in 1963 as *The Key to My Heart*, which consisted of the previously published title story and two new sequels, "Noisy Flushes the Birds" and "Noisy in the Doghouse." The book employs a tartly comic tone unique in Pritchett's work; the book jacket of the American edition of the tales blithely announces that they "will surprise and delight readers who may have forgotten the simple pleasure to be had from a work of fiction." Blithely and inexplicably, for the humor of *The Key to My Heart*, while it often produces laughter, is ultimately sardonic almost to the point of bleakness. The work sounds unlike most Pritchett because its voice is inspired by the comic novels of H. G. Wells and Arnold Bennett; it bears a particularly close resemblance to Bennett's hugely popular *The Card* (1911). But Pritchett uses this voice to narrate a tale that precisely reverses the hopeful fantasies on which such works as *The Card* are founded.

The Key to My Heart follows the changing fortunes of Bob Fraser, the young owner of a provincial bakery, as he pursues first a large debt owed his business since his father's time by an eccentric member of the failing local aristocracy, Mrs. Brackett, and then Mrs. Brackett herself. Fraser lives with his tart-tongued mother, a champion of traditional differences who discourages her son's pursuit of both the bill and the woman, in a state of affectionate antagonism clearly inspired by the relations between Denry Machin (the Card himself) and his mother. The movement of the three stories is, until its last few pages, highly reminiscent of the typical Wells-Bennett comic plot. In "The Key to My Heart," Fraser's attempt to collect his debt results in Mrs. Brackett's payment of the outstanding bills of every merchant in town except him, as she blames him for the desertion of her husband, Noisy Brackett, a penniless race-car driver and all-purpose gadabout. Such is the origin of a fascination.

In "Noisy Flushes the Birds," Mrs. Brackett's husband returns to "steal" a cage of stuffed birds (actually his all along) that he needs to sell in order to remain flush. Noisy's escapade disguises another plot that escapes Bob Fraser's notice until it is fortunately too late. His mother conspires with Mrs. Brackett to break up by devious means an entirely unsuitable engagement between Bob, a proposing sort, and Claudia Dingle, whose "finishing school had finished her" (p. 581). By the start of the third tale, "Noisy in the Doghouse," Bob has realized that the woman he really wants to court is Mrs. Brackett. For a time, the tale seems to trace in their relationship a comic reconciliation of old and new orders, of an old landed class and a new monied one, of aristocrat and merchant. Noisy and Bob even seem to be changing places, with Noisy acting as the charming irresponsible son to Mrs. Fraser that she had always wanted to indulge, while Bob assumes Noisy's role as the lover and opponent of Mrs. Brackett. Such a resolution would put the trilogy firmly in the camp of *The Card*, a sort of capitalist fantasy (that Bennett knew perfectly well to be a fantasy) in which the monetary savvy of the middle-class Denry Machin and the aristocratic charity of the Countess of Chell work together for the betterment and entertainment of the Five Towns: the self-interest of business is magically arranged so that everyone makes a profit and nobody gets hurt.

But Pritchett withdraws such a resolution at the last moment—the effect is like that of seeing a promised oasis dissolve into sand as one finally reaches it—harking back instead to the older and crueler comic form of the fabliau. Bob pulls one joke too many on Mrs. Brackett and is requited by her and Noisy, who roar off in his car together, never to be seen again. The problem is precisely that Bob identifies himself too closely with Noisy; he describes to Mrs. Brackett as if she were real the paper cutout of an Argentine airline stewardess that Noisy has declared his new girl. Mrs. Brackett is not amused, announcing that "I don't like being mocked. I had ten years of that kind of thing with Noisy" (p. 619). No comic marriage ensues; no one crosses class lines; no new order arises from a union of differences. What humor the end of the trilogy generates, it generates by its ironic revision of the very sort of Edwardian fable it continually evokes. Rather than ending with an assumed future order, the set of stories ends on a note of radical uncertainty: "And then she [Mrs. Fraser] gets on to Teddy Longfellow saying there isn't any future, and I tell her I agree with him. A few weeks ago, Heading [Mrs. Brackett's estate] came up for sale. Mother says the class of trade is changing in our town" (p. 625). While the trilogy may not support the weight of being read as a warning about the irreconcilability of England's past and present and the unlikelihood of noblesse oblige and the profit motive improving each other, it certainly offers none of the fairy-tale reconciliation that comedy traditionally offers.

BLIND LOVE

THE title story in *Blind Love and Other Stories*—indeed, the volume as a whole—marks Pritchett's most significant departure from earlier forms. It was published in 1969, when Pritchett was nearly seventy years old. He had previously written few love stories, and virtually none in which love demonstrated the power to heal, rather than being an affliction in itself. Tales like "Blind Love" and "The Skeleton" offer in terms of personal relations all the reconciliation that *The Key to My Heart* denies in public ones. Indeed, "Blind Love" is almost an allegory of reconciliation. It abandons realism, the attempt to disguise the rhetoric of art as the coincidences of life, more fully than any work Pritchett had previously done (excepting such special cases as "The Ape," a beast fable), offering us symbols for elements of the human condition rather than representations of it. Nowhere is Pritchett's lifelong obsession with the double and the other more openly played out.

The protagonists of "Blind Love" serve at once as parallels to and opposites of each other. Mr. Armitage, a renowned lawyer, and Mrs. Johnson, his personal secretary, both suffer a profound defect: Armitage is blind and Johnson has an enormous, livid birthmark, a patch of wrongly pigmented bloodred skin that covers most of the left half of her torso. Armitage's wife left him when his blindness descended; Johnson's husband left her shortly after they were married, being first exposed to the stain on the wedding night. At the same time, the two are opposites, Mr. Armitage's defect being open and Mrs. Johnson's hidden, Mr. Armitage's an abnormality in perception, Mrs. Johnson's in being perceived. Opposite and yet complementary—Mr. Armitage, after all, cannot see Mrs. Johnson's mark—the couple eventually unite by a difficult path through which Pritchett at last resolves the doubts about the possibility of true human contact that had so long haunted his writing.

Mr. Armitage is not merely a blind lawyer, he is an incarnation of blind law: "he was the still figure, the law-giver" (p. 633). Pritchett uses his blindness as a metaphor for the substitution of the theoretic values and positions of things, their abstract, mental status, for sensual experience of them, for life itself. Mr. Armitage, from Mrs. Johnson's sighted perspective, "never went out. He lived in a system of tunnels" (p. 648). Mr. Armitage, indeed, lives within his own systems, has his own methods for organizing experience. Literally, he functions by scrupulously memorizing the positions of every utile object in his house and demanding that they never be moved; figuratively, he represents the refusal to acknowledge life's fearful asymmetry. He describes his own life as being "like trying to remember a dream" (p. 655). Such blindness is, of course, particularly a blindness to the independent existence of other consciousnesses. Pritchett implicitly identifies this unseeing self-absorption with masculinity—both Mr. Armitage and Mr. Johnson use precisely the same words to reprove Mrs. Johnson for disturbing their dreams: "I told you to leave me alone" (p. 636). The self-protective masculine desire for solitude is the consequence of a need to assert the primacy of the self; Mrs. Johnson, Pritchett reports, "hated confession; to her it was the male weakness—self-love" (p. 656). Even the start of the couple's affair involves no real contact. Mrs. Johnson accepts it as a revenge against her former husband, while Mr. Armitage initiates it by wandering into her bedroom on the pretense of needing her to set his watch: "He had the habit of giving orders. They were orders spoken into space—and she was the space, non-existent" (p. 642).

It takes the offices of the faith healer Wolverhampton Smith to cure Mr. Armitage's blindness—though not his physical blindness, nor in the fashion that Smith expects. The faith healer is another of Pritchett's bevy of Christian Scientists (though he never so identifies the religion); Smith denies the very existence of the body, though he himself weighs a hefty 16 stone (224 pounds). Exposure to this denial begins the process of Armitage's recovery, as he comes to recognize, not the unreality of the body, but the life-denying dream of bodilessness in which he has himself been living. He must experience helplessness to complete his cure, to escape the confinement of his own mind. When his secretary and lover falls (or jumps) into his pool, Armitage can do nothing but call for others to find and help her. The moment is cathartic: "Armitage made an effort to recover his system, but it was lost" (p. 665). When the story flashes forward from Johnson's near-drowning to the couple's present happiness, we see an Armitage who has at last allowed himself to depend on another person, rather than his own systems. Mr. Armitage and Mrs. Johnson have lodged, of course, in Italy, the eternal English symbol for life-giving anarchism, where "his system has broken down completely" (p. 666).

Mrs. Johnson's defect is equally and oppositely suggestive; while Armitage denies tangible experience in his assertion of the organizing self, Johnson denies the self in her assertion of the primacy of tangible experience. Mrs. Johnson desires most of all "to be simply a body" (p. 646). Indeed, initially one of the most difficult aspects of her work is the need to act as an observing intelligence for Mr. Armitage: "He obviously liked her version of the world, but it was a strain having versions" (p. 632). Mrs. Johnson's birthmark is paradoxically a sign of the body's importance to her; after all, her life has been made by the way men perceive her female body, by her husband's estrangement from the too raw, too living appearance of her birthmark (which stands for her gender itself). That Pritchett associates masculinity with vision (and its absence) and femininity with the body (and its imperfections) is at best troubling, but as in "The Sniff," the representative of each sex must escape its traditional bounds in order for contact to occur.

At first, the affair with her employer involves as little real contact for Mrs. Johnson as for Mr. Armitage. Her pleasure comes from the implicit deception of her situation, from flaunting the "stain" that he cannot see; indeed, it is the "shamed insulted woman in her, that blotched inhabitant" (p. 642) that responds to his first deep kiss. She thus takes revenge on Armitage "for not being able to see her" precisely by remaining unseen, playing at being the perfect body she could not be for her first husband, "and when she was ashamed of doing this the shame itself would rouse her desire: two women uniting in her" (p. 646). She suspects that her lover does not truly meet her, "that he was just filing this affair away in one of the systems of his memory," but at the same time she uses his blindness to heighten her awareness of her own body by contrast with his abstraction: "It often terrified her at the height of her pleasure that she was being carried into the dark where he lived. She knew she was not but she could not resist the excitement of imagining it" (p. 646).

Wolverhampton Smith plays as unlikely a part in the redemption of Mrs. Johnson as of her lover. While Mr. Armitage needs to experience helplessness, Mrs. Johnson needs to experience exposure—self-exposure, the admission that her own personal, subjective viewpoint exists within, but not as a mere accessory to, the body she would be. Smith begins her journey toward achieving it. Having accidentally seen Mrs. Johnson lying naked by Armitage's pool, Smith uses her secret to work on the blind man, claiming that prayer "had revealed to him that the Devil had put his mark on Mrs. Johnson" (p. 660). For Smith, of course, the body itself is the devil's mark, the body of a woman in particular. Throughout her affair with Mr. Armitage, Mrs. Johnson has "dreaded the word 'love'" (p. 656). Smith's insistence that the power of divine love can cure Mr. Armitage so annoys Mrs. Johnson that she at last asserts that "I love Mr. Armitage as he is" (p. 662). When they have returned home, Mrs. Johnson soon lets out "the wronged inhabitant inside her" (p. 664), revealing not only the birthmark she has kept secret from Armitage, but articulating her larger grievance at her imprisonment in other people's (primarily males) misperception. "I'm fed up with you blind people," she announces, significantly using the plural although Mr. Armitage is the only literally blind character in the story. "All jealousy and malice, just childish . . . I don't wonder your wife walked out on you. Pity the poor blind! What about other people?" (p. 664). She then storms out and falls or throws herself in the pool, her emergence from which marks the beginning of the couple's real contact, as Mr. Armitage's earlier rescue from it had begun their sexual affair. In Italy, Mr. Armitage "depends on her entirely," and she declares to him: "I love you. I feel gaudy!" (p. 666).

THE CAMBERWELL BEAUTY

THE title story of Pritchett's next collection, *The Camberwell Beauty and Other Stories* (1974), concerns the very snare from which the protagonists of "Blind Love" escape: using the lover to indulge a private obsession, and so never emerging from self-delusion into contact with the other, with life, and, for that matter, with the self. The tale follows the rivalry of three antiques dealers, Pliny, August, and the narrator, over August's niece, Is-abel. The victim of August's periodic attempts at sexual abuse, Isabel marries the old man, Pliny, from whose possession the narrator's courtship fails to dislodge her. The plot of "The Camberwell Beauty" can be paraphrased in a sentence; its richness of significance derives from its setting and its mode of narration. The antiques trade provides a perfect analogy to Pliny's relationship with Isabel. As the narrator observes near the beginning of the tale, "At the heart of the trade is lust but a lust that is a dream paralyzed by itself" (p. 827). This thick prose requires some unwinding. The apotheosis of an antique, as described in "The Camberwell Beauty," is a piece that has passed from a functional to an aesthetic object, and that finally lacks even a commercial utility—the dealer pursues it for the sheer delight of possession, with no intention ever to sell. Such obsession, however, defeats itself; to possess is equally to be possessed by, to lose joy in the precious object in fear of its loss. While Pliny's marriage to Isabel brings him to life, the life to which it brings him is mere nervous reaction; "He seemed to be possessed by a demon," the narrator reports, "he looked like a man expecting to be robbed" (p. 844). Pliny does not, in fact, even sleep with Isabel, though he does ritually undress her at night, satisfying his bodily desires instead with a venerable prostitute named Lal Drake.

Such ambiguous care is the most Isabel has ever learned to expect. She twice declares to the narrator, with no trace of conscious irony, "I am the most precious thing he [Pliny] has" (pp. 853, 855). Isabel's acceptance of her role, however, does not stem merely from her comparison of it to August's attempts to get into her bed. Two other women also affirm that Pliny's treatment of women is admirable, interpreting as protection what men in the tale interpret as confinement. When August charges that Pliny kept his mother locked in, Mrs. Price (Isabel's aunt and August's common-law wife) insists, "It was kindness" (p. 833), citing a previous burglary in the area. The tobacconist from whom the narrator seeks information about Isabel claims that Pliny "keeps her locked up like his mother"; his wife responds, "He worships her" (p. 845). While the narrator assumes that Pliny locks Isabel in when she is alone, he finds when he visits the shop that the door is in fact open. The same illusion viewed from opposite perspectives appears as two different illusions—the men (especially the narrator) do not recognize themselves as threats and so fail to comprehend how Isabel could prefer the security of Pliny; the women, having themselves been objects of male pursuit, do not recognize Pliny's protectiveness as another form of objectification.

Isabel's value as a possession springs precisely from her vitality in a world of old, dead objects and frozen desires. For the narrator, Isabel's defining moment is one of indefinition; he sees her trace the first four letters of her name on the top of a dusty cabinet. In the antiques trade, dust is a reminder of death—"even the dust is the dust of families that have gone" (p. 829)—which is precisely what moves the narrator about the scene: "I S A B—half a name, written by a living finger in dust" (p. 840). Even having obtained the age of twenty-five, Isabel remains Isab, remains childlike and incomplete—the narrator twice moves her in the last ten pages of the story by addressing her as "Isab . . ." (pp. 847, 855). But Pritchett avoids implying that Isabel's incompletion is merely a matter of her probable virginity or that accepting the narrator's love would complete her. While the narrator recognizes Isabel's need to escape the illusion of safety, the objectification that keeps her identity half-formed, he fails to perceive his own illusion. Far from being Isabel's deliverer, in the end he appears more to be Pliny's younger double.

Throughout "The Camberwell Beauty," the narrator takes too-elaborate pains to distance himself from the antiques world, and even from his own narrative. He contrasts himself with other dealers, declaring "I was in it for the money" (p. 832), yet soon runs himself out of business by overbuying; he introduces Isabel casually, with no hint as to his future relation to her—only well into the story does one realize that the narrator is a chief agent in the plot, not merely an observer. While he notes that the antiques business "is a trade that feeds illusions" (p. 831), while he is ready with such apparently self-aware observations as "we live on myths" (p. 834), the narrator is remarkably obtuse as to his own motives. He initially makes a metonymous transfer of his desire for Isabel to the jug he had seen her holding, a Caughley, the products of which company he decides—ironically, with a "thrill of revelation" (p. 839)—will be his official obsession as an antiques dealer. He seems not to comprehend that his awakened lust for "things enshrined and inaccessible," his "longing for possession" (p. 840), applies equally to his feelings for Isabel. Even though he says of his "pas-

sion for the girl" that "the fever of the trade had come alive in me; Pliny had got something I wanted" (p. 846), he continues to judge himself as morally superior to Pliny. He persists in this illusion all the more when Isabel challenges it. Informed again of Pliny's worship for his wife, the narrator observes that Isabel "seemed to be illumined by the simple knowledge of her own value and looked at my love as if it were nothing at all" (p. 856). His reaction inadvertently proves how little his love in fact is and the extent to which Isabel has reason to desire Pliny's protection; in effect, he momentarily contemplates rape: "I looked at the sofa and was so mad that I thought of grabbing her and pulling her down there" (p. 856). The moment turns almost instantly from ugly to comic when a blast from Isabel's bugle frightens the lust out of the narrator, but no enlightenment follows. When, after a short, unheroic fight with the returning Pliny, the narrator finds himself on the street, separated from Isabel for good, he thinks, "How unreal people looked in the sodium light" (p. 857). The unreality of his self-image goes unremarked.

ON THE EDGE OF THE CLIFF *AND* CARELESS WIDOW

MANY of the stories in Pritchett's *On the Edge of the Cliff and Other Stories* (1979) and *A Careless Widow and Other Stories* (1989) work variations on the familiar theme of the plunge, taken or refused, out of the self and into a love whose form is never what one would have predicted. In the earlier volume's "Tea with Mrs. Bittell," for instance, two lonely churchgoers take risks to relieve their loneliness; Mrs. Bittell, an elderly matron, befriends a young man named Sidney, who works at the tea counter of a large emporium. Sidney has fallen for Rupert, a former coworker who has unfortunately departed the country. Sidney's despondence turns to joy, however, when his and Mrs. Bittell's united prayers apparently have an effect: Rupert comes back. Rupert, however, proves to be an aspiring art thief whom Mrs. Bittell surprises stealing her Psyche—a painting she has long disregarded, as she has disregarded the "thee" (p. 1072) within her—her own psyche; that is, the unfulfilled self with its inconvenient desires and needs (though she has begun to note an answering "thee" in Sidney). Beating off Rupert with a lamp, Mrs. Bittell momentarily becomes "as strong as History" (p. 1081), then faints. Hearing the noise, the doorman and others apprehend Rupert attempting to escape. At the end of the story, the doorman answers the phone as Mrs. Bittell is murmuring for Sidney to come; Sidney, in fact, is the caller. While the doorman hangs up the phone before contact can be made, the attachment between Sidney and Mrs. Bittell is clearly more "sincere" (the tale's repeated word) than that between Sidney and Rupert. While Rupert symbolizes elevation to Sidney, to such a point that Sidney cannot really perceive him, Sidney meets Mrs. Bittell much more truly.

In *A Careless Widow,* one finds a similar, but more unambiguously hopeful, tale of unpredictable love compensating for life's failure to provide security: "A Change of Policy." A printer named George, whose wife, Ethel, is not expected to emerge from a long coma, begins an affair with Paula, who, after years of service, has just left a journal that George once printed. The change of policy that has led Paula to leave the journal comes to stand not only for the unexpected events that prevent human security, but for the only possible response to them as well. George reconsiders his fidelity to his stricken wife, and Paula reconsiders her initial decision not to sleep with George. To change one's mind seems to be the only way to attain any harmony with the changing world. After George is killed in a particularly random fashion (a fall from a horse), Ethel coincidentally recovers. Instead of the two women remaining locked each in her private loneliness, they finally wind up taking a house together in the tale's final change of policy; from Pritchett's language it is often hard to tell which woman qualifies as George's wife. Having started his literary career over seventy years earlier from a position skeptical even of the possibility of human contact, Pritchett at last arrives at the idea that human contact is the sole good; one must accept it in whatever form it takes, accept even its changes of form, if one is to live well.

CONCLUSION

V. S. Pritchett has frequently been commended for the believability of his stories. Many of his finest stories, however, are among his least plausible. Is it likely that a blind male lawyer should unknow-

ingly hire a disfigured female secretary and the two should ultimately wind up conjugally united in Italy, as in "Blind Love"? Is it likely that, as in "The Camberwell Beauty," a young man, briefly an antiques dealer, should be so obsessed with an even younger woman (whom he has barely seen do more than write her name in the dust) that he should corner her in her husband's shop, only to discover that her asexual relationship with her husband suits her fine? Too much fits too well to accept these stories (or, indeed, any stories) as truth; while the asexual marriage of "The Camberwell Beauty" certainly resembles situations one may know from real life, its convenient proximity to the symbol-laden antiques trade does not.

Nevertheless, in declaring Pritchett's work believable, critics have hinted at a crucial feature of it. The air of believability comes not from the lifelike construction of Pritchett's plots or the behavior of his characters, but from the dazzling accuracy of observation the author unfailingly achieves in his work. When, for instance, the narrator of "The Camberwell Beauty" reports: "You rarely see an antique shop standing on its own. There are usually three or four together watching one another" (p. 828), readers know that Pritchett is a man who has looked at antique shops. This scrupulous exactitude of observation is important not because it makes the tales seem believable, but because observation and recognition are precisely what the stories are typically about. Again and again in Pritchett's fiction, characters face dilemmas that involve seeing themselves, seeing others, and, above all, seeing themselves in others. Again and again, Pritchett returns to the theme of the double, for self-knowledge in Pritchett's world is ultimately a matter of observation—one can only know oneself by recognizing one's otherness, by seeing from the outside perspective of the double.

Whether V. S. Pritchett will attain the status in academic circles that is presently the only way for writers who do not work in a popular genre to retain a readership is not yet clear. His work certainly has the multidimensionality that allows a variety of contemporary critical approaches to make use of it, but it seems unlikely to have a special appeal to any one. Further, the short story is not so widely taught as is the novel, nor does Pritchett ensure himself a place in future syllabi by stylistic innovation; he does not expand the fundamental resources of the language of fiction in the way that Joyce or Woolf, Dickens or Austen did. But he has done all any writer can do and done it supremely well: he has told the stories he is capable of telling. Pritchett has created an identity for himself as a writer, a fusion of motives, techniques, and material that marks his stories as his own. Some future writer may, of course, speak so much more compellingly in Pritchett's voice as to make that voice his or her own, make Pritchett seem a mere precursor. But unless that happens, it is likely that Pritchett will continue to be read for the pleasure of his being so himself, for contributing to the variety of experience of those who care to experience variety rather than to search vainly for the literary prophet who will word the world as it really is.

SELECTED BIBLIOGRAPHY

I. COLLECTED WORKS. *Collected Stories* (London, 1956); *Selected Stories* (London and New York, 1978); *Collected Stories* (London and New York, 1982); *More Collected Stories* (London and New York, 1983); *The Other Side of the Frontier: A V. S. Pritchett Reader* (London, 1984); *The Complete Short Stories* (London, 1990), also pub. as *Complete Collected Stories* (New York, 1991); *The Complete Essays* (London, 1991), also pub. as *Complete Collected Essays* (New York, 1991).

II. SHORT STORIES. *The Spanish Virgin and Other Stories* (London, 1930); *You Make Your Own Life* (London, 1938); *It May Never Happen and Other Stories* (London, 1945); *The Sailor, Sense of Humour, and Other Stories* (New York, 1956); *When My Girl Comes Home* (London and New York, 1961); *The Key to My Heart: A Comedy in Three Acts* (London, 1963); *The Saint and Other Stories* (Harmondsworth, Eng., 1966); *Blind Love and Other Stories* (London and New York, 1969); *The Camberwell Beauty and Other Stories* (London and New York, 1974); *On the Edge of the Cliff and Other Stories* (London and New York, 1979); *A Careless Widow and Other Stories* (London and New York, 1989).

III. NOVELS. *Clare Drummer* (London, 1929); *Shirley Sanz* (London, 1932), repub. as *Elopement into Exile* (Boston, 1932); *Nothing Like Leather* (London and New York, 1935); *Dead Man Leading* (London and New York, 1937); *Mr. Beluncle* (London and New York, 1951).

IV. TRAVEL. *Marching Spain* (London, 1928); *The Spanish Temper* (London, 1954); *London Perceived* (London and New York, 1962); *Foreign Faces* (London, 1964), repub. as *The Offensive Traveller* (New York, 1964); *New York Proclaimed* (London and New York, 1965); *Dublin: A Portrait* (London and New York, 1967); *At Home and Abroad* (San Francisco, 1989).

V. BIOGRAPHY. *Balzac* (London and New York, 1973); *The Gentle Barbarian: The Life and Work of Turgenev* (London and New York, 1977); *Chekhov: A Spirit Set Free* (London and New York, 1988).

VI. LITERARY CRITICISM. *In My Good Books* (London, 1942); *The Living Novel* (London, 1946), rev. ed. *The Living Novel and Other Appreciations* (New York, 1964); *Why Do I Write?: An Exchange of Views Between Elizabeth Bowen, Graham Greene, and V. S. Pritchett*, with Elizabeth Bowen and Graham Greene (London and New York, 1948); *Books in General* (London and New York, 1953); *Shakespeare: The Comprehensive Soul* (London, 1965); *The Working Novelist* (London and New York, 1965); "The Short Story," in *London Magazine* (September 1966); *George Meredith and English Comedy: The Clark Lectures for 1969* (London and New York, 1970); *The Myth Makers: Essays on European, Russian, and South American Novelists* (London, 1979), also pub. as *The Myth Makers: Literary Essays* (New York, 1979); *The Tale Bearers: Literary Essays* (London and New York, 1980); "The Writer's Tale," in *Vogue* (March 1981); *A Man of Letters: Selected Essays* (London, 1985); *Lasting Impressions: Selected Essays* (London, 1990).

VII. MEMOIRS. *A Cab at the Door* (London, 1968); *Midnight Oil* (London, 1971); *The Turn of the Years* (Wilton, U.K., 1981).

VIII. AS EDITOR. *This England* (London, 1937); *Robert Louis Stevenson, Novels and Stories* (London, 1945); *Turnstile One: A Literary Miscellany from the* New Statesman and Nation (London, 1948); *The Oxford Book of Short Stories* (New York, 1981).

IX. CRITICAL STUDIES. John Vickery and J'nan Sellery, eds., "Ritual in the Streets: A Study of Pritchett's 'The Scapegoat,'" in their *Ritual and Literature* (Boston, 1972); John Mellors, "V. S. Pritchett: Man on the Other Side of a Frontier," in *London Magazine* (April-May 1975); Clare Hanson, *Short Stories and Short Fictions, 1880–1980* (New York, 1980); Walter Allen, "V. S. Pritchett," in his *The Short Story in English* (New York, 1981); Dennis Vannatta, "V. S. Pritchett," in *Critical Survey of Short Fiction 6*, ed. by Frank N. Magill (Englewood Cliffs, N.J., 1981); Douglas A. Hughes, "The Eclipsing of V. S. Pritchett and H. E. Bates: A Representative Case of Critical Myopia," in *Studies in Short Fiction 19* (fall 1982); William Peden, "Realism and Anti-realism in the Modern Short Story," in *The Teller and the Tale: Aspects of the Short Story*, ed. by Wendell M. Aycock (Lubbock, Tex., 1982); Alain Theil, *Les Nouvelles de V. S. Pritchett* (Clermont-Ferrand, France, 1982); Susan Lohafer, "'The Wheelbarrow' by V. S. Pritchett," in her *Coming to Terms with the Short Story* (Baton Rouge, La., 1983); William Peden, "V. S. Pritchett," in *The English Short Story, 1880–1945: A Critical History*, ed. by Joseph M. Flora (Boston, 1985); Dennis Vannatta, ed., *The English Short Story, 1945–1980* (Boston, 1985); Pascal Aquien, "'The Diver'; or the Plunge into Fantasy," in *Journal of the Short Story in English 6* (spring 1986); Genevieve

Doze, "Two Tentative Readings of 'Many Are Disappointed' by V. S. Pritchett," in *Journal of the Short Story in English* 6 (spring 1986); Claire Larrière, "Explosions and Catharses," in *Journal of the Short Story in English* 6 (spring 1986); Cecile Oumhani, "Water in V. S. Pritchett's Art of Revealing," in *Journal of the Short Story in English* 6 (spring 1986); Michel Pouillard, "V. S. Pritchett's 'The Aristocrat' as a One-Act Comedy," in *Journal of the Short Story in English* 6 (spring 1986); Alain Theil, "V. S. Pritchett's Quiet Expressionism," in *Journal of the Short Story in English* 6 (spring 1986); Pierre Yvard, "V. S. Pritchett and the Short Narrative in 'A Fly in the Ointment,'" in *Journal of the Short Story in English* 6 (spring 1986); Dean R. Baldwin, *V. S. Pritchett* (Boston, 1987); John J. Stinson, *V. S. Pritchett: A Study of the Short Fiction* (New York, 1992).

DOROTHY L. SAYERS

(1893–1957)

David Glover

Cora Kaplan

ALTHOUGH DOROTHY SAYERS will probably always be best known for her detective fiction, she was one of the most versatile as well as one of the liveliest writers of her generation. A book of poems written while she was a student at Oxford became her first publication, and her final project was a strikingly original translation of Dante's *Divine Comedy*, for which she taught herself medieval Italian at the age of fifty-two, and which was still in print forty years after its publication. In the intervening decades her multifaceted career cut a path through the worlds of advertising, journalism, drama, broadcasting, and popular literature. Its variety was made possible by the expanding mass media in Britain, but Sayers was driven at all times by her restless desire to try something new, even if what was new was sometimes a modern reincarnation of traditional culture. A productive tension between progressive social ideas and a more conservative view of art and morality runs across and through her work in different genres and media. Passionate in her love of learning, frequently outspoken in her opinions, and immensely hardworking, in her later years Sayers developed into an important public intellectual whose influence stretched far beyond the large and devoted following she had won in the 1920s and 1930s for her crime novels. Grabbing with both hands and with an inventive zest the enlarged opportunities that full civic rights offered to women of her generation, she became a new kind of twentieth-century figure, a nationally respected woman of letters.

During the period between the two world wars, Sayers's formative years as a writer, every branch of the popular arts in Britain underwent a sea change. New media like film and radio started to play a central role in national life, and older industries like publishing experienced a steadily rising demand for fiction of all kinds. Even in the worst depths of the economic depression, annual book sales reached a record 7.2 million, a figure that had soared to 26.8 million by 1939. Then, as now, there was a huge audience for detective fiction, but in the 1920s a stylistic revolution took place, a transformation that led to what has been dubbed the genre's Golden Age. What defined this new era was not merely the rise of a new type of writer, including the growing prominence of women as authors. The very form taken by crime narratives began to change as the short story, epitomized by the adventures of Sir Arthur Conan Doyle's Sherlock Holmes, was rapidly eclipsed by a new streamlined version of the detective novel that bore little resemblance to its mid-nineteenth-century ancestors.

Much of the appeal of the short story had been based on its brisk pace and concentrated focus on a single problem, which tended to make the novel appear rambling and unwieldy by comparison. But once the economics of publishing had started to shift in favor of shorter novels at around the turn of the century, it became feasible to produce a novel-length detective narrative that still provided a tightly framed puzzle, with clues and plots far more intricate than anything the relatively compressed form of the short story could offer. The enjoyment of reading these new detective novels came from a sense of pitting one's wits against the author, sorting out the real clues from the red herrings, and piecing together the scattering of evidence that would infallibly reveal the identity of the guilty party. Sometimes these novels were promoted as competitions in which readers were offered cash prizes if they could work out the correct solution, and Sayers herself even toyed with the idea of putting part of the answer to one of her mysteries in a sealed envelope at the back of her novel *The Five Red Herrings*. Detective fiction was often half-seriously treated as a kind of game with ideal rules and conventions.

Sayers was one of the founding figures in the Golden Age, alongside her friend and rival Agatha Christie. Ironically, neither of their first novels sold particularly well, and both Christie's *The Mysterious Affair at Styles* (1920) and Sayers's *Whose Body?* (1923) at first had trouble finding publishers. Yet by the late 1920s Sayers and Christie had become "Queens of Crime," each in her different way opening up new directions for the detective novel. While Sayers never quite matched Christie in the ingenuity of her plots, her writing significantly raised the literary quality of crime fiction and brought it closer to the modern novel. Unlike the shy Christie, Sayers was an engaging public speaker who also acted as an eloquent and thoughtful advocate for her chosen genre, becoming one of its best-known and most well informed critics. By the summer of 1930, Sayers's work could be heard over the airwaves as part of the new public broadcasting service, and she was invited to give radio talks on aspects of the detective novel or on how she spent her working week. Between 1933 and 1935 Sayers wrote a weekly review of new detective fiction for the influential *Sunday Times,* a column that played a key role in helping to shape popular taste as the Golden Age neared its peak. The reviewer's importance in such a vast market was pivotal, for by the end of the 1930s detective fiction accounted for one-quarter of all fiction being published in Britain.

LIFE AND BACKGROUND

DOROTHY Leigh Sayers was born in Oxford on 13 June 1893. Her father was an Anglican clergyman and headmaster of the Christ Church Choir School, but toward the end of 1897 he took up a far better paid position as rector in the Cambridgeshire village of Bluntisham, a post that allowed him to provide adequate support and a spacious home for his grandmother and a maiden aunt. In his new role, the Reverend Henry Sayers was expected to be a pillar of what was a rather remote rural community. All the women in this extended household, especially his wife, Helen, helped him with his parish duties and responsibilities. Dorothy enjoyed a comfortable middle-class upbringing, though she later complained that it had been overprotective and sometimes lonely. She was educated at home until the age of fifteen, learning French and German from private tutors and Latin from her father, who started coaching her when she was six. When she did begin boarding school, her quick mind and her gift for languages had already made it clear to her parents that this would be a necessary stepping-stone to a university education. In March 1912 she won a scholarship to Somerville College in Oxford.

If English universities were the exclusive preserve of an elite, women university students were a minority within a minority, a situation that mirrored the wider social disadvantages experienced by women in that period. It took until 1918 for women over thirty to gain the right to vote and a further ten years before women were put on the same electoral footing as men. Although Somerville College had been founded in 1879, at the time Sayers was a student there women were still not allowed to receive degrees, despite following the same curriculum and taking the same examinations as men. Sayers proved herself a brilliant scholar, completing all the qualifications for a first-class honors degree in modern languages in 1915. Yet she had to wait until the rules were changed in 1920 before she could be awarded her B.A. and M.A. retroactively, which made her one of the first women officially to gain an Oxford degree. Oxford left a lasting impression on her, and Somerville served as the model for the women's college depicted in her finest novel, *Gaudy Night* (1935).

Upon leaving Oxford, Sayers tried her hand at a variety of jobs, but always with high hopes of a literary career of some kind. At first she found employment as a teacher of modern languages at a girls' school in Hull, but she did not enjoy the experience enough to stay long. She had been writing poetry since childhood and had begun to publish her work through the Oxford publisher Basil Blackwell, who later gave her a job editing new manuscripts. After a two-year stint with Blackwell, she worked briefly as an assistant to a friend who was teaching in a school in France, then returned to England, where she was eventually hired as a copywriter by the London advertising firm of S. H. Benson. Financially and personally, this was a very turbulent and uncertain period of her life. The early years in London were a struggle. There was fierce competition for jobs between the demobilized male soldiers returning from the war and the women who had replaced them. Once she had found employment at Benson's she did well, but her emotional life was less than stable. Early in 1924 she gave birth to an illegitimate son, a closely guarded secret she confided only to her cousin and childhood friend Ivy Shrimpton, whom she persuaded to act as the baby's foster mother. Sayers never told her parents what had happened, nor did she marry the boy's father. But in April 1926 her parents were surprised, and perhaps a little shocked, by her sudden announcement that she was about to marry a divorced Scottish journalist named Oswald Atherton Fleming, better known as Mac, who worked as the motoring correspondent for Britain's best-selling Sunday paper, the *News of the World*.

Sayers's rackety, unconventional years in London offer few hints of the respectable and rather conservative figure she was later to become. We see her riding round the city on her motorcycle, drinking with reporters in Fleet Street pubs, and playing the saxophone at the advertising agency's Christmas dances. The 1920s were also an extraordinarily productive period for Sayers. Before she landed the job at Benson's she had already completed the manuscript for her first detective novel starring Lord Peter Wimsey and was hard at work on a sequel. British publishers were slow to show an interest in her work, so she signed up with an enthusiastic literary agent shortly before starting her new career in advertising, and a few months later he found her a publisher in New York. A British contract quickly followed, and Sayers was on her way. She published three more Wimsey novels and a book of short stories in the 1920s, and in 1929 she signed a contract with an American publisher, which gave her a regular income without having to wait for royalties and advances. She was now making enough money to allow her to resign from Benson's and become a full-time writer.

In the 1930s seven more Wimsey novels and ten additional Wimsey short stories appeared, together with sundry other pieces of detective fiction, including a non-Wimsey novel entitled *The Documents in the Case* (1930), on which she worked with a doctor who specialized in providing crime writers with medical information for their books.

Other collaborative ventures followed. She had become a founding member of the Detection Club, a private society of mystery writers formed in 1929, to which some of the leading detective novelists of the period, including Agatha Christie and Anthony Berkeley, also belonged. Among the many activities of this group was the organization of collectively written serials, for which each individual author wrote an episode. The first of these, *Behind the Screen*, was broadcast over the radio in the summer of 1930, and three serials were published over the course of the decade with Sayers as coauthor. The Wimsey stories had become a huge success, but Sayers's literary ambitions drove her to extend the mystery format as far as she could until, impatient with what she felt to be the genre's limitations, she abandoned it. The last two Wimsey short stories to be published in her lifetime came out in 1939. They were later reissued in a posthumous collection entitled *Striding Folly* (1972), which also included a previously unpublished Wimsey story written in 1942. Her last Wimsey novel, *Busman's Honeymoon*, appeared in 1937, and despite rumors, entreaties from fans, and false starts, there were no more.

Meanwhile she was beginning to explore new territory. The enormous popularity of the Lord Peter Wimsey books brought Sayers many proposals to adapt her hero for stage and screen, and so in the early 1930s she tried her hand at scripting a Wimsey film. But when *The Silent Passenger* was shown in 1935, it was clear that Sayers's own work had been ignored in the final script and, worse still, Wimsey had been altered beyond all recognition. After this disastrous experience Sayers never wrote for the cinema again, and it was only with the encouragement of Muriel St. Clare Byrne, an old college friend who taught drama in London, that she was persuaded to attempt a play. The two women collaborated on *Busman's Honeymoon* in 1935, and Sayers turned the script into a novel while the play was awaiting production. First staged in Birmingham on 9 November 1936, *Busman's Honeymoon* played more than five hundred performances in London's West End and also went on tour.

Around the same time, Sayers was asked by the organizer of the Canterbury Festival if she would write one of the annual religious plays that were performed in the cathedral each summer. *The Zeal of Thy House* was staged in 1937, continuing a distinguished tradition that had begun with

T. S. Eliot's celebrated *Murder in the Cathedral* two years earlier. Sayers's historical drama examined the events leading up to the tragic accident suffered by William of Sens, the ambitious architect who took charge of the restoration of the cathedral after it had been partially destroyed by fire in 1174. The production was so successful that Sayers was commissioned to write a second play, and two years later *The Devil to Pay*, her version of the Faust legend, was also performed at Canterbury. Both plays dealt with the question of redemption, a subject that would figure strongly in her later religious drama, including *The Man Born to Be King*, a cycle of radio plays based on the life of Christ (which became a best-seller when it was released as a book in 1943); the Lichfield Cathedral miracle play *The Just Vengeance* (1946); and her theatrical chronicle *The Emperor Constantine*, for the 1951 Colchester Cathedral Festival.

Moral and religious issues preoccupied her increasingly during the Second World War, when she was extremely active as a lecturer and writer on Christian themes. The title of a collection of her talks published just after the war, *Creed or Chaos? and Other Essays in Popular Theology* (1947), captures the intent behind her spirited interventions and her commitment to making matters of church doctrine accessible to ordinary—though, in practice, largely middle-class—people. Although she continued to lecture on detective fiction from time to time, she was now more likely to be heard addressing ecclesiastical conferences on the relationship between church and state or speaking to British troops on the need for religious faith. Like T. S. Eliot and other intellectuals of her day, she became passionately involved in discussions of how best to build a new society when peace came. Early in the war she published *Begin Here: A War-Time Essay* (1940), in which she argued for the importance of men and women finding fulfillment and creativity in their work. Capitalizing on the popularity of her detective hero, she wrote a series of morale-boosting letters by members of the Wimsey family that engagingly described their wartime conditions; she also slipped in a plea to her readers on the urgency of thinking about future social reforms. Politically Sayers was strongly antisocialist, yet she was highly critical of what she considered capitalism's wastefulness and "soul-destroying" mass production, a view confirmed and intensified with the onset of the war. Though she was always predominantly a reli-

gious rather than a political thinker, she seems to have shared the widespread desire in the interwar years for an alternative economic system—a "third way" between state planning and the free market.

Once the war had ended most of her energies were absorbed in translating Dante, whose *Divine Comedy* she had discovered while sheltering from German missiles. She devoted the last fourteen years of her life to this project and would often give talks to both academic and popular audiences about translating or teaching Dante or on the meaning of his poetry. She could never quite shake her reputation as a writer of detective fiction, however. Though her English rendering of Dante could be heard on the radio, there was a continuing demand for readings and dramatizations of her Wimsey books, and early in October 1947 *Busman's Honeymoon* became one of the very first plays to be shown on British television. Sayers never lived to complete her translation of Dante, but by the time of her death she was firmly established as a widely respected, if somewhat eccentric, national figure. In her later years she showed signs of unease about the role she had assumed as a lay theologian, which she felt was a distraction from her real work as a creative writer. She declined the Church of England's offer of an honorary Doctorate of Divinity for precisely this reason, preferring to be known above all as a literary scholar. Endlessly fascinated by the ephemera of modern consumerism, from advertising jingles to cartoons, she looked to the church and the university as repositories of timeless values. She died from a stroke on 17 December 1957 at her home in Witham, Essex.

EARLY FICTION

Lord Peter Wimsey makes his first appearance in *Whose Body?* (1923), where he is introduced as a wealthy young aristocrat, excessively flippant in manner, yet highly cultured, living in a luxurious apartment in the heart of London with his manservant, Bunter. His irreverence is signaled by the opening words of the novel, Wimsey's exclamation of "Oh, damn!" as he instructs his taxi driver to make a U-turn in heavy traffic, "under the severe eye of a policeman" (chap. 1). This is Wimsey in hot pursuit, the enthusiastic amateur ready to bend the rules in a good cause, but here he is only tracking down a catalog he has forgotten to bring with him to a rare-book sale. In a few economical pages Sayers sketches in her hero's definitive attributes: his overelaborate courtesy, the light-hearted banter with his butler, his striking if less than dazzlingly handsome looks, with a "long, amiable face" that seems "as if it had generated spontaneously from his top hat, as white maggots breed from Gorgonzola" (chap. 1). But for all his slightly ironic attention to the niceties of dress and decorum we soon glimpse another, more serious side to Wimsey and quickly sense that his careless dilettantism is a kind of mask. Investigating murders may be his hobby, but when we observe his solitary preparations for starting a new case there is a speed and precision "one might not have expected from a man of his mannerisms" (chap. 1). He is, as he "whimsically" announces himself, "Sherlock Holmes, disguised as a walking gentleman" (chap. 1).

This tension between witty high spirits and a clear-eyed and altogether more sober outlook is characteristic of all the Wimsey books, though the balance between them varies considerably from novel to novel. By the time we have reached the conclusion of *Whose Body?*, Wimsey's studied elegance has been offset by the revelation that his nerves have suffered badly as a result of his experiences as a soldier in the First World War and that he is prone to debilitating nightmares that bring him to the point of breakdown. There are, then, several Wimseys, and if his different selves do not always quite add up, they are held together by the unflagging exuberance and inventiveness of Sayers's writing, which keeps the mystery bubbling along at a rapid pace. Some of the immediate influences on her work are not hard to spot. The jokey relationship between Wimsey and Bunter is in part a reincarnation of P. G. Wodehouse's comic creations Bertie Wooster and his butler Jeeves, and Sayers's light-handed touch with a detective narrative also borrows from *Trent's Last Case* (1913), E. C. Bentley's "well-thought-out little work" (chap. 13), which receives an approving nod in the final chapter. And the murder mystery itself has a paradoxical quality worthy of G. K. Chesterton, its title challenging the reader to find the missing link between the unidentified corpse found in an architect's bath and the powerful financier who has simultaneously disappeared without a trace in rather curi-

ous circumstances. Yet Sayers's resort to allusion and pastiche carries her far beyond mere eclecticism, and the use she makes of these borrowings is very much her own.

Whose Body? is an immensely confident first novel, its author not afraid to tease her readers by flaunting her predecessors or to construct an ingenious conjuring trick that emphasizes its own illusoriness. We are never allowed to forget that this is above all a literary performance, bookish and knowing, but full of fun. If detective fiction was developing a tendency toward academicism, which manifested itself in a near obsession with rules of evidence and logical procedure, Sayers accentuated the verbal exhilaration of mimicry and wordplay, so that in her novels language becomes as much of a game as is working out the solution to the mystery. Lord Peter's shrewdly scatter-brained mother, the Dowager Duchess of Denver, exemplifies this ebullient verbosity to perfection with her perceptive yet oddly rambling mode of delivery, twisting and turning as thought or word associations take her fancy, sounding like a parody of a stream-of-consciousness monologue. Imitating a coroner she has been observing in court, the Duchess describes "the little man, leaning forward and screaming" at a female witness who refuses to be intimidated, "and so crimson in the face and his ears sticking out so—just like a cherubim in that poem of Tennyson's—or is a cherub blue?—perhaps it's a seraphim I mean—anyway, you know what I mean, all eyes, with little wings on its head" (chap. 7).

In addition to such freewheeling literary allusions, the novel comes replete with footnotes, striking a mock-pedantic note that corrects Lord Peter's bibliographical errors, invents histories for some of the volumes in his valuable collection, or cites legal chapter and verse in support of his criminological theories. In fact, *Whose Body?* glitters with an awareness of its own artifice, and Wimsey himself is more than a little conscious that his mind "had been warped in its young growth by 'Raffles' and 'Sherlock Holmes,' or the sentiments for which they stand" (chap. 11), the inevitable legacy of an upper-class education. However, as the novel moves toward its denouement and the murderer has finally to be reckoned with, Wimsey's schoolboy romanticism starts to come under strain, momentarily puncturing the novel's air of innocent unreality. As Lord Peter's friend and colleague Charles Parker, a police officer from Scotland Yard, unpleasantly insists in one of the book's harsher passages: "you want to look pretty, you want to swagger debonairly through a comedy of puppets or else to stalk magnificently through a tragedy of human sorrows and things" (chap. 7). But this sort of elegant gamesmanship proves ultimately impossible. The moral solemnity of the law cannot be reduced to a sporting challenge, a round of hide-and-seek played by the criminal and the detective.

Of course, this tough-minded realism is far from being the dominant tone of the novel, but it does show that, even at this very early stage, Sayers was prepared to take her entertainments seriously, to give them a moral edge. One of the most significant lines of conflict in the book is between the religiously inspired moral vision articulated by Parker, a policeman who reads theology in his spare time, and the criminal psychology advanced by the surgeon Sir Julian Freke. Freke claims that the ordinary human ability to distinguish good from evil is merely a physiological property of the brain, which, like any other vital organ, is amenable to surgical intervention and modification. Contrary to the common assumption that our moral sense is an indispensable component of modern civilization, Freke suggests that the promptings of the human conscience may actually impede the survival of the fittest by arbitrarily restricting the range of possible individual behavior. Nothing could stand in greater contrast to Wimsey's fanciful verbal flights than the leaden cadences of Freke's controversial treatise, with its evasive abstractions and specious philosophical jargon. So it is no accident that when Wimsey suddenly sees how the pieces of the mystery fit together, his intuition is virtually a mystical experience, a kind of revelation in which he feels "as if he stood outside the world and saw it suspended in infinitely dimensional space" (chap. 8). Yet, as Sayers deliberately emphasizes in the very next paragraph, Wimsey's insight is also like the unconscious solving of a riddle, something that Freke, an avowed opponent of Sigmund Freud, could never hope to understand.

Sayers's other Wimsey novels from the 1920s continue to develop the characters she introduced in *Whose Body?* while drafting in some interesting new additions. In the first book, Wimsey's props—his monocle with its powerful magnifying lens, his silver matchbox that doubles as an electric flashlight, his silver-headed walking stick containing a sword and compass—all underscore the essential independence of the true hero, ably assisted by some occasional photography and below-stairs interrogations by the redoubtable Bunter. But, beginning with the sequel, *Clouds of Witness* (1926), Wimsey starts to acquire a network of confederates who help him in his work, including the family lawyer Mr. Murbles and the barrister Sir Impey Biggs, K.C. In the third book, *Unnatural Death* (1927), Sayers introduces one of her most important creations, Miss Alexandra Katherine Climpson, the spinster detective. At the same time, figures like the rather stolid Detective-Inspector Parker are more sympathetically treated, so that in *Clouds of Witness* we gain an appreciation of this provincial lower-middle-class police officer's need to escape to London from the north of England, where his unmarried elder sister still lives "a rather depressing life in Barrow-in-Furness" (chap. 5). Wimsey too takes on new qualities. In *Clouds of Witness* he is desperately trying to prove his brother innocent of murder, and his dashing manner becomes by turns abstracted, manic, and morose. By putting the spotlight on Lord Peter's family, the novel examines the peculiarities of the English nobility, revealing a strain of stubbornness in the Wimsey clan that is its greatest weakness as well as its greatest strength. After a climactic courtroom drama, the novel ends with a comic scene of aristocratic excess: Lord Peter perched drunkenly on a statue near the Houses of Parliament using an empty champagne bottle for a telescope.

As the series progressed, the Wimsey novels increasingly blended pointed social comment and satirical portraiture into the mystery format. *Unnatural Death*, for example, looks at the contemporary condition of women from a variety of angles. While Wimsey tracks down the murder suspects, Sayers gingerly and inconclusively explores the moral psychology of lesbianism through the juxtaposition of two very different lesbian couples, and a kind of protofeminist debate is staged as to the nature of women's friendships compared with those between men. References in the novel to "superfluous women" and "the flapper vote," phrases culled from the popular journalism of the period, indicate the wider context in which these issues were being posed. For the combination of a growing demographic imbalance between the numbers of men and women in the British population after the First World War, together with intense competition for jobs as soldiers were demobilized, exacerbated male fears of what might happen if the franchise were extended to younger women. Indeed, Sayers's own difficulties in finding employment in London in the early 1920s were in large measure a result of the decline in the female labor force when men began to return home from the war. When Lord Peter draws on the services of Miss Climpson in *Unnatural Death*, he offers a staunchly male feminist defense of the "superfluous women" whose "useful energy" is wasted "by our stupid social system" (chap. 3). Thanks to Wimsey's patrician concern, Miss Climpson is spared the feelings of redundancy experienced by Charles Parker's spinsterly sister.

By contrast, much of the pathos of *The Unpleasantness at the Bellona Club* (1928) stems from a concern with the plight of First World War veterans, military men who are no longer needed by the society for which they once risked their lives. George Fentiman, one of the suspects in the mysterious death of an aged general at the club, typifies the ex-soldier's dilemma. Fentiman, who is the general's grandson, gave up his job to volunteer for military service but was injured at the front and invalided out of the army. He is currently unemployed, in poor health, and has been reduced to renting a cheap two-room flat in a seedy part of London. Chronically short of money and dependent on his wife's meager earnings, he is touchy and quarrelsome and repeatedly blames "these hard-mouthed, cigarette-smoking females" for his inability to find "a decent job" (chap. 7). In fact, despite the customary verve of Sayers's writing, this is often a rather ill-tempered book. The euphemism "unpleasantness" runs like a distasteful leitmotif throughout the story and, among other unedifying incidents, we even see Wimsey and Parker squabbling.

The clash between the fusty but increasingly discontented world of military traditionalism and the arty young bohemians who congregate in fashionable Chelsea forms the ethical center of the book. Like her earlier lampooning of the leftist Soviet Club in *Clouds of Witness*, Sayers's portrayal of the youthful social whirl of studios and parties casts a critical eye on the pretensions of the younger generation, and she continues to satirize her contemporaries in the next Wimsey novel, *Strong Poison* (1930). In each instance, Sayers treads a careful path between the dead weight of

received morality and the misguided attempt to dispense with the lessons of the past completely. A key scene in *The Unpleasantness at the Bellona Club* comes when Lord Peter confronts the young and bitterly unhappy heiress Ann Dorland and talks about the effect the war has had on him as a way of getting her to open up about her own problems. He succeeds in dispelling her self-doubts and illusions and persuades her to let go of her romantic dreams of being dominated by a powerful man. Instead she needs to come to terms with her own resourceful intelligence and to recognize that in any partnership hers "will be the leading brain of the two" (chap. 21).

Sayers's attempts to reimagine the meaning of ordinary domesticity for women were never simple or easy, and however forthright her views on the relationship between the sexes could sometimes be, she was characteristically cautious and conservative in her response to the feminism of her period. Nevertheless, when Sayers writes as a moralist, whether in her popular fiction or in her later essays, her arguments are largely shaped by her engagement with the legacy of the early-twentieth-century women's movement.

GENRE AND ENGLISH LITERARY CULTURE

To read any of the Sayers Wimsey novels from the 1920s is to enter a densely structured textual field whose literary signposts seem to point in any number of directions. In *Clouds of Witness*, for example, each chapter has an epigraph that foreshadows what is to follow, and these quotations are from such varied sources as Shakespeare, Dickens, *Alice's Adventures in Wonderland*, and the *Adventures of Sexton Blake*. While the enjoyment of the mystery does not hinge upon appreciating the aptness of these oddly assorted references, Sayers's attempt to link her novels to a wider literary culture does shed an instructive light on the kind of audience she ideally sought—neither too snobbish to take pleasure in the more vulgar forms of popular fiction, nor lacking in the education required to recognize true literary worth. More than any other cultural marker in Sayers's novels, the books she invokes are meant to orient the reader's responses and judgments by underscoring the finer points of character and narrative or by standing in for a more complex set of values.

In *The Unpleasantness at the Bellona Club*, for example, the discovery that Ann Dorland has been reading D. H. Lawrence and Virginia Woolf indicates that part of her problem is that she has been stuffing her head with misguided ideas. Better to be like Detective-Inspector Parker, who, when he is not reading theology or Conan Doyle, is very fond of Thomas Hardy, a taste he shares with Miss Climpson.

If detective fiction offers an antidote to what Sayers felt to be the pretentiousness or irrationalism of literary modernism, what relationship do her own books bear to the traditions of the English novel? In the essays on the art of the mystery story she wrote during the late 1920s and early 1930s, we find Sayers trying to think through her position on this question, often changing her mind as she does so. In her editorial introduction to the first volume of *Great Short Stories of Detection, Mystery, and Horror* (1928), Sayers sketches out a brief history of detective fiction whose turning point comes, conventionally enough, in the 1840s, through the work of Edgar Allan Poe. Although it is possible to identify a multitude of social and cultural antecedents to the mystery story, Poe is the writer who effectively created the genre in the form we know today and who invented several of its most distinctive plots and variations. More critical, after Poe's death the different strands found in his writing tended to become polarized, as crime fiction began to pull in two opposite directions. Sayers labels these the "Sensational" and the "Intellectual." Usually known as the "thriller," the former emphasizes excitement and atmosphere, with one dramatic episode following rapidly upon another, pushing the narrative to the brink of incoherence in a bid to hold the reader's attention. In the intellectual detective story, by contrast, coherence is all, and in place of the thrill of the chase we are offered the "quiet enjoyment of the logical" (p. 15).

As her account of their respective pleasures suggests, Sayers makes no bones about which of these two developments she considers to be superior, explicitly referring to the intellectual branch of the genre as "the higher type" (p. 44). Throughout her essay, Sayers consistently aligns the detective story with the life of the mind, so that reading and reasoning become closely intertwined. In her stress on the modern doctrine of "fair play" (the insistence that the reader and the fictional detective have equal access to the same clues in getting

to the bottom of the mystery), Sayers was voicing the view that became the orthodoxy of the influential Detection Club. In the club's seriocomic initiation ceremony, largely drafted by Sayers, new members were required to recite an oath forswearing the use of such unfair practices as mysterious poisons unknown to science, concealed clues, or reliance on feminine intuition. Many of the highly popular Sherlock Holmes stories fail to meet this austere standard, for as Sayers is at pains to point out, Conan Doyle's narratives are hybrids that frequently withhold vital pieces of information in order to create sensational effects, and he employs the deductive method merely as a ruse to bamboozle his audience. Yet where the rules of the game are strictly observed, the detective story often finds itself confined to a purely formal perfection. Its logical, objective stance distances it from the extremes of human feeling and prevents it from reaching the heights of artistic achievement.

Sayers's essay contains many shrewd insights into the genre but, instructively, hardly any of her own work from the 1920s really fits the categories she devised. Novels like *Whose Body?* or *Unnatural Death* are too stylishly playful to be hobbled by literary convention, and Sayers plays fast and loose with the reader's expectations. In both books the manner in which the murder is committed is deliberately made far more mysterious than the murderer's identity, and Sayers's literary references, like the American hard-boiled crime magazine left behind at the scene of a murder in *Unnatural Death,* add an extra twist to the mystery's impenetrability. Although Sayers argues in her 1928 essay that the thriller is the pastime of the "uncritical" rather than the "educated" reader, there is plenty of evidence that her own imagination could readily be sparked by this type of writing. Neither the car chase at the end of *Unnatural Death* nor the elaborate secret society of supercriminals in the Lord Peter Wimsey short story "The Adventurous Exploit of the Cave of Ali Baba" in *Lord Peter Views the Body* (1928) would have seemed out of place in a 1920s thriller. Indeed, as Sayers makes clear in her first novel, the character of Wimsey owes something to Raffles, the gentleman-burglar hero of E. W. Hornung's adventure stories. But the more she gained in reputation and stature as a writer, the harder it became for Sayers to turn to the thriller for amusement and inspiration, and the more her anxieties began to focus on the future of the detective novel itself.

Foremost among Sayers's fears was that the rational type of detective story might reach a point where its own technical ingenuity would be exhausted, and all the tricks of the writer's trade would have become known and predictable. Looking for a way out of this impasse, she suggested that Wilkie Collins' *The Moonstone* (1868) was one of the few detective novels that genuinely extended the range of the genre by its successful combination of a mystery story with a romance. Collins was a model writer for Sayers, and during the late 1920s she wrote several chapters of a critical biography of Collins, which she was never able to finish. In the surviving manuscript she argues that Collins was a quintessentially English writer, hardheaded but possessing a flair for melodrama, and displaying what she regards as a typically English male ambivalence toward women—including a marked hostility to women intellectuals. Sayers traces Collins' gradual emergence as a professional man of letters, examines the influence of his family background, and assesses the strengths and weaknesses of his early literary successes. Her study comes to a halt in the mid-1850s, some years before his finest work had been produced, but already we can see the outline of a new history of popular literature beginning to appear, in which Collins stands with the ordinary reader against the highbrow or the literary critic. In Sayers's view, Collins is a much more important writer than had previously been recognized, one whose work encouraged his friend Charles Dickens to construct his plots in the more intricate mode of *Bleak House* and the unfinished *Mystery of Edwin Drood.*

Sayers's high regard for Collins was unusual for her time, and in some respects her judgment anticipates the reappraisal of this author that began gathering momentum in the late 1970s. She saw Collins' work as an essential resource for mystery writers and believed it suggested ways in which detective fiction might be brought closer to the mainstream novel without becoming trapped in what she regarded as the dead end of literary modernism. In her 1928 introduction to the first volume of *Great Short Stories of Detection, Mystery, and Horror,* Sayers floated the possibility of a rapprochement between the detective story and "the novel of manners" (p. 44) only in passing, but by the time she wrote her introduction to

the second volume in 1931 she thought she saw signs that this was really starting to happen. Sayers was not alone in this view. She quoted the prediction of her fellow Detection Club member Anthony Berkeley that the puzzle of character would increasingly displace the puzzle of time, place, motive, and opportunity, and that the genre would break away from the old rigid investigative formulas. Reviewing a number of recent books, Sayers noticed "a natural reaction against the extremely mathematical form of detective-problem" that had so far dominated the field and a resulting trend toward a greater psychological realism, in which guilt and innocence had ceased to be simple matters (p. 7). She praised these experiments, though she emphasized that they would eventually make it impossible for writers to fall back on the techniques that had once guaranteed them a living.

In her introduction to *Tales of Detection* (1936) just a few years later, Sayers was less sanguine about the genre's prospects. She still believed that the future lay with the fusion between the detective story and the novel of manners, but for all the experimentation that had taken place, she felt that no one had really discovered how to combine "the mechanical elements of the plot" with "a serious artistic treatment of the psychological elements" (p. xiii). Detective fiction remained an intellectual exercise, the lessons offered by Victorian writers like Collins remained unheeded, and her hope that readers from every segment of society might find "common ground" in a morally and aesthetically enriched detective fiction "as once they did in Greek or Elizabethan tragedy" remained unfulfilled (p. xiii). Sayers's skepticism bears a close relation to her own struggle to be a literary innovator who would heal the rift between reason and sentiment, between detection and romance, between serious fiction and entertainment. It is the fitful engagement in that struggle, in which technical puzzles alternate with the psychology of human desire, that marks her writing throughout the 1930s, culminating in the complex achievement of her novel *Gaudy Night.*

EXPERIMENTS IN NARRATIVE

DURING the 1930s, Sayers continued to experiment with the mystery genre. On the one hand, she sought to develop her ideal of a synthesis between crime fiction and the novel of manners, but she also tried out popular forms used by other writers of the period. Both of her books published in 1930, *The Documents in the Case* (coauthored with the poisons expert Dr. Eustace Barton, writing under the pen name Robert Eustace) and *Strong Poison,* are attempts to modify and complicate the mystery as an intellectual exercise, to combine it with an exploration of the kind of psychological and social questions that were proving so fascinating to the reading public. In her only non-Wimsey crime novel, *The Documents in the Case,* Sayers explores the different kinds of narratives that science and literature produce as ways of understanding human action. Instead of a traditional sequence of chapters, the novel consists of fifty-three consecutively numbered items including letters, telegrams, and newspaper reports, which are divided into two large sections under the scientific headings "Synthesis" and "Analysis." Out of this miscellany of information emerges a complex story about a married couple, the Harrisons, and two men, the writer Jack Munting and the artist Harwood Lathom, who move into the maisonette above the couple in London. Of all Sayers's texts, *The Documents in the Case* is the one most indebted to Wilkie Collins, particularly in the technique of collating multiple points of view also found in *The Moonstone.* By piecing the documents and testimony together, we follow the events leading up to and away from the mysterious death of George Harrison.

In this book, as elsewhere in her work, debates about literary genres and their content, particularly as these influence social behavior, individual identity, and moral choices, frequently crop up in the exchanges between the various characters. Thus Jack Munting, poet, novelist, biographer, and the main narrative voice in *The Documents in the Case,* warns his writer fiancée, Elizabeth Drake, not to "overdo the psycho-analytical part" of her work in progress on the grounds that it is not her "natural style" and that "pre-natal influences and childhood fears" have had their day as motives for characters' actions, now that "glands are the thing." Wary of such biological accounts of personality, Jack tells Elizabeth that he is worried by the view advanced in "Nicholson's book on *The Development of English Biography*" that "scientific biography" based on "studies of heredity and endocrine secretions" will make his own type of work redundant (document

6). Meanwhile, he struggles to make sense of "that curious Victorian blend of materialism and trust in a personally interfering Providence" displayed by the unnamed subject of his current biographical study (document 8). Like their creator, Sayers's writer-characters are trying to find successful literary frameworks through which the competing explanatory claims of natural science, psychology, and Christianity can be dramatized.

There are conflicts within each of these bodies of knowledge too, disputes as to the most useful branch of science, for example, or the best kind of psychological theory. As Jack Munting's warning to Elizabeth Drake suggests, psychoanalysis is one of the novel's obvious targets. Its association with the Harrisons' spinster housekeeper Aggie Milson, who keeps a "handbook to Freud" and patronizes the kind of psychiatrists who make their living from the imaginary ailments of gullible middle-aged women, serves to caricature psychoanalysis as a jargon-ridden pseudoscience (document 16). By contrast, the sciences that do pass muster as philosophically or practically sound are speculative physics and mathematics on the one hand and organic chemistry on the other. The penultimate document of the book involves a discussion between senior scientists about the origins of life, a discussion that leads by a train of associations to an experiment that provides the final solution to Harrison's murder.

Sayers has an easier time dismissing the more fashionable forms of psychology and the mechanistic and reductive applications of biology than she does playing off her own views against the psychological and sexual themes found in other popular novels of the period. The unhappiness of the Harrisons' marriage is partly conveyed through Margaret Harrison's choice of reading matter: this self-regarding "suburban vamp" (document 5) represents Sayers's image of the typical middlebrow reader of contemporary fiction. Margaret's favorite authors are the successful literary entrepreneurs of the early and mid-1920s: Arthur Hutchinson, Michael Arlen, and Margaret Kennedy, whose best-sellers *If Winter Comes* (1921), *The Green Hat* (1924), and *The Constant Nymph* (1924) chart the chaos of modern morals through their melodramatic plots, explicit references to sex, and often highly charged prose. Jack Munting, who functions as the mouthpiece for many of Sayers's ideas about literature and science, does not think that all these books are trash—he and Margaret Harrison share the then widely held opinion that *The Constant Nymph* "was a very good piece of work" (document 11)—but he aims for something both more substantial and less ponderous in his own writing. Although we are never told exactly what kind of novel Jack writes, it is clear that as a character and as a writer he rejects the posturing pretensions of these books and their readers, epitomized by the Emma Bovary–ish Margaret. With its explicit contrast between the cheerful, prosaic relationship between Jack and Elizabeth Drake and the disastrous romantic script followed by Margaret in her unfaithfulness to her husband George, it is tempting to see *The Documents in the Case* as a modest antidote to the worst excesses of the best-sellers of the 1920s.

At the same time, Sayers was developing her own kind of tragicomic mode within the crime genre. *Strong Poison* has Lord Peter Wimsey falling in love with Harriet Vane, a successful mystery writer who has been charged with murdering her writer lover, Philip Boyes, an accusation supported by the fact that she has purchased arsenic while researching poisons for her new novel. Completed and published in the same year, *Strong Poison* and *The Documents in the Case* are in many respects mirror images of each other, especially in their discussion of sexual politics and the arts. *Strong Poison* neatly reverses the ideal relationship between literary equals imagined in the non-Wimsey book: the affair between Harriet Vane and Philip Boyes is a miserable mésalliance. Whereas Jack Munting self-consciously fears that, however hard he tries, he will be less than the "new man" he believes Elizabeth Drake wants and deserves, the murdered Philip Boyes is revealed as a conventional prig and a sexist in bohemian clothing.

If *The Documents in the Case* reproduces certain long-standing stereotypes of women as vamps or dotty spinsters, and even defends a certain conservative masculinity in the figure of its murder victim, *Strong Poison* offers a welcome corrective. Miss Climpson, the spinster detective from *Unnatural Death*, is again brought in to play a major role in the investigation. She is now part of an organization of socially and economically marginal women employed by Wimsey to assist him in his work, a collection of widows, retirees, out-of-work actresses, and others of slender means, which he affectionately calls "My Cattery" (chap. 5). As in *The Documents in the Case*, though in a rather less well integrated manner, the mystery as to how the murder was committed requires specialized scientific knowledge. However, in *Strong Poison* the crucial evidence is supplied not by a group of male scientists, but by a young working woman, a typical 1920s flapper to whom, significantly, Wimsey very fully discloses the details of his investigation.

In spite of Wimsey's confident and expressive male feminism, the question of egalitarian relationships between men and women is also a more complex matter in this novel. Harriet had accepted Philip Boyes's suggestion that they live together without getting married, but she had left him when he later asked her to become his wife; she felt that his proposal showed that their unwedded liaison had only been a test of her suitability as a partner. Similarly, Harriet refuses Wimsey's offer of marriage because she is afraid that she would only be marrying him out of gratitude for proving her innocence and saving her from the gallows. Indeed, in its focus on "superfluous women" and the ethics of marriage, *Strong Poison*'s plot echoes such late-nineteenth-century novels as George Gissing's *The Odd Women* (1893) that were also concerned with critically examining the new dilemmas men and women were beginning to face in an earlier era. The difference between Sayers and Gissing, however, is that Sayers is considerably more optimistic about the emergence of a "new man." Read as they were written, in tandem, *Strong Poison* and *The Documents in the Case* expose the constant tension between Sayers's conservatism and her more progressive social beliefs. Compared to her earlier work, these two books make a much stronger case for the importance of crime fiction, and her own work in particular, in the development of the modern novel. While *The Documents in the Case* never received the recognition of her Wimsey books, Sayers came to see it as the first of her really "serious" novels, which paved the way for *The Nine Tailors* and *Gaudy Night*. Read in the context of the broad field of interwar fiction, to whose popular or modernist texts Sayers's own novels so frequently refer, her judgment seems to be amply confirmed.

Nevertheless, Sayers's writing was sometimes attacked by detective-fiction buffs as too discursive and lacking in suspense, criticisms she was unwilling to ignore. In *The Five Red Herrings* (1931) she therefore emphasized place and plot almost exclusively. She set her story in an artists' colony at Kirkcudbright in Scotland, where she had recently spent a very happy holiday with her husband Mac, who was then dabbling with painting. Neither psychology, science, nor romance is a topic in the novel, whose mystery superficially concerns painters and painting but whose solution turns on distances and timetables. Wimsey and Bunter are much reduced as characters; they figure as vehicles for the crime's detection and little else. The book sold well, and her letters to her publisher indicate that she was happy at having successfully tried this more limited but no less demanding form. She was particularly pleased and amused that her Scottish readers in Kirkcudbright enjoyed it. Yet for all its skillful handling of an intricate puzzle, *The Five Red Herrings* could have been written by virtually any competent crime writer of the period—indeed, Sayers noted in a letter that Freeman Wills Crofts had used the same part of Scotland and very similar kinds of plot devices in a mystery published in the same year.

Much more idiosyncratic and ambitious, her 1934 novel *The Nine Tailors* has become the favorite of many readers for whom neither sexual politics nor Wimsey in love are particularly compelling elements of Sayers's detective fiction. The fen country of her childhood in Bluntisham is lovingly memorialized and, like the "young cathedral" with its ancient bells and rectory at the center of the story, is lyrically evoked. So too is Sayers's father, in part the model for the gentle and scholarly rector, Mr. Venables, and the rural class system of her youth, including its squires, villagers, and domestic servants. Although ostensibly set in the interwar present, with the dislocations of World War I still keenly felt, the novel is in many respects a kind of hymn to an idealized prewar rural England. When Wimsey and Bunter arrive at the rectory with Venables, the old man tells his wife that he has "brought a guest," and Bunter, referred to by Mrs. Venables only as "your man," is firmly packed off to the servants' quarters. A subtler hint of this half-conscious anachronism appears in the novel through a minor character befriended by Wimsey: the fifteen-year-old daughter of the local gentry who aspires to an Oxford education and a writing career, greatly resembling in spirit and ambition the young Dorothy as she would have been in 1908.

Her detailed account of the British art of bell ringing (or campanology) is typical of the careful research found in all Sayers's novels, but in *The Nine Tailors* this arcane branch of knowledge is much more fully integrated symbolically into the plot than is the organic chemistry of her poison mysteries. Here campanology, with its national history and mathematical formulas, replaces both science and the literary quotations that Sayers used in other works to establish or breach distinctions of class and education. It is also deployed as a device for organizing the text, which is laid out in sections and chapters whose names and numbers draw extensively on the technical vocabulary of bell ringing. In *The Nine Tailors*, bell ringing represents the organic nation in miniature, right from the novel's opening sequence in which Wimsey, stranded by a car accident in the village of Fenchurch St. Paul one New Year's Eve, participates in a nine-hour performance of "no less than fifteen thousand, eight hundred and forty Kent Treble Bob Majors"—a feat that is, as Wimsey tells the rector, "equal to the great performance of the College Youths in eighteen hundred and something" ("The First Course"). The presence of an aristocrat among the village bell ringers, who include the rector, the blacksmith, the pub landlord, a gardener, and several other rural workmen, and whose age span runs from the septagenarian Hezekiah Lavender to the adolescent apprentice Walter Pratt, suggests not only the harmonious cross-class interdependence of the community, but also its innocent forms of male comradeship organized around a common skill. In a parallel way the bells themselves, each with a name and a history reaching back across the centuries, embody the village's still-active continuity with its English past.

Even the war, though it sets in motion the events that lie at the heart of the mystery, serves only as a minor interruption in what is an essentially stable society. Of course, Wimsey's methods and those of his Scotland Yard friend Charles Parker are as up-to-date as ever as they move outside English society to seek the cooperation of the French police. Yet in comparison with other village mysteries of the 1930s, especially those featuring Agatha Christie's spinster detective Miss Marple, *The Nine Tailors* seems deeply concerned to present a world only intermittently touched by modernity. While Wimsey must, in some sense, apologize for and send up his aristocratic origins and wealth in other novels, in *The Nine Tailors* his existence is portrayed as natural, as normal and as unremarkable a part of the English social land-scape as the fens are a part of its geography. In the end crime and justice are communal and self-enclosed. The church bells—Gaude, Sabaoth, John, Jericho, Jubilee, Dimity, Batty Thomas, and Tailor Paul—and their titled and plebeian ringers are shown to be the collective agents of the novel's unsolved murder. And meting out their own brand of retribution, beyond the justice of men, the floodwaters around the village bring death to the guilty; in Sayers's words, "the Fen had re-claimed its own" ("The Second Part: The Waters Are Called Home").

Murder Must Advertise (1933) takes for its close community of suspects a London advertising agency. One of the junior executives has mysteri-ously fallen to his death down a spiral staircase, and Wimsey is called in by the director of the firm to carry out an undercover investigation. In his guise as the agency's new copywriter, Wimsey gains access to the motives and alibis of the other employees, but his sleuthing soon takes him into the very different cultural milieu of the rich "bright young people" of the interwar years, with their drugs, parties, and fast cars. There is some-thing unreal about both these worlds, and in trac-ing the criminal links between them, Wimsey comes to feel that his life has acquired "an odd dreamlike quality," lacking any stable reference point (chap. 11). Ultimately, as Sayers herself later suggested in her study of creativity, *The Mind of the Maker* (1941), Wimsey's detective work also re-quires him to act as a social critic, and this pro-vides the book with a moral perspective. Yet one of *Murder Must Advertise*'s most remarkable fea-tures is how all-pervasive the sense of unreality becomes; it produces an eerily surrealistic effect with which Wimsey is curiously complicit. He en-ters into the wild nocturnal revels of Dian de Momerie's smart set in Harlequin's fancy dress and assumes the identity of this fabled character throughout his dealings with Dian, a role that re-calls Agatha Christie's use of the same figure in her book *The Mysterious Mr. Quin* (1930).

Sayers paints a vivid picture of office life in an advertising agency, its gossip, its rivalries, and its pleasures. Because of his wealth, Wimsey has paid scant attention to advertising in the past, and his detachment gives the reader an ironic view of the agency's work. As Wimsey soon realizes, advertis-ing campaigns create powerful and self-sustaining imaginary worlds that become a vital part of ev-eryday life. The grand scheme he devises for pro-moting cigarettes creates an alternative currency devoted to popular leisure; it uses a system of coupons that can be used to pay for travel, hotels, and theater tickets. This is Wimsey's first (and only) experience of paid work, and he is alarmed to discover that "a few idle words on a sheet of paper" can touch "the lives of millions" (chap. 21). Sayers implies that advertising is a necessary evil in an industrial society, an argument she subse-quently made more explicit in a 1937 essay on "The Psychology of Advertising," and she gently satirizes its absurdities and excesses. But she also seems at times to suggest that advertising is a symptom of what is wrong with the modern world, matching the mindless consumption its campaigns induce to the unrestrained hedonism of the drug-addicted young as sources of Wimsey's growing sense of unreality. It is perhaps no acci-dent that one of the products with which the agency is constantly involved is "Nutrax," a highly successful tonic for jaded nerves.

CRIME AND ROMANCE

Strong Poison brought a new breath of romance to Sayers's detective fiction, but the touchy relation-ship between Wimsey and Harriet Vane has reached an impasse by the end of the novel. Be-cause Harriet owes Wimsey everything, she can-not marry him without losing her self-respect. This difficulty evidently continued to haunt Sayers, and in the majority of the Wimsey novels written in the 1930s it is as if Harriet had never ex-isted. She appears again in *Have His Carcase* (1932), a more lighthearted book now that Harriet is a free woman. Yet the dilemma with which Sayers has saddled her heroine is as intractable as ever. When Harriet goes on a walking holiday and discovers the body of a man with his throat cut, she is immediately regarded with suspicion by the local police. The fact that Wimsey comes to her aid simply reanimates the earlier tension between them. For most of the investigation the couple manage to sustain a precarious truce and work to-gether to solve the mystery: a tangle of unshak-able alibis, overabundant motives, and coded messages whose complexity rivals that of its pre-decessor, *The Five Red Herrings*. Continuing her practice of experimenting with current narrative scenarios, Sayers produces her own version of the coastal resort town, a setting prominent in several of Christie's novels from the period, and uses it to create an atmosphere of rather dowdy provincial opulence. Wimsey ultimately cracks the case, but the romantic impasse remains. "I always did hate watering-places!" is his final, angry comment, which closes the novel (chap. 34).

Have His Carcase develops new possibilities for Harriet and sets the stage for the couple's reconciliation in *Gaudy Night* (1935). If Wimsey is the more experienced detective, Harriet is established in *Have His Carcase* as someone who is herself a credible investigator. She is quick-witted enough to take several photographs of the body on the beach, which provides crucial evidence since the corpse is immediately washed away by the tide. As a mystery writer she brings considerable insight to the investigation, and when she warns Wimsey that his reconstruction of the murder sounds "like a bad plot" he understands at once what she means (chap. 25). *Gaudy Night* takes her characterization a step further by effectively making her the detective. She is asked by the dean of her old Oxford college to undertake a discreet investigation of a series of unpleasant incidents, including vandalized manuscripts, obscene drawings, and poison-pen letters, which threaten its reputation and stability. The university is a world Harriet has avoided since her graduation, partly because she has been too busy making a career as a popular novelist, partly because of the events surrounding her own infamous murder trial, and partly because "she had loved the place too well" (chap. 1). *Gaudy Night* is a mystery that also serves as an extended meditation on women, education, and work. In turning detective, Harriet is forced to confront her ideals, her fears, and her hopes for the future. This is a novel that combines mystery and romance, but it is equally a novel of ideas.

Of all the settings in Sayers's books, the fictitious Shrewsbury College is the most fully realized portrayal of a world to which she had once belonged. But *Gaudy Night*'s underfunded, egalitarian college is probably closer in spirit to Somerville as Sayers experienced it in her undergraduate days than to Somerville as it was in 1935. This is more than a nostalgic re-creation, however, for Sayers was attempting to defend and honor what she believed to be the timeless values of university life. Wimsey himself testifies to their importance when he observes that there is "something about this place" that "alters all one's values," and in deference to its powerful presence he refrains from asking Harriet to marry him until the very end of the book (chap. 23). But by then Harriet has had a change of heart: about Oxford, about her own writing, and about Lord Peter Wimsey. One way in which Sayers attempts to show the difference the world of scholarship can make is through the effect it has on Harriet's thinking about her life and the choices before her. More significantly, however, Sayers also positions the college's work and its respect for truth and reason as a bulwark against the looming threat of fascism in continental Europe. Indeed, a crucial clue to the mystery's solution lies in the nature of the books and papers that are damaged or destroyed, one of which is a study of Nazi political thought and its justification of women's subordination. To reinforce this point, Wimsey is heavily involved in diplomatic missions abroad while the novel is unfolding, which removes him from the scene of the mystery for much of the time.

Wimsey's absence is essential to *Gaudy Night*'s exploration of the community of women academics and the personal sacrifices that their work has demanded of them, for the vandalism and poison-pen letters seem to come from inside the college. This threatens the trust and mutual respect on which its scholarship is founded and implies that something has gone horribly wrong with the institution itself. The obscene quality of the letters suggests both madness and sexual pathology, and even the celibate scholars are prepared to believe that they might have been written by someone who has been emotionally unhinged by pent-up sexuality. This theme recurs throughout *Gaudy Night*, and it is notable that when Wimsey comes back into the story his reappearance leads to an unpleasant outburst of jealousy against Harriet from one of the women lecturers who has fallen in love with him. The real explanation of the crimes comes to light when Wimsey puts all the pieces together, able to see what Harriet is much too close to see, despite her resourceful and courageous investigation. The unmasking of the guilty party is an extraordinary scene, unrivaled in Sayers's fiction for its sexual and political resonances.

The final explanation of the criminal's motive and method condenses into a single narrative all of the issues that have been raised in the novel and creates the conditions necessary for Harriet and Wimsey to reach a new understanding. Wimsey demonstrates that a college servant, whose husband had been exposed by one of Shrewsbury's lecturers for falsifying his academic work, has been attempting to ruin the college in revenge for her husband's subsequent suicide. The servant's grievance is shown to be rooted in the failings of her class: though she had married a man who was a cut above her socially, she had never really understood what a scholar's vocation meant. In her eyes the women of Shrewsbury are selfishly taking away men's jobs, not pursuing knowledge and truth. Her contempt for the world of learning, symbolized by her destruction of scholarly books and her trashing of the college library, aligns her with Nazi ideology, for she believes a woman's place is in the home, supporting her man. It is as if, in imagining a possible threat to the college from within, Sayers has immediately to keep it at a distance from the community of women scholars, as if the voice of fascism can most clearly be heard in the raw anger of an uneducated woman, too emotional to appreciate the hard-won achievements of her betters.

While the woman's crimes are part of a rational plan to discredit the college, her actions are made to represent the destructive, even the self-immolating, side of human passion. This is a grim reminder that Harriet and Peter are also trying to deal with the power of their emotions in arriving at what will have to be the "very delicate balance" between them. Harriet confesses that she is afraid that if she "once gave way to Peter, I should go up like straw" (chap. 22). One of the real strengths of *Gaudy Night*'s exploration of sexual politics is its willingness to probe deeply into the psychology of men's and women's relationships to themselves and each other and to link that discussion with questions of ethics and justice. It is therefore all the more disappointing, though not so unusual for her time, that in her resolution to the mystery Sayers's own myopic social prejudices make a working-class woman express in murderous excess sentiments that could be found at every level of British society.

Gaudy Night does succeed in bringing the romance and the mystery together generically: its virtues and faults are closely entwined in a way that *Busman's Honeymoon*, the final Wimsey novel, which takes Peter and Harriet through their wed-

ding and early months of married life, fails to achieve. Set mostly in Paggleham, a village adjacent to the one in which Harriet grew up, the novel's rural murder and the passionate working out of the Wimseys' romance coexist uneasily, a fact made into a running joke by having the most emotionally intense moments between Peter and Harriet constantly interrupted by the locals: aging spinster, comic charlady, ineffectual vicar, sullen gardener, salt-of-the-earth chimney sweep. While the murder of the little-mourned Noakes, the former owner of the old house Peter has bought Harriet as a wedding gift, is neatly plotted and concluded, there is a jarring dissonance between the dense moral, intellectual, and emotional language of the rich and educated and the superficial and stereotyped vernacular of those who are merely ordinary and poor. This gap makes itself felt uncomfortably in the writing: in the long untranslated passages in French, which clearly indicate the level of reader Sayers had in mind; in the contrast between the lyrical and sensual evocations of married love and the humdrum scenes of village life; and, most tellingly, in the different kinds of social comedy and tragedy that *Busman's Honeymoon* tries to orchestrate. At its best in following through on the questions about sexuality and emotional independence and interdependence posed in *Gaudy Night*, this final Wimsey book must have suggested to Sayers, as her essays on the subject indicate, how very difficult it was to integrate the mystery and the novel of manners—at least in the way in which she had chosen to imagine them.

FROM DRAMA TO DANTE

IN *The Mind of the Maker*, Sayers describes the exhilaration the writer experiences in moving from the novel to the stage, where the collaboration between playwright, producer, and actor brings into being "a living thing with a mind and will of its own" (p. 65). That transforming energy certainly affected her own experience of working in the theater, and it is undoubtedly among her plays that we find her most ambitious, if not always her most artistically successful, projects.

While the bulk of her dramatic work was specially devised for religious festivals or religious broadcasting, her first play, *Busman's Honeymoon*, was written for the commercial theater, as was her 1940 comedy *Love All*. Compared to her novels, these ventures were never very lucrative; the reward lay in the pleasure Sayers took in the production side of the theater. She saw it as her duty to attend the rehearsals, and her concern for the minutiae of performance is evidenced by the elaborate character sketches and production notes she sometimes appended to her scripts, which included alternative methods and set designs for amateur theater companies with smaller budgets.

Busman's Honeymoon, the only stage appearance of Lord Peter Wimsey, contains both the best and the worst of Sayers: intricate plotting, lively characterization, and spirited verbal jousting, marred by some flat-footed comedy and the resort to stock types. Despite some effervescent dialogue, the humor occasionally descends to such ludicrous working-class malapropisms or neologisms as "insinuendo" and "corpusses." Structurally, Sayers and her collaborator, Muriel St. Clare Byrne, were attempting to create a theatrical counterpart to the classic detective story. They scrupulously observed the rule of fair play by putting most of the major clues before the detective's and the audience's eyes in the first act and by gradually adding complications of motive and opportunity as the play developed. However, Sayers's typical emphasis on the "how" rather than the "why" of a murder, when focused on a single theatrical set, has a curiously stultifying effect upon the drama—an effect the ebullient wit or romantic interest can never quite alleviate. Sayers and Byrne's prefatory note to the play emphasizes its "highly experimental" nature. *Busman's Honeymoon* was well received, but it was an experiment she never tried to repeat.

However, once she had abandoned the constraints inherent in her conception of a good detective play, Sayers was able to turn her gift for banter and repartee to better use. The neatly satirical social comedy *Love All* is one of her most adroitly feminist works, mocking male self-centeredness and exuberantly underscoring the fulfillment that personal and economic independence can mean for a woman. The story sets up a conventional triangle: a romantic-novelist husband, Godfrey Daybrook, abandons his wife and child to run off to Venice with his actress mistress, Lydia Hillington. However, neither wife nor mistress is content to be either a victim or a dependent. Edith Daybrook uses her husband's desertion as an opportunity to

refashion herself as a popular playwright, and Lydia Hillington returns to London to resume her stage career. Predicated on a wildly improbable cluster of coincidences, the play mischievously but relentlessly undermines Godfrey's presumption that he can run the lives of his two "wives."

By ironically juxtaposing Godfrey's elegant apartment overlooking Venice's Grand Canal with Edith Daybrook's chaotically workaday flat close to London's much less salubrious Grand Junction Canal, Sayers contrasts the busy clutter of a hectic professional life with the orderly seclusion and unquestioning support the male novelist requires. The play portrays Godfrey as deeply shocked and incredulous that his wife can prefer the career she has made to the domestic duty handed down to her, but their differences about gender roles are characteristically represented by Sayers in terms of the meaning of creative work. When Edith earnestly asks Godfrey whether he would not much rather "be valued for your work than for yourself," Godfrey patronizingly replies that he sees his work as offering escapism, bringing "colour and romance into thousands of humdrum lives" (p. 174). In Edith's eyes it is Godfrey who has become a two-dimensional cliché, as "unreal" as his own fictions, little better than "an unconvincing character in a book" (p. 170).

Sayers was unlucky with the play. It opened in a small London theater club in the early months of the Second World War, just as the German offensive in Europe was beginning. Despite favorable reviews, the rapidly escalating conflict prevented it from reaching the big West End audience for whom it was designed. Sayers seems to have written it off as another experiment, a diversion from the more weighty religious dramas that were bringing her a new reputation as a serious writer.

Her earliest religious commission, *The Zeal of Thy House* (1937), does reveal some thematic continuities with Sayers's lighter work in its concern with questions of vocation and responsibility. It tells the story of a worldly twelfth-century architect and builder, William of Sens, a man whose tragically overconfident faith in his own judgment leads to his downfall. Although this is a tale of male hubris, of a man who treats people solely as the means to his own ends and whose uncompromising professional autonomy is echoed by the complete freedom he claims in his private life, its protagonist is treated sympathetically as well as punished. Throughout the play, William is an attractive figure with a warmth and directness that is conveyed even when we see him at his most irascible or despairing. Yet in the revealing episode when William first meets his future mistress, Lady Ursula De Warbois, Sayers brings out the masculine roots of William's vanity by having him boast that "the craftman's dream" is denied to women—only to be reminded by Ursula that it was Eve who first "snatched the torch / Of knowledge from the jealous hand of God / So that the fire runs in man's blood for ever" (p. 51). This finely matched exchange initiates a commentary on the theology of creativity by the play's chorus of angels, a theme that returns in the archangel Michael's closing speech. For, in spite of William's failings, his work will live on in the fabric of the very cathedral in which the play is being specially performed, just as the labor and imagination of humankind will continue to mirror and honor the creativity of God through the ages to come.

Sayers's desire to give her theological convictions a new human relevance was to dominate all her religious plays and was to be the source of her greatest problems as a dramatist. In *The Zeal of Thy House*, for example, the attempt to link the human and the divine through the presence of an angelic host produces a confusion of individual and supernatural motivations. When William is chosen as architect because an angel whispers his name in the ear of the cleric with the casting vote, it is hard not to feel that human beings are being reduced to divine puppets, and the drama of human responsibility is correspondingly weakened.

Sayers's second Canterbury play, *The Devil to Pay* (1939), suffers from a parallel flaw, for in it she seeks to preserve the sixteenth-century spirit of the story of Faust while at the same time exploring an acutely contemporary moral dilemma. The stage setting is taken directly from the early Renaissance, complete with the jaws of hell to the left and a staircase ascending to a heavenly pavilion on the right, with various "mansions" in between to represent the locations in which the drama takes place. Yet Sayers's Faustus is envisioned as a modern secular figure, "the impulsive reformer, over-sensitive to suffering, impatient of the facts, eager to set the world right by a sudden overthrow" (p. 10), a man whose high-minded obsessions cause him to lose his humanity. This conception quickly becomes obscured by the increasingly bombastic wrangles between Faustus and Mephistopheles, and when the rights and wrongs of Faustus' bargain with the devil become the subject of a legal suit in "the court of Heaven," much of the force of Sayers's original point is lost in a welter of theological niceties.

By the end of the 1930s the prestige of her Canterbury productions had firmly established her position as an important religious dramatist. Sayers's interpretations of her commissions in the following decade were characteristically bold and imaginative, painted on a much broader historical canvas than anything she had previously attempted. In the life of Christ she wrote for national public radio, for example, Sayers hoped to recapture the vivid immediacy of the Gospels in a single, integrated dramatic narrative. Originally intended for children, the scope of *The Man Born to Be King* (1943) broadened considerably while the final contract was being negotiated, and the conditions on which Sayers insisted guaranteed that her work would catch the attention of the widest possible public. By stipulating that her plays would portray "people painfully like us," Sayers planned to imbue historical events with a twentieth-century realism; she rounded out her characters by linking them to their latter-day counterparts and had them use the accents and idioms of modern speech. She wanted to bring home to her listeners the shocking truth about Christ's death, to make them recognize that "the Elders of the Synagogue . . . are to be found on every Parish Council—always highly respectable, often quarrelsome, and sometimes in a crucifying mood" (p. 23).

As she so often did in her work, Sayers turned the writing of *The Man Born to Be King* into a immense labor of scholarship. In order to re-create the freshness of the Gospels she went back to what she called the New Testament's "homely and vigorous Greek" (p. 23) and made new English translations that echoed the directness of the original sources. At the same time, she tried to provide intelligible causes and motivations where these are only hinted at in biblical accounts. Her most elaborate creative move appears in the character of Judas Iscariot, who emerges from the shadows of the Gospels as a man whose intellectual arrogance leads him to suspect that Christ has allowed himself to be duped by dangerous revolutionaries whose reckless actions will ruin and ultimately destroy Israel if they are not stopped. Throughout the cycle of twelve plays, political themes are frequently emphasized, and Sayers would sometimes draw disturbing parallels in her stage notes between those who collaborated with the occupying Roman forces and the Nazi sympathizers of her own day. There is a sense of urgency about these plays that stems partly from the presence of these menacing contemporary overtones and partly from the fact that each of these short dramatic pieces is broken down into a number of brief scenes or episodes, which produces a swiftly moving and hard-hitting progression of events. Only occasionally does the rapid deployment of a large cast of characters lead to confusion as to who is speaking or what is happening.

When Sayers tried to write a major historical play by transferring some of these dramatic techniques from radio to the stage, the results were far less successful. *The Emperor Constantine* (1951) was her enormously ambitious attempt to chart the growth of Christianity from a minority cult to the official religion of the Roman Empire. The play ranged over a twenty-one-year time span and used a cast of nearly a hundred, with additional guards, soldiers, slaves, attendants, and other nonspeaking characters. The action moves from England to Asia Minor and takes in battle scenes, court intrigues, and executions, leading up to the Council of Nicaea, which Constantine called in order to bring together the warring branches of the church and to persuade them to agree on a common creed, and which ended with the emperor's deathbed baptism. Here the erudition and historical detail in what is by far her longest play threaten to overwhelm the audience, and as in *The Devil to Pay*, it is easy to find oneself lost in the clash of theological ideas. Yet in the panoramic sweep of this work, from the coarse slang of its foot soldiers to the scholastic arguments of its bishops and clerics, one can also glimpse Sayers's dream of creating a new public forum that was both popular and vibrantly intellectual, like the "common ground" she had earlier desired for the newly imagined detective novel.

The same hopes animated her major translation of Dante's *Divine Comedy*, to which she devoted the last thirteen years of her life. In *Whose Body?* Lord Peter Wimsey was introduced as a collector of Dante, but Sayers's own knowledge of the poet's work was then only secondhand, despite her references to "Dantesque figures with pitchforks" at a somber graveyard exhumation (chap. 12). In her penultimate religious play, *The Just Vengeance* (1946), Sayers drew on Dante's poetry for her title and theme, which deals with the fate of a British pilot who has died after being shot down in World War II. Uncomprehending at first, the pilot gradually learns to make sense of his own suffering and the suffering that his bombs have caused to others through witnessing a reenactment of Christ's crucifixion in which the dead and martyred people of his hometown of Lichfield take part. Here Sayers's use of the doctrine of atonement, according to which humanity's sins constitute a debt that only God can repay by becoming a man, is taken directly from Dante's *Paradiso*.

Her paperback version of the first book of Dante's *Divine Comedy, Inferno*, which she bluntly translated as *Hell*, appeared in November 1949. It sold its first printing of fifty thousand copies by January of the following year. Although not the first post-Victorian English translation of Dante, Sayers produced an inventive and highly readable rendering of the classic narrative poem, one that managed to be both earthy and funny while preserving the tricky verse forms of the original. If Dante himself had chosen to write in the Italian vernacular in order to reach the common reader, Sayers was equally concerned to employ an English that was modern and vigorous enough to satisfy a new and expanding reading public. Steering a path between the medieval complexity of Dante's ideas and the charm and humor of his writing, Sayers stressed the subtle "self-mockery" of his verse, "a faintly ironic inflection in the voice" that to her own peculiarly English sensibility evoked echoes of another English woman author and moralist, Jane Austen (introduction, pp. 62–63).

CONCLUSION

SAYERS was a bold and imaginative writer who always wanted to reach a wide popular audience. But she was not prepared to court popularity at any price, and she could be uncompromising where the principles behind her work were at stake. So, despite strong objections from religious purists in the Lord's Day Observance Society who felt that it was near blasphemous to depict Christ as a very human figure using ordinary unbiblical language, Sayers insisted that it was necessary for Christ to appear as a character in her plays if the message of the Gospels was not to be lost. In a similar vein, she repeatedly refused lucrative offers for her Wimsey stories because she believed that the film companies would ruin them. But, for all her intellectual integrity, her writings contain many contradictions. While her work both extended and critiqued contemporary feminist agendas, and many of her most memorable characters are women, she could sometimes fall back on surprisingly crude misogynistic stereotypes. Moreover, the Sayers who defended the importance of the common touch in popular fiction was the same Sayers who larded her novels with learned quotations and untranslated passages in French and Latin. As a result, it seems that readers of Sayers must continue to try to reconcile the mannered, snobbish, and conservative aspects of her writing with her uncanny ability to break through the barriers of taste and genre, producing work that is provocative and refreshingly new.

While Sayers's writing has never lacked critics, her influence is undeniable. Just as she rescued Dante from the snares of Victorian sententiousness, she succeeded in transforming detective fiction from an intriguingly entertaining diversion to a richly varied form that could bear the weight of serious social and moral themes without becoming pompous or solemn. By focusing on the difficulty of changing the relationship between the sexes she gave the genre a new relevance to women authors, while setting a higher standard of excellence for the detective novel as a whole. Characters like Miss Climpson and Harriet Vane have permanently changed our conception of women sleuths, and if they had not existed few of our contemporary detective heroines would be quite the same. Lord Peter Wimsey too has proved to be a perennially popular figure, one of a handful of names like Holmes and Poirot that have become synonymous with the genre. With such a distinguished past and in such good company, Wimsey's reputation—like that of Sayers herself—seems certain to endure.

SELECTED BIBLIOGRAPHY

I. BIBLIOGRAPHIES. Robert B. Harmon and Margaret A. Burger, *An Annotated Guide to the Works of Dorothy L. Sayers* (New York, 1977); Colleen B. Gilbert, *A Bibliography of the Works of Dorothy L. Sayers* (Hamden, Conn., 1978); Ruth T. Youngberg, *Dorothy L. Sayers: A Reference Guide* (Boston, 1982).

II. COLLECTED WORKS. *Four Sacred Plays* (London, 1948), includes *The Zeal of Thy House, The Devil to Pay, He That Should Come,* and *The Just Vengeance; Lord Peter: A Collection of All the Lord Peter Wimsey Stories,* ed. by James Sandoe (New York, 1972), short stories.

III. DETECTIVE FICTION. *Whose Body?* (New York and London, 1923); *Clouds of Witness* (London, 1926), repub. as *Clouds of Witnesses* (New York, 1927); *Unnatural Death* (London, 1927), repub. as *The Dawson Pedigree* (New York, 1928); *The Unpleasantness at the Bellona Club* (London and New York, 1928).

The Documents in the Case, with Robert Eustace (London and New York, 1930); *Strong Poison* (London and New York, 1930); *The Five Red Herrings* (London, 1931), repub. as *Suspicious Characters* (New York, 1931); *The Floating Admiral,* with members of the Detection Club (London, 1931; New York, 1932); *Have His Carcase* (London and New York, 1932); *Ask a Policeman,* with members of the Detection Club (London and New York, 1933); *Murder Must Advertise: A Detective Story* (London and New York, 1933); *The Nine Tailors: Changes Rung on an Old Theme in Two Short Touches and Two Full Peals* (London and New York, 1934); *Gaudy Night* (London, 1935; New York, 1936); *Papers Relating to the Family of Wimsey,* with C. W. Scott-Giles, as Matthew Wimsey (London, 1936); *Busman's Honeymoon: A Love Story with Detective Interruptions* (New York and London, 1937); *Double Death: A Murder Story,* with members of the Detection Club (London, 1939); "Wimsey Papers I–XI," in the *Spectator* (November 1939–January 1940), fictional letters and documents.

IV. SHORT STORIES. *Lord Peter Views the Body* (London, 1928; New York, 1929); *Hangman's Holiday* (London and New York, 1933); "Blood Sacrifice," in *Six Against the Yard,* by Sayers and others (London, 1936), repub. as *Six Against Scotland Yard* (New York, 1936); *In the Teeth of the Evidence and Other Stories* (London, 1939; New York, 1940); *Striding Folly, Including Three Final Lord Peter Wimsey Stories* (London, 1973).

V. PLAYS. *Busman's Honeymoon,* with Muriel St. Clare Byrne (London 1937; New York, 1939); *The Zeal of Thy House* (New York and London, 1937); *The Devil to Pay* (London and New York, 1939); *He That Should Come: A Nativity Play in One Act* (London, 1939).

Love All (produced at the Torch Theatre, 8 April 1940), repub. as *Love All* with *Busman's Honeymoon* (Kent, Ohio, 1984); *The Man Born to Be King: A Play-Cycle on the Life of Our Lord and Savior, Jesus Christ* (London, 1943; New York, 1949); *The Just Vengeance* (London, 1946); *The Emperor Constantine: A Chronicle* (London and New York, 1951).

VI. POETRY. *Op. I* (Oxford, 1916); *Catholic Tales and Christian Songs* (Oxford, 1918).

VII. BOOKS FOR CHILDREN. *Even the Parrot: Exemplary Conversations for Enlightened Children* (London, 1944); *The Days of Christ's Coming* (London, 1953; New York, 1960).

VIII. ESSAYS AND MISCELLANEOUS NONFICTION. Intro. to *Great Short Stories of Detection, Mystery, and Horror* (London, 1928), repub. as *The Omnibus of Crime* (New York, 1929); intro. to *Great Short Stories of Detection, Mystery, and Horror, Second Series* (London, 1931), repub. as *The Second Omnibus of Crime: The World's Great Crime Stories* (New York, 1932); intro. to *Great Short Stories of Detection, Mystery, and Horror, Third Series* (London, 1934), repub. as *The Third Omnibus of Crime* (New York, 1935); "How I Came to Invent the Character of Lord Peter," in *Harcourt Brace News* 1 (15 July 1936); "The Murder of Julia Wallace," in *The Anatomy of Murder: Famous Crimes Critically Considered*, with members of the Detection Club (London, 1936; New York, 1937); intro. to *Tales of Detection* (London, 1936); "Gaudy Night," in Denys K. Roberts, ed., *Titles to Fame* (London, 1937); "The Psychology of Advertising," in the *Spectator* (19 November 1937); *The Greatest Drama Ever Staged* (London, 1938); *Strong Meat* (London, 1939).

Begin Here: A War-Time Essay (London, 1940; New York, 1941); *The Mind of the Maker* (London and New York, 1941); *Why Work?* (London, 1942); intro. to *The Moonstone*, by Wilkie Collins (London and New York, 1944); intro. to *A Time Is Born*, by Garet Garrett (Oxford, 1945); *Unpopular Opinions: Twenty-One Essays* (London, 1946; New York, 1947); *Creed or Chaos? and Other Essays in Popular Theology* (London, 1947; New York, 1949); *The Lost Tools of Learning* (London, 1948); *Introductory Papers on Dante* (London, 1954; New York, 1955); *Further Papers on Dante* (London and New York, 1957).

The Poetry of Search and the Poetry of Statement, and Other Posthumous Essays on Literature, Religion, and Language (London, 1963); *Christian Letters to a Post-Christian World: A Selection of Essays*, ed. by Roderick Jellema (Grand Rapids, Mich., 1969), repub. as *The Whimsical Christian: Eighteen Essays* (New York, 1978); *Wilkie Collins: A Critical and Biographical Study* (Toledo, Ohio, 1977); intro. to *Trent's Last Case*, by E. C. Bentley (New York, 1978); *Dorothy L. Sayers: Spiritual Writings*, ed. by Ann Loades (Boston, 1993), extracts from verse, drama and prose.

IX. TRANSLATIONS. *Tristan in Brittany* (London, 1929); *The Comedy of Dante Alighieri, the Florentine. Cantica I: Hell* (Harmondsworth, Eng., 1949); *The Comedy of Dante Alighieri, the Florentine. Cantica II: Purgatory* (Harmondsworth, Eng., 1955); *The Song of Roland: A New Translation* (Harmondsworth, Eng., 1957); *The Comedy of Dante Alighieri, the Florentine. Cantica III: Paradise*, completed by Barbara Reynolds (Harmondsworth, Eng., 1962).

X. INTERVIEWS. "Departure from Crime," in *Newsweek* 46 (22 August 1955); Val Gielgud, "Why I Killed Peter Wimsey—by Dorothy L. Sayers," in *Sunday Dispatch* (22 December 1957).

XI. BIOGRAPHICAL STUDIES. Janet Hitchman, *Such a Strange Lady: An Introduction to Dorothy L. Sayers (1893–1957)* (New York, 1975); Alzina Stone Dale, *Maker and Craftsman: The Story of Dorothy L. Sayers* (Grand Rapids, Mich., 1978; rev. ed., Wheaton, Ill., 1992); Ralph E. Hone, *Dorothy L. Sayers: A Literary Biography* (Kent, Ohio, 1979); Nancy M. Tischler, *Dorothy L. Sayers: A Pilgrim Soul* (Atlanta, 1980); James Brabazon, *Dorothy L. Sayers: A Biography* (New York, 1981); David Coomes, *Dorothy L. Sayers: A Careless Rage for Life* (Oxford, 1992); Barbara Reynolds, *Dorothy L. Sayers: Her Life and Soul* (London and New York, 1993).

XII. CRITICAL STUDIES. Queenie D. Leavis, "The Case of Miss Dorothy Sayers," in *Scrutiny* 6 (December 1937); Howard Haycraft, *Murder for Pleasure: The Life and Times of the Detective Story* (New York, 1941; rev. ed. 1968); Paul Foster, "Dorothy L. Sayers," in Denys V. Baker, ed., *Writers of Today* (London, 1946); H. P. Rickman, "From Detection to Theology: The Work of Dorothy Sayers," in *Hibbert Journal* 60 (July 1962); Martin Green, "The Detection of a Snob: Martin Green on Lord Peter Wimsey," in *The Listener* 69 (14 March 1963); Carolyn Heilbrun, "Reappraisals: Sayers, Lord Peter, and God," in *The American Scholar* 37 (spring 1968).

Fritz Wölken, "Dorothy Sayers," in Rudolf Sühnel and Dieter Riesner, eds., *Englische Dichter der Moderne* (Berlin, 1971); John G. Cawelti, *Adventure, Mystery, and Romance* (Chicago, 1976); Nancy Y. Hoffman, "Mistresses of Malfeasance," in L. N. Landrum, Pat Browne, and R. B. Browne, eds., *Dimensions of Detective Fiction* (Bowling Green, Ohio, 1976); Richard Tillinghast, "Dorothy L. Sayers: Murder and Whimsy," in *New Republic* 175 (31 July 1976); Alden B. Flanders, "Dorothy L. Sayers: The Holy Mysteries," in *Anglican Theological Review* 59 (October 1977); E. R. Gregory, "From Detective Stories to Dante: The Transitional Phase of Dorothy L. Sayers," in *Christianity and Literature* 26 (winter 1977); Barbara Reynolds, "The Origin of Lord Peter Wimsey," in *The Times Literary Supplement* (22 April 1977); C. W. Scott-Giles, *The Wimsey Family* (London and New York, 1977); Nina Auerbach, *Communities of Women: An Idea in Fiction* (Cambridge, Mass., 1978); Margaret P. Hannay, ed., *As Her Whimsey Took Her: Critical Essays on the Work of Dorothy L. Sayers* (Kent, Ohio, 1979).

Mary Durkin, *Dorothy L. Sayers* (Boston, 1980); Trevor H. Hall, *Dorothy L. Sayers: Nine Literary Studies* (London, 1980); Patricia Craig and Mary Cadogan, *The Lady Investigates: Women Detectives and Spies in Fiction* (New York, 1981); Dawson Gaillard, *Dorothy L. Sayers* (New York, 1981); Kathleen Gregory Klein, "Dorothy Sayers," in Earl F. Bargainnier, ed., *Ten Women of Mystery* (Bowling Green, Ohio, 1981); Carolyn Heilbrun, "Dorothy L. Sayers: Biography Between the Lines," in *The American Scholar* 51 (autumn 1982); C. S. Lewis, "A Panegyric for Dorothy L. Sayers," in Walter Hooper, ed., *On Stories, and Other Essays on Literature* (New York, 1982); SueEllen Campbell, "The Detective Heroine and the Death of Her Hero: Dorothy Sayers to P. D. James," in *Modern Fiction Studies* 29 (autumn 1983); Virginia B. Morris, "Arsenic and Blue Lace: Sayers' Criminal Women," in *Modern Fiction Studies* 29 (autumn 1983); Bruce Merry, "Dorothy L. Sayers: Mystery and Demystification," in Bernard Benstock, ed., *Essays on Detective Fiction* (New York, 1983); P. L. Scowcroft, "The Detective Fiction of Dorothy L. Sayers: A Source for the Social Historian?," in *Seven* 5 (April 1984); Miriam Brody, "The Haunting of *Gaudy Night:* Misreadings in a Work of Detective Fiction," in *Style* 19 (spring 1985); Valerie Pitt, "Dorothy L. Sayers: The Predicaments of Women," in *Literature and History* 14 (autumn 1988); Bernard Benstock, "Dorothy L. Sayers," in Bernard Benstock and Thomas F. Staley, eds., *Dictionary of Literary Biography 77: British Mystery Writers, 1920–1939* (Detroit, 1989); T. J. Binyon, *"Murder Will Out": The Detective in Fiction* (Oxford, 1989); Jim Collins, *Uncommon Cultures: Popular Culture and Post-Modernism* (London and New York, 1989); Susan J. Leonardi, *Dangerous by Degrees: Women at Oxford and the Somerville College Novelists* (New Brunswick, N.J., 1989); Barbara Reynolds, *The Passionate Intellect: Dorothy L. Sayers' Encounter with Dante* (Kent, Ohio, 1989).

Mitzi Brunsdale, *Dorothy L. Sayers, Solving the Mystery of Wickedness* (New York, 1990); Catherine Kenney, *The Remarkable Case of Dorothy L. Sayers* (Kent, Ohio, 1990); Valerie Pitt, "Dorothy Sayers: The Masks of Lord Peter," in Clive Bloom, ed., *Twentieth-Century Suspense: The Thriller Comes of Age* (New York, 1990); Janice Rossen, "Oxford in *Loco Parentis:* The College as Mother in Dorothy Sayers' *Gaudy Night,*" in David Bevan, ed., *University Fiction* (Amsterdam, 1990);

Catherine Kenney, "Detecting a Novel Use for Spinsters in Sayers's Fiction," in Laura L. Doan, ed., *Old Maids to Radical Spinsters: Unmarried Women in the Twentieth-Century Novel* (Urbana, Ill., 1991); Nicholas Freeling, "Gaudy Night in 1935," in Patricia Craig, ed., *Julian Symons at Eighty: A Tribute* (Helsinki, 1992); Alzina Stone Dale, ed., *Dorothy L. Sayers: The Centenary Celebration* (New York, 1993).

Note: Many of Dorothy L. Sayers's papers and manuscripts are in the Marion E. Wade Center at Wheaton College in Wheaton, Ill. The Dorothy L. Sayers Society also has a collection of Sayersiana.

MARY SHELLEY
(1797–1851)

Anne K. Mellor

WHEN MARY WOLLSTONECRAFT died of puerperal fever on 10 September 1797, she left her newborn daughter with a double burden: a powerful need to be mothered, which was never to be fulfilled, together with a name, Mary Wollstonecraft Godwin, that proclaimed this small child the fruit of the most famous radical literary marriage of eighteenth-century England. As we trace the growth of this baby girl into the author of *Frankenstein; or, The Modern Prometheus* (1818), we can never forget how much her desire for a loving and supportive family defined her character, shaped her fantasies, and structured her fictional idealizations of the nuclear family—idealizations so exaggerated that their impossibility is always apparent.

LIFE

LEFT with two infant daughters to raise, the austere philosopher William Godwin immediately hired a nanny, Louisa Jones, to care for Mary and her half sister Fanny Imlay (Wollstonecraft's daughter by Gilbert Imlay). For three years, Mary enjoyed a happy childhood, beloved both by Louisa and by Fanny. But when Louisa fell in love with George Dyson, one of Godwin's more tempestuous and irresponsible disciples, Godwin strongly objected; when she decided to live with Dyson, Godwin in July 1800 forbade her ever seeing the girls again. Thus, at the age of three, Mary lost the only mother she had ever known. Godwin, desperate to find a wife to care for his family, soon married Mary Jane Clairmont, the unmarried mother of two children, who deeply resented the special attention paid by visitors to Wollstonecraft's and Godwin's only daughter. She favored her own children, refused to provide any special lessons for Mary, and quarreled frequently with her. The tension between Mary Godwin and her stepmother was so severe that Mary suffered from psychosomatic skin boils at the age of thirteen, boils that disappeared when she and her stepmother were separated. Godwin then decided to send Mary away indefinitely, shipping her to Dundee, Scotland, to stay with the family of a near stranger, William Thomas Baxter, in June 1812.

An outsider in the happy home of the Baxters, Mary nonetheless learned to enjoy the bleak but beautiful landscape of the Tay estuary and gradually became close friends with the Baxter daughters. Nevertheless, she continued to yearn for her father, for whom she had developed by the age of twelve, as she later confessed to Maria Reveley Gisborne, an "excessive & romantic attachment" (letter to Gisborne, 30 October 1834). At the age of sixteen, she returned to London to discover that Godwin had acquired a new disciple, one whom she saw as a youthful incarnation of all she most admired in her father. Within two months, she and the married Percy Shelley had become lovers; on 28 July 1814, they eloped to Paris, taking Mrs. Godwin's daughter Jane Clairmont with them.

The Godwins were furious at this elopement; William Godwin refused to speak to Mary (although he continued to borrow money from Percy Shelley), especially after Jane insisted on living with Mary and Percy. The trio traveled across Europe to Lake Lucerne; Mary and Percy later published their letters describing the sublime landscapes they encountered on this trip in *History of a Six Weeks' Tour Through a Part of France, Switzerland, Germany, and Holland: With Letters Descriptive of a Sail Round the Lake of Geneva, and of the Glaciers of Chamouni* (1817). During this trip Mary became pregnant, Jane and Percy probably became lovers, and all three converted to Percy's fervent belief in free or nonpossessive love and universal benevolence as the solution to every social and political evil.

When they returned to England, Mary gave birth to a baby girl, christened Clara, who lived for only two weeks. After Clara's death on 6 March 1815, Mary had a recurrent dream that she recorded in her journal: "Dream that my little baby came to life again—that it had only been cold, and that we rubbed it before the fire, and it lived—I awake and find no baby—I think about the little thing all day—not in good spirits" (*Journal*, 19 March 1815). Increasingly resentful of Jane's presence in her household, Mary insisted that she leave; Jane then decided to find her own poet and set her cap for the most famous young poet of the day, Lord Byron. By April 1816, Jane (having changed her name to the more romantic Claire) had become Byron's lover, despite his obvious lack of affection for her. She then persuaded Percy (who wanted to meet Byron) and Mary to accompany her to Switzerland in pursuit of Byron. The four spent the summer of 1816, the coldest summer for a century, on the shores of Lake Geneva, engaging in intense conversation and reading ghost stories out loud. On the memorable night of 15 June, they decided to compete in writing the most frightening story each could imagine. The next day, Mary Godwin, as she later reported in her introduction to the 1831 edition of *Frankenstein*, having experienced a "reverie" or waking nightmare in which she saw "the pale student of unhallowed arts" create a living being from dead parts, began to write one of the most powerful horror stories of modern times.

FRANKENSTEIN; OR, THE MODERN PROMETHEUS

MARY Shelley's story of a scientist who creates a monster he cannot control can claim the status of a myth, so profoundly resonant are its implications for our understanding of the modern world. Of course, the media and the average person often mistakenly assign the name of Frankenstein not to the maker of the monster but to his creature. But as we shall see, this "mistake" derives from an intuitively correct reading of the final identity of the creator with his creation.

From the feminist perspective, which has dominated critical discussions of the novel since 1975, *Frankenstein* is in part a book about what happens when a man tries to have a baby without a woman. As such, the novel is concerned with natural as opposed to unnatural modes of reproduction. In 1976, in her *Literary Women*, Ellen Moers drew our attention to the novel's emphasis on birth and "the trauma of the after-birth." Since this is a novel about giving birth, let us first ask why the eighteen-year-old Mary Godwin gave birth to this novel on that night in 1816, the question so frequently put to her, "How I, then a young girl, came to think of, and to dilate upon, so very hideous an idea?" In her author's introduction to the revised edition of *Frankenstein* (1831), she tells us that the night before her dream, she had heard Byron and Shelley discussing certain scientific experiments by Erasmus Darwin, in which he was said to have animated a piece of vermicelli by sending an electrical current though it.

Mary's reverie of creation, which followed this discussion, also drew upon far more personal knowledge. More than fifteen years later, she claimed she could still see vividly the room to which she woke and feel "the thrill of fear" that ran through her. Why was she so frightened? Remember that she had eighteen months earlier given birth to a baby girl whom she had dreamed she had "rubbed . . . before the fire" and brought back to life. Here once again she dreamed of reanimating a corpse by warming it with "a spark of life." Only six months ago this night, Mary had given birth a second time, to a boy named William. And while she wrote out her novel, she was pregnant a third time, with a daughter, again named Clara, who was born in September 1817. Mary's waking dream unleashed her deepest subconscious anxieties, the anxieties of a very young, frequently pregnant mother.

The dream that gave birth to her novel also gave shape to what we might imagine to be her deepest fears: "What if my child is born deformed, a freak, a 'hideous' thing? Could I still love it, or would I be horrified and wish it were dead again (as the 'pale student' does)? What will happen if I cannot love my child? Am I capable of raising a normal, healthy child? Will my child die (as my first baby did)? Could I wish my own child to die, to destroy itself? Could I kill it? Could it kill me (as I killed my mother, Mary Wollstonecraft)?" One reason Mary Shelley's story reverberates so strongly is that it articulates, for perhaps the first time in Western literature, the most powerfully felt anxieties of pregnancy, a topic avoided by male writers and considered improper for women to discuss in public. Mary Shelley's focus on the birth process both educates a male readership about the ways in which pregnant women or new mothers may not desire their own babies, even as it reassures female readers that their fears and hostilities are shared by other women.

Her dream thus generates that dimension of the novel's plot that has been much discussed by feminist critics, Victor Frankenstein's total failure as a parent. Even though he has labored nine months to give birth to his Creature, Frankenstein flees from his child the moment it opens its eyes with the "convulsive motion" of birth. And when like a child, his Creature follows him, grinning, arms open to embrace him, Frankenstein can see his creation only as a devil, a wretch, whom he violently abandons. Throughout the novel, Frankenstein's inability to accept responsibility for his son, his Adam, is contrasted with the examples of two loving fathers, Alphonse Frankenstein and the father in the De Lacey family. Mary Shelley's ideal family, a community of equals joined by love and mutual respect, is represented in the novel especially by the De Laceys: Felix (whose name connotes happiness), Agatha (goodness), and Safie (Sophia or wisdom, a portrait of the liberated woman modeled on Mary Wollstonecraft).

As the novel develops, the author's attention focuses less on the feelings and experiences of Victor Frankenstein and more on those of his Creature, the abandoned child. Mary Shelley powerfully identified with this rejected child. The Creature spends two years peering in on the De Lacey family, just as Mary peered in on the Baxters; the Creature reads the same books as did Mary in 1814 and 1815 (*Paradise Lost*, *The Sorrows of Young Werther*, Plutarch's *Parallel Lives*, Volney's *Ruins of Empires*, the poetry of Coleridge and Byron); both lack a mother and suffer from distant fathers. The novel powerfully evokes the Creature's pain at the recognition that he will be alone, forever alone; equally powerfully, the novel evokes the anger and desire for revenge that such abandonment and isolation can produce. When the Creature finally loses his last hope of joining the De Lacey family, he commits his first act of violence and burns down their cottage.

Mary Shelley recognized that the experience of parental rejection can produce a desire to retaliate: it is no accident that the Creature's first victim is a young boy named William whom he wished to adopt. By naming this child William Frankenstein, Mary Shelley invoked her father William Godwin, her stepbrother William Godwin, Jr., who displaced her in her father's affections, and her own son William Shelley (of whom William Frankenstein is a portrait, possessing the same blue eyes and blond curls). At the psychological level, the Creature's murder of William Frankenstein manifests Mary Shelley's repressed patricidal, fratricidal, and even infanticidal urges, revealing her horrified recognition of her own capacity for aggression.

Mary Shelley's anxiety about her capacity to give birth to a normal, healthy child that she could mother lovingly surfaces in the novel in another way. In her introduction to the revised edition of *Frankenstein* (1831), she identifies the novel itself as her child, her "hideous progeny." For Mary Shelley, this metaphor of the book-as-baby articulates a double anxiety. In giving birth to a book, she has given birth to herself as an author, and specifically to herself as the author of horror. She is reinforcing the literary tradition of the female Gothic, the association of women with the expression of desire that might better remain hidden, repressed. She is thus defying the decorum of the "proper lady," the domestic ideology that insists that women should remain silent in public.

Mary Shelley's guilt at writing an "improper" book led to extensive self-censorship in her novel. Not only did she repress the female authorial voice, assigning her tale to three male narrators (Walton, Frankenstein, and the Creature), but she also gave her tale to a man, Percy Shelley, to "edit" and "correct." Percy Shelley made numerous changes to the manuscript of *Frankenstein*, changes that both improved and damaged the novel. He corrected occasional factual errors and misspellings, he substituted technical terms for Mary Shelley's less precise ones, and he sometimes improved the continuity of and clarified her text. Everywhere he "heightened" her diction and style, substituting polysyllabic, Latinate words and Miltonic inversions for her vernacular, Anglo-Saxon words and sentence constructions. He is thus responsible for that ornate, Ciceronian prose style employed by Frankenstein and his Creature, a style that many readers have found distancing and stilted, not to say improbable for a Creature who is only two years old!

Percy also distorted Mary Shelley's intentions in two important ways. He tended to see Victor

Frankenstein more sympathetically than did Mary. He called Victor an "author" and regarded him as a tragic hero, whereas Mary saw the scientist as an agent of evil and identified him with the hubristic overreachers Faust, Satan, and Prometheus. Similarly, Percy Shelley regarded the Creature more negatively and introduced the Creature as an "abortion." Finally, he changed the last line of the novel, from Mary Shelley's "I soon lost sight of him in the darkness and distance" to "[he was] lost in darkness and distance." Mary Shelley's ending leaves open the possibility that the Creature is still alive, the more so because his promise to build a funeral pyre at the North Pole is inherently incredible, given the lack of wood for such a pyre. Percy Shelley's ending gives a false sense of closure to the novel. Feminist critics have suggested that Mary Shelley's willingness to accept all of Percy's emendations reflected her sense of psychological and literary inferiority to her older, already published, mentor, father figure, and now husband (Percy and Mary were married on 30 December 1816, after his first wife, Harriet, committed suicide).

As its subtitle suggests and many critics have noted, *Frankenstein; or, The Modern Prometheus* functions as a political critique both of Romantic Prometheanism and of the ideology of the French Revolution. By naming her scientist a modern Prometheus, Mary Shelley called into question the fundamental project of the Romantic poets and philosophers she knew best (Godwin, Coleridge, Byron, Percy Shelley): their attempt to perfect mankind, to transform mortals into godlike creatures, to locate the divine in the human. Victor Frankenstein's quest, to "bestow animation upon lifeless matter" and thereby "renew life where death had apparently devoted the body to corruption," is in fact a quest to become God, the creator of life and the gratefully worshiped father of a new species of immortal beings. This quest parallels Godwin's theory of perfectibility through unfettered rationality, Coleridge's claim that the primary human imagination is an "echo of the Infinite I AM," Blake's vision of the human form divine, Wordsworth's insistence that the "higher minds" of poets "are truly from the Deity," and Percy Shelley's image of the poet as the savior and "unacknowledged legislator of the world."

Invoking the myths both of Prometheus plasticator (the maker of man) and of Prometheus pyr-phoros (the fire stealer), Mary Shelley identified her modern Prometheus explicitly with Byron and Percy Shelley. In 1816 she had copied out for his publisher Byron's poem "Prometheus" and verse-drama *Manfred,* in which the Faustian Manfred, who cannot escape his incestuous guilt, nonetheless defies the gods and insists that

> The mind, the spirit, the Promethean spark,
> The lightning of my being, is as bright,
> Pervading, and far-darting as your own,
> And shall not yield to yours, though coop'd in clay!
> (*Manfred*, I.i.154–157)

More immediately, she identified Victor Frankenstein with her husband. Percy Shelley had published his first volume of poems under the pen name Victor; like Frankenstein, he had a "sister" named Elizabeth; he had received the same education as Victor, reading Paracelsus, Albertus Magnus, Pliny, and Buffon, and specializing in alchemy, chemistry, and foreign languages; he shared Frankenstein's revolutionary ideals, which are signaled in the novel by Frankenstein's attending the University of Ingolstadt, home of the leading German Jacobin thinker, Adam Weishaupt. Most important, Frankenstein shared Percy Shelley's relative indifference to his children: Shelley had abandoned his first wife and their children and had not grieved for the death of Mary's first child, Clara.

Mary Shelley also included a positive portrait of her husband through the character of Clerval, Victor's other "self." Clerval is a poet who loves nature, is capable of empathy, of parenting others (he nurses Victor when Victor is sick), and does not disobey his father. But this positive image of an altruistic Percy Shelley is torn from the novel when Clerval is murdered, leaving behind only the egotistical, self-absorbed Victor.

As a modern Prometheus, Victor Frankenstein is a fire stealer, someone who usurps nature's "spark of life" to animate a dead corpse, but then refuses to accept responsibility for the Creature he has created. Mary Shelley rejected the Romantic dream of progressing ever upward to human perfection and immortality because she recognized that a commitment to a utopian, future ideal too often entailed an indifference to the responsibilities of the present. She concluded that a Romantic poetics that valued the creative process above the created product too often failed to acknowledge the predictable consequences of that product, once created—for example, the suffering caused by the political and social revolutions that the passionate words of the poet might inspire.

Imbedded in *Frankenstein* is an allegory of the French Revolution and the Terror. Mary Shelley encourages us to see the Creature as the embodiment of the entire progress of the French Revolution. The Creature first invokes Rousseau's noble savage, born free but everywhere in chains: "I was benevolent and good; misery made me a fiend," he claims (p. 95). Were he incorporated into the family of man, he would be entirely virtuous, he insists. But the Creature does not get the female companion he craves and is driven to violence. Just so the French Revolution was driven out of the hands of the well-intentioned Girondists (Mirabeau, Lafayette, Talleyrand) by the September massacres and the execution of Louis XVI and Marie Antoinette, and into the bloodthirsty arms of Marat, Saint-Just, and Robespierre. The identification of the French Revolution as a "monster" had been made by Edmund Burke and Abbé Barruel, both of whom Mary Shelley had read and admired; in his *Reflections on the Revolution in France* (1789), Burke had defined the Revolution as a "vast, tremendous, unformed spectre."

With this allegory, Mary Shelley offers a subtle political argument, crudely stated as "the end does not justify the means." An abstract cause can never be separated from its historical embodiment in events, nor can an ideology be separated from the class interests it serves. If Victor Frankenstein had loved and cared for his child, the Creature might never have become a monster; similarly, if the early leaders of the French Revolution had found a place for the aristocrats, clergy, and king and queen in their new republic, the Terror and the devastations of the Napoleonic campaigns might not have occurred. Mary Shelley sums up her political credo in a central passage in *Frankenstein*:

A human being in perfection ought always to preserve a calm and peaceful mind and never to allow passion or a transitory desire to disturb his tranquillity. I do not think that the pursuit of knowledge is an exception to this rule. If the study to which you apply yourself has a tendency to weaken your affections, and to destroy your taste for those simple pleasures in which no alloy can possibly mix, then that study is certainly unlawful, that is to say, not befitting the human mind. If this rule were always observed; if no man allowed any pursuit whatsoever to interfere with the tranquillity of his do-

mestic affections, Greece had not been enslaved; Caesar would have spared his country; America would have been discovered more gradually; and the empires of Mexico and Peru had not been destroyed.

(p. 51)

Mary Shelley was a political reformist, rather than a revolutionary. She believed that the nation-state ought to be modeled upon the "domestic affections," upon a loving family in which each member is valued and cared for equally. She shared this concept of "family politics" with other women writers of her day, with Mary Wollstonecraft, Maria Edgeworth, and Jane Austen, a concept of the ideal state as a socialist community grounded in an ethic of care that serves the needs of all the community's members.

Frankenstein offers a powerful critique both of scientific thought and of the psychology of the modern scientist. Mary Shelley may have been the first to question the commitment of science to the search for objective truth irrespective of the consequences. What science did Mary Shelley know? Clearly, she had no personal experience with scientific research; she envisioned Frankenstein's laboratory as a small attic room lit by a single candle! Nonetheless, she had a sound grasp of the concepts and implications of some of the most important scientific research of her day, namely the work of Sir Humphry Davy, Erasmus Darwin, and Luigi Galvani.

At the University of Ingolstadt, Victor Frankenstein chooses to specialize in the field of "natural philosophy," or chemical physiology, the field defined by Humphry Davy in his *A Discourse, Introductory to a Course of Lectures on Chemistry* (1802), the source for Professor Waldman's lecture in the novel. In this pamphlet, Davy insisted that modern chemistry had bestowed upon the chemist "powers which may be almost called creative; which have enabled him to modify and change the beings surrounding him, and by his experiments to interrogate nature with power, not simply as a scholar, passive and seeking only to understand her operations, but rather as a master, active with his own instruments" (p. 16). Gendering nature as female, Davy defined two scientific ways of dealing with her. A "descriptive" science would try to understand the workings of Mother Nature. An "interventionist" science, on the other hand, would be an effort to change the operations of nature. Davy clearly preferred the latter and hailed the scientist who modified nature as a "master." Similarly, Professor Waldman urges Victor Frankenstein to "penetrate into the recesses of nature, and show how she works in her hiding places" (p. 42), an effort Victor undertakes so that he might discover the "principle of life" (p. 46) and use it to his own ends. In Mary Shelley's view, such interventionist science is bad science, dangerous and self-serving.

In contrast, good science is that practiced by Erasmus Darwin, the first theorist of evolution and the grandfather of Charles Darwin. In *The Botanic Garden* (1789, 1791) and *Zoonomia; or, The Laws of Organic Life* (1794, 1801), Darwin had described the evolution of more complex life-forms from simpler ones and argued that dual-sex propagation is higher on the evolutionary ladder than single-sex propagation. From Darwin's perspective, Victor Frankenstein's experiment would reverse evolutionary progress, both because Frankenstein engages in single-sex propagation and because he constructs his new species from both human parts (collected from cemeteries and charnel houses) and animal parts (collected from slaughterhouses). Moreover, he defies the entire concept of evolution by attempting to create a "new" species all at once, rather than through the random mutation of existing species.

The scientist who had the most direct impact on Shelley's representation of Frankenstein's experiment was Luigi Galvani, who argued that electricity was the life force and who had performed numerous experiments conducting electrical currents through dead animals in order to revive them. His most notorious experiment was performed in public in London on 17 January 1803, by his nephew Giovanni Aldini. On that day Aldini applied galvanic electricity to the corpse of a human being. The body of the recently hanged criminal Thomas Forster was brought from Newgate Prison, where it had lain in the prison yard for one hour at thirty degrees Fahrenheit, to Mr. Wilson's Anatomical Theatre, where live wires attached to a pile composed of 120 plates of zinc and 120 plates of copper were connected to the ear and mouth of the dead man. At this moment, Aldini reported, "the jaw began to quiver, the adjoining muscles were horribly contorted, and the left eye actually opened." When the wires were applied to the dissected thumb muscles they "induced a forcible effort to clench the hand"; when applied to the ear and rectum, they "excited in the

muscles contractions much stronger. . . . The action even of those muscles furthest distant from the points of contact with the arc was so much increased as almost to give an appearance of re-animation." When volatile alkali was smeared on the nostrils and mouth before the galvanic stimulus was applied, "the convulsions appeared to be much increased . . . and extended from the muscles of the head, face, and neck, as far as the deltoid. The effect in this case surpassed our most sanguine expectations," Aldini exulted, and he concluded remarkably that "vitality might, perhaps, have been restored, if many circumstances had not rendered it impossible" (Giovanni Aldini, *An Account of the Late Improvements in Galvanism*, 1803, pp. 54, 193-194). Here is the scientific prototype for Victor Frankenstein, restoring life to dead human corpses.

By grounding her literary vision of a scientist animating a corpse upon the cutting-edge scientific research of her day, Mary Shelley initiated a new literary genre, what we now call "science fiction." As Brian Aldiss in *Billion Year Spree: The History of Science Fiction* (1973) and Robert Scholes and Eric Rabkin in *Science Fiction: History, Science, Vision* (1977) have argued, *Frankenstein* possesses the three characteristics essential to the genre of science fiction: (1) it is based on valid scientific research; (2) it gives a persuasive prediction of what science might achieve in the future; and (3) it offers a humanistic critique of the benefits and dangers of either a specific scientific discovery/invention or of the nature of scientific thought.

Frankenstein is notable both for its grasp of the nature of the scientific enterprise and for its searching analysis of the dangers inherent in that enterprise. Victor Frankenstein is our first literary portrait of what we might now call the "mad scientist," but it is a far more subtle portrait than that provided by such films as *Dr. Strangelove*. Mary Shelley recognized that Victor Frankenstein's passion for scientific research is a displacement of normal emotions and healthy affections. Significantly, when Victor is working on his experiment, he cannot love—he ignores his family, even his fiancée Elizabeth, and he takes no pleasure in the beauties of nature. Moreover, he becomes physically and mentally ill, subject to nervous fevers.

Mary Shelley also offers a critique of the nature of scientific thought. Inherent in the concept of science is a potent gender identification, as Sir Humphry Davy assumed: nature is female, the scientist is male. Therefore the scientist who analyzes, manipulates, and attempts to control nature is engaging in sexual politics. In his essay "Temporis Partus Masculus," Francis Bacon heralded the seventeenth-century scientific revolution with the words, "I am come in very truth leading to you Nature with all her children to bind her to your service and make her your slave." By constructing nature as female, the scientist feels entitled to exploit her to gratify his own desire for power, money, and status. Frankenstein's scientific quest is nothing less than an attempt to "penetrate into the recesses of nature, and show how she works in her hiding places," to penetrate the womb of nature and to appropriate that womb, to usurp the process of female biological reproduction. In effect, Frankenstein wishes to rape nature in order to gratify his own lust for power. Frankenstein fantasizes, "A new species would bless me as its creator and source; many happy and excellent natures would owe their being to me. No father could claim the gratitude of his child so completely as I should deserve theirs" (p. 49). If Frankenstein were to succeed in stealing the power of female biological reproduction, he would eliminate the biological necessity for females; the human race of males could survive by cloning. For women readers, this is perhaps the greatest horror of Mary Shelley's story: the implicit threat to the social and biological survival of the human female.

By constituting nature as female, Frankenstein participates in a gendered construction of both physical and social reality. Feminist critics have argued that his scientific endeavor to clone human males and eliminate human females reinforces the general devaluation of women in the nineteenth-century European society to which he belongs. The society of Geneva depicted in Shelley's novel is based on the doctrine of the separate spheres, the assumption that men should work outside the home in the public sphere, while women are confined in the private sphere within the home. Notably, the male characters in Shelley's novel all leave home, to go to university (Victor), to explore the planet (Walton), to work as businessmen (Clerval and his father), and to work as public servants (Alphonse Frankenstein). In contrast, the women are kept at home; as much as she would like to, Elizabeth is not permitted to attend university or travel. Inside the home, the women function as housewives (Caroline Beaufort, Margaret Saville),

as nurses, caregivers for children, servants (Justine), or as "pets" (Elizabeth).

Shelley's novel makes it clear that this division of labor on the basis of gender is destructive for both sexes. All of the women associated with Victor Frankenstein die: his mother sacrifices herself to nurse Elizabeth's scarlet fever, Justine is executed for a crime she did not commit, and Elizabeth is killed by Victor's Creature on her wedding night. Similarly, Victor, his father, and his best friend all die, killed by the results of Victor's reckless experiment. In contrast to this mutually destructive construction of gender is the egalitarian family of the De Laceys, in which both son and daughter contribute equally to the welfare of the family and hold all property in common. But this socialist, egalitarian community is wrenched from the novel, as it was from Mary Shelley's own life: in her view, such a social ideal could not survive in the nineteenth-century England she knew.

Why have women been oppressed, in Mary Shelley's view? She offers a particularly subtle answer to this question in the scene where Victor Frankenstein decides to destroy the female creature. His male Creature has begged him for a female companion. Acknowledging the justice of the Creature's claim that, as Adam, he deserves an Eve, Victor Frankenstein collects his instruments together on a desolate island off the coast of Scotland and proceeds to construct a female body. But halfway through his endeavor, he destroys this body and throws it away. He rationalizes his action thus:

I was now about to form another being, of whose dispositions I was alike ignorant; she might become ten thousand times more malignant than her mate, and delight, for its own sake, in murder and wretchedness. He had sworn to quit the neighbourhood of man, and hide himself in deserts; but she had not; and she, who in all probability was to become a thinking and reasoning animal, might refuse to comply with a compact made before her creation. They might even hate each other; the creature who already lived loathed his own deformity, and might he not conceive a greater abhorrence for it when it came before his eyes in the female form? She also might turn with disgust from him to the superior beauty of man; she might quit him, and he be again alone, exasperated by the fresh provocation of being deserted by one of his own species.

Even if they were to leave Europe, and inhabit the deserts of the new world, yet one of the first results of those sympathies for which the daemon thirsted would be children, and a race of devils would be propagated upon the earth, who might make the very existence of the species of man a condition precarious and full of terror. Had I a right, for my own benefit, to inflict this curse upon everlasting generations?

(p. 163)

What Frankenstein truly fears is that the female he will construct might be independent, that she might refuse to obey laws she did not make. She might be aggressive, ugly, and lustful. Worse, given that she too would be eight feet tall, she would have the physical strength to realize her sexual desires, perhaps even upon Victor Frankenstein himself. Most frightening, she would have the capacity to procreate. Frankenstein's deepest fear is of female sexuality. He evinces traditional patriarchal womb envy, which stems in part from the fact that a child's paternity can be called into question, whereas a female always knows that the child she carries is hers. In reaction to this masculine fear of an independent, uncontrollable female sexuality, Frankenstein rips up the female creature in an act that echoes a violent rape: "trembling with passion, [I] tore to pieces the thing on which I was engaged" (p. 164). Later, he remarks, "I almost felt as if I had mangled the living flesh of a human being" (p. 167).

In Mary Shelley's feminist novel, however, Victor Frankenstein does not succeed in creating a new race of supermen because nature fights back. She begins by plaguing Frankenstein with bad health. As he engages in his two experiments, he is tormented by fevers, heart palpitations, nervous fits, depression, and paranoia. His physical exhaustion is finally so great that he dies at the age of twenty-five. Nature further punishes Victor by preventing him from creating a normal child: his lack of empathy first causes him to create a giant (simply because the "minuteness of the [normal-sized] parts formed a great hindrance to my speed") and then leads to a series of disasters that prevent him from normal procreation with his bride Elizabeth. Finally, nature pursues Victor Frankenstein with the very electricity and fire he has stolen from her. The lightning, thunder, and rain that surround Victor as he carries on his experiments are not just the conventional atmospheric effects of the Gothic novel but also a manifestation of nature's elemental powers. Like the Furies, nature pursues Victor to his hiding places, destroying not only Victor but his family, friend, and servant. Finally, the penalty of violating nature is death.

Encoded in *Frankenstein* is an alternative to Victor's and Walton's view of nature as female and to be penetrated or as dead matter to be reassembled at will. Significantly, the only member of the Frankenstein family still alive at the end of the novel is Ernest, who, rather than becoming a lawyer like his father, wished to become a farmer. His survival, together with Clerval's enthusiastic love of the changing beauty of the seasons, reveals Mary Shelley's view of the appropriate relationship between human beings and nature: an ecological vision of nature as a person with rights and responsibilities who must be treated with respect, even reverence.

Frankenstein persistently raises the two philosophical questions that haunted all the Romantic writers of the period: What is being? And how do we know what we know? These are the ontological and epistemological questions David Hume and Immanuel Kant had tried to answer, and these are the questions with which both Victor Frankenstein and his Creature are wrestling. Victor sets out to answer the question "whence did the principle of life proceed?" And the Creature insistently demands, "Who was I? What was I? Whence did I come? What was my destination?" (p. 124).

As Shelley's characters struggle with these questions, the novel presents two diametrically opposed answers. The Creature, echoing Jean-Jacques Rousseau, insists that human nature is innately good: "I was benevolent and good; misery made me a fiend" (p. 95). On the other hand, Victor Frankenstein insists that the Creature is innately evil: "Abhorred monster! fiend that thou art!" (p. 94). Insofar as the Creature is frequently referred to in the text as "Being," his very existence poses this problem: is human nature innately good or evil?

This question is emphasized in the emblematic scene when the Creature first sees himself, in a forest pool: "At first I started back, unable to believe that it was indeed I who was reflected in the mirror; and when I became fully convinced that I was in reality the monster that I am, I was filled with the bitterest sensations of despondency and mortification" (p. 109). This scene suggests that in this novel, knowing (re-cognition) is a matter of seeing (perception)—the Creature is at first unable to believe that he is what he perceives himself to be. He then decides that he is "in reality" what he appears to be, what his mirror shows him to be, namely, a "monster." The Creature is as he is seen; he functions in the novel as the sign of the unknown, as that which does not exist until it is read or linguistically named. All the characters impose such names upon him; all immediately read this giant with yellow skin and black lips as the monstrous. The creature insists that such a reading is arbitrary; "'Thus I relieve thee, my creator,' he said, and placed his hated hands before my eyes" (p. 96), as if to suggest that when Victor ceases to see the Creature, he may be able to read him more correctly. Similarly, the father in the De Lacey family can interpret the Creature as "sincere" because he is blind. Walton also covers his eyes when he finally encounters the Creature, refusing to impose a single interpretation upon him, but even Walton then "lost sight" of him in "darkness and distance."

By refusing to tell us whether the Creature is innately good and driven to violence by social rejection, or innately evil, Mary Shelley constructs the Creature as the Kantian noumenon, the forever unknowable "thing-in-itself." She thus equates her Creature with the terror of the Romantic or Burkean sublime, that ultimate power in nature which overwhelms human cognition and consciousness. But, unlike Kant or Burke, or such Romantic poets as Wordsworth, Coleridge, and Percy Shelley, Mary Shelley does not represent the sublime as a moment when the mind of the (male) poet or philosopher comes to know its own creative, shaping powers.

Rather, she represents the sublime as posing an ethical problem. The way we read or interpret the Creature determines the way we treat him. Human beings typically construe the unique, the unfamiliar, and the abnormal as frightening, threatening, and evil. As Michel Foucault argues in *Madness and Civilization*, we use language to fix the boundaries between the acceptable and the unacceptable. Linguistic definitions of evil thus create evil. Because Victor Frankenstein reads his newborn child as a "miserable monster," he interprets the Creature as evil and thus becomes the author of evil.

In effect, Victor Frankenstein becomes the monster he constructs. By the end of the novel, Victor and his creature have been fused into one consciousness, each the hunter and the hunted, each driven equally by revenge and remorse. In their chase across the North Pole, both are identified with the fallen Adam and with Satan, until Victor in his nightmares experiences the Creature as "my own vampire" (p. 72)—"I felt the fiend's grasp *in* my neck" (p. 181), not "around" his neck, as we might expect. The Creature and Victor now inhabit the same body. This is the sense in which popular culture is correct in confounding the Creature with his creator.

Mary Shelley wants us to see that in a world created by linguistic constructions that code the unfamiliar as evil, we create the evil and injustice that we imagine. She is here criticizing the male Romantic poets' celebration of the imagination as divine. A promiscuous imagination is more likely to generate readings based on fear than on love, as Theseus says in Shakespeare's *A Midsummer Night's Dream*. Her answer to the philosophical questions posed in *Frankenstein* is a radical skepticism. Since we can never *know* the thing-in-itself, we must consciously control our interpretations of almighty nature with a nurturing love that can embrace even freaks and monsters. For as the Creature reminds Victor, "You are my creator but I am your master—obey!"

MATHILDA

SHORTLY after Mary Shelley completed *Frankenstein*, her second daughter, Clara Everina, died, on 24 September 1818, as a result of Percy Shelley's refusal to obtain adequate medical care for her; less than a year later, on 7 June 1819, her only surviving child, William, died in Rome of malaria. Mary Shelley entered a prolonged period of profound depression, blaming Percy (in part correctly) for both these deaths and refusing to be reconciled to him. She was roused from this depression only by the writing of her long novella *Mathilda*, which she began in August 1819, and by the birth of her second son, Percy Florence, on 12 November 1819. *Mathilda* is a powerful tale of incestuous father-daughter love and death in which Mary Shelley articulates her deepest and most ambivalent feelings toward both her father and her husband.

Her hostility to her father was immediately aroused by his failure to understand her despair at William's death. In a letter that may rank among the cruelest ever sent by a father to a bereaved daughter, Godwin had written on 9 September 1819:

I cannot but consider it as lowering your character in a memorable degree, and putting you among the commonality and mob of your sex, when I had thought you to be ranked among those noble spirits that do honour to our nature. Oh! What a falling off is here! . . . you have lost a child; and all the rest of the world, all that is beautiful, and all that has a claim upon your kindness, is nothing, because a child of three years old is dead!

(quoted in *Shelley and Mary*, ed. by Jane Shelley, 1882, I:104A)

In her novella, Shelley writes the story of a young man whose adored wife Diana dies in childbirth; he then abandons his baby daughter Mathilda for sixteen years, returning only to fall passionately in love with the girl who exactly resembles his dead wife. When he confesses his incestuous passion, Mathilda is horrified and immediately dreams of his suicide, only to awaken to find him gone. This novella thus uncovers Mary Shelley's deepest desire: to be passionately loved by the father who had rejected her, and at the same time to reject and even kill him.

Unlike representations of father-daughter incest by men, like Percy Shelley's *The Cenci*, in which incest is a trope for the domination of the tyrant-father over the rights of both his daughters and his sons (whose appropriate "brides" he usurps), Mary Shelley recognizes that in a relationship of incest the daughter may deeply love her father. Mathilda cannot survive her father's suicide; she stages her own suicide and then retires to live like a hermit, dressed as a nun, in a forsaken wood in Scotland. She regards herself as "the bride of death."

There she is found by an idealistic but lovelorn poet, Woodville (modeled on Percy Shelley), who urges her to rejoin the living but fails to understand the depths of her suffering. When she offers Woodville a drink of total communion, a poison, he refuses it, claiming that he must remain alive to give his poetry to the world. He abandons her, as Percy had emotionally abandoned Mary in her suffering. Mathilda then wanders in a storm at night until she becomes ill—she soon expires from self-induced consumption, penning the story of her life as she dies.

THE LAST MAN

MARY Shelley's sufferings were to continue. Her husband's sudden death by drowning on 8 July 1822, off the coast of Livorno, Italy, was a devastating blow to Mary Shelley and left her widowed at the age of twenty-five with a two-year-old son to raise. Worse, Percy Shelley's death followed a long period of emotional estrangement between the couple caused by Mary Shelley's conviction that Percy had been in part responsible for the prior deaths of both her daughter, Clara Everina, and her son, William. As Mary Shelley wrote bitterly to her good friend Marianne Hunt on 29 June 1819: "We came to Italy thinking to do Shelley's health good—but the Climate is not any means warm enough to be of benefit to him & yet it is that that has destroyed my two children" (*Letters*, vol. 1, p. 101). Confronted with his wife's depression and resentment, Percy Shelley had in the months prior to his death found consolation in the company of other women, of Maria Gisborne, Claire Clairmont, and Jane Williams. His death thus occurred at the worst possible time for Mary Shelley, when there was a great deal of emotional turmoil between them.

Overwhelmed by love, guilt, and remorse, blaming herself for having made his final months unhappy, Mary attempted to make reparation to her dead husband by giving him a posthumous life. She immediately collected his manuscripts and published texts for a complete edition of his works and began to write a hagiographic biography. When her father-in-law forebade its publication, she instead appended long biographical notes to her 1824 and 1839 editions of Percy Shelley's poems, notes in which she deified the poet and revised their past history together, asserting that his last two months on earth were "the happiest he had ever known" (1824). She used her fiction to present idealized portraits of Percy Shelley, first and most tellingly as Adrian in *The Last Man* (1826). In financially straitened circumstances, she managed to give her only surviving child the education and upbringing of a future baronet (he inherited his grandfather's title and estate in 1844) by writing novels, essays, and encyclopedia articles, by translating, and by living as economically as possible on her meager inheritance and allowance from Percy's father, Sir Timothy Shelley.

Published in 1826, *The Last Man* is a brilliantly prophetic novel. It draws on Mary Shelley's personal experiences of abandonment and isolation after the deaths of her husband and of Lord Byron, who died on 19 April 1824. At the same time, it articulates a profound critique of the dominant gender, cultural, and political ideologies of the Romantic era. Equally important, *The Last Man* explores the social significance of a worldwide plague that relentlessly annihilates the entire human race, leaving only one last man to tell the story.

At the biographical level, *The Last Man* is a roman à clef in which Mary Shelley projected and tried to come to terms with both Percy Shelley and Lord Byron, in the figures of Adrian, Earl of Windsor, and of Lord Raymond. Adrian, the "hero" of the novel, shares Percy Shelley's democratic principles as well as his face, form, and voice; he arouses universal affection, even among his enemies. But like the poet of Percy Shelley's "Alastor," he is driven mad by despair when his beloved Evadne rejects him, a madness from which he recovers only after a severe fever has permanently impaired his health.

Despite his physical weakness, Adrian ardently supports the cause of freedom, fights for a year with the Greeks against their Turkish oppressors, and urges his countrymen "to introduce a perfect system of republican government into England" (p. 30). But he refuses to use his position as Earl of Windsor to gain personal political power. Not until England is ravaged by the deadly plague does he determine to "sacrifice himself for the public good" (p. 182) and to accept the position of Lord Protector. With courage and unflagging energy, he then comforts the sick, takes what preventive measures he can against the unstoppable epidemic, and when factions develop among his followers, heroically hurls himself between their armed forces, eloquently reminding them that the plague is their common enemy and that each human life is sacred. Like "an angel of peace" (p. 277), he reunites and governs his countrymen.

Even as Mary Shelley lovingly portrays Adrian as a paragon of benevolence, idealism, courage, and self-sacrifice, her underlying resentment toward her husband cracks this perfect facade. Adrian never marries, never accepts responsibility for a family: "the sensitive and excellent Adrian, loving all, and beloved by all, yet seemed destined not to find the half of himself, which was to complete his happiness" (p. 65). Thus Mary Shelley alludes to the narcissistic egoism of her husband, his insatiable demand for that perfect soul mate who could only be his own self.

Moreover, Adrian is incapable of working pragmatically to achieve his political ideals. Only after the plague has brutally eliminated all distinctions of wealth and class can he assume leadership over a leveled, egalitarian society. As Hugh Luke has observed, he is subtly associated with Merrival, the old astronomer who is "too long sighted in his view of humanity to heed the casualties of the day" (p. 209) and who remains oblivious to the sufferings of his wife and children until poverty, hunger, and the plague have killed them all.

This oblique criticism of Percy Shelley's insensitivity to the needs of his wife and children is also expressed in the final fate of Adrian. After war, disease, and the plague have destroyed all but three of the human race, Adrian urges the reluctant Verney to accede to his niece Clara's request that the three of them sail to Greece to visit the tomb of her parents. Verney warns against the dangers of a storm at sea, but Adrian insists that they can easily make the journey. In the ensuing tempest, Adrian and Clara are both drowned, leaving only Verney alive on earth. Here Mary Shelley vividly focuses her persistent anger at her husband's irresponsibility concerning his family's welfare. Despite her overt celebration of her husband's genius and "angelic" character, Mary Shelley had not forgiven him for contributing to Clara Everina Shelley's death, or to his own.

This critique of male egoism also informs Shelley's characterization of Lord Raymond, in which she comes to terms with her fascination with Lord Byron. After the death of Percy Shelley, Mary had expected Byron to become her protector and eagerly welcomed his offers of help. But Byron disappointed her. Caught up in his plans to fight for Greek independence, Byron could not long be bothered with the distraught widow and abruptly withdrew his financial and emotional support. Nonetheless, Mary Shelley's emotions toward Byron remained charged. When she learned of his death at Missolonghi, she cried out to her journal (15 May 1824):

Byron has become one of the people of the grave— . . . Can I forget his attentions & consolations to me during my deepest misery?—Never.
Beauty sat on his countenance and power beamed from his eye—his faults being for the most part weaknesses induced one readily to pardon them. Albe [the Shelley circle's pun on L. B.]—the dear capricious fascinating Albe has left this desart [*sic*] world.

(*Journals*, vol. 2, p. 478)

Lord Raymond is presented as the antithesis of Adrian: a proud man of personal ambition, practical worldly knowledge, and intense sexual passions. After fighting heroically in the Greek wars of independence and successfully scheming to restore the British monarchy, Raymond throws over his worldly ambitions to marry the woman he loves, the impoverished Perdita Verney. Mary Shelley, who has given many of her own personality traits to Perdita, reveals through this character her own half-conscious fantasies: that Byron would give up his mistress Teresa Guiccioli and his dreams of military glory in order to marry her. Nevertheless, Raymond cannot long be content with a retired life of intellectually stimulating companionship and the domestic affections; drawn back into politics as Lord Protector (with Perdita as a successful hostess at his side), for three years he rules wisely and well.

But when Raymond falls half in love with the impoverished Evadne, he cannot acknowledge his feelings to his wife. Their perfect communion is destroyed, the foundation of their marriage wrecked. Still in love with Perdita but too proud to apologize, Raymond turns to dreams of military glory instead, heroically conquering Constantinople, only to die in a fatal explosion when he courageously enters its streets silenced by plague. In her portrait of Raymond, Mary Shelley reiterated the judgment of masculine political ambition she had earlier attributed to her protagonist, Castruccio, in her novel *Valperga* (1823): military and civic glory is too often won at the expense of family relationships and the suffering of the innocent. At the same time she exorcised her fascination with Byron: his pride and lack of control over his personal passions tainted even his most noble achievements.

The failures of both Adrian and Raymond to protect either their own or their children's lives again expresses Mary Shelley's political criticism of her contemporary society's division of labor on the basis of sex. Mary Shelley again suggests that the domination of such masculine values as ambition, competition, and heroism in the public realm can extinguish human life in both the public and the private sphere and even extinguish the human race itself. Implicit is the political argument that she had made earlier in *Frankenstein:* only if men as well as women define their primary personal and political responsibility as the nurturance and preservation of all human life, even abnormal monsters, will humanity survive.

In *The Last Man*, Mary Shelley further explores the specific consequences for women of the gen-

der ideology of her day. The female characters in *The Last Man* register her perception that the social roles assigned by her culture to women both cripple and destroy them. Perdita and Idris, both in part self-portraits of Mary Shelley, confine their lives to the domestic sphere; they thereby reveal the results of a society that defines women primarily as members of family units, as daughters, wives, or mothers.

Perdita, whose name is drawn from the outcast and "orphaned" child of Shakespeare's *Winter's Tale,* can conceive of herself only as a part of her husband's self: "Her whole existence was one sacrifice to him" (p. 84). When she discovers Raymond's secret visits to Evadne, she knows that they are no longer one. Mary Shelley explicitly denies her husband's self-serving declaration in "Epipsychidion" that "True Love in this differs from gold and clay / That to divide is not to take away" (pp. 160–161). As Perdita insists, the unique love between a devoted husband and wife cannot be shared without destroying the very intimacy and trust on which it is grounded.

Perdita cannot tolerate the sham of living a lost love and leaves Raymond, but her unwavering passion for him forces her back to his side, first to nurse him when he is wounded and then to die and be buried in his tomb in Greece. Perdita's suicide by drowning imaginatively realizes Mary Shelley's own guilt-ridden desire to rejoin her dead husband in a final act of atonement. But it also embodies her recognition that the role of devoted wife within the bourgeois family is inherently suicidal: the wife submerges her identity into that of her husband, sacrificing herself for his welfare.

Idris, Mary Shelley's second self-portrait in this novel, is portrayed almost exclusively as a mother. She is so idealized in her highborn beauty, sensitivity, and loyalty as to be almost an abstraction of female perfection. Idris becomes a rounded character only in her relationships with her children. Here she embodies the overriding maternal anxiety experienced by the very young Mary Shelley, who had been pregnant five times. As the plague advances, Idris is slowly destroyed by this maternal anxiety: "she compared this gnawing of sleepless expectation of evil, to the vulture that fed on the heart of Prometheus" (p. 219). Shelley identifies the modern Prometheus, not with the scientist/creator Victor Frankenstein, but with the biological creator, the mother. By implying that

Idris' maternal suffering is as intense and unending as that of Prometheus, Shelley underlines the heroic but self-destructive dimensions of motherhood. Because Idris identifies so closely with her children, she has no life of her own—her sons' deaths annihilate her as well.

In *The Last Man*, women can find fulfillment neither within the family nor outside it. In contrast to Perdita and Idris, who define themselves entirely as wives and mothers, the Countess of Windsor has strong political ambitions—she wishes to restore the monarchy and to rule over England. But she is defeated by her gender. The English would never accept her, a foreign woman, as monarch. Hence she must channel her ambitions through her son or her daughter's husband. Blocked by her husband's decision to abdicate, her son's republicanism, her daughter's rejection of Raymond, and Raymond's own desire for Perdita, she can never achieve her desires. After Idris' death, she acknowledges that her political ambition has been both futile and counterproductive and has cut her off from the love and nurturance of her children. While Mary Shelley makes it clear that the Countess of Windsor would have been a tyrannical ruler, she also emphasizes that a woman cannot even gain access to the corridors of political power: the countess is notably absent from the parliamentary debates concerning the protectorship.

Mary Shelley thus suggests that in both the future (the novel is set in the years 2073–2100) and the present, a rigid division of sex roles denies women full satisfaction in life. In the public realm, her female characters must depend on and serve men. In the private domestic realm, they again must depend on others, whether their children or their husbands, to gratify their emotional needs. Both in the public and the private spheres depicted in *The Last Man*, women have only a relational identity, as wife or mother. They are never self-centered or self-sufficient. And while this relational identity contributes positively to the welfare and survival of the family, it is also extremely precarious. It is easily destroyed by infidelity (the betrayal of Raymond) or by the greater power that rules over all human experience, that of chance, accident, and death. Mary Shelley here undermines the very ideology of the egalitarian family that she celebrated in her earlier novels *(Frankenstein, Valperga)* by acknowledging that it can oppress and even finally destroy the women who practice it.

This pessimistic assessment of the future of the family and domestic affection is summed up in the fate of Clara, a portrait of the ideal daughter that Mary Shelley desired. Sensitive, loving, exuberant, intelligent, devoted to her uncle, a second mother to her younger cousins, Clara suddenly becomes sad and withdrawn at the age of puberty. Clara's transformation is never explained but we can speculate as to its cause. With her dawning sexuality, Clara may have realized that her future—and the future of the human race—demanded her involvement in a sexual liaison and motherhood. With her choices limited to an incestuous union with her uncle or her cousin, or a legitimate union with Adrian, her inability to contemplate the latter with pleasure is final testimony to Mary Shelley's ambivalence toward Percy. She cannot imagine a satisfying relationship between Adrian and a woman, not even with her ideal future self. When she insists on visiting her parents' tomb, Clara shows that she feels more bonded to death than to Adrian. Significantly, our last glimpse of Clara is as a half-drowned virgin clasped to Adrian's breast (p. 323). But Adrian cannot support her; Lionel last sees Adrian alone, clinging not to Clara but to an oar. Clara's death is Mary Shelley's final comment in this novel on the possibility of female fulfillment and even survival in a family unit to which men do not make an equal commitment.

To the ideology of the domestic affections that sustained her earlier fiction, which she so effectively explodes in *The Last Man*, Mary Shelley offers but one alternative: a stoical solipsism rendered endurable by an optimistic imagination. We must look closely at the way Mary Shelley depicts the creative imagination in this novel, for she gives a far more devastating critique of Romantic poetics than she did in *Frankenstein*. When he loses his family, Lionel Verney becomes a writer, the narrator of the tale we read.

The last man, Lionel Verney, is also the last woman, Mary Shelley—she so identified herself in her journal on 14 May 1824: "The last man! Yes I may well describe that solitary being's feelings, feeling myself as the last relic of a beloved race, my companions, extinct before me" (*Journals*, vol. 2, pp. 476–477). There are numerous parallels between Verney's situation and Mary Shelley's. Both were "outcasts" in childhood, both possessed a scholarly temperament, a literary imagination, and a preference for domestic pleasures and affections. Both were in love with Adrian/Shelley and credited him with their salvation from intellectual ignorance and emotional misery. Both find themselves at last enduring an almost unimaginable experience of isolation and loneliness. As Mary Shelley recorded in the journal she addressed to her dead husband: "At the age of seven & twenty in the busy metropolis of native England I find myself alone—deserted by the few I knew—disdained—insulted" (3 December 1824; *Journals*, vol. 2, p. 487). Deprived of human companionship, Lionel Verney and Mary Shelley both turn to creative composition for comfort. Lionel Verney, inspired by the monuments of Rome and a desire to celebrate the "matchless specimens of humanity" that created such grandeur, receives momentary satisfaction from his decision to write an account of the end of mankind.

Significantly, Verney consciously works within a female literary tradition; he invokes both Ann Radcliffe's *The Italian* and Madame de Staël's *Corinne* as models. In the author's introduction to *The Last Man*, we are told that the author functioned merely as the collector and arranger of the fragmentary leaves of a prophecy found in the cave of the Cumaean Sibyl. Mary Shelley thus invokes the ultimate female literary authority, the oracle of the Sibyl, to authenticate her prophetic vision. Of course, the novel also identifies Verney with a male-authored literary tradition that focuses on the isolated hero: Charles Brockden Brown's egocentric Arthur Mervyn, Shakespeare's dying Macbeth, Defoe's stranded Robinson Crusoe, Coleridge's guilt-ridden and blasted Ancient Mariner. In contrast to these prototypes, Lionel Verney cannot even hope for human communication; he can dedicate his tale only to "the illustrious dead."

Explicit in Mary Shelley's account of the last man is the assertion that her tale has no living readership, no audience. Even as she constructs a female literary tradition, from the Sibyl through her own editorship, she terminates that tradition. Shelley's novel posits the end of writing. It is a manuscript left on the tombs of Rome for no one to read by a writer who has abandoned authorship in order to voyage aimlessly, an ancient mariner encountering no wedding guest but only life-in-death. Shelley thus implies that the female writer—like Lionel Verney—will not be read, her voice will not be heard, her discourse will be silenced forever.

Shelley further suggests that the products of the creative imagination so glorified by the male Romantic poets may be worthless. At best their consolation is temporary, if delusive, as Verney finds when he enters Constantinople, seeking the deceased Raymond: "For a moment I could yield to the creative power of the imagination, and for a moment was soothed by the sublime fictions it presented to me. The beatings of my human heart drew me back to blank reality" (p. 145).

Insubstantial dreams, such fictions become "tales of sound and fury, signifying nothing" when they can reach no living ear or mind. Here Shelley's philosophical skepticism becomes visible. She first posits the idealist epistemology endorsed by Berkeley, Kant, and Percy Shelley. If to be is to be perceived, if the human mind can never know the thing itself but only its own linguistic constructions of it, then reality exists only in the collective minds of all perceivers. As Percy Shelley had put it in "Mont Blanc," "The everlasting universe of things / Flows though the mind." Unlike Bishop Berkeley, Kant, or her husband, Mary Shelley posits no overarching mind of God, no transcendental subject, no eternal power, to guarantee the truth or endurance of mental things. Once all human perceivers are dead, history ends. The death of the last man is the death of consciousness. It is moreover the death of the universe, since the Cumaean Sibyl prophesies a point in the future, "2100 Last Year of the World," when time and space—as experienced duration and extension—terminate. Since reality is a set of language systems, the death of Lionel Verney is the death of narration, the final period.

Underlining her critique of Romantic idealism, Mary Shelley sets the final scene of the plague's devastation on the very banks of the Arve River in the valley of Chamonix where Percy Shelley wrote "Mont Blanc" and raised the epistemological question of whether the universe could have an existence not constituted by human thought:

And what were thou, and earth, and stars, and sea,
If to the human mind's imaginings
Silence and solitude were vacancy?
("Mont Blanc," ll. 142–145)

When Adrian and his few remaining followers cross into Switzerland, they are confronted with one of nature's most sublime Alpine landscapes. Overcome by the sheer grandeur of nature's beauty, many in the group are moved to tears and one cries out, "God reveals his heaven to us; we may die blessed" (p. 305). But Mary Shelley's allusions here to both Christian heavens and pagan naiads serve paradoxically to highlight the fact that no deity presides over this plague, only an indifferent nature. Human efforts to fit their experiences into a preexisting providential design or ontological moral absolutes are here rendered nugatory.

Mary Shelley's conception of the last man thus stands in deliberate contrast to her contemporaries' treatments of the same theme, all of which used the trope of the end of civilization to point to either an ethical or religious moral. Byron's "Darkness" (1816; itself derived from Alexander Pope's vision of chaotic night in "The Dunciad," 1728) and Thomas Hood's "The Last Man" (1826) had satirized mankind's greed, aggression, and cowardice as forceful enough to compel even the last two men on earth to turn against each other. In a more optimistic vein, the paintings of *The Deluge* and *The Last Man* by John Martin and Philippe de Loutherbourg, Cousin de Grainville's novel *The Last Man; or, Omegarious and Syderia, a Romance in Futurity* (1806), and Thomas Campbell's poem "The Last Man" (first published in 1823 and probably the immediate inspiration for Mary Shelley's 14 May 1824, journal entry and title) all invoke a Judeo-Christian framework and the possibility of a finer life elsewhere, either on earth or in heaven. Mary Shelley explicitly denies such theological or millennial interpretations of her plague. In her novel, the illiterate man who insists that the plague is God's punishment for human sin and that he and his followers constitute an "Elect" that will be saved is explicitly condemned as an "Imposter" who is finally driven to suicide and whose deceived followers perish along with everyone else.

Moreover, Shelley's intentions go far beyond satire. Implicit in *Frankenstein* is a belief in the primacy of the domestic affections and in the restorative power of a maternal, "beautiful" nature. But in *The Last Man,* all pastoral idylls—whether set among the woods of Windsor or on the shores of Lake Como—are abruptly shattered by the advent of the plague. Even though nature continues to provide scenes of sublime grandeur and beautiful delight that give pleasure to the human senses, it remains indifferent to the preservation of human life.

Therefore all human values must be engendered out of the human imagination. But such values, including the value of the domestic affections that Lionel Verney celebrates throughout *The Last Man,* finally depend entirely on individual commitment. And since individuals are mutable, often unable to control their passions (as in the case of Lord Raymond) and always unable to control their final destiny, such values are necessarily temporal and mutable. As Verney says at the very beginning of his tale, "My fortunes have been . . . an exemplification of the power that mutability may possess over the varied tenor of man's life" (p. 5). Mary Shelley's novel recognizes only one controlling power, death.

Moreover, when Mary Shelley defines nature (the plague) as the final arbiter of human destiny in *The Last Man,* she undercuts another fundamental Romantic assumption that she had endorsed in *Frankenstein:* the belief that nature can be the source of moral authority, a belief asserted by Wordsworth in *The Prelude* (1805, 1850). Mary Shelley explicitly denies Wordsworth's assertion by portraying her "child of nature," her orphaned narrator Lionel Verney, as an aggressive, embittered outcast, much like the rejected Creature in *Frankenstein.* Deliberately alluding to Wordsworth's celebrations of the life of the shepherd, Shelley portrays her Cumberland sheep boy as a savage whose only law "was that of the strongest" and whose only concept of virtue "was never to submit" (pp. 8–9). Verney eagerly abandons his lonely shepherd life to participate in the social pleasures offered by Adrian—friendship, learning, gamesmanship, military struggle, and politics. But all such social interactions terminate in the destructions of the plague. Verney ends in the solitude in which he began, but he bears it less well, since he has learned to appreciate the value of those social relationships that he can never know again.

Mary Shelley also undercuts the Romantic concept of nature as a source of cultural meaning. The nature imaged in *The Last Man* is closer to Alfred, Lord Tennyson's trope of "Nature, red in tooth and claw" in *In Memoriam* (1850) than to Mary Shelley's earlier image in *Frankenstein* of nature as a sacred female life force that man penetrates and violates at his peril. Here female nature is indifferent to mankind; her agent, the female plague, now "Queen of the World" (p. 252), is a juggernaut: "she proceeds crushing out the being of all who strew the high road of life" (p. 289). In a passage that explicitly refutes Percy Shelley's invocation of nature (in the shape of the west wind) as both destroyer and preserver in his "Ode to the West Wind" (1820), Lionel Verney addresses the omnipotent power of nature: "when any whole nation becomes the victim of the destructive powers of exterior agents, then indeed man shrinks into insignificance, he feels his tenure of life insecure, his inheritance on earth cut off" (pp. 166–167). In this central passage, Mary Shelley undercuts the Romantic assumption that language constructs and communicates meaning. If the human race can be eliminated, as it is in *The Last Man*, then the very concept of meaning is, finally, meaningless. Where human discourse cannot occur, linguistically constituted meaning cannot exist and human consciousness is annihilated. This is Mary Shelley's sweeping critique of the masculine Romantic poetic ideology promoted by Percy Shelley, Blake, Coleridge, and Wordsworth: the constructions of the imagination cannot transcend the human mind, which is inherently finite, mutable, and mortal.

From this position of radical skepticism, *The Last Man* generates a powerful political criticism. The first half of the novel pits Mary Shelley's earlier belief in the domestic affections as the model of good government and the source of human fulfillment against the forces that destroy it: the forces of male egotism, female masochism, and plague-induced death. In undermining the family as the preserver of cultural value and social stability, Shelley does more than undercut her own beliefs. She also reveals the failure of all the dominant political ideologies of her day—both radical (republican and democratic) and conservative (monarchical and theocratic). Ultimately, she denies the authority of all ideologies and systems of belief.

Both her father, the radical philosopher William Godwin, and his disciple Percy Shelley believed that mankind might be perfected through the improvement of reason and love under a democratic government or benevolent anarchy. This belief is tested by Mary Shelley in *The Last Man* through the actions of both Ryland, leader of the people's party, and Adrian, the ardent espouser of republican principles. Ryland, whose appearance and character are based on the radical British journalist and politician William Cobbett, eloquently defends the rights of the common man against Lord Raymond's attempts to restore the monarchy. But equal freedoms mean equal responsibilities, sacrifices, and limitations. In the period of economic expansion celebrated by Ryland, an egalitarian society can provide adequately for all its members. But in a time of scarcity, of restricted resources, all its members must be equally deprived. Mary Shelley subtly unmasks the inability of Ryland's democratic ideology to confront the necessity of distributing the burden of disaster equally. When the limited resource is life itself, freedom from plague, who is to be saved? Initially the wealthier members of English society willingly share their lands and goods with the refugees fleeing from the plague in Europe, even taking up the hoe and plow to till their own fields (p. 172). The plague thus brings about the social leveling advocated by democratic theory, but it also demands that all must die equally. When confronted with the brute reality that, in a classless society, all must suffer as well as benefit equally, Ryland abdicates the Lord Protectorship and barricades himself within his own estate in a futile attempt to save his own life. Ryland's frantic abdication of political responsibility expresses Mary Shelley's skeptical view of the excessive optimism inherent in a democratic ideology: a socialist government succeeds only if there is enough for every individual. In a scarcity economy, she implies, the equal distribution of resources may not be the best way to protect and preserve the human race.

Inherent in Godwin's and Percy Shelley's political ideology were more extreme utopian concepts that Mary Shelley's novel specifically challenges. Adrian repeats the visionary ideas that Godwin had propounded in his *Enquiry Concerning Political Justice* (1793) and that Percy Shelley had endorsed in his epic verse-drama *Prometheus Unbound* (1820): the conviction that the improved powers of the rational mind could conquer disease and even death. As Godwin argued, "we are sick and we die . . . because we consent to suffer these accidents." When the rational mind has achieved its full powers, Godwin claimed, "there will be no disease, no anguish, no melancholy and no resentment." At that point, he speculated, man "will perhaps be immortal" (II: 869, 872, 871).

Adrian endorses these utopian beliefs when he cries out to Verney: "the will of man is omnipotent, blunting the arrows of death, soothing the bed of disease, and wiping away the tears of agony" (pp. 53–54). But Mary Shelley shows that the powers of the human mind are feeble in comparison to those of all-controlling nature. In this novel, no one can determine the cause, the mode of transmission, or the cure of the fatal plague that sweeps across the earth.

Mary Shelley similarly undercuts the conservative political ideology most powerfully articulated during her lifetime by Edmund Burke. Initially, she invokes Burke's arguments for a constitutional monarchy and a traditional class system with approval, assigning them both to the successful politician Lord Raymond (p. 43) and to her narrator Lionel Verney (p. 165). Gazing on the playing fields of Eton, the source of "the future governors of England" (p. 165), Verney explicitly endorses Burke's view in *Reflections on the Revolution in France* that the human race is an organism in "a condition of unchangeable constancy" and "moves on through the varied tenors of perpetual decay, fall, renovation, and progression" (pp. 107–108). Mary Shelley clearly has more sympathy for Burke's vision of an organic society developing naturally toward an ever-higher form of being, guided by enlightened and benevolent rulers who institute gradual reforms in pragmatically effective ways, than she has for the impractical utopianism of Godwin and Percy Shelley.

Nonetheless, she recognizes that Burke's conservative ideology also rests on a heuristic fiction, a trope: the image of the body politic as a natural organism. If society is an organism, then it is subject to disease. Burke had defined this disease as the "plague" of revolution currently festering in France, a plague which "the precautions of the most severe quarantine ought to be established against" lest it infect that "course of succession [which] is the healthy habit of the British constitution" (Burke, pp. 107–108). In *The Last Man*, Mary Shelley takes Burke's metaphor literally. Even the healthy British constitution cannot long resist the ravages of a deadly plague that can be neither confined nor cured. The body politic, like all living organisms, can die as well as grow.

By taking Burke's figure of the plague and the body politic literally, Mary Shelley implies that human consciousness functions within a linguistic universe in which the figural and the literal are but differing signs or linguistic markers. Since in Shelley's radically skeptical view, there is no ontological distinction between the literal and the figurative, between the thing and the word, conscious experience can occur only within the prison house of language. Therefore the destruction of language—or of all speakers of language and recorded texts—is the destruction of human life. In place of the metaphor put forth by both Godwin and Burke, of history as progress toward perfection, Mary Shelley offers the alternative metaphor of human history as a motion that can suddenly stop. By the end of her novel, only one human being remains alive on earth. She thus introduces a powerful image that has increasingly dominated our cultural consciousness: the image of history as a narrative that reaches an abrupt and final conclusion, whether by biological epidemic, chemical warfare, invasion from outer space, or nuclear holocaust. Since this metaphor denies any ultimate significance to all human events, Shelley's novel is on the deepest level antipolitical and anti-ideological. Echoing the radical skepticism of David Hume, she suggests that all conceptions of human history, all ideologies, are grounded on metaphors or tropes that have no referent or authority outside of language.

The Last Man thus foreshadowed twentieth-century existentialism and nihilism. It anticipates the assertion in Albert Camus's *The Plague* (1947) that all meaning resides, not in an indifferent universe, but in human relationships that are inherently temporal and doomed to end. But *The Last Man* went further than Camus in extending this claim to language itself: it is the first literary text to base itself on the philosophical concept we now call deconstruction. It is the first text to demonstrate that all cultural ideologies and human interactions rest on nonreferential signs, signs written as literal but nonetheless inherently figural, signs no more stable or enduring than the mortal mind.

FINAL FICTIONS

IN the novels she wrote to support herself and her son—*Perkin Warbeck* (1830), *Lodore* (1835), and *Falkner* (1837)—Mary Shelley continued to explore the themes that had long obsessed her: the relation of the individual to history and the relationship of daughters to fathers. She details the ways in which daughters fail to escape their dependence on their fathers, marrying father figures and submitting to the demands of powerful men. Again and again, she uncovers the hierarchy implicit in the bourgeois family even as she idealizes the family as the only location in which a woman could find the love and companionship she craved.

Mary Shelley believed the egalitarian family to be the only social context in which both men and women could achieve emotional satisfaction, through powerful husband-wife and parent-child bonding. Such a loving family embodies an ethic of disinterested care that is in her view the necessary foundation of a healthy body politic. It is critical to recognize that, most explicitly in *Frankenstein* and *Lodore*, Shelley insisted that the role of the mother must also be filled by men if the family is to survive. Nevertheless, even as her novels celebrate the egalitarian bourgeois family and an ethic of care, they reveal the limits of her ideology. They consistently show that a woman who defines herself totally in terms of her family relationships is unhappy: either she is cruelly abandoned, or lacks any sense of autonomy or self-esteem, or loses those she loves to disease and death. Even as she overtly celebrates the egalitarian bourgeois family, Mary Shelley acknowledges that it has never existed. There are no detailed examinations of such a family in her novels.

Her lifelong search for a fulfilling family life was never successful. Her surviving son was devoted to her, but she found him dull. In 1848 she found him a satisfactory wife, Jane St. John, a young widow. She moved with them into Field Place, the Shelley estate in Bournemouth, Sussex, in 1849, ensured that a shrine to Percy Shelley would always be kept there, and soon after died of nervous attacks that had produced a partial paralysis, on 1 February 1851.

SELECTED BIBLIOGRAPHY

I. BIBLIOGRAPHY. "Current Bibliography," *Keats-Shelley Journal* (1952–present), an exceptionally complete annual and indexed bibliography to all publications on the Shelley circle; W. H. Lyles, *Mary Shelley: An Annotated Bibliography* (New York, 1975).

II. SEPARATE WORKS. *History of a Six Weeks' Tour Through a Part of France, Switzerland, Germany, and Holland: With Letters Descriptive of a Sail Round the Lake of Geneva, and of the Glaciers of Chamouni* (London, 1817), travel writing; *Frankenstein; or, The Modern Prometheus* (London, 1818; rev. ed. 1831), novel; *Mathilda* (1819), repr. ed. by Elizabeth Nitchie (Chapel Hill, N.C., 1959), novella; *Valperga; or, The Life and Adventures of Castruccio, Prince of Lucca* (London, 1823), historical novel; *The Last Man* (1826), repr. ed. by Hugh J. Luke, Jr. (Lincoln, Nebr., 1965, repr. 1993), novel; *The Fortunes of Perkin

Warbeck* (London, 1830), historical novel; *Lodore* (London, 1835), novel; *Falkner*, 3 vols. (London, 1837); *Lives of the Most Eminent Literary and Scientific Men of France*, for *Lardner's Cabinet Cyclopedia*, ed. by Rev. Dionysius Lardner (London, 1838–1839), encyclopedia entries; notes to *The Poetical Works of Percy Bysshe Shelley* (London, 1839), repr. in *The Complete Poetical Works of Percy Bysshe Shelley*, ed. by Thomas Hutchinson (London, 1905, 1960), biography; *Rambles in Germany and Italy in 1840, 1842, and 1843* (London, 1844), travel writing; *The Choice: A Poem on Shelley's Death*, ed. by H. Buxton Forman (London, 1876); *Proserpine and Midas: Two Unpublished Mythological Dramas by Mary Shelley*, ed. by André Koszul (London, 1922); *Mary Shelley, Collected Tales and Stories*, ed. by Charles E. Robinson (Baltimore and London, 1976).

III. LETTERS AND JOURNALS. Betty T. Bennett, ed., *The Letters of Mary Wollstonecraft Shelley*, 3 vols. (Baltimore, 1980, 1983, 1988); Paula R. Feldman and Diana Scott-Kilvert, eds., *The Journals of Mary Shelley, 1814–1844*, 2 vols. (Oxford, Eng., 1987).

IV. BIOGRAPHICAL STUDIES. Elizabeth Nitchie, *Mary Shelley: Author of* Frankenstein (New Brunswick, N.J., 1953); Emily W. Sunstein, *Mary Shelley: Romance and Reality* (Boston, 1989).

V. CRITICAL STUDIES. General: Jean de Palacio, *Mary Shelley dans son oeuvre* (Paris, 1969), phenomenological approach to Shelley's work; Mary Poovey, *The Proper Lady and the Woman Writer: Ideology as Style in the Works of Mary Wollstonecraft, Mary Shelley, and Jane Austen* (Chicago and London, 1984), thoughtful and perceptive analysis of Shelley's thought and style; Anne K. Mellor, *Mary Shelley: Her Life, Her Fiction, Her Monsters* (New York and London, 1988), feminist approach to life and works; Meena Alexander, *Mary Shelley* (New York, 1993), intelligent, brief overview; Audrey Fisch, Anne Mellor, and Esther Schor, *The Other Mary Shelley: Beyond Frankenstein* (New York, 1993), important collection of essays on Shelley's less familiar works.

On *Frankenstein*: Robert Kiely, *The Romantic Novel in England* (Cambridge, Mass., 1972), on Frankenstein as a tragic hero; Ellen Moers, *Literary Women* (Garden City, N.J., 1976), brilliant discussion of birth myth in *Frankenstein*; Marc A. Rubenstein, "'My Accursed Origin': The Search for the Mother in *Frankenstein*," in *Studies in Romanticism* 15 (1976), the best of the psychoanalytic readings of the novel; Martin Tropp, *Mary Shelley's Monster* (Boston, 1976), useful collection of historical documents; Sandra Gilbert and Susan Gubar, *The Madwoman in the Attic* (New Haven, Conn., 1979), excellent feminist discussion; David Ketterer, *Frankenstein's Creation: The Book, the Monster, and the Human Reality* (Victoria, B.C., 1979), on Frankenstein as a tragic hero; George Levine and U. C. Knoepflmacher, eds., *The Endurance of Frankenstein* (Berkeley, Calif., and London, 1979), extremely influential collection of essays; Jerrold E. Hogle,

"Otherness in *Frankenstein:* The Confinement/Autonomy of Fabrication," in *Structuralist Review* 2 (1980), interesting deconstructionist analysis; Barbara Johnson, "My Monster/Myself," in *Diacritics* 12 (1982), seminal feminist analysis; Franco Moretti, *Signs Taken for Wonders: Essays in the Sociology of Literary Forms* (London, 1983), interesting Marxist analysis; Paul A. Cantor, *Creature and Creator: Myth-making and English Romanticism* (New York, 1984), excellent analysis of Rousseau's influence; William Veeder, *Mary Shelley and* Frankenstein: *The Fate of Androgyny* (Chicago, 1986), Freudian and Lacanian approach; Chris Baldick, *In Frankenstein's Shadow: Myth, Monstrosity, and Nineteenth-Century Writing* (Oxford, 1987), fine study of the text and its impact on later works.

On *The Last Man:* A. J. Sambrook, "A Romantic Theme: The Last Man," in *Forum for Modern Language Studies* 2 (1966), useful treatment of other texts; Lee Sterrenburg, *"The Last Man:* Anatomy of Failed Revolutions," in *Nineteenth-Century Fiction* 33 (1978), superb analysis of politics in the novel; Morton D. Paley, "Mary Shelley's *The Last Man:* Apocalypse Without Millennium," in *Keats-Shelley Review* 4 (1989), excellent discussion of Romantic millenarian thought; Jane Aaron, "The Return of the Repressed: Reading Mary Shelley's *The Last Man,"* in Susan Sellers, ed., *Feminist Criticism: Theory and Practice* (New York and London, 1991), on the role of nature; Anne Mellor, introduction to *The Last Man* (Lincoln, Nebr., 1993), overview of the novel.

BRAM STOKER
(1847–1912)

Leonard Wolf

"MY DEAR, [*Dracula*] is splendid, a thousand miles beyond anything you have written before, and I feel certain will place you very high in the writers of the day. . . . No book since Mrs. Shelley's *Frankenstein* or indeed any other at all has come near yours in originality, or terror—Poe is nowhere" (quoted in Ludlam, pp. 108–109).

Leaving aside the charmingly maternal dismissal of Edgar Allan Poe, what is notable about the passage above, written to Bram Stoker by his mother, is how right she was in assessing both her son's book and what would become his place in literature.

But she was not right right away. When Stoker's novel was published in 1897, though the *London Daily Mail* saw it as a jewel in the crown of Gothic fiction, comparing *Dracula* with Ann Radcliffe's *The Mysteries of Udolpho*, Mary Shelley's *Frankenstein*, and Emily Brontë's *Wuthering Heights,* another paper, the *Athenaeum,* assigned the book to the subcellar of literature from which it has only in the late twentieth century begun to emerge. The book, said its reviewer, "is wanting in the constructive art as well as in the higher literary sense."

The novel, in the first decades of its existence, continued to sell, but the name "Dracula" did not become a household word until some thirty-five years later, when the second film treatment of the story, directed by Tod Browning and starring Bela Lugosi, appeared in 1931. That film, based more nearly on a theatrical adaptation by Hamilton Deane and John Balderston than on the novel, was, all by itself, responsible for the elevation of Count Dracula to the horror pantheon.

STAGE AND FILM ADAPTATIONS

THE first film, F. W. Murnau's silent *Nosferatu* (a Romanian word that means "the undead") was made in 1921 by Prana-Films in Germany. In Murnau's treatment, the vampire, instead of being an ally of the devil who can be combated by the use of holy symbols, is a secular being. Count Orlok, though he is identified as a vampire, clearly stands for a plague of some unknown sort. As the screen titles tell us, the count "leaves his castle to haunt the world. . . . Wherever he emerges, rats swarm out and people fall dead." Just after his ship docks in Bremen, we see brief sequences in which doors are marked with crosses to indicate the presence of plague, as well as scenes of funeral processions to convey the grim pervasiveness of death.

Contemporary audiences are likely to feel that the extreme gestures and the stylized posturing of the main characters in *Nosferatu* make them more comical than fearful. But once viewers accustom themselves to the film's mannerisms, its essential power takes over. Murnau did two things superbly well. First, he re-created the oppressive, irrational anxiety that characterizes nightmares. Second, he exploited the eroticism implicit in vampire imagery. This despite the fact that his vampire, Count Orlok, more resembles Thomas Pecket Prest's Varney the Vampire than the suave continental depicted in later films. Orlok is tall, skull-faced, and humpbacked, with pointed ears and fingernails so long as to make them useless for any human or bestial need. Still, when he lumbers up the stairs to enter Nina's bedroom, audiences lean forward in voyeuristic expectation, and when Orlok kneels beside Nina's bed, Murnau's camera is "busy . . . suggesting a couple, one of whom is engrossed in, while the other is enduring, an unspeakable erotic act" (Wolf, 1972, p. 281). The world came within an inch of losing Murnau's superb film when Florence Stoker, Bram Stoker's widow, sued the Prana production company for unauthorized use of the novel. The courts, ruling in Florence Stoker's favor, ordered that all copies of *Nosferatu* be destroyed. Fortunately the decree was unenforceable, and succeeding generations have had ample opportunity to rent or buy the film.

Bram Stoker, who had spent nearly thirty years in the world of theater, knew instinctively that there was theatrical stuff buried in his vampire tale. To ensure his ownership of the dramatic rights to his novel, he arranged a read-through performance of *Dracula* on the stage of the Lyceum Theatre on 18 May 1897. A true theatrical production of the story had, however, to wait until the British actor Hamilton Deane mounted his *Dracula* on the stage of the Grand Theatre in Derby in June 1924. The play became a popular offering of Deane's provincial company for the next several years. In 1927, with Raymond Huntley in the leading role, it opened in London at the Little Theatre. According to Stoker's biographer Daniel Farson, the play "ran for 391 performances after being transferred to two other theatres. Deane added to its success with the gimmick of placing a uniformed nurse in the theatre to scare the audience even more. One night, twenty-nine people fainted" (p. 165).

In 1927, Hamilton Deane's version of the play, considerably modified by the American writer John Balderston, opened on Broadway with the Hungarian-born actor Bela Lugosi in the title role. The Balderston-Deane production (which is still the basis for most popular presentations of *Dracula*) is notable for the skill with which its adapters sandwiched humorous—or downright slapstick—scenes between those that were meant to be horrific. Slapstick is indeed present in Stoker's novel, but it tends to be both heavy-handed and heavy-footed. Stoker thought his use of dialect was killingly funny, a view derived perhaps from his shrewd theatrical sense that in a culture where class and geographical origins are revealed by speech, the "other fellow's" dialect is a source of humor. Hence Dracula speaks a ponderous, bookish English; Van Helsing a mangled Dutch-English that does very little honor to either language; Quincey Morris has a Texas accent that no Texan would recognize; and various cockneys and Yorkshiremen sprinkle the text with their own parodic intonations.

But the mixture of fear and laughter was a magical formula for success on the Broadway stage. Crucial to that success was the performance of Bela Lugosi, who can hardly be thought of as a great actor, either before or after he took on the role of the count. Lugosi was stiff, uninsightful, melodramatic, and cold. However, he gave off an aura of malevolent command, which, coupled with his authentic Hungarian accent, made him an utterly believable and unforgettable Dracula. The play was such a tremendous success on Broadway that Lugosi was asked to play the title role in Universal Pictures' 1931 film version, directed by Tod Browning.

Most casual filmgoers would identify Browning's *Dracula* as the "first" of the film Draculas, and it is often honored as a classic despite its serious flaws. David J. Skal, in *Hollywood Gothic*, makes a convincing case that Tod Browning himself contributed to the film's deficiencies. Skal writes:

In scene after scene the script demonstrates just how much Browning cut, trimmed, ignored, and generally sabotaged the screenplay's visual potentials, insisting on static camera setups, eliminating reaction shots and special effects, and generally taking the lazy way out at every opportunity. . . . Indeed, there is one endless take in the finished film featuring [David] Manners, [Helen] Chandler, and [Edward] Van Sloan that runs 251 feet, nearly three minutes without a cut that was clearly meant to be broken up with close-ups and reaction shots. At one point Chandler tells Manners, "Oh, no—don't look at me like that," in an apparent reference to a dramatic change in his expression. The two-shot, however, shows Manners as motionless as a wax dummy—as if oblivious that the camera is even catching his face.

(p. 130)

The scenes of broad comic relief, which worked well on stage, feel mechanical and forced on the screen. The film has technical glitches that provoke audience laughter, such as the woefully unlifelike bat that flaps over the horses' heads during Renfield's journey to Dracula's castle. In a scene in which we are meant to be impressed by the hypnotic power of Lugosi's eyes, the pencil light meant to shine on the actor's pupils misses its mark and hovers near the bridge of his nose. Most egregious of all are the armadillos that wandered onto the set from a nearby soundstage.

But the impact of the Browning-Lugosi *Dracula* remains significant. It gave us Lugosi, with his accent, his courtly and powerful manner, and his incredible evening clothes, modernizing the "death and the maiden" imagery of the central European king vampire. There would be hundreds of film

Draculas to come in the seven decades left in the century. But there is not a single actor playing the title role whose performance is not compared with Lugosi's.

The film gave us several other magnificent images: there is Edward Van Sloan's chillingly precise portrayal of Dr. Van Helsing, who, if Dracula looms as the towering source of evil, is the equally towering source of good; and there is Dwight Frye, whose low, rising, mad chuckle as he comes up out of the hold of the ship is perhaps the ghastliest film laugh ever recorded. There are other great Lugosi moments, permanently etched into our memories: Dracula in Transylvania saying to Jonathan Harker, "Listen to them [the howling wolves], the children of the night. What music they make." Or, turning down Harker's invitation to join him in a glass of wine, "I do not drink—wine." The innocent simplicity of the film's plot serves, rather than interferes with, its dark theme. And, best of all, Browning had the good judgment to treat the symbolism of the vampire with respect. His *Dracula* feels like a gathering place of portentous personal, moral, and mythic confrontations.

Dracula films have proliferated since 1931, and there are now hundreds of them, most of them exploitation films of little interest to all but the most devoted fans of the vampire genre. There are, however, a few that deserve pausing over.

In 1936, Universal Pictures released *Dracula's Daughter* in which we see the Countess Marya Zaleska unsuccessfully trying to rid herself of the vampire curse she has inherited from her father. The film's power derives from the skill with which its director, Lambert Hillyer, turns his story of the reluctant vampire into a darkly brooding tale that seems to have emerged out of an ancient mythology.

In 1943, Robert Siodmak released *Son of Dracula*. This time the setting of the story is not Transylvania but Tennessee. A young woman named Katherine Caldwell has returned from Europe, where she met the fascinating Count Alucard ("Dracula" spelled backward), whom she invites back to her family home. When he and his earthboxes, filled with the native Transylvanian soil in which he is required to sleep, arrive in Tennessee, dreadful things follow quickly one after the other. Not a great film, *Son of Dracula* is worth seeing for the way that it expands the notion of Dracula as a family man. Beyond that, the film is

wonderfully atmospheric, and J. Salter's musical score is superb.

With the appearance of Hammer Films' *Horror of Dracula*, directed by Terence Fisher (1958), film versions of the novel took a sharp turn in the direction of the erotic. Filmed in color, Fisher's film has an intelligent script and is informed by a British sense of tradition. Christopher Lee's hauteur and imposing demeanor was of a quite different order of sinister from the one Lugosi had imprinted on our minds. The Hammer Dracula films that followed elaborated this style: lush color, bosomy heroines, expensive period sets, and an inescapable touch of sadism brightened, in a literal sense, the drama of Dracula for more than a decade, and Christopher Lee's performance of the title roles made his features almost as recognizably Dracula's as Bela Lugosi's.

In 1979, Klaus Kinski starred in Werner Herzog's remake of Murnau's *Nosferatu*. Herzog's film, though it does not succeed in scaring anyone, is one of the most beautifully filmed versions of the Dracula story ever made. Kinski gives a memorable performance as the vampire, infusing the role with a deep sense of weariness, which Herzog, who directed the film, understood as the primary experience of a human creature doomed to everlasting life.

That same year saw the Walter Mirisch–John Badham production of *Dracula*, starring Frank Langella, who had made a Broadway hit of the role. Langella turned Dracula into a Byronic threat to women, profoundly erotic, magnetic, and commanding. Langella's performance matched or perhaps even surpassed Christopher Lee's in the Hammer films' Draculas. Where Lee was distant and austere, Langella was overtly erotic and personally charming.

In 1993, Francis Ford Coppola released *Bram Stoker's "Dracula"* starring Gary Oldham. Coppola's self-indulgent treatment of Stoker's fiction makes for a visually baroque, Freudian, and thoroughly Coppolaesque production—which is to say that it is colorful, sensuous, exquisitely bizarre, and erotic enough to satisfy the most prurient of tastes.

LIFE

THERE is a poignant irony in the fact that Bram Stoker's own name and life have receded into the shadows while the name and story of the creature he imagined have become part of the folklore of the world. Indeed, the first full-length account of Stoker's life, by Harry Ludlam, is entitled *The Biography of Dracula*. The second biography, *The Man Who Wrote Dracula*, by Stoker's grandnephew, Daniel Farson, relegates Stoker's name to the subtitle. The jacket cover features a doctored photograph of Stoker in an unearthly green suit coat, the pupils of his eyes appearing as glaring white dots to make him seem close kin to his fictive monster.

The facts of Stoker's life, at least for its first three decades, are far removed from such cartoonish distortions. Bram Stoker ("Bram" is short for "Abraham," which was also his father's name) was born into a solid middle-class Dublin family on 8 November 1847. He was the third of seven children—five sons and two daughters. His father was a petty civil servant; his mother, Charlotte, twenty years his father's junior, was a strong-minded woman of whom the family, according to Daniel Farson, "were in awe . . . if not actually afraid of her. When one of the boys failed to come first in an examination, Charlotte did not conceal her resentment, even though he came second out of a thousand" (p. 13).

Until he was seven, Bram was a frequently bedridden child who suffered from an unspecified illness. Like many such afflicted children, books were an early consolation. Whatever the nature of his ailment, he grew up to be a robust, athletic man "who stood over six feet two in his stockings [and] weighed over twelve stone [168 pounds]. A rich auburn beard, contrasting with his brown hair, added to his strong presence, and he was as quick, confident and big in conversation as in build" (Ludlam, p. 32).

Stoker was seventeen when he entered Trinity College in Dublin, where it was expected that he would be trained to follow in his father's footsteps in the civil service. And indeed, after graduating with honors in history and mathematics, he did take a job as a clerk in Dublin Castle.

It was the pull of things theatrical that was to change Bram Stoker's life forever. In 1867, when he was nineteen, Stoker saw the actor Henry Irving in a performance of Richard Sheridan's *The Rivals* and was overwhelmed by the man, whom he described in *Personal Reminiscences of Henry Irving* (1906) as "a figure full of dash and fine irony, and whose ridicule seemed to *bite*; buoyant with the joy of life; self-conscious; an inoffensive egoist even in his love-making; of supreme and unsurpassable insolence, veiled and shrouded in his fine quality of manner" (p. 4).

Stoker saw Irving again three years later in the play *Two Roses*, and because "there was not a word in any of the papers of the acting of any of the accomplished players who took part in it" (*Personal Reminiscences*, p. 11), he obtained a job for himself as an unpaid drama reviewer for the *Dublin Mail*. When, in 1876, Henry Irving came once again to Dublin, Stoker was nearly thirty years old. This time, Irving performed *Hamlet* and Stoker reviewed the performance enthusiastically in the *Dublin Mail*. As a result, he found himself invited to supper after the play at the actor's hotel room. What happened then is both dramatic and baffling.

For some while, the two men discussed *Hamlet*. After dinner, Irving gave a dramatic reading of Thomas Hood's poem "The Dream of Eugene Aram" (1831):

'Twas in the prime of summer time,
  An evening calm and cool,
And four-and-twenty happy boys
  Came bounding out of school:
There were some that ran and some that leapt,
  Like troutlets in a pool.

The poem recounts that, not far away from the meadow where the boys are playing, Eugene Aram, an usher described as "a melancholy man," encounters a boy engrossed in the story of Cain and Abel. Aram talks with the boy about the history of murder that began with Cain. He then tells the boy about a dream he had in which he saw himself murdering an old man for his money and the struggles that followed as he tried to hide the victim's body. He finishes his tale, the two depart the scene, and the poem concludes,

That very night, while gentle sleep
  The urchin eyelids kiss'd,
Two stern-faced men set out from Lynn,
  Through the cold and heavy mist;
And Eugene Aram walked between,
  With gyves upon his wrist.

It is a poem bathetic enough, to be sure, and, no doubt, read by an actor of Irving's caliber, must have been very affecting. Stoker's response, however, was extreme. He writes in his memoir of Irving:

That experience I shall never—can never—forget . . . such was Irving's commanding force, so great was the magnetism of his genius, so profound was the sense of his dominance that I sat spellbound. Outwardly I was as of stone . . . here was incarnate power, incarnate passion. . . . Here was indeed Eugene Aram as he was face to face with his Lord; his very soul aflame in the light of his abiding horror.

When Irving finished his recitation, he was so overwhelmed with emotion that he collapsed. Stoker goes on, "I can only say that after a few seconds of stony silence following his collapse I burst into something like hysterics." As if aware that the behavior of both men was excessive, he feels obliged to say,

I was no hysterical subject. I was no green youth; no weak individual, yielding to a superior emotional force. I was as men go a strong man. . . .

When, therefore, after his recitation I became hysterical, it was distinctly a surprise to my friends; for myself surprise had no part in my then state of mind. Irving seemed much moved by the occurrence.

(pp. 31–32)

As Stoker tells the story, Irving then went off to his bedroom, returning with a signed photograph of himself that he presented to Stoker. "In those moments of our mutual emotion, he too had found a friend and knew it. Soul had looked into soul! From that hour began a friendship as profound, as close, as lasting as can be between two men."

The word "friendship" seems hardly to cover the case. Over the next couple of years, though they saw each other only at intervals, the relationship deepened. When Irving came to Dublin, the two men spent long nights in conversation. Then, in 1878, Stoker was summoned by telegram to Glasgow, where Irving offered Stoker the job of acting manager of the Lyceum, his theater in London. Given the intensity of their relationship, Stoker's decision was a foregone conclusion. He resigned the civil-service post he had held for thirteen years.

At this time, Stoker was courting a woman named Florence Balcombe, who, like himself, came from the Dublin suburb of Clontarf. Balcombe, whom Oscar Wilde described as "an exquisitely pretty girl," had been warmly courted by the poet before he married Constance Lloyd. Daniel Farson reports that the two men "knew each other, for Bram was a regular visitor to Wilde's home in Merrion Square, and a favourite of Sir William and

Lady Wilde. . . . Lady Wilde, who wrote poems under the name of 'Speranza,' welcomed Bram to their artistic circle" (p. 39). Even after Bram's marriage to Balcombe, the friendship between Wilde and the Stokers continued.

Florence Balcombe was twenty years old when she married Bram Stoker. Whatever life she may have imagined for herself as the wife of a civil servant, five days after her marriage to Stoker on 4 December 1878 the newlyweds were racing off to join Henry Irving in Birmingham, where Bram was about to assume his duties as, as Stoker's mother would have it, "manager to a strolling player."

Though David J. Skal, in *Hollywood Gothic*, writes that "it would become almost a cliché among his chroniclers that Stoker's 'real' marriage was to Irving and not to his bride" (p. 18), nothing in print suggests that Stoker ever understood himself as having fallen in love with Henry Irving, but everything we know about the subsequent years of his life tells us clearly just what his emotional priorities were.

After the birth of the Stokers' only child, Noel, in 1879, the marriage declined into a formal and somewhat chilly arrangement. Daniel Farson writes:

Florence Stoker was a beauty, and aware of it. This may explain why she was a cold woman. My family, speaking of her, gave me the impression of an elegant, aloof woman, more interested in her position in society than she was in her son. Her granddaughter Ann, Noel's daughter, confirms this. She told me that she doubted if "Granny Moo," as Florence was called, was really capable of love. "She was cursed with her great beauty and the need to maintain it. In my knowledge now, she was very anti-sex. After having my father [Noel Stoker] in her early twenties, I think she was quite put off."

(pp. 213–214)

Stoker's devotion to Irving, on the other hand, was complete. His days and many of his nights were spent in the service of his aloof master, who doted on the adoration of men, women, and dogs. Curiously enough, being at Irving's beck and call engaged those aspects of Stoker's character that had prompted him to write his first book, *The Duties of Clerks of Petty Sessions in Ireland* (1879). Stoker had a mind that could fasten on, and organize, multitudinous detail. When the Lyceum company traveled, it was Stoker who assumed, according to Laurence Irving, Henry Irving's grandson, "the burden of supervising the unloading and setting up within a few hours this quantity of scenery in unfamiliar theatres with comparatively untrained stage staffs and of recruiting and rehearsing in each town a regiment of local supers" (*Henry Irving*, 1951, pp. 481–482).

Stoker found it exhilarating to be behind the scenes, coordinating the work of 151 actors, carpenters, scene shifters, makeup artists, costumers, and stage designers who were involved in Irving's newly invigorated Lyceum Theatre. Stoker tells us that he learned to usher "five hundred guests to a buffet supper on stage" and that, over a twenty-seven-year period "I think I shall be very well within the mark when I say that during my time of working with Henry Irving I have written in his name nearer half a million than a quarter of a million letters" (*Personal Reminiscences*, p. 62).

His role as Irving's man-of-all-work did not always elicit admiration. An American reporter whom Stoker had offended described him as someone "who seems to occupy some anomalous position between secretary and valet. Whose manifest duties are to see that there is mustard in the sandwiches and to take the dogs out for a run; and who unites in his own person every vulgarity of the English speaking race" (quoted in Farson, p. 79).

One ought not, however, to think of Stoker as a mere flunky. For one thing, he was well paid; he and Florence were able to acquire a fine house in fashionable Chelsea. And there were prestige gains as well. Horace Wyndham, in *The Nineteen Hundreds* (1923), writes, "To see Stoker in his element was to see him standing at the top of the theater's stairs, surveying a 'first-night' crowd trooping up to them. There was no mistake about it—a Lyceum *premiere* did draw an audience that really was representative of the best of that period in the realms of art, literature, and society" (pp. 118–119). The young former civil servant from Dublin now moved in social circles that included "the likes of James McNeill Whistler, John Singer Sargent, Dante Gabriel Rossetti, W. S. Gilbert, Mark Twain, and Alfred, Lord Tennyson" (Skal, p. 19).

There was, also, the excitement of the American tours that the Lyceum company made and that Stoker coordinated. Stoker became an avid admirer of American life and culture, even giving a lecture at the London Institution that was published as *A Glimpse of America* (1886). He was an early admirer of Walt Whitman, to whom he wrote gushing letters in 1876, and whom he met in 1884. As readers of *Dracula* know, one of the heroes of that novel, Quincey Morris, is Stoker's version of the American frontiersman-knight-gentleman.

Henry Irving died on the night of 13 October 1905 after a performance of *Becket*. Stoker had one final opportunity to do his idol a service: he closed the dead man's eyes. With Irving gone, his life lost its center. Though for the next several years he continued to write and keep busy, like Chaucer's Merchant he "seemed busier than he was." There were other consequences of Irving's death. Despite the success of *Dracula*, neither it nor his subsequent books improved his financial fortunes significantly. Daniel Farson quotes "Reginald Auberon" (a pseudonym used by Horace Wyndham) on the matter: "Apart from the sudden severance of a close friendship between them . . . it meant the abrupt and entire cessation of his sole source of income. . . . on Irving's death, the problem of ways and means began to press rather hardly" (p. 226). Though Farson reports that a wealthy physician brother of Stoker's did not turn a hand to help Bram, Stoker's friends were sufficiently concerned about his welfare to help him get money from a literary fund for authors.

In his last years, Stoker suffered the symptoms incident to syphilis infection, which, Farson speculates, he caught at the turn of the century, "when his wife's frigidity drove him to other women, probably prostitutes among them" (p. 234). Farson's remarks can only be taken as conjecture. Stoker died on 20 April 1912. He was survived by his wife, Florence, and his son, Noel.

LITERARY CAREER

How, in the midst of his busy life as Henry Irving's aide-de-camp, right-hand man, and general gofer, Stoker found the time and mustered the energy to maintain a career as a fiction writer is a mystery, particularly since he had neither the insight nor the instinctive narrative gifts usually associated with literary achievement. His sensibility was crude; his mind, stocked with Victorian clichés of manhood, chivalry, Christian piety, and British class consciousness, was never first-rate. When he wrote romances or adventure novels, his prose, even in *Dracula*, tilted in the direction of the banal. His male heroes are in the standard Victorian mold: stalwart, fatuously noble, courageous, and patronizing of women.

The first fiction he published was a collection of stories for children called *Under the Sunset* (1881), which, though they are ostensibly moralizing tales, give glimpses of Stoker's morbidly bizarre imagination, particularly in the story the "Invisible Giant." In a shadowy anticipation of *Dracula*, this narrative concerns a plague that destroys all in its path except a single orphan girl. The tale derived from accounts Stoker's mother told him about an 1831 cholera epidemic in Sligo that she had survived.

Stoker's first novel, *The Snake's Pass*, an adventure tale set in Ireland, was published in 1890. It is an undistinguished romance with conventional male protagonists who vie for the love of the same woman. *The Watter's Mou'* appeared in 1894. Here, the plot turns on the conflict experienced by the gallant young heroine, Maggie, who is lost at sea in an attempt to warn her father, a fisherman turned smuggler, of an impending coast-guard trap. The complication in the plot is Maggie's romantic entanglement with Willy, a coastguardsman. Willy, seeing his beloved's body being tossed by the waves, leaps into the raging water. The story ends on an organ note: "The requiem of the twain was the roar of the breaking waves and the scream of the white birds that circled round the Watter's Mou'" (p. 82). In 1895, Stoker published *The Shoulder of Shasta*. Two years later there appeared *Dracula*, which was conceived in the course of long walks beside Cruden Bay, which is the setting for *The Watter's Mou'*.

After *Dracula* there followed eight more novels, most of which, says Daniel Farson, "might have been written by another author. There is throughout the most surprising contrast between florid romance and lurid horror" (p. 205). None of them requires to be taken seriously as literature.

They are terribly sincere books. Invariably sentimental, they breathe the humid air of British Decency. The men in them are (except when they are villains) gallant or dutiful or honorable or long-suffering, or patient. The women are not particularly complex either, but there is a difference. As in *Dracula*, where it is Mina who shines, whatever the sum of their positive virtues, they are stronger, smarter, braver and more believable than the men.

(Wolf, 1972, p. 254)

In 1905, after Irving's death, Stoker published *The Man*, which Les Daniels has called "a comparatively ordinary love story that shows some concern over the role of women in society" (*Supernatural Fiction Writers*, p. 378). The female protagonist of the novel, interestingly, is named Stephen. In 1908, he published *Lady Athlyne*, a romance, which, says Daniels, is "perhaps the weakest of Stoker's attempts at this genre." The two-volume *Personal Reminiscences of Henry Irving*, in which the details of Stoker's devoted life in the service of his hero are set down with considerable verve, was published in 1906.

In 1909, there appeared *The Lady of the Shroud*, which touches on vampiric matters briefly but devolves into a conventional romance with the single distinction that it contains an early battle scene involving the use of aircraft. Finally, in 1911, there is *The Lair of the White Worm*.

Outside of *Dracula*, few of the novels deserve comment, and then only to call attention to the way that Stoker, when he is describing love relationships, slips into revealing byways of description. In *The Mystery of the Sea* (1902), his typical protagonists, a gallant man, Archie, and a beautiful and "sweet" heroine, Marjory, spend a great deal of their time engaged in strenuous physical (but not erotic) activity. Marjory, on the afternoon of the day before her wedding, disguises herself as a boy and goes to the woods to meet Archie. Instead of a wedding-night scene of any kind, we see Archie hacking with a pickax at the rock floor of a cave beside the sea. When, later, Archie and Marjory are trapped inside that same cave as the tide begins to fill it, Archie offers to lie down in the icy waters so that Marjory may stand on his body and thus save herself. Later, after the danger has passed, Archie tells us, "I wanted to kiss her hand, but as I bent, her foot was temptingly near. I stooped lower to kiss it. She saw my intention and saying impulsively: 'Oh, Archie dear, not that wet, dirty shoe,' kicked it off. I stooped still lower and kissed her bare foot" (p. 301).

The most disturbing of Stoker's books—with the obvious exception of *Dracula*—is certainly *The Lair of the White Worm*. Stoker was sixty-four years old when he wrote it, and was undoubtedly by then suffering the effects of the syphilis that finally killed him. It may be for that reason that the novel has long sections of prose that seem more like the unshaped material squirming at the bottom of disturbed minds than the details a writer makes use of in the service of an artistic vision.

The word "worm" in the title has the archaic meaning of "serpent." The lamia creature who is the wer-serpent of the story is Lady Arabella March who, as a young woman, was bitten by a snake. Its essence possessed her and she assumes the forms of both woman and serpent. Stoker describes her as moving with a quick, gliding motion. She is, he says,

clad in some kind of soft white stuff, which clung close to her form, showing to the full every movement of her sinuous figure. . . . Her voice was peculiar, very low and sweet, and so soft that the dominant note was of sibilation. Her hands, too were peculiar—long, flexible, white, with a strange movement as of waving gently to and fro.

(p. 29)

However sweet her voice is, she is a dangerous foe. When a mongoose, whose natural instinct it is to attack snakes, rushes at her, she tears it apart with her bare hands. She kills another by shooting at the creature, breaking its back. She continues to shoot until the animal's body is mangled beyond recognition. More disturbing than any of this are the awkward, because only too apparent, displays of loathing of the physical realities that accompany human sexuality. Once Stoker has made it clear that Lady Arabella inhabits a deep, dark hole, he cannot seem to control the spume of revulsive language with which he describes it. That hole, he writes, has

a queer smell—yes! Like bilge or a rank swamp. It was distinctly nauseating . . . like nothing that Adam [the novel's protagonist] had ever met with. He compared it with all the noxious experiences he had ever had—the drainage of war hospitals, of slaughter-houses, the refuse of dissecting rooms . . . the sourness of chemical waste and the poisonous effluvium of the bilge of a water-logged ship whereon a multitude of rats had been drowned.

(p. 119)

When Adam blows the hole up with dynamite, "From [the well hole] agonized shrieks were rising, growing ever more terrible with each second that passed. . . . Once, in a sort of lull or pause, the seething contents of the hole rose . . . and Adam saw part of the thin form of Lady Arabella, forced up to the top amid a mass of slime" (p. 186).

In *Dracula*, the vampire plays his role as an eroticizing threat to women without making the reader wonder whether Stoker's mind was intact when he wrote it. *The Lair of the White Worm*, on the other hand, reads uncomfortably like journal entries dictated by someone whose personal disintegration is, at every instant, shaping his prose.

Besides the novels, Stoker wrote a number of short stories, several of which have become classics of the horror-fiction genre. The best of these, "The Judge's House," all but matches Poe's "The Pit and the Pendulum" for sheer horror. Malcolm Malcomson, a young scholar seeking a quiet place in which to prepare for his examinations, rents an old house. As in *Dracula*, where Jonathan Harker is warned not to go on to Dracula's castle, Malcolm is cautioned by the well-wishing landlady of the local inn to stay away from what she refers to as "the Judge's House." Malcolm, with the temerity of the young and the ignorant, condescends to Mrs. Witham, the landlady, and goes off to the judge's house to prepare for his mathematical tripos examinations. Soon, however, Malcolm becomes aware that he is not alone. There are rats in the old house, who keep up their noisy movements until dawn, when the house grows suddenly silent. Then he sees that "on the great high-backed carved oak chair by the right side of the fireplace sat an enormous rat steadily glaring at him with baleful eyes. He made a motion to it as though to hunt it away, but it did not stir."

Rats are a familiar icon of fear for Stoker. In "The Burial of the Rats" they swarm through the rubbish heaps of Paris. In *Dracula*, they appear as a sort of tidal wave of rodents flung magically across the path of the count's antagonists at Carfax Abbey.

In "The Squaw," another tale that owes much to Edgar Allan Poe, Stoker gives us the protagonist-villain Elias P. Hutchinson, a likable American who, to amuse a couple of fellow tourists in Heidelberg Castle, drops a pebble from a parapet, meaning only to frighten a cat and her kitten who are playing in the moat below. The pebble kills the kitten. The mother cat "seemed to realize that it [the kitten] was dead, and again threw her eyes up at us. I shall never forget the sight, for she looked the perfect incarnation of hate. Her green eyes blazed with lurid fire, and the white, sharp teeth seemed almost to shine through the blood which dabbled her mouth and whiskers."

From here on, a reader can guess that a revenge tragedy is about to be enacted, and when, later,

Hutchinson and his two friends visit the castle's torture chamber, we are not at all surprised by the story's bloody denouement. "The Squaw," written in unresonant, workmanlike prose, has only its plot to recommend it. Though it does not work at any symbolic or allegorical level, its central narrative situation is likely to linger in the reader's memory.

"Dracula's Guest," published in 1914 after Stoker's death, was evidently excised from an earlier version of *Dracula*. Here, the unnamed protagonist (presumably Jonathan Harker), who is on his way to see Dracula in Transylvania, stops off in Munich, where he insists on going for a ride in the country, though it is the day of Walpurgis Night, when, according to popular belief, the devil was abroad. Though his coachman pleads with Harker to return to Munich with him, Harker refuses and sets out on foot for what was once an "unholy" village where the living dead were said to have resided. As he walks, snow begins to fall, and the air turns perceptibly colder. He takes refuge in a grove of trees where, in his search for shelter, he comes upon a tomb in which a suicide, the Styrian Countess Dolingen of Gratz, is buried.

At this point, the storm bursts upon him with full force. To escape its fury, he enters the tomb. What happens then is, of course, the heart of the horrible matter and is best left to readers of the story. It is enough to say that Harker is saved from the consequences of his untoward curiosity by the intervention, though from a great distance, of the man who, in *Dracula*, will become first his client and then his foe.

As horror fiction, "Dracula's Guest" is comparatively inert, but it is interesting for readers of *Dracula* as an indication of how a fine book can emerge even after a most unfortunate start. Clearly, Stoker used good judgment in deleting it from the final manuscript.

THE GOTHIC PRECEDENT

Dracula is classed as a novel in the continuing Gothic tradition, which, in English literature, has its origins in the eighteenth century. Typically, novels of this genre have at their center a well-bred, beautiful heroine who is pursued by a tall, sinisterly handsome man who means to subject her to the "fate worse than death." The action takes place against a backdrop of ruined or dismal architecture: tumbledown castles, crumbling tombs, graveyards, monasteries, convents, subterranean corridors, secret rooms. As James B. Twitchell wrote in *Dreadful Pleasures*, "The image that was the most crucial, and still is, was the image of the active sexual molester. The old fustian fiends of Jacobean drama had finally dragged their clanking chains away and new, palpable antagonists were introduced" (p. 241). To make the fate of the unfortunate heroine even more frightening, her antagonist sometimes has the help of supernatural agencies. Still, however complicated her situation, the heroine is typically rescued by a handsome, marriageable young man who is far less interesting than the villain.

Horace Walpole's *The Castle of Otranto*, the first Gothic novel in English, was published in 1764. Walpole, a friend of the poet Thomas Gray, was an antiquary, a dramatist, and a distinguished letter writer, whom Byron praised as "the father of the first romance and of the last tragedy in our language and surely worthy of a higher place than any living writer be he who he may." Today, however, Walpole is more likely to be remembered as the obsessive owner of a Gothic mansion named Strawberry Hill and as the author of *The Castle of Otranto*. Like Mary Shelley, Robert Louis Stevenson, and Bram Stoker after him, Walpole claimed that his novel was instigated by a dream that so inspired him, he finished the book in the space of two months.

The novel is a particularly grotesque tale in which the despotic Manfred, prince of Otranto, undertakes to outwit a prophecy that says that his family's rule of the principality will be cut short "whenever the real owner should be grown too large to inhabit it." Manfred arranges the marriage of his sickly son Conrad to Princess Isabella of Vincenza, a descendant of Alphonso the Good. On the morning of the marriage, Conrad is found smashed to bits by a giant helmet that has fallen from a statue of Alphonso. Manfred, though married to the gentle Hippolita, casts his wife aside so he can marry Isabella himself. But Isabella, who is in love with Theodore, a handsome peasant, escapes from him.

From that point on, there are chase scenes through subterranean passages, supernatural events—other mysterious pieces of armor are found in the castle, a portrait steps from its frame, a statue bleeds. Finally, the castle itself collapses. Manfred, aiming a dagger blow at Isabella, kills his daughter, Matilda, instead. Her death shocks him to contrition. As the story ends, Theodore assumes the throne while Manfred and his wife devote themselves to lives of penitence.

A bare-bones plot summary can make *The Castle of Otranto* sound ridiculous. In fact, the novel is important because it created a blueprint for the settings and psychodynamic dilemmas that subsequent Gothic novelists would employ. Walpole deserves praise too for his adeptness at the kind of atmospheric writing that today we associate with surrealism.

Ann Radcliffe, the author of two of the most important of the eighteenth century's Gothic fictions, established her reputation as a Gothic novelist with *The Mysteries of Udolpho* (1794), the fourth of the five books she published in her short lifetime. It is a book that makes rich use of the genre's machinery: mysterious music, uncanny apparitions, lowering villains, gloomy castles, dangerous forests. Her heroine, Emily St. Aubert, is the quintessential Gothic heroine: she is orphaned, beautiful, delicate, sensitive, courageous. The villain who pursues her is Montoni, putatively her uncle by marriage. In the course of the story, the reader is treated to any number of mysteries: uncanny groans, disembodied music, flitting shapes, strange footsteps. And, of course, long, dark hallways and wild mountain scenery. Unfortunately, Ann Radcliffe dispels her "mysteries" at the end of the novel by revealing the reallife tricks that were performed to create them.

Her novel *The Italian* (1797) is far superior to *The Mysteries*. This time, the heroine is Ellena, her lover is Vivaldi, and the villain who pursues her is Father Schedoni. The plot, which involves an assassination attempt against Ellena's life, is intricate beyond easy summary, but the pervasive power of the story derives from its sharply delineated characterizations—especially of Father Schedoni—and the implications of incest that hover over the fiction.

With Matthew Lewis' *The Monk* (1796), eighteenth-century Gothic fiction reached an apogee of sorts. Byron called it a masturbative fiction; John Berryman compared *The Monk* with Thomas Mann's *Dr. Faustus*, to Mann's discredit. For contemporary readers, *The Monk* is likely to prove more fascinating than anything that either Walpole

or Radcliffe wrote. For one thing, Lewis' prose moves at a gallop. His scenes, both of violence and of eros, are graphic; his imagination is so enthusiastic that it feels sometimes beyond his control.

Lewis tells the story of Friar Ambrosio, who for thirty years led a life of unblemished purity. Seduced by the handsome young novice Rosario, who turns out to be the beautiful Matilda as well as a minion of the devil, Ambrosio enters upon a life of crime and lust, which Lewis describes with gleeful relish: "The hour was night. All was silence around. . . . No prying eye or curious ear was near the lovers: nothing was heard but Matilda's melodious accents. Ambrosio was in the full vigour of manhood . . . he clasped her rapturously in his arms; he forgot his vows, his sanctity, and his fame; he remembered nothing but the pleasure and opportunity" (1952 ed., p. 109). Before Ambrosio's rich career of sensuality and crime are done, he will have murdered his mother and raped and murdered his sister. But Lewis, who has chronicled his crimes with effervescent prose, saves his best writing for the novel's denouement, when Ambrosio, hoping to escape justice and the Inquisition, calls upon Satan for help—and gets it. The prose of the novel's final moments as Ambrosio, his shaven skull in the grip of the devil's claw, is carried heavenward only to be dropped into an appalling chasm are, stylistically, thematically, and, from the point of view of poetic justice, sublimely, apt.

Melmoth the Wanderer (1820), by Charles Maturin, is the most intellectually demanding of the Gothic fictions that precede *Dracula*. Maturin, like Bram Stoker an Irish writer, takes as his theme the moral uses of time. His eponymous protagonist is given a 150-year life span by Satan. Melmoth's curse is that, having bought time at the cost of his soul, he learns that the world in which he is destined to spend that time is essentially dreadful. Maturin's account of how his "wanderer" uses the devil's gift makes for an early and profound examination of the nature of personal evil. Like Lewis' Ambrosio, Melmoth comes to a dreadful end, falling from a precipice. But first, he dreams of the event:

His last despairing reverted glance was fixed on the clock of eternity—the upraised black arm seemed to push forward the hand—it arrived at its period—he fell—he sunk—he blazed—he shrieked! The burning waves boomed over his sinking head, and the clock of eternity rung out its awful chime—"Room for the soul of the Wanderer!"—and the waves of the burning ocean answered, as they lashed the adamantine rock—"There is room for more!"

(1989 ed., p. 539)

A brief overview of the vampire fictions that preceded *Dracula* must begin with John Polidori, credited with introducing the theme of the vampire into English literature. Polidori, Lord Byron's physician, was among the assembled on the famous night in 1816 when Byron assigned his friends, including Percy Bysshe Shelley and Mary Shelley, the task of writing a horror tale. Polidori and Mary Shelley took the assignment seriously enough to finish a book. In Polidori's case, it was *The Vampyre: A Tale* (1819). Mary Shelley, of course, produced *Frankenstein* (1818).

The Vampyre's protagonist is young Aubrey, who is a friend of Lord Ruthven's, with whom he sets out on a continental tour. Ruthven, we learn, is an absolute cad, who ruins his friends at the gambling table. In Athens, Aubrey learns to his horror that Ruthven is also a vampire. But Ruthven, fatally wounded by bandits, makes Aubrey swear not to reveal this knowledge for the space of one year.

In London, months later, Aubrey sees his resurrected friend moving about in search of fresh prey. When it turns out that Ruthven's next victim is Aubrey's sister, Aubrey faces a dilemma: he has sworn not to reveal Ruthven's proclivities for a year—and the year is not yet up. What's a gentleman to do? In fact, he lapses into incoherence. At the penultimate moment, on the midnight of the day preceding his sister's marriage to Ruthven, when his oath of silence has been fulfilled, Aubrey reveals the truth, but by then it is too late—"Lord Ruthven had disappeared and Aubrey's sister had glutted the thirst of a Vampyre."

There are only two reasons Polidori's fiction deserves study. There is, first of all, the Byronic context in which *The Vampyre* was written. But more important to our discussion is the characterization of Ruthven as a nobleman, aloof, brilliant, magnetic, fascinating to women, and coolly evil. Except that he is a British lord, he is an absolute precursor of Stoker's *Dracula*.

Varney the Vampire (1847), written, evidently, by many hands and attributed to Thomas Pecket Prest and James Malcolm Rymer, is of a different order of interest altogether. Its authors wrote the kind of prose that, had they lived in the era of motion pictures, would have fitted them to be screenwriters for what used to be called "serials" or "chapter movies," those cliff-hangers of the 1930s and 1940s that entranced generations of lucky children. *Varney the Vampyre* is pure Grand Guignol. Chapter 1 begins portentously with a verse:

> —"How graves give up their dead,
> And how the night air hideous grows
> With shrieks!"

And the chapter heading reads "Midnight.—The hailstorm.—The dreadful visitor.—The vampyre." Prest and Rymer, even more flamboyantly than Matthew Lewis, loved the pyrotechnic mixture of gore, concupiscence, and Gothic settings that animate *Varney*. The seemingly endless, chain-linked narrative contains thunder, lightning, death, blood, pistol shots, stabbings, caves, and resurrections. Varney is brought back to life so frequently that death itself takes on a thoroughly ludicrous aspect. He is shot, hanged, staked, and drowned, but a touch of light from a full moon enables him to resume his thirsty quest. Throughout, his motivation is fiendishly clear: "I was . . . ruminating what I should do, until a strange feeling crept over me that I should like—what? Blood!—raw blood, reeking and hot, bubbling and juicy, from the veins of some gasping victim."

Reading *Varney the Vampyre* is the literary equivalent of eating popcorn—hard to stop and not particularly nourishing, but, in defiance of one's own best judgment, tremendous fun. The book should not be overvalued, however. There is nothing in *Varney*, nothing at all, that compares with the resonant darkness of Stoker's *Dracula*.

Though it is often asserted that Bram Stoker was influenced by Joseph Sheridan Le Fanu's vampire tale, *Carmilla* (1872), it is harder to demonstrate where the influence lies. Certainly in his short story "Dracula's Guest," Stoker used the name "Styria," which can be traced to Le Fanu. And Lucy Westenra's flight through the yew trees and her execution presided over by two physicians in a family tomb have their analogues in *Carmilla*, but the authors' prose style, narrative technique, and vision have nothing in common.

Le Fanu, for one thing, is the finer prosodist. His tale, encompassed in a short story (or novella)

385

is more narrowly focused. Laura, the protagonist of Le Fanu's story, is the daughter of an Englishman who, having served in the Austrian army, has retired on his pension to a castle in Styria because "a small income, in that part of the world goes a long way." She describes her lonely childhood, with only her father and governesses for company, and tells of a frightening experience she had one night twelve years before:

[I] saw a solemn, but very pretty face looking at me from the side of the bed. . . . she caressed me with her hands, and lay down beside me on the bed, and drew me towards her again. I was awakened by a sensation as if two needles ran into my breast very deep at the same moment, and I cried loudly.

> (E. F. Bleiler, ed., *Best Ghost Stories*, 1964, p. 277)

Twelve years later, a coach breaks down in front of Laura's schloss. Its passenger, the mother of a beautiful young woman named Carmilla, pleads with Laura's father to allow her to leave her daughter in his care while she (the mother) goes off on a "journey of life and death." At first Laura is enchanted with the guest. Then, gradually, it becomes clear to her that it was Carmilla whom she had seen at the foot of her bed on that night twelve years ago. As the story progresses, it becomes increasingly sensuous, indeed languorous, even as Carmilla's true identity as the vampire daughter of a vampire clan is revealed.

Le Fanu's achievement, in an age when the word "lesbian" was hardly spoken, is that in his story of the relationship between two young women, he successfully linked lesbian experience with the vampire theme. Carmilla puts the matter directly when she says to Laura, "I cannot help it, as I draw near to you, you, in your turn, will draw near to others, and learn the rapture of that cruelty, which yet is love."

The rapture of that cruelty, which yet is love! On that note we turn, as on a hinge, to Bram Stoker's masterwork, for which Stoker may have made notes as early as 1890.

DRACULA

STOKER, borrowing from a procedure Wilkie Collins used in his 1860 novel *The Woman in White*, organized his narrative in *Dracula* to make full use of a variety of points of view. The story emerges from what purports to be a collection of letters, journals, business memoranda, and transcriptions of phonograph recordings. It is a technique that lends realism and urgency as well as depth to the actions described. The first seventy or so pages of the novel comprise excerpts from Jonathan Harker's journal as he describes his voyage from England to the Borgo Pass in Transylvania. Harker, a young British solicitor, is on his way to conclude a real estate transaction with the mysterious Count Dracula. After an ominous coach ride, he is set down somewhere in the Borgo Pass, and continues on to Castle Dracula in an eerie conveyance the count has sent to meet him. Once at the castle, Harker meets the count, whom he describes as

a tall old man, clean shaven save for a long white moustache, and clad in black from head to foot, without a single speck of colour about him anywhere. . . . [He] motioned me in with his right hand with a courtly gesture, saying in excellent English, but with a strange intonation:—

"Welcome to my house! Enter freely and of your own will! . . . Come freely. Go safely; and leave something of the happiness you bring!"

> (p. 23)[1]

We learn that Count Dracula has purchased property in London and plans to move there. Soon, Harker discovers the dreadful truth: the count is a vampire who lives in the castle with three beautiful—and ghastly—vampire women, and that he, Jonathan, is a prisoner, helpless to prevent the count from carrying out his plan to journey to England, where he means to prey on the blood of vital English womanhood. Harker, seeing the earth-boxes in which the count habitually sleeps being loaded for shipment to England, makes a desperate resolve:

I shall try to scale the castle wall farther than I have yet attempted. I shall take some of the gold with me, lest I want it later. . . .

And then away for home! away to the quickest and nearest train! away from this cursed spot, from this cursed land, where the devil and his children still walk with earthly feet!

---

[1]All quotes from the novel are taken from *The Essential Dracula*, edited by Leonard Wolf.

At least God's mercy is better than that of these monsters, and the precipice is steep and high. At its foot a man may sleep—as a man.

(p. 69)

At this point, the other protagonists of the story join the action. We meet Lucy Westenra, close friend and former schoolfellow of Mina Murray, Jonathan Harker's fiancée. We watch the nineteen-year-old Lucy being proposed to by three men: Arthur Holmwood, the future Lord Godalming, a wealthy nobleman; Dr. John Seward, a medical researcher and the keeper of a nearby madhouse; and Quincey Morris, an adventurous young Texan. Lucy chooses Godalming.

In Whitby, on the northwest coast of England, where Lucy, her houseguest Mina, and Lucy's mother are staying, a raging storm flings a Russian ship, the *Demeter*, aground. A great dog who, we will learn, is Dracula in one of his metamorphoses, is seen to run from the wreck. Soon after that, Lucy takes to sleepwalking. Her health begins to deteriorate because of the nighttime visits she is receiving from Dracula, who has taken refuge in a suicide's grave on the edge of a cliff near Whitby Abbey. In the midst of all this, we learn that Lucy's mother and Godalming's father are both fatally ill, and that fifty boxes, which are the earth-boxes Dracula needs to sustain himself in during the daylight hours, have been shipped to London.

When Mina Murray receives a letter from a Budapest hospital informing her that Jonathan Harker is being nursed back to health there, Mina instantly leaves for Budapest, where she and Jonathan are married. Meanwhile, Dr. John Seward, at the asylum in London, records the behavior of a patient named Renfield who talks agitatedly about the arrival of his "master." The message to the reader is clear: Dracula has arrived in London.

After a brief period of well-being in Whitby coinciding with Dracula's absence, Lucy and her mother return to London, where Lucy's illness reasserts itself. When Godalming calls Seward in to examine her, Seward, puzzled by a malady with no observable cause, sends for his old teacher, Dr. Van Helsing, in Amsterdam. On his second visit, Van Helsing performs a blood transfusion with Lucy's fiancé as the donor. Eventually all of her suitors, as well as Dr. Van Helsing, will have given her their blood. Van Helsing, suspecting a supernatural agency behind Lucy's illness, places garlic flowers around her bedroom. But Lucy's dying mother, unaware of the significance of the blooms, has them removed "to let in a little fresh air" (p. 173). Lucy, unprotected by the flowers, suffers a relapse. When the garlic is replaced, she is able to sleep peacefully, until the night Berserker, an escaped wolf from the London zoo who is under Dracula's control, smashes through her bedroom window. The shock of this event kills Lucy's mother. Lucy herself sinks into unconsciousness. Even a fourth transfusion, this time using Quincey Morris' blood, fails to save her. At the moment of her death, she becomes a creature as lascivious and lovely as the women Harker encountered at Castle Dracula. She calls to Arthur "in a soft, voluptuous voice . . . 'Arthur! . . . Kiss me!'" (p. 201), but Dr. Van Helsing, aware of the implications of her behavior, interposes to prevent their embrace.

Soon after her death, there are newspaper accounts of a "bloofer lady" (baby talk for "beautiful lady") who has been creating mysterious wounds on the throats of children on Hampstead Heath. Dr. Van Helsing understands the meaning of the stories and arranges for the hallowed destruction of the vampirized Lucy. In one of the most powerful scenes of the novel, the men gather in Lucy's tomb. As Van Helsing reads from a missal, Godalming, wielding a hammer, drives an oak stake through Lucy's heart. "The Thing in the coffin writhed; and a hideous, blood-curdling screech came from the opened red lips. The body shook and quivered and twisted in wild contortions. . . . But Arthur never faltered. . . . whilst the blood from the pierced heart welled and spurted. . . . His face was set, and high duty seemed to shine through it" (p. 262). When it is all over, "One and all we felt that the holy calm that lay . . . over the wasted face and form was only an earthly token and symbol of the calm that was to reign for ever" (p. 264).

Having destroyed Lucy, the band of men that now includes Jonathan Harker, Lord Godalming, Quincey Morris, and Dr. John Seward, with Dr. Van Helsing as its leader, turns to the destruction of Dracula in his residence at Carfax, the estate that is conveniently next door to Dr. Seward's madhouse. Seward continues his observation of Renfield, whose fixation it is that by ingesting living creatures (flies, spiders, mice, cats) he will enhance his own life force.

Dr. Seward, in a conversation with Renfield, learns that his patient is somehow involved with the king vampire. After Seward reports what he has learned to Van Helsing, Renfield is found in a pool of his own blood. Dracula, we learn, has smashed his skull and broken his neck and back. In his dying moments, Renfield tells of how Dracula used him to gain entry to Seward's hospital. He also informs his listeners that Mina, Jonathan Harker's wife, is already a victim of the vampire.

The four men, Van Helsing, Quincey Morris, Dr. John Seward, and Lord Godalming, hurry off to the guest bedroom in which the Harkers have been staying. When they break the door down, they witness the following:

On the bed beside the window lay Jonathan Harker, his face flushed and breathing heavily as though in a stupor. Kneeling on the near edge of the bed facing outwards was the white-clad figure of his wife. By her side stood a tall, thin man, clad in black. . . . With his left hand he held both Mrs. Harker's hands, keeping them away with her arms at full tension; his right hand gripped her by the back of the neck, forcing her face down on his bosom. Her white nightdress was smeared with blood, and a thin stream trickled down the man's bare breast which was shown by his torn-open dress. The attitude of the two had a terrible resemblance to a child forcing a kitten's nose into a saucer of milk to compel it to drink. . . . Mrs. Harker . . . lay in her helpless attitude and disarray. Her face was ghastly, with a pallor which was accentuated by the blood which smeared her lips and cheeks and chin; from her throat trickled a thin stream of blood.

(pp. 336–338)

Dracula manages to escape the men, who renew their hunt and destroy various of the vampire's lairs, but the count continues to elude them. "You think to baffle me," he sneers during one confrontation. "My revenge is just begun! I spread it over centuries, and time is on my side. Your girls that you all love are mine already; and through them you and others shall yet be mine" (p. 365).

When it becomes clear that Dracula has fled back to Transylvania, the pursuit of the vampire enters its final stage. Dracula's inert body is in a coffin in the hold of a ship on its way to Varna, a Romanian seaport. The avenging band, seeking to anticipate the arrival of his ship, take a train. In the course of their journey, Dr. Van Helsing, at the instigation of Mina Harker, who recognizes that the vampire taint in her blood may give her access to

Dracula's psyche, hypnotizes her. By that means, Mina is able to monitor Dracula's flight by sea.

Once Dracula's body is put ashore, not in Varna, as anticipated, but in Galatz, the pursuit intensifies. The group breaks up into three bands to follow Dracula to his castle: Godalming and Harker take a steam launch up the Siret River. Van Helsing and Mina take a train to Bistritza and then hire a coach. Morris and Seward ride on horseback upstream along the river's bank.

Van Helsing and Mina are the first to reach Castle Dracula. By then the vampire taint in her blood has produced palpable changes in Mina; Van Helsing fears that she may be imminently transformed into a vampire. To safeguard her from satanic influences, he encloses her in a holy circle made of crumbled Communion wafers. Later, when Dracula's vampiric harem beckon to her, Van Helsing drives them back with another holy wafer. At daylight, he enters the castle, finds the coffins of the three ghostly women, and begins the task of destruction. When he comes to the tomb of the most beautiful of the women, he is taken aback because "she was so fair to look on, so radiantly beautiful, so exquisitely voluptuous, that the very instinct of man in me, which calls some of my sex to love and to protect one of hers, made my head whirl with new emotion" (p. 437). Duty, however, is duty, and Van Helsing completes his sanctified "butcher work."

Now begins the climactic phase of the novel. It is late afternoon on 6 November. Mina and Dr. Van Helsing watch from a distance as two sets of horsemen, Quincey Morris and John Seward from the south, Jonathan Harker and Lord Godalming from the north, ride at a furious pace in an attempt to overtake a band of Gypsies who are driving the *leiter-waggon* bearing Dracula's inert body. The sun has all but set. When it does, Dracula's catalepsy will be at an end and he will come powerfully alive. From the rocks on the slopes of the pass, the howling of wolves is heard. Mina and Professor Van Helsing have their guns at the ready. Morris and Harker cry "Halt!" and the Gypsies rein in their horses just as Godalming and Seward converge on the scene.

What follows is a tight and bloody skirmish as the Gypsies defend themselves and their charge. In the melee, Quincey Morris and Jonathan Harker fight their way to the box in which Dracula's body lies. The two men get its lid off just as the sun sets. As Mina Harker recounts in her journal, the count's eyes opened, "but, on the instant, came the sweep and flash of Jonathan's great knife. I shrieked as I saw it shear through the throat; whilst at the same moment Mr. Morris's bowie knife plunged into the heart" (p. 443). And that is the end of the king vampire, but not before his face takes on "a look of peace" before "the whole body crumbled into dust" (p. 443). Dracula's death, however, is not without cost. Quincey Morris, though "only too happy to have been of any service" (p. 444) in the fight, is mortally wounded in the struggle.

The power of this strange novel defies the shibboleths available to a literary critic. Stoker is hardly a prose stylist, though mostly because of his exposure to the theater, his language occasionally reverberates with mock grandeur. His protagonists have little depth, though two of them, Dr. Van Helsing and Renfield, almost come to life. Van Helsing is at once a serious figure who is the source of all wisdom as "a philosopher and a metaphysician, and one of the most advanced scientists of his day" (p. 147), as well as a figure of fun with his stilted "Anglo-Dutch" speech. Still, that very mixture of wise crusader and tactless boor make for a memorable, even sympathetic, character.

Renfield is effectively portrayed as a man in profound intellectual and spiritual pain. He comes brilliantly into his own near the middle of the book when he is faced with the riddle of the relationship between lives and souls. In the course of the narrative, he passes through stages of madness, devotion to Satan, penitential Christianity, and, finally, redemptive suffering. When he dies, horribly mutilated by Dracula and unresponsive to Dr. Van Helsing's well-intentioned trephining operation, he dies as a sane man and a good Christian.

Both of the women in *Dracula* start out as types. Lucy is the nineteen-year-old hoyden, the quintessential flirt who preens herself on getting three proposals in the same day. Even though she is transformed in the novel into a parodic version of a scarlet woman, there is no significant growth in her character. She has been vampirized, but this incarnation of Lucy is no more nuanced than her former coquettish self.

The character of Mina Murray (later Harker) is somewhat more complex. Stoker cannot conceal his admiration for her. He has Van Helsing say of her, "Ah, that wonderful Madame Mina! She has man's brain . . . and woman's heart" (p. 284). And

indeed, Mina has virtues galore. She is inexhaustibly competent. She can type, studies shorthand, and has a head filled with train and steamship timetables. With all of that, she is still a model Victorian heroine: sweet, courageous, biddable, and good. Mina, unlike Lucy, must work for a living. Then, too, as a married woman, she has a greater range of emotional (and sexual) experience. The sacrament of matrimony provides her with the added spiritual strength she needs to resist Dracula.

The young men who are cast as the protectors of the women are all stalwart, decent, dependable, and brave; for the most part, they are differentiated from each other only by their professions: Harker is a solicitor; Quincey Morris is a Texas adventurer; John Seward is a doctor, while Lord Godalming, the most shadowy of the group, is merely rich.

What about the character of Dracula himself? His power has nothing to do with character. He is in no way a person who can or needs to be understood. His personality is not Stoker's problem. He is, rather, a force, a figure who represents absolute evil. Charged with satanic power, his evil is generic, not personal. Though he drinks his victims' blood, the act has nothing to do with mere thirst. His goal, rather, is to transform his victims into creatures of Satan.

But if Stoker is neither a prose stylist nor adept at characterization, how can one claim greatness for his *Dracula?* The answer is that Stoker's story—its sheer narrative design—manages to bear the weight of a multitude of powerful meanings. To the unsophisticated reader, *Dracula* is a rousing adventure tale in the Gothic tradition. Here there is not just one but two beautiful, innocent women who are pursued by a tall, dark, exotic figure of evil. The tension mounts as five courageous men succeed finally in defeating the monster. The novel, however, works equally well as a Christian allegory in the mode of the chivalric romance. Read that way, Dr. Van Helsing becomes the Merlin of the tale to whom the bewildered young knights come for counsel. When they learn that their antagonist is an instrument of Satan, they take an oath to do combat with him, aware now that they are fighting the Great Serpent (Dracula's name, in Romanian, means "son of the dragon") who threatens not only the lives of the women they love, but the eternal welfare of their souls.

We have, then, a fiction that is at once an exciting adventure tale and a Christian chivalric romance. But there is more to *Dracula* even than that. Twentieth-century readers, whose sensibilities have been affected by Freudian constructs, are able to see the narrative line of *Dracula* as supporting an extraordinary weight of sexual symbolism. The predominant image in the narrative, the blood exchange between Dracula and his victims, is particularly rich in such implication. As Dracula takes their blood, his chaste female victims become or are in danger of becoming lascivious women; the heroic band that set out to destroy him, led by their wise Dutch seer, are determined to resist the eroticization of their women. The vampire's embrace contains the entire range of human sexuality and is capable of standing for all unions: men with women, men with men, fathers with daughters, mothers with sons. After AIDS, the blood exchange has been reread as an allegorical warning about blood-transmissible disease.

Stoker's story, finally, transcends its Victorian origins as well as Stoker's understanding of his own achievement. *Dracula* is

a novel that lurches toward greatness. . . . This strange book . . . continues to pulse with sometimes incoherent, more often dismembered symbolic material of the sort that makes up what Jung has called "primordial experience which surpasses man's understanding, and to which he is therefore in danger of succumbing." Stoker's achievement is that he put all this *stuff* into his book with such skill that a headlong reader as well as one capable of worrying over the signs and portents is always in the grip of the narrative line.

(Wolf, 1972, p. 222)

Whether we read it as a straightforward adventure tale or as a Christian chivalric romance or as a psychological allegory with erotic implications or as all of these combined, what we are left with is a compelling sense of the urgency of the battle between love and death, the light and the dark.

SELECTED BIBLIOGRAPHY

I. NOVELS. *The Snake's Pass* (New York, 1890); *Crooken Sands* (New York, 1894); *The Watter's Mou'* (New York, 1894); *The Shoulder of Shasta* (Westminster, Eng., 1895); *Dracula* (Westminster, Eng., and Garden City, N.Y., 1897); *Miss Betty* (London, 1898); *The Mystery of the Sea* (New York, 1902); *The Jewel of Seven Stars* (London, 1904); *The Man* (London, 1905); *Lady Athlyne* (London and New York, 1908); *The Gates of Life* (New York, 1908); *The Lady of the Shroud* (London, 1909); *The Lair of the White Worm* (London, 1911).

II. SHORT STORIES. "The Spectre of Doom," in *Dublin Mail* (November 1880); *Under the Sunset* (London, 1882), collection; "The Dualists," in *Theatre Annual of 1887* (Christmas 1887); "Death in the Wings," in *Collier's Magazine* (November 1888); "The Gombeen Man," in *The Dramatic News* (Christmas 1893); "The Red Stockade," in *Cosmopolitan Magazine* (September 1894); "A Criminal Star," in *Collier's Magazine* (October 1904); *Dracula's Guest, and Other Weird Stories* (London, 1914), includes "Dracula's Guest," "The Judge's House," "The Squaw," and others; *Dracula's Guest* (New York, 1937); *Midnight Tales* (London, 1990), ed. by Peter Haining, includes "A Deal with the Devil," "The Funeral Party," and "Shakespeare Mystery."

III. NONFICTION. *The Duties of Clerks of Petty Sessions in Ireland* (Dublin, 1879); *A Glimpse of America* (London, 1886); *Personal Reminiscences of Henry Irving*, 2 vols. (London and New York, 1906); *Snowbound: The Record of a Theatrical Touring Party* (London, 1908); *Famous Impostors* (London and New York, 1910).

IV. ADAPTATION. Hamilton Deane, *Dracula, The Vampire Play in Three Acts, Dramatized by Hamilton Deane and John L. Balderston from Bram Stoker's World Famous Novel "Dracula"* (New York, Los Angeles, and London, 1933).

V. BIOGRAPHICAL AND CRITICAL STUDIES. Harry Ludlam, *A Biography of Dracula: The Life Story of Bram Stoker* (London, 1962); Thomas R. Thornburg, "The Quester and the Castle: The Gothic Novel as Myth, with Special Reference to Bram Stoker's *Dracula*" (Ph.D. diss., Ball State University, 1970); Devendra Varma, introduction to *Varney the Vampire; or, The Feast of Blood* by James M. Rymer or Thomas P. Prest (New York, 1970); Christopher Bentley, "The Monster in the Bedroom: Sexual Symbolism in Bram Stoker's *Dracula*," in *Literature and Psychology* 22, no. 1 (1972); Raymond T. McNally and Radu Florescu, *In Search of Dracula* (Greenwich, Conn., 1972); Leonard Wolf, *A Dream of Dracula* (Boston and Toronto, 1972); Donald F. Glut, *The Dracula Book* (Metuchen, N.J., 1975); Daniel Farson, *The Man Who Wrote Dracula: A Biography of Bram Stoker* (New York, 1976); Mark M. Hennelly, Jr., "*Dracula*: The Gnostic Quest and Victorian Wasteland," in *English Literature in Transition* 20, no. 1 (1977); Douglas O. Street, "Bram Stoker's *Under the Sunset*: An Edition with Introductory Biographical and Critical Material" (Ph.D. diss., University of Nebraska, 1977); Eric Irvin, "Dracula's Friends and Forerunner," in *Quadrant* 135 (1978).

Nina Auerbach, *Woman and the Demon: The Life of a Victorian Myth* (Cambridge, Mass., 1982); Phyllis A. Roth, *Bram Stoker* (Boston, 1982); Les Daniels, "Bram Stoker," in E. F. Bleiler, ed., *Supernatural Fiction Writers,*

2 vols. (New York, 1985); Clive Leatherdale, *Dracula, the Novel and the Legend: A Study of Bram Stoker's Gothic Masterpiece* (Northamptonshire, Eng., 1985); James B. Twitchell, *Dreadful Pleasures: An Anatomy of Modern Horror* (New York, 1985); Bram Dijkstra, *Idols of Perversity: Fantasies of Evil in Fin-de-Siècle Culture* (New York, 1986); Jacques Finne, *La Bibliographie de Dracula* (Paris, 1986); George Stade, "Dracula's Women, and Why Men Love to Hate Them," in *The Psychology of Men: New Psychoanalytic Perspectives*, ed. by Gerald I. Fogel, Frederick M. Lane, and Robert S. Liebert (New York, 1986); Clive Leatherdale, *The Origins of Dracula* (London, 1987); Margaret L. Carter, *The Vampire and the Critics* (Ann Arbor, 1988); Kelley Hurley, "The Novel of the Gothic Body: Deviance, Abjection, and Late-Victorian Popular Fiction" (Ph.D. diss., Stanford University, 1988); Margaret L. Carter, ed., *The Vampire in Literature: A Critical Bibliography* (Ann Arbor, Mich., 1989); Christopher C. Craft, "Another Kind of Love: Sodomy, Inversion, and Male Homosexual Desire in English Discourse, 1850–1897" (Ph.D. diss., University of California, Berkeley, 1989), on Tennyson, Wilde, Stoker, Ellis, Symonds; Rosemary Jann, "Saved by Science? The Mixed Messages of Stoker's *Dracula*," in *Texas Studies in Literature and Language* 31, no. 2 (summer 1989); Rebecca Stott, "The Kiss of Death: A Demystification of the Late Nineteenth Century 'Femme Fatale' in the Selected Works of Bram Stoker, Rider Haggard, Joseph Conrad, and Thomas Hardy" (Ph.D. diss., University of York, Eng., 1989); Kathleen M. Ward, "Dear Sir or Madame: The Epistolary Novel in Britain in the Nineteenth Century" (Ph.D. diss., University of Wisconsin, 1989).

David Skal, *Hollywood Gothic: The Tangled Web of Dracula from Novel to Stage to Screen* (New York, 1990); Marie N. Zeender, "L'Érotisme et la mort: Images de la mère dans trois oeuvres de Bram Stoker," in *Actes du XIe Colloque du CERLI* (26–27 January 1990); Christopher Frayling, ed., *Vampires: Lord Byron to Count Dracula* (London, 1991); Michelle J. Gardner, "The Vampire in English Literature" (Ph.D. diss., University of Waterloo, Canada, 1991); Anne Williams, "*Dracula*: Si(g)ns of the Fathers," in *Texas Studies in Literature and Language* 33, no. 4 (winter 1991); Donald T. Anderson, "The Female Vampire and the Politics of Gender" (Ph.D. diss., University of Alberta, 1992); Matthew C. Brennan, "Repression, Knowledge, and Saving Souls: The Role of the 'New Woman' in Stoker's *Dracula* and Murnau's *Nosferatu*," in *Studies in the Humanities* 19, no. 1 (June 1992); Alexandra C. Dence, "The Nineteenth-Century Novel's Divided Personality" (Ph.D. diss., University of Alberta, 1992); David Glover, "Bram Stoker and the Crisis of the Liberal Subject," in *New Literary History: A Journal of Theory and Interpretation* 23, no. 4 (autumn 1992); Mark M. Hennelly, Jr., "The Victorian Book of the Dead: *Dracula*," in *Journal of Evolutionary Psychology* 13, nos. 3–4 (August 1992); Richard L. Homan, "Freud's 'Seduction Theory' on Stage: Deane's and Balderston's *Dracula*," in *Literature and Psychology* 38, nos. 1–2 (1992); Beth E. McDonald, "The Vampire as Trickster Figure in Bram Stoker's *Dracula*," in *Extrapolation: A Journal of Science Fiction and Fantasy* 33, no. 2 (summer 1992); Kathleen L. Spencer, "Purity and Danger: *Dracula*, the Urban Gothic, and the Late Victorian Degeneracy Crisis," in *English Literary History* 59, no. 1 (spring 1992); Robert J. Lange, "Mad About Sex: Tropes of Gender and Madness in the American and British Novel" (Ph.D. diss., University of Kentucky, 1993); Lenora P. Ledwon, "Legal Fictions: Constructions of the Female Legal Subject in Nineteenth-Century Law and Literature" (Ph.D. diss., University of Notre Dame, 1993); Carol A. Senf, *The Critical Response to Bram Stoker* (Westport, Conn., 1993); Leonard Wolf, ed., *The Essential Dracula* (New York, 1993); Barbara Belford, *Bram Stoker: A Biography* (New York, forthcoming).

EDWARD THOMAS

(1878–1917)

Anthony Whiting

WHEN EDWARD THOMAS died on Easter Monday, 1917, one of the first casualties of the Battle of Arras, he was a well-known figure on the Georgian literary scene. In addition to reviewing for more than a half dozen journals, he had written a book of stories; essays; critical studies of figures such as Algernon Charles Swinburne and Walter Pater; a biography of the duke of Marlborough; introductions to the work of, among others, Christopher Marlowe and George Herbert; and edited an anthology of English writers. His work as editor and reviewer brought him into contact with many of the leading literary figures of the day: Ernest Rhys, Harold Monro, Edward Garnett, Hilaire Belloc, Ford Madox Ford, Robert Frost, Ezra Pound, John Galsworthy, and Joseph Conrad. He was acquainted with most of the "official" Georgian poets—those whose work appeared in *Georgian Poetry*—and was close friends with several of them: Ralph Hodgson, W. H. Davies, and Gordon Bottomley, who dedicated his volume of poetry, *The Riding to Lithend*, to Thomas.

Although it is for his verse that he is mainly remembered today, Thomas was almost unknown as a poet to the Georgian reading public. All of his poetry was written during the last two and a half years of his life, and the few poems that were published while he was alive appeared under a pseudonym, Edward Eastaway. A volume of poems, published under his own name, appeared the year after his death, and in 1920 *Collected Poems* was issued. Fame, though, did not come quickly to Thomas. In the introduction to the first volume of *Georgian Poetry* (1912), Edward Marsh wrote that English verse was once again putting on new strength and beauty. By the latter part of the decade, however, Georgian poetry appeared to many contemporary observers to be out of touch with postwar reality. High modernism was on the ascendancy, and by the early 1920s the Georgian movement had all but ended. Although Thomas' verse was not published in any of the five volumes of *Georgian Poetry*, interest in his work declined when Georgian poetry fell out of critical and popular favor. F. R. Leavis wrote appreciatively of Thomas' poetry in the 1930s, but it was not until the 1950s that his work began to receive sustained critical attention. He is regarded today as one of the best of the Georgian poets.

LIFE

PHILIP Edward Thomas was born in London on 3 March 1878, the oldest of six sons. Both his father, Philip Henry Thomas, and his mother, Mary Elizabeth Townsend Thomas, had been born and raised in Wales. Philip, a teacher in his hometown of Tredegar, came to London to join the Board of Trade as a clerk for light railways and tramways. He had a strong interest in politics and campaigned throughout his life for Liberal or Progressive candidates. He also had a lively interest in religion. Edward wrote in his autobiography, *The Childhood of Edward Thomas* (1938), that his father tried many different chapels and preachers. He settled for a time on the Unitarian Church but eventually gave up Unitarianism to become a minister in the Church of Humanity in Holborn.

Although Thomas became involved in his father's political activities during the Home Rule election, he did not share Philip Thomas' interest in politics. Nor did he share his father's religious enthusiasm. He looked on Sundays, he remarks in his autobiography, as a cruel punishment for the freedom he enjoyed during the rest of the week. Forced attendance at church and at various evening educational lectures contributed to the deep rift between father and son that is recorded in Thomas' poem "P. H. T.": "I may come near loving you / When you are dead / . . . / But not so long as you live / Can I love you at all."[1]

Thomas was a shy boy, and his free time was spent taking long walks, sometimes twenty or twenty-five miles, to explore the countryside around London. Similar explorations were made during visits to his relatives at Swindon. He began to write detailed descriptions of nature in the style of Richard Jefferies (1848–1887), a nature writer who first gained popularity with his sketches *The Gamekeeper at Home* (1878). (In 1909, Thomas published an appreciative study of Jefferies' work.) During a visit to Swindon, Thomas met and formed a lifelong friendship with David ("Dad") Uzzell. (As Thomas' biographer R. George Thomas notes, Thomas even spent his brief honeymoon in Uzzell's cottage.) Uzzell, a reformed poacher who lived close to the soil and had an extensive knowledge of nature, became in many ways an emotional surrogate for Thomas' father. Several of the themes of Thomas' poetry can be related to this early phase of his life. His poems often express a sense of alienation, the desire to find home, the satisfaction the spirit can take in nature, and the pleasure of the open road. "Dad" Uzzell can be seen behind the English country characters who are featured in "Man and Dog," "Bob's Lane," and, most famously, "Lob."

In 1894 the minister of the Unitarian Church that Thomas attended showed several of Thomas' essays to a distinguished member of his congregation, James Ashcroft Noble, former editor of the *Manchester Examiner* and literary critic for the *Spectator,* the *Academy,* and the *Daily Chronicle.* Noble encouraged Thomas to write and used his influence to help Thomas place his essays in *New Age,* the *Speaker,* and the *Globe.* He also encouraged Thomas to court his daughter, Helen, whom Thomas married on 20 June 1899, the year after he won a history scholarship to Lincoln College, Oxford. In January 1900 their son, Merfyn, was born, and Helen was forced to move in with the Thomas family in London while Edward completed his degree (June 1900). Thomas' second-class degree and his decision not to enter the Civil Service led to a serious quarrel with his father,

and Edward, his wife, and infant son left the elder Thomas' household.

They settled in a poor neighborhood in London, and for several years Thomas struggled to provide for his growing family. (His daughter, Rachel Mary Bronwen, was born in October 1902.) Work as a reviewer was unsteady, and Thomas had to sell some of the books he had acquired at Oxford to pay for household expenses. In 1902 his literary fortunes began to change. In November of that year, Lionel Johnson, who had been a reviewer for the *Daily Chronicle,* died. Thomas took his place and reviewed regularly for the *Chronicle* for the next ten years. Also in 1902, Duckworth published a volume of Thomas' essays under the title *Horae Solitariae.* The reader for Duckworth was Edward Garnett, and because of his support, Duckworth continued to publish Thomas' noncommercial prose books throughout his life. (Garnett also helped Thomas establish a relationship with J. M. Dent and Company, and he was instrumental in securing a government grant of £300 for Thomas in June 1916.) Thomas' income from reviewing was supplemented by writing books and essays and by editing. The pace was terrific. He sometimes reviewed as many as fifteen books a week, and between 1910 and 1912, he published twelve books of his own. The strain overwhelmed Thomas, and in 1911 he suffered a nervous breakdown. He went to West Wales to recover, and by December of that year had written a study of George Borrow and agreed to write books on Swinburne and Pater.

In October 1913, Thomas made the acquaintance of an American poet who was to have a profound effect on his professional and personal life, Robert Frost. Frost had come to England in 1912. His first two books of poetry, *A Boy's Will* (1913) and *North of Boston* (1914), were published in England, and Frost, a diligent propagandist for his own work, was assiduously cultivating English and American literary figures such as Ezra Pound, F. S. Flint, Harold Monro, Lascelles Abercrombie, Wilfred Gibson, and Ralph Hodgson. His acquaintance with the latter two led to an introduction to Thomas. Frost and Thomas met several times in London in December 1913. In April 1914, Thomas stayed with Frost at Little Iddens, where Frost was living near the Georgian poets Lascelles Abercrombie, John Drinkwater, and Gordon Bottomley, and Thomas and his family spent August of that year at Ledington, in a cottage near Frost. The two

---

[1] Edward Thomas, *The Collected Poems of Edward Thomas,* ed. by R. George Thomas (Oxford: 1978), 273. All quotations from Thomas' poetry have been taken from this edition.

became close friends. In his elegy to Thomas, "To E. T.," Frost calls Thomas a brother. Thomas' affection to Frost is recorded in his poem "The sun used to shine" (1916), which recalls their time together in the late summer of 1914.

> The sun used to shine while we two walked
> Slowly together, paused and started
> Again, and sometimes mused, sometimes talked
> As either pleased, and cheerfully parted
> Each night. We never disagreed
> Which gate to rest on.
>
> (p. 319)

This sense of relaxed intimacy with another person is not found often in Thomas' work. When World War I broke out, Frost decided to return to America. He urged Thomas to emigrate to New Hampshire, where he could lecture and continue to write. Thomas declined but sent his son, Merfyn, to stay with the Frosts from February to December 1915. (Thomas' poem "Parting," which examines the relationship between Merfyn and Thomas, was written in response to Merfyn's departure for America.)

The years 1913–1915 were particularly important in Frost's poetic development. As is evident from his letters to John Bartlett and Sidney Cox, Frost's theory of the sound of sense, a theory he had been mulling over since at least 1894, seemed to crystallize during this period. Frost's idea was that sound carried meaning apart from the words. His well-known example is of a conversation heard from behind a door. The words cannot be made out, but the sound of the words expresses meaning. An auditor, that is, can tell from the sound of the words what emotions—anger, fear, joy, sadness, and so on—are being expressed. Frost's intention was to bring into poetry the sound and rhythm of actual speech. But Frost was not advocating free verse. He wanted the poet to break the irregular accent of speech across a metrical scheme.

Thomas was an early champion of Frost's ideas. In his 22 July 1914 *Daily News* review of *North of Boston*, Thomas writes that Frost's "medium is common speech," a theme to which he returns in his 8 August 1914 review of the volume in the *New Weekly*. Frost's poetry, he writes, is full of "ordinary English speech." It is "more colloquial and idiomatic than the ordinary man dares to use even in a letter." But he emphasizes that Frost's work should not be mistaken for prose: "Whatever discipline . . . was necessary, [Frost] got from the use of the good old English medium of blank verse."

Thomas had been developing similar ideas on his own. In a 19 May 1914 letter to Frost, he playfully tells Frost that if Frost does not write a book on speech in literature, he will take Frost's ideas and write one himself. He adds on a more serious note that if Frost will look at Thomas' study of Pater (1913), he will see that Thomas had already been thinking about language along the same lines. Thomas' criticism of Pater—his bejeweled writing is cut off from the living, social world—had been anticipated in his studies of Swinburne (1912) and Lafcadio Hearn (1912) and in his 31 January 1913 article in *T. P.'s Weekly*, "How I Began," where he writes of the poet's connection with the thoughts of ordinary, rural inhabitants.

Frost wrote in a 28 June 1921 letter to the American poet Grace Walcott Conkling that he and Thomas gave each other a boost. Thomas, more than anyone else during the period 1913–1915, gave Frost standing as a poet, and Frost certainly stimulated Thomas' critical thinking about the language and rhythm of poetry. But Frost gave Thomas a boost in another way. Through the example of his own work, through his conversations with Thomas, and through encouragement and prodding (at one point Frost asked Thomas to rewrite certain paragraphs of his *In Pursuit of Spring* [1914] in verse form in the same cadence), Frost did for Thomas what Emerson had done for Whitman: brought him to a boil. In December 1914, Thomas completed the first of the 144 poems for which he is mainly remembered today.

In July 1915, Thomas enlisted in the British army. His motives were complex. In part he wanted to get away from what he described as the mess of journalism, in part he wanted to secure a pension for Helen, and in part he was motivated by the kind of unambiguous love of country he expresses in "This is no case of petty right or wrong":

> But with the best and meanest Englishmen
> I am one in crying, God save England, lest
> We lose what never slaves and cattle blessed.
> The ages made her that made us from the dust:
> She is all we know and live by, and we trust
> She is good and must endure, loving her so:
> And as we love ourselves we hate her foe.
>
> (p. 257)

He became a training instructor at Hare Hall Camp in Essex, where his duties included teaching map reading and the use of the protractor and compass. When his Civil List pension was turned down in June 1916, he almost immediately volunteered for duty in France. He joined the Royal Artillery and by August was training as an officer cadet at St. John's Wood. He completed his last poem on 13 January 1917, just before his departure for France. It is a farewell, probably to his wife, Helen. "The sorrow of true love is a great sorrow / And true love parting blackens a bright morrow" (p. 377). On 29 January he embarked for Le Havre. He was soon made an adjutant at headquarters at Arras, a position he held until 9 March 1917, when he rejoined his battery. He was given observation duty, supervised trench digging, and helped position the guns. He had a narrow escape on Easter Sunday when, he records in his diary, a German 5.9 shell fell within two yards of him but did not explode. The next morning, 9 April 1917, the Arras offensive began. At 7:36 A.M., at an observation post, Thomas was killed by an exploding shell. His unmarked body was recovered, and he was buried in a military cemetery at Agny, south of Arras.

THE GEORGIAN LITERARY SCENE

WITH the exception of Thomas Hardy, who published *Poems of the Past and the Present* in 1901, *The Dynasts* in the years 1903–1908, and *Time's Laughing-Stocks* in 1909, and William Butler Yeats, who published *In the Seven Woods* in 1904 and *The Green Helmet and Other Poems* in 1910, the first decade of the twentieth century was a relatively quiet one for English poetry. This changed dramatically at the end of the Edwardian and beginning of the Georgian periods, when new schools of poetry seemed to spring up (and disappear) almost overnight. At least four major groups vied for the attention of the poetry-reading public: the Georgians, the imagists, the vorticists, and the futurists. As an established member of the literary community, Thomas was undoubtedly acquainted with all of them. Several received close attention in reviews. A brief description of the differences and similarities among these groups will help to clarify Thomas' place in the Georgian literary scene.

One of the most colorful personalities in a period of colorful personalities was Filippo T. Marinetti, who published the first futurist manifesto in *Le Figaro* on 20 February 1909. Successive manifestos followed over the next several years. An anthology of Italian futurist verse, issued in 1912, was extremely successful. By 1913 it had sold 35,000 copies. Marinetti's impact on the London scene came not only from manifestos and verse but also from his lectures, which he gave between 1912 and 1914. These lectures were grand performances in which he was sometimes accompanied by an offstage drum, and he himself would on occasion imitate the sound of a machine gun.

Marinetti rejected symbolism, with its love of the immaterial and eternal, the cult of art, the Romantic imagination, and the worship of nature. Futurism celebrated the machine, especially the automobile, action, war, and love of danger. For Marinetti, only the most radical forms could embody these futurist concepts. In his "Technical Manifesto of Futurist Literature" (11 May 1912), he called for the destruction of syntax; the abolition of the adjective in order to allow the "naked noun to preserve its essential color"; the linking of nouns without conjunctions (man-torpedo-boat, for example); the elimination of punctuation; the use of mathematical symbols such as $+$, $-$, $\times$, $:$, and $=$; the abolition of the adverb because it preserves a tedious unity of tone; the destruction of the "I"; and the use of the infinitive to give a feeling of the continuity of life. He also called for the typographical harmony of the page to be destroyed by using various kinds of type and different colors of ink. London, as Richard Aldington remarked in the *New Freewoman* (1 December 1913), was both shocked and amused. Though Marinetti lived until 1944, futurism was effectively ended as a viable movement by World War I. The violence called for by the futurists could not survive the public reaction to the brutality of the war.

The futurists were vigorously opposed by the vorticists, a group of writers, painters, and sculptors that included Ezra Pound, Wyndham Lewis, and Henri Gaudier-Brzeska. On 5 May 1914 they heckled Marinetti at the Doré Gallery, where he was lecturing, and in June published a manifesto of their own in their short-lived periodical, *Blast*. The vorticist artist tried to locate himself or herself at the center of the vortex, a whirlpool of energy into and from which ideas and associations are continually moving. The vorticists believed that each art has a primary form: in poetry, image; in painting, color in position; in sculpture, form in three planes; in music, sound. Each artist, using the primary form of his or her art, expresses the energy concentrated at the center of the vortex. The essential thing is for the artist to be able to remain in the vortex, which changes over time. According to the vorticists, futurism and impressionism did not change and hence are the corpses of vortices. Though the vorticists rejected futurist art, they shared with the futurists a number of aesthetic biases: they rejected aestheticism; they called for an art of the present; and they invited extreme formal experimentation.

A third group, and one that was to have more influence than either the futurists or the vorticists on the development of modern poetry, was the imagists. According to its indefatigable publicist, Ezra Pound, imagism began in the spring or summer of 1912 when he, Hilda Doolittle ("H. D."), and Richard Aldington agreed to certain principles. Imagism called for economy of language, and clarity and precision of presentation. These two principles represented a rejection of the vagueness and wordiness of late Victorian poetry and of the kind of penumbral evocation of objects practiced by the symbolist poets. The imagists also rejected formal verse forms when the subject could not be rendered in them. They called instead for a fluid form that organically relates to the poem's subject. In their willingness to experiment with *vers libre*, the imagists shared common ground with the futurists and the vorticists. In 1914, Pound published an anthology of imagist poetry, *Des Imagistes: An Anthology*. The next year the group came under the leadership of Amy Lowell. Pound dubbed the group Amygists and withdrew from it. Lowell retaliated. In her chapter on the imagists in her 1917 survey of modern poetry, *Tendencies in Modern American Poetry*, Pound is mentioned only as the discoverer of H. D. and as the person who collected the poems published in the first imagist anthology. His own imagist poetry and his founding role in the movement are nowhere mentioned. Lowell published her own imagist anthologies, entitled *Some Imagist Poets*, in 1915, 1916, and 1917.

By far the most popular group of poets during this period was the Georgians. An anthology of Georgian poets, *Georgian Poetry, 1911–1912*, was published in 1912. Unlike the imagists, futurists,

and vorticists, the Georgians wrote no manifestos. The idea behind the anthology was to bring deserving but unnoticed poets to the attention of the public. Though the idea for the anthology was originally Rupert Brooke's, it was brought to life by Edward Marsh, private secretary to Winston Churchill, then first lord of the Admiralty. Marsh not only edited all of the volumes of *Georgian Poetry* but also provided financial guarantees to its publisher, Harold Monro, owner of the Poetry Bookshop and editor of the influential journal *Poetry and Drama*, should the venture not be a commercial success. Marsh, using his personal and professional contacts, waged a brilliant public relations campaign, and *Georgian Poetry* I was a tremendous success. Even the prime minister's car, as John Drinkwater comments in *Discovery*, was seen outside a bookshop on Oxford Street on the day *Georgian Poetry* I was published. By 1913 the volume had gone into a ninth edition. The first edition had a print run of 500. By 1919 the volume had sales of 13,000. A second *Georgian Poetry*, covering the years 1913–1915, was published in 1915; its sales eventually exceeded those of *Georgian Poetry* I. Three more anthologies were produced, *Georgian Poetry* III (1916–1917), *Georgian Poetry* IV (1918–1919), and *Georgian Poetry* V (1920–1922). All of the volumes sold extremely well.

Though the poets in the Georgian anthologies represented a wide range of sensibilities, they did share some characteristics. First, they rejected the lush Victorian vocabulary that Richard Aldington has called the cult of the painted adjective. They also rejected the language of the nineties poets and their attitude of world-weariness. Instead, the Georgians attempted to write in the accents of common speech, and they adopted an attitude of engagement with life and experience. In rejecting any Victorian elements in their verse, the Georgians shared ground with the imagists, futurists, and vorticists. As Robert Ross notes, some contemporary readers felt that the Georgians' attempt to escape from their Victorian predecessors was so extreme that they had become futurists.

In at least two ways, however, the Georgians differed from these other groups. First, in regard to rhythm and form, the Georgians were not as extreme in their experiments as were the imagists, vorticists, and futurists. The standard here was set by Edward Marsh, who strongly favored some discernible rhythmic and formal pattern in poetry. The rule was not absolute. D. H. Lawrence, for instance, who published a strong defense of *vers libre*, "Poetry of the Present," in the introduction to the American edition of *New Poems* (1918), was represented in four of the five Georgian anthologies. On the whole, however, selections in *Georgian Poetry* reflected Marsh's taste. Second, Georgian verse had a strong bias toward realism. Though it may be hard to imagine today, some Georgian verse—for example, Lascelles Abercrombie's "The Sale of St. Thomas," the lead poem in *Georgian Poetry* I—was criticized as the most brutal kind of realism. And it was the Georgians' realism that, as much as anything else, distinguished their verse from the verse of the imagists, futurists, and vorticists in the public's mind.

Thomas' views on modern poetry, as suggested in his reviews, were in many ways close to those of Marsh. In general, Thomas objected to obscurity, preferred some formal and rhythmic pattern to *vers libre*, eschewed antique diction and vocabulary, and liked directness and simplicity of style and poetry that reflects an engagement with life. Perhaps his central critical principle, though, was the Romantic and Victorian one of sincerity. When Thomas heard the accents of sincerity in a poet, he was quite open to experimentation in form. In Ezra Pound's *Personae* (1909), for example, Thomas found a good deal to criticize: "Let us straightway acknowledge the faults; the signs of conflict; the old and foreign words and old spellings that stand doubtless for much that the ordinary reader is not privileged to detect; the tricky use of inverted commas; the rhythms at one time so free as not to be distinguishable at first from prose, at another time so stiff that 'evanescent' becomes 'evan'scent'" (*English Review*, June 1909). Yet for Thomas, Pound was a sincere poet. In all of the forms he used, Pound "is true in his strength and weakness to himself" (*English Review*, June 1909). And Thomas singled out Pound's "In Praise of Ysolt" for commendation: "The beauty of it is the beauty of passion, sincerity and intensity" (*English Review*, June 1909). Experimentation for its own sake, however, drew Thomas' unequivocal censure. In Pound's *Exultations* (1909), Thomas found only a "turbulent opacity" (*Daily Chronicle*, 23 November 1909). When Pound wrote in the first person, he was "so obscure" that he was "incapable of self-expression" (*Daily Chronicle*, 23 November 1909). Even those verses where "the thought is simple and plain enough" expressed no "individual value as a cry of the heart" (*Daily Chronicle*, 23 November 1909).

Thomas found none of the obscurity or opacity that he felt marred Pound's *Exultations* in the work of W. H. Davies and Walter de la Mare, or in *Georgian Poetry* I. "There is a truth and freshness in the writing," Thomas commented about Davies' *Nature Poems*, "that is a pledge of the author's absolute sincerity" (*Morning Post*, 31 December 1908). Davies' *Autobiography of a Supertramp* was praised for "the ease and sincerity and inevitableness of [its] English" (*Daily Chronicle*, 23 April 1908). Thomas saw similar characteristics in Davies' second volume of poetry, *New Poems*, which he described as coming "straight from the spirit of a strange, vivid, unlearned, experienced man" (*Morning Post*, 3 January 1907). In de la Mare, Thomas heard sincerity "speaking, as sincerity always does, a strange new tongue" (*Daily Chronicle*, 9 November 1906). And in his review of *Georgian Poetry* I, he commented that the *Yellow Book* authors "would have contracted a chill from so much eagerness both to come at truth and to avoid the appearance of insincerity, the fidelity to crudest fact [that is found] in Messrs. Abercrombie, Gibson and Masefield" (*Bookman*, March 1913).

These critical judgments found a sympathetic ear in Harold Monro, and Thomas was asked by Monro to write reviews for his journal, *Poetry and Drama*. Thomas was also asked by Monro for comments on his own verse. In mid-1914, Thomas wrote to Monro inquiring whether he would be interested in publishing a work written by Thomas on from twelve to twenty modern poets. Probably because of World War I, however, the project never went beyond a few discussions.

Monro's response to Thomas' poetry was very different from his response to Thomas' criticism. In 1915, Thomas sent poems to a number of editors, including Monro, under the name of Edward Eastaway. He used the pseudonym because he did not want to be treated favorably by reviewers who were also friends. He need not have taken the trouble with Monro, who knew the true identity of Edward Eastaway and still rejected the poems. Nor did Thomas' work fare any better with Edward Marsh. In 1917, after Thomas' death, Walter de la Mare, John Freeman, and W. J. Turner suggested to Marsh that he include some of Thomas' verse in *Georgian Poetry* III. Though Marsh would later come to appreciate Thomas' work, he rejected their advice, and Thomas did not appear in that or any other volume of *Georgian Poetry*.

A few of Thomas' poems, though, did appear in his lifetime. All were printed under the pseudonym Edward Eastaway. He included two of his own poems, "The Manor Farm" and "Haymaking," in an anthology he edited in 1915. James Guthrie published *Six Poems* in 1916, and in 1917, Thomas' friend Gordon Bottomley selected eighteen poems for inclusion in *An Annual of New Poetry*. A wider audience for his work seemed assured in 1917 when Harriet Monroe accepted his verse for *Poetry* magazine and Selwyn and Blount decided to publish a volume of his poetry. Thomas did not live to see the volume through the press.

NON–WAR POETRY

ALTHOUGH Thomas wrote more than one million words of prose, he is remembered today for the poems he composed during the last two and a half years of his life. During this period T. S. Eliot and Pound were developing the high modernist mode in poetry. ("The Love Song of J. Alfred Prufrock" was published in Harriet Monroe's *Poetry* magazine in June 1915. Conrad Aiken had earlier shown the poem to Harold Monro, who rejected it.) Thomas' work differs from Eliot's and Pound's in several ways. While they strive for impersonality, Thomas' voice is unmistakably that of a particular individual. While their work is allusive (Thomas wrote that Pound's poetry is "dappled with French, Provençal, Spanish, Italian, Latin, and old English" [*Daily Chronicle*, 23 November 1909]), he uses colloquial, unaffected language that has proselike rhythms. And while high modernist poetry cultivates irony, Thomas generally avoids both rhetorical and philosophical irony. These characteristics also set Thomas' work apart from the extravagant formal experiments of the futurists and vorticists, from the lush rhetoric of high Victorian poetry, and from the polished, artificial verse of the decadent poets. Though his poems are realistic, Thomas does not strive for the kind of shock effects the Georgian public found in Lascelles Abercrombie or Rupert Brooke.

The popular audience for poetry may have found some Georgian verse to be rather shocking, but to modernists such as T. S. Eliot, J. Middleton Murry, and Edith Sitwell, to read Georgian poetry was to suffer death by insipid pleasantness. Perhaps this view of Georgian verse would have been different if Thomas had been included in the Georgian anthologies. The feelings of alienation, isolation, and self-doubt that are explored in his poetry are very far from the world of moonlight and nightingales that frequently is found in late Georgian verse. Thomas often explores his sense of isolation through the use of memory. "'Go now'" (p. 303), for instance, opens with his recollection of being surprised by a woman's love.

> Like the touch of rain she was
> On a man's flesh and hair and eyes
> When the joy of walking thus
> Has taken him by surprise.

He recounts his "love of the storm," but the poem closes with his irrevocable separation from his beloved. She says, "Go now." Those words "shut a door / Between me and the blessed rain / That was never shut before / And will not open again." The tone, characteristic in Thomas, is restrained. There is no self-pity, no Hopkins-like cry for relief, no Eliotic self-mockery, no direct expression of pain. Thomas' reserve, however, should not be mistaken for lack of feeling. In pointing to the almost sacred quality of her love, "blessed," Thomas also defines the profound nature of his loss.

If the past is the mirror that reflects the spiritual blankness of the present in "'Go now,'" in other poems the past actively intrudes upon the present. In "Two Houses" (p. 243), for instance, the past threatens the tranquillity of the present, which is represented by an ideal country house— "No other one / So pleasant to look at / And remember, for many miles." This house, however, was built on the site of one that "stood there long before." There is an eerie haunting of the present by the first house, which "Half yields the dead that never / More than half hidden lie: / And out they creep and back again for ever." In "The Cuckoo" (p. 81), the past again intrudes upon the present, this time separating Thomas from the pleasure of each returning spring, symbolized by the song of the cuckoo. He cannot hear the cuckoo, and he cannot even recall when he last heard it. But he does remember when he first failed to hear the bird. "It was drowned by my man groaning out to his sheep 'Ho! Ho!'" The man "died that Summer." But now the memory of the man blocks the cuckoo's song. "[E]ven if I could lose my deafness / The Cuckoo's note would be drowned by the voice of my dead."

Memory is also used by Thomas to define a kind of spiritual powerlessness or inability to overcome his isolation. "Over the Hills" (p. 77), for example, begins with Thomas' recollection of a visit to a "new country." He finds there an "inn where all were kind, / All were strangers." This vision of an ideal society where one is greeted as a friend even though one is a stranger is returned to in "Good-night" (p. 125). In that poem Thomas records his experience of "All Friends' Night." He comes into "unfamiliar streets," yet "The friendless town is friendly; homeless, I am not lost." In "Over the Hills," however, his memory of this ideal social moment leads to a recognition of his inability ever to cross the hills again to that new country. "It became / Almost a habit through the year for me / To lean and see it and think to do the same." But recollection is vain. He can no more go back than the "restless brook" could "turn back and climb the waterfall." Here, as in "'Go now,'" "Two Houses," and "The Cuckoo," the past serves to define a sense of alienation and diminishment. In none does memory lead to any sense of renewal or recovery.

These four poems also express several other characteristics that are typical of Thomas' verse. First, they seek no explanation for the situations they present. Thomas wrote in a review of Hardy's *Time's Laughing-Stocks and Other Poems* that "the obvious quality to point to in all the poems is the sense of the misery and fraudulence of life" (*Daily Chronicle*, 7 December 1909). Having given up the myth of an evil god, Hardy, in "Hap," can only offer chance as the cause of human unhappiness. In Thomas, not even chance is invoked to explain the diminishments of the present. Second, the poems are not judgmental. Thomas neither blames nor exonerates the woman for withdrawing from him in "'Go now,'" nor blames nor exonerates himself for not acting in "Over the Hills." Rather than explanations or judgments, Thomas strives in his work for a scrupulous fidelity to fact and feeling. It is perhaps the clarity and precision with which Thomas renders his experience that underlies a third characteristic of his poetry, the sense of balance or poise that the mind displays as it contemplates emotions—love that can never be renewed, the loss of a connection to nature, social acceptance

that will never recur—that might otherwise overwhelm it.

Thomas sometimes expresses a sense of openness to others even as he acknowledges his isolation from them. In "What will they do?" (p. 361), for example, Thomas flatly observes that his departure for France, and hence perhaps his death, will have no effect on those around him: "What will they do when I am gone? It is plain / That they will do without me as the rain / Can do without the flowers and the grass." Though they are indifferent to him, he acknowledges their deep influence on him, and he asks whether he has also influenced them: "But what if I in them as they in me / Nourished what has great value and no price?" A laugh from one of them, "one turned back and lightly laughed," answers his question in the negative. Though the poem records with unflinching directness Thomas' sense that he means nothing to them, it nowhere suggests that their influence on him has diminished. He remains open to them, even though he feels alienated from them.

The passive state of being open to the influence of others is exchanged for an active one of sympathy in "Rain" (p. 259). One of Thomas' darkest poems, "Rain" opens on "midnight rain," a "bleak hut," and Thomas "Remembering again that I shall die." Though utterly isolated, he reaches out to those whom once he loved.

> Blessed are the dead that the rain rains upon:
> But here I pray that none whom once I loved
> Is dying tonight or lying still awake
> Solitary, listening to the rain,
> Either in pain or thus in sympathy
> Helpless among the living and the dead.

The first act of sympathy is Thomas' blessing of the dead. Blessing gives way to prayer, and the dead give way to the living, those who are "lying still awake." The solemnity of the prayer is emphasized by Thomas' use of the phrase "the living and the dead," which echoes both the Bible (2 Timothy 4:1 and 1 Peter 4:5) and the Anglican Nicene Creed. This act of sympathy does not alleviate Thomas' own isolation. Though he reaches out toward others, he remains alone, in the "bleak hut," facing death.

Perhaps Thomas' most poignant expression of the sense of openness to and yet alienation from another is his poem to his wife, Helen. After

Thomas enlisted, he wrote poems to his father, his mother, his children, and his wife. These poems are a kind of emotional leave-taking, a settling of accounts before going to war. His estrangement from his father is recorded in "To P. H. T." His poem to his mother, "M. E. T.," expresses his deep love and devotion to her. To his wife and children, he offers gifts. He writes to Bronwen, his elder daughter, that he would buy "Codham, Cockridden, and Childerditch / Roses, Pyro, and Lapwater" (p. 291) and give them to her. To his son, Merfyn, he gives "the Tyes" (p. 293). His daughter Myfanwy (born in August 1910) is given "Steep and her own world" (p. 297). To Helen he offers "youth / All kinds of loveliness and truth / . . . / Lands, waters, flowers, wine." And he ends the poem by giving "myself, too, if I could find / Where it lay hidden" (p. 299). Here, as in "Rain" and "What will they do?," Thomas makes a gesture of sympathy and openness to others even as he points to his isolation from them.

F. R. Leavis argues that Thomas' work expresses a representative type of modern experience, and it is true that Thomas' poetry records a sense of isolation and alienation that to many is a defining feature of modernism. "To Helen," "Rain," and "What will they do?," however, seem closer in spirit to the Coleridge of "Frost at Midnight," "This Lime-Tree Bower My Prison," and "The Eolian Harp" than to "The Love Song of J. Alfred Prufrock." In these three poems, Thomas expresses a kind of spiritual generosity toward others even as he acknowledges his isolation from them that is similar to the way Coleridge sympathetically imagines for another possibilities—insight, happiness, release—that he himself will not experience.

Isolation in Thomas, however, is not always seen in negative terms. In "The Bridge" (p. 123), for example, Thomas remembers his "old friends" not with the sympathy of "Rain" but "without smile or moan." These friends are "all behind" him. They are "no more / Tonight than a dream." This poem was written in March 1915, four months before Thomas enlisted, and perhaps it records his sense of being poised between what the poem calls "two lives," his life as a husband, father, and man of letters, and his life as a soldier. The moment of being between future and past, "The dark-lit stream has drowned the Future and the Past," is not seen as a dark moment for the soul. Rather, the poem records the pleasure of this emotional weightlessness. "No traveller has rest more blest / Than this moment brief between / Two lives."

"The Bridge" looks forward to "Song [3]" (pp. 333–335), where Thomas writes not of the pleasure of being between two lives but of his desire to escape from social and personal entanglements. The poem begins with a jaunty celebration of wanderlust. The speaker sets out early one morning in May: "There was no wind to trouble the weathercocks. / I had burnt my letters and darned my socks." The exuberant freedom of the road is modified by an understanding that liberty also entails loss. "A gate banged in a fence and banged in my head / . . . / I could not return from my liberty, / To my youth and my love and my misery." Yet acknowledgment of loss does not curtail the desire for freedom, and the poem ends with the speaker reaffirming his desire for the road. "I'm bound away for ever, / Away somewhere, away for ever."

In "Lights Out" (p. 367), one of Thomas' last poems, he also writes of the desire to escape from society and personal relations. Unlike "Song [3]," however, Thomas' freedom is found not on the road but in the "unfathomable deep / Forest" of sleep. "There is not any book / Or face of dearest look / That I would not turn from now / To go into the unknown." As David Perkins points out, the poem fights the battle Keats fought in "Ode to a Nightingale." In contrast with Keats, who resisted the desire to leave the world, Thomas in "Lights Out" succumbs to the invitation to lose himself in the forest of sleep. "I hear and obey / That I may lose my way / And myself." In "The Lofty Sky" (p. 79), Thomas turns from the freedom of the road and the freedom offered in sleep to the limitless freedom of the sky. The poem records his disgust with earth, "I sicken of the woods / And all the multitudes / Of hedge-trees," and his desire for the ideal world, "sky, nothing but sky."

In addition to the self and the sky, nature in Thomas' work also offers a haven to the spirit. "Beauty" (p. 97), for example, opens with Thomas' acknowledgment of his estrangement from the world. "Tired, angry, and ill at ease, / No man, woman, or child alive could please / Me now." And he wryly imagines his own epitaph, "'Here lies all that no one loved of him / And that loved no one.'" The mood shifts—"Then in a trice that whim / Has wearied"—and Thomas describes the feeling of "home" and "love" that he finds in nature:

> This heart, some fraction of me, happily
> Floats through the window even now to a tree
> Down in the misting, dim-lit, quiet vale,
> Not like a pewit that returns to wail
> For something it has lost, but like a dove
> That slants unswerving to its home and love.

Nature provides a similar kind of solace in "The Unknown Bird" (pp. 85–87). In the woods four or five years before, he alone heard the song of a bird. "I alone could hear him / Though many listened." When he thinks back on the bird's matchless song, his spirit soars.

> This surely I know, that I who listened then,
> Happy sometimes, sometimes suffering
> A heavy body and a heavy heart,
> Now straightway, if I think of it, become
> Light as that bird wandering beyond my shore.

"The Unknown Bird" looks forward to "The Ash Grove" (p. 269), where Thomas records his experience of an unexplained gladness when he passed through a grove of ash trees: "I was glad without cause and delayed." In the grove "Not even the spirits of memory and fear with restless wing, / Could climb down in to molest me." Now the memory of that grove brings the same tranquillity: "I had what most I desired, without search or desert or cost."

Both "The Ash Grove" and "The Unknown Bird" express the kind of Romantic relation between the self and nature that can be seen, for example, in William Wordsworth's "Tintern Abbey." There, the recollection of the "beauteous forms" of nature provide solace to the mind and heart. "But oft, in lonely rooms, and 'mid the din / Of towns and cities, I have owed to them / In hours of weariness, sensations sweet" and "tranquil restoration." Though Thomas' poems do echo his Romantic heritage, he also, like Frost, questions this inheritance. "Old Man" (pp. 19–21), for instance, challenges the Romantic view of experience that is expressed in what M. H. Abrams has called the greater Romantic lyric. In this type of lyric, the reader typically overhears a speaker, often in an outdoor setting, carry on a conversation with himself, the scene, or another human being. This second person, though often present in the scene from the beginning, is sometimes not revealed to the reader until after the speaker has completed a part of his meditation. Some aspect of the landscape will evoke a train of thought, during the course of which the speaker will resolve a problem, confront a loss, or achieve an insight. The poem often ends by rounding back to where it began, but with a deepened sense of understanding or knowledge.

This pattern, which can be seen in Wordsworth's "Ode: Intimations of Immortality," and Percy Bysshe Shelley's "Stanzas Written in Dejection," also underlies Thomas' poem "Old Man." The poem opens with the speaker's observations on "Old Man, or Lad's-love," a mysterious "hoar-green feathery herb" that arouses ambivalent feelings in the speaker. "The herb itself I like not, but for certain / I love it." The scene widens outward, and the speaker observes a child who "plucks a feather from the door-side bush / Whenever she goes in or out of the house." The child shreds the plant "on to the path, perhaps / Thinking, perhaps of nothing, till she sniffs / Her fingers and runs off." The speaker asks how much the child will remember in later years when she sniffs the herb

> Of garden rows, and ancient damson-trees
> Topping a hedge, a bent path to a door,
> A low thick bush beside the door, and me
> Forbidding her to pick.

The meditation on what the child will remember leads the speaker to ask the same question of himself: "I, too, often shrivel the grey shreds, / Sniff them and think and sniff again and try / Once more to think what it is I am remembering." His attempt leads nowhere. He can think of nothing, hear nothing, see nothing. He has "mislaid the key."

> No garden appears, no path, no hoar-green bush
> Of Lad's-love or Old Man, no child beside,
> Neither father nor mother, nor any playmate;
> Only an avenue, dark, nameless, without end.

Since the child's actual later experience of sniffing the herb and trying to remember is not reported, the poem at least brings up the possibility that her adult experience will be the same as Thomas', that she will not recollect garden rows, ancient damson trees or Thomas forbidding her to pick the herb. Like him, she will have mislaid the key and will see only a dark avenue, nameless, without end. This poem writes the greater Romantic lyric backward. Thomas' meditation leads not toward but away from any sense of resolution, deeper understanding, or insight.

To be psychologically between two lives, as Thomas tells us he is in "The Bridge," is to have shed one identity and not yet taken on another. The feeling of being between, of not yet having a stable identity, is a recurrent theme in Thomas' work, particularly before his enlistment. In "The Signpost" (pp. 23–25), for example, he asks, "Which way shall I go?" Two voices debate the direction, but the poem concludes without resolution—"Wondering where he shall journey, O where?" In "House and Man" (p. 105), Thomas remembers leaving an old man. The memory is recalled because "I see / As then I saw—I at the gate and he / In the house darkness,—a magpie veering about, / A magpie like a weathercock in doubt." What links the two experiences is the sense of indirection. In "The Other" (pp. 27–33), Thomas' longest meditation on the search for identity, he utilizes the doppelgänger motif, which was popularized in England in Robert Louis Stevenson's *Dr. Jekyll and Mr. Hyde* (1886). The moral dimension of Stevenson's story, however, is not explored in Thomas' poem, which remains focused on the psychological implications of the motif. The speaker of the poem pursues the other to gain self-knowledge. "What to do / When caught, I planned not. I pursued / To prove the likeness, and, if true, / To watch until myself I knew." The speaker finally catches up with the other at an inn, but before confronting him, the double speaks "Of how I thought and dreamed and ran / After him thus, day after day: / He lived as one under a ban." This confession paralyzes the speaker—"I said nothing. I slipped away"—and the poem concludes with the speaker shadowing the other, "Dreading his frown and worse his laughter," until death. "He goes: I follow: no release / Until he ceases. Then I also shall cease." In having the speaker and the double still separated at death, Thomas suggests that unity, and the self-knowledge that comes when the divided self is reunited, may be unattainable.

Though Thomas' poems explore feelings of doubt, isolation, and indirection, there is also in his work a countering spirit. Particularly after his enlistment in July 1915, his poems seem to express a firmer sense of identity and purpose. This sea change in Thomas' work is perhaps best understood in the context of World War I.

THOMAS AS WAR POET

THOMAS was in France with the Royal Artillery from January to 9 April 1917, when he was killed. Unlike Wilfred Owen and Siegfried Sassoon, who wrote of the physical and psychological horrors of trench warfare (see, for example, Sassoon's "They" and Owen's "Dulce et decorum est"), Thomas did not write of his experience in France. All of his poems, however, were written during the war, and its presence in his work can be seen in a number of ways. At its most remote, in the pre-enlistment poems, the war is used sometimes simply to illustrate a larger theme. In "Fifty Faggots," for example, Thomas meditates on the unpredictability of fate. Before the fifty faggots have been used, "The war will have ended, many other things / Have ended, maybe, that I can no more / Foresee or more control than robin and wren" (p. 207). In other poems, the war is seen as part of the context of daily life. It comes up, for instance, in the conversation between the speaker and an itinerant English laborer in "Man and Dog" (pp. 93–95).

> "I'll get no shakedown with that bedfellow
> From farmers. Many a man sleeps worse tonight
> Than I shall." "In the trenches." "Yes, that's right.
> But they'll be out of that—I hope they be—
> This weather, marching after the enemy."
> "And so I hope. Good luck." And there I nodded
> "Good-night. You keep straight on."

After the expected sentiments are expressed about getting out of France, the subject of the war is dropped, even though, as we learn earlier in the poem, the old man has three sons who are fighting in France.

War moves from the wings to center stage in three other pre-enlistment poems. The four-line "In Memoriam" mourns the fallen in France, who, "with their sweethearts" (p. 173), should have gathered Easter flowers and will never do so again. In "A Private," a ploughman who slept under "None knew what bush" (p. 67) now lies in an unmarked grave in France. And in "The Owl" (p. 119), the speaker of the poem contrasts his own comfort with that of soldiers and the poor.

> Then at the inn I had food, fire, and rest,
> And salted was my food, and my repose,
> Salted and sobered, too, by the bird's voice
> Speaking for all who lay under the stars,
> Soldiers and poor, unable to rejoice.

Though the war is the subject of these three poems, it is seen in all of them from the point of view of an outsider, one back home who hears about the war but does not seem to have been touched by it personally.

In August 1914, Thomas broached to his agent, C. Frank Cazenove, the idea of writing a series of articles on the response in rural England to the war. Cazenove liked the idea, and Thomas eventually wrote four essays on the subject. "Tipperary," "It's a Long, Long Way," and "England," were published in *The English Review.* The fourth, "This England," was published in the *Nation* of 7 November 1914. In it Thomas describes his own feelings about the war:

At one stroke, I thought, like many other people, what things that same new moon sees eastward about the Meuse in France. . . . I was deluged, in a second stroke, by another thought, or something that overpowered thought. All I can tell is, it seemed to me that either I had never loved England, or I had loved it foolishly, aesthetically, like a slave, not having realized that it was not mine unless I were willing and prepared to die rather than leave it as Belgian women and old men and children had left their country. Something I had omitted. Something, I felt, had to be done before I could look again composedly at English landscape, at the elms and poplars about the houses, at the purple-headed wood-betony with two pairs of dark leaves on a stiff stem, who stood sentinel among the grasses or bracken by hedge-side or wood's-edge. What he stood sentinel for I did not know, any more than what I had got to do.

(p. 171)

Thomas decided what he had "got to do" by July of the next year. On the fourteenth of that month, he passed his enlistment medical exam.

Enlistment affected Thomas' poetry in several ways. For one thing, the war is no longer seen from the outside. In contrast to the pre-enlistment poem "In Memoriam," for example, where the speaker mourns for those who will not return from France, in "Bugle Call" (p. 323), written ten months after Thomas enlisted, the speaker wonders whether *he* will die in a foreign field. "Nobody knows but God / Whether I am destined to lie / Under a foreign clod." And in contrast to the pre-enlistment poem "The Owl," where a speaker who is housed at an inn contrasts his own comfort with soldiers and poor, in "Home [3]" (pp. 285–287), written at Hare Hall Camp, where he was a map-reading instructor, Thomas records his own sense of homelessness, of not being at an inn and safe.

The word "home" raised a smile in us all three,
And one repeated it, smiling just so
That all knew what he meant and none would say.

　　　　　　　. . .
　　　　　　　. . . [t]his captivity
Must somehow come to an end, else I should be
Another man, as often now I seem,
Or this life be only an evil dream.

If enlistment brought Thomas intimations of mortality, it also brought a sense of purpose, direction, and identity. "Roads" (pp. 263–267), for example, written seven months after Thomas enlisted, begins with an expression of the pedestrian pleasures of the road: "Often footsore, never / Yet of the road I weary, / Though long and steep and dreary / As it winds on for ever." But these wanderings are not aimless:

Now all roads lead to France
And heavy is the tread
Of the living; but the dead
Returning lightly dance
　　　　. . .
They keep me company
With their pattering.

(p. 267)

A similar sense of purpose is expressed in "There was a time" (p. 341), which begins with Thomas looking back over his carefree youth. His "heels hammered out a melody / From pavements of a city left behind." He realizes now that "there is something I could use / My youth and strength for"—that is, the war—and he dedicates himself to that purpose. "I . . . refuse / To admit I am unworthy of the wage / Paid to a man who gives up eyes and breath / For what can neither ask nor heed his death." Frost remarked in a letter to Lascelles Abercrombie (21 September 1915) that the war made a new man out of Thomas, and in neither of these poems is there any sense of the vacillation or indirection Thomas expresses in the pre-enlistment poems "The Signpost" and "House and Man," where he veers about like a magpie in doubt.

A third way that the war affected Thomas' poetry is suggested in the title of an anthology that he edited for Oxford University Press, *This England: An Anthology from Her Writers.* The phrase "this England," which Thomas also used as the title of his November 1914 article for the *Nation*, echoes John of Gaunt's speech in *Richard II*, where Gaunt movingly expresses his love for the enduring beauty and majesty of England, now threatened by war. It is a "fortress built by Nature for herself / Against the hand of war / . . . / This blessed plot, this earth, this realm, this England" (act 2, scene 1, ll. 43–44, 50). A number of Thomas' poems record his own attempt to find an enduring and permanent England that could be set against the disruptions brought about by the war. One of the finest of these poems is his 1916 lyric "As the team's head brass" (pp. 325–327). The poem, written when Thomas was considering applying for a commission in the Royal Artillery and hence, if accepted, would very likely go to France, is a dialogue between a speaker and a ploughman. The conversation takes place in the intervals between the ploughman's circuits in the field. "Every time the horses turned / Instead of treading me down, the ploughman leaned / Upon the handles to say or ask a word, / About the weather, next about the war." The speaker says he has not been to France but, quietly and without fanfare, expresses a willingness to go and to sacrifice even his life if need be. Thomas acknowledges in the poem that the war has interrupted daily life. Without it, "Everything / Would have been different." But the poem also suggests that life goes on, and it is this enduring rhythm of life that Thomas here sets against the hand of war.

"The Manor Farm," "Home [2]," and "Haymaking" also locate an enduring England. In "The Manor Farm" (p. 49), Thomas writes of a "season of bliss unchangeable / . . . / Safe under tile and thatch for ages since / This England, Old already, was called Merry." In "Home [2]" (p. 177), Thomas discovers an England that has been there all along:

> Often I had gone this way before:
> But now it seemed I never could be
> And never had been anywhere else;
> 'Twas home; one nationality
> We had, I and the birds that sang,
> One memory.

And in "Haymaking" (pp. 225–227), Thomas celebrates the timeless quality of an "old grange":

> A white house crouched at the foot of a great tree.
> Under the heavens that know not what years be

> The men, the beasts, the trees, the implements
> Uttered even what they will in times far hence—
> All of us gone out of the reach of change—
> Immortal in a picture of an old grange.

In none of these poems is the war mentioned. But in all of them, as in "As the team's head brass," the war is the context against which Thomas attempts to find an enduring sense of place.

Thomas' search for a sense of permanence extends to the English character as well as to the English landscape. He had a lively interest, perhaps because of his childhood friendship with "Dad" Uzzell, in the inhabitants of the English countryside. These include the itinerant workers seen in "Man and Dog," "Bob's Lane," and "May 23," and the kind of rural, cottage-dwelling laborer seen in "Home [2]." All of these figures are melded into the mythological Englishman that Thomas creates in "Lob" (pp. 159–167). Lob represents the spirit of England. "He is as English as this gate, these flowers, this mire. / . . . / He has been in England as long as dove and daw." Lob unites in himself opposing elements. He has "A land face" and is "sea-blue-eyed." Like Adam, he is a name giver: "'Twas he first called the Hog's Back the Hog's Back." He understands the language of nature: "Our blackbirds sang no English till his ear / Told him they call his Jan Toy 'Pretty Dear.'" Though untutored, he is wiser than a sage: "If ever a sage troubles him he will buzz / Like a beehive to conclude the tedious fray: / And the sage, who knows all languages, runs away." And he is unswervingly patriotic. He "was seen dying at Waterloo, / Hastings, Agincourt, and Sedgmoore, too." The reference to war is telling. The poem clearly implies that Lob will also be seen dying in various battles in World War I. Wise, at one with nature, deeply patriotic, Lob embodies what are for Thomas unchanging elements of the English character: "He will never admit he is dead / Till millers cease to grind men's bones for bread."

Thomas' response to the war can also be seen in poems that at first glance seem to be the most remote from it. Gordon Bottomley selected eighteen of Thomas' poems for inclusion in *An Annual of New Poetry*, which was published in March 1917. The *Annual* was reviewed in the *Times Literary Supplement* of 29 March 1917. The reviewer praises Edward Eastaway as "a real poet, with the truth in him." But he complains that Eastaway's work, like the work of many of his contemporaries, does not respond to the war. "At present, like most of his contemporaries, he has too little control over his eyes. . . . Or is the new method an unconscious survival of a materialism and naturalism which the tremendous life of the last three years has made an absurdity?" Thomas read the review and offered the counterargument in a letter to Bottomley:

I don't mind now being called inhuman & being told by a reviewer now that April's here—in England now—that I am blind to the "tremendous life of these 3 years." It would be the one consolation in finishing up out here to provide such reviewers with a conundrum, except that I know they would invent an answer if they saw that it was a conundrum. Why do the idiots accuse me of using my eyes? Must I only use them with fieldglasses & must I see only Huns in these beautiful hills eastwards & only hostile flashes in the night skies when I am at the Observation Post?[2]

Of the eighteen poems published in *An Annual of New Poetry*, a few, "A Private" and "Roads," for instance, speak directly of the war. Others, such as "Aspens," "After Rain," "Sedge-Warblers," and "The Word," speak of nature's beauty and unforgettable presence. "One name that I have not—/ . . . forgot," he writes in "The Word" (p. 221), "Never can die because Spring after Spring / Some thrushes learn to say it as they sing." These poems do not turn to nature to escape from the war. Rather, they assert the validity of a certain kind of response to the world in the face of war. To look through fieldglasses and see not just Huns but also beautiful hills to the east, to look in the night sky and see more than hostile flashes—these, too, might be considered heroic responses to the devastations of war.

CONCLUSION

AFTER World War I, Georgian poetry came under attack from several camps within the literary establishment. T. S. Eliot complained that the Georgians had developed their own set of emotions and that they caressed everything they touched. Edith Sitwell, editor of the avant-garde magazine *Wheels*, characterized the Georgians as weekend poets whose work expressed only pretended emotions. One of the most damaging attacks, however, came in the pages of a middle-of-the-road journal, the *Athenaeum*. In the 5 December 1919 issue, J. Middleton Murry wrote of the false simplicity and derivative quality of later Georgian verse. Nor did the Georgians escape the jibes of the more popular press. W. H. Davies, John Drinkwater, Walter de la Mare, and Ralph Hodgson were all satirized in *Punch*. In 1925, Harold Monro wrote to Edward Marsh about the possibility of doing one more volume of Georgian poetry. Marsh, wisely, declined. By the mid-1920s, high modernism dominated the literary scene. Major works by Wallace Stevens (*Harmonium*, 1923), William Carlos Williams (*Spring and All*, 1923), Ezra Pound (*Mauberly*, 1920; *Poems, 1918–1921*, 1921), and T. S. Eliot ("The Waste Land," 1922), had been published. The Georgian moment had passed. Acutely aware of the declining popularity of Georgian verse, Walter de la Mare wrote in the introduction to the 1920 edition of Thomas' poetry that Thomas' voice would be heard clearly only when the "noise of the present" had ended. It would be another thirty years before the "noise" of high modernism had quieted enough for Thomas' voice to begin to be audible. From the 1950s to the present, it has been listened to with increasing attention.

Thomas' work has not spawned a school of followers. But it would not be accurate to characterize him as a solitary genius, a kind of literary meteor that, without connection to what is around it, shines once brilliantly and then disappears into the night sky. Perhaps his closest affiliation is to Philip Larkin. As Edna Longley observes, in both poets there is a strong sense of being English. Both write of the alienation of the self from other humans and from nature, yet both entertain the possibility of belonging, of feeling "at home." And both Thomas and Larkin, unlike the Eliot of "The Waste Land," write of the deep connection between past and present. The tentative, open probing of experience in Thomas' verse also links his poetry to Frost, the late W. H. Auden, Charles Tomlinson, George Oppen, and Elizabeth Bishop.

SELECTED BIBLIOGRAPHY

I. POETRY. *Six Poems* (Flansham, Eng., 1916), under the name of Edward Eastaway; eighteen poems in *An Annual of New Poetry* (London, 1917), under the name of

[2]R. George Thomas, ed., *Letters from Edward Thomas to Gordon Bottomley*, pp. 282–283.

Eastaway; *Poems* (London, 1917), under the name of Eastaway; *Last Poems* (London, 1918); *Collected Poems* (London, 1920); *Collected Poems* (London, 1928); *Collected Poems* (London, 1936); *Poems and Last Poems,* ed. by Edna Longley (London, 1973); *The Collected Poems of Edward Thomas,* ed. by R. George Thomas (Oxford, 1978).

II. PROSE BY THOMAS. *The Woodland Life* (Edinburgh, 1897); *Horae Solitariae* (London, 1902); *Oxford* (London, 1903); *Rose Acre Papers* (London, 1904); *Beautiful Wales* (London, 1905); *The Heart of England* (London, 1906); *Richard Jefferies: His Life and Work* (London, 1909); *The South Country* (London, 1909); *Feminine Influence on the Poets* (London, 1910); *Rest and Unrest* (London, 1910); *Windsor Castle* (London, 1910); *Celtic Stories* (Oxford, 1911); *The Isle of Wight* (London, 1911); *Light and Twilight* (London, 1911); *Maurice Maeterlinck* (London, 1911); *The Tenth Muse* (London, 1911); *Algernon Charles Swinburne: A Critical Study* (London, 1912); *George Borrow: The Man and His Books* (London, 1912); *Lafcadio Hearn* (London, 1912); *Norse Tales* (Oxford, 1912); *The Country* (London, 1913); *The Happy-Go-Lucky Morgans* (London, 1913); *The Icknield Way* (London, 1913); *Walter Pater: A Critical Study* (London, 1913); *In Pursuit of Spring* (London, 1914); *Four-and-Twenty Blackbirds* (London, 1915); *The Life of the Duke of Marlborough* (London, 1915); *Keats* (London, 1916); *A Literary Pilgrim in England* (London, 1917); *The Friend of the Blackbird* (Flansham, Eng., 1938).

III. COLLECTED PROSE. *Cloud Castle and Other Papers* (London, 1922); *The Last Sheaf: Essays by Edward Thomas* (London, 1928); *The Prose of Edward Thomas,* ed. by Roland Gant (London, 1948); *Edward Thomas on the Countryside: A Selection of His Prose and Verse,* ed. by Roland Gant (London, 1977); *A Language Not to Be Betrayed: Selected Prose of Edward Thomas,* ed. by Edna Longley (New York, 1981); *Selected Poems and Prose,* ed. by David Wright (Harmondsworth, Eng., 1981).

IV. WORKS EDITED BY THOMAS. *The Poems of John Dyer* (London, 1903); *The Book of the Open Air* (London, 1907); *British Country Life in Spring and Summer: The Book of the Open Air* (London, 1907); *British Butterflies and Other Insects* (London, 1908); *British Country Life in Autumn and Winter: The Book of the Open Air* (London, 1908); *Some British Birds* (London, 1908).

V. INTRODUCTIONS BY THOMAS. *The Bible in Spain,* by George Borrow (London, 1906); *The Temple* and *A Priest to the Temple,* by George Herbert (London, 1908); *The Hills and the Vales,* by Richard Jefferies (London, 1909); *The Plays and Poems of Christopher Marlowe* (London, 1909); *Words and Places in Illustration of History, Ethnology, and Geography,* by Isaac Taylor (London, 1911); *Rural Rides,* by William Cobbett, 2 vols. (London, 1912); *The Zincali: An Account of the Gipsies of Spain,* by George Borrow (London, 1914).

VI. WORKS COMPILED BY THOMAS. *The Pocket Book of Poems and Songs for the Open Air* (London, 1907); *The Pocket George Borrow* (London, 1912); *This England: An Anthology from Her Writers* (London, 1915); *The Flowers I Love* (London, 1916; New York, 1917).

VII. BIOGRAPHICAL AND AUTOBIOGRAPHICAL WORKS. Helen Thomas, *As It Was and World Without End* (London, 1926); Robert P. Eckert, *Edward Thomas: A Biography and a Bibliography* (London, 1937); Edward Thomas, *The Childhood of Edward Thomas* (London, 1938); John Moore, *The Life and Letters of Edward Thomas* (London, 1939); Eleanor Farjeon, *Edward Thomas: The Last Four Years* (London, 1958); Edward Thomas, *Letters from Edward Thomas to Gordon Bottomley,* ed. by R. George Thomas (London, 1968); William Cooke, *Edward Thomas: A Portrait* (Bakewell, Eng., 1978); Helen Thomas, *Time and Again: Memoirs and Letters,* ed. by Myfanwy Thomas (Manchester, Eng., 1978); Myfanwy Thomas, *One of These Fine Days: Memoirs* (Manchester, Eng., 1982); Edward Thomas, *The Letters of Edward Thomas to Jesse Berridge,* ed. by Anthony Berridge (London, 1983); R. George Thomas, *Edward Thomas, A Portrait* (Oxford, 1985).

VIII. CRITICAL STUDIES. John Middleton Murry, "The Poetry of Edward Thomas," in his *Aspects of Literature* (London, 1920); F. R. Leavis, *New Bearings in English Poetry* (London, 1932); B. Rajan, "Georgian Poetry: A Retrospect," in *The Critic* 1, no. 2 (autumn 1947).

John Lehmann, "Edward Thomas," in his *The Open Night* (London, 1952); H. Coombes, "The Poetry of Edward Thomas," in *Essays in Criticism* 3 (April 1953), and *Edward Thomas: A Critical Study* (London, 1956; New York, 1973); C. Day Lewis, "The Poetry of Edward Thomas," in *Essays by Divers Hands: Transactions of the Royal Society of Literature* 28 (1956); John Burrow, "Keats and Edward Thomas," in *Essays in Criticism* 7 (October 1957); Louis Coxe, "Edward Thomas and the Real World," in his *Enabling Acts: Selected Essays in Criticism* (Columbia, Mo., 1959); John F. Danby, "Edward Thomas," in *Critical Quarterly* 1 (winter 1959).

Roland Mathias, "Edward Thomas," in *Anglo-Welsh Review* 10, no. 26 (1960); Philip Hobsbaum, "The Road Not Taken," in *Listener* 66 (23 November 1961); Vernon Scannell, "Content with Discontent: A Note on Edward Thomas," in *London Magazine* (January 1962); C. B. Cox and A. E. Dyson, "The Signpost," in C. B. Cox, *Modern Poetry: Studies in Practical Criticism* (London, 1963); Vernon Scannell, *Edward Thomas* (London, 1963); Robert H. Ross, *The Georgian Revolt: Rise and Fall of a Poetic Ideal* (Carbondale, Ill., 1965); R. George Thomas, "Edward Thomas: Poet and Critic," in *Essays and Studies* n.s. 21 (1968); Jeremy Hooker, "The Writings of Edward Thomas: I," in *Anglo-Welsh Review* 18 (summer 1969).

William Cooke, *Edward Thomas: A Critical Biography* (London, 1970); Jeremy Hooker, "The Writings of Edward Thomas: II, The Sad Passion," in *Anglo-Welsh Review* 19 (autumn 1970); R. George Thomas, *Edward Thomas* (Cardiff, Wales, 1972); Raymond Williams, *The Country and the City* (London, 1973); Hugh Underwood, "The Poetical Character of Edward Thomas," in *Essays in Criticism* 23 (July 1973); Edna Longley, "Larkin, Edward Thomas, and the Tradition," in *Phoenix* 11–12 (1973–1974); Marie Quinn, "The Personal Past in the Poetry of Thomas Hardy and Edward Thomas," in *Critical Quarterly* 16, no. 1 (1974); W. J. Keith, *The Rural Tradition* (Hassocks, Eng., 1975); Edna Longley, "Edward Thomas and the 'English' Line," in *New Review* 1 (February 1975); Peter T. Pienaar, "Edward Thomas: Poetic Premonitions in the Prose," in *Theoria* 44 (May 1975); Jonathan Dollimore, "The Poetry of Hardy and Edward Thomas," in *Critical Quarterly* 17 (autumn 1975); Michael Kirkham, "The Edwardian Critical Opposition," in *University of Toronto Quarterly* 45 (fall 1975); David Perkins, *A History of Modern Poetry: From the 1890s to the High Modernist Mode* (Cambridge, Mass., 1976); Edna Longley, "A Language Not to Be Betrayed: The Poetry of Edward Thomas," in *Poetry Wales* 12, no. 1 (summer 1976); Michael Black, "A Language Not to Be Betrayed," in *Use of English* 28 (autumn 1976 and summer 1977); Stan Smith, "'A Language Not to Be Betrayed': Language, Class, and History in the Work of Edward Thomas," in *Literature and History* no. 4 (autumn 1976); Jan Marsh, *Edward Thomas: A Poet for His Country* (London, 1978); Leslie Norris, "A Land Without a Name," in *Poetry Wales* 13, no. 4 (spring 1978); J. P. Ward, "The Solitary Note: Edward Thomas and Modernism," in *Poetry Wales* 13, no. 4 (spring 1978); Stan Smith, "Singular Men: Edward Thomas and Richard Jefferies," in *Delta,* no. 59 (1979); Ralph Lawrence, "Edward Thomas in Perspective," in *English* 12 (summer 1979); Donald Davie, "Lessons in Honesty," in *Times Literary Supplement* (23 November 1979).

W. J. Keith, *The Poetry of Nature* (Toronto, 1980); Andrew Motion, *The Poetry of Edward Thomas* (London, 1980); David Parker, "Edward Thomas: Tasting Deep the Hour," in *Critical Review* no. 22 (1980); Robert Richman, "In Search of Edward Thomas," in *The New Criterion* 1 (December 1982); Malcolm Pittock, "Knowledge and Experience in Wordsworth and Edward Thomas," in *Durham University Journal* 76 (June 1984); Jonathan Barker, ed., *The Art of Edward Thomas* (Bridgend, Wales, 1986); Michael Kirkham, *The Imagination of Edward Thomas* (Cambridge, 1986); Peter Mitchell, "Edward Thomas and the Georgians," in *University of Toronto Quarterly* 55 (1986); D. W. Harding, "A Note on Nostalgia," in *Scrutiny* 1, no. 1 (1989); Keith Clark, *The Muse Colony: Rupert Brooke, Edward Thomas, Robert Frost, and Friends. Dymock, 1914* (Bristol, Eng., 1992).

JAMES THOMSON

(1700–1748)

Frans De Bruyn

THE POETIC CAREER OF James Thomson poses something of a puzzle for the twentieth-century reader. He was an ambitious and innovative poet—Samuel Johnson credits him with creating poetry "of a new kind" (vol. 3, 1905 ed., p. 285) and with pursuing an original "mode of thinking and of expressing his thoughts" (p. 293)—yet many of his contemporaries sensed that he did not quite live up to the potential displayed in his early published poems. He was an enormously popular poet in his lifetime and for more than a century after his death, but his work is no longer widely read. *The Seasons*, the poem on which his literary reputation largely rests, went through several hundred separate editions in the eighteenth and nineteenth centuries; in the present century, by contrast, only a small handful of new editions have appeared. His influence on subsequent generations of poets, both in Britain and in Europe, was no less pervasive than the wide availability of his works, yet their acknowledgment of his achievement as a descriptive poet of nature was often double-edged. While hailing him as a pioneer of blank-verse nature poetry, they saw themselves as bringing to maturity his imperfectly realized poetic designs, which they viewed as anticipations of greater things to come. Thus, he was regarded by William Wordsworth and others as the literary equivalent of John the Baptist, a voice crying in the poetic wilderness, preparing the way for the Romantic writers of the early nineteenth century. Ironically, our own time has produced some of the most sympathetic and perceptive critical studies in the history of Thomson criticism, even as the common reader has largely forgotten his poetry.

These paradoxes in the literary life and afterlife of Thomson prompt a number of questions that demand to be addressed in any critical overview of the poet. Perhaps the most important of these for the general reader of literature (as opposed to the academic specialist) is what value his poetry holds for a late-twentieth-century audience. It clearly held great interest for his contemporaries, and we can turn to their responses to reconstruct the aesthetic and cultural context in which it flourished. But such a project of critical or historical excavation does not answer the question of its current poetic value. To understand Thomson's oeuvre historically is not necessarily to feel pleasure in perusing it.

Thomson's poetry does demand, nonetheless, to be read historically, for his work, like that of his contemporaries, was deeply implicated in the political struggles of his time. Given the system of literary patronage in Thomson's day and the government's manipulation of the press, it was difficult to be a poet without becoming involved in the topical political controversies of the moment. Thus, a poem like *Britannia* (1729), written in the heat of general public clamor for war with Spain, cannot be read very profitably without some knowledge of the circumstances that occasioned the poem. More significant, Thomson absorbed the cultural crosscurrents of his age so thoroughly that his writings can be regarded as an intellectual mirror of the early eighteenth century. His poems reflect new views about religion, science, nature, and aesthetics, and they incorporate a nascent humanitarian and sentimental strain that was to become increasingly powerful as the century wore on. Thomson inhabited a society undergoing dramatic change: his poetry celebrates the growing commercial, imperial, and scientific greatness of eighteenth-century Britain.

In reading Thomson's poetry, then, we must recover something of the historical context in which it was written. This is by no means an antiquarian exercise, for we live in a world that has been irrevocably shaped by the changes Thomson experi-

409

enced in his lifetime. His writings are not only a witness to historical change, but also an embodiment of that change as the poet experiments with language and form in order to find an "answerable style" to reflect a society in transition. Thomson's experiments with diction, metrics, and genre alert us to the fact that literary features and verse forms are acculturated: they are transformed as the writer's and society's perception of the world around them alters. The twentieth century has become accustomed to incessant and ever more rapid change; to observe an artist of an earlier time grappling with the consequences of these historical processes is to come to a clearer recognition of their impact on present-day life, art, and culture.

In *The Varied God,* Patricia Spacks encapsulates the paradox of James Thomson. Referring to *The Seasons,* she writes, "the puzzle . . . becomes only greater as we examine the poem. Why so many contradictory elements, why the promise of unity not quite fulfilled, why beauty remembered in individual sections rather than in the poem as a whole?" (p. 3). Spacks's question has been posed in a number of ways over the last two and a half centuries, and it has elicited various answers, including Ralph Cohen's detailed argument in *The Unfolding of* The Seasons for the poem's artistic unity. Perhaps it is time to let the gaps, contradictions, and silences in Thomson's poetry speak for themselves. No human being is entirely consistent, and the places where consistency breaks down can be particularly revealing of those ideological commitments or perceptual limitations that cause a writer to conceptualize the world in a particular way—even though that conception may not account for all that the writer sees and describes. Thomson's vision of social harmony in *The Seasons,* for instance, which is based on a hierarchical, patriarchal conception of society led by a wise elite or of retired, disinterested gentlemen, leads him to overlook other perspectives, such as those of women or town dwellers, that might call his vision into question. To read Thomson in this manner is not to arraign him as a failed writer, for other observers in his time, even those gifted with superior powers of discursive analysis, equally failed to see the blind alleys into which their assumptions sometimes led them. On the contrary, by confronting these points of "slippage," we gain a much richer sense of the complex, intricate ways in which Thomson's choices as a poet, whether his

diction, subject matter, or poetic form, reflect the reality of a culture experiencing dynamic growth and change.

LIFE

THOMSON was born on 11 September 1700 in the village of Ednam, Roxburghshire, in the Scottish Border region just north of England. The austere beauty of the Cheviot Hills, where he grew up, taught him to observe and appreciate nature with an exactness that was to bear literary fruit in his great descriptive-didactic poem, *The Seasons.* His childhood surroundings also supplied him with two other lifelong influences: his religious spirit and his Whiggism. The son of Thomas Thomson, a Presbyterian minister, James was intended from an early age to follow his father's footsteps into the ministry. Through his mother, Beatrix Trotter, he inherited social connections with Scottish Whig families, and he himself became staunchly Whig in his political outlook. Scottish Whigs supported the Protestant settlement establishing the German Hanoverian line on the throne (instead of the Scottish, but Roman Catholic, Stuarts) and promoted the Act of Union by which England and Scotland became a united kingdom in 1707.

As a boy Thomson was not a distinguished pupil, perhaps already preferring poetry to the mundane routine of the schoolroom. A number of his juvenile productions survive, in spite of a reported annual ritual in which he burned the previous year's compositions, "crowning the solemnity," according to Patrick Murdoch, a friend from Thomson's college days and his most authoritative early biographer, "with a copy of verses, in which were humorously recited the several grounds of their condemnation" (p. 7). In preparation for the ministry Thomson was sent to the College of Edinburgh, where he was introduced to the ideas of Isaac Newton and the new experimental science. He pursued his studies in divinity under William Hamilton, who taught a more moderate, liberal theology than the strict Presbyterianism of his boyhood. Both of these influences were to play a key role in shaping the intellectual outlook expressed in his poetry. In determining his future course, however, his informal education as a member of Edinburgh literary societies like the Grotesque Club proved to be more important than his formal studies. As time went on, his inclinations toward the ministry grew less and less strong, and in 1725 he sailed for London to try his fortune there.

Shortly after his arrival in London, Thomson began writing *Winter,* a poem that became the germ for *The Seasons,* but his most pressing problem was to make a living. Like most writers of his generation, he pursued several avenues of income. One of these was tutoring, a seemingly unpromising career but occasionally rewarding, as it was for Thomson when he accompanied Charles Richard Talbot, the son and heir of Solicitor-General (and subsequently Lord Chancellor) Charles Talbot, on his grand tour of Europe in 1730 and 1731. This position was typical of the kind of employments doled out to writers through the extensive system of patronage that flourished in the period. The elder Talbot, who subsequently found Thomson a lucrative sinecure in the government, was only one of several powerful connections he cultivated; others included George Bubb Dodington, his chief patron during his first decade in London; George Lyttelton, the patron of his later career; and even Frederick, Prince of Wales, to whom he dedicated the poem *Liberty* (1735–1736). Thomson wrote flattering dedications to his patrons and extolled their virtues fulsomely in his verse, but his correspondence reveals that he chafed under the restrictions of the patronage system. From patronage to active involvement in politics, as a paid writer for a political party, was only a small step in the mid-eighteenth century: Thomson took that step in the late 1730s when he enlisted actively in the service of the political opposition under Prince Frederick and Lyttelton.

If patronage meant security, but little independence, the world of publishing offered a scarcely better alternative. Rather than serve the bidding of the wealthy and powerful, the professional writer felt the vagaries of the literary marketplace and suffered the capricious patronage of the public. Thomson was acutely aware of the pressure to cater to popular taste, as he indicates in an August 1726 letter to his friend David Mallet describing his new poem *Summer:* "[These lines] contain a Panegyric on Brittain, which may perhaps contribute to make my Poem popular" (*James Thomson, 1700–1748: Letters and Documents,* p. 48). One way to secure both prestige and profit for one's writings was to publish a subscription edition. This Thomson did with his collected *Seasons* in

1730, a project that attracted a prestigious list of subscribers, including Queen Caroline, Sir Robert Walpole, Lord Burlington, and Alexander Pope. He also had a knack for identifying subjects topical with the public, as is evident in *A Poem Sacred to the Memory of Sir Isaac Newton* (1727), which commemorated the great scientist's death and proved popular enough to warrant four editions within a year, and in *Britannia* (1729), a poem intervening in the political debate over the advisability of war with Spain.

Thomson also cultivated literary friends, sometimes with the same obsequious flattery he used on his political connections. A lifelong friend and fellow litterateur who helped Thomson establish himself in London was David Mallet. Mallet in turn introduced him to Aaron Hill, a poet and playwright who cultivated a literary circle. Hill encouraged him to write for the theater, easily the most profitable form of literary activity in the period, and Thomson responded with *The Tragedy of Sophonisba* (1730), the first of five tragedies on classical themes. In turning to tragedy, he was following the accepted path of the poet in Britain's classically influenced culture: after cutting his teeth on the lesser genres (such as the descriptive poetry of *The Seasons*), the poet was expected to aspire to the culturally prestigious forms of tragedy and epic. Accordingly, four more tragedies appeared at intervals over the remaining years of Thomson's life: *Agamemnon* (1738), *Edward and Eleonora* (1739), *Tancred and Sigismunda* (1745), and *Coriolanus* (1749). Ironically, it was his experiments in *The Seasons* with the "lesser" genre of Virgilian georgic, rather than his tragedies, that were to prove most significant and enduring.

The same aspiration to literary prestige governed the choice of subject for Thomson's next great project, his political poem *Liberty.* On his travels through Europe, he had found political and economic conditions deplorable, especially in Italy, where modern squalor stood juxtaposed with the ruined monuments of Roman greatness. "Thomson," reports Samuel Johnson in *Lives of the English Poets,* "in his travels on the continent, found or fancied so many evils arising from the tyranny of other governments, that he resolved to write a very long poem, in five parts, upon *Liberty*" (p. 289). Though intended as a poem of epic scope and grandeur, *Liberty* was to prove unsuccessful with the public. But with its dedication to Prince Frederick, the poem marked Thomson's entrance into active politics on the side of the op position to Walpole. His political activities inspired at least one poem of enduring fame, his patriotic ode "Rule, Britannia," composed to climax *Alfred* (1740), a masque he wrote in collaboration with Mallet.

The failure of *Liberty* seemed to hobble Thomson's literary ambitions. He produced only one major new poem in the last years of his life, a Spenserian imitation entitled *The Castle of Indolence* (1748). Some critics have read a biographical significance into this title: certainly, the poet was reputed by his contemporaries to have given in to a mood of lethargy and self-indulgence in his later years. Lady Hertford, a friend from the time of his arrival in London, remarked in a letter that he had "quite drown'd his Genius"—presumably in drink. He was roused, however, from his mood of indolence by an intense passion he developed for Elizabeth Young, a feeling that resulted in a long but unsuccessful courtship. The character of Amanda in the extensively revised *Seasons* published in 1744 is based on his relationship with Young. The final literary task the poet undertook was to revise *The Castle of Indolence* for a second edition, but he did not live to see the poem reprinted. He died of pneumonia on 27 August 1748, shortly before his forty-eighth birthday, and was buried in St. Mary's Church, Richmond. His passing was sincerely mourned by his friends, who remembered him as an amiable and good-hearted man.

THE SEASONS *AND* NEWTON

The Seasons, Thomson's most ambitious, successful, and innovative poem, is also the earliest product of his poetic maturity. In April 1726, a little more than a year after his move from Edinburgh to London, the first edition of *Winter* was published. This poem, a mere 405 lines in its first version, was the beginning of a great work that grew and expanded over the years, appearing in numerous revised forms, until the final, definitive text totaling some 5,500 lines was published in 1746. The fact that *Winter* appeared so soon after Thomson's arrival in London lends credence to the view that the genesis of the poem lay in his formative experience of the Scottish climate and landscape. In a letter to his old friend William

Cranstoun written in the fall of 1725, Thomson makes reference to his new project:

Nature delights me in every form, I am just now painting her in her most lugubrious dress; for my own amusement, describing winter as it presents itself. [A]fter my first proposal of the subject,
> I sing of winter and his gelid reign;
> Nor let a riming insect of the spring
> Deem it a barren theme to me tis full
> Of manly charms; to me, who court the shade
> Whom the gay seasons suit not, and who shun
> The glare of summer. Welcom! kindred Glooms
> Drear awfull wintry horrors, welcome all, &c.
>> (*Letters*, pp. 16–17)

In his choice of subject, Thomson draws on Scottish literary tradition, in which depictions of the harshness of winter, inspired by Scotland's northern clime, were more of a thematic staple than in English poetry. Indeed, he credits a poem on winter by Robert Riccaltoun, a fellow Scot, as the immediate inspiration for his poem.

As his letter to Cranstoun suggests, Thomson adopts a pose of philosophic melancholy toward his subject, echoing John Milton's reflective, contemplative mood in his influential poem *Il Penseroso* (1631). But the poem soon outgrew its origins, with the addition of poems on the other three seasons (some of them reflecting the "gay" mood he had previously rejected), and with the extension of its subject matter to include wide-ranging religious, scientific, social, and political observation. His aim is to demonstrate that behind the bewildering variety of nature stands nature's "varied God": the changing faces of nature, its destructive and benign manifestations, form part of a harmonious, divinely ordained order that humanity, limited by its fragmentary knowledge and the anxieties of daily experience, often perceives only dimly:

> THESE, as they change, ALMIGHTY FATHER, these,
> Are but the *varied* GOD. The rolling Year
> Is full of Thee. Forth in the pleasing Spring
> THY Beauty walks, THY Tenderness and Love.
>> (*Hymn*, 1–4)

Thomson's own words in his preface to *Winter* convey both his enthusiasm for his subject and his larger purpose in writing *The Seasons*:

I know no Subject more elevating, more amusing; more ready to awake the poetical Enthusiasm, the philosophical Reflection, and the moral Sentiment, than the *Works of Nature*. Where can we meet with such Variety, such Beauty, such Magnificence? All that enlarges, and transports, the Soul? What more inspiring than a calm, wide, Survey of Them? In every Dress *Nature* is greatly charming! whether she puts on the Crimson Robes of the *Morning!* the strong Effulgence of *Noon!* the sober Suit of the *Evening!* or the deep Sables of *Blackness,* and *Tempest!* How gay looks the *Spring!* how glorious the *Summer!* how pleasing the *Autumn!* and how venerable the *Winter!*

The scope of this theme renders doubly ironic Thomson's ritual comment in his letter to Cranstoun that his poetic musings are intended merely as a casual diversion: "being only a present amusement, tis ten to one but I drop it when e'er another fancy come cross" (*Letters,* p. 17). That "present amusement" was to become his life's work.

Each of the four component sections of *The Seasons* is constructed in a like fashion. The primary unifying device in each instance is the season itself, which prompts appropriate associations in the mind of the poet-narrator. In *Summer,* much of the poem is devoted to a description of the Tropics, an imaginative excursion that is balanced in *Winter* by a journey to the "frigid zone" of the Arctic. These extremes of sublime power and destructiveness are contrasted with the more harmonious, moderate scenes of gentle *Spring* and receding *Autumn.* Thomson sometimes uses an internal structuring device, such as the rising "Chain of Being" in *Spring,* which describes the effects of spring and sexual awakening in turn on plants, birds, animals, and humans; and the progress of the day in *Summer,* from dawn to dusk and night. But the chief principle of organization in the poem is the associative mind of the poet-narrator, who moves back and forth, sometimes in a seemingly arbitrary way, between external observation and historical, social, or devotional reflection.

An enormous quantity of nature poetry has been written since Thomson's day, which makes it difficult to recognize just how innovative a contributor he was to this branch of writing. By no means was he the first poet in the English language to write about nature—one need only think of the opening lines of Geoffrey Chaucer's *Canterbury Tales*—but he broke new ground in the fusion he achieved between the observation of nature and the affirmation of an order and harmony behind nature's multifarious and seemingly contradictory faces.

The impetus for this linking of observation and faith lay in the intellectual currents of his time. Theologians and clergymen of the late seventeenth century, dazzled by the scientific discoveries of Isaac Newton, Robert Boyle, and others, argued that human reason could come to a knowledge of God's existence and providence by examining the evidence for divine order in the created universe. This "physico-theological" argument was taken up in such works as John Ray's *Wisdom of God Manifested in the Works of the Creation* (1691) and William Derham's *Physico-Theology* (1713). Joseph Addison summarizes the spirit of the age with his comment in *Spectator* 543, "The more extended our Reason is, and the more able to grapple with immense Objects, the greater still are those Discoveries which it makes of Wisdom and Providence in the Works of the Creation."

Before examining further Thomson's thematic use of the religious and scientific ideas of his age, it may be useful to consider the impact of those ideas on his poetic style, particularly his diction. For what strikes the modern reader as most foreign or strange in Thomson are precisely his experiments with language. The most notorious of these is his use of periphrasis or circumlocution, his referring to barnyard chickens as "household feathery people" or fish as "the finny tribe." To the twentieth-century reader, accustomed to spare, informal, understated poetic diction, these phrases seem to strain exaggeratedly for poetic effect. The present-day writer prefers to call a poetic spade a spade. But Thomson is not trying to be showy or clever in his choice of phrases. He is striving instead for a language precise enough to describe accurately and scientifically the teeming variety and complexity of the natural world. In a moment of despair at the daunting task he has set for himself, the narrator asks,

> But who can paint
> Like Nature? Can Imagination boast,
> Amid its gay Creation, Hues like hers?
> . . .
> Ah what shall Language do? Ah where find Words
> Ting'd with so many Colours; and whose Power,
> To Life approaching, may perfume my Lays?
> (*Spring,* 468–470, 475–477)

Thomson's solution is to devise a language that discriminates carefully, as a scientific observer would, among different objects or among the same objects in different contexts. In *Spring* the courting birds are variously referred to as "gay Troops" (584), "tuneful Nations" (594), "glossy Kind" (617), "soft Tribes" (711), and "soaring Race" (753). Each of these adjective-noun combinations emphasizes a specific characteristic of the birds and their behavior. In describing their mating rituals, Thomson uses the epithet "glossy" to stress their alluring appearance. In a passage condemning the caging of wild birds, he notes, by contrast, "their Plumage dull" (706) and substitutes the epithet "soft" to highlight their fragility and vulnerability. Similarly, in *Winter* he calls a flock of sheep the "bleating Kind" (261), the participle "bleating" underscoring their dependence on humans. The relationship is reversed in the sheepshearing scene in *Summer*, where phrases like "new-shorn Vagrant's heaving Side" (407) and "fleecy Stores" (398) emphasizes humanity's dependence on the sheep for their wool.

At the end of the sheepshearing passage, Thomson makes explicit the interdependence of human and beast: "Behold where bound, and of its Robe bereft, / By needy Man, that all-depending Lord, / How meek, how patient, the mild Creature lies!" (412–414). These lines, especially the oxymoronic phrase, "all-depending Lord," dramatize a paradoxical reciprocity between the two species, a local harmony that expands to include Britain's commerce and her imperial greatness: "A simple Scene! yet hence BRITANNIA sees / Her solid Grandeur rise: hence she commands / Th' exalted Stores of every brighter Clime" (423–425). Britain's agricultural pursuits are the foundation for her commercial success: her economic and political institutions are patriotically identified with the reciprocal concord between shepherd and sheep. Human activity is seen as part of a larger, harmonious order.

Thomson's persistent use of classifying nouns like "Race," "Nations," and "Tribes" to refer to both animals and humans calls further attention to the interrelatedness of the great chain of being, in which all species have their assigned places, like a huge extended family. Adjectives like "finny" and "feathery," meanwhile, pinpoint the place in the chain to which a group is adapted. Thus, what may appear as Thomson's awkward attempt to make his language more poetic is in fact a striving for scientific precision. The poet's choice of language, in this case his reliance on periphrasis, embodies cultural assumptions. As these assumptions change (such as our changed conception of scientific classification, which shies away from anthropomorphizing animals and rejects the existence of a chain of being), a language that was intended to be precise comes across as sentimental or unclear.

A similar problem arises with the heavily Latinate vocabulary and sentence structure that characterize *The Seasons*. Words like "umbrageous," "prelusive," "reluctant," and "detruded" seem to us unnecessarily inflated and pretentious, but to Thomson they came naturally. Latin had long been Scotland's second language and played a central role in Scottish education. English, by contrast, ran third, after Scots and Latin, as a literary language in Scotland. When Thomson moved to England, he relied on the familiar structures of Latin to bridge the many differences between his native Scots and standard English. At the same time, Latinate terminology allowed him great economy and precision in his poetic diction. In referring, for example, to a rainbow as an "amusive Arch" (*Spring*, 216), he is able to pack complex meanings into a single word. The rural rustic in *Spring* who chases after the rainbow is both pleased and taken in by the optical spectacle: this double attitude is perfectly captured by the term "amusive," which conveys the sense not only of affording amusement, but also of deceit and illusion. A single term thus expresses what would otherwise require a much more elaborate construction of words. Thomson's Latinate language also performs an allusive function, for it reminds the reader of the poet's relation to the past, the poetic tradition of Virgil and Milton to which he is indebted. Finally, it must be remembered that many of the Latinisms he uses, such as "effusive South" (*Spring*, 144), had a scientific meaning for him that we no longer recognize. The word "effusive," which we apply in a metaphorical sense to refer to a gushing or excessively demonstrative person, means, in the example above, "pouring freely" (as in "effusive liquid").

Perhaps the most innovative aspects of Thomson's diction are his habitual interchangings of parts of speech and his creative use of modifiers. Examples of the former include "serener Blue" (adjective used as noun), "looking lively gratitude" (intransitive verb used transitively), and "Fleeces unbounded Ether" (*Autumn*, 958) (noun used as verb). His use of modifiers is illustrated in the following passage describing a shower of autumn leaves:

But should a quicker Breeze amid the Boughs
Sob, o'er the Sky the leafy Deluge streams;
Till choak'd, and matted with the dreary Shower,
The Forest-Walks, at every rising Gale,
Roll wide the wither'd Waste, and whistle bleak.

(Autumn, 993–997)

In this passage Thomson uses a characteristically loose sentence structure, in which the most conspicuous element is the many nouns modified by adjectives, especially present and past participles. In other contexts, he intensifies his use of modifiers further by creating numerous compound epithets, such as "gay-shifting" and "many-twinkling." The effect of all these techniques is to approximate verbally a world in constant movement and change. Indeed, Thomson is very successful in conveying a sense of process and dynamic motion in nature. His description of the deceptive calm before a spring rain vibrates with suspense and tension: "Gradual, sinks the Breeze, / Into a perfect Calm . . . 'Tis Silence all, / And pleasing Expectation" (*Spring*, 155–162). His heavy reliance on modifiers, each of which specifies, defines, or qualifies an object or phenomenon, reflects the empirical bias of his age. John Locke, the leading philosopher of the period, argued that sense perception is the basis of all knowledge. Accordingly, the ability to compare and discriminate among objects, as the poet does with his carefully chosen modifiers, is essential in coming to understand the external world. Thomson's verbal art has thus appropriately been called an art of discrimination.

Closely related to Thomson's experiments with language are his experiments with literary form. He combines elements of several preexisting genres to create a form suitable to his own needs—a large-scale form capable of combining descriptive and didactic aims. His Latinate language points to his chief literary model, Virgil's *Georgics*, but he modifies the georgic form by adding features from many other sources, including John Milton's *Paradise Lost*, *L'Allegro*, and *Il Penseroso*; the Old Testament books of Job and Psalms; and the *De rerum natura* of Lucretius. Eighteenth-century writers accepted a hierarchy of genres, in which the greater, more prestigious forms, like epic and tragedy, were seen as including elements of lesser genres, like georgic and satire. Conversely, writers of satire and georgic (like Thomson) often claimed greater stature for their works by incorporating into them elements of the major genres. The struc-

ture of *The Seasons* reflects this inventive attitude toward genre so characteristic of the period.

Traces of Virgil's *Georgics* are to be found throughout *The Seasons*. Thomson chose the Virgilian model for its flexibility and its capacity to accommodate the miscellaneous topics he intended to address in his poem. At their simplest the four *Georgics* make up a poem of practical advice about matters agricultural. Information about weather forecasting, plowing, planting, livestock breeding, and even beekeeping is the stock-in-trade of Virgil's poem, and many of these features find their counterpart in *The Seasons*, such as the poet's advice on controlling noxious insects, the accounts of hay making and sheepshearing, and the prognostications of the weather. In addition, Thomson draws upon the Roman poet's patriotic sentiments, his mythic accounts of the origins of agriculture, and his mock-heroic, anthropomorphizing descriptions of animals. But Virgil moves beyond topics like these to consider deeper issues: the moral and social value of work, its key role in the formation of society and the advancement of culture, the central importance of agriculture in the economic life of the nation, the nature and purpose of the good polity, and the proper channeling of human energy and ingenuity.

The subjects Virgil addresses in his poem were very much on the minds of British thinkers in the seventeenth and eighteenth centuries. The civil war of the 1640s had laid open fundamental religious and political questions in British society, and the ensuing agricultural, scientific, and, eventually, industrial revolutions prompted equally searching inquiries into problems of economics, labor, and imperial expansion. Though Thomson and his contemporaries often understood only partly the forces at work in their society, they were keenly alive to the burgeoning, transforming energy around them and looked to Virgil for a literary mode capable of articulating their heady experience of change. Just as Virgil wonders about the effects of Rome's military conquests and imperial wealth upon her republican institutions and the public virtue of her citizens, so too Thomson contemplates the possible consequences of Britain's commercial and colonial growth—on the one hand, untold wealth and prosperity, or, on the other, political corruption and enervating luxury. Though these concerns are important features of *The Seasons*, they figure much more prominently in the political poem *Lib-*

erty and will be considered further below in connection with that poem.

As this brief survey of Virgilian elements in *The Seasons* indicates, Thomson's debt to Virgil is so thoroughgoing that the Roman poet's influence has been used as an explanation for the apparent contradictions in Thomson's poem. A good example is the thematic clash many readers have noted between ideas of primitivism and progress in *The Seasons*. On the one hand, Thomson celebrates in *Spring* a paradisiacal golden age at the dawn of history, when humans lived in harmony with one another and with nature. From this state of perfection human society has degenerated into conflict and disorder, resulting in "these iron Times, / These Dregs of Life" (274–275) that are the lot of modern humanity. On the other hand, he begins *Autumn* with an account of the misery, rather than the idyllic harmony, of primitive human existence, and of the progress achieved in later ages through labor and industry. John Chalker has suggested that these contradictory visions can be reconciled by turning to Thomson's source, where the same tension between nostalgia for an idealized past and pride in the accomplishments of the present can be found.

Yet why Thomson should choose to emphasize the Virgilian antithesis of progress versus decline to the extent that he does remains a problem, for a writer making use of existing literary forms is free to modify or reject preexisting features of a genre—as Thomson does elsewhere in *The Seasons*. The choices he makes must be understood, rather, in terms of their functional significance for him and his audience. When viewed in this light, the logical contradiction in which the poet entangles himself no longer looms so large because his real purpose in offering the two versions of human social origins is to make available for the reader several salient perspectives from which to judge the present. The passage extolling the golden age offers an ideal view of the past that serves as a moral and imaginative touchstone of human perfection and fulfillment against which the inadequacies of the present can be measured. The comparison is not flattering: the injustice, corruption, and privations of eighteenth-century Britain stand out glaringly when juxtaposed with the poet's vision of primal felicity. Viewed from the less absolute perspective of the history of human progress, however, modern society has made great strides over ancient times in its wealth, knowledge, and politi-

cal liberty. Thomson's contrasting myths of origin thus offer his readers interpretive fictions by which they can assess and evaluate the changes their society is undergoing.

Perhaps the most significant modification of the Virgilian georgic introduced by Thomson and his contemporaries is the prospect survey: passages of visual assessment in which the narrator stands back and takes a broad view of the landscape, examining it with the eye of a landscape painter like Claude Lorrain. In *Summer* the narrator calls this procedure an "equal, wide survey" (1617), vouchsafing him (and the reader) a glimpse of the order that underlies the welter of observed detail crowding the poem:

> Here let us sweep
> The boundless Landskip: now the raptur'd Eye,
> Exulting swift, to huge AUGUSTA send,
> 　　　. . .
> HEAVENS! what a goodly Prospect spreads around,
> Of Hills, and Dales, and Woods, and Lawns, and Spires,
> And glittering Towns, and gilded Streams, till all
> The stretching Landskip into Smoke decays!
> Happy BRITANNIA!
> 　　　　　　(*Summer*, 1408–1410, 1438–1442)

The natural and human worlds are brought together by the observer's eye, and compose a harmonious whole in which human activity reflects and forms part of the beauty and order of nature. The observer moves from an idealized description of an actual landscape (here the Thames river valley) to various topics of reflection prompted by the scene: peace, patriotism, and political liberty. The prospect before him exemplifies the Virgilian ideal of nature improved by art, but the improving art that transforms this landscape almost into an image of the golden age is, as the visual imagery and the emphasis on the viewing eye imply, very much an eighteenth-century conception of art, thoroughly grounded in the period's philosophical bias toward observation, experience, and experiment. (Throughout his poetry, Thomson uses the term "arts" in a broader sense than we understand it today: for him the term means not only what we would call the "fine" or aesthetic arts but also the "useful" arts, including skills and technology.)

But the question arises as to the identity of the privileged viewer whose gaze brings all the tumultuous variety of the world into a unified whole. The many prospect views Thomson describes in *The Seasons* are located on the estates of his various aristocratic friends and patrons, and he attributes the harmonious scenes described in his poem to their gentlemanly gaze. Only a gentleman like Bubb Dodington, who is characterized in "The Happy Man" (1729) as furnished with a mind "Where *Judgment* sits clear-sighted, and surveys / The Chain of *Reason* with unerring Gaze" (19–20), has the wealth, leisure, and impartial judgment to be able to perceive the underlying harmony of the world. Moreover, he achieves his harmonious view of the world by withdrawing from it: only the retired gentleman's country estate affords the prospects described by Thomson, not the city with all its bustle and squalor. Seen from a distance, the noisome smoke of the town blends aesthetically into the far horizon: "The stretching Landskip into Smoke decays!" Reduced to a smudge, the town can be assimilated into the design of the view.

The role of the gentleman that emerges from Thomson's poem is, as John Barrell notes in *English Literature in History*, a contradictory one. If the perceiver can achieve a unified view of things only by retiring from the hurly-burly of life to the country, then the comprehensiveness of his view is called into question. It does not include, for example, the getting and spending of urban England, where the pursuit of political power and material gain distracts the individual from pursuing a clear and disinterested vision of the world. But if calmness, benevolence, and philosophic rationality can only be found by retreating from the jarring world, then retirement becomes indistinguishable from detachment and disengagement. There remains, logically speaking, nothing for the gentleman to do, nothing to spur him to action, no urgent national priorities upon which to exercise his impartial public virtue because the world, from the vantage point of the country estate, appears to be altogether perfect:

> This is the Life which those who fret in Guilt,
> And guilty Cities never knew; the Life,
> Led by primeval Ages, uncorrupt,
> When Angels dwelt, and GOD himself, with Man!
> (*Autumn*, 1348–1351)

These lines appear at the end of a long passage in imitation of one of Virgil's most famous set pieces, his praise in *Georgics* II of the advantages and virtues of the country life. But whereas Virgil praises the frugality, healthiness, and virtue of the hardworking farmer's life, Thomson dwells on the gifts that nature showers unbidden upon the "hedonist-philosopher-poet," as James Sambrook characterizes the eighteenth-century gentleman. Virgil is significantly rewritten to fit the circumstances of eighteenth-century Britain.

The contradictions of Thomson's argument need not be dismissed as evidence of the poet's carelessness or lack of skill, for they mirror broader incongruities evident in the rapidly changing society around him. The traditional, inherited view of society and the gentleman's role in it had been of a congeries of warring and conflicting interests requiring the disinterested intervention of the gentleman to regulate competing claims. In the eighteenth century, however, these competing interests were increasingly seen in a more positive light: individuals pursuing their private economic ends were recognized as unwitting contributors to the public good. This new conception of national cohesion posed two acute problems for the gentleman: his adjudicative role seemed to become more and more irrelevant in a self-regulating political and economic system, and the increasing complexity of the system itself made less and less plausible the ideal that the gentleman could comprehend the "beauteous Whole" (*Winter*, 579). But Thomson, like many other writers in the period, remains committed to a hierarchical conception of the social order, with the gentleman at the head; thus, the ideal of retirement in *The Seasons*, exemplified in his revision of Virgil's praise of country life, is his attempt to find a mode of literary representation that reaffirms the gentleman's intellectual and political authority.

If Thomson retains an ideological commitment to the ideal of the retired gentleman-philosopher who is privileged to perceive the harmony of "Nature's boundless Frame" (*Winter*, 575), he also contrasts the ideal with the actual. The poem exhibits a constant tension between desired perfection and a disharmonious, unjust, cruel reality. This reality is most dramatically shown in the episode of Celadon and Amelia recounted in *Summer* (1171–1222). At the very moment that Celadon assures the innocent Amelia of the power of divine providence and justice, she is struck dead by a bolt of lightning. The untimely death of Amelia is the most vivid of many instances of suffering and destruction narrated in the poem. At these points Thomson turns away from the *Georgics* and toward his biblical models, particularly the Book of Job, which tells the story of a faithful man's confrontation with an inscrutable God who allows him to undergo tremendous suffering. The Book of Job concludes with God's assertion of his omnipotence, his control of the entire created universe, or, as Thomson puts it in his preface to *Winter*, "with a Description of the grand *Works of Nature* . . . from the Mouth of their ALMIGHTY AUTHOR." Job's suffering is part of a larger plan that he cannot fully understand.

The story of Job provides Thomson with his devotional theme, which he summarizes in the concluding lines of *Winter*:

> Ye good Distrest!
> Ye noble Few! who here unbending stand
> Beneath Life's Pressure, yet bear up a While,
> And what your bounded View, which only saw
> A little Part, deem'd *Evil* is no more:
> The Storms of WINTRY TIME will quickly pass
> And one unbounded SPRING encircle All.
>   (1063–1069)

As many readers of *The Seasons* have noted, these religious or philosophical generalizations (asserting, in Alexander Pope's memorable concluding words to *An Essay on Man*, book 1, that "whatever is, is right") ring with far less emotional conviction and imaginative truth than his graphic portrayals of the often destructive processes of nature. Thomson's explicit doctrinal formulations, in other words, seem rather feeble compared with the precision of his observation of nature and the enthusiasm of his search for knowledge and insight into natural processes. In *To the Palace of Wisdom*, Martin Price explains the poet's use of nature as a means of conveying religious feeling and contrasts his approach with the techniques of religious poets like John Donne in the previous century: "Thomson is finding new vehicles for religious experience and putting behind him the landscape of symbols we see in the Metaphysical poets. He insists upon a scientific understanding of the operations of nature; and this attempt to see the splendor that streams through natural process makes for a minuteness of detail and at times a deliberate pursuit of the 'unpoetic'" (pp. 356–357).

Thomson's devotional purpose in *The Seasons* raises the question of the temper of his religious beliefs, which have been characterized variously as deistic, pantheistic, and traditionally Christian and orthodox. The very fact that this question has elicited such a wide variety of responses implies that the poem is not terribly clear and consistent on the subject. His conception of God seems too providential and interventionist to be called deistic. Deists like the earl of Shaftesbury held that individuals could come to a knowledge of God through their own unaided reason, rather than divine revelation, and maintained that the Creator refrains from interfering with the laws of nature or the functioning of the universe. God was regarded by the deists as a divine engineer who created the machinery of the cosmos and set it in motion, but then left it to function on its own. This view does not altogether square with Thomson's characterization of God as "boundless Spirit" and "unremitting Energy," who "pervades, / Adjusts, sustains, and agitates the Whole" (*Spring*, 853–855). Yet the absence of any reference to explicitly orthodox Christian doctrines, such as the atonement of Christ, original sin, and divine revelation, makes implausible the claim that the religious orientation of *The Seasons* is orthodox. Indeed, Thomson's patron George Lyttelton, himself a devout Christian, went to great lengths to dispel the poet's religious doubt, as he states in a letter dated 21 May 1747: "My refuge and consolation is in philosophy—Christian philosophy, which I heartily wish you may be a disciple of, as well as myself" (*Letters*, p. 189).

Some sense of the extent to which Thomson strayed from the strict Presbyterianism of his youth can be gained by examining the view of divine revelation promulgated in the poem. In the conclusion to *Summer* he conceives of revelation as an ongoing process that spans a person's life on earth and the eternity to come. No mention is made of the Bible as the revealed word of God; instead, in a scenario that is fully fleshed out in his *Poem Sacred to the Memory of Sir Isaac Newton*, he traces the human mind in its stage by stage ascent through eternity, attaining an ever greater knowledge of the cosmos and its creator. In the commemorative poem to Newton, Thomson imagines him in endless, immortal pursuit of scientific knowledge, and he apotheosizes the great mathematician as a tutelary spirit presiding over his native land. Newton's apotheosis is equally an apotheosis of reason, which is capable of discerning the divinely instituted laws governing the universe. In *Summer*, Thomson describes Newton as enjoying direct access to divine wisdom. The great physicist is nothing less than, *"pure Intelligence, whom* GOD / *To Mortals lent, to trace his boundless Works"* (1560–1561).

Sir Isaac Newton died on 20 March 1727, a little more than a month after the initial publication of *Summer*, so it is not surprising that Thomson's poem to Newton, which he wrote rapidly in the weeks following the scientist's death, bears a strong thematic affinity with *The Seasons*. Thomson had been introduced to the new Newtonian science in his fourth year at Edinburgh, and he deploys his knowledge extensively in *Summer*, which includes passages on gravitation and projection, and light and color. Though Newton's fame for posterity rests primarily with his discovery of the laws of motion, his investigations of light and the spectrum were more immediately influential on the literary practice of the eighteenth century. Thomson's own fascination with color, evident in his highly visual poetic diction, is clearly attributable to Newton's ideas.

Beyond the immediate impact of his scientific discoveries, Newton exerted an extraordinary cultural influence on his time. Joseph Addison called him "the miracle of the present age," and Alexander Pope eulogized him in his memorable epigram, "Nature, and Nature's Laws lay hid in Night. / God said, *Let Newton be!* and All was *Light.*" He was a cultural and patriotic icon for the British people in the eighteenth century. Far from emptying the universe of meaning and mystery, his discoveries were hailed as proving the existence of order and purpose in the cosmos. Newton's work also contributed to the development of new aesthetic ideas that played an important role in shaping Thomson's poetry, which has often been called a poetry of the sublime. The term "sublime" was used in the eighteenth century to describe those sentiments (fear, awe, astonishment) raised by spectacular natural phenomena—storms, oceans, mountain ranges, or the infinite reaches of the Newtonian universe. As a poet of the sublime in *The Seasons*, Thomson makes the response of the perceiver (both the poet-narrator and the reader) a central focus of interest in the poem.

Finally, a brief word is in order about Thomson's habit of revision and expansion over the twenty or more years of his work on *The Seasons*. Each new edition of the poem in Thomson's lifetime was significantly longer than previous editions. From a purely practical point of view he needed to provide the public with a substantially new poem each time he came out with a new edition. These continual revisions need to be taken into account in any interpretation of the poem because they alter its form and thematic emphasis. Much of the political and intellectual material, for instance (as opposed to the more purely descriptive passages), is a later addition. A comparison of the many states of *The Seasons* thus provides a window into the process of artistic creation: the poem offers unusual insight into what might be called the aesthetics of revision. The process of revision, which is for Thomson largely an additive one, also encourages a reconsideration of the question of artistic unity. If a poem is composed of detachable sections, then a theory of "organic" unity, such as that championed by the Romantic poets of the early nineteenth century, is clearly inadequate to explain the structure and aesthetic power of a poem like *The Seasons*.

POLITICAL POETRY: BRITANNIA *AND* LIBERTY

THE success of *The Seasons* encouraged Thomson to try his hand at a more ambitious strain of poetry. In conformity with the critical orthodoxy of his time that tragedy and epic are the supreme forms of poetic expression, he went on to produce several neoclassical tragic dramas in the 1730s, and in *Liberty* (1735–1736) he attempted a theme epic in its grandeur and historical scope. His career as a dramatist, which will be traced further below, was, at least in his own time, reasonably successful; his five-part poem *Liberty*, by contrast, met with an indifferent reception that greatly disappointed the poet. Many reasons have been suggested for the failure of this poem, but perhaps the most plausible answer is to be found in the view of poetry championed in the work itself. In his review of the cultural flowering of ancient Athens, Thomson argues that the arts should serve as the "Handmaids" of "Public Virtue" (II.365–366), a doctrine that he appears to have taken too much to heart in his own poetic practice. In wedding his muse to public virtue, Thomson produced a poem heavily didactic and often excessively abstract. If the strength of *The Seasons* lies in his power to find a poetic style capable of capturing a world in constant motion and process, *Liberty* represents a yoking of this visual style to an abstract, intellectual subject matter resistant to visualization. Nor does Thomson supply human interest—an epic hero or a dramatic plot—to substitute for the descriptive movement of his earlier poem. Without plot or characters to help carry his theme, the poet relies heavily on personification: virtues or vices are lined up in the poem like the mute statues encountered in his surveys of ancient Greece and Rome.

A brief example will illustrate the problem that confronts the reader of *Liberty*. In the final section of the poem, the personified goddess Liberty, the narrator of the poem, stresses the importance of benevolence for others in the formation of a just and free society:

> An active Flood of *universal Love*
> Must swell the Beast.
> · · ·
>   Without This,
> This awful Pant, shook from sublimer Powers
> Than those of *Self*, this HEAVEN-infus'd Delight,
> This *moral Gravitation*, rushing prone
> To press the *public Good*, MY System soon,
> Traverse, to several *selfish* Centers drawn,
> Will reel to Ruin.
>   (V.245–246, 254–260)

In *The Seasons*, Thomson enlivens this doctrine of moral gravitation (note the use of scientific, Newtonian language to describe a moral principle) by illustrating it in action. The parental solicitude of the birds in *Spring*, as they build their nests and care for their young, enacts the fundamental benevolence built into the framework of things. In *Liberty*, the same point is asserted baldly, distanced from the emotional immediacy and concreteness of the illustrative episodes scattered through *The Seasons*.

Nonetheless, as this example indicates, many of the political ideas highlighted in *Liberty*, such as patriotism, public virtue, and the link between liberty, art, and commerce, are present in the earlier poem. Indeed, a passage near the beginning of *Autumn* in which Thomson traces the progress of human society from obscure, savage origins to civilized splendor encapsulates the movement or "plot" of the later poem. (The "progress," a common set piece in the poetry of the eighteenth century, typically traces the evolution of an idea or movement over time and space. Pope's *Essay on Criticism* [1711], for example, concludes with a history of the "progress" of criticism from ancient Greece and Rome to modern Britain.) As Thomson revised and expanded *The Seasons*, he included more and more political and social reflections in his scheme, inclusions that look forward to his later poetry. Moreover, the appearance of *Britannia* in 1729, while he was still hard at work on his great descriptive poem, attests that political concerns were never far from his mind.

Britannia anticipates Thomson's later political poem in a number of striking ways. The two poems employ an identical narrative frame: in each case a goddess (Britannia and Liberty, respectively) speaks out on urgent political subjects while the poet records her words. The goddess then vanishes, leaving the poet along with his thoughts in a desolate landscape. The poems rehearse many of the same ideas—the contrast of past glory and present decline, and the opposition between liberty and luxury—and in both instances, as Alan McKillop observes in *The Castle of Indolence and Other Poems*, "tendentious political utterances merge with universally acceptable political, moral, and social generalizations" (p. 164). This last point applies particularly to *Britannia*: patriotic utterances in that poem against Spanish tyranny and religious bigotry shade into jingoism. The modern reader is left with the question of how to respond to the rhetoric of the poem, a problem similar to that posed by the patriotic verse of Alfred, Lord Tennyson, or Rudyard Kipling in the nineteenth century. What to one person may sound like a defense of lofty ideals like liberty and national destiny will strike another as sophistry or even propaganda.

Liberty, for the most part, takes a higher road, though in the political atmosphere of the Walpole era it was often difficult to make a theoretical generalization about politics or history without having one's views read as a partisan argument. Thomson's political observations are, for the most part, political commonplaces of his time. He opens the poem with a view of contemporary Italy, a country sadly fallen away from its erstwhile Roman glory as arbiter of the world. The subsequent sections of the poem recount several visions of historical moments in the past, particularly in ancient Greece and Rome, when the flame of liberty burned most strongly. The history of liberty follows a repeating pattern that Thomson lays out at the beginning of the poem's second part. Like John Locke in his *The Second Treatise of Government* (1690), he imagines the human race at the dawn of time in a harmonious "state of nature," a state, however, that humanity is mysteriously prompted to abandon despite its apparent perfection. Needs and desires produce the arts of civilization and its accompanying wealth, which in turn leads to violence, the product of insatiable desire and laziness, and ultimately to the self-indulgent complacency of luxury. The circle is completed by the corruption, enervation, and social collapse to which luxury inevitably leads. Some readers in Thomson's day undoubtedly read this cyclical theory of history as an attack on Walpole's government, but the idea itself goes back to classical times and can thus also be read in a more general, theoretical sense. Whether the poem is read in a specific or general sense, it contains a warning for the British, who presumably still have time to change direction and to break out of the cycle in which they find themselves.

One way to counteract the effects of corruption, fortune, and human frailty was to establish a mixed government, as did Lycurgus in Sparta, "Where mix'd each Government, in such just Poise; / Each Power so checking, and supporting, Each; / That firm for Ages, and unmov'd, it stood" (II. 116–118). By the term "mixed government" was meant a polity containing elements of monarchy, aristocracy, and democracy, like the British constitution, which, in Thomson's time, divided political power among the Crown, the House of Lords, and the House of Commons. (The American constitutional system of checks and balances among the branches of government is a present-day version of this idea.) Each element in this balance of interests was meant to contribute to society as a whole its characteristic virtue, while checking the vices to which the other elements were subject (such as monarchy's tendency toward tyranny and democracy's drift toward demagoguery and mob rule). In this way, it was felt, the dangers of corruption and decline could be held at bay.

The reign of liberty was sustained in Sparta by a ruthless control of wealth and luxury: the austere Spartan ethic of the city ensured its continued freedom. But while the suppression of luxury prevented the growth of corruption, it also hindered the development of the arts. Athens, by contrast, took advantage of its state of liberty to encourage the growth of arts of all kinds. Like many of his contemporaries, Thomson regarded freedom as a necessary precondition for the flourishing of arts,

commerce, and technology. Paradoxically, however, the very arts that are the crowning achievement of a society also produce the wealth that becomes the undoing of that society—a conundrum that neither the poet nor the political thinkers of his time were able to resolve.

The safeguarding of public virtue, as Thomson emphasizes in the third and fourth parts of his poem, is essential in maintaining liberty. This was a favorite theme of the political opposition in the 1730s, who charged Walpole with systematically undermining both public virtue and the checks and balances of mixed government by bribing members of the House of Commons into supporting the administration. Here a problem emerges similar to that we have observed in Thomson's conception of the retired gentleman: If public virtue can be maintained only by a stance of complete independence from the messy business of commerce and political horse-trading, then the pursuit of power in Parliament serves to undermine the very ideal of public virtue to which one is committed. The standard of independence is set so high that it becomes available only to the wealthy landowner, whose landed income buys him freedom from the dictates of patrons or the temptations of bribes and business deals.

Many readers have observed that among the most successful passages in *Liberty* are those describing classical and Renaissance painting and sculpture (for example, IV.134–206). Because Thomson, like his fellow poets in the eighteenth century, especially Alexander Pope, associated the production of great art with political liberty, his discussion of the great achievements in the history of art acquires a political dimension. By extension, to bemoan the degenerate state of modern artistic endeavor, as Pope does in *The Dunciad* (1728), is to comment unfavorably on the political health of the country. Pope in fact argues that the writer must adopt the same stance of public-spirited independence as is required in the political sphere, insisting that any trace of indebtedness, whether to party, publisher, or patron, fatally undermines a writer's moral integrity. In book 4 of *The Dunciad* he recounts a dreamlike vision of a society so corrupt that the arts themselves have become prisoners of the goddess Dulness.

For his part, Thomson concludes *Liberty* with an analogous dream vision, though he couches his vision positively by projecting himself into a future time when the arts belong once again to Liberty rather than to Dulness: "BEHOLD! all *thine again* the SISTER-ARTS, / Thy *Graces* They, knit in harmonious Dance" (V.683–684). The ending of the poem is a kind of anti-Dunciad in which Pope's grotesque images of cultural decay have been banished from the scene:

Lo! vanish'd *Monster-land*. Lo! driven away
Those that *Apollo's* sacred Walks profane:
Their wild Creation scatter'd, where a World
Unknown to *Nature*, Chaos more confus'd,
O'er the brute Scene its *Ouran-Outangs* pours;
Detested Forms! that, on the Mind imprest,
Corrupt, confound and barbarize an Age.
(V. 676–682)

In contrast with Pope's gallery of hack writers and dunces, Thomson's closing lines hail a number of genuine contributors to the arts, including Pope himself and his friends Lord Burlington and Lord Bathurst, two men influential in propagating the latest ideas in architecture and landscape gardening. But lest the reader be transported by this glowing vision of future possibility, the poem concludes with a stern reminder of a more dismal fate that may yet befall Great Britain: "The VISION broke; And, on my waking Eye, / Rush'd the still RUINS of dejected ROME" (V.719–720).

THOMSON THE PLAYWRIGHT

PERHAPS the greatest irony of Thomson's poetic career was his failure to recognize that his true achievement as a poet lay with *The Seasons*, a poem focused on objects and ideas accessible to the immediate experience of his audience, rather than the more rarefied, heroic reaches of tragedy that he attempted to scale in the 1730s and 1740s. That "failure," however, is not so much a question of misdirected poetic talent as a consequence of a modern cultural climate increasingly uncongenial to tragic and heroic plays and increasingly partial to sentimental drama and literary realism. Nonetheless, it was assumed in the eighteenth century that any poet worthy of the name would rise in due course to the challenge of composing epics and tragedies, an ambition endorsed by a writer in the *Whitehall Evening-Post* of 19 March 1728, who prognosticated that Thomson would "prove" his readers' "*future* Entertainment in a nobler way; when the Author shall rise from the *still Life*

of Poetry, to represent the Passions of Mankind" (quoted in Sambrook, p. 81).

Yet if Thomson's attempts at serious drama have proved disappointing to posterity, he was by no means the only poet of his time to find his talents ill suited to the rigidity of the classical paradigm of the poetic career. Joseph Addison and Samuel Johnson, skilled poets both, met with failure in their attempts to write neoclassical tragedy. Even Alexander Pope, the greatest poet of Thomson's generation, who aspired to write an epic as the jewel in his poetic crown, produced instead memorable mock-epics and satires. The very forms that eighteenth-century writers venerated in theory proved elusive in practice: the period is remembered for its satires and georgics, its novels and biographies, rather than its epics and tragedies. Ironically, the fear and pity that the tragic writer was expected to arouse in his audience were more likely to be encountered in reading the sublime and sentimental passages for which *The Seasons* had become famous. Not only is the grandeur of the tragic hero displaced onto the natural scenery, but also the spirit of heroism, which was traditionally displayed and proved in action. The heroic spirit is transmuted into the elevated emotional responses of an essentially passive perceiver. In Thomson's first play, *Sophonisba*, the character of Scipio, whose heroic stature is demonstrated by the pity he feels for a captive princess, illustrates how greatness of soul is increasingly measured or proved by the hero's capacity for feeling, rather than action. The fear, awe, and astonishment that an Elizabethan audience had felt at the death of a tragic hero like Hamlet or Othello were increasingly experienced in the eighteenth century through an individual's "sublime" encounters, whether in real life or in verbal description, with the power of nature in its storms and earthquakes—its infinite vastness and unending variety.

Great tragedy is a rare poetic achievement. It enjoyed a brief flowering in ancient Athens and again in Renaissance Europe. These two periods are notable for producing tragedies of remarkable complexity and ambiguity, plays that typically highlight an irresoluble conflict between opposing values, such as personal nobility and honor on the one hand and public necessity or the demands of society on the other. What makes such a conflict tragic is the recognition that the opposing forces tugging at the protagonist are both valuable and estimable, even as they are mutually exclusive and irreconcilable. A good example is Shakespeare's *Coriolanus*, a play that was to provide Thomson with the inspiration for his final tragedy. In Shakespeare's play, Coriolanus is a Roman hero of almost godlike proportions who threatens to destroy his native city rather than violate his personal code of honor. But his mother confronts him with the fact that Rome also has legitimate claims upon him; indeed, it is Rome that has made him what he is, and without her historical record and collective memory his heroic name and reputation would soon be forgotten. He is not self-sufficient in his heroism. Though Coriolanus learns painfully that his heroic stance is limited by human finitude and though he dies in an irreconcilable clash between personal and public values, Shakespeare ends the play with an unmistakable affirmation of the worthiness of his heroic aspirations.

In Thomson's *Coriolanus*, the tragic conflict in the original version is largely short-circuited. The commonwealth or the public good, rather than an individual, has become the implicit protagonist of the drama. Thomson's Coriolanus defends and justifies his heroic integrity by associating it with the public virtues of Rome:

> Whate'er her Blots, whate'er her giddy Factions,
> There is more Virtue in one single Year
> Of Roman Story, than your Volscian Annals
> Can boast thro' all your creeping dark Duration!
>
> (V.ii.65–68)

Heroism no longer holds any intrinsic value as a private virtue, and Coriolanus is accordingly sacrificed on the altar of civic responsibility. The playwright concludes with a strong condemnation of Coriolanus' private aspirations and a pious assertion of public values: "*Above* ourselves *our* COUNTRY *should be dear*" (V.iv.40). Two opposing values are no longer held in balance; the tragic dilemma collapses into didacticism and moralizing.

This tendency to simplify tragic complexities is even more pronounced in *Sophonisba*, the work that introduced Thomson to the playgoing public. The title character, a Carthaginian queen, experiences no tragic conflict at all between her private desires and her public responsibilities. For Sophonisba, love of Carthage supersedes all else, and she feels no compunction in abandoning her husband, Syphax, and manipulating Masinissa's intense love for her in order to defend her country. When confronted by her outraged husband, she defends her actions by arguing that there can be no shame in preferring

> Thousands to one, a whole collected people,
> All nature's tenderness, whate'er is sacred,
> The liberty the welfare of a state,
> To one man's frantic happiness.
>
> (IV.ii.151–154)

In Sophonisba there is no tragic agonizing about ends and means: her mind is made up from the start. The only character in the play who grapples with a potentially tragic conflict between love and duty is Masinissa, who attempts unsuccessfully to balance his love for Sophonisba with his obligations to Rome. By contrast, Sophonisba proves to be a true Roman at heart, despite her African origins. "She had a *Roman* soul," Laelius states in the play's closing scene, "for every one / Who loves, like her, his country is a *Roman*" (V.ix.63–64). The untragic ease with which Sophonisba makes her choice and the play's insistent reiteration of the patriotic theme that love of country must take precedence over private affections explains Samuel Johnson's observation in his biography of Thomson "that nobody was much affected, and that the company rose as from a moral lecture" (p. 288).

The reasons literary forms that dominate in one period become impossible to sustain in another are as complex as the process of historical change itself, but part of the answer for the demise of tragedy in Thomson's day can be found in the vivid memory eighteenth-century Britain retained of the political disorder and social upheaval of the previous century, which had culminated in a bloody civil war and the execution of King Charles I. With the disastrous effects of civil disorder still fresh in memory, eighteenth-century writers and critics tended to the view that literature and art should serve the interests of state and society. Thus, in the dedication of *Tancred and Sigismunda*, addressed to the Prince of Wales, Thomson argues that the stage "most deserves the Attention of Princes, who by a judicious Approbation of such Pieces as tend to promote all Publick and Private Virtue, may . . . greatly advance the Morals and Politeness of their People." Elizabethan tragedy was capable of raising intractable ethical issues, including questions concerning the fundamental basis of society. Eighteenth-century tragic theory, by contrast, shied away from such ambiguities and insisted on a much more clear-cut, didactic conception of tragedy. Thus, the earl of Shaftesbury (among many others) argues that the purpose of tragedy is to promote social harmony, "to the end that the people . . . may be taught the better to content themselves with privacy, enjoy their safer state, and prize the equality and justice of their guardian laws."[1] Accordingly, eighteenth-century poets, in their professed desire to encourage civil harmony and order in place of factionalism and political strife, avoid the portrayal of heroes whose actions might raise questions about the foundations of society. In this regard, Thomson's Sophonisba is the exemplary heroic figure for the period.

The prologue to *Tancred and Sigismunda*, Thomson's next to last and, in many respects, most skillful play, acknowledges the pressure to move away from the traditional verbal, visual, and thematic trappings of heroic drama in favor of the bourgeois realism exemplified in the emerging form of the novel:

> *Our Spells are vanish'd, broke our magic Wand,*
> *That us'd to waft you over Sea and Land.*
>   · · ·
> *In vain of martial Scenes the loud Alarms,*
> *The mighty Prompter thundering out to Arms.*
>   · · ·
> *Your Taste rejects the glittering false Sublime,*
> *To sigh in Metaphor, and die in Rhime.*
> *High* Rant *is tumbled from his Gallery Throne.*

The fact that Henry Fielding, in his celebrated burlesque play *The Tragedy of Tragedies; or, The Life and Death of Tom Thumb the Great* (1731), was able to parody so successfully the action and diction of contemporary tragedy, including no fewer than a dozen spoofs of passages in *Sophonisba*, is a sure measure of the changing taste that Thomson acknowledges in the lines above. (One of Fielding's best hits is his parody of Masinissa's notorious emotional outburst, "Oh! *Sophonisba! Sophonisba!* Oh!"—an unfortunate line that, as Johnson reports, had given "occasion to a waggish parody: 'O, Jemmy Thomson, Jemmy Thomson, O!'") (p. 288). *Tancred and Sigismunda* moves closer than Thomson's other plays to a portrayal of "*the deep Recesses of the Heart,*" as he puts it in

the play's prologue. Though the struggle between private desire and public obligation remains central in the play, the emotional conflict within Tancred's breast is given greater emphasis and the interplay between private feelings and public virtue is taken more seriously. The tragic struggle is played out in a predominantly domestic rather than public sphere, with Siffredi, a well-meaning but misguided father, pitted against his daughter, Sigismunda, and her suitor, Tancred, who is like a surrogate son to Siffredi. This domestic focus gives greater scope to the melodramatic, the sentimental, and the pathetic; it plays down the heroic and historical emphasis of the previous plays.

The period of Thomson's activity as a playwright also saw his active involvement in partisan politics as a writer for the political opposition to Sir Robert Walpole. Consequently, while all of his plays deal with political themes, two of them, *Agamemnon* and *Edward and Eleonora*, written when his collaboration with opposition figures like Lyttelton and the Prince of Wales was at its peak, contain thinly disguised attacks upon Walpole and his political machinations. Though *Agamemnon* was permitted to be staged, *Edward and Eleonora* was banned by the licenser on the very day of its intended first performance, and it never saw the stage in Thomson's lifetime. In other respects, these two works are similar to his other plays in their neoclassical structure, emphasizing the unities of time, place, and action; their reliance on noble historical characters and subjects; and their avoidance of onstage action, spectacle, and violence in favor of elevated dialogue and debate. They also share the thematic preoccupations of the other plays, particularly the opposition between private affection, generally disparaged as a selfish passion, and social love, the basis of public virtue and the spur to public-spirited action.

Thomson deviates from the standard pattern of his tragic writing in only one dramatic production, the masque *Alfred*, written in collaboration with his longtime friend David Mallet. Composed in 1740 to celebrate the third birthday of Princess Augusta, daughter of Frederick, Prince of Wales, and the anniversary of the accession of George I to the British throne in 1714, the masque is a glowing tribute to Frederick and his family. Though *Alfred* differs from Thomson's other plays in form and tone, it reiterates a number of the political ideas explored in the tragedies. The masque presents these ideas, however, in an overtly partisan form,

---

[1]Anthony Ashley Cooper, Earl of Shaftesbury, *Characteristics of Men, Manners, Opinions, Times*, ed. by John M. Robertson (1711; repr. Indianapolis, Ind., 1964), p. 143.

as one might expect in a performance written to extol the royal leader of the political opposition to Walpole and George II. The great monarchs of England, a decidedly partisan opposition list including Alfred, Edward III, Elizabeth I, and William III, are summoned up as exemplary defenders of English liberty and as a collective pattern of the ideal figure of kingship: the public-spirited, selfless "patriot king." The reigning monarch, George II, who continued to hold Walpole in favor, is pointedly excluded from the list. The masque concludes with a vision of Britain's future under the promised reign of Frederick and beyond, a future heralded in optative strain in the great patriotic ode "Rule Britannia":

> To thee belongs the rural reign;
>   Thy cities shall with commerce shine:
> All thine shall be the subject main,
>   And every shore it circles thine.
>   "Rule, Britannia, rule the waves:
>   Britons never will be slaves."
>   (III.iv.146–151)

Of all Thomson's overtly political writings, this song is the most memorable and durable. Its continued popularity demonstrates that his exuberant patriotic sentiments could on occasion transcend the partisan fray of contemporary politics to express the patriotism of his fellow Britons, regardless of their political allegiance.

THE CASTLE OF INDOLENCE

DURING the years Thomson was pursuing the recognized path of the serious poet, addressing "nobler" themes in the "higher" forms of epic and tragedy, he also experimented with a poem written in the Spenserian manner, a mode that had fallen into disuse and some measure of disrepute by the early eighteenth century. The commonly held view of critics in the period was that their more polite, rational, perspicuous age had outgrown the "rude" diction and fairy-tale marvels of Spenserian romance. By the time Thomson began writing *The Castle of Indolence* in the 1730s, Spenser's poetic reputation was undergoing a significant rehabilitation; even so, adopting the Spenserian mode remained a sufficiently novel choice to prompt the question of Thomson's purpose in reviving it. One senses in his experimentation a continuing search

for form, a quest for a mode of representation capable of bringing to life the abstract formulations that weigh so heavily in the tragedies and *Liberty*. The result is a much more entertaining and poetically satisfying performance than many of his attempts in the more serious genres.

Whether *The Castle of Indolence* is an altogether successful poem, however, remains a matter of critical debate. Many readers have remarked that the poem's two cantos differ so much in subject and mood as to amount almost to two separate poems. The contrasting visions of indolence and industry that Thomson conjures up leave ample room for ambiguity and discontinuity, qualities critics have been quick to seize upon in their sometimes ponderous readings of the poem. Its allegorical structure, imitative of Edmund Spenser, admittedly encourages the political, religious, and ethical interpretations that have variously been advanced. That the poem can support such a broad and contradictory array of readings reflects, more than anything else, the tensions in outlook and thought that have been present in Thomson's poetry from the start.

But before loading down *The Castle of Indolence* with too much interpretive weight, it is worth recalling that the poem originated as a jeu d'esprit, a witty composition written in a form that eighteenth-century readers did not take altogether seriously. Patrick Murdoch remarks on the light-hearted origins of the poem: "It was, at first, little more than a few detached stanzas, in the way of raillery upon himself, and on some of his friends, who would reproach him with indolence; while he thought them, at least, as indolent as himself" (p. 17). Murdoch himself appears in the poem as one of the castle's sluggish inhabitants and is described with a touch of burlesque as "A little, round, fat, oily Man of God" (I.lxix). A number of Thomson's other friends, including Lyttelton and the actor James Quin, are also included among the ranks of the indolent, but the most interesting of the thumbnail sketches Thomson provides is a humorous yet revealing self-portrait:

> A Bard here dwelt, more fat than Bard beseems;
> Who void of Envy, Guile, and Lust of Gain,
> On Virtue still, and Nature's pleasing Themes,
> Pour'd forth his unpremeditated Strain.
>   . . .
> Oft moralizing sage; his Ditty sweet
> He loathed much to write, ne cared to repeat.
>   (I.lxviii)

Thomson's inclusion of himself among the inmates of the castle has led to a good deal of biographical speculation. Whatever else one may wish to infer, the chief autobiographical burden of these lines and of the poem as a whole is the conflict they voice about the writer's poetic vocation. The two cantos of *The Castle of Indolence* offer alternative models of poetry, the seductive, sensual, enchanting song of the Wizard in Canto I and the stern, didactic lays of the Bard in Canto II. The narrator laments to find that temptation can sing with such an inspired voice—"What pity base his Song who so divinely sings!" (II.xli)—yet it is clear that he finds the poetry of enchantment supremely attractive. Most readers of the poem, including many of the poet's friends, have concurred, finding the first canto more pleasing and convincing than the second. It is not difficult to see in this contrast an externalization of a deep conflict within Thomson himself about his role as a poet. While he feels duty bound to stoop to truth and moralize his song, his talent and bent incline much more to fancy's maze. Indeed, he has to bestir himself to escape the toils of poetic imagination: "No, fair Illusions! artful Phantoms, no! / My Muse will not attempt your Fairy-Land" (I.xlv). In Canto II he aligns himself with the poetry of reason and virtue, but here a more fundamental doubt about his poetic vocation emerges. When the Knight of Industry orders the Bard to sing and rouse the castle's inhabitants from their torpor, the Bard voices many of Thomson's favorite didactic themes, yet his song proves to be of severely limited power. Some of the "better Sort" shake off their enchantment, but "far the greater Part" curse the Bard for disturbing their rest (II.lxiv, lxvi). The Knight is forced to intervene with an "anti-magic" wand in order to rescue the vast majority from the Wizard of Indolence (II.lxvii). In the end the problem dramatized in the poem is not whether one has chosen to pursue the right kind of poetry, but whether poetry has any moral or spiritual efficacy at all.

These sorts of reflections take *The Castle of Indolence* a considerable way beyond its playful, burlesque origins. As Murdoch observes, when Thomson began writing, "he saw very soon, that the subject [of indolence] deserved to be treated more seriously, and in a form fitted to convey one of the most important moral lessons" (p. 17). In traditional Christian terms that lesson is clear: Thomson warns against sloth or acedia (lack of interest, care, or involvement), a condition traditionally viewed as one of the seven deadly sins. Yet, if indolence is redefined in terms of its Latin etymology as "freedom from pain," that capacity to rise above one's private passions and interests recommended by the ancient Stoics as the beginning of wisdom, then the life of retired ease is in some ways worth pursuing. And, as we have seen elsewhere in Thomson's writings, he values the life of the disinterested, retired gentleman as the breeding ground for public-spirited action in British society.

At this point, however, his ethical categories begin to contradict each other. If we are to derive an orthodox Christian moral from the poem, a life of ardent commitment is required, not one of impartiality and retirement. The Bible condemns those who are indifferent or lukewarm to a worse fate than those who are actively hot or cold. The Knight of Industry appears to represent just such commitment, but his purposeful activity culminates in a life of retirement and withdrawal: "Then sought he from the toilsome Scene to part, / And let Life's vacant Eve breathe Quiet through the Heart" (II.xxiv). The purpose of "industry" is to furnish the material conditions for a life of retired moderation and equipoise, a life in which philosophy and the arts can flourish, but what is to prevent that life from degenerating into a state of apathy and self-indulgence? And this is precisely what happens in Canto II, as the Wizard Indolence spreads his "curst influence" far and wide through the prosperous land the Knight has brought into existence (II.xxix). Even the Bard, who is charged with the task of breaking the Wizard's spell, partly succumbs to the ethical apathy he is sent to combat. "As God shall judge me, Knight," he exclaims,

> we must forgive
> . . .
> The frail good Man deluded here to live.
> . . .
> Ah, Nought is pure! It cannot be deny'd,
> That Virtue still some Tincture has of Vice,
> And Vice of Virtue.
>
> (II.xxxviii)

The Bard's unseemly eagerness to embrace prudence, his evasion of hard choices, helps explain why he is largely unsuccessful in freeing the Wizard's prisoners from their enthrallment.

The ethical dilemmas explored in *The Castle of Indolence* shade into social and political ones. Christine Gerrard observes in her essay on the political implications of the poem that the indolence afflicting the inhabitants of the castle is not simply a private neurosis affecting Thomson and his friends, but a national malaise that the opposition to Walpole saw as infecting the entire body politic, "a malaise of inertia, self-interest, hedonism, corruption, and loss of 'public spirit' which finds its supreme embodiment in the 'Dulness' of Pope's *Dunciad*" (p. 47). Thomson's alluring account of the land of indolence echoes the sort of oblique rhetoric the opposition repeatedly used in their attacks on Walpole. On 10 March 1729, for example, the chief opposition newspaper, the *Craftsman* (no. 27), published a diagnosis of Britain's ills that looks forward to Thomson's castle. The country is in the grip of a "POLITICAL LETHARGY, which lays all the noble faculties, generous passions, and social virtues, as it were by *Opium*, in a profound Trance, and thereby leaves publick Ministers at their discretion . . . to do whatever their ambition dictates." This lethargy "is occasioned by . . . a general spirit of luxury and profusion, or a prevailing appetite to soft effeminate inventions and wanton entertainments [which] tend to enervate the mind." The consequence is a people who have given "themselves up intirely to the pursuits of private pleasure." If one reads the poem allegorically along these lines (and the subtitle "An Allegorical Poem" does invite such readings), it is possible to see Walpole in the character of the Wizard and the opposition leader Lord Bollingbroke in the Knight. But if the poem is an allegory of Walpole's England, Thomson is honest enough to recognize that he and his friends are also beneficiaries of her misbegotten prosperity; they are, in Gerrard's phrase, "implicated, by their passivity, in the very regime they [have] criticized" (p. 61).

One of the great pleasures of an allegorical poem like *The Castle of Indolence* is that no single reading can be definitive. Spenser's *Faerie Queene* (1590) invites the reader to explore its romantic fables on the literal, moral, political, historical, and anagogical or spiritual levels. Similarly, the autobiographical, ethical, metapoetic, and political approaches already outlined by no means exhaust the many interpretive possibilities of Thomson's poem. If one pursues the implications of the Knight's name—Sir Industry—*The Castle of Indolence* offers a commentary on the changing economic arrangements of eighteenth-century Britain. These changes are mirrored in the rapidly shifting meanings of words like "industry," shifts that show a fascinating interplay between moral and economic concerns. The term traditionally conveyed the morally laudable meaning of "diligence" or "assiduous application," the habitual hard work required to accomplish things, but by midcentury it was acquiring the more modern, economic sense of "a branch of manufacture or trade"—a transfer of meaning from agent to object acted upon. The reverse movement can be observed in the word "improvement," which originally meant "to turn to profit" in the economic sense, but came in the eighteenth century to mean intellectual, moral, or aesthetic improvement, as in "improving one's mind."

These complex shifts of meaning are symptoms of a society attempting to negotiate dramatic economic and social change by marrying the new with the old, new economic activities and social pressures with traditional modes of ethical justification and social organization. This process can be seen in Thomson's description of the transforming effects of the Knight's industry, an account that idealizes the inevitable dislocations wrought by his insatiable energy:

> Then Towns he quicken'd by mechanic Arts,
> And bade the fervent City glow with Toil;
> Bade social Commerce raise renownèd Marts,
> Join Land to Land, and marry Soil to Soil,
> Unite the Poles, and without bloody Spoil
> Bring home of either *Ind* the gorgeous Stores.
>   (II.xx)

The poem as a whole exhibits a like impulse to justify the new—Britain's burgeoning commerce and industrial power—in terms of the old—the georgic and biblical accounts of the dignity and necessity of work. The first canto opens with a stern, Virgilian sermon on the advantages of a life of toil over one of enervating ease. The poor choose their life of backbreaking labor not because they would otherwise starve, but because they recognize the greater evils that a life of idle luxury would bring. In fact, one of the greatest threats posed by the Wizard's reign is to the existing order of social gradations and division of labor. Under the Wizard's influence, the poor begin to ask, "why should the vulgar Man, / The Lacquey, be more virtuous than his Lord?" (II.xxx). The

Knight's response to these rumblings of social discontent is to put everyone back to work at the tasks proper to his or her social station: "Some he will lead to Courts, and Some to Camps; / To Senates Some, and public sage Debates" (II.lx). Social inequality is justified as the necessary concomitant of a complex economic system that requires a division of labor in order for the whole to function. In the Knight's scheme the rich are no more idle than the poor; they simply perform different tasks. Read in this way, *The Castle of Indolence* offers an ideological justification for traditional social hierarchies as they are adapted to a new economic order.

CONCLUSION

IF for no other reason than the extraordinary strength of his influence in the century and a half following his death, Thomson's place in literary history is secure. *The Seasons* was rapidly translated into the major European languages, and many Continental writers acknowledged his importance in their poetic development. At home the judgment of Samuel Taylor Coleridge spoke for his contemporaries and for succeeding generations. On one occasion, reports William Hazlitt in "My First Acquaintance with Poets," when he and Coleridge came upon a well-worn copy of *The Seasons* in a remote country pub, Coleridge exclaimed, "*That* is true fame!" At the same time, speaking as a critic rather than a poet, Coleridge could not forbear qualifying his praise of Thomson, a pattern that has marked critical judgments of the poet since his death. "Thomson was a great poet, rather than a good one," he remarked to Hazlitt; "his style was as meretricious as his thoughts were natural." There may be a hint of professional jealousy in this and similar comments: Thomson has suffered some of the scorn high culture reserves for writers of broad popular appeal. The same pattern can be seen in the reception later accorded Henry Wadsworth Longfellow and Alfred, Lord Tennyson, two popular poets who inherited Thomson's broad audience in the nineteenth century.

The precipitous decline in Thomson's readership during the present century is most usefully measured against the equally sudden rehabilitation in the reputation of eighteenth-century writers like Jonathan Swift and Laurence Sterne. Our

age is suspicious of writing that tends to the sentimental or to the voicing of what at times may sound like an "official" line on politics, religion, and culture, preferring instead writing that is ironic, playful, oppositional, and skeptical. Many of the features of eighteenth-century Britain that Thomson lauds most loudly—its sentimentalist ethics, commercial optimism, and imperialist ambitions, to name but three—have come under severe attack in the twentieth century. Yet he remains a more complex figure than either the Victorians or we have tended to make of him. The paradoxes and contradictions we have traced in Thomson's life and poetry bear witness to a writer who, while accepting many of the orthodoxies of his age, also drew attention to the pressure points in his society, those places and occasions when consensual views break down. His career as a poet is itself the most eloquent testimony to this dimension of his writing, for in attempting to conform rigorously to the received, classical view of the poet's development, he ironically pointed to the radically new directions literary expression was taking in spite of the critical orthodoxy of his time. In this sense his work in a "played out" genre like tragedy is as interesting as his success with *The Seasons:* in both instances the artist's practice offers an early barometer to the direction of historical and cultural change—long before a conscious awareness of that change and its implications registered broadly in his society.

SELECTED BIBLIOGRAPHY

I. BIBLIOGRAPHIES. Ralph Cohen, "A Check List of Editions of *The Seasons*," in *The Art of Discrimination: Thomson's* The Seasons *and the Language of Criticism* (Berkeley and Los Angeles, 1964); Hilbert H. Campbell, *James Thomson, 1700–1748: An Annotated Bibliography of Selected Editions and the Important Criticism* (New York and London, 1976).

II. SEPARATE WORKS. POETRY. *Winter: A Poem* (London, 1726); *Summer: A Poem* (London, 1727); *A Poem Sacred to the Memory of Sir Isaac Newton* (London, 1727); *Spring: A Poem* (London, 1728); *Britannia* (London, 1729); *The Seasons* (London, 1730), the first collected edition of the poem, which includes significantly altered and expanded versions of *Winter, Summer,* and *Spring; Antient and Modern Italy Compared: Being the First Part of LIBERTY* (London, 1735); *Greece: Being the Second Part of LIBERTY* (London, 1735); *Rome: Being the Third Part of*

LIBERTY (London, 1735); *Britain: Being the Fourth Part of LIBERTY* (London, 1736); *The Prospect: Being the Fifth Part of LIBERTY* (London, 1736); *Poem to the Memory of the Right Honourable the Lord Talbot* (London, 1737); *The Seasons* (London, 1744), a significantly revised and enlarged version of the poem; *The Seasons* (London, 1746), the last edition of the poem published in Thomson's lifetime and considered by scholars to be the definitive text; *The Castle of Indolence: An Allegorical Poem Written in Imitation of Spenser* (London, 1748); *The Seasons,* ed. by Bolton Corney, (London, 1842), the first reliable posthumous edition, based on the 1746 text; *Thomson's Seasons: Critical Edition,* ed. by Otto Zippel, (Berlin, 1908), the first full collation of the various versions of the poem published in Thomson's lifetime; *The Seasons,* ed. by James Sambrook (Oxford, 1981).

PLAYS. *The Tragedy of Sophonisba* (London, 1730); *Agamemnon: A Tragedy* (London, 1738); *Edward and Eleonora: A Tragedy* (London, 1739); *Alfred: A Musque* (London, 1740); *Tancred and Sigismunda: A Tragedy* (London, 1745); *Coriolanus: A Tragedy* (London, 1749).

III. COLLECTED WORKS. *The Works of Mr. Thomson,* 2 vols. (London, 1738); *The Works of James Thomson,* ed. by George, Baron Lyttelton (London, 1750), an unreliable edition that includes many unauthorized revisions; *The Works of James Thomson,* ed. by Patrick Murdoch (London, 1762); *The Poetical Works of James Thomson,* ed. by Sir Harris Nicolas, 2 vols. (London, 1830), the popular "Aldine" edition, with a prefatory biography (the most complete to date) that was revised in 1860 and 1897; *The Complete Poetical Works of James Thomson,* ed. by J. Logie Robertson (Oxford, 1908); *James Thomson: The Castle of Indolence and Other Poems,* ed. by Alan D. McKillop (Lawrence, Kans., 1961); *The Seasons and the Castle of Indolence,* ed. by James Sambrook (Oxford, 1972); *The Plays of James Thomson,* ed. by Percy G. Adams (New York and London, 1979); *Liberty, The Castle of Indolence, and Other Poems,* ed. by James Sambrook (Oxford, 1986); *The Plays of James Thomson, 1700–1748: A Critical Edition,* ed. by John C. Greene, 2 vols. (New York and London, 1987).

IV. LETTERS. *James Thomson, 1700–1748: Letters and Documents,* ed. by Alan D. McKillop (Lawrence, Kans., 1958); Alan D. McKillop, "Two More Thomson Letters," in *Modern Philology* 60 (1962); A. S. Bell, "Three New Letters of James Thomson," in *Notes and Queries* 217 (October 1972).

V. BIOGRAPHICAL STUDIES. Patrick Murdoch, "An Account of the Life and Writings of Mr. James Thomson," in *The Works of James Thomson,* ed. by Patrick Murdoch (London, 1762), repr. in *The Seasons, Hymns, Ode, and Songs, of James Thomson: With His Life, by Mr. Murdoch* (Manchester, Eng., 1834); Samuel Johnson, "Thomson," in *Lives of the English Poets,* 4 vols. (London, 1781), repr. in 3 vols., ed. by G. B. Hill (Oxford, 1905); Léon Morel, *James Thomson: Sa vie et ses oeuvres* (Paris, 1895); George C. Macaulay, *James Thomson* (London, 1908); Douglas Grant, *James Thomson: Poet of* The Seasons (London, 1951); James Sambrook, *James Thomson 1700–1748: A Life* (Oxford, 1991).

VI. CRITICAL STUDIES. Alan D. McKillop, *The Background of Thomson's* Seasons (Minneapolis, Minn., 1942; repr., Hamden, Conn., 1961); Marjorie H. Nicolson, *Newton Demands the Muse: Newton's* Opticks *and the Eighteenth-Century Poets* (Princeton, N.J., 1946; repr., Hamden, Conn., 1963); John Arthos, *The Language of Natural Description in Eighteenth-Century Poetry* (Ann Arbor, Mich., 1949); Maren-Sofie Røstvig, "James Thomson," in *The Happy Man: Studies in the Metamorphoses of a Classical Ideal,* vol. 2 (Oslo, 1958); Patricia Meyer Spacks, *The Varied God: A Critical Study of Thomson's* The Seasons (Berkeley and Los Angeles, 1959).

Ralph Cohen, *The Art of Discrimination: Thomson's* The Seasons *and the Language of Criticism* (Berkeley and Los Angeles, 1964); Martin Price, *To the Palace of Wisdom: Studies in Order and Energy from Dryden to Blake* (New York, 1964); William Powell Jones, *The Rhetoric of Science: A Study of Scientific Ideas and Imagery in Eighteenth-Century Poetry* (Berkeley and Los Angeles, 1966); Patricia Meyer Spacks, *The Poetry of Vision: Five Eighteenth-Century Poets* (Cambridge, Mass., 1967); John Chalker, *The English Georgic: A Study in the Development of a Form* (London and Baltimore, 1969).

Ralph Cohen, *The Unfolding of* The Seasons (Baltimore, 1970); John Barrell, *The Idea of Landscape and the Sense of Place, 1730–1840* (Cambridge, Eng., 1972); Donald Greene, "From Accidie to Neurosis: *The Castle of Indolence* Revisited," in *English Literature in the Age of Disguise,* ed. by Maximilian Novak (Berkeley and Los Angeles, 1977); D. W. Jefferson, "The Place of James Thomson," in *Proceedings of the British Academy* 64 (1978); Hilbert H. Campbell, *James Thomson* (Boston, 1979).

John Barrell, *English Literature in History, 1730–1780: An Equal, Wide Survey* (London, 1983); Mary Jane W. Scott, *James Thomson, Anglo-Scot* (Athens, Ga., 1988); Christine Gerrard, "*The Castle of Indolence* and the Opposition to Walpole," in *Review of English Studies* n.s. 41 (1990); Eric Rothstein, "James Thomson," in *Eighteenth-Century British Poets,* 1st ser., ed. by John Sitter, *Dictionary of Literary Biography* 95 (Detroit, 1990).

REBECCA WEST

(1892–1983)

Gita May

REBECCA WEST WAS BORN Cicely Isabel Fairfield in London, on 21 December 1892, to Charles and Isabella Fairfield. Her father belonged to an Anglo-Irish army family with Scottish ancestors and aristocratic connections. A son of Major Charles George Fairfield of the Scots Guards, he served as an ensign in Prince Albert's Rifle Brigade, was sent to Canada, and from there to the United States, then in the midst of the Civil War. Upon returning to England, he resigned his commission and accepted the offer of an American friend to join him in a timber business in Virginia. He traveled to the western territory and became a mine manager. A stagecoach accident that orphaned the son of friends prompted him to sail for Australia to escort the boy to relatives in Melbourne. Fairfield, who had talent as a writer (he also liked to draw caricatures), got himself hired as a journalist by the *Melbourne Argus.*

Fairfield was a widely read man with brilliant intellectual gifts, but also with an erratic, restless streak. Upon his return to England, he served on the staff of the *Glasgow Herald* as chief leader-writer before moving back to London. His health began to deteriorate and his temperament became ever more volatile and unpredictable. He unsuccessfully tried various ventures in order to provide for his family. By the time of his death, in October 1906, he had deserted his wife and children. Cicely, the youngest of his three daughters, was nearly fourteen years of age.

Rebecca West had a strong affection tinged with a sense of awe for her father. She admired his intellectual brilliance and personal charm, while ruefully acknowledging his enigmatic restlessness and self-indulgent sexual appetite. The latter took the form of numerous marital infidelities, even with servants and nurses in the employ of the Fairfield household. She tended to romanticize his weaknesses and singularities, and in her *Family*

Memories (1987) she fondly evokes his many eccentricities, including his habit of becoming most active at night, when he seemed to come into his own. This nocturnal pattern at first greatly intrigued her as mysterious, and she soon made it her own, refusing to go to bed early like other children. For the rest of her life she would belong to what she described as a "breed of happy insomniacs who are glad of the peace which falls on the world when all that machinery stops clanking" (p. 205). That Charles Fairfield was also a great storyteller who liked to regale his family with tales of his adventures also contributed to the romantic aura with which he is endowed in *Family Memories,* a vivid account of Rebecca West's childhood and of her paternal and maternal ancestry, written intermittently during the last two decades of the writer's life.

But it is with her mother that Rebecca West most closely identified. Isabella Mackenzie came from Edinburgh and was of solid Scottish stock. She was an accomplished pianist, and West was convinced that, under more favorable circumstances, her mother could have become a concert pianist. Instead, she had to serve as "musical governess" to the daughters of a wealthy and cultivated London family, eventually returning to Edinburgh and going off to Australia in order to visit one of her brothers, John. There she met Charles Fairfield, whom she married in Melbourne on 17 December 1883. She later would manage to keep the family together during her husband's ill-fated adventures and financial enterprises, and eventual moral and physical disintegration.

In *The Fountain Overflows* (1956), a semifictionalized account of her early years, West presents these contrasting portraits of her parents:

We all knew that Mamma was not good-looking. She was too thin, her nose and forehead were shiny like

431

bone, and her features were disordered because her tortured nerves were always drawing a rake over her face. Also we were so poor that she never had new clothes. But we were conscious that our Papa was far handsomer than anybody else's. He was not tall, but he was slender and graceful, he stood like a fencer in a picture, and he was romantically dark.

(p. 5)

After Charles Fairfield's relations with the management of the *Melbourne Argus* soured, he and Isabella decided to return to Scotland, to be near her family. Charles was hired by the *Glasgow Herald* but invested most of the money he earned in speculative overseas copper-mining ventures. The Fairfields decided to move to London and try their luck there. The earliest memories of Cicely Fairfield, or Cissie as she was called by her intimates, were of living in a still-rural area of South London, where her parents had settled. This was the house, on 21 Streatham Place, off Brixton Hill, nostalgically depicted in *The Fountain Overflows*. It was a semidetached, early-nineteenth-century villa with an untended garden and a grove of chestnut trees. Despite its dilapidated furniture and faded family mementos, it turned out to be the coziest home the family ever managed to have, and it is also lovingly evoked in *Family Memories* as "a magical place" (p. 198).

By 1898 the Fairfields had to move from their pleasant home in Streatham Place to a less expensive but also less attractive house in Richmond, on the outer edge of London. West's last book published in her lifetime, *1900* (1982), is a tender, nostalgic remembrance of an era when the octogenarian Queen Victoria could be glimpsed in a horse-drawn carriage, when the far-off Boer War raged, when the Great Exhibition in Paris proudly displayed the stunning achievements of the West, and when powerful and seemingly indestructible European empires ruled most of the world.

The book opens with one of the walks the Fairfields liked to take to Richmond Hill, which afforded a spectacular vista: "The slope of the hill is set out as terraced gardens and the eye looks straight down on the green vale through which the silver Thames meanders towards Windsor Castle" (p. 5). There is no mention of family troubles or financial difficulties, and the accompanying photograph, showing little Cissie on one such outing being fed blackberries by one of her sisters, while the other sister and two cousins smilingly and so-

licitously look on, only reinforces the impression of innocence and happiness. In her other autobiographical writings, however, West was less reticent about her family's personal and financial difficulties, which cast a pall over her childhood.

West's *1900* is above all a celebration of a bygone era, which alongside venerable old institutions and traditions exhibited powerful evidence of momentous change and creativity. The turn of the century was marked by the deaths of Friedrich Nietzsche, Oscar Wilde, and John Ruskin, and by the excommunication of Leo Tolstoy from the Russian Orthodox Church for his writings. George Bernard Shaw and H. G. Wells advocated socialist ideals and pointed the way to a new, more equitable society. Joseph Conrad published his fourth novel, *Lord Jim,* in 1900, and Henri Bergson brought out *Le Rire* (*On Laughter*) that same year. In 1900, Anton Chekhov wrote *Uncle Vanya,* to be followed by such masterworks as *The Three Sisters* and *The Cherry Orchard.* Henrik Ibsen published the last of his plays, *When We Dead Awaken,* in 1899. Puccini's opera *Tosca* was first performed in 1900, Edward Elgar completed his oratorio, *The Dream of Gerontius,* Gustav Mahler wrote his Fourth Symphony, and Claude Debussy's *Pelléas et Mélisande,* begun in 1892, was finally performed in 1902. Henry James was bringing out a series of short, powerful novels, including *The Turn of the Screw* (1898) and *The Sacred Fount* (1901). In art, Pablo Picasso, Gustav Klimt, and Edvard Munch were asserting themselves, while the older generation of impressionists and postimpressionists including Pierre-Auguste Renoir, Claude Monet, and Henri de Toulouse-Lautrec continued to be vigorously productive. Max Planck elaborated the quantum theory in 1900, and that same year Sigmund Freud founded psychoanalysis and published *The Interpretation of Dreams.* West celebrates all these and other epoch-making achievements and brings back to life the turn of the century, which had cast off fin-de-siècle decadence and pessimism in favor of a confident, optimistic outlook on the future of the Western world.

The financial situation of the Fairfields worsened after their move to Richmond, and Charles left his family in 1901, ostensibly in order to launch a pharmaceutical factory in Sierra Leone, West Africa. This venture, like the previous ones, quickly foundered, and Charles returned to England. Instead of rejoining his family he settled alone in Liverpool, where his health steadily declined until he died in 1906, a lonely lodger in a boardinghouse. West always had some difficulty dealing with her father's estrangement and feckless conduct, probably because as a child she had experienced it as a painfully shameful but unacknowledged rejection. In her personal and autobiographical writings she always tried to put the best light on her father's behavior and last years. In *Family Memories* she notes "the disinclination of human beings to record their humiliations in full" (p. 53). This is of course not always the case, as Rousseau's autobiographical *Confessions* and their unabashed revelations amply attest. While truthfulness was West's goal in her autobiographical writings, she remained wary of the compulsion to tell all in the name of absolute veracity. Her concept of autobiography, unlike that of a Saint Augustine or a Rousseau, was that a personal memoir need not be confessional or even strictly factual. Furthermore, as a woman with a controversial reputation and her share of critics, she was probably disinclined to feed the public's morbid curiosity for sensational revelations. Besides, an attempt at total self-revelation can easily turn into a narcissistic form of self-indulgence. Since objective truth is unattainable in any case, for human experience is too mysterious, complex, and contradictory to be contained and compressed in a narrative, West, like all writers with a strong autobiographical impulse, rewrote the story of her life repeatedly and in various guises. Her own strategy as an autobiographer would freely combine revelation, reticence, and fictionalization.

It is therefore not too surprising that in *St. Augustine* (1933), West paid tribute to his *Confessions* as a work of unsurpassed literary achievement rather than as one of total truthfulness:

He is one of the greatest of all writers, and he works in the same introspective field as the moderns. In his short, violent sentences, which constantly break out in the rudest tricks of the rhetoricians, rhymes, puns, and assonances, he tries to do exactly what Proust tries to do in his long, reflective sentences. . . . Not only is the experience itself depicted with the clear colour and right form of master-painting, but a vast area of his temperament round the point of impact with this experience is illuminated also.

(quoted in *Rebecca West: A Celebration*, pp. 165–166)

Rebecca West maintained that "we must not take the *Confessions* as altogether faithful to reality.

It is too subjectively true to be objectively true" (p. 166). Besides, she was convinced that the *Confessions* "are not without gaps, understatements, and mis-statements" (p. 166).

At any rate, the painful story and tragic outcome of her parents' relationship left West with strongly ambivalent feelings toward marriage and men and a fierce desire to protect her independence and integrity as a woman. After Charles's departure for West Africa, the nearly destitute Isabella, who had fallen ill with hyperthyroidism, went back to Edinburgh with her daughters. Cissie had trouble adapting to her new surroundings and her generally dour Scottish relatives. Despite a bout with tuberculosis and having to care for her ailing mother, she finished her schooling with distinction on a scholarship at George Watson's Ladies' College. In 1908 she happily left Edinburgh and returned to London with her mother, whose health had improved considerably.

After seeing some of the most famous actresses of the time on stage, notably Sarah Bernhardt, Mrs. Patrick Campbell, and Ellen Terry, West developed an intense interest in the theater. A career on the stage soon proved irresistible; in April 1910 she auditioned and was accepted in the Academy of Dramatic Art. She was then seventeen years of age, a handsome, dark-haired young woman with a lively personality and a fiercely probing intelligence. Cicely attended the Academy of Dramatic Art for only one year, during which she quickly came to the realization that a career on the stage was not, after all, for her. She had in the meantime become attracted to writing and journalism, and in 1911 she decided to leave the theater and join the staff of the feminist journal *The Freewoman*. Her unconventional and insecure childhood, despite its veneer of genteel respectability, had imbued her with a passionate and lifelong sense of justice.

West's political involvement started early, when she was still a teenage student in Edinburgh. She began taking part in the movement for women's rights by distributing pamphlets and wearing a badge, to the consternation of some of her elders. Whereas her father had always been a conservative and antisocialist, she became not only a socialist, but a militant suffragist as well, for she eagerly identified with the feminist cause and considered exclusive male suffrage an intolerable inequity and an affront to women as well as to humanity.

H. G. WELLS AND HENRY MAXWELL ANDREWS

In September 1911, West reviewed H. G. Wells's latest novel, *Marriage,* in *The Freewoman.* Wells was a subscriber and occasional contributor to the journal, and West's provocative and critical review piqued his curiosity about the author. He therefore gallantly responded by inviting her to lunch at his country home, Little Easton Rectory, in Essex, where he was living with his second wife and their two sons. Wells was then in his mid-forties and a famous if controversial author who was also notorious for his tangled love life and marital infidelities, of which his wife, by mutual agreement, took no overt notice. Not surprisingly, he was immediately attracted by West's combination of youthful good looks and intellectual brilliance. She, for her part, was powerfully drawn to the older man, and they met again at his London house in Hampstead, seeing each other afterward often and with increasing intimacy. West was not yet twenty but determined to live according to her feminist principles and to disregard the Victorian rules of proper conduct still prevalent in Edwardian England. She strongly felt that sexual freedom would be part of her emancipation as a free, independent woman. The disastrous marriage of her parents also must have played a significant part in her rejection of accepted rules of social conduct, and at the age of eighteen she had already written scathingly against the institution of matrimony.

In June 1913, Wells, probably reconsidering the consequences of an amorous involvement with a woman half his age, decided to break off their relationship. West's emotions were thrown into a turmoil: she was devastated, infuriated, and even contemplated suicide. Men, she felt, were indeed a sorry lot, and her feminism was once more aroused. She finally found solace in her articles for *The New Freewoman* and the *Clarion* and in other writings, notably travel accounts of trips recently undertaken (including a one-month stay in Spain), to find relief and distraction from her anger and depression.

Before long, Wells, who had been reading her latest articles and had been greatly impressed by them, invited West to his new London flat, on St. James's Court. In the meantime, Rebecca had grown emotionally stronger and more self-reliant, so that when Wells resumed courting her she at first resisted his advances and offers of friendship and professional advice. Soon, however, they became lovers, and on 4 August 1914, a date that coincided with the outbreak of World War I, West gave birth to a son, Anthony West.

The dramatic circumstances of the birth of her illegitimate son are recounted by Gordon Ray in *H. G. Wells and Rebecca West* (1974): "This was motherhood with a difference. When the mists of chloroform cleared away and they held out her squealing son, she looked at him, not with the passive contentment of the mother at peace-time, but with the active and passionate intention: 'I must keep this thing safe'" (p. 54).

West tried her best to keep up with her professional career after the birth of her son, despite the additional strains on her time and energies and the continuing ups and downs of her stormy relationship with Wells. Repeated quarrels eventually resulted in a final break. On 1 November 1930, West married Henry Maxwell Andrews, whom she had met in 1928. In *Family Memories* she asserts that her marriage to Andrews "was certainly the most important thing in my life, though I never understood why it had that primacy" (p. 223). Perhaps the main reason for this assessment was that the marriage, based on the solid foundation of deep affection and mutual respect and understanding, provided her with the kind of emotional stability she had never known, either throughout her stressful childhood and early adolescence or during her trying years with Wells. Marrying Andrews may indeed have been a compromise on her part, but it turned out to be a happy one. They eventually settled in a large, comfortable country house, Ibstone, in Buckinghamshire, with fairly long stays in London, and made several journeys together, including the trip to Yugoslavia that would be the source of inspiration for *Black Lamb and Grey Falcon* (1941).

A departmental head at Schroders, the merchant bank, Andrews was courtly in manners and of a stable, even-tempered disposition. Two years younger than his wife, he had been born in 1894, in Rangoon, Burma. In *Family Memories*—written some time after his death in 1968, when she came upon a package of letters and documents—West gives a detailed and loving account of her husband's background and early life. We learn that his ancestry was far from that of the typical Englishman, whom he seemed to incarnate in his staid personality.

Andrews had in common with West broad intellectual and cultural interests. Further, his middle-European origins, familiarity with languages and cultures other than British, as well as a painful internment in Germany during World War I, had sensitized him to the meaning of injustice, estrangement, ostracism, and marginalization. This awareness was probably at the root of the generous efforts both he and West would later make on behalf of Jews and other victims of fascism.

THE JOURNALIST AND ESSAYIST

REBECCA West signed her first articles for *The Freewoman* with her real name, Cicely Fairfield. (Her name was often misspelled as "Cicily.") Among the parts she had been called upon to act at the Academy of Dramatic Art, that of Rebecca West, the tragic character in Ibsen's feminist drama *Rosmersholm*, struck her as an apt choice for her pseudonym. To be sure, the heroine in the Ibsen play turns out to be a rather melodramatic character, the mistress of a married man who ends up committing a double suicide with him by drowning. Yet Ibsen's Rebecca West embodies the rebellion of a woman against the stifling restrictions imposed upon her by society, a rebellion with which Cicely Fairfield wholeheartedly identified. The rejection of the all-too-proper name of Cicely Fairfield in favor of that of a heroine who symbolized a radical rejection of convention also signified that she was ready to create her own identity and construct a persona entirely of her own making. As a militantly emancipated young woman with literary ambitions, she was probably also concerned that keeping her real name would risk involving or embarrassing her family.

Unlike such other famous women writers as Madame de La Fayette, Madame de Sévigné, Madame de Staël, Jane Austen, Willa Cather, or Virginia Woolf, who did not change their names, or George Sand and George Eliot, who opted for masculine pen names, Cicely Fairfield chose a name clearly emblematic of her feminist concerns and determination to escape from her caste. As a woman born into a class with social and educational advantages (despite her family's near-poverty), she nevertheless felt a strong kinship with the countless members of her sex who could not claim any special distinction of birth, rank, or achievement. Yet she most strongly identified with the exceptional woman who is marked for unhappiness in a society hostile to individuals of superior talent or nonconformist ideas. It is, therefore, somewhat disconcerting that in his introduction to *Rebecca West: A Celebration* (1977), Samuel Hynes should state: "One must feel some discomfort in the fact that an appreciation of so considerable a talent as Dame Rebecca's should start, inevitably, with the problems arising from her sex" (p. x). An appreciation of West's talent is hardly diminished by an awareness of the daunting obstacles she had to overcome as a woman striving to achieve her full creative potential at a time when such aspirations met with open hostility or, at best, with condescending indifference.

The first review signed "Rebecca West" appeared in *The Freewoman* in February 1912. In her articles for *The Freewoman* and its successor, *The New Freewoman*, journals devoted to the cause of socialism and feminism, she combined fiery advocacy for women's rights with strong literary interests, deep political and social commitment, and equally intense involvement in the arts, thereby setting a pattern from which she would never swerve. Ideological and aesthetic concerns would always commingle in her writings, but at the same time she remained keenly aware that the overt hostility shown toward art by such figures as Saint Augustine and Tolstoy (and she might have added Rousseau) not only resulted from excessively ideological, religious, and moralistic preoccupations, but had deeper roots, as she noted in her essay on Saint Augustine, included in *Rebecca West: A Celebration*:

Art is bound to come under the censorship of our sense of guilt, which suspects all our activities if they are not part of processes that we hope will redeem us from our stains, not by giving pleasure but by withholding it; and it is bound to incur the disapproval of the death-wish we all have in varying degrees, since by analysing experience it makes us able to handle experience and increase our hold on life. But Augustine's hostility to art was given a special vigour, because it proceeded not only from these causes but from the political situation which had such a dynamic effect on him.

(p. 177)

Among the articles Rebecca West wrote for *The New Freewoman* was an impassioned tribute to Emily Wilding Davison, martyr to the suffragist cause. Davison was a B.A. of London University and had taken first-class honors at Oxford in English language and literature. The suffragist cause appealed to her so powerfully, however, that she set aside all other interests in order to become a suffragette. Repeatedly imprisoned, she went on many hunger strikes and, according to West's eulogy, was forcefed forty-nine times. This barbarous treatment had been made possible by what has become known as the Cat and Mouse Act of April 1913, a measure adopted by a Liberal government that heeded the home secretary's argument that the alternative to forcible feeding was to let the prisoners die of starvation. On one occasion, when Davison barricaded herself in the cell against the prison doctors, a hose was turned on her from the window, nearly drowning her. After these experiences, she became convinced that the best way to arouse the conscience of the public was through the sacrifice of a human life.

Davison tried to kill herself by throwing herself from one of the upper galleries in prison, but only managed to sustain serious injuries. In June 1913 she finally succeeded by rushing onto the Derby course at Ascot and snatching the bridle of Anmer, the king's horse, falling under its hooves and causing both the horse and its jockey, named Jones, to spill in full view of the horrified king and queen and a great multitude of onlookers. A famous photograph caught the dramatic moment after Anmer's fall, with Davison on the ground. Her skull was fractured, and she died on 8 June, without regaining consciousness. A massive solemn funeral procession, organized in her honor, has also been recorded by a contemporary photograph, which shows the densely lined streets and the suffragettes walking beside and behind the horse-drawn carriage bearing the coffin of the martyred heroine.

While writing for *The Freewoman* and *The New Freewoman*, West became a member of a new circle of friends, joined the Fabian Women's Group, and met George Bernard Shaw, whom she at first admired for his dazzling wit and masterful command of language, his eloquence as a speaker on behalf of socialism, as well as for his exceptionally lean, athletic bearing, so unlike that of most men of his class and time, whose portly corpulence bespoke overabundant meals and little physical activity (she photographed Shaw in bathing trunks at a Fabian summer school). Later on, however, she would express reservations about the way in which he put his great mind and brilliant style in service of "reactionary ideas" and about his am-

bivalent, manipulative relationship with the opposite sex.

Gradually, West, who had passionately espoused the cause of the women's rights movement since her early teenage years, began to distance herself somewhat from the Pankhursts and their Women's Social and Political Union (founded in 1903 by Emmeline Pankhurst, who had been disappointed by what she considered as the indifference to women's suffrage by the Fabian Society and the Liberal party), because of their dogmatic single-mindedness and increasing reliance on spectacular and even violent means and acts of terrorism. The passage of partial women's suffrage in 1917 also made the movement less urgently relevant. West would nevertheless always remain a fervent feminist. She fully appreciated the significance of Pankhurst's historical role, but she felt that great social changes do not happen overnight and cannot be forced through acts of vandalism and terrorism.

West also contributed articles to other feminist and socialist journals, notably the *Clarion*, articles in which she denounced politicians for their indifference to the cause of women and defended the trade unions by using satire and humor as potent weapons of attack against social injustice. Throughout her long, productive career, West would continue to write steadily for British and American journals. Her numerous reviews, articles, and book-length essays on politics, literary criticism, history, biography, travel, crime reportage, and coverage of treason as well as war trials are still highly readable today and attest to her indefatigable energy, astonishing range of interests, and sharpness of observation. Not least among her qualities is her exceptionally lively style, her terse, vivid descriptions, made even more striking with visual metaphors and similes, with sprightly dialogues, sketches, and narratives, frequently peppered with satirical barbs. Her essays, articles, and reviews demonstrate a unique ability to mingle the mundane, personal, everyday yet telling and revealing detail, anecdote, or story with broader historical, political, or moral considerations.

Early in her professional career, West acquired a deserved reputation as a daringly personal and independent-minded reviewer and essayist with forceful opinions and a strong moral stance. Not only did she consistently have something original and important to say about the books she was evaluating, she also soon demonstrated her exceptional skills as a prose stylist. From the outset, her range of subjects was awesome, from Saint Augustine to D. H. Lawrence (she was among the first to acknowledge Lawrence's genius). Her strong convictions and forceful rhetoric were especially effective in advocacy for controversial or misunderstood authors, an in the case of Lawrence. When he died in 1930, she paid him an eloquent tribute in an obituary essay that praised him for managing "to keep free from the shackles of civilization and the cant of literary cliques" (*D. H. Lawrence*, 1930, p. 43), for laying sex "before the consciousness of the world" (p. 40), and for an "apocalyptic vision of mankind that he registered again and again and again, always rising to a pitch of ecstatic agony" (p. 24). Turning combative, she rebuked and ridiculed the many unfair and untrue things that uncomprehending critics had said about both Lawrence the man and Lawrence the writer.

Her admiring, book-length study of Henry James in 1916 was her first literary monograph. It came out the year of the author's death, and by then his reputation was on the wane, as H. G. Wells's scathing attack in *Boon* shows. Defying adverse current opinion, West carefully probed each of the great novels. Hoping in *Henry James* to bring about a rediscovery and renewed appreciation of the master's innovations, narrative techniques, psychological subtleties, and distinctive, convoluted prose style, she had to admit that, in the final analysis, criticism is powerless to explain genius:

One pauses, horrified to find oneself ticking off these masterpieces on one's fingers, as though they were so many books by Mrs Humphry Ward or buns by Lyons. And yet what can one do? Criticism must break down when it comes to masterpieces. For if one is creative one wants to go away and spend oneself utterly on this sacred business of creation, wring out of oneself every drop of this inestimable thing art; and if one is not creative one can only put out a tremulous finger to touch the marvellous shining crystal, and be silent with wonder.

(pp. 98–99)

Despite the imposing body of highly sophisticated James criticism that has appeared since West's youthful essay, it retains its highly appealing qualities of freshness, fervor, and readability. When she embarked on a career as a novelist in her own right, Rebecca West would not forget the lessons learned from both D. H. Lawrence and Henry James, especially their total dedication to their mission as artists endowed with a unique vision of the world.

West wrote on a number of other literary figures. Her comments on such authors as James Joyce, Marcel Proust, Leo Tolstoy, Franz Kafka, and Charlotte Brontë remain remarkably apposite and timely, and her vigorous, frequently epigrammatic style plays a large part in the enduring appeal of her essays. As a fervent feminist she also paid special attention to women writers, notably Madame de La Fayette, Madame de Sévigné, Jane Austen, Colette, Willa Cather, and of course, Virginia Woolf and *A Room of One's Own*. She especially appreciated those women who attempted to steer clear of the values imposed by a society dominated by men and who, in their own works, dealt with those themes most familiar to them and closest to their own experience as women. This interest, genuine and serious though it was, may be considered insufficient by today's standards of feminism, since it remained somewhat peripheral to the central importance she accorded male authors. Neither did she attempt to elaborate a feminist theory or to probe the social and cultural reasons women have historically been impeded from achieving their creative potential.

To be sure, West would not be human if her judgments were invariably on the mark. She was too passionate and engaged to be coolly even-handed and objectively detached. For instance, one would wish that she had shown a fuller and more sympathetic understanding of Joyce, whose greatness she readily acknowledged but about whose radical literary techniques she at first had some serious reservations. She also initially recoiled before Joyce's use of obscenities and vulgarities in his fiction. She nevertheless staunchly defended him against his detractors, for she considered him a true, if raw, genius. When in 1933 the publication of *Ulysses* was banned for obscenity in America, her comments were quoted by the defense. Gradually, however, she came to admire Joyce more wholeheartedly, but never with the kind of special reverence she had for Proust, whom she regarded from the outset as a transcendent genius.

It is, of course, to be expected that the judgments of a critic are not always borne out by the test of time, but West's evaluations, even when we disagree with them, have lost little of their pungency. Her literary criticism rests on a generous capacity for empathy and admiration. An underlying theme that never changed over the decades was her unshakable belief that art cannot be divorced from ethics, that even a genius bears obligations to society and humanity. Transcendent masterpieces have in common that they convey an important spiritual message beyond their purely formal qualities. Art, in her view, occupies a vital part of life, and any society must nurture art for its own survival.

In 1928, West published *The Strange Necessity,* and in 1931 *Ending in Earnest.* Both books consist of previously published essays of literary criticism. *The Strange Necessity* comprises one long essay on Constant, Joyce, and Proust that had appeared in *The Bookman,* and shorter essays on such American writers as Theodore Dreiser, Ernest Hemingway, Sinclair Lewis, Sherwood Anderson, Edith Wharton, and Willa Cather, all previously published in the *New York Herald Tribune* and the *New Statesman. Ending in Earnest* is a collection of essays written for *The Bookman.* Even though time has not always ratified her opinions of individual writers, the essays republished in the two books are more than occasional pieces and have, for the most part, not become outdated because they deal not only with the authors at hand but also with more general issues regarding the respective and sometimes opposing concerns of art and science, the function of art in society, the relation of the artist to his culture and tradition, and the conditions of creativity.

The Court and the Castle, published in 1957, is a thoughtful and mature work of literary criticism spanning three centuries and ranging from Shakespeare's *Hamlet* to Kafka's *The Castle.* It focuses on the uneasy relation of the artist, and specifically the writer, to political power, as well as on the causes of the rise of the novel as the dominant genre, with stern caveats about the mediocrity, vulgarity, facility, and commercialism that lurk in so much modern fiction writing.

Rebecca West also wrote extensively on political topics and covered some of the great war-crime trials of her time. The unfolding twentieth century, which had begun on such a hopeful note, at least for the English and Western European middle and upper classes, tended to confirm Rebecca West in her pessimistic belief, probably also reinforced by her study of Saint Augustine, that there lurks in human nature a dark, irrational, self-destructive streak. That she wrote about some of the bloodiest events of her time, as her post–World War II trial books attest, could only heighten her awareness of the evils of modern Western civilization.

Indeed, some of Rebecca West's essays are astoundingly prophetic, as is especially the case of *Black Lamb and Grey Falcon* (1941). This highly personal, thoughtful travel account, interspersed with many historical segments, of two journeys undertaken to the Balkans and Yugoslavia in 1936 and 1937, was a result of an invitation to give a series of lectures under the aegis of the British Council. Her second trip, in 1937, had been undertaken at her own insistence; she believed that learning more about this part of Europe, with its long, painful history and tortuous relationships between different ethnic groups and the Roman Catholics, the Orthodox Church, and the Muslims, was vital for a better understanding of what was currently happening in the world.

Considered by many as West's masterwork, *Black Lamb and Grey Falcon* is a magnificently rich and wise book, replete with fascinating vignettes, sprightly dialogues, and thumbnail sketches, as well as thoughtful historical and political meditations on the dark sources of long-existing ethnic and religious quarrels, and of the explosive politics of festering old resentments, hatreds, and prejudices. Resorting to the travelogue, a literary genre that became popular at the end of the eighteenth century and that has endured throughout the nineteenth and twentieth centuries, West vividly relates her journeys through picturesque towns and landscapes and her encounters and conversations with the locals. She has a painter's eye and knows how to depict a scene in striking and colorful detail, but it is the human element rather than the setting, no matter how spectacular, that constantly solicits her sharp powers of observation.

At the same time, West expands the travel genre to include not only the usual personal impressions, observations, and anecdotes, but also more general considerations and reflections of a historical, political, and ethical nature. Her method often consists of starting with an apparently minor episode, which she recounts with typical gusto and alacrity, and then enlarging it into a broader meditation. Age-old rites, ceremonies, and customs hold a special fascination for her, both for their exotic appeal and for what they may reveal of a people's beliefs, aspirations, and fears. Even when a ritual involves the sacrifice of animals, as was the case when she came upon a Gypsy camp, she manages to overcome her revulsion at the sickening spectacle of blood spurting from the slaughtered lambs in order to observe the entire ceremony and learn about its meaning and why people "had done it for a very long time, for hundreds of years" (in *Rebecca West: A Celebration*, p. 689). She also draws the conclusion that the Muslim women putting out their arms to embrace a blood-soaked rock and bending down their heads to kiss it "made a gesture of the same nature, though not so absolute, as that which men and women make when they bend down to kiss the cloth which lies instead of Christ on the holy table at Easter" (p. 690).

In the course of her two trips to Yugoslavia, West, who by her own admission knew next to nothing about this far-off land, fell under its spell and became totally absorbed by its beauty, its people, and especially its tragic history, which she looked upon as a microcosm of Europe's. Indeed, she came to the realization that the course of European history, and even of her own life, had directly been affected by the events in Yugoslavia and the Balkans. Reading this work more than half a century after its publication, and with the benefit of hindsight, it is clear that she not only foresaw the imminent outbreak of World War II but also the ongoing civil war between the Muslims, Croats, and Bosnian Serbs.

The unforgiving hatreds dividing the different ethnic and religious groups were forcefully and repeatedly impressed upon her during her travels, and she shares these insights with her reader not only through erudite historical disquisitions, but also through specific and revealing anecdotes and incidents. The successive assassinations that had such disastrous repercussions on the course of European history, notably that of Archduke Franz Ferdinand and his wife in Sarajevo on 28 June 1914, which was the immediate cause of World War I, and that of the assassination in Marseilles of King Alexander I of Yugoslavia in 1934, also play a large part in the book. "My life," muses Rebecca West in the prologue of *Black Lamb and Grey Falcon*, "had been punctuated by the slaughter of royalties, by the shouting of newsboys who have run down the streets to tell me that someone has used a lethal weapon to turn over a new leaf in the book of history" (in *Rebecca West: A Celebration*, p. 552). It is through these concrete touches

that Rebecca West succeeds in personalizing and vivifying history.

In the epilogue that she added in 1941 to *Black Lamb and Grey Falcon*, she was in an understandably somber frame of mind. By then not only Yugoslavia but the whole of continental Europe had been overrun by Nazi Germany, and England was directly threatened. No wonder, therefore, that she would draw gloomy conclusions from her travels and observations; her view of human nature is perhaps especially predictable from a woman who had steeped herself in Saint Augustine:

Only part of us is sane: only part of us loves pleasure and the longer day of happiness, wants to live to our nineties and die in peace, in a house that we built, that shall shelter those who come after us. The other half is nearly mad. It prefers the disagreeable to the agreeable, loves pain and its darker night despair, and wants to die in a catastrophe that will set back life to its beginnings and leave nothing of our house save its blackened foundations.

(*Rebecca West: A Celebration*, p. 749)

The horrors of World War II, postwar hardships, and the ensuing Cold War absorbed West's talent and energies. In 1946 she attended the Nuremberg trial of Nazi war criminals and wrote a series of articles, reissued in *A Train of Powder* (1955). These remarkable and profound essays, which also offer a striking picture of postwar Germany and of such devastated cities as Berlin, eloquently and specifically deal with the problem of evil in terms of existing laws and of the means by which they can encompass an international recognition and condemnation of the Nazi crimes against humanity. And once more, her keen eye for the visual component and her mordant sense of humor served her well. This, for instance, is how she presents the Nazi war criminals at the Nuremberg trial:

The people in court who wanted the tedium to endure eternally were the twenty-one defendants in the dock, who disconcerted the spectator by presenting the blatant appearance that historical characters, particularly in distress, assume in bad pictures. They looked what they were as crudely as Mary Queen of Scots at Fotheringay or Napoleon on St Helena in a mid-Victorian Academy success. But it was, of course, an unusually ghastly picture. They were wreathed in suggestions of death.

(pp. 3–4)

Individualized portraits of such infamous and notorious figures as Rudolf Hess, Hjalmar Schacht, Julius Streicher, and Hermann Göring catch each of them in a revealing pose of repressed rage, feigned indifference, belligerent arrogance, or overwhelming stupor. Once more, West excels at commingling the concrete and the general, the specific and the broadly historical. In general, however, she has a difficult time being fairminded toward the Germans, although she tends to show greater sympathy for the Berliners.

The political, legal, and moral drama of the courtroom deeply stirred West, and she doggedly pursued her reportage of Nazi as well as Communist traitors and defectors. The resulting essays, which first appeared in American magazines, the *New Yorker* and *Harper's,* were collected in book form under the title of *The Meaning of Treason,* published in 1947 and reissued as *The New Meaning of Treason* in a revised and expanded edition in 1964. The nearly twenty-year time span between both editions enabled Rebecca West to cover a broad range of spies, from World War II Nazis to Cold War Communists.

The first, largest, and most engrossing section of the book, ironically titled "The Revolutionary," dwells on the complex and at times contradictory motives of one particular traitor and defector to Germany, William Joyce. Born in the United States of poor Irish parents, he was in awe of the English aristocracy and, once in Ireland, even sympathized with the British against the Sinn Fein nationalists. Intellectually gifted, but domineering and morally flawed, he was frustrated in his ambition for a military career and denied the opportunity for rank and position. He thereupon turned to the Fascists, by whom he felt appreciated. He also discovered that he could arouse the crowds not by his physical presence, which was unimpressive, but by his powerful, charismatic voice. When he defected to Germany, he offered his services to the Nazi propaganda machine as a radio broadcaster. After the war, he was caught, tried in 1946, and sentenced to death by hanging.

In many ways, the mentality that produced the Fascist spy also characterized the Communist infiltrator and secret agent of the Cold War period, although the latter had to possess far greater sophistication and scientific or technical knowledge than a crude demagogue like William Joyce. In dealing with the scientists and others who spied for Russia, and in reviewing some famous English and American cases, West shows keen insight into their motivations as well as into the reasons why postwar Western society fostered this new breed of intellectual, highly educated agent. Of course, spying thrives in a democratic, open society, and West fully appreciated and supported laws that protect the rights even of traitors. She also strongly felt that even when national security is at stake, vigilance must be exercised in order to protect those precious and hard-won freedoms of speech and expression without which democracy cannot survive.

Summing up her investigations at the end of *The Meaning of Treason,* Rebecca West has some sobering thoughts on what prompts some individuals to betray their country, and reminds us in passing that there is "a drop or two of treason" in all of us. Her concluding remarks make clear that, despite all the glamorous romanticizing in novels and films, the lot of the professional spy is indeed an unhappy one:

All the men described in this book were sad as they stood their trials, not only because they were going to be punished. They would have been sad even if they had never been brought to justice. They had forsaken the familiar medium; they had trusted themselves to the mercies of those who had no reason to care for them; knowing their custodians' indifference, they had lived for long in fear; and they were aware that they had thrown away their claim on those who might naturally have felt affection for them. Strangers, as King Solomon put it, were filled with their wealth, and their labours were in the house of a stranger, and they mourned at the last when their flesh and body were consumed.

(pp. 306–307)

THE NOVELIST

WRITING fiction was among Rebecca West's major interests, although one cannot consider her primarily as a novelist. Her first novel, *The Return of the Soldier,* serialized in the *Century,* was published in 1918, and she pursued her novelistic endeavors, albeit at uneven intervals, well into her seventies, when she brought out her last work of fiction, *The Birds Fall Down,* in 1966. Between these two dates she produced six novels and a volume of four short stories. While her novels and short stories were well received and widely read, and some have been reprinted in paperback, they did not gain the kind of special recognition and admiration earned by such noteworthy books of political reportage as *Black Lamb and Grey Falcon* and *The Meaning of Treason.*

The Return of the Soldier is a relatively short war novel with feminist overtones. Its publication in 1918 coincided with English women finally winning their suffrage. Two years earlier, in 1916, West had published her first book, her monograph on Henry James, and the Jamesian influence is unmistakable in the narrative techniques and general tone of this first novel. The story is set in a large, comfortable English country home, in 1916. The main character is a wounded soldier, Chris Baldry, who has returned to his estate to recuperate. He is shell-shocked and suffering from amnesia, a fifteen-year lapse in his memory. He is therefore totally oblivious of his wife and can only remember and love Margaret, a sweetheart of his youth, although by now she is a middle-aged married woman living in needy circumstances and marked by years of care and worry. She turns out to be far more admirable and generous than Chris's elegant, very proper but egotistical wife, Kitty.

The novel's interest lies in the way West has treated the war theme and introduced amnesia as the catalyst for a contrasting study of two types of women and for the depiction of the conflict in the soldier's psyche that pulls him in opposing directions: an idealistic love that defies social conventions, and the necessity to resume the obligations imposed by his class and to return to active military duty. Rather than dealing with the war directly, West has preferred the more subtle approach of showing its impact on individual lives. The story is related by Jenny, a cousin of Chris, who is a sympathetic but generally uninvolved observer, and it is enriched with aphoristic observations on the nature of love, on social mores, and on good and evil. The novel is also noteworthy as one of the first in which the Freudian influence is apparent through the theme of a soldier's psychological and emotional conflict, the resolution of which is contingent upon the cure of his amnesia. The book enjoyed considerable success and was adapted for the stage. (Henry Andrews, a fan of West even before meeting her, had seen the play several times by the time they were introduced to each other.)

The Judge, West's second novel, appeared in 1922. Longer than *The Return of the Soldier,* it is also Jamesian in its thematics and narrative techniques, and it stresses the psychological impact of events on individuals by shifting points of view and relating an occurrence as perceived by different characters. Bright dialogues alternate with narrative sequences and evocative descriptions. It focuses on two women, a young one, seventeen-year-old Ellen Melville, who works as a legal secretary and lives with her widowed mother in Edinburgh, and an older one, Marion Yaverland, who lives on her family farm, the mother of two sons, one illegitimate, Richard Yaverland. The title is explained in a suggestive epigraph: "Every mother is a judge who sentences the children for the sins of the father."

The novel is divided into two parts. The first part, which takes place in Edinburgh, depicts the maturing of headstrong Ellen into womanhood through her sexual relationship with the handsome and impulsive Richard, as well as her discovery of loss and sorrow through the death of her mother. The second part takes place in Essex, where the focus switches to the story of Marion Yaverland, Richard's mother, her pregnancy by a local squire, her unhappy marriage of convenience with the squire's butler, the birth of a second son, the dim-witted Roger, who becomes a fanatical evangelist, and her eventual suicide. The hatred between the two half brothers results in Richard's murder of Roger and, after a brief happy interlude with Ellen, his voluntary surrender to the police. Richard will probably pay for his crime with his life. He leaves behind a pregnant, forlorn, but wiser Ellen, who has learned the hard lesson that a woman's fate is determined by man's deceptions, mistakes, and weaknesses and that "though life at its beginning was lovely as a corn of wheat, it was ground down to flour that must make bitter bread between two human tendencies: the insane sexual caprice of men, the not less mad excessive steadfastness of women" (p. 490). *The Judge* has been widely praised as one of West's best novels, and it exemplifies, with impressive results, her superior gifts both as a literary artist and as polemicist.

After an interval of seven years, Rebecca West published her next novel, *Harriet Hume: A London Fantasy,* in 1929. *Harriet Hume* is an experiment in fantasy, as the subtitle indicates. Although departing from the fairly realistic settings of *The Return* of the Soldier and *The Judge*, it nevertheless deals with similar themes and concerns, mainly the tortuous relationship between men and women because of their opposing impulses and natures. The two main protagonists are lovers, Harriet Hume, a musician, and Arnold Condorex, a man with political ambitions who opts for a marriage that will advance his career. As an artist, Harriet is a free, generous spirit endowed with a superior gift of intuition that transcends rational thought. She even possesses the uncanny ability of reading the thoughts of those she loves. Arnold is of course her opposite, insecure and calculating, but hard experience will teach him the emptiness of success and wealth, and he will be driven back to Harriet, having realized too late that he has "been infected with the desire to rise in the world," and that he has sold his soul to "the abominable principle of negotiation" (p. 270). As a whole, however, *Harriet Hume*, probably because of its self-conscious mixture of realism and fantasy, is novelistically less successful and convincing than *The Return of the Soldier* and *The Judge*.

The Harsh Voice, published in 1935, brings together four short stories. Three had previously appeared in American magazines, "Life Sentence" and "There Is No Conversation" in the *Saturday Evening Post* and "The Salt of the Earth" in *Woman's Home Companion*. The fourth, "The Abiding Vision," was a previously unpublished novella. In 1923, West had gone to the United States on a lecture tour, and thereafter she would regularly contribute to American newspapers and magazines. Unlike her previous fictional work, which was entirely English in setting and tone, the stories in *The Harsh Voice* take place in America, and reflect her broadening experience and growing familiarity with places and people outside England.

The Harsh Voice conveys once more West's essentially dualistic outlook: good versus evil, love pitted against hate, and of course the uneasy relations between men and women. "Life Sentence" deals with a failed marriage between an American woman with entrepreneurial ambitions and her hapless mate. "There Is No Conversation" also features a shrewd American businesswoman who becomes estranged from her husband because of her overweening need to increase her wealth. "The Salt of the Earth" is a kind of American murder mystery, for its main protagonist is an insufferable meddler and fanatic of domestic or-

derliness who is slowly being poisoned by her long-suffering husband. "The Abiding Vision," the last of the four novellas, is the story of a man enthralled by the American myth of success who will eventually lose almost everything in his frantic quest for financial security. One must remember that these stark stories reflect West's acute observations of American society at a time when the dramatic economic collapse and ensuing years of depression seemed to have spelled the doom of unfettered capitalism and unrestrained individualistic enterprise.

The Thinking Reed, published in 1936 and dedicated to Henry Maxwell Andrews, is a satirical novel of upper-class manners just prior to the 1929 Wall Street crash, and features as its main protagonist the young, beautiful, and wealthy widow Isabelle Tarry, an expatriate American from St. Louis, Missouri, of French aristocratic descent, who is making the most of the high life in the most fashionable circles in France. Despite her obvious advantages, she is something of an outsider among the self-indulgent and wealthy aristocrats with whom she associates. In her private life, Isabelle remains emotionally unhappy and unfulfilled, even though she has admirers and a lover, the aristocratic, personable, but tyrannical and quarrelsome André de Verviers. She is also courted by Laurence Vernon, a proper Virginian, whom she almost marries. Eventually, out of pique rather than passion, she agrees to marry Marc Sallafranque, a successful, self-made Jewish automobile manufacturer who is not part of the idle, hard-drinking international set. This unlikely match turns out to be happier than Isabelle had expected, but she almost wrecks it by making a public scene when she finds Marc indulging his gambling compulsion in a Riviera casino (her outburst also causes her miscarriage and nearly ruins her health). A fourth man, Alan Fielding, a painter, enters Isabelle's life during this crisis, but she eventually comes to the realization that her best chance at happiness is to return to Marc.

The Thinking Reed continues to be one of Rebecca West's most widely read novels, probably because of its evocative and impressionistic descriptions of French and Swiss locales, its ironic depiction of a heedless, pleasure-loving society about to be hard hit by the stock market crash, and its convincing portrayal of the kind of attractively sophisticated and impulsive young woman reminiscent of such Henry James heroines as Isabel Archer in *The Portrait of a Lady* and made familiar to the public by Hollywood romantic comedies of the era.

West did not return to the novel for twenty years, for as we have seen, she became absorbed by the political conflict over Yugoslavia, by World War II and its aftermath, as well as by her postwar study of war criminals and traitors, and her Cold War investigation of spies and infiltrators. In 1956 she published *The Fountain Overflows*, a fictionalized account of her childhood years dedicated to her sister Letitia and first serialized in *Ladies' Home Journal*. It is full of nostalgic and tender evocations of life in an eccentric and financially hardpressed middle-class family, at the turn of the century and up to World War I, a period of which West was especially fond. It is well-nigh impossible to separate authentic reminiscences from imaginary elaborations in this engrossing story, narrated by young Rose Aubrey, but the essential features are strikingly close to what we know of West's own early years and family. The novel resurrects, with remarkable freshness and immediacy, the whole bygone Edwardian world, the mores and manners of its men and women, as perceived by Rose, who grows into adulthood as a talented concert pianist and who learns about the possibilities and limitations of life.

Piers Aubrey, Rose's father, a charming and quick-witted Anglo-Irishman who is also an inveterate gambler and speculator in stocks, marries a Scottish pianist of great talent, Clare Keith, who sacrifices her career in order to raise their four children, Cordelia, Mary, Rose (the narrator), and Richard Quin. Clare not only manages to keep the family together, she also instills a love of art and beauty, and especially music, in her children. Rose and her sister Mary grow up to be concert pianists; Cordelia makes a conventional marriage; their brother Richard Quin, after promising beginnings, will be killed in World War I; and Clare, their beloved mother, who had been the mainstay as well as moral and artistic conscience of the family, dies an agonizingly slow and painful death shortly thereafter.

The Fountain Overflows, written when West was in her sixties, was part of a trilogy of novels in progress to which she gave the overall working title of *Cousin Rosamund: A Saga of the Century*. The two remaining volumes were published posthumously and in uncompleted form: *This Real Night*, in 1984, which appropriately ends with the dramatic scenes of Clare's death (an abridged version of the first chapter first appeared in *Rebecca West: A Celebration* in 1977), and *Cousin Rosamund*, which appeared in 1985 and concludes with the 1929 Wall Street crash. There was a projected fourth volume, never written, which was to encompass World War II and the Nuremberg trials.

Once more a recurring theme in West's works of fiction surfaces in this partly autobiographical saga, the unfathomable nature of the relations between the sexes, the steadfastness of women contrasted with the restless unreliability of men. Doubtless, her resentment over her father's quasi-abandonment of his family had a great deal to do with West's negative view of men. Yet the portrait of Piers Aubrey, Rose's father, who so closely resembles Charles Fairfield, is a loving one, and it generously acknowledges his intellectual curiosities and love of ideas. Another theme is that of gifted women's painful choice between a career devoted to art and personal fulfillment through marriage and motherhood. It is revealing that Mary gives up her career as a concert pianist, withdraws into her own private world, and plays only for her own pleasure. As for Rose, the narrator, she at long last experiences sexual fulfillment and happiness and is also on the brink of sacrificing her successful career as a concert pianist at the end of *Cousin Rosamund*, at least in its published unfinished state.

Even though West never brought to completion her ambitious tetralogy of novels, the published volumes recount a richly detailed, insightful story of a family, its intimate joys and sorrows, its financial worries, and its involvement with art, politics, and war. The unfinished saga, with its strongly delineated characters, deals with the problems of growing up in a bewildering modern world, of trying to cope with urban, materialistic society, and of discovering sexual passion and the meaning of love. The reader is also made to share the exacting but exhilarating quest for achievement in art, as experienced and related in a strikingly vivid first-person narrative from the evolving vantage point of the musically gifted Rose Aubrey as child, adolescent, and adult. The depiction of a struggling family and the coming of age of a gifted young woman are effectively set against the background of a rapidly changing society and a Europe undergoing the upheavals of wars and revolutions. If time prevented West from finishing her tetralogy and from achieving her goal of emulating Proust in chronicling a whole era, she has nevertheless left a highly engrossing and readable work of fiction that brings back to life crucial decades of English history.

The Birds Fall Down, West's last work of fiction, appeared in 1966, two years after her masterful *The New Meaning of Treason*. There is a thematic identity between the two books, since both probe, albeit in different genres, the psychological characteristics and motivations of the traitor. Here West no longer relies on her own intimate experience for the material of her novel, but rather on the painstaking research and rich observations resulting from her years as a spy-trial reporter and investigator.

In the foreword we are told that the novel is essentially founded on history, that most of the characters are portraits of real people, and that only their names have been changed. It is essentially a suspenseful and highly readable spy thriller dealing with political terrorism, treachery, and perfidy, set in pre–World War I Paris. The story is related by Laura Rowan, the young daughter of Edward Rowan, an Englishman who is a member of Parliament, and his lovely but melancholy Russian wife, Tania. Their relationship is on the breaking point, primarily owing to Rowan's infidelities. Laura's grandfather, Count Nicolai Diakonov, is an aristocratic Russian émigré who had been minister of justice but had fallen in disfavor because of his failure to forestall a string of assassinations of Russian officials. Now living in Paris, he nevertheless remains fiercely loyal to the czar who has exiled him. He has as his trusted confidant a somewhat mysterious man always referred to as Monsieur Kamensky, who in actuality turns out to be a double agent responsible for double-crossing the count and causing his disgrace in the first place.

The Judas-like character of Kamensky, adept at disguising himself and wearing many masks, was inspired by a real-life double spy, the then-notorious Yevno-Meyer Fishelevich Azef, a member of a revolutionary terrorist group bent on destroying the aristocracy and czarist regime in Russia and involved in a series of political assassinations in the first decade of the twentieth century. The revelation that Azef was a czarist agent demoralized the revolutionaries. All these events contributed to opening the way for the 1917 revolution.

West's masterful portrayal of the malevolent Kamensky, who spies for both the czarists and the terrorists, no doubt owes a great deal to the insights she gained in her exhaustively researched inquiries into the motivations and behavior of traitors and conspirators. Count Diakonov and his daughter, Tania Rowan, are convincingly drawn as representative types of the romantic, idealistic Slav. Laura, the aristocratic, initially innocent and inexperienced narrator of the novel, quickly learns how to deal with her unusual and dangerous circumstances. Fearing that her life is threatened by Kamensky, who suspects that she knows the truth about him, she deliberately becomes the instrument of his death.

The Birds Fall Down, unlike the more hopeful *The Fountain Overflows*, is a novel about the darker side of human nature, and its underlying somber message is effectively conveyed through an understated narrative technique. It is at once suspenseful and richly evocative of the era that predated World War I and the Russian Revolution. From all accounts it was her most favorably received and most widely read novel, and in 1978 it was adapted for BBC television.

CONCLUSION

OFFICIAL recognition of Rebecca West's lifelong accomplishments came in the form of many honors: she was made a chevalier of the Legion of Honor in 1957, and a Dame of the British Empire in 1959, among numerous other distinctions.

In her private life, West sustained the loss of her husband, who died on 3 November 1968. They had been married for thirty-eight years. H. G. Wells had died in 1946. Her relation with her son Anthony, who had always resented his illegitimacy, had its ups and downs. In 1929 the stigma of illegitimacy was removed when West adopted him legally and designated Wells as his guardian. Their relations somewhat improved after Anthony's marriage in 1936 to Katharine Church, an artist, but deteriorated again after his divorce.

In her seventies and even eighties Dame Rebecca continued to be as active as ever, writing articles on such current events as the Watergate scandal and on such political figures as Margaret Thatcher, working on her memoirs and novels, pursuing a far-flung correspondence, and taking copious notes. Soon after her husband's death, she sold Ibstone, their large country house, and settled in a London flat. This move enabled her to frequent theaters and concerts and participate more fully in the rich cultural and social life of the city.

In 1977, Macmillan published a hefty anthology of West's works titled *Rebecca West: A Celebration.* In 1978, Virago, a feminist press, began reissuing her books, and in 1982 a selection of her early articles and essays appeared in a volume titled *The Young Rebecca: Writings of Rebecca West, 1911–1917.* In 1981 she completed her last book, *1900,* with its nostalgic personal reminiscences and its political, cultural, and social panorama of England and Europe at the turn of the century. She was able to remain in her London flat, where visitors from near and far paid her homage, until her death, at the age of ninety, on 15 March 1983.

Dame Rebecca richly earned the official recognition and widespread admiration that came to her at the end of her long, productive life. As a young woman living in pre–World War I England, she intrepidly defied current taboos in order to fight for such causes as women's suffrage and greater social justice. She also overcame the many obstacles set in the path of women of her time in order to achieve individual independence and self-reliance as a writer. Her unconventional relationship with H. G. Wells and her full acceptance of single parenthood were long held against her. Yet, despite all odds, she succeeded in achieving personal satisfaction through a solid, stable, and long-lasting marriage.

Rebecca West's richly diverse and important body of work, comprising critical essays, journalistic reportage, novels, and short stories, testifies to an extraordinarily fertile, resourceful, and multifaceted talent. Her uniqueness resides precisely in her uncanny ability to seize upon the great issues of her time, whether they be political or aesthetic, and treat them with singular lucidity and incisiveness. A powerful stylist, she knows how to grab and hold on to the reader's attention. While such masterworks as *Black Lamb and Grey Falcon* and *The Meaning of Treason* have received their critical due, her considerable novelistic achievement deserves fuller investigation and appreciation. Her important role as an early feminist also merits greater interest and scrutiny.

Dame Rebecca's lifelong courageous and generous impulses and constant striving for social progress and improvement are interestingly at odds with an underlying Manichaean or dualistic view of human nature, which was reinforced by the unfolding of twentieth-century history, with all its attending horrors. Her passionate commitment to all forms of artistic creativity and her fervent belief that the artist has a crucial role to play in society, the boldness with which she threw herself in the early struggle of women to gain full political and social recognition and participation, the special contribution she made as an exceptionally observant and clairvoyant, and at times uncannily prophetic, witness of our tragic century and its bloody wars and cruel treacheries, entitle her to a special place among the most important and influential British writers of our time.

SELECTED BIBLIOGRAPHY

I. BIBLIOGRAPHY. Evelyn G. Hutchinson, *A Preliminary List of the Writings of Rebecca West, 1912–1951* (New Haven, Conn., 1957).

II. INDIVIDUAL WORKS. *Henry James* (London and New York, 1916); *The Return of the Soldier* (London and New York, 1918); *The Judge* (London and New York, 1922); *The Strange Necessity: Essays by Rebecca West* (London and New York, 1928); *Harriet Hume: A London Fantasy* (London and New York, 1929); *D. H. Lawrence* (London and New York, 1930); *Ending in Earnest: A Literary Log* (London and New York, 1931); *St. Augustine* (London and New York, 1933); *The Harsh Voice: Four Short Novels* (London and New York, 1935); *The Thinking Reed* (London and New York, 1936); *Black Lamb and Grey Falcon: The Record of a Journey through Yugoslavia in 1937* (London and New York, 1941); *The Meaning of Treason* (New York, 1947; London, 1949); *A Train of Powder* (London and New York, 1955); *The Fountain Overflows* (New York, 1956; London, 1957); *The Court and the Castle: Some Treatments of a Recurrent Theme* (New Haven, Conn., 1957; London, 1958); *The New Meaning of Treason* (New York, 1964; London, 1965); *The Birds Fall Down* (London and New York, 1966); *1900* (London and New York, 1982); *This Real Night* (London, 1984; New York, 1985); *Cousin Rosamund* (London, 1985; New York, 1986); *Family Memories: An Autobiographical Journey* (London, 1987), with an intro. by Faith Evans.

III. COLLECTED WORKS. *Rebecca West: A Celebration, Selected by Her Publishers with Her Help* (New York, 1977), critical introduction by Samuel Hynes; Jane Marcus, ed., *The Young Rebecca: Writings of Rebecca West, 1911–1917* (New York and Bloomington, Ind., 1982)

IV. BIOGRAPHICAL AND CRITICAL STUDIES. Peter Wolfe, *Rebecca West: Artist and Thinker* (Carbondale, Ill., 1971); Verena Elsbeth Wolfer, *Rebecca West: Kunsttheorie und Romanschaffen* (Bern, 1972); Gordon N. Ray, *H. G. Wells and Rebecca West* (New Haven, Conn., 1974); Harold Orel, *The Literary Achievement of Rebecca West* (London and New York, 1986); Victoria Glendinning, *Rebecca West: A Life* (London and New York, 1987).

P. G. WODEHOUSE

(1881–1975)

David Damrosch

PELHAM GRENVILLE WODEHOUSE—"Plum" to his many friends—wrote ninety-eight books over a period of seventy-five years, virtually inventing the modern comic novel. In his fiction he developed an extraordinarily rich and supple prose, with which he detailed the adventures of a world of eccentric characters, most notably the bumbling Bertie Wooster and his masterful valet Jeeves, and the circle of friends and relations gathered around Clarence, the potty Earl of Emsworth, at his ancestral estate of Blandings Castle. Yet during the 1920s and 1930s Wodehouse was equally prominent as a writer for the stage, and he had a major influence on the development of the Broadway musical. He collaborated on the book and lyrics for thirty-one musicals, in addition to writing seventeen staged plays, not to mention occasional verse and essays for many newspapers and magazines.

Wodehouse's phenomenal output has been viewed in widely differing ways. Immensely popular from around 1915 onward—with sales of more than fifty million volumes at last count, in more than thirty languages—Wodehouse has been cherished by many intellectuals but dismissed by others, and his work has received little critical analysis. His readers are divided between those who admire him as the creator of a perfectly unreal comic universe, existing on its own terms and by its own laws, and those who see in his books a loving—or reactionary—recreation of the vanished late-Victorian and Edwardian world of his childhood and youth. Writing on the occasion of Wodehouse's eightieth birthday, Evelyn Waugh insisted that "Mr. Wodehouse's characters are not, as has been fatuously suggested, survivals of the Edwardian age. They are creations of pure fancy. . . . the language of the Drones was never heard on human lips. It is all Mr. Wodehouse's invention, or rather inspiration. . . . His characters have never tasted the forbidden fruit. They are still in Eden.

The Gardens of Blandings Castle are that original garden from which we are all exiled" (*The Sunday Times Magazine*, 16 July 1961). Against this view, others have observed that Wodehouse always based his locations on places he personally knew and drew many characters from life; while he took care not to specify dates, many details even in his late stories recall the turn of the century. George Orwell went so far as to describe him as "fixated" on his schooldays in the 1890s, and others have followed Orwell in seeing Wodehouse as a schoolboy who, like Peter Pan, refused ever to grow up.

The contradictions in Wodehouse's life began early. He always insisted that he had enjoyed a happy childhood, including a good relationship with a father who was "normal as rice pudding," and yet he was essentially abandoned by his parents during his childhood. His father, Henry Ernest Wodehouse, was a magistrate in Hong Kong; born on 15 October 1881 in the town of Guildford in Surrey, England, P. G. Wodehouse was taken to Hong Kong in infancy, but when he was two, his mother brought him and his two older brothers back to England. She rented a house for them in Bath and engaged a nanny to look after them. She then returned to Hong Kong; Wodehouse scarcely saw his parents during the ensuing dozen years. He was shuttled about among nannies, schools, and aunts and uncles—he had no fewer than fifteen uncles and twenty aunts, by birth or marriage—and his relations with his mother, Eleanor Deane Wodehouse, remained minimal for the rest of her life.

Parents are few and far between in Wodehouse's fiction, and mothers are almost unknown; most of his heroes and heroines are dependent upon their aunts and uncles, especially their aunts, most of whom are irritable, domineering figures. As Bertie Wooster remarks in a story called "The Aunt and the Sluggard" (1916):

It's a curious thing how many of my pals seem to have aunts and uncles who are their main source of supply. . . . These things cannot be mere coincidence. They must be meant. What I'm driving at is that Providence seems to look after the chumps of this world; and, personally, I'm all for it. I suppose the fact is that, having been snootered from infancy upwards by my own aunts, I like to see that it is possible for these relatives to have a better and a softer side.

(Carry On, Jeeves, 1956 repr., p. 93)

From an early age, Wodehouse took refuge in humorous fantasy. In later life, he supposed that he had spent his earliest years "just loafing" before he began to write—at age five. His earliest surviving story, written at the age of seven, already shows a sense of art as creating an enchanted world:

About five years ago in a wood there was a Thrush, who built her nest in a Poplar tree. and sang so beautifully that all the worms came up from their holes and the ants laid down their burdens. and the crickets stopped their mirth. and moths settled all in a row to hear her. she sang a song as if she were in heaven—going up higher and higher as she sang.

at last the song was done and the bird came down panting.

Thank you said all the creatures.

Now my story is ended.

Pelham G. Wodehouse
(Donaldson, p. 46)

In this story, Wodehouse already displays a developed sense of prose rhythm, together with a clear image of himself as author, an emphasis on pleasing the audience, and an ironic awareness of the sheer labor involved in the process.

After ten years of frequent changes of locale, Wodehouse and his older brother Armine were sent to board at Dulwich, a school that was to have a decisive influence on him. There, his schoolmates became a new and better extended family. Though shy and uncomfortable in less stylized social settings, Wodehouse throve on the fellowship and rituals of school life. He excelled at cricket and other sports, succeeded his brother as editor of the school paper, and performed in amateur theatricals. The school, located on extensive grounds in a suburb of London, had been founded by Edward Alleyn, a famous seventeenth-century actor, and it continued to attract children of artistic as well as professional families.

Wodehouse was popular with his teachers as well as with his classmates; though never highly studious, he found that his innate love of language stood him in good stead in the classically oriented curriculum of the day. By the end of his time, his friends later recalled, he could compose Latin and Greek verse as swiftly as he could write English, and the beautifully modulated sentences of his later comic style owe as much to his reading of Virgil and Apuleius as to Charles Dickens and Oscar Wilde. "To me, the years between 1894 and 1900 were like heaven," he later remarked (Donaldson, p. 52).

The influence of Dulwich remained strong for Wodehouse in part because it unexpectedly proved to mark the end of his formal education. Wodehouse came from a prominent family, which traced its lineage back to Bertram of Wodehouse Tower in Yorkshire, who was said to have been an ally of William the Conqueror. A third cousin, the Earl of Kimberly, was William Gladstone's foreign minister during the early 1890s, and three other Wodehouses were Members of Parliament during Wodehouse's adolescence. On his mother's side, Wodehouse had a number of prominent ancestors, including his great-uncle, Cardinal Newman, famous both as a theologian and as one of the great masters of Victorian prose style. Yet Wodehouse's parents were younger children of younger children, and they had no inheritance to look forward to. Wodehouse's father had an adequate salary as a magistrate, and Wodehouse assumed that he would follow his brother Armine to Oxford upon graduation in 1900. His father's fortunes took a turn for the worse in the late 1890s, though, and for an appropriately Wodehousian reason. He made a bet that he could walk all the way around the island of Hong Kong in a single day; in the course of accomplishing this feat, he suffered severe sunstroke. He returned to England on medical leave, at the age of forty-five; unable to resume his duties, he took a disability pension in 1898, and remained on pension for the remaining forty years of his life.

Through connections of his father's, Wodehouse found work as a clerk for the Hong Kong and Shanghai Bank. After three years in the London office, he would be sent East. Wodehouse hated the work, shuddered at the thought of a career as a bank manager in Hong Kong, and set himself to become an established writer before he would be sent away from England. Writing at night and on the weekends, he began sending out a stream of stories to magazines that catered to the market for stories of schoolboy life. He also wrote humorous verse for *Punch* and the *Daily Express* newspaper, and began to contribute topical anecdotes to a humorous column at another paper, the *Globe*. In the fall of 1902 the editor of that column took a five-week vacation, and Wodehouse was offered the chance to write the column for those weeks. Forced to choose between the bank and this very temporary job, Wodehouse resigned from the bank on the spot and never looked back.

THE SCHOOL STORIES

BETWEEN 1900 and 1913, Wodehouse wrote a total of nine volumes' worth of school stories, mostly short stories or novels that were serialized in the *Public School Magazine* and *The Captain*, magazines read both by schoolboys and by Old Boys in later life. Journeyman work, these stories are interesting for the glimpses they give of the later concerns and techniques of the mature Wodehouse. His school stories are at once realistic and stylized, steeped in the conventions of the genre and yet mocking those conventions at the same time. In "Mike: A Public School Story" (1909), a new arrival is asked, "Are you the Bully, the Pride of the School, or the Boy who is Led Astray and takes to Drink in Chapter Sixteen?" (quoted in Usborne, p. 52). Elsewhere in the same book, Wodehouse brings on a lisping younger sister. Prattling children were staples of the genre, but in Wodehouse's story little Gladys Maud Evangeline gets only a single sentence of baby talk before her brother Bob growls, "Oh, put a green baize cloth over that kid, somebody!"

Wodehouse had an equally keen impatience with melodrama, the heart and soul of most school stories, and of much popular fiction in general. In 1901, at the age of twenty, he published an essay titled "School Stories" in the *Public School Magazine*, in which he remarked that "the worst of school life, from the point of view of a writer, is that nothing happens. A time may come when a writer shall arise bold enough and independent enough to retail the speech of school as it really is, but that time is not yet." He goes on to mock stories that feature thirteen-year-olds who develop philosophies of

life as they die of consumption, and adds: "No, the worst thing that ought to happen to your hero is the loss of the form-prize. . . . There should be a rule that no one under the age of twenty-one be permitted to die, unless he can get the whole thing finished in a space of time not exceeding two minutes" (quoted in Usborne, pp. 49–50).

In his school stories, Wodehouse set himself to capture the genuine speech of schoolboys and to show them engaged in plausible activities: winning at sports, dealing with friendship and rivalry, trying to outfox headmasters at exam time. The stories collected in 1903 as *Tales of St. Austin's*, for example, already show Wodehouse's sense of the ironic distance between the elevated diction of boys' adventure stories and the true speech of adolescents. Confronted with the announcement of a surprise examination, one boy "would have liked to have stalked up to Mr. Mellish's desk, fixed him with a blazing eye, and remarked, 'Sir, withdraw that remark. Cancel that statement instantly, or—!' or words to that effect. What he did say was: 'Oo, si-i-r!!'" (p. 9).

Wodehouse also distanced himself from the moralizing emphasis of many school stories; in "The Tom Brown Question," parodying theories of Homeric composition, the narrator discovers that the edifying second half of *Tom Brown's Schooldays* was actually written by a committee known as the S.S.F.P.W.L.W.T.R.O.E.B.A.S.T.H.G.I—"the Secret Society for Putting Wholesome Literature Within The Reach Of Every Boy, And Seeing That He Gets It" (p. 161).

Yet Wodehouse's school stories display certain values that remain strong in his later fiction. Loyalty to friends is all-important, and so are generosity and tolerance. A love of order coexists alongside a mockery of conventionality, of rules for their own sake. Work and self-discipline are valued, so long as they are freely chosen; work under compulsion, serving the arbitrary dictates of figures in authority, is to be avoided by any possible means. People who have ambition and who want to do things for themselves are likely to triumph over all obstacles; people who want to get other people to do things for them are highly suspect. In a sharply drawn story, "How Pillingshot Scored," the title character is manipulated by a big man on campus, Scott, who "could always get people to do things for him." Scott befriends Pillingshot and brings him to his room for tea, simply because his servant is out sick: "'Oh, by the way,' he said, with a coolness which to Pillingshot appeared simply brazen, 'I'm afraid my fag won't be here today . . . So would you mind just lighting that stove? . . . You'll find the toasting-fork on the wall somewhere. It's hanging up. Got it? Good man'" (pp. 13–14).

The St. Austin's stories feature the first in the long series of Wodehouse's amoralists, comic heroes or antiheroes who exist outside the normal conventions of society. Unlike the basely manipulative Scott, Frederick Wackerbath Bradshaw acts—or more often, avoids action—for pure pleasure, the sheer challenge of the game: "he had reduced cribbing to such an exact science that he loved it for its own sake, and would no sooner have come tamely into school with a prepared lesson than a sportsman would shoot a sitting bird" (p. 40). True, in later life, these sterling qualities will render him conspicuous in "the now celebrated affair of the European, African, and Asiatic Pork Pie and Ham Sandwich Supply Company frauds," but in school Bradshaw devotes himself to helping his friends evade the watchful eyes of their masters.

Like Rudyard Kipling, with whom he became friends, Wodehouse continued to see the world in terms of a great game (though not, in Wodehouse's case, the "Great Game" of British imperialism). In his view, at once ironic and deeply serious, adults are always adolescents at heart. The essence of Wodehouse's comedy is the construction of absurd scenarios in which the veneer of adulthood is stripped off and a person's essential immaturity is openly brought into play.

UKRIDGE AND PSMITH

THE immoralist germ of Bradshaw developed into Wodehouse's first two memorable characters, Ukridge and Psmith. Stanley Featherstonehaugh Ukridge was based in part on a schoolmaster Wodehouse knew of who tried to run a struggling chicken farm. Ukridge served as the chief comic character in Wodehouse's first adult novel, *Love Among the Chickens* (1906), though his role in the plot was subordinate to the love interest of a young couple. He later became the hero of a series of short stories. A rogue and a swindler, yet generous in spirit, good with dogs, and an opponent of all conventionality, Ukridge becomes, above all, a great talker, always hatching implausible schemes that will surely save him from the indignity of taking a steady job, always borrowing from his friends against the day when he will come into real cash.

Ukridge is at his best in small doses; Wodehouse went further with Psmith, initially a secondary character in the later school stories, then a hero in his own right once he went off to Cambridge. Psmith—who has added the silent "P" to his name to make it more interesting—is a natural aristocrat, a sublime talker, disinclined to work except on his friends' behalf; he floats through life with amused detachment, parodying every style he encounters and every author he reads, unflappable even when confronted by a gangster's gat. This occurs in *Psmith Journalist* (1915), the most memorable of the Psmith stories. In this book, Psmith visits New York, where he unexpectedly becomes involved in championing slum reform, combating both the gangsters and the politicians who prefer business as usual. In the process, Wodehouse gives a detailed picture of the mixed motives of the publishers of muckraking journalism—sincerely reformist, yet also sensationalistic, ever concerned with audience and the bottom line. The book is also a bravura exercise in style, counterpointing Psmith's Oxbridge English against Brooklynese and several other versions of "ordinary" English. Wodehouse never again wrote such a realistic work, and yet the more fantastical worlds of Blandings Castle and the Drones Club are similarly grounded through Wodehouse's sharp eye for psychologically revealing detail and his flawless ear for the nuances of many-leveled speech.

AMERICA AND MUSICAL COMEDY

WODEHOUSE was drawn to the American setting of *Psmith Journalist* because he was living in New York when he wrote it. He had been making extended visits since 1909 and was there when war broke out in 1914, making trans-Atlantic travel difficult. He stayed until 1919. American magazines were paying much better than British publications, and Wodehouse rapidly found a steady market for fanciful tales with aristocratic English settings. He had already begun to be active in British theater in the previous decade, and during his time in New York he quickly established himself in the world of musical theater. He became theater critic for *Vanity Fair* in 1915, and in December of that year he reviewed a musical composed by Jerome Kern, with book and lyrics by Guy Bolton. Within days, he had become friendly with Kern and Bolton, and they soon agreed to collaborate, with Bolton and Wodehouse creating stories and dialogue, and Wodehouse writing the lyrics.

The trio produced eight musicals in the next eight years, most of them enormous successes. Before then, musicals had generally been comic revues, with musical numbers loosely connected to a contrived farcical plot. Wodehouse, Bolton, and Kern worked to integrate story and music much more fully, and Wodehouse soon became famous as one of Broadway's premier librettists. He approached the writing of lyrics very differently from his contemporaries, for whom the usual method was to have the librettist write the song lyrics, to which the composer would then set a tune. Wodehouse felt that song lyrics should not be conceived independently of the music; instead, he preferred for Kern to give him a melody, to which he would set words. The result was more fluid and ear-catching, and Wodehouse soon found himself in great demand. Within two years, he became the most active writer on Broadway, with no fewer than five shows performing simultaneously in 1917; he later collaborated with George and Ira Gershwin, among others.

Wodehouse's attachment to America was strengthened by the fact that in New York he met his future wife, Ethel Newton Rowley, an English widow with a charming young daughter, Leonora. The courtship resembled the love-at-first-sight plots that are common in Wodehouse's stories: he met Ethel in August 1914, and they were married in September.

For the next twenty-five years, Wodehouse and his family commuted back and forth across the Atlantic, their movements closely related to the timing of theatrical productions in New York and London. By contemporary standards, Wodehouse's musicals and plays are highly contrived, and they are rarely performed today, but they had important effects on his fiction. His stories and novels took on a new scenic coherence; his complex plots flow unusually well because they are visually conceived and readily take shape in the mind's eye as one reads. Wodehouse applied many lessons from stagecraft to his fiction, as can

be seen in a comment from 1923 on the actions that are appropriate to major and minor characters respectively:

It is an error, I think, ever to have your villain manhandled by a minor character. Just imagine Moriarty socked by Doctor Watson. A villain ought to be a sort of scarcely human invulnerable figure. The reader ought to be in a constant state of panic, saying to himself: "How the devil *is* this superman to be foiled?" The only person capable of hurting him should be the hero.

(Edwards, pp. 96–97)

Wodehouse would complain hilariously about the unreasonableness of producers' demands, as in a depiction, in "The Agonies of Writing a Musical Comedy," of writing for a pair of ballroom dancers who wish to become musical comedy stars—"both artistes, though extremely gifted northward as far as the ankle-bone, go all to pieces above that level, with the result that by the time you reach the zone where the brains and voice are located, there is nothing stirring whatever" (in *The Uncollected Wodehouse*, 1977, pp. 30–31). But all his life, Wodehouse loved the craftsmanship of writing, and he was often stimulated to his best work by the requirements of editors and producers.

The interplay between Wodehouse's dramatic and fictional work is well illustrated by the story of *Spring Fever*, published as a novel in 1948. An actor and producer wished to put on the story as a play in New York, and Wodehouse rewrote the novel into a play, changing its locale from England to Hollywood in the process. The production fell through; never one to waste his work, Wodehouse rewrote the play as a new novel, differing from *Spring Fever* largely in its Hollywood setting and the names of the characters; this was published as *The Old Reliable* in 1951.

Above all, Wodehouse's theatrical work led him to make a decisive shift from realistically based comic romance to the more farcical, uniquely Wodehousian world of his mature style. Wodehouse once wrote that "I believe there are only two ways of writing a novel. One is mine, making the thing a sort of musical comedy without music, ignoring real life altogether; the other is going right down deep into life and not caring a damn" (Donaldson, p. 11). Like many of Wodehouse's remarks, this is an exaggerated and self-deprecating contrast, for the fascination of Wodehouse's work lies in his ability to present his farcical world with remarkable realism, even as his prose style provides all the music one could wish for; yet it remains true that from 1915 onward his books become something new in humorous writing, novels that can well be described as musical comedies in prose.

BLANDINGS CASTLE AND ENVIRONS

DURING 1914, as Wodehouse was writing of Psmith's slum-clearing adventures in New York, he was also beginning a novel set at the imaginary Blandings Castle, home of Clarence, Earl of Emsworth, and his ludicrous family. *Something New* (1915; published in England as *Something Fresh*) was Wodehouse's first best-seller, and it marked the decisive emergence of his own comic world. This world, however, is actually the site at which several very different spheres collide. The aristocratic leisure of the absent-minded Earl and his empty-headed son Freddie Threepwood is counterpointed against the energy of the go-getting American tycoon J. Preston Peters and his daughter Aline, to whom Freddie is engaged. Caught in the middle is a hero who looks remarkably like the young Wodehouse himself: Ashe Marson, struggling writer of dime novels, whom the Mammoth Publishing Company pays poorly for monthly installments of the implausible adventures of Gridley Quayle, Investigator. The author is caught in a sort of indentured servitude to his own character:

The unholy alliance had been in progress now for more than two years, and it seemed to Ashe that Gridley grew less human each month. He was so complacent and so maddeningly blind to the fact that only the most amazing luck enabled him to detect anything. To depend on Gridley Quayle for one's income was like being chained to some horrible monster.

(pp. 14–15)

Wodehouse, who himself had been anonymously turning out quick detective stories among his other ventures, pairs Ashe up with Joan Valentine, an anonymous writer for Mammoth's weekly paper "Home Gossip," which Joan describes as "a horrid little paper, all brown-paper patterns and advice to the lovelorn. I do a short story for it every week, under various names. A duke or an earl goes with each story. I loathe it intensely" (p. 17). These two young writers soon find themselves involved in an absurd imbroglio involving theft and detection at the Earl of Emsworth's property, thereby bringing together the two genres in which they write. Lord Emsworth has wandered off with an ancient Egyptian scarab belonging to the tycoon Mr. Peters, believing it a gift, while Mr. Peters believes that Emsworth has stolen it from him. Joan and Ashe use their knowledge of the conventions of their own pulp fiction to sort out the tangled situation. In the process, they fall in love, and earn a reward that enables them to loosen the grip of their commercial writing.

Appropriately, this book that mocks the daily fare of the popular magazines sold for what was then an enormous sum, $3,500, to a leading popular magazine, the *Saturday Evening Post,* freeing Wodehouse himself to name his price and choose his audience for his work thereafter. So congenial did the world of Blandings prove that Wodehouse returned to it for a dozen later novels over the years; his last novel, uncompleted at his death at the age of ninety-three, was published posthumously under the title *Sunset at Blandings* (1977). Blandings mellowed somewhat over time, but for several decades there was a real edge to Wodehouse's depiction of this aristocratic world. When Ashe comes to Blandings on assignment from Mr. Peters to track down his missing scarab, his first view of the village of Market Blandings is none too encouraging:

The church is Norman, and the intelligence of the majority of the natives palaeozoic. To alight at Market Blandings Station in the dusk of a rather chilly Spring day, when the south-west wind has shifted to due east, and the thrifty inhabitants have not yet lit their windows, is to be smitten with the feeling that one is at the edge of the world with no friends near.

(p. 83)

The rolling acres of the Blandings estate are beautiful, but the host hides from his guests, who stroll listlessly around the grounds, having nothing in common and nothing to do but abuse their host. Both Ashe and Joan come to the estate in the guise of servants as they seek the scarab, and Wodehouse takes the opportunity to give a detailed picture of life in the servants' quarters. The servants are obsessed with hierarchy and status, snubbing or looking up to each other on the twin basis of their own duties and the social standing of their particular employer. Presiding over the servants' wing is the magisterial figure of Beach the butler, who "had that strained air of being on the very point of bursting which one sees in frogs and toy balloons" (p. 89). Butlers, Wodehouse continues, "seem to grow less and less like anything human in proportion to the magnificence of their surroundings. . . . Beach, accordingly, had acquired a dignified inertia which almost qualified him for inclusion in the vegetable kingdom." Beach's particular form of dignity is perfectly captured in his melancholy disquisitions on his health: "I Suffer Extremely From My Feet. Not only corns. I have but recently recovered from an Ingrowing Toe-Nail. . . . The Lining Of My Stomach is not what I could wish the Lining Of My Stomach to be" (pp. 90, 92–93).

Beach is a minor supporting character, a stock figure well known from the stage, but Wodehouse had found comrades among butlers and other servants during his childhood, when he was often sent off to play in the servants' hall while his aunts and uncles conversed in the drawing room; and he had observed his grown-up friends closely. Beach comes to life through brilliantly chosen descriptive touches: "Mr. Beach said grace somewhat patronizingly. The meal began" (p. 104); in *Pigs Have Wings* (1952), when someone ventures to address Beach as "Cocky," "ice formed on the butler's upper slopes" (p. 93).

Uneasily caught between the upper-class world where they are socially at home and the servants' world whose economic status is closer to their own, Ashe and Joan are fully alive to the incongruities of their situation. Hoping to garner the reward offered for the scarab's return, Joan proposes that her old school friend Aline, Mr. Peters' daughter, take her to Blandings in the guise of her maid. The wealthy Aline is unsure how she should treat Joan, so Joan instructs her to behave "kindly and yet distantly, as if I were a worm, but a worm for whom you felt a mild liking" (p. 65).

The master of Blandings is, nominally, the absent-minded Clarence; in actuality, the place is run by his strong-minded sister Constance, who treats Clarence in much the way an impatient aunt would treat a balky nephew. Inevitably, Emsworth heightens Constance's irritation by his very efforts to forestall it. Wodehouse developed a sly narrative voice, capable of underlining his characters' absurdity even as he seems to take their side. In the opening of *Pigs Have Wings*, Beach brings the mail in to Emsworth, who is ab-sorbed in reading his favorite book, Whiffle's *On the Care of the Pig.* "Ah, the afternoon post?" Emsworth observes. "'The afternoon post, eh? Quite. Quite.' His sister, Lady Constance Keeble, might, and frequently did, complain of his vagueness—('Oh, for goodness' sake, Clarence, don't *gape* like that!')—but he could on occasion be as quick on the uptake as the next man. 'Yes, yes, to be sure, the afternoon post,' he said, fully abreast" (p. 1).

Constance is only one of three major irritants in Clarence's life, the others being his personal secretary and his younger son Freddie. His secretary, the Efficient Baxter, is always trying to get Emsworth to organize his affairs, and generally to do things, while Freddie would prefer to do nothing whatsoever, other than acquire gambling debts from which his father must bail him out. Kindly and lovable as he is, Emsworth has no visible affection for Freddie. In the British system of primogeniture, in which the eldest son inherits the title and the bulk of the estate, Freddie illustrates "the problem of What To Do With The Younger Sons. It is useless to try to gloss over the fact, the younger son is not required" (*Something New*, p. 23). When Freddie manages to get engaged to the wealthy Aline Peters, "such was the relief [Clarence] experienced that he found himself feeling almost affectionate towards Freddie" (p. 24).

Edenic Blandings may be, but not to Freddie, who chafes at captivity there, mooning about "with an air of crushed gloom which would have caused comment in Siberia" (p. 24). The innocence many readers have celebrated in the portrayal of Blandings is a selective sort of innocence. Lively young heroes and heroines remain pure before marriage and chaste thereafter; death is unknown; endings are always happy. And yet family relations are deeply strained, comically though those strains may be manifested; in *Blandings Castle* (1935), Emsworth still regards his son as "a worse menace to the happy life of rural England than botts, green-fly, or foot-and-mouth disease. The prospect of having him at Blandings indefinitely affected Lord Emsworth like a blow on the base of the skull" (p. 45).

Relations among the older generation are similarly uneasy. Clarence's own younger brother Galahad, a free-living character, is a thorn in the side of their sister Constance. In *Pigs Have Wings*, she recalls an occasion when he came close to drowning: "'just as he was sinking for the last time, one of the gardeners came along and pulled him out,' she added, speaking with a sort of wild regret" (pp. 155–156). Wodehouse underscores this regret, having Constance pause for a moment, "brooding on the thoughtless folly of the chuckle-headed gardener."

Blandings, then, is not simply seen through rose-colored glasses; it is, in fact, seen through monocles, pince-nez, and horn-rimmed glasses as well. At the time he was writing *Something New,* Wodehouse published "In Defense of Astigmatism," an essay on the modern novel, in which he used eyeglasses as his example of the real-life details his supposedly bold contemporaries were too timid to take up: "This is peculiarly an age where novelists pride themselves on the breadth of their outlook and the courage with which they refuse to ignore the realities of life. . . . why, you can hardly hear yourself think for the uproar of earnest young novelists proclaiming how free and unfettered they are. And yet, no writer has had the pluck to make his hero wear glasses" (in *The Uncollected Wodehouse,* pp. 19–20). Wodehouse goes on to imagine a scene involving a young lover named Clarence, who polishes his pince-nez tenderly as he woos his sweetheart. Next, Wodehouse gives a dramatic scenario ("Clarence adjusted his tortoise-shell-rimmed spectacles with a careless gesture, and faced his assassins without a tremor"), pointing out the wealth of new situations such an accoutrement can offer the novelist: "Have you ever considered the latent possibilities for dramatic situations in short sight? You know how your glasses cloud over when you come into a warm room out of the cold? Well, imagine your hero in such a position" (p. 21). He then sketches two hilarious scenes based on this problem.

At Blandings, Clarence does indeed wear pince-nez; the urbane Galahad sports a monocle whose mocking glitter alone can drive Constance up to her room to bathe her temples with eau de Cologne; the Efficient Baxter's suspicious eyes peer through rimless glasses. The world of Blandings, grounded in realistic detail and more socially and psychologically layered than it first appears to be, is a highly conventional world whose true heroes and heroines revel in the absurdity of all convention. This is why Galahad is so irritating to Constance, and why the narrator of *Pigs Have Wings* describes him as "the only genuinely distinguished member of the family" (p. 9). He is distinguished by a zest for eating well, drinking abundantly, smoking profusely, and exerting himself endlessly on behalf of friends in need. "A pain in the neck to his sister Constance, his sister Julia, his sister Dora and all his other sisters, he was universally esteemed in less austere quarters, for his heart was of gold and his soul overflowing with the milk of human kindness" (p. 10).

Free of the class snobbery and money-consciousness of his sisters—perhaps just because, as a younger son, he has no secure social position and is always in need of cash—Gally befriends butlers, barmaids, and dukes alike. The plot of *Pigs Have Wings* turns on Lord Emsworth's anxiety that his scheming neighbor Sir Gregory Parsloe may steal his prize pig, the Empress of Blandings, so that his own pig can win first prize at an upcoming county fair. Gally rallies round to try to prevent this evil deed, moved both by pity for his brother and by his own financial interests, as he has wagered a hefty sum in Market Blandings that the Empress will carry the day. He is aided in his efforts by Beach the butler, who has evolved over the years into an almost friendly character, and who has also placed a substantial sum on the pig. Wodehouse portrays a sort of freemasonry of the enterprising, cash-starved soul; it is a mark of the sterling quality of the wealthy young heroine of this book, Penny Donaldson, that she too recognizes Beach as "a soulmate and a buddy" (p. 42).

The true coin of Wodehouse's realm is not cash at all but anecdotes; what his free spirits collect as they move through life is a fund of stories, and these tales bestow upon their owners both a wry detachment and also a toleration for the varieties of human conduct. Brought into contact with the earnest and humorless young Orlo Vosper, Gally Threepwood need not ignore him and go off in search of more congenial company, for to Gally all company is congenial: "Orlo Vosper belonged to the human race, and all members of the human race were to Gally a potential audience for his stories. It was possible, he felt, that the young man had not heard the one about the duke, the bottle of champagne and the female contortionist, so he welcomed him now with a cordial wave of his cigar" (p. 119).

Wodehouse had little patience for highbrow literature and satirized the exquisite aesthetes who were often producing it at the turn of the century; perhaps the early Marcel Proust stands behind the figure of Charleton (read: charlatan) Prout, author of *Grey Myrtles* and other Pastels in Prose (*Ukridge*, 1924, pp. 146–147). Yet the aristocratic world of Blandings had for Wodehouse something of the same attraction that the high society of the Guermantes had for Proust: an artificial world in which the social conventions are raised to a higher degree, susceptible of analysis and satire; freed of many of the constraints of ordinary life, the characters can pursue their desires, and vent their feelings, in an endless series of machinations and a constant stream of talk.

BERTIE AND JEEVES

THE snake-filled Eden of Blandings has an urban counterpart in the Drones Club, populated chiefly by the idle scions of aristocratic families and their sporadically active, impecunious younger brothers. The central figure in Wodehouse's Drones Club is Bertie Wooster, who first appeared in a short story in 1917; he soon became closely paired with his valet Jeeves in several stories (*My Man Jeeves*, 1919). Their relationship was fully developed in the stories collected in *Carry On, Jeeves* in 1925, and a full novel, *Thank You, Jeeves*, was devoted to their adventures in 1934. Thereafter Wodehouse returned regularly to them, up through his last completed novel, *Aunts Aren't Gentlemen* (1974; published in the United States as *The Cat Nappers*).

Closely similar in character to Freddie Threepwood, Bertie typically narrates his own adventures, giving Wodehouse the comic opportunity, and the challenge, of conveying complex events and the nuances of social interactions through the voice of an observer whose own devoted servant describes him as "mentally negligible." Bertie is often involved in helping his shiftless friends out of difficult situations, or in disentangling himself from problems, usually some social obligation foisted on him by an aunt, or an undesirable romantic involvement he has somehow backed into; over the years, Bertie is engaged at least nine times, never wisely.

Bertie and his friends are always bailed out by the brilliant counter-plotting of Jeeves, Bertie's valet or "gentleman's gentleman." Recounting his misadventures and Jeeves's miraculous solutions, Bertie plays Dr. Watson to Jeeves's Sherlock Holmes, a comparison often openly made in the stories themselves. Like Watson, Bertie is a kind of Everyman, through whose eyes the reader can indirectly appreciate the almost superhuman skills of the master detective; Bertie's own slowness on the uptake allows Wodehouse, like Conan Doyle, to have Watson/Bertie give the reader clues that he himself does not notice.

Unlike Watson, Bertie is wealthy, having been left a fortune by his deceased father—he never mentions his mother; yet Bertie's wealth earns him no respect. The censorious aunt of one of his friends views him as "a typical specimen of a useless and decaying aristocracy" ("The Aunt and the Sluggard," 1916, p. 110), while the celebrated loony-doctor Sir Roderick Glossop, no enemy to aristocrats in general, displays with Bertie "a knack of making a fellow feel like a waste-product" ("The Rummy Affair of Old Biffy," 1924, p. 133).[1] With the exception of his lively Aunt Dahlia, a sort of female Gally Threepwood, Bertie's own numerous aunts regard him with contempt. He lives in mortal fear of Aunt Agatha in particular, and will cross the Atlantic to avoid her.

Bertie himself is aware that he lacks a certain depth—"it was one of those jolly, peaceful mornings that make a chappie wish he'd got a soul or something" ("Jeeves and the Hard-Boiled Egg," p. 77)—and he becomes comically elated whenever he thinks that he has finally outflanked Jeeves. Though he is always wrong, he admits his failings with good grace, and he has many of the qualities that Wodehouse celebrates. He is intensely loyal to his friends and chivalrous to women—chivalrous to a fault, as he can never break even a dinner engagement, much less an engagement of marriage, however great a misunderstanding may be involved. He has no sense of snobbery and no love of money as such; he does love mystery novels, sunny weather, and the exquisite cooking of his Aunt Dahlia's French chef Anatole. Above all, he rebels instinctively against all sorts of pomposity, all adherence to conventionality for its own sake, all social duties that one is supposed to carry out simply because someone in authority says so.

Bertie's generosity and essential kindness do not prevent him from giving very pointed portraits of the less kindly souls he often encounters,

[1] Unless otherwise noted, page references to quoted passages from Wodehouse's short stories are from the 1956 reprint of *Carry On, Jeeves*.

and in Bertie's narratives Wodehouse carries to its highest level his ability to build comic scenes around a bumbling hero who can nonetheless give a very vivid account of his misadventures. By the 1920s, Wodehouse had succeeded in making far fuller use of farcical plots than the usual vaudeville pleasures that come from seeing stock figures stumbling through ridiculous situations. In Wodehouse's mature work, farcical plots work in parallel with the stylized aristocratic settings of Blandings and the Drones Club: absurd situations highlight the problems everyone finds in the stresses and strains of everyday life. When one story requires Bertie to stay at a country house in the guise of his friend Oliver Sipperley, Bertie comments, matter-of-factly, that "it is always a nervous job for a diffident and unassuming bloke to visit a strange house for the first time; and it doesn't make the thing any better when he goes there pretending to be another fellow. I was conscious of a rather pronounced sinking feeling, which the appearance of the Pringles did nothing to allay" ("Without the Option," 1925, p. 153).

Wodehouse's—and Bertie's—characterizations reinforce the effect of setting and plot. Bertie here finds himself in a house party from hell:

"No doubt you remember my mother?" said Professor Pringle mournfully, indicating Exhibit A.
"Oh—ah!" I said, achieving a bit of a beam.
"And my aunt," sighed the prof, as if things were getting worse and worse.
"Well, well, well!" I said, shooting another beam in the direction of Exhibit B.
"They were saying only this morning that they remembered you," groaned the prof, abandoning all hope.
(pp. 153–154)

These characters, moreover, express their inmost feelings with disorienting directness: "I remember Oliver," the mother says, believing Bertie to be Oliver; "she heaved a sigh. 'He was such a pretty child. What a pity!'" (p. 154). Her sister glares at Bertie, still burning with anger because the young Oliver had teased her cat many years before.

Wodehouse works the cat theme into the fabric of the scene: a cat appears, and when Bertie stoops to tickle it under its ear, the eighty-six-year-old aunt rushes forward to save the cat, crying "Stop him! Stop him!" A page later, Bertie backs into the cat and steps on its foot, confirming the aunt's worst fears; her now-justified loathing in turn figures in the denouement of the plot.

During the decade before he wrote these stories, Wodehouse had already begun to play down the romantic plot around which comedies were traditionally constructed: the efforts of two young lovers to overcome all obstacles and marry. Wodehouse continued to use the romance plot, but he gave less and less attention to detailing the stages of young love or the emotions of the hero and heroine, concentrating instead on social interactions and on the play of languages and viewpoints. In the Bertie Wooster stories, Wodehouse went further, creating an *anti*-marriage plot that revolves around the need to extricate Bertie (or one of his friends) from an unsuitable marriage.

These marriages are never unsuitable for the social or financial reasons that concern conventionally minded characters like Lady Constance Keeble; they are unsuitable because they involve the wrong sort of person. Wodehouse employs three basic types of young women in his stories: his favored heroines, who always get their man, are energetic, fun-loving, resourceful young women, often self-supporting, a little androgynous in character and typically bearing masculine-sounding names like Bobbie and Corky; these women, however, are drawn to young men with some talent or energy that Bertie apparently doesn't possess. Bertie always becomes engaged to one of Wodehouse's two other types of young woman: gooey, sensitive souls, like Madeline Bassett, who thinks the stars are God's daisy chain, or domineering types who want to reform Bertie and generally buck him up.

When Jeeves first enters Bertie's service, as recounted in a story aptly titled "Jeeves Takes Charge" (1916), Bertie is engaged to Florence Craye, an athletic, philosophically inclined woman. She has set Bertie to reading *Types of Ethical Theory* and plans to send him on to Nietzsche thereafter. Jeeves prevents this marriage from taking place, both for Bertie's sake ("You would not enjoy Nietzsche, sir. He is fundamentally unsound," p. 30), and also out of self-interest, as he has observed that when a bride comes in the front door, the valet of the groom's bachelor days is asked to leave by the back door.

The archetypal threat to Bertie's peace of mind is Honoria Glossop, daughter of the loony-doctor Sir Roderick:

Honoria, you see, is one of those robust, dynamic girls with the muscles of a welterweight and a laugh like a squadron of cavalry charging over a tin bridge. A beastly thing to have to face over the breakfast table. Brainy, moreover. The sort of girl who reduces you to pulp with sixteen sets of tennis and a few rounds of golf and then comes down to dinner as fresh as a daisy, expecting you to take an intelligent interest in Freud.

("The Rummy Affair of Old Biffy," p. 125)

Many of Wodehouse's stories feature clever and athletic young women who deservedly win the hands of relatively passive young men; what distinguishes the Florences and Honorias are three faults: first, the sheer excess to which they take their abilities; second, the degree of mismatch with Bertie, who is not just relatively but absolutely passive; third, the insistence by the activist Florence, Honoria, or Heloise that Bertie must transform himself into their own image.

Wodehouse's passive young men typically have to do some kind of real work in order to overcome the obstacles to their marriage, obstacles often raised by an aunt or a parent who has been hoping for a better match, financially or socially. Even Emsworth's idle son Freddie Threepwood, after marrying Niagara Donaldson, becomes a successful partner in his father-in-law's business. Yet the good heroine always has complete faith in her man from the beginning, schemes to help him meet whatever challenge is posed, and does not herself take social censure seriously except as a practical problem. Florence Craye, by contrast, actually shares her aunts' values, and she is the one who enjoins upon Bertie a heroic act, in the reduced form of the requirement that he steal the manuscript of an uncle's memoirs. In classic conventionalist fashion, Florence is concerned for the social embarrassment that will spread among her parents' friends if Uncle Willoughby's salacious memoirs reach print; equally, she really lacks respect for Bertie as he is: "You may look on it as a test, Bertie. If you have the resource and courage to carry this thing through, I will take it as evidence that you are not the vapid and shiftless person most people think you. If you fail, I shall know that your Aunt Agatha was right when she called you a spineless invertebrate and advised me strongly not to marry you" ("Jeeves Takes Charge," p. 17).

While staying at the Pringle household in the guise of Oliver Sipperley, Bertie finds himself wooed by the formidable Heloise Pringle, who is, naturally, a cousin of Honoria Glossop's. Heloise expresses her affection by suggesting that "Oliver" fire his valet Jeeves; then, in an eerie moment, she learns that "Oliver" is acquainted with Bertie Wooster, of whom she has heard so much from Honoria: "She gazed at me in a foul, motherly way. 'He can't be a good influence for you,' she said. 'I do wish you would drop him. Would you? . . . It only needs a little will-power'" (p. 161). Though she does not know it, Heloise's "foul, motherly" advice to Bertie is that he abandon himself, an all too accurate image of the effect she wishes to have on him. Her desire that he should exert a little "will-power" is, in reality, a demand that he surrender his will to hers.

When Jeeves intervenes to save Bertie or one of his friends from such a marriage, he displays many qualities in common with Sherlock Holmes: a vast knowledge of recondite information; a keen eye for clues and opportunities that others would miss; a focus on the psychology of the individual; an imperturbable calm even when things go awry. Yet he exercises his abilities very differently from Holmes: whereas Doyle's hero retraces and reveals a hidden plot, discovering what has happened to produce the crime or mystery, Jeeves acts above all to *keep* things from happening. Bertie's own love of inaction is considerable, and it can be carried even further among his friends, such as Rocky Todd in "The Aunt and the Sluggard." Rocky is a poet whose only wish is to stay at home and pen an occasional verse exhorting young people to live life to the fullest. Even Bertie's minimal occupations—dressing for dinner, going to nightclubs—strike Rocky as "a sort of St. Vitus's dance," since he prefers to stay in his pajamas until five in the afternoon, at which point he puts on an old sweater. ("I saw Jeeves wince, poor chap," Bertie comments; "this sort of revelation shocked his finest feelings," p. 98).

At times, characters rebel against the routines of life; at the extreme, they opt out of Wodehouse's world altogether, as in the notable instance of Florence Craye's father, Lord Worplesdon. First manifesting an impatient eccentricity by insisting on dressing for dinner in dress trousers, a flannel shirt, and a shooting coat, a few years later he "came down to breakfast one morning, lifted the first cover he saw, said 'Eggs! Eggs! Eggs! Damn all eggs!' in an overwrought sort of voice, and instantly legged it for France, never to return to the bosom of his family. This, mind you," Bertie adds, "being a bit of luck for the bosom of the family, for old Worplesdon had the worst temper in the county" ("Jeeves Takes Charge," p. 11).

Jeeves can always save the more temperate Bertie and his friends from the threat of change; typically, his method is psychological, grounded in analogy to someone else's response in a parallel situation. Jeeves's skills are less forensic than Holmes's and more narrative: he is a fund of stories of things that have happened to an aunt, a niece, a former employer, or a fellow valet's employer, and the resolutions to all these stories provide his chief resource in assessing unexpected situations. An aunt has been cured of a mania for driving about in hansom cabs; another relative has taken pride in having her stomach condition trumpeted in advertisements for a bromide; his uncle knew of a pair of cyclists named Nicholls and Jackson who were so badly mutilated by a truck that the coroners "collected as much as they could, and called it Nixon" (*Right Ho, Jeeves*, 1934, p. 232). All these anecdotes point the way at one or another difficult moment, and when stories fail, great literature can do the trick. Jeeves has read encyclopedically in Marcus Aurelius, the Bible, Shakespeare, and many more authors, and he always quotes from memory the passages Bertie can never quite dredge up from his school days.

Jeeves is variously compared to a father, mother, wife, and even a lover—Bertie pines for him when he is on vacation. Yet he is always also a servant, and he raises the servant's social invisibility to a semidivine level. In his preternatural skill at self-erasure he may even share traits with Wodehouse's older brother Armine, the one who went on to Oxford just before their father's fortunes faltered, and who became a theosophist and president of a theosophical college in India:

One of the rummy things about Jeeves is that, unless you watch like a hawk, you very seldom see him come into a room. He's like one of those weird birds in India who dissolve themselves into thin air and nip through space in a sort of disembodied way and assemble the parts again just where they want them. I've got a cousin who's what they call a Theosophist, and he says he's often nearly worked the thing himself, but couldn't quite bring it off, probably owing to having fed in his boyhood on the flesh of animals slain in anger, and pie.
("The Artistic Career of Corky," p. 37)

Jeeves is bound to his master by ties of affection and loyalty, by the frequent rewards paid him by Bertie and his grateful friends, and by the supreme malleability of his employer ("in an employer brains are not desirable," he tells us in "Bertie Changes His Mind," p. 230). Yet tensions occasionally arise between master and servant, for Jeeves is a stickler for propriety: not social or moral propriety as such, but the pure propriety of form, expressed above all in dress. He and Bertie recurrently disagree about some item of clothing that Bertie wishes to adopt; Jeeves's reward for solving the story's dilemma always includes—or even consists entirely of—Bertie's reluctant acquiescence to Jeeves's insistence that he give up the loud checked suit, or the soft collar, or even an unsightly moustache; "it seemed to me that it was getting a bit too thick if he was going to edit my face as well as my costume," Bertie complains ("Jeeves and the Hard-Boiled Egg," p. 73), but in the end he gives in.

Clothing displays the kind of order of which Wodehouse approves. The pleasures of dress, like those of the table at the hands of an inspired chef like Anatole, depend upon the creative modification of well-known recipes, the proper balance and harmonious concatenation of established ingredients. Like the detective fiction so many of Wodehouse's characters read and even write, clothes and meals provide pleasure for their own sake. The joy of clothing, like the joy of cooking, goes far beyond the simple provision of warmth or sustenance; in the hands of a Jeeves or an Anatole, it becomes a way of life. Sports work similarly. Wodehouse wrote many stories centered on golf, which becomes a virtual religion for its devotees, a religion with a self-sustaining code rather than divinely ordained commandments, a sublimely pointless and deeply gratifying pleasure.

Wrongly used—indeed, "used" for anything, even to promote good health—such pleasures become duties, ways to meet other people's expectations or else ostentatious signifiers of social status; rightly conceived, they cut across the divisions of society. In *Pigs Have Wings*, it is food that rekindles the love of the wealthy aristocrat Sir Gregory Parsloe for his long-lost sweetheart Maudie, a former barmaid who now heads a detective agency: "when I watched you wading into that Ambrosia Chiffon Pie, obviously enjoying it, I mean to say *understanding* it, not pecking at it the way most of these dashed women would have done but plainly getting its inner meaning and all that, I said to myself 'My mate!'" (p. 141). Food even crosses the boundaries separating species: Lord

Emsworth is never happier than when helping the Empress of Blandings to her daily 57,800 calories, and the rotund Sir Gregory must reject the dictates of an athletic aristocratic fiancée who has forced him onto a crash diet. As he bitterly reflects, "Why should there be one law for pigs and another for Baronets?" (p. 30).

WODEHOUSE AT WAR

IMMERSED in exploring the laws of his satirically skewed fictional world, Wodehouse took less and less interest in the outside world as such, apart from the hothouse worlds of the New York and London theater. In the spring of 1940, Wodehouse and his wife were living in a French village, in a beautiful half-timbered house conveniently located near a major casino; when the Germans occupied the area they were arrested, having resisted friends' appeals to come to safer territory in England, in part because of immunization problems involving their beloved Pekinese dogs. As an alien from a then-noncombatant nation, Wodehouse was interned by the Germans at a prisoner-of-war camp in Silesia for a little over a year; he was released just before his sixtieth birthday and allowed to stay in Berlin, joined by his wife and the dogs.

Wodehouse bore his internment with good humor, taking his share at peeling the few potatoes the prisoners were supplied and also writing away, not making any real concession to his uncomfortable environment. He wrote an entire novel, *Money in the Bank*, (1942), together with half of a second, *Full Moon* (1947); both are among his best books, showing no trace of the setting in which they were composed. Wodehouse seems actually to have enjoyed life in the camp. Refusing to dwell on the physical privation, the separation from his family, and worries about the future, Wodehouse enjoyed the camaraderie of the inmates and their covert resistance to their captors; the camp became for him a sort of adult boys' school.

His approach toward his situation made life there tolerable but caused enormous problems for him thereafter. While in the camp, he wrote a humorous sketch of camp life for an American magazine; getting wind of this, the German propaganda ministry inquired whether he might care to broadcast a few humorous talks to his American audi-

ence. Pleased at the chance to release some of his pent-up observations, Wodehouse never considered the fact that, as England by this time was locked in mortal combat with Germany, many of his countrymen would regard a humorous account of camp life as traitorous propaganda on behalf of the enemy, an implicit denial of the grim rumors that were beginning to circulate concerning the Nazi concentration camps.

Wodehouse made five radio broadcasts in the summer of 1941, which received little attention when broadcast to America but caused a storm of protest when they were rebroadcast to England. Wodehouse had no idea that people being nightly bombed by the Luftwaffe would take offense at an account of earnest, well-meaning German soldiers, described in a tone of ironic self-observation:

One's reactions on suddenly finding oneself surrounded by the armed strength of a hostile power are rather interesting. There is a sense of strain. The first time you see a German soldier over your garden fence, your impulse is to jump ten feet straight up into the air, and you do so. About a week later, you find that you are only jumping five feet. And then, after you have been living with him in a small village for two months, you inevitably begin to fraternize and to wish that you had learned German at school instead of Latin and Greek. All the German I know is *"Es ist schönes Wetter"* and this handicaps conversation with a Bavarian private who knows no English. After I had said *"Es ist schönes Wetter,"* I was a spent force and we used to take up the rest of the interview in beaming at one another.
(Donaldson, p. 224)

Unlike some of the British aristocracy who had been covertly or even overtly pro-fascist in the years before the war, Wodehouse was never a lover of authoritarianism in any form. In 1938 he had parodied the British fascist movement in his novel *The Code of the Woosters* (1938), in which Bertie sharply reproves Spode, a would-be dictator who has founded the Black Shorts party. Typically, Wodehouse focuses his satire on the fascists' clothing, which resembles the shorts worn by soccer players: "The trouble with you, Spode," Bertie remarks,

is that just because you have succeeded in inducing a handful of half-wits to disfigure the London scene by going about in black shorts, you think you're someone. You hear them shouting "Heil, Spode!" and you imagine it is the Voice of the People. That is where you make your bloomer. What the Voice of the People is saying is:

"Look at that frightful ass Spode swanking about in footer bags! Did you ever in your puff see such a perfect perisher?"

(p. 118)

Clear in his own mind about his scorn for Hitler and the whole Nazi ethos, Wodehouse saw nothing wrong with accounts of "beaming" at friendly young soldiers, to say nothing of the unfortunate choice of the term "fraternizing."

Bitter articles were written in England against his broadcasts; Sean O'Casey, for example, described the talks as "the pitiful antics of English Literature's performing flea." In a more measured vein, Malcolm Muggeridge, then a young intelligence officer, concluded that "it wasn't that he was other-worldly or un-worldly, as much as that he was a-worldly. Wodehouse's true offense was to have disinterested himself in the war" (Phelps, p. 223). The price of that disinterest was high. Questions were raised in Parliament, and for years thereafter, successive foreign ministers refused to rule out the possibility that Wodehouse might be tried for treason if he returned to England. He never did. He moved to New York in 1947; in 1955, he and his wife moved to a house on several wooded acres on Long Island, not far from the home of his close friend and theatrical collaborator Guy Bolton. Wodehouse lived there for the remaining twenty years of his life, rarely leaving home even for a night.

Wodehouse gradually came to understand the offense his broadcasts had caused, and he abandoned a book he had begun to write defending his talks, though he did continue to feel that the outcry had been excessive; he rejected out of hand the inflammatory accusations that had been made suggesting that he was a Nazi supporter. He even made an ironic point of pride of O'Casey's literary judgment of his work, and actually titled a 1953 volume of his theater correspondence *Performing Flea*.

Wodehouse's breach with England was symbolically healed in 1975, two months before his death, when he was made a Knight Commander of the British Empire.

THE LATER WODEHOUSE

WODEHOUSE wrote steadily to the end of his life, developing and refining his comic world, especially the worlds of Blandings and of Bertie Wooster and his circle of friends. Some of his best books appeared in his later years, such as *Ice in the Bedroom* (1961), *Galahad at Blandings* (1965; U.S. title *The Brinkmanship of Galahad Threepwood*), and *Much Obliged, Jeeves* (U.S. title *Jeeves and the Tie That Binds*), which he published in 1971 at the age of ninety. This remarkable late career—he published twenty-eight books after the age of seventy—involved mining familiar terrain rather than exploring new areas, but he could do so with considerable success, in part because he had always been inspired by the challenge of reworking established situations. In his early days, those situations were given to him by the conventions of existing popular fiction; from the late 1920s onward, the conventions were primarily those of his own creation or adaptation. As early as 1928, a critic accused him of virtual self-plagiarism, a charge that Wodehouse hilariously took up in the preface to his next novel, *Fish Preferred* (1929; published in London as *Summer Lightning*), a new Blandings story: "A certain critic—for such men, I regret to say, do exist—made a nasty remark about my last novel that it contained 'all the old Wodehouse characters under different names'. . . . With my superior intelligence I have outgeneralled the man this time by putting in all the old Wodehouse characters under the same names. Pretty silly it will make him feel, I rather fancy" (Phelps, p. 158).

In his later fiction, Wodehouse exploits to the full not only the charms of old acquaintance he can expect his characters to provide for his readers but also the surprises that can come when long-familiar characters appear in guises we never would have expected. Thus, in *How Right You Are, Jeeves* (1960), Sir Roderick Glossop surprises the reader no less than Bertie Wooster when he turns up at Aunt Dahlia's country house disguised as a butler named Swordfish. This apparition gives a severe jolt to the heroic sangfroid that Bertie believes himself to possess: "In the eyes of many people, I suppose, I seem one of those men of chilled steel you read about, and I'm not saying I'm not. But it is possible to find a chink in my armor, and this can be done by suddenly springing eminent loony-doctors on me in the guise of butlers" (p. 29). Bertie is somehow unprepared for this role change, even though in *Thank You, Jeeves* (1934), he and Sir Roderick had both donned blackface to disguise themselves as traveling minstrels. In *Uncle Fred in the Springtime* (1939), conversely, Frederick, fifth Earl of Ickenham and an inveterate impersonator, stays at Blandings Castle disguised as Sir Roderick himself.

In the late fiction, some of the emotional rough edges are smoothed; in *How Right You Are, Jeeves*, Bertie even discovers himself feeling fond of Sir Roderick a.k.a. Swordfish: "It seemed incredible that I could ever have looked on this admirable loony-doctor as the menace in the treatment" (p. 104). What has turned the tables for Bertie is a late-blooming sense of fellowship based on the fact that Sir Roderick's disguise, and the attendant plotting in which he becomes involved, restore the doctor to his youth, bringing back his school days, when he—like Bertie a generation later—would sneak into the headmaster's study late at night to steal some biscuits.

Even in this mellow late work, though, financial realities still assert themselves. The romantic lead in the story, "Kipper" Herring, hopes to marry Bobbie Wickham, one of Wodehouse's vivacious, mischief-making heroines, to whom Bertie once proposed but whom he came to see as "pure dynamite, and better kept at a distance by all those who aimed at leading the peaceful life" (p. 10). She and Kipper, however, are made for one another, but Kipper will be unable to marry if he loses his newspaper job. This will happen if his former headmaster sues the paper for libel on the basis of an article Kipper wrote concerning him. Kipper explains that if the suit should go forward, he would not only lose his job but be blacklisted among all the editors in London: "'Herring?' the latter [would] say when Kipper comes seeking employment. 'Isn't he the bimbo who took the bread out of the mouths of the *Thursday Review* people? Chuck the blighter out of the window and we want to see him bounce'" (p. 98). To the end, Wodehouse's artificial world was infused with a healthy dose of reality.

WODEHOUSE'S STYLE

THE paradox of Wodehouse's work is that his greatest gift, his magnificent style, came naturally and effortlessly to him. He labored at length over his plots, drafting and redrafting 30,000-word "treatments" of his novels; once the treatment was completed to his satisfaction, he wrote at great speed. As he remarked in a letter to a friend in 1944, "The actual writing of a story always gives me a guilty feeling, as if I were wasting my time. The only thing that matters is thinking the stuff out" (Donaldson, p. 30). Yet the result was anything but the forgettable, workmanlike prose that such methods would ordinarily produce; all his life, Wodehouse had an extraordinary stylistic gift, an ear for comical clashes of modes and manners of speech, a love of setting clichés and quotations askew, and the ability to convey action and character with great economy through long, hilarious sentences.

Like his plots and characterizations, Wodehouse's verbal play was grounded in close observation of reality. We may recall the early essay in which the twenty-year-old Wodehouse hoped for the day in which the real speech of schoolboys would be recorded in fiction; in his later work, his imaginary characters speak a highly realistic language in their unreal surroundings. Even their less articulate moments are rendered with precision: "Bicky laughed what I have sometimes seen described as a hollow, mocking laugh, a sort of bitter cackle from the back of the throat, rather like a gargle" (*Carry On, Jeeves*, p. 82). Later in the same book: "'On the liner going to New York I met a girl.' Biffy made a sort of curious gulping noise not unlike a bulldog trying to swallow half a cutlet in a hurry so as to be ready for the other half" (p. 121).

Wodehouse's own skill with metaphors is counterpointed against his characters' incompetence with them, and he specializes in circular conversations that occur when someone tries to use a comparison to clarify his meaning. In *Right Ho, Jeeves*, Bertie's shy friend Gussie Fink-Nottle wishes he were a male newt:

"Do you know how a male newt proposes, Bertie? He just stands in front of the female newt vibrating his tail and bending his body in a semicircle. I could do that on my head. No, you wouldn't find me grousing if I were a male newt."

"But if you were a male newt, Madeline Bassett wouldn't look at you. Not with the eye of love, I mean."

"She would, if she were a female newt."

"But she isn't a female newt."

"No, but suppose she was."

"Well, if she was, you wouldn't be in love with her."

"Yes I would, if I were a male newt."

A slight throbbing about the temples told me that this discussion had reached saturation point.

(p. 22)

Wodehouse's omniscient narrative voice often displays a sort of manic precision, and even Bertie and Emsworth regularly drift into woolly moments of reflection on phrases or quotations they don't understand. Comparing his Aunt Dahlia at one point to Lot's wife, turned into a pillar of salt, Bertie adds, "though what was the thought behind this I've never been able to understand. Salt, I mean. Seems so bizarre somehow and not at all what you would expect" (*How Right You Are, Jeeves*, p. 99). At the start of *Pigs Have Wings*, Lord Emsworth is told that his nemesis Sir Gregory Parsloe is about to walk over to Blandings to see him. Emsworth is startled, but not from any concern about Sir Gregory's intentions:

> Lord Emsworth blinked.
> "Walk?"
> "So Sir Gregory gave me to understand, m'lord."
> "What does he want to walk for?"
> "I could not say, m'lord."
> "It's three miles each way, and about the hottest day we've had this summer. The man's an ass."
>
> (pp. 1–2)

Clarence's insistent focus on the trivial detail of Sir Gregory's mode of arrival would give Lady Constance a headache, but Clarence's surprise has a logic of its own. Sir Gregory, like Clarence himself, is a rotund, elderly man who would not normally engage in any activity more strenuous than ordering food for himself or his prize pig. Something unnatural has, in fact, intruded into Sir Gregory's life: the athletic fiancée who has put him on a crash diet and who is insisting that he get regular exercise to boot.

Having introduced the theme of walking, Wodehouse keeps it in Emsworth's mind; two pages later, when Constance asks him whether he has seen Galahad and another houseguest, Emsworth replies that "'I was looking out of the window and they came past. Going for a walk or something. They were walking,' explained Lord Emsworth, making it clear that his brother and the young visitor from America had not been mounted on pogosticks" (p. 5). This absurd alternative suddenly presents itself to the reader's eye, with a momentary plausibility to those who know Gally; and after all, in Wodehouse's fluid style, characters rarely do anything so simple as walking, even when they are simply walking. They are more likely to toddle, bound, leg it, nip, or charge, to

take just one sequence from a single paragraph in *Carry On, Jeeves.*

Wodehouse's verbal brilliance won him many admirers among his contemporary writers; in 1936 Hilaire Belloc called him "the best writer of English now alive. The head of my profession" (Phelps, p. 200). He was awarded an honorary Doctor of Letters from Oxford University in 1939—to the distress of some; in 1941 Sean O'Casey wrote that "the civilization that could let Joyce die in poverty and crown with an Litt.D. a thing like Wodehouse, deserves fire and brimstone from heaven: and is getting it" (Phelps, pp. 203–204). Yet Wodehouse and Joyce had more in common than either might have supposed: each had an abiding interest in concrete physical realities and the comedy they can provoke; each was a master of a many-leveled modern English prose style; each was steeped both in classics and in popular culture, though Joyce preferred to view that culture from a distance and transform it while Wodehouse remained immersed within it, playing with an ever-ramifying stock of images, quotations, characters, and events.

The ambiguous literary position of Wodehouse's work is perhaps best summed up by one of his own characters, Vladimir Brusiloff, a tragic Russian novelist and secret golf enthusiast who is giving a lecture tour in America in a story called "The Clicking of Cuthbert." Like any great novelist, at heart Brusiloff despises all of his contemporaries, most of all his eminent compatriots Nastikoff and Sovietski. Yet, though Brusiloff specializes in gray studies of hopeless misery, where nothing happens until a muzhik commits suicide on page 380, he does admit to a grudging admiration for one great predecessor and one contemporary writer: "No novelists anywhere any good except me. P. G. Wodehouse and Tolstoi not bad. Not good, but not bad. No novelists any good except me" (in *The Most of P. G. Wodehouse*, 1960, p. 394).

Among the most popular of popular writers, a lover of Shakespeare and of detective thrillers, trained equally on the Greek and Latin classics and on the works of W. S. Gilbert, Conan Doyle, and Kipling, all of whom he knew in his youth, Wodehouse moved all his life along the border between highbrow and lowbrow, just as he crossed and recrossed the Atlantic and turned novels into plays and back into novels again. A master of convention and a mocker of conventionality, he used the time-bound materials of his late-Victorian childhood to create a strangely timeless world: an artificial paradise shot through with reality.

SELECTED BIBLIOGRAPHY

I. NOVELS AND VOLUMES OF SHORT STORIES. When published under different titles in England and America, the later, alternate title follows in parentheses. Later reprints are listed when they have been cited in the text.

The Pothunters (London, 1902); A Prefect's Uncle (London, 1903); Tales of St. Austin's (London, 1903; repr. London, 1972); The Gold Bat (London, 1904); William Tell Told Again (London, 1904); The Head of Kay's (London, 1905); Love Among the Chickens (London, 1906; New York, 1909); The White Feather (London, 1907); Not George Washington (London, 1907); The Swoop! or, How Clarence Saved England (London, 1909); Mike: A Public School Story (London, 1909).

The Intrusion of Jimmy (New York, 1910; A Gentleman of Leisure, London, 1910); Psmith in the City (London, 1910); The Prince and Betty (London and New York, 1912); The Little Nugget (London, 1913; New York, 1914); The Man Upstairs (London, 1914); Something New (London, 1915; Something Fresh, New York, 1915; repr. as Something New, New York, 1943, 1972); Psmith Journalist (London, 1915); Uneasy Money (New York, 1916; London, 1918); Piccadilly Jim (New York, 1917; London, 1918); The Man with Two Left Feet (London, 1917; New York, 1933); A Damsel in Distress (London and New York, 1919); My Man Jeeves (London, 1919); Their Mutual Child (New York, 1919; The Coming of Bill, London, 1920).

The Little Warrior (New York, 1920; Jill the Reckless, London, 1921); Indiscretions of Archie (London and New York, 1921); The Clicking of Cuthbert (London, 1922; Golf Without Tears, New York, 1924); Three Men and a Maid (New York, 1922; The Girl on the Boat, London, 1922); The Adventures of Sally (London, 1923; Mostly Sally, New York, 1923); The Inimitable Jeeves (London, 1923; Jeeves, New York, 1923); Leave It to Psmith (London, 1923; New York, 1924); Ukridge (London, 1924; He Rather Enjoyed It, New York, 1925); Bill, the Conqueror: His Invasion of England in the Springtime (London and New York, 1924); Carry On, Jeeves (London, 1925; New York, 1927; repr. Harmondsworth, Eng., 1956, including "Jeeves Takes Charge," "The Artistic Career of Corky," "Jeeves and the Unbidden Guest," "Jeeves and the Hard-Boiled Egg," "The Aunt and the Sluggard," "The Rummy Affair of Old Biffy," "Without the Option," and "Bertie Changes His Mind"); Sam the Sudden (London, 1925; Sam in the Suburbs, New York, 1925); The Heart of a Goof (London, 1926; Divots, New York, 1927); Meet Mr. Mulliner (London, 1927; New York, 1928); The Small Bachelor (London and New York, 1927); Money for Noth-

ing (London and New York, 1928); Mr. Mulliner Speaking (London, 1929; New York, 1930); Fish Preferred (New York, 1929; Summer Lightning, London, 1929).

Very Good, Jeeves (London and New York, 1930); Big Money (London and New York, 1931); If I Were You (London and New York, 1931); Doctor Sally (London, 1932); Hot Water (London and New York, 1932); Heavy Weather (London and New York, 1933); Mulliner Nights (London and New York, 1933); Thank You, Jeeves! (London and New York, 1934); Right Ho, Jeeves (London, 1934; repr. Harmondsworth, Eng., 1972); Brinkley Manor: A Novel About Jeeves (Boston, 1934); Blandings Castle (London and New York, 1935); The Luck of the Bodkins (London, 1935; New York, 1936); Young Men in Spats (London and New York, 1936); Laughing Gas (London and New York, 1936); Lord Emsworth and Others (London, 1937; The Crime Wave at Blandings, New York, 1937); Summer Moonshine (New York, 1937; London, 1938); The Code of the Woosters (London and New York, 1938); Uncle Fred in the Springtime (London and New York, 1939).

Eggs, Beans and Crumpets (London and New York, 1940); Quick Service (London and New York, 1940); Money in the Bank (New York, 1942; London, 1946); Joy in the Morning (New York, 1946; London, 1947); Full Moon (London and New York, 1947), illus. by Paul Galdone; Spring Fever (London and New York, 1948), illus. by Paul Galdone; Uncle Dynamite (London and New York, 1948); The Mating Season (London and New York, 1949).

Nothing Serious (London, 1950; New York, 1951); The Old Reliable (London and New York, 1951); Barmy in Wonderland (London, 1952; Angel Cake, New York, 1952); Pigs Have Wings (London and New York, 1952; repr. New York, 1977); Ring for Jeeves (London, 1953; The Return of Jeeves, New York, 1954); Jeeves and the Feudal Spirit (London, 1954; Bertie Wooster Sees It Through, New York, 1955); French Leave (London, 1955; New York, 1959); Something Fishy (London, 1957; The Butler Did It, New York, 1957); Cocktail Time (London and New York, 1958); A Few Quick Ones (London and New York, 1959).

How Right You Are, Jeeves (New York, 1960; repr., New York, 1966; Jeeves in the Offing, London, 1960); The Ice in the Bedroom (New York, 1961; Ice in the Bedroom, London, 1961); Service with a Smile (New York, 1961; London, 1962); Stiff Upper Lip, Jeeves (London and New York, 1963); Biffen's Millions (New York, 1964; Frozen Assets, London, 1964); The Brinkmanship of Galahad Threepwood (New York, 1965; Galahad at Blandings, London, 1965); The Purloined Paperweight (New York, 1967; Company for Henry, London, 1967; reissued in 1986 by the Paperweight Press of Santa Cruz, Calif., with a preface stressing that "today, interest in paperweights is at an all-time high"); Do Butlers Burgle Banks? (London and New York, 1968); A Pelican at Blandings (London, 1969; No Nudes Is Good Nudes, New York, 1970).

The Girl in Blue (London, 1970; New York, 1971); *Much Obliged, Jeeves* (London, 1971; *Jeeves and the Tie that Binds,* New York, 1971); *Pearls, Girls, and Monty Bodkin* (London, 1972; *The Plot That Thickened,* New York, 1973); *Bachelors Anonymous* (London, 1973; New York, 1974); *Aunts Aren't Gentlemen* (London, 1974; *The Cat Nappers,* New York, 1975); *Sunset at Blandings* (London and New York, 1977).

II. Selected Anthologies. *Jeeves Omnibus* (London, 1931); *Week-End Wodehouse* (London and New York, 1939); *Wodehouse on Golf* (New York, 1940); *The Best of Wodehouse* (New York, 1949), intro. by Scott Meredith; *Selected Stories by P. G. Wodehouse* (New York, 1958); intro. by John W. Albridge; *The Most of P. G. Wodehouse* (New York, 1960; including "The Clicking of Cuthbert"); *The World of Jeeves* (London, 1967); *Vintage Wodehouse* (London, 1977).

III. Selected Plays and Musicals. Complete bibliographies for Wodehouse's theater work can be found in the biographies by Donaldson and Phelps listed below.

Sergeant Brue (London, 1904; book and one lyric); *A Gentleman of Leisure* (New York, 1911; book); *Miss Springtime* (New York, 1916; book by Guy Bolton, lyrics by Wodehouse, music by Emmerich Kalman and Jerome Kern); *Oh, Boy!* (New York, 1917; book by Guy Bolton and Wodehouse, lyrics by Wodehouse, music by Jerome Kern; 475 performances); *Oh, Kay!* (New York, 1926; book by Guy Bolton and Wodehouse; lyrics by Ira Gershwin, music by George Gershwin; 256 performances); *The Play's the Thing* (New York, 1926; repr. with three other plays in *Four Plays,* London, 1983); *Rosalie* (New York, 1928; lyrics by Ira Gershwin and Wodehouse; music by George Gershwin and Sigmund Romberg; 335 performances).

IV. Essays and Letters. *The Globe by the Way Book* (London, 1908); *Louder and Funnier* (London, 1932); *Bring On the Girls* (New York, 1953; London, 1954); *Performing Flea* (London, 1953; *Author! Author!,* New York, 1962); *America, I Like You* (New York, 1956; *Over Seventy,* London, 1957); *Plum Pie* (London, 1966; New York, 1967); *The Uncollected Wodehouse* (New York, 1976, including "In Defense of Astigmatism" and "The Agonies of Writing a Musical Comedy"); *Wodehouse on Wodehouse* (London, 1980); *Yours, Plum* (London, 1990).

V. Biographical Studies. The two best biographies, giving very different views of Wodehouse, are Frances Donaldson, *P. G. Wodehouse: The Authorized Biography* (London, 1982), and Barry Phelps, *P. G. Wodehouse: Man and Myth* (London, 1992); both build on and quarrel with an earlier work, David A. Jasen, *P. G. Wodehouse: Portrait of a Master* (New York, 1974). Also of interest are Iain Sproat, *Wodehouse at War* (London, 1981), and N. T. P. Murphy, *In Search of Blandings* (London, repr. 1986).

VI. Critical Studies. The best analytical books on Wodehouse are Owen Dudley Edwards, *P. G. Wodehouse: A Critical and Historical Essay* (London, 1977), and Richard Usborne, *Wodehouse at Work to the End* (London, 1977, rev. ed. of his *Wodehouse at Work,* 1961). A general overview is provided by Richard J. Voorhees, *P. G. Wodehouse* (New York, 1966). Other studies are George Orwell, "In Defense of P. G. Wodehouse," in *Dickens, Dali, and Others* (London, 1946); Geoffrey Jaggard, *Wooster's World* (London, 1967) and *Blandings the Blest* (London, 1968); Herbert Warren Wind, *The World of P. G. Wodehouse* (New York, 1972); Robert A. Hall, Jr., *The Comic Style of P. G. Wodehouse* (Hamden, Conn., 1974); J. H. C. Morris and A. D. Macintyre, *Thank You, Wodehouse* (London, 1981); Charles E. Gould, Jr., *The Toad at Harrow* (London, 1982).

MARY WOLLSTONECRAFT

(1759–1797)

Mary Poovey

TODAY, MARY WOLLSTONECRAFT is most famous for *A Vindication of the Rights of Woman* (1792), which was one of the earliest statements of the principles of the modern feminist movement. In her own lifetime, however—and in the decades immediately following her death—Wollstonecraft was notorious for her unorthodox religious views, her unconventional sexual behavior, and her attempted suicides. Thanks largely to the posthumous publication of her husband's *Memoirs of the Author of* A Vindication of the Rights of Woman (1798), Mary Wollstonecraft provided subsequent generations with the type of an "unsex'd female." Espousing the principles that modern feminists take for granted, in other words, rendered Mary Wollstonecraft an object of ridicule and loathing to many of the women who most immediately followed her.

In order to understand Wollstonecraft's accomplishments and her vilification, it is important to reconstruct the cultural values by which middle-class English women were evaluated in the last quarter of the eighteenth century. These values can be encapsulated by the term "propriety": to fulfill the domestic roles God and nature had theoretically assigned them, women had to be self-denying, deferential, modest, and chaste; to be good wives and mothers, they had to be thrifty, disciplined, and responsive to their husbands' and children's every need. The complexities of late-eighteenth-century propriety begin to emerge in this last injunction, for, if a woman was too responsive to the needs of others, she might well prove too susceptible to other kinds of influences as well—including that of sentimental novels composed to awaken the emotional responsiveness that women ideally (but not necessarily) directed toward husbands and homes. Then, too, the injunction to be a modest lady was levied in a social context in which unmarried women had to compete with each other for suitable mates. In the often highly ritualized situations in which proper women could attract the notice of marriageable men, women had to find a way to display their modesty. In order to become what moralists claimed they were born to be—good wives and mothers—middle-class women had to assert and deny themselves at the same time.

Mary Wollstonecraft identified these contradictions in the contemporary code of propriety, and she argued that propriety was both unnatural and wrong. Yet in the course of recognizing the biases at the heart of her culture, Wollstonecraft became a lightning rod for the anger and anxieties that lay beneath the surface of propriety. Perhaps more to the point, she discovered that the complex investments others so obviously had in the contradictory code of propriety were echoed in her own attachment to a model of female feeling that kept Wollstonecraft vulnerable to confusion, disappointment, and pain.

EARLY LIFE

THE early stage of Wollstonecraft's life and writing is characterized by the persistence of two conflicting desires. On the one hand, she constantly craved the emotional rewards that propriety decreed were every woman's birthright: love, gratitude, and a sense of being necessary to someone else's happiness. On the other hand, she was driven by a fierce determination to be independent—free not just from financial debts but, more significantly, from feeling itself, from the emotional demands that were also considered a part of female "nature." Wollstonecraft's ambivalence toward feeling resurfaced in its most troubling form when she tried to cope with the emotions and sexual urges traditionally signified by the euphemism "sentiments."

For much of her life, Mary Wollstonecraft occupied a precarious social position, which made emotional vulnerability especially pernicious. She was born in London on 27 April 1759. Her father, Edward John Wollstonecraft, the eldest son of a well-to-do silk weaver, was able to purchase a considerable estate in 1765, when Mary was six years old. Within ten years, however, he had lost his estate and nearly destroyed his family, not only through financial mismanagement, but through drunkenness and a tyrannical temper. Largely because of their rapid social descent and her father's irresponsibility, Mary Wollstonecraft took the audacious step of leaving home at the age of nineteen to work as a lady's companion.

Even in her precarious position as a self-supporting working woman, Wollstonecraft remained—in some conflicting senses—a child of the middle classes. Two of the most dramatic incidents of Wollstonecraft's young adulthood reflect her remarkable determination and self-assertiveness. In 1783 she single-handedly rescued her sister Eliza from an unhappy marriage. Then, late in 1785, Wollstonecraft sailed to Lisbon to oversee the lying-in of her beloved friend Fanny Blood. She arrived in the foreign country only to watch her friend die soon after giving birth.

Despite their daring, Wollstonecraft's interventions focused on typical female concerns; this suggests that she had also internalized the expectations and self-definition of a proper middle-class young lady. She spent much of her young adulthood seeking the kind of emotional situation that would substitute for the unhappy family relationships she had left behind. Throughout her teens and late twenties she turned to a series of father figures and gathered about her, in addition to her two natural sisters, a flock of surrogate siblings—Jane Arden in her youth, then Fanny Blood and her brother George. When Wollstonecraft's mother, Elizabeth Dickson Wollstonecraft, fell ill in late 1780, Mary went home to nurse her until she died in April 1782. On her deathbed, as Wollstonecraft reconstructed the scene in her last work, *Maria* (published in *Posthumous Works*, 1798), Mary's mother bequeathed to her an ongoing domestic responsibility: "My mother . . . solemnly recommended my sisters to my care, and bid me be a mother to them."

Wollstonecraft's personal sense of the unreliability of domestic affections, however, contributed to her need to dictate the terms on which she would assume a traditional woman's role. Her anxiety about the possibility of domestic love led directly to an anxiety about the possibility of romantic love. Perhaps in defiance of the disappointment she had come to expect and fear, Wollstonecraft began to speak scornfully of romantic love even before the collapse of Eliza's marriage. As early as 1779, when she was just twenty, Wollstonecraft repudiated love and prided herself on having achieved "a kind of early old age" (*Collected Letters of Mary Wollstonecraft*,[1] p. 69; 17 October 1779). Wollstonecraft's wistful repudiation of emotional vulnerability was intensified by the helplessness and humiliation she associated with her social and economic dependence. Between 1778 and 1787 she tried virtually every honorable occupation open to middle-class women. For various periods of time, she served as a lady's companion, a seamstress, a schoolmistress, and, finally, a governess for the daughters of Irish aristocrats. During her stay in Ireland as a governess, Wollstonecraft's insecurity surfaced in nagging doubts that she was qualified for the job, fears that she was not well-dressed or pretty enough, and a perhaps defensive concern that the children were growing too fond of her. Inferior in status, she consoled herself with the thought that she was superior in "sensibility," in "real refinement."

In 1787, Wollstonecraft finally shed her dependence and moved to London, determined to become what she hyperbolically called "the first of a new genus"—a self-supporting, professional woman writer (*Letters*, p. 164; 7 November 1787). Although she began to describe herself as a professional writer only after moving to London, her literary career had actually already begun. By 1788 Wollstonecraft had published two books that epitomize the two poles that thus far had dominated the young woman's emotional struggle. The first, *Thoughts on the Education of Daughters: With Reflections on Female Conduct, in the More Important Duties of Life* (1787), advocates the ideal principles of self-control and submission that theoretically guaranteed a woman love. The second, *Mary, A Fiction* (1788), is a melodramatic heightening of Wollstonecraft's own love for Fanny Blood, her sense of loss, and the frustrated romantic expectations she had tried to renounce.

For Mary Wollstonecraft, the role of professional writer initially promised to resolve her emotional

[1]Referred to hereafter as *Letters*.

dilemma; it seemed to offer both independence and a means by which she could fulfill a woman's traditional responsibilities. As her familiarity with professional writing increased, however, she gradually began to believe that in order to escape the belittling stereotypes men (and many women) had canonized she would have to suppress those easily frustrated "mortal longings" she too associated with female emotion—and therefore with humiliation and weakness. Rapidly Wollstonecraft began to make herself over in the "masculine" image of an intellectual. Soon after her momentous move to London, she begged her sister Everina to contribute to her self-transformation "by gathering together all the news you can, with respect to literature." "Many motives impel me besides sheer love of knowledge, which however has ever been a predominate mover in my little world, it is the only way to destroy the worm that will gnaw the core—and make that being an isolé, whom nature made too susceptible of affections, which stray beyond the bounds, reason prescribes" (*Letters*, p. 173, 22 March 1788). Study would not finally banish the worm, however, nor would Mary Wollstonecraft rest content to become an "isolé," or solitary, isolated person. The tensions that characterized her early life would continue to plague the first efforts of her professional career. Gradually, however, by subjecting her "affections" to the scrutiny of her "reason," she would begin to understand the origin of the desires that still warred in her heart.

A VINDICATION OF THE RIGHTS OF MEN

WITHIN the group of radical artists, writers, and philosophers who frequented Joseph Johnson's publishing house in London, Wollstonecraft found reassuring proof that it *was* possible to be a "self-made" man, but she also encountered the more troubling problem that to be a "self-made" woman involved altogether different obstacles. As Dissenters, Johnson and most of his friends had to create careers according to unorthodox designs, doing battle with legal restrictions and educational disadvantages in the process. Having achieved a measure of security himself, Johnson was determined to help others gain intellectual independence. The position he offered Wollstonecraft, as reviewer for the *Analytical Review*, provided her

with the opportunity to begin in earnest the ambitious project of becoming a self-made intellectual.

Wollstonecraft's first work for Johnson consisted of reviewing and translating, but by 1790 she felt sufficiently self-confident to undertake an original composition. Significantly, her first extensive production as a self-supporting professional and self-proclaimed intellectual took the form that most people would have considered the least appropriate for a woman—the political disquisition. Requiring knowledge of government, analytical ability, and the ambition to participate directly in contemporary events, political disquisition was in every sense a masculine domain. Wollstonecraft's choice of a project, then, signals her determination to transcend the limitations she felt her sex had already imposed on her. In this first expression of her professional persona, Wollstonecraft actually aspires to *be* a man, for she suspects that the shortest way to success and equality is to hide what seemed to her a fatal female flaw beneath the mask of male discourse.

Wollstonecraft's *A Vindication of the Rights of Men* (1790) was the first English reply to Edmund Burke's *Reflections on the Revolution in France* (November 1790). Wollstonecraft's *Vindication*, written in fewer than thirty days and published anonymously, predates Thomas Paine's more famous *Rights of Man* (1791) by almost eleven months. The book was so popular that Johnson issued a second, signed edition by December 1790. Despite the bold, self-confident tone with which the book begins, however, *The Rights of Men* immediately betrays its writer's inexperience in political disquisition. Wollstonecraft's bravado masks her insecurity about both how to present the outrage she felt at Burke's defense of the monarchy, hereditary property, and manners, and how to give her largely subjective response authority. What we soon discover in *The Rights of Men* are the same tensions that had thus far marked Wollstonecraft's life. On the one hand she unleashes the emotionalism with which she feels most at home; on the other hand she invokes reason, which she believes to be a necessary control for feeling. She claims independence, especially from the roles assigned to women, but also resorts to the characteristically feminine posture of seeking shelter within the protective hierarchy of a paternal order.

The "Advertisement" at the beginning of *The Rights of Men* immediately announces Wollstonecraft's divided attitudes, for it both insists on the authority of feeling and lays claim to a rational authorization for this feeling. This "Advertisement" is both explicitly apologetic and decidedly assertive. In it Wollstonecraft depicts the book as a spontaneous outburst of indignant feeling, "the effusions of the moment," which has been published only at someone else's urging. By this aggressive "apology," Wollstonecraft not only deflects personal responsibility for the book but, by stressing the volatility of the emotion that inspired it, emphasizes the energy, hence the power, of that emotion. Wollstonecraft is also anxious to legitimize the prominent role that feeling plays in the organization of her text. *The Rights of Men* follows the associations of Wollstonecraft's own mind instead of presenting an orderly analysis of the topics discussed by Burke. The young writer explains this technique as necessary to her subject; alternately, she argues that slavish attention to particulars is unnecessary and that, given Burke's contradictions, such logic is impossible. Despite her reliance on the power of her subjective response to Burke, however, she clearly fears that feeling is not a legitimate authority for political disquisition. In order to bolster what at times becomes a completely subjective response, she repeatedly insists that her position is "obvious," that it is based on the absolute, objectively verifiable truth of God. Although she claims that this truth can be "demonstrated," she invokes "objective" principles only to ennoble her subjective responses. Her demonstration of self-evident "truths" is, in fact, no less subjective than Burke's defense of very different truths. What is interesting about Wollstonecraft's reply to Burke is that the manner in which she turns to the authority of these "fundamental truths" suggests that she is really battling not Burke's argument so much as her own old enemy, feeling.

In *The Rights of Men*, Wollstonecraft subordinates her objections to Burke's political argument to an attack on the hyperbolic rhetoric with which she believes he deliberately manipulates his audience. Ironically, she objects both to Burke's *lack* of feeling and to his tendency to get carried away by his argument: "Words are heaped on words, till the understanding is confused by endeavouring to disentangle the sense, and the memory by tracing contradictions . . . ; you have often sacrificed your sincerity to enforce your favourite arguments, and called in your judgement to adjust the arrangement of words that could not convey its dictates"

(facsimile ed., 1975, p. 127). Wollstonecraft's anger at Burke's acrobatic rhetoric is really only one aspect of what proves to be her most sweeping condemnation: the entire *Reflections*, she charges, contains no reasoned argument at all; it is merely an expression of Burke's obsessive vanity, a noisy appeal for public attention. Wollstonecraft also scorns what she calls Burke's "unmanly servility," for Wollstonecraft's primary target is Burke's tendency to universalize the attitude of "dignified obedience" that women are supposed to display (p. 50). Wollstonecraft despises the passivity of this posture; from her personal experience, she knows that "subordination of the heart," far from nourishing a "spirit of exalted freedom," brings only helplessness and pain. Intent on rejecting this psychological and political model, she substitutes for Burke's feminized paradigm a description of human nature anchored in "masculine" behavior, in confrontation and conquest.

Wollstonecraft's attack on submission is preeminently a middle-class assault made in the name of individual effort and proven merit against aristocratic privilege. Unlike the responses of many other middle-class liberals, however, Wollstonecraft's complaint also articulates the special frustrations of a woman. For, just as the wealthy inherit "privilege" as their "natural" birthright, so women acquire "privilege" through the education that renders "natural" their dependence on men. Unlike rich men, however, women do not have the self-confidence or power to transcend their "benumbed" existence. Women are debilitated by the privilege they are given because the virtue they are asked to embody discourages them from the intellectual exertion that would enable them to cultivate reason. The implication is that women are unwitting victims not only of Edmund Burke, but of all men who idealize virtuous women.

Despite Wollstonecraft's brief insight into the investment that women have in overthrowing propriety, she refuses in *The Rights of Men* to identify consistently with women or even to sympathize with the submissiveness they have been forced to assume. Instead, she rejects the female experience of helplessness and frustration for the defiant middle-class assertion that one can, in fact, be anything one wants. Wollstonecraft explicitly adopts an attitude that is implicitly at odds with feminine propriety and hence, with the typical female situation. She allies herself with the individualistic values of middle-class men and heaps scorn on the posture of helplessness, which she can see only as weakness and personal failure.

In one particularly significant passage, Wollstonecraft reveals that her rejection of the feminine position rests on a recognition that the acquiescence it requires is "dangerous." All "first principles" must be demonstrated, she insists, "and not determined by arbitrary authority and dark traditions, lest a dangerous supineness should take place; for probably, in ceasing to enquire, our reason would remain dormant and delivered up, without a curb, to every impulse of passion, we might soon lose sight of the clear light which the exercise of our understanding no longer kept alive" (pp. 37–38). For Wollstonecraft, to remain passive—whether before innate feelings or cultural authority—is to court an absolute loss of control, and, implicitly, it is to deliver oneself up to the threatening force of emotion itself.

Submissiveness to feelings is, of course, what Wollstonecraft had always feared in herself. "Reason" should be the active legislator of passion and thus the defense against vulnerability and pain. But the passage just quoted suggests that reason would "remain dormant" were it not for another faculty—desire or passion. Wollstonecraft does not want to abandon passion, for she feels too acutely the energy of her own feelings; but she does not quite trust passion either. Thus she tries to vindicate feeling without capitulating to it. Although she admits, in passing, that passion and reason bear a disconcerting likeness to each other, she argues for an authoritative system of values that will simultaneously distinguish between reason and passion and sanction feeling by making it part of a larger design. Interestingly, in order to vindicate feeling, Wollstonecraft inadvertently assumes the feminine position she has just attacked Burke for supporting; in endorsing Christianity, Wollstonecraft assumes the feminine stance of "proud submission."

Before coming to London, Wollstonecraft's religious practice had been basically Evangelical; as her friendship with Johnson and his circle developed, her Christianity was supplemented by the faith in reason that she announces in *The Rights of Men*. Even during the period in which she was most subject to their influence, however, Wollstonecraft never exchanged her religious faith for skepticism, for her particular beliefs served a crucial function in her developing self-image. For her, the authority of God, which can be "deduced" by

reason as well as intuited by the heart, reduces the pain that a dependent posture might otherwise entail. The "proof" that she offers for this objective authority, however, is finally only her own belief—or, more precisely, her own need.

I bend with awful reverence when I enquire on what my fear is built.—I fear that sublime power, whose motive for creating me must have been wise and good; and I submit to the moral laws which my reason deduces from this view of my dependence on him.—It is not his power that I fear—it is not to an arbitrary will, but to unerring *reason* I submit. . . .

This fear of God makes me reverence myself. . . . And this, enlightened self-love . . . forces me to see; and, if I may venture to borrow a prostituted term, to *feel* that happiness is reflected, and that, in communicating good, my soul receives its noble aliment.

(pp. 78–79)

Wollstonecraft "reverences" herself because she believes herself to be "a faint image" of a reasonable, benevolent God: she believes that her own rationality and benevolence reflect God's image because her "enlightened self-love" makes her feel that this is true. This circular logic is finally anchored in "fear" and "dependence," yet, because God must be just, such emotions can cause no pain.

Wollstonecraft's investment in Evangelical religion was profoundly influenced by her gender. Wollstonecraft's belief that a reasonable paternalistic order exists in the universe enables her to advocate self-assertion, confrontation, and a perpetual struggle after "higher attainments" *without* transgressing the fundamental posture of submissiveness that a woman was expected to maintain. *Because* she is a woman, Wollstonecraft conceives her religious faith primarily in terms of only one facet of the Protestant faith. In other words, because she has partially internalized the aspirations, expectations, and self-definition of a woman rather than a man, the work she imagines yields spiritual, not material, rewards; it is, in fact, conceived of in terms of self-denial and triumphant suffering rather than self-assertion in the name of spiritual gain.

The paternal authority exercised by God in Wollstonecraft's religious faith has a counterpart in her vision of a reformed society. In her utopia an entire army of father figures, both secular and religious, ensures happiness by anticipating every need. As a result, society can return to its prelapsarian—and presexual—harmony.

A garden more inviting than Eden would then meet the eye, and springs of joy murmur on every side. The clergyman would superintend his own flock, the shepherd would then love the sheep he daily tended; the school might rear its decent head, and the buzzing tribe, let loose to play, impart a portion of their vivacious spirits to the heart that longed to open their minds, and lead them to taste the pleasures of men. Domestic comfort, the civilizing relations of husband, brother, and father, would soften labour, and render life contented.

(p. 147)

Notice that there is no real equality in this garden. Nor are there, literally, any women. But women's presence is implied in the last sentence. Here women are the invisible center, the silent beings whose simple existence turns men into "husband, brother, and father" and whose actions epitomize indirection: they "soften" labor without working themselves; they "render life contented" and only presumably enjoy the "domestic comforts" that others' happiness yields.

In such passages Wollstonecraft obviously resorts to the same "pomp of words" for which she castigates Burke. Her rationale for employing such rhetoric differs significantly from his, however. Instead of controlling the response of the audience, Wollstonecraft's rhetoric helps control her own emotions. The rhetoric of the passages in which she invokes God and imagines utopia helps to give acceptable form to the passion that threatens to explode both language and logic. Reliance on rhetoric is for Wollstonecraft a form of indirection that distances her from her own unreliable emotion without sacrificing its force. At the same time, it permits her to project the appearance of masculine assertiveness without having to take personal responsibility for it. Just as Wollstonecraft's invocation of reason is really a transvaluation of feeling, so her masculine persona is really a cover for the feminine position she has all along retained.

The tension we see here between the masculine posture of direct confrontation and the feminine strategy of indirection, like the tension between reason and feeling, betrays Wollstonecraft's uncertainty about the nature of her voice and its authority. Not having fully grasped the relationship between any individual and his or her social situation, she has yet to identify either her own natural allies or the origin of her own volatile feelings. Not having fully worked out the connection between any individual position and cultural values, she still attacks Burke when she might well focus her discontent on the tradition behind him. In *The Rights of Men*, Wollstonecraft has not identified her place within the code of propriety that surrounds her, and, as a consequence, she still lacks the self-confidence truly to be the first of that hybrid "new genus," a self-expressive woman in a chorus of male voices.

A VINDICATION OF THE RIGHTS OF WOMAN

IN October 1791, Mary Wollstonecraft informed her new friend William Roscoe that she had begun sitting for the portrait he had commissioned. "I do not imagine that it will be a very striking likeness," she apologized playfully; "but, if you do not find me in it, I will send you a more faithful sketch—a book that I am now writing, in which *I* myself . . . shall certainly appear, head and heart" (*Letters*, pp. 202–203; 6 October 1791). The "sketch" was *A Vindication of the Rights of Woman* (1792), and, as this letter suggests, Wollstonecraft's second political tract proves that during the preceding year she had progressed considerably in her ability to understand not only political issues but also her own place within them. In discovering that her most natural allies in the debate conducted in *The Rights of Men* were women, Wollstonecraft was more nearly able to come to terms with the emotionalism that disrupted that argument. In learning to harness her emotion and by recognizing its fellow in the emotionalism of other women, she seems to have begun to perceive that the problem that had always undermined her self-confidence was collective rather than personal.

The first of Wollstonecraft's breakthroughs in *The Rights of Woman* was the insight that individual responses are, first and foremost, responses to situations and that, in a telling way, what deformed middle-class women was the code of propriety: women are "swallowed up . . . by *courtesy*." "Rest on yourself," Wollstonecraft replied to the request for advice from the young author Mary Hays, for special danger awaits the woman writer who, accustomed to "courtesy," can be placated by meaningless praise. "An author, especially a woman, should be cautious lest she too hastily swallows the crude praises which partial friend and polite acquaintance bestow thoughtlessly when the supplicating eye looks for them" (*Letters*, p. 219, 12 November 1792).

Wollstonecraft's second important realization in *The Rights of Woman* was that the attitudes and expectations that perpetuate female weakness are institutionalized by the texts that express masculine assumptions of what "feminine" behavior should be. Thus one major cause of the "barren blooming" that Wollstonecraft discerns in women is "a false system of education, gathered from the books written on this subject by men who, considering females rather as women than human creatures, have been more anxious to make them alluring mistresses than affectionate wives and rational mothers" (*A Vindication of the Rights of Woman*, p. 7). By teaching women to understand themselves solely by men's judgments, to submit to the restraint of propriety, and to pursue their educations only with regard to men's happiness, these male "authorities"—and the women who echo them—have deprived women of the opportunity for self-exertion and, therefore, of the possibility for self-improvement.

In *The Rights of Woman*, Wollstonecraft assumes that all human beings are equal in their fundamental capacity to reason; discriminatory education should thus be eliminated because it is detrimental to the improvement of humanity as a whole. Only when women are considered—and consider themselves—human beings rather than sexual objects, only when their education develops rather than suppresses their reason, only when they are granted the legal equality they by nature deserve, will they be able to contribute to this improvement. Wollstonecraft insists that her argument is not based on special interest; because she is intent on effacing all sexual discrimination, she declares herself "disinterested" and claims to speak with the neutral voice of the species, "the firm tone of humanity" (p. 3).

Perceiving her own voice as the generalized, ideal voice of collective humanity relieves Wollstonecraft of much of the insecurity that marked *The Rights of Men*. She claims that her admonitions now have the widest possible base; they transcend the charge of egotism or self-interest, and they derive their authority from the instances of reason that, as she continues to argue, are everywhere evident. This position gives Wollstonecraft the confidence to embark on the course of direct confrontation she advocated but did not pursue in *The Rights of Men*. In *The Rights of Woman* she is finally able to identify and aggressively challenge the "authorities" she holds most responsible for female education: Jean-Jacques Rousseau and eighteenth-century conduct-book writers.

The root of the wrongs of women, according to Wollstonecraft, is the general acceptance of the idea that women are essentially sexual beings—or, as Rousseau phrases it, "a male is only a male now and again, the female is always a female . . . ; everything reminds her of her sex" (*Émile*). Wollstonecraft's response to this sexual characterization of women is simply to reverse the charge: not women, she argues, but *men* are dominated by their sexual desires; men's insatiable appetites are the root of both economic inequality and social injustice. Arguments about women's "natural" inferiority, then, are only men's rationalizations for the superior social position they have unjustifiably seized, and their talk of "natural" female wantonness is merely a cover for the sexual appetite that men both fear and relish in themselves. Rousseau is the "sensualist" Wollstonecraft attacks most systematically for indulging in "voluptuous reveries": "Rousseau declares that a woman should never, for a moment, feel herself independent, that she should be governed by fear to exercise her natural cunning, and made a coquettish slave in order to render her a more alluring object of desire, a *sweeter* companion to man, whenever he chooses to relax himself" (p. 25). Thus Rousseau's "discovery" of the "natural law" governing women is simply a creation of his own repressed desire. Rousseau, as a "voluptuous tyrant," simultaneously rationalizes his own sensuality and gratifies it, and, at the same time, he punishes the being who tempts him to this self-indulgence by making her responsible for sexual control. Wollstonecraft is very close to perceiving how a set of beliefs can be generated from or adopted because of local needs and psychological imperatives. Moreover, she intuits the dynamics of repression and compensation at work in this production: as forbidden longings are censured, sexual desire erupts in other, more permissible forms like Rousseau's sensual reveries. When his imagination is "debauched" in the name of virtuous self-denial, Rousseau seduces his reader as he indulges himself: "And thus making us feel whilst dreaming that we reason, erroneous conclusions are left in the mind" (p. 91).

From the disguised but ever-present force of male desire, Wollstonecraft charges, all the evils that oppress women follow. Kept in a prolonged mental childhood to enhance the "innocence" men find so appealing, women are denied access to the personal experience necessary to the formation of a strong "human character" (p. 114). She clearly sees the paradox inherent in this deprivation: denied all challenging encounters and education, women are actually trapped within the narrow domain of their own personal, sensual experience. Consequently incapable of "generalizing ideas or drawing comprehensive conclusions from individual observations," women become obsessed with immediate impressions and gratifications. Because men indulge *their* sensual desires, women, trying to please, become slaves to their own senses and thus hostage to every transient emotion (p. 54).

So intent is Wollstonecraft to reject the prevalent stereotype of women as *all* sexuality that she comes close to arguing that women have no innate sexual desires at all. Repeatedly she implies that female sexuality is only a learned response to male sexuality. Promiscuity and repression surely exist; yet Wollstonecraft is at pains to argue that such responses to sexual agitation are rare and unnatural. She describes an ideal marriage as one without passion, for example, and she asserts with apparent assurance that women will easily be able to transform sexual desire into the more "serious" and "austere" emotions of friendship (p. 130).

The closer we read Wollstonecraft's *The Rights of Woman*, however, the clearer it becomes that her defensive denial of female sexuality is just that—a defense against what she feared: desire doomed to repeated frustration. Contrary to her assertions, Wollstonecraft's deepest fear centers not on the voraciousness of male sexual desire but on what she fears is its brevity. Thus, while she can insist that "in the exercise of their maternal feelings providence has furnished women with a natural substitute for love," this substitute turns out to be necessary because, inevitably, the "lover [will become] only a friend" (p. 152). The devoted mother she describes proves to be a "neglected wife," driven to seek from her children the gratification that her "unhappy marriage" no longer provides. And the heroism of the self-sacrificing widow, which she celebrates, turns out to be barren and decidedly equivocal: "Raised to heroism by misfortunes, she represses the first faint dawning of a natural inclination, before it ripens into love, and in the bloom of life forgets her sex" (pp. 50–51).

Such repression is necessary, Wollstonecraft implies, because, far from being the learned response she asserts it is, female sexuality is actually as demanding as male sexuality; perhaps it is even more urgent. In a remarkable passage Wollstonecraft betrays the fact that she shares the moralists' anxiety about female appetite. This passage begins with an indictment of indecorous eating habits. Men are the worst offenders on this score, but, she acknowledges, "some women, particularly French women, have also lost a sense of decency in this respect; for they will talk very calmly of an indigestion. It were to be wished that idleness was not allowed to generate, on the rank soil of wealth, those swarms of summer insects that feed on putrefaction, we should not then be disgusted by the sight of such brutal excesses" (p. 137). While Wollstonecraft's scorn for the idle rich accounts for part of her venom here, her subsequent association of the "refinement of eating" with the "refinements of love" more fully explains her vitriolic language. Until women can transcend their fleshly desires and fleshly forms, this passage suggests, they will be hostage to the body—a body that in demanding physical satisfaction makes itself vulnerable to frustration and pain.

The suspicion Wollstonecraft reveals here that female appetite might be the precipitating cause of women's cultural objectification also helps account for her vehement disgust with female physicality. Abhorring those "nasty, or immodest habits" that girls in boarding schools acquire, she goes on to attack the "gross degree of familiarity" that "sisters, female intimates, or ladies and their waiting women" exhibit toward one another (p. 127). She cautions all girls to wash and dress alone, lest they take up "some still more nasty customs, which men never fall into" (p. 128). Wollstonecraft's disgust involves female bodies and female desires—and all the ramifications of sexuality that she does not want to think about here.

In her attempt to control the emotional energy that threatened to explode her political argument in *The Rights of Men*, Wollstonecraft has turned her argument outward. The result is a more perceptive analysis both of the code of propriety and of her own position within it. But while her basic assumption—that women are primarily reasoning rather than sexual beings—enabled her to create a self-image sufficiently strong to attack prejudices that had traditionally blocked women's participation in political discussions, her inability to assimilate fully her own profoundly unreasonable emotions or bodily appetites weakens the argument she had so effectively begun. For Wollstonecraft does not extend to women the same insight she used in exploding Rousseau's euphemisms and evasions; that is, she does not develop the idea that women's volatile sensibility might be a sublimation of sexual energy. In order to sidestep the investigation of sexuality that this insight would necessitate—and the admission of "weakness" it would entail—Wollstonecraft repeatedly turns her argument away from the idea that women might have sexual or physical needs.

The most obvious consequence of Wollstonecraft's refusal to acknowledge female sexuality is her reluctance to consider women as a group capable of agency. Because she considers the root of culture's values to be *men's* sexual desire, she continues to portray social reform strictly in terms of individual men's acts of self-denial and self-control. Wollstonecraft generally does not challenge women to act. When she calls for a "revolution in female manners" (p. 45), for example, she is not advocating a feminist uprising to overthrow propriety but rather a general acquiescence in a gradual transformation, which was the meaning carried by the word "revolution" in the eighteenth century. Women are simply to wait for this revolution to be effected, for their dignity to *be* restored, for their reformation to be made necessary. Wollstonecraft defers her discussion of legal inequality to the promised second volume (which she never wrote) because, in her scheme, social legislation is less effective than individual self-control. And in *The Rights of Woman*, Wollstonecraft emphasizes independence rather than equality both because she conceives of society as a collection of individual attitudes rather than legal contracts and because she imagines relationships to be fundamentally antagonistic rather than cooperative. The major antagonism, however, is not against an external force but against one's own self—against fear and, especially, against desire.

From her evasions and her aspirations, it seems clear that the price Wollstonecraft felt her new profession exacted was her female sexuality. This was a price she thought she was willing to pay; for if the ideal writer has no sex, he or she is free from both the body's limitations and its demands. Adopting this characterization of the writer could theoretically protect Wollstonecraft from the pain-

ful vacillations of feeling she had alternately repressed and indulged during her youth. At the same time, this persona allowed her a certain amount of social self-confidence, especially in Joseph Johnson's circle, where feminine graces seemed irrelevant and such women as Anna Barbauld were acknowledged as intellectual equals by being criticized as such. But it also, of course, blinded Wollstonecraft to crucial emotional and physical needs—needs that were increasingly demanding attention in her own life. That she could mistake her growing passion for Henry Fuseli for a purely "rational desire"—even to the point of proposing, to his wife, that she, Wollstonecraft, should join the Fuseli household—attests to the power of the desire she tried to philosophize away.

Whether or not Wollstonecraft was correct in deducing a fundamentally nonsexual human essence is, of course, beside the point, for the tensions in her argument demonstrate that, even in her own terms, she had not resolved the complexities of the issue, either theoretically or practically. Clearly, simply to recognize the structure of sexual oppression and inequality, as Mary Wollstonecraft did, was not sufficient to achieve genuine freedom. The frustrations behind the contradictions evident in *A Vindication of the Rights of Woman*, her strongest polemic, would be dispelled only when she found a way to allow the writer and the woman to speak with one voice.

LETTERS WRITTEN DURING A SHORT RESIDENCE IN SWEDEN, NORWAY, AND DENMARK

In 1793, Wollstonecraft journeyed to France, partly to escape the pain of Fuseli's rejection and partly to witness the French Revolution firsthand. She arrived in time to see the revolutionary promises fall beneath the blade of the guillotine, but Wollstonecraft's political disappointment was soon offset by the passionate relationship she developed with Gilbert Imlay, an American entrepreneur. Her happiness was not long-lived, however. After their child was born, Imlay's interest in Wollstonecraft flagged, and she soon found herself not Imlay's lover but his employee and correspondent. Hoping to assess the business opportunities available in Scandinavia and to win financial independence from Imlay, Wollstonecraft traveled to Sweden, Norway, and Denmark in 1795. The epistolary travelogue she composed in Scandinavia did not reclaim Imlay's affection, but it accomplished a great deal for Wollstonecraft. William Godwin, for example, who was unmoved by the "harshness" and "ruggedness" of *The Rights of Woman*, found in *Letters Written During a Short Residence in Sweden, Norway, and Denmark* (1796) "genius" and "gentleness." "If ever there was a book calculated to make a man in love with its author," he wrote, "this appears to be the book" (*Memoirs*, p. 84).

Godwin was responding to the direct, unabashedly autobiographical voice that resounds from the first page of this very personal travelogue. Wollstonecraft openly appeals here to her readers' emotions because for the first time she openly acknowledges the power of her own feelings to engage and persuade. Immediately, the persona, who is, explicitly, "Mary," grants subjectivity the authority Wollstonecraft had previously reserved for the objective "clear truths" of reason.

In writing these desultory letters, I found I could not avoid being continually the first person—the little hero of each tale. I tried to correct this fault, if it be one . . . but in proportion as I arranged my thoughts, my letter, I found, became stiff and affected: I, therefore, determined to let my remarks and reflections flow unrestrained, as I perceived that I could not give a just description of what I saw, but by relating the effect different objects had produced on my mind and feelings, whilst the impression was still fresh.

(p. 5)

This passage announces both the form and the content of Wollstonecraft's new aesthetic program. "Desultory" is no longer a pejorative term, as it was when she accused Burke of being a "desultory writer" in *The Rights of Men*. Wollstonecraft constructs her narrative according to the "desultory" associations of her mind because she now believes that accuracy is measured by the subject's unfolding response rather than by some fixed, objective standard. Her own feelings also make up the content of her work because she now considers these feelings an integral part of the truths she wants to convey.

Wollstonecraft's new self-confidence is largely due to the relationship she now emphasizes between herself as a particular subject and humanity in general. As early as 1790, in *The Rights of Men*, she had implied that the development of the individual recapitulated that of civilization, but not until *Sweden* does she make use of this connection

to justify self-consciousness and self-expression. Although Wollstonecraft claims that her "favourite subject of contemplation" is "the future improvement of the world" (p. 182), she concentrates instead on the present improvement of a single individual—herself. By narrating the progress of her own expanding consciousness, she forecasts the course of social improvement. For, she argues, each nation, like an individual, has a collective "understanding" that evolves organically, "ripening" gradually to fruition (p. 198).

Because Wollstonecraft recognizes that all perception is inevitably subjective, she uses natural objects to mediate her relationship with her audience. Even though her "jaundiced eye of melancholy" may color every thought (p. 169), she is able to communicate her emotions because she anchors them in the specific physical settings to which they correspond. Nature serves as a common reference point, a touchstone shared by Wollstonecraft and her audience, even though the readers may never see the landscapes for themselves. And because nature facilitates communication, concrete descriptions also anchor the most important organizational unit in *Sweden*. In a typical episode, Wollstonecraft essentially duplicates the activity of her own mind: she observes a natural object or scene, is inspired to an imaginative or intellectual excursion, and then returns to "the straight road" of observing the natural world. The return is frequently abrupt, however, and Wollstonecraft often accomplishes it only by concluding a letter; for the imagination repeatedly strains away from the natural world or threatens to center obsessively on the self.

As a chronicle of her observations and imaginative formation, Wollstonecraft's *Sweden* resembles Wordsworth's *Prelude*. Whereas Wordsworth explicitly but unobtrusively uses his vocation as a poet to organize and justify his autobiographical excursion, however, Wollstonecraft uses what she now sees as the most important aspect of her self—her femaleness—to mediate her observations. Wollstonecraft introduces her gender less self-consciously here than in *The Rights of Woman*; she simply notes matter-of-factly her acquaintances' surprise that a woman should travel to such unusual places and ask *"men's questions"* (p. 15). Wollstonecraft now realizes that her position as a woman has all along dictated the nature of her experiences and her responses. Her emotion is a woman's emotion, and her thoughts spring from these depths, not simply from asexual reason. "We reason deeply," she comments, "when we forcibly feel" (p. 160).

In *Sweden*, Wollstonecraft is much less anxious to anchor her subjective judgments in external, objective authorities than she was in her political vindications. This is especially obvious in her presentation of her religious sentiments. *Sweden* is not without references to God, but Wollstonecraft is now much less orthodox in describing God's order, and much more inclined to substitute non-theological phrases like "a mighty whole" (p. 17) or "all that is great and beautiful" (p. 58) for more traditional monotheistic terms.

Wollstonecraft's *Sweden*, as the mirror of a maturing self and self-consciousness, does have a plot of sorts, although the most significant unit of action is not the volume as a whole but the movement from observation to imaginative speculation. Taken as a whole, however, *Sweden* details the narrator's passage from an initial state of poised expectation through a period of energetic exploration, observation, and self-discovery, to a gradual decline into melancholy and anger. Recognition of the death of her love affair with Imlay surfaces in her acute consciousness of the significance of separation ("always a most melancholy, death-like idea" [p. 176]) and her sensitivity to the transience of all joy. As Wollstonecraft's return to London looms closer, her ability to maintain perspective on her own situation diminishes, and her personal pain moves nearer to the center of her narrative. She cannot refrain from turning her general castigation of commerce into a personal warning to Imlay, as if hoping that heartfelt pleas in this public form will effect what all her private communications have failed to do. "But you will say that I am growing bitter, perhaps, personal. Ah! shall I whisper to you—that you—yourself, are strangely altered, since you have entered deeply into commerce—more than you are aware of" (p. 187). In Imlay's growing preoccupation with business Wollstonecraft confronts the logical extension of the bourgeois self-assertiveness that she celebrated in *The Rights of Men*; one measure of the change she has undergone is that she now cherishes emotional stability and domestic affection over this restless desire for "improvement." Such exertion she now sees as a kind of selfishness, which actually prevents the individual from self-improvement because it concentrates all interest and desire on the self.

Considering herself a sacrificial lamb not so much to Imlay but to the commercial spirit invading society, Wollstonecraft melodramatically casts herself as an unheard Cassandra (p. 190) and as a pathetic, betrayed child (p. 184). Despite her determination to conquer sorrow, Wollstonecraft comes very close in these last letters to lapsing into her old role of sentimental sufferer. Only by resolutely turning her attention outward once more, to initiate the confrontation that awaits her, is she able to regain sufficient energy to transform her bitterness into a blessing.

If Wollstonecraft does not achieve sufficient stability of character to weather the storm raging within her it is because she is no longer willing to purchase "philosophical contentment" at the price of felt needs. To a woman demanding emotional and sexual fulfillment as well as respect and intellectual independence, satisfaction did not come easily in the late eighteenth century. Indeed, given the tendency of English society to equate a woman's value to her passivity—her willingness to be an object of desire rather than a human being with needs—satisfaction on Wollstonecraft's terms was virtually unattainable. Her maturation as a self-made woman was taking her directly into the vortex of this contradiction, and the rapid growth of her self-consciousness during the last years of her life can be seen as a recognition of bourgeois society's pervasive devaluation of her sex. In *Sweden* the villain Wollstonecraft identifies is still an individual—Imlay—and the lust for wealth she attacks is only the faceless tyrant by whom she hopes to excuse his infidelity. But with the growth of her recognition that her own capacity for emotion could become an aggressive version of the emotionalism other women shared, Wollstonecraft comes face-to-face with the institutional force that stands behind every man. The villain she was to identify in her next work was bourgeois society itself and, more particularly, the institution of marriage. Within marriage, even the potential power of female feeling is twisted so as to silence the woman who tries to reveal society's wrongs.

MARIA; OR, THE WRONGS OF WOMAN

FOR most of Mary Wollstonecraft's life her uncommon energy seemed fated to be squandered in false pursuits and on inferior objects. For a while it even appeared that her resolution would make the characteristic female revolution: turning back on her self, she would determine to die. The inconstancy of her American lover twice drove Wollstonecraft to attempt suicide. Imlay saved her the first time and then sent her packing off to Sweden to recover her peace of mind. On her return, when she found him still evasive, still indecisive, she rowed to Putney Bridge, walked in the rain for an hour to soak her skirts, and threw herself in the Thames. Boatmen pulled her from the water, however, and gradually her determination and her strong emotions revived once more.

Wollstonecraft emerged from the Imlay affair still fixed on obtaining the happiness and fulfillment she considered the birthright of women as well as men. In the last year and a half of her life she fell in love with William Godwin, and, when she found herself pregnant once more, married the evangelist of reason in order to spare her unborn child shame. For at least this short period Wollstonecraft relished the joys of motherhood, marriage, *and* intellectual freedom.

Wollstonecraft's brief physical and intellectual independence, however, did not guarantee freedom from her society's system of values. Nor did her brief happiness blind her to the circumstances that continued to cause her pain. If anything, this respite from sorrow honed her anger and gave her sufficient self-possession to turn her wrath upon its proper object. In her last work she speaks with her newfound woman's voice and from a "full heart," but her message is that the struggle has just begun.

In *Maria; or, The Wrongs of Woman* (1798), Wollstonecraft sought to popularize the insights of *The Rights of Woman* by turning to a genre she felt confident women would read: the sentimental novel. But the attempt to fictionalize the "wrongs of woman" afflicted Wollstonecraft with writer's block. She had composed *The Rights of Men* in less than a month and *The Rights of Woman* in six weeks, but she spent a year working on *Maria*, only to leave the manuscript less than a third finished when she died. Almost any passage from this unfinished manuscript reflects the difficulty with which Wollstonecraft wrote it. Syntax is frequently incoherent, narratives are broken off literally in midsentence, and, most problematic of all, the relationship between the narrative consciousness and that of the heroine is inconsistent. Such

hesitations culminate in a conspicuous failure to establish a consistent or purposeful attitude toward the subject under consideration.

The problem was not simply that Wollstonecraft could not construct a successful narrative, for both her first novel, *Mary,* and the story of Jemima, contained within *Maria,* demonstrate her competence as a storyteller. The problem apparently lay in the difficulty she had in reconciling her intended purpose with the genre, which here shapes the structure of the work. According to her sketchy preface, Wollstonecraft's purpose was political, to show "the peculiar Wrongs of Woman." And her structure, like the structure of what she calls "our best novels," was intended to delineate "passions rather than manners" (1975 ed., pp. 8, 7). The problem here was not, as it was in *The Rights of Men,* that Wollstonecraft tried to suppress the emotion she feared was inappropriate to the genre she had chosen. Instead, the kind of feeling that was appropriate to this genre aborted her political purpose. For the emotionalism that had so long crippled Wollstonecraft, along with the sentimental structure developed to dramatize such "finer sensations," was deeply implicated in the values of bourgeois society. It is Wollstonecraft's recognition of the incompatibility and—equally to the point—her resistance to this recognition that account for both the hesitations of composition and the contradictions that mark the text. In this, her final work, Wollstonecraft identified one aspect of what she held to be the tyranny of eighteenth-century bourgeois institutions; yet, because her own self-definition was inextricably bound up with these values, she was unable to pursue her revolutionary insights to their logical conclusion.

Wollstonecraft's dilemma is epitomized by the uncertain perspective of the novel's omniscient narrator. In chapter 4, for example, which traces Maria's emotional surrender to Henry Darnford, a fellow inmate, the narrator moves from judgmental observer to unreflecting sympathizer. Maria has been imprisoned in a madhouse so that her avaricious husband can gain control of the independent fortunes of both Maria and their infant daughter. At the beginning of the chapter, the narrative voice comments authoritatively on this situation. "Pity," the narrator observes,

and the forlorn seriousness of adversity, have both been considered as dispositions favourable to love, while satirical writers have attributed the propensity to the relaxing effect of idleness; what chance then had Maria of escaping, when pity, sorrow, and solitude all conspired to soften her mind, and nourish romantic wishes, and, from a natural progress, romantic expectations?

(p. 48)

The most pressing question here is the narrator's attitude toward Maria's "romantic expectations." Even though the rhetoric of imprisonment suggests that Wollstonecraft understands such wishes both to originate in deprivation and confinement and to be delusive and degrading, the narrator remains curiously ambivalent about the desirability of Maria's romantic desires. The ambiguous origin of the sentiments expressed in the first part of this passage, for example, suggests that the narrator hopes that such romantic expectations might be fulfilled, and the enthusiastic rhetoric with which the chapter ends suggests that the narrator shares Maria's "romantic wishes" and perhaps her "romantic aspirations" as well: "So much of heaven did they enjoy, that paradise bloomed around them; or they, by a powerful spell, had been transported into Armida's garden. Love, the grand enchanter, 'lapt them in Elysium,' and every sense was harmonized to joy and social extacy" (p. 51).

This chapter is particularly revealing because the progression of the narrator from detached, critical observer to emotional participant recapitulates the movement that constitutes the organization and, theoretically, the target of criticism of the novel. The movement is the "fall" into female sexuality or, more precisely, the fall into the susceptibility to romantic expectations that eighteenth-century culture annexed to female sexuality. The problem here is that the narrator—and by implication, Wollstonecraft herself—has just fallen victim to the very delusion it is the object of this novel to criticize.

This seduction of the narrator constitutes the third occurrence of this pattern in the novel, and, taking all three together, we begin to glimpse both Wollstonecraft's insight and her dilemma, for the pander in each case is precisely the kind of sentimental story that Wollstonecraft is writing. In what is chronologically the first fall, the sentimental story involves Maria's uncle. Maria seeks from this uncle the love she does not receive from her parents. In return, he tries to teach her to defend herself against romantic expectations by telling of his own romantic disappointment. The effect of the uncle's story is the reverse of what he had in-

tended, however. Because Maria has not personally experienced her uncle's disillusionment, she responds to his story as moralists feared women naturally respond to sentimental novels; her imagination is aroused and she projects herself, a heroine, into his text.

Her uncle's sentiments, along with the books he lends Maria, "conspired to make [her] form an ideal picture of life" and to project this ideal onto a young neighbor, George Venables. Even Maria's wishful idealism, however, cannot survive the brutal reality of marriage with Venables. Soon after marrying, she discovers that what she had imagined to be his love was actually avarice; he really only wanted the £5,000 Maria's uncle had settled on her as a dowry.

In the madhouse in which Venables eventually confines his wife, the same pattern threatens Maria again. Despite the fact that she has now experienced sorrow, she is once more seduced by sentiment—this time by a sentimental novel. Once more the narrator suggests that Maria's reading leads to a dangerous kind of projection, which finds its object in Darnford, a fellow prisoner who owns the novel she has been reading. It comes as no surprise that the seduction of Maria's imagination culminates in her sexual acquiescence to Darnford—she receives him "as her husband" (p. 138), just as she had earlier received Venables.

What is surprising is that the narrator does not underscore the similarity of Maria's two falls. Instead of a consistent condemnation of Maria's situation, we get the narrative ambivalence we have already seen. In most of the six endings Wollstonecraft projected for the novel, she suggests that Darnford will betray Maria, yet the bleakness of these provisional conclusions is still qualified by the narrator's optimism. It is as if the narrator resists the implications of the very insight her story dramatizes, as if she would like to retain, for as long as possible, the idealism she has shown to cripple Maria. In order fully to understand the implications of Wollstonecraft's narrative hesitations we need to return to those insights, to see precisely how feminine romanticism blasts female sexuality, and how female sexuality, as Wollstonecraft depicts it, is defined by bourgeois society and by the narratives that inculcate its values.

Mary Wollstonecraft's fundamental insight in *Maria* concerns the way in which female sexuality is defined and controlled by bourgeois institutions, especially marriage. According to bourgeois conventions, female sexuality can be legitimately expressed—indeed, can exist as a positive cultural force—only within marriage. For, confined within marriage, female sexuality is deprived of its power both to devour a man sexually and to rob him of his ability to identify his heirs. Wollstonecraft recognizes not only the consequences of the code of propriety but also its roots and its institutional guardians. She sees that marriage makes women property, objectifies them, and deprives them of their rights—even, finally, the right to act upon their own desire: within marriage, as Maria phrases it, the woman is "required to moralize, sentimentalize herself to stone" (p. 102).

Because the kind of economically advantageous marriages that frequently took place in this period often entailed reducing women to carriers of property, such transactions had to be enforced not only by laws but by a set of values that naturalized inequality. In *Maria,* Wollstonecraft identifies sentimentalism as the agent of this naturalization. As Wollstonecraft depicts it here, sentimentalism constitutes a paradox: its role is both to arouse female sexuality and to control it. In the first of these two functions, exemplified by Maria's adolescence, sentimental stories arouse a young woman's imagination by engaging her vicariously in thinly disguised sexual exploits. But because the young girl is protected (or confined) by both ignorance and inexperience, the expectations generated by reading lead her to project her desire uncritically onto a "hero," with whom she then seeks to realize her imaginative and sexual desires—ideally, through marriage.

The irony (and tragedy) of this situation is that, as often as not, the desire so aroused exceeds the gratification offered women through marriage. Precisely because one effect of marriage was to limit desire, sentimentalism theoretically generated a clash between female desire and male will. For, once imprisoned within marriage, a woman existed in the same state of confinement that characterized her adolescence. Thus the desire could begin again and lead a woman to seek fulfillment outside the marriage bed. But the second effect of sentimental novels curtailed this threat. Despite the ominous specters of adultery and seduction in eighteenth-century sentimental novels, the function of such flirtations with transgression was actually to sublimate female desire, to provide vicarious gratification, which compensated for the diminished fulfillment of marriage. One function of sentimental novels, then, was actually to reinforce the institution that the desire they aroused also theoretically subverted.

This recognition of the sentimental ways and means of marital tyranny constitutes the most important insight of Wollstonecraft's last novel. Despite this insight, the heroine remains ominously attracted to the very sentimentalism that has twice ensnared her. Even after the scheming brutality of Venables theoretically opens her eyes to the naïveté of her initial attraction to sentimental novels, Maria continues to extol the selflessness of "*active* sensibility" and to encourage her infant daughter to perpetuate her own mistakes: "Whilst your own heart is sincere," she writes in the memoirs she intends for her daughter, "always expect to meet one glowing with the same sentiments" (p. 77).

Maria contains some suggestions that the heroine's sentimentalism is being presented ironically, foremost among which is the decidedly unsentimental narrative of Jemima, Maria's warden in the madhouse. Jemima's history begins not with romantic expectations but with sexual violation ("My father . . . seduced my mother"), and it details the events of a continuing victimization: Jemima is raped by her master when she is sixteen, and the ensuing pregnancy drives her into the streets. After a self-inflicted abortion, poverty forces Jemima into prostitution. As a self-sufficient prostitute, Jemima experiences an unorthodox, if momentary, freedom.

Wollstonecraft says that Jemima values her "independence," but this independence is not socially acceptable; night watchmen soon drive Jemima into institutionalized prostitution—first in a whorehouse, then in a relationship with a "worn-out votary of voluptuousness." Upon her lover's death, Jemima is reduced, in rapid order, to being a washerwoman, a thief, and a pauper before she finds employment in the madhouse to which Maria is confined.

Jemima's story—which is a radical critique of the oppression of women—has the potential to call into question both the organizational principles of bourgeois society and the sentimentalism that perpetuates romantic idealism. For the subversion implicit in Jemima's brief assertion of female autonomy combines with the stark realism of the narrative to explode the assumptions that tie female sexuality to romance and thus to the institutions men traditionally control. Wollstonecraft does *not* develop the revolutionary implications of Jemima's narrative, however. Instead, her story is quickly, ostentatiously, suppressed. Jemima's history occupies only one of the seventeen completed chapters of *Maria*, and it is suspended prematurely by an unspecified "indistinct noise" whose only function is to curtail this narrative. The abrupt manner in which Jemima's story ends and the thoroughness with which her tough attitude is reabsorbed into Maria's sentimentalism suggests that Wollstonecraft is not willing to endorse so radical an alternative to women's oppression. Such a solution would entail renouncing not only the bourgeois institution of marriage but also the romantic expectations that motivate Maria and, we must conclude, the narrator as well.

Despite the strong suggestions that Maria's incorrigible romanticism is being presented ironically, despite Wollstonecraft's emphasis on the pernicious effects of sentimentalism, the narrator herself repeatedly lapses back into sentimental jargon and romantic idealism. At such moments the theoretical wisdom of the narrator simply collapses into the longing of the character. These repeated collapses are characteristically marked by Wollstonecraft's insistence on semantic distinctions where substantial differences do not in fact exist. "The real affections of life," she comments in a typical passage, "when they are allowed to burst forth, are buds pregnant with joy and all the sweet emotions of the soul. . . . The substantial happiness, which enlarges and civilizes the mind, may be compared to the pleasure experienced in roving through nature at large, inhaling the sweet gale natural to the clime" (pp. 143–144). In keeping with the renewed faith in physicality she exhibited in *Sweden*, Wollstonecraft desperately wants happiness to be "substantial," "real," physically possible. But the metaphorical language she uses to depict that happiness in *Maria* ("buds pregnant with joy") calls attention only to the literariness, the patent immateriality, of this ideal. Despite her anxious assertions that such happiness is "substantial" and that the "real affections of life" and "true sensibility" somehow differ from the romantic delusions that twice ensnare Maria, Wollstonecraft actually reveals only that her own ideals are insubstantial—that they are, in fact, part and parcel of the romantic idealism they are meant to transcend. Repeatedly, then, the narrator falls victim to the same sentimental idealism that cripples Maria.

Wollstonecraft continues to cherish the belief that, by fidelity to personal feelings kept pure of the taint of self-interest and the "grossness of sensuality," an individual can express a sensibility "true" in the most idealistic sense of the word. Even Wollstonecraft knows that something is wrong, however. In the crucible of her novel, things just do not work out that way: Darnford's love is "volatile," Maria's happiness is less substantial than the bars of her madhouse cell. And the fiction that Wollstonecraft believed "capable of producing an important effect" repeatedly threatens to lose sight of its political purpose and become just another sentimental novel.

Even though Wollstonecraft tries to "restrain [her] fancy" in the novel's final chapter, the objective summary of women's wrongs that she presents here does not transcend the problem of women's ineffectualness. For the heart of the problem is not, as Wollstonecraft supposed, finding the proper form of expression for the feeling heart. Rather, the real problem lies in the very concept of the feeling heart itself. Basically, Maria's concluding argument, which she presents before a jury summoned to try her for adultery, foregrounds this feeling heart: she justifies her flight from Venables by an appeal to her own subjective judgment, and urges the members of the jury to consult their own feelings in deciding her case. Moreover, Maria's defense, for all its insight, simply strives to institutionalize female feeling as a new rationale for the old covenant of marriage. Even as she pleads for freedom from Venables, Maria calls Darnford her "husband" and declares that what she really wants is only a new marriage in which better to fulfill "the duties of a wife and mother" (p. 148). We are not really surprised that Maria's attempt to generalize and institutionalize feeling has no effect on the court, for in her argument Wollstonecraft fails once more to take her own insights to their logical conclusions. Just as she turned from exploring the radical implications of Jemima's narrative, she now stops short of exposing either the tyranny of the marriage contract or the price that sensibility extracts from female sexuality. Instead, the defiant Mary Wollstonecraft clings to that bedrock of bourgeois society—the belief in individual feeling—and in doing this her voice hesitates and finally falters into silence.

The twist given female sexuality by the contradictory combination of sensibility and propriety is the heart of darkness Mary Wollstonecraft never identified. Yet this contradiction helps explain why sentimentalism was so appealing and so fatal to her as well as to many less-thoughtful women of this period. Mary Wollstonecraft could not renounce "true sensibility" because it was the only form in which her society allowed her to express either her sexuality or her craving for transcendent meaning. Yet retaining that form of expression, those values, and that self-definition prohibited her from renouncing the institutions that governed femininity in the late eighteenth century. This contradiction also helps explain Wollstonecraft's self-contradictory presentation of sexuality in *Maria*. In this novel Wollstonecraft insists—to a degree remarkable for any late-eighteenth-century novelist—on the importance of female sexual expression; yet, despite her insistence that sexual fulfillment is not only necessary but possible, every sexual relationship she depicts is dehumanizing and revolting. Sexuality is virtually the only human quality that is described in this novel with any degree of physical detail, and the descriptions—like the one of Venables' "tainted breath, pimpled face, and blood-shot eyes"—suggest grotesqueness, violence, and contamination.

The problem that plagued Mary Wollstonecraft's final efforts to reconcile her intense female feeling with intellectual independence was simply an extreme version of what was, for women of this period, a general dilemma. Not only were late-eighteenth-century moralists virtually unanimous in pointing out the twin appeal and danger of sentimental novels for women readers and writers, but most of the examples we have of this genre reveal many of the same problems as *Maria*. Perhaps, in fact, the only effective way a woman who thought as well as felt could successfully deal with the issue of feeling was to satirize "true sensibility" as novelists like Jane Austen and Maria Edgeworth were soon to do.

CONCLUSION

Given Mary Wollstonecraft's political commitment to women's independence and her fictional portrayal of the injustices of marriage, it may seem ironic that Wollstonecraft finally found what she described as genuine happiness in her marriage to William Godwin, the radical author and political philosopher. The iconoclastic couple married in 1797, allegedly to spare the child with which Wollstonecraft was pregnant the disapproval her first illegitimate daughter had already received. Early in September the child was born safely, but the placenta was not completely expelled. After so few months of happiness and ten days of excruciating pain, Mary Wollstonecraft died on 10 September 1797. Her daughter, who was to elope with another radical author after a courtship largely conducted beside Wollstonecraft's grave, bore her mother's name, if not her political convictions. As the author of *Frankenstein*, Mary Wollstonecraft Godwin Shelley is one of Mary Wollstonecraft's most enduring legacies.

In 1871, almost seventy-five years after Mary Wollstonecraft's death, an even more successful woman writer paid tribute once more to Wollstonecraft's courage: the words are those of Mary Ann Evans:

Hopelessness has been to me, all through my life, but especially in painful years of my youth, the chief source of wasted energy with all the consequent bitterness of regret. Remember, it has happened to many to be glad they did not commit suicide, though they once ran for the final leap, or as Mary Wollstonecraft did, wetted their garments well in the rain hoping to sink the better when they plunged. She tells how it occurred to her as she was walking in the damp shroud, that she might live to be glad that she had not put an end to herself—and so it turned out. She lived to know some real joys, and death came in time to hinder the joys from being spoiled.[2]

It is significant that Mary Ann Evans/George Eliot generalizes Wollstonecraft's determined death-walk ("wetted their garments well"), then individualizes her second thoughts ("it occurred to her"): from the multitude of hopeless, death-bound women, one woman steps forth who is capable of imagining "real joys" even in her "damp shroud." Mary Wollstonecraft was nothing if she was not determined, and, even when it was unfashionable to be so determined or so outspoken, her example stood in for many a more retiring woman's fantasies of self-assertion. Thus women novelists like Maria Edgeworth and Fanny Burney, for whose novels Wollstonecraft provided the requisite monitory figure, also used these

[2]"Margaret Fuller and Mary Wollstonecraft," in *Essays of George Eliot*, ed. by Thomas Pinney (New York, 1963), pp. 199–200.

Wollstonecraft characters to voice what may have been their own staunchly denied desires. The words of the numerous Harriet Frekes (*Belinda*, 1801) and Elinor Joddrels (*The Wanderer; or, Female Difficulties*, 1814) of early-nineteenth-century novels have such resonance that one cannot help but wonder how their authors heard these voices in their own imaginations—whether there was not a secret thrill of kindred souls.

SELECTED BIBLIOGRAPHY

I. BIBLIOGRAPHIES. Janet M. Todd, *Mary Wollstonecraft: An Annotated Bibliography* (New York, 1976), includes Wollstonecraft materials through 1976 and an introduction that classifies Wollstonecraft criticism by categories. J. R. Windle, *Mary Wollstonecraft: A Bibliography of Her Writings, 1787–1982* (Los Angeles, 1988).

II. COLLECTED WORKS. *A Wollstonecraft Anthology* (Bloomington, Ind., 1977), ed. by Janet Todd; *The Works of Mary Wollstonecraft*, 7 vols. (London, 1989), ed. by Janet Todd and Marilyn Butler.

III. SEPARATE WORKS. *Thoughts on the Education of Daughters: With Reflections on Female Conduct, in the More Important Duties of Life* (London, 1787), conduct manual; *Mary, A Fiction* (London, 1788), novel; *Original Stories from Real Life: With Conversations, Calculated to Regulate the Affections, and Form the Mind to Truth and Goodness* (London, 1788), conduct manual for children; trans. of *On the Importance of Religious Opinions* by Jacques Necker (London, 1788); *The Female Reader; or, Miscellaneous-Pieces, in Prose and Verse, Selected from the Best Writers, and Disposed Under Proper Heads; for the Improvement of Young Women* (London, 1789); trans. of *Young Grandison* by Madame de Cambon, 2 vols. (London, 1790); *A Vindication of the Rights of Men, in a Letter to the Right Honourable Edmund Burke; Occasioned by His "Reflections on the Revolution in France"* (London, 1790), political tract; *Original Stories from Real Life* (London, 1791); *A Vindication of the Rights of Woman, with Strictures on Political and Moral Subjects* (London, 1792), political tract; *An Historical and Moral View of the Origin and Progress of the French Revolution, and the Effects It Has Produced in Europe* (London, 1794), history with political analysis; *Letters Written During a Short Residence in Sweden, Norway, and Denmark* (London, 1796).

Posthumous works include *Posthumous Works of the Author of* A Vindication of the Rights of Woman, 4 vols. (London, 1798), ed. by William Godwin, includes *The Wrongs of Woman; or, Maria: A Fragment; Letters to Gilbert Imlay; Extract of the Cave of Fancy: A Tale;* and *Fragment of Letters on the Management of Infants; Collected Letters of Mary Wollstonecraft* (Ithaca, N.Y., 1979), ed. by Ralph Wardle.

IV. MODERN EDITIONS. *A Vindication of the Rights of Men, in a Letter to the Right Honourable Edmund Burke; Occasioned by His "Reflections on the Revolution in France"* (Gainesville, Fla., 1960), ed. by Eleanor Louise Nicholes; *Posthumous Works of the Author of* A Vindication of the Rights of Woman (New York, 1974), modern repr. with an intro. by Gina Luria; *A Vindication of the Rights of Men* (Delmar, N.Y., 1975), facsimile with intro. by Eleanor Louise Nicholes; *An Historical and Moral View of the Origin and Progress of the French Revolution and the Effects It Has Produced in Europe* (Delmar, N.Y., 1975), facsimile reproduction, ed. and with intro. by Janet M. Todd; *Maria; or, The Wrongs of Woman* (New York, 1975), ed. by Moira Ferguson; *Letters Written During a Short Residence in Sweden, Norway, and Denmark* (Lincoln, Nebr., 1976), ed. and with intro. by Carol H. Poston; *Maria; or, The Wrongs of Woman* (London and New York, 1976), annotated ed. by Gary Kelly; *Mary, a Fiction* (London, 1976), annotated ed. with an intro. by Gary Kelly; *The Female Reader; or, Miscellaneous Pieces, in Prose and Verse; Selected from the Best Writers and Disposed Under Proper Heads; for the Improvement of Young Women* (Delmar, N.Y., 1980), facsimile ed. with intro. by Moira Ferguson; *A Vindication of the Rights of Woman, with Strictures on Political and Moral Subjects* (New York, 1982), modern ed. with intro. by Miriam Kramnick; *A Short Residence in Sweden and Memoirs of the Author of* A Vindication of the Rights of Woman (New York, 1987), ed. with intro. by Richard Holmes; *A Vindication of the Rights of Woman*, 2d ed. (New York, 1988), modern ed. with background, Wollstonecraft debate, and criticism, ed. by Carol H. Poston; *Original Stories from Real Life* (Oxford and New York, 1990), facsimile with intro. by Jonathan Wordsworth; *Mary and Maria; Matilda* (London, 1992), ed. by Janet Todd; William Godwin, *Memoirs of the Author of* A Vindication of the Rights of Woman (New York and Oxford, 1993), facsimile ed. with intro. by Jonathan Wordsworth; *Political Writings* (London, 1993), includes the two *Vindications* and *An Historical and Moral View of the French Revolution*, ed. by Janet Todd.

V. BIOGRAPHICAL AND CRITICAL STUDIES. William Godwin, *Memoirs of the Author of* A Vindication of the Rights of Woman (London, 1798); Mary Ann Evans [George Eliot], "Margaret Fuller and Mary Wollstonecraft" in Thomas Pinney, ed., *Essays of George Eliot* (New York, 1963); Margaret George, *One Woman's "Situation": A Study of Mary Wollstonecraft* (Urbana and Chicago, 1970); Eleanor Flexner, *Mary Wollstonecraft: A Biography* (New York, 1972); Janet Todd, "The Language of Sex in *A Vindication of the Rights of Woman*," in *Mary Wollstonecraft Newsletter* 1 (1973); Claire Tomalin, *The Life and Death of Mary Wollstonecraft* (London and New York, 1974); Ralph M. Wardle, "Mary Wollstonecraft, Analytical Reviewer," in *PMLA* 62 (1947); Emily Sunstein, *A Different Face: The Life of Mary Wollstonecraft* (New York, 1975); Janet Todd, "The Biographies of Mary Wollstonecraft" in *Signs* 1 (1976); Mitzi Myers,

"Politics from the Outside: Mary Wollstonecraft's First *Vindication*," in *Studies in Eighteenth-Century Culture* 6 (1977); Mitzi Myers, "Mary Wollstonecraft's *Letters Written . . . in Sweden:* Towards Romantic Autobiography," in *Studies in Eighteenth-Century Culture* 8 (1979); Felicity Nussbaum, "Eighteenth-Century Women," in *Studies in Burke and His Time* 19, no. 3 (autumn 1978); Gary Kelly, "Mary Wollstonecraft as Vir Bonus," in *English Studies in Canada* 5, no. 3 (autumn 1979); Mary Jacobus, "The Difference of View," in her *Women Writing and Writing About Women* (New York, 1979).

Joan Kelly, "Early Feminist Theory and the *Querrelles des femmes, 1400–1789,*" in *Signs* 8 (autumn 1982); Ronald Paulson, *Representations of Revolution, 1789–1820* (New Haven, Conn., 1983), chap. 3; Moira Ferguson and Janet Todd, *Mary Wollstonecraft* (Boston, 1984), criticism and interpretation; Mary Poovey, *The Proper Lady and the Woman Writer: Ideology as Style in the Works of Mary Wollstonecraft, Mary Shelley, and Jane Austen* (Chicago, 1984); Moira Ferguson, *First Feminists: British Women Writers, 1578–1799* (Bloomington, Ind., 1985); Meena Alexander, *Women in Romanticism: Mary Wollstonecraft, Dorothy Wordsworth, and Mary Shelley* (Savage, Md., 1989); G. J. Barker-Benfield, "Mary Wollstonecraft: Eighteenth-Century Commonwealthwoman," in *Journal of the History of Ideas* 50 (January/March 1989); William St. Clair, *The Godwins and the Shelleys: The Biography of a Family* (London, 1989).

Jennifer Lorch, *Mary Wollstonecraft: The Making of a Radical Feminist* (New York, 1990); Lucinda Cole, "(Anti) feminist Sympathies: The Politics of Relationship in Smith, Wollstonecraft, and More," in *English Literary History* 58 (spring 1991); Cy Frost, "Autocracy and the Matrix of Power: Issues of Propriety and Economics in the Work of Mary Wollstonecraft, Jane Austen, and Harriet Martineau," in *Tulsa Studies in Women's Literature* 10 (fall 1991); Moira Ferguson, "Mary Wollstonecraft and the Problematic of Slavery," in *Feminist Review* 42 (autumn 1992); Gary Kelly, *Revolutionary Feminism: The Mind and Career of Mary Wollstonecraft* (London and New York, 1992); Shawn Lisa Maurer, "The Female (as) Reader: Sex, Sensibility, and the Maternal in Wollstonecraft's Fictions," in *Essays in Literature* 19 (spring 1992); Virginia Sapiro, *A Vindication of Political Virtue: The Political Theory of Mary Wollstonecraft* (Chicago, 1992); Moira Ferguson, *Colonial and Gender Relations from Mary Wollstonecraft to Jamaica Kincaid: East Caribbean Connections* (New York, 1993); Catriona MacKenzie, "Reason and Sensibility: The Ideal of Women's Self-Governance in the Writings of Mary Wollstonecraft," in *Hypatia* 8 (fall 1993); J. McCrystal, "Revolting Women: The Use of Revolutionary Discourse in Mary Astell and Mary Wollstonecraft Compared," in *History of Political Thought* 14 (summer 1993); Patricia Howell Michaelson, "Religious Bases of Eighteenth-Century Feminism: Mary Wollstonecraft and the Quakers," in *Women's Studies* 22, no. 3 (1993); Janet Todd, *Gender, Art, and Death* (New York, 1993); Syndy M. Conger, *Mary Wollstonecraft and the Language of Sensibility* (Rutherford, N.J., and London, 1994).

MASTER INDEX

The following index covers the entire British Writers series through Supplement III. All references include volume numbers in boldface Roman numerals followed by page numbers within that volume. Extended treatment of a subject is indicated by boldface type.

"Recantation, A" (Kipling), **VI:** 192–193
"Receipt to Restore Stella's Youth…. A" (Swift), **III:** 32
"Recessional" (Kipling), **VI:** 203
Recklings (Hughes), **Supp. I:** 346, 348
"Recollections" (Pearsall Smith), **VI:** 76
Recollections of Christ's Hospital (Lamb), **IV:** 85
"Recollections of Solitude" (Bridges), **VI:** 74
Recollections of the Lake Poets (De Quincey), **IV:** 146n, 155
"Reconcilement between Jacob Tonson and Mr. Congreve, The" (Rowe), **II:** 324
"Record of Badalia Herodsfoot, The" (Kipling), **VI:** 167, 168
Record of Friendship, A (Swinburne), **V:** 333
Record of Friendship and Criticism, A (Srnith), **V:** 391, 396, 398
Records of a Family of Engineers (Stevenson), **V:** 387, 396
"Recovery, The" (Vaughan), **II:** 185
Recruiting Officer, The (Farquhar), **II:** 353, 358–359, 360, 361, 362, 364
Rectory Umbrella and Mischmasch, The (Carroll), **V:** 264, 273
Red Cotton Night-Cap Country (Browning), **IV:** 358, 369, 371, 374
Red Days and White Nights (Koestler), **Supp. I:** 23
Red Harvest (Hammett), **Supp. II:** 130
Red Peppers (Coward), **Supp. II:** 153
"Red, Red Rose, A" (Burns), **III:** 321
Red Roses for Me (O'Casey), **VII:** 9
"Redemption" (Herbert), **II:** 126–127
Redgauntlet (Scott), **IV:** xviii, 31, 35, 39
"Red-Headed League, The" (Doyle), **Supp. II:** 170
Reed, Henry, **VII:** 422–423, 449
Reed, J. W., **III:** 249
"Reed, A" (Browning), **IV:** 313
Rees-Mogg, W., **II:** 288
Reeve, C., **III:** 345
Reeve, Clara, **III:** 80
Reeve's Tale, The (Chaucer), **I:** 37, 41
"Reflection from Anita Loos" (Empson), **Supp. II:** 183–184
"Reflections on a Peninsula" (Koestler), **Supp. I:** 34
Reflections on Hanging (Koestler), **Supp. I:** 36
"Reflections on Leaving a Place of Retirement" (Coleridge), **IV:** 44
"Reflections on the Death of a Porcupine" (Lawrence), **VII:** 103–104, 110, 119
Reflections on the French Revolution (Burke), **III:** 195, 197, 201–205; **IV:** xv, 127; **Supp. III:** 371, 467, 468, 470
Reflections on the Late Alarming Bankruptcies in Scotland (Boswell), **III:** 248
Reflections on the Psalms (Lewis), **Supp. III:** 249, 264
Reflections upon Ancient and Modern Learning (Wotton), **III:** 23

Reflector (periodical), **IV:** 80
Reformation of Manners (Defoe), **III:** 12
"Refusal to mourn, A" (Thomas), **Supp. I:** 178
Refutation of Deism, in a Dialogue, A (Shelley), **IV:** 208
"Refutation of Philosophies" (Bacon), **I:** 263
"Regency Houses" (Day Lewis), **Supp. III:** 127–128
Regeneration (Haggard), **Supp. III:** 214
"Regeneration" (Vaughan), **II:** 185, 187
Regent, The (Bennett), **VI:** 259, 267
Regicide, The (Smollett), **III:** 158
"Regina Cara" (Bridges), **VI:** 81
"Regret" (Swinburne), **V:** 332
Rehabilitations (Lewis), **Supp. III:** 249
Rehearsal, The (Buckingham), **II:** 206, 294
Rehearsal Transpros'd, The (Marvell), **II:** 205, 206–207, 209, 218, 219
Reid, J. C., **IV:** 254, 267
Rejected Address (Smith), **IV:** 253
"Relapse, The" (Vaughan), **II:** 187
Relapse, The; or, Virtue in Danger (Vanbrugh), **II:** 324, 326–329, 332, 334, 335, 336; **III:** 253, 261
Relation Between Michael Angelo and Tintoret, The (Ruskin), **V:** 184
Relationship of the Imprisonment of Mr. John Bunyan, A, (Bunyan), **II:** 253
Relative Values (Coward), **Supp. II:** 155
"Relativity" (Empson), **Supp. II:** 182
Religio Laici; or, A Layman's Faith (Dryden), **I:** 176, 189; **II:** 291, 299, 304
Religio Medici (Browne), **II:** 146–148, 150, 152, 156, 185; **III:** 40; **VII:** 29
"Religion" (Vaughan), **II:** 189
Religious Courtship:…Historical Discourses on…Marrying…(Defoe), **III:** 13
"Religious Musings" (Coleridge), **IV:** 43
Reliques of Ancient English Poetry (Percy), **III:** 336; **IV:** 28–29
Reliquiae Wottonianae, **II:** 142
"Remain, ah not in youth alone" (Landor), **IV:** 99
Remains of Elmet (Hughes), **Supp. I:** 342
Remains of Sir Walter Ralegh, The, **I:** 146, 157
Remarks Upon a Late Disingenuous Discourse (Marvell), **II:** 219
"Remember" (Rossetti), **VII:** 64
"Remember Me When I Am Gone Away" (Rossetti), **V:** 249
Remembering Sion (Ryan), **VII:** 2
Remembrances of Words and Matter Against Richard Cholmeley, **I:** 277
Reminiscences (Carlyle), **IV:** 70n, 239, 240, 245, 250
"Reminiscences of Charlotte Brontë" (Nussey), **V:** 108, 109, 152
Reminiscences of the Impressionistic Painters (Moore), **VI:** 99
Remorse (Coleridge), **IV:** 56
Remorse: A Study in Saffron (Wilde), **V:** 419

Renaissance: Studies in Art and Poetry, The (Pater), *see Studies in the History of the Renaissance*
Renan, Joseph Ernest, **II:** 244
Renegade Poet, And Other Essays, A (Thompson), **V:** 451
"Repentance" (Herbert), **II:** 128
"Rephan" (Browning), **IV:** 365
Replication (Skelton), **I:** 93
Reply to the Essay on Population, by the Rev. T. R. Malthus, A (Hazlitt), **IV:** 127, 139
"Report from Below, A" (Hood), **IV:** 258
"Report on a Threatened City" (Lessing), **Supp. I:** 250n
"Report on Experience" (Blunden), **VI:** 428
Report on the Salvation Army Colonies (Haggard), **Supp. III:** 214
"Reported Missing" (Scannell), **VII:** 424
Reports on Elementary Schools, 1852–1882 (Arnold), **V:** 216
Reprinted Pieces (Dickens), **V:** 72
Reprisal, The (Smollett), **III:** 149, 158
Reproof: A Satire (Smollett), **III:** 158
"Requiem" (Stevenson), **V:** 383
"Requiescat" (Arnold), **V:** 211
"Requiescat" (Wilde), **V:** 400
Required Writing (Larkin), **Supp. I:** 286, 288
Rescue, The (Conrad), **VI:** 136, 147
"Resignation" (Arnold), **V:** 210
"Resolution and Independence" (Wordsworth), **IV:** 19–20, 22; **V:** 352
"Resound my voice, ye woods that hear me plain" (Wyatt), **I:** 110
Responsibilities (Yeats), **VI:** 213
Restoration (Bond), **Supp. I:** 423, 434, 435
Restoration of Arnold Middleton, The (Storey), **Supp. I:** 408, 411, 412–413, 414, 415, 417
"Resurrection, The" (Cowley), **II:** 200
Resurrection, The (Yeats), **VI:** xiv, 222
"Resurrection and Immortality" (Vaughan), **II:** 185, 186
Resurrection of the Dead, The,…(Bunyan), **II:** 253
"Retaliation" (Goldsmith), **III:** 181, 185, 191
"Retired Cat, The" (Cowper), **III:** 217
"Retirement" (Vaughan), **II:** 187, 188, 189
"Retreate, The" (Vaughan), **II:** 186, 188–189
"Retrospect" (Brooke), **Supp. III:** 56
"Retrospect: From a Street in Chelsea" (Day Lewis), **Supp. III:** 121
"Retrospective Review" (Hood), **IV:** 255
"Return, The" (Conrad), **VI:** 148
Return from Parnassus, The, part 2, **II:** 27
Return of Eva Peron, The (Naipaul), **Supp. I:** 396, 397, 398, 399
Return of the Druses, The (Browning), **IV:** 374